‹‹‹ GAME FREAK ›››
INTERVIEW & CONCEPT ART

Behind the scenes of *Pokémon Sun* and *Pokémon Moon*

Turn the page to read an exclusive interview with Shigeru Ohmori, the director of *Pokémon Sun* and *Pokémon Moon*, and Junichi Masuda, the director of GAME FREAK inc. In it, they reveal some of the secrets behind the games and the new Pokémon. Following the interview, you can see some of the concept art for the new Pokémon that appear in these titles. Creating new Pokémon is a dream job many Pokémon fans imagine doing, but for the artists at GAME FREAK inc., that's their real job! Each Pokémon is drawn in multiple poses with amazing details. Take an exclusive peek at the concept artwork pieces to see where the Pokémon from *Pokémon Sun* and *Pokémon Moon* first became a new addition to the ever-expanding Pokémon world!

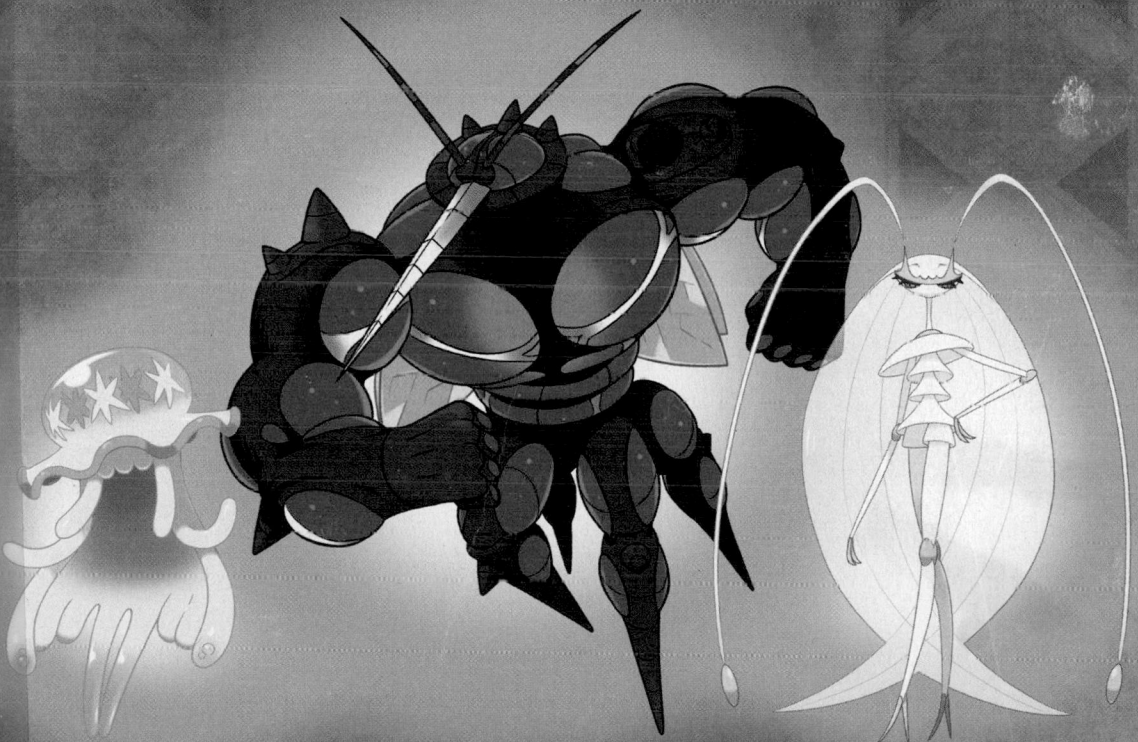

! CAUTION: Many details of the adventures that await you are discussed in these interviews and the design documents that follow. If you haven't completed the main story and you want to experience your adventures unspoiled, skip ahead to page 1 for now and come back to read this exclusive content after you've completed it all!

Pokémon Sun and *Pokémon Moon*
OFFICIAL CREATORS'
INTERVIEW

GAME FREAK

Pokémon Sun and *Pokémon Moon*
Producer

Junichi Masuda

Director of GAME FREAK inc.

Pokémon Sun and *Pokémon Moon*
Director

Shigeru Ohmori

General Manager
(Development Department 2)

In *Pokémon Sun* and *Pokémon Moon*, you can find the offices of the development company GAME FREAK in Akala Island's Heahea City. In the photo above, you get to see the actual face of the GAME FREAK inc. offices. And in the screenshot to the right, you can see GAME FREAK's offices as they appear in the world of the game. When you see how carefully they reproduced even the entrance to their office in the game, you can really appreciate the sense of fun you find at this company.

Interview conducted by Shusuke Motomiya (ONEUP, Inc.)

AS POKÉMON CELEBRATES 20 YEARS, THE ROLE OF DIRECTOR IS PASSED ON TO ANOTHER

So, Mr. Ohmori served as the director of *Pokémon Sun* and *Pokémon Moon*. He also served as the director of *Pokémon Omega Ruby* and *Pokémon Alpha Sapphire* (2014), but this was his first time serving as director on a completely new entry in the Pokémon series, wasn't it?

Masuda Yes. Up until now, I've been the one taking the role of director for any completely new titles. That means games like *Pokémon Black Version* and *Pokémon White Version* (2010), or *Pokémon X* and *Pokémon Y* (2013), to give a few recent examples. I've been in charge as the director of new titles for close to 20 years, but with 2016 being the 20th anniversary of Pokémon, it seemed like we had reached a turning point. It was the ideal timing to consider the future of Pokémon, and when I did so, I decided to entrust the directing of new titles in the Pokémon series to Ohmori here. *Pokémon Omega Ruby* and *Pokémon Alpha Sapphire* were also Ohmori's projects, and he worked hard to create good games and produced fine results.

THE THEME FOR DEVELOPMENT WAS "TRANSCENDENCE"

Mr. Ohmori, I'd love to hear about your reaction when you were first told that you would be the director of the new titles in the Pokémon series.

Ohmori To be honest, when I heard from Masuda that I'd continue on as the director of *Pokémon Sun* and *Pokémon Moon* after *Pokémon Omega Ruby* and *Pokémon Alpha Sapphire*, I had a lot of doubts. Creating new titles is a different beast than making games like *Pokémon Omega Ruby* and *Pokémon Alpha Sapphire*, where I already had a base to work from. But then I thought about what it meant to have the director's position change hands from Masuda to myself, and those feelings of unease changed to motivation to add some big changes to *Pokémon Sun* and *Pokémon Moon*. I made "transcendence" one of the themes of this project, and I started by questioning what Pokémon really is, so that I could try to rebuild the essential Pokémon experience from the ground up. A key example would be the Pokémon Gyms. I asked myself: are Pokémon Gyms really necessary? I reexamined the fundamental parts of playing a Pokémon game with questions like that. I was trying to rebuild Pokémon with my own hands, but I couldn't imagine everything that I would end up with when I remade Pokémon into what I wanted it to be. Of course, there were quite a lot of birth pangs that came along with the work of trying to rebuild Pokémon. I really tried to remake everything from the ground up, from the world building to the actual gameplay, and *Pokémon Sun* and *Pokémon Moon* became an extremely large project because of that.

Masuda When it comes to creating something completely new, there are always a huge number of decisions to be made. If you were to liken it to creating a new drink, for example, then new titles are like making a drink that doesn't even have a cup yet.

First, you have to decide the size of the cup and what it will look like. Then you go on to decide what you're going to pour into it: is it going to be orange juice or apple juice, or maybe even coffee? But take a game like *Pokémon Platinum Version*, which was already positioned as a sequel game. In that case, the cup you are going to use is already set, so all you have to decide is whether you want to swap orange juice in for coffee this time. The work is limited in scope. But for some of us, the development for *Pokémon Sun* and *Pokémon Moon* actually began back in the fall of 2013, as soon as *Pokémon X* and *Pokémon Y* were completed.

So the game had already progressed to a certain point, and then you added Mr. Ohmori into the mix as director. Did that create big changes in the game's content or how it is played?

Ohmori When I joined the *Pokémon Sun* and *Pokémon Moon* project, there had already been quite a bit of progress made. I gave a lot of careful consideration to how I could create a new Pokémon experience, while also taking that into account. Since I already had the materials that the other project members had created, I tried to mold them into something newer and even greater. I think that having to do that work is part of what has made *Pokémon Sun* and *Pokémon Moon* into such deep games.

Mr. Masuda, when you heard about Mr. Ohmori's desire to rebuild the very fundamentals that make up the core experience of the Pokémon series, what did you think?

Masuda Consider what Ohmori said about the existence of Pokémon Gyms. Whenever I was making new titles, I was always considering what I should change. Even if you got rid of Gyms, the players would still need some kind of goal to aim for. The conclusion that I came to was that if things aren't going to change in the essentials, then the usual pattern can already provide enough fun for the players. But in *Pokémon Sun* and *Pokémon Moon*, we had the idea that the player could battle against a Totem Pokémon instead of another Pokémon Trainer. Since that seemed like that could provide a lot of fun, I was all right with losing Gyms.

There are many other elements that were redesigned in these games, but can you give us an example of some that you really put particular energy into?

Ohmori The first would have to be the Pokédex. As the number of Pokémon increase, the hurdle of completing the Pokémon has grown too high. I really wanted to recreate the gameplay from the original *Pokémon Red* and *Pokémon Green* (1996), where you collected Pokémon and filled the Pokédex on your own. When I told the development team about those wishes, we ended up doing things like punching up the animations you see when you obtain a Pokémon for the first time, for example. When you evolved a Pokémon in the past, you didn't receive any message telling you that it had been registered in your Pokédex either, but with these titles, we made it so that you see the "REGISTERED!" screen when evolving Pokémon as well.

You also added animation for when you receive a Pokémon like Haunter in a trade and it evolves into Gengar, and both Haunter and Gengar are registered in the Pokédex. I really loved that touch the first time I saw it.

Ohmori Yes, we added that kind of scene because we wanted players to really experience the fun of collecting Pokémon once again, by making a system that really rewards them for their actions.

I was surprised by the addition of trials. That was a novel gameplay experience.

Ohmori The trials are one of those examples of how we really wanted to rebuild things. We made the trials as a result of wondering if we couldn't somehow express how Pokémon themselves can be threatening. These games are set in the Alola region, which is a place that is really rich in nature. We imagined that there could be these really powerful Pokémon that had come to live in the forests and mountains and other remote places, and we arrived at the idea that defeating such Pokémon in battle could become a goal for the player. I think that these trials, in which you have to defeat a powerful Pokémon called a Totem Pokémon, allowed us to introduce a new goal for players, in a different format than the old Gym battles.

AN ATMOSPHERE THAT MAKES YOU FEEL LIKE YOU REALLY ARE IN THE ALOLA REGION

Can you tell us what your keywords were when developing *Pokémon Sun* and *Pokémon Moon*?

Ohmori "Expressiveness"' and "atmosphere." By making the main characters' proportions closer to reality, I wanted players to be able to believe that the character they see in the game really is them and feel closer to the protagonists. And I wanted

to reduce the distance between the player and their Pokémon. Your Pokémon are your allies that travel around the islands together with you on your island challenge, and they respond to you in lively ways. With details like this, we can create the illusion that you really have gone to the Alola region yourself. Having players really feel that atmosphere for themselves was my number one goal in *Pokémon Sun* and *Pokémon Moon*.

What kind of meaning is included in the titles of *Pokémon Sun* and *Pokémon Moon*?

Ohmori The Earth orbits around the sun, and our moon orbits around Earth. Yet when seen from Earth, both the sun and the moon pass across the sky as though they share the same trajectory. But when you just change your point of view, you come to see that their orbits are completely different. The Earth and the sun and the moon—they all pull on each other and exert an influence on one another, and it is within this relationship that life has developed. In the same way, each one of us humans form relationships with and interact with various other people. You will exert an influence on someone, and you will be influenced in turn by someone else, and you are able to exist right there within this practically miraculous balance. In these titles, I wanted to express the brilliance of life and the relationships between people and Pokémon as they influence one another, and so I selected the names of the sun and the moon—which exert so much influence upon our Earth—for the titles of the games.

The way that time itself is separated by 12 hours between *Pokémon Sun* and *Pokémon Moon* is a vivid reminder of the relationship between the sun and the moon.

Ohmori That's right. There is the image that *Pokémon Sun* takes place during the day, while *Pokémon Moon* takes place at night. The origin of this idea came when I was traveling overseas with Masuda and experienced such time differences for myself. I really loved the idea of adding a time difference between two versions of a game, and I thought it would be a lot of fun. Then we decided that the setting of *Pokémon Sun* and *Pokémon Moon* would be inspired by the Hawaiian Islands, and I thought we could use the idea. So we tried fitting that idea into *Pokémon Sun* and *Pokémon Moon*, and we ended up with Yungoos being active during the day and Rattata's Alola Form being active at night. Even though you are in the same location, each player will meet different Pokémon. That makes the experience more fun, and offers a new way to play as you try to make up for all those differences for yourself. That kind of thinking is why we added the time difference to *Pokémon Sun* and *Pokémon Moon*.

Can you tell us about why you chose the Hawaiian Islands as the inspiration for the setting for these titles?

Ohmori There were a lot of things that I wanted to realize

> **"IT WAS THE IDEAL TIMING TO CONSIDER THE FUTURE OF POKÉMON, AND WHEN I DID SO, I DECIDED TO ENTRUST THE DIRECTING OF NEW TITLES IN THE POKÉMON SERIES TO OHMORI HERE."**
>
> –Junichi Masuda

"IN THESE TITLES, I WANTED TO EXPRESS THE BRILLIANCE OF LIFE AND THE RELATIONSHIPS BETWEEN PEOPLE AND POKÉMON AS THEY INFLUENCE ONE ANOTHER..."

—Shigeru Ohmori

with *Pokémon Sun* and *Pokémon Moon*, and one of those was the brilliance of life itself and that feeling of a pulsing, lively world. When you think of Hawaii, you may think of the beautiful beaches, but the islands also have a hugely diverse environment, including volcanoes and cold reaches and more. The fact that Hawaii is made up of a group of islands also helped the decision. Being able to enjoy adventures that differed from one island to another—with the excitement of moving from one island to the next, and the new encounters you can have on each island—was something we hadn't had in the regions that had been the setting of our past titles. So we thought it would convey an entirely new sense of fun.

Masuda You know, I once got the chance to experience flying around the island of Hawai'i in a helicopter. The scenery that I looked down upon from that helicopter window was not just a sea of green—there were lots of rocky areas and plenty of waterfalls, too. The energy that you find in the seas and land and creatures living in the Hawaiian Islands seemed like a great fit for the idea of "life" that is so pivotal to Pokémon, and that's why I agreed to using the islands as the inspiration for this setting.

When I hear you describing the Hawaiian Islands as a land full of energy, I can't help but think of the Hoenn region, which was the setting of *Pokémon Ruby* and *Pokémon Sapphire* (2002), as well as other games. What would you say are some of the defining characteristics of the Hoenn region versus the Alola region?

Masuda When I think of the Hoenn region, I think of the richness of the people and of a place where you can feel lush greenery surrounding you. For me, the Alola region has an image of each island giving off a powerful energy.

In *Pokémon Sun* and *Pokémon Moon*, the protagonist appears on the battle screen beside his or her Pokémon. It lets you feel like you really are battling right alongside your Pokémon. I was really impressed by seeing scenes like that.

Masuda It's taken us a long time to get to this point: the point at which we were able to create a screen where you see the protagonist and his or her Pokémon battling together. It began with *Pokémon X* and *Pokémon Y*. *Pokémon X* and *Pokémon Y* was a grandiose project, in which we had to create 3D models for the more than 700 Pokémon that already existed at that point. If we hadn't been successful, we never would have been able to create the battle screens you see in *Pokémon Sun* and *Pokémon Moon*. Then in *Pokémon Omega Ruby* and *Pokémon Alpha Sapphire*, we learned even more about expressing Pokémon in 3D and making them move. Even with all that, though, we still had a real challenge with creating a battle screen where you could see the protagonist and Pokémon together in these titles. That was because we had to completely remake the battle animation system we had used in *Pokémon X* and *Pokémon Y*. And that is why *Pokémon Sun* and *Pokémon Moon* can't communicate with *Pokémon X*, *Pokémon Y*, *Pokémon Omega Ruby*, or *Pokémon Alpha Sapphire*, even though they are all Nintendo 3DS titles.

You could say that this is the ultimate game for the Nintendo 3DS system, which really stretches its capabilities to the limit.

Masuda We had to decide: would we preserve compatibility between the games, and limit the graphics to the quality of our past titles? Or would we abandon cross-compatibility to create higher-quality graphics? It was a difficult decision. But since it had become possible to bring Pokémon with you to new titles, thanks to the Nintendo 3DS downloadable software *Pokémon Bank*, we committed to challenging ourselves to reach new levels of visual expression with these titles.

I was really surprised the first time I saw a regional variant. Where did that idea come from?

Ohmori The original idea came from the Galapagos Islands. These Pokémon have been separated from the mainland for many long years and changed to gain new forms. But for the people of Alola, the Alolan Rattata is completely normal, and maybe they've never even seen the Rattata that appear in other regions. We mentioned before the energy of the land, and it's the same sort of thing. Through the power of this land, even the Pokémon have taken on new forms that they don't have in other regions. We wanted to express the wonder of that to all of our players.

What were the standards you used for choosing which Pokémon would have new forms unique to the Alola region?

Ohmori The first regional variant that our graphic designers came up with was the Alolan Exeggutor. When I saw it, I felt it was a really great design. And that was the basis we used to create new designs for some of the Pokémon that so many

people have long loved since the days of *Pokémon Red* and *Pokémon Green*, so that they would be suited to the environment of the Alola region.

THE EMOTIONS EXPRESSED BY THE SUN AND THE MOON, AND LILLIE'S TALE OF PERSONAL GROWTH

The story of Lillie's growth really touched me deeply. Mr. Ohmori, what is it that you wanted to put into Lillie's character?

Ohmori What I really wanted to express through the story of *Pokémon Sun* and *Pokémon Moon* was how the various people we encounter really help us grow as individuals. That, and the way that your smile can inspire smiles in the people all around you. These two messages are what lie at the heart of the story. At the beginning of the story, Lillie is depicted as quite reticent, and you don't really understand what she is thinking. But as she goes along with the protagonist on their island challenge, Lillie is influenced a lot. You see her really begin to shine as this desire to try her hardest takes root within her. Seeing the protagonist's smiling face inspires Lillie to smile, and Lillie's smile brings a smile to the protagonist in turn. When the sun shines, so too does the moon. I wanted to show how all of the characters are full of light and glow with happiness.

So even Lillie's story of personal growth includes those elements of the sun and the moon!

Ohmori Yes. At the beginning of the story, Lillie takes on the characteristics of the moon, while Hau fits the image of the sun. But as the story progresses, those relationships slowly change. Lillie moves away from being the moon, and becomes the sun, shining with light.

Mr. Ohmori, you've designed a lot of the maps for the Pokémon series in the past. I'd be interested to think of what you wanted for the map of the Alola region.

Ohmori I was in charge of map design ever since I began working on the Pokémon series with *Pokémon Ruby* and *Pokémon Sapphire*, so I have a very deep appreciation for how important the map is to the game. By increasing the proportions of the main character in these titles, we became able to express things with more realism than before. But does that mean that you should aim for photorealism? We thought not. In the Pokémon series, the way that you play in the field has always been very important. In *Pokémon Sun* and *Pokémon Moon*, you still find the same collection of symbols as in past titles. As the protagonist travels down a route, you will see Pokémon Trainers you have to fight, and you will find items that have been dropped along the path, and the way you need to go will still be clearly marked. When it came to making the maps, we really tested every little detail to see how we could create a new expressiveness without losing the key gameplay experience that is central to the Pokémon series. Because of that, we spent an extraordinary time completing the maps for those four islands and one manmade island. It was a real headache. (Laughs.)

Z-MOVES: SO THAT EVERY POKÉMON CAN HAVE THE CHANCE TO SHINE

What did you want to express with Z-Moves?

Ohmori Every species of Pokémon has its own particular charms, so we thought we needed a feature that would make players think that they wanted to try battling together with them all. We wanted to make a system that would let any species of Pokémon contribute greatly to battle, depending on your strategy, and that was where the idea of Z-Moves first came from.

The debut of the Ultra Beasts was also quite shocking! What inspired their appearance?

Ohmori The idea first came from invasive species, which just keep increasing—even in the Hawaiian Islands. These invasive species cause a situation in which the animals that originally

lived in an area decrease in number. When I read about this phenomena, I wondered if we couldn't express invasive species in the Pokémon world as well, and the idea we came up with was the Ultra Beasts. But the truth is that the Ultra Beasts really are just Pokémon, too. (Laughs.) In these titles, we depict the existence of different worlds, and we created the beasts by imagining what kind of form Pokémon would take in different worlds. Normally, whenever we create a new Pokémon, we have a clear standard for "Pokémon-ness," but we really tried to take a big risk with our graphic designers to exceed the limits of what a Pokémon can be when it came to the beasts.

Mr. Masuda, when it came to your role as the producer of Pokémon Sun and Pokémon Moon, where did you find yourself making requests for how you wanted something to be?

Masuda The Rotom Dex. We had the idea, but really making it come to life was quite a process. But I was confident that we could make it into something really fun. You know that the Rotom Dex responds when you tap on the lower screen of your Nintendo 3DS system, right? That is because you can feel the joy of being together and experience an even greater feeling of adventuring together with Pokémon when it responds in a cute way.

It sounds like you were quite significantly involved in the overall game balance as well, Mr. Masuda. What area would you say you poured the most of your energy into?

Masuda The tempo of the gameplay. If there was something that was taking up time, I would work with the programmers to try to shave off even a frame or two. If it was hard to resolve the issue, then we would be sure to talk through the whole thing.

I remember you once mentioning, Mr. Masuda, that time is very important to you.

Masuda Pokémon is a game that you spend a lot of time playing. Even if it's just a tenth of a second, when you add that up over and over, you might waste more than an hour of your time, right? If you do that as a developer, then you've just wasted an hour of your players' precious time, so I take it very seriously. That's why I worked on adjusting things like the fade-in and fade-out you see when moving between screens, or the timing for going into and out of houses. All while saying to my staff, "Sorry, just let me handle this." (Laughs.)

Your care for the play experience is amazing, Mr. Masuda. And the user interface (UI) design that players interact with was also redesigned with these titles, wasn't it? Basically, the game is just plain easier to play.

Ohmori The redesign of the UI was something that we had been thinking about since development of these titles began. The location of the buttons had been carried over since the

Nintendo DS system days, but now we live in an age where everyone is accustomed to using smart phones and tablets with great UI design. We aimed to create a UI that could compare to such devices. One typical example would be the new feature that lets you throw a Poké Ball just by hitting the Y Button.

THE GAMES THAT COULD BECOME THE FOUNDATION OF THE FUTURE OF POKÉMON

When you consider Pokémon Sun and Pokémon Moon in relation to all of the Pokémon games that came before it, and all those that will come in the future, how do you think it will be positioned?

Ohmori There is a lot of new experimentation in these titles, so I think it may end up as a rather unique set of games. Among these new things we tried out, some may carry on and link to future titles, and some might change based on the reactions of our players. Or It might possibly become the basis of the next generation of the Pokémon series. The various challenges that we took on for these titles, and how they are received by fans, will have an effect on how we make our games in the future, so I think I can say that these games will play an important role in the Pokémon series.

Masuda I think that these titles have the greatest sense of drama within the Pokémon series. Like Ohmori said, these are games that try to rebuild what Pokémon is, and I think that the staff worked and suffered a lot to try to recreate everything from the ground up. I just want them all to know how much I appreciate how hard they worked.

The update to Pokémon Bank will link together the entire Pokémon series. As one of the original developers involved in Pokémon Red and Pokémon Green, how significant is that achievement for you, Mr. Masuda?

Masuda As you know, Pokémon Red, Pokémon Green, Pokémon Blue, and Pokémon Yellow: Special Pikachu Edition were all released for the Virtual Console at the beginning of 2016. I was actually the one who first proposed the idea. As for why I wanted to re-release the games on Virtual Console, it was precisely because we have Pokémon Bank and would be able to move Pokémon from Pokémon Red, Pokémon Green, Pokémon Blue, and Pokémon Yellow: Special Pikachu Edition to Pokémon Sun and Pokémon Moon. We have always placed importance on the ability to move Pokémon from previous generations to the newest generations of the Pokémon series, but we failed to make it possible to bring Pokémon from the Game Boy titles, so I thought that I really wanted to achieve that at last. I can't think of anything that would make me happier than to have players enjoy playing both Pokémon Red, Pokémon Green, Pokémon Blue, or Pokémon Yellow: Special Pikachu Edition on the Virtual Console and the newest titles, Pokémon Sun and Pokémon Moon.

> "EVEN IF IT'S JUST A TENTH OF A SECOND, WHEN YOU ADD THAT UP OVER AND OVER, YOU MIGHT WASTE MORE THAN AN HOUR OF YOUR TIME, RIGHT? IF YOU DO THAT AS A DEVELOPER, THEN YOU'VE JUST WASTED AN HOUR OF YOUR PLAYERS' PRECIOUS TIME, SO I TAKE IT VERY SERIOUSLY."
>
> –Junichi Masuda

ROWLET

1. Fluffs itself up when it's cold, when sleeping, or at other times **2.** Photosynthesis provides supplemental energy, but doesn't fill its tummy **3.** Got hit **4.** A silent leaf cutter that flies without making a noise—made up of a leaf blade and a feather **5.** Leaf pattern on its chest (these leaves aren't removable) **6.** What should we do? **7.** Rotates its head (nearly) 180 degrees to look behind itself

LITTEN

1. This is about the degree of its usual smile **2.** When it's really quite pleased **3.** Underside of foot **4.** Fiery fur ball **5.** Cleans its face **6.** (Can make hair balls)

 **POPPLIO**

1. It can run 2. Sniffle 3. Smiling 4. Ta-da! 5. It can stand upright

 **MIMIKYU**

1. When attacking 2. Wood 3. After taking damage 4. Expression never changes 5. From below 6. Tail, neck, and ears are not steady and wobble around a bit 7. Slithers along the ground 8. Jumps

ALOLAN RAICHU

1. Rides atop its tail as it floats 2. Side view 3. Ear 4. Head-on 5. Ear hole (only on the front side) 6. Sits on tail when sleeping, walking, or running, but it stands up on its tail during battle and flies about as though surfing 7. Volt Tackle 8. Able to control electricity with its psychic powers

ALOLAN EXEGGUTOR

1. Hu-yuk! 2. Just the middle head has changed from the normal form 3. Normal 4. Alola 5. Heads sway 6. It's actually set into the trunk a bit 7. Head can't be seen on the screen 8. Leaves and head are all three connected at the same point 9. Ten segments 10. Took damage 11. Eyes closed

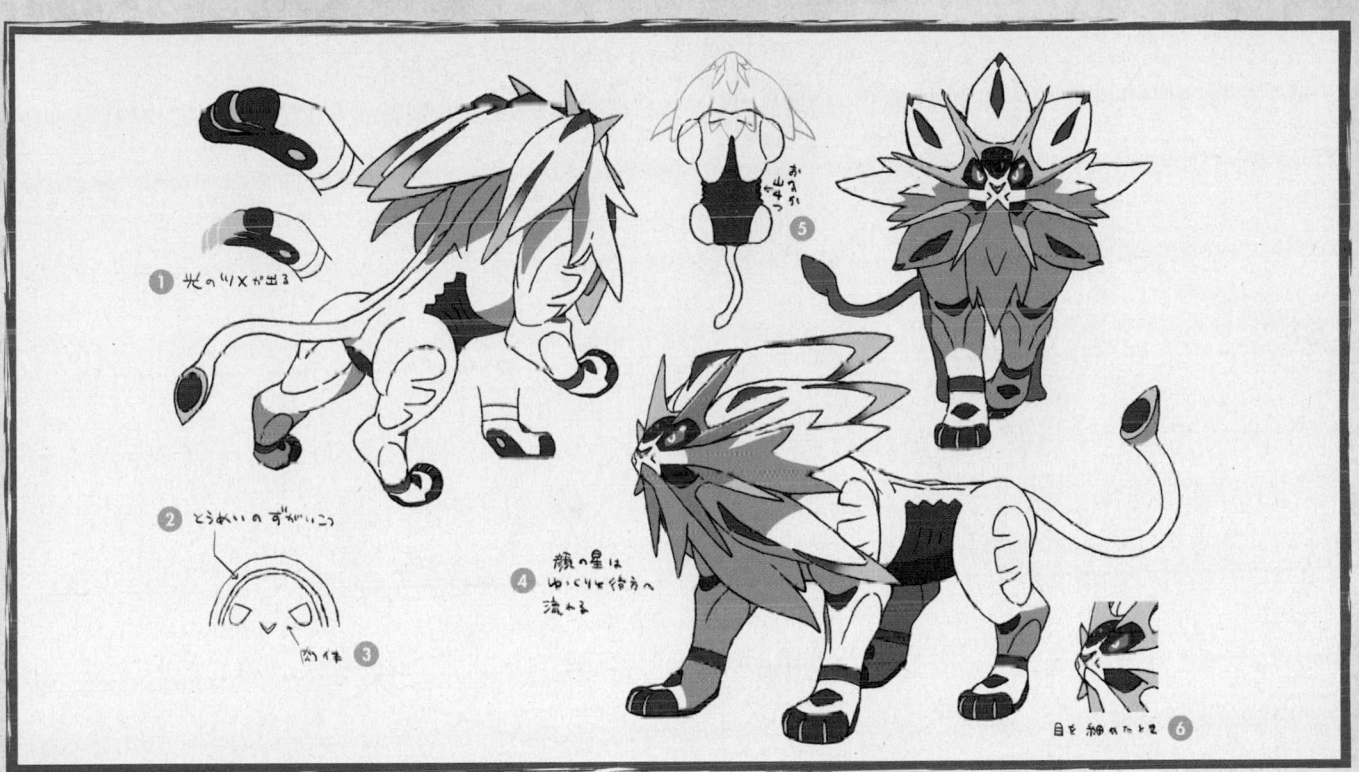

 SOLGALEO

1. Claws of light come out **2.** Transparent skull **3.** Flesh **4.** Stars in its face slowly streak backward **5.** Four ridges on stomach **6.** Eyes narrowed

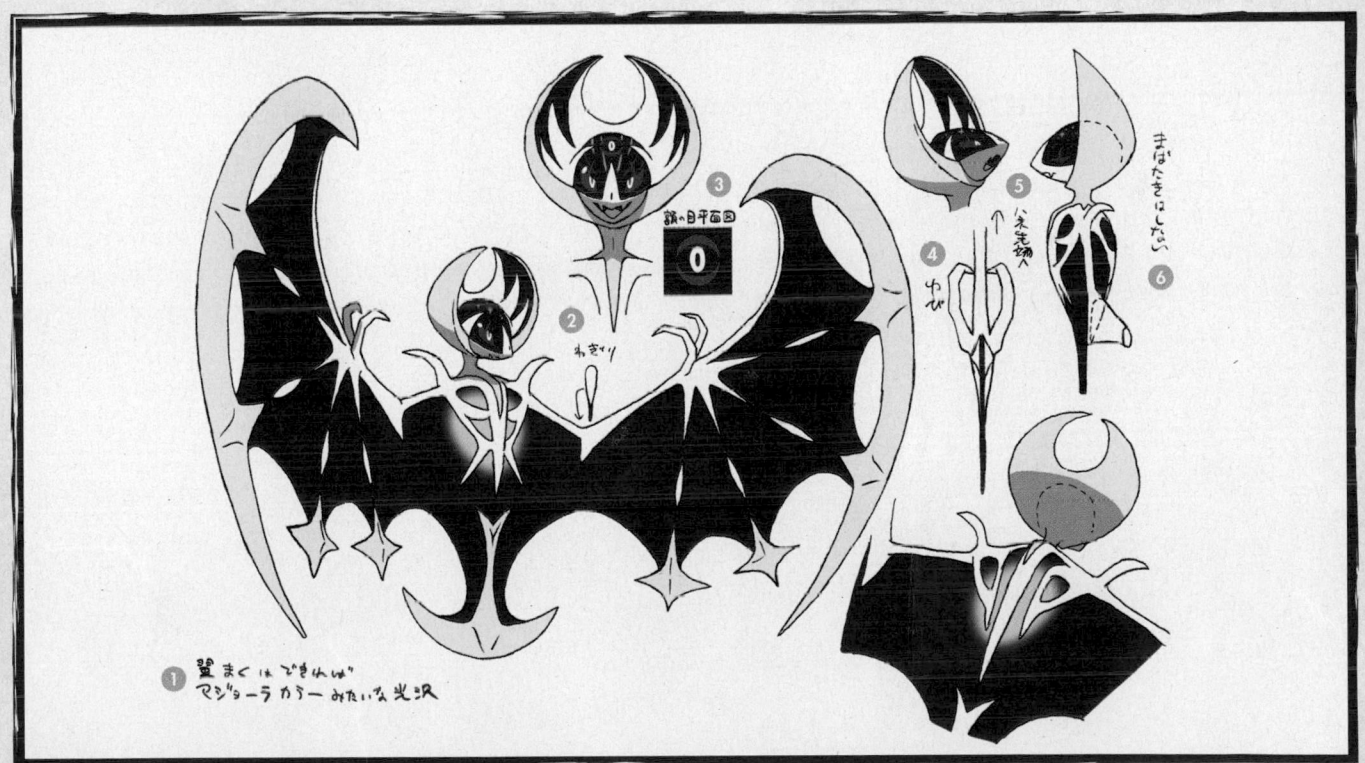

LUNALA

1. If possible, wings should have a sheen like color-shifting paint **2.** Cross section **3.** Flattened image of third eye **4.** Fingers **5.** Toward wing tip **6.** Does not blink

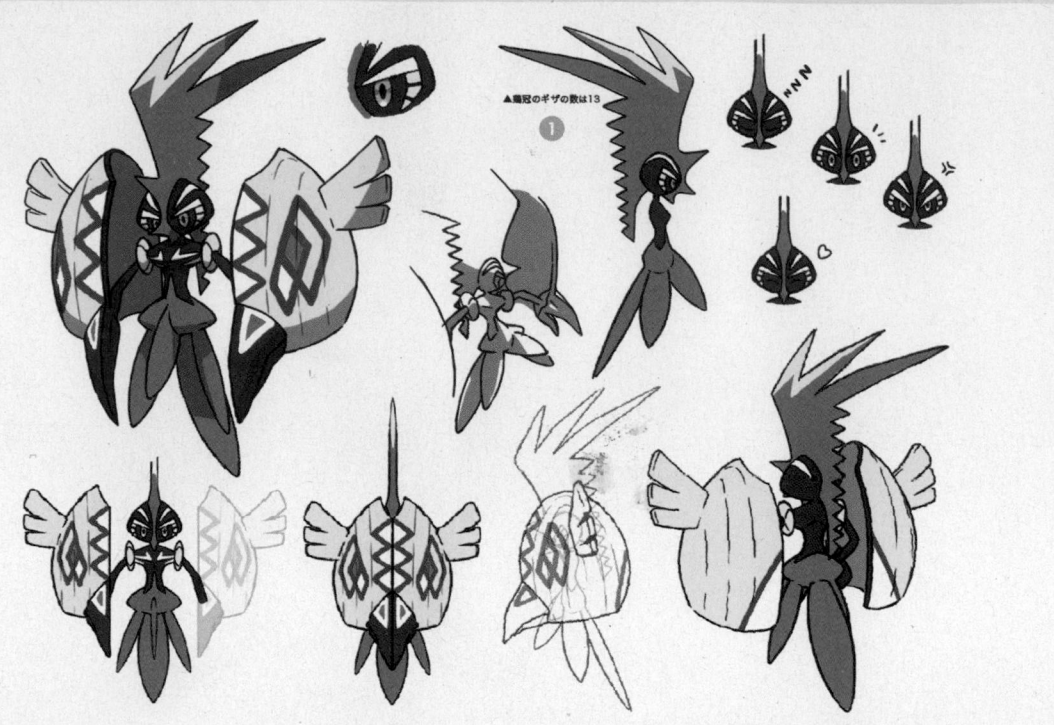

TAPU KOKO

1. Cockscomb has 13 spikes

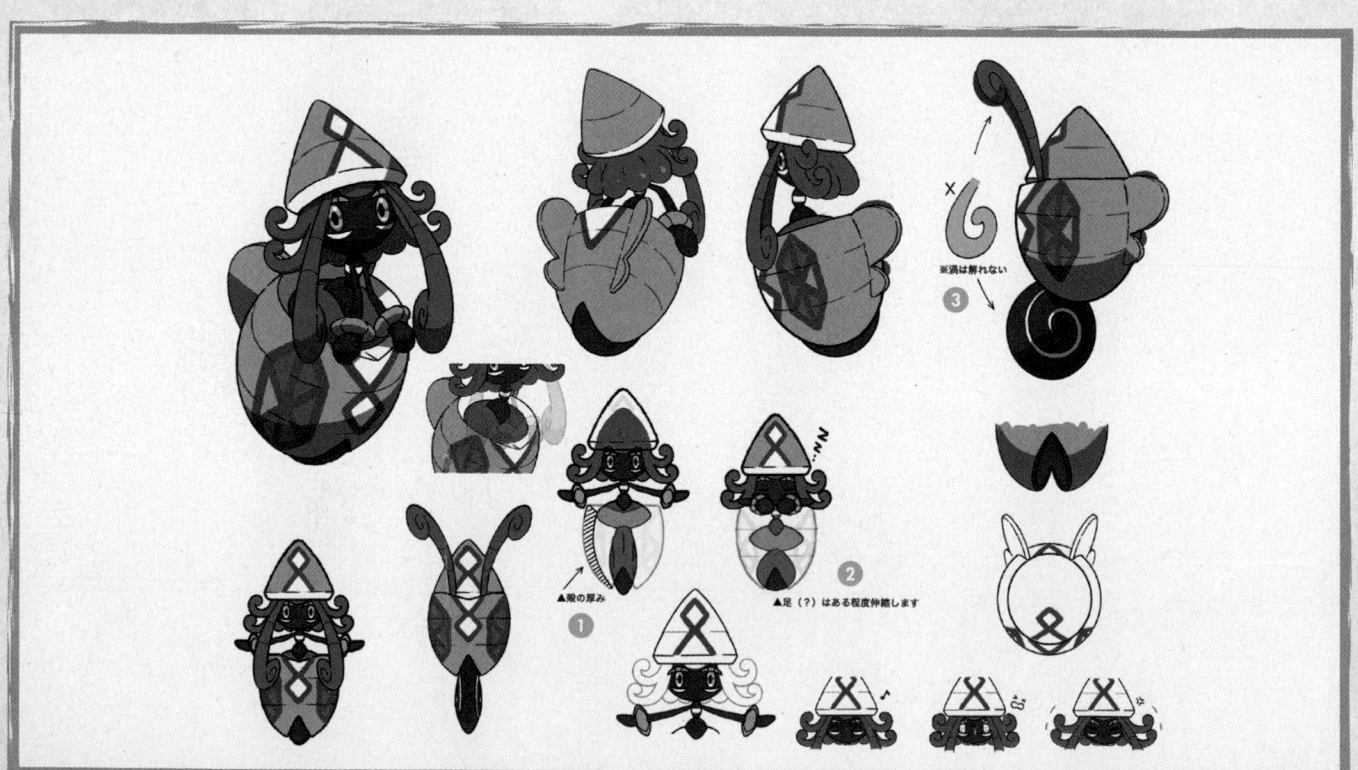

TAPU LELE

1. Thickness of shell 2. Legs (?) can expand and contract somewhat 3. The spiral stays wrapped up tight

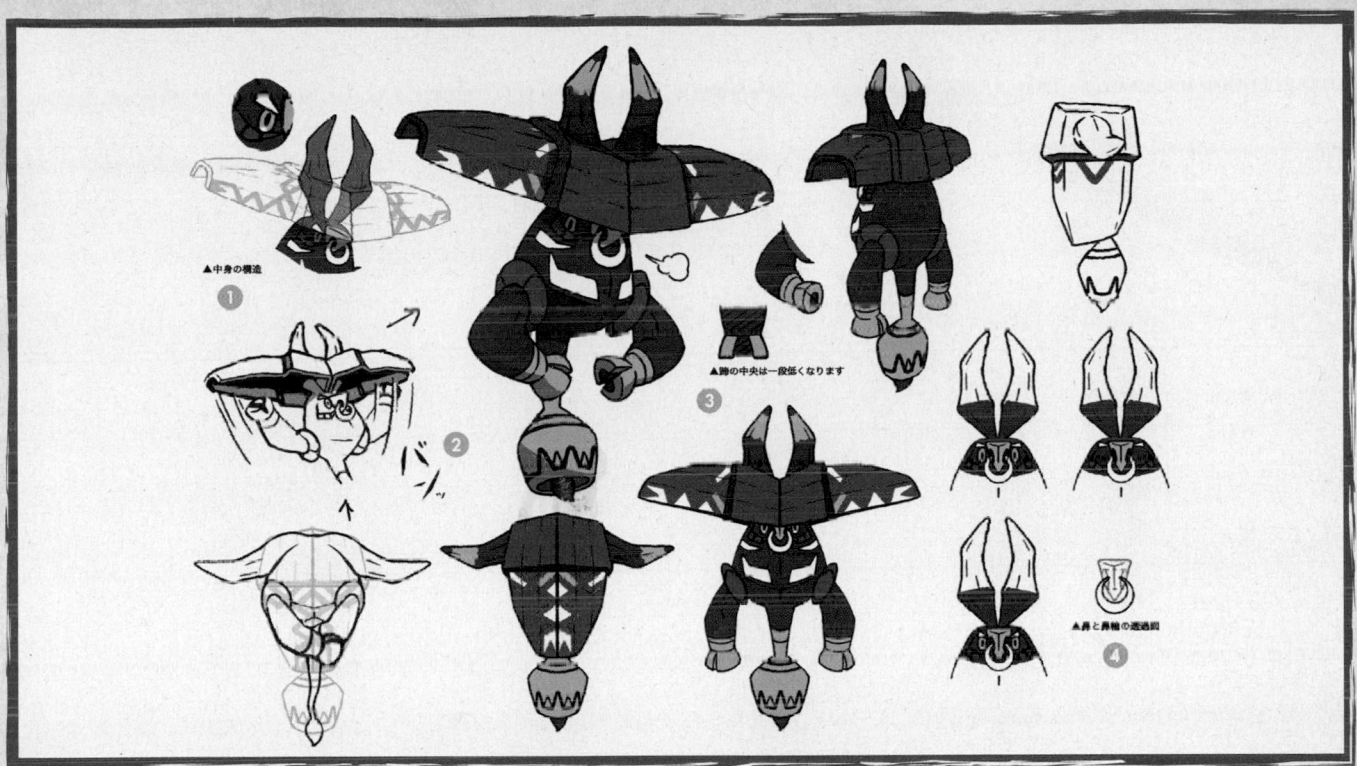

 TAPU BULU

1. Construction of the inside 2. Bam! 3. Center of the hooves is recessed a bit 4. Transparent view of nose and nose ring

 TAPU FINI

Pokémon Sun / Pokémon Moon

The Official Alola Region Pokédex & Postgame Adventure Guide

Table of Contents

Pokédex Article Index

Alola Region Pokédex Checklist

All of the Pokémon in the Alola Pokédex are listed below in Pokédex order. If you are looking for one Pokémon in particular that you already know the name of, you may want to check out the Alphabetical List of Alola Pokémon on page 4. Note that regional variants are listed by their species name—in other words, you will find the Alola Form of Raichu by looking for Raichu in these lists, not Alolan Raichu.

Key to Checklist

This checklist tells you which page to turn to if you want to find the Pokédex entry for a particular species of Pokémon, but that is not all. It also provides you with a quick reference to the ways that each Pokémon can be obtained.

Appears in the wild (IN THE WILD)

This Pokémon can be encountered through regular battles in the wild, triggered in locations like patches of tall grass or on the water surface, or through an ambush like the shadows that are sometimes cast from Pokémon flying overhead.

Only appears in SOS Battles in the wild (SOS BATTLE)

This Pokémon only ever appears in the wild if it is called on as an ally in an SOS Battle. SOS Battles are triggered when a wild Pokémon feels threatened and calls for help. Read more about them on pages 224–225.

Can be hatched from an Egg (HATCHED)

This Pokémon can be hatched from an Egg found at the Pokémon Nursery. Read more about Pokémon Eggs on pages 238–240.

Can be evolved from another Pokémon (EVOLVED)

This Pokémon is part of an evolutionary chain and it can be obtained through Evolution if you have caught the species that it evolves from.

Obtainable through an event (EVENT)

This Pokémon can be obtained through a special event, such as receiving it from someone in the game, completing some special mission, or receiving it as a special gift from The Pokémon Company.

Version Exclusive (EXCLUSIVE)

This Pokémon only appears in either *Pokémon Sun* ☀ or *Pokémon Moon* 🌙. If you are not playing the version of the game that it appears in, you will need to obtain it through a trade. Learn more about trading Pokémon with other players on pages 245–246.

ALOLA POKÉDEX NO.	POKÉMON SPECIES		IN THE WILD	SOS BATTLE	HATCHED	EVOLVED	EVENT	EXCLUSIVE
001	Rowlet	p. 12–13	—	—	•	—	•	—
002	Dartrix	p. 12–13	—	—	—	•	•	—
003	Decidueye	p. 12–13	—	—	—	•	•	—
004	Litten	p. 14–15	—	—	•	—	•	—
005	Torracat	p. 14–15	—	—	—	•	•	—
006	Incineroar	p. 14–15	—	—	—	•	•	—
007	Popplio	p. 16–17	—	—	•	—	•	—
008	Brionne	p. 16–17	—	—	—	•	•	—
009	Primarina	p. 16–17	—	—	—	•	•	—
010	Pikipek	p. 18–19	•	—	—	—	—	—
011	Trumbeak	p. 18–19	•	—	—	•	—	—
012	Toucannon	p. 18–19	•	—	—	•	—	—
013	Yungoos	p. 20	•	—	—	—	—	—
014	Gumshoos	p. 20	•	—	—	•	—	—
015	Rattata	p. 21	•	—	—	—	—	—
016	Raticate	p. 21	•	—	—	•	—	—
017	Caterpie	p. 22–23	•	—	•	—	—	—
018	Metapod	p. 22–23	•	—	—	•	—	—
019	Butterfree	p. 22–23	—	—	—	•	—	—
020	Ledyba	p. 24	•	—	•	—	—	—
021	Ledian	p. 24	•	—	—	•	—	—
022	Spinarak	p. 25	•	—	•	—	—	—
023	Ariados	p. 25	•	—	—	•	—	—
024	Pichu	p. 26–27	—	—	•	—	—	—
025	Pikachu	p. 26–27	•	—	•	•	—	—
026	Raichu	p. 26–27	—	—	—	•	—	—
027	Grubbin	p. 28–29	•	—	—	—	—	—
028	Charjabug	p. 28–29	•	—	—	•	—	—
029	Vikavolt	p. 28–29	•	—	—	•	—	—
030	Bonsly	p. 30	—	—	•	—	—	—

ALOLA POKÉDEX NO.	POKÉMON SPECIES		IN THE WILD	SOS BATTLE	HATCHED	EVOLVED	EVENT	EXCLUSIVE
031	Sudowoodo	p. 30	—	•	—	•	—	—
032	Happiny	p. 32–33	—	•	—	—	•	—
033	Chansey	p. 32–33	—	•	—	•	—	—
034	Blissey	p. 32–33	—	—	—	•	—	—
035	Munchlax	p. 34	•	—	•	—	—	—
036	Snorlax	p. 34	•	•	—	•	—	—
037	Slowpoke	p. 36–37	•	—	•	—	—	—
038	Slowbro	p. 36–37	•	—	—	•	—	—
039	Slowking	p. 36–37	—	—	—	•	—	—
040	Wingull	p. 38	•	—	—	—	—	—
041	Pelipper	p. 38	•	—	—	•	—	—
042	Abra	p. 40–41	•	—	—	—	—	—
043	Kadabra	p. 40–41	•	—	—	•	—	—
044	Alakazam	p. 40–41	—	—	—	•	—	—
045	Meowth	p. 42	•	—	•	—	—	—
046	Persian	p. 42	•	—	—	•	—	—
047	Magnemite	p. 44–45	•	—	—	—	—	—
048	Magneton	p. 44–45	•	—	—	•	—	—
049	Magnezone	p. 44–45	—	—	—	•	—	—
050	Grimer	p. 46	•	—	—	—	—	—
051	Muk	p. 46	—	—	—	•	•	—
052	Growlithe	p. 47	•	—	—	—	—	—
053	Arcanine	p. 47	•	—	—	•	—	—
054	Drowzee	p. 48	•	—	—	—	—	—
055	Hypno	p. 48	•	—	—	•	—	—
056	Makuhita	p. 49	•	—	—	—	—	—
057	Hariyama	p. 49	•	—	—	•	—	—
058	Smeargle	p. 50	•	—	—	—	—	—
059	Crabrawler	p. 51	•	—	—	—	—	—
060	Crabominable	p. 51	•	—	—	•	—	—
061	Gastly	p. 52–53	•	—	—	—	—	—
062	Haunter	p. 52–53	•	—	—	•	—	—
063	Gengar	p. 52–53	—	—	—	•	—	—
064	Drifloon	p. 54	•	—	—	—	—	—
065	Drifblim	p. 54	•	—	—	•	—	—

ALOLA POKÉDEX NO.	POKÉMON SPECIES		IN THE WILD	SOS BATTLE	HATCHED	EVOLVED	EVENT	EXCLUSIVE
066	Misdreavus	p. 55	•	—	•	—	—	—
067	Mismagius	p. 55	—	—	—	•	—	—
068	Zubat	p. 56–57	•	—	—	—	—	—
069	Golbat	p. 56–57	•	—	—	•	—	—
070	Crobat	p. 56–57	—	•	—	•	—	—
071	Diglett	p. 58	•	—	—	—	—	—
072	Dugtrio	p. 58	•	—	—	•	—	—
073	Spearow	p. 59	•	—	—	—	—	—
074	Fearow	p. 59	•	—	—	•	—	—
075	Rufflet	p. 60	•	—	—	—	—	☀
076	Braviary	p. 60	•	—	—	•	—	☀
077	Vullaby	p. 61	•	—	—	—	—	🌙
078	Mandibuzz	p. 61	•	—	—	•	—	🌙
079	Mankey	p. 62	•	—	—	—	—	—
080	Primeape	p. 62	•	—	—	•	—	—
081	Delibird	p. 63	•	—	—	—	—	—
082	Oricorio	p. 64–65	•	—	—	—	—	—
083	Cutiefly	p. 66	•	—	—	—	—	—
084	Ribombee	p. 66	•	—	—	•	—	—
085	Petilil	p. 67	•	—	—	—	—	🌙
086	Lilligant	p. 67	—	—	—	•	—	🌙
087	Cottonee	p. 68	•	—	—	—	—	☀
088	Whimsicott	p. 68	—	—	—	•	—	☀
089	Psyduck	p. 69	•	—	—	—	—	—
090	Golduck	p. 69	•	—	—	•	—	—
091	Magikarp	p. 70	•	—	—	—	—	—
092	Gyarados	p. 70	—	—	•	•	—	—
093	Barboach	p. 71	•	—	—	—	—	—
094	Whiscash	p. 71	•	—	—	•	—	—
095	Machop	p. 72–73	•	—	—	—	—	—
096	Machoke	p. 72–73	•	—	—	•	—	—
097	Machamp	p. 72–73	—	—	—	•	—	—
098	Roggenrola	p. 74–75	•	—	—	—	—	—
099	Boldore	p. 74–75	•	—	—	•	—	—
100	Gigalith	p. 74–75	—	—	—	•	—	—

101	Carbink	p. 76
102	Sableye	p. 76
103	Rockruff	p. 78–79
104	Lycanroc	p. 78–79
105	Spinda	p. 80
106	Tentacool	p. 81
107	Tentacruel	p. 81
108	Finneon	p. 82
109	Lumineon	p. 82
110	Wishiwashi	p. 83
111	Luvdisc	p. 84
112	Corsola	p. 84
113	Mareanie	p. 85
114	Toxapex	p. 85
115	Shellder	p. 86
116	Cloyster	p. 86
117	Bagon	p. 88–89
118	Shelgon	p. 88–89
119	Salamence	p. 88–89
120	Lillipup	p. 90–91
121	Herdier	p. 90–91
122	Stoutland	p. 90–91
123	Eevee	p. 92
124	Vaporeon	p. 93
125	Jolteon	p. 93
126	Flareon	p. 94
127	Espeon	p. 94
128	Umbreon	p. 95
129	Leafeon	p. 95
130	Glaceon	p. 96
131	Sylveon	p. 96
132	Mudbray	p. 97
133	Mudsdale	p. 97
134	Igglybuff	p. 98–99
135	Jigglypuff	p. 98–99
136	Wigglytuff	p. 98–99
137	Tauros	p. 100
138	Miltank	p. 100
139	Surskit	p. 101
140	Masquerain	p. 101
141	Dewpider	p. 102
142	Araquanid	p. 102
143	Fomantis	p. 103
144	Lurantis	p. 103
145	Morelull	p. 104
146	Shiinotic	p. 104
147	Paras	p. 105
148	Parasect	p. 105
149	Poliwag	p. 106
150	Poliwhirl	p. 106
151	Poliwrath	p. 107
152	Politoed	p. 107
153	Goldeen	p. 108
154	Seaking	p. 108
155	Feebas	p. 109
156	Milotic	p. 109
157	Alomomola	p. 110
158	Fletchling	p. 112–113
159	Fletchinder	p. 112–113
160	Talonflame	p. 112–113
161	Salandit	p. 114
162	Salazzle	p. 114
163	Cubone	p. 115
164	Marowak	p. 115
165	Kangaskhan	p. 116
166	Magby	p. 118–119
167	Magmar	p. 118–119
168	Magmortar	p. 118–119
169	Stufful	p. 120
170	Bewear	p. 120
171	Bounsweet	p. 122–123
172	Steenee	p. 122–123
173	Tsareena	p. 122–123
174	Comfey	p. 124
175	Pinsir	p. 124
176	Oranguru	p. 125
177	Passimian	p. 125
178	Goomy	p. 126–127
179	Sliggoo	p. 126–127
180	Goodra	p. 126–127
181	Castform	p. 128
182	Wimpod	p. 129
183	Golisopod	p. 129
184	Staryu	p. 130
185	Starmie	p. 130
186	Sandygast	p. 131
187	Palossand	p. 131
188	Cranidos	p. 132
189	Rampardos	p. 132
190	Shieldon	p. 133
191	Bastiodon	p. 133
192	Archen	p. 134
193	Archeops	p. 134
194	Tirtouga	p. 135
195	Carracosta	p. 135
196	Phantump	p. 136
197	Trevenant	p. 136
198	Nosepass	p. 137
199	Probopass	p. 137
200	Pyukumuku	p. 138
201	Chinchou	p. 139
202	Lanturn	p. 139
203	Type: Null	p. 140
204	Silvally	p. 141
205	Zygarde	p. 142–143
206	Trubbish	p. 144
207	Garbodor	p. 144
208	Skarmory	p. 145
209	Ditto	p. 145
210	Cleffa	p. 146–147
211	Clefairy	p. 146–147
212	Clefable	p. 146–147
213	Minior	p. 148
214	Beldum	p. 150–151
215	Metang	p. 150–151
216	Metagross	p. 150–151
217	Porygon	p. 152–153
218	Porygon2	p. 152–153
219	Porygon-Z	p. 152–153
220	Pancham	p. 155
221	Pangoro	p. 155
222	Komala	p. 156
223	Torkoal	p. 156
224	Turtonator	p. 157
225	Togedemaru	p. 157
226	Elekid	p. 158–159
227	Electabuzz	p. 158–159
228	Electivire	p. 158–159
229	Geodude	p. 160–161
230	Graveler	p. 160–161
231	Golem	p. 160–161
232	Sandile	p. 162–163
233	Krokorok	p. 162–163
234	Krookodile	p. 162–163
235	Trapinch	p. 164–165
236	Vibrava	p. 164–165
237	Flygon	p. 164–165
238	Gible	p. 166–167
239	Gabite	p. 166–167
240	Garchomp	p. 166–167
241	Klefki	p. 168
242	Mimikyu	p. 168
243	Bruxish	p. 170
244	Drampa	p. 170
245	Absol	p. 171
246	Snorunt	p. 172–173
247	Glalie	p. 172–173
248	Froslass	p. 172–173
249	Sneasel	p. 174
250	Weavile	p. 174
251	Sandshrew	p. 176
252	Sandslash	p. 176
253	Vulpix	p. 177
254	Ninetales	p. 177
255	Vanillite	p. 178–179
256	Vanillish	p. 178–179
257	Vanilluxe	p. 178–179
258	Snubbull	p. 180
259	Granbull	p. 180
260	Shellos	p. 181
261	Gastrodon	p. 181
262	Relicanth	p. 182
263	Dhelmise	p. 182
264	Carvanha	p. 183
265	Sharpedo	p. 183
266	Wailmer	p. 184
267	Wailord	p. 184
268	Lapras	p. 185
269	Exeggcute	p. 187
270	Exeggutor	p. 187
271	Jangmo-o	p. 188–189
272	Hakamo-o	p. 188–189
273	Kommo-o	p. 188–189
274	Emolga	p. 190
275	Scyther	p. 191
276	Scizor	p. 191
277	Murkrow	p. 192
278	Honchkrow	p. 192
279	Riolu	p. 193
280	Lucario	p. 193
281	Dratini	p. 194–195
282	Dragonair	p. 194–195
283	Dragonite	p. 194–195
284	Aerodactyl	p. 196
285	Tapu Koko	p. 197
286	Tapu Lele	p. 197
287	Tapu Bulu	p. 198
288	Tapu Fini	p. 198
289	Cosmog	p. 199
290	Cosmoem	p. 199
291	Solgaleo	p. 200
292	Lunala	p. 201
293	Nihilego	p. 202
294	Buzzwole	p. 202
295	Pheromosa	p. 203
296	Xurkitree	p. 203
297	Celesteela	p. 204
298	Kartana	p. 204
299	Guzzlord	p. 205
300	Necrozma	p. 205
301	Magearna	p. 206

Alphabetical List of Alola Pokémon

Alphabetical List of Mega-Evolved Pokémon

ALOLA REGION POKÉDEX
HOW TO COMPLETE THE ALOLA POKÉDEX
CHAMPION'S GUIDE TO ALOLA
ADVENTURE DATA

Alola Region Pokémon Maps

Along with Alola's various towns and routes, the following four maps also feature lists of the Pokémon that we recommend you try to catch at each location. Some Pokémon can also be found in other locations as well, so catch them whenever you encounter them! These lists are simply recommendations to help you most easily fill your Pokédex in the fewest number of stops, by catching the Pokémon you need to complete each Evolution chain. Then check out the Alola Region Pokédex Checklist on pages 2–3 to see which Pokémon can be obtained through Evolution or hatching Eggs, and you'll be on your way to completing your Island Pokédexes in no time. And note that Pokémon that appear as regional variants in Alola will always be found in their Alola Form in the wild.

Melemele Island

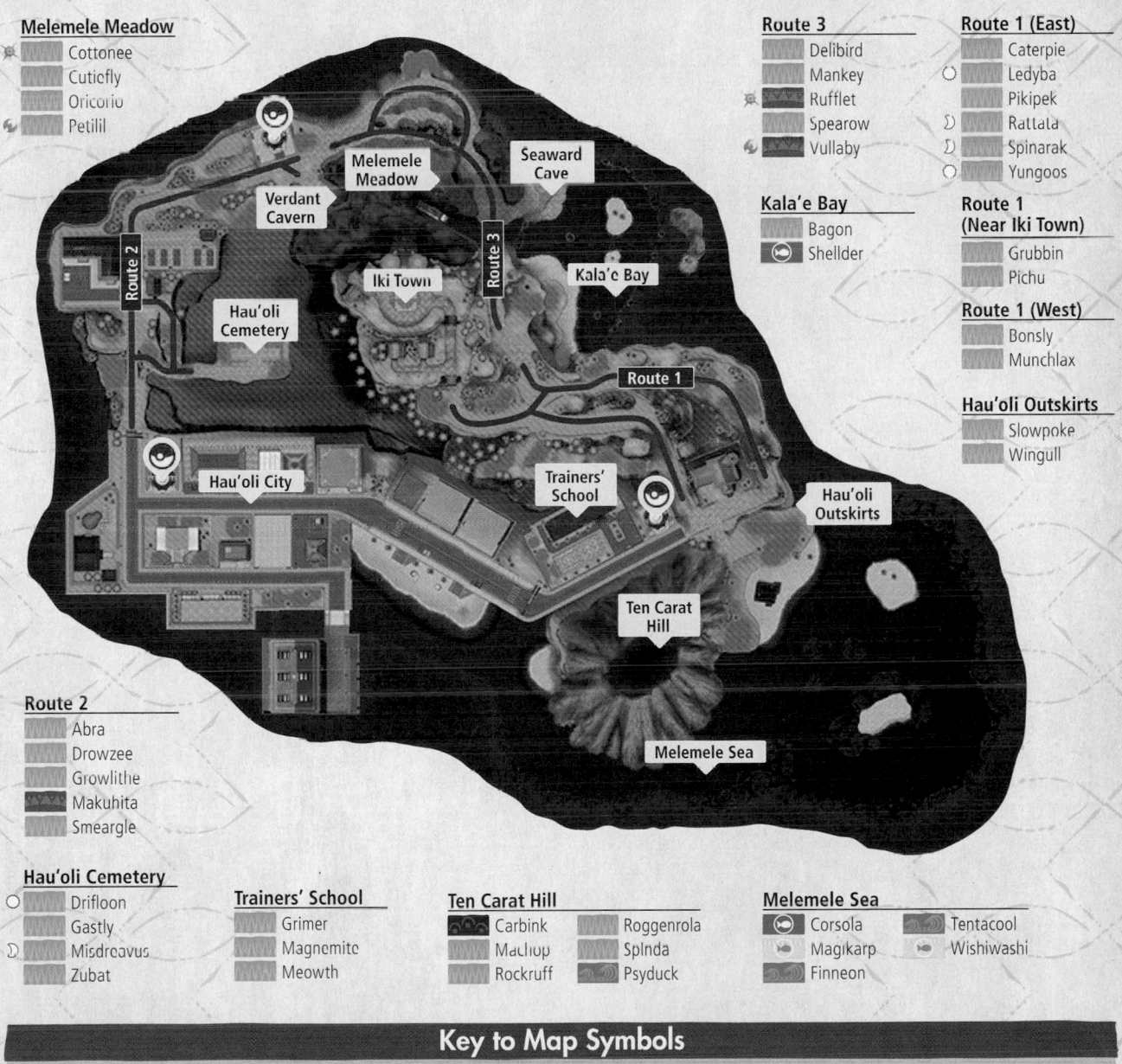

Melemele Meadow
- Cottonee
- Cutiefly
- Oricorio
- Petilil

Route 2
- Abra
- Drowzee
- Growlithe
- Makuhita
- Smeargle

Hau'oli Cemetery
- Drifloon
- Gastly
- Misdreavus
- Zubat

Trainers' School
- Grimer
- Magnemite
- Meowth

Ten Carat Hill
- Carbink
- Machop
- Rockruff
- Roggenrola
- Spinda
- Psyduck

Melemele Sea
- Corsola
- Magikarp
- Finneon
- Tentacool
- Wishiwashi

Route 3
- Delibird
- Mankey
- Rufflet
- Spearow
- Vullaby

Kala'e Bay
- Bagon
- Shellder

Route 1 (East)
- Caterpie
- Ledyba
- Pikipek
- Rattata
- Spinarak
- Yungoos

Route 1 (Near Iki Town)
- Grubbin
- Pichu

Route 1 (West)
- Bonsly
- Munchlax

Hau'oli Outskirts
- Slowpoke
- Wingull

Map labels: Melemele Meadow, Seaward Cave, Verdant Cavern, Route 2, Route 3, Iki Town, Kala'e Bay, Hau'oli Cemetery, Route 1, Hau'oli City, Trainers' School, Hau'oli Outskirts, Ten Carat Hill, Melemele Sea

Key to Map Symbols

Pokémon is encountered in tall grass or flowers	Pokémon can be encountered by fishing at a fishing spot
Pokémon will ambush you from rustling grass, shaking trees, or shadows overhead, and, for some, you will need to ambush them	Pokémon can be encountered by fishing at a rare fishing spot when bubbles can be seen (p. 110)
Pokémon can be encountered when traveling across the water surface on Lapras or Sharpedo	Pokémon can be encountered inside a cave or building

☀ When combined with any of the icons above, this indicates that the Pokémon can only be encountered in *Pokémon Sun*

🌙 When combined with any of the icons above, this indicates that the Pokémon can only be encountered in *Pokémon Moon*

○ When combined with any of the icons above, this indicates that the Pokémon can only be found during the day in your game

☽ When combined with any of the icons above, this indicates that the Pokémon can only be found during the nighttime in your game

Akala Island

Lush Jungle (North)
- Fomantis
- ☽ Morelull
- 🐾 Oranguru
- ◯ Paras
- ☀ Passimian
- Pinsir

Lush Jungle (West)
- Bounsweet
- Comfey

Route 8
- Salandit
- Stufful
- Wimpod

Wela Volcano Park
- Cubone
- Fletchling
- Kangaskhan
- Magby

Route 7
- Pyukumuku

Route 5
- Diglett

Brooklet Hill
- ◯ Dewpider
- Feebas
- ☽ Surskit

Brooklet Hill (Totem's Den)
- Alomomola

Paniola Ranch
- Lillipup
- Mudbray

Route 4
- Eevee
- ◯ Igglybuff

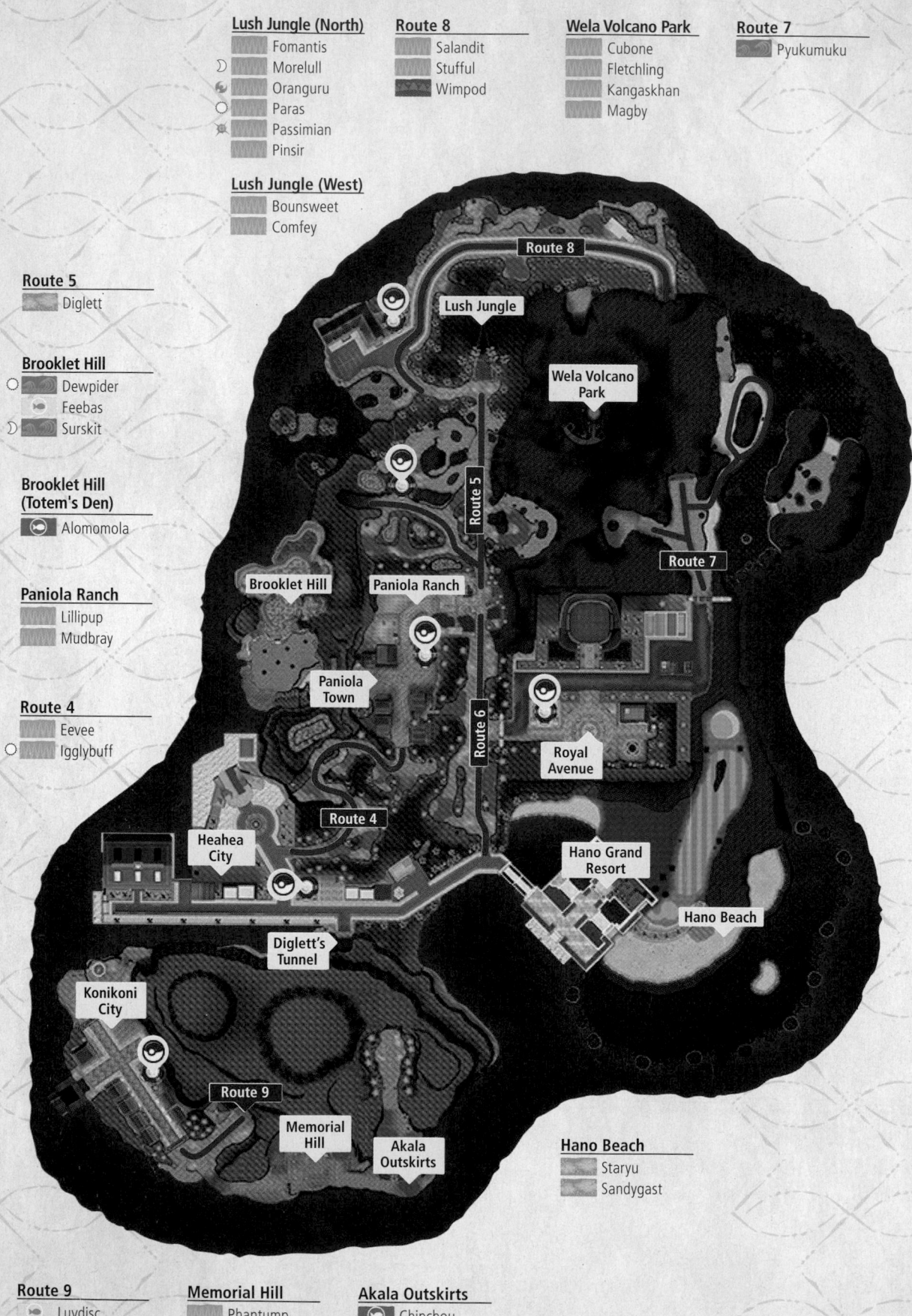

Route 8
Lush Jungle
Wela Volcano Park
Route 5
Route 7
Brooklet Hill
Paniola Ranch
Paniola Town
Route 6
Royal Avenue
Route 4
Heahea City
Hano Grand Resort
Hano Beach
Diglett's Tunnel
Konikoni City
Route 9
Memorial Hill
Akala Outskirts

Route 9
- Luvdisc

Memorial Hill
- Phantump

Akala Outskirts
- Chinchou
- Nosepass

Hano Beach
- Staryu
- Sandygast

Ula'ula Island

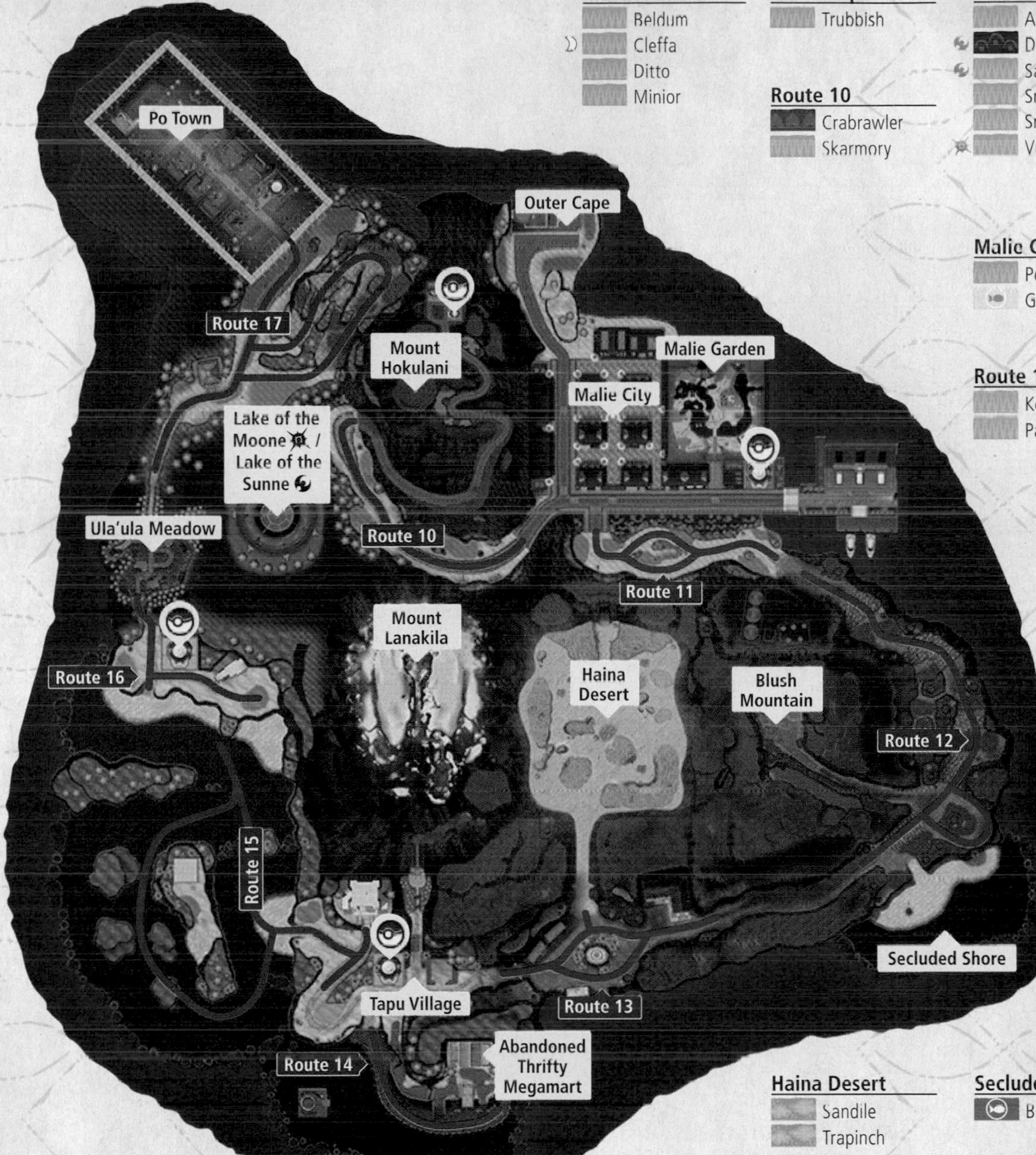

Mount Hokulani
- Beldum
- ☽ Cleffa
- Ditto
- Minior

Outer Cape
- Trubbish

Route 10
- Crabrawler
- Skarmory

Mount Lanakila
- Absol
- Drampa
- Sandshrew
- Sneasel
- Snorunt
- Vulpix

Malie Garden
- Poliwag
- Goldeen

Route 11
- Komala
- Pancham

Po Town

Outer Cape

Route 17

Mount Hokulani

Malie Garden

Malie City

Lake of the Moone ☼ / Lake of the Sunne ☽

Ula'ula Meadow

Route 10

Route 16

Mount Lanakila

Haina Desert

Blush Mountain

Route 11

Route 12

Route 15

Secluded Shore

Tapu Village

Route 13

Abandoned Thrifty Megamart

Route 14

Haina Desert
- Sandile
- Trapinch

Secluded Shore
- Bruxish

Blush Mountain
- Elekid
- Geodude
- Togedemaru
- Torkoal
- Turtonator

Abandoned Thrifty Megamart
- Klefki
- Mimikyu

Key to Map Symbols

- Pokémon is encountered in tall grass or flowers
- Pokémon will ambush you from rustling grass, shaking trees, or shadows overhead, and, for some, you will need to ambush them
- Pokémon will ambush you from within a cloud of dust or sand
- Pokémon can be encountered when traveling across the water surface on Lapras or Sharpedo

- Pokémon can be encountered by fishing at a fishing spot
- Pokémon can be encountered by fishing at a rare fishing spot when bubbles can be seen (p. 110)
- Pokémon can be encountered inside a cave or building
- Pokémon can be encountered when examining piles of Berries

- ☼ When combined with any of the icons above, this indicates that the Pokémon can only be encountered in *Pokémon Sun*
- ☽ When combined with any of the icons above, this indicates that the Pokémon can only be encountered in *Pokémon Moon*
- ○ When combined with any of the icons above, this indicates that the Pokémon can only be found during the day in your game
- ☽ When combined with any of the icons above, this indicates that the Pokémon can only be found during the nighttime in your game

Poni Island

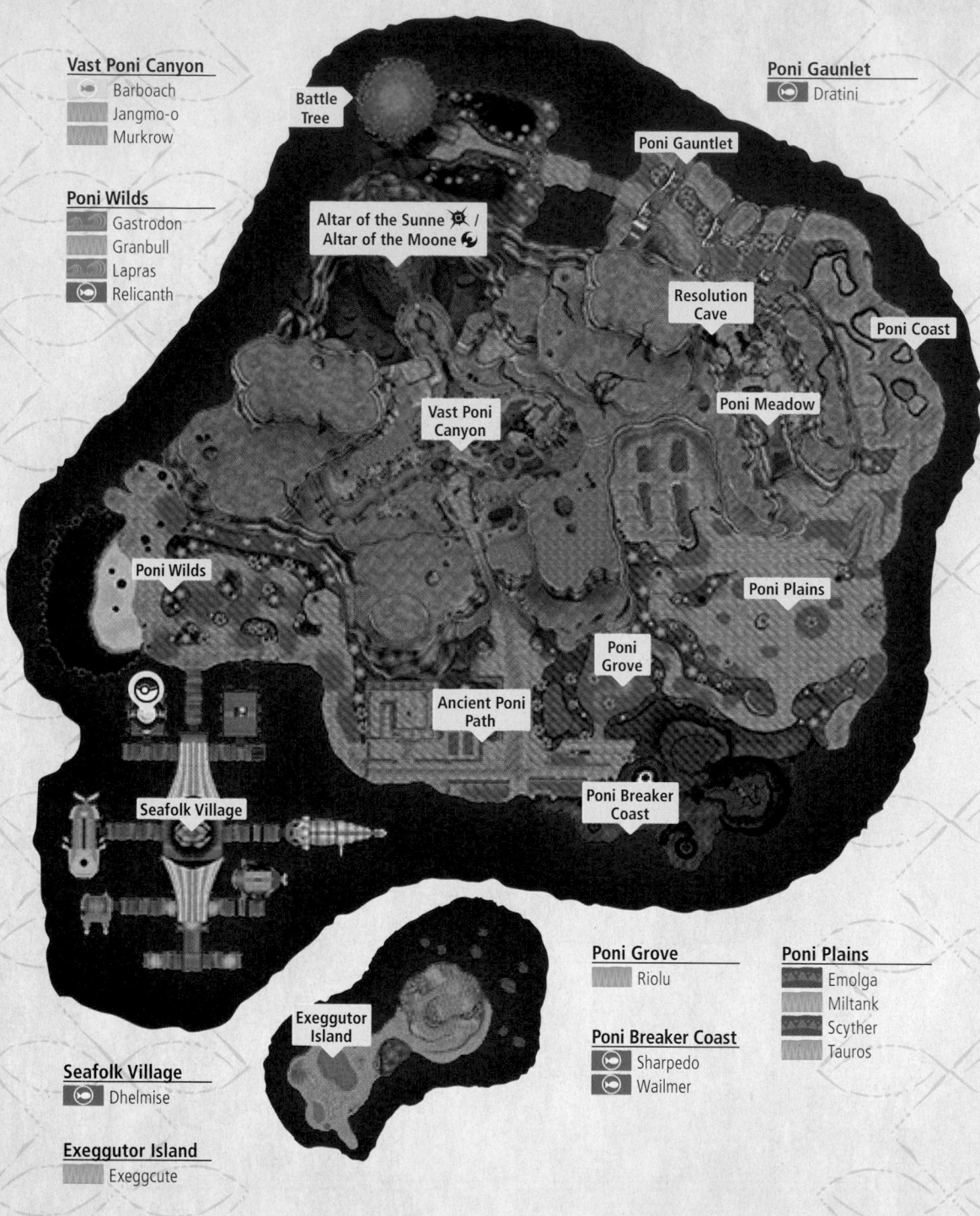

Vast Poni Canyon
- Barboach
- Jangmo-o
- Murkrow

Poni Wilds
- Gastrodon
- Granbull
- Lapras
- Relicanth

Battle Tree

Altar of the Sunne ☀ / Altar of the Moone 🌙

Vast Poni Canyon

Poni Wilds

Ancient Poni Path

Seafolk Village

Exeggutor Island

Poni Gauntlet
- Dratini

Poni Gauntlet

Resolution Cave

Poni Coast

Poni Meadow

Poni Plains

Poni Grove

Poni Breaker Coast

Poni Grove
- Riolu

Poni Breaker Coast
- Sharpedo
- Wailmer

Poni Plains
- Emolga
- Miltank
- Scyther
- Tauros

Seafolk Village
- Dhelmise

Exeggutor Island
- Exeggcute

Key to Map Symbols

Pokémon is encountered in tall grass or flowers

Pokémon will ambush you from rustling grass, shaking trees, or shadows overhead, and, for some, you will need to ambush them

Pokémon can be encountered when traveling across the water surface on Lapras or Sharpedo

Pokémon can be encountered by fishing at a fishing spot

Pokémon can be encountered by fishing at a rare fishing spot when bubbles can be seen (p. 110)

☀ When combined with any of the icons above, this indicates that the Pokémon can only be encountered in *Pokémon Sun*

🌙 When combined with any of the icons above, this indicates that the Pokémon can only be encountered in *Pokémon Moon*

○ When combined with any of the icons above, this indicates that the Pokémon can only be found during the day in your game

🌙 When combined with any of the icons above, this indicates that the Pokémon can only be found during the nighttime in your game

Alola Region Pokédex

How to Read the Pokédex Pages

Pokémon Pokédex Entry

When Pokémon are part of a 3-Evolution chain, their Pokédex entries may be laid out a little differently, but they still contain all of the same elements as are illustrated in the example to the right.

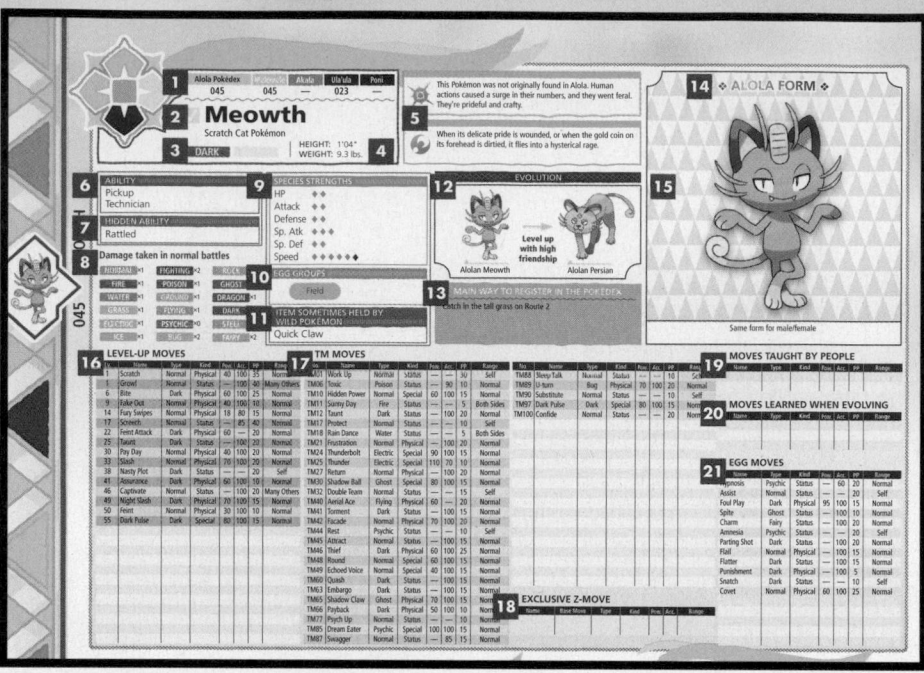

Mega-Evolved Pokémon Pokédex Entry

When Pokémon undergo Mega Evolution, they unleash new powers. Sometimes their types, Abilities, heights, and weights may change. If any of these do change, you will see that information highlighted in blue on these pages.

---

1 | Pokédex Numbers

Above each Pokémon's name you will see its number in the Alola Pokédex, as well as its number for any of the Island Pokédexes it may appear in. If it does not appear on a particular island, you will see — appear instead of a number and the corresponding petals in the flower to the left will also not be colored in.

2 | Pokémon's Name and Category

You will find the name of the Pokémon species here. In the case of a Mega-Evolving Pokémon, this will be the name of its form when it has Mega Evolved. Below this name is the Pokémon's category. A Pokémon's category may provide a pointer to its traits or attributes, and several Pokémon species may share the same category.

3 | Type

The Pokémon's type. Some Pokémon have two types.

4 | Height and Weight

The height and weight of the Pokémon is listed here.

5 | Pokédex Entries

You can reach the information provided by the Alola Pokédex about this Pokémon. The entries for both *Pokémon Sun* and *Pokémon Moon* are included, and they often differ somewhat.

6 | Ability

The Pokémon's Ability. If two Abilities are listed, then a Pokémon of this species may have either one of those two when encountered in the wild.

7 | Hidden Ability

Some Pokémon have Hidden Abilities. Hidden Abilities are rare Abilities that average Pokémon do not possess. In the Alola region, extraordinary specimens of Pokémon with Hidden Abilities sometimes appear as ally Pokémon in SOS battles.

8 | Damage Taken in Normal Battles

These tables provide a quick reference for how much damage each Pokémon will take by moves of the various types used in battles. If the effect of an Ability this Pokémon can have may affect how much damage the Pokémon takes from moves of a particular type, it will be marked ❶.

9 Species Strengths

On a scale of 1–10, the diamonds indicate how well this species' stats stack up when compared to the other Pokémon found in the Alola region. Pokémon with six diamonds or more for a certain stat have those diamonds shown in red so you can easily see which stats these Pokémon are strong in. Changes in Mega-Evolved Pokémon's stats are shown with blue diamonds. These species strengths are one of the three main factors that go into calculating a Pokémon's final stats, the other two being base stats and individual strengths. For more detailed strategy insights, check out *Pokémon Sun & Pokémon Moon: The Official Alola Region Strategy Guide*.

10 Egg Groups

The Egg Group the Pokémon belongs to. When two Egg Groups are listed, the Pokémon belongs to both. Two Pokémon left at the Pokémon Nursery together must share an Egg Group in order to find a Pokémon Egg.

11 Items Sometimes Held by Wild Pokémon

Wild Pokémon sometimes hold an item. If you catch the Pokémon, that item will become yours. Items that each particular species sometimes can be found holding are listed here. For more detail, see the table on page 313.

12 Evolution

If the Pokémon evolves, this box will show the course of Evolution for the Pokémon as well as any conditions governing its Evolution.

13 Main Way to Register in the Pokédex

This box gives you a recommended method to most easily register this Pokémon in your Alola Pokédex. There may be more than one way to register many Pokémon, such as catching them in the wild or having them evolve from another Pokémon. Some Pokémon cannot be obtained within both *Pokémon Sun* and *Pokémon Moon*, or must be traded to evolve. If a Pokémon must be traded to be obtained, that information will be included here.

14 Form

Some Pokémon can appear in more than one form. The form name will appear here to let you know which form exactly you are seeing.

15 Appearance and Gender Information

Here you will find an image of the Pokémon species. If it has different forms for each gender, then you will also see a small box with images of both male and female specimens. A description of any gender differences also appears in the small box below the Pokémon's image. You will also see a Mega Evolution symbol in this box if the Pokémon is capable of Mega Evolution.

p. 207

16 Level-Up Moves

A list of the moves that the Pokémon can learn by leveling up, as well as the levels at which they learn them.

17 TM Moves

A list of the moves the Pokémon can learn by using an item called a TM. TMs can be found all

around Alola, so check out the table on page 293 if you are looking for one in particular.

18 Exclusive Z-Move

Some Pokémon can use an exclusive Z-Move that no other Pokémon species can use. If so, it will be listed here along with the base move that the Pokémon must know in order to use this special Z-Move.

19 Moves Taught by People

These moves may be taught to the Pokémon by special Move Tutors. Some require special conditions be met before they can be learned. Learn more from the table on pages 294–295.

20 Moves Learned When Evolving

Some Pokémon may be able to learn a move when they evolve from their previous Evolution. Such moves will be listed in this table. These are often moves they would have otherwise been able to learn at Lv. 1.

21 Egg Moves

These moves may be learned by the Pokémon upon hatching from an Egg if they are known by one of the Pokémon you left at the Pokémon Nursery when finding an Egg.

22 Mega Evolution

The conditions for Mega Evolving the Pokémon, including its original form and a page reference to that species' Pokédex page.

23 Required Mega Stone

The Mega Stone required in order to Mega Evolve the Pokémon and how you can obtain it.

Move List Guide

Lv. The level at which the move can be learned.

No. The number of the TM that teaches the move.

Type The move's type.

Kind Whether the move is a physical, special, or status move.

- **Physical Move** Does more damage the higher the Attack stat is. Damage is lessened when the target has a high Defense stat.
- **Special Move** Does more damage the higher the Sp. Atk stat is. Damage is lessened when the target has a high Sp. Def stat.
- **Status Move** Affects stats or inflicts status condition on the target(s), or various other effects.

Pow. The move's power.

Acc. The move's accuracy (out of 100 maximum).

PP How many times the move can be used before the Pokémon must have its PP restored with an item or at a Pokémon Center.

Range The number and range of targets the move can affect.

Range Guide

Normal

The move affects the selected target. If the move is used by a Pokémon during a Double Battle, Multi Battle, or Battle Royal, the move can target any of the three other Pokémon (including an ally).

Self

The move affects only the user.

1 Ally

The move affects an adjacent Pokémon during a Double Battle, Multi Battle, or Battle Royal. It has no effect in a Single Battle.

Self/Ally

The move affects the user or one of its allies. In a Single Battle, it will only affect the user. In a Double Battle, Multi Battle, or Battle Royal, it can affect either the user or one of the other Pokémon.

Your Party

The move affects your entire party, including party Pokémon that are still in their Poké Balls.

1 Random

The move affects one of the opposing Pokémon at random.

Many Others

The move affects multiple Pokémon at the same time. If the move is used by a Pokémon during a Double Battle, Multi Battle, or Battle Royal, the move will affect all opposing Pokémon.

Adjacent

The move affects the surrounding Pokémon at the same time. If the move is used by a Pokémon during a Double Battle, Multi Battle, or Battle Royal, the move will affect the three surrounding Pokémon (including its ally) simultaneously.

Your Side

The move affects the side of the field where your Pokémon are in a Double Battle. It affects your Pokémon and its ally in a Multi Battle, but only affects your Pokémon in a Battle Royal. Since the move affects the field, the move's effects continue even if the Pokémon are swapped out (except for moves that only work for one turn).

Other Side

The move affects the opponent's side of the field. Since the move affects the field, the move's effects continue even if the Pokémon are swapped out (except for moves that only work for one turn).

Both Sides

The move affects the entire battle field and all Pokémon within it. Since the move affects the field, the move's effects continue even if Pokémon are swapped out.

Varies

The move is influenced by things such as the opposing Pokémon's move or the user's type, so the effect and range are not fixed.

Rowlet

Grass Quill Pokémon

GRASS FLYING

Alola Pokédex	Melemele	Akala	Ula'ula	Poni
001	001	—	—	—

HEIGHT: 1'00"
WEIGHT: 3.3 lbs.

This wary Pokémon uses photosynthesis to store up energy during the day, while becoming active at night.

Silently it glides, drawing near its targets. Before they even notice it, it begins to pelt them with vicious kicks.

ABILITY
Overgrow

HIDDEN ABILITY
—

Damage taken in normal battles

NORMAL	×1	FIGHTING	×0.5	ROCK	×2
FIRE	×2	POISON	×2	GHOST	×1
WATER	×0.5	GROUND	×0	DRAGON	×1
GRASS	×0.25	FLYING	×2	DARK	×1
ELECTRIC	×1	PSYCHIC	×1	STEEL	×1
ICE	×4	BUG	×1	FAIRY	×1

SPECIES STRENGTHS
HP ◆◆◆
Attack ◆◆◆
Defense ◆◆◆
Sp. Atk ◆◆◆
Sp. Def ◆◆◆
Speed ◆◆◆

EGG GROUPS
Flying

ITEM SOMETIMES HELD BY WILD POKÉMON
—

EVOLUTION

Rowlet → Lv. 17 → Dartrix → Lv. 34 → Decidueye

Same form for male/female

MAIN WAY TO REGISTER IN THE POKÉDEX
Receive from Kahuna Hala or receive in a trade from another player

---

Dartrix

Blade Quill Pokémon

GRASS FLYING

Alola Pokédex	Melemele	Akala	Ula'ula	Poni
002	002	—	—	—

HEIGHT: 2'04"
WEIGHT: 35.3 lbs.

A bit of a dandy, it spends its free time preening its wings. Its preoccupation with any dirt on its plumage can leave it unable to battle.

It throws sharp feathers called blade quills at enemies or prey. It seldom misses.

ABILITY
Overgrow

HIDDEN ABILITY
—

Damage taken in normal battles

NORMAL	×1	FIGHTING	×0.5	ROCK	×2
FIRE	×2	POISON	×2	GHOST	×1
WATER	×0.5	GROUND	×0	DRAGON	×1
GRASS	×0.25	FLYING	×2	DARK	×1
ELECTRIC	×1	PSYCHIC	×1	STEEL	×1
ICE	×4	BUG	×1	FAIRY	×1

SPECIES STRENGTHS
HP ◆◆◆
Attack ◆◆◆◆
Defense ◆◆◆◆
Sp. Atk ◆◆◆◆
Sp. Def ◆◆◆◆
Speed ◆◆◆

EGG GROUPS
Flying

ITEM SOMETIMES HELD BY WILD POKÉMON
—

EVOLUTION

Rowlet → Lv. 17 → Dartrix → Lv. 34 → Decidueye

Same form for male/female

MAIN WAY TO REGISTER IN THE POKÉDEX
Level up Rowlet to Lv. 17

Decidueye

Arrow Quill Pokémon

GRASS GHOST

Alola Pokédex	Melemele	Akala	Ula'ula	Poni
003	003	—	—	—

HEIGHT: 5'03"
WEIGHT: 80.7 lbs.

It fires arrow quills from its wings with such precision, they can pierce a pebble at distances over a hundred yards.

Although basically cool and cautious, when it's caught by surprise, it's seized by panic.

ABILITY
Overgrow

HIDDEN ABILITY
—

Damage taken in normal battles

NORMAL	×0	FIGHTING	×1	ROCK	×1
FIRE	×2	POISON	×1	GHOST	×2
WATER	×0.5	GROUND	×1	DRAGON	×1
GRASS	×0.5	FLYING	×2	DARK	×2
ELECTRIC	×0.5	PSYCHIC	×1	STEEL	×1
ICE	×2	BUG	×1	FAIRY	×1

SPECIES STRENGTHS
HP ◆◆◆
Attack ◆◆◆◆◆◆
Defense ◆◆◆◆
Sp. Atk ◆◆◆◆
Sp. Def ◆◆◆◆◆◆
Speed ◆◆◆◆◆

EGG GROUPS
Flying

ITEM SOMETIMES HELD BY WILD POKÉMON
—

EVOLUTION

Rowlet → Lv. 17 → Dartrix → Lv. 34 → Decidueye

Same form for male/female

MAIN WAY TO REGISTER IN THE POKÉDEX
Level up Dartrix to Lv. 34

ROWLET 001

LEVEL-UP MOVES

Lv.	Name	Type	Kind	Pow.	Acc.	PP	Range
1	Tackle	Normal	Physical	40	100	35	Normal
1	Leafage	Grass	Physical	40	100	40	Normal
4	Growl	Normal	Status	—	100	40	Many Others
8	Peck	Flying	Physical	35	100	35	Normal
11	Astonish	Ghost	Physical	30	100	15	Normal
15	Razor Leaf	Grass	Physical	55	95	25	Many Others
18	Foresight	Normal	Status	—	—	40	Normal
22	Pluck	Flying	Physical	60	100	20	Normal
25	Synthesis	Grass	Status	—	—	5	Self
29	Fury Attack	Normal	Physical	15	85	20	Normal
32	Sucker Punch	Dark	Physical	70	100	5	Normal
36	Leaf Blade	Grass	Physical	90	100	15	Normal
39	Feather Dance	Flying	Status	—	100	15	Normal
43	Brave Bird	Flying	Physical	120	100	15	Normal
46	Nasty Plot	Dark	Status	—	—	20	Self

TM MOVES

No.	Name	Type	Kind	Pow.	Acc.	PP	Range
TM01	Work Up	Normal	Status	—	—	30	Self
TM06	Toxic	Poison	Status	—	90	10	Normal
TM10	Hidden Power	Normal	Special	60	100	15	Normal
TM11	Sunny Day	Fire	Status	—	—	5	Both Sides
TM16	Light Screen	Psychic	Status	—	—	30	Your Side
TM17	Protect	Normal	Status	—	—	10	Self
TM19	Roost	Flying	Status	—	—	10	Self
TM20	Safeguard	Normal	Status	—	—	25	Your Side
TM21	Frustration	Normal	Physical	—	100	20	Normal
TM22	Solar Beam	Grass	Special	120	100	10	Normal
TM27	Return	Normal	Physical	—	100	20	Normal
TM32	Double Team	Normal	Status	—	—	15	Self
TM42	Facade	Normal	Physical	70	100	20	Normal
TM44	Rest	Psychic	Status	—	—	10	Self
TM45	Attract	Normal	Status	—	100	15	Normal
TM48	Round	Normal	Special	60	100	15	Normal
TM49	Echoed Voice	Normal	Special	40	100	15	Normal
TM51	Steel Wing	Steel	Physical	70	90	25	Normal
TM53	Energy Ball	Grass	Special	90	100	10	Normal
TM54	False Swipe	Normal	Physical	40	100	40	Normal
TM65	Shadow Claw	Ghost	Physical	70	100	15	Normal
TM75	Swords Dance	Normal	Status	—	—	20	Self
TM86	Grass Knot	Grass	Special	—	100	20	Normal
TM87	Swagger	Normal	Status	—	85	15	Normal
TM88	Sleep Talk	Normal	Status	—	—	10	Self
TM90	Substitute	Normal	Status	—	—	10	Self
TM96	Nature Power	Normal	Status	—	—	20	Normal
TM100	Confide	Normal	Status	—	—	20	Normal

MOVES TAUGHT BY PEOPLE

Name	Type	Kind	Pow.	Acc.	PP	Range
Grass Pledge	Grass	Special	80	100	10	Normal

MOVES LEARNED WHEN EVOLVING

Name	Type	Kind	Pow.	Acc.	PP	Range

EGG MOVES

Name	Type	Kind	Pow.	Acc.	PP	Range
Curse	Ghost	Status	—	—	10	Varies
Confuse Ray	Ghost	Status	—	100	10	Normal
Ominous Wind	Ghost	Special	60	100	5	Normal
Haze	Ice	Status	—	—	30	Both Sides
Baton Pass	Normal	Status	—	—	40	Self
Defog	Flying	Status	—	—	15	Normal

EXCLUSIVE Z-MOVE

Name	Base Move	Type	Kind	Pow.	Acc.	Range

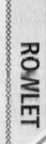

DARTRIX 002

LEVEL-UP MOVES

Lv.	Name	Type	Kind	Pow.	Acc.	PP	Range
1	Tackle	Normal	Physical	40	100	35	Normal
1	Leafage	Grass	Physical	40	100	40	Normal
1	Growl	Normal	Status	—	100	40	Many Others
1	Peck	Flying	Physical	35	100	35	Normal
4	Growl	Normal	Status	—	100	40	Many Others
8	Peck	Flying	Physical	35	100	35	Normal
11	Astonish	Ghost	Physical	30	100	15	Normal
15	Razor Leaf	Grass	Physical	55	95	25	Many Others
19	Foresight	Normal	Status	—	—	40	Normal
24	Pluck	Flying	Physical	60	100	20	Normal
28	Synthesis	Grass	Status	—	—	5	Self
33	Fury Attack	Normal	Physical	15	85	20	Normal
37	Sucker Punch	Dark	Physical	70	100	5	Normal
42	Leaf Blade	Grass	Physical	90	100	15	Normal
46	Feather Dance	Flying	Status	—	100	15	Normal
51	Brave Bird	Flying	Physical	120	100	15	Normal
55	Nasty Plot	Dark	Status	—	—	20	Self

TM MOVES

No.	Name	Type	Kind	Pow.	Acc.	PP	Range
TM01	Work Up	Normal	Status	—	—	30	Self
TM06	Toxic	Poison	Status	—	90	10	Normal
TM10	Hidden Power	Normal	Special	60	100	15	Normal
TM11	Sunny Day	Fire	Status	—	—	5	Both Sides
TM16	Light Screen	Psychic	Status	—	—	30	Your Side
TM17	Protect	Normal	Status	—	—	10	Self
TM19	Roost	Flying	Status	—	—	10	Self
TM20	Safeguard	Normal	Status	—	—	25	Your Side
TM21	Frustration	Normal	Physical	—	100	20	Normal
TM22	Solar Beam	Grass	Special	120	100	10	Normal
TM27	Return	Normal	Physical	—	100	20	Normal
TM32	Double Team	Normal	Status	—	—	15	Self
TM42	Facade	Normal	Physical	70	100	20	Normal
TM44	Rest	Psychic	Status	—	—	10	Self
TM45	Attract	Normal	Status	—	100	15	Normal
TM48	Round	Normal	Special	60	100	15	Normal
TM49	Echoed Voice	Normal	Special	40	100	15	Normal
TM51	Steel Wing	Steel	Physical	70	90	25	Normal
TM53	Energy Ball	Grass	Special	90	100	10	Normal
TM54	False Swipe	Normal	Physical	40	100	40	Normal
TM65	Shadow Claw	Ghost	Physical	70	100	15	Normal
TM75	Swords Dance	Normal	Status	—	—	20	Self
TM86	Grass Knot	Grass	Special	—	100	20	Normal
TM87	Swagger	Normal	Status	—	85	15	Normal
TM88	Sleep Talk	Normal	Status	—	—	10	Self
TM90	Substitute	Normal	Status	—	—	10	Self
TM96	Nature Power	Normal	Status	—	—	20	Normal
TM100	Confide	Normal	Status	—	—	20	Normal

MOVES TAUGHT BY PEOPLE

Name	Type	Kind	Pow.	Acc.	PP	Range
Grass Pledge	Grass	Special	80	100	10	Normal

MOVES LEARNED WHEN EVOLVING

Name	Type	Kind	Pow.	Acc.	PP	Range

EGG MOVES

Name	Type	Kind	Pow.	Acc.	PP	Range

EXCLUSIVE Z-MOVE

Name	Base Move	Type	Kind	Pow.	Acc.	Range

DECIDUEYE 003

LEVEL-UP MOVES

Lv.	Name	Type	Kind	Pow.	Acc.	PP	Range
1	Spirit Shackle	Ghost	Physical	80	100	10	Normal
1	U-turn	Bug	Physical	70	100	20	Normal
1	Tackle	Normal	Physical	40	100	35	Normal
1	Leafage	Grass	Physical	40	100	40	Normal
1	Growl	Normal	Status	—	100	40	Many Others
1	Peck	Flying	Physical	35	100	35	Normal
4	Growl	Normal	Status	—	100	40	Many Others
8	Peck	Flying	Physical	35	100	35	Normal
11	Astonish	Ghost	Physical	30	100	15	Normal
15	Razor Leaf	Grass	Physical	55	95	25	Many Others
19	Foresight	Normal	Status	—	—	40	Normal
24	Pluck	Flying	Physical	60	100	20	Normal
28	Synthesis	Grass	Status	—	—	5	Self
33	Fury Attack	Normal	Physical	15	85	20	Normal
38	Sucker Punch	Dark	Physical	70	100	5	Normal
44	Leaf Blade	Grass	Physical	90	100	15	Normal
49	Feather Dance	Flying	Status	—	100	15	Normal
55	Brave Bird	Flying	Physical	120	100	15	Normal
60	Nasty Plot	Dark	Status	—	—	20	Self

TM MOVES

No.	Name	Type	Kind	Pow.	Acc.	PP	Range
TM01	Work Up	Normal	Status	—	—	30	Self
TM06	Toxic	Poison	Status	—	90	10	Normal
TM10	Hidden Power	Normal	Special	60	100	15	Normal
TM11	Sunny Day	Fire	Status	—	—	5	Both Sides
TM16	Light Screen	Psychic	Status	—	—	30	Your Side
TM17	Protect	Normal	Status	—	—	10	Self
TM19	Roost	Flying	Status	—	—	10	Self
TM20	Safeguard	Normal	Status	—	—	25	Your Side
TM21	Frustration	Normal	Physical	—	100	20	Normal
TM22	Solar Beam	Grass	Special	120	100	10	Normal
TM23	Smack Down	Rock	Physical	50	100	15	Normal
TM27	Return	Normal	Physical	—	100	20	Normal
TM30	Shadow Ball	Ghost	Special	80	100	15	Normal
TM32	Double Team	Normal	Status	—	—	15	Self
TM42	Facade	Normal	Physical	70	100	20	Normal
TM44	Rest	Psychic	Status	—	—	10	Self
TM45	Attract	Normal	Status	—	100	15	Normal
TM47	Low Sweep	Fighting	Physical	65	100	20	Normal
TM48	Round	Normal	Special	60	100	15	Normal
TM49	Echoed Voice	Normal	Special	40	100	15	Normal
TM51	Steel Wing	Steel	Physical	70	90	25	Normal
TM53	Energy Ball	Grass	Special	90	100	10	Normal
TM54	False Swipe	Normal	Physical	40	100	40	Normal
TM62	Acrobatics	Flying	Physical	55	100	15	Normal
TM65	Shadow Claw	Ghost	Physical	70	100	15	Normal
TM68	Giga Impact	Normal	Physical	150	90	5	Normal
TM75	Swords Dance	Normal	Status	—	—	20	Self
TM86	Grass Knot	Grass	Special	—	100	20	Normal
TM87	Swagger	Normal	Status	—	85	15	Normal
TM88	Sleep Talk	Normal	Status	—	—	10	Self
TM89	U-turn	Bug	Physical	70	100	20	Normal
TM90	Substitute	Normal	Status	—	—	10	Self
TM96	Nature Power	Normal	Status	—	—	20	Normal
TM100	Confide	Normal	Status	—	—	20	Normal

MOVES TAUGHT BY PEOPLE

Name	Type	Kind	Pow.	Acc.	PP	Range
Grass Pledge	Grass	Special	80	100	10	Normal
Frenzy Plant	Grass	Special	150	90	5	Normal

MOVES LEARNED WHEN EVOLVING

Name	Type	Kind	Pow.	Acc.	PP	Range
Spirit Shackle	Ghost	Physical	80	100	10	Normal

EGG MOVES

Name	Type	Kind	Pow.	Acc.	PP	Range

EXCLUSIVE Z-MOVE

Name	Base Move	Type	Kind	Pow.	Acc.	Range
Sinister Arrow Raid	Spirit Shackle	Ghost	Physical	180	—	Normal

Alola Pokédex	Melemele	Akala	Ula'ula	Poni
004	004	—	—	—

☑ **Litten**

Fire Cat Pokémon

FIRE

HEIGHT: 1'04"
WEIGHT: 9.5 lbs.

While grooming itself, it builds up fur inside its stomach. It sets the fur alight and spews fiery attacks, which change based on how it coughs.

It doesn't allow its emotions to be easily seen. Earning its trust takes time. It prefers solitude.

ABILITY
Blaze

HIDDEN ABILITY
—

Damage taken in normal battles

NORMAL	×1	FIGHTING	×1	ROCK	×1
FIRE	×0.5	POISON	×1	GHOST	×1
WATER	×2	GROUND	×2	DRAGON	×1
GRASS	×0.5	FLYING	×1	DARK	×1
ELECTRIC	×1	PSYCHIC	×1	STEEL	×0.5
ICE	×0.5	BUG	×0.5	FAIRY	×0.5

SPECIES STRENGTHS

HP	◆◆
Attack	◆◆◆◆
Defense	◆◆
Sp. Atk	◆◆◆
Sp. Def	◆◆
Speed	◆◆◆◆◆

EGG GROUPS
Field

ITEM SOMETIMES HELD BY WILD POKÉMON
—

EVOLUTION

Litten → Torracat Lv. 17 → Incineroar Lv. 34

MAIN WAY TO REGISTER IN THE POKÉDEX
Receive from Kahuna Hala or receive in a trade from another player

Same form for male/female

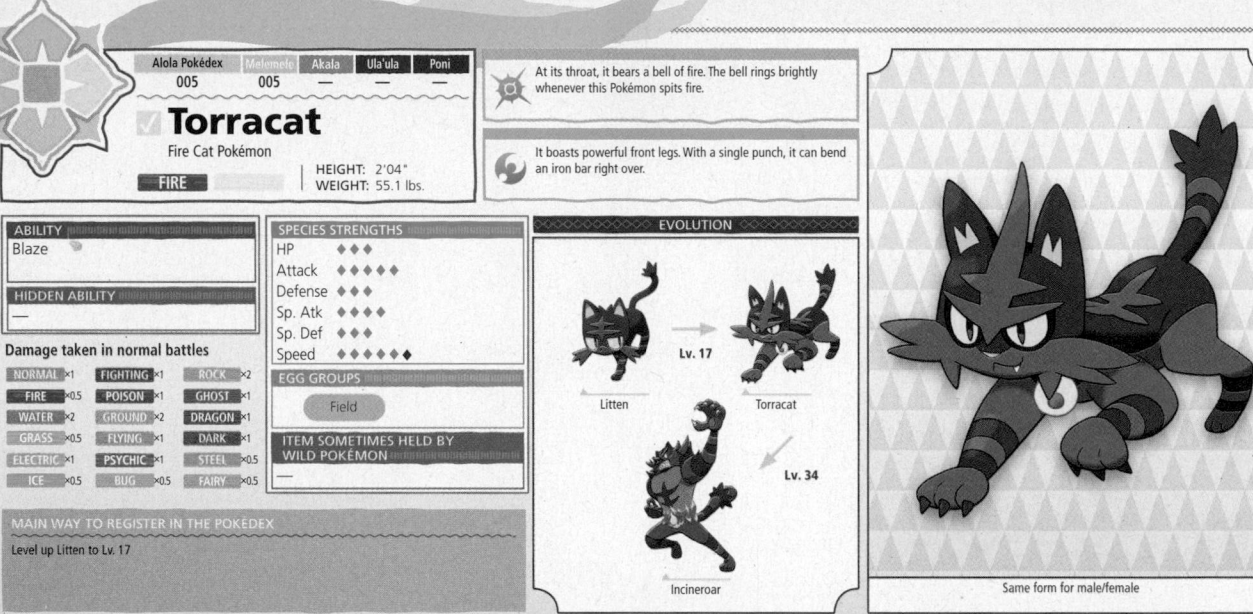

Alola Pokédex	Melemele	Akala	Ula'ula	Poni
005	005	—	—	—

☑ **Torracat**

Fire Cat Pokémon

FIRE

HEIGHT: 2'04"
WEIGHT: 55.1 lbs.

At its throat, it bears a bell of fire. The bell rings brightly whenever this Pokémon spits fire.

It boasts powerful front legs. With a single punch, it can bend an iron bar right over.

ABILITY
Blaze

HIDDEN ABILITY
—

Damage taken in normal battles

NORMAL	×1	FIGHTING	×1	ROCK	×1
FIRE	×0.5	POISON	×1	GHOST	×1
WATER	×2	GROUND	×2	DRAGON	×1
GRASS	×0.5	FLYING	×1	DARK	×1
ELECTRIC	×1	PSYCHIC	×1	STEEL	×0.5
ICE	×0.5	BUG	×0.5	FAIRY	×0.5

SPECIES STRENGTHS

HP	◆◆◆
Attack	◆◆◆◆◆
Defense	◆◆◆
Sp. Atk	◆◆◆◆
Sp. Def	◆◆◆
Speed	◆◆◆◆◆◆

EGG GROUPS
Field

ITEM SOMETIMES HELD BY WILD POKÉMON
—

EVOLUTION

Litten → Torracat Lv. 17 → Incineroar Lv. 34

MAIN WAY TO REGISTER IN THE POKÉDEX
Level up Litten to Lv. 17

Same form for male/female

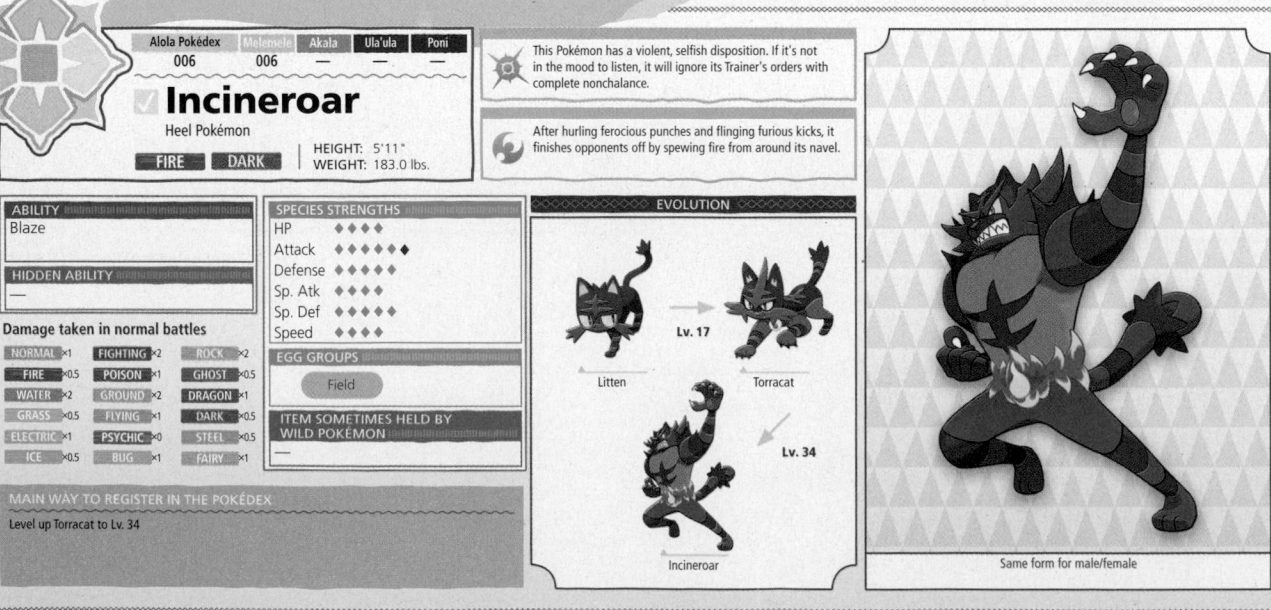

Alola Pokédex	Melemele	Akala	Ula'ula	Poni
006	006	—	—	—

☑ **Incineroar**

Heel Pokémon

FIRE **DARK**

HEIGHT: 5'11"
WEIGHT: 183.0 lbs.

This Pokémon has a violent, selfish disposition. If it's not in the mood to listen, it will ignore its Trainer's orders with complete nonchalance.

After hurling ferocious punches and flinging furious kicks, it finishes opponents off by spewing fire from around its navel.

ABILITY
Blaze

HIDDEN ABILITY
—

Damage taken in normal battles

NORMAL	×1	FIGHTING	×2	ROCK	×1
FIRE	×0.5	POISON	×1	GHOST	×2
WATER	×2	GROUND	×2	DRAGON	×1
GRASS	×0.5	FLYING	×1	DARK	×1
ELECTRIC	×1	PSYCHIC	×0	STEEL	×1
ICE	×0.5	BUG	×1	FAIRY	×1

SPECIES STRENGTHS

HP	◆◆◆◆
Attack	◆◆◆◆◆◆
Defense	◆◆◆◆◆
Sp. Atk	◆◆◆
Sp. Def	◆◆◆◆◆
Speed	◆◆◆◆

EGG GROUPS
Field

ITEM SOMETIMES HELD BY WILD POKÉMON
—

EVOLUTION

Litten → Torracat Lv. 17 → Incineroar Lv. 34

MAIN WAY TO REGISTER IN THE POKÉDEX
Level up Torracat to Lv. 34

Same form for male/female

LITTEN 004

❖ LEVEL-UP MOVES

Lv.	Name	Type	Kind	Pow.	Acc.	PP	Range
1	Scratch	Normal	Physical	40	100	35	Normal
1	Ember	Fire	Special	40	100	25	Normal
4	Growl	Normal	Status	—	100	40	Many Others
8	Lick	Ghost	Physical	30	100	30	Normal
11	Leer	Normal	Status	—	100	30	Many Others
15	Fire Fang	Fire	Physical	65	95	15	Normal
18	Roar	Normal	Status	—	—	20	Normal
22	Bite	Dark	Physical	60	100	25	Normal
25	Swagger	Normal	Status	—	85	15	Normal
29	Fury Swipes	Normal	Physical	18	80	15	Normal
32	Thrash	Normal	Physical	120	100	10	1 Random
36	Flamethrower	Fire	Special	90	100	15	Normal
39	Scary Face	Normal	Status	—	100	10	Normal
43	Flare Blitz	Fire	Physical	120	100	15	Normal
46	Outrage	Dragon	Physical	120	100	10	1 Random

❖ TM MOVES

No.	Name	Type	Kind	Pow.	Acc.	PP	Range
TM01	Work Up	Normal	Status	—	—	30	Self
TM05	Roar	Normal	Status	—	—	20	Normal
TM06	Toxic	Poison	Status	—	90	10	Normal
TM08	Bulk Up	Fighting	Status	—	—	20	Self
TM10	Hidden Power	Normal	Special	60	100	15	Normal
TM11	Sunny Day	Fire	Status	—	—	5	Both Sides
TM12	Taunt	Dark	Status	—	100	20	Normal
TM17	Protect	Normal	Status	—	—	10	Self
TM21	Frustration	Normal	Physical	—	100	20	Normal
TM27	Return	Normal	Physical	—	100	20	Normal
TM28	Leech Life	Bug	Physical	80	100	10	Normal
TM32	Double Team	Normal	Status	—	—	15	Self
TM35	Flamethrower	Fire	Special	90	100	15	Normal
TM38	Fire Blast	Fire	Special	110	85	5	Normal
TM41	Torment	Dark	Status	—	100	15	Normal
TM42	Facade	Normal	Physical	70	100	20	Normal
TM43	Flame Charge	Fire	Physical	50	100	20	Normal
TM44	Rest	Psychic	Status	—	—	10	Self
TM45	Attract	Normal	Status	—	100	15	Normal
TM48	Round	Normal	Special	60	100	15	Normal
TM50	Overheat	Fire	Special	130	90	5	Normal
TM61	Will-O-Wisp	Fire	Status	—	85	15	Normal
TM62	Acrobatics	Flying	Physical	55	100	15	Normal
TM65	Shadow Claw	Ghost	Physical	70	100	15	Normal
TM75	Swords Dance	Normal	Status	—	—	20	Self
TM87	Swagger	Normal	Status	—	85	15	Normal
TM88	Sleep Talk	Normal	Status	—	—	10	Self
TM89	U-turn	Bug	Physical	70	100	20	Normal
TM90	Substitute	Normal	Status	—	—	10	Self
TM100	Confide	Normal	Status	—	—	20	Normal

❖ EXCLUSIVE Z-MOVE

Name	Base Move	Type	Kind	Pow.	Acc.	Range

❖ MOVES TAUGHT BY PEOPLE

Name	Type	Kind	Pow.	Acc.	PP	Range
Fire Pledge	Fire	Special	80	100	10	Normal

❖ MOVES LEARNED WHEN EVOLVING

Name	Type	Kind	Pow.	Acc.	PP	Range

❖ EGG MOVES

Name	Type	Kind	Pow.	Acc.	PP	Range
Nasty Plot	Dark	Status	—	—	20	Self
Body Slam	Normal	Physical	85	100	15	Normal
Crunch	Dark	Physical	80	100	15	Normal
Fake Out	Normal	Physical	40	100	10	Normal
Revenge	Fighting	Physical	60	100	10	Normal
Heat Wave	Fire	Special	95	90	10	Many Others

TORRACAT 005

❖ LEVEL-UP MOVES

Lv.	Name	Type	Kind	Pow.	Acc.	PP	Range
1	Scratch	Normal	Physical	40	100	35	Normal
1	Ember	Fire	Special	40	100	25	Normal
1	Growl	Normal	Status	—	100	40	Many Others
1	Lick	Ghost	Physical	30	100	30	Normal
4	Growl	Normal	Status	—	100	40	Many Others
8	Lick	Ghost	Physical	30	100	30	Normal
11	Leer	Normal	Status	—	100	30	Many Others
15	Fire Fang	Fire	Physical	65	95	15	Normal
19	Roar	Normal	Status	—	—	20	Normal
24	Bite	Dark	Physical	60	100	25	Normal
28	Swagger	Normal	Status	—	85	15	Normal
33	Fury Swipes	Normal	Physical	18	80	15	Normal
37	Thrash	Normal	Physical	120	100	10	1 Random
42	Flamethrower	Fire	Special	90	100	15	Normal
46	Scary Face	Normal	Status	—	100	10	Normal
51	Flare Blitz	Fire	Physical	120	100	15	Normal
55	Outrage	Dragon	Physical	120	100	10	1 Random

❖ TM MOVES

No.	Name	Type	Kind	Pow.	Acc.	PP	Range
TM01	Work Up	Normal	Status	—	—	30	Self
TM05	Roar	Normal	Status	—	—	20	Normal
TM06	Toxic	Poison	Status	—	90	10	Normal
TM08	Bulk Up	Fighting	Status	—	—	20	Self
TM10	Hidden Power	Normal	Special	60	100	15	Normal
TM11	Sunny Day	Fire	Status	—	—	5	Both Sides
TM12	Taunt	Dark	Status	—	100	20	Normal
TM17	Protect	Normal	Status	—	—	10	Self
TM21	Frustration	Normal	Physical	—	100	20	Normal
TM27	Return	Normal	Physical	—	100	20	Normal
TM28	Leech Life	Bug	Physical	80	100	10	Normal
TM32	Double Team	Normal	Status	—	—	15	Self
TM35	Flamethrower	Fire	Special	90	100	15	Normal
TM38	Fire Blast	Fire	Special	110	85	5	Normal
TM41	Torment	Dark	Status	—	100	15	Normal
TM42	Facade	Normal	Physical	70	100	20	Normal
TM43	Flame Charge	Fire	Physical	50	100	20	Normal
TM44	Rest	Psychic	Status	—	—	10	Self
TM45	Attract	Normal	Status	—	100	15	Normal
TM48	Round	Normal	Special	60	100	15	Normal
TM50	Overheat	Fire	Special	130	90	5	Normal
TM61	Will-O-Wisp	Fire	Status	—	85	15	Normal
TM62	Acrobatics	Flying	Physical	55	100	15	Normal
TM65	Shadow Claw	Ghost	Physical	70	100	15	Normal
TM75	Swords Dance	Normal	Status	—	—	20	Self
TM87	Swagger	Normal	Status	—	85	15	Normal
TM88	Sleep Talk	Normal	Status	—	—	10	Self
TM89	U-turn	Bug	Physical	70	100	20	Normal
TM90	Substitute	Normal	Status	—	—	10	Self
TM100	Confide	Normal	Status	—	—	20	Normal

❖ EXCLUSIVE Z-MOVE

Name	Base Move	Type	Kind	Pow.	Acc.	Range

❖ MOVES TAUGHT BY PEOPLE

Name	Type	Kind	Pow.	Acc.	PP	Range
Fire Pledge	Fire	Special	80	100	10	Normal

❖ MOVES LEARNED WHEN EVOLVING

Name	Type	Kind	Pow.	Acc.	PP	Range

❖ EGG MOVES

Name	Type	Kind	Pow.	Acc.	PP	Range

INCINEROAR 006

❖ LEVEL-UP MOVES

Lv.	Name	Type	Kind	Pow.	Acc.	PP	Range
1	Darkest Lariat	Dark	Physical	85	100	10	Normal
1	Bulk Up	Fighting	Status	—	—	20	Self
1	Throat Chop	Dark	Physical	80	100	15	Normal
1	Scratch	Normal	Physical	40	100	35	Normal
1	Ember	Fire	Special	40	100	25	Normal
1	Growl	Normal	Status	—	100	40	Many Others
1	Lick	Ghost	Physical	30	100	30	Normal
4	Growl	Normal	Status	—	100	40	Many Others
8	Lick	Ghost	Physical	30	100	30	Normal
11	Leer	Normal	Status	—	100	30	Many Others
15	Fire Fang	Fire	Physical	65	95	15	Normal
19	Roar	Normal	Status	—	—	20	Normal
24	Bite	Dark	Physical	60	100	25	Normal
28	Swagger	Normal	Status	—	85	15	Normal
33	Fury Swipes	Normal	Physical	18	80	15	Normal
38	Thrash	Normal	Physical	120	100	10	1 Random
44	Flamethrower	Fire	Special	90	100	15	Normal
49	Scary Face	Normal	Status	—	100	10	Normal
55	Flare Blitz	Fire	Physical	120	100	15	Normal
60	Outrage	Dragon	Physical	120	100	10	1 Random
66	Cross Chop	Fighting	Physical	100	80	5	Normal

❖ TM MOVES

No.	Name	Type	Kind	Pow.	Acc.	PP	Range
TM01	Work Up	Normal	Status	—	—	30	Self
TM05	Roar	Normal	Status	—	—	20	Normal
TM06	Toxic	Poison	Status	—	90	10	Normal
TM08	Bulk Up	Fighting	Status	—	—	20	Self
TM10	Hidden Power	Normal	Special	60	100	15	Normal
TM11	Sunny Day	Fire	Status	—	—	5	Both Sides
TM12	Taunt	Dark	Status	—	100	20	Normal
TM15	Hyper Beam	Normal	Special	150	90	5	Normal
TM17	Protect	Normal	Status	—	—	10	Self
TM21	Frustration	Normal	Physical	—	100	20	Normal
TM26	Earthquake	Ground	Physical	100	100	10	Adjacent
TM27	Return	Normal	Physical	—	100	20	Normal
TM28	Leech Life	Bug	Physical	80	100	10	Normal
TM31	Brick Break	Fighting	Physical	75	100	15	Normal
TM32	Double Team	Normal	Status	—	—	15	Self
TM35	Flamethrower	Fire	Special	90	100	15	Normal
TM38	Fire Blast	Fire	Special	110	85	5	Normal
TM41	Torment	Dark	Status	—	100	15	Normal
TM42	Facade	Normal	Physical	70	100	20	Normal
TM43	Flame Charge	Fire	Physical	50	100	20	Normal
TM44	Rest	Psychic	Status	—	—	10	Self
TM45	Attract	Normal	Status	—	100	15	Normal
TM47	Low Sweep	Fighting	Physical	65	100	20	Normal
TM48	Round	Normal	Special	60	100	15	Normal
TM50	Overheat	Fire	Special	130	90	5	Normal
TM52	Focus Blast	Fighting	Special	120	70	5	Normal
TM56	Fling	Dark	Physical	—	100	10	Normal
TM59	Brutal Swing	Dark	Physical	60	100	20	Adjacent
TM60	Quash	Dark	Status	—	100	15	Normal
TM61	Will-O-Wisp	Fire	Status	—	85	15	Normal
TM62	Acrobatics	Flying	Physical	55	100	15	Normal
TM63	Embargo	Dark	Status	—	100	15	Normal
TM65	Shadow Claw	Ghost	Physical	70	100	15	Normal
TM68	Giga Impact	Normal	Physical	150	90	5	Normal
TM75	Swords Dance	Normal	Status	—	—	20	Self
TM78	Bulldoze	Ground	Physical	60	100	20	Adjacent
TM87	Swagger	Normal	Status	—	85	15	Normal
TM88	Sleep Talk	Normal	Status	—	—	10	Self
TM89	U-turn	Bug	Physical	70	100	20	Normal
TM90	Substitute	Normal	Status	—	—	10	Self
TM95	Snarl	Dark	Special	55	95	15	Many Others
TM97	Dark Pulse	Dark	Special	80	100	15	Normal
TM100	Confide	Normal	Status	—	—	20	Normal

❖ EXCLUSIVE Z-MOVE

Name	Base Move	Type	Kind	Pow.	Acc.	Range
Malicious Moonsault	Darkest Lariat	Dark	Physical	180	—	Normal

❖ MOVES TAUGHT BY PEOPLE

Name	Type	Kind	Pow.	Acc.	PP	Range
Fire Pledge	Fire	Special	80	100	10	Normal
Blast Burn	Fire	Special	150	90	5	Normal

❖ MOVES LEARNED WHEN EVOLVING

Name	Type	Kind	Pow.	Acc.	PP	Range
Darkest Lariat	Dark	Physical	85	100	10	Normal

❖ EGG MOVES

Name	Type	Kind	Pow.	Acc.	PP	Range

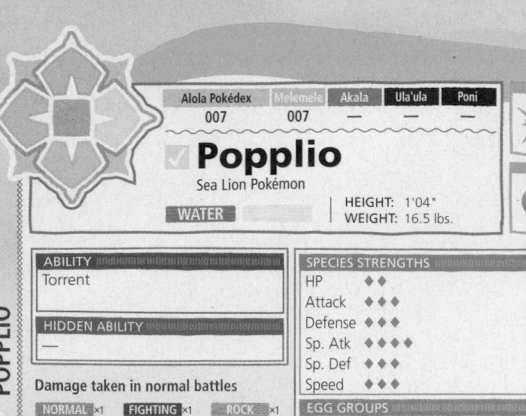

Popplio

Sea Lion Pokémon

Alola Pokédex	Melemele	Akala	Ula'ula	Poni
007	007	—	—	—

WATER

HEIGHT: 1'04"
WEIGHT: 16.5 lbs.

This Pokémon snorts body fluids from its nose, blowing balloons to smash into its foes. It's famous for being a hard worker.

This Pokémon can control water bubbles. It practices diligently so it can learn to make big bubbles.

ABILITY
Torrent

HIDDEN ABILITY
—

SPECIES STRENGTHS
HP ◆◆
Attack ◆◆
Defense ◆◆◆
Sp. Atk ◆◆◆◆
Sp. Def ◆◆◆
Speed ◆◆◆

EGG GROUPS
Water 1 | Field

ITEM SOMETIMES HELD BY WILD POKÉMON
—

Damage taken in normal battles

NORMAL	×1	FIGHTING	×1	ROCK	×1
FIRE	×0.5	POISON	×1	GHOST	×1
WATER	×0.5	GROUND	×1	DRAGON	×1
GRASS	×2	FLYING	×1	DARK	×1
ELECTRIC	×2	PSYCHIC	×1	STEEL	×0.5
ICE	×0.5	BUG	×1	FAIRY	×1

EVOLUTION

Popplio → Lv. 17 → Brionne
Lv. 34 → Primarina

MAIN WAY TO REGISTER IN THE POKÉDEX
Receive from Kahuna Hala or receive in a trade from another player

Same form for male/female

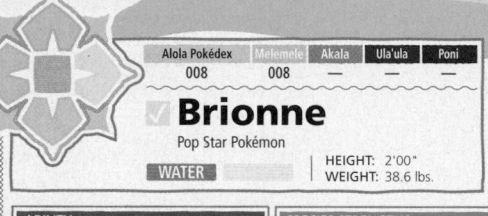

Brionne

Pop Star Pokémon

Alola Pokédex	Melemele	Akala	Ula'ula	Poni
008	008	—	—	—

WATER

HEIGHT: 2'00"
WEIGHT: 38.6 lbs.

A skillful dancer, it creates a sequence of water balloons as it dances, and briskly bombards its enemies.

It cares deeply for its companions. When its Trainer is feeling down, it performs a cheery dance to try and help.

ABILITY
Torrent

HIDDEN ABILITY
—

SPECIES STRENGTHS
HP ◆◆
Attack ◆◆◆◆
Defense ◆◆◆◆
Sp. Atk ◆◆◆◆
Sp. Def ◆◆◆◆◆
Speed ◆◆◆

EGG GROUPS
Water 1 | Field

ITEM SOMETIMES HELD BY WILD POKÉMON
—

Damage taken in normal battles

NORMAL	×1	FIGHTING	×1	ROCK	×1
FIRE	×0.5	POISON	×1	GHOST	×1
WATER	×0.5	GROUND	×1	DRAGON	×1
GRASS	×2	FLYING	×1	DARK	×1
ELECTRIC	×2	PSYCHIC	×1	STEEL	×0.5
ICE	×0.5	BUG	×1	FAIRY	×1

EVOLUTION

Popplio → Lv. 17 → Brionne
Lv. 34 → Primarina

MAIN WAY TO REGISTER IN THE POKÉDEX
Level up Popplio to Lv. 17

Same form for male/female

Primarina

Soloist Pokémon

Alola Pokédex	Melemele	Akala	Ula'ula	Poni
009	009	—	—	—

WATER | FAIRY

HEIGHT: 5'11"
WEIGHT: 97.0 lbs.

It controls its water balloons with song. The melody is learned from others of its kind and is passed down from one generation to the next.

Its singing voice is its chief weapon in battle. This Pokémon's Trainer must prioritize the daily maintenance of its throat at all costs.

ABILITY
Torrent

HIDDEN ABILITY
—

SPECIES STRENGTHS
HP ◆◆◆
Attack ◆◆◆◆
Defense ◆◆◆◆ ◆◆
Sp. Atk ◆◆◆◆◆◆ ◆◆
Sp. Def ◆◆◆◆◆◆ ◆◆
Speed ◆◆◆◆

EGG GROUPS
Water 1 | Field

ITEM SOMETIMES HELD BY WILD POKÉMON
—

Damage taken in normal battles

NORMAL	×1	FIGHTING	×0.5	ROCK	×1
FIRE	×0.5	POISON	×1	GHOST	×1
WATER	×0.5	GROUND	×1	DRAGON	×0
GRASS	×2	FLYING	×1	DARK	×0.5
ELECTRIC	×2	PSYCHIC	×1	STEEL	×1
ICE	×0.5	BUG	×0.5	FAIRY	×1

EVOLUTION
Popplio → Lv. 17 → Brionne
Lv. 34 → Primarina

MAIN WAY TO REGISTER IN THE POKÉDEX
Level up Brionne to Lv. 34

Same form for male/female

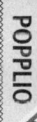

❖ LEVEL-UP MOVES

Lv.	Name	Type	Kind	Pow.	Acc.	PP	Range
1	Pound	Normal	Physical	40	100	35	Normal
1	Water Gun	Water	Special	40	100	25	Normal
4	Growl	Normal	Status	—	100	40	Many Others
8	Disarming Voice	Fairy	Special	40	—	15	Many Others
11	Baby-Doll Eyes	Fairy	Status	—	100	30	Normal
15	Aqua Jet	Water	Physical	40	100	20	Normal
18	Encore	Normal	Status	—	100	5	Normal
22	Bubble Beam	Water	Special	65	100	20	Normal
25	Sing	Normal	Status	—	55	15	Normal
29	Double Slap	Normal	Physical	15	85	10	Normal
32	Hyper Voice	Normal	Special	90	100	10	Many Others
36	Moonblast	Fairy	Special	95	100	15	Normal
39	Captivate	Normal	Status	—	100	20	Many Others
43	Hydro Pump	Water	Special	110	80	5	Normal
46	Misty Terrain	Fairy	Status	—	—	10	Both Sides

❖ TM MOVES

No.	Name	Type	Kind	Pow.	Acc.	PP	Range
TM01	Work Up	Normal	Status	—	—	30	Self
TM06	Toxic	Poison	Status	—	90	10	Normal
TM07	Hail	Ice	Status	—	—	10	Both Sides
TM10	Hidden Power	Normal	Special	60	100	15	Normal
TM13	Ice Beam	Ice	Special	90	100	10	Normal
TM14	Blizzard	Ice	Special	110	70	5	Many Others
TM17	Protect	Normal	Status	—	—	10	Self
TM18	Rain Dance	Water	Status	—	—	5	Both Sides
TM21	Frustration	Normal	Physical	—	100	20	Normal
TM27	Return	Normal	Physical	—	100	20	Normal
TM32	Double Team	Normal	Status	—	—	15	Self
TM42	Facade	Normal	Physical	70	100	20	Normal
TM44	Rest	Psychic	Status	—	—	10	Self
TM45	Attract	Normal	Status	—	100	15	Normal
TM48	Round	Normal	Special	60	100	15	Normal
TM49	Echoed Voice	Normal	Special	40	100	15	Normal
TM55	Scald	Water	Special	80	100	15	Normal
TM62	Acrobatics	Flying	Physical	55	100	15	Normal
TM87	Swagger	Normal	Status	—	85	15	Normal
TM88	Sleep Talk	Normal	Status	—	—	10	Self
TM90	Substitute	Normal	Status	—	—	10	Self
TM94	Surf	Water	Special	90	100	15	Adjacent
TM98	Waterfall	Water	Physical	80	100	15	Normal
TM100	Confide	Normal	Status	—	—	20	Normal

❖ MOVES TAUGHT BY PEOPLE

Name	Type	Kind	Pow.	Acc.	PP	Range
Water Pledge	Water	Special	80	100	10	Normal

❖ MOVES LEARNED WHEN EVOLVING

Name	Type	Kind	Pow.	Acc.	PP	Range

❖ EGG MOVES

Name	Type	Kind	Pow.	Acc.	PP	Range
Charm	Fairy	Status	—	100	20	Normal
Amnesia	Psychic	Status	—	—	20	Self
Aqua Ring	Water	Status	—	—	20	Self
Aromatic Mist	Fairy	Status	—	—	20	1 Ally
Perish Song	Normal	Status	—	—	5	Adjacent
Wonder Room	Psychic	Status	—	—	10	Both Sides

❖ EXCLUSIVE Z-MOVE

Name	Base Move	Type	Kind	Pow.	Acc.	Range

❖ LEVEL-UP MOVES

Lv.	Name	Type	Kind	Pow.	Acc.	PP	Range
1	Pound	Normal	Physical	40	100	35	Normal
1	Water Gun	Water	Special	40	100	25	Normal
1	Growl	Normal	Status	—	100	40	Many Others
1	Disarming Voice	Fairy	Special	40	—	15	Many Others
4	Growl	Normal	Status	—	100	40	Many Others
8	Disarming Voice	Fairy	Special	40	—	15	Many Others
11	Baby-Doll Eyes	Fairy	Status	—	100	30	Normal
15	Aqua Jet	Water	Physical	40	100	20	Normal
19	Encore	Normal	Status	—	100	5	Normal
24	Bubble Beam	Water	Special	65	100	20	Normal
28	Sing	Normal	Status	—	55	15	Normal
33	Double Slap	Normal	Physical	15	85	10	Normal
37	Hyper Voice	Normal	Special	90	100	10	Many Others
42	Moonblast	Fairy	Special	95	100	15	Normal
46	Captivate	Normal	Status	—	100	20	Many Others
51	Hydro Pump	Water	Special	110	80	5	Normal
55	Misty Terrain	Fairy	Status	—	—	10	Both Sides

❖ TM MOVES

No.	Name	Type	Kind	Pow.	Acc.	PP	Range
TM01	Work Up	Normal	Status	—	—	30	Self
TM06	Toxic	Poison	Status	—	90	10	Normal
TM07	Hail	Ice	Status	—	—	10	Both Sides
TM10	Hidden Power	Normal	Special	60	100	15	Normal
TM13	Ice Beam	Ice	Special	90	100	10	Normal
TM14	Blizzard	Ice	Special	110	70	5	Many Others
TM17	Protect	Normal	Status	—	—	10	Self
TM18	Rain Dance	Water	Status	—	—	5	Both Sides
TM21	Frustration	Normal	Physical	—	100	20	Normal
TM27	Return	Normal	Physical	—	100	20	Normal
TM32	Double Team	Normal	Status	—	—	15	Self
TM42	Facade	Normal	Physical	70	100	20	Normal
TM44	Rest	Psychic	Status	—	—	10	Self
TM45	Attract	Normal	Status	—	100	15	Normal
TM48	Round	Normal	Special	60	100	15	Normal
TM49	Echoed Voice	Normal	Special	40	100	15	Normal
TM55	Scald	Water	Special	80	100	15	Normal
TM62	Acrobatics	Flying	Physical	55	100	15	Normal
TM87	Swagger	Normal	Status	—	85	15	Normal
TM88	Sleep Talk	Normal	Status	—	—	10	Self
TM90	Substitute	Normal	Status	—	—	10	Self
TM94	Surf	Water	Special	90	100	15	Adjacent
TM98	Waterfall	Water	Physical	80	100	15	Normal
TM100	Confide	Normal	Status	—	—	20	Normal

❖ MOVES TAUGHT BY PEOPLE

Name	Type	Kind	Pow.	Acc.	PP	Range
Water Pledge	Water	Special	80	100	10	Normal

❖ MOVES LEARNED WHEN EVOLVING

Name	Type	Kind	Pow.	Acc.	PP	Range

❖ EGG MOVES

Name	Type	Kind	Pow.	Acc.	PP	Range

❖ EXCLUSIVE Z-MOVE

Name	Base Move	Type	Kind	Pow.	Acc.	Range

❖ LEVEL-UP MOVES

Lv.	Name	Type	Kind	Pow.	Acc.	PP	Range
1	Sparkling Aria	Water	Special	90	100	10	Adjacent
1	Pound	Normal	Physical	40	100	35	Normal
1	Water Gun	Water	Special	40	100	25	Normal
1	Growl	Normal	Status	—	100	40	Many Others
1	Disarming Voice	Fairy	Special	40	—	15	Many Others
4	Growl	Normal	Status	—	100	40	Many Others
9	Disarming Voice	Fairy	Special	40	—	15	Many Others
11	Baby-Doll Eyes	Fairy	Status	—	100	30	Normal
15	Aqua Jet	Water	Physical	40	100	20	Normal
19	Encore	Normal	Status	—	100	5	Normal
24	Bubble Beam	Water	Special	65	100	20	Normal
28	Sing	Normal	Status	—	55	15	Normal
33	Double Slap	Normal	Physical	15	85	10	Normal
38	Hyper Voice	Normal	Special	90	100	10	Many Others
44	Moonblast	Fairy	Special	95	100	15	Normal
49	Captivate	Normal	Status	—	100	20	Many Others
55	Hydro Pump	Water	Special	110	80	5	Normal
60	Misty Terrain	Fairy	Status	—	—	10	Both Sides

❖ TM MOVES

No.	Name	Type	Kind	Pow.	Acc.	PP	Range
TM01	Work Up	Normal	Status	—	—	30	Self
TM06	Toxic	Poison	Status	—	90	10	Normal
TM07	Hail	Ice	Status	—	—	10	Both Sides
TM10	Hidden Power	Normal	Special	60	100	15	Normal
TM13	Ice Beam	Ice	Special	90	100	10	Normal
TM14	Blizzard	Ice	Special	110	70	5	Many Others
TM16	Light Screen	Psychic	Status	—	—	30	Your Side
TM17	Protect	Normal	Status	—	—	10	Self
TM18	Rain Dance	Water	Status	—	—	5	Both Sides
TM21	Frustration	Normal	Physical	—	100	20	Normal
TM27	Return	Normal	Physical	—	100	20	Normal
TM29	Psychic	Psychic	Special	90	100	10	Normal
TM30	Shadow Ball	Ghost	Special	80	100	15	Normal
TM32	Double Team	Normal	Status	—	—	15	Self
TM33	Reflect	Psychic	Status	—	—	20	Your Side
TM42	Facade	Normal	Physical	70	100	20	Normal
TM44	Rest	Psychic	Status	—	—	10	Self
TM45	Attract	Normal	Status	—	100	15	Normal
TM48	Round	Normal	Special	60	100	15	Normal
TM49	Echoed Voice	Normal	Special	40	100	15	Normal
TM53	Energy Ball	Grass	Special	90	100	10	Normal
TM55	Scald	Water	Special	80	100	15	Normal
TM62	Acrobatics	Flying	Physical	55	100	15	Normal
TM68	Giga Impact	Normal	Physical	150	90	5	Normal
TM77	Psych Up	Normal	Status	—	—	10	Normal
TM87	Swagger	Normal	Status	—	85	15	Normal
TM88	Sleep Talk	Normal	Status	—	—	10	Self

No.	Name	Type	Kind	Pow.	Acc.	PP	Range
TM90	Substitute	Normal	Status	—	—	10	Self
TM94	Surf	Water	Special	90	100	15	Adjacent
TM98	Waterfall	Water	Physical	80	100	15	Normal
TM99	Dazzling Gleam	Fairy	Special	80	100	10	Many Others
TM100	Confide	Normal	Status	—	—	20	Normal

❖ MOVES TAUGHT BY PEOPLE

Name	Type	Kind	Pow.	Acc.	PP	Range
Water Pledge	Water	Special	80	100	10	Normal
Hydro Cannon	Water	Special	150	90	5	Normal

❖ MOVES LEARNED WHEN EVOLVING

Name	Type	Kind	Pow.	Acc.	PP	Range
Sparkling Aria	Water	Special	90	100	10	Adjacent

❖ EGG MOVES

Name	Type	Kind	Pow.	Acc.	PP	Range

❖ EXCLUSIVE Z-MOVE

Name	Base Move	Type	Kind	Pow.	Acc.	Range
Oceanic Operetta	Sparkling Aria	Water	Special	195	—	Normal

Pikipek

Alola Pokédex	Melemele	Akala	Ula'ula	Poni
010	010	001	001	001

Woodpecker Pokémon

NORMAL FLYING

HEIGHT: 1'00"
WEIGHT: 2.6 lbs.

It can peck at a rate of 16 times a second to drill holes in trees. It uses the holes for food storage and for nesting.

This Pokémon feeds on berries, whose leftover seeds become the ammunition for the attacks it fires off from its mouth.

ABILITY
Keen Eye
Skill Link

HIDDEN ABILITY
Pickup

Damage taken in normal battles

NORMAL ×1	FIGHTING ×1	ROCK ×1			
FIRE ×1	POISON ×1	GHOST ×0			
WATER ×1	GROUND ×0	DRAGON ×1			
GRASS ×0.5	FLYING ×1	DARK ×1			
ELECTRIC ×2	PSYCHIC ×1	STEEL ×1			
ICE ×2	BUG ×0.5	FAIRY ×1			

SPECIES STRENGTHS
HP ◆
Attack ◆◆◆◆
Defense ◆◆
Sp. Atk ◆◆
Sp. Def ◆
Speed ◆◆◆◆

EGG GROUPS
Flying

ITEM SOMETIMES HELD BY WILD POKÉMON
Oran Berry

MAIN WAY TO REGISTER IN THE POKÉDEX
Catch in the tall grass on Route 1

EVOLUTION

Pikipek — Lv. 14 → Trumbeak — Lv. 28 → Toucannon

Same form for male/female

Trumbeak

Alola Pokédex	Melemele	Akala	Ula'ula	Poni
011	011	002	002	002

Bugle Beak Pokémon

NORMAL FLYING

HEIGHT: 2'00"
WEIGHT: 32.6 lbs.

It eats berries and stores their seeds in its beak. When it encounters enemies or prey, it fires off all the seeds in a burst.

By bending its beak, it can produce a variety of calls and brand itself a noisy nuisance for its neighbors.

ABILITY
Keen Eye
Skill Link

HIDDEN ABILITY
Pickup

Damage taken in normal battles

NORMAL ×1	FIGHTING ×1	ROCK ×1			
FIRE ×1	POISON ×1	GHOST ×0			
WATER ×1	GROUND ×0	DRAGON ×1			
GRASS ×0.5	FLYING ×1	DARK ×1			
ELECTRIC ×2	PSYCHIC ×1	STEEL ×1			
ICE ×2	BUG ×0.5	FAIRY ×1			

SPECIES STRENGTHS
HP ◆◆
Attack ◆◆◆◆◆
Defense ◆◆◆
Sp. Atk ◆◆
Sp. Def ◆◆◆
Speed ◆◆◆◆◆

EGG GROUPS
Flying

ITEM SOMETIMES HELD BY WILD POKÉMON
Sitrus Berry

MAIN WAY TO REGISTER IN THE POKÉDEX
Catch in the tall grass on Route 8

EVOLUTION

Pikipek — Lv. 14 → Trumbeak — Lv. 28 → Toucannon

Same form for male/female

Toucannon

Alola Pokédex	Melemele	Akala	Ula'ula	Poni
012	012	003	003	003

Cannon Pokémon

NORMAL FLYING

HEIGHT: 3'07"
WEIGHT: 57.3 lbs.

When it battles, its beak heats up. The temperature can easily exceed 212 degrees Fahrenheit, causing severe burns when it hits.

Within its beak, its internal gas ignites, explosively launching seeds with enough power to pulverize boulders.

ABILITY
Keen Eye
Skill Link

HIDDEN ABILITY
Sheer Force

Damage taken in normal battles

NORMAL ×1	FIGHTING ×1	ROCK ×1			
FIRE ×1	POISON ×1	GHOST ×0			
WATER ×1	GROUND ×0	DRAGON ×1			
GRASS ×0.5	FLYING ×1	DARK ×1			
ELECTRIC ×2	PSYCHIC ×1	STEEL ×1			
ICE ×2	BUG ×0.5	FAIRY ×1			

SPECIES STRENGTHS
HP ◆◆◆
Attack ◆◆◆◆◆◆◆◆
Defense ◆◆◆◆
Sp. Atk ◆◆◆
Sp. Def ◆◆◆◆
Speed ◆◆◆◆

EGG GROUPS
Flying

ITEM SOMETIMES HELD BY WILD POKÉMON
—

MAIN WAY TO REGISTER IN THE POKÉDEX
Level up Trumbeak to Lv. 28

EVOLUTION

Pikipek — Lv. 14 → Trumbeak — Lv. 28 → Toucannon

Same form for male/female

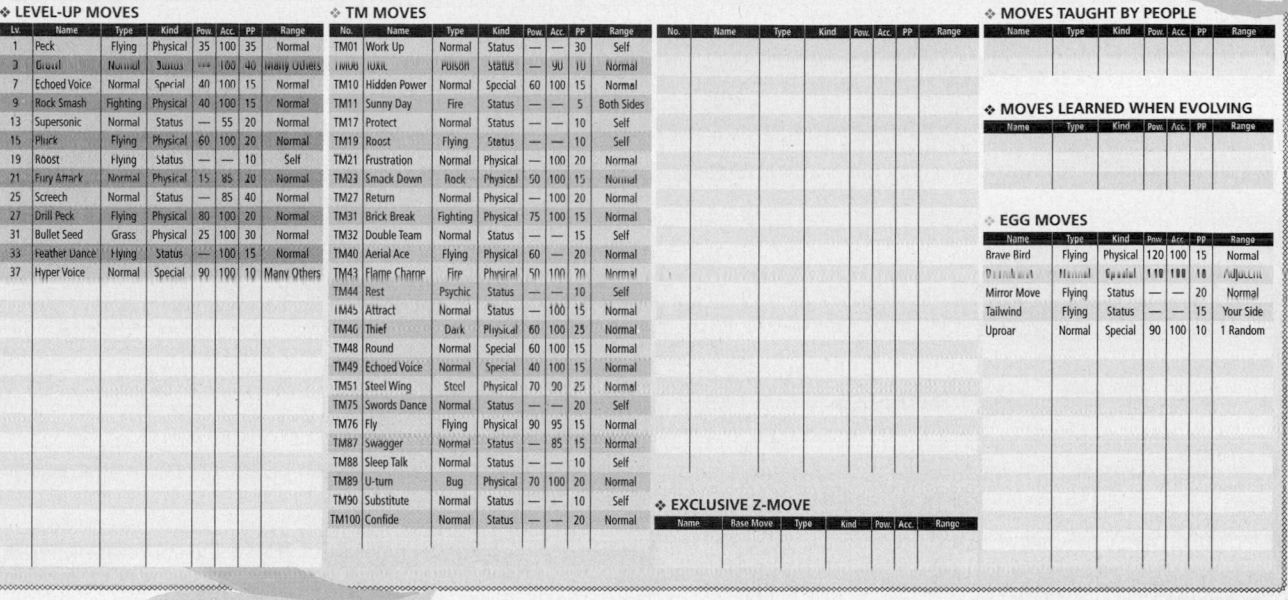

PIKIPEK 010

❖ LEVEL-UP MOVES

Lv.	Name	Type	Kind	Pow.	Acc.	PP	Range
1	Peck	Flying	Physical	35	100	35	Normal
3	Growl	Normal	Status	—	100	40	Many Others
7	Echoed Voice	Normal	Special	40	100	15	Normal
9	Rock Smash	Fighting	Physical	40	100	15	Normal
13	Supersonic	Normal	Status	—	55	20	Normal
15	Pluck	Flying	Physical	60	100	20	Normal
19	Roost	Flying	Status	—	—	10	Self
21	Fury Attack	Normal	Physical	15	85	20	Normal
25	Screech	Normal	Status	—	85	40	Normal
27	Drill Peck	Flying	Physical	80	100	20	Normal
31	Bullet Seed	Grass	Physical	25	100	30	Normal
33	Feather Dance	Flying	Status	—	100	15	Normal
37	Hyper Voice	Normal	Special	90	100	10	Many Others

❖ TM MOVES

No.	Name	Type	Kind	Pow.	Acc.	PP	Range
TM01	Work Up	Normal	Status	—	—	30	Self
TM06	Toxic	Poison	Status	—	90	10	Normal
TM10	Hidden Power	Normal	Special	60	100	15	Normal
TM11	Sunny Day	Fire	Status	—	—	5	Both Sides
TM17	Protect	Normal	Status	—	—	10	Self
TM19	Roost	Flying	Status	—	—	10	Self
TM21	Frustration	Normal	Physical	—	100	20	Normal
TM23	Smack Down	Rock	Physical	50	100	15	Normal
TM27	Return	Normal	Physical	—	100	20	Normal
TM31	Brick Break	Fighting	Physical	75	100	15	Normal
TM32	Double Team	Normal	Status	—	—	15	Self
TM40	Aerial Ace	Flying	Physical	60	—	20	Normal
TM43	Flame Charge	Fire	Physical	50	100	20	Normal
TM44	Rest	Psychic	Status	—	—	10	Self
TM45	Attract	Normal	Status	—	100	15	Normal
TM46	Thief	Dark	Physical	60	100	25	Normal
TM48	Round	Normal	Special	60	100	15	Normal
TM49	Echoed Voice	Normal	Special	40	100	15	Normal
TM51	Steel Wing	Steel	Physical	70	90	25	Normal
TM75	Swords Dance	Normal	Status	—	—	20	Self
TM76	Fly	Flying	Physical	90	95	15	Normal
TM87	Swagger	Normal	Status	—	85	15	Normal
TM88	Sleep Talk	Normal	Status	—	—	10	Self
TM89	U-turn	Bug	Physical	70	100	20	Normal
TM90	Substitute	Normal	Status	—	—	10	Self
TM100	Confide	Normal	Status	—	—	20	Normal

❖ MOVES TAUGHT BY PEOPLE

Name	Type	Kind	Pow.	Acc.	PP	Range

❖ MOVES LEARNED WHEN EVOLVING

Name	Type	Kind	Pow.	Acc.	PP	Range

❖ EGG MOVES

Name	Type	Kind	Pow.	Acc.	PP	Range
Brave Bird	Flying	Physical	120	100	15	Normal
Ominous Wind	Normal	Special	110	100	10	Adjacent
Mirror Move	Flying	Status	—	—	20	Normal
Tailwind	Flying	Status	—	—	15	Your Side
Uproar	Normal	Special	90	100	10	1 Random

❖ EXCLUSIVE Z-MOVE

Name	Base Move	Type	Kind	Pow.	Acc.	Range

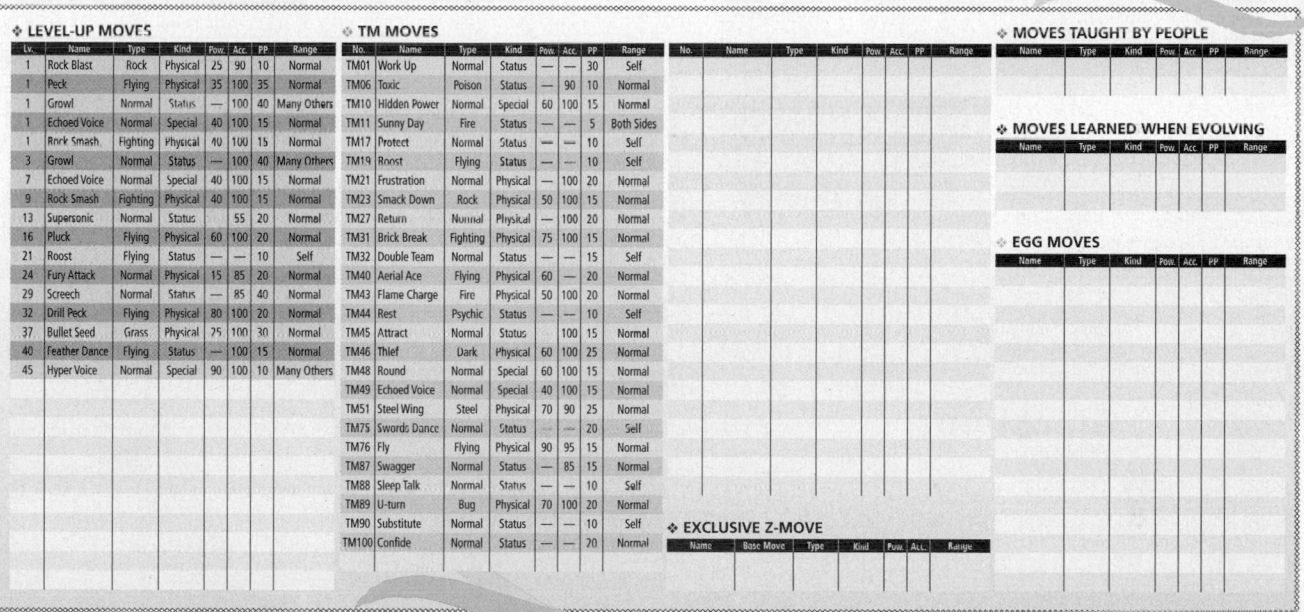

TRUMBEAK 011

❖ LEVEL-UP MOVES

Lv.	Name	Type	Kind	Pow.	Acc.	PP	Range
1	Rock Blast	Rock	Physical	25	90	10	Normal
1	Peck	Flying	Physical	35	100	35	Normal
1	Growl	Normal	Status	—	100	40	Many Others
1	Echoed Voice	Normal	Special	40	100	15	Normal
1	Rock Smash	Fighting	Physical	40	100	15	Normal
3	Growl	Normal	Status	—	100	40	Many Others
7	Echoed Voice	Normal	Special	40	100	15	Normal
9	Rock Smash	Fighting	Physical	40	100	15	Normal
13	Supersonic	Normal	Status	—	55	20	Normal
16	Pluck	Flying	Physical	60	100	20	Normal
21	Roost	Flying	Status	—	—	10	Self
24	Fury Attack	Normal	Physical	15	85	20	Normal
29	Screech	Normal	Status	—	85	40	Normal
32	Drill Peck	Flying	Physical	80	100	20	Normal
37	Bullet Seed	Grass	Physical	25	100	30	Normal
40	Feather Dance	Flying	Status	—	100	15	Normal
45	Hyper Voice	Normal	Special	90	100	10	Many Others

❖ TM MOVES

No.	Name	Type	Kind	Pow.	Acc.	PP	Range
TM01	Work Up	Normal	Status	—	—	30	Self
TM06	Toxic	Poison	Status	—	90	10	Normal
TM10	Hidden Power	Normal	Special	60	100	15	Normal
TM11	Sunny Day	Fire	Status	—	—	5	Both Sides
TM17	Protect	Normal	Status	—	—	10	Self
TM19	Roost	Flying	Status	—	—	10	Self
TM21	Frustration	Normal	Physical	—	100	20	Normal
TM23	Smack Down	Rock	Physical	50	100	15	Normal
TM27	Return	Normal	Physical	—	100	20	Normal
TM31	Brick Break	Fighting	Physical	75	100	15	Normal
TM32	Double Team	Normal	Status	—	—	15	Self
TM40	Aerial Ace	Flying	Physical	60	—	20	Normal
TM43	Flame Charge	Fire	Physical	50	100	20	Normal
TM44	Rest	Psychic	Status	—	—	10	Self
TM45	Attract	Normal	Status	—	100	15	Normal
TM46	Thief	Dark	Physical	60	100	25	Normal
TM48	Round	Normal	Special	60	100	15	Normal
TM49	Echoed Voice	Normal	Special	40	100	15	Normal
TM51	Steel Wing	Steel	Physical	70	90	25	Normal
TM75	Swords Dance	Normal	Status	—	—	20	Self
TM76	Fly	Flying	Physical	90	95	15	Normal
TM87	Swagger	Normal	Status	—	85	15	Normal
TM88	Sleep Talk	Normal	Status	—	—	10	Self
TM89	U-turn	Bug	Physical	70	100	20	Normal
TM90	Substitute	Normal	Status	—	—	10	Self
TM100	Confide	Normal	Status	—	—	20	Normal

❖ MOVES TAUGHT BY PEOPLE

No.	Name	Type	Kind	Pow.	Acc.	PP	Range

❖ MOVES LEARNED WHEN EVOLVING

Name	Type	Kind	Pow.	Acc.	PP	Range

❖ EGG MOVES

Name	Type	Kind	Pow.	Acc.	PP	Range

❖ EXCLUSIVE Z-MOVE

Name	Base Move	Type	Kind	Pow.	Acc.	Range

TOUCANNON 012

❖ LEVEL-UP MOVES

Lv.	Name	Type	Kind	Pow.	Acc.	PP	Range
1	Beak Blast	Flying	Physical	100	100	15	Normal
1	Rock Blast	Rock	Physical	25	90	10	Normal
1	Peck	Flying	Physical	35	100	35	Normal
1	Growl	Normal	Status	—	100	40	Many Others
1	Echoed Voice	Normal	Special	40	100	15	Normal
1	Rock Smash	Fighting	Physical	40	100	15	Normal
3	Growl	Normal	Status	—	100	40	Many Others
7	Echoed Voice	Normal	Special	40	100	15	Normal
9	Rock Smash	Fighting	Physical	40	100	15	Normal
13	Supersonic	Normal	Status	—	55	20	Normal
16	Pluck	Flying	Physical	60	100	20	Normal
21	Roost	Flying	Status	—	—	10	Self
24	Fury Attack	Normal	Physical	15	85	20	Normal
30	Screech	Normal	Status	—	85	40	Normal
34	Drill Peck	Flying	Physical	80	100	20	Normal
40	Bullet Seed	Grass	Physical	25	100	30	Normal
44	Feather Dance	Flying	Status	—	100	15	Normal
50	Hyper Voice	Normal	Special	90	100	10	Many Others

❖ TM MOVES

No.	Name	Type	Kind	Pow.	Acc.	PP	Range
TM01	Work Up	Normal	Status	—	—	30	Self
TM06	Toxic	Poison	Status	—	90	10	Normal
TM10	Hidden Power	Normal	Special	60	100	15	Normal
TM11	Sunny Day	Fire	Status	—	—	5	Both Sides
TM17	Protect	Normal	Status	—	—	10	Self
TM19	Roost	Flying	Status	—	—	10	Self
TM21	Frustration	Normal	Physical	—	100	20	Normal
TM23	Smack Down	Rock	Physical	50	100	15	Normal
TM27	Return	Normal	Physical	—	100	20	Normal
TM31	Brick Break	Fighting	Physical	75	100	15	Normal
TM32	Double Team	Normal	Status	—	—	15	Self
TM40	Aerial Ace	Flying	Physical	60	—	20	Normal
TM43	Flame Charge	Fire	Physical	50	100	20	Normal
TM44	Rest	Psychic	Status	—	—	10	Self
TM45	Attract	Normal	Status	—	100	15	Normal
TM46	Thief	Dark	Physical	60	100	25	Normal
TM48	Round	Normal	Special	60	100	15	Normal
TM49	Echoed Voice	Normal	Special	40	100	15	Normal
TM50	Overheat	Fire	Special	130	90	10	Normal
TM51	Steel Wing	Steel	Physical	70	90	25	Normal
TM75	Swords Dance	Normal	Status	—	—	20	Self
TM76	Fly	Flying	Physical	90	95	15	Normal
TM87	Swagger	Normal	Status	—	85	15	Normal
TM88	Sleep Talk	Normal	Status	—	—	10	Self
TM89	U-turn	Bug	Physical	70	100	20	Normal
TM90	Substitute	Normal	Status	—	—	10	Self
TM91	Flash Cannon	Steel	Special	80	100	10	Normal

❖ MOVES TAUGHT BY PEOPLE

No.	Name	Type	Kind	Pow.	Acc.	PP	Range
TM100	Confide	Normal	Status	—	—	20	Normal

❖ MOVES LEARNED WHEN EVOLVING

Name	Type	Kind	Pow.	Acc.	PP	Range
Beak Blast	Flying	Physical	100	100	15	Normal

❖ EGG MOVES

Name	Type	Kind	Pow.	Acc.	PP	Range

❖ EXCLUSIVE Z-MOVE

Name	Base Move	Type	Kind	Pow.	Acc.	Range

Yungoos
Loitering Pokémon

Alola Pokédex	Melemele	Akala	Ula'ula	Poni
013	013	004	004	004

NORMAL

HEIGHT: 1'04"
WEIGHT: 13.2 lbs.

With its sharp fangs, it will bite anything. It did not originally live in Alola but was imported from another region.

It wanders around in a never-ending search for food. At dusk, it collapses from exhaustion and falls asleep on the spot.

ABILITY
Stakeout
Strong Jaw

HIDDEN ABILITY
Adaptability

SPECIES STRENGTHS
HP ◆◆
Attack ◆◆◆◆
Defense ◆◆
Sp. Atk ◆◆
Sp. Def ◆◆
Speed ◆◆◆

Damage taken in normal battles

NORMAL ×1	FIGHTING ×2	ROCK ×1
FIRE ×1	POISON ×1	GHOST ×0
WATER ×1	GROUND ×1	DRAGON ×1
GRASS ×1	FLYING ×1	DARK ×1
ELECTRIC ×1	PSYCHIC ×1	STEEL ×1
ICE ×1	BUG ×1	FAIRY ×1

EGG GROUPS
Field

ITEM SOMETIMES HELD BY WILD POKÉMON
Pecha Berry

EVOLUTION

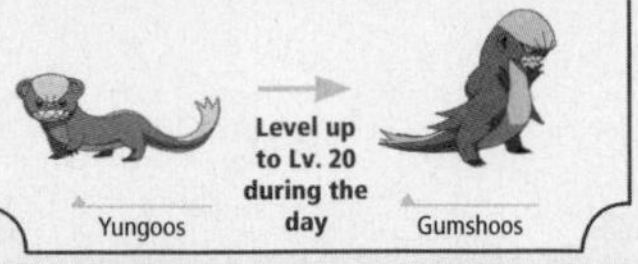

Yungoos → Level up to Lv. 20 during the day → Gumshoos

MAIN WAY TO REGISTER IN THE POKÉDEX
Catch in the tall grass on Route 1 when it is daytime in your game

Same form for male/female

❖ LEVEL-UP MOVES

Lv.	Name	Type	Kind	Pow.	Acc.	PP	Range
1	Tackle	Normal	Physical	40	100	35	Normal
3	Leer	Normal	Status	—	100	30	Many Others
7	Pursuit	Dark	Physical	40	100	20	Normal
10	Sand Attack	Ground	Status	—	100	15	Normal
13	Odor Sleuth	Normal	Status	—	—	40	Normal
16	Bide	Normal	Physical	—	—	10	Self
19	Bite	Dark	Physical	60	100	25	Normal
22	Mud-Slap	Ground	Special	20	100	10	Normal
25	Super Fang	Normal	Physical	—	90	10	Normal
28	Take Down	Normal	Physical	90	85	20	Normal
31	Scary Face	Normal	Status	—	100	10	Normal
34	Crunch	Dark	Physical	80	100	15	Normal
37	Hyper Fang	Normal	Physical	80	90	15	Normal
40	Yawn	Normal	Status	—	—	10	Normal
43	Thrash	Normal	Physical	120	100	10	1 Random
46	Rest	Psychic	Status	—	—	10	Self

❖ TM MOVES

No.	Name	Type	Kind	Pow.	Acc.	PP	Range
TM01	Work Up	Normal	Status	—	—	30	Self
TM06	Toxic	Poison	Status	—	90	10	Normal
TM10	Hidden Power	Normal	Special	60	100	15	Normal
TM12	Taunt	Dark	Status	—	100	20	Normal
TM17	Protect	Normal	Status	—	—	10	Self
TM21	Frustration	Normal	Physical	—	100	20	Normal
TM26	Earthquake	Ground	Physical	100	100	10	Adjacent
TM27	Return	Normal	Physical	—	100	20	Normal
TM32	Double Team	Normal	Status	—	—	15	Self
TM37	Sandstorm	Rock	Status	—	—	10	Both Sides
TM39	Rock Tomb	Rock	Physical	60	95	15	Normal
TM41	Torment	Dark	Status	—	100	15	Normal
TM42	Facade	Normal	Physical	70	100	20	Normal
TM44	Rest	Psychic	Status	—	—	10	Self
TM45	Attract	Normal	Status	—	100	15	Normal
TM46	Thief	Dark	Physical	60	100	25	Normal
TM48	Round	Normal	Special	60	100	15	Normal
TM49	Echoed Voice	Normal	Special	40	100	15	Normal
TM66	Payback	Dark	Physical	50	100	10	Normal
TM87	Swagger	Normal	Status	—	85	15	Normal
TM88	Sleep Talk	Normal	Status	—	—	10	Self
TM89	U-turn	Bug	Physical	70	100	20	Normal
TM90	Substitute	Normal	Status	—	—	10	Self
TM100	Confide	Normal	Status	—	—	20	Normal

❖ MOVES TAUGHT BY PEOPLE

Name	Type	Kind	Pow.	Acc.	PP	Range

❖ MOVES LEARNED WHEN EVOLVING

Name	Type	Kind	Pow.	Acc.	PP	Range

❖ EGG MOVES

Name	Type	Kind	Pow.	Acc.	PP	Range
Revenge	Fighting	Physical	60	100	10	Normal
Last Resort	Normal	Physical	140	100	5	Normal

❖ EXCLUSIVE Z-MOVE

Name	Base Move	Type	Kind	Pow.	Acc.	Range

Gumshoos
Stakeout Pokémon

Alola Pokédex	Melemele	Akala	Ula'ula	Poni
014	014	005	005	005

NORMAL

HEIGHT: 2'04"
WEIGHT: 31.3 lbs.

When it finds a trace of its prey, it patiently stakes out the location...but it's always snoozing by nightfall.

It adores having Rattata and Raticate for dinner, but as it's diurnal, it never encounters them. This Pokémon boasts incredible patience.

ABILITY
Stakeout
Strong Jaw

HIDDEN ABILITY
Adaptability

SPECIES STRENGTHS
HP ◆◆◆
Attack ◆◆◆◆◆◆◆◆
Defense ◆◆◆
Sp. Atk ◆◆◆
Sp. Def ◆◆◆
Speed ◆◆◆

Damage taken in normal battles

NORMAL ×1	FIGHTING ×2	ROCK ×1
FIRE ×1	POISON ×1	GHOST ×0
WATER ×1	GROUND ×1	DRAGON ×1
GRASS ×1	FLYING ×1	DARK ×1
ELECTRIC ×1	PSYCHIC ×1	STEEL ×1
ICE ×1	BUG ×1	FAIRY ×1

EGG GROUPS
Field

ITEM SOMETIMES HELD BY WILD POKÉMON
Pecha Berry

EVOLUTION

Yungoos → Level up to Lv. 20 during the day → Gumshoos

MAIN WAY TO REGISTER IN THE POKÉDEX
Catch in the tall grass in Akala Outskirts when it is daytime in your game

Same form for male/female

❖ LEVEL-UP MOVES

Lv.	Name	Type	Kind	Pow.	Acc.	PP	Range
1	Tackle	Normal	Physical	40	100	35	Normal
1	Leer	Normal	Status	—	100	30	Many Others
1	Pursuit	Dark	Physical	40	100	20	Normal
1	Sand Attack	Ground	Status	—	100	15	Normal
3	Leer	Normal	Status	—	100	30	Many Others
7	Pursuit	Dark	Physical	40	100	20	Normal
10	Sand Attack	Ground	Status	—	100	15	Normal
13	Odor Sleuth	Normal	Status	—	—	40	Normal
16	Bide	Normal	Physical	—	—	10	Self
19	Bite	Dark	Physical	60	100	25	Normal
23	Mud-Slap	Ground	Special	20	100	10	Normal
27	Super Fang	Normal	Physical	—	90	10	Normal
31	Take Down	Normal	Physical	90	85	20	Normal
35	Scary Face	Normal	Status	—	100	10	Normal
39	Crunch	Dark	Physical	80	100	15	Normal
43	Hyper Fang	Normal	Physical	80	90	15	Normal
47	Yawn	Normal	Status	—	—	10	Normal
51	Thrash	Normal	Physical	120	100	10	1 Random
55	Rest	Psychic	Status	—	—	10	Self

❖ TM MOVES

No.	Name	Type	Kind	Pow.	Acc.	PP	Range
TM01	Work Up	Normal	Status	—	—	30	Self
TM05	Roar	Normal	Status	—	—	20	Normal
TM06	Toxic	Poison	Status	—	90	10	Normal
TM10	Hidden Power	Normal	Special	60	100	15	Normal
TM12	Taunt	Dark	Status	—	100	20	Normal
TM17	Protect	Normal	Status	—	—	10	Self
TM21	Frustration	Normal	Physical	—	100	20	Normal
TM26	Earthquake	Ground	Physical	100	100	10	Adjacent
TM27	Return	Normal	Physical	—	100	20	Normal
TM32	Double Team	Normal	Status	—	—	15	Self
TM37	Sandstorm	Rock	Status	—	—	10	Both Sides
TM39	Rock Tomb	Rock	Physical	60	95	15	Normal
TM41	Torment	Dark	Status	—	100	15	Normal
TM42	Facade	Normal	Physical	70	100	20	Normal
TM44	Rest	Psychic	Status	—	—	10	Self
TM45	Attract	Normal	Status	—	100	15	Normal
TM46	Thief	Dark	Physical	60	100	25	Normal
TM48	Round	Normal	Special	60	100	15	Normal
TM49	Echoed Voice	Normal	Special	40	100	15	Normal
TM56	Fling	Dark	Physical	—	100	10	Normal
TM66	Payback	Dark	Physical	50	100	10	Normal
TM78	Bulldoze	Ground	Physical	60	100	20	Adjacent
TM87	Swagger	Normal	Status	—	85	15	Normal
TM88	Sleep Talk	Normal	Status	—	—	10	Self
TM89	U-turn	Bug	Physical	70	100	20	Normal
TM90	Substitute	Normal	Status	—	—	10	Self
TM100	Confide	Normal	Status	—	—	20	Normal

❖ MOVES TAUGHT BY PEOPLE

Name	Type	Kind	Pow.	Acc.	PP	Range

❖ MOVES LEARNED WHEN EVOLVING

Name	Type	Kind	Pow.	Acc.	PP	Range

❖ EGG MOVES

Name	Type	Kind	Pow.	Acc.	PP	Range

❖ EXCLUSIVE Z-MOVE

Name	Base Move	Type	Kind	Pow.	Acc.	Range

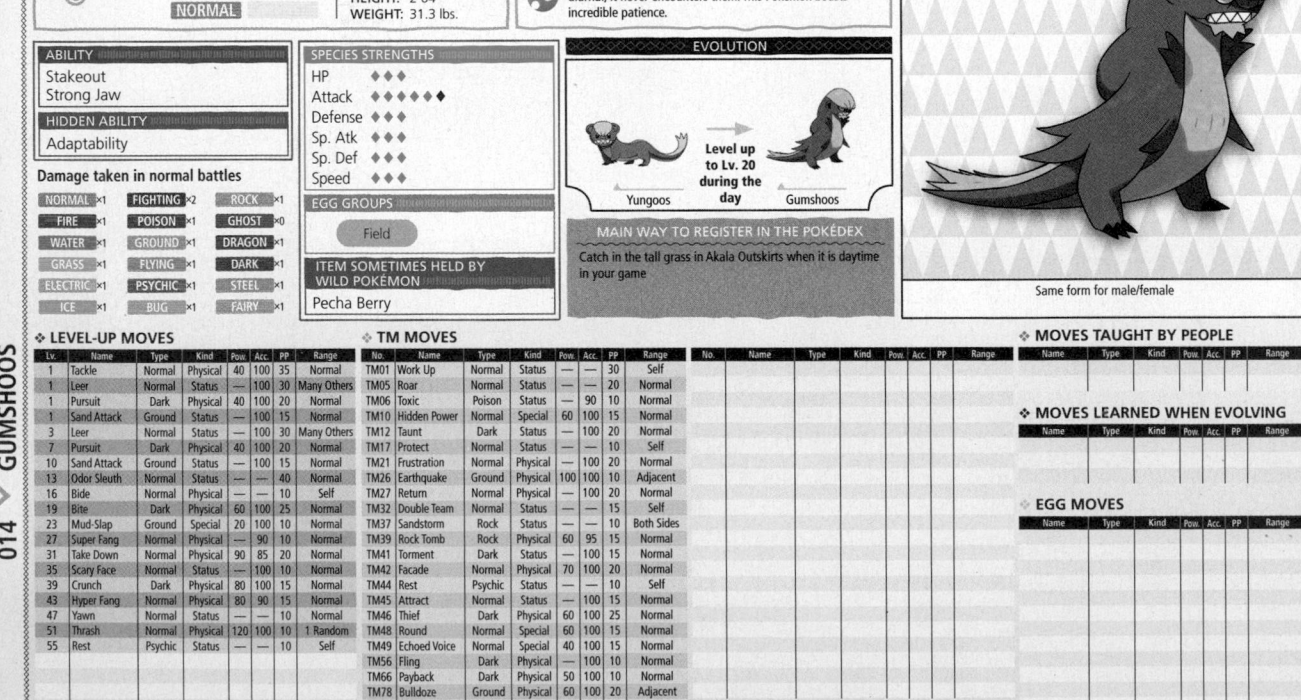

Rattata

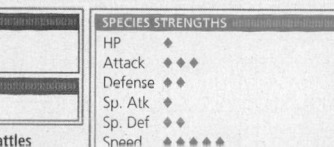

Alola Pokédex	Melemele	Akala	Ula'ula	Poni
015	015	006	006	006

Mouse Pokémon

DARK **NORMAL**

HEIGHT: 1'00"
WEIGHT: 8.4 lbs.

With its incisors, it gnaws through doors and infiltrates people's homes. Then, with a twitch of its whiskers, it steals whatever food it finds.

When the sun goes down, it becomes active. It runs around town on a chase for good food for the boss of its nest—Raticate.

ABILITY
Gluttony
Hustle

HIDDEN ABILITY
Thick Fat

SPECIES STRENGTHS
HP	◆
Attack	◆◆◆
Defense	◆◆
Sp. Atk	◆
Sp. Def	◆
Speed	◆◆◆◆

EGG GROUPS
Field

ITEM SOMETIMES HELD BY WILD POKÉMON
Pecha Berry

Damage taken in normal battles
NORMAL ×1	FIGHTING ×4	ROCK ×1
FIRE ×1	POISON ×1	GHOST ×0
WATER ×1	GROUND ×1	DRAGON ×1
GRASS ×1	FLYING ×1	DARK ×0.5
ELECTRIC ×1	PSYCHIC ×0	STEEL ×1
ICE ×1	BUG ×2	FAIRY ×1

EVOLUTION
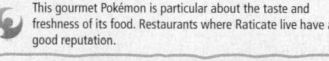
Alolan Rattata → Level up to Lv. 20 at night → Alolan Raticate

MAIN WAY TO REGISTER IN THE POKÉDEX
Catch in the tall grass on Route 1 when it is nighttime in your game.

❖ ALOLA FORM ❖

Same form for male/female

❖ LEVEL-UP MOVES

Lv.	Name	Type	Kind	Pow.	Acc.	PP	Range
1	Tackle	Normal	Physical	40	100	35	Normal
1	Tail Whip	Normal	Status	—	100	30	Many Others
4	Quick Attack	Normal	Physical	40	100	30	Normal
7	Focus Energy	Normal	Status	—	—	30	Self
10	Bite	Dark	Physical	60	100	25	Normal
13	Pursuit	Dark	Physical	40	100	20	Normal
16	Hyper Fang	Normal	Physical	80	90	15	Normal
19	Assurance	Dark	Physical	60	100	10	Normal
22	Crunch	Dark	Physical	80	100	15	Normal
25	Sucker Punch	Dark	Physical	70	100	5	Normal
28	Super Fang	Normal	Physical	—	90	10	Normal
31	Double-Edge	Normal	Physical	120	100	15	Normal
34	Endeavor	Normal	Physical	—	100	5	Normal

❖ TM MOVES

No.	Name	Type	Kind	Pow.	Acc.	PP	Range
TM06	Toxic	Poison	Status	—	90	10	Normal
TM10	Hidden Power	Normal	Special	60	100	15	Normal
TM11	Sunny Day	Fire	Status	—	—	5	Both Sides
TM12	Taunt	Dark	Status	—	100	20	Normal
TM13	Ice Beam	Ice	Special	90	100	10	Normal
TM14	Blizzard	Ice	Special	110	70	5	Many Others
TM17	Protect	Normal	Status	—	—	10	Self
TM18	Rain Dance	Water	Status	—	—	5	Both Sides
TM21	Frustration	Normal	Physical	—	100	20	Normal
TM27	Return	Normal	Physical	—	100	20	Normal
TM30	Shadow Ball	Ghost	Special	80	100	15	Normal
TM32	Double Team	Normal	Status	—	—	15	Self
TM36	Sludge Bomb	Poison	Special	90	100	10	Normal
TM41	Torment	Dark	Status	—	100	15	Normal
TM42	Facade	Normal	Physical	70	100	20	Normal
TM44	Rest	Psychic	Status	—	—	10	Self
TM45	Attract	Normal	Status	—	100	15	Normal
TM46	Thief	Dark	Physical	60	100	25	Normal
TM48	Round	Normal	Special	60	100	15	Normal
TM60	Quash	Dark	Status	—	100	15	Normal
TM63	Embargo	Dark	Status	—	100	15	Normal
TM65	Shadow Claw	Ghost	Physical	70	100	15	Normal
TM86	Grass Knot	Grass	Special	—	100	20	Normal
TM87	Swagger	Normal	Status	—	85	15	Normal
TM88	Sleep Talk	Normal	Status	—	—	10	Self
TM89	U-turn	Bug	Physical	70	100	20	Normal
TM90	Substitute	Normal	Status	—	—	10	Self
TM95	Snarl	Dark	Special	55	95	15	Many Others

No.	Name	Type	Kind	Pow.	Acc.	PP	Range
TM97	Dark Pulse	Dark	Special	80	100	15	Normal
TM100	Confide	Normal	Status	—	—	20	Normal

❖ MOVES TAUGHT BY PEOPLE
Name	Type	Kind	Pow.	Acc.	PP	Range

❖ MOVES LEARNED WHEN EVOLVING
Name	Type	Kind	Pow.	Acc.	PP	Range

❖ EGG MOVES
Name	Type	Kind	Pow.	Acc.	PP	Range
Snatch	Dark	Status	—	—	10	Self
Stockpile	Normal	Status	—	—	20	Self
Fury Swipes	Normal	Physical	18	80	15	Normal
Switcheroo	Dark	Status	—	100	10	Normal
Counter	Fighting	Physical	—	100	20	Varies
Reversal	Fighting	Physical	—	100	15	Normal
Uproar	Normal	Special	90	100	10	1 Random
Swallow	Normal	Status	—	—	10	Self
Me First	Normal	Status	—	—	20	Varies
Revenge	Fighting	Physical	60	100	10	Normal
Final Gambit	Fighting	Special	—	100	5	Normal

❖ EXCLUSIVE Z-MOVE
Name	Base Move	Type	Kind	Pow.	Acc.	Range

Raticate

Alola Pokédex	Melemele	Akala	Ula'ula	Poni
016	016	007	007	007

Mouse Pokémon

DARK **NORMAL**

HEIGHT: 2'04"
WEIGHT: 56.2 lbs.

It forms a group of Rattata, which it assumes command of. Each group has its own territory, and disputes over food happen often.

This gourmet Pokémon is particular about the taste and freshness of its food. Restaurants where Raticate live have a good reputation.

ABILITY
Gluttony
Hustle

HIDDEN ABILITY
Thick Fat

SPECIES STRENGTHS
HP	◆◆◆
Attack	◆◆◆◆
Defense	◆◆◆◆
Sp. Atk	◆◆
Sp. Def	◆◆◆◆◆
Speed	◆◆◆◆◆

EGG GROUPS
Field

ITEM SOMETIMES HELD BY WILD POKÉMON
Pecha Berry

Damage taken in normal battles
NORMAL ×1	FIGHTING ×1	ROCK ×1
FIRE ×1	POISON ×1	GHOST ×0
WATER ×1	GROUND ×1	DRAGON ×1
GRASS ×1	FLYING ×1	DARK ×0.5
ELECTRIC ×1	PSYCHIC ×0	STEEL ×1
ICE ×1	BUG ×2	FAIRY ×1

EVOLUTION

Alolan Rattata → Level up to Lv. 20 at night → Alolan Raticate

MAIN WAY TO REGISTER IN THE POKÉDEX
Catch in the tall grass at Akala Outskirts when it is nighttime in your game.

❖ ALOLA FORM ❖

Same form for male/female

❖ LEVEL-UP MOVES

Lv.	Name	Type	Kind	Pow.	Acc.	PP	Range
1	Scary Face	Normal	Status	—	100	10	Normal
1	Swords Dance	Normal	Status	—	—	20	Self
1	Tackle	Normal	Physical	40	100	35	Normal
1	Tail Whip	Normal	Status	—	100	30	Many Others
1	Quick Attack	Normal	Physical	40	100	30	Normal
1	Focus Energy	Normal	Status	—	—	30	Self
4	Quick Attack	Normal	Physical	40	100	30	Normal
7	Focus Energy	Normal	Status	—	—	30	Self
10	Bite	Dark	Physical	60	100	25	Normal
13	Pursuit	Dark	Physical	40	100	20	Normal
16	Hyper Fang	Normal	Physical	80	90	15	Normal
19	Assurance	Dark	Physical	60	100	10	Normal
24	Crunch	Dark	Physical	80	100	15	Normal
29	Sucker Punch	Dark	Physical	70	100	5	Normal
34	Super Fang	Normal	Physical	—	90	10	Normal
39	Double-Edge	Normal	Physical	120	100	15	Normal
44	Endeavor	Normal	Physical	—	100	5	Normal

❖ TM MOVES

No.	Name	Type	Kind	Pow.	Acc.	PP	Range
TM05	Roar	Normal	Status	—	—	20	Normal
TM06	Toxic	Poison	Status	—	90	10	Normal
TM08	Bulk Up	Fighting	Status	—	—	20	Self
TM09	Venoshock	Poison	Special	65	100	10	Normal
TM10	Hidden Power	Normal	Special	60	100	15	Normal
TM11	Sunny Day	Fire	Status	—	—	5	Both Sides
TM12	Taunt	Dark	Status	—	100	20	Normal
TM13	Ice Beam	Ice	Special	90	100	10	Normal
TM14	Blizzard	Ice	Special	110	70	5	Many Others
TM15	Hyper Beam	Normal	Special	150	90	5	Normal
TM17	Protect	Normal	Status	—	—	10	Self
TM18	Rain Dance	Water	Status	—	—	5	Both Sides
TM21	Frustration	Normal	Physical	—	100	20	Normal
TM27	Return	Normal	Physical	—	100	20	Normal
TM30	Shadow Ball	Ghost	Special	80	100	15	Normal
TM32	Double Team	Normal	Status	—	—	15	Self
TM34	Sludge Wave	Poison	Special	95	100	10	Adjacent
TM36	Sludge Bomb	Poison	Special	90	100	10	Normal
TM41	Torment	Dark	Status	—	100	15	Normal
TM42	Facade	Normal	Physical	70	100	20	Normal
TM44	Rest	Psychic	Status	—	—	10	Self
TM45	Attract	Normal	Status	—	100	15	Normal
TM46	Thief	Dark	Physical	60	100	25	Normal
TM48	Round	Normal	Special	60	100	15	Normal
TM60	Quash	Dark	Status	—	100	15	Normal
TM63	Embargo	Dark	Status	—	100	15	Normal
TM65	Shadow Claw	Ghost	Physical	70	100	15	Normal
TM68	Giga Impact	Normal	Physical	150	90	5	Normal

No.	Name	Type	Kind	Pow.	Acc.	PP	Range
TM75	Swords Dance	Normal	Status	—	—	20	Self
TM86	Grass Knot	Grass	Special	—	100	20	Normal
TM87	Swagger	Normal	Status	—	85	15	Normal
TM88	Sleep Talk	Normal	Status	—	—	10	Self
TM89	U-turn	Bug	Physical	70	100	20	Normal
TM90	Substitute	Normal	Status	—	—	10	Self
TM95	Snarl	Dark	Special	55	95	15	Many Others
TM97	Dark Pulse	Dark	Special	80	100	15	Normal
TM100	Confide	Normal	Status	—	—	20	Normal

❖ MOVES TAUGHT BY PEOPLE
Name	Type	Kind	Pow.	Acc.	PP	Range

❖ MOVES LEARNED WHEN EVOLVING
Name	Type	Kind	Pow.	Acc.	PP	Range
Scary Face	Normal	Status	—	100	10	Normal

❖ EGG MOVES
Name	Type	Kind	Pow.	Acc.	PP	Range

❖ EXCLUSIVE Z-MOVE
Name	Base Move	Type	Kind	Pow.	Acc.	Range

Caterpie
Worm Pokémon

Alola Pokédex	Melemele	Akala	Ula'ula	Poni
017	017	008	—	—

BUG

HEIGHT: 1'00"
WEIGHT: 6.4 lbs.

When attacked by bird Pokémon, it resists by releasing a terrifically strong odor from its antennae, but it often becomes their prey.

It's easy to catch, and it grows quickly, making it one of the top recommendations for novice Pokémon Trainers.

Same form for male/female

ABILITY
Shield Dust

HIDDEN ABILITY
Run Away

Damage taken in normal battles

NORMAL	×1	FIGHTING	×0.5	ROCK	×1
FIRE	×2	POISON	×1	GHOST	×1
WATER	×1	GROUND	×1	DRAGON	×1
GRASS	×0.5	FLYING	×2	DARK	×1
ELECTRIC	×1	PSYCHIC	×1	STEEL	×1
ICE	×1	BUG	×1	FAIRY	×1

SPECIES STRENGTHS
HP ◆◆
Attack ◆◆
Defense ◆◆
Sp. Atk ◆
Sp. Def ◆◆
Speed ◆◆◆

EGG GROUPS
Bug

ITEM SOMETIMES HELD BY WILD POKÉMON
—

EVOLUTION
Caterpie → Lv. 7 → Metapod → Lv. 10 → Butterfree

MAIN WAY TO REGISTER IN THE POKÉDEX
Catch in the tall grass on the east side of Route 1

Metapod
Cocoon Pokémon

Alola Pokédex	Melemele	Akala	Ula'ula	Poni
018	018	009	—	—

BUG

HEIGHT: 2'04"
WEIGHT: 21.8 lbs.

Its shell is filled with its soft innards. It doesn't move much because of the risk it might carelessly spill its innards out.

Its shell is hard, but it's still just a bug shell. It's been known to break, so intense battles with it should be avoided.

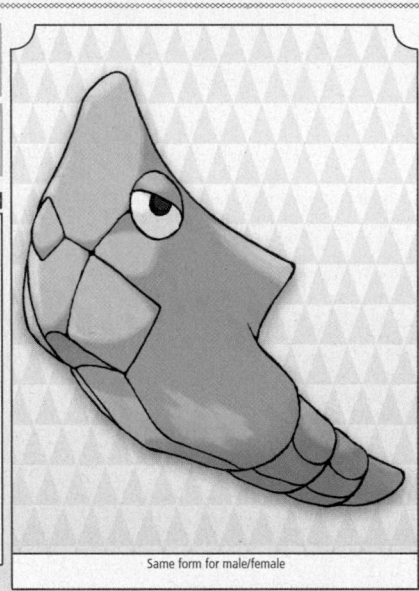

Same form for male/female

ABILITY
Shed Skin

HIDDEN ABILITY
—

Damage taken in normal battles

NORMAL	×1	FIGHTING	×0.5	ROCK	×1
FIRE	×2	POISON	×1	GHOST	×1
WATER	×1	GROUND	×0.5	DRAGON	×1
GRASS	×0.5	FLYING	×2	DARK	×1
ELECTRIC	×1	PSYCHIC	×1	STEEL	×1
ICE	×1	BUG	×1	FAIRY	×1

SPECIES STRENGTHS
HP ◆◆
Attack ◆
Defense ◆◆◆
Sp. Atk ◆
Sp. Def ◆
Speed ◆◆

EGG GROUPS
Bug

ITEM SOMETIMES HELD BY WILD POKÉMON
—

EVOLUTION
Caterpie → Lv. 7 → Metapod → Lv. 10 → Butterfree

MAIN WAY TO REGISTER IN THE POKÉDEX
Level up Caterpie to Lv. 7

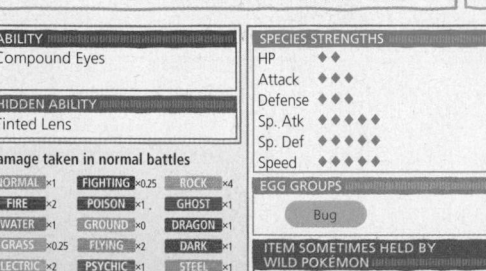

Butterfree
Butterfly Pokémon

Alola Pokédex	Melemele	Akala	Ula'ula	Poni
019	019	010	—	—

BUG | FLYING

HEIGHT: 3'07"
WEIGHT: 70.5 lbs.

Close examination of its large eyes reveals that each eye is composed of a myriad of tiny eyes.

When attacked by other Pokémon, it defends itself by scattering its poisonous scales and fluttering its wings.

The base of the male's lower wings is white, while the female's is black.

ABILITY
Compound Eyes

HIDDEN ABILITY
Tinted Lens

Damage taken in normal battles

NORMAL	×1	FIGHTING	×0.25	ROCK	×4
FIRE	×2	POISON	×1	GHOST	×1
WATER	×1	GROUND	×0	DRAGON	×1
GRASS	×0.25	FLYING	×2	DARK	×1
ELECTRIC	×2	PSYCHIC	×1	STEEL	×1
ICE	×2	BUG	×0.5	FAIRY	×1

SPECIES STRENGTHS
HP ◆◆
Attack ◆◆◆
Defense ◆◆◆
Sp. Atk ◆◆◆◆◆
Sp. Def ◆◆◆◆◆
Speed ◆◆◆◆◆

EGG GROUPS
Bug

ITEM SOMETIMES HELD BY WILD POKÉMON
Silver Powder

EVOLUTION
Caterpie → Lv. 7 → Metapod → Lv. 10 → Butterfree

MAIN WAY TO REGISTER IN THE POKÉDEX
Level up Metapod to Lv. 10

❖ LEVEL-UP MOVES

Lv.	Name	Type	Kind	Pow.	Acc.	PP	Range
1	Tackle	Normal	Physical	40	100	35	Normal
1	String Shot	Bug	Status	—	95	40	Many Others
9	Bug Bite	Bug	Physical	60	100	20	Normal

❖ TM MOVES

No.	Name	Type	Kind	Pow.	Acc.	PP	Range

No.	Name	Type	Kind	Pow.	Acc.	PP	Range

❖ MOVES TAUGHT BY PEOPLE

Name	Type	Kind	Pow.	Acc.	PP	Range

❖ MOVES LEARNED WHEN EVOLVING

Name	Type	Kind	Pow.	Acc.	PP	Range

❖ EGG MOVES

Name	Type	Kind	Pow.	Acc.	PP	Range

❖ EXCLUSIVE Z-MOVE

Name	Base Move	Type	Kind	Pow.	Acc.	Range

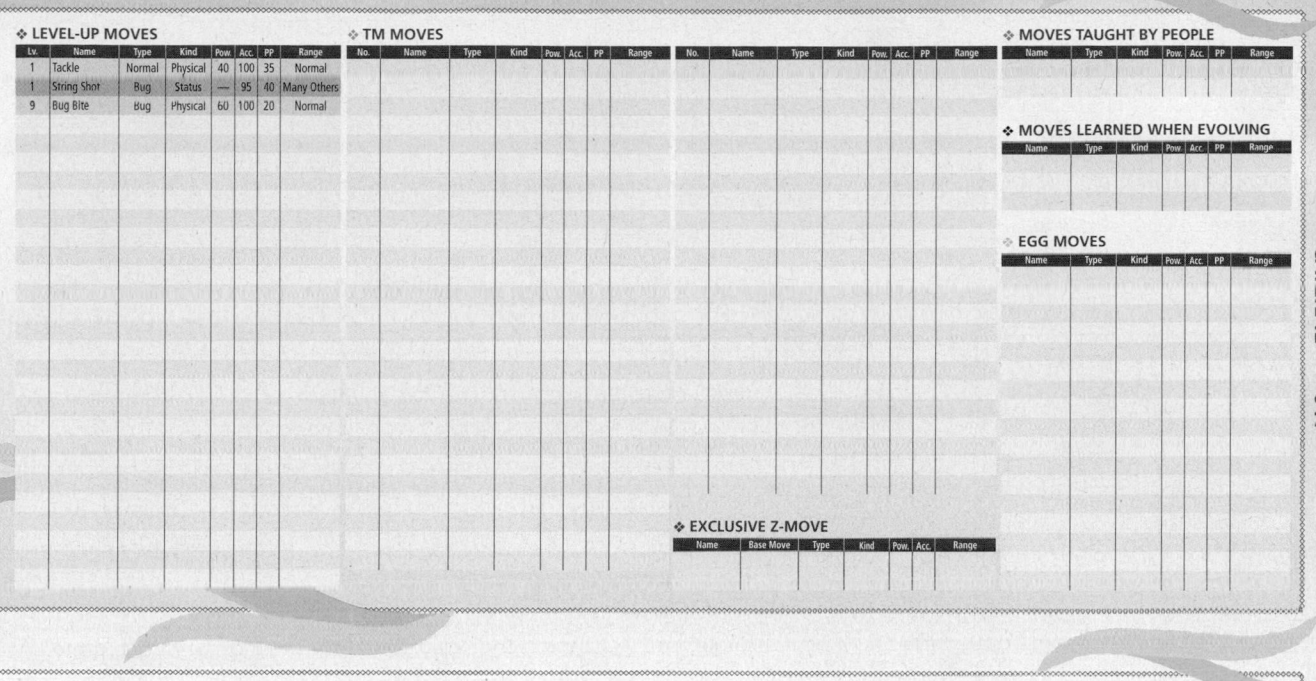

❖ LEVEL-UP MOVES

Lv.	Name	Type	Kind	Pow.	Acc.	PP	Range
1	Harden	Normal	Status	—	—	30	Self

❖ TM MOVES

No.	Name	Type	Kind	Pow.	Acc.	PP	Range

No.	Name	Type	Kind	Pow.	Acc.	PP	Range

❖ MOVES TAUGHT BY PEOPLE

Name	Type	Kind	Pow.	Acc.	PP	Range

❖ MOVES LEARNED WHEN EVOLVING

Name	Type	Kind	Pow.	Acc.	PP	Range
Harden	Normal	Status	—	—	30	Self

❖ EGG MOVES

Name	Type	Kind	Pow.	Acc.	PP	Range

❖ EXCLUSIVE Z-MOVE

Name	Base Move	Type	Kind	Pow.	Acc.	Range

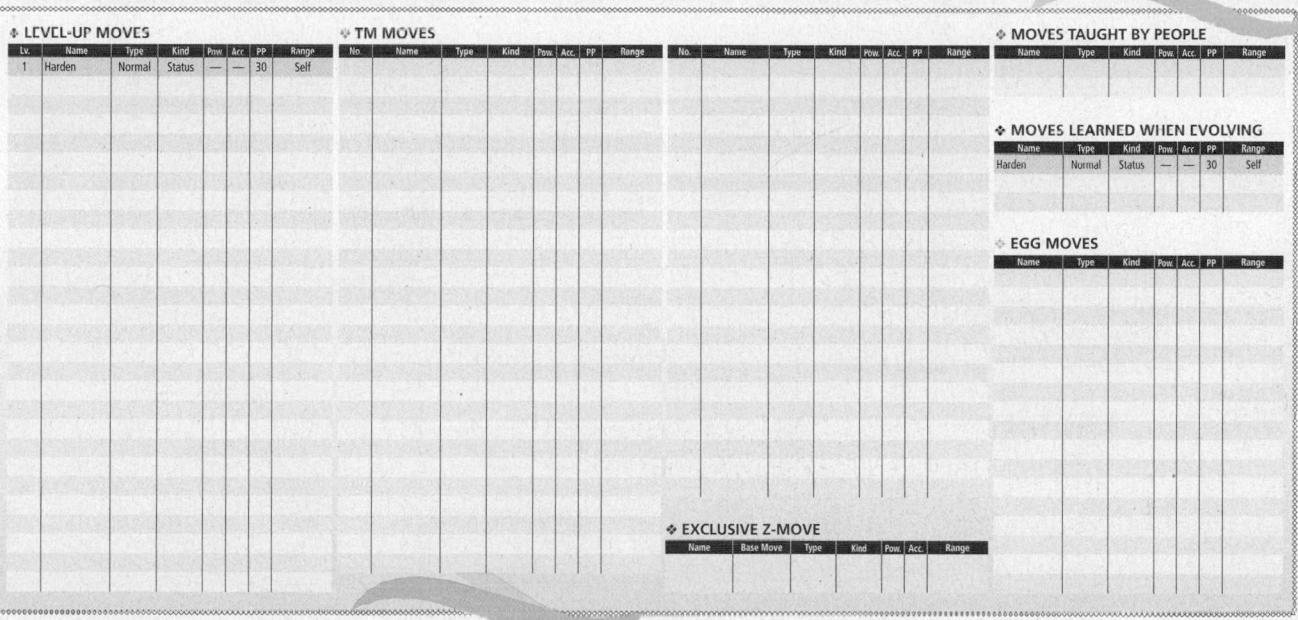

❖ LEVEL-UP MOVES

Lv.	Name	Type	Kind	Pow.	Acc.	PP	Range
1	Gust	Flying	Special	40	100	35	Normal
1	Confusion	Psychic	Special	50	100	25	Normal
11	Confusion	Psychic	Special	50	100	25	Normal
13	Poison Powder	Poison	Status	—	75	35	Normal
13	Stun Spore	Grass	Status	—	75	30	Normal
13	Sleep Powder	Grass	Status	—	75	15	Normal
17	Psybeam	Psychic	Special	65	100	20	Normal
19	Silver Wind	Bug	Special	60	100	5	Normal
23	Supersonic	Normal	Status	—	55	20	Normal
25	Safeguard	Normal	Status	—	—	25	Your Side
29	Whirlwind	Normal	Status	—	—	20	Normal
31	Bug Buzz	Bug	Special	90	100	10	Normal
35	Rage Powder	Bug	Status	—	—	20	Self
37	Captivate	Normal	Status	—	100	20	Many Others
41	Tailwind	Flying	Status	—	—	15	Your Side
43	Air Slash	Flying	Special	75	95	15	Normal
47	Quiver Dance	Bug	Status	—	—	20	Self

❖ TM MOVES

No.	Name	Type	Kind	Pow.	Acc.	PP	Range
TM06	Toxic	Poison	Status	—	90	10	Normal
TM09	Venoshock	Poison	Special	65	100	10	Normal
TM10	Hidden Power	Normal	Special	60	100	15	Normal
TM11	Sunny Day	Fire	Status	—	—	5	Both Sides
TM15	Hyper Beam	Normal	Special	150	90	5	Normal
TM17	Protect	Normal	Status	—	—	10	Self
TM18	Rain Dance	Water	Status	—	—	5	Both Sides
TM19	Roost	Flying	Status	—	—	10	Self
TM20	Safeguard	Normal	Status	—	—	25	Your Side
TM21	Frustration	Normal	Physical	—	100	20	Normal
TM22	Solar Beam	Grass	Special	120	100	10	Normal
TM27	Return	Normal	Physical	—	100	20	Normal
TM29	Psychic	Psychic	Special	90	100	10	Normal
TM30	Shadow Ball	Ghost	Special	80	100	15	Normal
TM32	Double Team	Normal	Status	—	—	15	Self
TM40	Aerial Ace	Flying	Physical	60	—	20	Normal
TM42	Facade	Normal	Physical	70	100	20	Normal
TM44	Rest	Psychic	Status	—	—	10	Self
TM45	Attract	Normal	Status	—	100	15	Normal
TM46	Thief	Dark	Physical	60	100	25	Normal
TM48	Round	Normal	Special	60	100	15	Normal
TM53	Energy Ball	Grass	Special	90	100	10	Normal
TM62	Acrobatics	Flying	Physical	55	100	15	Normal
TM68	Giga Impact	Normal	Physical	150	90	5	Normal
TM77	Psych Up	Normal	Status	—	—	10	Normal
TM83	Infestation	Bug	Special	20	100	20	Normal
TM85	Dream Eater	Psychic	Special	100	100	15	Normal

No.	Name	Type	Kind	Pow.	Acc.	PP	Range
TM87	Swagger	Normal	Status	—	85	15	Normal
TM88	Sleep Talk	Normal	Status	—	—	10	Self
TM89	U-turn	Bug	Physical	70	100	20	Normal
TM90	Substitute	Normal	Status	—	—	10	Self
TM100	Confide	Normal	Status	—	—	20	Normal

❖ MOVES TAUGHT BY PEOPLE

Name	Type	Kind	Pow.	Acc.	PP	Range

❖ MOVES LEARNED WHEN EVOLVING

Name	Type	Kind	Pow.	Acc.	PP	Range
Gust	Flying	Special	40	100	35	Normal

❖ EGG MOVES

Name	Type	Kind	Pow.	Acc.	PP	Range

❖ EXCLUSIVE Z-MOVE

Name	Base Move	Type	Kind	Pow.	Acc.	Range

Ledyba

Five Star Pokémon

Alola Pokédex	Melemele	Akala	Ula'ula	Poni
020	020	—	008	—

BUG · FLYING

HEIGHT: 3'03"
WEIGHT: 23.8 lbs.

They are timid and grow uneasy when not in a swarm with others of their kind. The pattern on their backs differs slightly from one to another.

They communicate with one another using bodily fluids that give off odors. When they're angry, their odor smells sour.

ABILITY
Swarm
Early Bird

HIDDEN ABILITY
Rattled

Damage taken in normal battles

NORMAL ×1	FIGHTING ×0.25	ROCK ×4	
FIRE ×2	POISON ×1	GHOST ×1	
WATER ×1	GROUND ×0	DRAGON ×1	
GRASS ×0.25	FLYING ×2	DARK ×1	
ELECTRIC ×2	PSYCHIC ×1	STEEL ×1	
ICE ×2	BUG ×0.5	FAIRY ×1	

SPECIES STRENGTHS
HP ◆◆
Attack ◆
Defense ◆◆
Sp. Atk ◆◆
Sp. Def ◆◆◆◆◆
Speed ◆◆◆◆

EGG GROUPS
Bug

ITEM SOMETIMES HELD BY WILD POKÉMON
—

EVOLUTION

Ledyba → (Lv. 18) → Ledian

MAIN WAY TO REGISTER IN THE POKÉDEX
Catch in the tall grass on Route 1 when it is daytime in your game

The male has longer antennae. The female has shorter antennae.

◆ LEVEL-UP MOVES

Lv.	Name	Type	Kind	Pow.	Acc.	PP	Range
1	Tackle	Normal	Physical	40	100	35	Normal
5	Supersonic	Normal	Status	—	55	20	Normal
8	Swift	Normal	Special	60	—	20	Many Others
12	Light Screen	Psychic	Status	—	—	30	Your Side
12	Reflect	Psychic	Status	—	—	20	Your Side
12	Safeguard	Normal	Status	—	—	25	Your Side
15	Mach Punch	Fighting	Physical	40	100	30	Normal
19	Silver Wind	Bug	Special	60	100	5	Normal
22	Comet Punch	Normal	Physical	18	85	15	Normal
26	Baton Pass	Normal	Status	—	—	40	Self
29	Agility	Psychic	Status	—	—	30	Self
33	Bug Buzz	Bug	Special	90	100	10	Normal
36	Air Slash	Flying	Special	75	95	15	Normal
40	Double-Edge	Normal	Physical	120	100	15	Normal

◆ TM MOVES

No.	Name	Type	Kind	Pow.	Acc.	PP	Range
TM06	Toxic	Poison	Status	—	90	10	Normal
TM10	Hidden Power	Normal	Special	60	100	15	Normal
TM11	Sunny Day	Fire	Status	—	—	5	Both Sides
TM16	Light Screen	Psychic	Status	—	—	30	Your Side
TM17	Protect	Normal	Status	—	—	10	Self
TM19	Roost	Flying	Status	—	—	10	Self
TM20	Safeguard	Normal	Status	—	—	25	Your Side
TM21	Frustration	Normal	Physical	—	100	20	Normal
TM22	Solar Beam	Grass	Special	120	100	10	Normal
TM27	Return	Normal	Physical	—	100	20	Normal
TM31	Brick Break	Fighting	Physical	75	100	15	Normal
TM32	Double Team	Normal	Status	—	—	15	Self
TM33	Reflect	Psychic	Status	—	—	20	Your Side
TM40	Aerial Ace	Flying	Physical	60	—	20	Normal
TM42	Facade	Normal	Physical	70	100	20	Normal
TM44	Rest	Psychic	Status	—	—	10	Self
TM45	Attract	Normal	Status	—	100	15	Normal
TM46	Thief	Dark	Physical	60	100	25	Normal
TM48	Round	Normal	Special	60	100	15	Normal
TM56	Fling	Dark	Physical	—	100	10	Normal
TM62	Acrobatics	Flying	Physical	55	100	15	Normal
TM75	Swords Dance	Normal	Status	—	—	20	Self
TM83	Infestation	Bug	Special	20	100	20	Normal
TM87	Swagger	Normal	Status	—	85	15	Normal
TM88	Sleep Talk	Normal	Status	—	—	10	Self
TM89	U-turn	Bug	Physical	70	100	20	Normal
TM90	Substitute	Normal	Status	—	—	10	Self
TM100	Confide	Normal	Status	—	—	20	Normal

◆ MOVES TAUGHT BY PEOPLE

Name	Type	Kind	Pow.	Acc.	PP	Range

◆ MOVES LEARNED WHEN EVOLVING

Name	Type	Kind	Pow.	Acc.	PP	Range

◆ EGG MOVES

Name	Type	Kind	Pow.	Acc.	PP	Range
Psybeam	Psychic	Special	65	100	20	Normal
Bide	Normal	Physical	—	—	10	Self
Silver Wind	Bug	Special	60	100	5	Normal
Bug Buzz	Bug	Special	90	100	10	Normal
Screech	Normal	Status	—	85	40	Normal
Encore	Normal	Status	—	100	5	Normal
Knock Off	Dark	Physical	65	100	20	Normal
Bug Bite	Bug	Physical	60	100	20	Normal
Focus Punch	Fighting	Physical	150	100	20	Normal
Drain Punch	Fighting	Physical	75	100	10	Normal
Dizzy Punch	Normal	Physical	70	100	10	Normal
Tailwind	Flying	Status	—	—	15	Your Side

◆ EXCLUSIVE Z-MOVE

Name	Base Move	Type	Kind	Pow.	Acc.	Range

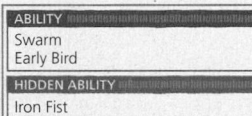

Ledian

Five Star Pokémon

Alola Pokédex	Melemele	Akala	Ula'ula	Poni
021	021	—	009	—

BUG · FLYING

HEIGHT: 4'07"
WEIGHT: 78.5 lbs.

While it's believed that starlight provides it with energy, this Pokémon also loves to eat berries. In the daytime, it curls up in the grass to sleep.

In battle, it throws punches with all four arms. The power of each individual blow is piddly, so it aims to win by quantity rather than quality.

ABILITY
Swarm
Early Bird

HIDDEN ABILITY
Iron Fist

Damage taken in normal battles

NORMAL ×1	FIGHTING ×0.25	ROCK ×4	
FIRE ×2	POISON ×1	GHOST ×1	
WATER ×1	GROUND ×0	DRAGON ×1	
GRASS ×0.25	FLYING ×2	DARK ×1	
ELECTRIC ×2	PSYCHIC ×1	STEEL ×1	
ICE ×2	BUG ×0.5	FAIRY ×1	

SPECIES STRENGTHS
HP ◆◆
Attack ◆◆
Defense ◆◆◆
Sp. Atk ◆◆◆
Sp. Def ◆◆◆◆◆◆◆
Speed ◆◆◆◆◆

EGG GROUPS
Bug

ITEM SOMETIMES HELD BY WILD POKÉMON
—

EVOLUTION

Ledyba → (Lv. 18) → Ledian

MAIN WAY TO REGISTER IN THE POKÉDEX
Catch in the tall grass on Route 10 when it is daytime in your game

The male has longer antennae. The female has shorter antennae.

◆ LEVEL-UP MOVES

Lv.	Name	Type	Kind	Pow.	Acc.	PP	Range
1	Tackle	Normal	Physical	40	100	35	Normal
1	Supersonic	Normal	Status	—	55	20	Normal
1	Swift	Normal	Special	60	—	20	Many Others
5	Supersonic	Normal	Status	—	55	20	Normal
8	Swift	Normal	Special	60	—	20	Many Others
12	Light Screen	Psychic	Status	—	—	30	Your Side
12	Reflect	Psychic	Status	—	—	20	Your Side
12	Safeguard	Normal	Status	—	—	25	Your Side
15	Mach Punch	Fighting	Physical	40	100	30	Normal
20	Silver Wind	Bug	Special	60	100	5	Normal
24	Comet Punch	Normal	Physical	18	85	15	Normal
29	Baton Pass	Normal	Status	—	—	40	Self
33	Agility	Psychic	Status	—	—	30	Self
38	Bug Buzz	Bug	Special	90	100	10	Normal
42	Air Slash	Flying	Special	75	95	15	Normal
47	Double-Edge	Normal	Physical	120	100	15	Normal

◆ TM MOVES

No.	Name	Type	Kind	Pow.	Acc.	PP	Range
TM06	Toxic	Poison	Status	—	90	10	Normal
TM10	Hidden Power	Normal	Special	60	100	15	Normal
TM11	Sunny Day	Fire	Status	—	—	5	Both Sides
TM15	Hyper Beam	Normal	Special	150	90	5	Normal
TM16	Light Screen	Psychic	Status	—	—	30	Your Side
TM17	Protect	Normal	Status	—	—	10	Self
TM19	Roost	Flying	Status	—	—	10	Self
TM20	Safeguard	Normal	Status	—	—	25	Your Side
TM21	Frustration	Normal	Physical	—	100	20	Normal
TM22	Solar Beam	Grass	Special	120	100	10	Normal
TM27	Return	Normal	Physical	—	100	20	Normal
TM31	Brick Break	Fighting	Physical	75	100	15	Normal
TM32	Double Team	Normal	Status	—	—	15	Self
TM33	Reflect	Psychic	Status	—	—	20	Your Side
TM40	Aerial Ace	Flying	Physical	60	—	20	Normal
TM42	Facade	Normal	Physical	70	100	20	Normal
TM44	Rest	Psychic	Status	—	—	10	Self
TM45	Attract	Normal	Status	—	100	15	Normal
TM46	Thief	Dark	Physical	60	100	25	Normal
TM48	Round	Normal	Special	60	100	15	Normal
TM52	Focus Blast	Fighting	Special	120	70	5	Normal
TM56	Fling	Dark	Physical	—	100	10	Normal
TM62	Acrobatics	Flying	Physical	55	100	15	Normal
TM68	Giga Impact	Normal	Physical	150	90	5	Normal
TM75	Swords Dance	Normal	Status	—	—	20	Self
TM83	Infestation	Bug	Special	20	100	20	Normal
TM87	Swagger	Normal	Status	—	85	15	Normal
TM88	Sleep Talk	Normal	Status	—	—	10	Self

◆ MOVES TAUGHT BY PEOPLE

No.	Name	Type	Kind	Pow.	Acc.	PP	Range
TM89	U-turn	Bug	Physical	70	100	20	Normal
TM90	Substitute	Normal	Status	—	—	10	Self
TM100	Confide	Normal	Status	—	—	20	Normal

◆ MOVES LEARNED WHEN EVOLVING

Name	Type	Kind	Pow.	Acc.	PP	Range

◆ EGG MOVES

Name	Type	Kind	Pow.	Acc.	PP	Range

◆ EXCLUSIVE Z-MOVE

Name	Base Move	Type	Kind	Pow.	Acc.	Range

Spinarak

String Spit Pokémon

BUG · **POISON**

HEIGHT: 1'08"
WEIGHT: 18.7 lbs.

Alola Pokédex	Melemele	Akala	Ula'ula	Poni
022	022	—	010	

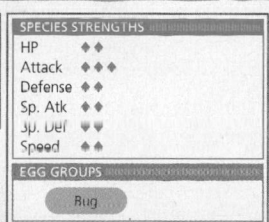

It waits intently until its preferred prey, Cutiefly, gets caught in its web. In fact, it's quite a patient Pokémon.

Some fishermen weave its sturdy thread into nets to catch fish Pokémon.

Same form for male/female

ABILITY
Swarm
Insomnia

HIDDEN ABILITY
Sniper

Damage taken in normal battles

NORMAL ×1	FIGHTING ×0.25	ROCK ×2
FIRE ×2	POISON ×0.5	GHOST ×1
WATER ×1	GROUND ×1	DRAGON ×1
GRASS ×0.25	FLYING ×2	DARK ×1
ELECTRIC ×1	PSYCHIC ×2	STEEL ×1
ICE ×1	BUG ×0.5	FAIRY ×0.5

SPECIES STRENGTHS
HP	◆◆
Attack	◆◆◆
Defense	◆◆
Sp. Atk	◆◆
Sp. Def	◆◆
Speed	◆◆

EGG GROUPS
Bug

ITEM SOMETIMES HELD BY WILD POKÉMON
—

EVOLUTION
Spinarak → (Lv. 22) → Ariados

MAIN WAY TO REGISTER IN THE POKÉDEX
Catch in the tall grass on Route 1 when it is nighttime in your game

◆ LEVEL-UP MOVES

Lv.	Name	Type	Kind	Pow.	Acc.	PP	Range
1	Poison Sting	Poison	Physical	15	100	35	Normal
1	String Shot	Bug	Status	—	95	40	Many Others
1	Constrict	Normal	Physical	10	100	35	Normal
5	Absorb	Grass	Special	20	100	25	Normal
8	Infestation	Bug	Special	20	100	20	Normal
12	Scary Face	Normal	Status	—	100	10	Normal
15	Night Shade	Ghost	Special	—	100	15	Normal
19	Shadow Sneak	Ghost	Physical	40	100	30	Normal
22	Fury Swipes	Normal	Physical	18	80	15	Normal
26	Sucker Punch	Dark	Physical	70	100	5	Normal
29	Spider Web	Bug	Status	—	—	10	Normal
33	Agility	Psychic	Status	—	—	30	Self
36	Pin Missile	Bug	Physical	25	95	20	Normal
40	Psychic	Psychic	Special	90	100	10	Normal
43	Poison Jab	Poison	Physical	80	100	20	Normal
47	Cross Poison	Poison	Physical	70	100	20	Normal
50	Sticky Web	Bug	Status	—	—	20	Other Side
54	Toxic Thread	Poison	Status	—	100	20	Normal

◆ TM MOVES

No.	Name	Type	Kind	Pow.	Acc.	PP	Range
TM06	Toxic	Poison	Status	—	90	10	Normal
TM09	Venoshock	Poison	Special	65	100	10	Normal
TM10	Hidden Power	Normal	Special	60	100	15	Normal
TM11	Sunny Day	Fire	Status	—	—	5	Both Sides
TM17	Protect	Normal	Status	—	—	10	Self
TM21	Frustration	Normal	Physical	—	100	20	Normal
TM22	Solar Beam	Grass	Special	120	100	10	Normal
TM27	Return	Normal	Physical	—	100	20	Normal
TM28	Leech Life	Bug	Physical	80	100	10	Normal
TM29	Psychic	Psychic	Special	90	100	10	Normal
TM32	Double Team	Normal	Status	—	—	15	Self
TM36	Sludge Bomb	Poison	Special	90	100	10	Normal
TM42	Facade	Normal	Physical	70	100	20	Normal
TM44	Rest	Psychic	Status	—	—	10	Self
TM45	Attract	Normal	Status	—	100	15	Normal
TM46	Thief	Dark	Physical	60	100	25	Normal
TM48	Round	Normal	Special	60	100	15	Normal
TM81	X-Scissor	Bug	Physical	80	100	15	Normal
TM83	Infestation	Bug	Special	20	100	20	Normal
TM84	Poison Jab	Poison	Physical	80	100	20	Normal
TM87	Swagger	Normal	Status	—	85	15	Normal
TM88	Sleep Talk	Normal	Status	—	—	10	Self
TM90	Substitute	Normal	Status	—	—	10	Self
TM100	Confide	Normal	Status	—	—	20	Normal

◆ MOVES TAUGHT BY PEOPLE

◆ MOVES LEARNED WHEN EVOLVING

◆ EGG MOVES

Name	Type	Kind	Pow.	Acc.	PP	Range
Psybeam	Psychic	Special	65	100	20	Normal
Disable	Normal	Status	—	100	20	Normal
Sonic Boom	Normal	Special	—	90	20	Normal
Baton Pass	Normal	Status	—	—	40	Self
Pursuit	Dark	Physical	40	100	20	Normal
Signal Beam	Bug	Special	75	100	15	Normal
Toxic Spikes	Poison	Status	—	—	20	Other Side
Twineedle	Bug	Physical	25	100	20	Normal
Electroweb	Electric	Special	55	95	15	Many Others
Rage Powder	Bug	Status	—	—	20	Self
Night Slash	Dark	Physical	70	100	15	Normal
Megahorn	Bug	Physical	120	85	10	Normal

◆ EXCLUSIVE Z-MOVE

Name	Base Move	Type	Kind	Pow.	Acc.	Range

Ariados

Long Leg Pokémon

BUG · **POISON**

HEIGHT: 3'07"
WEIGHT: 73.9 lbs.

Alola Pokédex	Melemele	Akala	Ula'ula	Poni
023	023	—	011	

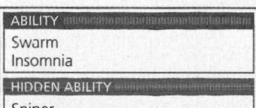

There are some areas where people use the string Ariados spins for their own weaving. The resulting cloth is popular for its strength.

It spins thread from both its rear and its mouth. Then it wraps its prey up in thread and sips their bodily fluids at its leisure.

Same form for male/female

ABILITY
Swarm
Insomnia

HIDDEN ABILITY
Sniper

Damage taken in normal battles

NORMAL ×1	FIGHTING ×0.25	ROCK ×2
FIRE ×2	POISON ×0.5	GHOST ×1
WATER ×1	GROUND ×1	DRAGON ×1
GRASS ×0.25	FLYING ×2	DARK ×1
ELECTRIC ×1	PSYCHIC ×2	STEEL ×1
ICE ×1	BUG ×0.5	FAIRY ×0.5

SPECIES STRENGTHS
HP	◆◆◆
Attack	◆◆◆◆◆
Defense	◆◆◆◆
Sp. Atk	◆◆◆
Sp. Def	◆◆◆◆
Speed	◆◆◆

EGG GROUPS
Bug

ITEM SOMETIMES HELD BY WILD POKÉMON
—

EVOLUTION
Spinarak → (Lv. 22) → Ariados

MAIN WAY TO REGISTER IN THE POKÉDEX
Catch in the tall grass on Route 10 when it is nighttime in your game

◆ LEVEL-UP MOVES

Lv.	Name	Type	Kind	Pow.	Acc.	PP	Range
1	Swords Dance	Normal	Status	—	—	20	Self
1	Focus Energy	Normal	Status	—	—	30	Self
1	Venom Drench	Poison	Status	—	100	20	Many Others
1	Fell Stinger	Bug	Physical	50	100	25	Normal
1	Bug Bite	Bug	Physical	60	100	20	Normal
1	Poison Sting	Poison	Physical	15	100	35	Normal
1	String Shot	Bug	Status	—	95	40	Many Others
1	Constrict	Normal	Physical	10	100	35	Normal
1	Absorb	Grass	Special	20	100	25	Normal
5	Absorb	Grass	Special	20	100	25	Normal
8	Infestation	Bug	Special	20	100	20	Normal
12	Scary Face	Normal	Status	—	100	10	Normal
15	Night Shade	Ghost	Special	—	100	15	Normal
19	Shadow Sneak	Ghost	Physical	40	100	30	Normal
23	Fury Swipes	Normal	Physical	18	80	15	Normal
28	Sucker Punch	Dark	Physical	70	100	5	Normal
32	Spider Web	Bug	Status	—	—	10	Normal
37	Agility	Psychic	Status	—	—	30	Self
41	Pin Missile	Bug	Physical	25	95	20	Normal
46	Psychic	Psychic	Special	90	100	10	Normal
50	Poison Jab	Poison	Physical	80	100	20	Normal
55	Cross Poison	Poison	Physical	70	100	20	Normal
58	Sticky Web	Bug	Status	—	—	20	Other Side
63	Toxic Thread	Poison	Status	—	100	20	Normal

◆ TM MOVES

No.	Name	Type	Kind	Pow.	Acc.	PP	Range
TM06	Toxic	Poison	Status	—	90	10	Normal
TM09	Venoshock	Poison	Special	65	100	10	Normal
TM10	Hidden Power	Normal	Special	60	100	15	Normal
TM11	Sunny Day	Fire	Status	—	—	5	Both Sides
TM15	Hyper Beam	Normal	Special	150	90	5	Normal
TM17	Protect	Normal	Status	—	—	10	Self
TM21	Frustration	Normal	Physical	—	100	20	Normal
TM22	Solar Beam	Grass	Special	120	100	10	Normal
TM27	Return	Normal	Physical	—	100	20	Normal
TM28	Leech Life	Bug	Physical	80	100	10	Normal
TM29	Psychic	Psychic	Special	90	100	10	Normal
TM32	Double Team	Normal	Status	—	—	15	Self
TM36	Sludge Bomb	Poison	Special	90	100	10	Normal
TM42	Facade	Normal	Physical	70	100	20	Normal
TM44	Rest	Psychic	Status	—	—	10	Self
TM45	Attract	Normal	Status	—	100	15	Normal
TM46	Thief	Dark	Physical	60	100	25	Normal
TM48	Round	Normal	Special	60	100	15	Normal
TM67	Smart Strike	Steel	Physical	70	—	10	Normal
TM68	Giga Impact	Normal	Physical	150	90	5	Normal
TM75	Swords Dance	Normal	Status	—	—	20	Self
TM81	X-Scissor	Bug	Physical	80	100	15	Normal
TM83	Infestation	Bug	Special	20	100	20	Normal
TM84	Poison Jab	Poison	Physical	80	100	20	Normal
TM87	Swagger	Normal	Status	—	85	15	Normal
TM88	Sleep Talk	Normal	Status	—	—	10	Self
TM90	Substitute	Normal	Status	—	—	10	Self
TM100	Confide	Normal	Status	—	—	20	Normal

◆ MOVES TAUGHT BY PEOPLE

◆ MOVES LEARNED WHEN EVOLVING

Name	Type	Kind	Pow.	Acc.	PP	Range
Swords Dance	Normal	Status	—	—	20	Self

◆ EGG MOVES

◆ EXCLUSIVE Z-MOVE

Name	Base Move	Type	Kind	Pow.	Acc.	Range

PICHU
024

Alola Pokédex	Melemele	Akala	Ula'ula	Poni
024	024	—		

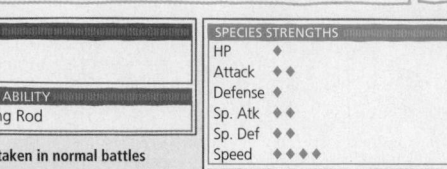

☑ **Pichu**
Tiny Mouse Pokémon

ELECTRIC

HEIGHT: 1'00"
WEIGHT: 4.4 lbs.

It is not yet skilled at controlling electricity. If you take your eyes off it, it may shock itself.

Despite this Pokémon's cute appearance, those who want to live with one should prepare to be on the receiving end of its electric jolts.

ABILITY
Static

HIDDEN ABILITY
Lightning Rod

Damage taken in normal battles

NORMAL	×1	FIGHTING	×1	ROCK	×1
FIRE	×1	POISON	×1	GHOST	×1
WATER	×1	GROUND	×2	DRAGON	×1
GRASS	×1	FLYING	×0.5	DARK	×1
⚡ELECTRIC	×0.5	PSYCHIC	×1	STEEL	×0.5
ICE	×1	BUG	×1	FAIRY	×1

SPECIES STRENGTHS

HP	◆
Attack	◆◆
Defense	◆
Sp. Atk	◆◆
Sp. Def	◆◆
Speed	◆◆◆

EGG GROUPS
No Eggs Discovered

ITEM SOMETIMES HELD BY WILD POKÉMON
—

MAIN WAY TO REGISTER IN THE POKÉDEX
Catch in the tall grass on Route 1 near Iki Town

EVOLUTION

Pichu → **Level up with high friendship** → Pikachu
→ **Use a Thunder Stone on a Pikachu in Alola** → Alolan Raichu

Same form for male/female

PIKACHU
025

Alola Pokédex	Melemele	Akala	Ula'ula	Poni
025	025	—		

☑ **Pikachu**
Mouse Pokémon

ELECTRIC

HEIGHT: 1'04"
WEIGHT: 13.2 lbs.

A plan was recently announced to gather many Pikachu and make an electric power plant.

It's in its nature to store electricity. It feels stressed now and then if it's unable to fully discharge the electricity.

ABILITY
Static

HIDDEN ABILITY
Lightning Rod

Damage taken in normal battles

NORMAL	×1	FIGHTING	×1	ROCK	×1
FIRE	×1	POISON	×1	GHOST	×1
WATER	×1	GROUND	×2	DRAGON	×1
GRASS	×1	FLYING	×0.5	DARK	×1
⚡ELECTRIC	×0.5	PSYCHIC	×1	STEEL	×0.5
ICE	×1	BUG	×1	FAIRY	×1

SPECIES STRENGTHS

HP	◆
Attack	◆◆◆
Defense	◆◆
Sp. Atk	◆◆◆
Sp. Def	◆◆◆
Speed	◆◆◆◆◆◆

EGG GROUPS
Field   Fairy

ITEM SOMETIMES HELD BY WILD POKÉMON
Light Ball

MAIN WAY TO REGISTER IN THE POKÉDEX
Level up Pichu with high friendship

EVOLUTION

Pichu → **Level up with high friendship** → Pikachu
→ **Use a Thunder Stone on a Pikachu in Alola** → Alolan Raichu

The tip of the male's tail is straight.
The female has a notch at the end of its tail.

RAICHU
026

Alola Pokédex	Melemele	Akala	Ula'ula	Poni
026	026	—		

☑ **Raichu**
Mouse Pokémon

ELECTRIC **PSYCHIC**

HEIGHT: 2'04"
WEIGHT: 46.3 lbs.

It only evolves to this form in the Alola region. According to researchers, its diet is one of the causes of this change.

It uses psychokinesis to control electricity. It hops aboard its own tail, using psychic power to lift the tail and move about while riding it.

ABILITY
Surge Surfer

HIDDEN ABILITY
—

Damage taken in normal battles

NORMAL	×1	FIGHTING	×0.5	ROCK	×1
FIRE	×1	POISON	×1	GHOST	×2
WATER	×1	GROUND	×2	DRAGON	×1
GRASS	×1	FLYING	×0.5	DARK	×1
ELECTRIC	×0.5	PSYCHIC	×1	STEEL	×0.5
ICE	×1	BUG	×1	FAIRY	×1

SPECIES STRENGTHS

HP	◆◆
Attack	◆◆◆◆◆
Defense	◆◆◆
Sp. Atk	◆◆◆◆
Sp. Def	◆◆◆◆◆
Speed	◆◆◆◆◆◆◆

EGG GROUPS
Field   Fairy

ITEM SOMETIMES HELD BY WILD POKÉMON
—

MAIN WAY TO REGISTER IN THE POKÉDEX
Use a Thunder Stone on a Pikachu in the Alola region

EVOLUTION

Pichu → **Level up with high friendship** → Pikachu
→ **Use a Thunder Stone on a Pikachu in Alola** → Alolan Raichu

❖ ALOLA FORM ❖

Same form for male/female

PICHU 024

LEVEL-UP MOVES

Lv.	Name	Type	Kind	Pow.	Acc.	PP	Range
1	Thunder Shock	Electric	Special	40	100	30	Normal
1	Charm	Fairy	Status	—	100	20	Normal
5	Tail Whip	Normal	Status	—	100	30	Many Others
10	Sweet Kiss	Fairy	Status	—	75	10	Normal
13	Nasty Plot	Dark	Status	—	—	20	Self
18	Thunder Wave	Electric	Status	—	90	20	Normal

TM MOVES

No.	Name	Type	Kind	Pow.	Acc.	PP	Range
TM06	Toxic	Poison	Status	—	90	10	Normal
TM10	Hidden Power	Normal	Special	60	100	15	Normal
TM16	Light Screen	Psychic	Status	—	—	30	Your Side
TM17	Protect	Normal	Status	—	—	10	Self
TM18	Rain Dance	Water	Status	—	—	5	Both Sides
TM21	Frustration	Normal	Physical	—	100	20	Normal
TM24	Thunderbolt	Electric	Special	90	100	15	Normal
TM25	Thunder	Electric	Special	110	70	10	Normal
TM27	Return	Normal	Physical	—	100	20	Normal
TM32	Double Team	Normal	Status	—	—	15	Self
TM42	Facade	Normal	Physical	70	100	20	Normal
TM44	Rest	Psychic	Status	—	—	10	Self
TM45	Attract	Normal	Status	—	100	15	Normal
TM48	Round	Normal	Special	60	100	15	Normal
TM49	Echoed Voice	Normal	Special	40	100	15	Normal
TM56	Fling	Dark	Physical	—	100	10	Normal
TM57	Charge Beam	Electric	Special	50	90	10	Normal
TM72	Volt Switch	Electric	Special	70	100	20	Normal
TM73	Thunder Wave	Electric	Status	—	90	20	Normal
TM86	Grass Knot	Grass	Special	—	100	20	Normal
TM87	Swagger	Normal	Status	—	85	15	Normal
TM88	Sleep Talk	Normal	Status	—	—	10	Self
TM90	Substitute	Normal	Status	—	—	10	Self
TM93	Wild Charge	Electric	Physical	90	100	15	Normal
TM100	Confide	Normal	Status	—	—	20	Normal

MOVES TAUGHT BY PEOPLE

Name	Type	Kind	Pow.	Acc.	PP	Range

MOVES LEARNED WHEN EVOLVING

Name	Type	Kind	Pow.	Acc.	PP	Range

EGG MOVES

Name	Type	Kind	Pow.	Acc.	PP	Range
Reversal	Fighting	Physical	—	100	15	Normal
Bide	Normal	Physical	—	—	10	Self
Present	Normal	Physical	—	90	15	Normal
Encore	Normal	Status	—	100	5	Normal
Double Slap	Normal	Physical	15	85	10	Normal
Wish	Normal	Status	—	—	10	Self
Charge	Electric	Status	—	—	20	Self
Fake Out	Normal	Physical	40	100	10	Normal
Thunder Punch	Electric	Physical	75	100	15	Normal
Tickle	Normal	Status	—	100	20	Normal
Flail	Normal	Physical	—	100	15	Normal
Endure	Normal	Status	—	—	10	Self
Lucky Chant	Normal	Status	—	—	30	Your Side
Bestow	Normal	Status	—	—	15	Normal
Disarming Voice	Fairy	Special	40	—	15	Many Others
Electric Terrain	Electric	Status	—	—	10	Both Sides
Volt Tackle	Electric	Physical	120	100	15	Normal

Note: For Pichu to inherit the Egg Move Volt Tackle, one of the Pokémon you leave at the Pokémon Nursery must be holding a Light Ball. You can find a Light Ball in Resolution Cave's interior, and wild Pikachu are sometimes found holding them.

PIKACHU 025

LEVEL-UP MOVES

Lv.	Name	Type	Kind	Pow.	Acc.	PP	Range
1	Tail Whip	Normal	Status	—	100	30	Many Others
1	Thunder Shock	Electric	Special	40	100	30	Normal
5	Growl	Normal	Status	—	100	40	Many Others
7	Play Nice	Normal	Status	—	—	20	Normal
10	Quick Attack	Normal	Physical	40	100	30	Normal
13	Electro Ball	Electric	Special	—	100	10	Normal
18	Thunder Wave	Electric	Status	—	90	20	Normal
21	Feint	Normal	Physical	30	100	10	Normal
23	Double Team	Normal	Status	—	—	15	Self
26	Spark	Electric	Physical	65	100	20	Normal
29	Nuzzle	Electric	Physical	20	100	20	Normal
34	Discharge	Electric	Special	80	100	15	Adjacent
37	Slam	Normal	Physical	80	75	20	Normal
42	Thunderbolt	Electric	Special	90	100	15	Normal
45	Agility	Psychic	Status	—	—	30	Self
50	Wild Charge	Electric	Physical	90	100	15	Normal
53	Light Screen	Psychic	Status	—	—	30	Your Side
58	Thunder	Electric	Special	110	70	10	Normal

TM MOVES

No.	Name	Type	Kind	Pow.	Acc.	PP	Range
TM06	Toxic	Poison	Status	—	90	10	Normal
TM10	Hidden Power	Normal	Special	60	100	15	Normal
TM16	Light Screen	Psychic	Status	—	—	30	Your Side
TM17	Protect	Normal	Status	—	—	10	Self
TM18	Rain Dance	Water	Status	—	—	5	Both Sides
TM21	Frustration	Normal	Physical	—	100	20	Normal
TM24	Thunderbolt	Electric	Special	90	100	15	Normal
TM25	Thunder	Electric	Special	110	70	10	Normal
TM27	Return	Normal	Physical	—	100	20	Normal
TM31	Brick Break	Fighting	Physical	75	100	15	Normal
TM32	Double Team	Normal	Status	—	—	15	Self
TM42	Facade	Normal	Physical	70	100	20	Normal
TM44	Rest	Psychic	Status	—	—	10	Self
TM45	Attract	Normal	Status	—	100	15	Normal
TM48	Round	Normal	Special	60	100	15	Normal
TM49	Echoed Voice	Normal	Special	40	100	15	Normal
TM56	Fling	Dark	Physical	—	100	10	Normal
TM57	Charge Beam	Electric	Special	50	90	10	Normal
TM72	Volt Switch	Electric	Special	70	100	20	Normal
TM73	Thunder Wave	Electric	Status	—	90	20	Normal
TM86	Grass Knot	Grass	Special	—	100	20	Normal
TM87	Swagger	Normal	Status	—	85	15	Normal
TM88	Sleep Talk	Normal	Status	—	—	10	Self
TM90	Substitute	Normal	Status	—	—	10	Self
TM93	Wild Charge	Electric	Physical	90	100	15	Normal
TM100	Confide	Normal	Status	—	—	20	Normal

MOVES TAUGHT BY PEOPLE

Name	Type	Kind	Pow.	Acc.	PP	Range
Volt Tackle	Electric	Physical	120	100	15	Normal

MOVES LEARNED WHEN EVOLVING

Name	Type	Kind	Pow.	Acc.	PP	Range

EGG MOVES

Name	Type	Kind	Pow.	Acc.	PP	Range

EXCLUSIVE Z-MOVE

Name	Base Move	Type	Kind	Pow.	Acc.	Range
Catastropika	Volt Tackle	Electric	Physical	210	—	Normal

RAICHU 026

LEVEL-UP MOVES

Lv.	Name	Type	Kind	Pow.	Acc.	PP	Range
1	Psychic	Psychic	Special	90	100	10	Normal
1	Speed Swap	Psychic	Status	—	—	10	Normal
1	Thunder Shock	Electric	Special	40	100	30	Normal
1	Tail Whip	Normal	Status	—	100	30	Many Others
1	Quick Attack	Normal	Physical	40	100	30	Normal
1	Thunderbolt	Electric	Special	90	100	15	Normal

TM MOVES

No.	Name	Type	Kind	Pow.	Acc.	PP	Range
TM03	Psyshock	Psychic	Special	80	100	10	Normal
TM04	Calm Mind	Psychic	Status	—	—	20	Self
TM06	Toxic	Poison	Status	—	90	10	Normal
TM10	Hidden Power	Normal	Special	60	100	15	Normal
TM15	Hyper Beam	Normal	Special	150	90	5	Normal
TM16	Light Screen	Psychic	Status	—	—	30	Your Side
TM17	Protect	Normal	Status	—	—	10	Self
TM18	Rain Dance	Water	Status	—	—	5	Both Sides
TM20	Safeguard	Normal	Status	—	—	25	Your Side
TM21	Frustration	Normal	Physical	—	100	20	Normal
TM24	Thunderbolt	Electric	Special	90	100	15	Normal
TM25	Thunder	Electric	Special	110	70	10	Normal
TM27	Return	Normal	Physical	—	100	20	Normal
TM29	Psychic	Psychic	Special	90	100	10	Normal
TM31	Brick Break	Fighting	Physical	75	100	15	Normal
TM32	Double Team	Normal	Status	—	—	15	Self
TM33	Reflect	Psychic	Status	—	—	20	Your Side
TM42	Facade	Normal	Physical	70	100	20	Normal
TM44	Rest	Psychic	Status	—	—	10	Self
TM45	Attract	Normal	Status	—	100	15	Normal
TM46	Thief	Dark	Physical	60	100	25	Normal
TM48	Round	Normal	Special	60	100	15	Normal
TM49	Echoed Voice	Normal	Special	40	100	15	Normal
TM52	Focus Blast	Fighting	Special	120	70	5	Normal
TM56	Fling	Dark	Physical	—	100	10	Normal
TM57	Charge Beam	Electric	Special	50	90	10	Normal
TM68	Giga Impact	Normal	Physical	150	90	5	Normal
TM72	Volt Switch	Electric	Special	70	100	20	Normal
TM73	Thunder Wave	Electric	Status	—	90	20	Normal
TM86	Grass Knot	Grass	Special	—	100	20	Normal
TM87	Swagger	Normal	Status	—	85	15	Normal
TM88	Sleep Talk	Normal	Status	—	—	10	Self
TM90	Substitute	Normal	Status	—	—	10	Self
TM93	Wild Charge	Electric	Physical	90	100	15	Normal
TM100	Confide	Normal	Status	—	—	20	Normal

MOVES TAUGHT BY PEOPLE

Name	Type	Kind	Pow.	Acc.	PP	Range

MOVES LEARNED WHEN EVOLVING

Name	Type	Kind	Pow.	Acc.	PP	Range
Psychic	Psychic	Special	90	100	10	Normal

EGG MOVES

Name	Type	Kind	Pow.	Acc.	PP	Range

EXCLUSIVE Z-MOVE

Name	Base Move	Type	Kind	Pow.	Acc.	Range
Stoked Sparksurfer	Thunderbolt	Electric	Special	175	—	Normal

Grubbin

Alola Pokédex	Melemele	Akala	Ula'ula	Poni
027	027	011	012	—

☑ **Grubbin**

Larva Pokémon

BUG

HEIGHT: 1'04"
WEIGHT: 9.7 lbs.

Its strong jaw enables it to scrape trees and slurp out the sap. It normally lives underground.

They often gather near places frequented by electric Pokémon in order to avoid being attacked by bird Pokémon.

ABILITY
Swarm

HIDDEN ABILITY
—

Damage taken in normal battles

NORMAL ×1	FIGHTING ×0.5	ROCK ×1
FIRE ×2	POISON ×1	GHOST ×1
WATER ×1	GROUND ×0.5	DRAGON ×1
GRASS ×0.5	FLYING ×2	DARK ×1
ELECTRIC ×1	PSYCHIC ×1	STEEL ×1
ICE ×1	BUG ×1	FAIRY ×1

SPECIES STRENGTHS
HP ◆◆
Attack ◆◆◆
Defense ◆◆◆
Sp. Atk ◆◆◆
Sp. Def ◆◆◆
Speed ◆◆◆

EGG GROUPS
Bug

ITEM SOMETIMES HELD BY WILD POKÉMON
—

EVOLUTION

Grubbin → Lv. 20 → Charjabug

Level up in Vast Poni Canyon

Vikavolt

MAIN WAY TO REGISTER IN THE POKÉDEX
Catch in the tall grass on Route 1 near Iki Town

Same form for male/female

Charjabug

Alola Pokédex	Melemele	Akala	Ula'ula	Poni
028	028	012	013	—

☑ **Charjabug**

Battery Pokémon

BUG ELECTRIC

HEIGHT: 1'08"
WEIGHT: 23.1 lbs.

Its body is capable of storing electricity. On camping trips, people are grateful to have one around.

From the food it digests, it generates electricity, and it stores this energy in its electric sac.

ABILITY
Battery

HIDDEN ABILITY
—

Damage taken in normal battles

NORMAL ×1	FIGHTING ×0.5	ROCK ×1
FIRE ×2	POISON ×1	GHOST ×1
WATER ×1	GROUND ×1	DRAGON ×1
GRASS ×0.5	FLYING ×1	DARK ×1
ELECTRIC ×0.5	PSYCHIC ×1	STEEL ×0.5
ICE ×1	BUG ×1	FAIRY ×1

SPECIES STRENGTHS
HP ◆◆
Attack ◆◆◆◆
Defense ◆◆◆◆◆
Sp. Atk ◆◆◆
Sp. Def ◆◆◆◆
Speed ◆◆

EGG GROUPS
Bug

ITEM SOMETIMES HELD BY WILD POKÉMON
Cell Battery

EVOLUTION

Grubbin → Lv. 20 → Charjabug

Level up in Vast Poni Canyon

Vikavolt

MAIN WAY TO REGISTER IN THE POKÉDEX
Catch in the tall grass on Blush Mountain

Same form for male/female

Vikavolt

Alola Pokédex	Melemele	Akala	Ula'ula	Poni
029	029	013	014	—

☑ **Vikavolt**

Stag Beetle Pokémon

BUG ELECTRIC

HEIGHT: 4'11"
WEIGHT: 99.2 lbs.

It zips around, on sharp lookout for an opening. It concentrates electrical energy within its large jaws and uses it to zap its enemies.

It produces electricity via an electrical organ in its abdomen. It overwhelms bird Pokémon with shocking beams of electrical energy.

ABILITY
Levitate

HIDDEN ABILITY
—

Damage taken in normal battles

NORMAL ×1	FIGHTING ×0.5	ROCK ×1
FIRE ×2	POISON ×1	GHOST ×1
WATER ×1	GROUND ×0	DRAGON ×1
GRASS ×0.5	FLYING ×1	DARK ×1
ELECTRIC ×0.5	PSYCHIC ×1	STEEL ×0.5
ICE ×1	BUG ×1	FAIRY ×1

SPECIES STRENGTHS
HP ◆◆◆
Attack ◆◆◆◆
Defense ◆◆◆◆◆
Sp. Atk ◆◆◆◆◆◆◆
Sp. Def ◆◆◆◆
Speed ◆◆◆

EGG GROUPS
Bug

ITEM SOMETIMES HELD BY WILD POKÉMON
—

EVOLUTION

Grubbin → Lv. 20 → Charjabug

Level up in Vast Poni Canyon

Vikavolt

MAIN WAY TO REGISTER IN THE POKÉDEX
Level up Charjabug in Vast Poni Canyon

Same form for male/female

GRUBBIN 027

❖ LEVEL-UP MOVES

Lv.	Name	Type	Kind	Pow.	Acc.	PP	Range
1	Vice Grip	Normal	Physical	55	100	30	Normal
4	String Shot	Bug	Status	—	95	40	Many Others
7	Mud-Slap	Ground	Special	20	100	10	Normal
10	Bite	Dark	Physical	60	100	25	Normal
13	Bug Bite	Bug	Physical	60	100	20	Normal
16	Spark	Electric	Physical	65	100	20	Normal
19	Acrobatics	Flying	Physical	55	100	15	Normal
22	Crunch	Dark	Physical	80	100	15	Normal
25	X-Scissor	Bug	Physical	80	100	15	Normal
28	Dig	Ground	Physical	80	100	10	Normal

❖ TM MOVES

No.	Name	Type	Kind	Pow.	Acc.	PP	Range
TM06	Toxic	Poison	Status	—	90	10	Normal
TM10	Hidden Power	Normal	Special	60	100	15	Normal
TM16	Light Screen	Psychic	Status	—	—	30	Your Side
TM17	Protect	Normal	Status	—	—	10	Self
TM18	Rain Dance	Water	Status	—	—	5	Both Sides
TM21	Frustration	Normal	Physical	—	100	20	Normal
TM24	Thunderbolt	Electric	Special	90	100	15	Normal
TM27	Return	Normal	Physical	—	100	20	Normal
TM32	Double Team	Normal	Status	—	—	15	Self
TM42	Facade	Normal	Physical	70	100	20	Normal
TM44	Rest	Psychic	Status	—	—	10	Self
TM45	Attract	Normal	Status	—	100	15	Normal
TM48	Round	Normal	Special	60	100	15	Normal
TM57	Charge Beam	Electric	Special	50	90	10	Normal
TM62	Acrobatics	Flying	Physical	55	100	15	Normal
TM72	Volt Switch	Electric	Special	70	100	20	Normal
TM73	Thunder Wave	Electric	Status	—	90	20	Normal
TM81	X-Scissor	Bug	Physical	80	100	15	Normal
TM84	Poison Jab	Poison	Physical	80	100	20	Normal
TM87	Swagger	Normal	Status	—	85	15	Normal
TM88	Sleep Talk	Normal	Status	—	—	10	Self
TM90	Substitute	Normal	Status	—	—	10	Self
TM93	Wild Charge	Electric	Physical	90	100	15	Normal
TM100	Confide	Normal	Status	—	—	20	Normal

❖ MOVES TAUGHT BY PEOPLE

Name	Type	Kind	Pow.	Acc.	PP	Range

❖ MOVES LEARNED WHEN EVOLVING

Name	Type	Kind	Pow.	Acc.	PP	Range

❖ EGG MOVES

Name	Type	Kind	Pow.	Acc.	PP	Range
Harden	Normal	Status	—	—	30	Self
Electroweb	Electric	Special	55	95	15	Many Others
Mud Shot	Ground	Special	55	95	15	Normal
Endure	Normal	Status	—	—	10	Self

❖ EXCLUSIVE Z-MOVE

Name	Base Move	Type	Kind	Pow.	Acc.	Range

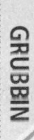

CHARJABUG 028

❖ LEVEL-UP MOVES

Lv.	Name	Type	Kind	Pow.	Acc.	PP	Range
1	Charge	Electric	Status	—	—	20	Self
1	Vice Grip	Normal	Physical	55	100	30	Normal
1	String Shot	Bug	Status	—	95	40	Many Others
1	Mud-Slap	Ground	Special	20	100	10	Normal
1	Bite	Dark	Physical	60	100	25	Normal
4	String Shot	Bug	Status	—	95	40	Many Others
7	Mud-Slap	Ground	Special	20	100	10	Normal
10	Bite	Dark	Physical	60	100	25	Normal
13	Bug Bite	Bug	Physical	60	100	20	Normal
16	Spark	Electric	Physical	65	100	20	Normal
19	Acrobatics	Flying	Physical	55	100	15	Normal
25	Crunch	Dark	Physical	80	100	15	Normal
31	X-Scissor	Bug	Physical	80	100	15	Normal
37	Dig	Ground	Physical	80	100	10	Normal
43	Discharge	Electric	Special	80	100	15	Adjacent
49	Iron Defense	Steel	Status	—	—	15	Self

❖ TM MOVES

No.	Name	Type	Kind	Pow.	Acc.	PP	Range
TM06	Toxic	Poison	Status	—	90	10	Normal
TM10	Hidden Power	Normal	Special	60	100	15	Normal
TM16	Light Screen	Psychic	Status	—	—	30	Your Side
TM17	Protect	Normal	Status	—	—	10	Self
TM18	Rain Dance	Water	Status	—	—	5	Both Sides
TM21	Frustration	Normal	Physical	—	100	20	Normal
TM24	Thunderbolt	Electric	Special	90	100	15	Normal
TM27	Return	Normal	Physical	—	100	20	Normal
TM32	Double Team	Normal	Status	—	—	15	Self
TM42	Facade	Normal	Physical	70	100	20	Normal
TM44	Rest	Psychic	Status	—	—	10	Self
TM45	Attract	Normal	Status	—	100	15	Normal
TM48	Round	Normal	Special	60	100	15	Normal
TM57	Charge Beam	Electric	Special	50	90	10	Normal
TM62	Acrobatics	Flying	Physical	55	100	15	Normal
TM72	Volt Switch	Electric	Special	70	100	20	Normal
TM73	Thunder Wave	Electric	Status	—	90	20	Normal
TM81	X-Scissor	Bug	Physical	80	100	15	Normal
TM84	Poison Jab	Poison	Physical	80	100	20	Normal
TM87	Swagger	Normal	Status	—	85	15	Normal
TM88	Sleep Talk	Normal	Status	—	—	10	Self
TM90	Substitute	Normal	Status	—	—	10	Self
TM93	Wild Charge	Electric	Physical	90	100	15	Normal
TM100	Confide	Normal	Status	—	—	20	Normal

❖ MOVES TAUGHT BY PEOPLE

Name	Type	Kind	Pow.	Acc.	PP	Range

❖ MOVES LEARNED WHEN EVOLVING

Name	Type	Kind	Pow.	Acc.	PP	Range
Charge	Electric	Status	—	—	20	Self

❖ EGG MOVES

Name	Type	Kind	Pow.	Acc.	PP	Range

❖ EXCLUSIVE Z-MOVE

Name	Base Move	Type	Kind	Pow.	Acc.	Range

VIKAVOLT 029

❖ LEVEL-UP MOVES

Lv.	Name	Type	Kind	Pow.	Acc.	PP	Range
1	Thunderbolt	Electric	Special	90	100	15	Normal
1	Air Slash	Flying	Special	75	95	15	Normal
1	Charge	Electric	Status	—	—	20	Self
1	Vice Grip	Normal	Physical	55	100	30	Normal
1	String Shot	Bug	Status	—	95	40	Many Others
1	Mud-Slap	Ground	Special	20	100	10	Normal
1	Bite	Dark	Physical	60	100	25	Normal
4	String Shot	Bug	Status	—	95	40	Many Others
7	Mud-Slap	Ground	Special	20	100	10	Normal
10	Bite	Dark	Physical	60	100	25	Normal
13	Bug Bite	Bug	Physical	60	100	20	Normal
16	Spark	Electric	Physical	65	100	20	Normal
19	Acrobatics	Flying	Physical	55	100	15	Normal
25	Guillotine	Normal	Physical	—	30	5	Normal
31	Bug Buzz	Bug	Special	90	100	10	Normal
37	Dig	Ground	Physical	80	100	10	Normal
41	Zap Cannon	Electric	Special	120	50	5	Normal
49	Agility	Psychic	Status	—	—	30	Self

❖ TM MOVES

No.	Name	Type	Kind	Pow.	Acc.	PP	Range
TM06	Toxic	Poison	Status	—	90	10	Normal
TM10	Hidden Power	Normal	Special	60	100	15	Normal
TM15	Hyper Beam	Normal	Special	150	90	5	Normal
TM16	Light Screen	Psychic	Status	—	—	30	Your Side
TM17	Protect	Normal	Status	—	—	10	Self
TM18	Rain Dance	Water	Status	—	—	5	Both Sides
TM19	Roost	Flying	Status	—	—	10	Self
TM21	Frustration	Normal	Physical	—	100	20	Normal
TM22	Solar Beam	Grass	Special	120	100	10	Normal
TM24	Thunderbolt	Electric	Special	90	100	15	Normal
TM25	Thunder	Electric	Special	110	70	10	Normal
TM27	Return	Normal	Physical	—	100	20	Normal
TM32	Double Team	Normal	Status	—	—	15	Self
TM42	Facade	Normal	Physical	70	100	20	Normal
TM44	Rest	Psychic	Status	—	—	10	Self
TM45	Attract	Normal	Status	—	100	15	Normal
TM48	Round	Normal	Special	60	100	15	Normal
TM53	Energy Ball	Grass	Special	90	100	10	Normal
TM57	Charge Beam	Electric	Special	50	90	10	Normal
TM58	Sky Drop	Flying	Physical	60	100	10	Normal
TM62	Acrobatics	Flying	Physical	55	100	15	Normal
TM68	Giga Impact	Normal	Physical	150	90	5	Normal
TM72	Volt Switch	Electric	Special	70	100	20	Normal
TM73	Thunder Wave	Electric	Status	—	90	20	Normal
TM81	X-Scissor	Bug	Physical	80	100	15	Normal
TM84	Poison Jab	Poison	Physical	80	100	20	Normal
TM87	Swagger	Normal	Status	—	85	15	Normal

❖ MOVES TAUGHT BY PEOPLE

No.	Name	Type	Kind	Pow.	Acc.	PP	Range
TM88	Sleep Talk	Normal	Status	—	—	10	Self
TM90	Substitute	Normal	Status	—	—	10	Self
TM91	Flash Cannon	Steel	Special	80	100	10	Normal
TM93	Wild Charge	Electric	Physical	90	100	15	Normal
TM100	Confide	Normal	Status	—	—	20	Normal

❖ MOVES LEARNED WHEN EVOLVING

Name	Type	Kind	Pow.	Acc.	PP	Range
Thunderbolt	Electric	Special	90	100	15	Normal

❖ EGG MOVES

Name	Type	Kind	Pow.	Acc.	PP	Range

❖ EXCLUSIVE Z-MOVE

Name	Base Move	Type	Kind	Pow.	Acc.	Range

Bonsly
Bonsai Pokémon

Alola Pokédex	Melemele	Akala	Ula'ula	Poni
030	030	014	—	—

ROCK

HEIGHT: 1'08"
WEIGHT: 33.1 lbs.

It does not deal well with water, so it lives in dry locales. Since its surroundings tend to lack greenery, it stands out noticeably.

From its eyes, it can expel excess moisture from its body. This liquid is similar in composition to human sweat.

ABILITY
Sturdy
Rock Head

HIDDEN ABILITY
Rattled

SPECIES STRENGTHS
HP	◆◆
Attack	◆◆◆◆
Defense	◆◆◆◆◆
Sp. Atk	◆◆
Sp. Def	◆◆
Speed	◆

EVOLUTION
Bonsly → Level up after learning Mimic → Sudowoodo

MAIN WAY TO REGISTER IN THE POKÉDEX
Catch in the tall grass on the west side of Route 1

Damage taken in normal battles
NORMAL ×0.5	FIGHTING ×2	ROCK ×1			
FIRE ×0.5	POISON ×0.5	GHOST ×1			
WATER ×2	GROUND ×1	DRAGON ×1			
GRASS ×2	FLYING ×0.5	DARK ×1			
ELECTRIC ×1	PSYCHIC ×1	STEEL ×1			
ICE ×1	BUG ×1	FAIRY ×1			

EGG GROUPS
No Eggs Discovered

ITEM SOMETIMES HELD BY WILD POKÉMON
—

Same form for male/female

❖ LEVEL-UP MOVES
Lv.	Name	Type	Kind	Pow.	Acc.	PP	Range
1	Fake Tears	Dark	Status	—	100	20	Normal
1	Copycat	Normal	Status	—	—	20	Self
5	Flail	Normal	Physical	—	100	15	Normal
8	Low Kick	Fighting	Physical	—	100	20	Normal
12	Rock Throw	Rock	Physical	50	90	15	Normal
15	Mimic	Normal	Status	—	—	10	Normal
19	Feint Attack	Dark	Physical	60	—	20	Normal
22	Tearful Look	Normal	Status	—	—	20	Normal
26	Rock Tomb	Rock	Physical	60	95	15	Normal
29	Block	Normal	Status	—	—	5	Normal
33	Rock Slide	Rock	Physical	75	90	10	Many Others
36	Counter	Fighting	Physical	—	100	20	Varies
40	Sucker Punch	Dark	Physical	70	100	5	Normal
43	Double-Edge	Normal	Physical	120	100	15	Normal

❖ TM MOVES
No.	Name	Type	Kind	Pow.	Acc.	PP	Range
TM04	Calm Mind	Psychic	Status	—	—	20	Self
TM06	Toxic	Poison	Status	—	90	10	Normal
TM10	Hidden Power	Normal	Special	60	100	15	Normal
TM11	Sunny Day	Fire	Status	—	—	5	Both Sides
TM17	Protect	Normal	Status	—	—	10	Self
TM21	Frustration	Normal	Physical	—	100	20	Normal
TM23	Smack Down	Rock	Physical	50	100	15	Normal
TM27	Return	Normal	Physical	—	100	20	Normal
TM31	Brick Break	Fighting	Physical	75	100	15	Normal
TM32	Double Team	Normal	Status	—	—	15	Self
TM37	Sandstorm	Rock	Status	—	—	10	Both Sides
TM39	Rock Tomb	Rock	Physical	60	95	15	Normal
TM42	Facade	Normal	Physical	70	100	20	Normal
TM44	Rest	Psychic	Status	—	—	10	Self
TM45	Attract	Normal	Status	—	100	15	Normal
TM46	Thief	Dark	Physical	60	100	25	Normal
TM48	Round	Normal	Special	60	100	15	Normal
TM64	Explosion	Normal	Physical	250	100	5	Adjacent
TM69	Rock Polish	Rock	Status	—	—	20	Self
TM77	Psych Up	Normal	Status	—	—	10	Normal
TM80	Rock Slide	Rock	Physical	75	90	10	Many Others
TM87	Swagger	Normal	Status	—	85	15	Normal
TM88	Sleep Talk	Normal	Status	—	—	10	Self
TM90	Substitute	Normal	Status	—	—	10	Self
TM96	Nature Power	Normal	Status	—	—	20	Normal
TM100	Confide	Normal	Status	—	—	20	Normal

❖ MOVES TAUGHT BY PEOPLE
Name	Type	Kind	Pow.	Acc.	PP	Range

❖ MOVES LEARNED WHEN EVOLVING
Name	Type	Kind	Pow.	Acc.	PP	Range

❖ EGG MOVES
Name	Type	Kind	Pow.	Acc.	PP	Range
Self-Destruct	Normal	Physical	200	100	5	Adjacent
Headbutt	Normal	Physical	70	100	15	Normal
Harden	Normal	Status	—	—	30	Self
Defense Curl	Normal	Status	—	—	40	Self
Rollout	Rock	Physical	30	90	20	Normal
Sand Tomb	Ground	Physical	35	85	15	Normal
Stealth Rock	Rock	Status	—	—	20	Other Side
Curse	Ghost	Status	—	—	10	Varies
Endure	Normal	Status	—	—	10	Self

❖ EXCLUSIVE Z-MOVE
Name	Base Move	Type	Kind	Pow.	Acc.	Range

Note: To find a Pokémon Egg that will hatch into a Bonsly, have Sudowoodo hold a Rock Incense when you leave it at the Pokémon Nursery.

Sudowoodo
Imitation Pokémon

Alola Pokédex	Melemele	Akala	Ula'ula	Poni
031	031	015	—	—

ROCK

HEIGHT: 3'11"
WEIGHT: 83.8 lbs.

To avoid attack, it mimics a tree. It will run off if splashed with water, which it hates.

Apparently, the larger the green parts of this Pokémon, the more collectors value it. It's a particular favorite among elderly people.

ABILITY
Sturdy
Rock Head

HIDDEN ABILITY
Rattled

SPECIES STRENGTHS
HP	◆◆◆
Attack	◆◆◆◆
Defense	◆◆◆◆◆◆
Sp. Atk	◆◆
Sp. Def	◆◆◆
Speed	◆◆

EVOLUTION
Bonsly → Level up after learning Mimic → Sudowoodo

MAIN WAY TO REGISTER IN THE POKÉDEX
Level up Bonsly to Lv. 15 and have it learn Mimic, or teach it Mimic later and then level it up again

Damage taken in normal battles
NORMAL ×0.5	FIGHTING ×2	ROCK ×1			
FIRE ×0.5	POISON ×0.5	GHOST ×1			
WATER ×2	GROUND ×1	DRAGON ×1			
GRASS ×2	FLYING ×0.5	DARK ×1			
ELECTRIC ×1	PSYCHIC ×1	STEEL ×2			
ICE ×1	BUG ×1	FAIRY ×1			

EGG GROUPS
Mineral

ITEM SOMETIMES HELD BY WILD POKÉMON
—

The male has larger horns. The female has smaller horns.

❖ LEVEL-UP MOVES
Lv.	Name	Type	Kind	Pow.	Acc.	PP	Range
1	Slam	Normal	Physical	80	75	20	Normal
1	Wood Hammer	Grass	Physical	120	100	15	Normal
1	Copycat	Normal	Status	—	—	20	Self
1	Flail	Normal	Physical	—	100	15	Normal
1	Low Kick	Fighting	Physical	—	100	20	Normal
1	Rock Throw	Rock	Physical	50	90	15	Normal
5	Flail	Normal	Physical	—	100	15	Normal
8	Low Kick	Fighting	Physical	—	100	20	Normal
12	Rock Throw	Rock	Physical	50	90	15	Normal
15	Mimic	Normal	Status	—	—	10	Normal
19	Feint Attack	Dark	Physical	60	—	20	Normal
22	Tearful Look	Normal	Status	—	—	20	Normal
26	Rock Tomb	Rock	Physical	60	95	15	Normal
29	Block	Normal	Status	—	—	5	Normal
33	Rock Slide	Rock	Physical	75	90	10	Many Others
36	Counter	Fighting	Physical	—	100	20	Varies
40	Sucker Punch	Dark	Physical	70	100	5	Normal
43	Double-Edge	Normal	Physical	120	100	15	Normal
47	Stone Edge	Rock	Physical	100	80	5	Normal
50	Hammer Arm	Fighting	Physical	100	90	10	Normal
54	Head Smash	Rock	Physical	150	80	5	Normal

❖ TM MOVES
No.	Name	Type	Kind	Pow.	Acc.	PP	Range
TM04	Calm Mind	Psychic	Status	—	—	20	Self
TM06	Toxic	Poison	Status	—	90	10	Normal
TM10	Hidden Power	Normal	Special	60	100	15	Normal
TM11	Sunny Day	Fire	Status	—	—	5	Both Sides
TM12	Taunt	Dark	Status	—	100	20	Normal
TM17	Protect	Normal	Status	—	—	10	Self
TM21	Frustration	Normal	Physical	—	100	20	Normal
TM23	Smack Down	Rock	Physical	50	100	15	Normal
TM26	Earthquake	Ground	Physical	100	100	10	Adjacent
TM27	Return	Normal	Physical	—	100	20	Normal
TM31	Brick Break	Fighting	Physical	75	100	15	Normal
TM32	Double Team	Normal	Status	—	—	15	Self
TM37	Sandstorm	Rock	Status	—	—	10	Both Sides
TM39	Rock Tomb	Rock	Physical	60	95	15	Normal
TM41	Torment	Dark	Status	—	100	15	Normal
TM42	Facade	Normal	Physical	70	100	20	Normal
TM44	Rest	Psychic	Status	—	—	10	Self
TM45	Attract	Normal	Status	—	100	15	Normal
TM46	Thief	Dark	Physical	60	100	25	Normal
TM48	Round	Normal	Special	60	100	15	Normal
TM56	Fling	Dark	Physical	—	100	10	Normal
TM64	Explosion	Normal	Physical	250	100	5	Adjacent
TM69	Rock Polish	Rock	Status	—	—	20	Self
TM71	Stone Edge	Rock	Physical	100	80	5	Normal
TM77	Psych Up	Normal	Status	—	—	10	Normal
TM78	Bulldoze	Ground	Physical	60	100	20	Adjacent
TM80	Rock Slide	Rock	Physical	75	90	10	Many Others
TM87	Swagger	Normal	Status	—	85	15	Normal
TM88	Sleep Talk	Normal	Status	—	—	10	Self
TM90	Substitute	Normal	Status	—	—	10	Self
TM96	Nature Power	Normal	Status	—	—	20	Normal
TM100	Confide	Normal	Status	—	—	20	Normal

❖ MOVES TAUGHT BY PEOPLE
Name	Type	Kind	Pow.	Acc.	PP	Range

❖ MOVES LEARNED WHEN EVOLVING
Name	Type	Kind	Pow.	Acc.	PP	Range
Slam	Normal	Physical	80	75	20	Normal

❖ EGG MOVES
Name	Type	Kind	Pow.	Acc.	PP	Range
Self-Destruct	Normal	Physical	200	100	5	Adjacent
Headbutt	Normal	Physical	70	100	15	Normal
Harden	Normal	Status	—	—	30	Self
Defense Curl	Normal	Status	—	—	40	Self
Rollout	Rock	Physical	30	90	20	Normal
Sand Tomb	Ground	Physical	35	85	15	Normal
Stealth Rock	Rock	Status	—	—	20	Other Side
Curse	Ghost	Status	—	—	10	Varies
Endure	Normal	Status	—	—	10	Self

❖ EXCLUSIVE Z-MOVE
Name	Base Move	Type	Kind	Pow.	Acc.	Range

BONSLY
030
SUDOWOODO
031

30

Even More Pokémon Exist Outside of Alola!

There are over 300 Pokémon to be found and caught in the Alola region, which is quite a large number for a few small islands. But there are even more Pokémon to be found in the other regions of the Pokémon world, which you may have visited in previous Pokémon titles. To date, there are more than 800 known species of Pokémon, and the number just keeps on growing. But not all of these Pokémon live in Alola, so how can you get them for your teams? There are two handy tools that can definitely help with that!

Pokémon Bank and Poké Transporter

Pokémon Bank is an application and service that lets you deposit, store, and manage your Pokémon in private Boxes on the Internet for an annual charge. In addition to allowing you to store a greater number of Pokémon than any single game can contain, it will also allow you to bring Pokémon from other Pokémon games to *Pokémon Sun* and *Pokémon Moon*! You can transfer Pokémon directly from *Pokémon X*, *Pokémon Y*, *Pokémon Omega Ruby*, and *Pokémon Alpha Sapphire* using *Pokémon Bank*, as well as from the virtual console versions of *Pokémon Red*, *Pokémon Blue*, and *Pokémon Yellow: Special Pikachu Edition*. You can even transfer Pokémon from older games using the linked application *Poké Transporter*, which is available to *Pokémon Bank* subscribers free of charge. Visit the *Pokémon Bank* official website, www.pokemon.com/bank, for more instructions on how to bring your old pals to the latest Pokémon games!

The Global Trade System (GTS)

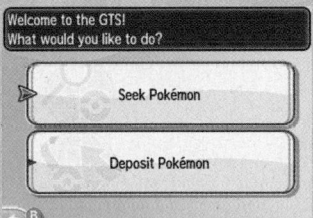

If you don't have a copy of *Pokémon Bank*, any previous titles to transfer Pokémon from, or are missing certain Pokémon, then turn to the GTS! With the GTS, you can trade Pokémon with people all over the world via the Internet. You can search for the exact Pokémon you want from all the many Pokémon that other players have offered. If you have the Pokémon another player wants and you're willing to trade it, go ahead and make the trade! You can also deposit a Pokémon for trading and input certain conditions for the Pokémon you would like to receive in return. To use the GTS, open up Festival Plaza from your X menu, tap "Trade" on the lower screen, and select "GTS." You'll then have two ways to trade: Seek Pokémon or Deposit Pokémon.

Seek Pokémon

This function lets you search for a desired Pokémon by name. If you are looking for a Pokémon you haven't seen before in Alola, you'll want to choose "What Pokémon?" and then type in its name. Once you're done specifying conditions you're looking for, tap "Search with these conditions!" Players who've offered Pokémon that match the conditions you've specified will be displayed. Browse through your options, and pick a player you want to trade with.

Deposit Pokémon

This function lets you deposit Pokémon for other players to browse over the GTS. Choose a Pokémon you want to deposit from your party or PC Boxes, then select "Deposit." You can specify which Pokémon you want in return, so choose "What Pokémon?" and enter the name of a Pokémon you can't find in Alola. If you're lucky, someone will choose to trade you one in return for the Pokémon you've put on offer!

Happiny

Playhouse Pokémon

Alola Pokédex	Melemele	Akala	Ula'ula	Poni
032	032	016	015	008

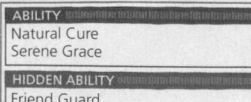

NORMAL

HEIGHT: 2'00"
WEIGHT: 53.8 lbs.

It carries a round white rock in its belly pouch. If it gets along well with someone, it will sometimes give that person the rock.

It's too small to lay eggs yet. As a surrogate, it searches out round white stones.

ABILITY
Natural Cure
Serene Grace

HIDDEN ABILITY
Friend Guard

SPECIES STRENGTHS
HP ◆◆◆◆
Attack ◆
Defense ◆
Sp. Atk ◆
Sp. Def ◆◆◆◆
Speed ◆◆

Damage taken in normal battles

NORMAL ×1	FIGHTING ×2	ROCK ×1			
FIRE ×1	POISON ×1	GHOST ×0			
WATER ×1	GROUND ×1	DRAGON ×1			
GRASS ×1	FLYING ×1	DARK ×1			
ELECTRIC ×1	PSYCHIC ×1	STEEL ×1			
ICE ×1	BUG ×1	FAIRY ×1			

EGG GROUPS
No Eggs Discovered

ITEM SOMETIMES HELD BY WILD POKÉMON
Oval Stone

MAIN WAY TO REGISTER IN THE POKÉDEX
Receive in exchange for Pancham at Sushi High Roller in Malie City

EVOLUTION

Happiny → Level up during the day while holding an Oval Stone → Chansey → Level up with high friendship → Blissey

Female only

Chansey

Egg Pokémon

Alola Pokédex	Melemele	Akala	Ula'ula	Poni
033	033	017	016	009

NORMAL

HEIGHT: 3'07"
WEIGHT: 76.3 lbs.

The eggs laid by Chansey are rich in nutrients and a favorite food of many Pokémon.

Not only are these Pokémon fast runners, they're also few in number, so anyone who finds one must be lucky indeed.

ABILITY
Natural Cure
Serene Grace

HIDDEN ABILITY
Healer

SPECIES STRENGTHS
HP ◆◆◆◆◆◆◆◆◆
Attack ◆
Defense ◆
Sp. Atk ◆
Sp. Def ◆◆◆◆◆◆
Speed ◆◆◆

Damage taken in normal battles

NORMAL ×1	FIGHTING ×2	ROCK ×1			
FIRE ×1	POISON ×1	GHOST ×0			
WATER ×1	GROUND ×1	DRAGON ×1			
GRASS ×1	FLYING ×1	DARK ×1			
ELECTRIC ×1	PSYCHIC ×1	STEEL ×1			
ICE ×1	BUG ×1	FAIRY ×1			

EGG GROUPS
Fairy

ITEM SOMETIMES HELD BY WILD POKÉMON
Lucky Punch

MAIN WAY TO REGISTER IN THE POKÉDEX
Catch in SOS battles against Elekid in the tall grass on Route 12

EVOLUTION

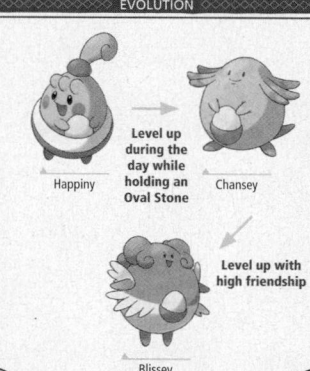

Happiny → Level up during the day while holding an Oval Stone → Chansey → Level up with high friendship → Blissey

Female only

Blissey

Happiness Pokémon

Alola Pokédex	Melemele	Akala	Ula'ula	Poni
034	034	018	017	010

NORMAL

HEIGHT: 4'11"
WEIGHT: 103.2 lbs.

Even the most ferocious Pokémon become calm when they eat Blissey's egg, which is said to be filled with happiness.

Its fluffy fur coat acts as a sensor, enabling it to read the feelings of people and Pokémon.

ABILITY
Natural Cure
Serene Grace

HIDDEN ABILITY
Healer

SPECIES STRENGTHS
HP ◆◆◆◆◆◆◆◆◆
Attack ◆
Defense ◆
Sp. Atk ◆◆◆◆
Sp. Def ◆◆◆◆◆◆◆
Speed ◆◆◆◆

Damage taken in normal battles

NORMAL ×1	FIGHTING ×2	ROCK ×1			
FIRE ×1	POISON ×1	GHOST ×0			
WATER ×1	GROUND ×1	DRAGON ×1			
GRASS ×1	FLYING ×1	DARK ×1			
ELECTRIC ×1	PSYCHIC ×1	STEEL ×1			
ICE ×1	BUG ×1	FAIRY ×1			

EGG GROUPS
Fairy

ITEM SOMETIMES HELD BY WILD POKÉMON
—

MAIN WAY TO REGISTER IN THE POKÉDEX
Level up Chansey with high friendship

EVOLUTION

Happiny → Level up during the day while holding an Oval Stone → Chansey → Level up with high friendship → Blissey

Female only

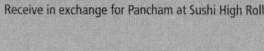

HAPPINY 032

❖ LEVEL-UP MOVES

Lv.	Name	Type	Kind	Pow.	Acc.	PP	Range
1	Pound	Normal	Physical	40	100	35	Normal
1	Charm	Fairy	Status	—	100	20	Normal
5	Copycat	Normal	Status	—	—	20	Self
9	Refresh	Normal	Status	—	—	20	Self
12	Sweet Kiss	Fairy	Status	—	75	10	Normal

❖ TM MOVES

No.	Name	Type	Kind	Pow.	Acc.	PP	Range
TM01	Work Up	Normal	Status	—	—	30	Self
TM06	Toxic	Poison	Status	—	90	10	Normal
TM07	Hail	Ice	Status	—	—	10	Both Sides
TM10	Hidden Power	Normal	Special	60	100	15	Normal
TM11	Sunny Day	Fire	Status	—	—	5	Both Sides
TM16	Light Screen	Psychic	Status	—	—	30	Your Side
TM17	Protect	Normal	Status	—	—	10	Self
TM18	Rain Dance	Water	Status	—	—	5	Both Sides
TM20	Safeguard	Normal	Status	—	—	25	Your Side
TM21	Frustration	Normal	Physical	—	100	20	Normal
TM22	Solar Beam	Grass	Special	120	100	10	Normal
TM27	Return	Normal	Physical	—	100	20	Normal
TM29	Psychic	Psychic	Special	90	100	10	Normal
TM30	Shadow Ball	Ghost	Special	80	100	15	Normal
TM32	Double Team	Normal	Status	—	—	15	Self
TM35	Flamethrower	Fire	Special	90	100	15	Normal
TM38	Fire Blast	Fire	Special	110	85	5	Normal
TM42	Facade	Normal	Physical	70	100	20	Normal
TM44	Rest	Psychic	Status	—	—	10	Self
TM45	Attract	Normal	Status	—	100	15	Normal
TM48	Round	Normal	Special	60	100	15	Normal
TM49	Echoed Voice	Normal	Special	40	100	15	Normal
TM56	Fling	Dark	Physical	—	100	10	Normal
TM73	Thunder Wave	Electric	Status	—	90	20	Normal
TM77	Psych Up	Normal	Status	—	—	10	Normal
TM85	Dream Eater	Psychic	Special	100	100	15	Normal
TM86	Grass Knot	Grass	Special	—	100	20	Normal
TM87	Swagger	Normal	Status	—	85	15	Normal
TM88	Sleep Talk	Normal	Status	—	—	10	Self
TM90	Substitute	Normal	Status	—	—	10	Self
TM100	Confide	Normal	Status	—	—	20	Normal

❖ EXCLUSIVE Z-MOVE

Name	Base Move	Type	Kind	Pow.	Acc.	Range

❖ MOVES TAUGHT BY PEOPLE

Name	Type	Kind	Pow.	Acc.	PP	Range

❖ MOVES LEARNED WHEN EVOLVING

Name	Type	Kind	Pow.	Acc.	PP	Range

❖ EGG MOVES

Name	Type	Kind	Pow.	Acc.	PP	Range
Present	Normal	Physical	—	90	15	Normal
Metronome	Normal	Status	—	—	10	Self
Heal Bell	Normal	Status	—	—	5	Your Party
Aromatherapy	Grass	Status	—	—	5	Your Party
Counter	Fighting	Physical	—	100	20	Varies
Helping Hand	Normal	Status	—	—	20	1 Ally
Gravity	Psychic	Status	—	—	5	Both Sides
Last Resort	Normal	Physical	140	100	5	Normal
Mud Bomb	Ground	Special	65	85	10	Normal
Natural Gift	Normal	Physical	—	100	15	Normal
Endure	Normal	Status	—	—	10	Self

Note: To find a Pokémon Egg that will hatch into a Happiny, have Chansey or Blissey hold a Luck Incense when you leave it at the Pokémon Nursery.

CHANSEY 033

❖ LEVEL-UP MOVES

Lv.	Name	Type	Kind	Pow.	Acc.	PP	Range
1	Double-Edge	Normal	Physical	120	100	15	Normal
1	Defense Curl	Normal	Status	—	—	40	Self
1	Pound	Normal	Physical	40	100	35	Normal
1	Growl	Normal	Status	—	100	40	Many Others
5	Tail Whip	Normal	Status	—	100	30	Many Others
9	Refresh	Normal	Status	—	—	20	Self
12	Double Slap	Normal	Physical	15	85	10	Normal
16	Soft-Boiled	Normal	Status	—	—	10	Self
20	Bestow	Normal	Status	—	—	15	Normal
23	Minimize	Normal	Status	—	—	10	Self
27	Take Down	Normal	Physical	90	85	20	Normal
31	Sing	Normal	Status	—	55	15	Normal
34	Fling	Dark	Physical	—	100	10	Normal
38	Heal Pulse	Psychic	Status	—	—	10	Normal
42	Egg Bomb	Normal	Physical	100	75	10	Normal
46	Light Screen	Psychic	Status	—	—	30	Your Side
50	Healing Wish	Psychic	Status	—	—	10	Self
54	Double-Edge	Normal	Physical	120	100	15	Normal

❖ TM MOVES

No.	Name	Type	Kind	Pow.	Acc.	PP	Range
TM01	Work Up	Normal	Status	—	—	30	Self
TM04	Calm Mind	Psychic	Status	—	—	20	Self
TM06	Toxic	Poison	Status	—	90	10	Normal
TM07	Hail	Ice	Status	—	—	10	Both Sides
TM10	Hidden Power	Normal	Special	60	100	15	Normal
TM11	Sunny Day	Fire	Status	—	—	5	Both Sides
TM13	Ice Beam	Ice	Special	90	100	10	Normal
TM14	Blizzard	Ice	Special	110	70	5	Many Others
TM15	Hyper Beam	Normal	Special	150	90	5	Normal
TM16	Light Screen	Psychic	Status	—	—	30	Your Side
TM17	Protect	Normal	Status	—	—	10	Self
TM18	Rain Dance	Water	Status	—	—	5	Both Sides
TM20	Safeguard	Normal	Status	—	—	25	Your Side
TM21	Frustration	Normal	Physical	—	100	20	Normal
TM22	Solar Beam	Grass	Special	120	100	10	Normal
TM24	Thunderbolt	Electric	Special	90	100	15	Normal
TM25	Thunder	Electric	Special	110	70	10	Normal
TM26	Earthquake	Ground	Physical	100	100	10	Adjacent
TM27	Return	Normal	Physical	—	100	20	Normal
TM29	Psychic	Psychic	Special	90	100	10	Normal
TM30	Shadow Ball	Ghost	Special	80	100	15	Normal
TM31	Brick Break	Fighting	Physical	75	100	15	Normal
TM32	Double Team	Normal	Status	—	—	15	Self
TM35	Flamethrower	Fire	Special	90	100	15	Normal
TM37	Sandstorm	Rock	Status	—	—	10	Both Sides
TM38	Fire Blast	Fire	Special	110	85	5	Normal
TM39	Rock Tomb	Rock	Physical	60	95	15	Normal
TM42	Facade	Normal	Physical	70	100	20	Normal
TM44	Rest	Psychic	Status	—	—	10	Self
TM45	Attract	Normal	Status	—	100	15	Normal
TM48	Round	Normal	Special	60	100	15	Normal
TM49	Echoed Voice	Normal	Special	40	100	15	Normal
TM56	Fling	Dark	Physical	—	100	10	Normal
TM57	Charge Beam	Electric	Special	50	90	10	Normal
TM68	Giga Impact	Normal	Physical	150	90	5	Normal
TM73	Thunder Wave	Electric	Status	—	90	20	Normal
TM77	Psych Up	Normal	Status	—	—	10	Normal
TM78	Bulldoze	Ground	Physical	60	100	20	Adjacent
TM80	Rock Slide	Rock	Physical	75	90	10	Many Others
TM85	Dream Eater	Psychic	Special	100	100	15	Normal
TM86	Grass Knot	Grass	Special	—	100	20	Normal
TM87	Swagger	Normal	Status	—	85	15	Normal
TM88	Sleep Talk	Normal	Status	—	—	10	Self
TM90	Substitute	Normal	Status	—	—	10	Self
TM93	Wild Charge	Electric	Physical	90	100	15	Normal
TM99	Dazzling Gleam	Fairy	Special	80	100	10	Many Others
TM100	Confide	Normal	Status	—	—	20	Normal

❖ EXCLUSIVE Z-MOVE

Name	Base Move	Type	Kind	Pow.	Acc.	Range

❖ MOVES TAUGHT BY PEOPLE

Name	Type	Kind	Pow.	Acc.	PP	Range

❖ MOVES LEARNED WHEN EVOLVING

Name	Type	Kind	Pow.	Acc.	PP	Range

❖ EGG MOVES

Name	Type	Kind	Pow.	Acc.	PP	Range
Present	Normal	Physical	—	90	15	Normal
Metronome	Normal	Status	—	—	10	Self
Heal Bell	Normal	Status	—	—	5	Your Party
Aromatherapy	Grass	Status	—	—	5	Your Party
Counter	Fighting	Physical	—	100	20	Varies
Helping Hand	Normal	Status	—	—	20	1 Ally
Gravity	Psychic	Status	—	—	5	Both Sides
Mud Bomb	Ground	Special	65	85	10	Normal
Natural Gift	Normal	Physical	—	100	15	Normal
Endure	Normal	Status	—	—	10	Self
Seismic Toss	Fighting	Physical	—	100	20	Normal

BLISSEY 034

❖ LEVEL-UP MOVES

Lv.	Name	Type	Kind	Pow.	Acc.	PP	Range
1	Double-Edge	Normal	Physical	120	100	15	Normal
1	Defense Curl	Normal	Status	—	—	40	Self
1	Pound	Normal	Physical	40	100	35	Normal
1	Growl	Normal	Status	—	100	40	Many Others
5	Tail Whip	Normal	Status	—	100	30	Many Others
9	Refresh	Normal	Status	—	—	20	Self
12	Double Slap	Normal	Physical	15	85	10	Normal
16	Soft-Boiled	Normal	Status	—	—	10	Self
20	Bestow	Normal	Status	—	—	15	Normal
23	Minimize	Normal	Status	—	—	10	Self
27	Take Down	Normal	Physical	90	85	20	Normal
31	Sing	Normal	Status	—	55	15	Normal
34	Fling	Dark	Physical	—	100	10	Normal
38	Heal Pulse	Psychic	Status	—	—	10	Normal
42	Egg Bomb	Normal	Physical	100	75	10	Normal
46	Light Screen	Psychic	Status	—	—	30	Your Side
50	Healing Wish	Psychic	Status	—	—	10	Self
54	Double-Edge	Normal	Physical	120	100	15	Normal

❖ TM MOVES

No.	Name	Type	Kind	Pow.	Acc.	PP	Range
TM01	Work Up	Normal	Status	—	—	30	Self
TM04	Calm Mind	Psychic	Status	—	—	20	Self
TM06	Toxic	Poison	Status	—	90	10	Normal
TM07	Hail	Ice	Status	—	—	10	Both Sides
TM10	Hidden Power	Normal	Special	60	100	15	Normal
TM11	Sunny Day	Fire	Status	—	—	5	Both Sides
TM13	Ice Beam	Ice	Special	90	100	10	Normal
TM14	Blizzard	Ice	Special	110	70	5	Many Others
TM15	Hyper Beam	Normal	Special	150	90	5	Normal
TM16	Light Screen	Psychic	Status	—	—	30	Your Side
TM17	Protect	Normal	Status	—	—	10	Self
TM18	Rain Dance	Water	Status	—	—	5	Both Sides
TM20	Safeguard	Normal	Status	—	—	25	Your Side
TM21	Frustration	Normal	Physical	—	100	20	Normal
TM22	Solar Beam	Grass	Special	120	100	10	Normal
TM24	Thunderbolt	Electric	Special	90	100	15	Normal
TM25	Thunder	Electric	Special	110	70	10	Normal
TM26	Earthquake	Ground	Physical	100	100	10	Adjacent
TM27	Return	Normal	Physical	—	100	20	Normal
TM29	Psychic	Psychic	Special	90	100	10	Normal
TM30	Shadow Ball	Ghost	Special	80	100	15	Normal
TM31	Brick Break	Fighting	Physical	75	100	15	Normal
TM32	Double Team	Normal	Status	—	—	15	Self
TM35	Flamethrower	Fire	Special	90	100	15	Normal
TM37	Sandstorm	Rock	Status	—	—	10	Both Sides
TM38	Fire Blast	Fire	Special	110	85	5	Normal
TM39	Rock Tomb	Rock	Physical	60	95	15	Normal
TM42	Facade	Normal	Physical	70	100	20	Normal
TM44	Rest	Psychic	Status	—	—	10	Self
TM45	Attract	Normal	Status	—	100	15	Normal
TM48	Round	Normal	Special	60	100	15	Normal
TM49	Echoed Voice	Normal	Special	40	100	15	Normal
TM52	Focus Blast	Fighting	Special	120	70	5	Normal
TM56	Fling	Dark	Physical	—	100	10	Normal
TM57	Charge Beam	Electric	Special	50	90	10	Normal
TM68	Giga Impact	Normal	Physical	150	90	5	Normal
TM73	Thunder Wave	Electric	Status	—	90	20	Normal
TM77	Psych Up	Normal	Status	—	—	10	Normal
TM78	Bulldoze	Ground	Physical	60	100	20	Adjacent
TM80	Rock Slide	Rock	Physical	75	90	10	Many Others
TM85	Dream Eater	Psychic	Special	100	100	15	Normal
TM86	Grass Knot	Grass	Special	—	100	20	Normal
TM87	Swagger	Normal	Status	—	85	15	Normal
TM88	Sleep Talk	Normal	Status	—	—	10	Self
TM90	Substitute	Normal	Status	—	—	10	Self
TM93	Wild Charge	Electric	Physical	90	100	15	Normal
TM99	Dazzling Gleam	Fairy	Special	80	100	10	Many Others
TM100	Confide	Normal	Status	—	—	20	Normal

❖ EXCLUSIVE Z-MOVE

Name	Base Move	Type	Kind	Pow.	Acc.	Range

❖ MOVES TAUGHT BY PEOPLE

Name	Type	Kind	Pow.	Acc.	PP	Range

❖ MOVES LEARNED WHEN EVOLVING

Name	Type	Kind	Pow.	Acc.	PP	Range

❖ EGG MOVES

Name	Type	Kind	Pow.	Acc.	PP	Range

Alola Pokédex	Melemele	Akala	Ula'ula	Poni
035	035	—	—	—

Munchlax

Big Eater Pokémon

NORMAL

HEIGHT: 2'00"
WEIGHT: 231.5 lbs.

It needs to consume its own weight in food every day. As far as flavor is concerned, it's indifferent.

When it finds something that looks like it might be edible, it goes right ahead and swallows it whole. That's why it gets fatter day by day.

Same form for male/female

ABILITY
Pickup
Thick Fat

HIDDEN ABILITY
Gluttony

Damage taken in normal battles

NORMAL	×1	FIGHTING	×2	ROCK	×1
FIRE	×1	POISON	×1	GHOST	×0
WATER	×1	GROUND	×1	DRAGON	×1
GRASS	×1	FLYING	×1	DARK	×1
ELECTRIC	×1	PSYCHIC	×1	STEEL	×1
ICE	×1	BUG	×1	FAIRY	×1

SPECIES STRENGTHS
HP ◆◆◆◆◆
Attack ◆◆◆◆◆
Defense ◆◆
Sp. Atk ◆◆
Sp. Def ◆◆◆◆◆
Speed ◆

EGG GROUPS
No Eggs Discovered

ITEM SOMETIMES HELD BY WILD POKÉMON
Leftovers

EVOLUTION

MAIN WAY TO REGISTER IN THE POKÉDEX
Catch in the tall grass on the west side of Route 1

❖ LEVEL-UP MOVES

Lv.	Name	Type	Kind	Pow.	Acc.	PP	Range
1	Last Resort	Normal	Physical	140	100	5	Normal
1	Recycle	Normal	Status	—	—	10	Self
1	Lick	Ghost	Physical	30	100	30	Normal
1	Metronome	Normal	Status	—	—	10	Self
1	Odor Sleuth	Normal	Status	—	—	40	Normal
1	Tackle	Normal	Physical	40	100	35	Normal
4	Defense Curl	Normal	Status	—	—	40	Self
9	Amnesia	Psychic	Status	—	—	20	Self
12	Lick	Ghost	Physical	30	100	30	Normal
17	Chip Away	Normal	Physical	70	100	20	Normal
20	Screech	Normal	Status	—	85	40	Normal
25	Body Slam	Normal	Physical	85	100	15	Normal
28	Stockpile	Normal	Status	—	—	20	Self
33	Swallow	Normal	Status	—	—	10	Self
36	Rollout	Rock	Physical	30	90	20	Normal
41	Fling	Dark	Physical	—	100	10	Normal
44	Belly Drum	Normal	Status	—	—	10	Self
49	Natural Gift	Normal	Physical	—	100	15	Normal
50	Snatch	Dark	Status	—	—	10	Self
57	Last Resort	Normal	Physical	140	100	5	Normal

❖ TM MOVES

No.	Name	Type	Kind	Pow.	Acc.	PP	Range
TM01	Work Up	Normal	Status	—	—	30	Self
TM06	Toxic	Poison	Status	—	90	10	Normal
TM10	Hidden Power	Normal	Special	60	100	15	Normal
TM11	Sunny Day	Fire	Status	—	—	5	Both Sides
TM13	Ice Beam	Ice	Special	90	100	10	Normal
TM14	Blizzard	Ice	Special	110	70	5	Many Others
TM17	Protect	Normal	Status	—	—	10	Self
TM18	Rain Dance	Water	Status	—	—	5	Both Sides
TM21	Frustration	Normal	Physical	—	100	20	Normal
TM22	Solar Beam	Grass	Special	120	100	10	Normal
TM24	Thunderbolt	Electric	Special	90	100	15	Normal
TM25	Thunder	Electric	Special	110	70	10	Normal
TM26	Earthquake	Ground	Physical	100	100	10	Adjacent
TM27	Return	Normal	Physical	—	100	20	Normal
TM29	Psychic	Psychic	Special	90	100	10	Normal
TM30	Shadow Ball	Ghost	Special	80	100	15	Normal
TM31	Brick Break	Fighting	Physical	75	100	15	Normal
TM32	Double Team	Normal	Status	—	—	15	Self
TM35	Flamethrower	Fire	Special	90	100	15	Normal
TM37	Sandstorm	Rock	Status	—	—	10	Both Sides
TM38	Fire Blast	Fire	Special	110	85	5	Normal
TM39	Rock Tomb	Rock	Physical	60	95	15	Normal
TM42	Facade	Normal	Physical	70	100	20	Normal
TM44	Rest	Psychic	Status	—	—	10	Self
TM45	Attract	Normal	Status	—	100	15	Normal
TM48	Round	Normal	Special	60	100	15	Normal
TM56	Fling	Dark	Physical	—	100	10	Normal
TM78	Bulldoze	Ground	Physical	60	100	20	Adjacent
TM80	Rock Slide	Rock	Physical	75	90	10	Many Others
TM87	Swagger	Normal	Status	—	85	15	Normal
TM88	Sleep Talk	Normal	Status	—	—	10	Self
TM90	Substitute	Normal	Status	—	—	10	Self
TM94	Surf	Water	Special	90	100	15	Adjacent
TM100	Confide	Normal	Status	—	—	20	Normal

❖ EXCLUSIVE Z-MOVE

Name	Base Move	Type	Kind	Pow.	Acc.	Range

❖ MOVES TAUGHT BY PEOPLE

Name	Type	Kind	Pow.	Acc.	PP	Range

❖ MOVES LEARNED WHEN EVOLVING

Name	Type	Kind	Pow.	Acc.	PP	Range

❖ EGG MOVES

Name	Type	Kind	Pow.	Acc.	PP	Range
Lick	Ghost	Physical	30	100	30	Normal
Charm	Fairy	Status	—	100	20	Normal
Double-Edge	Normal	Physical	120	100	15	Normal
Curse	Ghost	Status	—	—	10	Varies
Whirlwind	Normal	Status	—	—	20	Normal
Pursuit	Dark	Physical	40	100	20	Normal
Zen Headbutt	Psychic	Physical	80	90	15	Normal
Counter	Fighting	Physical	—	100	20	Varies
Natural Gift	Normal	Physical	—	100	15	Normal
After You	Normal	Status	—	—	15	Normal
Self-Destruct	Normal	Physical	200	100	5	Adjacent
Belch	Poison	Special	120	90	10	Normal

Note: To find a Pokémon Egg that will hatch into a Munchlax, have Snorlax hold a Lax Incense when you leave it at the Pokémon Nursery.

Alola Pokédex	Melemele	Akala	Ula'ula	Poni
036	036	—	—	—

Snorlax

Sleeping Pokémon

NORMAL

HEIGHT: 6'11"
WEIGHT: 1014.1 lbs.

Its stomach is said to be incomparably strong. Even Muk's poison is nothing more than a hint of spice on Snorlax's tongue.

It eats nearly 900 pounds of food every day. It starts nodding off while eating—and continues to eat even while it's asleep.

Same form for male/female

ABILITY
Immunity
Thick Fat

HIDDEN ABILITY
Gluttony

Damage taken in normal battles

NORMAL	×1	FIGHTING	×2	ROCK	×1
FIRE	×1	POISON	×1	GHOST	×0
WATER	×1	GROUND	×1	DRAGON	×1
GRASS	×1	FLYING	×1	DARK	×1
ELECTRIC	×1	PSYCHIC	×1	STEEL	×1
ICE	×1	BUG	×1	FAIRY	×1

SPECIES STRENGTHS
HP ◆◆◆◆◆◆
Attack ◆◆◆◆◆◆
Defense ◆◆◆◆
Sp. Atk ◆◆◆◆
Sp. Def ◆◆◆◆◆◆◆
Speed ◆◆

EGG GROUPS
Monster

ITEM SOMETIMES HELD BY WILD POKÉMON
Leftovers

EVOLUTION

MAIN WAY TO REGISTER IN THE POKÉDEX
Level up Munchlax with high friendship

❖ LEVEL-UP MOVES

Lv.	Name	Type	Kind	Pow.	Acc.	PP	Range
1	Tackle	Normal	Physical	40	100	35	Normal
4	Defense Curl	Normal	Status	—	—	40	Self
9	Amnesia	Psychic	Status	—	—	20	Self
12	Lick	Ghost	Physical	30	100	30	Normal
17	Chip Away	Normal	Physical	70	100	20	Normal
20	Yawn	Normal	Status	—	—	10	Normal
25	Body Slam	Normal	Physical	85	100	15	Normal
28	Rest	Psychic	Status	—	—	10	Self
28	Snore	Normal	Special	50	100	15	Normal
33	Sleep Talk	Normal	Status	—	—	10	Self
35	Giga Impact	Normal	Physical	150	90	5	Normal
36	Rollout	Rock	Physical	30	90	20	Normal
41	Block	Normal	Status	—	—	5	Normal
44	Belly Drum	Normal	Status	—	—	10	Self
49	Crunch	Dark	Physical	80	100	15	Normal
50	Heavy Slam	Steel	Physical	—	100	10	Normal
57	High Horsepower	Ground	Physical	95	95	10	Normal

❖ TM MOVES

No.	Name	Type	Kind	Pow.	Acc.	PP	Range
TM01	Work Up	Normal	Status	—	—	30	Self
TM06	Toxic	Poison	Status	—	90	10	Normal
TM10	Hidden Power	Normal	Special	60	100	15	Normal
TM11	Sunny Day	Fire	Status	—	—	5	Both Sides
TM13	Ice Beam	Ice	Special	90	100	10	Normal
TM14	Blizzard	Ice	Special	110	70	5	Many Others
TM15	Hyper Beam	Normal	Special	150	90	5	Normal
TM17	Protect	Normal	Status	—	—	10	Self
TM18	Rain Dance	Water	Status	—	—	5	Both Sides
TM21	Frustration	Normal	Physical	—	100	20	Normal
TM22	Solar Beam	Grass	Special	120	100	10	Normal
TM23	Smack Down	Rock	Physical	50	100	15	Normal
TM24	Thunderbolt	Electric	Special	90	100	15	Normal
TM25	Thunder	Electric	Special	110	70	10	Normal
TM26	Earthquake	Ground	Physical	100	100	10	Adjacent
TM27	Return	Normal	Physical	—	100	20	Normal
TM29	Psychic	Psychic	Special	90	100	10	Normal
TM30	Shadow Ball	Ghost	Special	80	100	15	Normal
TM31	Brick Break	Fighting	Physical	75	100	15	Normal
TM32	Double Team	Normal	Status	—	—	15	Self
TM35	Flamethrower	Fire	Special	90	100	15	Normal
TM37	Sandstorm	Rock	Status	—	—	10	Both Sides
TM38	Fire Blast	Fire	Special	110	85	5	Normal
TM39	Rock Tomb	Rock	Physical	60	95	15	Normal
TM42	Facade	Normal	Physical	70	100	20	Normal
TM44	Rest	Psychic	Status	—	—	10	Self
TM45	Attract	Normal	Status	—	100	15	Normal
TM48	Round	Normal	Special	60	100	15	Normal
TM52	Focus Blast	Fighting	Special	120	70	5	Normal
TM56	Fling	Dark	Physical	—	100	10	Normal
TM68	Giga Impact	Normal	Physical	150	90	5	Normal
TM78	Bulldoze	Ground	Physical	60	100	20	Adjacent
TM80	Rock Slide	Rock	Physical	75	90	10	Many Others
TM87	Swagger	Normal	Status	—	85	15	Normal
TM88	Sleep Talk	Normal	Status	—	—	10	Self
TM90	Substitute	Normal	Status	—	—	10	Self
TM93	Wild Charge	Electric	Physical	90	100	15	Normal
TM94	Surf	Water	Special	90	100	15	Adjacent
TM100	Confide	Normal	Status	—	—	20	Normal

❖ EXCLUSIVE Z-MOVE

Name	Base Move	Type	Kind	Pow.	Acc.	Range
Pulverizing Pancake	Giga Impact	Normal	Physical	210	—	Normal

❖ MOVES TAUGHT BY PEOPLE

Name	Type	Kind	Pow.	Acc.	PP	Range

❖ MOVES LEARNED WHEN EVOLVING

Name	Type	Kind	Pow.	Acc.	PP	Range

❖ EGG MOVES

Name	Type	Kind	Pow.	Acc.	PP	Range
Lick	Ghost	Physical	30	100	30	Normal
Charm	Fairy	Status	—	100	20	Normal
Double-Edge	Normal	Physical	120	100	15	Normal
Curse	Ghost	Status	—	—	10	Varies
Fissure	Ground	Physical	—	30	5	Normal
Whirlwind	Normal	Status	—	—	20	Normal
Pursuit	Dark	Physical	40	100	20	Normal
Counter	Fighting	Physical	—	100	20	Varies
Natural Gift	Normal	Physical	—	100	15	Normal
After You	Normal	Status	—	—	15	Normal
Belch	Poison	Special	120	90	10	Normal

Snorlax's Exclusive Z-Move

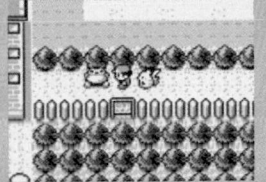

Pokémon Red and *Pokémon Blue*

Pokémon HeartGold and
Pokémon SoulSilver

Pokémon X and *Pokémon Y*

Snorlax is known as the Sleeping Pokémon and for good reason—it loves to sleep! It has been snoozing its way through Pokémon games for twenty years, but it is finally ready to get serious with its own exclusive Z-Move: Pulverizing Pancake! To use it, you will need a piece of Snorlium Z, a Z-Crystal that you cannot obtain through regular gameplay in *Pokémon Sun* and *Pokémon Moon*. It was available as a gift to players who purchased a copy of either game early enough to receive it by January 11, 2017. If you missed your chance during that period, then keep an eye on the official Pokémon website (Pokemon.com) for announcements about future distributions. Unfortunately, Z-Crystals can't be passed along via Link Trades or the GTS (p. 31), so you won't be able to get your hands on a pulverizingly powerful Snorlax that way!

Slowpoke
Dopey Pokémon

WATER **PSYCHIC**

Alola Pokédex	Melemele	Akala	Ula'ula	Poni
037	037	—	018	

HEIGHT: 3'11"
WEIGHT: 79.4 lbs.

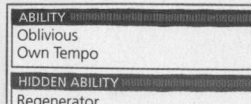
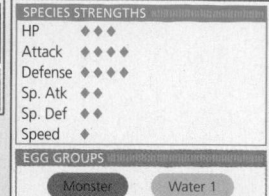

Its long tail often breaks off. It doesn't really feel any pain, though, and the tail grows back, so Slowpoke isn't particularly bothered.

Alolan home cooking involves drying Slowpoke tails and then simmering them into a salty stew.

ABILITY
Oblivious
Own Tempo

HIDDEN ABILITY
Regenerator

Damage taken in normal battles

NORMAL	×1	FIGHTING	×0.5	ROCK	×1
FIRE	×0.5	POISON	×1	GHOST	×2
WATER	×0.5	GROUND	×1	DRAGON	×1
GRASS	×2	FLYING	×1	DARK	×1
ELECTRIC	×2	PSYCHIC	×0.5	STEEL	×0.5
ICE	×0.5	BUG	×2	FAIRY	×1

SPECIES STRENGTHS
HP ◆◆◆
Attack ◆◆◆◆
Defense ◆◆◆◆
Sp. Atk ◆◆
Sp. Def ◆◆◆
Speed ◆

EGG GROUPS
Monster   Water 1

ITEM SOMETIMES HELD BY WILD POKÉMON
Lagging Tail

MAIN WAY TO REGISTER IN THE POKÉDEX
Catch in the tall grass in Hau'oli Outskirts

EVOLUTION

Slowpoke → Lv. 37 → Slowbro

Trade while holding a King's Rock → Slowking

Same form for male/female

Slowbro
Hermit Crab Pokémon

WATER **PSYCHIC**

Alola Pokédex	Melemele	Akala	Ula'ula	Poni
038	038	—	019	

HEIGHT: 5'03"
WEIGHT: 173.1 lbs.

It spaces out while gazing at the sea. With Shellder's poison flowing through its body, it becomes even spacier.

Whenever Shellder bites down hard on its tail, it gives Slowbro a flash of inspiration...which it forgets a moment later.

ABILITY
Oblivious
Own Tempo

HIDDEN ABILITY
Regenerator

Damage taken in normal battles

NORMAL	×1	FIGHTING	×0.5	ROCK	×1
FIRE	×0.5	POISON	×1	GHOST	×2
WATER	×0.5	GROUND	×1	DRAGON	×1
GRASS	×2	FLYING	×1	DARK	×1
ELECTRIC	×2	PSYCHIC	×0.5	STEEL	×1
ICE	×0.5	BUG	×2	FAIRY	×1

SPECIES STRENGTHS
HP ◆◆◆◆
Attack ◆◆◆◆
Defense ◆◆◆◆◆◆
Sp. Atk ◆◆◆◆
Sp. Def ◆◆◆◆◆
Speed ◆◆

EGG GROUPS
Monster   Water 1

ITEM SOMETIMES HELD BY WILD POKÉMON
King's Rock

MAIN WAY TO REGISTER IN THE POKÉDEX
Catch in SOS battles against Slowpoke in the tall grass by Kala'e Bay

EVOLUTION

Slowpoke → Lv. 37 → Slowbro

Same form for male/female

p. 207

Slowking
Royal Pokémon

WATER **PSYCHIC**

Alola Pokédex	Melemele	Akala	Ula'ula	Poni
039	039	—	020	

HEIGHT: 6'07"
WEIGHT: 175.3 lbs.

A poisonous bite reacted with its system, blessing it with the enhanced intellect of a genius. It has full control of its psychic powers.

This Pokémon is so famed for its intellect that a proverb still persists in some regions: "When in doubt, ask Slowking."

ABILITY
Oblivious
Own Tempo

HIDDEN ABILITY
Regenerator

Damage taken in normal battles

NORMAL	×1	FIGHTING	×0.5	ROCK	×1
FIRE	×0.5	POISON	×1	GHOST	×2
WATER	×0.5	GROUND	×1	DRAGON	×1
GRASS	×2	FLYING	×1	DARK	×1
ELECTRIC	×2	PSYCHIC	×0.5	STEEL	×0.5
ICE	×0.5	BUG	×2	FAIRY	×1

SPECIES STRENGTHS
HP ◆◆◆◆
Attack ◆◆◆◆
Defense ◆◆◆◆
Sp. Atk ◆◆◆◆◆
Sp. Def ◆◆◆◆◆◆◆
Speed ◆◆

EGG GROUPS
Monster   Water 1

ITEM SOMETIMES HELD BY WILD POKÉMON

MAIN WAY TO REGISTER IN THE POKÉDEX
Receive a Slowpoke holding a King's Rock in a trade and it will evolve

EVOLUTION

Slowpoke → Trade while holding a King's Rock → Slowking

Same form for male/female

SLOWPOKE 037

❖ LEVEL-UP MOVES

Lv.	Name	Type	Kind	Pow.	Acc.	PP	Range
1	Curse	Ghost	Status	—	—	10	Varies
1	Yawn	Normal	Status	—	—	10	Normal
1	Tackle	Normal	Physical	40	100	35	Normal
5	Growl	Normal	Status	—	100	40	Many Others
9	Water Gun	Water	Special	40	100	25	Normal
14	Confusion	Psychic	Special	50	100	25	Normal
19	Disable	Normal	Status	—	100	20	Normal
23	Headbutt	Normal	Physical	70	100	15	Normal
28	Water Pulse	Water	Special	60	100	20	Normal
32	Zen Headbutt	Psychic	Physical	80	90	15	Normal
36	Slack Off	Normal	Status	—	—	10	Self
41	Amnesia	Psychic	Status	—	—	20	Self
45	Psychic	Psychic	Special	90	100	10	Normal
49	Rain Dance	Water	Status			5	Both Sides
54	Psych Up	Normal	Status	—	—	10	Normal
58	Heal Pulse	Psychic	Status	—	—	10	Normal

❖ TM MOVES

No.	Name	Type	Kind	Pow.	Acc.	PP	Range
TM03	Psyshock	Psychic	Special	80	100	10	Normal
TM04	Calm Mind	Psychic	Status	—	—	20	Self
TM06	Toxic	Poison	Status	—	90	10	Normal
TM07	Hail	Ice	Status	—	—	10	Both Sides
TM10	Hidden Power	Normal	Special	60	100	15	Normal
TM11	Sunny Day	Fire	Status	—	—	5	Both Sides
TM13	Ice Beam	Ice	Special	90	100	10	Normal
TM14	Blizzard	Ice	Special	110	70	5	Many Others
TM16	Light Screen	Psychic	Status	—	—	30	Your Side
TM17	Protect	Normal	Status	—	—	10	Self
TM18	Rain Dance	Water	Status	—	—	5	Both Sides
TM20	Safeguard	Normal	Status	—	—	25	Your Side
TM21	Frustration	Normal	Physical	—	100	20	Normal
TM26	Earthquake	Ground	Physical	100	100	10	Adjacent
TM27	Return	Normal	Physical	—	100	20	Normal
TM29	Psychic	Psychic	Special	90	100	10	Normal
TM30	Shadow Ball	Ghost	Special	80	100	15	Normal
TM32	Double Team	Normal	Status	—	—	15	Self
TM35	Flamethrower	Fire	Special	90	100	15	Normal
TM38	Fire Blast	Fire	Special	110	85	5	Normal
TM42	Facade	Normal	Physical	70	100	20	Normal
TM44	Rest	Psychic	Status	—	—	10	Self
TM45	Attract	Normal	Status	—	100	15	Normal
TM48	Round	Normal	Special	60	100	15	Normal
TM49	Echoed Voice	Normal	Special	40	100	15	Normal
TM55	Scald	Water	Special	80	100	15	Normal
TM73	Thunder Wave	Electric	Status	—	90	20	Normal
TM77	Psych Up	Normal	Status	—	—	10	Normal
TM78	Bulldoze	Ground	Physical	60	100	20	Adjacent
TM85	Dream Eater	Psychic	Special	100	100	15	Normal
TM86	Grass Knot	Grass	Special	—	100	20	Normal
TM87	Swagger	Normal	Status	—	85	15	Normal
TM88	Sleep Talk	Normal	Status	—	—	10	Self
TM90	Substitute	Normal	Status	—	—	10	Self
TM92	Trick Room	Psychic	Status	—	—	5	Both Sides
TM94	Surf	Water	Special	90	100	15	Adjacent
TM100	Confide	Normal	Status	—	—	20	Normal

❖ EXCLUSIVE Z-MOVE

Name	Base Move	Type	Kind	Pow.	Acc.	Range

❖ MOVES TAUGHT BY PEOPLE

Name	Type	Kind	Pow.	Acc.	PP	Range

❖ MOVES LEARNED WHEN EVOLVING

Name	Type	Kind	Pow.	Acc.	PP	Range

❖ EGG MOVES

Name	Type	Kind	Pow.	Acc.	PP	Range
Belly Drum	Normal	Status	—	—	10	Self
Future Sight	Psychic	Special	120	100	10	Normal
Stomp	Normal	Physical	65	100	20	Normal
Mud Sport	Ground	Status	—	—	15	Both Sides
Sleep Talk	Normal	Status	—	—	10	Self
Snore	Normal	Special	50	100	15	Normal
Me First	Normal	Status	—	—	20	Varies
Block	Normal	Status	—	—	5	Normal
Zen Headbutt	Psychic	Physical	80	90	15	Normal
Wonder Room	Psychic	Status	—	—	10	Both Sides
Belch	Poison	Special	120	90	10	Normal

SLOWBRO 038

❖ LEVEL-UP MOVES

Lv.	Name	Type	Kind	Pow.	Acc.	PP	Range
1	Withdraw	Water	Status	—	—	40	Self
1	Heal Pulse	Psychic	Status	—	—	10	Normal
1	Curse	Ghost	Status			10	Varies
1	Yawn	Normal	Status	—	—	10	Normal
1	Tackle	Normal	Physical	40	100	35	Normal
1	Growl	Normal	Status	—	100	40	Many Others
5	Growl	Normal	Status	—	100	40	Many Others
9	Water Gun	Water	Special	40	100	25	Normal
14	Confusion	Psychic	Special	50	100	25	Normal
19	Disable	Normal	Status	—	100	20	Normal
23	Headbutt	Normal	Physical	70	100	15	Normal
28	Water Pulse	Water	Special	60	100	20	Normal
32	Zen Headbutt	Psychic	Physical	80	90	15	Normal
36	Slack Off	Normal	Status	—	—	10	Self
43	Amnesia	Psychic	Status			20	Self
49	Psychic	Psychic	Special	90	100	10	Normal
55	Rain Dance	Water	Status	—	—	5	Both Sides
62	Psych Up	Normal	Status	—	—	10	Normal
68	Heal Pulse	Psychic	Status	—	—	10	Normal

❖ TM MOVES

No.	Name	Type	Kind	Pow.	Acc.	PP	Range
TM03	Psyshock	Psychic	Special	80	100	10	Normal
TM04	Calm Mind	Psychic	Status	—	—	20	Self
TM06	Toxic	Poison	Status	—	90	10	Normal
TM07	Hail	Ice	Status	—	—	10	Both Sides
TM10	Hidden Power	Normal	Special	60	100	15	Normal
TM11	Sunny Day	Fire	Status			5	Both Sides
TM13	Ice Beam	Ice	Special	90	100	10	Normal
TM14	Blizzard	Ice	Special	110	70	5	Many Others
TM15	Hyper Beam	Normal	Special	150	90	5	Normal
TM16	Light Screen	Psychic	Status	—	—	30	Your Side
TM17	Protect	Normal	Status	—	—	10	Self
TM18	Rain Dance	Water	Status	—	—	5	Both Sides
TM20	Safeguard	Normal	Status	—	—	25	Your Side
TM21	Frustration	Normal	Physical	—	100	20	Normal
TM26	Earthquake	Ground	Physical	100	100	10	Adjacent
TM27	Return	Normal	Physical	—	100	20	Normal
TM29	Psychic	Psychic	Special	90	100	10	Normal
TM30	Shadow Ball	Ghost	Special	80	100	15	Normal
TM31	Brick Break	Fighting	Physical	75	100	15	Normal
TM32	Double Team	Normal	Status	—	—	15	Self
TM35	Flamethrower	Fire	Special	90	100	15	Normal
TM38	Fire Blast	Fire	Special	110	85	5	Normal
TM40	Aerial Ace	Flying	Physical	60	—	20	Normal
TM42	Facade	Normal	Physical	70	100	20	Normal
TM44	Rest	Psychic	Status	—	—	10	Self
TM45	Attract	Normal	Status	—	100	15	Normal
TM48	Round	Normal	Special	60	100	15	Normal
TM49	Echoed Voice	Normal	Special	40	100	15	Normal
TM52	Focus Blast	Fighting	Special	120	70	5	Normal
TM55	Scald	Water	Special	80	100	15	Normal
TM56	Fling	Dark	Physical	—	100	10	Normal
TM68	Giga impact	Normal	Physical	150	90	5	Normal
TM73	Thunder Wave	Electric	Status	—	90	20	Normal
TM77	Psych Up	Normal	Status	—	—	10	Normal
TM78	Bulldoze	Ground	Physical	60	100	20	Adjacent
TM85	Dream Eater	Psychic	Special	100	100	15	Normal
TM86	Grass Knot	Grass	Special	—	100	20	Normal
TM87	Swagger	Normal	Status	—	85	15	Normal
TM88	Sleep Talk	Normal	Status	—	—	10	Self
TM90	Substitute	Normal	Status	—	—	10	Self
TM92	Trick Room	Psychic	Status	—	—	5	Both Sides
TM94	Surf	Water	Special	90	100	15	Adjacent
TM100	Confide	Normal	Status	—	—	20	Normal

❖ EXCLUSIVE Z-MOVE

Name	Base Move	Type	Kind	Pow.	Acc.	Range

❖ MOVES TAUGHT BY PEOPLE

Name	Type	Kind	Pow.	Acc.	PP	Range

❖ MOVES LEARNED WHEN EVOLVING

Name	Type	Kind	Pow.	Acc.	PP	Range
Withdraw	Water	Status	—	—	40	Self

❖ EGG MOVES

Name	Type	Kind	Pow.	Acc.	PP	Range

SLOWKING 039

❖ LEVEL-UP MOVES

Lv.	Name	Type	Kind	Pow.	Acc.	PP	Range
1	Heal Pulse	Psychic	Status	—	—	10	Normal
1	Power Gem	Rock	Special	80	100	20	Normal
1	Hidden Power	Normal	Special	60	100	15	Normal
1	Curse	Ghost	Status	—	—	10	Varies
1	Yawn	Normal	Status	—	—	10	Normal
1	Tackle	Normal	Physical	40	100	35	Normal
5	Growl	Normal	Status	—	100	40	Many Others
9	Water Gun	Water	Special	40	100	25	Normal
14	Confusion	Psychic	Special	50	100	25	Normal
19	Disable	Normal	Status	—	100	20	Normal
23	Headbutt	Normal	Physical	70	100	15	Normal
28	Water Pulse	Water	Special	60	100	20	Normal
32	Zen Headbutt	Psychic	Physical	80	90	15	Normal
36	Nasty Plot	Dark	Status	—	—	20	Self
41	Swagger	Normal	Status	—	85	15	Normal
45	Psychic	Psychic	Special	90	100	10	Normal
49	Trump Card	Normal	Special	—	—	5	Normal
54	Psych Up	Normal	Status	—	—	10	Normal
58	Heal Pulse	Psychic	Status	—	—	10	Normal

❖ TM MOVES

No.	Name	Type	Kind	Pow.	Acc.	PP	Range
TM03	Psyshock	Psychic	Special	80	100	10	Normal
TM04	Calm Mind	Psychic	Status	—	—	20	Self
TM06	Toxic	Poison	Status	—	90	10	Normal
TM07	Hail	Ice	Status	—	—	10	Both Sides
TM10	Hidden Power	Normal	Special	60	100	15	Normal
TM11	Sunny Day	Fire	Status	—	—	5	Both Sides
TM13	Ice Beam	Ice	Special	90	100	10	Normal
TM14	Blizzard	Ice	Special	110	70	5	Many Others
TM15	Hyper Beam	Normal	Special	150	90	5	Normal
TM16	Light Screen	Psychic	Status	—	—	30	Your Side
TM17	Protect	Normal	Status	—	—	10	Self
TM18	Rain Dance	Water	Status	—	—	5	Both Sides
TM20	Safeguard	Normal	Status	—	—	25	Your Side
TM21	Frustration	Normal	Physical	—	100	20	Normal
TM26	Earthquake	Ground	Physical	100	100	10	Adjacent
TM27	Return	Normal	Physical	—	100	20	Normal
TM29	Psychic	Psychic	Special	90	100	10	Normal
TM30	Shadow Ball	Ghost	Special	80	100	15	Normal
TM31	Brick Break	Fighting	Physical	75	100	15	Normal
TM32	Double Team	Normal	Status	—	—	15	Self
TM35	Flamethrower	Fire	Special	90	100	15	Normal
TM38	Fire Blast	Fire	Special	110	85	5	Normal
TM42	Facade	Normal	Physical	70	100	20	Normal
TM44	Rest	Psychic	Status	—	—	10	Self
TM45	Attract	Normal	Status	—	100	15	Normal
TM48	Round	Normal	Special	60	100	15	Normal
TM49	Echoed Voice	Normal	Special	40	100	15	Normal
TM52	Focus Blast	Fighting	Special	120	70	5	Normal
TM55	Scald	Water	Special	80	100	15	Normal
TM56	Fling	Dark	Physical	—	100	10	Normal
TM60	Quash	Dark	Status	—	100	15	Normal
TM68	Giga Impact	Normal	Physical	150	90	5	Normal
TM73	Thunder Wave	Electric	Status	—	90	20	Normal
TM77	Psych Up	Normal	Status	—	—	10	Normal
TM78	Bulldoze	Ground	Physical	60	100	20	Adjacent
TM82	Dragon Tail	Dragon	Physical	60	90	10	Normal
TM85	Dream Eater	Psychic	Special	100	100	15	Normal
TM86	Grass Knot	Grass	Special	—	100	20	Normal
TM87	Swagger	Normal	Status	—	85	15	Normal
TM88	Sleep Talk	Normal	Status	—	—	10	Self
TM90	Substitute	Normal	Status	—	—	10	Self
TM92	Trick Room	Psychic	Status	—	—	5	Both Sides
TM94	Surf	Water	Special	90	100	15	Adjacent
TM100	Confide	Normal	Status	—	—	20	Normal

❖ EXCLUSIVE Z-MOVE

Name	Base Move	Type	Kind	Pow.	Acc.	Range

❖ MOVES TAUGHT BY PEOPLE

Name	Type	Kind	Pow.	Acc.	PP	Range

❖ MOVES LEARNED WHEN EVOLVING

Name	Type	Kind	Pow.	Acc.	PP	Range

❖ EGG MOVES

Name	Type	Kind	Pow.	Acc.	PP	Range

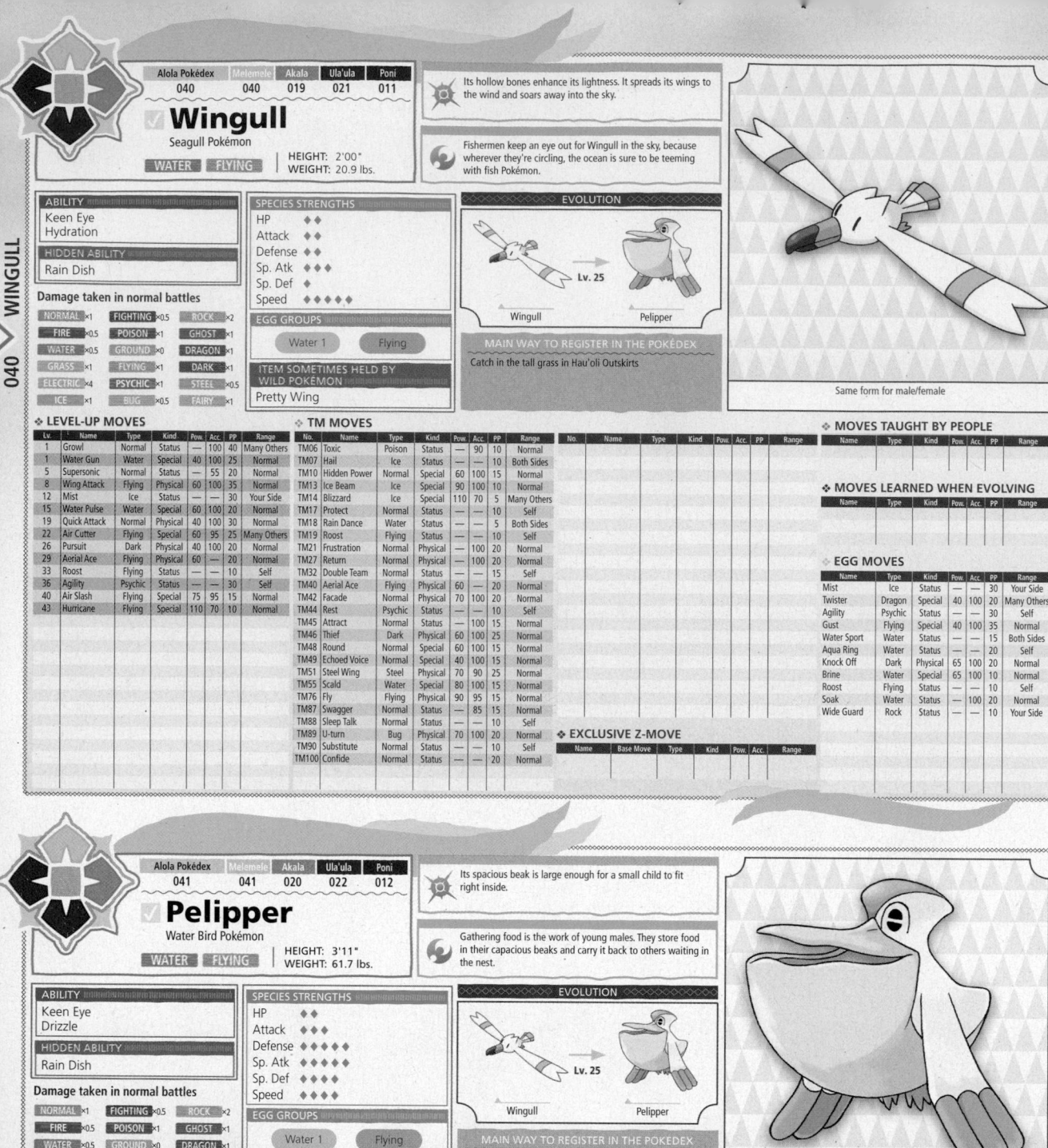

Wingull

Seagull Pokémon

Alola Pokédex	Melemele	Akala	Ula'ula	Poni
040	040	019	021	011

WATER FLYING

HEIGHT: 2'00"
WEIGHT: 20.9 lbs.

Its hollow bones enhance its lightness. It spreads its wings to the wind and soars away into the sky.

Fishermen keep an eye out for Wingull in the sky, because wherever they're circling, the ocean is sure to be teeming with fish Pokémon.

ABILITY
Keen Eye
Hydration

HIDDEN ABILITY
Rain Dish

SPECIES STRENGTHS
HP	◆◆
Attack	◆◆
Defense	◆◆
Sp. Atk	◆◆◆
Sp. Def	◆
Speed	◆◆◆◆

EGG GROUPS
Water 1   Flying

ITEM SOMETIMES HELD BY WILD POKÉMON
Pretty Wing

EVOLUTION
Wingull — Lv. 25 → Pelipper

MAIN WAY TO REGISTER IN THE POKÉDEX
Catch in the tall grass in Hau'oli Outskirts

Same form for male/female

Damage taken in normal battles
NORMAL	×1	FIGHTING	×0.5	ROCK	×1
FIRE	×0.5	POISON	×1	GHOST	×1
WATER	×0.5	GROUND	×0	DRAGON	×1
GRASS	×1	FLYING	×1	DARK	×1
ELECTRIC	×4	PSYCHIC	×1	STEEL	×0.5
ICE	×1	BUG	×0.5	FAIRY	×1

LEVEL-UP MOVES
Lv.	Name	Type	Kind	Pow.	Acc.	PP	Range
1	Growl	Normal	Status	—	100	40	Many Others
1	Water Gun	Water	Special	40	100	25	Normal
5	Supersonic	Normal	Status	—	55	20	Normal
8	Wing Attack	Flying	Physical	60	100	35	Normal
12	Mist	Ice	Status	—	—	30	Your Side
15	Water Pulse	Water	Special	60	100	20	Normal
19	Quick Attack	Normal	Physical	40	100	30	Normal
22	Air Cutter	Flying	Special	60	95	25	Many Others
26	Pursuit	Dark	Physical	40	100	20	Normal
29	Aerial Ace	Flying	Physical	60	—	20	Normal
33	Roost	Flying	Status	—	—	10	Self
36	Agility	Psychic	Status	—	—	30	Self
40	Air Slash	Flying	Special	75	95	15	Normal
43	Hurricane	Flying	Special	110	70	10	Normal

TM MOVES
No.	Name	Type	Kind	Pow.	Acc.	PP	Range
TM06	Toxic	Poison	Status	—	90	10	Normal
TM07	Hail	Ice	Status	—	—	10	Both Sides
TM10	Hidden Power	Normal	Special	60	100	15	Normal
TM13	Ice Beam	Ice	Special	90	100	10	Normal
TM14	Blizzard	Ice	Special	110	70	5	Many Others
TM17	Protect	Normal	Status	—	—	10	Self
TM18	Rain Dance	Water	Status	—	—	5	Both Sides
TM19	Roost	Flying	Status	—	—	10	Self
TM21	Frustration	Normal	Physical	—	100	20	Normal
TM27	Return	Normal	Physical	—	100	20	Normal
TM32	Double Team	Normal	Status	—	—	15	Self
TM40	Aerial Ace	Flying	Physical	60	—	20	Normal
TM42	Facade	Normal	Physical	70	100	20	Normal
TM44	Rest	Psychic	Status	—	—	10	Self
TM45	Attract	Normal	Status	—	100	15	Normal
TM46	Thief	Dark	Physical	60	100	25	Normal
TM48	Round	Normal	Special	60	100	15	Normal
TM49	Echoed Voice	Normal	Special	40	100	15	Normal
TM51	Steel Wing	Steel	Physical	70	90	25	Normal
TM55	Scald	Water	Special	80	100	15	Normal
TM76	Fly	Flying	Physical	90	95	15	Normal
TM87	Swagger	Normal	Status	—	85	15	Normal
TM88	Sleep Talk	Normal	Status	—	—	10	Self
TM89	U-turn	Bug	Physical	70	100	20	Normal
TM90	Substitute	Normal	Status	—	—	10	Self
TM100	Confide	Normal	Status	—	—	20	Normal

MOVES TAUGHT BY PEOPLE
Name	Type	Kind	Pow.	Acc.	PP	Range

MOVES LEARNED WHEN EVOLVING
Name	Type	Kind	Pow.	Acc.	PP	Range

EGG MOVES
Name	Type	Kind	Pow.	Acc.	PP	Range
Mist	Ice	Status	—	—	30	Your Side
Twister	Dragon	Special	40	100	20	Many Others
Agility	Psychic	Status	—	—	30	Self
Gust	Flying	Special	40	100	35	Normal
Water Sport	Water	Status	—	—	15	Both Sides
Aqua Ring	Water	Status	—	—	20	Self
Knock Off	Dark	Physical	65	100	20	Normal
Brine	Water	Special	65	100	10	Normal
Roost	Flying	Status	—	—	10	Self
Soak	Water	Status	—	100	20	Normal
Wide Guard	Rock	Status	—	—	10	Your Side

EXCLUSIVE Z-MOVE
Name	Base Move	Type	Kind	Pow.	Acc.	Range

Pelipper

Water Bird Pokémon

Alola Pokédex	Melemele	Akala	Ula'ula	Poni
041	041	020	022	012

WATER FLYING

HEIGHT: 3'11"
WEIGHT: 61.7 lbs.

Its spacious beak is large enough for a small child to fit right inside.

Gathering food is the work of young males. They store food in their capacious beaks and carry it back to others waiting in the nest.

ABILITY
Keen Eye
Drizzle

HIDDEN ABILITY
Rain Dish

SPECIES STRENGTHS
HP	◆◆
Attack	◆◆◆
Defense	◆◆◆◆
Sp. Atk	◆◆◆◆
Sp. Def	◆◆◆
Speed	◆◆◆

EGG GROUPS
Water 1   Flying

ITEM SOMETIMES HELD BY WILD POKÉMON
Pretty Wing

EVOLUTION
Wingull — Lv. 25 → Pelipper

MAIN WAY TO REGISTER IN THE POKÉDEX
Catch in the tall grass on Route 15

Same form for male/female

Damage taken in normal battles
NORMAL	×1	FIGHTING	×0.5	ROCK	×2
FIRE	×0.5	POISON	×1	GHOST	×1
WATER	×0.5	GROUND	×0	DRAGON	×1
GRASS	×1	FLYING	×1	DARK	×1
ELECTRIC	×4	PSYCHIC	×1	STEEL	×0.5
ICE	×1	BUG	×0.5	FAIRY	×1

LEVEL-UP MOVES
Lv.	Name	Type	Kind	Pow.	Acc.	PP	Range
1	Protect	Normal	Status	—	—	10	Self
1	Hurricane	Flying	Special	110	70	10	Normal
1	Hydro Pump	Water	Special	110	80	5	Normal
1	Tailwind	Flying	Status	—	—	15	Your Side
1	Soak	Water	Status	—	100	20	Normal
1	Growl	Normal	Status	—	100	40	Many Others
1	Water Gun	Water	Special	40	100	25	Normal
1	Water Sport	Water	Status	—	—	15	Both Sides
1	Wing Attack	Flying	Physical	60	100	35	Normal
5	Supersonic	Normal	Status	—	55	20	Normal
8	Wing Attack	Flying	Physical	60	100	35	Normal
12	Mist	Ice	Status	—	—	30	Your Side
15	Water Pulse	Water	Special	60	100	20	Normal
19	Payback	Dark	Physical	50	100	10	Normal
22	Brine	Water	Special	65	100	10	Normal
28	Fling	Dark	Physical	—	100	10	Normal
33	Stockpile	Normal	Status	—	—	20	Self
33	Swallow	Normal	Status	—	—	10	Self
33	Spit Up	Normal	Special	—	100	10	Normal
39	Roost	Flying	Status	—	—	10	Self
44	Tailwind	Flying	Status	—	—	15	Your Side
50	Hydro Pump	Water	Special	110	80	5	Normal
55	Hurricane	Flying	Special	110	70	10	Normal

TM MOVES
No.	Name	Type	Kind	Pow.	Acc.	PP	Range
TM06	Toxic	Poison	Status	—	90	10	Normal
TM07	Hail	Ice	Status	—	—	10	Both Sides
TM10	Hidden Power	Normal	Special	60	100	15	Normal
TM13	Ice Beam	Ice	Special	90	100	10	Normal
TM14	Blizzard	Ice	Special	110	70	5	Many Others
TM15	Hyper Beam	Normal	Special	150	90	5	Normal
TM17	Protect	Normal	Status	—	—	10	Self
TM18	Rain Dance	Water	Status	—	—	5	Both Sides
TM19	Roost	Flying	Status	—	—	10	Self
TM21	Frustration	Normal	Physical	—	100	20	Normal
TM27	Return	Normal	Physical	—	100	20	Normal
TM32	Double Team	Normal	Status	—	—	15	Self
TM40	Aerial Ace	Flying	Physical	60	—	20	Normal
TM42	Facade	Normal	Physical	70	100	20	Normal
TM44	Rest	Psychic	Status	—	—	10	Self
TM45	Attract	Normal	Status	—	100	15	Normal
TM46	Thief	Dark	Physical	60	100	25	Normal
TM48	Round	Normal	Special	60	100	15	Normal
TM49	Echoed Voice	Normal	Special	40	100	15	Normal
TM51	Steel Wing	Steel	Physical	70	90	25	Normal
TM55	Scald	Water	Special	80	100	15	Normal
TM56	Fling	Dark	Physical	—	100	10	Normal
TM58	Sky Drop	Flying	Physical	60	100	10	Normal
TM66	Payback	Dark	Physical	50	100	10	Normal
TM68	Giga Impact	Normal	Physical	150	90	5	Normal
TM76	Fly	Flying	Physical	90	95	15	Normal
TM87	Swagger	Normal	Status	—	85	15	Normal
TM88	Sleep Talk	Normal	Status	—	—	10	Self
TM89	U-turn	Bug	Physical	70	100	20	Normal
TM90	Substitute	Normal	Status	—	—	10	Self
TM94	Surf	Water	Special	90	100	15	Adjacent
TM100	Confide	Normal	Status	—	—	20	Normal

MOVES TAUGHT BY PEOPLE
Name	Type	Kind	Pow.	Acc.	PP	Range

MOVES LEARNED WHEN EVOLVING
Name	Type	Kind	Pow.	Acc.	PP	Range
Protect	Normal	Status	—	—	10	Self

EGG MOVES
Name	Type	Kind	Pow.	Acc.	PP	Range

EXCLUSIVE Z-MOVE
Name	Base Move	Type	Kind	Pow.	Acc.	Range

Wild Pokémon Encounters

You will encounter many Pokémon on your adventures in the Alola region, but have you ever wanted to encounter fewer—or more? There are a few ways that you can affect the encounter rate with which you run into wild Pokémon when you are out and about.

Use items and Abilities to increase encounters

An item called Honey can help increase encounters with wild Pokémon, and you can purchase it at any Poké Mart once you've cleared at least two trials. Or when your lead Pokémon has the Ability Swarm, No Guard, Illuminate, or Arena Trap you'll find yourself fighting them off in no time! Suction Cups or Sticky Hold will increase your success at reeling in Pokémon when fishing, as well. And then there are Abilities that will only attract certain kinds of Pokémon. Synchronize makes you more likely to encounter Pokémon with the same Nature as the lead Pokémon in your party, while Cute Charm makes it more likely you will encounter a Pokémon of the opposite gender. Compound Eyes increases your chances of encountering wild Pokémon that are holding items. Static attracts Electric-type Pokémon and Magnet Pull attracts Steel-type Pokémon, while Hustle, Pressure, and Vital Spirit all make you more likely to encounter high-level Pokémon. Just remember that the Pokémon with any of these Abilities has to be placed as the lead of your party if you want to receive these benefits!

Use consumable items to avoid encounters

What if you want to encounter fewer wild Pokémon? The most common strategy to avoid encounters is to use items like Repels, Super Repels, and Max Repels. Each wears off after a certain amount of time, but they guarantee that you will not be attacked by weak wild Pokémon for as long as they are in effect.

Use held items to avoid encounters

Have the lead Pokémon in your team hold a Cleanse Tag or Pure Incense, and you'll soon find that you're encountering wild Pokémon less often than before. These items aren't as effective as Repel items, but they also don't need to be constantly replaced. Instead you can simply set and forget them if you want to move around a bit more easily.

Use Abilities to avoid encounters

Having lead Pokémon with certain Abilities can also affect how often you encounter wild Pokémon. Stench, Quick Feet, and White Smoke all lower the chance that you will encounter wild Pokémon when you are out and about. Snow Cloak and Sand Veil also keep wild Pokémon away, but only in certain weather conditions—hail and sandstorm, respectively. Finally, Keen Eye and Intimidate won't keep all Pokémon away, but they do decrease the chance that you'll encounter low-level Pokémon. (To find Pokémon with Abilities like these, refer to the Pokémon Abilities Reverse Lookup tables beginning on page 360.)

Use Ride Pokémon to avoid encounters

Most Ride Pokémon make it less likely that you'll encounter wild Pokémon when you're traveling through Alola's wild spaces. Some reduce your chances of being attacked by a wild Pokémon just a bit, while others can have a serious effect on your encounters!

Ride Pokémon	Effects on Encounter Rates
Tauros	Half as likely as usual to encounter wild Pokémon on land
Stoutland	About half as likely as usual to encounter wild Pokémon on land
Mudsdale	About two-thirds as likely as usual to encounter wild Pokémon on land
Machamp	No less likely than usual to encounter wild Pokémon
Lapras	Less likely than usual to encounter wild Pokémon on water
Sharpedo	Much less likely than usual to encounter wild Pokémon on water

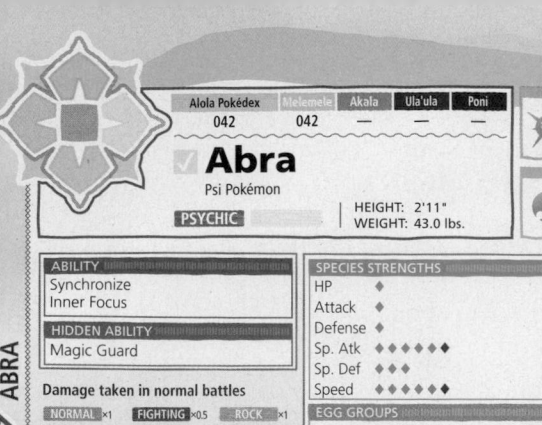

Abra

Alola Pokédex 042 | **Melemele** 042 | **Akala** — | **Ula'ula** — | **Poni** —

Psi Pokémon

PSYCHIC

HEIGHT: 2'11"
WEIGHT: 43.0 lbs.

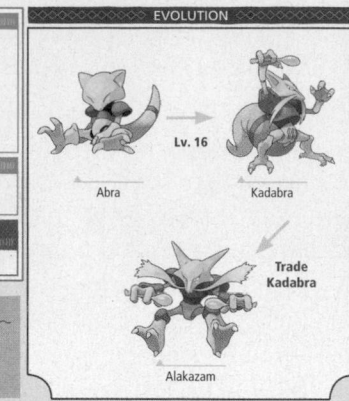

It sleeps 18 hours a day. Even while sleeping, it will teleport itself to treetops and pick and eat berries there.

It can teleport itself to safety while it's asleep, but when it wakes, it doesn't know where it is, so it panics.

ABILITY
Synchronize
Inner Focus

HIDDEN ABILITY
Magic Guard

Damage taken in normal battles

NORMAL	×1	FIGHTING	×0.5	ROCK	×1
FIRE	×1	POISON	×1	GHOST	×1
WATER	×1	GROUND	×1	DRAGON	×1
GRASS	×1	FLYING	×1	DARK	×1
ELECTRIC	×1	PSYCHIC	×0.5	STEEL	×1
ICE	×1	BUG	×2	FAIRY	×1

MAIN WAY TO REGISTER IN THE POKÉDEX
Catch in the tall grass on the south end of Route 2

SPECIES STRENGTHS
HP ◆
Attack ◆
Defense ◆
Sp. Atk ◆◆◆◆◆◆
Sp. Def ◆◆◆◆
Speed ◆◆◆◆◆◆

EGG GROUPS
Human-Like

ITEM SOMETIMES HELD BY WILD POKÉMON
Twisted Spoon

EVOLUTION

Abra → **Lv. 16** → Kadabra → **Trade Kadabra** → Alakazam

Same form for male/female

Kadabra

Alola Pokédex 043 | **Melemele** 043 | **Akala** — | **Ula'ula** — | **Poni** —

Psi Pokémon

PSYCHIC

HEIGHT: 4'03"
WEIGHT: 124.6 lbs.

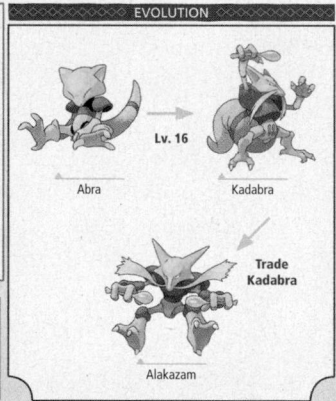

A theory exists that this Pokémon was a young boy who couldn't control his psychic powers and ended up transformed into this Pokémon.

Kadabra's presence infests televisions and monitors with creepy shadows that bring bad luck.

ABILITY
Synchronize
Inner Focus

HIDDEN ABILITY
Magic Guard

Damage taken in normal battles

NORMAL	×1	FIGHTING	×0.5	ROCK	×1
FIRE	×1	POISON	×1	GHOST	×1
WATER	×1	GROUND	×1	DRAGON	×1
GRASS	×1	FLYING	×1	DARK	×1
ELECTRIC	×1	PSYCHIC	×0.5	STEEL	×1
ICE	×1	BUG	×2	FAIRY	×1

MAIN WAY TO REGISTER IN THE POKÉDEX
Level up Abra to Lv. 16

SPECIES STRENGTHS
HP ◆◆
Attack ◆◆
Defense ◆◆
Sp. Atk ◆◆◆◆◆◆
Sp. Def ◆◆◆◆
Speed ◆◆◆◆◆◆

EGG GROUPS
Human-Like

ITEM SOMETIMES HELD BY WILD POKÉMON
—

EVOLUTION

Abra → **Lv. 16** → Kadabra → **Trade Kadabra** → Alakazam

The male has longer whiskers than the female.

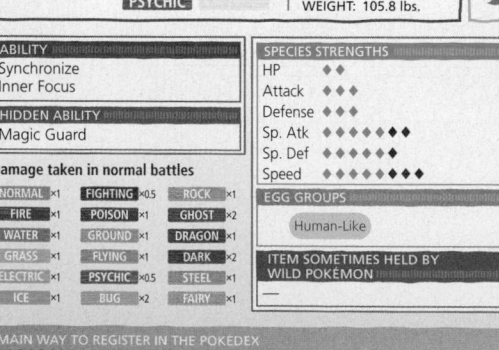

Alakazam

Alola Pokédex 044 | **Melemele** 044 | **Akala** — | **Ula'ula** — | **Poni** —

Psi Pokémon

PSYCHIC

HEIGHT: 4'11"
WEIGHT: 105.8 lbs.

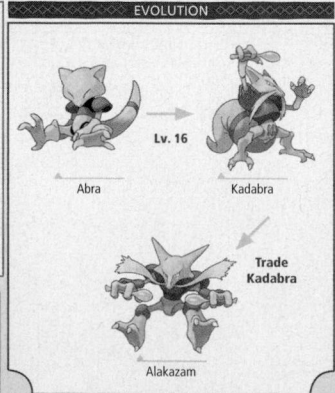

It is said to have an IQ of approximately 5,000. Its overflowing psychokinetic powers cause headaches to anyone nearby.

Its brain cells continue to increase in number until its death. The older the Alakazam, the larger its head.

ABILITY
Synchronize
Inner Focus

HIDDEN ABILITY
Magic Guard

Damage taken in normal battles

NORMAL	×1	FIGHTING	×0.5	ROCK	×1
FIRE	×1	POISON	×1	GHOST	×1
WATER	×1	GROUND	×1	DRAGON	×1
GRASS	×1	FLYING	×1	DARK	×2
ELECTRIC	×1	PSYCHIC	×0.5	STEEL	×1
ICE	×1	BUG	×2	FAIRY	×1

MAIN WAY TO REGISTER IN THE POKÉDEX
Receive a Kadabra in a trade and it will evolve

SPECIES STRENGTHS
HP ◆◆
Attack ◆◆◆
Defense ◆◆◆
Sp. Atk ◆◆◆◆◆◆◆
Sp. Def ◆◆◆◆◆◆
Speed ◆◆◆◆◆◆◆

EGG GROUPS
Human-Like

ITEM SOMETIMES HELD BY WILD POKÉMON
—

EVOLUTION

Abra → **Lv. 16** → Kadabra → **Trade Kadabra** → Alakazam

The male has longer whiskers than the female.

p. 207

ABRA 042

LEVEL-UP MOVES

Lv.	Name	Type	Kind	Pow.	Acc.	PP	Range
1	Teleport	Psychic	Status	—	—	20	Self

TM MOVES

No.	Name	Type	Kind	Pow.	Acc.	PP	Range
TM03	Psyshock	Psychic	Special	80	100	10	Normal
TM04	Calm Mind	Psychic	Status	—	—	20	Self
TM06	Toxic	Poison	Status	—	90	10	Normal
TM10	Hidden Power	Normal	Special	60	100	15	Normal
TM11	Sunny Day	Fire	Status	—	—	5	Both Sides
TM12	Taunt	Dark	Status	—	100	20	Normal
TM16	Light Screen	Psychic	Status	—	—	30	Your Side
TM17	Protect	Normal	Status	—	—	10	Self
TM18	Rain Dance	Water	Status	—	—	5	Both Sides
TM20	Safeguard	Normal	Status	—	—	25	Your Side
TM21	Frustration	Normal	Physical	—	100	20	Normal
TM27	Return	Normal	Physical	—	100	20	Normal
TM29	Psychic	Psychic	Special	90	100	10	Normal
TM30	Shadow Ball	Ghost	Special	80	100	15	Normal
TM32	Double Team	Normal	Status	—	—	15	Self
TM33	Reflect	Psychic	Status	—	—	20	Your Side
TM41	Torment	Dark	Status	—	100	15	Normal
TM42	Facade	Normal	Physical	70	100	20	Normal
TM44	Rest	Psychic	Status	—	—	10	Self
TM45	Attract	Normal	Status	—	100	15	Normal
TM46	Thief	Dark	Physical	60	100	25	Normal
TM48	Round	Normal	Special	60	100	15	Normal
TM53	Energy Ball	Grass	Special	90	100	10	Normal
TM56	Fling	Dark	Physical	—	100	10	Normal
TM57	Charge Beam	Electric	Special	50	90	10	Normal
TM63	Embargo	Dark	Status	—	100	15	Normal
TM73	Thunder Wave	Electric	Status	—	90	20	Normal
TM77	Psych Up	Normal	Status	—	—	10	Normal
TM85	Dream Eater	Psychic	Special	100	100	15	Normal
TM86	Grass Knot	Grass	Special	—	100	20	Normal
TM87	Swagger	Normal	Status	—	85	15	Normal
TM88	Sleep Talk	Normal	Status	—	—	10	Self
TM90	Substitute	Normal	Status	—	—	10	Self
TM92	Trick Room	Psychic	Status	—	—	5	Both Sides
TM99	Dazzling Gleam	Fairy	Special	80	100	10	Many Others
TM100	Confide	Normal	Status	—	—	20	Normal

MOVES TAUGHT BY PEOPLE

Name	Type	Kind	Pow.	Acc.	PP	Range

MOVES LEARNED WHEN EVOLVING

Name	Type	Kind	Pow.	Acc.	PP	Range

EGG MOVES

Name	Type	Kind	Pow.	Acc.	PP	Range
Encore	Normal	Status	—	100	5	Normal
Barrier	Psychic	Status	—	—	20	Self
Knock Off	Dark	Physical	65	100	20	Normal
Fire Punch	Fire	Physical	75	100	15	Normal
Thunder Punch	Electric	Physical	75	100	15	Normal
Ice Punch	Ice	Physical	75	100	15	Normal
Power Trick	Psychic	Status	—	—	10	Self
Guard Swap	Psychic	Status	—	—	10	Normal
Skill Swap	Psychic	Status	—	—	10	Normal
Guard Split	Psychic	Status	—	—	10	Normal
Psycho Shift	Psychic	Status	—	100	10	Normal
Ally Switch	Psychic	Status	—	—	15	Self

EXCLUSIVE Z-MOVE

Name	Base Move	Type	Kind	Pow.	Acc.	Range

KADABRA 043

LEVEL-UP MOVES

Lv.	Name	Type	Kind	Pow.	Acc.	PP	Range
1	Kinesis	Psychic	Status	—	80	15	Normal
1	Teleport	Psychic	Status	—	—	20	Self
1	Confusion	Psychic	Special	50	100	25	Normal
16	Confusion	Psychic	Special	50	100	25	Normal
18	Disable	Normal	Status	—	100	20	Normal
21	Psybeam	Psychic	Special	65	100	20	Normal
23	Miracle Eye	Psychic	Status	—	—	40	Normal
26	Reflect	Psychic	Status	—	—	20	Your Side
28	Psycho Cut	Psychic	Physical	70	100	20	Normal
31	Recover	Normal	Status	—	—	10	Self
33	Telekinesis	Psychic	Status	—	—	15	Normal
36	Ally Switch	Psychic	Status	—	—	15	Self
38	Psychic	Psychic	Special	90	100	10	Normal
41	Role Play	Psychic	Status	—	—	10	Normal
43	Future Sight	Psychic	Special	120	100	10	Normal
46	Trick	Psychic	Status	—	100	10	Normal

TM MOVES

No.	Name	Type	Kind	Pow.	Acc.	PP	Range
TM03	Psyshock	Psychic	Special	80	100	10	Normal
TM04	Calm Mind	Psychic	Status	—	—	20	Self
TM06	Toxic	Poison	Status	—	90	10	Normal
TM10	Hidden Power	Normal	Special	60	100	15	Normal
TM11	Sunny Day	Fire	Status	—	—	5	Both Sides
TM12	Taunt	Dark	Status	—	100	20	Normal
TM16	Light Screen	Psychic	Status	—	—	30	Your Side
TM17	Protect	Normal	Status	—	—	10	Self
TM18	Rain Dance	Water	Status	—	—	5	Both Sides
TM20	Safeguard	Normal	Status	—	—	25	Your Side
TM21	Frustration	Normal	Physical	—	100	20	Normal
TM27	Return	Normal	Physical	—	100	20	Normal
TM29	Psychic	Psychic	Special	90	100	10	Normal
TM30	Shadow Ball	Ghost	Special	80	100	15	Normal
TM32	Double Team	Normal	Status	—	—	15	Self
TM33	Reflect	Psychic	Status	—	—	20	Your Side
TM41	Torment	Dark	Status	—	100	15	Normal
TM42	Facade	Normal	Physical	70	100	20	Normal
TM44	Rest	Psychic	Status	—	—	10	Self
TM45	Attract	Normal	Status	—	100	15	Normal
TM46	Thief	Dark	Physical	60	100	25	Normal
TM48	Round	Normal	Special	60	100	15	Normal
TM53	Energy Ball	Grass	Special	90	100	10	Normal
TM56	Fling	Dark	Physical	—	100	10	Normal
TM57	Charge Beam	Electric	Special	50	90	10	Normal
TM63	Embargo	Dark	Status	—	100	15	Normal
TM73	Thunder Wave	Electric	Status	—	90	20	Normal
TM77	Psych Up	Normal	Status	—	—	10	Normal
TM85	Dream Eater	Psychic	Special	100	100	15	Normal
TM86	Grass Knot	Grass	Special	—	100	20	Normal
TM87	Swagger	Normal	Status	—	85	15	Normal
TM88	Sleep Talk	Normal	Status	—	—	10	Self
TM90	Substitute	Normal	Status	—	—	10	Self
TM92	Trick Room	Psychic	Status	—	—	5	Both Sides
TM99	Dazzling Gleam	Fairy	Special	80	100	10	Many Others
TM100	Confide	Normal	Status	—	—	20	Normal

MOVES TAUGHT BY PEOPLE

Name	Type	Kind	Pow.	Acc.	PP	Range

MOVES LEARNED WHEN EVOLVING

Name	Type	Kind	Pow.	Acc.	PP	Range
Kinesis	Psychic	Status	—	80	15	Normal

EGG MOVES

Name	Type	Kind	Pow.	Acc.	PP	Range

EXCLUSIVE Z-MOVE

Name	Base Move	Type	Kind	Pow.	Acc.	Range

ALAKAZAM 044

LEVEL-UP MOVES

Lv.	Name	Type	Kind	Pow.	Acc.	PP	Range
1	Kinesis	Psychic	Status	—	80	15	Normal
1	Teleport	Psychic	Status	—	—	20	Self
1	Confusion	Psychic	Special	50	100	25	Normal
16	Confusion	Psychic	Special	50	100	25	Normal
18	Disable	Normal	Status	—	100	20	Normal
21	Psybeam	Psychic	Special	65	100	20	Normal
23	Miracle Eye	Psychic	Status	—	—	40	Normal
26	Reflect	Psychic	Status	—	—	20	Your Side
28	Psycho Cut	Psychic	Physical	70	100	20	Normal
31	Recover	Normal	Status	—	—	10	Self
33	Telekinesis	Psychic	Status	—	—	15	Normal
36	Ally Switch	Psychic	Status	—	—	15	Self
38	Psychic	Psychic	Special	90	100	10	Normal
41	Calm Mind	Psychic	Status	—	—	20	Self
43	Future Sight	Psychic	Special	120	100	10	Normal
46	Trick	Psychic	Status	—	100	10	Normal

TM MOVES

No.	Name	Type	Kind	Pow.	Acc.	PP	Range
TM03	Psyshock	Psychic	Special	80	100	10	Normal
TM04	Calm Mind	Psychic	Status	—	—	20	Self
TM06	Toxic	Poison	Status	—	90	10	Normal
TM10	Hidden Power	Normal	Special	60	100	15	Normal
TM11	Sunny Day	Fire	Status	—	—	5	Both Sides
TM12	Taunt	Dark	Status	—	100	20	Normal
TM15	Hyper Beam	Normal	Special	150	90	5	Normal
TM16	Light Screen	Psychic	Status	—	—	30	Your Side
TM17	Protect	Normal	Status	—	—	10	Self
TM18	Rain Dance	Water	Status	—	—	5	Both Sides
TM20	Safeguard	Normal	Status	—	—	25	Your Side
TM21	Frustration	Normal	Physical	—	100	20	Normal
TM27	Return	Normal	Physical	—	100	20	Normal
TM29	Psychic	Psychic	Special	90	100	10	Normal
TM30	Shadow Ball	Ghost	Special	80	100	15	Normal
TM32	Double Team	Normal	Status	—	—	15	Self
TM33	Reflect	Psychic	Status	—	—	20	Your Side
TM41	Torment	Dark	Status	—	100	15	Normal
TM42	Facade	Normal	Physical	70	100	20	Normal
TM44	Rest	Psychic	Status	—	—	10	Self
TM45	Attract	Normal	Status	—	100	15	Normal
TM46	Thief	Dark	Physical	60	100	25	Normal
TM48	Round	Normal	Special	60	100	15	Normal
TM52	Focus Blast	Fighting	Special	120	70	5	Normal
TM53	Energy Ball	Grass	Special	90	100	10	Normal
TM56	Fling	Dark	Physical	—	100	10	Normal
TM57	Charge Beam	Electric	Special	50	90	10	Normal
TM63	Embargo	Dark	Status	—	100	15	Normal
TM68	Giga Impact	Normal	Physical	150	90	5	Normal
TM73	Thunder Wave	Electric	Status	—	90	20	Normal
TM77	Psych Up	Normal	Status	—	—	10	Normal
TM85	Dream Eater	Psychic	Special	100	100	15	Normal
TM86	Grass Knot	Grass	Special	—	100	20	Normal
TM87	Swagger	Normal	Status	—	85	15	Normal
TM88	Sleep Talk	Normal	Status	—	—	10	Self
TM90	Substitute	Normal	Status	—	—	10	Self
TM92	Trick Room	Psychic	Status	—	—	5	Both Sides
TM99	Dazzling Gleam	Fairy	Special	80	100	10	Many Others
TM100	Confide	Normal	Status	—	—	20	Normal

MOVES TAUGHT BY PEOPLE

Name	Type	Kind	Pow.	Acc.	PP	Range

MOVES LEARNED WHEN EVOLVING

Name	Type	Kind	Pow.	Acc.	PP	Range
Kinesis	Psychic	Status	—	80	15	Normal

EGG MOVES

Name	Type	Kind	Pow.	Acc.	PP	Range

EXCLUSIVE Z-MOVE

Name	Base Move	Type	Kind	Pow.	Acc.	Range

Meowth

Alola Pokédex	Melemele	Akala	Ula'ula	Poni
045	045	—	023	

Meowth
Scratch Cat Pokémon

DARK

HEIGHT: 1'04"
WEIGHT: 9.3 lbs.

This Pokémon was not originally found in Alola. Human actions caused a surge in their numbers, and they went feral. They're prideful and crafty.

When its delicate pride is wounded, or when the gold coin on its forehead is dirtied, it flies into a hysterical rage.

❖ ALOLA FORM ❖

Same form for male/female

ABILITY
Pickup
Technician

HIDDEN ABILITY
Rattled

Damage taken in normal battles
NORMAL ×1	FIGHTING ×2	ROCK ×1			
FIRE ×1	POISON ×1	GHOST ×0.5			
WATER ×1	GROUND ×1	DRAGON ×1			
GRASS ×1	FLYING ×1	DARK ×0.5			
ELECTRIC ×1	PSYCHIC ×0	STEEL ×1			
ICE ×1	BUG ×2	FAIRY ×2			

SPECIES STRENGTHS
HP ◆◆
Attack ◆◆
Defense ◆◆
Sp. Atk ◆◆◆
Sp. Def ◆◆
Speed ◆◆◆◆◆◆

EGG GROUPS
Field

ITEM SOMETIMES HELD BY WILD POKÉMON
Quick Claw

EVOLUTION
Alolan Meowth → **Level up with high friendship** → Alolan Persian

MAIN WAY TO REGISTER IN THE POKÉDEX
Catch in the tall grass on Route 2

❖ LEVEL-UP MOVES

Lv.	Name	Type	Kind	Pow.	Acc.	PP	Range
1	Scratch	Normal	Physical	40	100	35	Normal
1	Growl	Normal	Status	—	100	40	Many Others
6	Bite	Dark	Physical	60	100	25	Normal
9	Fake Out	Normal	Physical	40	100	10	Normal
14	Fury Swipes	Normal	Physical	18	80	15	Normal
17	Screech	Normal	Status	—	85	40	Normal
22	Feint Attack	Dark	Physical	60	—	20	Normal
25	Taunt	Dark	Status	—	100	20	Normal
30	Pay Day	Normal	Physical	40	100	20	Normal
33	Slash	Normal	Physical	70	100	20	Normal
38	Nasty Plot	Dark	Status	—	—	20	Self
41	Assurance	Dark	Physical	60	100	10	Normal
46	Captivate	Normal	Status	—	100	20	Many Others
49	Night Slash	Dark	Physical	70	100	15	Normal
50	Feint	Normal	Physical	30	100	10	Normal
55	Dark Pulse	Dark	Special	80	100	15	Normal

❖ TM MOVES

No.	Name	Type	Kind	Pow.	Acc.	PP	Range
TM01	Work Up	Normal	Status	—	—	30	Self
TM06	Toxic	Poison	Status	—	90	10	Normal
TM10	Hidden Power	Normal	Special	60	100	15	Normal
TM11	Sunny Day	Fire	Status	—	—	5	Both Sides
TM12	Taunt	Dark	Status	—	100	20	Normal
TM17	Protect	Normal	Status	—	—	10	Self
TM18	Rain Dance	Water	Status	—	—	5	Both Sides
TM21	Frustration	Normal	Physical	—	100	20	Normal
TM24	Thunderbolt	Electric	Special	90	100	15	Normal
TM25	Thunder	Electric	Special	110	70	10	Normal
TM27	Return	Normal	Physical	—	100	20	Normal
TM30	Shadow Ball	Ghost	Special	80	100	15	Normal
TM32	Double Team	Normal	Status	—	—	15	Self
TM40	Aerial Ace	Flying	Physical	60	—	20	Normal
TM41	Torment	Dark	Status	—	100	15	Normal
TM42	Facade	Normal	Physical	70	100	20	Normal
TM44	Rest	Psychic	Status	—	—	10	Self
TM45	Attract	Normal	Status	—	100	15	Normal
TM46	Thief	Dark	Physical	60	100	25	Normal
TM48	Round	Normal	Special	60	100	15	Normal
TM49	Echoed Voice	Normal	Special	40	100	15	Normal
TM60	Quash	Dark	Status	—	100	15	Normal
TM63	Embargo	Dark	Status	—	100	15	Normal
TM65	Shadow Claw	Ghost	Physical	70	100	15	Normal
TM66	Payback	Dark	Physical	50	100	10	Normal
TM77	Psych Up	Normal	Status	—	—	10	Self
TM85	Dream Eater	Psychic	Special	100	100	15	Normal
TM87	Swagger	Normal	Status	—	85	15	Normal
TM88	Sleep Talk	Normal	Status	—	—	10	Self
TM89	U-turn	Bug	Physical	70	100	20	Normal
TM90	Substitute	Normal	Status	—	—	10	Self
TM97	Dark Pulse	Dark	Special	80	100	15	Normal
TM100	Confide	Normal	Status	—	—	20	Normal

❖ MOVES TAUGHT BY PEOPLE

Name	Type	Kind	Pow.	Acc.	PP	Range

❖ MOVES LEARNED WHEN EVOLVING

Name	Type	Kind	Pow.	Acc.	PP	Range

❖ EGG MOVES

Name	Type	Kind	Pow.	Acc.	PP	Range
Hypnosis	Psychic	Status	—	60	20	Normal
Assist	Normal	Status	—	—	20	Self
Foul Play	Dark	Physical	95	100	15	Normal
Spite	Ghost	Status	—	100	10	Normal
Charm	Fairy	Status	—	100	20	Normal
Amnesia	Psychic	Status	—	—	20	Self
Parting Shot	Dark	Status	—	100	20	Normal
Flail	Normal	Physical	—	100	15	Normal
Flatter	Dark	Status	—	100	15	Normal
Punishment	Dark	Physical	—	100	5	Normal
Snatch	Dark	Status	—	—	10	Self
Covet	Normal	Physical	60	100	25	Normal

❖ EXCLUSIVE Z-MOVE

Name	Base Move	Type	Kind	Pow.	Acc.	Range

Persian

Alola Pokédex	Melemele	Akala	Ula'ula	Poni
046	046	—	024	

Persian
Classy Cat Pokémon

DARK

HEIGHT: 3'07"
WEIGHT: 72.8 lbs.

Its round face and smooth coat—softer than the most high-class velvet—have made this a very popular Pokémon in Alola.

It looks down on everyone other than itself. Its preferred tactics are sucker punches and blindside attacks.

❖ ALOLA FORM ❖

Same form for male/female

ABILITY
Fur Coat
Technician

HIDDEN ABILITY
Rattled

Damage taken in normal battles
NORMAL ×1	FIGHTING ×2	ROCK ×1
FIRE ×1	POISON ×1	GHOST ×0.5
WATER ×1	GROUND ×1	DRAGON ×1
GRASS ×1	FLYING ×1	DARK ×0.5
ELECTRIC ×1	PSYCHIC ×0	STEEL ×1
ICE ×1	BUG ×2	FAIRY ×2

SPECIES STRENGTHS
HP ◆◆◆
Attack ◆◆◆
Defense ◆◆◆
Sp. Atk ◆◆◆◆
Sp. Def ◆◆◆◆
Speed ◆◆◆◆◆◆◆

EGG GROUPS
Field

ITEM SOMETIMES HELD BY WILD POKÉMON

EVOLUTION
Alolan Meowth → **Level up with high friendship** → Alolan Persian

MAIN WAY TO REGISTER IN THE POKÉDEX
Level up Alolan Meowth with high friendship

❖ LEVEL-UP MOVES

Lv.	Name	Type	Kind	Pow.	Acc.	PP	Range
1	Swift	Normal	Special	60	—	20	Many Others
1	Quash	Dark	Status	—	100	15	Normal
1	Play Rough	Fairy	Physical	90	90	10	Normal
1	Switcheroo	Dark	Status	—	100	10	Normal
1	Scratch	Normal	Physical	40	100	35	Normal
1	Growl	Normal	Status	—	100	40	Many Others
1	Bite	Dark	Physical	60	100	25	Normal
1	Fake Out	Normal	Physical	40	100	10	Normal
6	Bite	Dark	Physical	60	100	25	Normal
9	Fake Out	Normal	Physical	40	100	10	Normal
14	Fury Swipes	Normal	Physical	18	80	15	Normal
17	Screech	Normal	Status	—	85	40	Normal
22	Feint Attack	Dark	Physical	60	—	20	Normal
25	Taunt	Dark	Status	—	100	20	Normal
32	Power Gem	Rock	Special	80	100	20	Normal
37	Slash	Normal	Physical	70	100	20	Normal
44	Nasty Plot	Dark	Status	—	—	20	Self
49	Assurance	Dark	Physical	60	100	10	Normal
56	Captivate	Normal	Status	—	100	20	Many Others
61	Night Slash	Dark	Physical	70	100	15	Normal
65	Feint	Normal	Physical	30	100	10	Normal
69	Dark Pulse	Dark	Special	80	100	15	Normal

❖ TM MOVES

No.	Name	Type	Kind	Pow.	Acc.	PP	Range
TM01	Work Up	Normal	Status	—	—	30	Self
TM05	Roar	Normal	Status	—	—	20	Normal
TM06	Toxic	Poison	Status	—	90	10	Normal
TM10	Hidden Power	Normal	Special	60	100	15	Normal
TM11	Sunny Day	Fire	Status	—	—	5	Both Sides
TM12	Taunt	Dark	Status	—	100	20	Normal
TM15	Hyper Beam	Normal	Special	150	90	5	Normal
TM17	Protect	Normal	Status	—	—	10	Self
TM18	Rain Dance	Water	Status	—	—	5	Both Sides
TM21	Frustration	Normal	Physical	—	100	20	Normal
TM24	Thunderbolt	Electric	Special	90	100	15	Normal
TM25	Thunder	Electric	Special	110	70	10	Normal
TM27	Return	Normal	Physical	—	100	20	Normal
TM30	Shadow Ball	Ghost	Special	80	100	15	Normal
TM32	Double Team	Normal	Status	—	—	15	Self
TM40	Aerial Ace	Flying	Physical	60	—	20	Normal
TM41	Torment	Dark	Status	—	100	15	Normal
TM42	Facade	Normal	Physical	70	100	20	Normal
TM44	Rest	Psychic	Status	—	—	10	Self
TM45	Attract	Normal	Status	—	100	15	Normal
TM46	Thief	Dark	Physical	60	100	25	Normal
TM48	Round	Normal	Special	60	100	15	Normal
TM49	Echoed Voice	Normal	Special	40	100	15	Normal
TM60	Quash	Dark	Status	—	100	15	Normal
TM63	Embargo	Dark	Status	—	100	15	Normal
TM65	Shadow Claw	Ghost	Physical	70	100	15	Normal
TM66	Payback	Dark	Physical	50	100	10	Normal
TM68	Giga Impact	Normal	Physical	150	90	5	Normal
TM77	Psych Up	Normal	Status	—	—	10	Self
TM85	Dream Eater	Psychic	Special	100	100	15	Normal
TM87	Swagger	Normal	Status	—	85	15	Normal
TM88	Sleep Talk	Normal	Status	—	—	10	Self
TM89	U-turn	Bug	Physical	70	100	20	Normal
TM90	Substitute	Normal	Status	—	—	10	Self
TM95	Snarl	Dark	Special	55	95	15	Many Others
TM97	Dark Pulse	Dark	Special	80	100	15	Normal
TM100	Confide	Normal	Status	—	—	20	Normal

❖ MOVES TAUGHT BY PEOPLE

Name	Type	Kind	Pow.	Acc.	PP	Range

❖ MOVES LEARNED WHEN EVOLVING

Name	Type	Kind	Pow.	Acc.	PP	Range
Swift	Normal	Special	60	—	20	Many Others

❖ EGG MOVES

Name	Type	Kind	Pow.	Acc.	PP	Range

❖ EXCLUSIVE Z-MOVE

Name	Base Move	Type	Kind	Pow.	Acc.	Range

Pokémon Adapted to the Alola Region

Some Pokémon have adapted to the distinctive microclimates of the Alola region, taking on different forms than they have in other regions. These Pokémon are called regional variants. Taking root in the Alola region, they live like native Pokémon. These regional variant Pokémon can have different appearances and types, and their ways of living can also differ from that of the forms previously known. Meowth is just one of the many Pokémon that have taken on a new form in the Alola region.

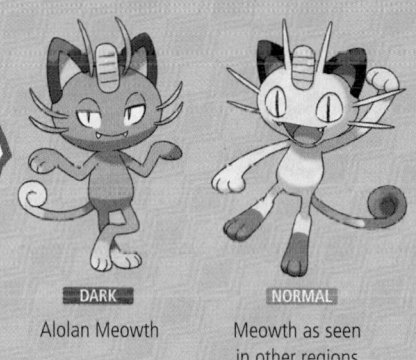

DARK
Alolan Meowth

NORMAL
Meowth as seen
in other regions

It's said that the Meowth that were offered to the royal family lived a life of luxury and pampering, which led them to have a selfish and prideful attitude. This caused Meowth's form to change. The once-rare Alolan Meowth became feral when the monarchy was destroyed, and they have now become regular Pokémon, seen as commonly in the Alola region as elsewhere.

ICE
Alolan Vulpix

FIRE
Vulpix as seen
in other regions

It is said that Vulpix came to the Alola region together with humans, but the Fox Pokémon moved to the snowy mountain peaks to avoid the normal habitats of other Pokémon, and thus it ended up taking on this form. These Alolan Vulpix live on high mountains that remain covered in snow year round. They live in small packs of two to five individuals, helping one another survive.

GRASS DRAGON
Alolan Exeggutor

GRASS PSYCHIC
Exeggutor as seen
in other regions

The environment of the Alola region, where strong sunlight pours down all year round, brought about this change in Exeggutor's form. The people of Alola boast that the Alolan Exeggutor is the true form of Exeggutor. It is...tall! And unlike other Exeggutor, the Alolan Exeggutor has a fourth head—on its tail! This fourth head controls the tail independently and can take on opponents to the rear that can't be reached by the main heads' attacks.

DARK NORMAL
Alolan Rattata

NORMAL
Rattata as seen
in other regions

As a countermeasure to the exploding Rattata population in Alola, Yungoos were imported and released around the region. Yungoos are by nature diurnal creatures, meaning they are active during the day and sleeping at night. To better avoid Yungoos, Rattata changed their preferred environments and circadian rhythms, taking on a nocturnal lifestyle to avoid run-ins with Yungoos. These adaptations to their changed environment led to this new form.

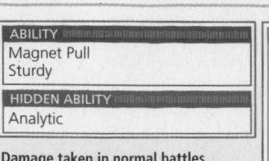

Alola Pokédex	Melemele	Akala	Ula'ula	Poni
047	047	—	025	—

Magnemite
Magnet Pokémon

ELECTRIC **STEEL**

HEIGHT: 1'00"
WEIGHT: 13.2 lbs.

They gather in places where electricity is available. They can be found clinging to the steel towers used to support power lines.

It sends out electromagnetic waves, which let it float through the air. Touching it while it's eating electricity will give you a full-body shock.

ABILITY
Magnet Pull
Sturdy

HIDDEN ABILITY
Analytic

Damage taken in normal battles

NORMAL ×0.5	FIGHTING ×2	ROCK ×0.5
FIRE ×2	POISON ×0	GHOST ×1
WATER ×1	GROUND ×4	DRAGON ×0.5
GRASS ×0.5	FLYING ×0.25	DARK ×1
ELECTRIC ×0.5	PSYCHIC ×0.5	STEEL ×1
ICE ×0.5	BUG ×0.5	FAIRY ×0.5

SPECIES STRENGTHS
HP ◆
Attack ◆◆
Defense ◆◆◆◆
Sp. Atk ◆◆◆◆◆
Sp. Def ◆◆◆
Speed ◆◆◆

EGG GROUPS
Mineral

ITEM SOMETIMES HELD BY WILD POKÉMON
Metal Coat

MAIN WAY TO REGISTER IN THE POKÉDEX
Catch in the tall grass in the Trainers' School

EVOLUTION
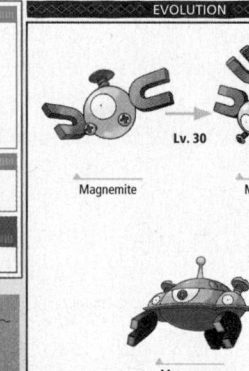
Magnemite → Lv. 30 → Magneton
Level up in Vast Poni Canyon
Magnezone

Gender unknown

047 MAGNEMITE

048 MAGNETON

Alola Pokédex	Melemele	Akala	Ula'ula	Poni
048	048	—	026	—

Magneton
Magnet Pokémon

ELECTRIC **STEEL**

HEIGHT: 3'03"
WEIGHT: 132.3 lbs.

When three Magnemite link together, their brains also become one. They do not become three times more intelligent.

It has about three times the electrical power of Magnemite. For some reason, outbreaks of this Pokémon happen when lots of sunspots appear.

ABILITY
Magnet Pull
Sturdy

HIDDEN ABILITY
Analytic

Damage taken in normal battles

NORMAL ×0.5	FIGHTING ×2	ROCK ×0.5
FIRE ×2	POISON ×0	GHOST ×1
WATER ×1	GROUND ×4	DRAGON ×0.5
GRASS ×0.5	FLYING ×0.25	DARK ×1
ELECTRIC ×0.5	PSYCHIC ×0.5	STEEL ×0.25
ICE ×0.5	BUG ×0.5	FAIRY ×0.5

SPECIES STRENGTHS
HP ◆◆
Attack ◆◆◆
Defense ◆◆◆◆
Sp. Atk ◆◆◆◆◆◆◆
Sp. Def ◆◆◆
Speed ◆◆◆◆

EGG GROUPS
Mineral

ITEM SOMETIMES HELD BY WILD POKÉMON
—

MAIN WAY TO REGISTER IN THE POKÉDEX
Level up Magnemite to Lv. 30

EVOLUTION
Magnemite → Lv. 30 → Magneton
Level up in Vast Poni Canyon
Magnezone

Gender unknown

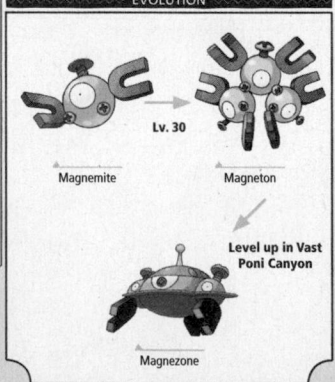

Alola Pokédex	Melemele	Akala	Ula'ula	Poni
049	049	—	027	—

Magnezone
Magnet Area Pokémon

ELECTRIC **STEEL**

HEIGHT: 3'11"
WEIGHT: 396.8 lbs.

Three units generate magnetism. There have been many mistaken reports of UFO sightings when Magnezone flies through the night sky.

As it zooms through the sky, this Pokémon seems to be receiving signals of unknown origin, while transmitting signals of unknown purpose.

ABILITY
Magnet Pull
Sturdy

HIDDEN ABILITY
Analytic

Damage taken in normal battles

NORMAL ×0.5	FIGHTING ×2	ROCK ×0.5
FIRE ×2	POISON ×0	GHOST ×1
WATER ×1	GROUND ×4	DRAGON ×0.5
GRASS ×0.5	FLYING ×0.25	DARK ×1
ELECTRIC ×0.5	PSYCHIC ×0.5	STEEL ×0.25
ICE ×0.5	BUG ×0.5	FAIRY ×0.5

SPECIES STRENGTHS
HP ◆◆◆
Attack ◆◆◆◆
Defense ◆◆◆◆◆◆
Sp. Atk ◆◆◆◆◆◆◆
Sp. Def ◆◆◆◆
Speed ◆◆◆◆

EGG GROUPS
Mineral

ITEM SOMETIMES HELD BY WILD POKÉMON
—

MAIN WAY TO REGISTER IN THE POKÉDEX
Level up Magneton in Vast Poni Canyon

EVOLUTION
Magnemite → Lv. 30 → Magneton
Level up in Vast Poni Canyon
Magnezone

Gender unknown

049 MAGNEZONE

MAGNEMITE 047

❖ LEVEL-UP MOVES

Lv.	Name	Type	Kind	Pow.	Acc.	PP	Range
1	Tackle	Normal	Physical	40	100	35	Normal
1	Supersonic	Normal	Status	—	55	20	Normal
5	Thunder Shock	Electric	Special	40	100	30	Normal
7	Magnet Bomb	Steel	Physical	60	—	20	Normal
11	Thunder Wave	Electric	Status	—	90	20	Normal
13	Light Screen	Psychic	Status	—	—	30	Your Side
17	Sonic Boom	Normal	Special	—	90	20	Normal
19	Spark	Electric	Physical	65	100	20	Normal
23	Mirror Shot	Steel	Special	65	85	10	Normal
25	Metal Sound	Steel	Status	—	85	40	Normal
29	Electro Ball	Electric	Special	—	100	10	Normal
31	Flash Cannon	Steel	Special	80	100	10	Normal
35	Screech	Normal	Status	—	85	40	Normal
37	Discharge	Electric	Special	80	100	15	Adjacent
41	Lock-On	Normal	Status	—	—	5	Normal
43	Magnet Rise	Electric	Status	—	—	10	Self
47	Gyro Ball	Steel	Physical	—	100	5	Normal
49	Zap Cannon	Electric	Special	120	50	5	Normal

❖ TM MOVES

No.	Name	Type	Kind	Pow.	Acc.	PP	Range
TM06	Toxic	Poison	Status	—	90	10	Normal
TM10	Hidden Power	Normal	Special	60	100	15	Normal
TM11	Sunny Day	Fire	Status	—	—	5	Both Sides
TM16	Light Screen	Psychic	Status	—	—	30	Your Side
TM17	Protect	Normal	Status	—	—	10	Self
TM18	Rain Dance	Water	Status	—	—	5	Both Sides
TM21	Frustration	Normal	Physical	—	100	20	Normal
TM24	Thunderbolt	Electric	Special	90	100	15	Normal
TM25	Thunder	Electric	Special	110	70	10	Normal
TM27	Return	Normal	Physical	—	100	20	Normal
TM32	Double Team	Normal	Status	—	—	15	Self
TM33	Reflect	Psychic	Status	—	—	20	Your Side
TM42	Facade	Normal	Physical	70	100	20	Normal
TM44	Rest	Psychic	Status	—	—	10	Self
TM48	Round	Normal	Special	60	100	15	Normal
TM57	Charge Beam	Electric	Special	50	90	10	Normal
TM64	Explosion	Normal	Physical	250	100	5	Adjacent
TM72	Volt Switch	Electric	Special	70	100	20	Normal
TM73	Thunder Wave	Electric	Status	—	90	20	Normal
TM74	Gyro Ball	Steel	Physical	—	100	5	Normal
TM77	Psych Up	Normal	Status	—	—	10	Normal
TM87	Swagger	Normal	Status	—	85	15	Normal
TM88	Sleep Talk	Normal	Status	—	—	10	Self
TM90	Substitute	Normal	Status	—	—	10	Self
TM91	Flash Cannon	Steel	Special	80	100	10	Normal
TM93	Wild Charge	Electric	Physical	90	100	15	Normal
TM100	Confide	Normal	Status	—	—	20	Normal

No.	Name	Type	Kind	Pow.	Acc.	PP	Range

❖ EXCLUSIVE Z-MOVE

Name	Base Move	Type	Kind	Pow.	Acc.	Range

❖ MOVES TAUGHT BY PEOPLE

Name	Type	Kind	Pow.	Acc.	PP	Range

❖ MOVES LEARNED WHEN EVOLVING

Name	Type	Kind	Pow.	Acc.	PP	Range

❖ EGG MOVES

Name	Type	Kind	Pow.	Acc.	PP	Range

MAGNETON 048

❖ LEVEL-UP MOVES

Lv.	Name	Type	Kind	Pow.	Acc.	PP	Range
1	Tri Attack	Normal	Special	80	100	10	Normal
1	Zap Cannon	Electric	Special	120	50	5	Normal
1	Electric Terrain	Electric	Status	—	—	10	Both Sides
1	Tackle	Normal	Physical	40	100	35	Normal
1	Supersonic	Normal	Status	—	55	20	Normal
1	Thunder Shock	Electric	Special	40	100	30	Normal
1	Magnet Bomb	Steel	Physical	60	—	20	Normal
5	Thunder Shock	Electric	Special	40	100	30	Normal
7	Magnet Bomb	Steel	Physical	60	—	20	Normal
11	Thunder Wave	Electric	Status	—	90	20	Normal
13	Light Screen	Psychic	Status	—	—	30	Your Side
17	Sonic Boom	Normal	Special	—	90	20	Normal
19	Spark	Electric	Physical	65	100	20	Normal
23	Mirror Shot	Steel	Special	65	85	10	Normal
25	Metal Sound	Steel	Status	—	85	40	Normal
29	Electro Ball	Electric	Special	—	100	10	Normal
33	Flash Cannon	Steel	Special	80	100	10	Normal
39	Screech	Normal	Status	—	85	40	Normal
43	Discharge	Electric	Special	80	100	15	Adjacent
49	Lock-On	Normal	Status	—	—	5	Normal
53	Magnet Rise	Electric	Status	—	—	10	Self
59	Gyro Ball	Steel	Physical	—	100	5	Normal
63	Zap Cannon	Electric	Special	120	50	5	Normal

❖ TM MOVES

No.	Name	Type	Kind	Pow.	Acc.	PP	Range
TM06	Toxic	Poison	Status	—	90	10	Normal
TM10	Hidden Power	Normal	Special	60	100	15	Normal
TM11	Sunny Day	Fire	Status	—	—	5	Both Sides
TM15	Hyper Beam	Normal	Special	150	90	5	Normal
TM16	Light Screen	Psychic	Status	—	—	30	Your Side
TM17	Protect	Normal	Status	—	—	10	Self
TM18	Rain Dance	Water	Status	—	—	5	Both Sides
TM21	Frustration	Normal	Physical	—	100	20	Normal
TM24	Thunderbolt	Electric	Special	90	100	15	Normal
TM25	Thunder	Electric	Special	110	70	10	Normal
TM27	Return	Normal	Physical	—	100	20	Normal
TM32	Double Team	Normal	Status	—	—	15	Self
TM33	Reflect	Psychic	Status	—	—	20	Your Side
TM42	Facade	Normal	Physical	70	100	20	Normal
TM44	Rest	Psychic	Status	—	—	10	Self
TM48	Round	Normal	Special	60	100	15	Normal
TM57	Charge Beam	Electric	Special	50	90	10	Normal
TM64	Explosion	Normal	Physical	250	100	5	Adjacent
TM68	Giga Impact	Normal	Physical	150	90	5	Normal
TM72	Volt Switch	Electric	Special	70	100	20	Normal
TM73	Thunder Wave	Electric	Status	—	90	20	Normal
TM74	Gyro Ball	Steel	Physical	—	100	5	Normal
TM77	Psych Up	Normal	Status	—	—	10	Normal
TM87	Swagger	Normal	Status	—	85	15	Normal
TM88	Sleep Talk	Normal	Status	—	—	10	Self
TM90	Substitute	Normal	Status	—	—	10	Self
TM91	Flash Cannon	Steel	Special	80	100	10	Normal

No.	Name	Type	Kind	Pow.	Acc.	PP	Range
TM93	Wild Charge	Electric	Physical	90	100	15	Normal
TM100	Confide	Normal	Status	—	—	20	Normal

❖ EXCLUSIVE Z-MOVE

Name	Base Move	Type	Kind	Pow.	Acc.	Range

❖ MOVES TAUGHT BY PEOPLE

Name	Type	Kind	Pow.	Acc.	PP	Range

❖ MOVES LEARNED WHEN EVOLVING

Name	Type	Kind	Pow.	Acc.	PP	Range
Tri Attack	Normal	Special	80	100	10	Normal

❖ EGG MOVES

Name	Type	Kind	Pow.	Acc.	PP	Range

MAGNEZONE 049

❖ LEVEL-UP MOVES

Lv.	Name	Type	Kind	Pow.	Acc.	PP	Range
1	Tri Attack	Normal	Special	80	100	10	Normal
1	Zap Cannon	Electric	Special	120	50	5	Normal
1	Magnetic Flux	Electric	Status	—	—	20	Your Party
1	Mirror Coat	Psychic	Special	—	100	20	Varies
1	Barrier	Psychic	Status	—	—	20	Self
1	Electric Terrain	Electric	Status	—	—	10	Both Sides
1	Tackle	Normal	Physical	40	100	35	Normal
1	Supersonic	Normal	Status	—	55	20	Normal
1	Thunder Shock	Electric	Special	40	100	30	Normal
1	Magnet Bomb	Steel	Physical	60	—	20	Normal
5	Thunder Shock	Electric	Special	40	100	30	Normal
7	Magnet Bomb	Steel	Physical	60	—	20	Normal
11	Thunder Wave	Electric	Status	—	90	20	Normal
13	Light Screen	Psychic	Status	—	—	30	Your Side
17	Sonic Boom	Normal	Special	—	90	20	Normal
19	Spark	Electric	Physical	65	100	20	Normal
23	Mirror Shot	Steel	Special	65	85	10	Normal
25	Metal Sound	Steel	Status	—	85	40	Normal
29	Electro Ball	Electric	Special	—	100	10	Normal
33	Flash Cannon	Steel	Special	80	100	10	Normal
39	Screech	Normal	Status	—	85	40	Normal
43	Discharge	Electric	Special	80	100	15	Adjacent
49	Lock-On	Normal	Status	—	—	5	Normal
53	Magnet Rise	Electric	Status	—	—	10	Self
59	Gyro Ball	Steel	Physical	—	100	5	Normal
63	Zap Cannon	Electric	Special	120	50	5	Normal

❖ TM MOVES

No.	Name	Type	Kind	Pow.	Acc.	PP	Range
TM06	Toxic	Poison	Status	—	90	10	Normal
TM10	Hidden Power	Normal	Special	60	100	15	Normal
TM11	Sunny Day	Fire	Status	—	—	5	Both Sides
TM15	Hyper Beam	Normal	Special	150	90	5	Normal
TM16	Light Screen	Psychic	Status	—	—	30	Your Side
TM17	Protect	Normal	Status	—	—	10	Self
TM18	Rain Dance	Water	Status	—	—	5	Both Sides
TM21	Frustration	Normal	Physical	—	100	20	Normal
TM24	Thunderbolt	Electric	Special	90	100	15	Normal
TM25	Thunder	Electric	Special	110	70	10	Normal
TM27	Return	Normal	Physical	—	100	20	Normal
TM32	Double Team	Normal	Status	—	—	15	Self
TM33	Reflect	Psychic	Status	—	—	20	Your Side
TM42	Facade	Normal	Physical	70	100	20	Normal
TM44	Rest	Psychic	Status	—	—	10	Self
TM48	Round	Normal	Special	60	100	15	Normal
TM57	Charge Beam	Electric	Special	50	90	10	Normal
TM64	Explosion	Normal	Physical	250	100	5	Adjacent
TM68	Giga Impact	Normal	Physical	150	90	5	Normal
TM72	Volt Switch	Electric	Special	70	100	20	Normal
TM73	Thunder Wave	Electric	Status	—	90	20	Normal
TM74	Gyro Ball	Steel	Physical	—	100	5	Normal
TM77	Psych Up	Normal	Status	—	—	10	Normal
TM87	Swagger	Normal	Status	—	85	15	Normal
TM88	Sleep Talk	Normal	Status	—	—	10	Self
TM90	Substitute	Normal	Status	—	—	10	Self
TM91	Flash Cannon	Steel	Special	80	100	10	Normal

No.	Name	Type	Kind	Pow.	Acc.	PP	Range
TM93	Wild Charge	Electric	Physical	90	100	15	Normal
TM100	Confide	Normal	Status	—	—	20	Normal

❖ EXCLUSIVE Z-MOVE

Name	Base Move	Type	Kind	Pow.	Acc.	Range

❖ MOVES TAUGHT BY PEOPLE

Name	Type	Kind	Pow.	Acc.	PP	Range

❖ MOVES LEARNED WHEN EVOLVING

Name	Type	Kind	Pow.	Acc.	PP	Range

❖ EGG MOVES

Name	Type	Kind	Pow.	Acc.	PP	Range

Alola Pokédex	Melemele	Akala	Ula'ula	Poni
050	050	—	028	—

Grimer

Sludge Pokémon

POISON DARK

HEIGHT: 2'04"
WEIGHT: 92.6 lbs.

A Grimer, which had been brought in to solve a problem with garbage, developed over time into this form.

The crystals on Grimer's body are lumps of toxins. If one falls off, lethal poisons leak out.

❖ ALOLA FORM ❖

Same form for male/female

ABILITY
Poison Touch
Gluttony

HIDDEN ABILITY
Power of Alchemy

Damage taken in normal battles

NORMAL	×1	FIGHTING	×1	ROCK	×1
FIRE	×1	POISON	×0.5	GHOST	×0.5
WATER	×1	GROUND	×2	DRAGON	×1
GRASS	×0.5	FLYING	×1	DARK	×0.5
ELECTRIC	×1	PSYCHIC	×0	STEEL	×1
ICE	×1	BUG	×1	FAIRY	×1

SPECIES STRENGTHS
HP ◆◆◆
Attack ◆◆◆◆
Defense ◆◆◆
Sp. Atk ◆◆
Sp. Def ◆◆◆
Speed ◆◆

EGG GROUPS
Amorphous

ITEM SOMETIMES HELD BY WILD POKÉMON
Black Sludge

EVOLUTION

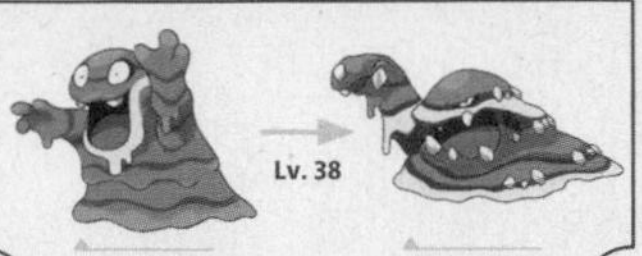

Alolan Grimer → Alolan Muk

MAIN WAY TO REGISTER IN THE POKÉDEX
Catch in the tall grass in the Trainers' School

❖ LEVEL-UP MOVES

Lv.	Name	Type	Kind	Pow.	Acc.	PP	Range
1	Pound	Normal	Physical	40	100	35	Normal
1	Poison Gas	Poison	Status	—	90	40	Many Others
4	Harden	Normal	Status	—	—	30	Self
7	Bite	Dark	Physical	60	100	25	Normal
12	Disable	Normal	Status	—	100	20	Normal
15	Acid Spray	Poison	Special	40	100	20	Normal
18	Poison Fang	Poison	Physical	50	100	15	Normal
21	Minimize	Normal	Status	—	—	10	Self
26	Fling	Dark	Physical	—	100	10	Normal
29	Knock Off	Dark	Physical	65	100	20	Normal
32	Crunch	Dark	Physical	80	100	15	Normal
37	Screech	Normal	Status	—	85	40	Normal
40	Gunk Shot	Poison	Physical	120	80	5	Normal
43	Acid Armor	Poison	Status	—	—	20	Self
46	Belch	Poison	Special	120	90	10	Normal
48	Memento	Dark	Status	—	100	10	Normal

❖ TM MOVES

No.	Name	Type	Kind	Pow.	Acc.	PP	Range
TM06	Toxic	Poison	Status	—	90	10	Normal
TM09	Venoshock	Poison	Special	65	100	10	Normal
TM10	Hidden Power	Normal	Special	60	100	15	Normal
TM11	Sunny Day	Fire	Status	—	—	5	Both Sides
TM12	Taunt	Dark	Status	—	100	20	Normal
TM17	Protect	Normal	Status	—	—	10	Self
TM18	Rain Dance	Water	Status	—	—	5	Both Sides
TM21	Frustration	Normal	Physical	—	100	20	Normal
TM27	Return	Normal	Physical	—	100	20	Normal
TM30	Shadow Ball	Ghost	Special	80	100	15	Normal
TM32	Double Team	Normal	Status	—	—	15	Self
TM34	Sludge Wave	Poison	Special	95	100	10	Adjacent
TM35	Flamethrower	Fire	Special	90	100	15	Normal
TM36	Sludge Bomb	Poison	Special	90	100	10	Normal
TM38	Fire Blast	Fire	Special	110	85	5	Normal
TM39	Rock Tomb	Rock	Physical	60	95	15	Normal
TM41	Torment	Dark	Status	—	100	15	Normal
TM42	Facade	Normal	Physical	70	100	20	Normal
TM44	Rest	Psychic	Status	—	—	10	Self
TM45	Attract	Normal	Status	—	100	15	Normal
TM46	Thief	Dark	Physical	60	100	25	Normal
TM48	Round	Normal	Special	60	100	15	Normal
TM56	Fling	Dark	Physical	—	100	10	Normal
TM59	Brutal Swing	Dark	Physical	60	100	20	Adjacent
TM60	Quash	Dark	Status	—	100	15	Normal
TM63	Embargo	Dark	Status	—	100	15	Normal
TM64	Explosion	Normal	Physical	250	100	5	Adjacent
TM66	Payback	Dark	Physical	50	100	10	Normal
TM69	Rock Polish	Rock	Status	—	—	20	Self
TM71	Stone Edge	Rock	Physical	100	80	5	Normal
TM80	Rock Slide	Rock	Physical	75	90	10	Many Others
TM83	Infestation	Bug	Special	20	100	20	Normal
TM84	Poison Jab	Poison	Physical	80	100	20	Normal
TM87	Swagger	Normal	Status	—	85	15	Normal
TM88	Sleep Talk	Normal	Status	—	—	10	Self
TM90	Substitute	Normal	Status	—	—	10	Self
TM95	Snarl	Dark	Special	55	95	15	Many Others
TM100	Confide	Normal	Status	—	—	20	Normal

❖ EXCLUSIVE Z-MOVE

Name	Base Move	Type	Kind	Pow.	Acc.	Range

❖ MOVES TAUGHT BY PEOPLE

Name	Type	Kind	Pow.	Acc.	PP	Range

❖ MOVES LEARNED WHEN EVOLVING

Name	Type	Kind	Pow.	Acc.	PP	Range

❖ EGG MOVES

Name	Type	Kind	Pow.	Acc.	PP	Range
Clear Smog	Poison	Special	50	—	15	Normal
Mean Look	Normal	Status	—	—	5	Normal
Pursuit	Dark	Physical	40	100	20	Normal
Imprison	Psychic	Status	—	—	10	Self
Curse	Ghost	Status	—	—	10	Varies
Assurance	Dark	Physical	60	100	10	Normal
Shadow Sneak	Ghost	Physical	40	100	30	Normal
Stockpile	Normal	Status	—	—	20	Self
Swallow	Normal	Status	—	—	10	Self
Spit Up	Normal	Special	—	100	10	Normal
Scary Face	Normal	Status	—	100	10	Normal
Spite	Ghost	Status	—	100	10	Normal

Alola Pokédex	Melemele	Akala	Ula'ula	Poni
051	051	—	029	—

Muk

Sludge Pokémon

POISON DARK

HEIGHT: 3'03"
WEIGHT: 114.6 lbs.

The garbage it eats causes continuous chemical changes in its body, which produce its exceedingly vivid coloration.

While it's unexpectedly quiet and friendly, if it's not fed any trash for a while, it will smash its Trainer's furnishings and eat up the fragments.

❖ ALOLA FORM ❖

Same form for male/female

ABILITY
Poison Touch
Gluttony

HIDDEN ABILITY
Power of Alchemy

Damage taken in normal battles

NORMAL	×1	FIGHTING	×1	ROCK	×1
FIRE	×1	POISON	×0.5	GHOST	×0.5
WATER	×1	GROUND	×2	DRAGON	×1
GRASS	×0.5	FLYING	×1	DARK	×0.5
ELECTRIC	×1	PSYCHIC	×0	STEEL	×1
ICE	×1	BUG	×1	FAIRY	×1

SPECIES STRENGTHS
HP ◆◆◆◆
Attack ◆◆◆◆◆◆
Defense ◆◆◆◆
Sp. Atk ◆◆◆◆
Sp. Def ◆◆◆◆◆◆
Speed ◆◆◆

EGG GROUPS
Amorphous

ITEM SOMETIMES HELD BY WILD POKÉMON
—

EVOLUTION

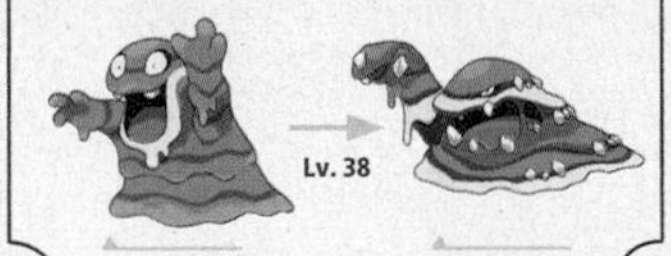

Alolan Grimer → Alolan Muk

MAIN WAY TO REGISTER IN THE POKÉDEX
Level up Alolan Grimer to Lv. 38

❖ LEVEL-UP MOVES

Lv.	Name	Type	Kind	Pow.	Acc.	PP	Range
1	Venom Drench	Poison	Status	—	100	20	Many Others
1	Pound	Normal	Physical	40	100	35	Normal
1	Poison Gas	Poison	Status	—	90	40	Many Others
1	Harden	Normal	Status	—	—	30	Self
1	Bite	Dark	Physical	60	100	25	Normal
4	Harden	Normal	Status	—	—	30	Self
7	Bite	Dark	Physical	60	100	25	Normal
12	Disable	Normal	Status	—	100	20	Normal
15	Acid Spray	Poison	Special	40	100	20	Normal
18	Poison Fang	Poison	Physical	50	100	15	Normal
21	Minimize	Normal	Status	—	—	10	Self
26	Fling	Dark	Physical	—	100	10	Normal
29	Knock Off	Dark	Physical	65	100	20	Normal
32	Crunch	Dark	Physical	80	100	15	Normal
37	Screech	Normal	Status	—	85	40	Normal
40	Gunk Shot	Poison	Physical	120	80	5	Normal
46	Acid Armor	Poison	Status	—	—	20	Self
52	Belch	Poison	Special	120	90	10	Normal
57	Memento	Dark	Status	—	100	10	Normal

❖ TM MOVES

No.	Name	Type	Kind	Pow.	Acc.	PP	Range
TM06	Toxic	Poison	Status	—	90	10	Normal
TM09	Venoshock	Poison	Special	65	100	10	Normal
TM10	Hidden Power	Normal	Special	60	100	15	Normal
TM11	Sunny Day	Fire	Status	—	—	5	Both Sides
TM12	Taunt	Dark	Status	—	100	20	Normal
TM15	Hyper Beam	Normal	Special	150	90	5	Normal
TM17	Protect	Normal	Status	—	—	10	Self
TM18	Rain Dance	Water	Status	—	—	5	Both Sides
TM21	Frustration	Normal	Physical	—	100	20	Normal
TM27	Return	Normal	Physical	—	100	20	Normal
TM30	Shadow Ball	Ghost	Special	80	100	15	Normal
TM31	Brick Break	Fighting	Physical	75	100	15	Normal
TM32	Double Team	Normal	Status	—	—	15	Self
TM34	Sludge Wave	Poison	Special	95	100	10	Adjacent
TM35	Flamethrower	Fire	Special	90	100	15	Normal
TM36	Sludge Bomb	Poison	Special	90	100	10	Normal
TM38	Fire Blast	Fire	Special	110	85	5	Normal
TM39	Rock Tomb	Rock	Physical	60	95	15	Normal
TM41	Torment	Dark	Status	—	100	15	Normal
TM42	Facade	Normal	Physical	70	100	20	Normal
TM44	Rest	Psychic	Status	—	—	10	Self
TM45	Attract	Normal	Status	—	100	15	Normal
TM46	Thief	Dark	Physical	60	100	25	Normal
TM48	Round	Normal	Special	60	100	15	Normal
TM52	Focus Blast	Fighting	Special	120	70	5	Normal
TM56	Fling	Dark	Physical	—	100	10	Normal
TM59	Brutal Swing	Dark	Physical	60	100	20	Adjacent
TM60	Quash	Dark	Status	—	100	15	Normal
TM63	Embargo	Dark	Status	—	100	15	Normal
TM64	Explosion	Normal	Physical	250	100	5	Adjacent
TM66	Payback	Dark	Physical	50	100	10	Normal
TM68	Giga Impact	Normal	Physical	150	90	5	Normal
TM69	Rock Polish	Rock	Status	—	—	20	Self
TM71	Stone Edge	Rock	Physical	100	80	5	Normal
TM80	Rock Slide	Rock	Physical	75	90	10	Many Others
TM83	Infestation	Bug	Special	20	100	20	Normal
TM84	Poison Jab	Poison	Physical	80	100	20	Normal
TM87	Swagger	Normal	Status	—	85	15	Normal
TM88	Sleep Talk	Normal	Status	—	—	10	Self
TM90	Substitute	Normal	Status	—	—	10	Self
TM95	Snarl	Dark	Special	55	95	15	Many Others
TM97	Dark Pulse	Dark	Special	80	100	15	Normal
TM100	Confide	Normal	Status	—	—	20	Normal

❖ EXCLUSIVE Z-MOVE

Name	Base Move	Type	Kind	Pow.	Acc.	Range

❖ MOVES TAUGHT BY PEOPLE

Name	Type	Kind	Pow.	Acc.	PP	Range

❖ MOVES LEARNED WHEN EVOLVING

Name	Type	Kind	Pow.	Acc.	PP	Range
Venom Drench	Poison	Status	—	100	20	Many Others

❖ EGG MOVES

Name	Type	Kind	Pow.	Acc.	PP	Range

Growlithe

	Melemele	Akala	Ula'ula	Poni
052	052	—	—	—

Puppy Pokémon

FIRE

HEIGHT: 2'04"
WEIGHT: 41.9 lbs.

It's both clever and loyal, but if a stranger tries to invade its territory, it barks threateningly.

It looks cute, but when you approach another Trainer's Growlithe, it will bark at you and bite.

ABILITY
Intimidate
Flash Fire

HIDDEN ABILITY
Justified

Damage taken in normal battles

NORMAL ×1	FIGHTING ×1	ROCK ×2			
FIRE ×0.5	POISON ×1	GHOST ×1			
WATER ×2	GROUND ×2	DRAGON ×1			
GRASS ×0.5	FLYING ×1	DARK ×1			
ELECTRIC ×1	PSYCHIC ×1	STEEL ×0.5			
ICE ×0.5	BUG ×0.5	FAIRY ×0.5			

SPECIES STRENGTHS
HP ◆◆
Attack ◆◆◆◆
Defense ◆◆◆
Sp. Atk ◆◆◆◆
Sp. Def ◆◆◆
Speed ◆◆◆◆

EGG GROUPS
Field

ITEM SOMETIMES HELD BY WILD POKÉMON
—

EVOLUTION

Growlithe → [Fire Stone] → Arcanine

MAIN WAY TO REGISTER IN THE POKÉDEX
Catch in the tall grass on the north end of Route 2

Same form for male/female

❖ LEVEL-UP MOVES

Lv.	Name	Type	Kind	Pow.	Acc.	PP	Range
1	Bite	Dark	Physical	60	100	25	Normal
1	Roar	Normal	Status	—	—	20	Normal
6	Ember	Fire	Special	40	100	25	Normal
8	Leer	Normal	Status	—	100	30	Many Others
10	Odor Sleuth	Normal	Status	—	—	40	Normal
12	Helping Hand	Normal	Status	—	—	20	1 Ally
17	Flame Wheel	Fire	Physical	60	100	25	Normal
19	Reversal	Fighting	Physical	—	100	15	Normal
21	Fire Fang	Fire	Physical	65	95	15	Normal
23	Take Down	Normal	Physical	90	85	20	Normal
28	Flame Burst	Fire	Special	70	100	15	Normal
30	Agility	Psychic	Status	—	—	30	Self
32	Retaliate	Normal	Physical	70	100	5	Normal
34	Flamethrower	Fire	Special	90	100	15	Normal
39	Crunch	Dark	Physical	80	100	15	Normal
41	Heat Wave	Fire	Special	95	90	10	Many Others
43	Outrage	Dragon	Physical	120	100	10	1 Random
45	Flare Blitz	Fire	Physical	120	100	15	Normal

❖ TM MOVES

No.	Name	Type	Kind	Pow.	Acc.	PP	Range
TM05	Roar	Normal	Status	—	—	20	Normal
TM06	Toxic	Poison	Status	—	90	10	Normal
TM10	Hidden Power	Normal	Special	60	100	15	Normal
TM11	Sunny Day	Fire	Status	—	—	5	Both Sides
TM17	Protect	Normal	Status	—	—	10	Self
TM20	Safeguard	Normal	Status	—	—	25	Your Side
TM21	Frustration	Normal	Physical	—	100	20	Normal
TM27	Return	Normal	Physical	—	100	20	Normal
TM32	Double Team	Normal	Status	—	—	15	Self
TM35	Flamethrower	Fire	Special	90	100	15	Normal
TM38	Fire Blast	Fire	Special	110	85	5	Normal
TM40	Aerial Ace	Flying	Physical	60	—	20	Normal
TM42	Facade	Normal	Physical	70	100	20	Normal
TM43	Flame Charge	Fire	Physical	50	100	20	Normal
TM44	Rest	Psychic	Status	—	—	10	Self
TM45	Attract	Normal	Status	—	100	15	Normal
TM46	Thief	Dark	Physical	60	100	25	Normal
TM48	Round	Normal	Special	60	100	15	Normal
TM50	Overheat	Fire	Special	130	90	5	Normal
TM61	Will-O-Wisp	Fire	Status	—	85	15	Normal
TM87	Swagger	Normal	Status	—	85	15	Normal
TM88	Sleep Talk	Normal	Status	—	—	10	Self
TM90	Substitute	Normal	Status	—	—	10	Self
TM93	Wild Charge	Electric	Physical	90	100	15	Normal
TM95	Snarl	Dark	Special	55	95	15	Many Others
TM100	Confide	Normal	Status	—	—	20	Normal

❖ MOVES TAUGHT BY PEOPLE

Name	Type	Kind	Pow.	Acc.	PP	Range

❖ MOVES LEARNED WHEN EVOLVING

Name	Type	Kind	Pow.	Acc.	PP	Range

❖ EGG MOVES

Name	Type	Kind	Pow.	Acc.	PP	Range
Body Slam	Normal	Physical	85	100	15	Normal
Crunch	Dark	Physical	80	100	15	Normal
Thrash	Normal	Physical	120	100	10	1 Random
Fire Spin	Fire	Special	35	85	15	Normal
Howl	Normal	Status	—	—	40	Self
Heat Wave	Fire	Special	95	90	10	Many Others
Double-Edge	Normal	Physical	120	100	15	Normal
Flare Blitz	Fire	Physical	120	100	15	Normal
Morning Sun	Normal	Status	—	—	5	Self
Covet	Normal	Physical	60	100	25	Normal
Iron Tail	Steel	Physical	100	75	15	Normal
Double Kick	Fighting	Physical	30	100	30	Normal
Close Combat	Fighting	Physical	120	100	5	Normal
Burn Up	Fire	Special	130	100	5	Normal

❖ EXCLUSIVE Z-MOVE

Name	Base Move	Type	Kind	Pow.	Acc.	Range

Arcanine

	Melemele	Akala	Ula'ula	Poni
053	053	—	—	—

Legendary Pokémon

FIRE

HEIGHT: 6'03"
WEIGHT: 341.7 lbs.

Overflowing with beauty and majesty, this strong Pokémon appears in ancient Eastern folklore.

The fire burning inside its body serves as the energy to fuel it as it runs great distances. It appears in many legends.

ABILITY
Intimidate
Flash Fire

HIDDEN ABILITY
Justified

Damage taken in normal battles

NORMAL ×1	FIGHTING ×1	ROCK ×2			
FIRE ×0.5	POISON ×1	GHOST ×1			
WATER ×2	GROUND ×2	DRAGON ×1			
GRASS ×0.5	FLYING ×1	DARK ×1			
ELECTRIC ×1	PSYCHIC ×1	STEEL ×0.5			
ICE ×0.5	BUG ×0.5	FAIRY ×0.5			

SPECIES STRENGTHS
HP ◆◆◆
Attack ◆◆◆◆◆◆
Defense ◆◆◆◆
Sp. Atk ◆◆◆◆◆
Sp. Def ◆◆◆◆◆
Speed ◆◆◆◆◆◆

EGG GROUPS
Field

ITEM SOMETIMES HELD BY WILD POKÉMON
—

EVOLUTION

Growlithe → [Fire Stone] → Arcanine

MAIN WAY TO REGISTER IN THE POKÉDEX
Use a Fire Stone on Growlithe

Same form for male/female

❖ LEVEL-UP MOVES

Lv.	Name	Type	Kind	Pow.	Acc.	PP	Range
1	Thunder Fang	Electric	Physical	65	95	15	Normal
1	Bite	Dark	Physical	60	100	25	Normal
1	Roar	Normal	Status	—	—	20	Normal
1	Odor Sleuth	Normal	Status	—	—	40	Normal
1	Fire Fang	Fire	Physical	65	95	15	Normal
34	Extreme Speed	Normal	Physical	80	100	5	Normal

❖ TM MOVES

No.	Name	Type	Kind	Pow.	Acc.	PP	Range
TM05	Roar	Normal	Status	—	—	20	Normal
TM06	Toxic	Poison	Status	—	90	10	Normal
TM10	Hidden Power	Normal	Special	60	100	15	Normal
TM11	Sunny Day	Fire	Status	—	—	5	Both Sides
TM15	Hyper Beam	Normal	Special	150	90	5	Normal
TM17	Protect	Normal	Status	—	—	10	Self
TM20	Safeguard	Normal	Status	—	—	25	Your Side
TM21	Frustration	Normal	Physical	—	100	20	Normal
TM22	Solar Beam	Grass	Special	120	100	10	Normal
TM27	Return	Normal	Physical	—	100	20	Normal
TM32	Double Team	Normal	Status	—	—	15	Self
TM35	Flamethrower	Fire	Special	90	100	15	Normal
TM38	Fire Blast	Fire	Special	110	85	5	Normal
TM40	Aerial Ace	Flying	Physical	60	—	20	Normal
TM42	Facade	Normal	Physical	70	100	20	Normal
TM43	Flame Charge	Fire	Physical	50	100	20	Normal
TM44	Rest	Psychic	Status	—	—	10	Self
TM45	Attract	Normal	Status	—	100	15	Normal
TM46	Thief	Dark	Physical	60	100	25	Normal
TM48	Round	Normal	Special	60	100	15	Normal
TM50	Overheat	Fire	Special	130	90	5	Normal
TM61	Will-O-Wisp	Fire	Status	—	85	15	Normal
TM68	Giga Impact	Normal	Physical	150	90	5	Normal
TM78	Bulldoze	Ground	Physical	60	100	20	Adjacent
TM87	Swagger	Normal	Status	—	85	15	Normal
TM88	Sleep Talk	Normal	Status	—	—	10	Self
TM90	Substitute	Normal	Status	—	—	10	Self
TM93	Wild Charge	Electric	Physical	90	100	15	Normal

❖ MOVES TAUGHT BY PEOPLE

No.	Name	Type	Kind	Pow.	Acc.	PP	Range
TM95	Snarl	Dark	Special	55	95	15	Many Others
TM100	Confide	Normal	Status	—	—	20	Normal

❖ MOVES LEARNED WHEN EVOLVING

Name	Type	Kind	Pow.	Acc.	PP	Range

❖ EGG MOVES

Name	Type	Kind	Pow.	Acc.	PP	Range

❖ EXCLUSIVE Z-MOVE

Name	Base Move	Type	Kind	Pow.	Acc.	Range

Drowzee

Hypnosis Pokémon

PSYCHIC

Alola Pokédex	Melemele	Akala	Ula'ula	Poni
054	054	—	—	013

HEIGHT: 3'03"
WEIGHT: 71.4 lbs.

A Pokémon that nourishes itself by eating dreams, it is thought to share common ancestry with Munna and Musharna.

It finds really fun dreams tasty. When it makes friends with people, it may show them the most delicious dreams it's ever eaten.

ABILITY
Insomnia
Forewarn

HIDDEN ABILITY
Inner Focus

SPECIES STRENGTHS
HP ◆◆
Attack ◆◆
Defense ◆◆◆
Sp. Atk ◆◆
Sp. Def ◆◆◆◆◆
Speed ◆◆◆

EGG GROUPS
Human-Like

ITEM SOMETIMES HELD BY WILD POKÉMON
—

Damage taken in normal battles
NORMAL ×1	FIGHTING ×0.5	ROCK ×1
FIRE ×1	POISON ×1	GHOST ×2
WATER ×1	GROUND ×1	DRAGON ×1
GRASS ×1	FLYING ×1	DARK ×2
ELECTRIC ×1	PSYCHIC ×0.5	STEEL ×1
ICE ×1	BUG ×2	FAIRY ×1

EVOLUTION
Drowzee → Lv. 26 → Hypno

MAIN WAY TO REGISTER IN THE POKÉDEX
Catch in the tall grass on the south end of Route 2

Same form for male/female

❖ LEVEL-UP MOVES
Lv.	Name	Type	Kind	Pow.	Acc.	PP	Range
1	Pound	Normal	Physical	40	100	35	Normal
1	Hypnosis	Psychic	Status	—	60	20	Normal
5	Disable	Normal	Status	—	100	20	Normal
9	Confusion	Psychic	Special	50	100	25	Normal
13	Headbutt	Normal	Physical	70	100	15	Normal
17	Poison Gas	Poison	Status	—	90	40	Many Others
21	Meditate	Psychic	Status	—	—	40	Self
25	Psybeam	Psychic	Special	65	100	20	Normal
29	Headbutt	Normal	Physical	70	100	15	Normal
33	Psych Up	Normal	Status	—	—	10	Normal
37	Synchronoise	Psychic	Special	120	100	10	Adjacent
41	Zen Headbutt	Psychic	Physical	80	90	15	Normal
45	Swagger	Normal	Status	—	85	15	Normal
49	Psychic	Psychic	Special	90	100	10	Normal
53	Nasty Plot	Dark	Status	—	—	20	Self
57	Psyshock	Psychic	Special	80	100	10	Normal
61	Future Sight	Psychic	Special	120	100	10	Normal

❖ TM MOVES
No.	Name	Type	Kind	Pow.	Acc.	PP	Range
TM03	Psyshock	Psychic	Special	80	100	10	Normal
TM04	Calm Mind	Psychic	Status	—	—	20	Self
TM06	Toxic	Poison	Status	—	90	10	Normal
TM10	Hidden Power	Normal	Special	60	100	15	Normal
TM11	Sunny Day	Fire	Status	—	—	5	Both Sides
TM12	Taunt	Dark	Status	—	100	20	Normal
TM16	Light Screen	Psychic	Status	—	—	30	Your Side
TM17	Protect	Normal	Status	—	—	10	Self
TM18	Rain Dance	Water	Status	—	—	5	Both Sides
TM20	Safeguard	Normal	Status	—	—	25	Your Side
TM21	Frustration	Normal	Physical	—	100	20	Normal
TM27	Return	Normal	Physical	—	100	20	Normal
TM29	Psychic	Psychic	Special	90	100	10	Normal
TM30	Shadow Ball	Ghost	Special	80	100	15	Normal
TM31	Brick Break	Fighting	Physical	75	100	15	Normal
TM32	Double Team	Normal	Status	—	—	15	Self
TM33	Reflect	Psychic	Status	—	—	20	Your Side
TM41	Torment	Dark	Status	—	100	15	Normal
TM42	Facade	Normal	Physical	70	100	20	Normal
TM44	Rest	Psychic	Status	—	—	10	Self
TM45	Attract	Normal	Status	—	100	15	Normal
TM46	Thief	Dark	Physical	60	100	25	Normal
TM47	Low Sweep	Fighting	Physical	65	100	20	Normal
TM48	Round	Normal	Special	60	100	15	Normal
TM56	Fling	Dark	Physical	—	100	10	Normal
TM73	Thunder Wave	Electric	Status	—	90	20	Normal
TM77	Psych Up	Normal	Status	—	—	10	Normal
TM85	Dream Eater	Psychic	Special	100	100	15	Normal

No.	Name	Type	Kind	Pow.	Acc.	PP	Range
TM86	Grass Knot	Grass	Special	—	100	20	Normal
TM87	Swagger	Normal	Status	—	85	15	Normal
TM88	Sleep Talk	Normal	Status	—	—	10	Self
TM90	Substitute	Normal	Status	—	—	10	Self
TM92	Trick Room	Psychic	Status	—	—	5	Both Sides
TM99	Dazzling Gleam	Fairy	Special	80	100	10	Many Others
TM100	Confide	Normal	Status	—	—	20	Normal

❖ MOVES TAUGHT BY PEOPLE
Name	Type	Kind	Pow.	Acc.	PP	Range

❖ MOVES LEARNED WHEN EVOLVING
Name	Type	Kind	Pow.	Acc.	PP	Range

❖ EGG MOVES
Name	Type	Kind	Pow.	Acc.	PP	Range
Barrier	Psychic	Status	—	—	20	Self
Assist	Normal	Status	—	—	20	Normal
Role Play	Psychic	Status	—	—	10	Normal
Fire Punch	Fire	Physical	75	100	15	Normal
Thunder Punch	Electric	Physical	75	100	15	Normal
Ice Punch	Ice	Physical	75	100	15	Normal
Nasty Plot	Dark	Status	—	—	20	Self
Flatter	Dark	Status	—	100	15	Normal
Psycho Cut	Psychic	Physical	70	100	20	Normal
Guard Swap	Psychic	Status	—	—	10	Normal
Secret Power	Normal	Physical	70	100	20	Normal
Skill Swap	Psychic	Status	—	—	10	Normal

❖ EXCLUSIVE Z-MOVE
Name	Base Move	Type	Kind	Pow.	Acc.	Range

Hypno

Hypnosis Pokémon

PSYCHIC

Alola Pokédex	Melemele	Akala	Ula'ula	Poni
055	055	—	—	014

HEIGHT: 5'03"
WEIGHT: 166.7 lbs.

While it is an extremely dangerous Pokémon, people who are in need of a good, sound sleep call it their savior.

As a matter of course, it makes anyone it meets fall asleep and has a taste of their dreams. Anyone having a good dream, it carries off.

ABILITY
Insomnia
Forewarn

HIDDEN ABILITY
Inner Focus

SPECIES STRENGTHS
HP ◆◆◆
Attack ◆◆◆◆
Defense ◆◆◆◆
Sp. Atk ◆◆◆◆
Sp. Def ◆◆◆◆◆◆ ◆◆
Speed ◆◆◆◆

EGG GROUPS
Human-Like

ITEM SOMETIMES HELD BY WILD POKÉMON
—

Damage taken in normal battles
NORMAL ×1	FIGHTING ×0.5	ROCK ×1
FIRE ×1	POISON ×1	GHOST ×2
WATER ×1	GROUND ×1	DRAGON ×1
GRASS ×1	FLYING ×1	DARK ×2
ELECTRIC ×1	PSYCHIC ×0.5	STEEL ×1
ICE ×1	BUG ×2	FAIRY ×1

EVOLUTION
Drowzee → Lv. 26 → Hypno

MAIN WAY TO REGISTER IN THE POKÉDEX
Level up Drowzee to Lv. 26

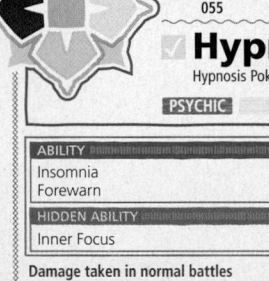

The fur around the male's neck is shorter.
The fur around the female's neck is longer.

❖ LEVEL-UP MOVES
Lv.	Name	Type	Kind	Pow.	Acc.	PP	Range
1	Future Sight	Psychic	Special	120	100	10	Normal
1	Nasty Plot	Dark	Status	—	—	20	Self
1	Nightmare	Ghost	Status	—	100	15	Normal
1	Switcheroo	Dark	Status	—	100	10	Normal
1	Pound	Normal	Physical	40	100	35	Normal
1	Hypnosis	Psychic	Status	—	60	20	Normal
1	Disable	Normal	Status	—	100	20	Normal
1	Confusion	Psychic	Special	50	100	25	Normal
5	Disable	Normal	Status	—	100	20	Normal
9	Confusion	Psychic	Special	50	100	25	Normal
13	Headbutt	Normal	Physical	70	100	15	Normal
17	Poison Gas	Poison	Status	—	90	40	Many Others
21	Meditate	Psychic	Status	—	—	40	Self
25	Psybeam	Psychic	Special	65	100	20	Normal
29	Headbutt	Normal	Physical	70	100	15	Normal
33	Psych Up	Normal	Status	—	—	10	Normal
37	Synchronoise	Psychic	Special	120	100	10	Adjacent
41	Zen Headbutt	Psychic	Physical	80	90	15	Normal
45	Swagger	Normal	Status	—	85	15	Normal
49	Psychic	Psychic	Special	90	100	10	Normal
53	Nasty Plot	Dark	Status	—	—	20	Self
57	Psyshock	Psychic	Special	80	100	10	Normal
61	Future Sight	Psychic	Special	120	100	10	Normal

❖ TM MOVES
No.	Name	Type	Kind	Pow.	Acc.	PP	Range
TM03	Psyshock	Psychic	Special	80	100	10	Normal
TM04	Calm Mind	Psychic	Status	—	—	20	Self
TM06	Toxic	Poison	Status	—	90	10	Normal
TM10	Hidden Power	Normal	Special	60	100	15	Normal
TM11	Sunny Day	Fire	Status	—	—	5	Both Sides
TM12	Taunt	Dark	Status	—	100	20	Normal
TM15	Hyper Beam	Normal	Special	150	90	5	Normal
TM16	Light Screen	Psychic	Status	—	—	30	Your Side
TM17	Protect	Normal	Status	—	—	10	Self
TM18	Rain Dance	Water	Status	—	—	5	Both Sides
TM20	Safeguard	Normal	Status	—	—	25	Your Side
TM21	Frustration	Normal	Physical	—	100	20	Normal
TM27	Return	Normal	Physical	—	100	20	Normal
TM29	Psychic	Psychic	Special	90	100	10	Normal
TM30	Shadow Ball	Ghost	Special	80	100	15	Normal
TM31	Brick Break	Fighting	Physical	75	100	15	Normal
TM32	Double Team	Normal	Status	—	—	15	Self
TM33	Reflect	Psychic	Status	—	—	20	Your Side
TM41	Torment	Dark	Status	—	100	15	Normal
TM42	Facade	Normal	Physical	70	100	20	Normal
TM44	Rest	Psychic	Status	—	—	10	Self
TM45	Attract	Normal	Status	—	100	15	Normal
TM46	Thief	Dark	Physical	60	100	25	Normal
TM47	Low Sweep	Fighting	Physical	65	100	20	Normal
TM48	Round	Normal	Special	60	100	15	Normal
TM52	Focus Blast	Fighting	Special	120	70	5	Normal
TM56	Fling	Dark	Physical	—	100	10	Normal
TM68	Giga Impact	Normal	Physical	150	90	5	Normal

No.	Name	Type	Kind	Pow.	Acc.	PP	Range
TM73	Thunder Wave	Electric	Status	—	90	20	Normal
TM77	Psych Up	Normal	Status	—	—	10	Normal
TM85	Dream Eater	Psychic	Special	100	100	15	Normal
TM86	Grass Knot	Grass	Special	—	100	20	Normal
TM87	Swagger	Normal	Status	—	85	15	Normal
TM88	Sleep Talk	Normal	Status	—	—	10	Self
TM90	Substitute	Normal	Status	—	—	10	Self
TM92	Trick Room	Psychic	Status	—	—	5	Both Sides
TM99	Dazzling Gleam	Fairy	Special	80	100	10	Many Others
TM100	Confide	Normal	Status	—	—	20	Normal

❖ MOVES TAUGHT BY PEOPLE
Name	Type	Kind	Pow.	Acc.	PP	Range

❖ MOVES LEARNED WHEN EVOLVING
Name	Type	Kind	Pow.	Acc.	PP	Range

❖ EGG MOVES
Name	Type	Kind	Pow.	Acc.	PP	Range

❖ EXCLUSIVE Z-MOVE
Name	Base Move	Type	Kind	Pow.	Acc.	Range

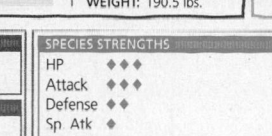

Makuhita

Guts Pokémon

Alola Pokédex

	Melemele Akala	Ula'ula	Poni
056	056	—	015

It was originally brought in from another region, but now Makuhita from Alola are more famous.

Their daily routine consists of training together first thing in the morning, eating and napping in the afternoon, and then more training afterward.

FIGHTING

HEIGHT: 3'03"
WEIGHT: 190.5 lbs.

ABILITY
Thick Fat
Guts

HIDDEN ABILITY
Sheer Force

SPECIES STRENGTHS
HP ♦♦♦
Attack ♦♦♦
Defense ♦♦
Sp. Atk ♦
Sp. Def ♦
Speed ♦♦

EGG GROUPS
Human-Like

ITEM SOMETIMES HELD BY WILD POKÉMON
Black Belt

EVOLUTION
Makuhita → Lv. 24 → Hariyama

MAIN WAY TO REGISTER IN THE POKÉDEX
Catch in a patch of rustling grass on Route 2

Same form for male/female

Damage taken in normal battles
NORMAL ×1	FIGHTING ×1	ROCK ×0.5			
FIRE ×1	POISON ×1	GHOST ×1			
WATER ×1	GROUND ×1	DRAGON ×1			
GRASS ×1	FLYING ×2	DARK ×0.5			
ELECTRIC ×1	PSYCHIC ×2	STEEL ×1			
ICE ×1	BUG ×0.5	FAIRY ×2			

❖ LEVEL-UP MOVES
Lv.	Name	Type	Kind	Pow.	Acc.	PP	Range
1	Tackle	Normal	Physical	40	100	35	Normal
1	Focus Energy	Normal	Status	—	—	30	Self
4	Sand Attack	Ground	Status	—	100	15	Normal
7	Arm Thrust	Fighting	Physical	15	100	20	Normal
10	Fake Out	Normal	Physical	40	100	10	Normal
13	Force Palm	Fighting	Physical	60	100	10	Normal
16	Whirlwind	Normal	Status	—	—	20	Normal
19	Knock Off	Dark	Physical	65	100	20	Normal
22	Vital Throw	Fighting	Physical	70	—	10	Normal
25	Belly Drum	Normal	Status	—	—	10	Self
28	Smelling Salts	Normal	Physical	70	100	10	Normal
31	Seismic Toss	Fighting	Physical	—	100	20	Normal
34	Wake-Up Slap	Fighting	Physical	70	100	10	Normal
37	Endure	Normal	Status	—	—	10	Self
40	Close Combat	Fighting	Physical	120	100	5	Normal
43	Reversal	Fighting	Physical	—	100	15	Normal
46	Heavy Slam	Steel	Physical	—	100	10	Normal

❖ TM MOVES
No.	Name	Type	Kind	Pow.	Acc.	PP	Range
TM01	Work Up	Normal	Status	—	—	30	Self
TM06	Toxic	Poison	Status	—	90	10	Normal
TM08	Bulk Up	Fighting	Status	—	—	20	Self
TM10	Hidden Power	Normal	Special	60	100	15	Normal
TM11	Sunny Day	Fire	Status	—	—	5	Both Sides
TM17	Protect	Normal	Status	—	—	10	Self
TM18	Rain Dance	Water	Status	—	—	5	Both Sides
TM21	Frustration	Normal	Physical	—	100	20	Normal
TM23	Smack Down	Rock	Physical	50	100	15	Normal
TM26	Earthquake	Ground	Physical	100	100	10	Adjacent
TM27	Return	Normal	Physical	—	100	20	Normal
TM31	Brick Break	Fighting	Physical	75	100	15	Normal
TM32	Double Team	Normal	Status	—	—	15	Self
TM39	Rock Tomb	Rock	Physical	60	95	15	Normal
TM42	Facade	Normal	Physical	70	100	20	Normal
TM44	Rest	Psychic	Status	—	—	10	Self
TM45	Attract	Normal	Status	—	100	15	Normal
TM47	Low Sweep	Fighting	Physical	65	100	20	Normal
TM48	Round	Normal	Special	60	100	15	Normal
TM52	Focus Blast	Fighting	Special	120	70	5	Normal
TM56	Fling	Dark	Physical	—	100	10	Normal
TM78	Bulldoze	Ground	Physical	60	100	20	Adjacent
TM80	Rock Slide	Rock	Physical	75	90	10	Many Others
TM84	Poison Jab	Poison	Physical	80	100	20	Normal
TM87	Swagger	Normal	Status	—	85	15	Normal
TM88	Sleep Talk	Normal	Status	—	—	10	Self
TM90	Substitute	Normal	Status	—	—	10	Self
TM94	Surf	Water	Special	90	100	15	Adjacent

No.	Name	Type	Kind	Pow.	Acc.	PP	Range
TM100	Confide	Normal	Status	—	—	20	Normal

❖ MOVES TAUGHT BY PEOPLE

❖ MOVES LEARNED WHEN EVOLVING

❖ EGG MOVES
Name	Type	Kind	Pow.	Acc.	PP	Range
Feint Attack	Dark	Physical	60	—	20	Normal
Detect	Fighting	Status	—	—	5	Self
Foresight	Normal	Status	—	—	40	Normal
Helping Hand	Normal	Status	—	—	20	1 Ally
Cross Chop	Fighting	Physical	100	80	5	Normal
Revenge	Fighting	Physical	60	100	10	Normal
Dynamic Punch	Fighting	Physical	100	50	5	Normal
Counter	Fighting	Physical	—	100	20	Varies
Wake-Up Slap	Fighting	Physical	70	100	10	Normal
Bullet Punch	Steel	Physical	40	100	30	Normal
Feint	Normal	Physical	30	—	10	Normal
Wide Guard	Rock	Status	—	—	10	Your Side
Focus Punch	Fighting	Physical	150	100	20	Normal
Chip Away	Normal	Physical	70	100	20	Normal

❖ EXCLUSIVE Z-MOVE
Name	Base Move	Type	Kind	Pow.	Acc.	Range

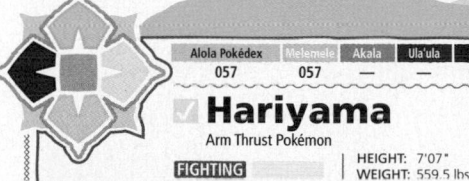
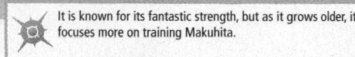

Hariyama

Arm Thrust Pokémon

Alola Pokédex

	Melemele Akala	Ula'ula	Poni
057	057	—	016

It is known for its fantastic strength, but as it grows older, it focuses more on training Makuhita.

They love to compare their freakish strength—strength enough to send a truck flying with a single slap.

FIGHTING

HEIGHT: 7'07"
WEIGHT: 559.5 lbs.

ABILITY
Thick Fat
Guts

HIDDEN ABILITY
Sheer Force

SPECIES STRENGTHS
HP ♦♦♦♦♦
Attack ♦♦♦♦♦♦
Defense ♦♦♦
Sp. Atk ♦♦
Sp. Def ♦♦♦
Speed ♦♦♦

EGG GROUPS
Human-Like

ITEM SOMETIMES HELD BY WILD POKÉMON
King's Rock

EVOLUTION
Makuhita → Lv. 24 → Hariyama

MAIN WAY TO REGISTER IN THE POKÉDEX
Level up Makuhita to Lv. 24

Same form for male/female

Damage taken in normal battles
NORMAL ×1	FIGHTING ×1	ROCK ×0.5			
FIRE ×1	POISON ×1	GHOST ×1			
WATER ×1	GROUND ×1	DRAGON ×1			
GRASS ×1	FLYING ×2	DARK ×0.5			
ELECTRIC ×1	PSYCHIC ×2	STEEL ×1			
ICE ×1	BUG ×0.5	FAIRY ×2			

❖ LEVEL-UP MOVES
Lv.	Name	Type	Kind	Pow.	Acc.	PP	Range
1	Brine	Water	Special	65	100	10	Normal
1	Tackle	Normal	Physical	40	100	35	Normal
1	Focus Energy	Normal	Status	—	—	30	Self
1	Sand Attack	Ground	Status	—	100	15	Normal
1	Arm Thrust	Fighting	Physical	15	100	20	Normal
4	Sand Attack	Ground	Status	—	100	15	Normal
7	Arm Thrust	Fighting	Physical	15	100	20	Normal
10	Fake Out	Normal	Physical	40	100	10	Normal
13	Force Palm	Fighting	Physical	60	100	10	Normal
16	Whirlwind	Normal	Status	—	—	20	Normal
19	Knock Off	Dark	Physical	65	100	20	Normal
22	Vital Throw	Fighting	Physical	70	—	10	Normal
26	Belly Drum	Normal	Status	—	—	10	Self
30	Smelling Salts	Normal	Physical	70	100	10	Normal
34	Seismic Toss	Fighting	Physical	—	100	20	Normal
38	Wake-Up Slap	Fighting	Physical	70	100	10	Normal
42	Endure	Normal	Status	—	—	10	Self
46	Close Combat	Fighting	Physical	120	100	5	Normal
50	Reversal	Fighting	Physical	—	100	15	Normal
54	Heavy Slam	Steel	Physical	—	100	10	Normal

❖ TM MOVES
No.	Name	Type	Kind	Pow.	Acc.	PP	Range
TM01	Work Up	Normal	Status	—	—	30	Self
TM06	Toxic	Poison	Status	—	90	10	Normal
TM08	Bulk Up	Fighting	Status	—	—	20	Self
TM10	Hidden Power	Normal	Special	60	100	15	Normal
TM11	Sunny Day	Fire	Status	—	—	5	Both Sides
TM15	Hyper Beam	Normal	Special	150	90	5	Normal
TM17	Protect	Normal	Status	—	—	10	Self
TM18	Rain Dance	Water	Status	—	—	5	Both Sides
TM21	Frustration	Normal	Physical	—	100	20	Normal
TM23	Smack Down	Rock	Physical	50	100	15	Normal
TM26	Earthquake	Ground	Physical	100	100	10	Adjacent
TM27	Return	Normal	Physical	—	100	20	Normal
TM31	Brick Break	Fighting	Physical	75	100	15	Normal
TM32	Double Team	Normal	Status	—	—	15	Self
TM39	Rock Tomb	Rock	Physical	60	95	15	Normal
TM42	Facade	Normal	Physical	70	100	20	Normal
TM44	Rest	Psychic	Status	—	—	10	Self
TM45	Attract	Normal	Status	—	100	15	Normal
TM47	Low Sweep	Fighting	Physical	65	100	20	Normal
TM48	Round	Normal	Special	60	100	15	Normal
TM52	Focus Blast	Fighting	Special	120	70	5	Normal
TM56	Fling	Dark	Physical	—	100	10	Normal
TM66	Payback	Dark	Physical	50	100	10	Normal
TM68	Giga Impact	Normal	Physical	150	90	5	Normal
TM71	Stone Edge	Rock	Physical	100	80	5	Normal
TM78	Bulldoze	Ground	Physical	60	100	20	Adjacent
TM80	Rock Slide	Rock	Physical	75	90	10	Many Others
TM84	Poison Jab	Poison	Physical	80	100	20	Normal

No.	Name	Type	Kind	Pow.	Acc.	PP	Range
TM87	Swagger	Normal	Status	—	85	15	Normal
TM88	Sleep Talk	Normal	Status	—	—	10	Self
TM90	Substitute	Normal	Status	—	—	10	Self
TM94	Surf	Water	Special	90	100	15	Adjacent
TM100	Confide	Normal	Status	—	—	20	Normal

❖ MOVES TAUGHT BY PEOPLE

❖ MOVES LEARNED WHEN EVOLVING

❖ EGG MOVES

❖ EXCLUSIVE Z-MOVE
Name	Base Move	Type	Kind	Pow.	Acc.	Range

Alola Pokédex	Melemele	Akala	Ula'ula	Poni
058	058	—	—	—

☑ **Smeargle**

Painter Pokémon

NORMAL

HEIGHT: 3'11"
WEIGHT: 127.9 lbs.

The unique creations produced by each Smeargle are painted using the fluid that oozes from its tail. This is how it marks its territory.

It draws symbols all over the place to mark its territory. In towns with many Smeargle, the walls are covered in graffiti.

ABILITY
Own Tempo
Technician

HIDDEN ABILITY
Moody

Damage taken in normal battles

NORMAL ×1	FIGHTING ×2	ROCK ×1	
FIRE ×1	POISON ×1	GHOST ×0	
WATER ×1	GROUND ×1	DRAGON ×1	
GRASS ×1	FLYING ×1	DARK ×1	
ELECTRIC ×1	PSYCHIC ×1	STEEL ×1	
ICE ×1	BUG ×1	FAIRY ×1	

SPECIES STRENGTHS

HP	◆◆
Attack	◆
Defense	◆◆
Sp. Atk	◆
Sp. Def	◆◆
Speed	◆◆◆◆◆

EGG GROUPS

Field

ITEM SOMETIMES HELD BY WILD POKÉMON

—

EVOLUTION

Does not evolve

MAIN WAY TO REGISTER IN THE POKÉDEX
Catch in the tall grass on Route 2

Same form for male/female

❖ LEVEL-UP MOVES

Lv.	Name	Type	Kind	Pow.	Acc.	PP	Range
1	Sketch	Normal	Status	—	—	1	Normal
11	Sketch	Normal	Status	—	—	1	Normal
21	Sketch	Normal	Status	—	—	1	Normal
31	Sketch	Normal	Status	—	—	1	Normal
41	Sketch	Normal	Status	—	—	1	Normal
51	Sketch	Normal	Status	—	—	1	Normal
61	Sketch	Normal	Status	—	—	1	Normal
71	Sketch	Normal	Status	—	—	1	Normal
81	Sketch	Normal	Status	—	—	1	Normal
91	Sketch	Normal	Status	—	—	1	Normal

❖ TM MOVES

No.	Name	Type	Kind	Pow.	Acc.	PP	Range

No.	Name	Type	Kind	Pow.	Acc.	PP	Range

❖ MOVES TAUGHT BY PEOPLE

Name	Type	Kind	Pow.	Acc.	PP	Range

❖ MOVES LEARNED WHEN EVOLVING

Name	Type	Kind	Pow.	Acc.	PP	Range

❖ EGG MOVES

Name	Type	Kind	Pow.	Acc.	PP	Range

❖ EXCLUSIVE Z-MOVE

Name	Base Move	Type	Kind	Pow.	Acc.	Range

Smeargle's Sketch

What is going on with Smeargle's move tables? They are filled with a single move: Sketch! Sketch is a move that only Smeargle is able to learn and is quite unique among Pokémon moves. It allows Smeargle to copy the last move that its opponent used in battle, permanently replacing Sketch with that move. With very few exceptions, Smeargle can learn practically every known Pokémon move! And what's more, it can then pass those moves onto Pokémon as Egg Moves.

Smeargle learned Hyper Fang!

Once Smeargle copies a move with Sketch, the new move will take Sketch's place in Smeargle's move set. But lucky for you—Smeargle will keep learning Sketch again and again every 10 levels, so you can keep on copying other moves as well! The one trick here is that Smeargle will only learn Sketch again if it has replaced its old Sketch with another move (i.e., if it has used Sketch to copy an opponent's move). A Pokémon cannot learn the same move twice, so you can't get around the low PP count of some powerful moves by trying to double the number of times you can use it!

Crabrawler

Alola Pokédex	Melemele	Akala	Ula'ula	Poni
059	059	021	030	017

Boxing Pokémon

✔ FIGHTING

HEIGHT: 2'00"
WEIGHT: 15.4 lbs.

While guarding its weak points with its pincers, it looks for an opening and unleashes punches. When it loses, it foams at the mouth and faints.

It punches so much, its pincers often come off from overuse, but they grow back quickly. What little meat they contain is rich and delicious.

ABILITY
Hyper Cutter
Iron Fist

HIDDEN ABILITY
Anger Point

SPECIES STRENGTHS
HP	◆◆
Attack	◆◆◆◆
Defense	◆◆◆
Sp. Atk	◆◆
Sp. Def	◆◆
Speed	◆◆◆◆

EGG GROUPS
Water 3

ITEM SOMETIMES HELD BY WILD POKÉMON
—

EVOLUTION

Crabrawler → Level up on Mount Lanakila → Crabominable

MAIN WAY TO REGISTER IN THE POKÉDEX
Catch in the pile of Berries on Route 10

Same form for male/female

Damage taken in normal battles
NORMAL ×1	FIGHTING ×1	ROCK ×0.5
FIRE ×1	POISON ×1	GHOST ×1
WATER ×1	GROUND ×1	DRAGON ×1
GRASS ×1	FLYING ×2	DARK ×1
ELECTRIC ×1	PSYCHIC ×2	STEEL ×1
ICE ×1	BUG ×0.5	FAIRY ×1

❖ LEVEL-UP MOVES
Lv.	Name	Type	Kind	Pow.	Acc.	PP	Range
1	Bubble	Water	Special	40	100	30	Many Others
5	Rock Smash	Fighting	Physical	40	100	15	Normal
9	Leer	Normal	Status	—	100	30	Many Others
13	Pursuit	Dark	Physical	40	100	20	Normal
17	Bubble Beam	Water	Special	65	100	20	Normal
22	Power-Up Punch	Fighting	Physical	40	100	20	Normal
25	Dizzy Punch	Normal	Physical	70	100	10	Normal
29	Payback	Dark	Physical	50	100	10	Normal
33	Reversal	Fighting	Physical	—	100	15	Normal
37	Crabhammer	Water	Physical	100	90	10	Normal
42	Iron Defense	Steel	Status	—	—	15	Self
45	Dynamic Punch	Fighting	Physical	100	50	5	Normal
49	Close Combat	Fighting	Physical	120	100	5	Normal

❖ TM MOVES
No.	Name	Type	Kind	Pow.	Acc.	PP	Range
TM01	Work Up	Normal	Status	—	—	30	Self
TM06	Toxic	Poison	Status	—	90	10	Normal
TM08	Bulk Up	Fighting	Status	—	—	20	Self
TM10	Hidden Power	Normal	Special	60	100	15	Normal
TM11	Sunny Day	Fire	Status	—	—	5	Both Sides
TM17	Protect	Normal	Status	—	—	10	Self
TM18	Rain Dance	Water	Status	—	—	5	Both Sides
TM21	Frustration	Normal	Physical	—	100	20	Normal
TM26	Earthquake	Ground	Physical	100	100	10	Adjacent
TM27	Return	Normal	Physical	—	100	20	Normal
TM31	Brick Break	Fighting	Physical	75	100	15	Normal
TM32	Double Team	Normal	Status	—	—	15	Self
TM39	Rock Tomb	Rock	Physical	60	95	15	Normal
TM42	Facade	Normal	Physical	70	100	20	Normal
TM44	Rest	Psychic	Status	—	—	10	Self
TM45	Attract	Normal	Status	—	100	15	Normal
TM46	Thief	Dark	Physical	60	100	25	Normal
TM48	Round	Normal	Special	60	100	15	Normal
TM52	Focus Blast	Fighting	Special	120	70	5	Normal
TM55	Scald	Water	Special	80	100	15	Normal
TM56	Fling	Dark	Physical	—	100	10	Normal
TM59	Brutal Swing	Dark	Physical	60	100	20	Adjacent
TM66	Payback	Dark	Physical	50	100	10	Normal
TM71	Stone Edge	Rock	Physical	100	80	5	Normal
TM78	Bulldoze	Ground	Physical	60	100	20	Adjacent
TM79	Frost Breath	Ice	Special	60	90	10	Normal
TM80	Rock Slide	Rock	Physical	75	90	10	Many Others
TM87	Swagger	Normal	Status	—	85	15	Normal
TM88	Sleep Talk	Normal	Status	—	—	10	Self
TM90	Substitute	Normal	Status	—	—	10	Self
TM100	Confide	Normal	Status	—	—	20	Normal

❖ MOVES TAUGHT BY PEOPLE
Name	Type	Kind	Pow.	Acc.	PP	Range

❖ MOVES LEARNED WHEN EVOLVING
Name	Type	Kind	Pow.	Acc.	PP	Range

❖ EGG MOVES
Name	Type	Kind	Pow.	Acc.	PP	Range
Wide Guard	Rock	Status	—	—	10	Your Side
Superpower	Fighting	Physical	120	100	5	Normal
Endeavor	Normal	Physical	—	100	5	Normal
Amnesia	Psychic	Status	—	—	20	Self

❖ EXCLUSIVE Z-MOVE
Name	Base Move	Type	Kind	Pow.	Acc.	Range

Crabominable

Alola Pokédex	Melemele	Akala	Ula'ula	Poni
060	060	022	031	018

Woolly Crab Pokémon

✔ FIGHTING ICE

HEIGHT: 5'07"
WEIGHT: 396.8 lbs.

It aimed for the top but got lost and ended up on a snowy mountain. Being forced to endure the cold, this Pokémon evolved and grew fur.

It just throws punches indiscriminately. In times of desperation, it can lop off its own pincers and fire them like rockets.

ABILITY
Hyper Cutter
Iron Fist

HIDDEN ABILITY
Anger Point

SPECIES STRENGTHS
HP	◆◆◆◆
Attack	◆◆◆◆◆◆◆
Defense	◆◆◆◆
Sp. Atk	◆◆
Sp. Def	◆◆◆
Speed	◆◆◆

EGG GROUPS
Water 3

ITEM SOMETIMES HELD BY WILD POKÉMON
—

EVOLUTION
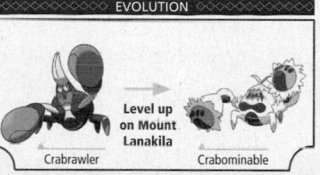
Crabrawler → Level up on Mount Lanakila → Crabominable

MAIN WAY TO REGISTER IN THE POKÉDEX
Level up Crabrawler on Mount Lanakila

Same form for male/female

Damage taken in normal battles
NORMAL ×1	FIGHTING ×2	ROCK ×1
FIRE ×2	POISON ×1	GHOST ×1
WATER ×1	GROUND ×1	DRAGON ×1
GRASS ×1	FLYING ×2	DARK ×0.5
ELECTRIC ×1	PSYCHIC ×2	STEEL ×1
ICE ×0.5	BUG ×0.5	FAIRY ×2

❖ LEVEL-UP MOVES
Lv.	Name	Type	Kind	Pow.	Acc.	PP	Range
1	Ice Punch	Ice	Physical	75	100	15	Normal
1	Bubble	Water	Special	40	100	30	Many Others
1	Rock Smash	Fighting	Physical	40	100	15	Normal
1	Leer	Normal	Status	—	100	30	Many Others
1	Pursuit	Dark	Physical	40	100	20	Normal
5	Rock Smash	Fighting	Physical	40	100	15	Normal
9	Leer	Normal	Status	—	100	30	Many Others
13	Pursuit	Dark	Physical	40	100	20	Normal
17	Bubble Beam	Water	Special	65	100	20	Normal
22	Power-Up Punch	Fighting	Physical	40	100	20	Normal
25	Dizzy Punch	Normal	Physical	70	100	10	Normal
29	Avalanche	Ice	Physical	60	100	10	Normal
33	Reversal	Fighting	Physical	—	100	15	Normal
37	Ice Hammer	Ice	Physical	100	90	10	Normal
42	Iron Defense	Steel	Status	—	—	15	Self
45	Dynamic Punch	Fighting	Physical	100	50	5	Normal
49	Close Combat	Fighting	Physical	120	100	5	Normal

❖ TM MOVES
No.	Name	Type	Kind	Pow.	Acc.	PP	Range
TM01	Work Up	Normal	Status	—	—	30	Self
TM06	Toxic	Poison	Status	—	90	10	Normal
TM07	Hail	Ice	Status	—	—	10	Both Sides
TM08	Bulk Up	Fighting	Status	—	—	20	Self
TM10	Hidden Power	Normal	Special	60	100	15	Normal
TM11	Sunny Day	Fire	Status	—	—	5	Both Sides
TM13	Ice Beam	Ice	Special	90	100	10	Normal
TM14	Blizzard	Ice	Special	110	70	5	Many Others
TM17	Protect	Normal	Status	—	—	10	Self
TM18	Rain Dance	Water	Status	—	—	5	Both Sides
TM21	Frustration	Normal	Physical	—	100	20	Normal
TM26	Earthquake	Ground	Physical	100	100	10	Adjacent
TM27	Return	Normal	Physical	—	100	20	Normal
TM31	Brick Break	Fighting	Physical	75	100	15	Normal
TM32	Double Team	Normal	Status	—	—	15	Self
TM39	Rock Tomb	Rock	Physical	60	95	15	Normal
TM42	Facade	Normal	Physical	70	100	20	Normal
TM44	Rest	Psychic	Status	—	—	10	Self
TM45	Attract	Normal	Status	—	100	15	Normal
TM46	Thief	Dark	Physical	60	100	25	Normal
TM48	Round	Normal	Special	60	100	15	Normal
TM52	Focus Blast	Fighting	Special	120	70	5	Normal
TM55	Scald	Water	Special	80	100	15	Normal
TM56	Fling	Dark	Physical	—	100	10	Normal
TM59	Brutal Swing	Dark	Physical	60	100	20	Adjacent
TM66	Payback	Dark	Physical	50	100	10	Normal
TM68	Giga Impact	Normal	Physical	150	90	5	Normal
TM71	Stone Edge	Rock	Physical	100	80	5	Normal
TM78	Bulldoze	Ground	Physical	60	100	20	Adjacent
TM79	Frost Breath	Ice	Special	60	90	10	Normal
TM80	Rock Slide	Rock	Physical	75	90	10	Many Others
TM87	Swagger	Normal	Status	—	85	15	Normal
TM00	Sleep Talk	Normal	Status	—	—	10	Self
TM90	Substitute	Normal	Status	—	—	10	Self
TM100	Confide	Normal	Status	—	—	20	Normal

❖ MOVES TAUGHT BY PEOPLE
Name	Type	Kind	Pow.	Acc.	PP	Range

❖ MOVES LEARNED WHEN EVOLVING
Name	Type	Kind	Pow.	Acc.	PP	Range
Ice Punch	Ice	Physical	75	100	15	Normal

❖ EGG MOVES
Name	Type	Kind	Pow.	Acc.	PP	Range

❖ EXCLUSIVE Z-MOVE
Name	Base Move	Type	Kind	Pow.	Acc.	Range

Alola Pokédex	Melemele	Akala	Ula'ula	Poni
061	061	023	032	—

☑ Gastly

Gas Pokémon

GHOST **POISON**

HEIGHT: 4'03"
WEIGHT: 0.2 lbs.

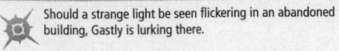 Should a strange light be seen flickering in an abandoned building, Gastly is lurking there.

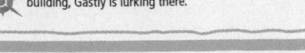 Although Gastly is barely visible, when it's near, a faint sweet smell lingers.

ABILITY
Levitate

HIDDEN ABILITY
—

SPECIES STRENGTHS
HP	◆
Attack	◆◆
Defense	◆◆
Sp. Atk	◆◆◆◆
Sp. Def	◆◆
Speed	◆◆◆◆◆

EGG GROUPS
Amorphous

ITEM SOMETIMES HELD BY WILD POKÉMON
—

Damage taken in normal battles
NORMAL	×0	FIGHTING	×0	ROCK	×1
FIRE	×1	POISON	×0.25	GHOST	×2
WATER	×1	GROUND	×2	DRAGON	×1
GRASS	×0.5	FLYING	×1	DARK	×2
ELECTRIC	×1	PSYCHIC	×2	STEEL	×1
ICE	×1	BUG	×0.25	FAIRY	×0.5

MAIN WAY TO REGISTER IN THE POKÉDEX
Catch in the tall grass in Hau'oli Cemetery

EVOLUTION

Gastly → Lv. 25 → Haunter
Gengar — Trade Haunter

Same form for male/female

Alola Pokédex	Melemele	Akala	Ula'ula	Poni
062	062	024	033	—

☑ Haunter

Gas Pokémon

GHOST **POISON**

HEIGHT: 5'03"
WEIGHT: 0.2 lbs.

It strikes at humans from total darkness. Those licked by its cold tongue grow weaker with each passing day until they die.

It fears the light and revels in the dark. It may be on the verge of extinction in cities that stay brightly lit at night.

ABILITY
Levitate

HIDDEN ABILITY
—

SPECIES STRENGTHS
HP	◆◆
Attack	◆◆◆
Defense	◆◆◆
Sp. Atk	◆◆◆◆◆◆
Sp. Def	◆◆◆
Speed	◆◆◆◆◆◆

EGG GROUPS
Amorphous

ITEM SOMETIMES HELD BY WILD POKÉMON
—

Damage taken in normal battles
NORMAL	×0	FIGHTING	×0	ROCK	×1
FIRE	×1	POISON	×0.25	GHOST	×2
WATER	×1	GROUND	×2	DRAGON	×1
GRASS	×0.5	FLYING	×1	DARK	×2
ELECTRIC	×1	PSYCHIC	×2	STEEL	×1
ICE	×1	BUG	×0.25	FAIRY	×0.5

MAIN WAY TO REGISTER IN THE POKÉDEX
Catch in the abandoned Thrifty Megamart off of Route 14

EVOLUTION

Gastly → Lv. 25 → Haunter
Gengar — Trade Haunter

Same form for male/female

Alola Pokédex	Melemele	Akala	Ula'ula	Poni
063	063	025	034	—

☑ Gengar

Shadow Pokémon

GHOST **POISON**

HEIGHT: 4'11"
WEIGHT: 89.3 lbs.

Should you feel yourself attacked by a sudden chill, it is evidence of an approaching Gengar. There is no escaping it. Give up.

It apparently wishes for a traveling companion. Since it was once human itself, it tries to create one by taking the lives of other humans.

ABILITY
Cursed Body

HIDDEN ABILITY
—

SPECIES STRENGTHS
HP	◆◆◆
Attack	◆◆◆◆
Defense	◆◆◆
Sp. Atk	◆◆◆◆◆◆◆
Sp. Def	◆◆◆
Speed	◆◆◆◆◆◆◆

EGG GROUPS
Amorphous

ITEM SOMETIMES HELD BY WILD POKÉMON
—

Damage taken in normal battles
NORMAL	×0	FIGHTING	×0	ROCK	×1
FIRE	×1	POISON	×0.25	GHOST	×2
WATER	×1	GROUND	×2	DRAGON	×1
GRASS	×0.5	FLYING	×1	DARK	×2
ELECTRIC	×1	PSYCHIC	×2	STEEL	×1
ICE	×1	BUG	×0.25	FAIRY	×0.5

MAIN WAY TO REGISTER IN THE POKÉDEX
Receive a Haunter in a trade and it will evolve

EVOLUTION

Gastly → Lv. 25 → Haunter
Gengar — Trade Haunter

p. 208

Same form for male/female

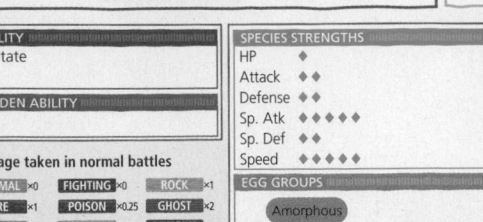
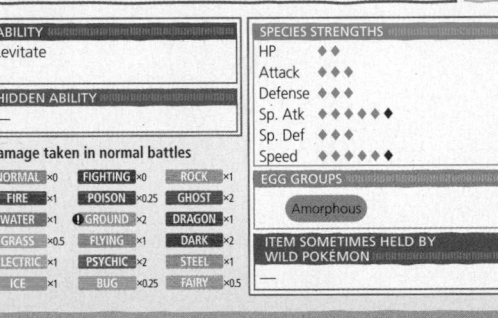
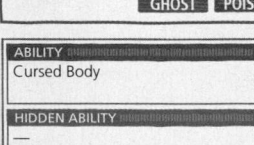
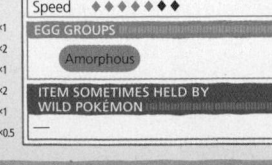

GASTLY 061

❖ LEVEL-UP MOVES

Lv.	Name	Type	Kind	Pow.	Acc.	PP	Range
1	Hypnosis	Psychic	Status	—	60	20	Normal
1	Lick	Ghost	Physical	30	100	30	Normal
5	Spite	Ghost	Status	—	100	10	Normal
8	Mean Look	Normal	Status	—	—	5	Normal
12	Curse	Ghost	Status	—	—	10	Varies
15	Night Shade	Ghost	Special	—	100	15	Normal
19	Confuse Ray	Ghost	Status	—	100	10	Normal
22	Sucker Punch	Dark	Physical	70	100	5	Normal
26	Payback	Dark	Physical	50	100	10	Normal
29	Shadow Ball	Ghost	Special	80	100	15	Normal
33	Dream Eater	Psychic	Special	100	100	15	Normal
36	Dark Pulse	Dark	Special	80	100	15	Normal
40	Destiny Bond	Ghost	Status	—	—	5	Self
43	Hex	Ghost	Special	65	100	10	Normal
47	Nightmare	Ghost	Status	—	100	15	Normal

❖ TM MOVES

No.	Name	Type	Kind	Pow.	Acc.	PP	Range
TM06	Toxic	Poison	Status	—	90	10	Normal
TM09	Venoshock	Poison	Special	65	100	10	Normal
TM10	Hidden Power	Normal	Special	60	100	15	Normal
TM11	Sunny Day	Fire	Status	—	—	5	Both Sides
TM12	Taunt	Dark	Status	—	100	20	Normal
TM17	Protect	Normal	Status	—	—	10	Self
TM18	Rain Dance	Water	Status	—	—	5	Both Sides
TM21	Frustration	Normal	Physical	—	100	20	Normal
TM24	Thunderbolt	Electric	Special	90	100	15	Normal
TM27	Return	Normal	Physical	—	100	20	Normal
TM29	Psychic	Psychic	Special	90	100	10	Normal
TM30	Shadow Ball	Ghost	Special	80	100	15	Normal
TM32	Double Team	Normal	Status	—	—	15	Self
TM36	Sludge Bomb	Poison	Special	90	100	10	Normal
TM41	Torment	Dark	Status	—	100	15	Normal
TM42	Facade	Normal	Physical	70	100	20	Normal
TM44	Rest	Psychic	Status	—	—	10	Self
TM45	Attract	Normal	Status	—	100	15	Normal
TM46	Thief	Dark	Physical	60	100	25	Normal
TM48	Round	Normal	Special	60	100	15	Normal
TM53	Energy Ball	Grass	Special	90	100	10	Normal
TM61	Will-O-Wisp	Fire	Status	—	85	15	Normal
TM63	Embargo	Dark	Status	—	100	15	Normal
TM64	Explosion	Normal	Physical	250	100	5	Adjacent
TM66	Payback	Dark	Physical	50	100	10	Normal
TM77	Psych Up	Normal	Status	—	—	10	Normal
TM83	Infestation	Bug	Special	20	100	20	Normal
TM85	Dream Eater	Psychic	Special	100	100	15	Normal
TM87	Swagger	Normal	Status	—	85	15	Normal
TM88	Sleep Talk	Normal	Status	—	—	10	Self
TM90	Substitute	Normal	Status	—	—	10	Self
TM92	Trick Room	Psychic	Status	—	—	5	Both Sides
TM97	Dark Pulse	Dark	Special	80	100	15	Normal
TM99	Dazzling Gleam	Fairy	Special	80	100	10	Many Others
TM100	Confide	Normal	Status	—	—	20	Normal

❖ EXCLUSIVE Z-MOVE

Name	Base Move	Type	Kind	Pow.	Acc.	Range

❖ MOVES TAUGHT BY PEOPLE

Name	Type	Kind	Pow.	Acc.	PP	Range

❖ MOVES LEARNED WHEN EVOLVING

Name	Type	Kind	Pow.	Acc.	PP	Range

❖ EGG MOVES

Name	Type	Kind	Pow.	Acc.	PP	Range
Psywave	Psychic	Special	—	100	15	Normal
Perish Song	Normal	Status	—	—	5	Adjacent
Haze	Ice	Status	—	—	30	Both Sides
Astonish	Ghost	Physical	30	100	15	Normal
Grudge	Ghost	Status	—	—	5	Self
Fire Punch	Fire	Physical	75	100	15	Normal
Ice Punch	Ice	Physical	75	100	15	Normal
Thunder Punch	Electric	Physical	75	100	15	Normal
Disable	Normal	Status	—	100	20	Normal
Scary Face	Normal	Status	—	100	10	Normal
Clear Smog	Poison	Special	50	—	15	Normal
Smog	Poison	Special	30	70	20	Normal
Reflect Type	Normal	Status	—	—	15	Normal

HAUNTER 062

❖ LEVEL-UP MOVES

Lv.	Name	Type	Kind	Pow.	Acc.	PP	Range
1	Shadow Punch	Ghost	Physical	60	—	20	Normal
1	Hypnosis	Psychic	Status	—	60	20	Normal
1	Lick	Ghost	Physical	30	100	30	Normal
1	Spite	Ghost	Status	—	100	10	Normal
5	Spite	Ghost	Status	—	100	10	Normal
8	Mean Look	Normal	Status	—	—	5	Normal
12	Curse	Ghost	Status	—	—	10	Varies
15	Night Shade	Ghost	Special	—	100	15	Normal
19	Confuse Ray	Ghost	Status	—	100	10	Normal
22	Sucker Punch	Dark	Physical	70	100	5	Normal
28	Payback	Dark	Physical	50	100	10	Normal
33	Shadow Ball	Ghost	Special	80	100	15	Normal
39	Dream Eater	Psychic	Special	100	100	15	Normal
44	Dark Pulse	Dark	Special	80	100	15	Normal
50	Destiny Bond	Ghost	Status	—	—	5	Self
55	Hex	Ghost	Special	65	100	10	Normal
61	Nightmare	Ghost	Status	—	100	15	Normal

❖ TM MOVES

No.	Name	Type	Kind	Pow.	Acc.	PP	Range
TM06	Toxic	Poison	Status	—	90	10	Normal
TM09	Venoshock	Poison	Special	65	100	10	Normal
TM10	Hidden Power	Normal	Special	60	100	15	Normal
TM11	Sunny Day	Fire	Status	—	—	5	Both Sides
TM12	Taunt	Dark	Status	—	100	20	Normal
TM17	Protect	Normal	Status	—	—	10	Self
TM18	Rain Dance	Water	Status	—	—	5	Both Sides
TM21	Frustration	Normal	Physical	—	100	20	Normal
TM24	Thunderbolt	Electric	Special	90	100	15	Normal
TM27	Return	Normal	Physical	—	100	20	Normal
TM29	Psychic	Psychic	Special	90	100	10	Normal
TM30	Shadow Ball	Ghost	Special	80	100	15	Normal
TM32	Double Team	Normal	Status	—	—	15	Self
TM36	Sludge Bomb	Poison	Special	90	100	10	Normal
TM41	Torment	Dark	Status	—	100	15	Normal
TM42	Facade	Normal	Physical	70	100	20	Normal
TM44	Rest	Psychic	Status	—	—	10	Self
TM45	Attract	Normal	Status	—	100	15	Normal
TM46	Thief	Dark	Physical	60	100	25	Normal
TM48	Round	Normal	Special	60	100	15	Normal
TM53	Energy Ball	Grass	Special	90	100	10	Normal
TM56	Fling	Dark	Physical	—	100	10	Normal
TM61	Will-O-Wisp	Fire	Status	—	85	15	Normal
TM63	Embargo	Dark	Status	—	100	15	Normal
TM64	Explosion	Normal	Physical	250	100	5	Adjacent
TM65	Shadow Claw	Ghost	Physical	70	100	15	Normal
TM66	Payback	Dark	Physical	50	100	10	Normal
TM77	Psych Up	Normal	Status	—	—	10	Normal
TM83	Infestation	Bug	Special	20	100	20	Normal
TM84	Poison Jab	Poison	Physical	80	100	20	Normal
TM85	Dream Eater	Psychic	Special	100	100	15	Normal
TM87	Swagger	Normal	Status	—	85	15	Normal
TM88	Sleep Talk	Normal	Status	—	—	10	Self
TM90	Substitute	Normal	Status	—	—	10	Self
TM92	Trick Room	Psychic	Status	—	—	5	Both Sides
TM97	Dark Pulse	Dark	Special	80	100	15	Normal
TM99	Dazzling Gleam	Fairy	Special	80	100	10	Many Others
TM100	Confide	Normal	Status	—	—	20	Normal

❖ EXCLUSIVE Z-MOVE

Name	Base Move	Type	Kind	Pow.	Acc.	Range

❖ MOVES TAUGHT BY PEOPLE

Name	Type	Kind	Pow.	Acc.	PP	Range

❖ MOVES LEARNED WHEN EVOLVING

Name	Type	Kind	Pow.	Acc.	PP	Range
Shadow Punch	Ghost	Physical	60	—	20	Normal

❖ EGG MOVES

Name	Type	Kind	Pow.	Acc.	PP	Range

GENGAR 063

❖ LEVEL-UP MOVES

Lv.	Name	Type	Kind	Pow.	Acc.	PP	Range
1	Shadow Punch	Ghost	Physical	60	—	20	Normal
1	Hypnosis	Psychic	Status	—	60	20	Normal
1	Lick	Ghost	Physical	30	100	30	Normal
1	Spite	Ghost	Status	—	100	10	Normal
5	Spite	Ghost	Status	—	100	10	Normal
8	Mean Look	Normal	Status	—	—	5	Normal
12	Curse	Ghost	Status	—	—	10	Varies
15	Night Shade	Ghost	Special	—	100	15	Normal
19	Confuse Ray	Ghost	Status	—	100	10	Normal
22	Sucker Punch	Dark	Physical	70	100	5	Normal
28	Payback	Dark	Physical	50	100	10	Normal
33	Shadow Ball	Ghost	Special	80	100	15	Normal
39	Dream Eater	Psychic	Special	100	100	15	Normal
44	Dark Pulse	Dark	Special	80	100	15	Normal
50	Destiny Bond	Ghost	Status	—	—	5	Self
55	Hex	Ghost	Special	65	100	10	Normal
61	Nightmare	Ghost	Status	—	100	15	Normal

❖ TM MOVES

No.	Name	Type	Kind	Pow.	Acc.	PP	Range
TM06	Toxic	Poison	Status	—	90	10	Normal
TM09	Venoshock	Poison	Special	65	100	10	Normal
TM10	Hidden Power	Normal	Special	60	100	15	Normal
TM11	Sunny Day	Fire	Status	—	—	5	Both Sides
TM12	Taunt	Dark	Status	—	100	20	Normal
TM15	Hyper Beam	Normal	Special	150	90	5	Normal
TM17	Protect	Normal	Status	—	—	10	Self
TM18	Rain Dance	Water	Status	—	—	5	Both Sides
TM21	Frustration	Normal	Physical	—	100	20	Normal
TM24	Thunderbolt	Electric	Special	90	100	15	Normal
TM25	Thunder	Electric	Special	110	70	10	Normal
TM27	Return	Normal	Physical	—	100	20	Normal
TM29	Psychic	Psychic	Special	90	100	10	Normal
TM30	Shadow Ball	Ghost	Special	80	100	15	Normal
TM31	Brick Break	Fighting	Physical	75	100	15	Normal
TM32	Double Team	Normal	Status	—	—	15	Self
TM36	Sludge Bomb	Poison	Special	90	100	10	Normal
TM41	Torment	Dark	Status	—	100	15	Normal
TM42	Facade	Normal	Physical	70	100	20	Normal
TM44	Rest	Psychic	Status	—	—	10	Self
TM45	Attract	Normal	Status	—	100	15	Normal
TM46	Thief	Dark	Physical	60	100	25	Normal
TM48	Round	Normal	Special	60	100	15	Normal
TM52	Focus Blast	Fighting	Special	120	70	5	Normal
TM53	Energy Ball	Grass	Special	90	100	10	Normal
TM56	Fling	Dark	Physical	—	100	10	Normal
TM61	Will-O-Wisp	Fire	Status	—	85	15	Normal
TM63	Embargo	Dark	Status	—	100	15	Normal
TM64	Explosion	Normal	Physical	250	100	5	Adjacent
TM65	Shadow Claw	Ghost	Physical	70	100	15	Normal
TM66	Payback	Dark	Physical	50	100	10	Normal
TM68	Giga Impact	Normal	Physical	150	90	5	Normal
TM77	Psych Up	Normal	Status	—	—	10	Normal
TM83	Infestation	Bug	Special	20	100	20	Normal
TM84	Poison Jab	Poison	Physical	80	100	20	Normal
TM85	Dream Eater	Psychic	Special	100	100	15	Normal
TM87	Swagger	Normal	Status	—	85	15	Normal
TM88	Sleep Talk	Normal	Status	—	—	10	Self
TM90	Substitute	Normal	Status	—	—	10	Self
TM92	Trick Room	Psychic	Status	—	—	5	Both Sides
TM97	Dark Pulse	Dark	Special	80	100	15	Normal
TM99	Dazzling Gleam	Fairy	Special	80	100	10	Many Others
TM100	Confide	Normal	Status	—	—	20	Normal

❖ EXCLUSIVE Z-MOVE

Name	Base Move	Type	Kind	Pow.	Acc.	Range

❖ MOVES TAUGHT BY PEOPLE

Name	Type	Kind	Pow.	Acc.	PP	Range

❖ MOVES LEARNED WHEN EVOLVING

Name	Type	Kind	Pow.	Acc.	PP	Range
Shadow Punch	Ghost	Physical	60	—	20	Normal

❖ EGG MOVES

Name	Type	Kind	Pow.	Acc.	PP	Range

Driploon

Balloon Pokémon

Alola Pokédex	Melemele	Akala	Ula'ula	Poni
064	064	—	—	—

☑ **Drifloon**

GHOST FLYING

HEIGHT: 1'04"
WEIGHT: 2.6 lbs.

Stories go that it grabs the hands of small children and drags them away to the afterlife. It dislikes heavy children.

If for some reason its body bursts, its soul spills out with a screaming sound.

ABILITY
Aftermath
Unburden

HIDDEN ABILITY
Flare Boost

Damage taken in normal battles

NORMAL	×0	FIGHTING	×0	ROCK	×2
FIRE	×1	POISON	×0.5	GHOST	×1
WATER	×1	GROUND	×0	DRAGON	×1
GRASS	×0.5	FLYING	×1	DARK	×1
ELECTRIC	×2	PSYCHIC	×1	STEEL	×1
ICE	×2	BUG	×0.25	FAIRY	×1

SPECIES STRENGTHS
HP ◆◆◆
Attack ◆◆
Defense ◆◆
Sp. Atk ◆◆◆
Sp. Def ◆◆
Speed ◆◆◆◆◆

EGG GROUPS
Amorphous

ITEM SOMETIMES HELD BY WILD POKÉMON
—

EVOLUTION

Drifloon → Lv. 28 → Drifblim

MAIN WAY TO REGISTER IN THE POKÉDEX
Catch in the tall grass in Hau'oli Cemetery when it is daytime in your game

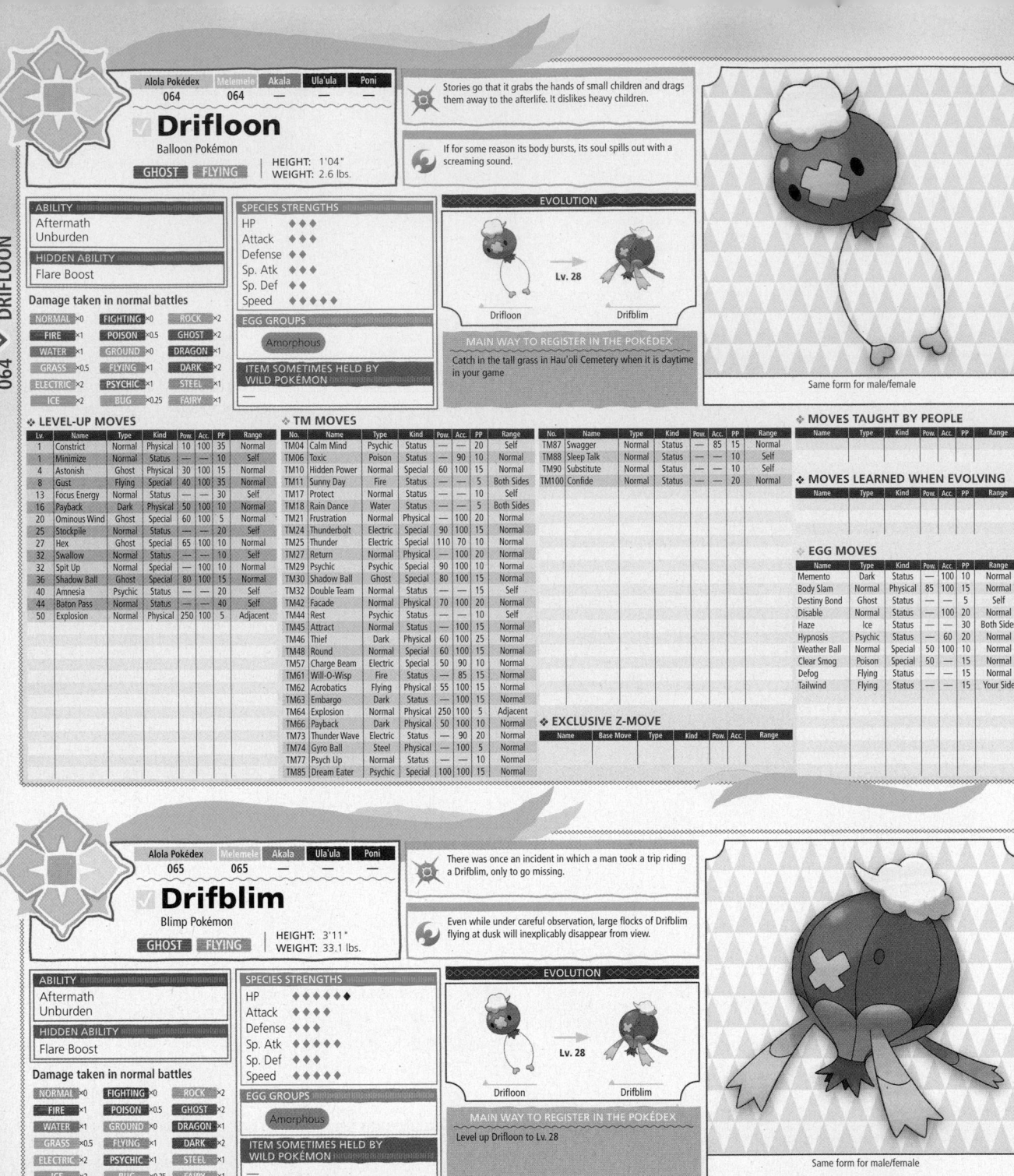

Same form for male/female

❖ LEVEL-UP MOVES

Lv.	Name	Type	Kind	Pow.	Acc.	PP	Range
1	Constrict	Normal	Physical	10	100	35	Normal
1	Minimize	Normal	Status	—	—	10	Self
4	Astonish	Ghost	Physical	30	100	15	Normal
8	Gust	Flying	Special	40	100	35	Normal
13	Focus Energy	Normal	Status	—	—	30	Self
16	Payback	Dark	Physical	50	100	10	Normal
20	Ominous Wind	Ghost	Special	60	100	5	Normal
25	Stockpile	Normal	Status	—	—	20	Self
27	Hex	Ghost	Special	65	100	10	Normal
32	Swallow	Normal	Status	—	—	10	Self
32	Spit Up	Normal	Special	—	100	10	Normal
36	Shadow Ball	Ghost	Special	80	100	15	Normal
40	Amnesia	Psychic	Status	—	—	20	Self
44	Baton Pass	Normal	Status	—	—	40	Self
50	Explosion	Normal	Physical	250	100	5	Adjacent

❖ TM MOVES

No.	Name	Type	Kind	Pow.	Acc.	PP	Range
TM04	Calm Mind	Psychic	Status	—	—	20	Self
TM06	Toxic	Poison	Status	—	90	10	Normal
TM10	Hidden Power	Normal	Special	60	100	15	Normal
TM11	Sunny Day	Fire	Status	—	—	5	Both Sides
TM17	Protect	Normal	Status	—	—	10	Self
TM18	Rain Dance	Water	Status	—	—	5	Both Sides
TM21	Frustration	Normal	Physical	—	100	20	Normal
TM24	Thunderbolt	Electric	Special	90	100	15	Normal
TM25	Thunder	Electric	Special	110	70	10	Normal
TM27	Return	Normal	Physical	—	100	20	Normal
TM29	Psychic	Psychic	Special	90	100	10	Normal
TM30	Shadow Ball	Ghost	Special	80	100	15	Normal
TM32	Double Team	Normal	Status	—	—	15	Self
TM42	Facade	Normal	Physical	70	100	20	Normal
TM44	Rest	Psychic	Status	—	—	10	Self
TM45	Attract	Normal	Status	—	100	15	Normal
TM46	Thief	Dark	Physical	60	100	25	Normal
TM48	Round	Normal	Special	60	100	15	Normal
TM57	Charge Beam	Electric	Special	50	90	10	Normal
TM61	Will-O-Wisp	Fire	Status	—	85	15	Normal
TM62	Acrobatics	Flying	Physical	55	100	15	Normal
TM63	Embargo	Dark	Status	—	100	15	Normal
TM64	Explosion	Normal	Physical	250	100	5	Adjacent
TM66	Payback	Dark	Physical	50	100	10	Normal
TM73	Thunder Wave	Electric	Status	—	90	20	Normal
TM74	Gyro Ball	Steel	Physical	—	100	5	Normal
TM77	Psych Up	Normal	Status	—	—	10	Normal
TM85	Dream Eater	Psychic	Special	100	100	15	Normal

❖ MOVES TAUGHT BY PEOPLE

Name	Type	Kind	Pow.	Acc.	PP	Range
TM87	Swagger	Normal	Status	—	85	15	Normal
TM88	Sleep Talk	Normal	Status	—	—	10	Self
TM90	Substitute	Normal	Status	—	—	10	Self
TM100	Confide	Normal	Status	—	—	20	Normal

❖ MOVES LEARNED WHEN EVOLVING

Name	Type	Kind	Pow.	Acc.	PP	Range

❖ EGG MOVES

Name	Type	Kind	Pow.	Acc.	PP	Range
Memento	Dark	Status	—	100	10	Normal
Body Slam	Normal	Physical	85	100	15	Normal
Destiny Bond	Ghost	Status	—	—	5	Self
Disable	Normal	Status	—	100	20	Normal
Haze	Ice	Status	—	—	30	Both Sides
Hypnosis	Psychic	Status	—	60	20	Normal
Weather Ball	Normal	Special	50	100	10	Normal
Clear Smog	Poison	Special	50	—	15	Normal
Defog	Flying	Status	—	—	15	Normal
Tailwind	Flying	Status	—	—	15	Your Side

❖ EXCLUSIVE Z-MOVE

Name	Base Move	Type	Kind	Pow.	Acc.	Range

Alola Pokédex	Melemele	Akala	Ula'ula	Poni
065	065	—	—	—

☑ **Drifblim**

Blimp Pokémon

GHOST FLYING

HEIGHT: 3'11"
WEIGHT: 33.1 lbs.

There was once an incident in which a man took a trip riding a Drifblim, only to go missing.

Even while under careful observation, large flocks of Drifblim flying at dusk will inexplicably disappear from view.

ABILITY
Aftermath
Unburden

HIDDEN ABILITY
Flare Boost

Damage taken in normal battles

NORMAL	×0	FIGHTING	×0	ROCK	×2
FIRE	×1	POISON	×0.5	GHOST	×1
WATER	×1	GROUND	×0	DRAGON	×1
GRASS	×0.5	FLYING	×1	DARK	×1
ELECTRIC	×2	PSYCHIC	×1	STEEL	×1
ICE	×2	BUG	×0.25	FAIRY	×1

SPECIES STRENGTHS
HP ◆◆◆◆◆◆◆
Attack ◆◆◆◆
Defense ◆◆◆
Sp. Atk ◆◆◆◆◆
Sp. Def ◆◆◆◆
Speed ◆◆◆◆◆

EGG GROUPS
Amorphous

ITEM SOMETIMES HELD BY WILD POKÉMON
—

EVOLUTION

Drifloon → Lv. 28 → Drifblim

MAIN WAY TO REGISTER IN THE POKÉDEX
Level up Drifloon to Lv. 28

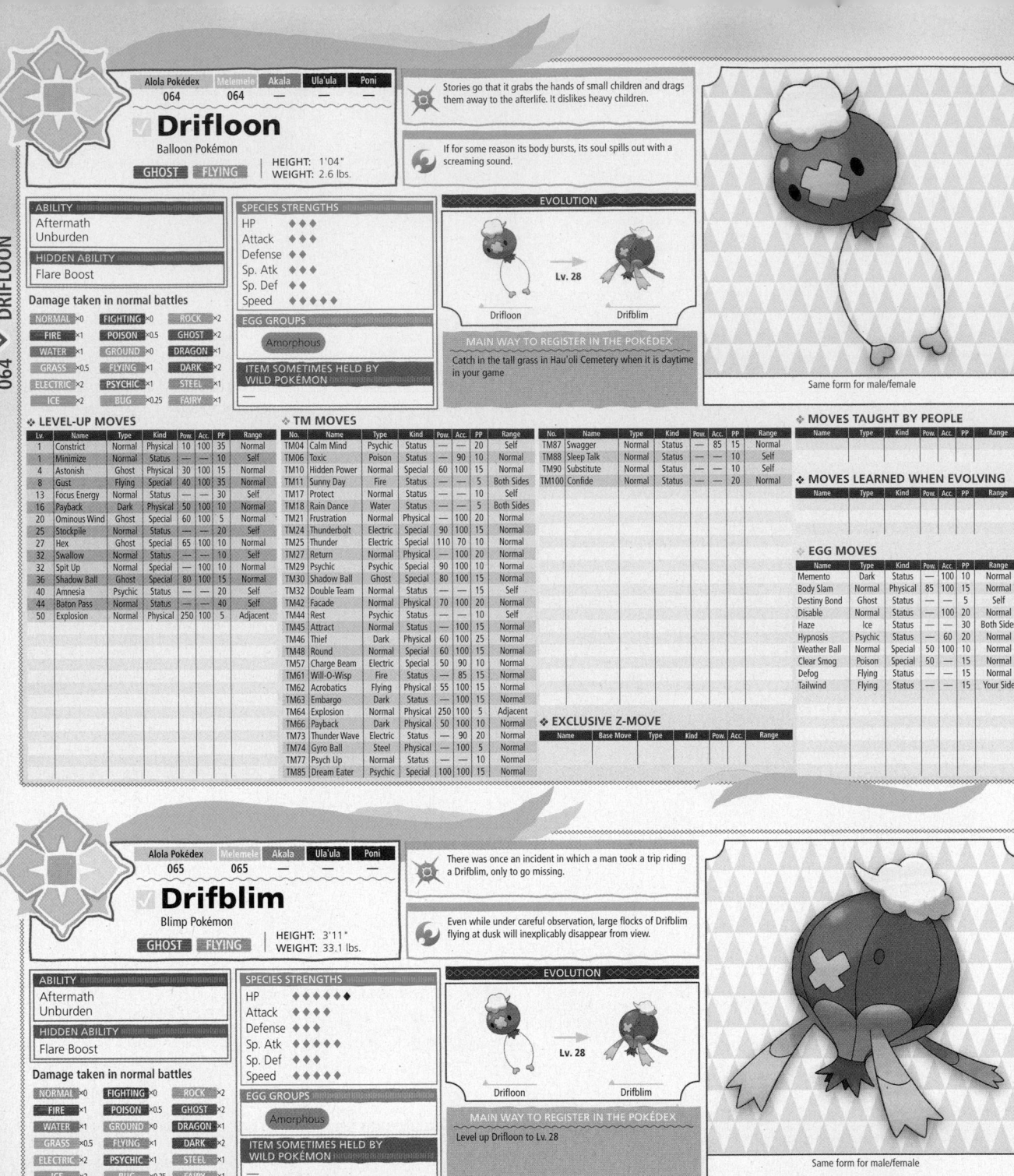

Same form for male/female

❖ LEVEL-UP MOVES

Lv.	Name	Type	Kind	Pow.	Acc.	PP	Range
1	Phantom Force	Ghost	Physical	90	100	10	Normal
1	Constrict	Normal	Physical	10	100	35	Normal
1	Minimize	Normal	Status	—	—	10	Self
1	Astonish	Ghost	Physical	30	100	15	Normal
4	Astonish	Ghost	Physical	30	100	15	Normal
8	Gust	Flying	Special	40	100	35	Normal
13	Focus Energy	Normal	Status	—	—	30	Self
16	Payback	Dark	Physical	50	100	10	Normal
20	Ominous Wind	Ghost	Special	60	100	5	Normal
25	Stockpile	Normal	Status	—	—	20	Self
27	Hex	Ghost	Special	65	100	10	Normal
34	Swallow	Normal	Status	—	—	10	Self
34	Spit Up	Normal	Special	—	100	10	Normal
40	Shadow Ball	Ghost	Special	80	100	15	Normal
46	Amnesia	Psychic	Status	—	—	20	Self
52	Baton Pass	Normal	Status	—	—	40	Self
60	Explosion	Normal	Physical	250	100	5	Adjacent
65	Phantom Force	Ghost	Physical	90	100	10	Normal

❖ TM MOVES

No.	Name	Type	Kind	Pow.	Acc.	PP	Range
TM04	Calm Mind	Psychic	Status	—	—	20	Self
TM06	Toxic	Poison	Status	—	90	10	Normal
TM10	Hidden Power	Normal	Special	60	100	15	Normal
TM11	Sunny Day	Fire	Status	—	—	5	Both Sides
TM15	Hyper Beam	Normal	Special	150	90	5	Normal
TM17	Protect	Normal	Status	—	—	10	Self
TM18	Rain Dance	Water	Status	—	—	5	Both Sides
TM21	Frustration	Normal	Physical	—	100	20	Normal
TM24	Thunderbolt	Electric	Special	90	100	15	Normal
TM25	Thunder	Electric	Special	110	70	10	Normal
TM27	Return	Normal	Physical	—	100	20	Normal
TM29	Psychic	Psychic	Special	90	100	10	Normal
TM30	Shadow Ball	Ghost	Special	80	100	15	Normal
TM32	Double Team	Normal	Status	—	—	15	Self
TM42	Facade	Normal	Physical	70	100	20	Normal
TM44	Rest	Psychic	Status	—	—	10	Self
TM45	Attract	Normal	Status	—	100	15	Normal
TM46	Thief	Dark	Physical	60	100	25	Normal
TM48	Round	Normal	Special	60	100	15	Normal
TM57	Charge Beam	Electric	Special	50	90	10	Normal
TM61	Will-O-Wisp	Fire	Status	—	85	15	Normal
TM62	Acrobatics	Flying	Physical	55	100	15	Normal
TM63	Embargo	Dark	Status	—	100	15	Normal
TM64	Explosion	Normal	Physical	250	100	5	Adjacent
TM66	Payback	Dark	Physical	50	100	10	Normal
TM68	Giga Impact	Normal	Physical	150	90	5	Normal
TM73	Thunder Wave	Electric	Status	—	90	20	Normal
TM74	Gyro Ball	Steel	Physical	—	100	5	Normal

❖ MOVES TAUGHT BY PEOPLE

No.	Name	Type	Kind	Pow.	Acc.	PP	Range
TM76	Fly	Flying	Physical	90	95	15	Normal
TM77	Psych Up	Normal	Status	—	—	10	Normal
TM85	Dream Eater	Psychic	Special	100	100	15	Normal
TM87	Swagger	Normal	Status	—	85	15	Normal
TM88	Sleep Talk	Normal	Status	—	—	10	Self
TM90	Substitute	Normal	Status	—	—	10	Self
TM100	Confide	Normal	Status	—	—	20	Normal

❖ MOVES LEARNED WHEN EVOLVING

Name	Type	Kind	Pow.	Acc.	PP	Range

❖ EGG MOVES

Name	Type	Kind	Pow.	Acc.	PP	Range

❖ EXCLUSIVE Z-MOVE

Name	Base Move	Type	Kind	Pow.	Acc.	Range

Misdreavus
Screech Pokémon

GHOST

Alola Pokédex	Melemele	Akala	Ula'ula	Poni
066	066	—	—	—

HEIGHT: 2'04"
WEIGHT: 2.2 lbs.

It will use any means necessary to frighten people and absorb their life energy. It practices constantly to hone its skill in causing fear.

If you hear a sobbing sound emanating from a vacant room, it's undoubtedly a bit of mischief from Misdreavus.

ABILITY
Levitate

HIDDEN ABILITY
—

SPECIES STRENGTHS
HP	◆◆
Attack	◆◆
Defense	◆◆◆
Sp. Atk	◆◆◆◆◆
Sp. Def	◆◆◆◆
Speed	◆◆◆◆◆

EGG GROUPS
Amorphous

ITEM SOMETIMES HELD BY WILD POKÉMON
—

EVOLUTION
Misdreavus → (Dusk Stone) → Mismagius

MAIN WAY TO REGISTER IN THE POKEDEX
Catch in the tall grass in Hau'oli Cemetery when it is nighttime in your game

Same form for male/female

Damage taken in normal battles
NORMAL ×0	FIGHTING ×0	ROCK ×1	
FIRE ×1	POISON ×0.5	GHOST ×2	DRAGON ×1
WATER ×1	GROUND ×1	DARK ×2	
GRASS ×1	FLYING ×1	STEEL ×1	
ELECTRIC ×1	PSYCHIC ×1	FAIRY ×1	
ICE ×1	BUG ×0.5		

LEVEL-UP MOVES
Lv.	Name	Type	Kind	Pow.	Acc.	PP	Range
1	Growl	Normal	Status	—	100	40	Many Others
1	Psywave	Psychic	Special	—	100	15	Normal
5	Spite	Ghost	Status	—	100	10	Normal
10	Astonish	Ghost	Physical	30	100	15	Normal
14	Confuse Ray	Ghost	Status	—	100	10	Normal
19	Mean Look	Normal	Status	—	—	5	Normal
73	Hex	Ghost	Special	65	100	10	Normal
28	Psybeam	Psychic	Special	65	100	20	Normal
32	Pain Split	Normal	Status	—	—	20	Normal
37	Payback	Dark	Physical	50	100	10	Normal
41	Shadow Ball	Ghost	Special	80	100	15	Normal
46	Perish Song	Normal	Status	—	—	5	Adjacent
50	Grudge	Ghost	Status	—	—	5	Self
55	Power Gem	Rock	Special	80	100	20	Normal

TM MOVES
No.	Name	Type	Kind	Pow.	Acc.	PP	Range
TM04	Calm Mind	Psychic	Status	—	—	20	Self
TM06	Toxic	Poison	Status	—	90	10	Normal
TM10	Hidden Power	Normal	Special	60	100	15	Normal
TM11	Sunny Day	Fire	Status	—	—	5	Both Sides
TM12	Taunt	Dark	Status	—	100	20	Normal
TM17	Protect	Normal	Status	—	—	10	Self
TM18	Rain Dance	Water	Status	—	—	5	Both Sides
TM21	Frustration	Normal	Physical	—	100	20	Normal
TM74	Thunderbolt	Electric	Special	90	100	15	Normal
TM25	Thunder	Electric	Special	110	70	10	Normal
TM27	Return	Normal	Physical	—	100	20	Normal
TM29	Psychic	Psychic	Special	90	100	10	Normal
TM30	Shadow Ball	Ghost	Special	80	100	15	Normal
TM32	Double Team	Normal	Status	—	—	15	Self
TM40	Aerial Ace	Flying	Physical	60	—	20	Normal
TM41	Torment	Dark	Status	—	100	15	Normal
TM42	Facade	Normal	Physical	70	100	20	Normal
TM44	Rest	Psychic	Status	—	—	10	Self
TM45	Attract	Normal	Status	—	100	15	Normal
TM46	Thief	Dark	Physical	60	100	25	Normal
TM48	Round	Normal	Special	60	100	15	Normal
TM49	Echoed Voice	Normal	Special	40	100	15	Normal
TM57	Charge Beam	Electric	Special	50	90	10	Normal
TM61	Will-O-Wisp	Fire	Status	—	85	15	Normal
TM63	Embargo	Dark	Status	—	100	15	Normal
TM66	Payback	Dark	Physical	50	100	10	Normal
TM73	Thunder Wave	Electric	Status	—	90	20	Normal
TM77	Psych Up	Normal	Status	—	—	10	Normal

No.	Name	Type	Kind	Pow.	Acc.	PP	Range
TM85	Dream Eater	Psychic	Special	100	100	15	Normal
TM87	Swagger	Normal	Status	—	85	15	Normal
TM88	Sleep Talk	Normal	Status	—	—	10	Self
TM90	Substitute	Normal	Status	—	—	10	Self
TM92	Trick Room	Psychic	Status	—	—	5	Both Sides
TM97	Dark Pulse	Dark	Special	80	100	15	Normal
TM99	Dazzling Gleam	Fairy	Special	80	100	10	Many Others
TM100	Confide	Normal	Status	—	—	20	Normal

MOVES TAUGHT BY PEOPLE
Name	Type	Kind	Pow.	Acc.	PP	Range

MOVES LEARNED WHEN EVOLVING
Name	Type	Kind	Pow.	Acc.	PP	Range

EGG MOVES
Name	Type	Kind	Pow.	Acc.	PP	Range
Screech	Normal	Status	—	85	40	Normal
Destiny Bond	Ghost	Status	—	—	5	Self
Imprison	Psychic	Status	—	—	10	Self
Memento	Dark	Status	—	100	10	Normal
Sucker Punch	Dark	Physical	70	100	5	Normal
Shadow Sneak	Ghost	Physical	40	100	30	Normal
Curse	Ghost	Status	—	—	10	Varies
Spite	Ghost	Status	—	100	10	Normal
Ominous Wind	Ghost	Special	60	100	5	Normal
Nasty Plot	Dark	Status	—	—	20	Self
Skill Swap	Psychic	Status	—	—	10	Normal
Wonder Room	Psychic	Status	—	—	10	Both Sides
Me First	Normal	Status	—	—	20	Varies

EXCLUSIVE Z-MOVE
Name	Base Move	Type	Kind	Pow.	Acc.	Range

Mismagius
Magical Pokémon

GHOST

Alola Pokédex	Melemele	Akala	Ula'ula	Poni
067	067	—	—	—

HEIGHT: 2'11"
WEIGHT: 9.7 lbs.

It appears as if from nowhere—muttering incantations, placing curses, and giving people terrifying visions.

Mismagius have been known to cast spells to make people fall in love, so some people search for this Pokémon as if their life depended on it.

ABILITY
Levitate

HIDDEN ABILITY
—

SPECIES STRENGTHS
HP	◆◆
Attack	◆◆◆
Defense	◆◆◆
Sp. Atk	◆◆◆◆◆
Sp. Def	◆◆◆◆◆◆
Speed	◆◆◆◆◆◆

EGG GROUPS
Amorphous

ITEM SOMETIMES HELD BY WILD POKÉMON
—

EVOLUTION
Misdreavus → (Dusk Stone) → Mismagius

MAIN WAY TO REGISTER IN THE POKEDEX
Use a Dusk Stone on Misdreavus

Same form for male/female

Damage taken in normal battles
NORMAL ×0	FIGHTING ×0	ROCK ×1	
FIRE ×1	POISON ×0.5	GHOST ×2	DRAGON ×1
WATER ×1	GROUND ×1	DARK ×2	
GRASS ×1	FLYING ×1	STEEL ×1	
ELECTRIC ×1	PSYCHIC ×1	FAIRY ×1	
ICE ×1	BUG ×0.5		

LEVEL-UP MOVES
Lv.	Name	Type	Kind	Pow.	Acc.	PP	Range
1	Mystical Fire	Fire	Special	75	100	10	Normal
1	Power Gem	Rock	Special	80	100	20	Normal
1	Phantom Force	Ghost	Physical	90	100	10	Normal
1	Lucky Chant	Normal	Status	—	—	30	Your Side
1	Magical Leaf	Grass	Special	60	—	20	Normal
1	Growl	Normal	Status	—	100	40	Many Others
1	Psywave	Psychic	Special	—	100	15	Normal
1	Spite	Ghost	Status	—	100	10	Normal
1	Astonish	Ghost	Physical	30	100	15	Normal

TM MOVES
No.	Name	Type	Kind	Pow.	Acc.	PP	Range
TM04	Calm Mind	Psychic	Status	—	—	20	Self
TM06	Toxic	Poison	Status	—	90	10	Normal
TM10	Hidden Power	Normal	Special	60	100	15	Normal
TM11	Sunny Day	Fire	Status	—	—	5	Both Sides
TM12	Taunt	Dark	Status	—	100	20	Normal
TM15	Hyper Beam	Normal	Special	150	90	5	Normal
TM17	Protect	Normal	Status	—	—	10	Self
TM18	Rain Dance	Water	Status	—	—	5	Both Sides
TM21	Frustration	Normal	Physical	—	100	20	Normal
TM24	Thunderbolt	Electric	Special	90	100	15	Normal
TM25	Thunder	Electric	Special	110	70	10	Normal
TM27	Return	Normal	Physical	—	100	20	Normal
TM29	Psychic	Psychic	Special	90	100	10	Normal
TM30	Shadow Ball	Ghost	Special	80	100	15	Normal
TM32	Double Team	Normal	Status	—	—	15	Self
TM40	Aerial Ace	Flying	Physical	60	—	20	Normal
TM41	Torment	Dark	Status	—	100	15	Normal
TM42	Facade	Normal	Physical	70	100	20	Normal
TM44	Rest	Psychic	Status	—	—	10	Self
TM45	Attract	Normal	Status	—	100	15	Normal
TM46	Thief	Dark	Physical	60	100	25	Normal
TM48	Round	Normal	Special	60	100	15	Normal
TM49	Echoed Voice	Normal	Special	40	100	15	Normal
TM53	Energy Ball	Grass	Special	90	100	10	Normal
TM57	Charge Beam	Electric	Special	50	90	10	Normal
TM61	Will-O-Wisp	Fire	Status	—	85	15	Normal
TM63	Embargo	Dark	Status	—	100	15	Normal
TM66	Payback	Dark	Physical	50	100	10	Normal

No.	Name	Type	Kind	Pow.	Acc.	PP	Range
TM68	Giga Impact	Normal	Physical	150	90	5	Normal
TM73	Thunder Wave	Electric	Status	—	90	20	Normal
TM77	Psych Up	Normal	Status	—	—	10	Normal
TM85	Dream Eater	Psychic	Special	100	100	15	Normal
TM87	Swagger	Normal	Status	—	85	15	Normal
TM88	Sleep Talk	Normal	Status	—	—	10	Self
TM90	Substitute	Normal	Status	—	—	10	Self
TM92	Trick Room	Psychic	Status	—	—	5	Both Sides
TM97	Dark Pulse	Dark	Special	80	100	15	Normal
TM99	Dazzling Gleam	Fairy	Special	80	100	10	Many Others
TM100	Confide	Normal	Status	—	—	20	Normal

MOVES TAUGHT BY PEOPLE
Name	Type	Kind	Pow.	Acc.	PP	Range

MOVES LEARNED WHEN EVOLVING
Name	Type	Kind	Pow.	Acc.	PP	Range

EGG MOVES
Name	Type	Kind	Pow.	Acc.	PP	Range

EXCLUSIVE Z-MOVE
Name	Base Move	Type	Kind	Pow.	Acc.	Range

Zubat
Bat Pokémon

POISON | FLYING

HEIGHT: 2'07"
WEIGHT: 16.5 lbs.

Alola Pokédex	Melemele	Akala	Ula'ula	Poni
068	068	026	035	019

It sleeps in caves during the day. It has no eyes, so to check its surroundings while flying, it emits ultrasonic waves.

When exposed to sunlight, they suffer burns. The frequency of their ultrasonic waves can differ slightly from colony to colony.

ABILITY
Inner Focus

HIDDEN ABILITY
Infiltrator

Damage taken in normal battles

NORMAL	×1	FIGHTING	×0.25	ROCK	×1
FIRE	×1	POISON	×0.5	GHOST	×1
WATER	×1	GROUND	×0	DRAGON	×1
GRASS	×0.25	FLYING	×1	DARK	×1
ELECTRIC	×2	PSYCHIC	×2	STEEL	×1
ICE	×2	BUG	×0.25	FAIRY	×0.5

SPECIES STRENGTHS
HP ◆◆
Attack ◆◆◆
Defense ◆◆
Sp. Atk ◆◆
Sp. Def ◆◆
Speed ◆◆◆◆

EGG GROUPS
Flying

ITEM SOMETIMES HELD BY WILD POKÉMON
—

MAIN WAY TO REGISTER IN THE POKÉDEX
Catch in Verdant Cavern

EVOLUTION
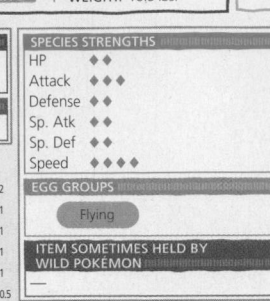
Zubat → Lv. 22 → Golbat
Level up with high friendship
Crobat

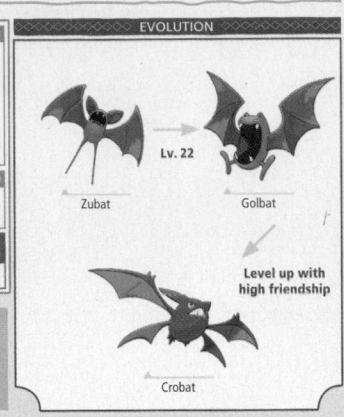

The male has larger fangs. The female has smaller fangs.

Golbat
Bat Pokémon

POISON | FLYING

HEIGHT: 5'03"
WEIGHT: 121.3 lbs.

Alola Pokédex	Melemele	Akala	Ula'ula	Poni
069	069	027	036	020

Its thick fangs are hollow like straws, making them unexpectedly fragile. These fangs are specialized for sucking blood.

Sometimes they drink so much blood, they can't fly anymore. Then they fall to the ground and become food for other Pokémon.

ABILITY
Inner Focus

HIDDEN ABILITY
Infiltrator

Damage taken in normal battles

NORMAL	×1	FIGHTING	×0.25	ROCK	×1
FIRE	×1	POISON	×0.5	GHOST	×1
WATER	×1	GROUND	×0	DRAGON	×1
GRASS	×0.25	FLYING	×1	DARK	×1
ELECTRIC	×2	PSYCHIC	×2	STEEL	×1
ICE	×2	BUG	×0.25	FAIRY	×0.5

SPECIES STRENGTHS
HP ◆◆◆
Attack ◆◆◆◆
Defense ◆◆◆◆
Sp. Atk ◆◆◆◆
Sp. Def ◆◆◆◆
Speed ◆◆◆◆◆◆

EGG GROUPS
Flying

ITEM SOMETIMES HELD BY WILD POKÉMON
—

MAIN WAY TO REGISTER IN THE POKÉDEX
Catch in the abandoned Thrifty Megamart off of Route 14

EVOLUTION
Zubat → Lv. 22 → Golbat
Level up with high friendship
Crobat

The male has larger fangs. The female has smaller fangs.

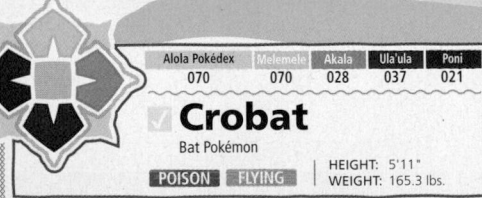

Crobat
Bat Pokémon

POISON | FLYING

HEIGHT: 5'11"
WEIGHT: 165.3 lbs.

Alola Pokédex	Melemele	Akala	Ula'ula	Poni
070	070	028	037	021

Both its legs became wings, and as a result, it can't move well on the ground. All it can do is crawl around.

Silent and swift in its four-winged flight, it bites down on its prey before they realize what's happening. In a heartbeat, it drains their blood.

ABILITY
Inner Focus

HIDDEN ABILITY
Infiltrator

Damage taken in normal battles

NORMAL	×1	FIGHTING	×0.25	ROCK	×1
FIRE	×1	POISON	×0.5	GHOST	×1
WATER	×1	GROUND	×0	DRAGON	×1
GRASS	×0.25	FLYING	×1	DARK	×1
ELECTRIC	×2	PSYCHIC	×2	STEEL	×1
ICE	×2	BUG	×0.25	FAIRY	×0.5

SPECIES STRENGTHS
HP ◆◆◆
Attack ◆◆◆◆◆
Defense ◆◆◆◆
Sp. Atk ◆◆◆◆
Sp. Def ◆◆◆◆◆
Speed ◆◆◆◆◆◆◆◆

EGG GROUPS
Flying

ITEM SOMETIMES HELD BY WILD POKÉMON
—

MAIN WAY TO REGISTER IN THE POKÉDEX
Level up Golbat with high friendship

EVOLUTION
Zubat → Lv. 22 → Golbat
Level up with high friendship
Crobat

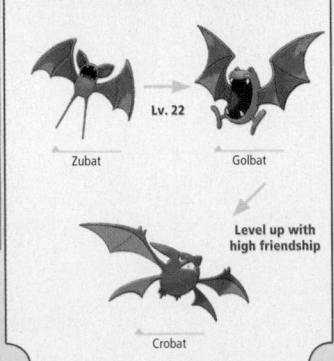

Same form for male/female

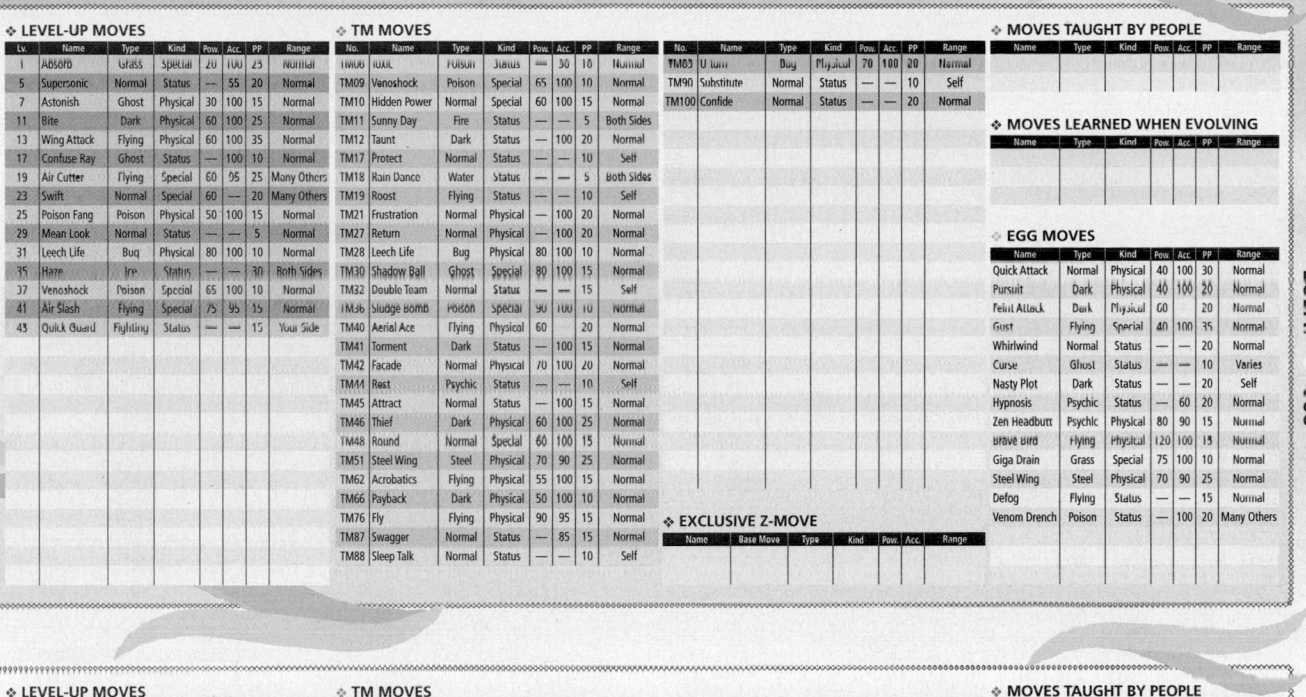

ZUBAT 068

❖ LEVEL-UP MOVES

Lv.	Name	Type	Kind	Pow.	Acc.	PP	Range
1	Absorb	Grass	Special	20	100	25	Normal
5	Supersonic	Normal	Status	—	55	20	Normal
7	Astonish	Ghost	Physical	30	100	15	Normal
11	Bite	Dark	Physical	60	100	25	Normal
13	Wing Attack	Flying	Physical	60	100	35	Normal
17	Confuse Ray	Ghost	Status	—	100	10	Normal
19	Air Cutter	Flying	Special	60	95	25	Many Others
23	Swift	Normal	Special	60	—	20	Many Others
25	Poison Fang	Poison	Physical	50	100	15	Normal
29	Mean Look	Normal	Status	—	—	5	Normal
31	Leech Life	Bug	Physical	80	100	10	Normal
35	Haze	Ice	Status	—	—	30	Both Sides
37	Venoshock	Poison	Special	65	100	10	Normal
41	Air Slash	Flying	Special	75	95	15	Normal
43	Quick Guard	Fighting	Status	—	—	15	Your Side

❖ TM MOVES

No.	Name	Type	Kind	Pow.	Acc.	PP	Range
TM06	Toxic	Poison	Status	—	90	10	Normal
TM09	Venoshock	Poison	Special	65	100	10	Normal
TM10	Hidden Power	Normal	Special	60	100	15	Normal
TM11	Sunny Day	Fire	Status	—	—	5	Both Sides
TM12	Taunt	Dark	Status	—	100	20	Normal
TM17	Protect	Normal	Status	—	—	10	Self
TM18	Rain Dance	Water	Status	—	—	5	Both Sides
TM19	Roost	Flying	Status	—	—	10	Self
TM21	Frustration	Normal	Physical	—	100	20	Normal
TM27	Return	Normal	Physical	—	100	20	Normal
TM28	Leech Life	Bug	Physical	80	100	10	Normal
TM30	Shadow Ball	Ghost	Special	80	100	15	Normal
TM32	Double Team	Normal	Status	—	—	15	Self
TM36	Sludge Bomb	Poison	Special	90	100	10	Normal
TM40	Aerial Ace	Flying	Physical	60		20	Normal
TM41	Torment	Dark	Status	—	100	15	Normal
TM42	Facade	Normal	Physical	70	100	20	Normal
TM44	Rest	Psychic	Status	—	—	10	Self
TM45	Attract	Normal	Status	—	100	15	Normal
TM46	Thief	Dark	Physical	60	100	25	Normal
TM48	Round	Normal	Special	60	100	15	Normal
TM51	Steel Wing	Steel	Physical	70	90	25	Normal
TM62	Acrobatics	Flying	Physical	55	100	15	Normal
TM66	Payback	Dark	Physical	50	100	10	Normal
TM76	Fly	Flying	Physical	90	95	15	Normal
TM87	Swagger	Normal	Status	—	85	15	Normal
TM88	Sleep Talk	Normal	Status	—	—	10	Self
TM89	U-turn	Bug	Physical	70	100	20	Normal
TM90	Substitute	Normal	Status	—	—	10	Self
TM100	Confide	Normal	Status	—	—	20	Normal

❖ EXCLUSIVE Z-MOVE

Name	Base Move	Type	Kind	Pow.	Acc.	Range

❖ MOVES TAUGHT BY PEOPLE

Name	Type	Kind	Pow.	Acc.	PP	Range

❖ MOVES LEARNED WHEN EVOLVING

Name	Type	Kind	Pow.	Acc.	PP	Range

❖ EGG MOVES

Name	Type	Kind	Pow.	Acc.	PP	Range
Quick Attack	Normal	Physical	40	100	30	Normal
Pursuit	Dark	Physical	40	100	20	Normal
Feint Attack	Dark	Physical	60		20	Normal
Gust	Flying	Special	40	100	35	Normal
Whirlwind	Normal	Status	—	—	20	Normal
Curse	Ghost	Status	—	—	10	Varies
Nasty Plot	Dark	Status	—	—	20	Self
Hypnosis	Psychic	Status	—	60	20	Normal
Zen Headbutt	Psychic	Physical	80	90	15	Normal
Brave Bird	Flying	Physical	120	100	15	Normal
Giga Drain	Grass	Special	75	100	10	Normal
Steel Wing	Steel	Physical	70	90	25	Normal
Defog	Flying	Status	—	—	15	Normal
Venom Drench	Poison	Status	—	100	20	Many Others

GOLBAT 069

❖ LEVEL-UP MOVES

Lv.	Name	Type	Kind	Pow.	Acc.	PP	Range
1	Screech	Normal	Status	—	85	40	Normal
1	Absorb	Grass	Special	20	100	25	Normal
1	Supersonic	Normal	Status	—	55	20	Normal
1	Astonish	Ghost	Physical	30	100	15	Normal
1	Bite	Dark	Physical	60	100	25	Normal
5	Supersonic	Normal	Status	—	55	20	Normal
7	Astonish	Ghost	Physical	30	100	15	Normal
11	Bite	Dark	Physical	60	100	25	Normal
13	Wing Attack	Flying	Physical	60	100	35	Normal
17	Confuse Ray	Ghost	Status	—	100	10	Normal
19	Air Cutter	Flying	Special	60	95	25	Many Others
24	Swift	Normal	Special	60	—	20	Many Others
27	Poison Fang	Poison	Physical	50	100	15	Normal
32	Mean Look	Normal	Status	—	—	5	Normal
35	Leech Life	Bug	Physical	80	100	10	Normal
40	Haze	Ice	Status	—	—	30	Both Sides
43	Venoshock	Poison	Special	65	100	10	Normal
48	Air Slash	Flying	Special	75	95	15	Normal
51	Quick Guard	Fighting	Status	—	—	15	Your Side

❖ TM MOVES

No.	Name	Type	Kind	Pow.	Acc.	PP	Range
TM06	Toxic	Poison	Status	—	90	10	Normal
TM09	Venoshock	Poison	Special	65	100	10	Normal
TM10	Hidden Power	Normal	Special	60	100	15	Normal
TM11	Sunny Day	Fire	Status	—	—	5	Both Sides
TM12	Taunt	Dark	Status	—	100	20	Normal
TM15	Hyper Beam	Normal	Special	150	90	5	Normal
TM17	Protect	Normal	Status	—	—	10	Self
TM18	Rain Dance	Water	Status	—	—	5	Both Sides
TM19	Roost	Flying	Status	—	—	10	Self
TM21	Frustration	Normal	Physical	—	100	20	Normal
TM27	Return	Normal	Physical	—	100	20	Normal
TM28	Leech Life	Bug	Physical	80	100	10	Normal
TM30	Shadow Ball	Ghost	Special	80	100	15	Normal
TM32	Double Team	Normal	Status	—	—	15	Self
TM36	Sludge Bomb	Poison	Special	90	100	10	Normal
TM40	Aerial Ace	Flying	Physical	60	—	20	Normal
TM41	Torment	Dark	Status	—	100	15	Normal
TM42	Facade	Normal	Physical	70	100	20	Normal
TM44	Rest	Psychic	Status	—	—	10	Self
TM45	Attract	Normal	Status	—	100	15	Normal
TM46	Thief	Dark	Physical	60	100	25	Normal
TM48	Round	Normal	Special	60	100	15	Normal
TM51	Steel Wing	Steel	Physical	70	90	25	Normal
TM62	Acrobatics	Flying	Physical	55	100	15	Normal
TM66	Payback	Dark	Physical	50	100	10	Normal
TM68	Giga Impact	Normal	Physical	150	90	5	Normal
TM76	Fly	Flying	Physical	90	95	15	Normal
TM87	Swagger	Normal	Status	—	85	15	Normal
TM88	Sleep Talk	Normal	Status	—	—	10	Self
TM89	U-turn	Bug	Physical	70	100	20	Normal
TM90	Substitute	Normal	Status	—	—	10	Self
TM100	Confide	Normal	Status	—	—	20	Normal

❖ EXCLUSIVE Z-MOVE

Name	Base Move	Type	Kind	Pow.	Acc.	Range

❖ MOVES TAUGHT BY PEOPLE

Name	Type	Kind	Pow.	Acc.	PP	Range

❖ MOVES LEARNED WHEN EVOLVING

Name	Type	Kind	Pow.	Acc.	PP	Range

❖ EGG MOVES

Name	Type	Kind	Pow.	Acc.	PP	Range

CROBAT 070

❖ LEVEL-UP MOVES

Lv.	Name	Type	Kind	Pow.	Acc.	PP	Range
1	Cross Poison	Poison	Physical	70	100	20	Normal
1	Screech	Normal	Status	—	85	40	Normal
1	Absorb	Grass	Special	20	100	25	Normal
1	Supersonic	Normal	Status	—	55	20	Normal
1	Astonish	Ghost	Physical	30	100	15	Normal
1	Bite	Dark	Physical	60	100	25	Normal
5	Supersonic	Normal	Status	—	55	20	Normal
7	Astonish	Ghost	Physical	30	100	15	Normal
11	Bite	Dark	Physical	60	100	25	Normal
13	Wing Attack	Flying	Physical	60	100	35	Normal
17	Confuse Ray	Ghost	Status	—	100	10	Normal
19	Air Cutter	Flying	Special	60	95	25	Many Others
24	Swift	Normal	Special	60	—	20	Many Others
27	Poison Fang	Poison	Physical	50	100	15	Normal
32	Mean Look	Normal	Status	—	—	5	Normal
35	Leech Life	Bug	Physical	80	100	10	Normal
40	Haze	Ice	Status	—	—	30	Both Sides
43	Venoshock	Poison	Special	65	100	10	Normal
48	Air Slash	Flying	Special	75	95	15	Normal
51	Quick Guard	Fighting	Status	—	—	15	Your Side

❖ TM MOVES

No.	Name	Type	Kind	Pow.	Acc.	PP	Range
TM06	Toxic	Poison	Status	—	90	10	Normal
TM09	Venoshock	Poison	Special	65	100	10	Normal
TM10	Hidden Power	Normal	Special	60	100	15	Normal
TM11	Sunny Day	Fire	Status	—	—	5	Both Sides
TM12	Taunt	Dark	Status	—	100	20	Normal
TM15	Hyper Beam	Normal	Special	150	90	5	Normal
TM17	Protect	Normal	Status	—	—	10	Self
TM18	Rain Dance	Water	Status	—	—	5	Both Sides
TM19	Roost	Flying	Status	—	—	10	Self
TM21	Frustration	Normal	Physical	—	100	20	Normal
TM27	Return	Normal	Physical	—	100	20	Normal
TM28	Leech Life	Bug	Physical	80	100	10	Normal
TM30	Shadow Ball	Ghost	Special	80	100	15	Normal
TM32	Double Team	Normal	Status	—	—	15	Self
TM36	Sludge Bomb	Poison	Special	90	100	10	Normal
TM40	Aerial Ace	Flying	Physical	60	—	20	Normal
TM41	Torment	Dark	Status	—	100	15	Normal
TM42	Facade	Normal	Physical	70	100	20	Normal
TM44	Rest	Psychic	Status	—	—	10	Self
TM45	Attract	Normal	Status	—	100	15	Normal
TM46	Thief	Dark	Physical	60	100	25	Normal
TM48	Round	Normal	Special	60	100	15	Normal
TM51	Steel Wing	Steel	Physical	70	90	25	Normal
TM62	Acrobatics	Flying	Physical	55	100	15	Normal
TM66	Payback	Dark	Physical	50	100	10	Normal
TM68	Giga Impact	Normal	Physical	150	90	5	Normal
TM76	Fly	Flying	Physical	90	95	15	Normal
TM81	X-Scissor	Bug	Physical	80	100	15	Normal
TM87	Swagger	Normal	Status	—	85	15	Normal
TM88	Sleep Talk	Normal	Status	—	—	10	Self
TM89	U-turn	Bug	Physical	70	100	20	Normal
TM90	Substitute	Normal	Status	—	—	10	Self
TM97	Dark Pulse	Dark	Special	80	100	15	Normal
TM100	Confide	Normal	Status	—	—	20	Normal

❖ EXCLUSIVE Z-MOVE

Name	Base Move	Type	Kind	Pow.	Acc.	Range

❖ MOVES TAUGHT BY PEOPLE

Name	Type	Kind	Pow.	Acc.	PP	Range

❖ MOVES LEARNED WHEN EVOLVING

Name	Type	Kind	Pow.	Acc.	PP	Range
Cross Poison	Poison	Physical	70	100	20	Normal

❖ EGG MOVES

Name	Type	Kind	Pow.	Acc.	PP	Range

Diglett

Alola Pokédex	Melemele	Akala	Ula'ula	Poni
071	071	029	038	022

☑ **Diglett**
Mole Pokémon

GROUND STEEL

HEIGHT: 0'08"
WEIGHT: 2.2 lbs.

Its head sports an altered form of whiskers made of metal. When in communication with its comrades, its whiskers wobble to and fro.

Its golden hairs function as sensors. It pokes them out of its burrow to monitor its surroundings.

ABILITY
Sand Veil
Tangling Hair

HIDDEN ABILITY
Sand Force

Damage taken in normal battles

NORMAL ×0.5	FIGHTING ×2	ROCK ×0.25			
FIRE ×2	POISON ×0	GHOST ×1			
WATER ×2	GROUND ×1	DRAGON ×1			
GRASS ×1	FLYING ×0.5	DARK ×1			
ELECTRIC ×0	PSYCHIC ×0.5	STEEL ×0.5			
ICE ×1	BUG ×0.5	FAIRY ×1			

SPECIES STRENGTHS
HP ◆
Attack ◆◆◆
Defense ◆◆
Sp. Atk ◆
Sp. Def ◆◆
Speed ◆◆◆◆◆◆◆

EGG GROUPS
Field

ITEM SOMETIMES HELD BY WILD POKÉMON
Soft Sand

EVOLUTION

Alolan Diglett → Lv. 26 → Alolan Dugtrio

MAIN WAY TO REGISTER IN THE POKÉDEX
Catch in the dust clouds on Route 5

❖ ALOLA FORM ❖

Same form for male/female

❖ LEVEL-UP MOVES

Lv.	Name	Type	Kind	Pow.	Acc.	PP	Range
1	Sand Attack	Ground	Status	—	100	15	Normal
1	Metal Claw	Steel	Physical	50	95	35	Normal
4	Growl	Normal	Status	—	100	40	Many Others
7	Astonish	Ghost	Physical	30	100	15	Normal
10	Mud-Slap	Ground	Special	20	100	10	Normal
14	Magnitude	Ground	Physical	—	100	30	Adjacent
18	Bulldoze	Ground	Physical	60	100	20	Adjacent
22	Sucker Punch	Dark	Physical	70	100	5	Normal
25	Mud Bomb	Ground	Special	65	85	10	Normal
28	Earth Power	Ground	Special	90	100	10	Normal
31	Dig	Ground	Physical	80	100	10	Normal
35	Iron Head	Steel	Physical	80	100	15	Normal
39	Earthquake	Ground	Physical	100	100	10	Adjacent
43	Fissure	Ground	Physical	—	30	5	Normal

❖ TM MOVES

No.	Name	Type	Kind	Pow.	Acc.	PP	Range
TM01	Work Up	Normal	Status	—	—	30	Self
TM06	Toxic	Poison	Status	—	90	10	Normal
TM10	Hidden Power	Normal	Special	60	100	15	Normal
TM11	Sunny Day	Fire	Status	—	—	5	Both Sides
TM17	Protect	Normal	Status	—	—	10	Self
TM21	Frustration	Normal	Physical	—	100	20	Normal
TM26	Earthquake	Ground	Physical	100	100	10	Adjacent
TM27	Return	Normal	Physical	—	100	20	Normal
TM32	Double Team	Normal	Status	—	—	15	Self
TM36	Sludge Bomb	Poison	Special	90	100	10	Normal
TM37	Sandstorm	Rock	Status	—	—	10	Both Sides
TM39	Rock Tomb	Rock	Physical	60	95	15	Normal
TM40	Aerial Ace	Flying	Physical	60	—	20	Normal
TM42	Facade	Normal	Physical	70	100	20	Normal
TM44	Rest	Psychic	Status	—	—	10	Self
TM45	Attract	Normal	Status	—	100	15	Normal
TM46	Thief	Dark	Physical	60	100	25	Normal
TM48	Round	Normal	Special	60	100	15	Normal
TM49	Echoed Voice	Normal	Special	40	100	15	Normal
TM65	Shadow Claw	Ghost	Physical	70	100	15	Normal
TM78	Bulldoze	Ground	Physical	60	100	20	Adjacent
TM80	Rock Slide	Rock	Physical	75	90	10	Many Others
TM87	Swagger	Normal	Status	—	85	15	Normal
TM88	Sleep Talk	Normal	Status	—	—	10	Self
TM90	Substitute	Normal	Status	—	—	10	Self
TM91	Flash Cannon	Steel	Special	80	100	10	Normal
TM100	Confide	Normal	Status	—	—	20	Normal

❖ MOVES TAUGHT BY PEOPLE

Name	Type	Kind	Pow.	Acc.	PP	Range

❖ MOVES LEARNED WHEN EVOLVING

Name	Type	Kind	Pow.	Acc.	PP	Range

❖ EGG MOVES

Name	Type	Kind	Pow.	Acc.	PP	Range
Feint Attack	Dark	Physical	60	—	20	Normal
Metal Sound	Steel	Status	—	85	40	Normal
Ancient Power	Rock	Special	60	100	5	Normal
Pursuit	Dark	Physical	40	100	20	Normal
Beat Up	Dark	Physical	—	100	10	Normal
Thrash	Normal	Physical	120	100	10	1 Random
Reversal	Fighting	Physical	—	100	15	Normal
Headbutt	Normal	Physical	70	100	15	Normal
Endure	Normal	Status	—	—	10	Self
Final Gambit	Fighting	Special	—	100	5	Normal
Memento	Dark	Status	—	100	10	Normal

❖ EXCLUSIVE Z-MOVE

Name	Base Move	Type	Kind	Pow.	Acc.	Range

Dugtrio

Alola Pokédex	Melemele	Akala	Ula'ula	Poni
072	072	030	039	023

☑ **Dugtrio**
Mole Pokémon

GROUND STEEL

HEIGHT: 2'04"
WEIGHT: 146.8 lbs.

Its shining gold hair provides it with protection. It's reputed that keeping any of its fallen hairs will bring bad luck.

These Pokémon are cherished in the Alola region, where they are thought to be feminine deities of the land incarnate.

ABILITY
Sand Veil
Tangling Hair

HIDDEN ABILITY
Sand Force

Damage taken in normal battles

NORMAL ×0.5	FIGHTING ×2	ROCK ×0.25			
FIRE ×2	POISON ×0	GHOST ×1			
WATER ×2	GROUND ×1	DRAGON ×0.5			
GRASS ×1	FLYING ×0.5	DARK ×1			
ELECTRIC ×0	PSYCHIC ×0.5	STEEL ×0.5			
ICE ×1	BUG ×0.5	FAIRY ×1			

SPECIES STRENGTHS
HP ◆
Attack ◆◆◆◆
Defense ◆◆
Sp. Atk ◆◆◆
Sp. Def ◆◆◆◆
Speed ◆◆◆◆◆◆◆

EGG GROUPS
Field

ITEM SOMETIMES HELD BY WILD POKÉMON
Soft Sand

EVOLUTION

Alolan Diglett → Lv. 26 → Alolan Dugtrio

MAIN WAY TO REGISTER IN THE POKÉDEX
Catch in the dust clouds in Vast Poni Canyon

❖ ALOLA FORM ❖

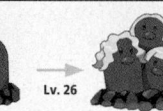

Same form for male/female

❖ LEVEL-UP MOVES

Lv.	Name	Type	Kind	Pow.	Acc.	PP	Range
1	Sand Tomb	Ground	Physical	35	85	15	Normal
1	Rototiller	Ground	Status	—	—	10	Adjacent
1	Night Slash	Dark	Physical	70	100	15	Normal
1	Tri Attack	Normal	Special	80	100	10	Normal
1	Sand Attack	Ground	Status	—	100	15	Normal
1	Metal Claw	Steel	Physical	50	95	35	Normal
1	Growl	Normal	Status	—	100	40	Many Others
4	Growl	Normal	Status	—	100	40	Many Others
7	Astonish	Ghost	Physical	30	100	15	Normal
10	Mud-Slap	Ground	Special	20	100	10	Normal
14	Magnitude	Ground	Physical	—	100	30	Adjacent
18	Bulldoze	Ground	Physical	60	100	20	Adjacent
22	Sucker Punch	Dark	Physical	70	100	5	Normal
25	Mud Bomb	Ground	Special	65	85	10	Normal
30	Earth Power	Ground	Special	90	100	10	Normal
35	Dig	Ground	Physical	80	100	10	Normal
41	Iron Head	Steel	Physical	80	100	15	Normal
47	Earthquake	Ground	Physical	100	100	10	Adjacent
53	Fissure	Ground	Physical	—	30	5	Normal

❖ TM MOVES

No.	Name	Type	Kind	Pow.	Acc.	PP	Range
TM01	Work Up	Normal	Status	—	—	30	Self
TM06	Toxic	Poison	Status	—	90	10	Normal
TM10	Hidden Power	Normal	Special	60	100	15	Normal
TM11	Sunny Day	Fire	Status	—	—	5	Both Sides
TM15	Hyper Beam	Normal	Special	150	90	5	Normal
TM17	Protect	Normal	Status	—	—	10	Self
TM21	Frustration	Normal	Physical	—	100	20	Normal
TM26	Earthquake	Ground	Physical	100	100	10	Adjacent
TM27	Return	Normal	Physical	—	100	20	Normal
TM32	Double Team	Normal	Status	—	—	15	Self
TM34	Sludge Wave	Poison	Special	95	100	10	Adjacent
TM36	Sludge Bomb	Poison	Special	90	100	10	Normal
TM37	Sandstorm	Rock	Status	—	—	10	Both Sides
TM39	Rock Tomb	Rock	Physical	60	95	15	Normal
TM40	Aerial Ace	Flying	Physical	60	—	20	Normal
TM42	Facade	Normal	Physical	70	100	20	Normal
TM44	Rest	Psychic	Status	—	—	10	Self
TM45	Attract	Normal	Status	—	100	15	Normal
TM46	Thief	Dark	Physical	60	100	25	Normal
TM48	Round	Normal	Special	60	100	15	Normal
TM49	Echoed Voice	Normal	Special	40	100	15	Normal
TM65	Shadow Claw	Ghost	Physical	70	100	15	Normal
TM68	Giga Impact	Normal	Physical	150	90	5	Normal
TM71	Stone Edge	Rock	Physical	100	80	5	Normal
TM78	Bulldoze	Ground	Physical	60	100	20	Adjacent
TM80	Rock Slide	Rock	Physical	75	90	10	Many Others
TM87	Swagger	Normal	Status	—	85	15	Normal
TM88	Sleep Talk	Normal	Status	—	—	10	Self

❖ MOVES TAUGHT BY PEOPLE

No.	Name	Type	Kind	Pow.	Acc.	PP	Range
TM90	Substitute	Normal	Status	—	—	10	Self
TM91	Flash Cannon	Steel	Special	80	100	10	Normal
TM100	Confide	Normal	Status	—	—	20	Normal

❖ MOVES LEARNED WHEN EVOLVING

Name	Type	Kind	Pow.	Acc.	PP	Range
Sand Tomb	Ground	Physical	35	85	15	Normal

❖ EGG MOVES

Name	Type	Kind	Pow.	Acc.	PP	Range

❖ EXCLUSIVE Z-MOVE

Name	Base Move	Type	Kind	Pow.	Acc.	Range

DIGLETT
071

DUGTRIO
072

Spearow
Tiny Bird Pokémon

Alola Pokédex	Melemele	Akala	Ula'ula	Poni
073	073	—	040	024

NORMAL FLYING

HEIGHT: 1'00"
WEIGHT: 4.4 lbs.

Its short wings make it inept at flying. It moves about hurriedly and pecks at Bug-type Pokémon in the tall grass.

Farmers whose fields are troubled by bug Pokémon appreciate Spearow for its vigorous appetite and look after it.

Same form for male/female

ABILITY
Keen Eye

HIDDEN ABILITY
Sniper

Damage taken in normal battles

NORMAL	×1	FIGHTING	×1	ROCK	×2
FIRE	×1	POISON	×1	GHOST	×0
WATER	×1	GROUND	×0	DRAGON	×1
GRASS	×0.5	FLYING	×1	DARK	×1
ELECTRIC	×2	PSYCHIC	×1	STEEL	×1
ICE	×2	BUG	×0.5	FAIRY	×1

SPECIES STRENGTHS
HP ◆◆
Attack ◆◆
Defense ◆◆
Sp. Atk ◆
Sp. Def ◆
Speed ◆◆◆◆

EGG GROUPS
Flying

ITEM SOMETIMES HELD BY WILD POKÉMON
Sharp Beak

EVOLUTION

Spearow → Lv. 20 → Fearow

MAIN WAY TO REGISTER IN THE POKÉDEX
Catch in the tall grass on the north end of Route 2

❖ LEVEL-UP MOVES

Lv.	Name	Type	Kind	Pow.	Acc.	PP	Range
1	Peck	Flying	Physical	35	100	35	Normal
1	Growl	Normal	Status	—	100	40	Many Others
4	Leer	Normal	Status	—	100	30	Many Others
8	Pursuit	Dark	Physical	40	100	20	Normal
11	Fury Attack	Normal	Physical	15	85	20	Normal
15	Aerial Ace	Flying	Physical	60	—	20	Normal
18	Mirror Move	Flying	Status	—	—	20	Normal
22	Assurance	Dark	Physical	60	100	10	Normal
25	Agility	Psychic	Status	—	—	30	Self
29	Focus Energy	Normal	Status	—	—	30	Self
32	Roost	Flying	Status	—	—	10	Self
36	Drill Peck	Flying	Physical	80	100	20	Normal

❖ TM MOVES

No.	Name	Type	Kind	Pow.	Acc.	PP	Range
TM01	Work Up	Normal	Status	—	—	30	Self
TM06	Toxic	Poison	Status	—	90	10	Normal
TM10	Hidden Power	Normal	Special	60	100	15	Normal
TM11	Sunny Day	Fire	Status	—	—	5	Both Sides
TM17	Protect	Normal	Status	—	—	10	Self
TM18	Rain Dance	Water	Status	—	—	5	Both Sides
TM19	Roost	Flying	Status	—	—	10	Self
TM21	Frustration	Normal	Physical	—	100	20	Normal
TM27	Return	Normal	Physical	—	100	20	Normal
TM32	Double Team	Normal	Status	—	—	15	Self
TM40	Aerial Ace	Flying	Physical	60	—	20	Normal
TM42	Facade	Normal	Physical	70	100	20	Normal
TM44	Rest	Psychic	Status	—	—	10	Self
TM45	Attract	Normal	Status	—	100	15	Normal
TM46	Thief	Dark	Physical	60	100	25	Normal
TM48	Round	Normal	Special	60	100	15	Normal
TM49	Echoed Voice	Normal	Special	40	100	15	Normal
TM51	Steel Wing	Steel	Physical	70	90	25	Normal
TM54	False Swipe	Normal	Physical	40	100	40	Normal
TM76	Fly	Flying	Physical	90	95	15	Normal
TM87	Swagger	Normal	Status	—	85	15	Normal
TM88	Sleep Talk	Normal	Status	—	—	10	Self
TM89	U-turn	Bug	Physical	70	100	20	Normal
TM90	Substitute	Normal	Status	—	—	10	Self
TM100	Confide	Normal	Status	—	—	20	Normal

❖ MOVES TAUGHT BY PEOPLE

Name	Type	Kind	Pow.	Acc.	PP	Range

❖ MOVES LEARNED WHEN EVOLVING

Name	Type	Kind	Pow.	Acc.	PP	Range

❖ EGG MOVES

Name	Type	Kind	Pow.	Acc.	PP	Range
Feint Attack	Dark	Physical	60	—	20	Normal
Scary Face	Normal	Status	—	100	10	Normal
Quick Attack	Normal	Physical	40	100	30	Normal
Tri Attack	Normal	Special	80	100	10	Normal
Astonish	Ghost	Physical	30	100	15	Normal
Sky Attack	Flying	Physical	140	90	5	Normal
Whirlwind	Normal	Status	—	—	20	Normal
Uproar	Normal	Special	90	100	10	1 Random
Feather Dance	Flying	Status	—	100	15	Normal
Steel Wing	Steel	Physical	70	90	25	Normal
Razor Wind	Normal	Special	80	100	10	Many Others

❖ EXCLUSIVE Z-MOVE

Name	Base Move	Type	Kind	Pow.	Acc.	Range

Fearow
Beak Pokémon

Alola Pokédex	Melemele	Akala	Ula'ula	Poni
074	074	—	041	025

NORMAL FLYING

HEIGHT: 3'11"
WEIGHT: 83.8 lbs.

It's tough and has excellent stamina. It has no problem flying continuously for a whole day carrying a heavy load.

Drawings of a Pokémon resembling Fearow can be seen in murals from deep in ancient history.

Same form for male/female

ABILITY
Keen Eye

HIDDEN ABILITY
Sniper

Damage taken in normal battles

NORMAL	×1	FIGHTING	×1	ROCK	×2
FIRE	×1	POISON	×1	GHOST	×0
WATER	×1	GROUND	×0	DRAGON	×1
GRASS	×0.5	FLYING	×1	DARK	×1
ELECTRIC	×2	PSYCHIC	×1	STEEL	×1
ICE	×2	BUG	×0.5	FAIRY	×1

SPECIES STRENGTHS
HP ◆◆◆
Attack ◆◆◆◆◆
Defense ◆◆◆◆
Sp. Atk ◆◆◆
Sp. Def ◆◆◆
Speed ◆◆◆◆◆◆

EGG GROUPS
Flying

ITEM SOMETIMES HELD BY WILD POKÉMON
Sharp Beak

EVOLUTION

Spearow → Lv. 20 → Fearow

MAIN WAY TO REGISTER IN THE POKÉDEX
Catch from the shaking trees on Route 10

❖ LEVEL-UP MOVES

Lv.	Name	Type	Kind	Pow.	Acc.	PP	Range
1	Drill Run	Ground	Physical	80	95	10	Normal
1	Pluck	Flying	Physical	60	100	20	Normal
1	Peck	Flying	Physical	35	100	35	Normal
1	Growl	Normal	Status	—	100	40	Many Others
1	Leer	Normal	Status	—	100	30	Many Others
1	Pursuit	Dark	Physical	40	100	20	Normal
4	Leer	Normal	Status	—	100	30	Many Others
8	Pursuit	Dark	Physical	40	100	20	Normal
11	Fury Attack	Normal	Physical	15	85	20	Normal
15	Aerial Ace	Flying	Physical	60	—	20	Normal
18	Mirror Move	Flying	Status	—	—	20	Normal
23	Assurance	Dark	Physical	60	100	10	Normal
27	Agility	Psychic	Status	—	—	30	Self
32	Focus Energy	Normal	Status	—	—	30	Self
36	Roost	Flying	Status	—	—	10	Self
41	Drill Peck	Flying	Physical	80	100	20	Normal
45	Drill Run	Ground	Physical	80	95	10	Normal

❖ TM MOVES

No.	Name	Type	Kind	Pow.	Acc.	PP	Range
TM01	Work Up	Normal	Status	—	—	30	Self
TM06	Toxic	Poison	Status	—	90	10	Normal
TM10	Hidden Power	Normal	Special	60	100	15	Normal
TM11	Sunny Day	Fire	Status	—	—	5	Both Sides
TM15	Hyper Beam	Normal	Special	150	90	5	Normal
TM17	Protect	Normal	Status	—	—	10	Self
TM18	Rain Dance	Water	Status	—	—	5	Both Sides
TM19	Roost	Flying	Status	—	—	10	Self
TM21	Frustration	Normal	Physical	—	100	20	Normal
TM27	Return	Normal	Physical	—	100	20	Normal
TM32	Double Team	Normal	Status	—	—	15	Self
TM40	Aerial Ace	Flying	Physical	60	—	20	Normal
TM42	Facade	Normal	Physical	70	100	20	Normal
TM44	Rest	Psychic	Status	—	—	10	Self
TM45	Attract	Normal	Status	—	100	15	Normal
TM46	Thief	Dark	Physical	60	100	25	Normal
TM48	Round	Normal	Special	60	100	15	Normal
TM49	Echoed Voice	Normal	Special	40	100	15	Normal
TM51	Steel Wing	Steel	Physical	70	90	25	Normal
TM54	False Swipe	Normal	Physical	40	100	40	Normal
TM68	Giga Impact	Normal	Physical	150	90	5	Normal
TM76	Fly	Flying	Physical	90	95	15	Normal
TM87	Swagger	Normal	Status	—	85	15	Normal
TM88	Sleep Talk	Normal	Status	—	—	10	Self
TM89	U-turn	Bug	Physical	70	100	20	Normal
TM90	Substitute	Normal	Status	—	—	10	Self
TM100	Confide	Normal	Status	—	—	20	Normal

❖ MOVES TAUGHT BY PEOPLE

Name	Type	Kind	Pow.	Acc.	PP	Range

❖ MOVES LEARNED WHEN EVOLVING

Name	Type	Kind	Pow.	Acc.	PP	Range

❖ EGG MOVES

Name	Type	Kind	Pow.	Acc.	PP	Range

❖ EXCLUSIVE Z-MOVE

Name	Base Move	Type	Kind	Pow.	Acc.	Range

Rufflet

Alola Pokédex				
	Melemele	Akala	Ula'ula	Poni
	075	075	—	026

☑ **Rufflet**

Eaglet Pokémon

NORMAL · FLYING

HEIGHT: 1'08"
WEIGHT: 23.1 lbs.

They pick fights indiscriminately. They grow stronger and more powerful each time they faint or are injured.

With its sharp claws, this Pokémon pierces its prey, and then it pecks at them. Although it also consumes berries, it's a carnivore at heart.

ABILITY
Keen Eye
Sheer Force

HIDDEN ABILITY
Hustle

Damage taken in normal battles

NORMAL ×1	FIGHTING ×1	ROCK ×1
FIRE ×1	POISON ×1	GHOST ×0
WATER ×1	GROUND ×0	DRAGON ×1
GRASS ×0.5	FLYING ×1	DARK ×1
ELECTRIC ×2	PSYCHIC ×1	STEEL ×1
ICE ×2	BUG ×0.5	FAIRY ×1

SPECIES STRENGTHS
HP ◆◆◆
Attack ◆◆◆
Defense ◆◆◆
Sp. Atk ◆◆
Sp. Def ◆◆◆
Speed ◆◆◆◆

EGG GROUPS
Flying

ITEM SOMETIMES HELD BY WILD POKÉMON
—

EVOLUTION

Rufflet → Lv. 54 → Braviary

MAIN WAY TO REGISTER IN THE POKÉDEX
Catch from a Pokémon shadow on Route 3 in *Pokémon Sun* / Obtain in a trade in *Pokémon Moon*

Male only

❖ LEVEL-UP MOVES

Lv.	Name	Type	Kind	Pow.	Acc.	PP	Range
1	Peck	Flying	Physical	35	100	35	Normal
1	Leer	Normal	Status	—	100	30	Many Others
5	Fury Attack	Normal	Physical	15	85	20	Normal
10	Wing Attack	Flying	Physical	60	100	35	Normal
14	Hone Claws	Dark	Status	—	—	15	Self
19	Scary Face	Normal	Status	—	100	10	Normal
23	Aerial Ace	Flying	Physical	60	—	20	Normal
28	Slash	Normal	Physical	70	100	20	Normal
32	Defog	Flying	Status	—	—	15	Normal
37	Tailwind	Flying	Status	—	—	15	Your Side
41	Air Slash	Flying	Special	75	95	15	Normal
46	Crush Claw	Normal	Physical	75	95	10	Normal
50	Sky Drop	Flying	Physical	60	100	10	Normal
55	Whirlwind	Normal	Status	—	—	20	Normal
59	Brave Bird	Flying	Physical	120	100	15	Normal
64	Thrash	Normal	Physical	120	100	10	1 Random

❖ TM MOVES

No.	Name	Type	Kind	Pow.	Acc.	PP	Range
TM01	Work Up	Normal	Status	—	—	30	Self
TM06	Toxic	Poison	Status	—	90	10	Normal
TM08	Bulk Up	Fighting	Status	—	—	20	Self
TM10	Hidden Power	Normal	Special	60	100	15	Normal
TM11	Sunny Day	Fire	Status	—	—	5	Both Sides
TM17	Protect	Normal	Status	—	—	10	Self
TM18	Rain Dance	Water	Status	—	—	5	Both Sides
TM19	Roost	Flying	Status	—	—	10	Self
TM21	Frustration	Normal	Physical	—	100	20	Normal
TM27	Return	Normal	Physical	—	100	20	Normal
TM32	Double Team	Normal	Status	—	—	15	Self
TM39	Rock Tomb	Rock	Physical	60	95	15	Normal
TM40	Aerial Ace	Flying	Physical	60	—	20	Normal
TM42	Facade	Normal	Physical	70	100	20	Normal
TM44	Rest	Psychic	Status	—	—	10	Self
TM45	Attract	Normal	Status	—	100	15	Normal
TM48	Round	Normal	Special	60	100	15	Normal
TM51	Steel Wing	Steel	Physical	70	90	25	Normal
TM58	Sky Drop	Flying	Physical	60	100	10	Normal
TM65	Shadow Claw	Ghost	Physical	70	100	15	Normal
TM76	Fly	Flying	Physical	90	95	15	Normal
TM80	Rock Slide	Rock	Physical	75	90	10	Many Others
TM87	Swagger	Normal	Status	—	85	15	Normal
TM88	Sleep Talk	Normal	Status	—	—	10	Self
TM89	U-turn	Bug	Physical	70	100	20	Normal
TM90	Substitute	Normal	Status	—	—	10	Self
TM100	Confide	Normal	Status	—	—	20	Normal

❖ MOVES TAUGHT BY PEOPLE

Name	Type	Kind	Pow.	Acc.	PP	Range

❖ MOVES LEARNED WHEN EVOLVING

Name	Type	Kind	Pow.	Acc.	PP	Range

❖ EGG MOVES

Name	Type	Kind	Pow.	Acc.	PP	Range

❖ EXCLUSIVE Z-MOVE

Name	Base Move	Type	Kind	Pow.	Acc.	Range

Braviary

Alola Pokédex				
	Melemele	Akala	Ula'ula	Poni
	076	076	—	027

☑ **Braviary**

Valiant Pokémon

NORMAL · FLYING

HEIGHT: 4'11"
WEIGHT: 90.4 lbs.

With its brave disposition, it fears nothing—not even death. Ancient Alolan people respected it, referring to it as "the hero of the sky."

It's thought that people disturbed their habitats in the past, so Braviary banded together to fight back.

ABILITY
Keen Eye
Sheer Force

HIDDEN ABILITY
Defiant

Damage taken in normal battles

NORMAL ×1	FIGHTING ×1	ROCK ×1
FIRE ×1	POISON ×1	GHOST ×0
WATER ×1	GROUND ×0	DRAGON ×1
GRASS ×0.5	FLYING ×1	DARK ×1
ELECTRIC ×2	PSYCHIC ×1	STEEL ×1
ICE ×2	BUG ×0.5	FAIRY ×1

SPECIES STRENGTHS
HP ◆◆◆◆
Attack ◆◆◆◆◆◆◆
Defense ◆◆◆◆
Sp. Atk ◆◆◆
Sp. Def ◆◆◆◆
Speed ◆◆◆◆◆

EGG GROUPS
Flying

ITEM SOMETIMES HELD BY WILD POKÉMON
—

EVOLUTION

Rufflet → Lv. 54 → Braviary

MAIN WAY TO REGISTER IN THE POKÉDEX
Level up Rufflet to Lv. 54

Male only

❖ LEVEL-UP MOVES

Lv.	Name	Type	Kind	Pow.	Acc.	PP	Range
1	Superpower	Fighting	Physical	120	100	5	Normal
1	Thrash	Normal	Physical	120	100	10	1 Random
1	Brave Bird	Flying	Physical	120	100	15	Normal
1	Whirlwind	Normal	Status	—	—	20	Normal
1	Peck	Flying	Physical	35	100	35	Normal
1	Leer	Normal	Status	—	100	30	Many Others
1	Fury Attack	Normal	Physical	15	85	20	Normal
1	Wing Attack	Flying	Physical	60	100	35	Normal
5	Fury Attack	Normal	Physical	15	85	20	Normal
10	Wing Attack	Flying	Physical	60	100	35	Normal
14	Hone Claws	Dark	Status	—	—	15	Self
19	Scary Face	Normal	Status	—	100	10	Normal
23	Aerial Ace	Flying	Physical	60	—	20	Normal
28	Slash	Normal	Physical	70	100	20	Normal
32	Defog	Flying	Status	—	—	15	Normal
37	Tailwind	Flying	Status	—	—	15	Your Side
41	Air Slash	Flying	Special	75	95	15	Normal
46	Crush Claw	Normal	Physical	75	95	10	Normal
50	Sky Drop	Flying	Physical	60	100	10	Normal
57	Whirlwind	Normal	Status	—	—	20	Normal
63	Brave Bird	Flying	Physical	120	100	15	Normal
70	Thrash	Normal	Physical	120	100	10	1 Random

❖ TM MOVES

No.	Name	Type	Kind	Pow.	Acc.	PP	Range
TM01	Work Up	Normal	Status	—	—	30	Self
TM06	Toxic	Poison	Status	—	90	10	Normal
TM08	Bulk Up	Fighting	Status	—	—	20	Self
TM10	Hidden Power	Normal	Special	60	100	15	Normal
TM11	Sunny Day	Fire	Status	—	—	5	Both Sides
TM15	Hyper Beam	Normal	Special	150	90	5	Normal
TM17	Protect	Normal	Status	—	—	10	Self
TM18	Rain Dance	Water	Status	—	—	5	Both Sides
TM19	Roost	Flying	Status	—	—	10	Self
TM21	Frustration	Normal	Physical	—	100	20	Normal
TM27	Return	Normal	Physical	—	100	20	Normal
TM32	Double Team	Normal	Status	—	—	15	Self
TM39	Rock Tomb	Rock	Physical	60	95	15	Normal
TM40	Aerial Ace	Flying	Physical	60	—	20	Normal
TM42	Facade	Normal	Physical	70	100	20	Normal
TM44	Rest	Psychic	Status	—	—	10	Self
TM45	Attract	Normal	Status	—	100	15	Normal
TM48	Round	Normal	Special	60	100	15	Normal
TM51	Steel Wing	Steel	Physical	70	90	25	Normal
TM58	Sky Drop	Flying	Physical	60	100	10	Normal
TM65	Shadow Claw	Ghost	Physical	70	100	15	Normal
TM68	Giga Impact	Normal	Physical	150	90	5	Normal
TM76	Fly	Flying	Physical	90	95	15	Normal
TM80	Rock Slide	Rock	Physical	75	90	10	Many Others
TM87	Swagger	Normal	Status	—	85	15	Normal
TM88	Sleep Talk	Normal	Status	—	—	10	Self
TM89	U-turn	Bug	Physical	70	100	20	Normal
TM90	Substitute	Normal	Status	—	—	10	Self

❖ MOVES TAUGHT BY PEOPLE

No.	Name	Type	Kind	Pow.	Acc.	PP	Range
TM100	Confide	Normal	Status	—	—	20	Normal

❖ MOVES LEARNED WHEN EVOLVING

Name	Type	Kind	Pow.	Acc.	PP	Range
Superpower	Fighting	Physical	120	100	5	Normal

❖ EGG MOVES

Name	Type	Kind	Pow.	Acc.	PP	Range

❖ EXCLUSIVE Z-MOVE

Name	Base Move	Type	Kind	Pow.	Acc.	Range

Vullaby

Diapered Pokémon

Alola Pokédex	Melemele	Akala	Ula'ula	Poni
077	077	—	—	028

DARK · FLYING

HEIGHT: 1'08"
WEIGHT: 19.8 lbs.

> It protects its plump posterior with the bones of prey it has consumed. As it grows, it replaces the bones.

> It can't fly yet and must wait until its wings have developed more. Since it's still at a playful age, it hops around friskily.

ABILITY
Big Pecks
Overcoat

HIDDEN ABILITY
Weak Armor

SPECIES STRENGTHS
HP	◆◆◆
Attack	◆◆◆
Defense	◆◆◆◆
Sp. Atk	◆◆◆
Sp. Def	◆◆◆◆
Speed	◆◆◆

EGG GROUPS
Flying

ITEM SOMETIMES HELD BY WILD POKÉMON
—

Damage taken in normal battles
NORMAL ×1	FIGHTING ×1	ROCK ×1
FIRE ×1	POISON ×1	GHOST ×0.5
WATER ×1	GROUND ×0	DRAGON ×1
GRASS ×0.5	FLYING ×1	DARK ×1
ELECTRIC ×1	PSYCHIC ×0	STEEL ×1
ICE ×2	BUG ×1	FAIRY ×1

EVOLUTION

Vullaby → Lv. 54 → Mandibuzz

MAIN WAY TO REGISTER IN THE POKÉDEX
Obtain in a trade in *Pokémon Sun* / Catch from a Pokémon shadow on Route 3 in *Pokémon Moon*

Female only

❖ LEVEL-UP MOVES
Lv.	Name	Type	Kind	Pow.	Acc.	PP	Range
1	Gust	Flying	Special	40	100	35	Normal
1	Leer	Normal	Status	—	100	30	Many Others
5	Fury Attack	Normal	Physical	15	85	20	Normal
10	Pluck	Flying	Physical	60	100	20	Normal
14	Nasty Plot	Dark	Status	—	—	20	Self
19	Flatter	Dark	Status	—	100	15	Normal
23	Feint Attack	Dark	Physical	60	—	20	Normal
28	Punishment	Dark	Physical	—	100	5	Normal
32	Defog	Flying	Status	—	—	15	Normal
37	Tailwind	Flying	Status	—	—	15	Your Side
41	Air Slash	Flying	Special	75	95	15	Normal
46	Dark Pulse	Dark	Special	80	100	15	Normal
50	Embargo	Dark	Status	—	100	15	Normal
55	Whirlwind	Normal	Status	—	—	20	Normal
59	Brave Bird	Flying	Physical	120	100	15	Normal
64	Mirror Move	Flying	Status	—	—	20	Normal

❖ TM MOVES
No.	Name	Type	Kind	Pow.	Acc.	PP	Range
TM06	Toxic	Poison	Status	—	90	10	Normal
TM10	Hidden Power	Normal	Special	60	100	15	Normal
TM11	Sunny Day	Fire	Status	—	—	5	Both Sides
TM12	Taunt	Dark	Status	—	100	20	Normal
TM17	Protect	Normal	Status	—	—	10	Self
TM18	Rain Dance	Water	Status	—	—	5	Both Sides
TM19	Roost	Flying	Status	—	—	10	Self
TM21	Frustration	Normal	Physical	—	100	20	Normal
TM27	Return	Normal	Physical	—	100	20	Normal
TM30	Shadow Ball	Ghost	Special	80	100	15	Normal
TM32	Double Team	Normal	Status	—	—	15	Self
TM39	Rock Tomb	Rock	Physical	60	95	15	Normal
TM40	Aerial Ace	Flying	Physical	60	—	20	Normal
TM41	Torment	Dark	Status	—	100	15	Normal
TM42	Facade	Normal	Physical	70	100	20	Normal
TM44	Rest	Psychic	Status	—	—	10	Self
TM45	Attract	Normal	Status	—	100	15	Normal
TM46	Thief	Dark	Physical	60	100	25	Normal
TM48	Round	Normal	Special	60	100	15	Normal
TM51	Steel Wing	Steel	Physical	70	90	25	Normal
TM63	Embargo	Dark	Status	—	100	15	Normal
TM66	Payback	Dark	Physical	50	100	10	Normal
TM76	Fly	Flying	Physical	90	95	15	Normal
TM77	Psych Up	Normal	Status	—	—	10	Normal
TM87	Swagger	Normal	Status	—	85	15	Normal
TM88	Sleep Talk	Normal	Status	—	—	10	Self
TM89	U-turn	Bug	Physical	70	100	20	Normal
TM90	Substitute	Normal	Status	—	—	10	Self
TM95	Snarl	Dark	Special	55	95	15	Many Others
TM97	Dark Pulse	Dark	Special	80	100	15	Normal
TM100	Confide	Normal	Status	—	—	20	Normal

❖ MOVES TAUGHT BY PEOPLE
Name	Type	Kind	Pow.	Acc.	PP	Range

❖ MOVES LEARNED WHEN EVOLVING
Name	Type	Kind	Pow.	Acc.	PP	Range

❖ EGG MOVES
Name	Type	Kind	Pow.	Acc.	PP	Range
Steel Wing	Steel	Physical	70	90	25	Normal
Mean Look	Normal	Status	—	—	5	Normal
Roost	Flying	Status	—	—	10	Self
Scary Face	Normal	Status	—	100	10	Normal
Knock Off	Dark	Physical	65	100	20	Normal
Fake Tears	Dark	Status	—	100	20	Normal
Foul Play	Dark	Physical	95	100	15	Normal

❖ EXCLUSIVE Z-MOVE
Name	Base Move	Type	Kind	Pow.	Acc.	Range

Mandibuzz

Bone Vulture Pokémon

Alola Pokédex	Melemele	Akala	Ula'ula	Poni
078	078	—	—	029

DARK · FLYING

HEIGHT: 3'11"
WEIGHT: 87.1 lbs.

> They adorn themselves beautifully with bones. This is supposedly an effort to attract males, but no male Mandibuzz have ever been found.

> It circles in the sky, keeping a keen eye out for Pokémon in a weakened state. Its choicest food is Cubone.

ABILITY
Big Pecks
Overcoat

HIDDEN ABILITY
Weak Armor

SPECIES STRENGTHS
HP	◆◆◆◆
Attack	◆◆◆◆
Defense	◆◆◆◆◆◆
Sp. Atk	◆◆◆
Sp. Def	◆◆◆◆◆◆
Speed	◆◆◆◆

EGG GROUPS
Flying

ITEM SOMETIMES HELD BY WILD POKÉMON
—

Damage taken in normal battles
NORMAL ×1	FIGHTING ×1	ROCK ×2
FIRE ×1	POISON ×1	GHOST ×1
WATER ×1	GROUND ×0	DRAGON ×1
GRASS ×0.5	FLYING ×1	DARK ×1
ELECTRIC ×2	PSYCHIC ×0	STEEL ×1
ICE ×2	BUG ×1	FAIRY ×2

EVOLUTION

Vullaby → Lv. 54 → Mandibuzz

MAIN WAY TO REGISTER IN THE POKÉDEX
Level up Vullaby to Lv. 54

Female only

❖ LEVEL-UP MOVES
Lv.	Name	Type	Kind	Pow.	Acc.	PP	Range
1	Bone Rush	Ground	Physical	25	90	10	Normal
1	Mirror Move	Flying	Status	—	—	20	Normal
1	Brave Bird	Flying	Physical	120	100	15	Normal
1	Whirlwind	Normal	Status	—	—	20	Normal
1	Gust	Flying	Special	40	100	35	Normal
1	Leer	Normal	Status	—	100	30	Many Others
1	Fury Attack	Normal	Physical	15	85	20	Normal
1	Pluck	Flying	Physical	60	100	20	Normal
5	Fury Attack	Normal	Physical	15	85	20	Normal
10	Pluck	Flying	Physical	60	100	20	Normal
14	Nasty Plot	Dark	Status	—	—	20	Self
19	Flatter	Dark	Status	—	100	15	Normal
23	Feint Attack	Dark	Physical	60	—	20	Normal
28	Punishment	Dark	Physical	—	100	5	Normal
32	Defog	Flying	Status	—	—	15	Normal
37	Tailwind	Flying	Status	—	—	15	Your Side
41	Air Slash	Flying	Special	75	95	15	Normal
46	Dark Pulse	Dark	Special	80	100	15	Normal
50	Embargo	Dark	Status	—	100	15	Normal
57	Whirlwind	Normal	Status	—	—	20	Normal
63	Brave Bird	Flying	Physical	120	100	15	Normal
70	Mirror Move	Flying	Status	—	—	20	Normal

❖ TM MOVES
No.	Name	Type	Kind	Pow.	Acc.	PP	Range
TM06	Toxic	Poison	Status	—	90	10	Normal
TM10	Hidden Power	Normal	Special	60	100	15	Normal
TM11	Sunny Day	Fire	Status	—	—	5	Both Sides
TM12	Taunt	Dark	Status	—	100	20	Normal
TM15	Hyper Beam	Normal	Special	150	90	5	Normal
TM17	Protect	Normal	Status	—	—	10	Self
TM18	Rain Dance	Water	Status	—	—	5	Both Sides
TM19	Roost	Flying	Status	—	—	10	Self
TM21	Frustration	Normal	Physical	—	100	20	Normal
TM27	Return	Normal	Physical	—	100	20	Normal
TM30	Shadow Ball	Ghost	Special	80	100	15	Normal
TM32	Double Team	Normal	Status	—	—	15	Self
TM39	Rock Tomb	Rock	Physical	60	95	15	Normal
TM40	Aerial Ace	Flying	Physical	60	—	20	Normal
TM41	Torment	Dark	Status	—	100	15	Normal
TM42	Facade	Normal	Physical	70	100	20	Normal
TM44	Rest	Psychic	Status	—	—	10	Self
TM45	Attract	Normal	Status	—	100	15	Normal
TM46	Thief	Dark	Physical	60	100	25	Normal
TM48	Round	Normal	Special	60	100	15	Normal
TM51	Steel Wing	Steel	Physical	70	90	25	Normal
TM63	Embargo	Dark	Status	—	100	15	Normal
TM66	Payback	Dark	Physical	50	100	10	Normal
TM68	Giga Impact	Normal	Physical	150	90	5	Normal
TM76	Fly	Flying	Physical	90	95	15	Normal
TM77	Psych Up	Normal	Status	—	—	10	Normal
TM87	Swagger	Normal	Status	—	85	15	Normal
TM88	Sleep Talk	Normal	Status	—	—	10	Self
TM89	U-turn	Bug	Physical	70	100	20	Normal
TM90	Substitute	Normal	Status	—	—	10	Self
TM95	Snarl	Dark	Special	55	95	15	Many Others
TM97	Dark Pulse	Dark	Special	80	100	15	Normal
TM100	Confide	Normal	Status	—	—	20	Normal

❖ MOVES TAUGHT BY PEOPLE
Name	Type	Kind	Pow.	Acc.	PP	Range

❖ MOVES LEARNED WHEN EVOLVING
Name	Type	Kind	Pow.	Acc.	PP	Range
Bone Rush	Ground	Physical	25	90	10	Normal

❖ EGG MOVES
Name	Type	Kind	Pow.	Acc.	PP	Range

❖ EXCLUSIVE Z-MOVE
Name	Base Move	Type	Kind	Pow.	Acc.	Range

Mankey

Pig Monkey Pokémon

Alola Pokédex	Melemele	Akala	Ula'ula	Poni
079	079	—	—	030

FIGHTING

HEIGHT: 1'08"
WEIGHT: 61.7 lbs.

It can spontaneously become enraged. Everyone near it clears out as it rampages, and the resulting loneliness makes it angrier still.

Its raging tires it out and causes it to fall asleep, but the anger resonating in its dreams causes it to wake up—which infuriates it all over again.

ABILITY
Vital Spirit
Anger Point

HIDDEN ABILITY
Defiant

SPECIES STRENGTHS
HP ◆◆
Attack ◆◆◆◆
Defense ◆◆
Sp. Atk ◆◆
Sp. Def ◆◆
Speed ◆◆◆◆

EGG GROUPS
Field

ITEM SOMETIMES HELD BY WILD POKÉMON
—

Damage taken in normal battles

NORMAL ×1	FIGHTING ×1	ROCK ×0.5
FIRE ×1	POISON ×1	GHOST ×1
WATER ×1	GROUND ×1	DRAGON ×1
GRASS ×1	FLYING ×2	DARK ×1
ELECTRIC ×1	PSYCHIC ×2	STEEL ×1
ICE ×1	BUG ×0.5	FAIRY ×2

EVOLUTION

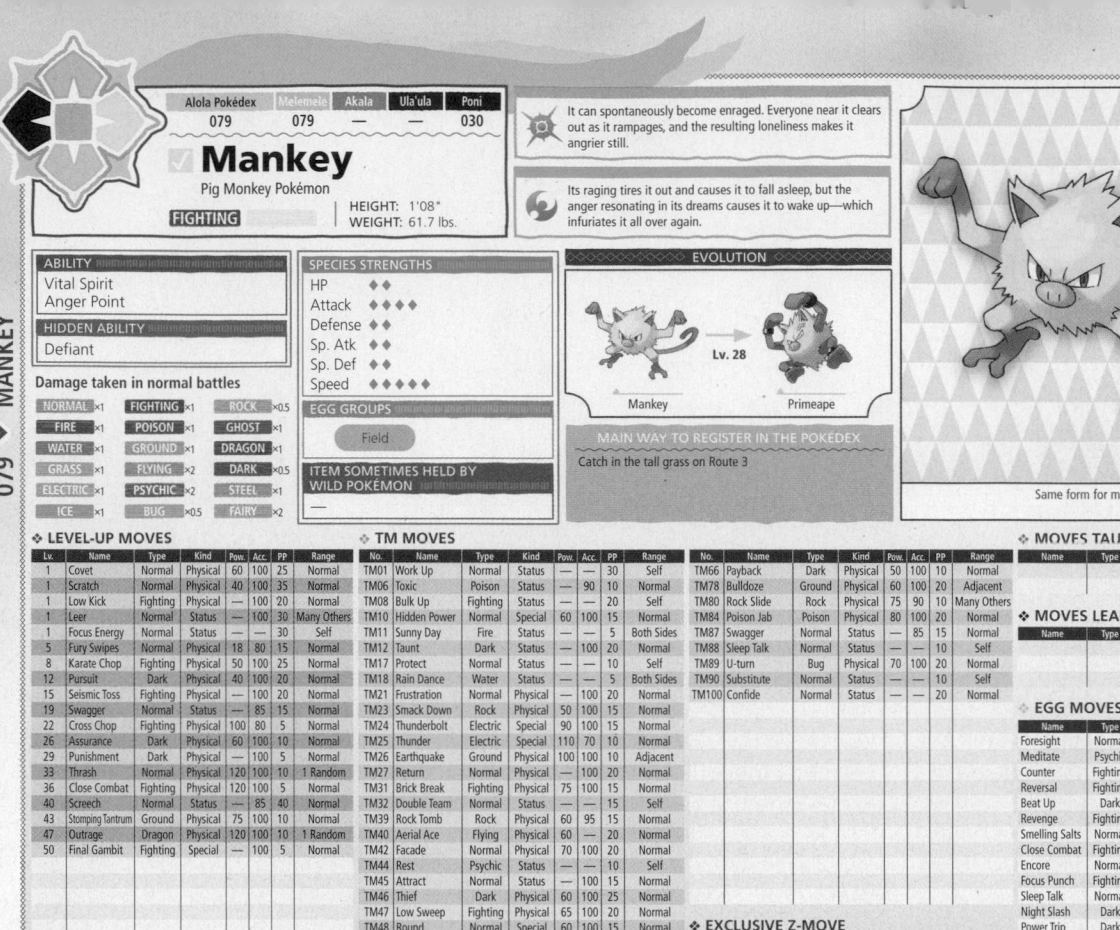

Mankey — Lv. 28 → Primeape

MAIN WAY TO REGISTER IN THE POKÉDEX
Catch in the tall grass on Route 3

Same form for male/female

◆ LEVEL-UP MOVES

Lv.	Name	Type	Kind	Pow.	Acc.	PP	Range
1	Covet	Normal	Physical	60	100	25	Normal
1	Scratch	Normal	Physical	40	100	35	Normal
1	Low Kick	Fighting	Physical	—	100	20	Normal
1	Leer	Normal	Status	—	100	30	Many Others
1	Focus Energy	Normal	Status	—	—	30	Self
5	Fury Swipes	Normal	Physical	18	80	15	Normal
8	Karate Chop	Fighting	Physical	50	100	25	Normal
12	Pursuit	Dark	Physical	40	100	20	Normal
15	Seismic Toss	Fighting	Physical	—	100	20	Normal
19	Swagger	Normal	Status	—	85	15	Normal
22	Cross Chop	Fighting	Physical	100	80	5	Normal
26	Assurance	Dark	Physical	60	100	10	Normal
29	Punishment	Dark	Physical	—	100	5	Normal
33	Thrash	Normal	Physical	120	100	10	1 Random
36	Close Combat	Fighting	Physical	120	100	5	Normal
40	Screech	Normal	Status	—	85	40	Normal
43	Stomping Tantrum	Ground	Physical	75	100	10	Normal
47	Outrage	Dragon	Physical	120	100	10	1 Random
50	Final Gambit	Fighting	Special	—	100	5	Normal

◆ TM MOVES

No.	Name	Type	Kind	Pow.	Acc.	PP	Range
TM01	Work Up	Normal	Status	—	—	30	Self
TM06	Toxic	Poison	Status	—	90	10	Normal
TM08	Bulk Up	Fighting	Status	—	—	20	Self
TM10	Hidden Power	Normal	Special	60	100	15	Normal
TM11	Sunny Day	Fire	Status	—	—	5	Both Sides
TM12	Taunt	Dark	Status	—	100	20	Normal
TM17	Protect	Normal	Status	—	—	10	Self
TM18	Rain Dance	Water	Status	—	—	5	Both Sides
TM21	Frustration	Normal	Physical	—	100	20	Normal
TM23	Smack Down	Rock	Physical	50	100	15	Normal
TM24	Thunderbolt	Electric	Special	90	100	15	Normal
TM25	Thunder	Electric	Special	110	70	10	Normal
TM26	Earthquake	Ground	Physical	100	100	10	Adjacent
TM27	Return	Normal	Physical	—	100	20	Normal
TM31	Brick Break	Fighting	Physical	75	100	15	Normal
TM32	Double Team	Normal	Status	—	—	15	Self
TM39	Rock Tomb	Rock	Physical	60	95	15	Normal
TM40	Aerial Ace	Flying	Physical	60	—	20	Normal
TM42	Facade	Normal	Physical	70	100	20	Normal
TM44	Rest	Psychic	Status	—	—	10	Self
TM45	Attract	Normal	Status	—	100	15	Normal
TM46	Thief	Dark	Physical	60	100	25	Normal
TM47	Low Sweep	Fighting	Physical	65	100	20	Normal
TM48	Round	Normal	Special	60	100	15	Normal
TM50	Overheat	Fire	Special	130	90	5	Normal
TM52	Focus Blast	Fighting	Special	120	70	5	Normal
TM56	Fling	Dark	Physical	—	100	10	Normal
TM62	Acrobatics	Flying	Physical	55	100	15	Normal
TM66	Payback	Dark	Physical	50	100	10	Normal
TM78	Bulldoze	Ground	Physical	60	100	20	Adjacent
TM80	Rock Slide	Rock	Physical	75	90	10	Many Others
TM84	Poison Jab	Poison	Physical	80	100	20	Normal
TM87	Swagger	Normal	Status	—	85	15	Normal
TM88	Sleep Talk	Normal	Status	—	—	10	Self
TM89	U-turn	Bug	Physical	70	100	20	Normal
TM90	Substitute	Normal	Status	—	—	10	Self
TM100	Confide	Normal	Status	—	—	20	Normal

◆ MOVES TAUGHT BY PEOPLE

Name	Type	Kind	Pow.	Acc.	PP	Range

◆ MOVES LEARNED WHEN EVOLVING

Name	Type	Kind	Pow.	Acc.	PP	Range

◆ EGG MOVES

Name	Type	Kind	Pow.	Acc.	PP	Range
Foresight	Normal	Status	—	—	40	Normal
Meditate	Psychic	Status	—	—	40	Self
Counter	Fighting	Physical	—	100	20	Varies
Reversal	Fighting	Physical	—	100	15	Normal
Beat Up	Dark	Physical	—	100	10	Normal
Revenge	Fighting	Physical	60	100	10	Normal
Smelling Salts	Normal	Physical	70	100	10	Normal
Close Combat	Fighting	Physical	120	100	5	Normal
Encore	Normal	Status	—	100	5	Normal
Focus Punch	Fighting	Physical	150	100	20	Normal
Sleep Talk	Normal	Status	—	—	10	Self
Night Slash	Dark	Physical	70	100	15	Normal
Power Trip	Dark	Physical	20	100	10	Normal

◆ EXCLUSIVE Z-MOVE

Name	Base Move	Type	Kind	Pow.	Acc.	Range

Primeape

Pig Monkey Pokémon

Alola Pokédex	Melemele	Akala	Ula'ula	Poni
080	080	—	—	031

FIGHTING

HEIGHT: 3'03"
WEIGHT: 70.5 lbs.

It has been known to become so angry that it dies as a result. Its face looks peaceful in death, however.

Some researchers theorize that Primeape remains angry even when inside a Poké Ball.

ABILITY
Vital Spirit
Anger Point

HIDDEN ABILITY
Defiant

SPECIES STRENGTHS
HP ◆◆◆
Attack ◆◆◆◆◆◆
Defense ◆◆◆
Sp. Atk ◆◆
Sp. Def ◆◆◆
Speed ◆◆◆◆◆◆

EGG GROUPS
Field

ITEM SOMETIMES HELD BY WILD POKÉMON
—

Damage taken in normal battles

NORMAL ×1	FIGHTING ×1	ROCK ×0.5
FIRE ×1	POISON ×1	GHOST ×1
WATER ×1	GROUND ×1	DRAGON ×1
GRASS ×1	FLYING ×2	DARK ×1
ELECTRIC ×1	PSYCHIC ×2	STEEL ×1
ICE ×1	BUG ×0.5	FAIRY ×2

EVOLUTION

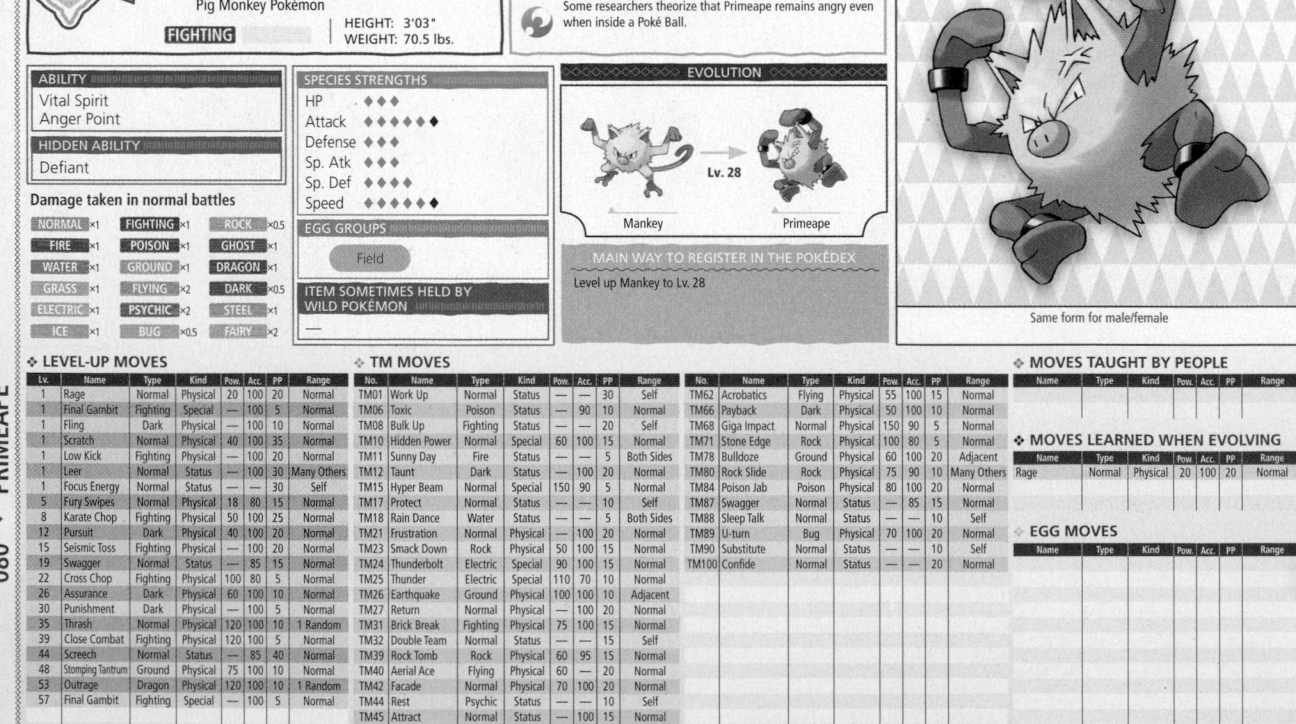

Mankey — Lv. 28 → Primeape

MAIN WAY TO REGISTER IN THE POKÉDEX
Level up Mankey to Lv. 28

Same form for male/female

◆ LEVEL-UP MOVES

Lv.	Name	Type	Kind	Pow.	Acc.	PP	Range
1	Rage	Normal	Physical	20	100	20	Normal
1	Final Gambit	Fighting	Special	—	100	5	Normal
1	Fling	Dark	Physical	—	100	10	Normal
1	Scratch	Normal	Physical	40	100	35	Normal
1	Low Kick	Fighting	Physical	—	100	20	Normal
1	Leer	Normal	Status	—	100	30	Many Others
1	Focus Energy	Normal	Status	—	—	30	Self
5	Fury Swipes	Normal	Physical	18	80	15	Normal
8	Karate Chop	Fighting	Physical	50	100	25	Normal
12	Pursuit	Dark	Physical	40	100	20	Normal
15	Seismic Toss	Fighting	Physical	—	100	20	Normal
19	Swagger	Normal	Status	—	85	15	Normal
22	Cross Chop	Fighting	Physical	100	80	5	Normal
26	Assurance	Dark	Physical	60	100	10	Normal
30	Punishment	Dark	Physical	—	100	5	Normal
35	Thrash	Normal	Physical	120	100	10	1 Random
39	Close Combat	Fighting	Physical	120	100	5	Normal
44	Screech	Normal	Status	—	85	40	Normal
48	Stomping Tantrum	Ground	Physical	75	100	10	Normal
53	Outrage	Dragon	Physical	120	100	10	1 Random
57	Final Gambit	Fighting	Special	—	100	5	Normal

◆ TM MOVES

No.	Name	Type	Kind	Pow.	Acc.	PP	Range
TM01	Work Up	Normal	Status	—	—	30	Self
TM06	Toxic	Poison	Status	—	90	10	Normal
TM08	Bulk Up	Fighting	Status	—	—	20	Self
TM10	Hidden Power	Normal	Special	60	100	15	Normal
TM11	Sunny Day	Fire	Status	—	—	5	Both Sides
TM12	Taunt	Dark	Status	—	100	20	Normal
TM15	Hyper Beam	Normal	Special	150	90	5	Normal
TM17	Protect	Normal	Status	—	—	10	Self
TM18	Rain Dance	Water	Status	—	—	5	Both Sides
TM21	Frustration	Normal	Physical	—	100	20	Normal
TM23	Smack Down	Rock	Physical	50	100	15	Normal
TM24	Thunderbolt	Electric	Special	90	100	15	Normal
TM25	Thunder	Electric	Special	110	70	10	Normal
TM26	Earthquake	Ground	Physical	100	100	10	Adjacent
TM27	Return	Normal	Physical	—	100	20	Normal
TM31	Brick Break	Fighting	Physical	75	100	15	Normal
TM32	Double Team	Normal	Status	—	—	15	Self
TM39	Rock Tomb	Rock	Physical	60	95	15	Normal
TM40	Aerial Ace	Flying	Physical	60	—	20	Normal
TM42	Facade	Normal	Physical	70	100	20	Normal
TM44	Rest	Psychic	Status	—	—	10	Self
TM45	Attract	Normal	Status	—	100	15	Normal
TM46	Thief	Dark	Physical	60	100	25	Normal
TM47	Low Sweep	Fighting	Physical	65	100	20	Normal
TM48	Round	Normal	Special	60	100	15	Normal
TM50	Overheat	Fire	Special	130	90	5	Normal
TM52	Focus Blast	Fighting	Special	120	70	5	Normal
TM56	Fling	Dark	Physical	—	100	10	Normal
TM62	Acrobatics	Flying	Physical	55	100	15	Normal
TM66	Payback	Dark	Physical	50	100	10	Normal
TM68	Giga Impact	Normal	Physical	150	90	5	Normal
TM71	Stone Edge	Rock	Physical	100	80	5	Normal
TM78	Bulldoze	Ground	Physical	60	100	20	Adjacent
TM80	Rock Slide	Rock	Physical	75	90	10	Many Others
TM84	Poison Jab	Poison	Physical	80	100	20	Normal
TM87	Swagger	Normal	Status	—	85	15	Normal
TM88	Sleep Talk	Normal	Status	—	—	10	Self
TM89	U-turn	Bug	Physical	70	100	20	Normal
TM90	Substitute	Normal	Status	—	—	10	Self
TM100	Confide	Normal	Status	—	—	20	Normal

◆ MOVES TAUGHT BY PEOPLE

Name	Type	Kind	Pow.	Acc.	PP	Range

◆ MOVES LEARNED WHEN EVOLVING

Name	Type	Kind	Pow.	Acc.	PP	Range
Rage	Normal	Physical	20	100	20	Normal

◆ EGG MOVES

Name	Type	Kind	Pow.	Acc.	PP	Range

◆ EXCLUSIVE Z-MOVE

Name	Base Move	Type	Kind	Pow.	Acc.	Range

Delibird

Alola Pokédex 081 081 — —
Melemele Akala Ula'ula Poni

Delivery Pokémon

ICE **FLYING**

HEIGHT: 2'11"
WEIGHT: 35.3 lbs.

Although it naturally prefers colder locales, Delibird in Alola seem able to withstand the heat to a certain extent.

It has a generous habit of sharing its food with people and Pokémon, so it's always scrounging around for more food.

Same form for male/female

ABILITY
Vital Spirit
Hustle

HIDDEN ABILITY
Insomnia

Damage taken in normal battles

NORMAL	×1	FIGHTING	×1	ROCK	×4
FIRE	×2	POISON	×1	GHOST	×1
WATER	×1	GROUND	×0	DRAGON	×1
GRASS	×0.5	FLYING	×1	DARK	×1
ELECTRIC	×2	PSYCHIC	×1	STEEL	×2
ICE	×1	BUG	×0.5	FAIRY	×1

SPECIES STRENGTHS
HP ◆◆
Attack ◆◆
Defense ◆◆◆
Sp. Atk ◆◆◆◆
Sp. Def ◆◆◆
Speed ◆◆◆◆◆

EGG GROUPS
Water 1 Field

ITEM SOMETIMES HELD BY WILD POKÉMON
—

EVOLUTION
Does not evolve

MAIN WAY TO REGISTER IN THE POKÉDEX
Catch in the tall grass on the north end of Route 3

❖ LEVEL-UP MOVES

Lv.	Name	Type	Kind	Pow.	Acc.	PP	Range
1	Present	Normal	Physical	—	90	15	Normal
25	Drill Peck	Flying	Physical	80	100	20	Normal

❖ TM MOVES

No.	Name	Type	Kind	Pow.	Acc.	PP	Range
TM06	Toxic	Poison	Status	—	90	10	Normal
TM07	Hail	Ice	Status	—	—	10	Both Sides
TM10	Hidden Power	Normal	Special	60	100	15	Normal
TM13	Ice Beam	Ice	Special	90	100	10	Normal
TM14	Blizzard	Ice	Special	110	70	5	Many Others
TM17	Protect	Normal	Status	—	—	10	Self
TM18	Rain Dance	Water	Status	—	—	5	Both Sides
TM21	Frustration	Normal	Physical	—	100	20	Normal
TM27	Return	Normal	Physical	—	100	20	Normal
TM31	Brick Break	Fighting	Physical	75	100	15	Normal
TM32	Double Team	Normal	Status	—	—	15	Self
TM40	Aerial Ace	Flying	Physical	60	—	20	Normal
TM42	Facade	Normal	Physical	70	100	20	Normal
TM44	Rest	Psychic	Status	—	—	10	Self
TM45	Attract	Normal	Status	—	100	15	Normal
TM46	Thief	Dark	Physical	60	100	25	Normal
TM48	Round	Normal	Special	60	100	15	Normal
TM56	Fling	Dark	Physical	—	100	10	Normal
TM59	Brutal Swing	Dark	Physical	60	100	20	Adjacent
TM70	Aurora Veil	Ice	Status	—	—	20	Your Side
TM76	Fly	Flying	Physical	90	95	15	Normal
TM79	Frost Breath	Ice	Special	60	90	10	Normal
TM87	Swagger	Normal	Status	—	85	15	Normal
TM88	Sleep Talk	Normal	Status	—	—	10	Self
TM90	Substitute	Normal	Status	—	—	10	Self
TM100	Confide	Normal	Status	—	—	20	Normal

❖ EXCLUSIVE Z-MOVE

Name	Base Move	Type	Kind	Pow.	Acc.	Range

❖ MOVES TAUGHT BY PEOPLE

Name	Type	Kind	Pow.	Acc.	PP	Range

❖ MOVES LEARNED WHEN EVOLVING

Name	Type	Kind	Pow.	Acc.	PP	Range

❖ EGG MOVES

Name	Type	Kind	Pow.	Acc.	PP	Range
Aurora Beam	Ice	Special	65	100	20	Normal
Quick Attack	Normal	Physical	40	100	30	Normal
Future Sight	Psychic	Special	120	100	10	Normal
Splash	Normal	Status	—	—	40	Self
Rapid Spin	Normal	Physical	20	100	40	Normal
Ice Ball	Ice	Physical	30	90	20	Normal
Ice Shard	Ice	Physical	40	100	30	Normal
Ice Punch	Ice	Physical	75	100	15	Normal
Take Out	Normal	Physical	40	100	10	Normal
Bestow	Normal	Status	—	—	15	Normal
Icy Wind	Ice	Special	55	95	15	Many Others
Freeze-Dry	Ice	Special	70	100	20	Normal
Destiny Bond	Ghost	Status	—	—	5	Normal
Spikes	Ground	Status	—	—	20	Other Side

Items Held by Wild Pokémon in Alola

Wild Pokémon in Alola sometimes hold an item you get when you catch them. Some of these items can be obtained in other ways, but these listed below can't be obtained in any other way in Alola.

Item	Pokémon that holds the item	Effects
Absorb Bulb	Petilil or Cottonee	Raises the holder's Sp. Atk by 1 when it is hit by a Water-type move. It goes away after use.
Black Belt	Makuhita	When held by a Pokémon, it boosts the power of Fighting-type moves by 20%.
Black Sludge	Alolan Grimer or Garbodor	If the holder is a Poison-type Pokémon, it restores 1/16 of its maximum HP every turn. If the holder is any other type, it loses 1/8 of its maximum HP every turn.
Cell Battery	Charjabug, Geodude, or Graveler	Increases Attack by 1 when the holder is hit with Electric-type moves. It goes away after use.
Electric Seed	Togedemaru	It boosts Defense of a Pokémon on Electric Terrain by 1 during battle. It can only be used once.
Grip Claw	Alolan Sandshrew	Extends the duration of moves like Bind and Wrap to seven turns.
Lagging Tail	Slowpoke	When held by a Pokémon, it makes it move later.
Luminous Moss	Corsola	Increases Sp. Def by 1 when the holder is hit with Water-type moves. It goes away after use.
Metal Coat	Magnemite, Skarmory, or Beldum	When held by a Pokémon, it boosts the power of Steel-type moves by 20%. Trade Onix or Scyther while they hold a Metal Coat to evolve them.
Metal Powder	Ditto	When held by Ditto, Defense doubles.
Psychic Seed	Exeggcute	It boosts Sp. Def of a Pokémon on Psychic Terrain by 1 during battle. It can only be used once.
Quick Powder	Ditto	When held by Ditto, Speed doubles.
Razor Claw	Kommo-o	Boosts the holder's critical-hit ratio.
Razor Fang	Bruxish	When the holder hits a target with an attack, there is a 10% chance the target will flinch.
Snowball	Snorunt or Alolan Vulpix	Increases Attack by 1 when the holder is hit with Ice-type moves. It goes away after use.
Thick Club	Cubone	When held by Cubone or Marowak, the power of physical moves is doubled.

These are useful items for battle. Some increase stats in certain conditions and some increase the power of certain moves. (See page 313 for a complete list of items held by wild Pokémon.)

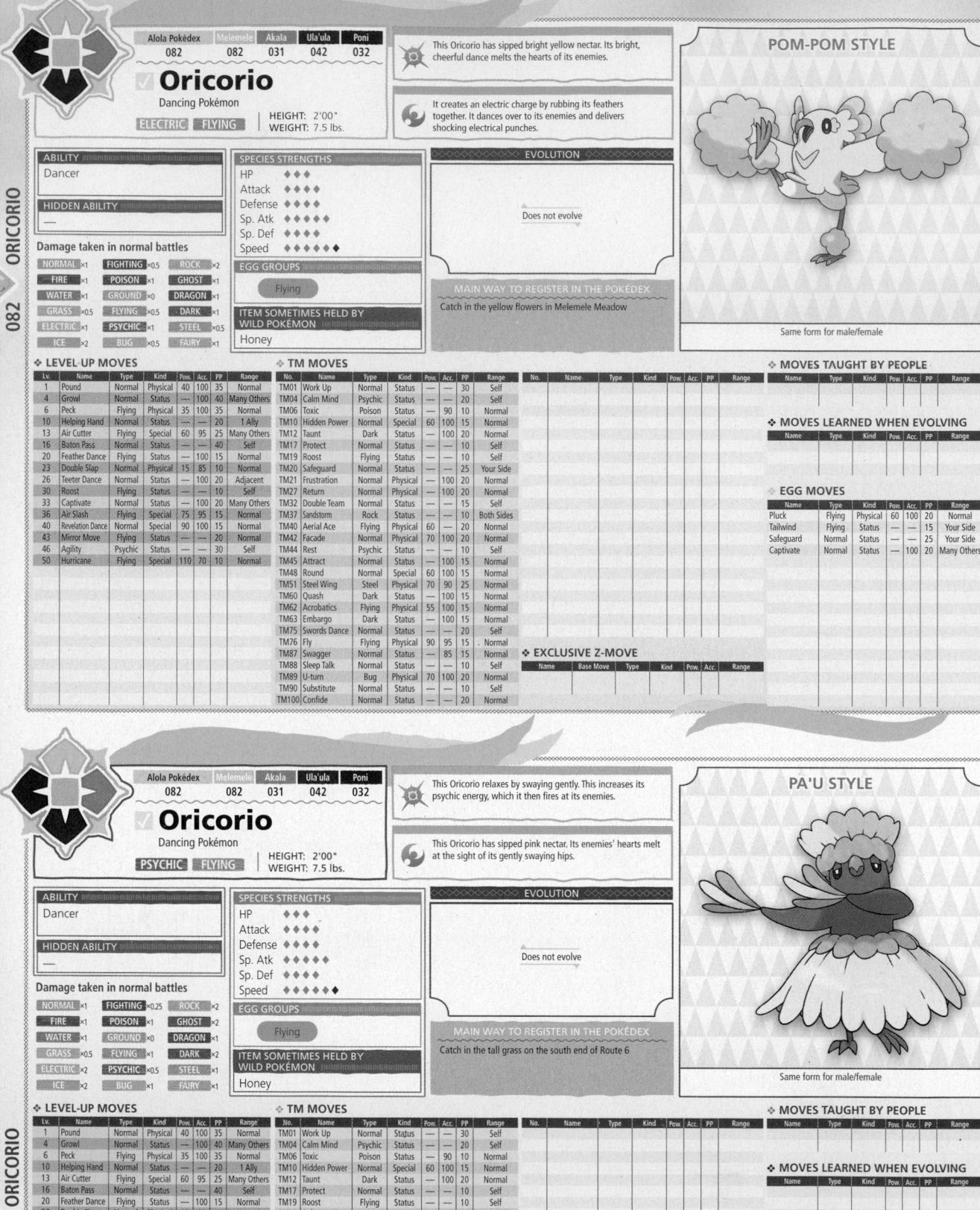

ORICORIO

POM-POM STYLE

Alola Pokédex	Melemele	Akala	Ula'ula	Poni
082	082	031	042	032

☑ **Oricorio**
Dancing Pokémon

ELECTRIC FLYING

HEIGHT: 2'00"
WEIGHT: 7.5 lbs.

This Oricorio has sipped bright yellow nectar. Its bright, cheerful dance melts the hearts of its enemies.

It creates an electric charge by rubbing its feathers together. It dances over to its enemies and delivers shocking electrical punches.

ABILITY
Dancer

HIDDEN ABILITY
—

SPECIES STRENGTHS
HP ◆◆◆
Attack ◆◆◆
Defense ◆◆◆◆
Sp. Atk ◆◆◆◆
Sp. Def ◆◆◆◆
Speed ◆◆◆◆◆◆

EVOLUTION
Does not evolve

MAIN WAY TO REGISTER IN THE POKÉDEX
Catch in the yellow flowers in Melemele Meadow

Same form for male/female

Damage taken in normal battles

NORMAL	×1	FIGHTING	×0.5	ROCK	×2
FIRE	×1	POISON	×1	GHOST	×1
WATER	×1	GROUND	×0	DRAGON	×1
GRASS	×0.5	FLYING	×0.5	DARK	×1
ELECTRIC	×1	PSYCHIC	×1	STEEL	×0.5
ICE	×2	BUG	×0.5	FAIRY	×1

EGG GROUPS
Flying

ITEM SOMETIMES HELD BY WILD POKÉMON
Honey

◆ LEVEL-UP MOVES

Lv.	Name	Type	Kind	Pow.	Acc.	PP	Range
1	Pound	Normal	Physical	40	100	35	Normal
4	Growl	Normal	Status	—	100	40	Many Others
6	Peck	Flying	Physical	35	100	35	Normal
10	Helping Hand	Normal	Status	—	—	20	1 Ally
13	Air Cutter	Flying	Special	60	95	25	Many Others
16	Baton Pass	Normal	Status	—	—	40	Self
20	Feather Dance	Flying	Status	—	100	15	Normal
23	Double Slap	Normal	Physical	15	85	10	Normal
26	Teeter Dance	Normal	Status	—	100	20	Adjacent
30	Roost	Flying	Status	—	—	10	Self
33	Captivate	Normal	Status	—	100	20	Many Others
36	Air Slash	Flying	Special	75	95	15	Normal
40	Revelation Dance	Normal	Special	90	100	15	Normal
43	Mirror Move	Flying	Status	—	—	20	Normal
46	Agility	Psychic	Status	—	—	30	Self
50	Hurricane	Flying	Special	110	70	10	Normal

◆ TM MOVES

No.	Name	Type	Kind	Pow.	Acc.	PP	Range
TM01	Work Up	Normal	Status	—	—	30	Self
TM04	Calm Mind	Psychic	Status	—	—	20	Self
TM06	Toxic	Poison	Status	—	90	10	Normal
TM10	Hidden Power	Normal	Special	60	100	15	Normal
TM12	Taunt	Dark	Status	—	100	20	Normal
TM17	Protect	Normal	Status	—	—	10	Self
TM19	Roost	Flying	Status	—	—	10	Self
TM20	Safeguard	Normal	Status	—	—	25	Your Side
TM21	Frustration	Normal	Physical	—	100	20	Normal
TM27	Return	Normal	Physical	—	100	20	Normal
TM32	Double Team	Normal	Status	—	—	15	Self
TM37	Sandstorm	Rock	Status	—	—	10	Both Sides
TM40	Aerial Ace	Flying	Physical	60	—	20	Normal
TM42	Facade	Normal	Physical	70	100	20	Normal
TM44	Rest	Psychic	Status	—	—	10	Self
TM45	Attract	Normal	Status	—	100	15	Normal
TM48	Round	Normal	Special	60	100	15	Normal
TM51	Steel Wing	Steel	Physical	70	90	25	Normal
TM60	Quash	Dark	Status	—	100	15	Normal
TM62	Acrobatics	Flying	Physical	55	100	15	Normal
TM63	Embargo	Dark	Status	—	100	15	Normal
TM75	Swords Dance	Normal	Status	—	—	20	Self
TM76	Fly	Flying	Physical	90	95	15	Normal
TM87	Swagger	Normal	Status	—	85	15	Normal
TM88	Sleep Talk	Normal	Status	—	—	10	Self
TM89	U-turn	Bug	Physical	70	100	20	Normal
TM90	Substitute	Normal	Status	—	—	10	Self
TM100	Confide	Normal	Status	—	—	20	Normal

◆ MOVES TAUGHT BY PEOPLE

Name	Type	Kind	Pow.	Acc.	PP	Range

◆ MOVES LEARNED WHEN EVOLVING

Name	Type	Kind	Pow.	Acc.	PP	Range

◆ EGG MOVES

Name	Type	Kind	Pow.	Acc.	PP	Range
Pluck	Flying	Physical	60	100	20	Normal
Tailwind	Flying	Status	—	—	15	Your Side
Safeguard	Normal	Status	—	—	25	Your Side
Captivate	Normal	Status	—	100	20	Many Others

◆ EXCLUSIVE Z-MOVE

Name	Base Move	Type	Kind	Pow.	Acc.	Range

PA'U STYLE

Alola Pokédex	Melemele	Akala	Ula'ula	Poni
082	082	031	042	032

☑ **Oricorio**
Dancing Pokémon

PSYCHIC FLYING

HEIGHT: 2'00"
WEIGHT: 7.5 lbs.

This Oricorio relaxes by swaying gently. This increases its psychic energy, which it then fires at its enemies.

This Oricorio has sipped pink nectar. Its enemies' hearts melt at the sight of its gently swaying hips.

ABILITY
Dancer

HIDDEN ABILITY
—

SPECIES STRENGTHS
HP ◆◆◆
Attack ◆◆◆◆
Defense ◆◆◆◆
Sp. Atk ◆◆◆◆◆
Sp. Def ◆◆◆◆
Speed ◆◆◆◆◆◆

EVOLUTION
Does not evolve

MAIN WAY TO REGISTER IN THE POKÉDEX
Catch in the tall grass on the south end of Route 6

Same form for male/female

Damage taken in normal battles

NORMAL	×1	FIGHTING	×0.25	ROCK	×2
FIRE	×1	POISON	×1	GHOST	×1
WATER	×1	GROUND	×0	DRAGON	×1
GRASS	×0.5	FLYING	×0.5	DARK	×1
ELECTRIC	×2	PSYCHIC	×0.5	STEEL	×1
ICE	×2	BUG	×1	FAIRY	×1

EGG GROUPS
Flying

ITEM SOMETIMES HELD BY WILD POKÉMON
Honey

◆ LEVEL-UP MOVES

Lv.	Name	Type	Kind	Pow.	Acc.	PP	Range
1	Pound	Normal	Physical	40	100	35	Normal
4	Growl	Normal	Status	—	100	40	Many Others
6	Peck	Flying	Physical	35	100	35	Normal
10	Helping Hand	Normal	Status	—	—	20	1 Ally
13	Air Cutter	Flying	Special	60	95	25	Many Others
16	Baton Pass	Normal	Status	—	—	40	Self
20	Feather Dance	Flying	Status	—	100	15	Normal
23	Double Slap	Normal	Physical	15	85	10	Normal
26	Teeter Dance	Normal	Status	—	100	20	Adjacent
30	Roost	Flying	Status	—	—	10	Self
33	Captivate	Normal	Status	—	100	20	Many Others
36	Air Slash	Flying	Special	75	95	15	Normal
40	Revelation Dance	Normal	Special	90	100	15	Normal
43	Mirror Move	Flying	Status	—	—	20	Normal
46	Agility	Psychic	Status	—	—	30	Self
50	Hurricane	Flying	Special	110	70	10	Normal

◆ TM MOVES

No.	Name	Type	Kind	Pow.	Acc.	PP	Range
TM01	Work Up	Normal	Status	—	—	30	Self
TM04	Calm Mind	Psychic	Status	—	—	20	Self
TM06	Toxic	Poison	Status	—	90	10	Normal
TM10	Hidden Power	Normal	Special	60	100	15	Normal
TM12	Taunt	Dark	Status	—	100	20	Normal
TM17	Protect	Normal	Status	—	—	10	Self
TM19	Roost	Flying	Status	—	—	10	Self
TM20	Safeguard	Normal	Status	—	—	25	Your Side
TM21	Frustration	Normal	Physical	—	100	20	Normal
TM27	Return	Normal	Physical	—	100	20	Normal
TM32	Double Team	Normal	Status	—	—	15	Self
TM37	Sandstorm	Rock	Status	—	—	10	Both Sides
TM40	Aerial Ace	Flying	Physical	60	—	20	Normal
TM42	Facade	Normal	Physical	70	100	20	Normal
TM44	Rest	Psychic	Status	—	—	10	Self
TM45	Attract	Normal	Status	—	100	15	Normal
TM48	Round	Normal	Special	60	100	15	Normal
TM51	Steel Wing	Steel	Physical	70	90	25	Normal
TM60	Quash	Dark	Status	—	100	15	Normal
TM62	Acrobatics	Flying	Physical	55	100	15	Normal
TM63	Embargo	Dark	Status	—	100	15	Normal
TM75	Swords Dance	Normal	Status	—	—	20	Self
TM76	Fly	Flying	Physical	90	95	15	Normal
TM87	Swagger	Normal	Status	—	85	15	Normal
TM88	Sleep Talk	Normal	Status	—	—	10	Self
TM89	U-turn	Bug	Physical	70	100	20	Normal
TM90	Substitute	Normal	Status	—	—	10	Self
TM100	Confide	Normal	Status	—	—	20	Normal

◆ MOVES TAUGHT BY PEOPLE

Name	Type	Kind	Pow.	Acc.	PP	Range

◆ MOVES LEARNED WHEN EVOLVING

Name	Type	Kind	Pow.	Acc.	PP	Range

◆ EGG MOVES

Name	Type	Kind	Pow.	Acc.	PP	Range
Pluck	Flying	Physical	60	100	20	Normal
Tailwind	Flying	Status	—	—	15	Your Side
Safeguard	Normal	Status	—	—	25	Your Side
Captivate	Normal	Status	—	100	20	Many Others

◆ EXCLUSIVE Z-MOVE

Name	Base Move	Type	Kind	Pow.	Acc.	Range

BAILE STYLE

✓ Oricorio
Dancing Pokémon

FIRE FLYING

HEIGHT: 2'00"
WEIGHT: 7.5 lbs.

It beats its wings together to create fire. As it moves in the steps of its beautiful dance, it bathes opponents in intense flames.

This Oricorio has sipped red nectar. Its passionate dance moves cause its enemies to combust in both body and mind.

ABILITY
Dancer

HIDDEN ABILITY
—

Damage taken in normal battles

NORMAL ×1	FIGHTING ×0.5	ROCK ×4
FIRE ×0.5	POISON ×1	GHOST ×1
WATER ×2	GROUND ×0	DRAGON ×1
GRASS ×0.25	FLYING ×1	DARK ×1
ELECTRIC ×2	PSYCHIC ×1	STEEL ×0.5
ICE ×2	BUG ×0.25	FAIRY ×0.5

SPECIES STRENGTHS
HP ◆◆◆
Attack ◆◆◆◆
Defense ◆◆◆◆
Sp. Atk ◆◆◆◆
Sp. Def ◆◆◆◆
Speed ◆◆◆◆◆◆

EGG GROUPS
Flying

ITEM SOMETIMES HELD BY WILD POKÉMON
Honey

EVOLUTION
Does not evolve

MAIN WAY TO REGISTER IN THE POKÉDEX
Catch in the tall grass or red flowers in Ula'ula Meadow

Same form for male/female

❖ LEVEL-UP MOVES

Lv.	Name	Type	Kind	Pow.	Acc.	PP	Range
1	Pound	Normal	Physical	40	100	35	Normal
4	Growl	Normal	Status	—	100	40	Many Others
6	Peck	Flying	Physical	35	100	35	Normal
10	Helping Hand	Normal	Status	—	—	20	1 Ally
13	Air Cutter	Flying	Special	60	95	25	Many Others
16	Baton Pass	Normal	Status	—	—	40	Self
20	Feather Dance	Flying	Status	—	100	15	Normal
23	Double Slap	Normal	Physical	15	85	10	Normal
26	Teeter Dance	Normal	Status	—	100	20	Adjacent
30	Roost	Flying	Status	—	—	10	Self
33	Captivate	Normal	Status	—	100	20	Many Others
36	Air Slash	Flying	Special	75	95	15	Normal
40	Revelation Dance	Normal	Special	90	100	15	Normal
43	Mirror Move	Flying	Status	—	—	20	Normal
46	Agility	Psychic	Status	—	—	30	Self
50	Hurricane	Flying	Special	110	70	10	Normal

❖ TM MOVES

No.	Name	Type	Kind	Pow.	Acc.	PP	Range
TM01	Work Up	Normal	Status	—	—	30	Self
TM04	Calm Mind	Psychic	Status	—	—	20	Self
TM06	Toxic	Poison	Status	—	90	10	Normal
TM10	Hidden Power	Normal	Special	60	100	15	Normal
TM12	Taunt	Dark	Status	—	100	20	Normal
TM17	Protect	Normal	Status	—	—	10	Self
TM19	Roost	Flying	Status	—	—	10	Self
TM20	Safeguard	Normal	Status	—	—	25	Your Side
TM21	Frustration	Normal	Physical	—	100	20	Normal
TM27	Return	Normal	Physical	—	100	20	Normal
TM32	Double Team	Normal	Status	—	—	15	Self
TM37	Sandstorm	Rock	Status	—	—	10	Both Sides
TM40	Aerial Ace	Flying	Physical	60	—	20	Normal
TM42	Facade	Normal	Physical	70	100	20	Normal
TM44	Rest	Psychic	Status	—	—	10	Self
TM45	Attract	Normal	Status	—	100	15	Normal
TM48	Round	Normal	Special	60	100	15	Normal
TM51	Steel Wing	Steel	Physical	70	90	25	Normal
TM60	Quash	Dark	Status	—	100	15	Normal
TM62	Acrobatics	Flying	Physical	55	100	15	Normal
TM63	Embargo	Dark	Status	—	100	15	Normal
TM75	Swords Dance	Normal	Status	—	—	20	Self
TM76	Fly	Flying	Physical	90	95	15	Normal
TM87	Swagger	Normal	Status	—	85	15	Normal
TM88	Sleep Talk	Normal	Status	—	—	10	Self
TM89	U-turn	Bug	Physical	70	100	20	Normal
TM90	Substitute	Normal	Status	—	—	10	Self
TM100	Confide	Normal	Status	—	—	20	Normal

❖ MOVES TAUGHT BY PEOPLE

Name	Type	Kind	Pow.	Acc.	PP	Range

❖ MOVES LEARNED WHEN EVOLVING

Name	Type	Kind	Pow.	Acc.	PP	Range

❖ EGG MOVES

Name	Type	Kind	Pow.	Acc.	PP	Range
Pluck	Flying	Physical	60	100	20	Normal
Tailwind	Flying	Status	—	—	15	Your Side
Safeguard	Normal	Status	—	—	25	Your Side
Captivate	Normal	Status	—	100	20	Many Others

❖ EXCLUSIVE Z-MOVE

Name	Base Move	Type	Kind	Pow.	Acc.	Range

SENSU STYLE

✓ Oricorio
Dancing Pokémon

GHOST FLYING

HEIGHT: 2'00"
WEIGHT: 7.5 lbs.

This Oricorio has sipped purple nectar. Its elegant, attractive dance will send the minds and hearts of its enemies to another world.

It summons the dead with its dreamy dancing. From their malice, it draws power with which to curse its enemies.

ABILITY
Dancer

HIDDEN ABILITY
—

Damage taken in normal battles

NORMAL ×0	FIGHTING ×0	ROCK ×2
FIRE ×1	POISON ×0.5	GHOST ×2
WATER ×1	GROUND ×0	DRAGON ×1
GRASS ×0.5	FLYING ×1	DARK ×1
ELECTRIC ×2	PSYCHIC ×1	STEEL ×1
ICE ×2	BUG ×0.25	FAIRY ×1

SPECIES STRENGTHS
HP ◆◆◆
Attack ◆◆◆◆
Defense ◆◆◆◆
Sp. Atk ◆◆◆◆◆
Sp. Def ◆◆◆◆
Speed ◆◆◆◆◆◆

EGG GROUPS
Flying

ITEM SOMETIMES HELD BY WILD POKÉMON
Honey

EVOLUTION
Does not evolve

MAIN WAY TO REGISTER IN THE POKÉDEX
Catch in the tall grass in Poni Meadow

Same form for male/female

❖ LEVEL-UP MOVES

Lv.	Name	Type	Kind	Pow.	Acc.	PP	Range
1	Pound	Normal	Physical	40	100	35	Normal
4	Growl	Normal	Status	—	100	40	Many Others
6	Peck	Flying	Physical	35	100	35	Normal
10	Helping Hand	Normal	Status	—	—	20	1 Ally
13	Air Cutter	Flying	Special	60	95	25	Many Others
16	Baton Pass	Normal	Status	—	—	40	Self
20	Feather Dance	Flying	Status	—	100	15	Normal
23	Double Slap	Normal	Physical	15	85	10	Normal
26	Teeter Dance	Normal	Status	—	100	20	Adjacent
30	Roost	Flying	Status	—	—	10	Self
33	Captivate	Normal	Status	—	100	20	Many Others
36	Air Slash	Flying	Special	75	95	15	Normal
40	Revelation Dance	Normal	Special	90	100	15	Normal
43	Mirror Move	Flying	Status	—	—	20	Normal
46	Agility	Psychic	Status	—	—	30	Self
50	Hurricane	Flying	Special	110	70	10	Normal

❖ TM MOVES

No.	Name	Type	Kind	Pow.	Acc.	PP	Range
TM01	Work Up	Normal	Status	—	—	30	Self
TM04	Calm Mind	Psychic	Status	—	—	20	Self
TM06	Toxic	Poison	Status	—	90	10	Normal
TM10	Hidden Power	Normal	Special	60	100	15	Normal
TM12	Taunt	Dark	Status	—	100	20	Normal
TM17	Protect	Normal	Status	—	—	10	Self
TM19	Roost	Flying	Status	—	—	10	Self
TM20	Safeguard	Normal	Status	—	—	25	Your Side
TM21	Frustration	Normal	Physical	—	100	20	Normal
TM27	Return	Normal	Physical	—	100	20	Normal
TM32	Double Team	Normal	Status	—	—	15	Self
TM37	Sandstorm	Rock	Status	—	—	10	Both Sides
TM40	Aerial Ace	Flying	Physical	60	—	20	Normal
TM42	Facade	Normal	Physical	70	100	20	Normal
TM44	Rest	Psychic	Status	—	—	10	Self
TM45	Attract	Normal	Status	—	100	15	Normal
TM48	Round	Normal	Special	60	100	15	Normal
TM51	Steel Wing	Steel	Physical	70	90	25	Normal
TM60	Quash	Dark	Status	—	100	15	Normal
TM62	Acrobatics	Flying	Physical	55	100	15	Normal
TM63	Embargo	Dark	Status	—	100	15	Normal
TM75	Swords Dance	Normal	Status	—	—	20	Self
TM76	Fly	Flying	Physical	90	95	15	Normal
TM87	Swagger	Normal	Status	—	85	15	Normal
TM88	Sleep Talk	Normal	Status	—	—	10	Self
TM89	U-turn	Bug	Physical	70	100	20	Normal
TM90	Substitute	Normal	Status	—	—	10	Self
TM100	Confide	Normal	Status	—	—	20	Normal

❖ MOVES TAUGHT BY PEOPLE

Name	Type	Kind	Pow.	Acc.	PP	Range

❖ MOVES LEARNED WHEN EVOLVING

Name	Type	Kind	Pow.	Acc.	PP	Range

❖ EGG MOVES

Name	Type	Kind	Pow.	Acc.	PP	Range
Pluck	Flying	Physical	60	100	20	Normal
Tailwind	Flying	Status	—	—	15	Your Side
Safeguard	Normal	Status	—	—	25	Your Side
Captivate	Normal	Status	—	100	20	Many Others

❖ EXCLUSIVE Z-MOVE

Name	Base Move	Type	Kind	Pow.	Acc.	Range

Alola Pokédex	Melemele	Akala	Ula'ula	Poni
083	083	—	043	033

☑ Cutiefly
Bee Fly Pokémon

BUG **FAIRY**

HEIGHT: 0'04"
WEIGHT: 0.4 lbs.

It feeds on the nectar and pollen of flowers. Because it's able to sense auras, it can identify which flowers are about to bloom.

Myriads of Cutiefly flutter above the heads of people who have auras resembling those of flowers.

ABILITY
Honey Gather
Shield Dust

HIDDEN ABILITY
Sweet Veil

Damage taken in normal battles

NORMAL ×1	FIGHTING ×0.25	ROCK ×2
FIRE ×2	POISON ×2	GHOST ×1
WATER ×1	GROUND ×0.5	DRAGON ×1
GRASS ×0.5	FLYING ×2	DARK ×0.5
ELECTRIC ×1	PSYCHIC ×1	STEEL ×2
ICE ×1	BUG ×0.5	FAIRY ×1

SPECIES STRENGTHS
HP ◆◆
Attack ◆◆◆
Defense ◆◆
Sp. Atk ◆◆◆
Sp. Def ◆◆
Speed ◆◆◆◆

EGG GROUPS
Bug · Fairy

ITEM SOMETIMES HELD BY WILD POKÉMON
Honey

EVOLUTION

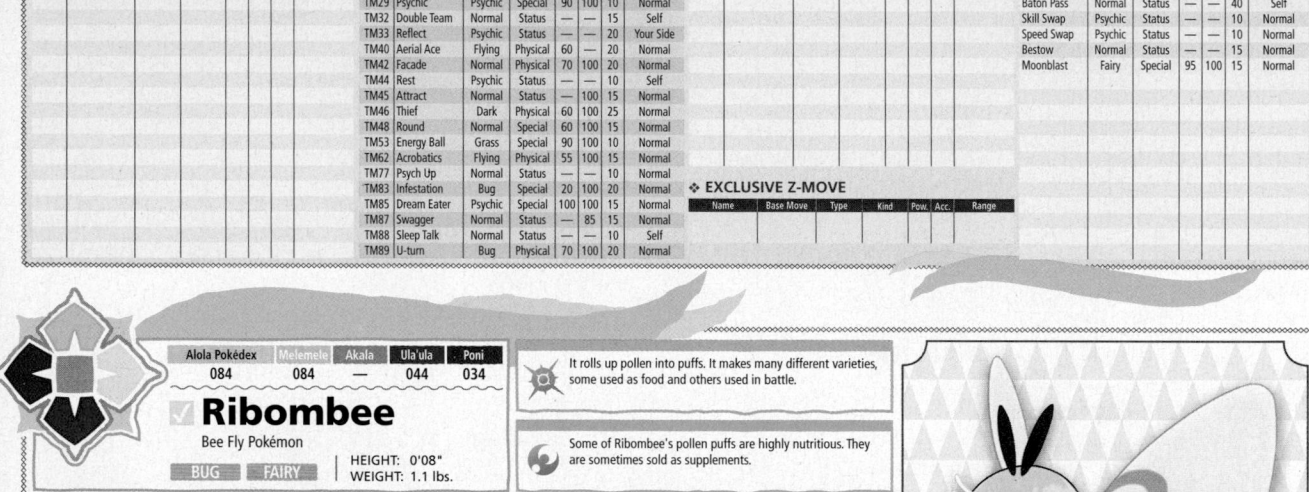

Cutiefly → (Lv. 25) → Ribombee

MAIN WAY TO REGISTER IN THE POKÉDEX
Catch in the tall grass on the north end of Route 3

Same form for male/female

◆ LEVEL-UP MOVES

Lv.	Name	Type	Kind	Pow.	Acc.	PP	Range
1	Absorb	Grass	Special	20	100	25	Normal
4	Fairy Wind	Fairy	Special	40	100	30	Normal
7	Stun Spore	Grass	Status	—	75	30	Normal
10	Struggle Bug	Bug	Special	50	100	20	Many Others
13	Silver Wind	Bug	Special	60	100	5	Normal
16	Draining Kiss	Fairy	Special	50	100	10	Normal
21	Sweet Scent	Normal	Status	—	100	20	Many Others
26	Bug Buzz	Bug	Special	90	100	10	Normal
31	Dazzling Gleam	Fairy	Special	80	100	10	Many Others
36	Aromatherapy	Grass	Status	—	—	5	Your Party
41	Quiver Dance	Bug	Status	—	—	20	Self

◆ TM MOVES

No.	Name	Type	Kind	Pow.	Acc.	PP	Range
TM04	Calm Mind	Psychic	Status	—	—	20	Self
TM06	Toxic	Poison	Status	—	90	10	Normal
TM10	Hidden Power	Normal	Special	60	100	15	Normal
TM11	Sunny Day	Fire	Status	—	—	5	Both Sides
TM16	Light Screen	Psychic	Status	—	—	30	Your Side
TM17	Protect	Normal	Status	—	—	10	Self
TM19	Roost	Flying	Status	—	—	10	Self
TM20	Safeguard	Normal	Status	—	—	25	Your Side
TM21	Frustration	Normal	Physical	—	100	20	Normal
TM27	Return	Normal	Physical	—	100	20	Normal
TM28	Leech Life	Bug	Physical	80	100	10	Normal
TM29	Psychic	Psychic	Special	90	100	10	Normal
TM32	Double Team	Normal	Status	—	—	15	Self
TM33	Reflect	Psychic	Status	—	—	20	Your Side
TM40	Aerial Ace	Flying	Physical	60	—	20	Normal
TM42	Facade	Normal	Physical	70	100	20	Normal
TM44	Rest	Psychic	Status	—	—	10	Self
TM45	Attract	Normal	Status	—	100	15	Normal
TM46	Thief	Dark	Physical	60	100	25	Normal
TM48	Round	Normal	Special	60	100	15	Normal
TM53	Energy Ball	Grass	Special	90	100	10	Normal
TM62	Acrobatics	Flying	Physical	55	100	15	Normal
TM77	Psych Up	Normal	Status	—	—	10	Normal
TM83	Infestation	Bug	Special	20	100	20	Normal
TM85	Dream Eater	Psychic	Special	100	100	15	Normal
TM87	Swagger	Normal	Status	—	85	15	Normal
TM88	Sleep Talk	Normal	Status	—	—	10	Self
TM89	U-turn	Bug	Physical	70	100	20	Normal
TM90	Substitute	Normal	Status	—	—	10	Self
TM99	Dazzling Gleam	Fairy	Special	80	100	10	Many Others
TM100	Confide	Normal	Status	—	—	20	Normal

◆ MOVES TAUGHT BY PEOPLE

Name	Type	Kind	Pow.	Acc.	PP	Range

◆ MOVES LEARNED WHEN EVOLVING

Name	Type	Kind	Pow.	Acc.	PP	Range

◆ EGG MOVES

Name	Type	Kind	Pow.	Acc.	PP	Range
Baton Pass	Normal	Status	—	—	40	Self
Skill Swap	Psychic	Status	—	—	10	Normal
Speed Swap	Psychic	Status	—	—	10	Normal
Bestow	Normal	Status	—	—	15	Normal
Moonblast	Fairy	Special	95	100	15	Normal

◆ EXCLUSIVE Z-MOVE

Name	Base Move	Type	Kind	Pow.	Acc.	Range

Alola Pokédex	Melemele	Akala	Ula'ula	Poni
084	084	—	044	034

☑ Ribombee
Bee Fly Pokémon

BUG **FAIRY**

HEIGHT: 0'08"
WEIGHT: 1.1 lbs.

It rolls up pollen into puffs. It makes many different varieties, some used as food and others used in battle.

Some of Ribombee's pollen puffs are highly nutritious. They are sometimes sold as supplements.

ABILITY
Honey Gather
Shield Dust

HIDDEN ABILITY
Sweet Veil

Damage taken in normal battles

NORMAL ×1	FIGHTING ×0.25	ROCK ×2
FIRE ×2	POISON ×2	GHOST ×1
WATER ×1	GROUND ×0.5	DRAGON ×0
GRASS ×0.5	FLYING ×2	DARK ×0.5
ELECTRIC ×1	PSYCHIC ×1	STEEL ×2
ICE ×1	BUG ×0.5	FAIRY ×1

SPECIES STRENGTHS
HP ◆◆
Attack ◆◆◆
Defense ◆◆◆
Sp. Atk ◆◆◆◆◆
Sp. Def ◆◆◆◆
Speed ◆◆◆◆◆◆◆

EGG GROUPS
Bug · Fairy

ITEM SOMETIMES HELD BY WILD POKÉMON
Honey

EVOLUTION

Cutiefly → (Lv. 25) → Ribombee

MAIN WAY TO REGISTER IN THE POKÉDEX
Catch in the tall grass or red flowers in Ula'ula Meadow

Same form for male/female

◆ LEVEL-UP MOVES

Lv.	Name	Type	Kind	Pow.	Acc.	PP	Range
1	Pollen Puff	Bug	Special	90	100	15	Normal
1	Absorb	Grass	Special	20	100	25	Normal
1	Fairy Wind	Fairy	Special	40	100	30	Normal
1	Stun Spore	Grass	Status	—	75	30	Normal
1	Struggle Bug	Bug	Special	50	100	20	Many Others
4	Fairy Wind	Fairy	Special	40	100	30	Normal
7	Stun Spore	Grass	Status	—	75	30	Normal
10	Struggle Bug	Bug	Special	50	100	20	Many Others
13	Silver Wind	Bug	Special	60	100	5	Normal
16	Draining Kiss	Fairy	Special	50	100	10	Normal
21	Sweet Scent	Normal	Status	—	100	20	Many Others
28	Bug Buzz	Bug	Special	90	100	10	Normal
35	Dazzling Gleam	Fairy	Special	80	100	10	Many Others
42	Aromatherapy	Grass	Status	—	—	5	Your Party
49	Quiver Dance	Bug	Status	—	—	20	Self

◆ TM MOVES

No.	Name	Type	Kind	Pow.	Acc.	PP	Range
TM04	Calm Mind	Psychic	Status	—	—	20	Self
TM06	Toxic	Poison	Status	—	90	10	Normal
TM10	Hidden Power	Normal	Special	60	100	15	Normal
TM11	Sunny Day	Fire	Status	—	—	5	Both Sides
TM16	Light Screen	Psychic	Status	—	—	30	Your Side
TM17	Protect	Normal	Status	—	—	10	Self
TM19	Roost	Flying	Status	—	—	10	Self
TM20	Safeguard	Normal	Status	—	—	25	Your Side
TM21	Frustration	Normal	Physical	—	100	20	Normal
TM22	Solar Beam	Grass	Special	120	100	10	Normal
TM27	Return	Normal	Physical	—	100	20	Normal
TM28	Leech Life	Bug	Physical	80	100	10	Normal
TM29	Psychic	Psychic	Special	90	100	10	Normal
TM32	Double Team	Normal	Status	—	—	15	Self
TM33	Reflect	Psychic	Status	—	—	20	Your Side
TM40	Aerial Ace	Flying	Physical	60	—	20	Normal
TM42	Facade	Normal	Physical	70	100	20	Normal
TM44	Rest	Psychic	Status	—	—	10	Self
TM45	Attract	Normal	Status	—	100	15	Normal
TM46	Thief	Dark	Physical	60	100	25	Normal
TM48	Round	Normal	Special	60	100	15	Normal
TM53	Energy Ball	Grass	Special	90	100	10	Normal
TM62	Acrobatics	Flying	Physical	55	100	15	Normal
TM77	Psych Up	Normal	Status	—	—	10	Normal
TM83	Infestation	Bug	Special	20	100	20	Normal
TM85	Dream Eater	Psychic	Special	100	100	15	Normal
TM87	Swagger	Normal	Status	—	85	15	Normal
TM88	Sleep Talk	Normal	Status	—	—	10	Self
TM89	U-turn	Bug	Physical	70	100	20	Normal
TM90	Substitute	Normal	Status	—	—	10	Self
TM96	Nature Power	Normal	Status	—	—	20	Normal
TM99	Dazzling Gleam	Fairy	Special	80	100	10	Many Others
TM100	Confide	Normal	Status	—	—	20	Normal

◆ MOVES TAUGHT BY PEOPLE

Name	Type	Kind	Pow.	Acc.	PP	Range

◆ MOVES LEARNED WHEN EVOLVING

Name	Type	Kind	Pow.	Acc.	PP	Range
Pollen Puff	Bug	Special	90	100	15	Normal

◆ EGG MOVES

Name	Type	Kind	Pow.	Acc.	PP	Range

◆ EXCLUSIVE Z-MOVE

Name	Base Move	Type	Kind	Pow.	Acc.	Range

Alola Pokédex	Melemele	Akala	Ula'ula	Poni
085	085	—	045	035

☑ Petilil

Bulb Pokémon

GRASS

HEIGHT: 1'08"
WEIGHT: 14.6 lbs.

Although the leaves on its head are bitter enough to cause dizziness, they provide relief from weariness—even more so when boiled.

By pruning the leaves on its head with regularity, this Pokémon can be grown into a fine plump shape.

Female only

ABILITY
Chlorophyll
Own Tempo

HIDDEN ABILITY
Leaf Guard

SPECIES STRENGTHS
HP ◆◆
Attack ◆◆
Defense ◆◆◆
Sp. Atk ◆◆◆◆
Sp. Def ◆◆◆
Speed ◆◆

EGG GROUPS
Grass

ITEM SOMETIMES HELD BY WILD POKÉMON
Absorb Bulb

EVOLUTION
Petilil → (Sun Stone) → Lilligant

MAIN WAY TO REGISTER IN THE POKÉDEX
Obtain in a trade in *Pokémon Sun* / Catch in Melemele Meadow in *Pokémon Moon*

Damage taken in normal battles
NORMAL ×1	FIGHTING ×1	ROCK ×1
FIRE ×2	POISON ×2	GHOST ×1
WATER ×0.5	GROUND ×0.5	DRAGON ×1
GRASS ×0.5	FLYING ×2	DARK ×1
ELECTRIC ×0.5	PSYCHIC ×1	STEEL ×1
ICE ×2	BUG ×2	FAIRY ×1

◆ LEVEL-UP MOVES
Lv.	Name	Type	Kind	Pow.	Acc.	PP	Range
1	Absorb	Grass	Special	20	100	25	Normal
4	Growth	Normal	Status	—	—	20	Self
8	Leech Seed	Grass	Status	—	90	10	Normal
10	Sleep Powder	Grass	Status	—	75	15	Normal
13	Mega Drain	Grass	Special	40	100	15	Normal
17	Synthesis	Grass	Status	—	—	5	Self
19	Magical Leaf	Grass	Special	60	—	20	Normal
22	Stun Spore	Grass	Status	—	75	30	Normal
26	Giga Drain	Grass	Special	75	100	10	Normal
28	Aromatherapy	Grass	Status	—	—	5	Your Party
31	Helping Hand	Normal	Status	—	—	20	1 Ally
35	Energy Ball	Grass	Special	90	100	10	Normal
37	Entrainment	Normal	Status	—	100	15	Normal
40	Sunny Day	Fire	Status	—	—	5	Both Sides
44	After You	Normal	Status	—	—	15	Normal
46	Leaf Storm	Grass	Special	130	90	5	Normal

◆ TM MOVES
No.	Name	Type	Kind	Pow.	Acc.	PP	Range
TM06	Toxic	Poison	Status	—	90	10	Normal
TM10	Hidden Power	Normal	Special	60	100	15	Normal
TM11	Sunny Day	Fire	Status	—	—	5	Both Sides
TM17	Protect	Normal	Status	—	—	10	Self
TM20	Safeguard	Normal	Status	—	—	25	Your Side
TM21	Frustration	Normal	Physical	—	100	20	Normal
TM22	Solar Beam	Grass	Special	120	100	10	Normal
TM27	Return	Normal	Physical	—	100	20	Normal
TM32	Double Team	Normal	Status	—	—	15	Self
TM42	Facade	Normal	Physical	70	100	20	Normal
TM44	Rest	Psychic	Status	—	—	10	Self
TM45	Attract	Normal	Status	—	100	15	Normal
TM48	Round	Normal	Special	60	100	15	Normal
TM53	Energy Ball	Grass	Special	90	100	10	Normal
TM85	Dream Eater	Psychic	Special	100	100	15	Normal
TM86	Grass Knot	Grass	Special	—	100	20	Normal
TM87	Swagger	Normal	Status	—	85	15	Normal
TM88	Sleep Talk	Normal	Status	—	—	10	Self
TM90	Substitute	Normal	Status	—	—	10	Self
TM96	Nature Power	Normal	Status	—	—	20	Normal
TM100	Confide	Normal	Status	—	—	20	Normal

◆ MOVES TAUGHT BY PEOPLE
Name	Type	Kind	Pow.	Acc.	PP	Range

◆ MOVES LEARNED WHEN EVOLVING
Name	Type	Kind	Pow.	Acc.	PP	Range

◆ EGG MOVES
Name	Type	Kind	Pow.	Acc.	PP	Range
Natural Gift	Normal	Physical	—	100	15	Normal
Charm	Fairy	Status	—	100	20	Normal
Endure	Normal	Status	—	—	10	Self
Ingrain	Grass	Status	—	—	20	Self
Worry Seed	Grass	Status	—	100	10	Normal
Grass Whistle	Grass	Status	—	55	15	Normal
Sweet Scent	Normal	Status	—	100	20	Many Others
Bide	Normal	Physical	—	—	10	Self
Healing Wish	Psychic	Status	—	—	10	Self

◆ EXCLUSIVE Z-MOVE
Name	Base Move	Type	Kind	Pow.	Acc.	Range

Alola Pokédex	Melemele	Akala	Ula'ula	Poni
086	086	—	046	036

☑ Lilligant

Flowering Pokémon

GRASS

HEIGHT: 3'07"
WEIGHT: 35.9 lbs.

No matter how much time and money is spent raising it, its flowers are the most beautiful when they bloom in the wild.

As soon as it finds a male to be its partner, the beautiful flower on its head darkens, droops, and withers away.

Female only

ABILITY
Chlorophyll
Own Tempo

HIDDEN ABILITY
Leaf Guard

SPECIES STRENGTHS
HP ◆◆◆
Attack ◆◆◆
Defense ◆◆◆◆
Sp. Atk ◆◆◆◆◆◆
Sp. Def ◆◆◆◆◆
Speed ◆◆◆◆◆◆

EGG GROUPS
Grass

ITEM SOMETIMES HELD BY WILD POKÉMON
—

EVOLUTION
Petilil → (Sun Stone) → Lilligant

MAIN WAY TO REGISTER IN THE POKÉDEX
Use a Sun Stone on Petilil

Damage taken in normal battles
NORMAL ×1	FIGHTING ×1	ROCK ×1
FIRE ×2	POISON ×2	GHOST ×1
WATER ×0.5	GROUND ×0.5	DRAGON ×1
GRASS ×0.5	FLYING ×2	DARK ×1
ELECTRIC ×0.5	PSYCHIC ×1	STEEL ×1
ICE ×2	BUG ×2	FAIRY ×1

◆ LEVEL-UP MOVES
Lv.	Name	Type	Kind	Pow.	Acc.	PP	Range
1	Growth	Normal	Status	—	—	20	Self
1	Leech Seed	Grass	Status	—	90	10	Normal
1	Mega Drain	Grass	Special	40	100	15	Normal
1	Synthesis	Grass	Status	—	—	5	Self
10	Teeter Dance	Normal	Status	—	100	20	Adjacent
28	Quiver Dance	Bug	Status	—	—	20	Self
46	Petal Dance	Grass	Special	120	100	10	1 Random
50	Petal Blizzard	Grass	Physical	90	100	15	Adjacent

◆ TM MOVES
No.	Name	Type	Kind	Pow.	Acc.	PP	Range
TM06	Toxic	Poison	Status	—	90	10	Normal
TM10	Hidden Power	Normal	Special	60	100	15	Normal
TM11	Sunny Day	Fire	Status	—	—	5	Both Sides
TM15	Hyper Beam	Normal	Special	150	90	5	Normal
TM16	Light Screen	Psychic	Status	—	—	30	Your Side
TM17	Protect	Normal	Status	—	—	10	Self
TM20	Safeguard	Normal	Status	—	—	25	Your Side
TM21	Frustration	Normal	Physical	—	100	20	Normal
TM22	Solar Beam	Grass	Special	120	100	10	Normal
TM27	Return	Normal	Physical	—	100	20	Normal
TM32	Double Team	Normal	Status	—	—	15	Self
TM42	Facade	Normal	Physical	70	100	20	Normal
TM44	Rest	Psychic	Status	—	—	10	Self
TM45	Attract	Normal	Status	—	100	15	Normal
TM48	Round	Normal	Special	60	100	15	Normal
TM53	Energy Ball	Grass	Special	90	100	10	Normal
TM68	Giga Impact	Normal	Physical	150	90	5	Normal
TM75	Swords Dance	Normal	Status	—	—	20	Self
TM85	Dream Eater	Psychic	Special	100	100	15	Normal
TM86	Grass Knot	Grass	Special	—	100	20	Normal
TM87	Swagger	Normal	Status	—	85	15	Normal
TM88	Sleep Talk	Normal	Status	—	—	10	Self
TM90	Substitute	Normal	Status	—	—	10	Self
TM96	Nature Power	Normal	Status	—	—	20	Normal
TM100	Confide	Normal	Status	—	—	20	Normal

◆ MOVES TAUGHT BY PEOPLE
Name	Type	Kind	Pow.	Acc.	PP	Range

◆ MOVES LEARNED WHEN EVOLVING
Name	Type	Kind	Pow.	Acc.	PP	Range

◆ EGG MOVES
Name	Type	Kind	Pow.	Acc.	PP	Range

◆ EXCLUSIVE Z-MOVE
Name	Base Move	Type	Kind	Pow.	Acc.	Range

Cottonee

Cotton Puff Pokémon

Alola Pokédex	Melemele	Akala	Ula'ula	Poni
087	087	—	047	037

GRASS | FAIRY

HEIGHT: 1'00"
WEIGHT: 1.3 lbs.

When it finds others of its kind, they all stick together. When enough of them have collected, the mass resembles a cumulonimbus cloud.

Pillows and beds stuffed with cotton exhaled by Cottonee are soft and puffy, light and airy—altogether top quality.

ABILITY
Prankster
Infiltrator

HIDDEN ABILITY
Chlorophyll

SPECIES STRENGTHS
HP	◆◆
Attack	◆◆
Defense	◆◆◆
Sp. Atk	◆◆
Sp. Def	◆◆◆
Speed	◆◆◆◆

Damage taken in normal battles
NORMAL ×1	FIGHTING ×0.5	ROCK ×1	
FIRE ×2	POISON ×4	GHOST ×1	
WATER ×0.5	GROUND ×0.5	DRAGON ×1	
GRASS ×0.5	FLYING ×2	DARK ×1	
ELECTRIC ×0.5	PSYCHIC ×1	STEEL ×1	
ICE ×2	BUG ×1	FAIRY ×1	

EGG GROUPS
Grass | Fairy

ITEM SOMETIMES HELD BY WILD POKÉMON
Absorb Bulb

EVOLUTION
Cottonee → (Sun Stone) → Whimsicott

MAIN WAY TO REGISTER IN THE POKÉDEX
Catch in Melemele Meadow in *Pokémon Sun* / Obtain in a trade in *Pokémon Moon*

Same form for male/female

◆ LEVEL-UP MOVES
Lv.	Name	Type	Kind	Pow.	Acc.	PP	Range
1	Absorb	Grass	Special	20	100	25	Normal
1	Fairy Wind	Fairy	Special	40	100	30	Normal
4	Growth	Normal	Status	—	—	20	Self
8	Leech Seed	Grass	Status	—	90	10	Normal
10	Stun Spore	Grass	Status	—	75	30	Normal
13	Mega Drain	Grass	Special	40	100	15	Normal
17	Cotton Spore	Grass	Status	—	100	40	Many Others
19	Razor Leaf	Grass	Physical	55	95	25	Many Others
22	Poison Powder	Poison	Status	—	75	35	Normal
26	Giga Drain	Grass	Special	75	100	10	Normal
28	Charm	Fairy	Status	—	100	20	Normal
31	Helping Hand	Normal	Status	—	—	20	1 Ally
35	Energy Ball	Grass	Special	90	100	10	Normal
37	Cotton Guard	Grass	Status	—	—	10	Self
40	Sunny Day	Fire	Status	—	—	5	Both Sides
44	Endeavor	Normal	Physical	—	100	5	Normal
46	Solar Beam	Grass	Special	120	100	10	Normal

◆ TM MOVES
No.	Name	Type	Kind	Pow.	Acc.	PP	Range
TM06	Toxic	Poison	Status	—	90	10	Normal
TM10	Hidden Power	Normal	Special	60	100	15	Normal
TM11	Sunny Day	Fire	Status	—	—	5	Both Sides
TM12	Taunt	Dark	Status	—	100	20	Normal
TM17	Protect	Normal	Status	—	—	10	Self
TM20	Safeguard	Normal	Status	—	—	25	Your Side
TM21	Frustration	Normal	Physical	—	100	20	Normal
TM22	Solar Beam	Grass	Special	120	100	10	Normal
TM27	Return	Normal	Physical	—	100	20	Normal
TM32	Double Team	Normal	Status	—	—	15	Self
TM42	Facade	Normal	Physical	70	100	20	Normal
TM44	Rest	Psychic	Status	—	—	10	Self
TM45	Attract	Normal	Status	—	100	15	Normal
TM48	Round	Normal	Special	60	100	15	Normal
TM53	Energy Ball	Grass	Special	90	100	10	Normal
TM85	Dream Eater	Psychic	Special	100	100	15	Normal
TM86	Grass Knot	Grass	Special	—	100	20	Normal
TM87	Swagger	Normal	Status	—	85	15	Normal
TM88	Sleep Talk	Normal	Status	—	—	10	Self
TM90	Substitute	Normal	Status	—	—	10	Self
TM96	Nature Power	Normal	Status	—	—	20	Normal
TM99	Dazzling Gleam	Fairy	Special	80	100	10	Many Others
TM100	Confide	Normal	Status	—	—	20	Normal

◆ MOVES TAUGHT BY PEOPLE
Name	Type	Kind	Pow.	Acc.	PP	Range

◆ MOVES LEARNED WHEN EVOLVING
Name	Type	Kind	Pow.	Acc.	PP	Range

◆ EGG MOVES
Name	Type	Kind	Pow.	Acc.	PP	Range
Natural Gift	Normal	Physical	—	100	15	Normal
Encore	Normal	Status	—	100	5	Normal
Tickle	Normal	Status	—	100	20	Normal
Fake Tears	Dark	Status	—	100	20	Normal
Grass Whistle	Grass	Status	—	55	15	Normal
Memento	Dark	Status	—	100	10	Normal
Beat Up	Dark	Physical	—	100	10	Normal
Switcheroo	Dark	Status	—	100	10	Normal
Worry Seed	Grass	Status	—	100	10	Normal
Captivate	Normal	Status	—	100	20	Many Others

◆ EXCLUSIVE Z-MOVE
Name	Base Move	Type	Kind	Pow.	Acc.	Range

Whimsicott

Windveiled Pokémon

Alola Pokédex	Melemele	Akala	Ula'ula	Poni
088	088	—	048	038

GRASS | FAIRY

HEIGHT: 2'04"
WEIGHT: 14.6 lbs.

It rides on the wind and slips into people's homes. After it has turned a room into a cotton-filled mess, it giggles to itself and takes off.

This Pokémon appears, riding upon the wind. But if the wind gusts up, it'll blow the cotton on this Pokémon's head clean off.

ABILITY
Prankster
Infiltrator

HIDDEN ABILITY
Chlorophyll

SPECIES STRENGTHS
HP	◆◆
Attack	◆◆◆◆
Defense	◆◆◆◆◆
Sp. Atk	◆◆◆◆
Sp. Def	◆◆◆◆
Speed	◆◆◆◆◆◆◆

Damage taken in normal battles
NORMAL ×1	FIGHTING ×0.5	ROCK ×1	
FIRE ×2	POISON ×4	GHOST ×1	
WATER ×0.5	GROUND ×0.5	DRAGON ×0	
GRASS ×0.5	FLYING ×2	DARK ×0.5	
ELECTRIC ×0.5	PSYCHIC ×1	STEEL ×1	
ICE ×2	BUG ×1	FAIRY ×1	

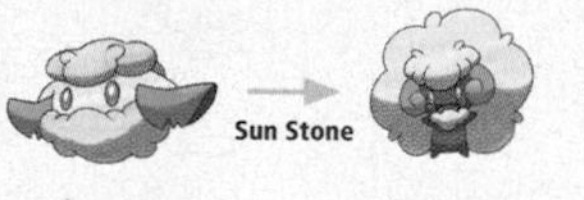

EGG GROUPS
Grass | Fairy

ITEM SOMETIMES HELD BY WILD POKÉMON
—

EVOLUTION
Cottonee → (Sun Stone) → Whimsicott

MAIN WAY TO REGISTER IN THE POKÉDEX
Use a Sun Stone on Cottonee

Same form for male/female

◆ LEVEL-UP MOVES
Lv.	Name	Type	Kind	Pow.	Acc.	PP	Range
1	Growth	Normal	Status	—	—	20	Self
1	Leech Seed	Grass	Status	—	90	10	Normal
1	Mega Drain	Grass	Special	40	100	15	Normal
1	Cotton Spore	Grass	Status	—	100	40	Many Others
10	Gust	Flying	Special	40	100	35	Normal
28	Tailwind	Flying	Status	—	—	15	Your Side
46	Hurricane	Flying	Special	110	70	10	Normal
50	Moonblast	Fairy	Special	95	100	15	Normal

◆ TM MOVES
No.	Name	Type	Kind	Pow.	Acc.	PP	Range
TM06	Toxic	Poison	Status	—	90	10	Normal
TM10	Hidden Power	Normal	Special	60	100	15	Normal
TM11	Sunny Day	Fire	Status	—	—	5	Both Sides
TM12	Taunt	Dark	Status	—	100	20	Normal
TM15	Hyper Beam	Normal	Special	150	90	5	Normal
TM16	Light Screen	Psychic	Status	—	—	30	Your Side
TM17	Protect	Normal	Status	—	—	10	Self
TM20	Safeguard	Normal	Status	—	—	25	Your Side
TM21	Frustration	Normal	Physical	—	100	20	Normal
TM22	Solar Beam	Grass	Special	120	100	10	Normal
TM27	Return	Normal	Physical	—	100	20	Normal
TM29	Psychic	Psychic	Special	90	100	10	Normal
TM30	Shadow Ball	Ghost	Special	80	100	15	Normal
TM32	Double Team	Normal	Status	—	—	15	Self
TM42	Facade	Normal	Physical	70	100	20	Normal
TM44	Rest	Psychic	Status	—	—	10	Self
TM45	Attract	Normal	Status	—	100	15	Normal
TM46	Thief	Dark	Physical	60	100	25	Normal
TM48	Round	Normal	Special	60	100	15	Normal
TM53	Energy Ball	Grass	Special	90	100	10	Normal
TM56	Fling	Dark	Physical	—	100	10	Normal
TM68	Giga Impact	Normal	Physical	150	90	5	Normal
TM85	Dream Eater	Psychic	Special	100	100	15	Normal
TM86	Grass Knot	Grass	Special	—	100	20	Normal
TM87	Swagger	Normal	Status	—	85	15	Normal
TM88	Sleep Talk	Normal	Status	—	—	10	Self
TM89	U-turn	Bug	Physical	70	100	20	Normal
TM90	Substitute	Normal	Status	—	—	10	Self

◆ MOVES TAUGHT BY PEOPLE
No.	Name	Type	Kind	Pow.	Acc.	PP	Range
TM92	Trick Room	Psychic	Status	—	—	5	Both Sides
TM96	Nature Power	Normal	Status	—	—	20	Normal
TM99	Dazzling Gleam	Fairy	Special	80	100	10	Many Others
TM100	Confide	Normal	Status	—	—	20	Normal

◆ MOVES LEARNED WHEN EVOLVING
Name	Type	Kind	Pow.	Acc.	PP	Range

◆ EGG MOVES
Name	Type	Kind	Pow.	Acc.	PP	Range

◆ EXCLUSIVE Z-MOVE
Name	Base Move	Type	Kind	Pow.	Acc.	Range

Psyduck
Duck Pokémon

Alola Pokédex		Melemele	Akala	Ula'ula	Poni
089		089	032	049	039

WATER

HEIGHT: 2'07"
WEIGHT: 43.2 lbs.

As a result of headaches so fierce they cause it to cry, it sometimes uses psychokinesis without meaning to.

This Pokémon is troubled by constant headaches. The more pain it's in, the more powerful its psychokinesis becomes.

ABILITY
Damp
Cloud Nine

HIDDEN ABILITY
Swift Swim

SPECIES STRENGTHS
HP ◆◆
Attack ◆◆◆
Defense ◆◆◆
Sp. Atk ◆◆◆◆
Sp. Def ◆◆◆
Speed ◆◆◆◆

EVOLUTION

Psyduck → Goalduck Lv. 33

Psyduck   Golduck

MAIN WAY TO REGISTER IN THE POKÉDEX
Catch on the water surface on Ten Carat Hill

Same form for male/female

Damage taken in normal battles

NORMAL	×1	FIGHTING	×1	ROCK	×1
FIRE	×0.5	POISON	×1	GHOST	×1
WATER	×0.5	GROUND	×1	DRAGON	×1
GRASS	×2	FLYING	×1	DARK	×1
ELECTRIC	×2	PSYCHIC	×1	STEEL	×0.5
ICE	×0.5	BUG	×1	FAIRY	×1

EGG GROUPS
Water 1   Field

ITEM SOMETIMES HELD BY WILD POKÉMON
—

❖ LEVEL-UP MOVES

Lv.	Name	Type	Kind	Pow.	Acc.	PP	Range
1	Water Sport	Water	Status	—	—	15	Both Sides
1	Scratch	Normal	Physical	40	100	35	Normal
4	Tail Whip	Normal	Status	—	100	30	Many Others
7	Water Gun	Water	Special	40	100	25	Normal
10	Confusion	Psychic	Special	50	100	25	Normal
13	Fury Swipes	Normal	Physical	18	80	15	Normal
16	Water Pulse	Water	Special	60	100	20	Normal
19	Disable	Normal	Status	—	100	20	Normal
22	Screech	Normal	Status	—	85	40	Normal
25	Zen Headbutt	Psychic	Physical	80	90	15	Normal
28	Aqua Tail	Water	Physical	90	90	10	Normal
31	Soak	Water	Status	—	100	20	Normal
34	Psych Up	Normal	Status	—	—	10	Normal
37	Amnesia	Psychic	Status	—	—	20	Self
40	Hydro Pump	Water	Special	110	80	5	Normal
43	Wonder Room	Psychic	Status	—	—	10	Both Sides

❖ TM MOVES

No.	Name	Type	Kind	Pow.	Acc.	PP	Range
TM03	Psyshock	Psychic	Special	80	100	10	Normal
TM04	Calm Mind	Psychic	Status	—	—	20	Self
TM06	Toxic	Poison	Status	—	90	10	Normal
TM07	Hail	Ice	Status	—	—	10	Both Sides
TM10	Hidden Power	Normal	Special	60	100	15	Normal
TM11	Ice Beam	Ice	Special	90	100	10	Normal
TM14	Blizzard	Ice	Special	110	70	5	Many Others
TM16	Light Screen	Psychic	Status	—	—	30	Your Side
TM17	Protect	Normal	Status	—	—	10	Self
TM18	Rain Dance	Water	Status	—	—	5	Both Sides
TM21	Frustration	Normal	Physical	—	100	20	Normal
TM27	Return	Normal	Physical	—	100	20	Normal
TM29	Psychic	Psychic	Special	90	100	10	Normal
TM31	Brick Break	Fighting	Physical	75	100	15	Normal
TM32	Double Team	Normal	Status	—	—	15	Self
TM40	Aerial Ace	Flying	Physical	60	—	20	Normal
TM42	Facade	Normal	Physical	70	100	20	Normal
TM44	Rest	Psychic	Status	—	—	10	Self
TM45	Attract	Normal	Status	—	100	15	Normal
TM48	Round	Normal	Special	60	100	15	Normal
TM55	Scald	Water	Special	80	100	15	Normal
TM56	Fling	Dark	Physical	—	100	10	Normal
TM65	Shadow Claw	Ghost	Physical	70	100	15	Normal
TM77	Psych Up	Normal	Status	—	—	10	Normal
TM87	Swagger	Normal	Status	—	85	15	Normal
TM88	Sleep Talk	Normal	Status	—	—	10	Self
TM90	Substitute	Normal	Status	—	—	10	Self
TM94	Surf	Water	Special	90	100	15	Adjacent

No.	Name	Type	Kind	Pow.	Acc.	PP	Range
TM98	Waterfall	Water	Physical	80	100	15	Normal
TM100	Confide	Normal	Status	—	—	20	Normal

❖ MOVES TAUGHT BY PEOPLE

Name	Type	Kind	Pow.	Acc.	PP	Range

❖ MOVES LEARNED WHEN EVOLVING

Name	Type	Kind	Pow.	Acc.	PP	Range

❖ EGG MOVES

Name	Type	Kind	Pow.	Acc.	PP	Range
Hypnosis	Psychic	Status	—	60	20	Normal
Psybeam	Psychic	Special	65	100	20	Normal
Foresight	Normal	Status	—	—	40	Normal
Future Sight	Psychic	Special	120	100	10	Normal
Cross Chop	Fighting	Physical	100	80	5	Normal
Refresh	Normal	Status	—	—	20	Self
Confuse Ray	Ghost	Status	—	100	10	Normal
Yawn	Normal	Status	—	—	10	Normal
Mud Bomb	Ground	Special	65	85	10	Normal
Encore	Normal	Status	—	100	5	Normal
Secret Power	Normal	Physical	70	100	20	Normal
Sleep Talk	Normal	Status	—	—	10	Self
Synchronoise	Psychic	Special	120	100	10	Adjacent
Simple Beam	Normal	Status	—	100	15	Normal
Clear Smog	Poison	Special	50	—	15	Normal

❖ EXCLUSIVE Z-MOVE

Name	Base Move	Type	Kind	Pow.	Acc.	Range

Golduck
Duck Pokémon

Alola Pokédex		Melemele	Akala	Ula'ula	Poni
090		090	033	050	040

WATER

HEIGHT: 5'07"
WEIGHT: 168.9 lbs.

It is said that the red part of its forehead grants supernatural powers to those who possess one, so it was over-hunted in the past.

It swims along the banks of lakes and catches fish Pokémon. It takes them to the shore and quietly eats them up.

ABILITY
Damp
Cloud Nine

HIDDEN ABILITY
Swift Swim

SPECIES STRENGTHS
HP ◆◆◆
Attack ◆◆◆
Defense ◆◆◆◆
Sp. Atk ◆◆◆◆◆
Sp. Def ◆◆◆◆◆
Speed ◆◆◆◆◆

EVOLUTION

Psyduck → Golduck Lv. 33

Psyduck   Golduck

MAIN WAY TO REGISTER IN THE POKÉDEX
Catch on the water surface in the caves of Vast Poni Canyon

Same form for male/female

Damage taken in normal battles

NORMAL	×1	FIGHTING	×1	ROCK	×1
FIRE	×0.5	POISON	×1	GHOST	×1
WATER	×0.5	GROUND	×1	DRAGON	×1
GRASS	×2	FLYING	×1	DARK	×1
ELECTRIC	×2	PSYCHIC	×1	STEEL	×0.5
ICE	×0.5	BUG	×1	FAIRY	×1

EGG GROUPS
Water 1   Field

ITEM SOMETIMES HELD BY WILD POKÉMON
—

❖ LEVEL-UP MOVES

Lv.	Name	Type	Kind	Pow.	Acc.	PP	Range
1	Me First	Normal	Status	—	—	20	Varies
1	Aqua Jet	Water	Physical	40	100	20	Normal
1	Water Sport	Water	Status	—	—	15	Both Sides
1	Scratch	Normal	Physical	40	100	35	Normal
1	Tail Whip	Normal	Status	—	100	30	Many Others
1	Water Gun	Water	Special	40	100	25	Normal
4	Tail Whip	Normal	Status	—	100	30	Many Others
7	Water Gun	Water	Special	40	100	25	Normal
10	Confusion	Psychic	Special	50	100	25	Normal
13	Fury Swipes	Normal	Physical	18	80	15	Normal
16	Water Pulse	Water	Special	60	100	20	Normal
19	Disable	Normal	Status	—	100	20	Normal
22	Screech	Normal	Status	—	85	40	Normal
25	Zen Headbutt	Psychic	Physical	80	90	15	Normal
28	Aqua Tail	Water	Physical	90	90	10	Normal
31	Soak	Water	Status	—	100	20	Normal
36	Psych Up	Normal	Status	—	—	10	Normal
41	Amnesia	Psychic	Status	—	—	20	Self
46	Hydro Pump	Water	Special	110	80	5	Normal
51	Wonder Room	Psychic	Status	—	—	10	Both Sides

❖ TM MOVES

No.	Name	Type	Kind	Pow.	Acc.	PP	Range
TM03	Psyshock	Psychic	Special	80	100	10	Normal
TM04	Calm Mind	Psychic	Status	—	—	20	Self
TM06	Toxic	Poison	Status	—	90	10	Normal
TM07	Hail	Ice	Status	—	—	10	Both Sides
TM10	Hidden Power	Normal	Special	60	100	15	Normal
TM13	Ice Beam	Ice	Special	90	100	10	Normal
TM14	Blizzard	Ice	Special	110	70	5	Many Others
TM15	Hyper Beam	Normal	Special	150	90	5	Normal
TM16	Light Screen	Psychic	Status	—	—	30	Your Side
TM17	Protect	Normal	Status	—	—	10	Self
TM18	Rain Dance	Water	Status	—	—	5	Both Sides
TM21	Frustration	Normal	Physical	—	100	20	Normal
TM27	Return	Normal	Physical	—	100	20	Normal
TM29	Psychic	Psychic	Special	90	100	10	Normal
TM31	Brick Break	Fighting	Physical	75	100	15	Normal
TM32	Double Team	Normal	Status	—	—	15	Self
TM40	Aerial Ace	Flying	Physical	60	—	20	Normal
TM42	Facade	Normal	Physical	70	100	20	Normal
TM44	Rest	Psychic	Status	—	—	10	Self
TM45	Attract	Normal	Status	—	100	15	Normal
TM47	Low Sweep	Fighting	Physical	65	100	20	Normal
TM48	Round	Normal	Special	60	100	15	Normal
TM52	Focus Blast	Fighting	Special	120	70	5	Normal
TM55	Scald	Water	Special	80	100	15	Normal
TM56	Fling	Dark	Physical	—	100	10	Normal
TM65	Shadow Claw	Ghost	Physical	70	100	15	Normal
TM68	Giga Impact	Normal	Physical	150	90	5	Normal
TM77	Psych Up	Normal	Status	—	—	10	Normal

No.	Name	Type	Kind	Pow.	Acc.	PP	Range
TM87	Swagger	Normal	Status	—	85	15	Normal
TM88	Sleep Talk	Normal	Status	—	—	10	Self
TM90	Substitute	Normal	Status	—	—	10	Self
TM94	Surf	Water	Special	90	100	15	Adjacent
TM98	Waterfall	Water	Physical	80	100	15	Normal
TM100	Confide	Normal	Status	—	—	20	Normal

❖ MOVES TAUGHT BY PEOPLE

Name	Type	Kind	Pow.	Acc.	PP	Range

❖ MOVES LEARNED WHEN EVOLVING

Name	Type	Kind	Pow.	Acc.	PP	Range

❖ EGG MOVES

Name	Type	Kind	Pow.	Acc.	PP	Range

❖ EXCLUSIVE Z-MOVE

Name	Base Move	Type	Kind	Pow.	Acc.	Range

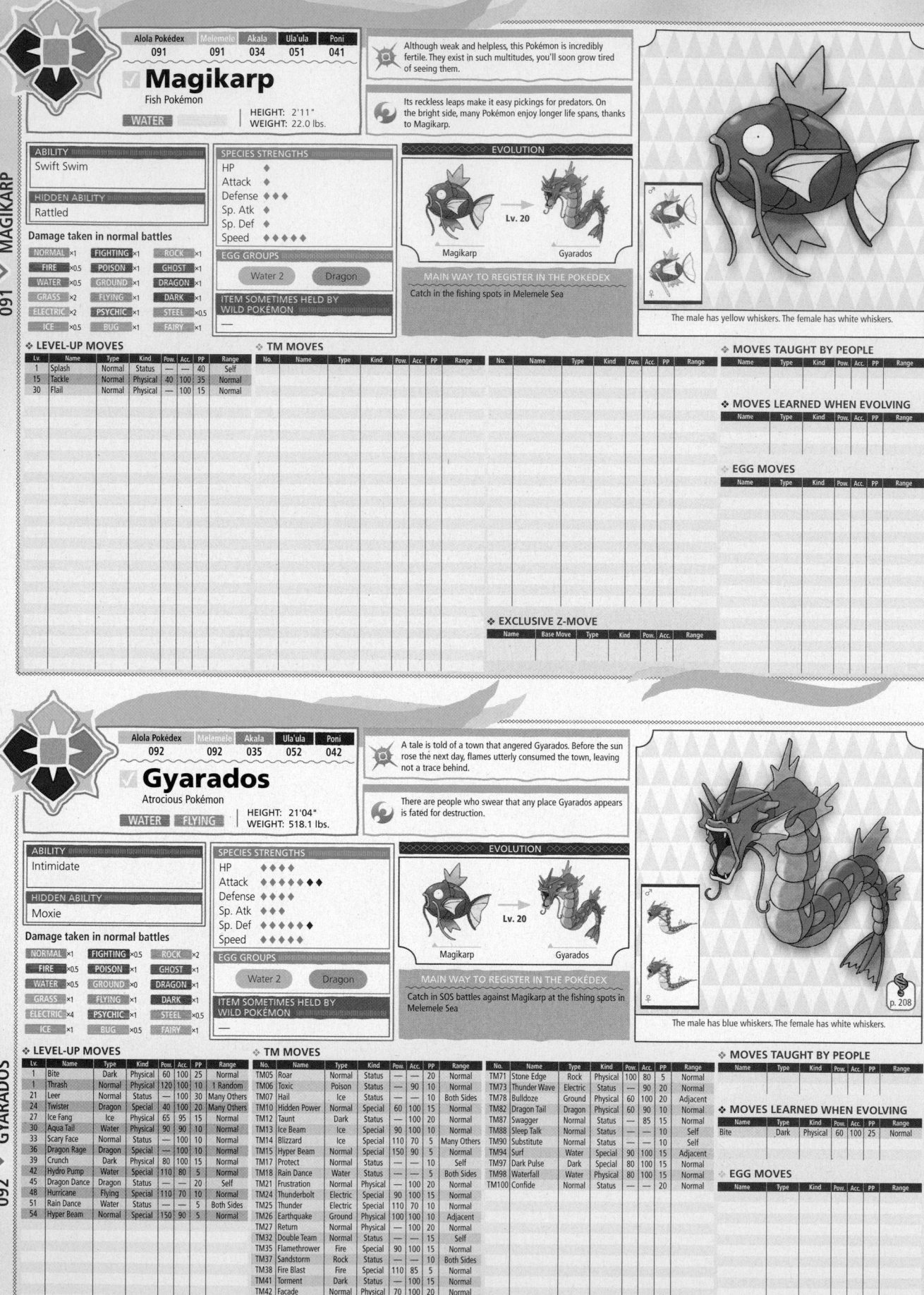

Alola Pokédex	Melemele	Akala	Ula'ula	Poni
091	091	034	051	041

☑ Magikarp
Fish Pokémon

WATER

HEIGHT: 2'11"
WEIGHT: 22.0 lbs.

Although weak and helpless, this Pokémon is incredibly fertile. They exist in such multitudes, you'll soon grow tired of seeing them.

Its reckless leaps make it easy pickings for predators. On the bright side, many Pokémon enjoy longer life spans, thanks to Magikarp.

ABILITY
Swift Swim

HIDDEN ABILITY
Rattled

SPECIES STRENGTHS
HP ◆
Attack ◆
Defense ◆◆◆
Sp. Atk ◆
Sp. Def ◆
Speed ◆◆◆◆◆

Damage taken in normal battles

NORMAL	×1	FIGHTING	×1	ROCK	×1
FIRE	×0.5	POISON	×1	GHOST	×1
WATER	×0.5	GROUND	×1	DRAGON	×1
GRASS	×2	FLYING	×1	DARK	×1
ELECTRIC	×2	PSYCHIC	×1	STEEL	×0.5
ICE	×0.5	BUG	×1	FAIRY	×1

EGG GROUPS
Water 2 | Dragon

ITEM SOMETIMES HELD BY WILD POKÉMON
—

EVOLUTION
Magikarp → (Lv. 20) → Gyarados

MAIN WAY TO REGISTER IN THE POKÉDEX
Catch in the fishing spots in Melemele Sea

The male has yellow whiskers. The female has white whiskers.

❖ LEVEL-UP MOVES

Lv.	Name	Type	Kind	Pow.	Acc.	PP	Range
1	Splash	Normal	Status	—	—	40	Self
15	Tackle	Normal	Physical	40	100	35	Normal
30	Flail	Normal	Physical	—	100	15	Normal

❖ TM MOVES

❖ MOVES TAUGHT BY PEOPLE
Name	Type	Kind	Pow.	Acc.	PP	Range

❖ MOVES LEARNED WHEN EVOLVING
Name	Type	Kind	Pow.	Acc.	PP	Range

❖ EGG MOVES
Name	Type	Kind	Pow.	Acc.	PP	Range

❖ EXCLUSIVE Z-MOVE
Name	Base Move	Type	Kind	Pow.	Acc.	Range

Alola Pokédex	Melemele	Akala	Ula'ula	Poni
092	092	035	052	042

☑ Gyarados
Atrocious Pokémon

WATER **FLYING**

HEIGHT: 21'04"
WEIGHT: 518.1 lbs.

A tale is told of a town that angered Gyarados. Before the sun rose the next day, flames utterly consumed the town, leaving not a trace behind.

There are people who swear that any place Gyarados appears is fated for destruction.

ABILITY
Intimidate

HIDDEN ABILITY
Moxie

SPECIES STRENGTHS
HP ◆◆◆◆
Attack ◆◆◆◆◆◆◆◆
Defense ◆◆◆◆
Sp. Atk ◆◆◆
Sp. Def ◆◆◆◆◆◆
Speed ◆◆◆◆◆

Damage taken in normal battles

NORMAL	×1	FIGHTING	×0.5	ROCK	×2
FIRE	×0.5	POISON	×1	GHOST	×1
WATER	×0.5	GROUND	×0	DRAGON	×1
GRASS	×1	FLYING	×1	DARK	×1
ELECTRIC	×4	PSYCHIC	×1	STEEL	×0.5
ICE	×1	BUG	×0.5	FAIRY	×1

EGG GROUPS
Water 2 | Dragon

ITEM SOMETIMES HELD BY WILD POKÉMON
—

EVOLUTION
Magikarp → (Lv. 20) → Gyarados

MAIN WAY TO REGISTER IN THE POKÉDEX
Catch in SOS battles against Magikarp at the fishing spots in Melemele Sea

p. 208

The male has blue whiskers. The female has white whiskers.

❖ LEVEL-UP MOVES

Lv.	Name	Type	Kind	Pow.	Acc.	PP	Range
1	Bite	Dark	Physical	60	100	25	Normal
1	Thrash	Normal	Physical	120	100	10	1 Random
21	Leer	Normal	Status	—	100	30	Many Others
24	Twister	Dragon	Special	40	100	20	Many Others
27	Ice Fang	Ice	Physical	65	95	15	Normal
30	Aqua Tail	Water	Physical	90	90	10	Normal
33	Scary Face	Normal	Status	—	100	10	Normal
36	Dragon Rage	Dragon	Special	—	100	10	Normal
39	Crunch	Dark	Physical	80	100	15	Normal
42	Hydro Pump	Water	Special	110	80	5	Normal
45	Dragon Dance	Dragon	Status	—	—	20	Self
48	Hurricane	Flying	Special	110	70	10	Normal
51	Rain Dance	Water	Status	—	—	5	Both Sides
54	Hyper Beam	Normal	Special	150	90	5	Normal

❖ TM MOVES

No.	Name	Type	Kind	Pow.	Acc.	PP	Range
TM05	Roar	Normal	Status	—	—	20	Normal
TM06	Toxic	Poison	Status	—	90	10	Normal
TM07	Hail	Ice	Status	—	—	10	Both Sides
TM10	Hidden Power	Normal	Special	60	100	15	Normal
TM12	Taunt	Dark	Status	—	100	20	Normal
TM13	Ice Beam	Ice	Special	90	100	10	Normal
TM14	Blizzard	Ice	Special	110	70	5	Many Others
TM15	Hyper Beam	Normal	Special	150	90	5	Normal
TM17	Protect	Normal	Status	—	—	10	Self
TM18	Rain Dance	Water	Status	—	—	5	Both Sides
TM21	Frustration	Normal	Physical	—	100	20	Normal
TM24	Thunderbolt	Electric	Special	90	100	15	Normal
TM25	Thunder	Electric	Special	110	70	10	Normal
TM26	Earthquake	Ground	Physical	100	100	10	Adjacent
TM27	Return	Normal	Physical	—	100	20	Normal
TM32	Double Team	Normal	Status	—	—	15	Self
TM35	Flamethrower	Fire	Special	90	100	15	Normal
TM37	Sandstorm	Rock	Status	—	—	10	Both Sides
TM38	Fire Blast	Fire	Special	110	85	5	Normal
TM41	Torment	Dark	Status	—	100	15	Normal
TM42	Facade	Normal	Physical	70	100	20	Normal
TM44	Rest	Psychic	Status	—	—	10	Self
TM45	Attract	Normal	Status	—	100	15	Normal
TM48	Round	Normal	Special	60	100	15	Normal
TM55	Scald	Water	Special	80	100	15	Normal
TM59	Brutal Swing	Dark	Physical	60	100	20	Adjacent
TM66	Payback	Dark	Physical	50	100	10	Normal
TM68	Giga Impact	Normal	Physical	150	90	5	Normal
TM71	Stone Edge	Rock	Physical	100	80	5	Normal
TM73	Thunder Wave	Electric	Status	—	90	20	Normal
TM78	Bulldoze	Ground	Physical	60	100	20	Adjacent
TM82	Dragon Tail	Dragon	Physical	60	90	10	Normal
TM87	Swagger	Normal	Status	—	85	15	Normal
TM88	Sleep Talk	Normal	Status	—	—	10	Self
TM90	Substitute	Normal	Status	—	—	10	Self
TM94	Surf	Water	Special	90	100	15	Adjacent
TM97	Dark Pulse	Dark	Special	80	100	15	Normal
TM98	Waterfall	Water	Physical	80	100	15	Normal
TM100	Confide	Normal	Status	—	—	20	Normal

❖ MOVES TAUGHT BY PEOPLE
Name	Type	Kind	Pow.	Acc.	PP	Range

❖ MOVES LEARNED WHEN EVOLVING
Name	Type	Kind	Pow.	Acc.	PP	Range
Bite	Dark	Physical	60	100	25	Normal

❖ EGG MOVES
Name	Type	Kind	Pow.	Acc.	PP	Range

❖ EXCLUSIVE Z-MOVE
Name	Base Move	Type	Kind	Pow.	Acc.	Range

Barboach

Whiskers Pokémon

Alola Pokédex	Melemele	Akala	Ula'ula	Poni
093	093	036	—	043

☑ WATER GROUND

HEIGHT: 1'04"
WEIGHT: 4.2 lbs.

Its two whiskers provide a sensitive radar. Even in muddy waters, it can detect its prey's location.

Its slippery body is hard to grasp, so much so that there are festivals where people compete to see how many they can catch barehanded.

ABILITY
Oblivious
Anticipation

HIDDEN ABILITY
Hydration

Damage taken in normal battles

NORMAL ×1	FIGHTING ×1	ROCK ×1			
FIRE ×0.5	POISON ×1	GHOST ×1			
WATER ×1	GROUND ×1	DRAGON ×1			
GRASS ×4	FLYING ×1	DARK ×1			
ELECTRIC ×0	PSYCHIC ×1	STEEL ×0.5			
ICE ×1	BUG ×1	FAIRY ×1			

SPECIES STRENGTHS
HP ◆◆
Attack ◆◆◆
Defense ◆◆
Sp. Atk ◆◆
Sp. Def ◆◆
Speed ◆◆◆◆

EGG GROUPS
Water 2

ITEM SOMETIMES HELD BY WILD POKÉMON
—

EVOLUTION

Barboach → (Lv. 30) → Whiscash

MAIN WAY TO REGISTER IN THE POKÉDEX
Catch in the fishing spot in Seaward Cave

Same form for male/female

❖ LEVEL-UP MOVES

Lv.	Name	Type	Kind	Pow.	Acc.	PP	Range
1	Mud-Slap	Ground	Special	20	100	10	Normal
6	Mud Sport	Ground	Status	—	—	15	Both Sides
6	Water Sport	Water	Status	—	—	15	Both Sides
9	Water Gun	Water	Special	40	100	25	Normal
13	Mud Bomb	Ground	Special	65	85	10	Normal
15	Amnesia	Psychic	Status	—	—	20	Self
17	Water Pulse	Water	Special	60	100	20	Normal
20	Magnitude	Ground	Physical	—	100	30	Adjacent
25	Rest	Psychic	Status	—	—	10	Self
25	Snore	Normal	Special	50	100	15	Normal
28	Aqua Tail	Water	Physical	90	90	10	Normal
32	Earthquake	Ground	Physical	100	100	10	Adjacent
35	Muddy Water	Water	Special	90	85	10	Many Others
39	Future Sight	Psychic	Special	120	100	10	Normal
44	Fissure	Ground	Physical	—	30	5	Normal

❖ TM MOVES

No.	Name	Type	Kind	Pow.	Acc.	PP	Range
TM06	Toxic	Poison	Status	—	90	10	Normal
TM07	Hail	Ice	Status	—	—	10	Both Sides
TM10	Hidden Power	Normal	Special	60	100	15	Normal
TM13	Ice Beam	Ice	Special	90	100	10	Normal
TM14	Blizzard	Ice	Special	110	70	5	Many Others
TM17	Protect	Normal	Status	—	—	10	Self
TM18	Rain Dance	Water	Status	—	—	5	Both Sides
TM21	Frustration	Normal	Physical	—	100	20	Normal
TM26	Earthquake	Ground	Physical	100	100	10	Adjacent
TM27	Return	Normal	Physical	—	100	20	Normal
TM32	Double Team	Normal	Status	—	—	15	Self
TM37	Sandstorm	Rock	Status	—	—	10	Both Sides
TM39	Rock Tomb	Rock	Physical	60	95	15	Normal
TM42	Facade	Normal	Physical	70	100	20	Normal
TM44	Rest	Psychic	Status	—	—	10	Self
TM45	Attract	Normal	Status	—	100	15	Normal
TM48	Round	Normal	Special	60	100	15	Normal
TM55	Scald	Water	Special	80	100	15	Normal
TM78	Bulldoze	Ground	Physical	60	100	20	Adjacent
TM87	Swagger	Normal	Status	—	85	15	Normal
TM88	Sleep Talk	Normal	Status	—	—	10	Self
TM90	Substitute	Normal	Status	—	—	10	Self
TM94	Surf	Water	Special	90	100	15	Adjacent
TM98	Waterfall	Water	Physical	80	100	15	Normal
TM100	Confide	Normal	Status	—	—	20	Normal

❖ MOVES TAUGHT BY PEOPLE

Name	Type	Kind	Pow.	Acc.	PP	Range

❖ MOVES LEARNED WHEN EVOLVING

Name	Type	Kind	Pow.	Acc.	PP	Range

❖ EGG MOVES

Name	Type	Kind	Pow.	Acc.	PP	Range
Thrash	Normal	Physical	120	100	10	1 Random
Whirlpool	Water	Special	35	85	15	Normal
Spark	Electric	Physical	65	100	20	Normal
Hydro Pump	Water	Special	110	80	5	Normal
Flail	Normal	Physical	—	100	15	Normal
Take Down	Normal	Physical	90	85	20	Normal
Dragon Dance	Dragon	Status	—	—	20	Self
Earth Power	Ground	Special	90	100	10	Normal
Mud Shot	Ground	Special	55	95	15	Normal
Muddy Water	Water	Special	90	85	10	Many Others

❖ EXCLUSIVE Z-MOVE

Name	Base Move	Type	Kind	Pow.	Acc.	Range

Whiscash

Whiskers Pokémon

Alola Pokédex	Melemele	Akala	Ula'ula	Poni
094	094	037	—	044

☑ WATER GROUND

HEIGHT: 2'11"
WEIGHT: 52.0 lbs.

A glutton that devours anything that moves, it quietly lurks at the bottom of swamps, lying in wait for prey.

Sighting Whiscash leaping from the water is believed to herald an earthquake.

ABILITY
Oblivious
Anticipation

HIDDEN ABILITY
Hydration

Damage taken in normal battles

NORMAL ×1	FIGHTING ×1	ROCK ×0.5			
FIRE ×0.5	POISON ×0.5	GHOST ×1			
WATER ×1	GROUND ×1	DRAGON ×1			
GRASS ×4	FLYING ×1	DARK ×1			
ELECTRIC ×0	PSYCHIC ×1	STEEL ×0.5			
ICE ×1	BUG ×1	FAIRY ×1			

SPECIES STRENGTHS
HP ◆◆◆◆
Attack ◆◆◆◆
Defense ◆◆◆◆
Sp. Atk ◆◆◆◆
Sp. Def ◆◆◆◆
Speed ◆◆◆◆

EGG GROUPS
Water 2

ITEM SOMETIMES HELD BY WILD POKÉMON
—

EVOLUTION

Barboach → (Lv. 30) → Whiscash

MAIN WAY TO REGISTER IN THE POKÉDEX
Catch in SOS battles against Barboach at the fishing spot in Seaward Cave

Same form for male/female

❖ LEVEL-UP MOVES

Lv.	Name	Type	Kind	Pow.	Acc.	PP	Range
1	Thrash	Normal	Physical	120	100	10	1 Random
1	Belch	Poison	Special	120	90	10	Normal
1	Zen Headbutt	Psychic	Physical	80	90	15	Normal
1	Tickle	Normal	Status	—	100	20	Normal
1	Mud-Slap	Ground	Special	20	100	10	Normal
1	Mud Sport	Ground	Status	—	—	15	Both Sides
1	Water Sport	Water	Status	—	—	15	Both Sides
1	Water Gun	Water	Special	40	100	25	Normal
6	Mud Sport	Ground	Status	—	—	15	Both Sides
6	Water Sport	Water	Status	—	—	15	Both Sides
9	Water Gun	Water	Special	40	100	25	Normal
13	Mud Bomb	Ground	Special	65	85	10	Normal
15	Amnesia	Psychic	Status	—	—	20	Self
17	Water Pulse	Water	Special	60	100	20	Normal
20	Magnitude	Ground	Physical	—	100	30	Adjacent
25	Rest	Psychic	Status	—	—	10	Self
25	Snore	Normal	Special	50	100	15	Normal
28	Aqua Tail	Water	Physical	90	90	10	Normal
34	Earthquake	Ground	Physical	100	100	10	Adjacent
39	Muddy Water	Water	Special	90	85	10	Many Others
45	Future Sight	Psychic	Special	120	100	10	Normal
52	Fissure	Ground	Physical	—	30	5	Normal

❖ TM MOVES

No.	Name	Type	Kind	Pow.	Acc.	PP	Range
TM06	Toxic	Poison	Status	—	90	10	Normal
TM07	Hail	Ice	Status	—	—	10	Both Sides
TM10	Hidden Power	Normal	Special	60	100	15	Normal
TM13	Ice Beam	Ice	Special	90	100	10	Normal
TM14	Blizzard	Ice	Special	110	70	5	Many Others
TM15	Hyper Beam	Normal	Special	150	90	5	Normal
TM17	Protect	Normal	Status	—	—	10	Self
TM18	Rain Dance	Water	Status	—	—	5	Both Sides
TM21	Frustration	Normal	Physical	—	100	20	Normal
TM26	Earthquake	Ground	Physical	100	100	10	Adjacent
TM27	Return	Normal	Physical	—	100	20	Normal
TM32	Double Team	Normal	Status	—	—	15	Self
TM37	Sandstorm	Rock	Status	—	—	10	Both Sides
TM39	Rock Tomb	Rock	Physical	60	95	15	Normal
TM42	Facade	Normal	Physical	70	100	20	Normal
TM44	Rest	Psychic	Status	—	—	10	Self
TM45	Attract	Normal	Status	—	100	15	Normal
TM48	Round	Normal	Special	60	100	15	Normal
TM55	Scald	Water	Special	80	100	15	Normal
TM68	Giga Impact	Normal	Physical	150	90	5	Normal
TM71	Stone Edge	Rock	Physical	100	80	5	Normal
TM78	Bulldoze	Ground	Physical	60	100	20	Adjacent
TM80	Rock Slide	Rock	Physical	75	90	10	Many Others
TM87	Swagger	Normal	Status	—	85	15	Normal
TM88	Sleep Talk	Normal	Status	—	—	10	Self
TM90	Substitute	Normal	Status	—	—	10	Self
TM94	Surf	Water	Special	90	100	15	Adjacent
TM98	Waterfall	Water	Physical	80	100	15	Normal

❖ MOVES TAUGHT BY PEOPLE

No.	Name	Type	Kind	Pow.	Acc.	PP	Range
TM100	Confide	Normal	Status	—	—	20	Normal

❖ MOVES LEARNED WHEN EVOLVING

Name	Type	Kind	Pow.	Acc.	PP	Range
Thrash	Normal	Physical	120	100	10	1 Random

❖ EGG MOVES

Name	Type	Kind	Pow.	Acc.	PP	Range

❖ EXCLUSIVE Z-MOVE

Name	Base Move	Type	Kind	Pow.	Acc.	Range

Machop

Superpower Pokémon

Alola Pokédex	Melemele	Akala	Ula'ula	Poni
095	095	—	—	045

FIGHTING

HEIGHT: 2'07"
WEIGHT: 43.0 lbs.

It loves working out. As it gazes at its muscles, which continue to swell day by day, it becomes more and more dedicated to its training.

With its superhuman strength, it's able to throw a hundred people all at the same time. Its strength comes from lifting Graveler every day.

ABILITY
Guts
No Guard

HIDDEN ABILITY
Steadfast

SPECIES STRENGTHS
HP ◆◆◆
Attack ◆◆◆◆
Defense ◆◆◆
Sp. Atk ◆◆
Sp. Def ◆◆
Speed ◆◆

Damage taken in normal battles

NORMAL	×1	FIGHTING	×1	ROCK	×0.5
FIRE	×1	POISON	×1	GHOST	×1
WATER	×1	GROUND	×1	DRAGON	×1
GRASS	×1	FLYING	×2	DARK	×0.5
ELECTRIC	×1	PSYCHIC	×2	STEEL	×1
ICE	×1	BUG	×0.5	FAIRY	×2

EGG GROUPS
Human-Like

ITEM SOMETIMES HELD BY WILD POKÉMON
Focus Band

EVOLUTION

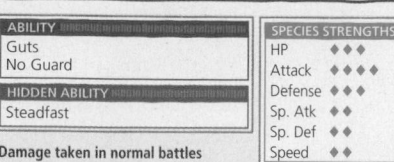

Machop → Lv. 28 → Machoke → Trade Machoke → Machamp

MAIN WAY TO REGISTER IN THE POKÉDEX
Receive in exchange for Spearow in the Pokémon Center on Route 2

Same form for male/female

Machoke

Superpower Pokémon

Alola Pokédex	Melemele	Akala	Ula'ula	Poni
096	096	—	—	046

FIGHTING

HEIGHT: 4'11"
WEIGHT: 155.4 lbs.

As a result of its continual workouts, it has developed tremendous power. It uses that power to help people with their work.

It willingly assists with hard labor because it knows the work is good training for its muscles.

ABILITY
Guts
No Guard

HIDDEN ABILITY
Steadfast

SPECIES STRENGTHS
HP ◆◆◆
Attack ◆◆◆◆◆
Defense ◆◆◆◆
Sp. Atk ◆◆◆
Sp. Def ◆◆◆
Speed ◆◆◆

Damage taken in normal battles

NORMAL	×1	FIGHTING	×1	ROCK	×0.5
FIRE	×1	POISON	×1	GHOST	×1
WATER	×1	GROUND	×1	DRAGON	×1
GRASS	×1	FLYING	×2	DARK	×0.5
ELECTRIC	×1	PSYCHIC	×2	STEEL	×1
ICE	×1	BUG	×0.5	FAIRY	×2

EGG GROUPS
Human-Like

ITEM SOMETIMES HELD BY WILD POKÉMON
Focus Band

EVOLUTION

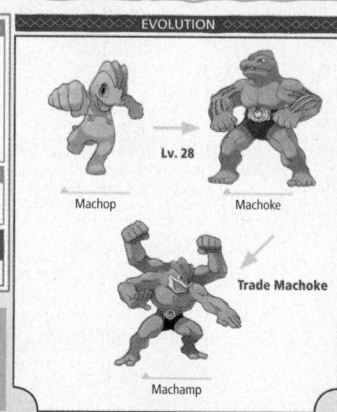

Machop → Lv. 28 → Machoke → Trade Machoke → Machamp

MAIN WAY TO REGISTER IN THE POKÉDEX
Catch in the tall grass in Vast Poni Canyon

Same form for male/female

Machamp

Superpower Pokémon

Alola Pokédex	Melemele	Akala	Ula'ula	Poni
097	097	—	—	047

FIGHTING

HEIGHT: 5'03"
WEIGHT: 286.6 lbs.

It unleashes megaton-level punches that send opponents flying clear over the horizon.

It can lift heavy loads with the greatest of ease. It can even heft dump trucks. But its clumsy fingers prevent it from doing any precision work.

ABILITY
Guts
No Guard

HIDDEN ABILITY
Steadfast

SPECIES STRENGTHS
HP ◆◆◆
Attack ◆◆◆◆◆◆◆
Defense ◆◆◆◆
Sp. Atk ◆◆◆
Sp. Def ◆◆◆◆
Speed ◆◆◆◆

Damage taken in normal battles

NORMAL	×1	FIGHTING	×1	ROCK	×0.5
FIRE	×1	POISON	×1	GHOST	×1
WATER	×1	GROUND	×1	DRAGON	×1
GRASS	×1	FLYING	×2	DARK	×0.5
ELECTRIC	×1	PSYCHIC	×2	STEEL	×1
ICE	×1	BUG	×0.5	FAIRY	×2

EGG GROUPS
Human-Like

ITEM SOMETIMES HELD BY WILD POKÉMON
—

EVOLUTION

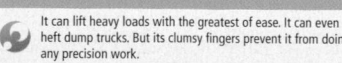

Machop → Lv. 28 → Machoke → Trade Machoke → Machamp

MAIN WAY TO REGISTER IN THE POKÉDEX
Receive a Machoke in a trade and it will evolve

Same form for male/female

MACHOP 095

MACHOKE 096

MACHAMP 097

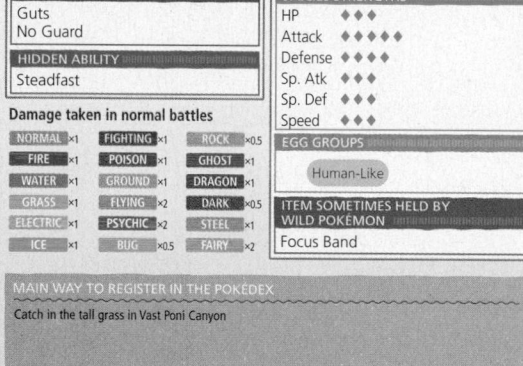

MACHOP 095

❖ LEVEL-UP MOVES

Lv.	Name	Type	Kind	Pow.	Acc.	PP	Range
1	Low Kick	Fighting	Physical	—	100	20	Normal
1	Leer	Normal	Status	—	100	30	Many Others
3	Focus Energy	Normal	Status	—	—	30	Self
7	Karate Chop	Fighting	Physical	50	100	25	Normal
9	Foresight	Normal	Status	—	—	40	Normal
13	Low Kick	Fighting	Physical	65	100	20	Normal
15	Seismic Toss	Fighting	Physical	—	100	20	Normal
19	Revenge	Fighting	Physical	60	100	10	Normal
21	Knock Off	Dark	Physical	65	100	20	Normal
25	Vital Throw	Fighting	Physical	70	—	10	Normal
27	Wake-Up Slap	Fighting	Physical	70	100	10	Normal
31	Dual Chop	Dragon	Physical	40	90	15	Normal
33	Submission	Fighting	Physical	80	80	20	Normal
37	Bulk Up	Fighting	Status	—	—	20	Self
39	Cross Chop	Fighting	Physical	100	80	5	Normal
43	Scary Face	Normal	Status	—	100	10	Normal
45	Dynamic Punch	Fighting	Physical	100	50	5	Normal

❖ TM MOVES

No.	Name	Type	Kind	Pow.	Acc.	PP	Range
TM01	Work Up	Normal	Status	—	—	30	Self
TM06	Toxic	Poison	Status	—	90	10	Normal
TM08	Bulk Up	Fighting	Status	—	—	20	Self
TM10	Hidden Power	Normal	Special	60	100	15	Normal
TM11	Sunny Day	Fire	Status	—	—	5	Both Sides
TM16	Light Screen	Psychic	Status	—	—	30	Your Side
TM17	Protect	Normal	Status	—	—	10	Self
TM18	Rain Dance	Water	Status	—	—	5	Both Sides
TM21	Frustration	Normal	Physical	—	100	20	Normal
TM23	Smack Down	Rock	Physical	50	100	15	Normal
TM26	Earthquake	Ground	Physical	100	100	10	Adjacent
TM27	Return	Normal	Physical	—	100	20	Normal
TM31	Brick Break	Fighting	Physical	75	100	15	Normal
TM32	Double Team	Normal	Status	—	—	15	Self
TM35	Flamethrower	Fire	Special	90	100	15	Normal
TM38	Fire Blast	Fire	Special	110	85	5	Normal
TM39	Rock Tomb	Rock	Physical	60	95	15	Normal
TM42	Facade	Normal	Physical	70	100	20	Normal
TM44	Rest	Psychic	Status	—	—	10	Self
TM45	Attract	Normal	Status	—	100	15	Normal
TM46	Thief	Dark	Physical	60	100	25	Normal
TM47	Low Sweep	Fighting	Physical	65	100	20	Normal
TM48	Round	Normal	Special	60	100	15	Normal
TM52	Focus Blast	Fighting	Special	120	70	5	Normal
TM56	Fling	Dark	Physical	—	100	10	Normal
TM66	Payback	Dark	Physical	50	100	10	Normal
TM78	Bulldoze	Ground	Physical	60	100	20	Adjacent

❖ MOVES TAUGHT BY PEOPLE

No.	Name	Type	Kind	Pow.	Acc.	PP	Range
TM80	Rock Slide	Rock	Physical	75	90	10	Many Others
TM84	Poison Jab	Poison	Physical	80	100	20	Normal
TM87	Swagger	Normal	Status	—	85	15	Normal
TM88	Sleep Talk	Normal	Status	—	—	10	Self
TM90	Substitute	Normal	Status	—	—	10	Self
TM100	Confide	Normal	Status	—	—	20	Normal

❖ MOVES LEARNED WHEN EVOLVING

Name	Type	Kind	Pow.	Acc.	PP	Range

❖ EGG MOVES

Name	Type	Kind	Pow.	Acc.	PP	Range
Meditate	Psychic	Status	—	—	40	Self
Rolling Kick	Fighting	Physical	60	85	15	Normal
Encore	Normal	Status	—	100	5	Normal
Smelling Salts	Normal	Physical	70	100	10	Normal
Counter	Fighting	Physical	—	100	20	Varies
Close Combat	Fighting	Physical	120	100	5	Normal
Fire Punch	Fire	Physical	75	100	15	Normal
Thunder Punch	Electric	Physical	75	100	15	Normal
Ice Punch	Ice	Physical	75	100	15	Normal
Bullet Punch	Steel	Physical	40	100	30	Normal
Power Trick	Psychic	Status	—	—	10	Self
Heavy Slam	Steel	Physical	—	100	10	Normal
Knock Off	Dark	Physical	65	100	20	Normal
Tickle	Normal	Status	—	—	20	Normal
Quick Guard	Fighting	Status	—	—	15	Your Side

❖ EXCLUSIVE Z-MOVE

Name	Base Move	Type	Kind	Pow.	Acc.	Range

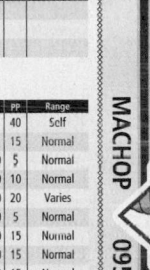

MACHOKE 096

❖ LEVEL-UP MOVES

Lv.	Name	Type	Kind	Pow.	Acc.	PP	Range
1	Low Kick	Fighting	Physical	—	100	20	Normal
1	Leer	Normal	Status	—	100	30	Many Others
1	Focus Energy	Normal	Status	—	—	30	Self
1	Karate Chop	Fighting	Physical	50	100	25	Normal
3	Focus Energy	Normal	Status	—	—	30	Self
7	Karate Chop	Fighting	Physical	50	100	25	Normal
9	Foresight	Normal	Status	—	—	40	Normal
13	Low Sweep	Fighting	Physical	65	100	20	Normal
15	Seismic Toss	Fighting	Physical	—	100	20	Normal
19	Revenge	Fighting	Physical	60	100	10	Normal
21	Knock Off	Dark	Physical	65	100	20	Normal
25	Vital Throw	Fighting	Physical	70	—	10	Normal
27	Wake-Up Slap	Fighting	Physical	70	100	10	Normal
33	Dual Chop	Dragon	Physical	40	90	15	Normal
37	Submission	Fighting	Physical	80	80	20	Normal
43	Bulk Up	Fighting	Status	—	—	20	Self
47	Cross Chop	Fighting	Physical	100	80	5	Normal
53	Scary Face	Normal	Status	—	100	10	Normal
57	Dynamic Punch	Fighting	Physical	100	50	5	Normal

❖ TM MOVES

No.	Name	Type	Kind	Pow.	Acc.	PP	Range
TM01	Work Up	Normal	Status	—	—	30	Self
TM06	Toxic	Poison	Status	—	90	10	Normal
TM08	Bulk Up	Fighting	Status	—	—	20	Self
TM10	Hidden Power	Normal	Special	60	100	15	Normal
TM11	Sunny Day	Fire	Status	—	—	5	Both Sides
TM16	Light Screen	Psychic	Status	—	—	30	Your Side
TM17	Protect	Normal	Status	—	—	10	Self
TM18	Rain Dance	Water	Status	—	—	5	Both Sides
TM21	Frustration	Normal	Physical	—	100	20	Normal
TM23	Smack Down	Rock	Physical	50	100	15	Normal
TM26	Earthquake	Ground	Physical	100	100	10	Adjacent
TM27	Return	Normal	Physical	—	100	20	Normal
TM31	Brick Break	Fighting	Physical	75	100	15	Normal
TM32	Double Team	Normal	Status	—	—	15	Self
TM35	Flamethrower	Fire	Special	90	100	15	Normal
TM38	Fire Blast	Fire	Special	110	85	5	Normal
TM39	Rock Tomb	Rock	Physical	60	95	15	Normal
TM42	Facade	Normal	Physical	70	100	20	Normal
TM44	Rest	Psychic	Status	—	—	10	Self
TM45	Attract	Normal	Status	—	100	15	Normal
TM46	Thief	Dark	Physical	60	100	25	Normal
TM47	Low Sweep	Fighting	Physical	65	100	20	Normal
TM48	Round	Normal	Special	60	100	15	Normal
TM52	Focus Blast	Fighting	Special	120	70	5	Normal
TM56	Fling	Dark	Physical	—	100	10	Normal
TM66	Payback	Dark	Physical	50	100	10	Normal
TM78	Bulldoze	Ground	Physical	60	100	20	Adjacent

❖ MOVES TAUGHT BY PEOPLE

No.	Name	Type	Kind	Pow.	Acc.	PP	Range
TM80	Rock Slide	Rock	Physical	75	90	10	Many Others
TM84	Poison Jab	Poison	Physical	80	100	20	Normal
TM87	Swagger	Normal	Status	—	85	15	Normal
TM88	Sleep Talk	Normal	Status	—	—	10	Self
TM90	Substitute	Normal	Status	—	—	10	Self
TM100	Confide	Normal	Status	—	—	20	Normal

❖ MOVES LEARNED WHEN EVOLVING

Name	Type	Kind	Pow.	Acc.	PP	Range

❖ EGG MOVES

Name	Type	Kind	Pow.	Acc.	PP	Range

❖ EXCLUSIVE Z-MOVE

Name	Base Move	Type	Kind	Pow.	Acc.	Range

MACHAMP 097

❖ LEVEL-UP MOVES

Lv.	Name	Type	Kind	Pow.	Acc.	PP	Range
1	Strength	Normal	Physical	80	100	15	Normal
1	Wide Guard	Rock	Status	—	—	10	Your Side
1	Low Kick	Fighting	Physical	—	100	20	Normal
1	Leer	Normal	Status	—	100	30	Many Others
1	Focus Energy	Normal	Status	—	—	30	Self
1	Karate Chop	Fighting	Physical	50	100	25	Normal
3	Focus Energy	Normal	Status	—	—	30	Self
7	Karate Chop	Fighting	Physical	50	100	25	Normal
9	Foresight	Normal	Status	—	—	40	Normal
13	Low Sweep	Fighting	Physical	65	100	20	Normal
15	Seismic Toss	Fighting	Physical	—	100	20	Normal
19	Revenge	Fighting	Physical	60	100	10	Normal
21	Knock Off	Dark	Physical	65	100	20	Normal
25	Vital Throw	Fighting	Physical	70	—	10	Normal
27	Wake-Up Slap	Fighting	Physical	70	100	10	Normal
33	Dual Chop	Dragon	Physical	40	90	15	Normal
37	Submission	Fighting	Physical	80	80	20	Normal
43	Bulk Up	Fighting	Status	—	—	20	Self
47	Cross Chop	Fighting	Physical	100	80	5	Normal
53	Scary Face	Normal	Status	—	100	10	Normal
57	Dynamic Punch	Fighting	Physical	100	50	5	Normal

❖ TM MOVES

No.	Name	Type	Kind	Pow.	Acc.	PP	Range
TM01	Work Up	Normal	Status	—	—	30	Self
TM06	Toxic	Poison	Status	—	90	10	Normal
TM08	Bulk Up	Fighting	Status	—	—	20	Self
TM10	Hidden Power	Normal	Special	60	100	15	Normal
TM11	Sunny Day	Fire	Status	—	—	5	Both Sides
TM15	Hyper Beam	Normal	Special	150	90	5	Normal
TM16	Light Screen	Psychic	Status	—	—	30	Your Side
TM17	Protect	Normal	Status	—	—	10	Self
TM18	Rain Dance	Water	Status	—	—	5	Both Sides
TM21	Frustration	Normal	Physical	—	100	20	Normal
TM23	Smack Down	Rock	Physical	50	100	15	Normal
TM26	Earthquake	Ground	Physical	100	100	10	Adjacent
TM27	Return	Normal	Physical	—	100	20	Normal
TM31	Brick Break	Fighting	Physical	75	100	15	Normal
TM32	Double Team	Normal	Status	—	—	15	Self
TM35	Flamethrower	Fire	Special	90	100	15	Normal
TM38	Fire Blast	Fire	Special	110	85	5	Normal
TM39	Rock Tomb	Rock	Physical	60	95	15	Normal
TM42	Facade	Normal	Physical	70	100	20	Normal
TM44	Rest	Psychic	Status	—	—	10	Self
TM45	Attract	Normal	Status	—	100	15	Normal
TM46	Thief	Dark	Physical	60	100	25	Normal
TM47	Low Sweep	Fighting	Physical	65	100	20	Normal
TM48	Round	Normal	Special	60	100	15	Normal
TM52	Focus Blast	Fighting	Special	120	70	5	Normal
TM56	Fling	Dark	Physical	—	100	10	Normal
TM66	Payback	Dark	Physical	50	100	10	Normal

❖ MOVES TAUGHT BY PEOPLE

No.	Name	Type	Kind	Pow.	Acc.	PP	Range
TM68	Giga Impact	Normal	Physical	150	90	5	Normal
TM71	Stone Edge	Rock	Physical	100	80	5	Normal
TM78	Bulldoze	Ground	Physical	60	100	20	Adjacent
TM80	Rock Slide	Rock	Physical	75	90	10	Many Others
TM84	Poison Jab	Poison	Physical	80	100	20	Normal
TM87	Swagger	Normal	Status	—	85	15	Normal
TM88	Sleep Talk	Normal	Status	—	—	10	Self
TM90	Substitute	Normal	Status	—	—	10	Self
TM100	Confide	Normal	Status	—	—	20	Normal

❖ MOVES LEARNED WHEN EVOLVING

Name	Type	Kind	Pow.	Acc.	PP	Range
Strength	Normal	Physical	80	100	15	Normal

❖ EGG MOVES

Name	Type	Kind	Pow.	Acc.	PP	Range

❖ EXCLUSIVE Z-MOVE

Name	Base Move	Type	Kind	Pow.	Acc.	Range

Alola Pokédex	Melemele	Akala	Ula'ula	Poni
098	098	—	—	048

☑ Roggenrola
Mantle Pokémon

`ROCK`

HEIGHT: 1'04"
WEIGHT: 39.7 lbs.

Born deep within the ground, it compares itself with similar species, such as Geodude and Carbink, to settle which has the hardest body.

The hexagonal cavity is its ear. It walks in the direction of sounds it hears, but if the sounds cease, it panics and topples over.

ABILITY
Sturdy
Weak Armor

HIDDEN ABILITY
Sand Force

SPECIES STRENGTHS
HP ◆◆
Attack ◆◆◆◆
Defense ◆◆◆◆◆
Sp. Atk ◆
Sp. Def ◆
Speed ◆

Damage taken in normal battles

NORMAL ×0.5	FIGHTING ×2	ROCK ×1
FIRE ×0.5	POISON ×0.5	GHOST ×1
WATER ×2	GROUND ×2	DRAGON ×1
GRASS ×2	FLYING ×1	DARK ×1
ELECTRIC ×1	PSYCHIC ×1	STEEL ×1
ICE ×1	BUG ×1	FAIRY ×1

EGG GROUPS
Mineral

ITEM SOMETIMES HELD BY WILD POKÉMON
Everstone / Hard Stone

EVOLUTION
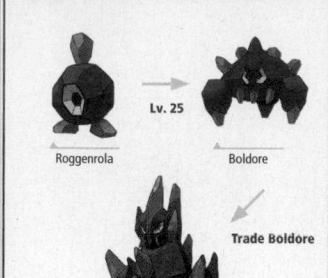
Roggenrola — **Lv. 25** → Boldore
↘ **Trade Boldore**
Gigalith

MAIN WAY TO REGISTER IN THE POKÉDEX
Catch in the tall grass or the cave on Ten Carat Hill

Same form for male/female

Alola Pokédex	Melemele	Akala	Ula'ula	Poni
099	099	—	—	049

☑ Boldore
Ore Pokémon

`ROCK`

HEIGHT: 2'11"
WEIGHT: 224.9 lbs.

Its orange crystal is a mass of energy. Just one crystal fragment would provide enough fuel for a hundred dump trucks.

It explores caves in search of underground water. It's not comfortable around water, so this Pokémon takes great care in lapping it up.

ABILITY
Sturdy
Weak Armor

HIDDEN ABILITY
Sand Force

SPECIES STRENGTHS
HP ◆◆◆
Attack ◆◆◆◆◆◆
Defense ◆◆◆◆◆◆
Sp. Atk ◆◆◆
Sp. Def ◆◆
Speed ◆

Damage taken in normal battles

NORMAL ×0.5	FIGHTING ×2	ROCK ×1
FIRE ×0.5	POISON ×0.5	GHOST ×1
WATER ×2	GROUND ×2	DRAGON ×0.5
GRASS ×2	FLYING ×1	DARK ×1
ELECTRIC ×1	PSYCHIC ×1	STEEL ×2
ICE ×1	BUG ×1	FAIRY ×1

EGG GROUPS
Mineral

ITEM SOMETIMES HELD BY WILD POKÉMON
Everstone / Hard Stone

EVOLUTION
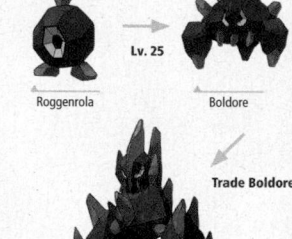
Roggenrola — **Lv. 25** → Boldore
↘ **Trade Boldore**
Gigalith

MAIN WAY TO REGISTER IN THE POKÉDEX
Catch in the caves in Vast Poni Canyon

Same form for male/female

Alola Pokédex	Melemele	Akala	Ula'ula	Poni
100	100	—	—	050

☑ Gigalith
Compressed Pokémon

`ROCK`

HEIGHT: 5'07"
WEIGHT: 573.2 lbs.

The blasts of energy it makes from sunbeams have terrifying power. However, it's not able to fire its blasts at night or on rainy days.

Known for its hefty horsepower, this Pokémon is a popular partner for construction workers.

ABILITY
Sturdy
Sand Stream

HIDDEN ABILITY
Sand Force

SPECIES STRENGTHS
HP ◆◆◆
Attack ◆◆◆◆◆◆
Defense ◆◆◆◆◆◆◆
Sp. Atk ◆◆◆
Sp. Def ◆◆◆◆◆
Speed ◆◆

Damage taken in normal battles

NORMAL ×0.5	FIGHTING ×2	ROCK ×1
FIRE ×0.5	POISON ×0.5	GHOST ×1
WATER ×2	GROUND ×2	DRAGON ×1
GRASS ×2	FLYING ×0.5	DARK ×1
ELECTRIC ×1	PSYCHIC ×1	STEEL ×2
ICE ×1	BUG ×1	FAIRY ×1

EGG GROUPS
Mineral

ITEM SOMETIMES HELD BY WILD POKÉMON
—

EVOLUTION
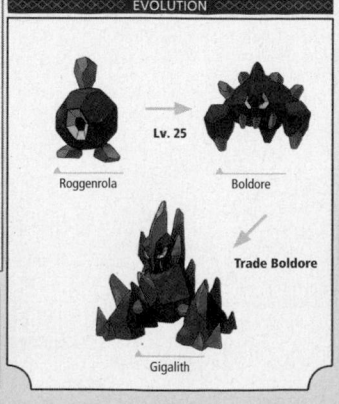
Roggenrola — **Lv. 25** → Boldore
↘ **Trade Boldore**
Gigalith

MAIN WAY TO REGISTER IN THE POKÉDEX
Receive a Boldore in a trade and it will evolve

Same form for male/female

ROGGENROLA 098

❖ LEVEL-UP MOVES

Lv.	Name	Type	Kind	Pow.	Acc.	PP	Range
1	Tackle	Normal	Physical	40	100	35	Normal
4	Harden	Normal	Status	—	—	30	Self
7	Sand Attack	Ground	Status	—	100	15	Normal
10	Headbutt	Normal	Physical	70	100	15	Normal
14	Rock Blast	Rock	Physical	25	90	10	Normal
17	Mud-Slap	Ground	Special	20	100	10	Normal
20	Iron Defense	Steel	Status	—	—	15	Self
23	Smack Down	Rock	Physical	50	100	15	Normal
27	Rock Slide	Rock	Physical	75	90	10	Many Others
30	Stealth Rock	Rock	Status	—	—	20	Other Side
33	Sandstorm	Rock	Status	—	—	10	Both Sides
36	Stone Edge	Rock	Physical	100	80	5	Normal
40	Explosion	Normal	Physical	250	100	5	Adjacent

❖ TM MOVES

No.	Name	Type	Kind	Pow.	Acc.	PP	Range
TM06	Toxic	Poison	Status	—	90	10	Normal
TM10	Hidden Power	Normal	Special	60	100	15	Normal
TM17	Protect	Normal	Status	—	—	10	Self
TM21	Frustration	Normal	Physical	—	100	20	Normal
TM23	Smack Down	Rock	Physical	50	100	15	Normal
TM26	Earthquake	Ground	Physical	100	100	10	Adjacent
TM27	Return	Normal	Physical	—	100	20	Normal
TM32	Double Team	Normal	Status	—	—	15	Self
TM37	Sandstorm	Rock	Status	—	—	10	Both Sides
TM39	Rock Tomb	Rock	Physical	60	95	15	Normal
TM42	Facade	Normal	Physical	70	100	20	Normal
TM44	Rest	Psychic	Status	—	—	10	Self
TM45	Attract	Normal	Status	—	100	15	Normal
TM48	Round	Normal	Special	60	100	15	Normal
TM64	Explosion	Normal	Physical	250	100	5	Adjacent
TM69	Rock Polish	Rock	Status	—	—	20	Self
TM71	Stone Edge	Rock	Physical	100	80	5	Normal
TM78	Bulldoze	Ground	Physical	60	100	20	Adjacent
TM80	Rock Slide	Rock	Physical	75	90	10	Many Others
TM87	Swagger	Normal	Status	—	85	15	Normal
TM88	Sleep Talk	Normal	Status	—	—	10	Self
TM90	Substitute	Normal	Status	—	—	10	Self
TM91	Flash Cannon	Steel	Special	80	100	10	Normal
TM96	Nature Power	Normal	Status	—	—	20	Normal
TM100	Confide	Normal	Status	—	—	20	Normal

❖ MOVES TAUGHT BY PEOPLE

Name	Type	Kind	Pow.	Acc.	PP	Range

❖ MOVES LEARNED WHEN EVOLVING

Name	Type	Kind	Pow.	Acc.	PP	Range

❖ EGG MOVES

Name	Type	Kind	Pow.	Acc.	PP	Range
Magnitude	Ground	Physical	—	100	30	Adjacent
Curse	Ghost	Status	—	—	10	Varies
Autotomize	Steel	Status	—	—	15	Self
Rock Tomb	Rock	Physical	60	95	15	Normal
Lock-On	Normal	Status	—	—	5	Normal
Heavy Slam	Steel	Physical	—	100	10	Normal
Take Down	Normal	Physical	90	85	20	Normal
Gravity	Psychic	Status	—	—	5	Both Sides
Wide Guard	Rock	Status	—	—	10	Your Side

❖ EXCLUSIVE Z-MOVE

Name	Base Move	Type	Kind	Pow.	Acc.	Range

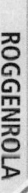

BOLDORE 099

❖ LEVEL-UP MOVES

Lv.	Name	Type	Kind	Pow.	Acc.	PP	Range
1	Power Gem	Rock	Special	80	100	20	Normal
1	Tackle	Normal	Physical	40	100	35	Normal
1	Harden	Normal	Status	—	—	30	Self
1	Sand Attack	Ground	Status	—	100	15	Normal
1	Headbutt	Normal	Physical	70	100	15	Normal
4	Harden	Normal	Status	—	—	30	Self
7	Sand Attack	Ground	Status	—	100	15	Normal
10	Headbutt	Normal	Physical	70	100	15	Normal
14	Rock Blast	Rock	Physical	25	90	10	Normal
17	Mud-Slap	Ground	Special	20	100	10	Normal
20	Iron Defense	Steel	Status	—	—	15	Self
23	Smack Down	Rock	Physical	50	100	15	Normal
30	Rock Slide	Rock	Physical	75	90	10	Many Others
36	Stealth Rock	Rock	Status	—	—	20	Other Side
42	Sandstorm	Rock	Status	—	—	10	Both Sides
48	Stone Edge	Rock	Physical	100	80	5	Normal
55	Explosion	Normal	Physical	250	100	5	Adjacent

❖ TM MOVES

No.	Name	Type	Kind	Pow.	Acc.	PP	Range
TM06	Toxic	Poison	Status	—	90	10	Normal
TM10	Hidden Power	Normal	Special	60	100	15	Normal
TM17	Protect	Normal	Status	—	—	10	Self
TM21	Frustration	Normal	Physical	—	100	20	Normal
TM23	Smack Down	Rock	Physical	50	100	15	Normal
TM26	Earthquake	Ground	Physical	100	100	10	Adjacent
TM27	Return	Normal	Physical	—	100	20	Normal
TM32	Double Team	Normal	Status	—	—	15	Self
TM37	Sandstorm	Rock	Status	—	—	10	Both Sides
TM39	Rock Tomb	Rock	Physical	60	95	15	Normal
TM42	Facade	Normal	Physical	70	100	20	Normal
TM44	Rest	Psychic	Status	—	—	10	Self
TM45	Attract	Normal	Status	—	100	15	Normal
TM48	Round	Normal	Special	60	100	15	Normal
TM64	Explosion	Normal	Physical	250	100	5	Adjacent
TM69	Rock Polish	Rock	Status	—	—	20	Self
TM71	Stone Edge	Rock	Physical	100	80	5	Normal
TM78	Bulldoze	Ground	Physical	60	100	20	Adjacent
TM80	Rock Slide	Rock	Physical	75	90	10	Many Others
TM87	Swagger	Normal	Status	—	85	15	Normal
TM88	Sleep Talk	Normal	Status	—	—	10	Self
TM90	Substitute	Normal	Status	—	—	10	Self
TM91	Flash Cannon	Steel	Special	80	100	10	Normal
TM96	Nature Power	Normal	Status	—	—	20	Normal
TM100	Confide	Normal	Status	—	—	20	Normal

❖ MOVES TAUGHT BY PEOPLE

Name	Type	Kind	Pow.	Acc.	PP	Range

❖ MOVES LEARNED WHEN EVOLVING

Name	Type	Kind	Pow.	Acc.	PP	Range
Power Gem	Rock	Special	80	100	20	Normal

❖ EGG MOVES

Name	Type	Kind	Pow.	Acc.	PP	Range

❖ EXCLUSIVE Z-MOVE

Name	Base Move	Type	Kind	Pow.	Acc.	Range

GIGALITH 100

❖ LEVEL-UP MOVES

Lv.	Name	Type	Kind	Pow.	Acc.	PP	Range
1	Power Gem	Rock	Special	80	100	20	Normal
1	Tackle	Normal	Physical	40	100	35	Normal
1	Harden	Normal	Status	—	—	30	Self
1	Sand Attack	Ground	Status	—	100	15	Normal
1	Headbutt	Normal	Physical	70	100	15	Normal
4	Harden	Normal	Status	—	—	30	Self
7	Sand Attack	Ground	Status	—	100	15	Normal
10	Headbutt	Normal	Physical	70	100	15	Normal
14	Rock Blast	Rock	Physical	25	90	10	Normal
17	Mud-Slap	Ground	Special	20	100	10	Normal
20	Iron Defense	Steel	Status	—	—	15	Self
23	Smack Down	Rock	Physical	50	100	15	Normal
30	Rock Slide	Rock	Physical	75	90	10	Many Others
36	Stealth Rock	Rock	Status	—	—	20	Other Side
42	Sandstorm	Rock	Status	—	—	10	Both Sides
48	Stone Edge	Rock	Physical	100	80	5	Normal
55	Explosion	Normal	Physical	250	100	5	Adjacent

❖ TM MOVES

No.	Name	Type	Kind	Pow.	Acc.	PP	Range
TM06	Toxic	Poison	Status	—	90	10	Normal
TM10	Hidden Power	Normal	Special	60	100	15	Normal
TM15	Hyper Beam	Normal	Special	150	90	5	Normal
TM17	Protect	Normal	Status	—	—	10	Self
TM21	Frustration	Normal	Physical	—	100	20	Normal
TM22	Solar Beam	Grass	Special	120	100	10	Normal
TM23	Smack Down	Rock	Physical	50	100	15	Normal
TM26	Earthquake	Ground	Physical	100	100	10	Adjacent
TM27	Return	Normal	Physical	—	100	20	Normal
TM32	Double Team	Normal	Status	—	—	15	Self
TM37	Sandstorm	Rock	Status	—	—	10	Both Sides
TM39	Rock Tomb	Rock	Physical	60	95	15	Normal
TM42	Facade	Normal	Physical	70	100	20	Normal
TM44	Rest	Psychic	Status	—	—	10	Self
TM45	Attract	Normal	Status	—	100	15	Normal
TM48	Round	Normal	Special	60	100	15	Normal
TM64	Explosion	Normal	Physical	250	100	5	Adjacent
TM68	Giga Impact	Normal	Physical	150	90	5	Normal
TM69	Rock Polish	Rock	Status	—	—	20	Self
TM71	Stone Edge	Rock	Physical	100	80	5	Normal
TM78	Bulldoze	Ground	Physical	60	100	20	Adjacent
TM80	Rock Slide	Rock	Physical	75	90	10	Many Others
TM87	Swagger	Normal	Status	—	85	15	Normal
TM88	Sleep Talk	Normal	Status	—	—	10	Self
TM90	Substitute	Normal	Status	—	—	10	Self
TM91	Flash Cannon	Steel	Special	80	100	10	Normal
TM96	Nature Power	Normal	Status	—	—	20	Normal

❖ MOVES TAUGHT BY PEOPLE

No.	Name	Type	Kind	Pow.	Acc.	PP	Range
TM100	Confide	Normal	Status	—	—	20	Normal

❖ MOVES LEARNED WHEN EVOLVING

Name	Type	Kind	Pow.	Acc.	PP	Range

❖ EGG MOVES

Name	Type	Kind	Pow.	Acc.	PP	Range

❖ EXCLUSIVE Z-MOVE

Name	Base Move	Type	Kind	Pow.	Acc.	Range

Carbink

Jewel Pokémon

Alola Pokédex	Melemele	Akala	Ula'ula	Poni
101	101	—	—	051

ROCK FAIRY

HEIGHT: 1'00"
WEIGHT: 12.6 lbs.

Born from the high temperatures and pressures deep underground, it defends itself by firing beams from the jewel part of its body.

Although this Pokémon is not especially rare, its glittering, jewel-draped body draws attention from people.

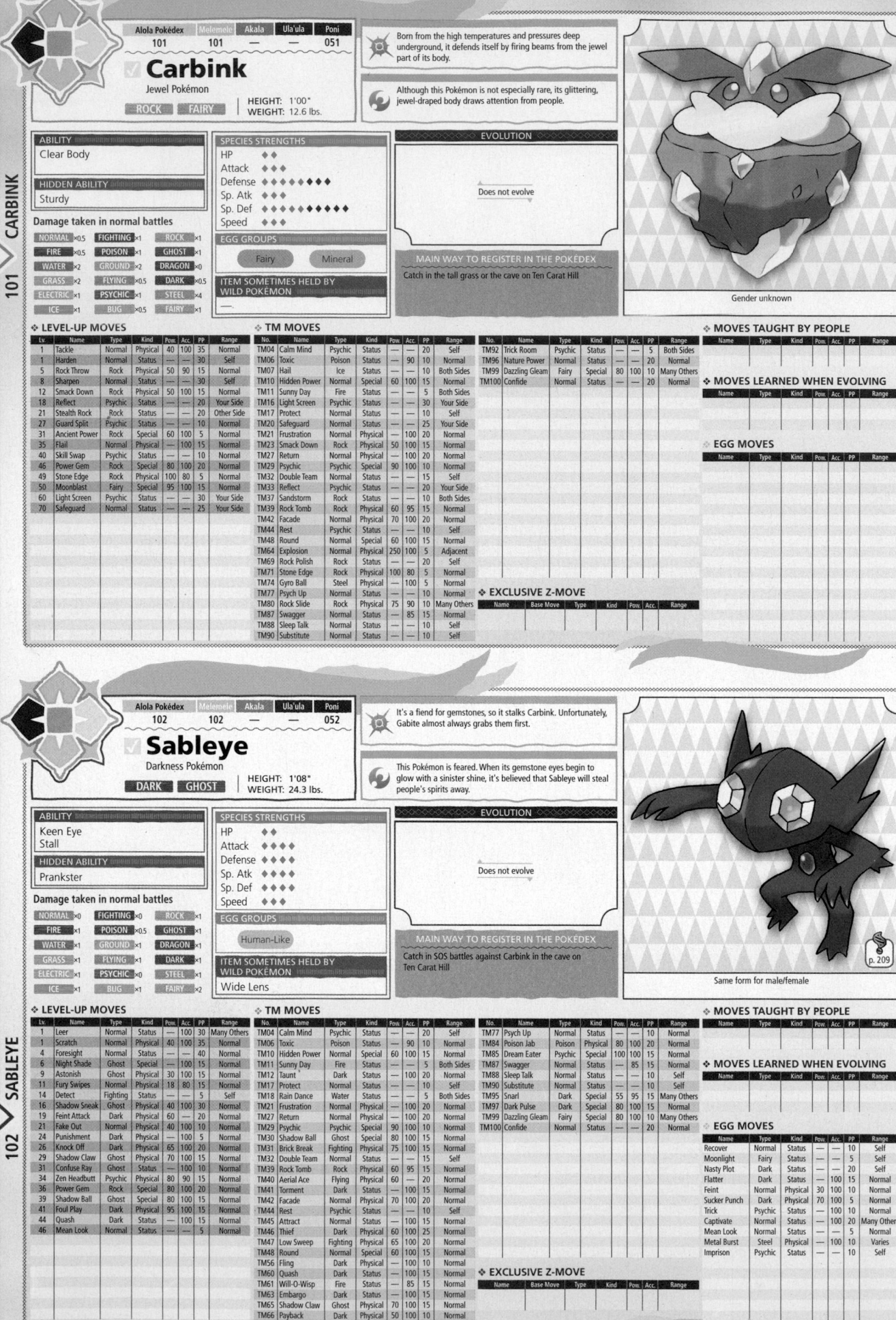

Gender unknown

ABILITY
Clear Body

HIDDEN ABILITY
Sturdy

SPECIES STRENGTHS
HP ◆◆
Attack ◆◆◆
Defense ◆◆◆◆◆◆◆◆
Sp. Atk ◆◆◆
Sp. Def ◆◆◆◆◆◆◆◆
Speed ◆◆◆

Damage taken in normal battles

NORMAL ×0.5	FIGHTING ×1	ROCK ×1
FIRE ×0.5	POISON ×1	GHOST ×1
WATER ×2	GROUND ×2	DRAGON ×0
GRASS ×2	FLYING ×0.5	DARK ×0.5
ELECTRIC ×1	PSYCHIC ×1	STEEL ×4
ICE ×1	BUG ×0.5	FAIRY ×1

EGG GROUPS
Fairy Mineral

ITEM SOMETIMES HELD BY WILD POKÉMON
—

EVOLUTION
Does not evolve

MAIN WAY TO REGISTER IN THE POKÉDEX
Catch in the tall grass or the cave on Ten Carat Hill

❖ LEVEL-UP MOVES

Lv.	Name	Type	Kind	Pow.	Acc.	PP	Range
1	Tackle	Normal	Physical	40	100	35	Normal
1	Harden	Normal	Status	—	—	30	Self
5	Rock Throw	Rock	Physical	50	90	15	Normal
8	Sharpen	Normal	Status	—	—	30	Self
12	Smack Down	Rock	Physical	50	100	15	Normal
18	Reflect	Psychic	Status	—	—	20	Your Side
21	Stealth Rock	Rock	Status	—	—	20	Other Side
27	Guard Split	Psychic	Status	—	—	10	Normal
31	Ancient Power	Rock	Special	60	100	5	Normal
35	Flail	Normal	Physical	—	100	15	Normal
40	Skill Swap	Psychic	Status	—	—	10	Normal
46	Power Gem	Rock	Special	80	100	20	Normal
49	Stone Edge	Rock	Physical	100	80	5	Normal
50	Moonblast	Fairy	Special	95	100	15	Normal
60	Light Screen	Psychic	Status	—	—	30	Your Side
70	Safeguard	Normal	Status	—	—	25	Your Side

❖ TM MOVES

No.	Name	Type	Kind	Pow.	Acc.	PP	Range
TM04	Calm Mind	Psychic	Status	—	—	20	Self
TM06	Toxic	Poison	Status	—	90	10	Normal
TM07	Hail	Ice	Status	—	—	10	Both Sides
TM10	Hidden Power	Normal	Special	60	100	15	Normal
TM11	Sunny Day	Fire	Status	—	—	5	Both Sides
TM16	Light Screen	Psychic	Status	—	—	30	Your Side
TM17	Protect	Normal	Status	—	—	10	Self
TM20	Safeguard	Normal	Status	—	—	25	Your Side
TM21	Frustration	Normal	Physical	—	100	20	Normal
TM23	Smack Down	Rock	Physical	50	100	15	Normal
TM27	Return	Normal	Physical	—	100	20	Normal
TM29	Psychic	Psychic	Special	90	100	10	Normal
TM32	Double Team	Normal	Status	—	—	15	Self
TM33	Reflect	Psychic	Status	—	—	20	Your Side
TM37	Sandstorm	Rock	Status	—	—	10	Both Sides
TM39	Rock Tomb	Rock	Physical	60	95	15	Normal
TM42	Facade	Normal	Physical	70	100	20	Normal
TM44	Rest	Psychic	Status	—	—	10	Self
TM48	Round	Normal	Special	60	100	15	Normal
TM64	Explosion	Normal	Physical	250	100	5	Adjacent
TM69	Rock Polish	Rock	Status	—	—	20	Self
TM71	Stone Edge	Rock	Physical	100	80	5	Normal
TM74	Gyro Ball	Steel	Physical	—	100	5	Normal
TM77	Psych Up	Normal	Status	—	—	10	Self
TM80	Rock Slide	Rock	Physical	75	90	10	Many Others
TM87	Swagger	Normal	Status	—	85	15	Normal
TM88	Sleep Talk	Normal	Status	—	—	10	Self
TM90	Substitute	Normal	Status	—	—	10	Self

No.	Name	Type	Kind	Pow.	Acc.	PP	Range
TM92	Trick Room	Psychic	Status	—	—	5	Both Sides
TM96	Nature Power	Normal	Status	—	—	20	Normal
TM99	Dazzling Gleam	Fairy	Special	80	100	10	Many Others
TM100	Confide	Normal	Status	—	—	20	Normal

❖ MOVES TAUGHT BY PEOPLE

Name	Type	Kind	Pow.	Acc.	PP	Range

❖ MOVES LEARNED WHEN EVOLVING

Name	Type	Kind	Pow.	Acc.	PP	Range

❖ EGG MOVES

Name	Type	Kind	Pow.	Acc.	PP	Range

❖ EXCLUSIVE Z-MOVE

Name	Base Move	Type	Kind	Pow.	Acc.	Range

Sableye

Darkness Pokémon

Alola Pokédex	Melemele	Akala	Ula'ula	Poni
102	102	—	—	052

DARK GHOST

HEIGHT: 1'08"
WEIGHT: 24.3 lbs.

It's a fiend for gemstones, so it stalks Carbink. Unfortunately, Gabite almost always grabs them first.

This Pokémon is feared. When its gemstone eyes begin to glow with a sinister shine, it's believed that Sableye will steal people's spirits away.

Same form for male/female

p. 209

ABILITY
Keen Eye
Stall

HIDDEN ABILITY
Prankster

SPECIES STRENGTHS
HP ◆◆
Attack ◆◆◆◆
Defense ◆◆◆◆
Sp. Atk ◆◆◆◆
Sp. Def ◆◆◆◆
Speed ◆◆◆

Damage taken in normal battles

NORMAL ×0	FIGHTING ×0	ROCK ×1
FIRE ×1	POISON ×0.5	GHOST ×1
WATER ×1	GROUND ×1	DRAGON ×1
GRASS ×1	FLYING ×1	DARK ×1
ELECTRIC ×1	PSYCHIC ×0	STEEL ×1
ICE ×1	BUG ×1	FAIRY ×2

EGG GROUPS
Human-Like

ITEM SOMETIMES HELD BY WILD POKÉMON
Wide Lens

EVOLUTION
Does not evolve

MAIN WAY TO REGISTER IN THE POKÉDEX
Catch in SOS battles against Carbink in the cave on Ten Carat Hill

❖ LEVEL-UP MOVES

Lv.	Name	Type	Kind	Pow.	Acc.	PP	Range
1	Leer	Normal	Status	—	100	30	Many Others
1	Scratch	Normal	Physical	40	100	35	Normal
4	Foresight	Normal	Status	—	—	40	Normal
6	Night Shade	Ghost	Special	—	100	15	Normal
9	Astonish	Ghost	Physical	30	100	15	Normal
11	Fury Swipes	Normal	Physical	18	80	15	Normal
14	Detect	Fighting	Status	—	—	5	Self
16	Shadow Sneak	Ghost	Physical	40	100	30	Normal
19	Feint Attack	Dark	Physical	60	—	20	Normal
21	Fake Out	Normal	Physical	40	100	10	Normal
24	Punishment	Dark	Physical	—	100	5	Normal
26	Knock Off	Dark	Physical	65	100	20	Normal
29	Shadow Claw	Ghost	Physical	70	100	15	Normal
31	Confuse Ray	Ghost	Status	—	100	10	Normal
34	Zen Headbutt	Psychic	Physical	80	90	15	Normal
36	Power Gem	Rock	Special	80	100	20	Normal
39	Shadow Ball	Ghost	Special	80	100	15	Normal
41	Foul Play	Dark	Physical	95	100	15	Normal
44	Quash	Dark	Status	—	100	15	Normal
46	Mean Look	Normal	Status	—	—	5	Normal

❖ TM MOVES

No.	Name	Type	Kind	Pow.	Acc.	PP	Range
TM04	Calm Mind	Psychic	Status	—	—	20	Self
TM06	Toxic	Poison	Status	—	90	10	Normal
TM10	Hidden Power	Normal	Special	60	100	15	Normal
TM11	Sunny Day	Fire	Status	—	—	5	Both Sides
TM12	Taunt	Dark	Status	—	100	20	Normal
TM17	Protect	Normal	Status	—	—	10	Self
TM18	Rain Dance	Water	Status	—	—	5	Both Sides
TM21	Frustration	Normal	Physical	—	100	20	Normal
TM27	Return	Normal	Physical	—	100	20	Normal
TM29	Psychic	Psychic	Special	90	100	10	Normal
TM30	Shadow Ball	Ghost	Special	80	100	15	Normal
TM31	Brick Break	Fighting	Physical	75	100	15	Normal
TM32	Double Team	Normal	Status	—	—	15	Self
TM39	Rock Tomb	Rock	Physical	60	95	15	Normal
TM40	Aerial Ace	Flying	Physical	60	—	20	Normal
TM41	Torment	Dark	Status	—	100	15	Normal
TM42	Facade	Normal	Physical	70	100	20	Normal
TM44	Rest	Psychic	Status	—	—	10	Self
TM45	Attract	Normal	Status	—	100	15	Normal
TM46	Thief	Dark	Physical	60	100	25	Normal
TM47	Low Sweep	Fighting	Physical	65	100	20	Normal
TM48	Round	Normal	Special	60	100	15	Normal
TM56	Fling	Dark	Physical	—	100	10	Normal
TM60	Quash	Dark	Status	—	100	15	Normal
TM61	Will-O-Wisp	Fire	Status	—	85	15	Normal
TM63	Embargo	Dark	Status	—	100	15	Normal
TM65	Shadow Claw	Ghost	Physical	70	100	15	Normal
TM66	Payback	Dark	Physical	50	100	10	Normal

No.	Name	Type	Kind	Pow.	Acc.	PP	Range
TM77	Psych Up	Normal	Status	—	—	10	Self
TM84	Poison Jab	Poison	Physical	80	100	20	Normal
TM85	Dream Eater	Psychic	Special	100	100	15	Normal
TM87	Swagger	Normal	Status	—	85	15	Normal
TM88	Sleep Talk	Normal	Status	—	—	10	Self
TM90	Substitute	Normal	Status	—	—	10	Self
TM95	Snarl	Dark	Special	55	95	15	Many Others
TM97	Dark Pulse	Dark	Special	80	100	15	Normal
TM99	Dazzling Gleam	Fairy	Special	80	100	10	Many Others
TM100	Confide	Normal	Status	—	—	20	Normal

❖ MOVES TAUGHT BY PEOPLE

Name	Type	Kind	Pow.	Acc.	PP	Range

❖ MOVES LEARNED WHEN EVOLVING

Name	Type	Kind	Pow.	Acc.	PP	Range

❖ EGG MOVES

Name	Type	Kind	Pow.	Acc.	PP	Range
Recover	Normal	Status	—	—	10	Self
Moonlight	Fairy	Status	—	—	5	Self
Nasty Plot	Dark	Status	—	—	20	Self
Flatter	Dark	Status	—	100	15	Normal
Feint	Normal	Physical	30	100	10	Normal
Sucker Punch	Dark	Physical	70	100	5	Normal
Trick	Psychic	Status	—	100	10	Normal
Captivate	Normal	Status	—	100	20	Many Others
Mean Look	Normal	Status	—	—	5	Normal
Metal Burst	Steel	Physical	—	100	10	Varies
Imprison	Psychic	Status	—	—	10	Self

❖ EXCLUSIVE Z-MOVE

Name	Base Move	Type	Kind	Pow.	Acc.	Range

Day and Night Exclusives

Whether it is daytime or nighttime affects various things in Alola. For example, certain Pokémon appear or evolve only during the daytime or the nighttime. Some Pokémon appear at photo spots only at certain times. Some items are also only found during the daytime or nighttime.

Note: Daytime will last from 6:00 a.m. until 5:59 p.m. in *Pokémon Sun,* and nighttime lasts from 6:00 p.m. until 5:59 a.m. The time in your game will be based on the time set for your Nintendo 3DS system. But time is reversed in *Pokémon Moon.* In *Pokémon Moon,* daytime starts at 6:00 p.m. and lasts until 5:59 a.m., according to the time set on your system, and nighttime lasts from 6:00 a.m. until 5:59 p.m.

Pokémon that can be caught only during the daytime or nighttime

The following Pokémon can only be encountered and caught in the wild when it is daytime in your copy of *Pokémon Sun* or *Pokémon Moon.*

| Yungoos | Gumshoos | Ledyba | Ledian | Drifloon | Lycanroc (Midday Form) | Espeon |

| Igglybuff | Jigglypuff | Dewpider | Araquanid | Paras | Poliwrath |

The Pokémon below, however, can only be encountered and caught in the wild when it is nighttime in your game.

| Alolan Rattata | Alolan Raticate | Spinarak | Ariados | Misdreavus | Lycanroc (Midnight Form) |

| Umbreon | Surskit | Masquerain | Morelull | Politoed | Cleffa | Clefairy |

Pokémon that evolve only during daytime or nighttime

The following Pokémon will only evolve if they meet all of the conditions for their Evolution during the daytime in your game.

| Yungoos evolves into Gumshoos | Happiny evolves into Chansey | Rockruff evolves into Lycanroc (Midday Form) ☀ | Eevee evolves into Espeon | Fomantis evolves into Lurantis | Riolu evolves into Lucario |

Meanwhile some Pokémon only evolve during the dark of night. The following Pokémon Evolutions are only possible if all conditions for Evolution are met when it is nighttime in your game.

| Alolan Rattata evolves into Alolan Raticate | Rockruff evolves into Lycanroc (Midnight Form) ☾ | Eevee evolves into Umbreon | Cubone evolves into Alolan Marowak | Sneasel evolves into Weavile |

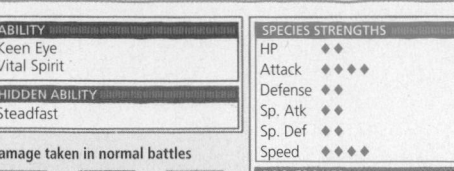

Rockruff

Alola Pokédex	Melemele	Akala	Ula'ula	Poni
103	103	—	—	053

Puppy Pokémon

ROCK

HEIGHT: 1'08"
WEIGHT: 20.3 lbs.

It's considered to be a good Pokémon for beginners because of its friendliness, but its disposition grows rougher as it grows up.

This Pokémon has lived with people since times long ago. It can sense when its Trainer is in the dumps and will stick close by its Trainer's side.

ABILITY
Keen Eye
Vital Spirit

HIDDEN ABILITY
Steadfast

Damage taken in normal battles

NORMAL	×0.5	FIGHTING	×2	ROCK	×1
FIRE	×0.5	POISON	×0.5	GHOST	×1
WATER	×2	GROUND	×2	DRAGON	×1
GRASS	×2	FLYING	×0.5	DARK	×1
ELECTRIC	×1	PSYCHIC	×1	STEEL	×1
ICE	×1	BUG	×1	FAIRY	×1

SPECIES STRENGTHS
HP ◆◆
Attack ◆◆◆◆
Defense ◆◆
Sp. Atk ◆◆
Sp. Def ◆◆
Speed ◆◆◆◆

EGG GROUPS
Field

ITEM SOMETIMES HELD BY WILD POKÉMON
—

MAIN WAY TO REGISTER IN THE POKÉDEX
Catch in the tall grass in the Farthest Hollow on Ten Carat Hill

EVOLUTION

Rockruff → Level up to Lv. 25 in *Pokémon Sun* when it is daytime in your game → Midday Form Lycanroc

Level up to Lv. 25 in *Pokémon Moon* when it is nighttime in your game → Midnight Form Lycanroc

Same form for male/female

Lycanroc

Alola Pokédex	Melemele	Akala	Ula'ula	Poni
104	104	—	—	054

Wolf Pokémon

ROCK

HEIGHT: 2'07"
WEIGHT: 55.1 lbs.

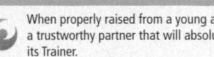

Its quick movements confuse its enemies. Well equipped with claws and fangs, it also uses the sharp rocks in its mane as weapons.

When properly raised from a young age, it will become a trustworthy partner that will absolutely never betray its Trainer.

ABILITY
Keen Eye
Sand Rush

HIDDEN ABILITY
Steadfast

Damage taken in normal battles

NORMAL	×0.5	FIGHTING	×2	ROCK	×1
FIRE	×0.5	POISON	×0.5	GHOST	×1
WATER	×2	GROUND	×2	DRAGON	×1
GRASS	×2	FLYING	×0.5	DARK	×1
ELECTRIC	×1	PSYCHIC	×1	STEEL	×1
ICE	×1	BUG	×1	FAIRY	×1

SPECIES STRENGTHS
HP ◆◆◆
Attack ◆◆◆◆◆◆
Defense ◆◆◆◆
Sp. Atk ◆◆◆
Sp. Def ◆◆◆
Speed ◆◆◆◆◆◆◆

EGG GROUPS
Field

ITEM SOMETIMES HELD BY WILD POKÉMON
—

MAIN WAY TO REGISTER IN THE POKÉDEX
Catch in the tall grass in Vast Poni Canyon when it is daytime in your game

EVOLUTION

Rockruff → Level up to Lv. 25 in *Pokémon Sun* when it is daytime in your game → Midday Form Lycanroc

MIDDAY FORM

Same form for male/female

Lycanroc

Alola Pokédex	Melemele	Akala	Ula'ula	Poni
104	104	—	—	054

Wolf Pokémon

ROCK

HEIGHT: 3'07"
WEIGHT: 55.1 lbs.

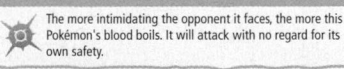

The more intimidating the opponent it faces, the more this Pokémon's blood boils. It will attack with no regard for its own safety.

It goads its enemies into attacking, withstands the hits, and in return, delivers a headbutt, crushing their bones with its rocky mane.

ABILITY
Keen Eye
Vital Spirit

HIDDEN ABILITY
No Guard

Damage taken in normal battles

NORMAL	×0.5	FIGHTING	×2	ROCK	×1
FIRE	×0.5	POISON	×0.5	GHOST	×1
WATER	×2	GROUND	×2	DRAGON	×1
GRASS	×2	FLYING	×0.5	DARK	×1
ELECTRIC	×1	PSYCHIC	×1	STEEL	×1
ICE	×1	BUG	×1	FAIRY	×1

SPECIES STRENGTHS
HP ◆◆◆
Attack ◆◆◆◆◆◆
Defense ◆◆◆◆
Sp. Atk ◆◆◆
Sp. Def ◆◆◆
Speed ◆◆◆◆◆

EGG GROUPS
Field

ITEM SOMETIMES HELD BY WILD POKÉMON
—

MAIN WAY TO REGISTER IN THE POKÉDEX
Catch in the tall grass in Vast Poni Canyon when it is nighttime in your game

EVOLUTION

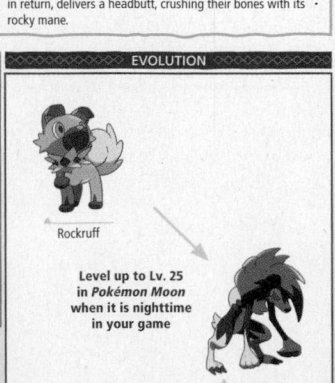

Rockruff → Level up to Lv. 25 in *Pokémon Moon* when it is nighttime in your game → Midnight Form Lycanroc

MIDNIGHT FORM

Same form for male/female

ROCKRUFF 103

LYCANROC 104

LYCANROC 104

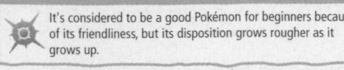

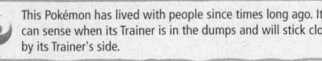

ROCKRUFF 103

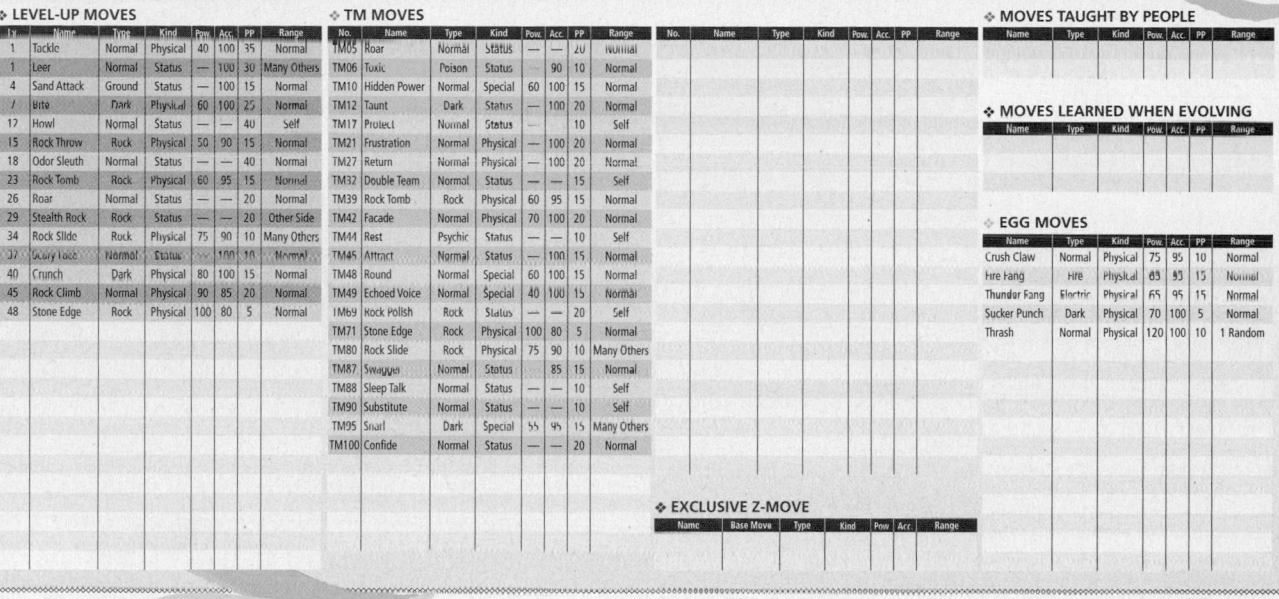

❖ LEVEL-UP MOVES

Lv.	Name	Type	Kind	Pow.	Acc.	PP	Range
1	Tackle	Normal	Physical	40	100	35	Normal
1	Leer	Normal	Status	—	100	30	Many Others
4	Sand Attack	Ground	Status	—	100	15	Normal
7	Bite	Dark	Physical	60	100	25	Normal
17	Howl	Normal	Status	—	—	40	Self
15	Rock Throw	Rock	Physical	50	90	15	Normal
18	Odor Sleuth	Normal	Status	—	—	40	Normal
23	Rock Tomb	Rock	Physical	60	95	15	Normal
26	Roar	Normal	Status	—	—	20	Normal
29	Stealth Rock	Rock	Status	—	—	20	Other Side
34	Rock Slide	Rock	Physical	75	90	10	Many Others
37	Scary Face	Normal	Status	—	100	10	Normal
40	Crunch	Dark	Physical	80	100	15	Normal
45	Rock Climb	Normal	Physical	90	85	20	Normal
48	Stone Edge	Rock	Physical	100	80	5	Normal

❖ TM MOVES

No.	Name	Type	Kind	Pow.	Acc.	PP	Range
TM05	Roar	Normal	Status	—	—	20	Normal
TM06	Toxic	Poison	Status	—	90	10	Normal
TM10	Hidden Power	Normal	Special	60	100	15	Normal
TM12	Taunt	Dark	Status	—	100	20	Normal
TM17	Protect	Normal	Status	—	—	10	Self
TM21	Frustration	Normal	Physical	—	100	20	Normal
TM27	Return	Normal	Physical	—	100	20	Normal
TM32	Double Team	Normal	Status	—	—	15	Self
TM39	Rock Tomb	Rock	Physical	60	95	15	Normal
TM42	Facade	Normal	Physical	70	100	20	Normal
TM44	Rest	Psychic	Status	—	—	10	Self
TM45	Attract	Normal	Status	—	100	15	Normal
TM48	Round	Normal	Special	60	100	15	Normal
TM49	Echoed Voice	Normal	Special	40	100	15	Normal
TM69	Rock Polish	Rock	Status	—	—	20	Self
TM71	Stone Edge	Rock	Physical	100	80	5	Normal
TM80	Rock Slide	Rock	Physical	75	90	10	Many Others
TM87	Swagger	Normal	Status	—	85	15	Normal
TM88	Sleep Talk	Normal	Status	—	—	10	Self
TM90	Substitute	Normal	Status	—	—	10	Self
TM95	Snarl	Dark	Special	55	95	15	Many Others
TM100	Confide	Normal	Status	—	—	20	Normal

❖ MOVES TAUGHT BY PEOPLE

Name	Type	Kind	Pow.	Acc.	PP	Range

❖ MOVES LEARNED WHEN EVOLVING

Name	Type	Kind	Pow.	Acc.	PP	Range

❖ EGG MOVES

Name	Type	Kind	Pow.	Acc.	PP	Range
Crush Claw	Normal	Physical	75	95	10	Normal
Fire Fang	Fire	Physical	65	95	15	Normal
Thunder Fang	Electric	Physical	65	95	15	Normal
Sucker Punch	Dark	Physical	70	100	5	Normal
Thrash	Normal	Physical	120	100	10	1 Random

❖ EXCLUSIVE Z-MOVE

Name	Base Move	Type	Kind	Pow.	Acc.	Range

LYCANROC 104

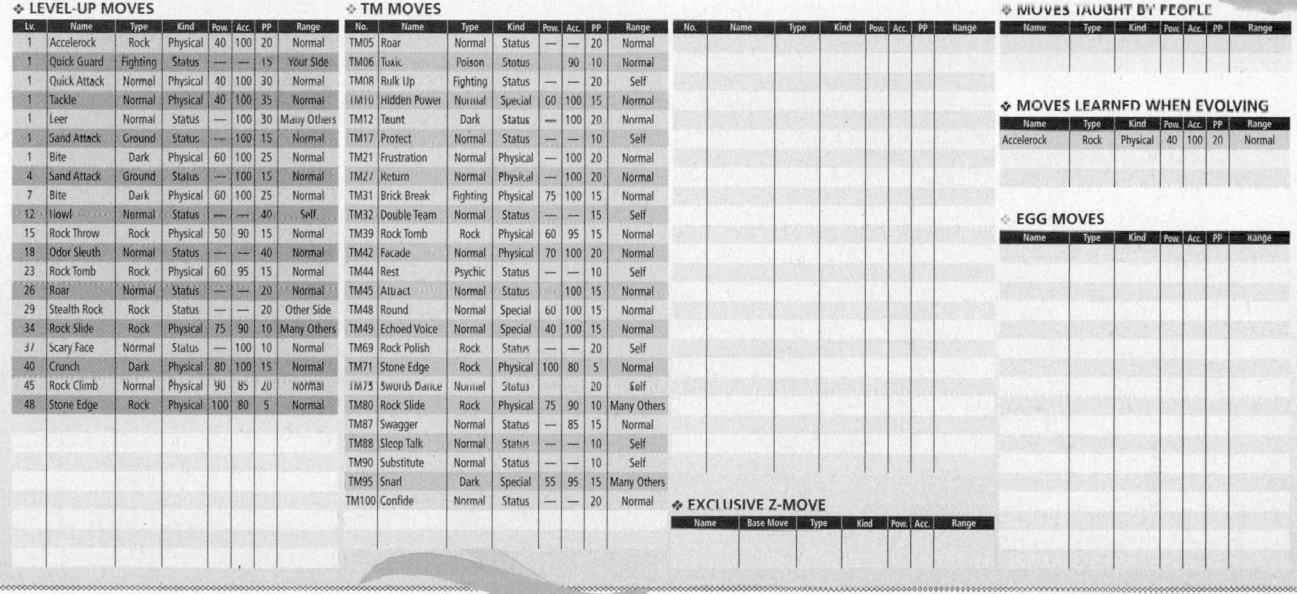

❖ LEVEL-UP MOVES

Lv.	Name	Type	Kind	Pow.	Acc.	PP	Range
1	Accelerock	Rock	Physical	40	100	20	Normal
1	Quick Guard	Fighting	Status	—	—	15	Your Side
1	Quick Attack	Normal	Physical	40	100	30	Normal
1	Tackle	Normal	Physical	40	100	35	Normal
1	Leer	Normal	Status	—	100	30	Many Others
1	Sand Attack	Ground	Status	—	100	15	Normal
1	Bite	Dark	Physical	60	100	25	Normal
4	Sand Attack	Ground	Status	—	100	15	Normal
7	Bite	Dark	Physical	60	100	25	Normal
12	Howl	Normal	Status	—	—	40	Self
15	Rock Throw	Rock	Physical	50	90	15	Normal
18	Odor Sleuth	Normal	Status	—	—	40	Normal
23	Rock Tomb	Rock	Physical	60	95	15	Normal
26	Roar	Normal	Status	—	—	20	Normal
29	Stealth Rock	Rock	Status	—	—	20	Other Side
34	Rock Slide	Rock	Physical	75	90	10	Many Others
37	Scary Face	Normal	Status	—	100	10	Normal
40	Crunch	Dark	Physical	80	100	15	Normal
45	Rock Climb	Normal	Physical	90	85	20	Normal
48	Stone Edge	Rock	Physical	100	80	5	Normal

❖ TM MOVES

No.	Name	Type	Kind	Pow.	Acc.	PP	Range
TM05	Roar	Normal	Status	—	—	20	Normal
TM06	Toxic	Poison	Status	—	90	10	Normal
TM08	Bulk Up	Fighting	Status	—	—	20	Self
TM10	Hidden Power	Normal	Special	60	100	15	Normal
TM12	Taunt	Dark	Status	—	100	20	Normal
TM17	Protect	Normal	Status	—	—	10	Self
TM21	Frustration	Normal	Physical	—	100	20	Normal
TM27	Return	Normal	Physical	—	100	20	Normal
TM31	Brick Break	Fighting	Physical	75	100	15	Normal
TM32	Double Team	Normal	Status	—	—	15	Self
TM39	Rock Tomb	Rock	Physical	60	95	15	Normal
TM42	Facade	Normal	Physical	70	100	20	Normal
TM44	Rest	Psychic	Status	—	—	10	Self
TM45	Attract	Normal	Status	—	100	15	Normal
TM48	Round	Normal	Special	60	100	15	Normal
TM49	Echoed Voice	Normal	Special	40	100	15	Normal
TM69	Rock Polish	Rock	Status	—	—	20	Self
TM71	Stone Edge	Rock	Physical	100	80	5	Normal
TM75	Swords Dance	Normal	Status	—	—	20	Self
TM80	Rock Slide	Rock	Physical	75	90	10	Many Others
TM87	Swagger	Normal	Status	—	85	15	Normal
TM88	Sleep Talk	Normal	Status	—	—	10	Self
TM90	Substitute	Normal	Status	—	—	10	Self
TM95	Snarl	Dark	Special	55	95	15	Many Others
TM100	Confide	Normal	Status	—	—	20	Normal

❖ MOVES TAUGHT BY PEOPLE

Name	Type	Kind	Pow.	Acc.	PP	Range

❖ MOVES LEARNED WHEN EVOLVING

Name	Type	Kind	Pow.	Acc.	PP	Range
Accelerock	Rock	Physical	40	100	20	Normal

❖ EGG MOVES

Name	Type	Kind	Pow.	Acc.	PP	Range

❖ EXCLUSIVE Z-MOVE

Name	Base Move	Type	Kind	Pow.	Acc.	Range

LYCANROC 104

❖ LEVEL-UP MOVES

Lv.	Name	Type	Kind	Pow.	Acc.	PP	Range
1	Counter	Fighting	Physical	—	100	20	Varies
1	Reversal	Fighting	Physical	—	100	15	Normal
1	Taunt	Dark	Status	—	100	20	Normal
1	Tackle	Normal	Physical	40	100	35	Normal
1	Leer	Normal	Status	—	100	30	Many Others
1	Sand Attack	Ground	Status	—	100	15	Normal
1	Bite	Dark	Physical	60	100	25	Normal
4	Sand Attack	Ground	Status	—	100	15	Normal
7	Bite	Dark	Physical	60	100	25	Normal
12	Howl	Normal	Status	—	—	40	Self
15	Rock Throw	Rock	Physical	50	90	15	Normal
18	Odor Sleuth	Normal	Status	—	—	40	Normal
23	Rock Tomb	Rock	Physical	60	95	15	Normal
26	Roar	Normal	Status	—	—	20	Normal
29	Stealth Rock	Rock	Status	—	—	20	Other Side
34	Rock Slide	Rock	Physical	75	90	10	Many Others
37	Scary Face	Normal	Status	—	100	10	Normal
40	Crunch	Dark	Physical	80	100	15	Normal
45	Rock Climb	Normal	Physical	90	85	20	Normal
48	Stone Edge	Rock	Physical	100	80	5	Normal

❖ TM MOVES

No.	Name	Type	Kind	Pow.	Acc.	PP	Range
TM05	Roar	Normal	Status	—	—	20	Normal
TM06	Toxic	Poison	Status	—	90	10	Normal
TM08	Bulk Up	Fighting	Status	—	—	20	Self
TM10	Hidden Power	Normal	Special	60	100	15	Normal
TM12	Taunt	Dark	Status	—	100	20	Normal
TM17	Protect	Normal	Status	—	—	10	Self
TM21	Frustration	Normal	Physical	—	100	20	Normal
TM27	Return	Normal	Physical	—	100	20	Normal
TM31	Brick Break	Fighting	Physical	75	100	15	Normal
TM32	Double Team	Normal	Status	—	—	15	Self
TM39	Rock Tomb	Rock	Physical	60	95	15	Normal
TM42	Facade	Normal	Physical	70	100	20	Normal
TM44	Rest	Psychic	Status	—	—	10	Self
TM45	Attract	Normal	Status	—	100	15	Normal
TM48	Round	Normal	Special	60	100	15	Normal
TM49	Echoed Voice	Normal	Special	40	100	15	Normal
TM69	Rock Polish	Rock	Status	—	—	20	Self
TM71	Stone Edge	Rock	Physical	100	80	5	Normal
TM75	Swords Dance	Normal	Status	—	—	20	Self
TM80	Rock Slide	Rock	Physical	75	90	10	Many Others
TM87	Swagger	Normal	Status	—	85	15	Normal
TM88	Sleep Talk	Normal	Status	—	—	10	Self
TM90	Substitute	Normal	Status	—	—	10	Self
TM95	Snarl	Dark	Special	55	95	15	Many Others
TM100	Confide	Normal	Status	—	—	20	Normal

❖ MOVES TAUGHT BY PEOPLE

Name	Type	Kind	Pow.	Acc.	PP	Range

❖ MOVES LEARNED WHEN EVOLVING

Name	Type	Kind	Pow.	Acc.	PP	Range
Counter	Fighting	Physical	—	100	20	Varies

❖ EGG MOVES

Name	Type	Kind	Pow.	Acc.	PP	Range

❖ EXCLUSIVE Z-MOVE

Name	Base Move	Type	Kind	Pow.	Acc.	Range

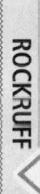

Alola Pokédex	Melemele	Akala	Ula'ula	Poni
105	105	—	—	—

Spinda
Spot Panda Pokémon

NORMAL

HEIGHT: 3'07"
WEIGHT: 11.0 lbs.

Its steps are staggering and unsteady, but Spinda thinks it's walking in a straight line.

Each and every Spinda has a slightly different configuration of spots. There are collectors who enjoy the tiny differences in their spot patterns.

ABILITY
Own Tempo
Tangled Feet

HIDDEN ABILITY
Contrary

Damage taken in normal battles

NORMAL ×1	FIGHTING ×2	ROCK ×1			
FIRE ×1	POISON ×1	GHOST ×0			
WATER ×1	GROUND ×1	DRAGON ×1			
GRASS ×1	FLYING ×1	DARK ×1			
ELECTRIC ×1	PSYCHIC ×1	STEEL ×1			
ICE ×1	BUG ×1	FAIRY ×1			

SPECIES STRENGTHS
HP	◆◆
Attack	◆◆
Defense	◆◆◆
Sp. Atk	◆◆
Sp. Def	◆◆◆
Speed	◆◆◆◆

EGG GROUPS
Field   Human-Like

ITEM SOMETIMES HELD BY WILD POKÉMON
—

EVOLUTION
Does not evolve

MAIN WAY TO REGISTER IN THE POKÉDEX
Catch in the tall grass in the Farthest Hollow on Ten Carat Hill

Same form for male/female

❖ LEVEL-UP MOVES

Lv.	Name	Type	Kind	Pow.	Acc.	PP	Range
1	Tackle	Normal	Physical	40	100	35	Normal
5	Copycat	Normal	Status	—	—	20	Self
10	Feint Attack	Dark	Physical	60	—	20	Normal
14	Psybeam	Psychic	Special	65	100	20	Normal
19	Hypnosis	Psychic	Status	—	60	20	Normal
23	Dizzy Punch	Normal	Physical	70	100	10	Normal
28	Sucker Punch	Dark	Physical	70	100	5	Normal
32	Teeter Dance	Normal	Status	—	100	20	Adjacent
37	Uproar	Normal	Special	90	100	10	1 Random
41	Psych Up	Normal	Status	—	—	10	Normal
46	Double-Edge	Normal	Physical	120	100	15	Normal
50	Flail	Normal	Physical	—	100	15	Normal
55	Thrash	Normal	Physical	120	100	10	1 Random

❖ TM MOVES

No.	Name	Type	Kind	Pow.	Acc.	PP	Range
TM01	Work Up	Normal	Status	—	—	30	Self
TM04	Calm Mind	Psychic	Status	—	—	20	Self
TM06	Toxic	Poison	Status	—	90	10	Normal
TM10	Hidden Power	Normal	Special	60	100	15	Normal
TM11	Sunny Day	Fire	Status	—	—	5	Both Sides
TM17	Protect	Normal	Status	—	—	10	Self
TM18	Rain Dance	Water	Status	—	—	5	Both Sides
TM20	Safeguard	Normal	Status	—	—	25	Your Side
TM21	Frustration	Normal	Physical	—	100	20	Normal
TM27	Return	Normal	Physical	—	100	20	Normal
TM29	Psychic	Psychic	Special	90	100	10	Normal
TM30	Shadow Ball	Ghost	Special	80	100	15	Normal
TM31	Brick Break	Fighting	Physical	75	100	15	Normal
TM32	Double Team	Normal	Status	—	—	15	Self
TM39	Rock Tomb	Rock	Physical	60	95	15	Normal
TM42	Facade	Normal	Physical	70	100	20	Normal
TM44	Rest	Psychic	Status	—	—	10	Self
TM45	Attract	Normal	Status	—	100	15	Normal
TM46	Thief	Dark	Physical	60	100	25	Normal
TM48	Round	Normal	Special	60	100	15	Normal
TM56	Fling	Dark	Physical	—	100	10	Normal
TM77	Psych Up	Normal	Status	—	—	10	Normal
TM80	Rock Slide	Rock	Physical	75	90	10	Many Others
TM85	Dream Eater	Psychic	Special	100	100	15	Normal
TM87	Swagger	Normal	Status	—	85	15	Normal
TM88	Sleep Talk	Normal	Status	—	—	10	Self
TM90	Substitute	Normal	Status	—	—	10	Self
TM92	Trick Room	Psychic	Status	—	—	5	Both Sides

No.	Name	Type	Kind	Pow.	Acc.	PP	Range
TM93	Wild Charge	Electric	Physical	90	100	15	Normal
TM100	Confide	Normal	Status	—	—	20	Normal

❖ MOVES TAUGHT BY PEOPLE

Name	Type	Kind	Pow.	Acc.	PP	Range

❖ MOVES LEARNED WHEN EVOLVING

Name	Type	Kind	Pow.	Acc.	PP	Range

❖ EGG MOVES

Name	Type	Kind	Pow.	Acc.	PP	Range
Encore	Normal	Status	—	100	5	Normal
Assist	Normal	Status	—	—	20	Self
Disable	Normal	Status	—	100	20	Normal
Baton Pass	Normal	Status	—	—	40	Self
Wish	Normal	Status	—	—	10	Self
Trick	Psychic	Status	—	100	10	Normal
Smelling Salts	Normal	Physical	70	100	10	Normal
Fake Out	Normal	Physical	40	100	10	Normal
Role Play	Psychic	Status	—	—	10	Normal
Psycho Cut	Psychic	Physical	70	100	20	Normal
Fake Tears	Dark	Status	—	100	20	Normal
Rapid Spin	Normal	Physical	20	100	40	Normal
Icy Wind	Ice	Special	55	95	15	Many Others
Water Pulse	Water	Special	60	100	20	Normal
Psycho Shift	Psychic	Status	—	100	10	Normal
Guard Split	Psychic	Status	—	—	10	Normal
Spotlight	Normal	Status	—	—	15	Normal

❖ EXCLUSIVE Z-MOVE

Name	Base Move	Type	Kind	Pow.	Acc.	Range

Spinda's Spots

Each Spinda's face has a slightly different pattern of spots on it. You can encounter Spinda in Ten Carat Hill's Farthest Hollow. Try to catch a bunch and see if any two look just alike. People say that the chances of catching two Spinda with identical spot patterns are less than 1 in 4 billion, though, so you'll need to get incredibly lucky or catch a huge number of Spinda before you ever see the same pattern twice! Use some Repeat Balls if you'd like to catch a lot of Spinda a bit more easily. Who knows, maybe you'll finally be the Trainer who catches two identical Spinda!

Can you spot the difference?

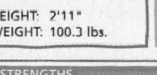

Alola Pokédex	Melemele	Akala	Ula'ula	Poni
106	106	038	053	055

Tentacool

Jellyfish Pokémon

WATER POISON

HEIGHT: 2'11"
WEIGHT: 100.3 lbs.

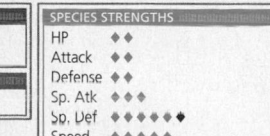

They can be found lying dehydrated on beaches, but they are often still alive. When soaked in water, they will revive.

It drifts in shallow seas, such as the areas near beaches. If you get bitten or stabbed by its toxic tentacles, rush to the hospital.

Same form for male/female

ABILITY
Clear Body
Liquid Ooze

HIDDEN ABILITY
Rain Dish

SPECIES STRENGTHS
HP ◆◆
Attack ◆◆
Defense ◆◆
Sp. Atk ◆◆◆
Sp. Def ◆◆◆◆◆◆
Speed ◆◆◆◆◆

EGG GROUPS
Water 3

ITEM SOMETIMES HELD BY WILD POKÉMON
Poison Barb

EVOLUTION

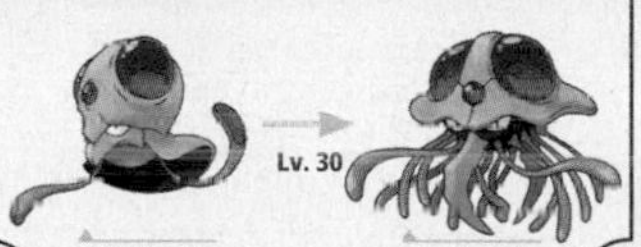

MAIN WAY TO REGISTER IN THE POKÉDEX
Catch on the water surface in Melemele Sea

Damage taken in normal battles

NORMAL	×1	FIGHTING	×0.5	ROCK	×1
FIRE	×0.5	POISON	×0.5	GHOST	×1
WATER	×0.5	GROUND	×2	DRAGON	×1
GRASS	×1	FLYING	×1	DARK	×1
ELECTRIC	×2	PSYCHIC	×2	STEEL	×0.5
ICE	×0.5	BUG	×0.5	FAIRY	×0.5

❖ LEVEL-UP MOVES

Lv.	Name	Type	Kind	Pow.	Acc.	PP	Range
1	Poison Sting	Poison	Physical	15	100	35	Normal
4	Supersonic	Normal	Status	—	55	20	Normal
7	Constrict	Normal	Physical	10	100	35	Normal
10	Acid	Poison	Special	40	100	30	Many Others
13	Toxic Spikes	Poison	Status	—	—	20	Other Side
16	Water Pulse	Water	Special	60	100	20	Normal
19	Wrap	Normal	Physical	15	90	20	Normal
22	Acid Spray	Poison	Special	40	100	20	Normal
25	Bubble Beam	Water	Special	65	100	20	Normal
28	Barrier	Psychic	Status	—	—	20	Self
31	Poison Jab	Poison	Physical	80	100	20	Normal
34	Brine	Water	Special	65	100	10	Normal
37	Screech	Normal	Status	—	85	40	Normal
40	Hex	Ghost	Special	65	100	10	Normal
43	Sludge Wave	Poison	Special	95	100	10	Adjacent
46	Hydro Pump	Water	Special	110	80	5	Normal
49	Wring Out	Normal	Special	—	100	5	Normal

❖ TM MOVES

No.	Name	Type	Kind	Pow.	Acc.	PP	Range
TM06	Toxic	Poison	Status	—	90	10	Normal
TM07	Hail	Ice	Status	—	—	10	Both Sides
TM09	Venoshock	Poison	Special	65	100	10	Normal
TM10	Hidden Power	Normal	Special	60	100	15	Normal
TM13	Ice Beam	Ice	Special	90	100	10	Normal
TM14	Blizzard	Ice	Special	110	70	5	Many Others
TM17	Protect	Normal	Status	—	—	10	Self
TM18	Rain Dance	Water	Status	—	—	5	Both Sides
TM20	Safeguard	Normal	Status	—	—	25	Your Side
TM21	Frustration	Normal	Physical	—	100	20	Normal
TM27	Return	Normal	Physical	—	100	20	Normal
TM32	Double Team	Normal	Status	—	—	15	Self
TM34	Sludge Wave	Poison	Special	95	100	10	Adjacent
TM36	Sludge Bomb	Poison	Special	90	100	10	Normal
TM42	Facade	Normal	Physical	70	100	20	Normal
TM44	Rest	Psychic	Status	—	—	10	Self
TM45	Attract	Normal	Status	—	100	15	Normal
TM46	Thief	Dark	Physical	60	100	25	Normal
TM48	Round	Normal	Special	60	100	15	Normal
TM55	Scald	Water	Special	80	100	15	Normal
TM66	Payback	Dark	Physical	50	100	10	Normal
TM75	Swords Dance	Normal	Status	—	—	20	Self
TM83	Infestation	Bug	Special	20	100	20	Normal
TM84	Poison Jab	Poison	Physical	80	100	20	Normal
TM87	Swagger	Normal	Status	—	85	15	Normal
TM88	Sleep Talk	Normal	Status	—	—	10	Self
TM90	Substitute	Normal	Status	—	—	10	Self
TM94	Surf	Water	Special	90	100	15	Adjacent
TM98	Waterfall	Water	Physical	80	100	15	Normal
TM99	Dazzling Gleam	Fairy	Special	80	100	10	Many Others
TM100	Confide	Normal	Status	—	—	20	Normal

❖ EXCLUSIVE Z-MOVE

Name	Base Move	Type	Kind	Pow.	Acc.	Range

❖ MOVES TAUGHT BY PEOPLE

Name	Type	Kind	Pow.	Acc.	PP	Range

❖ MOVES LEARNED WHEN EVOLVING

Name	Type	Kind	Pow.	Acc.	PP	Range

❖ EGG MOVES

Name	Type	Kind	Pow.	Acc.	PP	Range
Aurora Beam	Ice	Special	65	100	20	Normal
Mirror Coat	Psychic	Special	—	100	20	Varies
Rapid Spin	Normal	Physical	20	100	40	Normal
Haze	Ice	Status	—	—	30	Both Sides
Confuse Ray	Ghost	Status	—	100	10	Normal
Knock Off	Dark	Physical	65	100	20	Normal
Acupressure	Normal	Status	—	—	30	Self / Ally
Muddy Water	Water	Special	90	85	10	Many Others
Bubble	Water	Special	40	100	30	Many Others
Aqua Ring	Water	Status	—	—	20	Self
Tickle	Normal	Status	—	100	20	Normal

Alola Pokédex	Melemele	Akala	Ula'ula	Poni
107	107	039	054	056

Tentacruel

Jellyfish Pokémon

WATER POISON

HEIGHT: 5'03"
WEIGHT: 121.3 lbs.

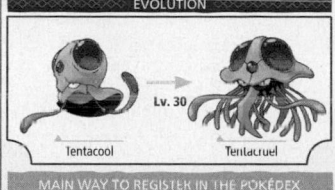

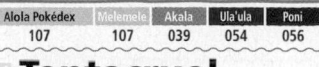

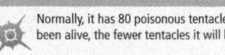

Normally, it has 80 poisonous tentacles. The longer one has been alive, the fewer tentacles it will have.

Although these Pokémon are rare, when a large outbreak of them occurs, all fish Pokémon disappear from the surrounding sea.

Same form for male/female

ABILITY
Clear Body
Liquid Ooze

HIDDEN ABILITY
Rain Dish

SPECIES STRENGTHS
HP ◆◆◆
Attack ◆◆◆◆
Defense ◆◆◆◆
Sp. Atk ◆◆◆◆
Sp. Def ◆◆◆◆◆◆◆
Speed ◆◆◆◆◆◆

EGG GROUPS
Water 3

ITEM SOMETIMES HELD BY WILD POKÉMON
Poison Barb

EVOLUTION

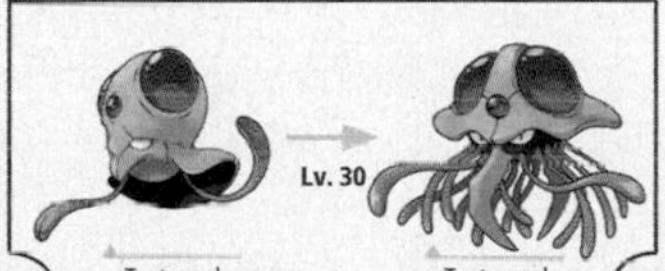

MAIN WAY TO REGISTER IN THE POKÉDEX
Catch on the water surface in Poni Wilds

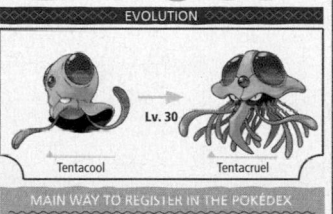

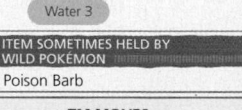

Damage taken in normal battles

NORMAL	×1	FIGHTING	×0.5	ROCK	×1
FIRE	×0.5	POISON	×0.5	GHOST	×1
WATER	×0.5	GROUND	×2	DRAGON	×1
GRASS	×1	FLYING	×1	DARK	×1
ELECTRIC	×2	PSYCHIC	×2	STEEL	×0.5
ICE	×0.5	BUG	×0.5	FAIRY	×0.5

❖ LEVEL-UP MOVES

Lv.	Name	Type	Kind	Pow.	Acc.	PP	Range
1	Reflect Type	Normal	Status	—	—	15	Normal
1	Wring Out	Normal	Special	—	100	5	Normal
1	Poison Sting	Poison	Physical	15	100	35	Normal
1	Supersonic	Normal	Status	—	55	20	Normal
1	Constrict	Normal	Physical	10	100	35	Normal
1	Acid	Poison	Special	40	100	30	Many Others
4	Supersonic	Normal	Status	—	55	20	Normal
7	Constrict	Normal	Physical	10	100	35	Normal
10	Acid	Poison	Special	40	100	30	Many Others
13	Toxic Spikes	Poison	Status	—	—	20	Other Side
16	Water Pulse	Water	Special	60	100	20	Normal
19	Wrap	Normal	Physical	15	90	20	Normal
22	Acid Spray	Poison	Special	40	100	20	Normal
25	Bubble Beam	Water	Special	65	100	20	Normal
28	Barrier	Psychic	Status	—	—	20	Self
32	Poison Jab	Poison	Physical	80	100	20	Normal
36	Brine	Water	Special	65	100	10	Normal
40	Screech	Normal	Status	—	85	40	Normal
44	Hex	Ghost	Special	65	100	10	Normal
48	Sludge Wave	Poison	Special	95	100	10	Adjacent
52	Hydro Pump	Water	Special	110	80	5	Normal
56	Wring Out	Normal	Special	—	100	5	Normal

❖ TM MOVES

No.	Name	Type	Kind	Pow.	Acc.	PP	Range
TM06	Toxic	Poison	Status	—	90	10	Normal
TM07	Hail	Ice	Status	—	—	10	Both Sides
TM09	Venoshock	Poison	Special	65	100	10	Normal
TM10	Hidden Power	Normal	Special	60	100	15	Normal
TM13	Ice Beam	Ice	Special	90	100	10	Normal
TM14	Blizzard	Ice	Special	110	70	5	Many Others
TM15	Hyper Beam	Normal	Special	150	90	5	Normal
TM17	Protect	Normal	Status	—	—	10	Self
TM18	Rain Dance	Water	Status	—	—	5	Both Sides
TM20	Safeguard	Normal	Status	—	—	25	Your Side
TM21	Frustration	Normal	Physical	—	100	20	Normal
TM27	Return	Normal	Physical	—	100	20	Normal
TM32	Double Team	Normal	Status	—	—	15	Self
TM34	Sludge Wave	Poison	Special	95	100	10	Adjacent
TM36	Sludge Bomb	Poison	Special	90	100	10	Normal
TM42	Facade	Normal	Physical	70	100	20	Normal
TM44	Rest	Psychic	Status	—	—	10	Self
TM45	Attract	Normal	Status	—	100	15	Normal
TM46	Thief	Dark	Physical	60	100	25	Normal
TM48	Round	Normal	Special	60	100	15	Normal
TM55	Scald	Water	Special	80	100	15	Normal
TM66	Payback	Dark	Physical	50	100	10	Normal
TM68	Giga Impact	Normal	Physical	150	90	5	Normal
TM75	Swords Dance	Normal	Status	—	—	20	Self
TM83	Infestation	Bug	Special	20	100	20	Normal
TM84	Poison Jab	Poison	Physical	80	100	20	Normal
TM87	Swagger	Normal	Status	—	85	15	Normal
TM88	Sleep Talk	Normal	Status	—	—	10	Self
TM90	Substitute	Normal	Status	—	—	10	Self
TM94	Surf	Water	Special	90	100	15	Adjacent
TM98	Waterfall	Water	Physical	80	100	15	Normal
TM99	Dazzling Gleam	Fairy	Special	80	100	10	Many Others
TM100	Confide	Normal	Status	—	—	20	Normal

❖ EXCLUSIVE Z-MOVE

Name	Base Move	Type	Kind	Pow.	Acc.	Range

❖ MOVES TAUGHT BY PEOPLE

Name	Type	Kind	Pow.	Acc.	PP	Range

❖ MOVES LEARNED WHEN EVOLVING

Name	Type	Kind	Pow.	Acc.	PP	Range

❖ EGG MOVES

Name	Type	Kind	Pow.	Acc.	PP	Range

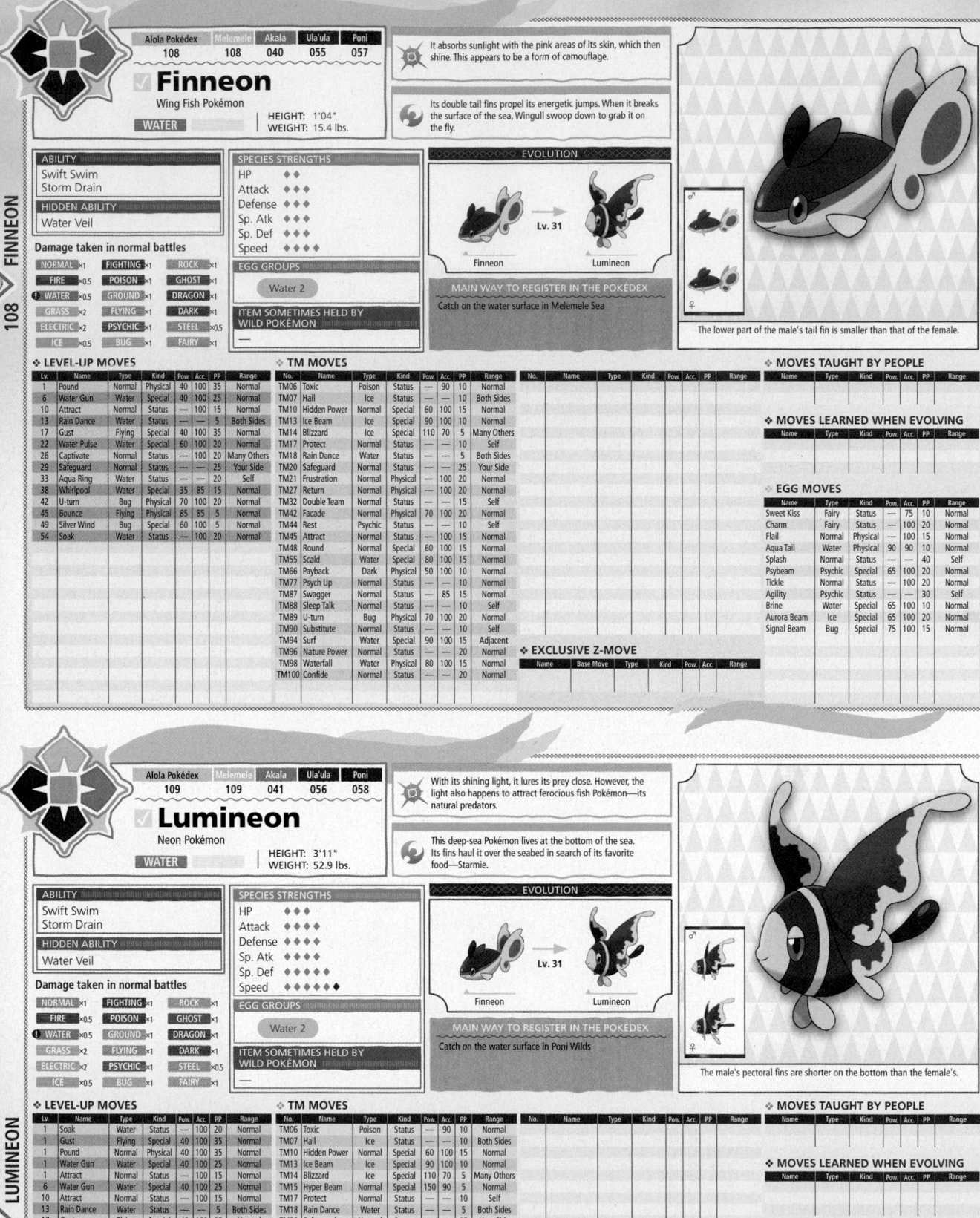

Finneon

Alola Pokédex	Melemele	Akala	Ula'ula	Poni
108	108	040	055	057

☑ **Finneon**

Wing Fish Pokémon

WATER

HEIGHT: 1'04"
WEIGHT: 15.4 lbs.

It absorbs sunlight with the pink areas of its skin, which then shine. This appears to be a form of camouflage.

Its double tail fins propel its energetic jumps. When it breaks the surface of the sea, Wingull swoop down to grab it on the fly.

ABILITY
Swift Swim
Storm Drain

HIDDEN ABILITY
Water Veil

SPECIES STRENGTHS
HP	◆◆
Attack	◆◆◆
Defense	◆◆◆
Sp. Atk	◆◆◆
Sp. Def	◆◆◆
Speed	◆◆◆◆

EGG GROUPS
Water 2

ITEM SOMETIMES HELD BY WILD POKÉMON
—

Damage taken in normal battles
NORMAL ×1	FIGHTING ×1	ROCK ×1
FIRE ×0.5	POISON ×1	GHOST ×1
WATER ×0.5	GROUND ×1	DRAGON ×1
GRASS ×2	FLYING ×1	DARK ×1
ELECTRIC ×2	PSYCHIC ×1	STEEL ×0.5
ICE ×1	BUG ×1	FAIRY ×1

EVOLUTION
Finneon → Lv. 31 → Lumineon

MAIN WAY TO REGISTER IN THE POKÉDEX
Catch on the water surface in Melemele Sea

The lower part of the male's tail fin is smaller than that of the female.

❖ LEVEL-UP MOVES
Lv.	Name	Type	Kind	Pow.	Acc.	PP	Range
1	Pound	Normal	Physical	40	100	35	Normal
6	Water Gun	Water	Special	40	100	25	Normal
10	Attract	Normal	Status	—	100	15	Normal
13	Rain Dance	Water	Status	—	—	5	Both Sides
17	Gust	Flying	Special	40	100	35	Normal
22	Water Pulse	Water	Special	60	100	20	Normal
26	Captivate	Normal	Status	—	100	20	Many Others
29	Safeguard	Normal	Status	—	—	25	Your Side
33	Aqua Ring	Water	Status	—	—	20	Self
38	Whirlpool	Water	Special	35	85	15	Normal
42	U-turn	Bug	Physical	70	100	20	Normal
45	Bounce	Flying	Physical	85	85	5	Normal
49	Silver Wind	Bug	Special	60	100	5	Normal
54	Soak	Water	Status	—	100	20	Normal

❖ TM MOVES
No.	Name	Type	Kind	Pow.	Acc.	PP	Range
TM06	Toxic	Poison	Status	—	90	10	Normal
TM07	Hail	Ice	Status	—	—	10	Both Sides
TM10	Hidden Power	Normal	Special	60	100	15	Normal
TM13	Ice Beam	Ice	Special	90	100	10	Normal
TM14	Blizzard	Ice	Special	110	70	5	Many Others
TM17	Protect	Normal	Status	—	—	10	Self
TM18	Rain Dance	Water	Status	—	—	5	Both Sides
TM20	Safeguard	Normal	Status	—	—	25	Your Side
TM21	Frustration	Normal	Physical	—	100	20	Normal
TM27	Return	Normal	Physical	—	100	20	Normal
TM32	Double Team	Normal	Status	—	—	15	Self
TM42	Facade	Normal	Physical	70	100	20	Normal
TM44	Rest	Psychic	Status	—	—	10	Self
TM45	Attract	Normal	Status	—	100	15	Normal
TM48	Round	Normal	Special	60	100	15	Normal
TM55	Scald	Water	Special	80	100	15	Normal
TM66	Payback	Dark	Physical	50	100	10	Normal
TM77	Psych Up	Normal	Status	—	—	10	Normal
TM87	Swagger	Normal	Status	—	85	15	Normal
TM88	Sleep Talk	Normal	Status	—	—	10	Self
TM89	U-turn	Bug	Physical	70	100	20	Normal
TM90	Substitute	Normal	Status	—	—	10	Self
TM94	Surf	Water	Special	90	100	15	Adjacent
TM96	Nature Power	Normal	Status	—	—	20	Normal
TM98	Waterfall	Water	Physical	80	100	15	Normal
TM100	Confide	Normal	Status	—	—	20	Normal

❖ MOVES TAUGHT BY PEOPLE
Name	Type	Kind	Pow.	Acc.	PP	Range

❖ MOVES LEARNED WHEN EVOLVING
Name	Type	Kind	Pow.	Acc.	PP	Range

❖ EGG MOVES
Name	Type	Kind	Pow.	Acc.	PP	Range
Sweet Kiss	Fairy	Status	—	75	10	Normal
Charm	Fairy	Status	—	100	20	Normal
Flail	Normal	Physical	—	100	15	Normal
Aqua Tail	Water	Physical	90	90	10	Normal
Splash	Normal	Status	—	—	40	Self
Psybeam	Psychic	Special	65	100	20	Normal
Tickle	Normal	Status	—	100	20	Normal
Agility	Psychic	Status	—	—	30	Self
Brine	Water	Special	65	100	10	Normal
Aurora Beam	Ice	Special	65	100	20	Normal
Signal Beam	Bug	Special	75	100	15	Normal

❖ EXCLUSIVE Z-MOVE
Name	Base Move	Type	Kind	Pow.	Acc.	Range

Lumineon

Alola Pokédex	Melemele	Akala	Ula'ula	Poni
109	109	041	056	058

☑ **Lumineon**

Neon Pokémon

WATER

HEIGHT: 3'11"
WEIGHT: 52.9 lbs.

With its shining light, it lures its prey close. However, the light also happens to attract ferocious fish Pokémon—its natural predators.

This deep-sea Pokémon lives at the bottom of the sea. Its fins haul it over the seabed in search of its favorite food—Starmie.

ABILITY
Swift Swim
Storm Drain

HIDDEN ABILITY
Water Veil

SPECIES STRENGTHS
HP	◆◆◆
Attack	◆◆◆
Defense	◆◆◆◆
Sp. Atk	◆◆◆◆
Sp. Def	◆◆◆◆◆
Speed	◆◆◆◆◆◆◆

EGG GROUPS
Water 2

ITEM SOMETIMES HELD BY WILD POKÉMON
—

Damage taken in normal battles
NORMAL ×1	FIGHTING ×1	ROCK ×1
FIRE ×0.5	POISON ×1	GHOST ×1
WATER ×0.5	GROUND ×1	DRAGON ×1
GRASS ×2	FLYING ×1	DARK ×1
ELECTRIC ×2	PSYCHIC ×1	STEEL ×0.5
ICE ×1	BUG ×1	FAIRY ×1

EVOLUTION
Finneon → Lv. 31 → Lumineon

MAIN WAY TO REGISTER IN THE POKÉDEX
Catch on the water surface in Poni Wilds

The male's pectoral fins are shorter on the bottom than the female's.

❖ LEVEL-UP MOVES
Lv.	Name	Type	Kind	Pow.	Acc.	PP	Range
1	Soak	Water	Status	—	100	20	Normal
1	Gust	Flying	Special	40	100	35	Normal
1	Pound	Normal	Physical	40	100	35	Normal
1	Water Gun	Water	Special	40	100	25	Normal
1	Attract	Normal	Status	—	100	15	Normal
6	Water Gun	Water	Special	40	100	25	Normal
10	Attract	Normal	Status	—	100	15	Normal
13	Rain Dance	Water	Status	—	—	5	Both Sides
17	Gust	Flying	Special	40	100	35	Normal
22	Water Pulse	Water	Special	60	100	20	Normal
26	Captivate	Normal	Status	—	100	20	Many Others
29	Safeguard	Normal	Status	—	—	25	Your Side
35	Aqua Ring	Water	Status	—	—	20	Self
42	Whirlpool	Water	Special	35	85	15	Normal
48	U-turn	Bug	Physical	70	100	20	Normal
53	Bounce	Flying	Physical	85	85	5	Normal
59	Silver Wind	Bug	Special	60	100	5	Normal
66	Soak	Water	Status	—	100	20	Normal

❖ TM MOVES
No.	Name	Type	Kind	Pow.	Acc.	PP	Range
TM06	Toxic	Poison	Status	—	90	10	Normal
TM07	Hail	Ice	Status	—	—	10	Both Sides
TM10	Hidden Power	Normal	Special	60	100	15	Normal
TM13	Ice Beam	Ice	Special	90	100	10	Normal
TM14	Blizzard	Ice	Special	110	70	5	Many Others
TM15	Hyper Beam	Normal	Special	150	90	5	Normal
TM17	Protect	Normal	Status	—	—	10	Self
TM18	Rain Dance	Water	Status	—	—	5	Both Sides
TM20	Safeguard	Normal	Status	—	—	25	Your Side
TM21	Frustration	Normal	Physical	—	100	20	Normal
TM27	Return	Normal	Physical	—	100	20	Normal
TM32	Double Team	Normal	Status	—	—	15	Self
TM42	Facade	Normal	Physical	70	100	20	Normal
TM44	Rest	Psychic	Status	—	—	10	Self
TM45	Attract	Normal	Status	—	100	15	Normal
TM48	Round	Normal	Special	60	100	15	Normal
TM55	Scald	Water	Special	80	100	15	Normal
TM66	Payback	Dark	Physical	50	100	10	Normal
TM68	Giga Impact	Normal	Physical	150	90	5	Normal
TM77	Psych Up	Normal	Status	—	—	10	Normal
TM87	Swagger	Normal	Status	—	85	15	Normal
TM88	Sleep Talk	Normal	Status	—	—	10	Self
TM89	U-turn	Bug	Physical	70	100	20	Normal
TM90	Substitute	Normal	Status	—	—	10	Self
TM94	Surf	Water	Special	90	100	15	Adjacent
TM98	Waterfall	Water	Physical	80	100	15	Normal
TM100	Confide	Normal	Status	—	—	20	Normal

❖ MOVES TAUGHT BY PEOPLE
Name	Type	Kind	Pow.	Acc.	PP	Range

❖ MOVES LEARNED WHEN EVOLVING
Name	Type	Kind	Pow.	Acc.	PP	Range

❖ EGG MOVES
Name	Type	Kind	Pow.	Acc.	PP	Range

❖ EXCLUSIVE Z-MOVE
Name	Base Move	Type	Kind	Pow.	Acc.	Range

Alola Pokédex	Melemele	Akala	Ula'ula	Poni
110	110	042	057	—

Wishiwashi
Small Fry Pokémon

WATER

HEIGHT: 0'08"
WEIGHT: 0.7 lbs.

When it's in trouble, its eyes moisten and begin to shine. The shining light attracts its comrades, and they stand together against their enemies.

It's awfully weak and notably tasty, so everyone is always out to get it. As it happens, anyone trying to bully it receives a painful lesson.

SOLO FORM

Same form for male/female

ABILITY
Schooling

HIDDEN ABILITY
—

SPECIES STRENGTHS
HP	◆◆
Attack	◆
Defense	◆
Sp. Atk	◆
Sp. Def	◆
Speed	◆◆◆

EGG GROUPS
Water 2

ITEM SOMETIMES HELD BY WILD POKÉMON
—

EVOLUTION
Does not evolve

MAIN WAY TO REGISTER IN THE POKÉDEX
Catch in the fishing spots in Melemele Sea

Damage taken in normal battles
NORMAL ×1	FIGHTING ×1	ROCK ×1			
FIRE ×0.5	POISON ×1	GHOST ×1			
WATER ×0.5	GROUND ×1	DRAGON ×1			
GRASS ×2	FLYING ×1	DARK ×1			
ELECTRIC ×2	PSYCHIC ×1	STEEL ×0.5			
ICE ×1	BUG ×1	FAIRY ×1			

✦ LEVEL-UP MOVES
Lv.	Name	Type	Kind	Pow.	Acc.	PP	Range
1	Water Gun	Water	Special	40	100	25	Normal
1	Growl	Normal	Status	—	100	40	Many Others
6	Helping Hand	Normal	Status	—	—	20	1 Ally
9	Feint Attack	Dark	Physical	60	—	20	Normal
14	Brine	Water	Special	65	100	10	Normal
17	Aqua Ring	Water	Status	—	—	20	Self
22	Tearful Look	Normal	Status	—	—	20	Normal
25	Take Down	Normal	Physical	90	85	20	Normal
30	Dive	Water	Physical	80	100	10	Normal
33	Beat Up	Dark	Physical	—	100	10	Normal
38	Aqua Tail	Water	Physical	90	90	10	Normal
41	Double-Edge	Normal	Physical	120	100	15	Normal
46	Soak	Water	Status	—	100	20	Normal
49	Endeavor	Normal	Physical	—	100	5	Normal
54	Hydro Pump	Water	Special	110	80	5	Normal

✦ TM MOVES
No.	Name	Type	Kind	Pow.	Acc.	PP	Range
TM06	Toxic	Poison	Status	—	90	10	Normal
TM07	Hail	Ice	Status	—	—	10	Both Sides
TM10	Hidden Power	Normal	Special	60	100	15	Normal
TM13	Ice Beam	Ice	Special	90	100	10	Normal
TM17	Protect	Normal	Status	—	—	10	Self
TM18	Rain Dance	Water	Status	—	—	5	Both Sides
TM21	Frustration	Normal	Physical	—	100	20	Normal
TM26	Earthquake	Ground	Physical	100	100	10	Adjacent
TM27	Return	Normal	Physical	—	100	20	Normal
TM32	Double Team	Normal	Status	—	—	15	Self
TM42	Facade	Normal	Physical	70	100	20	Normal
TM44	Rest	Psychic	Status	—	—	10	Self
TM45	Attract	Normal	Status	—	100	15	Normal
TM48	Round	Normal	Special	60	100	15	Normal
TM55	Scald	Water	Special	80	100	15	Normal
TM78	Bulldoze	Ground	Physical	60	100	20	Adjacent
TM87	Swagger	Normal	Status	—	85	15	Normal
TM88	Sleep Talk	Normal	Status	—	—	10	Self
TM89	U-turn	Bug	Physical	70	100	20	Normal
TM90	Substitute	Normal	Status	—	—	10	Self
TM94	Surf	Water	Special	90	100	15	Adjacent
TM98	Waterfall	Water	Physical	80	100	15	Normal
TM100	Confide	Normal	Status	—	—	20	Normal

✦ MOVES TAUGHT BY PEOPLE
Name	Type	Kind	Pow.	Acc.	PP	Range

✦ MOVES LEARNED WHEN EVOLVING
Name	Type	Kind	Pow.	Acc.	PP	Range

✦ EGG MOVES
Name	Type	Kind	Pow.	Acc.	PP	Range
Muddy Water	Water	Special	90	85	10	Many Others
Mist	Ice	Status	—	—	30	Your Side
Water Pulse	Water	Special	60	100	20	Normal
Water Sport	Water	Status	—	—	15	Both Sides

✦ EXCLUSIVE Z-MOVE
Name	Base Move	Type	Kind	Pow.	Acc.	Range

Get Ready to Get Schooled!

Once Wishiwashi reaches Lv. 20, its Schooling Ability allows it to call for help from its fellow Wishiwashi to take on its School Form. If its HP drops to less than ¼ of its maximum HP during a battle, though, it will stop schooling and return to its Solo Form. If you're able to restore your Wishiwashi's HP back up to higher than 25%, it will start schooling again at the end of the turn during which it was healed. You'll want to keep your Wishiwashi in School Form most of the time as most of its species strengths are much higher than they are when it's in Solo Form—except for its HP, which remains the same, and Speed, which is lower.

SCHOOL FORM

HEIGHT: 26'11"
WEIGHT: 173.3 lbs.

Same form for male/female

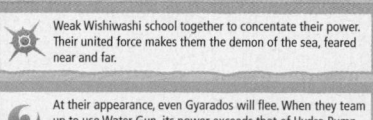

Weak Wishiwashi school together to concentrate their power. Their united force makes them the demon of the sea, feared near and far.

At their appearance, even Gyarados will flee. When they team up to use Water Gun, its power exceeds that of Hydro Pump.

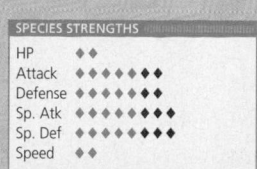

SPECIES STRENGTHS
HP	◆◆
Attack	◆◆◆◆◆◆
Defense	◆◆◆◆◆◆
Sp. Atk	◆◆◆◆◆◆
Sp. Def	◆◆◆◆◆◆
Speed	◆◆

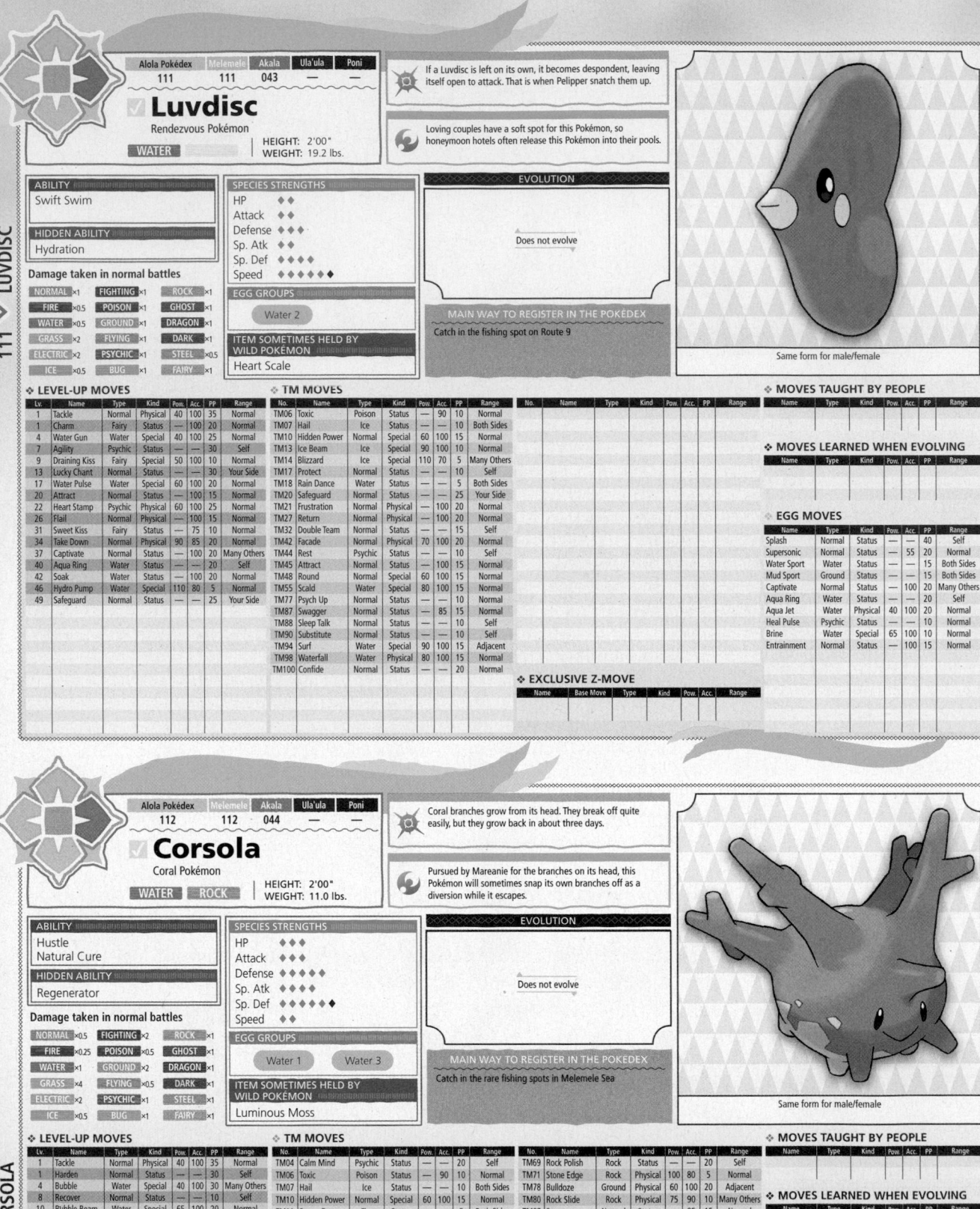

Luvdisc

Alola Pokédex	Melemele	Akala	Ula'ula	Poni
111	111	043	—	—

Luvdisc
Rendezvous Pokémon

WATER

HEIGHT: 2'00"
WEIGHT: 19.2 lbs.

If a Luvdisc is left on its own, it becomes despondent, leaving itself open to attack. That is when Pelipper snatch them up.

Loving couples have a soft spot for this Pokémon, so honeymoon hotels often release this Pokémon into their pools.

ABILITY
Swift Swim

HIDDEN ABILITY
Hydration

SPECIES STRENGTHS
HP ◆◆
Attack ◆◆
Defense ◆◆◆
Sp. Atk ◆◆
Sp. Def ◆◆◆◆
Speed ◆◆◆◆◆◆

EGG GROUPS
Water 2

ITEM SOMETIMES HELD BY WILD POKÉMON
Heart Scale

EVOLUTION
Does not evolve

MAIN WAY TO REGISTER IN THE POKÉDEX
Catch in the fishing spot on Route 9

Same form for male/female

Damage taken in normal battles

NORMAL ×1	FIGHTING ×1	ROCK ×1			
FIRE ×0.5	POISON ×1	GHOST ×1			
WATER ×0.5	GROUND ×1	DRAGON ×1			
GRASS ×2	FLYING ×1	DARK ×1			
ELECTRIC ×2	PSYCHIC ×1	STEEL ×0.5			
ICE ×0.5	BUG ×1	FAIRY ×1			

❖ LEVEL-UP MOVES

Lv.	Name	Type	Kind	Pow.	Acc.	PP	Range
1	Tackle	Normal	Physical	40	100	35	Normal
1	Charm	Fairy	Status	—	100	20	Normal
4	Water Gun	Water	Special	40	100	25	Normal
7	Agility	Psychic	Status	—	—	30	Self
9	Draining Kiss	Fairy	Special	50	100	10	Normal
13	Lucky Chant	Normal	Status	—	—	30	Your Side
17	Water Pulse	Water	Special	60	100	20	Normal
20	Attract	Normal	Status	—	100	15	Normal
22	Heart Stamp	Psychic	Physical	60	100	25	Normal
26	Flail	Normal	Physical	—	100	15	Normal
31	Sweet Kiss	Fairy	Status	—	75	10	Normal
34	Take Down	Normal	Physical	90	85	20	Normal
37	Captivate	Normal	Status	—	100	20	Many Others
40	Aqua Ring	Water	Status	—	—	20	Self
42	Soak	Water	Status	—	100	20	Normal
46	Hydro Pump	Water	Special	110	80	5	Normal
49	Safeguard	Normal	Status	—	—	25	Your Side

❖ TM MOVES

No.	Name	Type	Kind	Pow.	Acc.	PP	Range
TM06	Toxic	Poison	Status	—	90	10	Normal
TM07	Hail	Ice	Status	—	—	10	Both Sides
TM10	Hidden Power	Normal	Special	60	100	15	Normal
TM13	Ice Beam	Ice	Special	90	100	10	Normal
TM14	Blizzard	Ice	Special	110	70	5	Many Others
TM17	Protect	Normal	Status	—	—	10	Self
TM18	Rain Dance	Water	Status	—	—	5	Both Sides
TM20	Safeguard	Normal	Status	—	—	25	Your Side
TM21	Frustration	Normal	Physical	—	100	20	Normal
TM27	Return	Normal	Physical	—	100	20	Normal
TM32	Double Team	Normal	Status	—	—	15	Self
TM42	Facade	Normal	Physical	70	100	20	Normal
TM44	Rest	Psychic	Status	—	—	10	Self
TM45	Attract	Normal	Status	—	100	15	Normal
TM48	Round	Normal	Special	60	100	15	Normal
TM55	Scald	Water	Special	80	100	15	Normal
TM77	Psych Up	Normal	Status	—	—	10	Normal
TM87	Swagger	Normal	Status	—	85	15	Normal
TM88	Sleep Talk	Normal	Status	—	—	10	Self
TM90	Substitute	Normal	Status	—	—	10	Self
TM94	Surf	Water	Special	90	100	15	Adjacent
TM98	Waterfall	Water	Physical	80	100	15	Normal
TM100	Confide	Normal	Status	—	—	20	Normal

❖ MOVES TAUGHT BY PEOPLE

Name	Type	Kind	Pow.	Acc.	PP	Range

❖ MOVES LEARNED WHEN EVOLVING

Name	Type	Kind	Pow.	Acc.	PP	Range

❖ EGG MOVES

Name	Type	Kind	Pow.	Acc.	PP	Range
Splash	Normal	Status	—	—	40	Self
Supersonic	Normal	Status	—	55	20	Normal
Water Sport	Water	Status	—	—	15	Both Sides
Mud Sport	Ground	Status	—	—	15	Both Sides
Captivate	Normal	Status	—	100	20	Many Others
Aqua Ring	Water	Status	—	—	20	Self
Aqua Jet	Water	Physical	40	100	20	Normal
Heal Pulse	Psychic	Status	—	—	10	Normal
Brine	Water	Special	65	100	10	Normal
Entrainment	Normal	Status	—	100	15	Normal

❖ EXCLUSIVE Z-MOVE

Name	Base Move	Type	Kind	Pow.	Acc.	Range

Corsola

Alola Pokédex	Melemele	Akala	Ula'ula	Poni
112	112	044	—	—

Corsola
Coral Pokémon

WATER ROCK

HEIGHT: 2'00"
WEIGHT: 11.0 lbs.

Coral branches grow from its head. They break off quite easily, but they grow back in about three days.

Pursued by Mareanie for the branches on its head, this Pokémon will sometimes snap its own branches off as a diversion while it escapes.

ABILITY
Hustle
Natural Cure

HIDDEN ABILITY
Regenerator

SPECIES STRENGTHS
HP ◆◆◆
Attack ◆◆◆
Defense ◆◆◆◆◆
Sp. Atk ◆◆◆◆
Sp. Def ◆◆◆◆◆◆
Speed ◆◆

EGG GROUPS
Water 1   Water 3

ITEM SOMETIMES HELD BY WILD POKÉMON
Luminous Moss

EVOLUTION
Does not evolve

MAIN WAY TO REGISTER IN THE POKÉDEX
Catch in the rare fishing spots in Melemele Sea

Same form for male/female

Damage taken in normal battles

NORMAL ×0.5	FIGHTING ×2	ROCK ×1			
FIRE ×0.25	POISON ×0.5	GHOST ×1			
WATER ×1	GROUND ×2	DRAGON ×1			
GRASS ×4	FLYING ×0.5	DARK ×1			
ELECTRIC ×2	PSYCHIC ×1	STEEL ×1			
ICE ×0.5	BUG ×1	FAIRY ×1			

❖ LEVEL-UP MOVES

Lv.	Name	Type	Kind	Pow.	Acc.	PP	Range
1	Tackle	Normal	Physical	40	100	35	Normal
1	Harden	Normal	Status	—	—	30	Self
4	Bubble	Water	Special	40	100	30	Many Others
8	Recover	Normal	Status	—	—	10	Self
10	Bubble Beam	Water	Special	65	100	20	Normal
13	Refresh	Normal	Status	—	—	20	Self
17	Ancient Power	Rock	Special	60	100	5	Normal
20	Spike Cannon	Normal	Physical	20	100	15	Normal
23	Lucky Chant	Normal	Status	—	—	30	Your Side
27	Brine	Water	Special	65	100	10	Normal
29	Iron Defense	Steel	Status	—	—	15	Self
31	Rock Blast	Rock	Physical	25	90	10	Normal
35	Endure	Normal	Status	—	—	10	Self
38	Aqua Ring	Water	Status	—	—	20	Self
41	Power Gem	Rock	Special	80	100	20	Normal
45	Mirror Coat	Psychic	Special	—	100	20	Varies
47	Earth Power	Ground	Special	90	100	10	Normal
50	Flail	Normal	Physical	—	100	15	Normal

❖ TM MOVES

No.	Name	Type	Kind	Pow.	Acc.	PP	Range
TM04	Calm Mind	Psychic	Status	—	—	20	Self
TM06	Toxic	Poison	Status	—	90	10	Normal
TM07	Hail	Ice	Status	—	—	10	Both Sides
TM10	Hidden Power	Normal	Special	60	100	15	Normal
TM11	Sunny Day	Fire	Status	—	—	5	Both Sides
TM13	Ice Beam	Ice	Special	90	100	10	Normal
TM14	Blizzard	Ice	Special	110	70	5	Many Others
TM16	Light Screen	Psychic	Status	—	—	30	Your Side
TM17	Protect	Normal	Status	—	—	10	Self
TM18	Rain Dance	Water	Status	—	—	5	Both Sides
TM20	Safeguard	Normal	Status	—	—	25	Your Side
TM21	Frustration	Normal	Physical	—	100	20	Normal
TM26	Earthquake	Ground	Physical	100	100	10	Adjacent
TM27	Return	Normal	Physical	—	100	20	Normal
TM29	Psychic	Psychic	Special	90	100	10	Normal
TM30	Shadow Ball	Ghost	Special	80	100	15	Normal
TM32	Double Team	Normal	Status	—	—	15	Self
TM33	Reflect	Psychic	Status	—	—	20	Your Side
TM37	Sandstorm	Rock	Status	—	—	10	Both Sides
TM39	Rock Tomb	Rock	Physical	60	95	15	Normal
TM42	Facade	Normal	Physical	70	100	20	Normal
TM44	Rest	Psychic	Status	—	—	10	Self
TM45	Attract	Normal	Status	—	100	15	Normal
TM48	Round	Normal	Special	60	100	15	Normal
TM55	Scald	Water	Special	80	100	15	Normal
TM64	Explosion	Normal	Physical	250	100	5	Adjacent
TM69	Rock Polish	Rock	Status	—	—	20	Self
TM71	Stone Edge	Rock	Physical	100	80	5	Normal
TM78	Bulldoze	Ground	Physical	60	100	20	Adjacent
TM80	Rock Slide	Rock	Physical	75	90	10	Many Others
TM87	Swagger	Normal	Status	—	85	15	Normal
TM88	Sleep Talk	Normal	Status	—	—	10	Self
TM90	Substitute	Normal	Status	—	—	10	Self
TM94	Surf	Water	Special	90	100	15	Adjacent
TM96	Nature Power	Normal	Status	—	—	20	Normal
TM100	Confide	Normal	Status	—	—	20	Normal

❖ MOVES TAUGHT BY PEOPLE

Name	Type	Kind	Pow.	Acc.	PP	Range

❖ MOVES LEARNED WHEN EVOLVING

Name	Type	Kind	Pow.	Acc.	PP	Range

❖ EGG MOVES

Name	Type	Kind	Pow.	Acc.	PP	Range
Screech	Normal	Status	—	85	40	Normal
Mist	Ice	Status	—	—	30	Your Side
Amnesia	Psychic	Status	—	—	20	Self
Barrier	Psychic	Status	—	—	20	Self
Ingrain	Grass	Status	—	—	20	Self
Confuse Ray	Ghost	Status	—	100	10	Normal
Icicle Spear	Ice	Physical	25	100	30	Normal
Nature Power	Normal	Status	—	—	20	Normal
Aqua Ring	Water	Status	—	—	20	Self
Curse	Ghost	Status	—	—	10	Varies
Bide	Normal	Physical	—	—	10	Self
Water Pulse	Water	Special	60	100	20	Normal
Head Smash	Rock	Physical	150	80	5	Normal
Camouflage	Normal	Status	—	—	20	Self
Liquidation	Water	Physical	85	100	10	Normal

❖ EXCLUSIVE Z-MOVE

Name	Base Move	Type	Kind	Pow.	Acc.	Range

Mareanie

Alola Pokédex	Melemele	Akala	Ula'ula	Poni
113	113	045	—	—

Brutal Star Pokémon

POISON · WATER

HEIGHT: 1'04"
WEIGHT: 17.6 lbs.

It plunges the poison spike on its head into its prey. When the prey has weakened, Mareanie deals the finishing blow with its 10 tentacles.

It's found crawling on beaches and seafloors. The coral that grows on Corsola's head is as good as a five-star banquet to this Pokémon.

ABILITY
Merciless
Limber

HIDDEN ABILITY
Regenerator

SPECIES STRENGTHS
HP	◆◆
Attack	◆◆◆
Defense	◆◆◆
Sp. Atk	◆◆
Sp. Def	◆◆
Speed	◆◆◆

Damage taken in normal battles
NORMAL ×1	FIGHTING ×0.5	ROCK ×1
FIRE ×0.5	POISON ×0.5	GHOST ×1
WATER ×0.5	GROUND ×2	DRAGON ×1
GRASS ×1	FLYING ×1	DARK ×1
ELECTRIC ×2	PSYCHIC ×2	STEEL ×0.5
ICE ×1	BUG ×0.5	FAIRY ×0.5

EGG GROUPS
Water 1

ITEM SOMETIMES HELD BY WILD POKÉMON
Poison Barb

EVOLUTION
Mareanie → Lv. 38 → Toxapex

MAIN WAY TO REGISTER IN THE POKÉDEX
Catch in SOS battles against Corsola in Melemele Sea

Same form for male/female

LEVEL-UP MOVES
Lv.	Name	Type	Kind	Pow.	Acc.	PP	Range
1	Poison Sting	Poison	Physical	15	100	35	Normal
5	Peck	Flying	Physical	35	100	35	Normal
9	Bite	Dark	Physical	60	100	25	Normal
13	Toxic Spikes	Poison	Status	—	—	20	Other Side
17	Wide Guard	Rock	Status	—	—	10	Your Side
21	Toxic	Poison	Status	—	90	10	Normal
25	Venoshock	Poison	Special	65	100	10	Normal
29	Spike Cannon	Normal	Physical	20	100	15	Normal
33	Recover	Normal	Status	—	—	10	Self
37	Poison Jab	Poison	Physical	80	100	20	Normal
41	Venom Drench	Poison	Status	—	100	20	Many Others
45	Pin Missile	Bug	Physical	25	95	20	Normal
49	Liquidation	Water	Physical	85	100	10	Normal

TM MOVES
No.	Name	Type	Kind	Pow.	Acc.	PP	Range
TM06	Toxic	Poison	Status	—	90	10	Normal
TM07	Hail	Ice	Status	—	—	10	Both Sides
TM09	Venoshock	Poison	Special	65	100	10	Normal
TM10	Hidden Power	Normal	Special	60	100	15	Normal
TM13	Ice Beam	Ice	Special	90	100	10	Normal
TM14	Blizzard	Ice	Special	110	70	5	Many Others
TM17	Protect	Normal	Status	—	—	10	Self
TM18	Rain Dance	Water	Status	—	—	5	Both Sides
TM20	Safeguard	Normal	Status	—	—	25	Your Side
TM21	Frustration	Normal	Physical	—	100	20	Normal
TM27	Return	Normal	Physical	—	100	20	Normal
TM32	Double Team	Normal	Status	—	—	15	Self
TM34	Sludge Wave	Poison	Special	95	100	10	Adjacent
TM36	Sludge Bomb	Poison	Special	90	100	10	Normal
TM42	Facade	Normal	Physical	70	100	20	Normal
TM44	Rest	Psychic	Status	—	—	10	Self
TM45	Attract	Normal	Status	—	100	15	Normal
TM48	Round	Normal	Special	60	100	15	Normal
TM55	Scald	Water	Special	80	100	15	Normal
TM66	Payback	Dark	Physical	50	100	10	Normal
TM79	Frost Breath	Ice	Special	60	90	10	Normal
TM83	Infestation	Bug	Special	20	100	20	Normal
TM84	Poison Jab	Poison	Physical	80	100	20	Normal
TM87	Swagger	Normal	Status	—	85	15	Normal
TM88	Sleep Talk	Normal	Status	—	—	10	Self
TM90	Substitute	Normal	Status	—	—	10	Self
TM94	Surf	Water	Special	90	100	15	Adjacent
TM100	Confide	Normal	Status	—	—	20	Normal

MOVES TAUGHT BY PEOPLE
Name	Type	Kind	Pow.	Acc.	PP	Range

MOVES LEARNED WHEN EVOLVING
Name	Type	Kind	Pow.	Acc.	PP	Range

EGG MOVES
Name	Type	Kind	Pow.	Acc.	PP	Range
Stockpile	Normal	Status	—	—	20	Self
Swallow	Normal	Status	—	—	10	Self
Spit Up	Normal	Special	—	100	10	Normal
Haze	Ice	Status	—	—	30	Both Sides

EXCLUSIVE Z-MOVE
Name	Base Move	Type	Kind	Pow.	Acc.	Range

Toxapex

Alola Pokédex	Melemele	Akala	Ula'ula	Poni
114	114	046	—	—

Brutal Star Pokémon

POISON · WATER

HEIGHT: 2'04"
WEIGHT: 32.0 lbs.

Toxapex crawls along the ocean floor on its 12 legs. It leaves a trail of Corsola bits scattered in its wake.

Those attacked by Toxapex's poison will suffer intense pain for three days and three nights. Post-recovery, there will be some aftereffects.

ABILITY
Merciless
Limber

HIDDEN ABILITY
Regenerator

SPECIES STRENGTHS
HP	◆◆
Attack	◆◆◆
Defense	◆◆◆◆◆◆◆
Sp. Atk	◆◆◆
Sp. Def	◆◆◆◆◆◆◆
Speed	◆◆

Damage taken in normal battles
NORMAL ×1	FIGHTING ×0.5	ROCK ×1
FIRE ×0.5	POISON ×0.5	GHOST ×1
WATER ×0.5	GROUND ×2	DRAGON ×1
GRASS ×1	FLYING ×1	DARK ×1
ELECTRIC ×2	PSYCHIC ×2	STEEL ×0.5
ICE ×0.5	BUG ×0.5	FAIRY ×0.5

EGG GROUPS
Water 1

ITEM SOMETIMES HELD BY WILD POKÉMON
—

EVOLUTION
Mareanie → Lv. 38 → Toxapex

MAIN WAY TO REGISTER IN THE POKÉDEX
Level up Mareanie to Lv. 38

Same form for male/female

LEVEL-UP MOVES
Lv.	Name	Type	Kind	Pow.	Acc.	PP	Range
1	Baneful Bunker	Poison	Status	—	—	10	Self
1	Poison Sting	Poison	Physical	15	100	35	Normal
1	Peck	Flying	Physical	35	100	35	Normal
1	Bite	Dark	Physical	60	100	25	Normal
1	Toxic Spikes	Poison	Status	—	—	20	Other Side
5	Peck	Flying	Physical	35	100	35	Normal
9	Bite	Dark	Physical	60	100	25	Normal
13	Toxic Spikes	Poison	Status	—	—	20	Other Side
17	Wide Guard	Rock	Status	—	—	10	Your Side
21	Toxic	Poison	Status	—	90	10	Normal
25	Venoshock	Poison	Special	65	100	10	Normal
29	Spike Cannon	Normal	Physical	20	100	15	Normal
33	Recover	Normal	Status	—	—	10	Self
37	Poison Jab	Poison	Physical	80	100	20	Normal
44	Venom Drench	Poison	Status	—	100	20	Many Others
51	Pin Missile	Bug	Physical	25	95	20	Normal
58	Liquidation	Water	Physical	85	100	10	Normal

TM MOVES
No.	Name	Type	Kind	Pow.	Acc.	PP	Range
TM06	Toxic	Poison	Status	—	90	10	Normal
TM07	Hail	Ice	Status	—	—	10	Both Sides
TM09	Venoshock	Poison	Special	65	100	10	Normal
TM10	Hidden Power	Normal	Special	60	100	15	Normal
TM13	Ice Beam	Ice	Special	90	100	10	Normal
TM14	Blizzard	Ice	Special	110	70	5	Many Others
TM16	Light Screen	Psychic	Status	—	—	30	Your Side
TM17	Protect	Normal	Status	—	—	10	Self
TM18	Rain Dance	Water	Status	—	—	5	Both Sides
TM20	Safeguard	Normal	Status	—	—	25	Your Side
TM21	Frustration	Normal	Physical	—	100	20	Normal
TM23	Smack Down	Rock	Physical	50	100	15	Normal
TM27	Return	Normal	Physical	—	100	20	Normal
TM32	Double Team	Normal	Status	—	—	15	Self
TM34	Sludge Wave	Poison	Special	95	100	10	Adjacent
TM36	Sludge Bomb	Poison	Special	90	100	10	Normal
TM42	Facade	Normal	Physical	70	100	20	Normal
TM44	Rest	Psychic	Status	—	—	10	Self
TM45	Attract	Normal	Status	—	100	15	Normal
TM48	Round	Normal	Special	60	100	15	Normal
TM55	Scald	Water	Special	80	100	15	Normal
TM66	Payback	Dark	Physical	50	100	10	Normal
TM79	Frost Breath	Ice	Special	60	90	10	Normal
TM83	Infestation	Bug	Special	20	100	20	Normal
TM84	Poison Jab	Poison	Physical	80	100	20	Normal
TM87	Swagger	Normal	Status	—	85	15	Normal
TM88	Sleep Talk	Normal	Status	—	—	10	Self
TM90	Substitute	Normal	Status	—	—	10	Self

MOVES TAUGHT BY PEOPLE
No.	Name	Type	Kind	Pow.	Acc.	PP	Range
TM94	Surf	Water	Special	90	100	15	Adjacent
TM100	Confide	Normal	Status	—	—	20	Normal

MOVES LEARNED WHEN EVOLVING
Name	Type	Kind	Pow.	Acc.	PP	Range
Baneful Bunker	Poison	Status	—	—	10	Self

EGG MOVES
Name	Type	Kind	Pow.	Acc.	PP	Range

EXCLUSIVE Z-MOVE
Name	Base Move	Type	Kind	Pow.	Acc.	Range

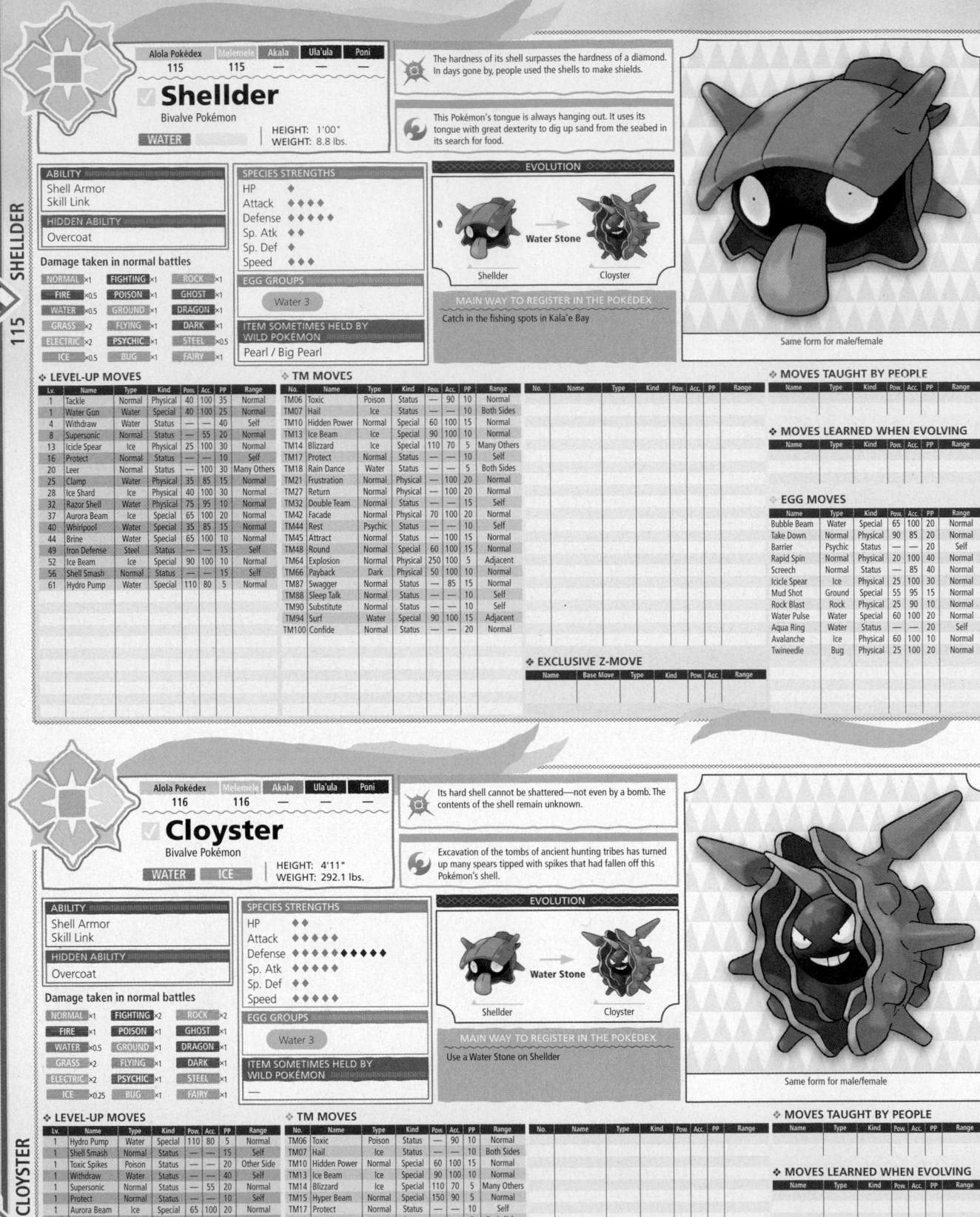

Alola Pokédex	Melemele	Akala	Ula'ula	Poni
115	115	—	—	—

☑ **Shellder**

Bivalve Pokémon

WATER

HEIGHT: 1'00"
WEIGHT: 8.8 lbs.

The hardness of its shell surpasses the hardness of a diamond. In days gone by, people used the shells to make shields.

This Pokémon's tongue is always hanging out. It uses its tongue with great dexterity to dig up sand from the seabed in its search for food.

ABILITY
Shell Armor
Skill Link

HIDDEN ABILITY
Overcoat

Damage taken in normal battles

NORMAL ×1	FIGHTING ×1	ROCK ×1	
FIRE ×0.5	POISON ×1	GHOST ×1	
WATER ×0.5	GROUND ×1	DRAGON ×1	
GRASS ×2	FLYING ×1	DARK ×1	
ELECTRIC ×2	PSYCHIC ×1	STEEL ×0.5	
BUG ×1		FAIRY ×1	

SPECIES STRENGTHS
HP ◆
Attack ◆◆◆◆
Defense ◆◆◆◆◆
Sp. Atk ◆◆
Sp. Def ◆◆
Speed ◆◆◆

EGG GROUPS
Water 3

ITEM SOMETIMES HELD BY WILD POKÉMON
Pearl / Big Pearl

EVOLUTION

Shellder → (Water Stone) → Cloyster

MAIN WAY TO REGISTER IN THE POKÉDEX
Catch in the fishing spots in Kala'e Bay

Same form for male/female

❖ LEVEL-UP MOVES

Lv.	Name	Type	Kind	Pow.	Acc.	PP	Range
1	Tackle	Normal	Physical	40	100	35	Normal
1	Water Gun	Water	Special	40	100	25	Normal
4	Withdraw	Water	Status	—	—	40	Self
8	Supersonic	Normal	Status	—	55	20	Normal
13	Icicle Spear	Ice	Physical	25	100	30	Normal
16	Protect	Normal	Status	—	—	10	Self
20	Leer	Normal	Status	—	100	30	Many Others
25	Clamp	Water	Physical	35	85	15	Normal
28	Ice Shard	Ice	Physical	40	100	30	Normal
32	Razor Shell	Water	Physical	75	95	10	Normal
37	Aurora Beam	Ice	Special	65	100	20	Normal
40	Whirlpool	Water	Special	35	85	15	Normal
44	Brine	Water	Special	65	100	10	Normal
49	Iron Defense	Steel	Status	—	—	15	Self
52	Ice Beam	Ice	Special	90	100	10	Normal
56	Shell Smash	Normal	Status	—	—	15	Self
61	Hydro Pump	Water	Special	110	80	5	Normal

❖ TM MOVES

No.	Name	Type	Kind	Pow.	Acc.	PP	Range
TM06	Toxic	Poison	Status	—	90	10	Normal
TM07	Hail	Ice	Status	—	—	10	Both Sides
TM10	Hidden Power	Normal	Special	60	100	15	Normal
TM13	Ice Beam	Ice	Special	90	100	10	Normal
TM14	Blizzard	Ice	Special	110	70	5	Many Others
TM17	Protect	Normal	Status	—	—	10	Self
TM18	Rain Dance	Water	Status	—	—	5	Both Sides
TM21	Frustration	Normal	Physical	—	100	20	Normal
TM27	Return	Normal	Physical	—	100	20	Normal
TM32	Double Team	Normal	Status	—	—	15	Self
TM42	Facade	Normal	Physical	70	100	20	Normal
TM44	Rest	Psychic	Status	—	—	10	Self
TM45	Attract	Normal	Status	—	100	15	Normal
TM48	Round	Normal	Special	60	100	15	Normal
TM64	Explosion	Normal	Physical	250	100	5	Adjacent
TM66	Payback	Dark	Physical	50	100	10	Normal
TM87	Swagger	Normal	Status	—	85	15	Normal
TM88	Sleep Talk	Normal	Status	—	—	10	Self
TM90	Substitute	Normal	Status	—	—	10	Self
TM94	Surf	Water	Special	90	100	15	Adjacent
TM100	Confide	Normal	Status	—	—	20	Normal

❖ MOVES TAUGHT BY PEOPLE

Name	Type	Kind	Pow.	Acc.	PP	Range

❖ MOVES LEARNED WHEN EVOLVING

Name	Type	Kind	Pow.	Acc.	PP	Range

❖ EGG MOVES

Name	Type	Kind	Pow.	Acc.	PP	Range
Bubble Beam	Water	Special	65	100	20	Normal
Take Down	Normal	Physical	90	85	20	Normal
Barrier	Psychic	Status	—	—	20	Self
Rapid Spin	Normal	Physical	20	100	40	Normal
Screech	Normal	Status	—	85	40	Normal
Icicle Spear	Ice	Physical	25	100	30	Normal
Mud Shot	Ground	Special	55	95	15	Normal
Rock Blast	Rock	Physical	25	90	10	Normal
Water Pulse	Water	Special	60	100	20	Normal
Aqua Ring	Water	Status	—	—	20	Self
Avalanche	Ice	Physical	60	100	10	Normal
Twineedle	Bug	Physical	25	100	20	Normal

❖ EXCLUSIVE Z-MOVE

Name	Base Move	Type	Kind	Pow.	Acc.	Range

Alola Pokédex	Melemele	Akala	Ula'ula	Poni
116	116	—	—	—

☑ **Cloyster**

Bivalve Pokémon

WATER · ICE

HEIGHT: 4'11"
WEIGHT: 292.1 lbs.

Its hard shell cannot be shattered—not even by a bomb. The contents of the shell remain unknown.

Excavation of the tombs of ancient hunting tribes has turned up many spears tipped with spikes that had fallen off this Pokémon's shell.

ABILITY
Shell Armor
Skill Link

HIDDEN ABILITY
Overcoat

Damage taken in normal battles

NORMAL ×1	FIGHTING ×2	ROCK ×2	
FIRE ×1	POISON ×1	GHOST ×1	
WATER ×0.5	GROUND ×1	DRAGON ×1	
GRASS ×2	FLYING ×1	DARK ×1	
ELECTRIC ×2	PSYCHIC ×1	STEEL ×1	
ICE ×0.25		FAIRY ×1	

SPECIES STRENGTHS
HP ◆◆
Attack ◆◆◆◆◆
Defense ◆◆◆◆◆◆◆◆◆◆
Sp. Atk ◆◆◆◆◆
Sp. Def ◆◆
Speed ◆◆◆◆

EGG GROUPS
Water 3

ITEM SOMETIMES HELD BY WILD POKÉMON

EVOLUTION

Shellder → (Water Stone) → Cloyster

MAIN WAY TO REGISTER IN THE POKÉDEX
Use a Water Stone on Shellder

Same form for male/female

❖ LEVEL-UP MOVES

Lv.	Name	Type	Kind	Pow.	Acc.	PP	Range
1	Hydro Pump	Water	Special	110	80	5	Normal
1	Shell Smash	Normal	Status	—	—	15	Self
1	Toxic Spikes	Poison	Status	—	—	20	Other Side
1	Withdraw	Water	Status	—	—	40	Self
1	Supersonic	Normal	Status	—	55	20	Normal
1	Protect	Normal	Status	—	—	10	Self
1	Aurora Beam	Ice	Special	65	100	20	Normal
13	Spike Cannon	Normal	Physical	20	100	15	Normal
28	Spikes	Ground	Status	—	—	20	Other Side
50	Icicle Crash	Ice	Physical	85	90	10	Normal

❖ TM MOVES

No.	Name	Type	Kind	Pow.	Acc.	PP	Range
TM06	Toxic	Poison	Status	—	90	10	Normal
TM07	Hail	Ice	Status	—	—	10	Both Sides
TM10	Hidden Power	Normal	Special	60	100	15	Normal
TM13	Ice Beam	Ice	Special	90	100	10	Normal
TM14	Blizzard	Ice	Special	110	70	5	Many Others
TM15	Hyper Beam	Normal	Special	150	90	5	Normal
TM17	Protect	Normal	Status	—	—	10	Self
TM18	Rain Dance	Water	Status	—	—	5	Both Sides
TM21	Frustration	Normal	Physical	—	100	20	Normal
TM27	Return	Normal	Physical	—	100	20	Normal
TM32	Double Team	Normal	Status	—	—	15	Self
TM41	Torment	Dark	Status	—	100	15	Normal
TM42	Facade	Normal	Physical	70	100	20	Normal
TM44	Rest	Psychic	Status	—	—	10	Self
TM45	Attract	Normal	Status	—	100	15	Normal
TM48	Round	Normal	Special	60	100	15	Normal
TM64	Explosion	Normal	Physical	250	100	5	Adjacent
TM66	Payback	Dark	Physical	50	100	10	Normal
TM67	Smart Strike	Steel	Physical	70	—	10	Normal
TM68	Giga Impact	Normal	Physical	150	90	5	Normal
TM79	Frost Breath	Ice	Special	60	90	10	Normal
TM84	Poison Jab	Poison	Physical	80	100	20	Normal
TM87	Swagger	Normal	Status	—	85	15	Normal
TM88	Sleep Talk	Normal	Status	—	—	10	Self
TM90	Substitute	Normal	Status	—	—	10	Self
TM94	Surf	Water	Special	90	100	15	Adjacent
TM100	Confide	Normal	Status	—	—	20	Normal

❖ MOVES TAUGHT BY PEOPLE

Name	Type	Kind	Pow.	Acc.	PP	Range

❖ MOVES LEARNED WHEN EVOLVING

Name	Type	Kind	Pow.	Acc.	PP	Range

❖ EGG MOVES

Name	Type	Kind	Pow.	Acc.	PP	Range

❖ EXCLUSIVE Z-MOVE

Name	Base Move	Type	Kind	Pow.	Acc.	Range

Making Money in Alola

If you are short of prize money, there are many ways to make it in Alola! Whether you want to stock up on the perfect kind of Poké Ball or just buy up every outfit at the apparel shops, with these tricks you should find that you're never low on funds again.

Sell items at a Poké Mart

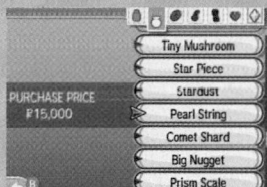

You can sell most items at any Poké Mart, except for certain exceptions, such as TMs, key items, and Z-Crystals. Get the following valuable items, and sell them at a Poké Mart. They don't have any practical use, but they can be sold at shops, and usually for a high price. Here are some examples of how to obtain them.

Item	How to Obtain	Value When Sold
Balm Mushroom	Sometimes picked up by a Pokémon with the Pickup Ability (p. 297)	₽7,500
Big Nugget	Defeat five Trainers on a bridge in Malie Garden (after defeating the Team Skull Boss there) / Sometimes picked up by a Pokémon with the Pickup Ability	₽20,000
Big Pearl	Find on Route 8 and Poni Gauntlet / Reel it in at fishing spots (p. 226)	₽4,000
Comet Shard	Find on Poni Coast and in Haina Desert / Sometimes found after Tauros or Sharpedo breaks rocks on Poni Island	₽30,000
Nugget	Find on Route 1, Ten Carat Hill, or Malie City's Outer Cape / Sometimes picked up by a Pokémon with the Pickup Ability	₽5,000
Pearl	Reel it in at fishing spots / Often held by wild Shellder	₽1,000
Pearl String	Find on Hano Beach or in Poni Wilds / Reel it in at fishing spots on Melemele Island / Sometimes picked up by a Pokémon with the Pickup Ability	₽15,000
Rare Bone	Sometimes found by your Pokémon on Isle Aphun in Poké Pelago	₽2,500
Star Piece	Find on Route 2 or in Poni Plains / Sometimes found after Tauros or Sharpedo breaks rocks on Ula'ula Island and Poni Island	₽6,000
Stardust	Often held by wild Staryu or Starmie / Sometimes found after Tauros or Sharpedo breaks rocks on all four islands	₽1,500

Do favors for people

Some people in Alola ask you to show them certain Pokémon or find runaway Pokémon. There is also a part-time job as a Pyukumuku chucker at Hano Beach. Do favors for people or chuck Pyukumuku to earn some cash. Most of these tasks can only be done once, but you can work as a Pyukumuku chucker over and over if you come back once a day!

Location	Request	Reward
Hau'oli City	Show the Beauty in the Pokémon Center a Drifloon	₽10,000
Route 2	Show the Sightseer in the Pokémon Center a Cutiefly	₽3,000
Route 3	Show the Sightseer at the east end a Rockruff	₽3,000
Heahea City	Show the Fisherman in the apparel shop a Pyukumuku	₽10,000
Route 5	Show the Scientist in the Pokémon Center a Feebas	₽3,000
Route 8	Show the Aether Foundation Employee in the Aether Base a Stufful	₽5,000
Konikoni City	Show the Aether Foundation Employee in the Pokémon Center a Passimian ☀ or Oranguru ☽	₽5,000
Malie City	Show the Collector in the apparel shop a Togedemaru	₽10,000
Hano Beach	Find and chuck back Pyukumuku into the sea each day	₽20,000
Route 10	Find runaway Stufful for a Never-Melt Ice and some cash	₽15,000
Route 16	Show the Aether Foundation Employee in the Pokémon Center a Mimikyu	₽20,000

Alola Pokédex	Melemele	Akala	Ula'ula	Poni
117	117	—	—	—

Bagon
Rock Head Pokémon

DRAGON

HEIGHT: 2'00"
WEIGHT: 92.8 lbs.

Its belief that it will be able to fly one day is apparently the influence of information carried in its genes.

With its steel-hard stone head, it headbutts indiscriminately. This is because of the stress it feels at being unable to fly.

ABILITY
Rock Head

HIDDEN ABILITY
Sheer Force

Damage taken in normal battles

NORMAL	×1	FIGHTING	×1	ROCK	×1
FIRE	×0.5	POISON	×1	GHOST	×1
WATER	×0.5	GROUND	×1	DRAGON	×2
GRASS	×0.5	FLYING	×1	DARK	×1
ELECTRIC	×0.5	PSYCHIC	×1	STEEL	×1
ICE	×2	BUG	×1	FAIRY	×1

SPECIES STRENGTHS
HP	◆◆
Attack	◆◆◆◆
Defense	◆◆◆
Sp. Atk	◆◆
Sp. Def	◆
Speed	◆◆◆

EGG GROUPS
Dragon

ITEM SOMETIMES HELD BY WILD POKÉMON
Dragon Fang

EVOLUTION

Bagon → Lv. 30 → Shelgon → Lv. 50 → Salamence

MAIN WAY TO REGISTER IN THE POKÉDEX
Catch in the tall grass on Route 3

Same form for male/female

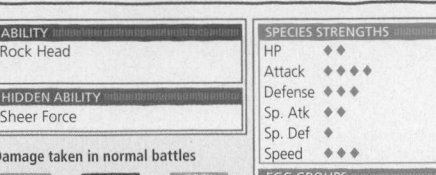

Alola Pokédex	Melemele	Akala	Ula'ula	Poni
118	118	—	—	—

Shelgon
Endurance Pokémon

DRAGON

HEIGHT: 3'07"
WEIGHT: 243.6 lbs.

The cells within its shell transform with explosive speed, preparing it for evolution.

They lurk deep within caves—motionless, neither eating nor drinking. Why they don't die is not known.

ABILITY
Rock Head

HIDDEN ABILITY
Overcoat

Damage taken in normal battles

NORMAL	×1	FIGHTING	×1	ROCK	×1
FIRE	×0.5	POISON	×1	GHOST	×1
WATER	×0.5	GROUND	×1	DRAGON	×2
GRASS	×0.5	FLYING	×1	DARK	×1
ELECTRIC	×0.5	PSYCHIC	×1	STEEL	×1
ICE	×2	BUG	×1	FAIRY	×1

SPECIES STRENGTHS
HP	◆◆◆
Attack	◆◆◆◆◆
Defense	◆◆◆◆◆
Sp. Atk	◆◆◆
Sp. Def	◆◆
Speed	◆◆◆

EGG GROUPS
Dragon

ITEM SOMETIMES HELD BY WILD POKÉMON
Dragon Fang

EVOLUTION
Bagon → Lv. 30 → Shelgon → Lv. 50 → Salamence

MAIN WAY TO REGISTER IN THE POKÉDEX
Catch in SOS battles against Bagon in the tall grass by Kala'e Bay

Same form for male/female

Alola Pokédex	Melemele	Akala	Ula'ula	Poni
119	119	—	—	—

Salamence
Dragon Pokémon

DRAGON **FLYING**

HEIGHT: 4'11"
WEIGHT: 226.2 lbs.

When angered, it loses all sense of itself and destroys everything around it. The destruction will continue until Salamence has tired itself out.

It flies around on its wings, which have grown in at last. In its happiness, it gushes hot flames, burning up the fields it passes over.

ABILITY
Intimidate

HIDDEN ABILITY
Moxie

Damage taken in normal battles

NORMAL	×1	FIGHTING	×0.5	ROCK	×1
FIRE	×0.5	POISON	×1	GHOST	×1
WATER	×0.5	GROUND	×0	DRAGON	×2
GRASS	×0.25	FLYING	×1	DARK	×1
ELECTRIC	×1	PSYCHIC	×1	STEEL	×1
ICE	×4	BUG	×0.5	FAIRY	×1

SPECIES STRENGTHS
HP	◆◆◆◆
Attack	◆◆◆◆◆◆◆
Defense	◆◆◆◆
Sp. Atk	◆◆◆◆◆◆
Sp. Def	◆◆◆◆
Speed	◆◆◆◆◆◆

EGG GROUPS
Dragon

ITEM SOMETIMES HELD BY WILD POKÉMON
Dragon Fang

EVOLUTION

Bagon → Lv. 30 → Shelgon → Lv. 50 → Salamence

MAIN WAY TO REGISTER IN THE POKÉDEX
Catch in SOS battles against Bagon in the tall grass on Route 3

Same form for male/female

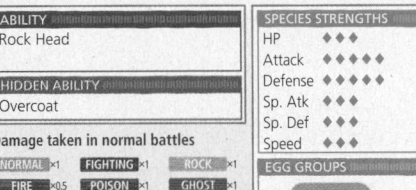
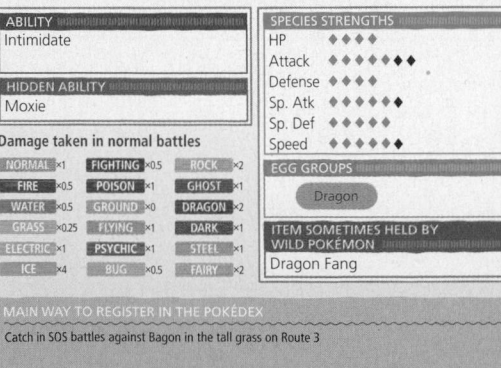

p. 209

BAGON 117

❖ LEVEL-UP MOVES

Lv.	Name	Type	Kind	Pow.	Acc.	PP	Range
1	Rage	Normal	Physical	20	100	20	Normal
4	Ember	Fire	Special	40	100	25	Normal
7	Leer	Normal	Status	—	100	30	Many Others
10	Bite	Dark	Physical	60	100	25	Normal
13	Dragon Breath	Dragon	Special	60	100	20	Normal
17	Headbutt	Normal	Physical	70	100	15	Normal
21	Focus Energy	Normal	Status	—	—	30	Self
25	Crunch	Dark	Physical	80	100	15	Normal
29	Dragon Claw	Dragon	Physical	80	100	15	Normal
34	Zen Headbutt	Psychic	Physical	80	90	15	Normal
39	Scary Face	Normal	Status	—	100	10	Normal
44	Flamethrower	Fire	Special	90	100	15	Normal
49	Double-Edge	Normal	Physical	120	100	15	Normal

❖ TM MOVES

No.	Name	Type	Kind	Pow.	Acc.	PP	Range
TM02	Dragon Claw	Dragon	Physical	80	100	15	Normal
TM05	Roar	Normal	Status	—	—	20	Normal
TM06	Toxic	Poison	Status	—	90	10	Normal
TM10	Hidden Power	Normal	Special	60	100	15	Normal
TM11	Sunny Day	Fire	Status	—	—	5	Both Sides
TM17	Protect	Normal	Status	—	—	10	Self
TM18	Rain Dance	Water	Status	—	—	5	Both Sides
TM21	Frustration	Normal	Physical	—	100	20	Normal
TM27	Return	Normal	Physical	—	100	15	Normal
TM31	Brick Break	Fighting	Physical	75	100	15	Normal
TM32	Double Team	Normal	Status	—	—	15	Self
TM35	Flamethrower	Fire	Special	90	100	15	Normal
TM38	Fire Blast	Fire	Special	110	85	5	Normal
TM39	Rock Tomb	Rock	Physical	60	95	15	Normal
TM40	Aerial Ace	Flying	Physical	60	—	20	Normal
TM42	Facade	Normal	Physical	70	100	20	Normal
TM44	Rest	Psychic	Status	—	—	10	Self
TM45	Attract	Normal	Status	—	100	15	Normal
TM48	Round	Normal	Special	60	100	15	Normal
TM65	Shadow Claw	Ghost	Physical	70	100	15	Normal
TM80	Rock Slide	Rock	Physical	75	90	10	Many Others
TM87	Swagger	Normal	Status	—	85	15	Normal
TM88	Sleep Talk	Normal	Status	—	—	10	Self
TM90	Substitute	Normal	Status	—	—	10	Self
TM100	Confide	Normal	Status	—	—	20	Normal

❖ MOVES TAUGHT BY PEOPLE

Name	Type	Kind	Pow.	Acc.	PP	Range
Draco Meteor	Dragon	Special	130	90	5	Normal

❖ MOVES LEARNED WHEN EVOLVING

Name	Type	Kind	Pow.	Acc.	PP	Range

❖ EGG MOVES

Name	Type	Kind	Pow.	Acc.	PP	Range
Hydro Pump	Water	Special	110	80	5	Normal
Thrash	Normal	Physical	120	100	10	1 Random
Dragon Rage	Dragon	Special		100	10	Normal
Twister	Dragon	Special	40	100	20	Many Others
Dragon Dance	Dragon	Status			20	Self
Fire Fang	Fire	Physical	65	95	15	Normal
Dragon Rush	Dragon	Physical	100	75	10	Normal
Dragon Pulse	Dragon	Special	85	100	10	Normal
Endure	Normal	Status			10	Self
Defense Curl	Normal	Status			40	Self

❖ EXCLUSIVE Z-MOVE

Name	Base Move	Type	Kind	Pow.	Acc.	Range

SHELGON 118

❖ LEVEL-UP MOVES

Lv.	Name	Type	Kind	Pow.	Acc.	PP	Range
1	Protect	Normal	Status	—	—	10	Self
1	Rage	Normal	Physical	20	100	20	Normal
1	Ember	Fire	Special	40	100	25	Normal
1	Leer	Normal	Status	—	100	30	Many Others
1	Bite	Dark	Physical	60	100	25	Normal
4	Ember	Fire	Special	40	100	25	Normal
7	Leer	Normal	Status	—	100	30	Many Others
10	Bite	Dark	Physical	60	100	25	Normal
13	Dragon Breath	Dragon	Special	60	100	20	Normal
17	Headbutt	Normal	Physical	70	100	15	Normal
21	Focus Energy	Normal	Status	—	—	30	Self
25	Crunch	Dark	Physical	80	100	15	Normal
29	Dragon Claw	Dragon	Physical	80	100	15	Normal
35	Zen Headbutt	Psychic	Physical	80	90	15	Normal
42	Scary Face	Normal	Status	—	100	10	Normal
49	Flamethrower	Fire	Special	90	100	15	Normal
56	Double-Edge	Normal	Physical	120	100	15	Normal

❖ TM MOVES

No.	Name	Type	Kind	Pow.	Acc.	PP	Range
TM02	Dragon Claw	Dragon	Physical	80	100	15	Normal
TM05	Roar	Normal	Status	—	—	20	Normal
TM06	Toxic	Poison	Status	—	90	10	Normal
TM10	Hidden Power	Normal	Special	60	100	15	Normal
TM11	Sunny Day	Fire	Status	—	—	5	Both Sides
TM17	Protect	Normal	Status	—	—	10	Self
TM18	Rain Dance	Water	Status	—	—	5	Both Sides
TM21	Frustration	Normal	Physical	—	100	20	Normal
TM27	Return	Normal	Physical	—	100	15	Normal
TM31	Brick Break	Fighting	Physical	75	100	15	Normal
TM32	Double Team	Normal	Status	—	—	15	Self
TM35	Flamethrower	Fire	Special	90	100	15	Normal
TM38	Fire Blast	Fire	Special	110	85	5	Normal
TM39	Rock Tomb	Rock	Physical	60	95	15	Normal
TM40	Aerial Ace	Flying	Physical	60	—	20	Normal
TM42	Facade	Normal	Physical	70	100	20	Normal
TM44	Rest	Psychic	Status	—	—	10	Self
TM45	Attract	Normal	Status	—	100	15	Normal
TM48	Round	Normal	Special	60	100	15	Normal
TM65	Shadow Claw	Ghost	Physical	70	100	15	Normal
TM80	Rock Slide	Rock	Physical	75	90	10	Many Others
TM87	Swagger	Normal	Status	—	85	15	Normal
TM88	Sleep Talk	Normal	Status	—	—	10	Self
TM90	Substitute	Normal	Status	—	—	10	Self
TM100	Confide	Normal	Status	—	—	20	Normal

❖ MOVES TAUGHT BY PEOPLE

Name	Type	Kind	Pow.	Acc.	PP	Range
Draco Meteor	Dragon	Special	130	90	5	Normal

❖ MOVES LEARNED WHEN EVOLVING

Name	Type	Kind	Pow.	Acc.	PP	Range
Protect	Normal	Status	—	—	10	Self

❖ EGG MOVES

Name	Type	Kind	Pow.	Acc.	PP	Range

❖ EXCLUSIVE Z-MOVE

Name	Base Move	Type	Kind	Pow.	Acc.	Range

SALAMENCE 119

❖ LEVEL-UP MOVES

Lv.	Name	Type	Kind	Pow.	Acc.	PP	Range
1	Fly	Flying	Physical	90	95	15	Normal
1	Protect	Normal	Status	—	—	10	Self
1	Dragon Tail	Dragon	Physical	60	90	15	Normal
1	Fire Fang	Fire	Physical	65	95	15	Normal
1	Thunder Fang	Electric	Physical	65	95	15	Normal
1	Rage	Normal	Physical	20	100	20	Normal
1	Ember	Fire	Special	40	100	25	Normal
1	Leer	Normal	Status	—	100	30	Many Others
1	Bite	Dark	Physical	60	100	25	Normal
4	Ember	Fire	Special	40	100	25	Normal
7	Leer	Normal	Status	—	100	30	Many Others
10	Bite	Dark	Physical	60	100	25	Normal
13	Dragon Breath	Dragon	Special	60	100	20	Normal
17	Headbutt	Normal	Physical	70	100	15	Normal
21	Focus Energy	Normal	Status	—	—	30	Self
25	Crunch	Dark	Physical	80	100	15	Normal
29	Dragon Claw	Dragon	Physical	80	100	15	Normal
35	Zen Headbutt	Psychic	Physical	80	90	15	Normal
42	Scary Face	Normal	Status	—	100	10	Normal
49	Flamethrower	Fire	Special	90	100	15	Normal
63	Double-Edge	Normal	Physical	120	100	15	Normal

❖ TM MOVES

No.	Name	Type	Kind	Pow.	Acc.	PP	Range
TM02	Dragon Claw	Dragon	Physical	80	100	15	Normal
TM05	Roar	Normal	Status	—	—	20	Normal
TM06	Toxic	Poison	Status	—	90	10	Normal
TM10	Hidden Power	Normal	Special	60	100	15	Normal
TM11	Sunny Day	Fire	Status	—	—	5	Both Sides
TM15	Hyper Beam	Normal	Special	150	90	5	Normal
TM17	Protect	Normal	Status	—	—	10	Self
TM18	Rain Dance	Water	Status	—	—	5	Both Sides
TM19	Roost	Flying	Status	—	—	10	Self
TM21	Frustration	Normal	Physical	—	100	20	Normal
TM26	Earthquake	Ground	Physical	100	100	10	Adjacent
TM27	Return	Normal	Physical	—	100	15	Normal
TM31	Brick Break	Fighting	Physical	75	100	15	Normal
TM32	Double Team	Normal	Status	—	—	15	Self
TM35	Flamethrower	Fire	Special	90	100	15	Normal
TM38	Fire Blast	Fire	Special	110	85	5	Normal
TM39	Rock Tomb	Rock	Physical	60	95	15	Normal
TM40	Aerial Ace	Flying	Physical	60	—	20	Normal
TM42	Facade	Normal	Physical	70	100	20	Normal
TM44	Rest	Psychic	Status	—	—	10	Self
TM45	Attract	Normal	Status	—	100	15	Normal
TM48	Round	Normal	Special	60	100	15	Normal
TM51	Steel Wing	Steel	Physical	70	90	25	Normal
TM59	Brutal Swing	Dark	Physical	60	100	20	Adjacent
TM65	Shadow Claw	Ghost	Physical	70	100	15	Normal
TM68	Giga Impact	Normal	Physical	150	90	5	Normal
TM71	Stone Edge	Rock	Physical	100	80	5	Normal
TM76	Fly	Flying	Physical	90	95	15	Normal
TM78	Bulldoze	Ground	Physical	60	100	20	Adjacent
TM80	Rock Slide	Rock	Physical	75	90	10	Many Others
TM82	Dragon Tail	Dragon	Physical	60	90	10	Normal
TM87	Swagger	Normal	Status	—	85	15	Normal
TM88	Sleep Talk	Normal	Status	—	—	10	Self
TM90	Substitute	Normal	Status	—	—	10	Self
TM100	Confide	Normal	Status	—	—	20	Normal

❖ MOVES TAUGHT BY PEOPLE

Name	Type	Kind	Pow.	Acc.	PP	Range
Draco Meteor	Dragon	Special	130	90	5	Normal

❖ MOVES LEARNED WHEN EVOLVING

Name	Type	Kind	Pow.	Acc.	PP	Range
Fly	Flying	Physical	90	95	15	Normal

❖ EGG MOVES

Name	Type	Kind	Pow.	Acc.	PP	Range

❖ EXCLUSIVE Z-MOVE

Name	Base Move	Type	Kind	Pow.	Acc.	Range

Lillipup

Alola Pokédex	Melemele	Akala	Ula'ula	Poni
120	—	047	—	—

Puppy Pokémon

NORMAL

HEIGHT: 1'04"
WEIGHT: 9.0 lbs.

Because it doesn't yelp, it's extremely popular with Trainers who live in apartment buildings.

The long fur surrounding its face functions as radar, enabling it to probe the condition of its battle opponents.

ABILITY
Vital Spirit
Pickup

HIDDEN ABILITY
Run Away

Damage taken in normal battles

NORMAL ×1	FIGHTING ×2	ROCK ×1
FIRE ×1	POISON ×1	GHOST ×0
WATER ×1	GROUND ×1	DRAGON ×1
GRASS ×1	FLYING ×1	DARK ×1
ELECTRIC ×1	PSYCHIC ×1	STEEL ×1
ICE ×1	BUG ×1	FAIRY ×1

SPECIES STRENGTHS
HP ◆◆
Attack ◆◆◆
Defense ◆◆◆
Sp. Atk ◆
Sp. Def ◆◆
Speed ◆◆◆◆

EGG GROUPS
Field

ITEM SOMETIMES HELD BY WILD POKÉMON
—

MAIN WAY TO REGISTER IN THE POKÉDEX
Catch in the tall grass in Paniola Ranch

EVOLUTION

Lillipup → Lv. 16 → Herdier → Lv. 32 → Stoutland

Same form for male/female

Herdier

Alola Pokédex	Melemele	Akala	Ula'ula	Poni
121	—	048	—	—

Loyal Dog Pokémon

NORMAL

HEIGHT: 2'11"
WEIGHT: 32.4 lbs.

Its dense black fur grows continuously. The high cost of keeping its hard fur properly groomed makes this a troublesome Pokémon to train.

This Pokémon obeys its master's orders faithfully. However, it refuses to listen to anything said by a person it doesn't respect.

ABILITY
Intimidate
Sand Rush

HIDDEN ABILITY
Scrappy

Damage taken in normal battles

NORMAL ×1	FIGHTING ×2	ROCK ×1
FIRE ×1	POISON ×1	GHOST ×0
WATER ×1	GROUND ×1	DRAGON ×1
GRASS ×1	FLYING ×1	DARK ×1
ELECTRIC ×1	PSYCHIC ×1	STEEL ×1
ICE ×1	BUG ×1	FAIRY ×1

SPECIES STRENGTHS
HP ◆◆◆
Attack ◆◆◆◆
Defense ◆◆◆◆
Sp. Atk ◆◆
Sp. Def ◆◆
Speed ◆◆◆◆

EGG GROUPS
Field

ITEM SOMETIMES HELD BY WILD POKÉMON
—

MAIN WAY TO REGISTER IN THE POKÉDEX
Level up Lillipup to Lv. 16

EVOLUTION

Lillipup → Lv. 16 → Herdier → Lv. 32 → Stoutland

Same form for male/female

Stoutland

Alola Pokédex	Melemele	Akala	Ula'ula	Poni
122	—	049	—	—

Big-Hearted Pokémon

NORMAL

HEIGHT: 3'11"
WEIGHT: 134.5 lbs.

Intelligent, good-natured, and valiant, it's a trustworthy partner on rescue teams.

With this wise Pokémon, there could be no concern that it would ever attack people. Some parents even trust it to babysit.

ABILITY
Intimidate
Sand Rush

HIDDEN ABILITY
Scrappy

Damage taken in normal battles

NORMAL ×1	FIGHTING ×2	ROCK ×1
FIRE ×1	POISON ×1	GHOST ×0
WATER ×1	GROUND ×1	DRAGON ×1
GRASS ×1	FLYING ×1	DARK ×1
ELECTRIC ×1	PSYCHIC ×1	STEEL ×1
ICE ×1	BUG ×1	FAIRY ×1

SPECIES STRENGTHS
HP ◆◆◆
Attack ◆◆◆◆◆◆
Defense ◆◆◆◆◆◆
Sp. Atk ◆◆
Sp. Def ◆◆◆◆
Speed ◆◆◆◆◆

EGG GROUPS
Field

ITEM SOMETIMES HELD BY WILD POKÉMON
—

MAIN WAY TO REGISTER IN THE POKÉDEX
Level up Herdier to Lv. 32

EVOLUTION

Lillipup → Lv. 16 → Herdier → Lv. 32 → Stoutland

Same form for male/female

LILLIPUP 120

LEVEL-UP MOVES

Lv.	Name	Type	Kind	Pow.	Acc.	PP	Range
1	Leer	Normal	Status	—	100	30	Many Others
1	Tackle	Normal	Physical	40	100	35	Normal
5	Odor Sleuth	Normal	Status	—	—	40	Normal
8	Bite	Dark	Physical	60	100	25	Normal
10	Baby-Doll Eyes	Fairy	Status	—	100	30	Normal
12	Helping Hand	Normal	Status	—	—	20	1 Ally
15	Take Down	Normal	Physical	90	85	20	Normal
19	Work Up	Normal	Status	—	—	30	Self
22	Crunch	Dark	Physical	80	100	15	Normal
26	Roar	Normal	Status	—	—	20	Normal
29	Retaliate	Normal	Physical	70	100	5	Normal
33	Reversal	Fighting	Physical	—	100	15	Normal
36	Last Resort	Normal	Physical	140	100	5	Normal
40	Giga Impact	Normal	Physical	150	90	5	Normal
45	Play Rough	Fairy	Physical	90	90	10	Normal

TM MOVES

No.	Name	Type	Kind	Pow.	Acc.	PP	Range
TM01	Work Up	Normal	Status	—	—	30	Self
TM05	Roar	Normal	Status	—	—	20	Normal
TM06	Toxic	Poison	Status	—	—	10	Normal
TM10	Hidden Power	Normal	Special	60	100	15	Normal
TM11	Sunny Day	Fire	Status	—	—	5	Both Sides
TM17	Protect	Normal	Status	—	—	10	Self
TM18	Rain Dance	Water	Status	—	—	5	Both Sides
TM21	Frustration	Normal	Physical	—	100	20	Normal
TM24	Thunderbolt	Electric	Special	90	100	15	Normal
TM27	Return	Normal	Physical	—	100	15	Normal
TM30	Shadow Ball	Ghost	Special	80	100	15	Normal
TM32	Double Team	Normal	Status	—	—	15	Self
TM39	Rock Tomb	Rock	Physical	60	95	15	Normal
TM40	Aerial Ace	Flying	Physical	60	—	20	Normal
TM42	Facade	Normal	Physical	70	100	20	Normal
TM44	Rest	Psychic	Status	—	—	10	Self
TM45	Attract	Normal	Status	—	100	15	Normal
TM48	Round	Normal	Special	60	100	15	Normal
TM68	Giga Impact	Normal	Physical	150	90	5	Normal
TM73	Thunder Wave	Electric	Status	—	90	20	Normal
TM87	Swagger	Normal	Status	—	85	15	Normal
TM88	Sleep Talk	Normal	Status	—	—	10	Self
TM90	Substitute	Normal	Status	—	—	10	Self
TM93	Wild Charge	Electric	Physical	90	100	15	Normal
TM95	Snarl	Dark	Special	55	95	15	Many Others
TM100	Confide	Normal	Status	—	—	20	Normal

MOVES TAUGHT BY PEOPLE

Name	Type	Kind	Pow.	Acc.	PP	Range

MOVES LEARNED WHEN EVOLVING

Name	Type	Kind	Pow.	Acc.	PP	Range

EGG MOVES

Name	Type	Kind	Pow.	Acc.	PP	Range
Howl	Normal	Status	—	—	40	Self
Sand Attack	Ground	Status	—	100	15	Normal
Mud-Slap	Ground	Special	20	100	10	Normal
Lick	Ghost	Physical	30	100	30	Normal
Charm	Fairy	Status	—	100	20	Normal
Endure	Normal	Status	—	—	10	Self
Yawn	Normal	Status	—	—	10	Normal
Pursuit	Dark	Physical	40	100	20	Normal
Fire Fang	Fire	Physical	65	95	15	Normal
Thunder Fang	Electric	Physical	65	95	15	Normal
Ice Fang	Ice	Physical	65	95	15	Normal
After You	Normal	Status	—	—	15	Normal
Psychic Fangs	Psychic	Physical	85	100	10	Normal

EXCLUSIVE Z-MOVE

Name	Base Move	Type	Kind	Pow.	Acc.	Range

HERDIER 121

LEVEL-UP MOVES

Lv.	Name	Type	Kind	Pow.	Acc.	PP	Range
1	Leer	Normal	Status	—	100	30	Many Others
1	Tackle	Normal	Physical	40	100	35	Normal
1	Odor Sleuth	Normal	Status	—	—	40	Normal
1	Bite	Dark	Physical	60	100	25	Normal
5	Odor Sleuth	Normal	Status	—	—	40	Normal
8	Bite	Dark	Physical	60	100	25	Normal
12	Helping Hand	Normal	Status	—	—	20	1 Ally
15	Take Down	Normal	Physical	90	85	20	Normal
20	Work Up	Normal	Status	—	—	30	Self
24	Crunch	Dark	Physical	80	100	15	Normal
29	Roar	Normal	Status	—	—	20	Normal
33	Retaliate	Normal	Physical	70	100	5	Normal
38	Reversal	Fighting	Physical	—	100	15	Normal
42	Last Resort	Normal	Physical	140	100	15	Normal
47	Giga Impact	Normal	Physical	150	90	5	Normal
52	Play Rough	Fairy	Physical	90	90	10	Normal

TM MOVES

No.	Name	Type	Kind	Pow.	Acc.	PP	Range
TM01	Work Up	Normal	Status	—	—	30	Self
TM05	Roar	Normal	Status	—	—	20	Normal
TM06	Toxic	Poison	Status	—	90	10	Normal
TM10	Hidden Power	Normal	Special	60	100	15	Normal
TM11	Sunny Day	Fire	Status	—	—	5	Both Sides
TM17	Protect	Normal	Status	—	—	10	Self
TM18	Rain Dance	Water	Status	—	—	5	Both Sides
TM21	Frustration	Normal	Physical	—	100	20	Normal
TM24	Thunderbolt	Electric	Special	90	100	15	Normal
TM27	Return	Normal	Physical	—	100	15	Normal
TM30	Shadow Ball	Ghost	Special	80	100	15	Normal
TM32	Double Team	Normal	Status	—	—	15	Self
TM39	Rock Tomb	Rock	Physical	60	95	15	Normal
TM40	Aerial Ace	Flying	Physical	60	—	20	Normal
TM42	Facade	Normal	Physical	70	100	20	Normal
TM44	Rest	Psychic	Status	—	—	10	Self
TM45	Attract	Normal	Status	—	100	15	Normal
TM48	Round	Normal	Special	60	100	15	Normal
TM66	Payback	Dark	Physical	50	100	10	Normal
TM68	Giga Impact	Normal	Physical	150	90	5	Normal
TM73	Thunder Wave	Electric	Status	—	90	20	Normal
TM87	Swagger	Normal	Status	—	85	15	Normal
TM88	Sleep Talk	Normal	Status	—	—	10	Self
TM90	Substitute	Normal	Status	—	—	10	Self
TM93	Wild Charge	Electric	Physical	90	100	15	Normal
TM94	Surf	Water	Special	90	100	15	Adjacent
TM95	Snarl	Dark	Special	55	95	15	Many Others

MOVES TAUGHT BY PEOPLE

No.	Name	Type	Kind	Pow.	Acc.	PP	Range
TM100	Confide	Normal	Status	—	—	20	Normal

MOVES LEARNED WHEN EVOLVING

Name	Type	Kind	Pow.	Acc.	PP	Range

EGG MOVES

Name	Type	Kind	Pow.	Acc.	PP	Range

EXCLUSIVE Z-MOVE

Name	Base Move	Type	Kind	Pow.	Acc.	Range

STOUTLAND 122

LEVEL-UP MOVES

Lv.	Name	Type	Kind	Pow.	Acc.	PP	Range
1	Ice Fang	Ice	Physical	65	95	15	Normal
1	Fire Fang	Fire	Physical	65	95	15	Normal
1	Thunder Fang	Electric	Physical	65	95	15	Normal
1	Leer	Normal	Status	—	100	30	Many Others
1	Tackle	Normal	Physical	40	100	35	Normal
1	Odor Sleuth	Normal	Status	—	—	40	Normal
1	Bite	Dark	Physical	60	100	25	Normal
5	Odor Sleuth	Normal	Status	—	—	40	Normal
8	Bite	Dark	Physical	60	100	25	Normal
12	Helping Hand	Normal	Status	—	—	20	1 Ally
15	Take Down	Normal	Physical	90	85	20	Normal
20	Work Up	Normal	Status	—	—	30	Self
24	Crunch	Dark	Physical	80	100	15	Normal
29	Roar	Normal	Status	—	—	20	Normal
36	Retaliate	Normal	Physical	70	100	5	Normal
42	Reversal	Fighting	Physical	—	100	15	Normal
51	Last Resort	Normal	Physical	140	100	5	Normal
59	Giga Impact	Normal	Physical	150	90	5	Normal
63	Play Rough	Fairy	Physical	90	90	10	Normal

TM MOVES

No.	Name	Type	Kind	Pow.	Acc.	PP	Range
TM01	Work Up	Normal	Status	—	—	30	Self
TM05	Roar	Normal	Status	—	—	20	Normal
TM06	Toxic	Poison	Status	—	90	10	Normal
TM10	Hidden Power	Normal	Special	60	100	15	Normal
TM11	Sunny Day	Fire	Status	—	—	5	Both Sides
TM15	Hyper Beam	Normal	Special	150	90	5	Normal
TM17	Protect	Normal	Status	—	—	10	Self
TM18	Rain Dance	Water	Status	—	—	5	Both Sides
TM21	Frustration	Normal	Physical	—	100	20	Normal
TM24	Thunderbolt	Electric	Special	90	100	15	Normal
TM25	Thunder	Electric	Special	110	70	10	Normal
TM27	Return	Normal	Physical	—	100	20	Normal
TM30	Shadow Ball	Ghost	Special	80	100	15	Normal
TM32	Double Team	Normal	Status	—	—	15	Self
TM39	Rock Tomb	Rock	Physical	60	95	15	Normal
TM40	Aerial Ace	Flying	Physical	60	—	20	Normal
TM42	Facade	Normal	Physical	70	100	20	Normal
TM44	Rest	Psychic	Status	—	—	10	Self
TM45	Attract	Normal	Status	—	100	15	Normal
TM48	Round	Normal	Special	60	100	15	Normal
TM66	Payback	Dark	Physical	50	100	10	Normal
TM68	Giga Impact	Normal	Physical	150	90	5	Normal
TM73	Thunder Wave	Electric	Status	—	90	20	Normal
TM87	Swagger	Normal	Status	—	85	15	Normal
TM88	Sleep Talk	Normal	Status	—	—	10	Self
TM90	Substitute	Normal	Status	—	—	10	Self
TM93	Wild Charge	Electric	Physical	90	100	15	Normal

MOVES TAUGHT BY PEOPLE

No.	Name	Type	Kind	Pow.	Acc.	PP	Range
TM94	Surf	Water	Special	90	100	15	Adjacent
TM95	Snarl	Dark	Special	55	95	15	Many Others
TM100	Confide	Normal	Status	—	—	20	Normal

MOVES LEARNED WHEN EVOLVING

Name	Type	Kind	Pow.	Acc.	PP	Range

EGG MOVES

Name	Type	Kind	Pow.	Acc.	PP	Range

EXCLUSIVE Z-MOVE

Name	Base Move	Type	Kind	Pow.	Acc.	Range

Alola Pokédex	Melemele	Akala	Ula'ula	Poni
123	—	050	—	—

Eevee
Evolution Pokémon

NORMAL

HEIGHT: 1'00"
WEIGHT: 14.3 lbs.

Possessing an unbalanced and unstable genetic makeup, it conceals many possible evolutions.

Current studies show it can evolve into an incredible eight different species of Pokémon.

ABILITY
Run Away
Adaptability

HIDDEN ABILITY
Anticipation

Damage taken in normal battles

NORMAL	×1	FIGHTING	×2	ROCK	×1
FIRE	×1	POISON	×1	GHOST	×0
WATER	×1	GROUND	×1	DRAGON	×1
GRASS	×1	FLYING	×1	DARK	×1
ELECTRIC	×1	PSYCHIC	×1	STEEL	×1
ICE	×1	BUG	×1	FAIRY	×1

SPECIES STRENGTHS
HP	◆◆
Attack	◆◆◆
Defense	◆◆◆
Sp. Atk	◆◆
Sp. Def	◆◆◆◆
Speed	◆◆◆◆

EGG GROUPS
Field

ITEM SOMETIMES HELD BY WILD POKÉMON
—

EVOLUTION
See below

MAIN WAY TO REGISTER IN THE POKÉDEX
Catch in the tall grass on Route 4

Same form for male/female

❖ LEVEL-UP MOVES

Lv.	Name	Type	Kind	Pow.	Acc.	PP	Range
1	Covet	Normal	Physical	60	100	25	Normal
1	Helping Hand	Normal	Status	—	—	20	1 Ally
1	Growl	Normal	Status	—	100	40	Many Others
1	Tackle	Normal	Physical	40	100	35	Normal
1	Tail Whip	Normal	Status	—	100	30	Many Others
5	Sand Attack	Ground	Status	—	100	15	Normal
9	Baby-Doll Eyes	Fairy	Status	—	100	30	Normal
13	Quick Attack	Normal	Physical	40	100	30	Normal
17	Bite	Dark	Physical	60	100	25	Normal
17	Swift	Normal	Special	60	—	20	Many Others
20	Refresh	Normal	Status	—	—	20	Self
25	Take Down	Normal	Physical	90	85	20	Normal
29	Charm	Fairy	Status	—	100	20	Normal
33	Baton Pass	Normal	Status	—	—	40	Self
37	Double-Edge	Normal	Physical	120	100	15	Normal
41	Last Resort	Normal	Physical	140	100	5	Normal
45	Trump Card	Normal	Special	—	—	5	Normal

❖ TM MOVES

No.	Name	Type	Kind	Pow.	Acc.	PP	Range
TM01	Work Up	Normal	Status	—	—	30	Self
TM06	Toxic	Poison	Status	—	90	10	Normal
TM10	Hidden Power	Normal	Special	60	100	15	Normal
TM11	Sunny Day	Fire	Status	—	—	5	Both Sides
TM17	Protect	Normal	Status	—	—	10	Self
TM18	Rain Dance	Water	Status	—	—	5	Both Sides
TM21	Frustration	Normal	Physical	—	100	20	Normal
TM27	Return	Normal	Physical	—	100	20	Normal
TM30	Shadow Ball	Ghost	Special	80	100	15	Normal
TM32	Double Team	Normal	Status	—	—	15	Self
TM42	Facade	Normal	Physical	70	100	20	Normal
TM44	Rest	Psychic	Status	—	—	10	Self
TM45	Attract	Normal	Status	—	100	15	Normal
TM48	Round	Normal	Special	60	100	15	Normal
TM49	Echoed Voice	Normal	Special	40	100	15	Normal
TM87	Swagger	Normal	Status	—	85	15	Normal
TM88	Sleep Talk	Normal	Status	—	—	10	Self
TM90	Substitute	Normal	Status	—	—	10	Self
TM100	Confide	Normal	Status	—	—	20	Normal

❖ MOVES TAUGHT BY PEOPLE

Name	Type	Kind	Pow.	Acc.	PP	Range

❖ MOVES LEARNED WHEN EVOLVING

Name	Type	Kind	Pow.	Acc.	PP	Range

❖ EGG MOVES

Name	Type	Kind	Pow.	Acc.	PP	Range
Charm	Fairy	Status	—	100	20	Normal
Flail	Normal	Physical	—	100	15	Normal
Endure	Normal	Status	—	—	10	Self
Curse	Ghost	Status	—	—	10	Varies
Tickle	Normal	Status	—	100	20	Normal
Wish	Normal	Status	—	—	10	Self
Yawn	Normal	Status	—	—	10	Normal
Fake Tears	Dark	Status	—	100	20	Normal
Covet	Normal	Physical	60	100	25	Normal
Detect	Fighting	Status	—	—	5	Self
Natural Gift	Normal	Physical	—	100	15	Normal
Stored Power	Psychic	Special	20	100	10	Normal
Synchronoise	Psychic	Special	120	100	10	Adjacent
Captivate	Normal	Status	—	100	20	Many Others

❖ EXCLUSIVE Z-MOVE

Name	Base Move	Type	Kind	Pow.	Acc.	Range
Extreme Evoboost	Last Resort	Normal	Status	—	—	Self

Eevee's Evolutions

Vaporeon — Water Stone

Jolteon — Thunder Stone

Flareon — Fire Stone

Espeon — Level up during the day with high friendship

Umbreon — Level up during the night with high friendship

Leafeon — Level up near the mossy stone in Lush Jungle

Glaceon — Level up near the icy stone in Mount Lanakila's cave

Sylveon — Level up affectionate Eevee that knows a Fairy-type move

Eevee

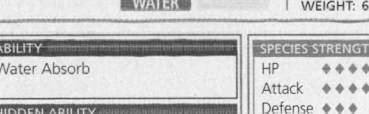

Alola Pokédex	Melemele	Akala	Ula'ula	Poni
124	—	051		

Vaporeon
Bubble Jet Pokémon

WATER

HEIGHT: 3'03"
WEIGHT: 63.9 lbs.

Its cells are composed of units much like water molecules. It lives close to water and is often mistaken for a mermaid.

Blending in with the water and erasing all signs of its presence, it patiently waits for its prey, fish Pokémon.

ABILITY
Water Absorb

HIDDEN ABILITY
Hydration

Damage taken in normal battles

NORMAL ×1	FIGHTING ×1	ROCK ×1			
FIRE ×0.5	POISON ×1	GHOST ×1			
WATER ×0.5	GROUND ×1	DRAGON ×1			
GRASS ×2	FLYING ×1	DARK ×1			
ELECTRIC ×2	PSYCHIC ×1	STEEL ×0.5			
ICE ×0.5	BUG ×1	FAIRY ×1			

SPECIES STRENGTHS
HP ◆◆◆◆◆
Attack ◆◆◆◆
Defense ◆◆◆
Sp. Atk ◆◆◆◆◆◆
Sp. Def ◆◆◆◆◆◆
Speed ◆◆◆◆

EGG GROUPS
Field

ITEM SOMETIMES HELD BY WILD POKÉMON
—

EVOLUTION

Eevee → **Water Stone** → Vaporeon

MAIN WAY TO REGISTER IN THE POKÉDEX
Use a Water Stone on Eevee

Same form for male/female

◆ LEVEL-UP MOVES

Lv.	Name	Type	Kind	Pow.	Acc.	PP	Range
1	Water Gun	Water	Special	40	100	25	Normal
1	Helping Hand	Normal	Status	—	—	20	1 Ally
1	Tackle	Normal	Physical	40	100	35	Normal
1	Tail Whip	Normal	Status	—	100	30	Many Others
5	Sand Attack	Ground	Status	—	100	15	Normal
9	Baby-Doll Eyes	Fairy	Status	—	100	30	Normal
13	Quick Attack	Normal	Physical	40	100	30	Normal
17	Water Pulse	Water	Special	60	100	20	Normal
20	Aurora Beam	Ice	Special	65	100	20	Normal
25	Aqua Ring	Water	Status	—	—	20	Self
29	Acid Armor	Poison	Status	—	—	20	Self
33	Haze	Ice	Status	—	—	30	Both Sides
37	Muddy Water	Water	Special	90	85	10	Many Others
41	Last Resort	Normal	Physical	140	100	5	Normal
45	Hydro Pump	Water	Special	110	80	5	Normal

◆ TM MOVES

No.	Name	Type	Kind	Pow.	Acc.	PP	Range
TM01	Work Up	Normal	Status	—	—	30	Self
TM05	Roar	Normal	Status	—	—	20	Normal
TM06	Toxic	Poison	Status	—	90	10	Normal
TM07	Hail	Ice	Status	—	—	10	Both Sides
TM10	Hidden Power	Normal	Special	60	100	15	Normal
TM11	Sunny Day	Fire	Status	—	—	5	Both Sides
TM13	Ice Beam	Ice	Special	90	100	10	Normal
TM14	Blizzard	Ice	Special	110	70	5	Many Others
TM15	Hyper Beam	Normal	Special	150	90	5	Normal
TM17	Protect	Normal	Status	—	—	10	Self
TM18	Rain Dance	Water	Status	—	—	5	Both Sides
TM21	Frustration	Normal	Physical	—	100	20	Normal
TM27	Return	Normal	Physical	—	100	20	Normal
TM30	Shadow Ball	Ghost	Special	80	100	15	Normal
TM32	Double Team	Normal	Status	—	—	15	Self
TM42	Facade	Normal	Physical	70	100	20	Normal
TM44	Rest	Psychic	Status	—	—	10	Self
TM45	Attract	Normal	Status	—	100	15	Normal
TM48	Round	Normal	Special	60	100	15	Normal
TM49	Echoed Voice	Normal	Special	40	100	15	Normal
TM55	Scald	Water	Special	80	100	15	Normal
TM68	Giga Impact	Normal	Physical	150	90	5	Normal
TM87	Swagger	Normal	Status	—	85	15	Normal
TM88	Sleep Talk	Normal	Status	—	—	10	Self
TM90	Substitute	Normal	Status	—	—	10	Self
TM94	Surf	Water	Special	90	100	15	Adjacent
TM98	Waterfall	Water	Physical	80	100	15	Normal
TM100	Confide	Normal	Status	—	—	20	Normal

◆ MOVES TAUGHT BY PEOPLE

Name	Type	Kind	Pow.	Acc.	PP	Range

◆ MOVES LEARNED WHEN EVOLVING

Name	Type	Kind	Pow.	Acc.	PP	Range
Water Gun	Water	Special	40	100	25	Normal

◆ EGG MOVES

Name	Type	Kind	Pow.	Acc.	PP	Range

◆ EXCLUSIVE Z-MOVE

Name	Base Move	Type	Kind	Pow.	Acc.	Range

Alola Pokédex	Melemele	Akala	Ula'ula	Poni
125	—	052		

Jolteon
Lightning Pokémon

ELECTRIC

HEIGHT: 2'07"
WEIGHT: 54.0 lbs.

They send out electrical charges of about 10,000 volts. Because they are high-strung, it can be difficult to grow close to them.

When its fur stands on end, that's a sign it's about to give off a jolt of electricity. Take care, as sometimes lightning strikes next to it, too.

ABILITY
Volt Absorb

HIDDEN ABILITY
Quick Feet

Damage taken in normal battles

NORMAL ×1	FIGHTING ×1	ROCK ×1			
FIRE ×1	POISON ×1	GHOST ×1			
WATER ×1	GROUND ×2	DRAGON ×1			
GRASS ×1	FLYING ×0.5	DARK ×1			
ELECTRIC ×0.5	PSYCHIC ×1	STEEL ×0.5			
ICE ×1	BUG ×1	FAIRY ×1			

SPECIES STRENGTHS
HP ◆◆◆
Attack ◆◆◆
Defense ◆◆◆
Sp. Atk ◆◆◆◆◆◆
Sp. Def ◆◆◆◆◆
Speed ◆◆◆◆◆◆◆

EGG GROUPS
Field

ITEM SOMETIMES HELD BY WILD POKÉMON
—

EVOLUTION

Eevee → **Thunder Stone** → Jolteon

MAIN WAY TO REGISTER IN THE POKÉDEX
Use a Thunder Stone on Eevee

Same form for male/female

◆ LEVEL-UP MOVES

Lv.	Name	Type	Kind	Pow.	Acc.	PP	Range
1	Thunder Shock	Electric	Special	40	100	30	Normal
1	Helping Hand	Normal	Status	—	—	20	1 Ally
1	Tackle	Normal	Physical	40	100	35	Normal
1	Tail Whip	Normal	Status	—	100	30	Many Others
5	Sand Attack	Ground	Status	—	100	15	Normal
9	Baby-Doll Eyes	Fairy	Status	—	100	30	Normal
13	Quick Attack	Normal	Physical	40	100	30	Normal
17	Double Kick	Fighting	Physical	30	100	30	Normal
20	Thunder Fang	Electric	Physical	65	95	15	Normal
25	Pin Missile	Bug	Physical	25	95	20	Normal
29	Agility	Psychic	Status	—	—	30	Self
33	Thunder Wave	Electric	Status	—	90	20	Normal
37	Discharge	Electric	Special	80	100	15	Adjacent
41	Last Resort	Normal	Physical	140	100	5	Normal
45	Thunder	Electric	Special	110	70	10	Normal

◆ TM MOVES

No.	Name	Type	Kind	Pow.	Acc.	PP	Range
TM01	Work Up	Normal	Status	—	—	30	Self
TM05	Roar	Normal	Status	—	—	20	Normal
TM06	Toxic	Poison	Status	—	90	10	Normal
TM10	Hidden Power	Normal	Special	60	100	15	Normal
TM11	Sunny Day	Fire	Status	—	—	5	Both Sides
TM13	Hyper Beam	Normal	Special	150	90	5	Normal
TM16	Light Screen	Psychic	Status	—	—	30	Your Side
TM17	Protect	Normal	Status	—	—	10	Self
TM18	Rain Dance	Water	Status	—	—	5	Both Sides
TM21	Frustration	Normal	Physical	—	100	20	Normal
TM24	Thunderbolt	Electric	Special	90	100	15	Normal
TM25	Thunder	Electric	Special	110	70	10	Normal
TM27	Return	Normal	Physical	—	100	20	Normal
TM30	Shadow Ball	Ghost	Special	80	100	15	Normal
TM32	Double Team	Normal	Status	—	—	15	Self
TM42	Facade	Normal	Physical	70	100	20	Normal
TM44	Rest	Psychic	Status	—	—	10	Self
TM45	Attract	Normal	Status	—	100	15	Normal
TM48	Round	Normal	Special	60	100	15	Normal
TM49	Echoed Voice	Normal	Special	40	100	15	Normal
TM57	Charge Beam	Electric	Special	50	90	10	Normal
TM68	Giga Impact	Normal	Physical	150	90	5	Normal
TM72	Volt Switch	Electric	Special	70	100	20	Normal
TM73	Thunder Wave	Electric	Status	—	90	20	Normal
TM87	Swagger	Normal	Status	—	85	15	Normal
TM88	Sleep Talk	Normal	Status	—	—	10	Self
TM90	Substitute	Normal	Status	—	—	10	Self
TM93	Wild Charge	Electric	Physical	90	100	15	Normal

◆ MOVES TAUGHT BY PEOPLE

No.	Name	Type	Kind	Pow.	Acc.	PP	Range
TM100	Confide	Normal	Status	—	—	20	Normal

◆ MOVES LEARNED WHEN EVOLVING

Name	Type	Kind	Pow.	Acc.	PP	Range
Thunder Shock	Electric	Special	40	100	30	Normal

◆ EGG MOVES

Name	Type	Kind	Pow.	Acc.	PP	Range

◆ EXCLUSIVE Z-MOVE

Name	Base Move	Type	Kind	Pow.	Acc.	Range

VAPOREON 124

JOLTEON 125

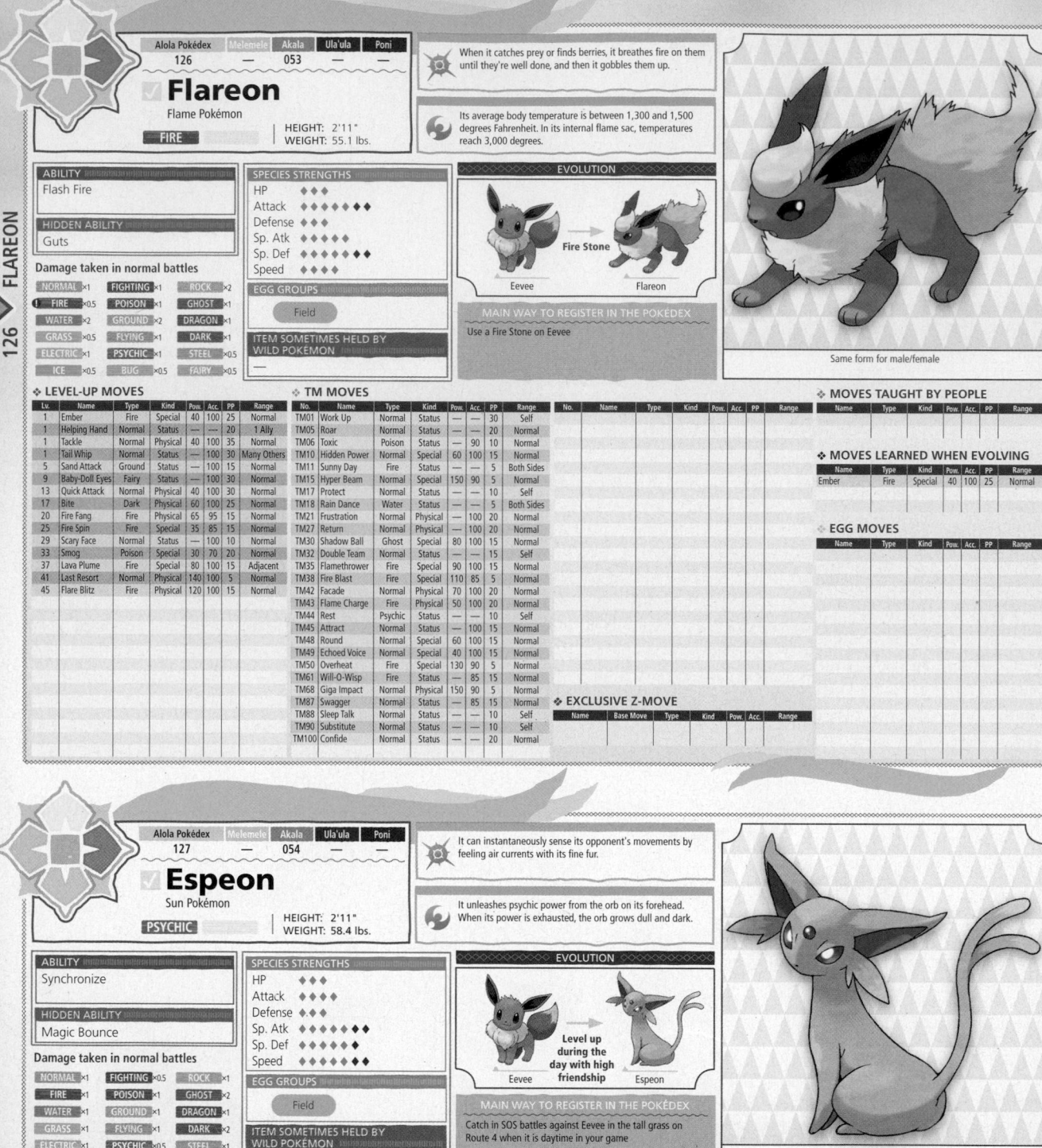

Flareon

Alola Pokédex	Melemele	Akala	Ula'ula	Poni
126	—	053	—	—

Flareon
Flame Pokémon

FIRE

HEIGHT: 2'11"
WEIGHT: 55.1 lbs.

When it catches prey or finds berries, it breathes fire on them until they're well done, and then it gobbles them up.

Its average body temperature is between 1,300 and 1,500 degrees Fahrenheit. In its internal flame sac, temperatures reach 3,000 degrees.

ABILITY
Flash Fire

HIDDEN ABILITY
Guts

SPECIES STRENGTHS
HP	◆◆◆
Attack	◆◆◆◆◆◆
Defense	◆◆◆
Sp. Atk	◆◆◆◆◆
Sp. Def	◆◆◆◆◆◆
Speed	◆◆◆

Damage taken in normal battles
NORMAL ×1	FIGHTING ×1	ROCK ×2			
FIRE ×0.5	POISON ×1	GHOST ×1			
WATER ×2	GROUND ×1	DRAGON ×1			
GRASS ×0.5	FLYING ×1	DARK ×1			
ELECTRIC ×1	PSYCHIC ×1	STEEL ×0.5			
ICE ×0.5	BUG ×0.5	FAIRY ×0.5			

EGG GROUPS
Field

ITEM SOMETIMES HELD BY WILD POKÉMON
—

EVOLUTION
Eevee → **Fire Stone** → Flareon

MAIN WAY TO REGISTER IN THE POKÉDEX
Use a Fire Stone on Eevee

Same form for male/female

❖ LEVEL-UP MOVES
Lv.	Name	Type	Kind	Pow.	Acc.	PP	Range
1	Ember	Fire	Special	40	100	25	Normal
1	Helping Hand	Normal	Status	—	—	20	1 Ally
1	Tackle	Normal	Physical	40	100	35	Normal
1	Tail Whip	Normal	Status	—	100	30	Many Others
5	Sand Attack	Ground	Status	—	100	15	Normal
9	Baby-Doll Eyes	Fairy	Status	—	100	30	Normal
13	Quick Attack	Normal	Physical	40	100	30	Normal
17	Bite	Dark	Physical	60	100	25	Normal
20	Fire Fang	Fire	Physical	65	95	15	Normal
25	Fire Spin	Fire	Special	35	85	15	Normal
29	Scary Face	Normal	Status	—	100	10	Normal
33	Smog	Poison	Special	30	70	20	Normal
37	Lava Plume	Fire	Special	80	100	15	Adjacent
41	Last Resort	Normal	Physical	140	100	5	Normal
45	Flare Blitz	Fire	Physical	120	100	15	Normal

❖ TM MOVES
No.	Name	Type	Kind	Pow.	Acc.	PP	Range
TM01	Work Up	Normal	Status	—	—	30	Self
TM05	Roar	Normal	Status	—	—	20	Normal
TM06	Toxic	Poison	Status	—	90	10	Normal
TM10	Hidden Power	Normal	Special	60	100	15	Normal
TM11	Sunny Day	Fire	Status	—	—	5	Both Sides
TM15	Hyper Beam	Normal	Special	150	90	5	Normal
TM17	Protect	Normal	Status	—	—	10	Self
TM18	Rain Dance	Water	Status	—	—	5	Both Sides
TM21	Frustration	Normal	Physical	—	100	20	Normal
TM27	Return	Normal	Physical	—	100	20	Normal
TM30	Shadow Ball	Ghost	Special	80	100	15	Normal
TM32	Double Team	Normal	Status	—	—	15	Self
TM35	Flamethrower	Fire	Special	90	100	15	Normal
TM38	Fire Blast	Fire	Special	110	85	5	Normal
TM42	Facade	Normal	Physical	70	100	20	Normal
TM43	Flame Charge	Fire	Physical	50	100	20	Normal
TM44	Rest	Psychic	Status	—	—	10	Self
TM45	Attract	Normal	Status	—	100	15	Normal
TM48	Round	Normal	Special	60	100	15	Normal
TM49	Echoed Voice	Normal	Special	40	100	15	Normal
TM50	Overheat	Fire	Special	130	90	5	Normal
TM61	Will-O-Wisp	Fire	Status	—	85	15	Normal
TM68	Giga Impact	Normal	Physical	150	90	5	Normal
TM87	Swagger	Normal	Status	—	85	15	Normal
TM88	Sleep Talk	Normal	Status	—	—	10	Self
TM90	Substitute	Normal	Status	—	—	10	Self
TM100	Confide	Normal	Status	—	—	20	Normal

❖ MOVES TAUGHT BY PEOPLE
No.	Name	Type	Kind	Pow.	Acc.	PP	Range

❖ MOVES LEARNED WHEN EVOLVING
Name	Type	Kind	Pow.	Acc.	PP	Range
Ember	Fire	Special	40	100	25	Normal

❖ EGG MOVES
Name	Type	Kind	Pow.	Acc.	PP	Range

❖ EXCLUSIVE Z-MOVE
Name	Base Move	Type	Kind	Pow.	Acc.	Range

Espeon

Alola Pokédex	Melemele	Akala	Ula'ula	Poni
127	—	054	—	—

Espeon
Sun Pokémon

PSYCHIC

HEIGHT: 2'11"
WEIGHT: 58.4 lbs.

It can instantaneously sense its opponent's movements by feeling air currents with its fine fur.

It unleashes psychic power from the orb on its forehead. When its power is exhausted, the orb grows dull and dark.

ABILITY
Synchronize

HIDDEN ABILITY
Magic Bounce

SPECIES STRENGTHS
HP	◆◆◆
Attack	◆◆◆
Defense	◆◆◆
Sp. Atk	◆◆◆◆◆◆◆
Sp. Def	◆◆◆◆◆◆
Speed	◆◆◆◆◆◆

Damage taken in normal battles
NORMAL ×1	FIGHTING ×0.5	ROCK ×1	
FIRE ×1	POISON ×1	GHOST ×2	
WATER ×1	GROUND ×1	DRAGON ×1	
GRASS ×1	FLYING ×1	DARK ×2	
ELECTRIC ×1	PSYCHIC ×0.5	STEEL ×1	
ICE ×1	BUG ×2	FAIRY ×1	

EGG GROUPS
Field

ITEM SOMETIMES HELD BY WILD POKÉMON
—

EVOLUTION
Eevee → **Level up during the day with high friendship** → Espeon

MAIN WAY TO REGISTER IN THE POKÉDEX
Catch in SOS battles against Eevee in the tall grass on Route 4 when it is daytime in your game

Same form for male/female

❖ LEVEL-UP MOVES
Lv.	Name	Type	Kind	Pow.	Acc.	PP	Range
1	Confusion	Psychic	Special	50	100	25	Normal
1	Helping Hand	Normal	Status	—	—	20	1 Ally
1	Tackle	Normal	Physical	40	100	35	Normal
1	Tail Whip	Normal	Status	—	100	30	Many Others
5	Sand Attack	Ground	Status	—	100	15	Normal
9	Baby-Doll Eyes	Fairy	Status	—	100	30	Normal
13	Quick Attack	Normal	Physical	40	100	30	Normal
17	Swift	Normal	Special	60	—	20	Many Others
20	Psybeam	Psychic	Special	65	100	20	Normal
25	Future Sight	Psychic	Special	120	100	10	Normal
29	Psych Up	Normal	Status	—	—	10	Normal
33	Morning Sun	Normal	Status	—	—	5	Self
37	Psychic	Psychic	Special	90	100	10	Normal
41	Last Resort	Normal	Physical	140	100	5	Normal
45	Power Swap	Psychic	Status	—	—	10	Normal

❖ TM MOVES
No.	Name	Type	Kind	Pow.	Acc.	PP	Range
TM01	Work Up	Normal	Status	—	—	30	Self
TM03	Psyshock	Psychic	Special	80	100	10	Normal
TM04	Calm Mind	Psychic	Status	—	—	20	Self
TM06	Toxic	Poison	Status	—	90	10	Normal
TM10	Hidden Power	Normal	Special	60	100	15	Normal
TM11	Sunny Day	Fire	Status	—	—	5	Both Sides
TM15	Hyper Beam	Normal	Special	150	90	5	Normal
TM16	Light Screen	Psychic	Status	—	—	30	Your Side
TM17	Protect	Normal	Status	—	—	10	Self
TM18	Rain Dance	Water	Status	—	—	5	Both Sides
TM21	Frustration	Normal	Physical	—	100	20	Normal
TM27	Return	Normal	Physical	—	100	20	Normal
TM29	Psychic	Psychic	Special	90	100	10	Normal
TM30	Shadow Ball	Ghost	Special	80	100	15	Normal
TM32	Double Team	Normal	Status	—	—	15	Self
TM33	Reflect	Psychic	Status	—	—	20	Your Side
TM42	Facade	Normal	Physical	70	100	20	Normal
TM44	Rest	Psychic	Status	—	—	10	Self
TM45	Attract	Normal	Status	—	100	15	Normal
TM48	Round	Normal	Special	60	100	15	Normal
TM49	Echoed Voice	Normal	Special	40	100	15	Normal
TM68	Giga Impact	Normal	Physical	150	90	5	Normal
TM77	Psych Up	Normal	Status	—	—	10	Normal
TM85	Dream Eater	Psychic	Special	100	100	15	Normal
TM86	Grass Knot	Grass	Special	—	100	20	Normal
TM87	Swagger	Normal	Status	—	85	15	Normal
TM88	Sleep Talk	Normal	Status	—	—	10	Self
TM90	Substitute	Normal	Status	—	—	10	Self

❖ MOVES TAUGHT BY PEOPLE
No.	Name	Type	Kind	Pow.	Acc.	PP	Range
TM92	Trick Room	Psychic	Status	—	—	5	Both Sides
TM99	Dazzling Gleam	Fairy	Special	80	100	10	Many Others
TM100	Confide	Normal	Status	—	—	20	Normal

❖ MOVES LEARNED WHEN EVOLVING
Name	Type	Kind	Pow.	Acc.	PP	Range
Confusion	Psychic	Special	50	100	25	Normal

❖ EGG MOVES
Name	Type	Kind	Pow.	Acc.	PP	Range

❖ EXCLUSIVE Z-MOVE
Name	Base Move	Type	Kind	Pow.	Acc.	Range

Same form for male/female

Umbreon

Moonlight Pokémon

Alola Pokédex	Melemele	Akala	Ula'ula	Poni
128	—	055	—	—

DARK

HEIGHT: 3'03"
WEIGHT: 59.5 lbs.

When this Pokémon becomes angry, its pores secrete a poisonous sweat, which it sprays at its opponent's eyes.

With its black fur, it blends into the darkness. It bides its time, and when prey appears, this Pokémon goes for its throat, and then eats it.

ABILITY
Synchronize

HIDDEN ABILITY
Inner Focus

Damage taken in normal battles

NORMAL ×1	FIGHTING ×2	ROCK ×1
FIRE ×1	POISON ×1	GHOST ×0.5
WATER ×1	GROUND ×1	DRAGON ×1
GRASS ×1	FLYING ×1	DARK ×0.5
ELECTRIC ×1	PSYCHIC ×0	STEEL ×1
ICE ×1	BUG ×2	FAIRY ×2

SPECIES STRENGTHS
HP ◆◆◆◆
Attack ◆◆◆◆
Defense ◆◆◆◆◆◆
Sp. Atk ◆◆◆
Sp. Def ◆◆◆◆◆◆◆
Speed ◆◆◆◆

EGG GROUPS
Field

ITEM SOMETIMES HELD BY WILD POKEMON
—

EVOLUTION

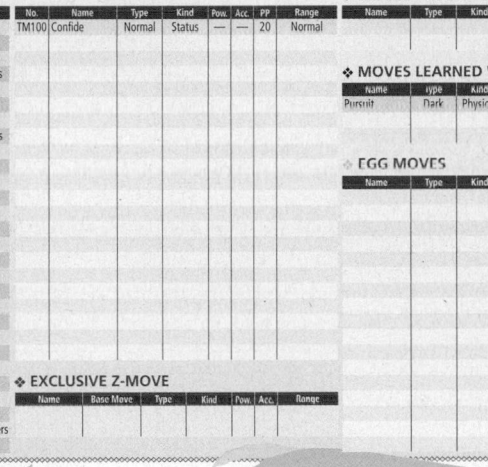

Eevee → Umbreon

Level up during the night with high friendship

MAIN WAY TO REGISTER IN THE POKÉDEX
Catch in SOS battles against Eevee in the tall grass on Route 4 when it is nighttime in your game

✦ LEVEL-UP MOVES

Lv.	Name	Type	Kind	Pow.	Acc.	PP	Range
1	Pursuit	Dark	Physical	40	100	20	Normal
1	Helping Hand	Normal	Status	—	—	20	1 Ally
1	Tackle	Normal	Physical	40	100	35	Normal
1	Tail Whip	Normal	Status	—	100	30	Many Others
5	Sand Attack	Ground	Status	—	100	15	Normal
9	Baby-Doll Eyes	Fairy	Status	—	100	30	Normal
13	Quick Attack	Normal	Physical	40	100	30	Normal
17	Confuse Ray	Ghost	Status	—	100	10	Normal
20	Feint Attack	Dark	Physical	60	—	20	Normal
25	Assurance	Dark	Physical	60	100	10	Normal
29	Screech	Normal	Status	—	85	40	Normal
33	Moonlight	Fairy	Status	—	—	5	Self
37	Mean Look	Normal	Status	—	—	5	Normal
41	Last Resort	Normal	Physical	140	100	5	Normal
45	Guard Swap	Psychic	Status	—	—	10	Normal

✦ TM MOVES

No.	Name	Type	Kind	Pow.	Acc.	PP	Range
TM01	Work Up	Normal	Status	—	—	30	Self
TM06	Toxic	Poison	Status	—	90	10	Normal
TM10	Hidden Power	Normal	Special	60	100	15	Normal
TM11	Sunny Day	Fire	Status	—	—	5	Both Sides
TM12	Taunt	Dark	Status	—	100	20	Normal
TM15	Hyper Beam	Normal	Special	150	90	5	Normal
TM17	Protect	Normal	Status	—	—	10	Self
TM18	Rain Dance	Water	Status	—	—	5	Both Sides
TM21	Frustration	Normal	Physical	—	100	20	Normal
TM27	Return	Normal	Physical	—	100	20	Normal
TM29	Psychic	Psychic	Special	90	100	10	Normal
TM30	Shadow Ball	Ghost	Special	80	100	15	Normal
TM32	Double Team	Normal	Status	—	—	15	Self
TM41	Torment	Dark	Status	—	100	15	Normal
TM42	Facade	Normal	Physical	70	100	20	Normal
TM44	Rest	Psychic	Status	—	—	10	Self
TM45	Attract	Normal	Status	—	100	15	Normal
TM48	Round	Normal	Special	60	100	15	Normal
TM49	Echoed Voice	Normal	Special	40	100	15	Normal
TM66	Payback	Dark	Physical	50	100	10	Normal
TM68	Giga Impact	Normal	Physical	150	90	5	Normal
TM77	Psych Up	Normal	Status	—	—	10	Self
TM85	Dream Eater	Psychic	Special	100	100	15	Normal
TM87	Swagger	Normal	Status	—	85	15	Normal
TM88	Sleep Talk	Normal	Status	—	—	10	Self
TM90	Substitute	Normal	Status	—	—	10	Self
TM95	Snarl	Dark	Special	55	95	15	Many Others
TM97	Dark Pulse	Dark	Special	80	100	15	Normal

No.	Name	Type	Kind	Pow.	Acc.	PP	Range
TM100	Confide	Normal	Status	—	—	20	Normal

✦ MOVES TAUGHT BY PEOPLE

Name	Type	Kind	Pow.	Acc.	PP	Range

✦ MOVES LEARNED WHEN EVOLVING

Name	Type	Kind	Pow.	Acc.	PP	Range
Pursuit	Dark	Physical	40	100	20	Normal

✦ EGG MOVES

Name	Type	Kind	Pow.	Acc.	PP	Range

✦ EXCLUSIVE Z-MOVE

Name	Base Move	Type	Kind	Pow.	Acc.	Range

Same form for male/female

LEAFEON 129

Leafeon

Verdant Pokémon

Alola Pokédex	Melemele	Akala	Ula'ula	Poni
129	—	056	—	—

GRASS

HEIGHT: 3'03"
WEIGHT: 56.2 lbs.

Its cellular composition is closer to that of a plant than an animal. It uses photosynthesis to produce its energy supply without eating food.

The younger they are, the more they smell like fresh grass. With age, their fragrance takes on the odor of fallen leaves.

ABILITY
Leaf Guard

HIDDEN ABILITY
Chlorophyll

Damage taken in normal battles

NORMAL ×1	FIGHTING ×1	ROCK ×1
FIRE ×2	POISON ×1	GHOST ×1
WATER ×0.5	GROUND ×0.5	DRAGON ×1
GRASS ×0.5	FLYING ×1	DARK ×1
ELECTRIC ×0.5	PSYCHIC ×1	STEEL ×1
ICE ×2	BUG ×2	FAIRY ×1

SPECIES STRENGTHS
HP ◆◆◆
Attack ◆◆◆◆◆
Defense ◆◆◆◆◆◆◆
Sp. Atk ◆◆◆
Sp. Def ◆◆◆
Speed ◆◆◆◆◆◆

EGG GROUPS
Field

ITEM SOMETIMES HELD BY WILD POKEMON
—

EVOLUTION

Eevee → Umbreon

Level up near the mossy stone in Lush Jungle

MAIN WAY TO REGISTER IN THE POKÉDEX
Level up Eevee near the moss-covered rock in Lush Jungle

✦ LEVEL-UP MOVES

Lv.	Name	Type	Kind	Pow.	Acc.	PP	Range
1	Razor Leaf	Grass	Physical	55	95	25	Many Others
1	Helping Hand	Normal	Status	—	—	20	1 Ally
1	Tackle	Normal	Physical	40	100	35	Normal
1	Tail Whip	Normal	Status	—	100	30	Many Others
5	Sand Attack	Ground	Status	—	100	15	Normal
9	Baby-Doll Eyes	Fairy	Status	—	100	30	Normal
13	Quick Attack	Normal	Physical	40	100	30	Normal
17	Grass Whistle	Grass	Status	—	55	15	Normal
20	Magical Leaf	Grass	Special	60	—	20	Normal
25	Giga Drain	Grass	Special	75	100	10	Normal
29	Swords Dance	Normal	Status	—	—	20	Self
33	Synthesis	Grass	Status	—	—	5	Self
37	Sunny Day	Fire	Status	—	—	5	Both Sides
41	Last Resort	Normal	Physical	140	100	5	Normal
45	Leaf Blade	Grass	Physical	90	100	15	Normal

✦ TM MOVES

No.	Name	Type	Kind	Pow.	Acc.	PP	Range
TM01	Work Up	Normal	Status	—	—	30	Self
TM05	Roar	Normal	Status	—	—	20	Normal
TM06	Toxic	Poison	Status	—	90	10	Normal
TM10	Hidden Power	Normal	Special	60	100	15	Normal
TM11	Sunny Day	Fire	Status	—	—	5	Both Sides
TM15	Hyper Beam	Normal	Special	150	90	5	Normal
TM17	Protect	Normal	Status	—	—	10	Self
TM18	Rain Dance	Water	Status	—	—	5	Both Sides
TM21	Frustration	Normal	Physical	—	100	20	Normal
TM22	Solar Beam	Grass	Special	120	100	10	Normal
TM27	Return	Normal	Physical	—	100	20	Normal
TM30	Shadow Ball	Ghost	Special	80	100	15	Normal
TM32	Double Team	Normal	Status	—	—	15	Self
TM40	Aerial Ace	Flying	Physical	60	—	20	Normal
TM42	Facade	Normal	Physical	70	100	20	Normal
TM44	Rest	Psychic	Status	—	—	10	Self
TM45	Attract	Normal	Status	—	100	15	Normal
TM48	Round	Normal	Special	60	100	15	Normal
TM49	Echoed Voice	Normal	Special	40	100	15	Normal
TM53	Energy Ball	Grass	Special	90	100	10	Normal
TM68	Giga Impact	Normal	Physical	150	90	5	Normal
TM75	Swords Dance	Normal	Status	—	—	20	Self
TM81	X-Scissor	Bug	Physical	80	100	15	Normal
TM86	Grass Knot	Grass	Special	—	100	20	Normal
TM87	Swagger	Normal	Status	—	85	15	Normal
TM88	Sleep Talk	Normal	Status	—	—	10	Self
TM90	Substitute	Normal	Status	—	—	10	Self
TM96	Nature Power	Normal	Status	—	—	20	Normal

No.	Name	Type	Kind	Pow.	Acc.	PP	Range
TM100	Confide	Normal	Status	—	—	20	Normal

✦ MOVES TAUGHT BY PEOPLE

Name	Type	Kind	Pow.	Acc.	PP	Range

✦ MOVES LEARNED WHEN EVOLVING

Name	Type	Kind	Pow.	Acc.	PP	Range
Razor Leaf	Grass	Physical	55	95	25	Many Others

✦ EGG MOVES

Name	Type	Kind	Pow.	Acc.	PP	Range

✦ EXCLUSIVE Z-MOVE

Name	Base Move	Type	Kind	Pow.	Acc.	Range

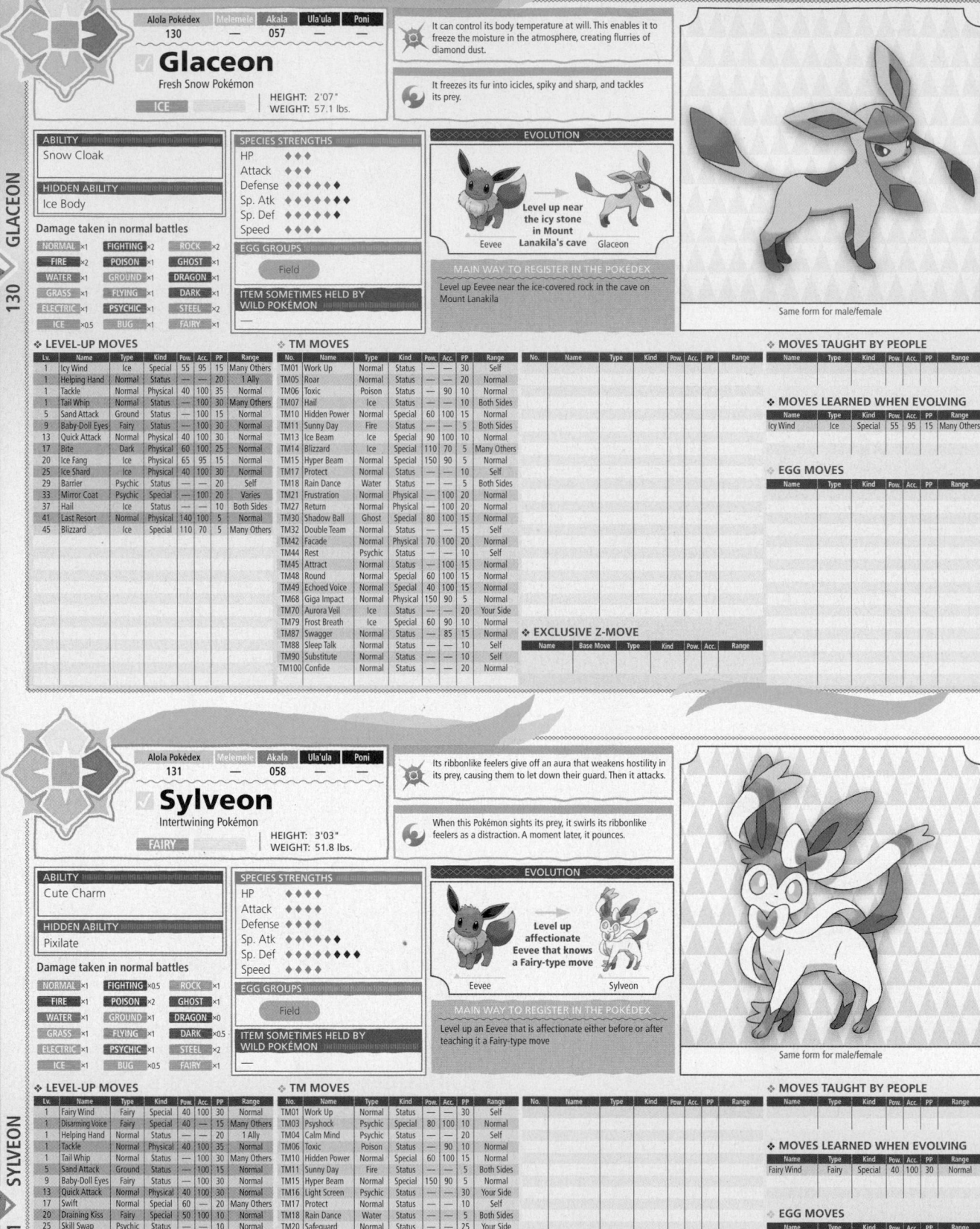

Glaceon
Fresh Snow Pokémon

ICE

Alola Pokédex	Melemele	Akala	Ula'ula	Poni
130	—	057	—	—

HEIGHT: 2'07"
WEIGHT: 57.1 lbs.

It can control its body temperature at will. This enables it to freeze the moisture in the atmosphere, creating flurries of diamond dust.

It freezes its fur into icicles, spiky and sharp, and tackles its prey.

ABILITY
Snow Cloak

HIDDEN ABILITY
Ice Body

SPECIES STRENGTHS
HP	◆◆◆
Attack	◆◆◆
Defense	◆◆◆◆
Sp. Atk	◆◆◆◆◆◆
Sp. Def	◆◆◆◆◆
Speed	◆◆◆◆

EGG GROUPS
Field

ITEM SOMETIMES HELD BY WILD POKÉMON
—

Damage taken in normal battles
NORMAL	×1	FIGHTING	×2	ROCK	×1
FIRE	×2	POISON	×1	GHOST	×1
WATER	×1	GROUND	×1	DRAGON	×1
GRASS	×1	FLYING	×1	DARK	×1
ELECTRIC	×1	PSYCHIC	×1	STEEL	×1
ICE	×0.5	BUG	×1	FAIRY	×1

EVOLUTION
Eevee → Level up near the icy stone in Mount Lanakila's cave → Glaceon

MAIN WAY TO REGISTER IN THE POKÉDEX
Level up Eevee near the ice-covered rock in the cave on Mount Lanakila

Same form for male/female

❖ LEVEL-UP MOVES
Lv.	Name	Type	Kind	Pow.	Acc.	PP	Range
1	Icy Wind	Ice	Special	55	95	15	Many Others
1	Helping Hand	Normal	Status	—	—	20	1 Ally
1	Tackle	Normal	Physical	40	100	35	Normal
1	Tail Whip	Normal	Status	—	100	30	Many Others
5	Sand Attack	Ground	Status	—	100	15	Normal
9	Baby-Doll Eyes	Fairy	Status	—	100	30	Normal
13	Quick Attack	Normal	Physical	40	100	30	Normal
17	Bite	Dark	Physical	60	100	25	Normal
20	Ice Fang	Ice	Physical	65	95	15	Normal
25	Ice Shard	Ice	Physical	40	100	30	Normal
29	Barrier	Psychic	Status	—	—	20	Self
33	Mirror Coat	Psychic	Special	—	100	20	Varies
37	Hail	Ice	Status	—	—	10	Both Sides
41	Last Resort	Normal	Physical	140	100	5	Normal
45	Blizzard	Ice	Special	110	70	5	Many Others

❖ TM MOVES
No.	Name	Type	Kind	Pow.	Acc.	PP	Range
TM01	Work Up	Normal	Status	—	—	30	Self
TM05	Roar	Normal	Status	—	—	20	Normal
TM06	Toxic	Poison	Status	—	90	10	Normal
TM07	Hail	Ice	Status	—	—	10	Both Sides
TM10	Hidden Power	Normal	Special	60	100	15	Normal
TM11	Sunny Day	Fire	Status	—	—	5	Both Sides
TM13	Ice Beam	Ice	Special	90	100	10	Normal
TM14	Blizzard	Ice	Special	110	70	5	Many Others
TM15	Hyper Beam	Normal	Special	150	90	5	Normal
TM17	Protect	Normal	Status	—	—	10	Self
TM18	Rain Dance	Water	Status	—	—	5	Both Sides
TM21	Frustration	Normal	Physical	—	100	20	Normal
TM27	Return	Normal	Physical	—	100	20	Normal
TM30	Shadow Ball	Ghost	Special	80	100	15	Normal
TM32	Double Team	Normal	Status	—	—	15	Self
TM42	Facade	Normal	Physical	70	100	20	Normal
TM44	Rest	Psychic	Status	—	—	10	Self
TM45	Attract	Normal	Status	—	100	15	Normal
TM48	Round	Normal	Special	60	100	15	Normal
TM49	Echoed Voice	Normal	Special	40	100	15	Normal
TM68	Giga Impact	Normal	Physical	150	90	5	Normal
TM70	Aurora Veil	Ice	Status	—	—	20	Your Side
TM79	Frost Breath	Ice	Special	60	90	10	Normal
TM87	Swagger	Normal	Status	—	85	15	Normal
TM88	Sleep Talk	Normal	Status	—	—	10	Self
TM90	Substitute	Normal	Status	—	—	10	Self
TM100	Confide	Normal	Status	—	—	20	Normal

❖ MOVES TAUGHT BY PEOPLE
Name	Type	Kind	Pow.	Acc.	PP	Range

❖ MOVES LEARNED WHEN EVOLVING
Name	Type	Kind	Pow.	Acc.	PP	Range
Icy Wind	Ice	Special	55	95	15	Many Others

❖ EGG MOVES
Name	Type	Kind	Pow.	Acc.	PP	Range

❖ EXCLUSIVE Z-MOVE
Name	Base Move	Type	Kind	Pow.	Acc.	Range

Sylveon
Intertwining Pokémon

FAIRY

Alola Pokédex	Melemele	Akala	Ula'ula	Poni
131	—	058	—	—

HEIGHT: 3'03"
WEIGHT: 51.8 lbs.

Its ribbonlike feelers give off an aura that weakens hostility in its prey, causing them to let down their guard. Then it attacks.

When this Pokémon sights its prey, it swirls its ribbonlike feelers as a distraction. A moment later, it pounces.

ABILITY
Cute Charm

HIDDEN ABILITY
Pixilate

SPECIES STRENGTHS
HP	◆◆◆◆
Attack	◆◆◆◆
Defense	◆◆◆◆
Sp. Atk	◆◆◆◆◆◆
Sp. Def	◆◆◆◆◆◆◆
Speed	◆◆◆◆

EGG GROUPS
Field

ITEM SOMETIMES HELD BY WILD POKÉMON
—

Damage taken in normal battles
NORMAL	×1	FIGHTING	×0.5	ROCK	×1
FIRE	×1	POISON	×2	GHOST	×1
WATER	×1	GROUND	×1	DRAGON	×0
GRASS	×1	FLYING	×1	DARK	×0.5
ELECTRIC	×1	PSYCHIC	×1	STEEL	×2
ICE	×1	BUG	×0.5	FAIRY	×1

EVOLUTION
Eevee → Level up affectionate Eevee that knows a Fairy-type move → Sylveon

MAIN WAY TO REGISTER IN THE POKÉDEX
Level up an Eevee that is affectionate either before or after teaching it a Fairy-type move

Same form for male/female

❖ LEVEL-UP MOVES
Lv.	Name	Type	Kind	Pow.	Acc.	PP	Range
1	Fairy Wind	Fairy	Special	40	100	30	Normal
1	Disarming Voice	Fairy	Special	40	—	15	Many Others
1	Helping Hand	Normal	Status	—	—	20	1 Ally
1	Tackle	Normal	Physical	40	100	35	Normal
1	Tail Whip	Normal	Status	—	100	30	Many Others
5	Sand Attack	Ground	Status	—	100	15	Normal
9	Baby-Doll Eyes	Fairy	Status	—	100	30	Normal
13	Quick Attack	Normal	Physical	40	100	30	Normal
17	Swift	Normal	Special	60	—	20	Many Others
20	Draining Kiss	Fairy	Special	50	100	10	Normal
25	Skill Swap	Psychic	Status	—	—	10	Normal
29	Misty Terrain	Fairy	Status	—	—	10	Both Sides
33	Light Screen	Psychic	Status	—	—	30	Your Side
37	Moonblast	Fairy	Special	95	100	15	Normal
41	Last Resort	Normal	Physical	140	100	5	Normal
45	Psych Up	Normal	Status	—	—	10	Normal

❖ TM MOVES
No.	Name	Type	Kind	Pow.	Acc.	PP	Range
TM01	Work Up	Normal	Status	—	—	30	Self
TM03	Psyshock	Psychic	Special	80	100	10	Normal
TM04	Calm Mind	Psychic	Status	—	—	20	Self
TM06	Toxic	Poison	Status	—	90	10	Normal
TM10	Hidden Power	Normal	Special	60	100	15	Normal
TM11	Sunny Day	Fire	Status	—	—	5	Both Sides
TM15	Hyper Beam	Normal	Special	150	90	5	Normal
TM16	Light Screen	Psychic	Status	—	—	30	Your Side
TM17	Protect	Normal	Status	—	—	10	Self
TM18	Rain Dance	Water	Status	—	—	5	Both Sides
TM20	Safeguard	Normal	Status	—	—	25	Your Side
TM21	Frustration	Normal	Physical	—	100	20	Normal
TM27	Return	Normal	Physical	—	100	20	Normal
TM30	Shadow Ball	Ghost	Special	80	100	15	Normal
TM32	Double Team	Normal	Status	—	—	15	Self
TM33	Reflect	Psychic	Status	—	—	20	Your Side
TM42	Facade	Normal	Physical	70	100	20	Normal
TM44	Rest	Psychic	Status	—	—	10	Self
TM45	Attract	Normal	Status	—	100	15	Normal
TM48	Round	Normal	Special	60	100	15	Normal
TM49	Echoed Voice	Normal	Special	40	100	15	Normal
TM68	Giga Impact	Normal	Physical	150	90	5	Normal
TM77	Psych Up	Normal	Status	—	—	10	Normal
TM87	Swagger	Normal	Status	—	85	15	Normal
TM88	Sleep Talk	Normal	Status	—	—	10	Self
TM90	Substitute	Normal	Status	—	—	10	Self
TM99	Dazzling Gleam	Fairy	Special	80	100	10	Many Others
TM100	Confide	Normal	Status	—	—	20	Normal

❖ MOVES TAUGHT BY PEOPLE
Name	Type	Kind	Pow.	Acc.	PP	Range

❖ MOVES LEARNED WHEN EVOLVING
Name	Type	Kind	Pow.	Acc.	PP	Range
Fairy Wind	Fairy	Special	40	100	30	Normal

❖ EGG MOVES
Name	Type	Kind	Pow.	Acc.	PP	Range

❖ EXCLUSIVE Z-MOVE
Name	Base Move	Type	Kind	Pow.	Acc.	Range

Alola Pokédex	Melemele	Akala	Ula'ula	Poni
132	—	059	058	059

Mudbray

Donkey Pokémon

GROUND

HEIGHT: 3'03"
WEIGHT: 242.5 lbs.

 The mud stuck to Mudbray's hooves enhances its grip and its powerful running gait.

It has a stubborn, individualistic disposition. Eating dirt, making mud, and playing in the mire all form part of its daily routine.

ABILITY
Own Tempo
Stamina

HIDDEN ABILITY
Inner Focus

Damage taken in normal battles

NORMAL ×1	FIGHTING ×1	ROCK ×1	
FIRE ×1	POISON ×0.5	GHOST ×1	
WATER ×2	GROUND ×1	DRAGON ×1	
GRASS ×2	FLYING ×1	DARK ×1	
ELECTRIC ×0	PSYCHIC ×1	STEEL ×1	
ICE ×2	BUG ×1	FAIRY ×1	

SPECIES STRENGTHS
HP ◆◆◆
Attack ◆◆◆◆◆
Defense ◆◆◆◆
Sp. Atk ◆◆
Sp. Def ◆◆◆
Speed ◆◆◆

EGG GROUPS
Field

ITEM SOMETIMES HELD BY WILD POKÉMON
Light Clay

EVOLUTION
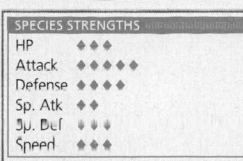

Mudbray — Lv. 30 → Mudsdale

MAIN WAY TO REGISTER IN THE POKÉDEX
Catch in the tall grass in Paniola Ranch

Same form for male/female

❖ LEVEL-UP MOVES

Lv.	Name	Type	Kind	Pow.	Acc.	PP	Range
1	Mud-Slap	Ground	Special	20	100	10	Normal
3	Mud Sport	Ground	Status	—	—	15	Both Sides
8	Rototiller	Ground	Status	—	—	10	Adjacent
10	Bulldoze	Ground	Physical	60	100	20	Adjacent
15	Double Kick	Fighting	Physical	30	100	30	Normal
17	Stomp	Normal	Physical	65	100	20	Normal
22	Bide	Normal	Physical	—	—	10	Self
24	High Horsepower	Ground	Physical	95	95	10	Normal
29	Iron Defense	Steel	Status	—	—	15	Self
31	Heavy Slam	Steel	Physical	—	100	10	Normal
36	Counter	Fighting	Physical	—	100	20	Varies
38	Earthquake	Ground	Physical	100	100	10	Adjacent
43	Mega Kick	Normal	Physical	120	75	5	Normal
45	Superpower	Fighting	Physical	120	100	5	Normal

❖ TM MOVES

No.	Name	Type	Kind	Pow.	Acc.	PP	Range
TM05	Roar	Normal	Status	—	—	20	Normal
TM06	Toxic	Poison	Status	—	90	10	Normal
TM10	Hidden Power	Normal	Special	60	100	15	Normal
TM17	Protect	Normal	Status	—	—	10	Self
TM21	Frustration	Normal	Physical	—	100	20	Normal
TM26	Earthquake	Ground	Physical	100	100	10	Adjacent
TM27	Return	Normal	Physical	—	100	20	Normal
TM32	Double Team	Normal	Status	—	—	15	Self
TM37	Sandstorm	Rock	Status	—	—	10	Both Sides
TM39	Rock Tomb	Rock	Physical	60	95	15	Normal
TM42	Facade	Normal	Physical	70	100	20	Normal
TM44	Rest	Psychic	Status	—	—	10	Self
TM45	Attract	Normal	Status	—	100	15	Normal
TM47	Low Sweep	Fighting	Physical	65	100	20	Normal
TM48	Round	Normal	Special	60	100	15	Normal
TM66	Payback	Dark	Physical	50	100	10	Normal
TM78	Bulldoze	Ground	Physical	60	100	20	Adjacent
TM80	Rock Slide	Rock	Physical	75	90	10	Many Others
TM87	Swagger	Normal	Status	—	85	15	Normal
TM88	Sleep Talk	Normal	Status	—	—	10	Self
TM90	Substitute	Normal	Status	—	—	10	Self
TM100	Confide	Normal	Status	—	—	20	Normal

❖ MOVES TAUGHT BY PEOPLE

Name	Type	Kind	Pow.	Acc.	PP	Range

❖ MOVES LEARNED WHEN EVOLVING

Name	Type	Kind	Pow.	Acc.	PP	Range

❖ EGG MOVES

Name	Type	Kind	Pow.	Acc.	PP	Range
Body Slam	Normal	Physical	85	100	15	Normal
Double-Edge	Normal	Physical	120	100	15	Normal
Magnitude	Ground	Physical	—	100	30	Adjacent
Close Combat	Fighting	Physical	120	100	5	Normal
Mud Bomb	Ground	Special	65	85	10	Normal

❖ EXCLUSIVE Z-MOVE

Name	Base Move	Type	Kind	Pow.	Acc.	Range

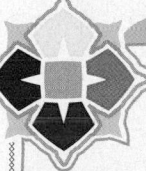

Alola Pokédex	Melemele	Akala	Ula'ula	Poni
133	—	060	059	060

Mudsdale

Draft Horse Pokémon

GROUND

HEIGHT: 8'02"
WEIGHT: 2028.3 lbs.

It spits a mud that provides resistance to both wind and rain, so the walls of old houses were often coated with it.

Its heavy, mud-covered kicks are its best means of attack, and it can reduce large trucks to scrap without breaking a sweat.

ABILITY
Own Tempo
Stamina

HIDDEN ABILITY
Inner Focus

Damage taken in normal battles

NORMAL ×1	FIGHTING ×1	ROCK ×0.5	
FIRE ×1	POISON ×0.5	GHOST ×1	
WATER ×2	GROUND ×1	DRAGON ×1	
GRASS ×2	FLYING ×1	DARK ×1	
ELECTRIC ×0	PSYCHIC ×1	STEEL ×1	
ICE ×2	BUG ×1	FAIRY ×1	

SPECIES STRENGTHS
HP ◆◆◆◆
Attack ◆◆◆◆◆◆◆
Defense ◆◆◆◆◆
Sp. Atk ◆◆◆
Sp. Def ◆◆◆
Speed ◆◆

EGG GROUPS
Field

ITEM SOMETIMES HELD BY WILD POKÉMON
Light Clay

EVOLUTION
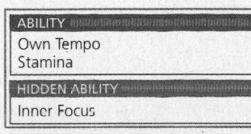

Mudbray — Lv. 30 → Mudsdale

MAIN WAY TO REGISTER IN THE POKÉDEX
Level up Mudbray to Lv. 30

Same form for male/female

❖ LEVEL-UP MOVES

Lv.	Name	Type	Kind	Pow.	Acc.	PP	Range
1	Mud-Slap	Ground	Special	20	100	10	Normal
1	Mud Sport	Ground	Status	—	—	15	Both Sides
1	Rototiller	Ground	Status	—	—	10	Adjacent
1	Bulldoze	Ground	Physical	60	100	20	Adjacent
3	Mud Sport	Ground	Status	—	—	15	Both Sides
8	Rototiller	Ground	Status	—	—	10	Adjacent
10	Bulldoze	Ground	Physical	60	100	20	Adjacent
15	Double Kick	Fighting	Physical	30	100	30	Normal
17	Stomp	Normal	Physical	65	100	20	Normal
22	Bide	Normal	Physical	—	—	10	Self
24	High Horsepower	Ground	Physical	95	95	10	Normal
29	Iron Defense	Steel	Status	—	—	15	Self
34	Heavy Slam	Steel	Physical	—	100	10	Normal
42	Counter	Fighting	Physical	—	100	20	Varies
47	Earthquake	Ground	Physical	100	100	10	Adjacent
55	Mega Kick	Normal	Physical	120	75	5	Normal
60	Superpower	Fighting	Physical	120	100	5	Normal

❖ TM MOVES

No.	Name	Type	Kind	Pow.	Acc.	PP	Range
TM05	Roar	Normal	Status	—	—	20	Normal
TM06	Toxic	Poison	Status	—	90	10	Normal
TM10	Hidden Power	Normal	Special	60	100	15	Normal
TM17	Protect	Normal	Status	—	—	10	Self
TM21	Frustration	Normal	Physical	—	100	20	Normal
TM26	Earthquake	Ground	Physical	100	100	10	Adjacent
TM27	Return	Normal	Physical	—	100	20	Normal
TM32	Double Team	Normal	Status	—	—	15	Self
TM37	Sandstorm	Rock	Status	—	—	10	Both Sides
TM39	Rock Tomb	Rock	Physical	60	95	15	Normal
TM42	Facade	Normal	Physical	70	100	20	Normal
TM44	Rest	Psychic	Status	—	—	10	Self
TM45	Attract	Normal	Status	—	100	15	Normal
TM47	Low Sweep	Fighting	Physical	65	100	20	Normal
TM48	Round	Normal	Special	60	100	15	Normal
TM52	Focus Blast	Fighting	Special	120	70	5	Normal
TM66	Payback	Dark	Physical	50	100	10	Normal
TM68	Giga Impact	Normal	Physical	150	90	5	Normal
TM78	Bulldoze	Ground	Physical	60	100	20	Adjacent
TM80	Rock Slide	Rock	Physical	75	90	10	Many Others
TM87	Swagger	Normal	Status	—	85	15	Normal
TM88	Sleep Talk	Normal	Status	—	—	10	Self
TM90	Substitute	Normal	Status	—	—	10	Self
TM100	Confide	Normal	Status	—	—	20	Normal

❖ MOVES TAUGHT BY PEOPLE

Name	Type	Kind	Pow.	Acc.	PP	Range

❖ MOVES LEARNED WHEN EVOLVING

Name	Type	Kind	Pow.	Acc.	PP	Range

❖ EGG MOVES

Name	Type	Kind	Pow.	Acc.	PP	Range

❖ EXCLUSIVE Z-MOVE

Name	Base Move	Type	Kind	Pow.	Acc.	Range

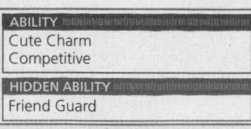

IGGLYBUFF — 134

Alola Pokédex	Melemele	Akala	Ula'ula	Poni
134	—	061	—	—

Igglybuff
Balloon Pokémon

NORMAL   FAIRY

HEIGHT: 1'00"
WEIGHT: 2.2 lbs.

It likes to sing but is not yet good at it. With praise and encouragement, it will get better little by little.

It moves by bouncing along. As it moves a lot, it sweats, and its body gives off a sweet aroma.

ABILITY
Cute Charm
Competitive

HIDDEN ABILITY
Friend Guard

SPECIES STRENGTHS
HP ◆◆◆
Attack ◆◆
Defense ◆
Sp. Atk ◆◆
Sp. Def ◆◆
Speed ◆

Damage taken in normal battles

NORMAL ×1	FIGHTING ×1	ROCK ×1
FIRE ×1	POISON ×2	GHOST ×0
WATER ×1	GROUND ×1	DRAGON ×1
GRASS ×1	FLYING ×1	DARK ×0.5
ELECTRIC ×1	PSYCHIC ×1	STEEL ×2
ICE ×1	BUG ×0.5	FAIRY ×1

EGG GROUPS
No Eggs Discovered

ITEM SOMETIMES HELD BY WILD POKÉMON
—

EVOLUTION

Igglybuff → Level up with high friendship → Jigglypuff
Moon Stone → Wigglytuff

Same form for male/female

MAIN WAY TO REGISTER IN THE POKÉDEX
Catch in the tall grass on Route 4 when it is daytime in your game

---

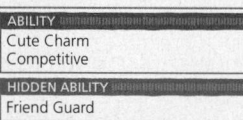

JIGGLYPUFF — 135

Alola Pokédex	Melemele	Akala	Ula'ula	Poni
135	—	062	—	—

Jigglypuff
Balloon Pokémon

NORMAL   FAIRY

HEIGHT: 1'08"
WEIGHT: 12.1 lbs.

It hugely inflates its stomach and sings a mysterious melody. If you hear this melody, you'll become sleepy right away.

Jigglypuff possess a vocal range that exceeds 12 octaves, but each individual's singing skill depends on its own effort.

ABILITY
Cute Charm
Competitive

HIDDEN ABILITY
Friend Guard

SPECIES STRENGTHS
HP ◆◆◆◆
Attack ◆◆◆
Defense ◆
Sp. Atk ◆◆
Sp. Def ◆
Speed ◆

Damage taken in normal battles

NORMAL ×1	FIGHTING ×1	ROCK ×1
FIRE ×1	POISON ×2	GHOST ×0
WATER ×1	GROUND ×1	DRAGON ×0
GRASS ×1	FLYING ×1	DARK ×0.5
ELECTRIC ×1	PSYCHIC ×1	STEEL ×2
ICE ×1	BUG ×0.5	FAIRY ×1

EGG GROUPS
Fairy

ITEM SOMETIMES HELD BY WILD POKÉMON
Moon Stone

EVOLUTION

Igglybuff → Level up with high friendship → Jigglypuff
Moon Stone → Wigglytuff

Same form for male/female

MAIN WAY TO REGISTER IN THE POKÉDEX
Catch in SOS battles against Igglybuff in the tall grass on Route 4 when it is daytime in your game

---

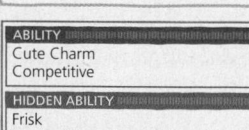

WIGGLYTUFF — 136

Alola Pokédex	Melemele	Akala	Ula'ula	Poni
136	—	063	—	—

Wigglytuff
Balloon Pokémon

NORMAL   FAIRY

HEIGHT: 3'03"
WEIGHT: 26.5 lbs.

It sheds its fine fur when the seasons change. The fur is gathered and spun into a luxurious yarn.

As it inhales, it expands...and expands...and expands. Wigglytuff compete to see which one can inflate itself the most.

ABILITY
Cute Charm
Competitive

HIDDEN ABILITY
Frisk

SPECIES STRENGTHS
HP ◆◆◆◆◆
Attack ◆◆◆◆
Defense ◆◆◆
Sp. Atk ◆◆◆◆◆
Sp. Def ◆◆◆
Speed ◆◆◆

Damage taken in normal battles

NORMAL ×1	FIGHTING ×1	ROCK ×1
FIRE ×1	POISON ×2	GHOST ×0
WATER ×1	GROUND ×1	DRAGON ×0
GRASS ×1	FLYING ×1	DARK ×0.5
ELECTRIC ×1	PSYCHIC ×1	STEEL ×2
ICE ×1	BUG ×0.5	FAIRY ×1

EGG GROUPS
Fairy

ITEM SOMETIMES HELD BY WILD POKÉMON
—

EVOLUTION

Igglybuff → Level up with high friendship → Jigglypuff
Moon Stone → Wigglytuff

Same form for male/female

MAIN WAY TO REGISTER IN THE POKÉDEX
Use a Moon Stone on Jigglypuff

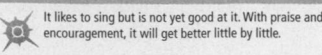

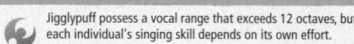

IGGLYBUFF

❖ LEVEL-UP MOVES

Lv.	Name	Type	Kind	Pow.	Acc.	PP	Range
1	Sing	Normal	Status	—	55	15	Normal
1	Charm	Fairy	Status	—	100	20	Normal
3	Defense Curl	Normal	Status	—	—	40	Self
5	Pound	Normal	Physical	40	100	35	Normal
9	Sweet Kiss	Fairy	Status	—	75	10	Normal
11	Copycat	Normal	Status	—	—	20	Self

❖ TM MOVES

No.	Name	Type	Kind	Pow.	Acc.	PP	Range
TM01	Work Up	Normal	Status	—	—	30	Self
TM06	Toxic	Poison	Status	—	90	10	Normal
TM10	Hidden Power	Normal	Special	60	100	15	Normal
TM11	Sunny Day	Fire	Status	—	—	5	Both Sides
TM17	Light Screen	Psychic	Status	—	—	30	Your Side
TM17	Protect	Normal	Status	—	—	10	Self
TM18	Rain Dance	Water	Status	—	—	5	Both Sides
TM20	Safeguard	Normal	Status	—	—	25	Your Side
TM21	Frustration	Normal	Physical	—	100	20	Normal
TM22	Solar Beam	Grass	Special	120	100	10	Normal
TM27	Return	Normal	Physical	—	100	20	Normal
TM29	Psychic	Psychic	Special	90	100	10	Normal
TM30	Shadow Ball	Ghost	Special	80	100	15	Normal
TM32	Double Team	Normal	Status	—	—	15	Self
TM33	Reflect	Psychic	Status	—	—	20	Your Side
TM35	Flamethrower	Fire	Special	90	100	15	Normal
TM38	Fire Blast	Fire	Special	110	85	5	Normal
TM42	Facade	Normal	Physical	70	100	20	Normal
TM44	Rest	Psychic	Status	—	—	10	Self
TM45	Attract	Normal	Status	—	100	15	Normal
TM48	Round	Normal	Special	60	100	15	Normal
TM49	Echoed Voice	Normal	Special	40	100	15	Normal
TM56	Fling	Dark	Physical	—	100	10	Normal
TM73	Thunder Wave	Electric	Status	—	90	20	Normal
TM77	Psych Up	Normal	Status	—	—	10	Normal
TM85	Dream Eater	Psychic	Special	100	100	15	Normal
TM86	Grass Knot	Grass	Special	—	100	20	Normal
TM87	Swagger	Normal	Status	—	85	15	Normal
TM88	Sleep Talk	Normal	Status	—	—	10	Self
TM90	Substitute	Normal	Status	—	—	10	Self
TM93	Wild Charge	Electric	Physical	90	100	15	Normal
TM100	Confide	Normal	Status	—	—	20	Normal

❖ MOVES TAUGHT BY PEOPLE

Name	Type	Kind	Pow.	Acc.	PP	Range

❖ MOVES LEARNED WHEN EVOLVING

Name	Type	Kind	Pow.	Acc.	PP	Range

❖ EGG MOVES

Name	Type	Kind	Pow.	Acc.	PP	Range
Perish Song	Normal	Status	—	—	5	Adjacent
Present	Normal	Physical	—	90	15	Normal
Feint Attack	Dark	Physical	60	—	20	Normal
Wish	Normal	Status	—	—	10	Self
Fake Tears	Dark	Status	—	100	20	Normal
Last Resort	Normal	Physical	140	100	5	Normal
Covet	Normal	Physical	60	100	25	Normal
Gravity	Psychic	Status	—	—	5	Both Sides
Sleep Talk	Normal	Status	—	—	10	Self
Captivate	Normal	Status	—	100	20	Many Others
Punishment	Dark	Physical	—	100	5	Normal
Misty Terrain	Fairy	Status	—	—	10	Both Sides
Heal Pulse	Psychic	Status	—	—	10	Normal

❖ EXCLUSIVE Z-MOVE

Name	Base Move	Type	Kind	Pow.	Acc.	Range

JIGGLYPUFF

❖ LEVEL-UP MOVES

Lv.	Name	Type	Kind	Pow.	Acc.	PP	Range
1	Sing	Normal	Status	—	55	15	Normal
3	Defense Curl	Normal	Status	—	—	40	Self
5	Pound	Normal	Physical	40	100	35	Normal
9	Play Nice	Normal	Status	—	—	20	Normal
11	Disarming Voice	Fairy	Special	40	—	15	Many Others
14	Disable	Normal	Status	—	100	20	Normal
17	Double Slap	Normal	Physical	15	85	10	Normal
20	Rollout	Rock	Physical	30	90	20	Normal
22	Round	Normal	Special	60	100	15	Normal
25	Stockpile	Normal	Status	—	—	20	Self
25	Swallow	Normal	Status	—	—	10	Self
25	Spit Up	Normal	Special	—	100	10	Normal
27	Wake-Up Slap	Fighting	Physical	70	100	10	Normal
30	Rest	Psychic	Status	—	—	10	Self
32	Body Slam	Normal	Physical	85	100	15	Normal
35	Gyro Ball	Steel	Physical	—	100	5	Normal
38	Mimic	Normal	Status	—	—	10	Normal
41	Hyper Voice	Normal	Special	90	100	10	Many Others
45	Double-Edge	Normal	Physical	120	100	15	Normal

❖ TM MOVES

No.	Name	Type	Kind	Pow.	Acc.	PP	Range
TM01	Work Up	Normal	Status	—	—	30	Self
TM06	Toxic	Poison	Status	—	90	10	Normal
TM10	Hidden Power	Normal	Special	60	100	15	Normal
TM11	Sunny Day	Fire	Status	—	—	5	Both Sides
TM13	Ice Beam	Ice	Special	90	100	10	Normal
TM14	Blizzard	Ice	Special	110	70	5	Many Others
TM16	Light Screen	Psychic	Status	—	—	30	Your Side
TM17	Protect	Normal	Status	—	—	10	Self
TM18	Rain Dance	Water	Status	—	—	5	Both Sides
TM20	Safeguard	Normal	Status	—	—	25	Your Side
TM21	Frustration	Normal	Physical	—	100	20	Normal
TM22	Solar Beam	Grass	Special	120	100	10	Normal
TM24	Thunderbolt	Electric	Special	90	100	15	Normal
TM25	Thunder	Electric	Special	110	70	10	Normal
TM27	Return	Normal	Physical	—	100	20	Normal
TM29	Psychic	Psychic	Special	90	100	10	Normal
TM30	Shadow Ball	Ghost	Special	80	100	15	Normal
TM31	Brick Break	Fighting	Physical	75	100	15	Normal
TM32	Double Team	Normal	Status	—	—	15	Self
TM33	Reflect	Psychic	Status	—	—	20	Your Side
TM35	Flamethrower	Fire	Special	90	100	15	Normal
TM38	Fire Blast	Fire	Special	110	85	5	Normal
TM42	Facade	Normal	Physical	70	100	20	Normal
TM44	Rest	Psychic	Status	—	—	10	Self
TM45	Attract	Normal	Status	—	100	15	Normal
TM48	Round	Normal	Special	60	100	15	Normal
TM49	Echoed Voice	Normal	Special	40	100	15	Normal
TM56	Fling	Dark	Physical	—	100	10	Normal
TM57	Charge Beam	Electric	Special	50	90	10	Normal
TM73	Thunder Wave	Electric	Status	—	90	20	Normal
TM74	Gyro Ball	Steel	Physical	—	100	5	Normal
TM77	Psych Up	Normal	Status	—	—	10	Normal
TM85	Dream Eater	Psychic	Special	100	100	15	Normal
TM86	Grass Knot	Grass	Special	—	100	20	Normal
TM87	Swagger	Normal	Status	—	85	15	Normal
TM88	Sleep Talk	Normal	Status	—	—	10	Self
TM90	Substitute	Normal	Status	—	—	10	Self
TM93	Wild Charge	Electric	Physical	90	100	15	Normal
TM99	Dazzling Gleam	Fairy	Special	80	100	10	Many Others
TM100	Confide	Normal	Status	—	—	20	Normal

❖ MOVES TAUGHT BY PEOPLE

Name	Type	Kind	Pow.	Acc.	PP	Range

❖ MOVES LEARNED WHEN EVOLVING

Name	Type	Kind	Pow.	Acc.	PP	Range

❖ EGG MOVES

Name	Type	Kind	Pow.	Acc.	PP	Range

❖ EXCLUSIVE Z-MOVE

Name	Base Move	Type	Kind	Pow.	Acc.	Range

WIGGLYTUFF

❖ LEVEL-UP MOVES

Lv.	Name	Type	Kind	Pow.	Acc.	PP	Range
1	Double-Edge	Normal	Physical	120	100	15	Normal
1	Play Rough	Fairy	Physical	90	90	10	Normal
1	Sing	Normal	Status	—	55	15	Normal
1	Defense Curl	Normal	Status	—	—	40	Self
1	Disable	Normal	Status	—	100	20	Normal
1	Double Slap	Normal	Physical	15	85	10	Normal

❖ TM MOVES

No.	Name	Type	Kind	Pow.	Acc.	PP	Range
TM01	Work Up	Normal	Status	—	—	30	Self
TM06	Toxic	Poison	Status	—	90	10	Normal
TM10	Hidden Power	Normal	Special	60	100	15	Normal
TM11	Sunny Day	Fire	Status	—	—	5	Both Sides
TM13	Ice Beam	Ice	Special	90	100	10	Normal
TM14	Blizzard	Ice	Special	110	70	5	Many Others
TM15	Hyper Beam	Normal	Special	150	90	5	Normal
TM16	Light Screen	Psychic	Status	—	—	30	Your Side
TM17	Protect	Normal	Status	—	—	10	Self
TM18	Rain Dance	Water	Status	—	—	5	Both Sides
TM20	Safeguard	Normal	Status	—	—	25	Your Side
TM21	Frustration	Normal	Physical	—	100	20	Normal
TM22	Solar Beam	Grass	Special	120	100	10	Normal
TM24	Thunderbolt	Electric	Special	90	100	15	Normal
TM25	Thunder	Electric	Special	110	70	10	Normal
TM27	Return	Normal	Physical	—	100	20	Normal
TM29	Psychic	Psychic	Special	90	100	10	Normal
TM30	Shadow Ball	Ghost	Special	80	100	15	Normal
TM31	Brick Break	Fighting	Physical	75	100	15	Normal
TM32	Double Team	Normal	Status	—	—	15	Self
TM33	Reflect	Psychic	Status	—	—	20	Your Side
TM35	Flamethrower	Fire	Special	90	100	15	Normal
TM38	Fire Blast	Fire	Special	110	85	5	Normal
TM42	Facade	Normal	Physical	70	100	20	Normal
TM44	Rest	Psychic	Status	—	—	10	Self
TM45	Attract	Normal	Status	—	100	15	Normal
TM48	Round	Normal	Special	60	100	15	Normal
TM49	Echoed Voice	Normal	Special	40	100	15	Normal
TM52	Focus Blast	Fighting	Special	120	70	5	Normal
TM56	Fling	Dark	Physical	—	100	10	Normal
TM57	Charge Beam	Electric	Special	50	90	10	Normal
TM68	Giga Impact	Normal	Physical	150	90	5	Normal
TM73	Thunder Wave	Electric	Status	—	90	20	Normal
TM74	Gyro Ball	Steel	Physical	—	100	5	Normal
TM77	Psych Up	Normal	Status	—	—	10	Normal
TM85	Dream Eater	Psychic	Special	100	100	15	Normal
TM86	Grass Knot	Grass	Special	—	100	20	Normal
TM87	Swagger	Normal	Status	—	85	15	Normal
TM88	Sleep Talk	Normal	Status	—	—	10	Self
TM90	Substitute	Normal	Status	—	—	10	Self
TM93	Wild Charge	Electric	Physical	90	100	15	Normal
TM99	Dazzling Gleam	Fairy	Special	80	100	10	Many Others
TM100	Confide	Normal	Status	—	—	20	Normal

❖ MOVES TAUGHT BY PEOPLE

Name	Type	Kind	Pow.	Acc.	PP	Range

❖ MOVES LEARNED WHEN EVOLVING

Name	Type	Kind	Pow.	Acc.	PP	Range

❖ EGG MOVES

Name	Type	Kind	Pow.	Acc.	PP	Range

❖ EXCLUSIVE Z-MOVE

Name	Base Move	Type	Kind	Pow.	Acc.	Range

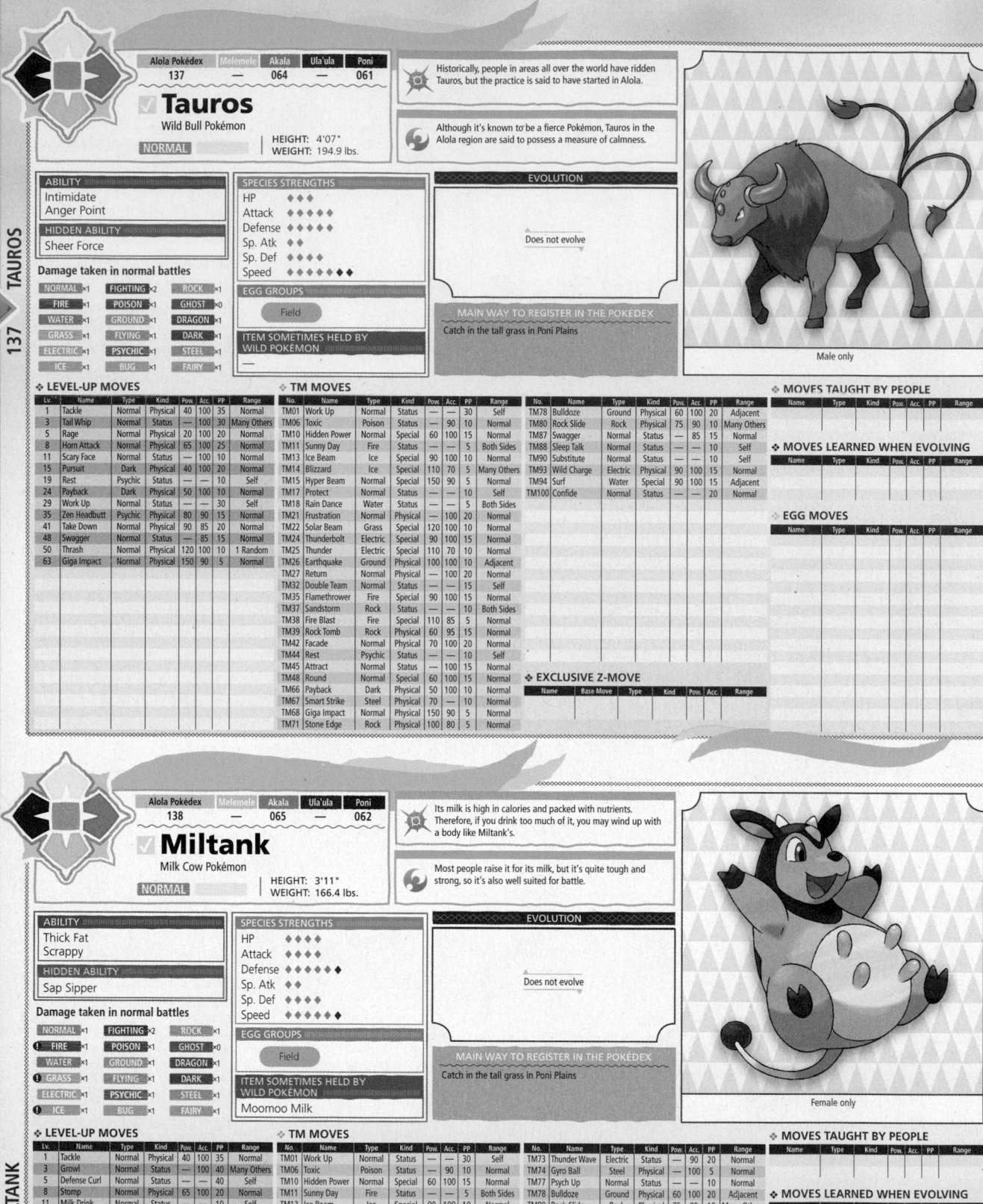

Tauros

Wild Bull Pokémon

Alola Pokédex	Melemele	Akala	Ula'ula	Poni
137	—	064	—	061

NORMAL

HEIGHT: 4'07"
WEIGHT: 194.9 lbs.

Historically, people in areas all over the world have ridden Tauros, but the practice is said to have started in Alola.

Although it's known to be a fierce Pokémon, Tauros in the Alola region are said to possess a measure of calmness.

ABILITY
Intimidate
Anger Point

HIDDEN ABILITY
Sheer Force

Damage taken in normal battles

NORMAL ×1	FIGHTING ×2	ROCK ×1
FIRE ×1	POISON ×1	GHOST ×1
WATER ×1	GROUND ×1	DRAGON ×1
GRASS ×1	FLYING ×1	DARK ×1
ELECTRIC ×1	PSYCHIC ×1	STEEL ×1
ICE ×1	BUG ×1	FAIRY ×1

SPECIES STRENGTHS
HP ♦♦♦
Attack ♦♦♦♦♦
Defense ♦♦♦♦
Sp. Atk ♦♦
Sp. Def ♦♦♦♦
Speed ♦♦♦♦♦♦♦

EGG GROUPS
Field

ITEM SOMETIMES HELD BY WILD POKÉMON

EVOLUTION
Does not evolve

MAIN WAY TO REGISTER IN THE POKÉDEX
Catch in the tall grass in Poni Plains

Male only

❖ LEVEL-UP MOVES

Lv.	Name	Type	Kind	Pow.	Acc.	PP	Range
1	Tackle	Normal	Physical	40	100	35	Normal
3	Tail Whip	Normal	Status	—	100	30	Many Others
5	Rage	Normal	Physical	20	100	20	Normal
8	Horn Attack	Normal	Physical	65	100	25	Normal
11	Scary Face	Normal	Status	—	100	10	Normal
15	Pursuit	Dark	Physical	40	100	20	Normal
19	Rest	Psychic	Status	—	—	10	Self
24	Payback	Dark	Physical	50	100	10	Normal
29	Work Up	Normal	Status	—	—	30	Self
35	Zen Headbutt	Psychic	Physical	80	90	15	Normal
41	Take Down	Normal	Physical	90	85	20	Normal
48	Swagger	Normal	Status	—	85	15	Normal
50	Thrash	Normal	Physical	120	100	10	1 Random
63	Giga Impact	Normal	Physical	150	90	5	Normal

❖ TM MOVES

No.	Name	Type	Kind	Pow.	Acc.	PP	Range
TM01	Work Up	Normal	Status	—	—	30	Self
TM06	Toxic	Poison	Status	—	90	10	Normal
TM10	Hidden Power	Normal	Special	60	100	15	Normal
TM11	Sunny Day	Fire	Status	—	—	5	Both Sides
TM13	Ice Beam	Ice	Special	90	100	10	Normal
TM14	Blizzard	Ice	Special	110	70	5	Many Others
TM15	Hyper Beam	Normal	Special	150	90	5	Normal
TM17	Protect	Normal	Status	—	—	10	Self
TM18	Rain Dance	Water	Status	—	—	5	Both Sides
TM21	Frustration	Normal	Physical	—	100	20	Normal
TM22	Solar Beam	Grass	Special	120	100	10	Normal
TM24	Thunderbolt	Electric	Special	90	100	15	Normal
TM25	Thunder	Electric	Special	110	70	10	Normal
TM26	Earthquake	Ground	Physical	100	100	10	Adjacent
TM27	Return	Normal	Physical	—	100	20	Normal
TM32	Double Team	Normal	Status	—	—	15	Self
TM35	Flamethrower	Fire	Special	90	100	15	Normal
TM37	Sandstorm	Rock	Status	—	—	10	Both Sides
TM38	Fire Blast	Fire	Special	110	85	5	Normal
TM39	Rock Tomb	Rock	Physical	60	95	15	Normal
TM42	Facade	Normal	Physical	70	100	20	Normal
TM44	Rest	Psychic	Status	—	—	10	Self
TM45	Attract	Normal	Status	—	100	15	Normal
TM48	Round	Normal	Special	60	100	15	Normal
TM66	Payback	Dark	Physical	50	100	10	Normal
TM67	Smart Strike	Steel	Physical	70	—	10	Normal
TM68	Giga Impact	Normal	Physical	150	90	5	Normal
TM71	Stone Edge	Rock	Physical	100	80	5	Normal

No.	Name	Type	Kind	Pow.	Acc.	PP	Range
TM78	Bulldoze	Ground	Physical	60	100	20	Adjacent
TM80	Rock Slide	Rock	Physical	75	90	10	Many Others
TM87	Swagger	Normal	Status	—	85	15	Normal
TM88	Sleep Talk	Normal	Status	—	—	10	Self
TM90	Substitute	Normal	Status	—	—	10	Self
TM93	Wild Charge	Electric	Physical	90	100	15	Normal
TM94	Surf	Water	Special	90	100	15	Adjacent
TM100	Confide	Normal	Status	—	—	20	Normal

❖ MOVES TAUGHT BY PEOPLE

Name	Type	Kind	Pow.	Acc.	PP	Range

❖ MOVES LEARNED WHEN EVOLVING

Name	Type	Kind	Pow.	Acc.	PP	Range

❖ EGG MOVES

Name	Type	Kind	Pow.	Acc.	PP	Range

❖ EXCLUSIVE Z-MOVE

Name	Base Move	Type	Kind	Pow.	Acc.	Range

Miltank

Milk Cow Pokémon

Alola Pokédex	Melemele	Akala	Ula'ula	Poni
138	—	065	—	062

NORMAL

HEIGHT: 3'11"
WEIGHT: 166.4 lbs.

Its milk is high in calories and packed with nutrients. Therefore, if you drink too much of it, you may wind up with a body like Miltank's.

Most people raise it for its milk, but it's quite tough and strong, so it's also well suited for battle.

ABILITY
Thick Fat
Scrappy

HIDDEN ABILITY
Sap Sipper

Damage taken in normal battles

NORMAL ×1	FIGHTING ×2	ROCK ×1
FIRE ×1	POISON ×1	GHOST ×0
WATER ×1	GROUND ×1	DRAGON ×1
GRASS ×1	FLYING ×1	DARK ×1
ELECTRIC ×1	PSYCHIC ×1	STEEL ×1
ICE ×1	BUG ×1	FAIRY ×1

SPECIES STRENGTHS
HP ♦♦♦♦
Attack ♦♦♦
Defense ♦♦♦♦♦♦
Sp. Atk ♦♦
Sp. Def ♦♦♦
Speed ♦♦♦♦♦

EGG GROUPS
Field

ITEM SOMETIMES HELD BY WILD POKÉMON
Moomoo Milk

EVOLUTION
Does not evolve

MAIN WAY TO REGISTER IN THE POKÉDEX
Catch in the tall grass in Poni Plains

Female only

❖ LEVEL-UP MOVES

Lv.	Name	Type	Kind	Pow.	Acc.	PP	Range
1	Tackle	Normal	Physical	40	100	35	Normal
3	Growl	Normal	Status	—	100	40	Many Others
5	Defense Curl	Normal	Status	—	—	40	Self
8	Stomp	Normal	Physical	65	100	20	Normal
11	Milk Drink	Normal	Status	—	—	10	Self
15	Bide	Normal	Physical	—	—	10	Self
19	Rollout	Rock	Physical	30	90	20	Normal
24	Body Slam	Normal	Physical	85	100	15	Normal
29	Zen Headbutt	Psychic	Physical	80	90	15	Normal
35	Captivate	Normal	Status	—	100	20	Many Others
41	Gyro Ball	Steel	Physical	—	100	5	Normal
48	Heal Bell	Normal	Status	—	—	5	Your Party
50	Wake-Up Slap	Fighting	Physical	70	100	10	Normal

❖ TM MOVES

No.	Name	Type	Kind	Pow.	Acc.	PP	Range
TM01	Work Up	Normal	Status	—	—	30	Self
TM06	Toxic	Poison	Status	—	90	10	Normal
TM10	Hidden Power	Normal	Special	60	100	15	Normal
TM11	Sunny Day	Fire	Status	—	—	5	Both Sides
TM13	Ice Beam	Ice	Special	90	100	10	Normal
TM14	Blizzard	Ice	Special	110	70	5	Many Others
TM15	Hyper Beam	Normal	Special	150	90	5	Normal
TM17	Protect	Normal	Status	—	—	10	Self
TM18	Rain Dance	Water	Status	—	—	5	Both Sides
TM21	Frustration	Normal	Physical	—	100	20	Normal
TM22	Solar Beam	Grass	Special	120	100	10	Normal
TM24	Thunderbolt	Electric	Special	90	100	15	Normal
TM25	Thunder	Electric	Special	110	70	10	Normal
TM26	Earthquake	Ground	Physical	100	100	10	Adjacent
TM27	Return	Normal	Physical	—	100	20	Normal
TM30	Shadow Ball	Ghost	Special	80	100	15	Normal
TM31	Brick Break	Fighting	Physical	75	100	15	Normal
TM32	Double Team	Normal	Status	—	—	15	Self
TM37	Sandstorm	Rock	Status	—	—	10	Both Sides
TM39	Rock Tomb	Rock	Physical	60	95	15	Normal
TM42	Facade	Normal	Physical	70	100	20	Normal
TM44	Rest	Psychic	Status	—	—	10	Self
TM45	Attract	Normal	Status	—	100	15	Normal
TM48	Round	Normal	Special	60	100	15	Normal
TM49	Echoed Voice	Normal	Special	40	100	15	Normal
TM52	Focus Blast	Fighting	Special	120	70	5	Normal
TM56	Fling	Dark	Physical	—	100	10	Normal
TM68	Giga Impact	Normal	Physical	150	90	5	Normal

No.	Name	Type	Kind	Pow.	Acc.	PP	Range
TM73	Thunder Wave	Electric	Status	—	90	20	Normal
TM74	Gyro Ball	Steel	Physical	—	100	5	Normal
TM77	Psych Up	Normal	Status	—	—	10	Normal
TM78	Bulldoze	Ground	Physical	60	100	20	Adjacent
TM80	Rock Slide	Rock	Physical	75	90	10	Many Others
TM87	Swagger	Normal	Status	—	85	15	Normal
TM88	Sleep Talk	Normal	Status	—	—	10	Self
TM90	Substitute	Normal	Status	—	—	10	Self
TM94	Surf	Water	Special	90	100	15	Adjacent
TM100	Confide	Normal	Status	—	—	20	Normal

❖ MOVES TAUGHT BY PEOPLE

Name	Type	Kind	Pow.	Acc.	PP	Range

❖ MOVES LEARNED WHEN EVOLVING

Name	Type	Kind	Pow.	Acc.	PP	Range

❖ EGG MOVES

Name	Type	Kind	Pow.	Acc.	PP	Range
Present	Normal	Physical	—	90	15	Normal
Reversal	Fighting	Physical	—	100	15	Normal
Seismic Toss	Fighting	Physical	—	100	20	Normal
Endure	Normal	Status	—	—	10	Self
Curse	Ghost	Status	—	—	10	Varies
Helping Hand	Normal	Status	—	—	20	1 Ally
Sleep Talk	Normal	Status	—	—	10	Self
Dizzy Punch	Normal	Physical	70	100	10	Normal
Hammer Arm	Fighting	Physical	100	90	10	Normal
Double-Edge	Normal	Physical	120	100	15	Normal
Punishment	Dark	Physical	—	100	5	Normal
Natural Gift	Normal	Physical	—	100	15	Normal
Heart Stamp	Psychic	Physical	60	100	25	Normal
Belch	Poison	Special	120	90	10	Normal

❖ EXCLUSIVE Z-MOVE

Name	Base Move	Type	Kind	Pow.	Acc.	Range

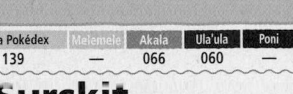

Surskit
Pond Skater Pokémon

Alola Pokédex	Melemele	Akala	Ula'ula	Poni
139	—	066	060	—

BUG　WATER

HEIGHT: 1'08"
WEIGHT: 3.7 lbs.

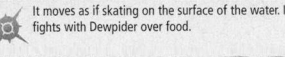 It moves as if skating on the surface of the water. It often fights with Dewpider over food.

When this Pokémon senses danger, a sweet fluid oozes from the tip of its head. The taste of it disgusts bird Pokémon.

ABILITY
Swift Swim

HIDDEN ABILITY
Rain Dish

Damage taken in normal battles

NORMAL ×1	FIGHTING ×½	ROCK ×2
FIRE ×1	POISON ×1	GHOST ×1
WATER ×0.5	GROUND ×0.5	DRAGON ×1
GRASS ×1	FLYING ×2	DARK ×1
ELECTRIC ×2	PSYCHIC ×1	STEEL ×0.5
ICE ×0.5	BUG ×1	FAIRY ×1

SPECIES STRENGTHS
HP	◆◆
Attack	◆◆
Defense	◆◆
Sp. Atk	◆◆◆
Sp. Def	◆◆◆
Speed	◆◆◆◆

EGG GROUPS
Water 1　Bug

ITEM SOMETIMES HELD BY WILD POKÉMON

EVOLUTION
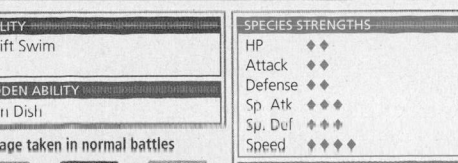
Surskit　→ Lv. 22 →　Masquerain

MAIN WAY TO REGISTER IN THE POKÉDEX
Catch on the water surface on Brooklet Hill when it is nighttime in your game.

Same form for male/female

❖ LEVEL-UP MOVES

Lv.	Name	Type	Kind	Pow.	Acc.	PP	Range
1	Bubble	Water	Special	40	100	30	Many Others
6	Quick Attack	Normal	Physical	40	100	30	Normal
9	Sweet Scent	Normal	Status	—	100	20	Many Others
14	Water Sport	Water	Status	—	—	15	Both Sides
17	Bubble Beam	Water	Special	65	100	20	Normal
21	Agility	Psychic	Status	—	—	30	Self
25	Mist	Ice	Status	—	—	30	Your Side
25	Haze	Ice	Status	—	—	30	Both Sides
30	Aqua Jet	Water	Physical	40	100	20	Normal
35	Baton Pass	Normal	Status	—	—	40	Self
38	Sticky Web	Bug	Status	—	—	20	Other Side

❖ TM MOVES

No.	Name	Type	Kind	Pow.	Acc.	PP	Range
TM06	Toxic	Poison	Status	—	90	10	Normal
TM10	Hidden Power	Normal	Special	60	100	15	Normal
TM11	Sunny Day	Fire	Status	—	—	5	Both Sides
TM13	Ice Beam	Ice	Special	90	100	10	Normal
TM14	Blizzard	Ice	Special	110	70	5	Many Others
TM17	Protect	Normal	Status	—	—	10	Self
TM18	Rain Dance	Water	Status	—	—	5	Both Sides
TM21	Frustration	Normal	Physical	—	100	20	Normal
TM22	Solar Beam	Grass	Special	120	100	10	Normal
TM27	Return	Normal	Physical	—	100	20	Normal
TM30	Shadow Ball	Ghost	Special	80	100	15	Normal
TM32	Double Team	Normal	Status	—	—	15	Self
TM42	Facade	Normal	Physical	70	100	20	Normal
TM44	Rest	Psychic	Status	—	—	10	Self
TM45	Attract	Normal	Status	—	100	15	Normal
TM46	Thief	Dark	Physical	60	100	25	Normal
TM48	Round	Normal	Special	60	100	15	Normal
TM55	Scald	Water	Special	80	100	15	Normal
TM77	Psych Up	Normal	Status	—	—	10	Normal
TM90	Infestation	Bug	Special	20	100	20	Normal
TM87	Swagger	Normal	Status	—	85	15	Normal
TM88	Sleep Talk	Normal	Status	—	—	10	Self
TM90	Substitute	Normal	Status	—	—	10	Self
TM100	Confide	Normal	Status	—	—	20	Normal

❖ MOVES TAUGHT BY PEOPLE

No.	Name	Type	Kind	Pow.	Acc.	PP	Range

❖ MOVES LEARNED WHEN EVOLVING

Name	Type	Kind	Pow.	Acc.	PP	Range

❖ EGG MOVES

Name	Type	Kind	Pow.	Acc.	PP	Range
Foresight	Normal	Status	—	—	40	Normal
Mud Shot	Ground	Special	55	95	15	Normal
Psybeam	Psychic	Special	65	100	20	Normal
Hydro Pump	Water	Special	110	80	5	Normal
Mind Reader	Normal	Status	—	—	5	Normal
Signal Beam	Bug	Special	75	100	15	Normal
Bug Bite	Bug	Physical	60	100	20	Normal
Aqua Jet	Water	Physical	40	100	20	Normal
Endure	Normal	Status	—	—	10	Self
Fell Stinger	Bug	Physical	50	100	25	Normal
Power Split	Psychic	Status	—	—	10	Normal
Lunge	Bug	Physical	80	100	15	Normal

❖ EXCLUSIVE Z-MOVE

Name	Base Move	Type	Kind	Pow.	Acc.	Range

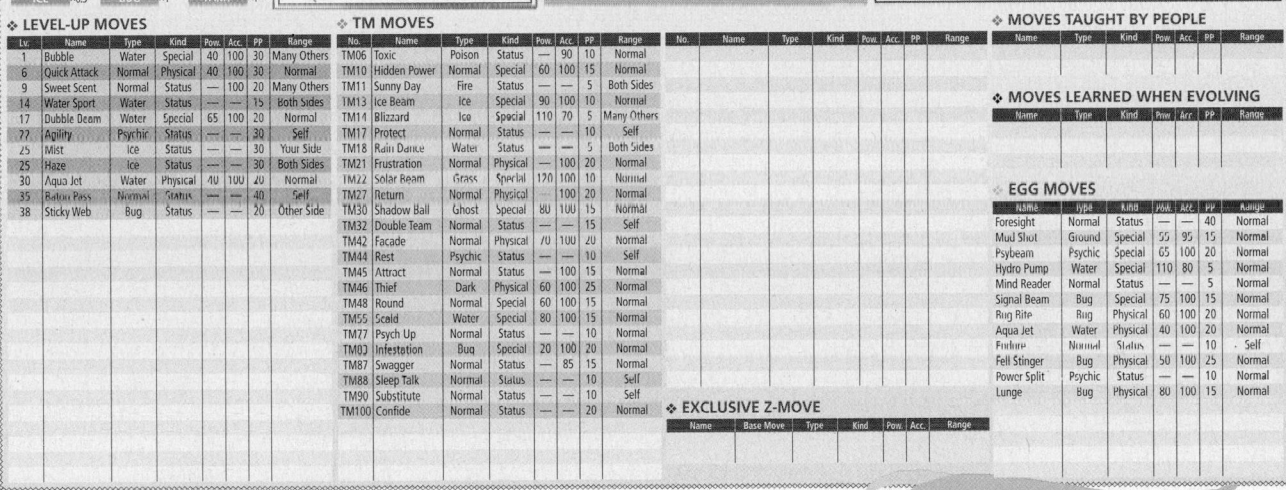

Masquerain
Eyeball Pokémon

Alola Pokédex	Melemele	Akala	Ula'ula	Poni
140	—	067	061	—

BUG　FLYING

HEIGHT: 2'07"
WEIGHT: 7.9 lbs.

It intimidates enemies with the eye-like patterns on its antennae. Its four wings allow it to fly in any direction.

Its wings and antennae don't cope well with moisture. After a rain, it faces sunward to dry off.

ABILITY
Intimidate

HIDDEN ABILITY
Unnerve

Damage taken in normal battles

NORMAL ×1	FIGHTING ×0.25	ROCK ×4
FIRE ×2	POISON ×1	GHOST ×1
WATER ×1	GROUND ×0	DRAGON ×1
GRASS ×0.25	FLYING ×1	DARK ×1
ELECTRIC ×2	PSYCHIC ×1	STEEL ×1
ICE ×2	BUG ×0.5	FAIRY ×1

SPECIES STRENGTHS
HP	◆◆◆
Attack	◆◆◆
Defense	◆◆◆
Sp. Atk	◆◆◆◆◆
Sp. Def	◆◆◆◆
Speed	◆◆◆◆

EGG GROUPS
Water 1　Bug

ITEM SOMETIMES HELD BY WILD POKÉMON
Silver Powder

EVOLUTION
Surskit　→ Lv. 22 →　Masquerain

MAIN WAY TO REGISTER IN THE POKÉDEX
Catch in the tall grass in Malie Garden when it is nighttime in your game.

Same form for male/female

❖ LEVEL-UP MOVES

Lv.	Name	Type	Kind	Pow.	Acc.	PP	Range
1	Quiver Dance	Bug	Status	—	—	20	Self
1	Whirlwind	Normal	Status	—	—	20	Normal
1	Bug Buzz	Bug	Special	90	100	10	Normal
1	Ominous Wind	Ghost	Special	60	100	5	Normal
1	Bubble	Water	Special	40	100	30	Many Others
1	Quick Attack	Normal	Physical	40	100	30	Normal
1	Sweet Scent	Normal	Status	—	100	20	Many Others
1	Water Sport	Water	Status	—	—	15	Both Sides
6	Quick Attack	Normal	Physical	40	100	30	Normal
9	Sweet Scent	Normal	Status	—	100	20	Many Others
14	Water Sport	Water	Status	—	—	15	Both Sides
17	Gust	Flying	Special	40	100	35	Normal
22	Scary Face	Normal	Status	—	100	10	Normal
22	Air Cutter	Flying	Special	60	95	25	Many Others
26	Stun Spore	Grass	Status	—	75	30	Normal
32	Silver Wind	Bug	Special	60	100	5	Normal
38	Air Slash	Flying	Special	75	95	15	Normal
42	Bug Buzz	Bug	Special	90	100	10	Normal
48	Whirlwind	Normal	Status	—	—	20	Normal
52	Quiver Dance	Bug	Status	—	—	20	Self

❖ TM MOVES

No.	Name	Type	Kind	Pow.	Acc.	PP	Range
TM06	Toxic	Poison	Status	—	90	10	Normal
TM10	Hidden Power	Normal	Special	60	100	15	Normal
TM11	Sunny Day	Fire	Status	—	—	5	Both Sides
TM13	Ice Beam	Ice	Special	90	100	10	Normal
TM14	Blizzard	Ice	Special	110	70	5	Many Others
TM15	Hyper Beam	Normal	Special	150	90	5	Normal
TM17	Protect	Normal	Status	—	—	10	Self
TM18	Rain Dance	Water	Status	—	—	5	Both Sides
TM19	Roost	Flying	Status	—	—	10	Self
TM21	Frustration	Normal	Physical	—	100	20	Normal
TM22	Solar Beam	Grass	Special	120	100	10	Normal
TM27	Return	Normal	Physical	—	100	20	Normal
TM30	Shadow Ball	Ghost	Special	80	100	15	Normal
TM32	Double Team	Normal	Status	—	—	15	Self
TM40	Aerial Ace	Flying	Physical	60	—	20	Normal
TM42	Facade	Normal	Physical	70	100	20	Normal
TM44	Rest	Psychic	Status	—	—	10	Self
TM45	Attract	Normal	Status	—	100	15	Normal
TM46	Thief	Dark	Physical	60	100	25	Normal
TM48	Round	Normal	Special	60	100	15	Normal
TM53	Energy Ball	Grass	Special	90	100	10	Normal
TM55	Scald	Water	Special	80	100	15	Normal
TM68	Giga Impact	Normal	Physical	150	90	5	Normal
TM77	Psych Up	Normal	Status	—	—	10	Normal
TM83	Infestation	Bug	Special	20	100	20	Normal
TM87	Swagger	Normal	Status	—	85	15	Normal
TM88	Sleep Talk	Normal	Status	—	—	10	Self
TM89	U-turn	Bug	Physical	70	100	20	Normal

❖ MOVES TAUGHT BY PEOPLE

No.	Name	Type	Kind	Pow.	Acc.	PP	Range
TM90	Substitute	Normal	Status	—	—	10	Self
TM100	Confide	Normal	Status	—	—	20	Normal

❖ MOVES LEARNED WHEN EVOLVING

Name	Type	Kind	Pow.	Acc.	PP	Range

❖ EGG MOVES

Name	Type	Kind	Pow.	Acc.	PP	Range

❖ EXCLUSIVE Z-MOVE

Name	Base Move	Type	Kind	Pow.	Acc.	Range

Dewpider

Water Bubble Pokémon

WATER · BUG

Alola Pokédex	Melemele	Akala	Ula'ula	Poni
141	—	068	062	—

HEIGHT: 1'00"
WEIGHT: 8.8 lbs.

It crawls onto the land in search of food. Its water bubble allows it to breathe and protects its soft head.

When it comes across enemies or potential prey, this Pokémon smashes its water-bubble-covered head into them.

ABILITY
Water Bubble

HIDDEN ABILITY
Water Absorb

Damage taken in normal battles

NORMAL ×1	FIGHTING ×0.5	ROCK ×1
FIRE ×1	POISON ×1	GHOST ×1
WATER ×0.5	GROUND ×0.5	DRAGON ×1
GRASS ×1	FLYING ×1	DARK ×1
ELECTRIC ×2	PSYCHIC ×1	STEEL ×0.5
ICE ×0.5	BUG ×1	FAIRY ×1

SPECIES STRENGTHS
HP ◆◆
Attack ◆◆
Defense ◆◆◆
Sp. Atk ◆◆
Sp. Def ◆◆◆◆
Speed ◆◆

EGG GROUPS
Water 1 · Bug

ITEM SOMETIMES HELD BY WILD POKÉMON
Mystic Water

EVOLUTION

Dewpider — Lv. 22 → Araquanid

MAIN WAY TO REGISTER IN THE POKÉDEX
Catch on the water surface on Brooklet Hill when it is daytime in your game

Same form for male/female

LEVEL-UP MOVES

Lv.	Name	Type	Kind	Pow.	Acc.	PP	Range
1	Water Sport	Water	Status	—	—	15	Both Sides
1	Bubble	Water	Special	40	100	30	Many Others
5	Infestation	Bug	Special	20	100	20	Normal
8	Spider Web	Bug	Status	—	—	10	Normal
13	Bug Bite	Bug	Physical	60	100	20	Normal
16	Bubble Beam	Water	Special	65	100	20	Normal
21	Bite	Dark	Physical	60	100	25	Normal
24	Aqua Ring	Water	Status	—	—	20	Self
29	Leech Life	Bug	Physical	80	100	10	Normal
32	Crunch	Dark	Physical	80	100	15	Normal
37	Lunge	Bug	Physical	80	100	15	Normal
40	Mirror Coat	Psychic	Special	—	100	20	Varies
45	Liquidation	Water	Physical	85	100	10	Normal
48	Entrainment	Normal	Status	—	100	15	Normal

TM MOVES

No.	Name	Type	Kind	Pow.	Acc.	PP	Range
TM06	Toxic	Poison	Status	—	90	10	Normal
TM10	Hidden Power	Normal	Special	60	100	15	Normal
TM13	Ice Beam	Ice	Special	90	100	10	Normal
TM14	Blizzard	Ice	Special	110	70	5	Many Others
TM17	Protect	Normal	Status	—	—	10	Self
TM18	Rain Dance	Water	Status	—	—	5	Both Sides
TM21	Frustration	Normal	Physical	—	100	20	Normal
TM27	Return	Normal	Physical	—	100	20	Normal
TM28	Leech Life	Bug	Physical	80	100	10	Normal
TM32	Double Team	Normal	Status	—	—	15	Self
TM42	Facade	Normal	Physical	70	100	20	Normal
TM44	Rest	Psychic	Status	—	—	10	Self
TM45	Attract	Normal	Status	—	100	15	Normal
TM48	Round	Normal	Special	60	100	15	Normal
TM55	Scald	Water	Special	80	100	15	Normal
TM79	Frost Breath	Ice	Special	60	90	10	Normal
TM81	X-Scissor	Bug	Physical	80	100	15	Normal
TM83	Infestation	Bug	Special	20	100	20	Normal
TM84	Poison Jab	Poison	Physical	80	100	20	Normal
TM87	Swagger	Normal	Status	—	85	15	Normal
TM88	Sleep Talk	Normal	Status	—	—	10	Self
TM90	Substitute	Normal	Status	—	—	10	Self
TM94	Surf	Water	Special	90	100	15	Adjacent
TM98	Waterfall	Water	Physical	80	100	15	Normal
TM100	Confide	Normal	Status	—	—	20	Normal

MOVES TAUGHT BY PEOPLE

Name	Type	Kind	Pow.	Acc.	PP	Range

MOVES LEARNED WHEN EVOLVING

Name	Type	Kind	Pow.	Acc.	PP	Range

EGG MOVES

Name	Type	Kind	Pow.	Acc.	PP	Range
Power Split	Psychic	Status	—	—	10	Normal
Aurora Beam	Ice	Special	65	100	20	Normal
Stockpile	Normal	Status	—	—	20	Self
Spit Up	Normal	Special	—	100	10	Normal

EXCLUSIVE Z-MOVE

Name	Base Move	Type	Kind	Pow.	Acc.	Range

Araquanid

Water Bubble Pokémon

WATER · BUG

Alola Pokédex	Melemele	Akala	Ula'ula	Poni
142	—	069	063	—

HEIGHT: 5'11"
WEIGHT: 180.8 lbs.

It delivers headbutts with the water bubble on its head. Small Pokémon get sucked into the bubble, where they drown.

Despite what its appearance suggests, it cares for others. If it finds vulnerable, weak Pokémon, it protectively brings them into its water bubble.

ABILITY
Water Bubble

HIDDEN ABILITY
Water Absorb

Damage taken in normal battles

NORMAL ×1	FIGHTING ×0.5	ROCK ×2
FIRE ×1	POISON ×1	GHOST ×1
WATER ×0.5	GROUND ×0.5	DRAGON ×1
GRASS ×1	FLYING ×2	DARK ×1
ELECTRIC ×2	PSYCHIC ×1	STEEL ×0.5
ICE ×0.5	BUG ×1	FAIRY ×1

SPECIES STRENGTHS
HP ◆◆◆
Attack ◆◆◆◆
Defense ◆◆◆◆◆
Sp. Atk ◆◆◆
Sp. Def ◆◆◆◆◆◆◆
Speed ◆◆◆

EGG GROUPS
Water 1 · Bug

ITEM SOMETIMES HELD BY WILD POKÉMON
Mystic Water

EVOLUTION

Dewpider — Lv. 22 → Araquanid

MAIN WAY TO REGISTER IN THE POKÉDEX
Catch in the tall grass in Malie Garden when it is daytime in your game

Same form for male/female

LEVEL-UP MOVES

Lv.	Name	Type	Kind	Pow.	Acc.	PP	Range
1	Wide Guard	Rock	Status	—	—	10	Your Side
1	Soak	Water	Status	—	100	20	Normal
1	Bubble	Water	Special	40	100	30	Many Others
1	Infestation	Bug	Special	20	100	20	Normal
1	Spider Web	Bug	Status	—	—	10	Normal
1	Bug Bite	Bug	Physical	60	100	20	Normal
5	Infestation	Bug	Special	20	100	20	Normal
8	Spider Web	Bug	Status	—	—	10	Normal
13	Bug Bite	Bug	Physical	60	100	20	Normal
16	Bubble Beam	Water	Special	65	100	20	Normal
21	Bite	Dark	Physical	60	100	25	Normal
26	Aqua Ring	Water	Status	—	—	20	Self
33	Leech Life	Bug	Physical	80	100	10	Normal
38	Crunch	Dark	Physical	80	100	15	Normal
45	Lunge	Bug	Physical	80	100	15	Normal
50	Mirror Coat	Psychic	Special	—	100	20	Varies
57	Liquidation	Water	Physical	85	100	10	Normal
62	Entrainment	Normal	Status	—	100	15	Normal

TM MOVES

No.	Name	Type	Kind	Pow.	Acc.	PP	Range
TM06	Toxic	Poison	Status	—	90	10	Normal
TM10	Hidden Power	Normal	Special	60	100	15	Normal
TM13	Ice Beam	Ice	Special	90	100	10	Normal
TM14	Blizzard	Ice	Special	110	70	5	Many Others
TM17	Protect	Normal	Status	—	—	10	Self
TM18	Rain Dance	Water	Status	—	—	5	Both Sides
TM20	Safeguard	Normal	Status	—	—	25	Your Side
TM21	Frustration	Normal	Physical	—	100	20	Normal
TM27	Return	Normal	Physical	—	100	20	Normal
TM28	Leech Life	Bug	Physical	80	100	10	Normal
TM32	Double Team	Normal	Status	—	—	15	Self
TM33	Reflect	Psychic	Status	—	—	20	Your Side
TM42	Facade	Normal	Physical	70	100	20	Normal
TM44	Rest	Psychic	Status	—	—	10	Self
TM45	Attract	Normal	Status	—	100	15	Normal
TM48	Round	Normal	Special	60	100	15	Normal
TM55	Scald	Water	Special	80	100	15	Normal
TM79	Frost Breath	Ice	Special	60	90	10	Normal
TM81	X-Scissor	Bug	Physical	80	100	15	Normal
TM83	Infestation	Bug	Special	20	100	20	Normal
TM84	Poison Jab	Poison	Physical	80	100	20	Normal
TM87	Swagger	Normal	Status	—	85	15	Normal
TM88	Sleep Talk	Normal	Status	—	—	10	Self
TM90	Substitute	Normal	Status	—	—	10	Self
TM94	Surf	Water	Special	90	100	15	Adjacent
TM98	Waterfall	Water	Physical	80	100	15	Normal
TM100	Confide	Normal	Status	—	—	20	Normal

MOVES TAUGHT BY PEOPLE

Name	Type	Kind	Pow.	Acc.	PP	Range

MOVES LEARNED WHEN EVOLVING

Name	Type	Kind	Pow.	Acc.	PP	Range

EGG MOVES

Name	Type	Kind	Pow.	Acc.	PP	Range

EXCLUSIVE Z-MOVE

Name	Base Move	Type	Kind	Pow.	Acc.	Range

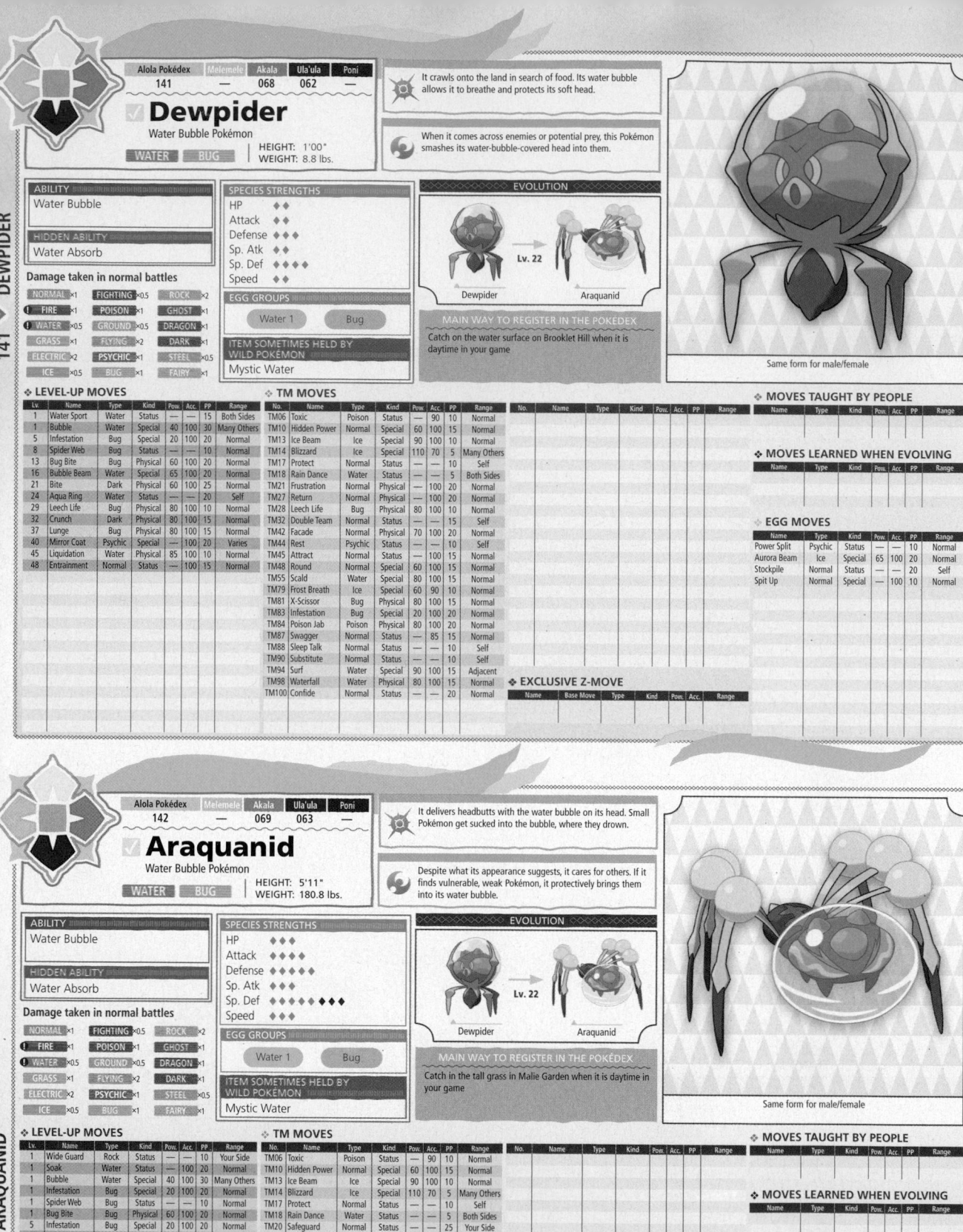

Fomantis

Alola Pokédex	Melemele	Akala	Ula'ula	Poni
143	—	070	—	—

Fomantis
Sickle Grass Pokémon

GRASS

HEIGHT: 1'00"
WEIGHT: 3.3 lbs.

During the day, it sleeps and soaks up light. When night falls, it walks around looking for a safer place to sleep.

They give off a sweet and refreshing scent. Cutieflies often gather near the tall grass where Fomantis are hiding.

ABILITY
Leaf Guard

HIDDEN ABILITY
Contrary

SPECIES STRENGTHS
HP ◆◆
Attack ◆◆◆
Defense ◆◆
Sp. Atk ◆◆◆
Sp. Def ◆◆
Speed ◆◆

EGG GROUPS
Grass

ITEM SOMETIMES HELD BY WILD POKÉMON
Miracle Seed

EVOLUTION

Fomantis → Level up to Lv. 34 during the day → Lurantis

MAIN WAY TO REGISTER IN THE POKÉDEX
Catch from a shaking tree in Lush Jungle

Same form for male/female

Damage taken in normal battles

NORMAL ×1	FIGHTING ×1	ROCK ×1
FIRE ×2	POISON ×2	GHOST ×1
WATER ×0.5	GROUND ×0.5	DRAGON ×1
GRASS ×0.5	FLYING ×2	DARK ×1
ELECTRIC ×0.5	PSYCHIC ×1	STEEL ×1
ICE ×2	BUG ×2	FAIRY ×1

❖ LEVEL-UP MOVES

Lv.	Name	Type	Kind	Pow.	Acc.	PP	Range
1	Fury Cutter	Bug	Physical	40	95	20	Normal
5	Leafage	Grass	Physical	40	100	40	Normal
10	Razor Leaf	Grass	Physical	55	95	25	Many Others
14	Growth	Normal	Status	—	—	20	Self
19	Ingrain	Grass	Status	—	—	20	Self
23	Leaf Blade	Grass	Physical	90	100	15	Normal
28	Synthesis	Grass	Status	—	—	5	Self
32	Slash	Normal	Physical	70	100	20	Normal
37	Sweet Scent	Normal	Status	—	100	20	Many Others
41	Solar Beam	Grass	Special	120	100	10	Normal
46	Sunny Day	Fire	Status	—	—	5	Both Sides

❖ TM MOVES

No.	Name	Type	Kind	Pow.	Acc.	PP	Range
TM06	Toxic	Poison	Status	—	90	10	Normal
TM10	Hidden Power	Normal	Special	60	100	15	Normal
TM11	Sunny Day	Fire	Status	—	—	5	Both Sides
TM17	Protect	Normal	Status	—	—	10	Self
TM20	Safeguard	Normal	Status	—	—	25	Your Side
TM21	Frustration	Normal	Physical	—	100	20	Normal
TM22	Solar Beam	Grass	Special	120	100	10	Normal
TM27	Return	Normal	Physical	—	100	20	Normal
TM28	Leech Life	Bug	Physical	80	100	10	Normal
TM32	Double Team	Normal	Status	—	—	15	Self
TM42	Facade	Normal	Physical	70	100	20	Normal
TM44	Rest	Psychic	Status	—	—	10	Self
TM45	Attract	Normal	Status	—	100	15	Normal
TM48	Round	Normal	Special	60	100	15	Normal
TM53	Energy Ball	Grass	Special	90	100	10	Normal
TM54	False Swipe	Normal	Physical	40	100	40	Normal
TM56	Fling	Dark	Physical	—	100	10	Normal
TM66	Payback	Dark	Physical	50	100	10	Normal
TM75	Swords Dance	Normal	Status	—	—	20	Self
TM81	X-Scissor	Bug	Physical	80	100	15	Normal
TM84	Poison Jab	Poison	Physical	80	100	20	Normal
TM86	Grass Knot	Grass	Special	—	100	20	Normal
TM87	Swagger	Normal	Status	—	85	15	Normal
TM88	Sleep Talk	Normal	Status	—	—	10	Self
TM90	Substitute	Normal	Status	—	—	10	Self
TM96	Nature Power	Normal	Status	—	—	20	Normal
TM100	Confide	Normal	Status	—	—	20	Normal

❖ MOVES TAUGHT BY PEOPLE

Name	Type	Kind	Pow.	Acc.	PP	Range

❖ MOVES LEARNED WHEN EVOLVING

Name	Type	Kind	Pow.	Acc.	PP	Range

❖ EGG MOVES

Name	Type	Kind	Pow.	Acc.	PP	Range
Weather Ball	Normal	Special	50	100	10	Normal
Giga Drain	Grass	Special	75	100	10	Normal
Aromatherapy	Grass	Status	—	—	5	Your Party
Defog	Flying	Status	—	—	15	Normal
Leaf Storm	Grass	Special	130	90	5	Normal

❖ EXCLUSIVE Z-MOVE

Name	Base Move	Type	Kind	Pow.	Acc.	Range

Lurantis

Alola Pokédex	Melemele	Akala	Ula'ula	Poni
144	—	071	—	—

Lurantis
Bloom Sickle Pokémon

GRASS

HEIGHT: 2'11"
WEIGHT: 40.8 lbs.

It requires a lot of effort to maintain Lurantis's vivid coloring, but some collectors enjoy this work and treat it as their hobby.

It fires beams from its sickle-shaped petals. These beams are powerful enough to cleave through thick metal plates.

ABILITY
Leaf Guard

HIDDEN ABILITY
Contrary

SPECIES STRENGTHS
HP ◆◆◆
Attack ◆◆◆◆◆◆◆
Defense ◆◆◆◆◆
Sp. Atk ◆◆◆◆
Sp. Def ◆◆◆◆◆
Speed ◆◆◆

EGG GROUPS
Grass

ITEM SOMETIMES HELD BY WILD POKÉMON
—

EVOLUTION

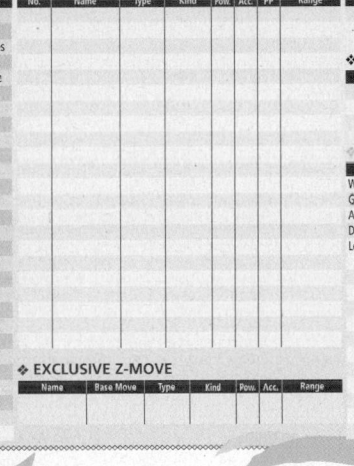

Fomantis → Level up to Lv. 34 during the day → Lurantis

MAIN WAY TO REGISTER IN THE POKÉDEX
Level up Fomantis to Lv. 34 when it is daytime in your game

Same form for male/female

Damage taken in normal battles

NORMAL ×1	FIGHTING ×1	ROCK ×1
FIRE ×2	POISON ×2	GHOST ×1
WATER ×0.5	GROUND ×0.5	DRAGON ×1
GRASS ×0.5	FLYING ×2	DARK ×1
ELECTRIC ×0.5	PSYCHIC ×1	STEEL ×1
ICE ×2	BUG ×2	FAIRY ×1

❖ LEVEL-UP MOVES

Lv.	Name	Type	Kind	Pow.	Acc.	PP	Range
1	Petal Blizzard	Grass	Physical	90	100	15	Adjacent
1	X-Scissor	Bug	Physical	80	100	15	Normal
1	Fury Cutter	Bug	Physical	40	95	20	Normal
1	Leafage	Grass	Physical	40	100	40	Normal
1	Razor Leaf	Grass	Physical	55	95	25	Many Others
1	Growth	Normal	Status	—	—	20	Self
5	Leafage	Grass	Physical	40	100	40	Normal
10	Razor Leaf	Grass	Physical	55	95	25	Many Others
14	Growth	Normal	Status	—	—	20	Self
19	Ingrain	Grass	Status	—	—	20	Self
23	Leaf Blade	Grass	Physical	90	100	15	Normal
28	Synthesis	Grass	Status	—	—	5	Self
32	Slash	Normal	Physical	70	100	20	Normal
40	Sweet Scent	Normal	Status	—	100	20	Many Others
47	Solar Blade	Grass	Physical	125	100	10	Normal
55	Sunny Day	Fire	Status	—	—	5	Both Sides

❖ TM MOVES

No.	Name	Type	Kind	Pow.	Acc.	PP	Range
TM06	Toxic	Poison	Status	—	90	10	Normal
TM10	Hidden Power	Normal	Special	60	100	15	Normal
TM11	Sunny Day	Fire	Status	—	—	5	Both Sides
TM15	Hyper Beam	Normal	Special	150	90	5	Normal
TM17	Protect	Normal	Status	—	—	10	Self
TM20	Safeguard	Normal	Status	—	—	25	Your Side
TM21	Frustration	Normal	Physical	—	100	20	Normal
TM22	Solar Beam	Grass	Special	120	100	10	Normal
TM27	Return	Normal	Physical	—	100	20	Normal
TM28	Leech Life	Bug	Physical	80	100	10	Normal
TM31	Brick Break	Fighting	Physical	75	100	15	Normal
TM32	Double Team	Normal	Status	—	—	15	Self
TM40	Aerial Ace	Flying	Physical	60	—	20	Normal
TM42	Facade	Normal	Physical	70	100	20	Normal
TM44	Rest	Psychic	Status	—	—	10	Self
TM45	Attract	Normal	Status	—	100	15	Normal
TM47	Low Sweep	Fighting	Physical	65	100	20	Normal
TM48	Round	Normal	Special	60	100	15	Normal
TM53	Energy Ball	Grass	Special	90	100	10	Normal
TM54	False Swipe	Normal	Physical	40	100	40	Normal
TM56	Fling	Dark	Physical	—	100	10	Normal
TM66	Payback	Dark	Physical	50	100	10	Normal
TM68	Giga Impact	Normal	Physical	150	90	5	Normal
TM75	Swords Dance	Normal	Status	—	—	20	Self
TM81	X-Scissor	Bug	Physical	80	100	15	Normal
TM84	Poison Jab	Poison	Physical	80	100	20	Normal
TM86	Grass Knot	Grass	Special	—	100	20	Normal
TM87	Swagger	Normal	Status	—	85	15	Normal
TM88	Sleep Talk	Normal	Status	—	—	10	Self
TM90	Substitute	Normal	Status	—	—	10	Self
TM96	Nature Power	Normal	Status	—	—	20	Normal
TM100	Confide	Normal	Status	—	—	20	Normal

❖ MOVES TAUGHT BY PEOPLE

Name	Type	Kind	Pow.	Acc.	PP	Range

❖ MOVES LEARNED WHEN EVOLVING

Name	Type	Kind	Pow.	Acc.	PP	Range
Petal Blizzard	Grass	Physical	90	100	15	Adjacent

❖ EGG MOVES

Name	Type	Kind	Pow.	Acc.	PP	Range

❖ EXCLUSIVE Z-MOVE

Name	Base Move	Type	Kind	Pow.	Acc.	Range

Morelull
Illuminating Pokémon

GRASS · FAIRY

HEIGHT: 0'08"
WEIGHT: 3.3 lbs.

It scatters spores that flicker and glow. Anyone seeing these lights falls into a deep slumber.

As it drowses the day away, it nourishes itself by sucking from tree roots. It wakens at the fall of night, wandering off in search of a new tree.

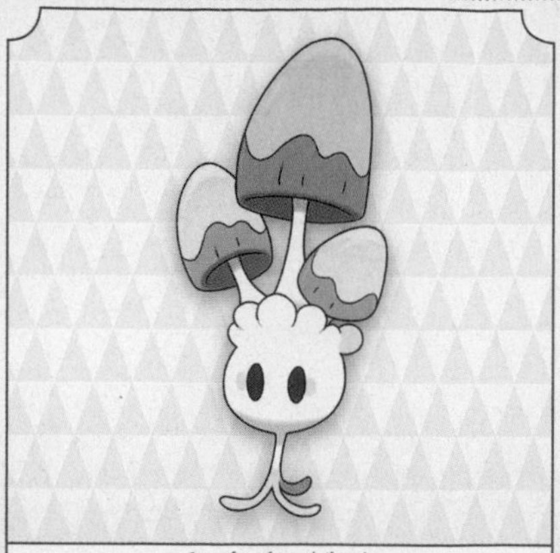

ABILITY
Illuminate
Effect Spore

HIDDEN ABILITY
Rain Dish

SPECIES STRENGTHS
HP	◆◆
Attack	◆◆
Defense	◆◆
Sp. Atk	◆◆◆◆
Sp. Def	◆◆◆◆
Speed	◆

Damage taken in normal battles
NORMAL ×1	FIGHTING ×0.5	ROCK ×1			
FIRE ×2	POISON ×4	GHOST ×1			
WATER ×0.5	GROUND ×0.5	DRAGON ×1			
GRASS ×0.5	FLYING ×2	DARK ×1			
ELECTRIC ×0.5	PSYCHIC ×1	STEEL ×2			
ICE ×2	BUG ×1	FAIRY ×1			

EGG GROUPS
Grass

ITEM SOMETIMES HELD BY WILD POKÉMON
Tiny Mushroom / Big Mushroom

EVOLUTION
Morelull → (Lv. 24) → Shiinotic

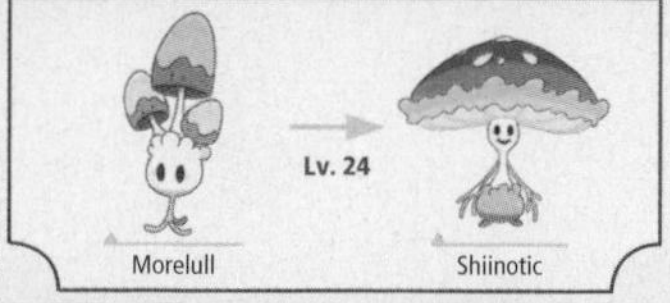

MAIN WAY TO REGISTER IN THE POKÉDEX
Catch in the tall grass on Brooklet Hill when it is nighttime in your game

Same form for male/female

❖ LEVEL-UP MOVES
Lv.	Name	Type	Kind	Pow.	Acc.	PP	Range
1	Absorb	Grass	Special	20	100	25	Normal
4	Astonish	Ghost	Physical	30	100	15	Normal
8	Flash	Normal	Status	—	100	20	Normal
11	Moonlight	Fairy	Status	—	—	5	Self
15	Mega Drain	Grass	Special	40	100	15	Normal
18	Sleep Powder	Grass	Status	—	75	15	Normal
22	Ingrain	Grass	Status	—	—	20	Self
25	Confuse Ray	Ghost	Status	—	100	10	Normal
29	Giga Drain	Grass	Special	75	100	10	Normal
32	Strength Sap	Grass	Status	—	100	10	Normal
36	Spore	Grass	Status	—	100	15	Normal
39	Moonblast	Fairy	Special	95	100	15	Normal
43	Dream Eater	Psychic	Special	100	100	15	Normal
46	Spotlight	Normal	Status	—	—	15	Normal

❖ TM MOVES
No.	Name	Type	Kind	Pow.	Acc.	PP	Range
TM06	Toxic	Poison	Status	—	90	10	Normal
TM10	Hidden Power	Normal	Special	60	100	15	Normal
TM11	Sunny Day	Fire	Status	—	—	5	Both Sides
TM16	Light Screen	Psychic	Status	—	—	30	Your Side
TM17	Protect	Normal	Status	—	—	10	Self
TM20	Safeguard	Normal	Status	—	—	25	Your Side
TM21	Frustration	Normal	Physical	—	100	20	Normal
TM22	Solar Beam	Grass	Special	120	100	10	Normal
TM27	Return	Normal	Physical	—	100	20	Normal
TM32	Double Team	Normal	Status	—	—	15	Self
TM36	Sludge Bomb	Poison	Special	90	100	10	Normal
TM44	Rest	Psychic	Status	—	—	10	Self
TM45	Attract	Normal	Status	—	100	15	Normal
TM48	Round	Normal	Special	60	100	15	Normal
TM53	Energy Ball	Grass	Special	90	100	10	Normal
TM73	Thunder Wave	Electric	Status	—	90	20	Normal
TM85	Dream Eater	Psychic	Special	100	100	15	Normal
TM86	Grass Knot	Grass	Special	—	100	20	Normal
TM87	Swagger	Normal	Status	—	85	15	Normal
TM88	Sleep Talk	Normal	Status	—	—	10	Self
TM90	Substitute	Normal	Status	—	—	10	Self
TM96	Nature Power	Normal	Status	—	—	20	Normal
TM99	Dazzling Gleam	Fairy	Special	80	100	10	Many Others
TM100	Confide	Normal	Status	—	—	20	Normal

❖ MOVES TAUGHT BY PEOPLE
Name	Type	Kind	Pow.	Acc.	PP	Range

❖ MOVES LEARNED WHEN EVOLVING
Name	Type	Kind	Pow.	Acc.	PP	Range

❖ EGG MOVES
Name	Type	Kind	Pow.	Acc.	PP	Range
Amnesia	Psychic	Status	—	—	20	Self
Poison Powder	Poison	Status	—	75	35	Normal
Stun Spore	Grass	Status	—	75	30	Normal
Growth	Normal	Status	—	—	20	Self
Leech Seed	Grass	Status	—	90	10	Normal

❖ EXCLUSIVE Z-MOVE
Name	Base Move	Type	Kind	Pow.	Acc.	Range

Shiinotic
Illuminating Pokémon

GRASS · FAIRY

HEIGHT: 3'03"
WEIGHT: 25.4 lbs.

Forests where Shiinotic live are treacherous to enter at night. People confused by its strange lights can never find their way home again.

It emits flickering spores that cause drowsiness. When its prey succumb to sleep, this Pokémon feeds on them by sucking in their energy.

ABILITY
Illuminate
Effect Spore

HIDDEN ABILITY
Rain Dish

SPECIES STRENGTHS
HP	◆◆
Attack	◆◆◆
Defense	◆◆◆◆
Sp. Atk	◆◆◆◆◆
Sp. Def	◆◆◆◆◆◆
Speed	◆◆

Damage taken in normal battles
NORMAL ×1	FIGHTING ×0.5	ROCK ×1			
FIRE ×2	POISON ×4	GHOST ×1			
WATER ×0.5	GROUND ×0.5	DRAGON ×1			
GRASS ×0.5	FLYING ×2	DARK ×1			
ELECTRIC ×0.5	PSYCHIC ×1	STEEL ×2			
ICE ×2	BUG ×1	FAIRY ×1			

EGG GROUPS
Grass

ITEM SOMETIMES HELD BY WILD POKÉMON
—

EVOLUTION
Morelull → (Lv. 24) → Shiinotic

MAIN WAY TO REGISTER IN THE POKÉDEX
Level up Morelull to Lv. 24

Same form for male/female

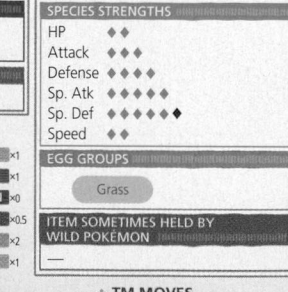
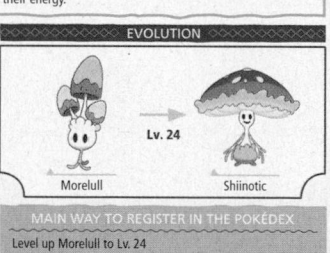

❖ LEVEL-UP MOVES
Lv.	Name	Type	Kind	Pow.	Acc.	PP	Range
1	Absorb	Grass	Special	20	100	25	Normal
1	Astonish	Ghost	Physical	30	100	15	Normal
1	Ingrain	Grass	Status	—	—	20	Self
1	Flash	Normal	Status	—	100	20	Normal
4	Astonish	Ghost	Physical	30	100	15	Normal
8	Flash	Normal	Status	—	100	20	Normal
11	Moonlight	Fairy	Status	—	—	5	Self
15	Mega Drain	Grass	Special	40	100	15	Normal
18	Sleep Powder	Grass	Status	—	75	15	Normal
22	Ingrain	Grass	Status	—	—	20	Self
26	Confuse Ray	Ghost	Status	—	100	10	Normal
31	Giga Drain	Grass	Special	75	100	10	Normal
35	Strength Sap	Grass	Status	—	100	10	Normal
40	Spore	Grass	Status	—	100	15	Normal
44	Moonblast	Fairy	Special	95	100	15	Normal
49	Dream Eater	Psychic	Special	100	100	15	Normal
53	Spotlight	Normal	Status	—	—	15	Normal

❖ TM MOVES
No.	Name	Type	Kind	Pow.	Acc.	PP	Range
TM06	Toxic	Poison	Status	—	90	10	Normal
TM10	Hidden Power	Normal	Special	60	100	15	Normal
TM16	Light Screen	Psychic	Status	—	—	30	Your Side
TM17	Protect	Normal	Status	—	—	10	Self
TM20	Safeguard	Normal	Status	—	—	25	Your Side
TM21	Frustration	Normal	Physical	—	100	20	Normal
TM22	Solar Beam	Grass	Special	120	100	10	Normal
TM27	Return	Normal	Physical	—	100	20	Normal
TM32	Double Team	Normal	Status	—	—	15	Self
TM36	Sludge Bomb	Poison	Special	90	100	10	Normal
TM44	Rest	Psychic	Status	—	—	10	Self
TM45	Attract	Normal	Status	—	100	15	Normal
TM48	Round	Normal	Special	60	100	15	Normal
TM53	Energy Ball	Grass	Special	90	100	10	Normal
TM57	Charge Beam	Electric	Special	50	90	10	Normal
TM68	Giga Impact	Normal	Physical	150	90	5	Normal
TM73	Thunder Wave	Electric	Status	—	90	20	Normal
TM85	Dream Eater	Psychic	Special	100	100	15	Normal
TM86	Grass Knot	Grass	Special	—	100	20	Normal
TM87	Swagger	Normal	Status	—	85	15	Normal
TM90	Substitute	Normal	Status	—	—	10	Self
TM96	Nature Power	Normal	Status	—	—	20	Normal
TM99	Dazzling Gleam	Fairy	Special	80	100	10	Many Others
TM100	Confide	Normal	Status	—	—	20	Normal

❖ MOVES TAUGHT BY PEOPLE
Name	Type	Kind	Pow.	Acc.	PP	Range

❖ MOVES LEARNED WHEN EVOLVING
Name	Type	Kind	Pow.	Acc.	PP	Range

❖ EGG MOVES
Name	Type	Kind	Pow.	Acc.	PP	Range

❖ EXCLUSIVE Z-MOVE
Name	Base Move	Type	Kind	Pow.	Acc.	Range

Paras

Alola Pokédex	Melemele	Akala	Ula'ula	Poni
147	—	074	066	—

Mushroom Pokémon

BUG **GRASS**

HEIGHT: 1'00"
WEIGHT: 11.9 lbs.

No matter how much it eats, the mushrooms growing on its back steal away most of the nutrients it consumes.

Mushrooms called tochukaso sprout from its back. They can be dried and powdered to make a medicine used to extend life.

ABILITY
Effect Spore
Dry Skin

HIDDEN ABILITY
Damp

SPECIES STRENGTHS
HP	◆
Attack	◆◆◆◆
Defense	◆◆◆
Sp. Atk	◆◆
Sp. Def	◆◆◆
Speed	◆◆

EGG GROUPS
Bug · Grass

ITEM SOMETIMES HELD BY WILD POKÉMON
Tiny Mushroom / Big Mushroom

Damage taken in normal battles
NORMAL ×1	FIGHTING ×0.5	ROCK ×2			
FIRE ×4	POISON ×2	GHOST ×1			
WATER ×0.5	GROUND ×0.25	DRAGON ×1			
GRASS ×0.25	FLYING ×4	DARK ×1			
ELECTRIC ×0.5	PSYCHIC ×1	STEEL ×1			
ICE ×2	BUG ×1	FAIRY ×1			

EVOLUTION
Paras → Lv. 24 → Parasect

MAIN WAY TO REGISTER IN THE POKÉDEX
Catch in the tall grass in Lush Jungle when it is daytime in your game

Same form for male/female

❖ LEVEL-UP MOVES
Lv.	Name	Type	Kind	Pow.	Acc.	PP	Range
1	Scratch	Normal	Physical	40	100	35	Normal
6	Stun Spore	Grass	Status	—	75	30	Normal
6	Poison Powder	Poison	Status	—	75	35	Normal
11	Absorb	Grass	Special	20	100	25	Normal
17	Fury Cutter	Bug	Physical	40	95	20	Normal
22	Spore	Grass	Status	—	100	15	Normal
27	Slash	Normal	Physical	70	100	20	Normal
33	Growth	Normal	Status	—	—	20	Self
38	Giga Drain	Grass	Special	75	100	10	Normal
43	Aromatherapy	Grass	Status	—	—	5	Your Party
49	Rage Powder	Bug	Status	—	—	20	Self
54	X-Scissor	Bug	Physical	80	100	15	Normal

❖ TM MOVES
No.	Name	Type	Kind	Pow.	Acc.	PP	Range
TM06	Toxic	Poison	Status	—	90	10	Normal
TM09	Venoshock	Poison	Special	65	100	10	Normal
TM10	Hidden Power	Normal	Special	60	100	15	Normal
TM11	Sunny Day	Fire	Status	—	—	5	Both Sides
TM16	Light Screen	Psychic	Status	—	—	30	Your Side
TM17	Protect	Normal	Status	—	—	10	Self
TM21	Frustration	Normal	Physical	—	100	20	Normal
TM22	Solar Beam	Grass	Special	120	100	10	Normal
TM27	Return	Normal	Physical	—	100	20	Normal
TM28	Leech Life	Bug	Physical	80	100	10	Normal
TM31	Brick Break	Fighting	Physical	75	100	15	Normal
TM32	Double Team	Normal	Status	—	—	15	Self
TM36	Sludge Bomb	Poison	Special	90	100	10	Normal
TM40	Aerial Ace	Flying	Physical	60	—	20	Normal
TM42	Facade	Normal	Physical	70	100	20	Normal
TM44	Rest	Psychic	Status	—	—	10	Self
TM45	Attract	Normal	Status	—	100	15	Normal
TM46	Thief	Dark	Physical	60	100	25	Normal
TM48	Round	Normal	Special	60	100	15	Normal
TM53	Energy Ball	Grass	Special	90	100	10	Normal
TM54	False Swipe	Normal	Physical	40	100	40	Normal
TM75	Swords Dance	Normal	Status	—	—	20	Self
TM81	X-Scissor	Bug	Physical	80	100	15	Normal
TM86	Grass Knot	Grass	Special	—	100	20	Normal
TM87	Swagger	Normal	Status	—	85	15	Normal
TM88	Sleep Talk	Normal	Status	—	—	10	Self
TM90	Substitute	Normal	Status	—	—	10	Self
TM96	Nature Power	Normal	Status	—	—	20	Normal

❖ MOVES TAUGHT BY PEOPLE
No.	Name	Type	Kind	Pow.	Acc.	PP	Range
TM100	Confide	Normal	Status	—	—	20	Normal

❖ MOVES LEARNED WHEN EVOLVING
Name	Type	Kind	Pow.	Acc.	PP	Range

❖ EGG MOVES
Name	Type	Kind	Pow.	Acc.	PP	Range
Screech	Normal	Status	—	85	40	Normal
Counter	Fighting	Physical	—	100	20	Varies
Psybeam	Psychic	Special	65	100	20	Normal
Flail	Normal	Physical	—	100	15	Normal
Sweet Scent	Normal	Status	—	100	20	Many Others
Pursuit	Dark	Physical	40	100	20	Normal
Metal Claw	Steel	Physical	50	95	35	Normal
Bug Bite	Bug	Physical	60	100	20	Normal
Cross Poison	Poison	Physical	70	100	20	Normal
Agility	Psychic	Status	—	—	30	Self
Endure	Normal	Status	—	—	10	Self
Natural Gift	Normal	Physical	—	100	15	Normal
Leech Seed	Grass	Status	—	90	10	Normal
Wide Guard	Rock	Status	—	—	10	Your Side
Rototiller	Ground	Status	—	—	10	Adjacent
Fell Stinger	Bug	Physical	50	100	25	Normal

❖ EXCLUSIVE Z-MOVE
Name	Base Move	Type	Kind	Pow.	Acc.	Range

Parasect

Alola Pokédex	Melemele	Akala	Ula'ula	Poni
148	—	075	067	—

Mushroom Pokémon

BUG **GRASS**

HEIGHT: 3'03"
WEIGHT: 65.0 lbs.

The large mushroom on its back controls it. It often fights over territory with Shiinotic.

It scatters toxic spores from its mushroom cap. Once harvested, these spores can be steeped and boiled down to prepare herbal medicines.

ABILITY
Effect Spore
Dry Skin

HIDDEN ABILITY
Damp

SPECIES STRENGTHS
HP	◆◆
Attack	◆◆
Defense	◆◆◆◆
Sp. Atk	◆◆◆
Sp. Def	◆◆◆◆◆
Speed	◆◆

EGG GROUPS
Bug · Grass

ITEM SOMETIMES HELD BY WILD POKÉMON
—

Damage taken in normal battles
NORMAL ×1	FIGHTING ×0.5	ROCK ×2			
FIRE ×4	POISON ×2	GHOST ×1			
WATER ×0.5	GROUND ×0.25	DRAGON ×1			
GRASS ×0.25	FLYING ×4	DARK ×1			
ELECTRIC ×0.5	PSYCHIC ×1	STEEL ×1			
ICE ×2	BUG ×2	FAIRY ×1			

EVOLUTION
Paras → Lv. 24 → Parasect

MAIN WAY TO REGISTER IN THE POKÉDEX
Level up Paras to Lv. 24

Same form for male/female

❖ LEVEL-UP MOVES
Lv.	Name	Type	Kind	Pow.	Acc.	PP	Range
1	Cross Poison	Poison	Physical	70	100	20	Normal
1	Scratch	Normal	Physical	40	100	35	Normal
1	Stun Spore	Grass	Status	—	75	30	Normal
1	Poison Powder	Poison	Status	—	75	35	Normal
1	Absorb	Grass	Special	20	100	25	Normal
6	Stun Spore	Grass	Status	—	75	30	Normal
6	Poison Powder	Poison	Status	—	75	35	Normal
11	Absorb	Grass	Special	20	100	25	Normal
17	Fury Cutter	Bug	Physical	40	95	20	Normal
22	Spore	Grass	Status	—	100	15	Normal
29	Slash	Normal	Physical	70	100	20	Normal
37	Growth	Normal	Status	—	—	20	Self
44	Giga Drain	Grass	Special	75	100	10	Normal
51	Aromatherapy	Grass	Status	—	—	5	Your Party
59	Rage Powder	Bug	Status	—	—	20	Self
66	X-Scissor	Bug	Physical	80	100	15	Normal

❖ TM MOVES
No.	Name	Type	Kind	Pow.	Acc.	PP	Range
TM06	Toxic	Poison	Status	—	90	10	Normal
TM09	Venoshock	Poison	Special	65	100	10	Normal
TM10	Hidden Power	Normal	Special	60	100	15	Normal
TM11	Sunny Day	Fire	Status	—	—	5	Both Sides
TM15	Hyper Beam	Normal	Special	150	90	5	Normal
TM16	Light Screen	Psychic	Status	—	—	30	Your Side
TM17	Protect	Normal	Status	—	—	10	Self
TM21	Frustration	Normal	Physical	—	100	20	Normal
TM22	Solar Beam	Grass	Special	120	100	10	Normal
TM27	Return	Normal	Physical	—	100	20	Normal
TM28	Leech Life	Bug	Physical	80	100	10	Normal
TM31	Brick Break	Fighting	Physical	75	100	15	Normal
TM32	Double Team	Normal	Status	—	—	15	Self
TM36	Sludge Bomb	Poison	Special	90	100	10	Normal
TM40	Aerial Ace	Flying	Physical	60	—	20	Normal
TM42	Facade	Normal	Physical	70	100	20	Normal
TM44	Rest	Psychic	Status	—	—	10	Self
TM45	Attract	Normal	Status	—	100	15	Normal
TM46	Thief	Dark	Physical	60	100	25	Normal
TM48	Round	Normal	Special	60	100	15	Normal
TM53	Energy Ball	Grass	Special	90	100	10	Normal
TM54	False Swipe	Normal	Physical	40	100	40	Normal
TM68	Giga Impact	Normal	Physical	150	90	5	Normal
TM75	Swords Dance	Normal	Status	—	—	20	Self
TM81	X-Scissor	Bug	Physical	80	100	15	Normal
TM86	Grass Knot	Grass	Special	—	100	20	Normal
TM87	Swagger	Normal	Status	—	85	15	Normal
TM88	Sleep Talk	Normal	Status	—	—	10	Self

❖ MOVES TAUGHT BY PEOPLE
No.	Name	Type	Kind	Pow.	Acc.	PP	Range
TM90	Substitute	Normal	Status	—	—	10	Self
TM96	Nature Power	Normal	Status	—	—	20	Normal
TM100	Confide	Normal	Status	—	—	20	Normal

❖ MOVES LEARNED WHEN EVOLVING
Name	Type	Kind	Pow.	Acc.	PP	Range

❖ EGG MOVES
Name	Type	Kind	Pow.	Acc.	PP	Range

❖ EXCLUSIVE Z-MOVE
Name	Base Move	Type	Kind	Pow.	Acc.	Range

PARAS 147
PARASECT 148

105

Poliwag

Alola Pokédex	Melemele	Akala	Ula'ula	Poni
149	—	076	068	—

Tadpole Pokémon

WATER

HEIGHT: 2'00"
WEIGHT: 27.3 lbs.

The swirl on its belly is its internal organs showing through. If the swirl is tinged white, that means it's affected by some disease.

It's still not very good at walking. Its Trainers should train this Pokémon to walk every day.

ABILITY
Water Absorb
Damp

HIDDEN ABILITY
Swift Swim

Damage taken in normal battles
NORMAL ×1	FIGHTING ×1	ROCK ×1
FIRE ×0.5	POISON ×1	GHOST ×1
WATER ×0.5	GROUND ×1	DRAGON ×1
GRASS ×2	FLYING ×1	DARK ×1
ELECTRIC ×2	PSYCHIC ×1	STEEL ×0.5
ICE ×0.5	BUG ×1	FAIRY ×1

SPECIES STRENGTHS
HP	◆◆
Attack	◆◆◆
Defense	◆◆
Sp. Atk	◆◆
Sp. Def	◆◆
Speed	◆◆◆◆◆◆

EGG GROUPS
Water 1

ITEM SOMETIMES HELD BY WILD POKÉMON
—

EVOLUTION
Poliwag → (Lv. 25) Poliwhirl → (Water Stone) Poliwrath
Poliwhirl → (Trade while holding a King's Rock) Politoed

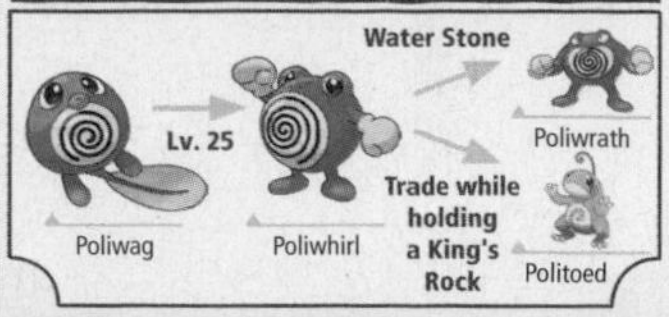

MAIN WAY TO REGISTER IN THE POKÉDEX
Catch on the water surface on Brooklet Hill

Same form for male/female

❖ LEVEL-UP MOVES
Lv.	Name	Type	Kind	Pow.	Acc.	PP	Range
1	Water Sport	Water	Status	—	—	15	Both Sides
5	Water Gun	Water	Special	40	100	25	Normal
8	Hypnosis	Psychic	Status	—	60	20	Normal
11	Bubble	Water	Special	40	100	30	Many Others
15	Double Slap	Normal	Physical	15	85	10	Normal
18	Rain Dance	Water	Status	—	—	5	Both Sides
21	Body Slam	Normal	Physical	85	100	15	Normal
25	Bubble Beam	Water	Special	65	100	20	Normal
28	Mud Shot	Ground	Special	55	95	15	Normal
31	Belly Drum	Normal	Status	—	—	10	Self
35	Wake-Up Slap	Fighting	Physical	70	100	10	Normal
38	Hydro Pump	Water	Special	110	80	5	Normal
41	Mud Bomb	Ground	Special	65	85	10	Normal

❖ TM MOVES
No.	Name	Type	Kind	Pow.	Acc.	PP	Range
TM06	Toxic	Poison	Status	—	90	10	Normal
TM07	Hail	Ice	Status	—	—	10	Both Sides
TM10	Hidden Power	Normal	Special	60	100	15	Normal
TM13	Ice Beam	Ice	Special	90	100	10	Normal
TM14	Blizzard	Ice	Special	110	70	5	Many Others
TM17	Protect	Normal	Status	—	—	10	Self
TM18	Rain Dance	Water	Status	—	—	5	Both Sides
TM21	Frustration	Normal	Physical	—	100	20	Normal
TM27	Return	Normal	Physical	—	100	20	Normal
TM29	Psychic	Psychic	Special	90	100	10	Normal
TM32	Double Team	Normal	Status	—	—	15	Self
TM42	Facade	Normal	Physical	70	100	20	Normal
TM44	Rest	Psychic	Status	—	—	10	Self
TM45	Attract	Normal	Status	—	100	15	Normal
TM46	Thief	Dark	Physical	60	100	25	Normal
TM48	Round	Normal	Special	60	100	15	Normal
TM55	Scald	Water	Special	80	100	15	Normal
TM87	Swagger	Normal	Status	—	85	15	Normal
TM88	Sleep Talk	Normal	Status	—	—	10	Self
TM90	Substitute	Normal	Status	—	—	10	Self
TM94	Surf	Water	Special	90	100	15	Adjacent
TM98	Waterfall	Water	Physical	80	100	15	Normal
TM100	Confide	Normal	Status	—	—	20	Normal

❖ MOVES TAUGHT BY PEOPLE
Name	Type	Kind	Pow.	Acc.	PP	Range

❖ MOVES LEARNED WHEN EVOLVING
Name	Type	Kind	Pow.	Acc.	PP	Range

❖ EGG MOVES
Name	Type	Kind	Pow.	Acc.	PP	Range
Mist	Ice	Status	—	—	30	Your Side
Splash	Normal	Status	—	—	40	Self
Bubble Beam	Water	Special	65	100	20	Normal
Haze	Ice	Status	—	—	30	Both Sides
Mind Reader	Normal	Status	—	—	5	Normal
Water Sport	Water	Status	—	—	15	Both Sides
Ice Ball	Ice	Physical	30	90	20	Normal
Mud Shot	Ground	Special	55	95	15	Normal
Refresh	Normal	Status	—	—	20	Self
Endeavor	Normal	Physical	—	100	5	Normal
Encore	Normal	Status	—	100	5	Normal
Endure	Normal	Status	—	—	10	Self
Water Pulse	Water	Special	60	100	20	Normal

❖ EXCLUSIVE Z-MOVE
Name	Base Move	Type	Kind	Pow.	Acc.	Range

Poliwhirl

Alola Pokédex	Melemele	Akala	Ula'ula	Poni
150	—	077	069	—

Tadpole Pokémon

WATER

HEIGHT: 3'03"
WEIGHT: 44.1 lbs.

Although it can live on land, it prefers to stay in the water, where it has fewer natural enemies.

It marches over the land in search of bug Pokémon to eat. Then it takes them underwater so it can dine on them where it's safe.

ABILITY
Water Absorb
Damp

HIDDEN ABILITY
Swift Swim

Damage taken in normal battles
NORMAL ×1	FIGHTING ×1	ROCK ×1
FIRE ×0.5	POISON ×1	GHOST ×1
WATER ×0.5	GROUND ×1	DRAGON ×1
GRASS ×2	FLYING ×1	DARK ×1
ELECTRIC ×2	PSYCHIC ×1	STEEL ×0.5
ICE ×0.5	BUG ×1	FAIRY ×1

SPECIES STRENGTHS
HP	◆◆◆
Attack	◆◆◆◆
Defense	◆◆◆◆
Sp. Atk	◆◆◆
Sp. Def	◆◆◆
Speed	◆◆◆◆◆◆

EGG GROUPS
Water 1

ITEM SOMETIMES HELD BY WILD POKÉMON
King's Rock

EVOLUTION
Poliwag → (Lv. 25) Poliwhirl → (Water Stone) Poliwrath
Poliwhirl → (Trade while holding a King's Rock) Politoed

MAIN WAY TO REGISTER IN THE POKÉDEX
Receive in exchange for Zubat in the Pokémon Center in Konikoni City

Same form for male/female

❖ LEVEL-UP MOVES
Lv.	Name	Type	Kind	Pow.	Acc.	PP	Range
1	Water Sport	Water	Status	—	—	15	Both Sides
1	Water Gun	Water	Special	40	100	25	Normal
1	Hypnosis	Psychic	Status	—	60	20	Normal
5	Water Gun	Water	Special	40	100	25	Normal
8	Hypnosis	Psychic	Status	—	60	20	Normal
11	Bubble	Water	Special	40	100	30	Many Others
15	Double Slap	Normal	Physical	15	85	10	Normal
18	Rain Dance	Water	Status	—	—	5	Both Sides
21	Body Slam	Normal	Physical	85	100	15	Normal
27	Bubble Beam	Water	Special	65	100	20	Normal
32	Mud Shot	Ground	Special	55	95	15	Normal
37	Belly Drum	Normal	Status	—	—	10	Self
43	Wake-Up Slap	Fighting	Physical	70	100	10	Normal
48	Hydro Pump	Water	Special	110	80	5	Normal
53	Mud Bomb	Ground	Special	65	85	10	Normal

❖ TM MOVES
No.	Name	Type	Kind	Pow.	Acc.	PP	Range
TM06	Toxic	Poison	Status	—	90	10	Normal
TM07	Hail	Ice	Status	—	—	10	Both Sides
TM10	Hidden Power	Normal	Special	60	100	15	Normal
TM13	Ice Beam	Ice	Special	90	100	10	Normal
TM14	Blizzard	Ice	Special	110	70	5	Many Others
TM17	Protect	Normal	Status	—	—	10	Self
TM18	Rain Dance	Water	Status	—	—	5	Both Sides
TM21	Frustration	Normal	Physical	—	100	20	Normal
TM26	Earthquake	Ground	Physical	100	100	10	Adjacent
TM27	Return	Normal	Physical	—	100	20	Normal
TM29	Psychic	Psychic	Special	90	100	10	Normal
TM31	Brick Break	Fighting	Physical	75	100	15	Normal
TM32	Double Team	Normal	Status	—	—	15	Self
TM42	Facade	Normal	Physical	70	100	20	Normal
TM44	Rest	Psychic	Status	—	—	10	Self
TM45	Attract	Normal	Status	—	100	15	Normal
TM46	Thief	Dark	Physical	60	100	25	Normal
TM48	Round	Normal	Special	60	100	15	Normal
TM55	Scald	Water	Special	80	100	15	Normal
TM56	Fling	Dark	Physical	—	100	10	Normal
TM78	Bulldoze	Ground	Physical	60	100	20	Adjacent
TM87	Swagger	Normal	Status	—	85	15	Normal
TM88	Sleep Talk	Normal	Status	—	—	10	Self
TM90	Substitute	Normal	Status	—	—	10	Self
TM94	Surf	Water	Special	90	100	15	Adjacent
TM98	Waterfall	Water	Physical	80	100	15	Normal
TM100	Confide	Normal	Status	—	—	20	Normal

❖ MOVES TAUGHT BY PEOPLE
Name	Type	Kind	Pow.	Acc.	PP	Range

❖ MOVES LEARNED WHEN EVOLVING
Name	Type	Kind	Pow.	Acc.	PP	Range

❖ EGG MOVES
Name	Type	Kind	Pow.	Acc.	PP	Range

❖ EXCLUSIVE Z-MOVE
Name	Base Move	Type	Kind	Pow.	Acc.	Range

Poliwrath

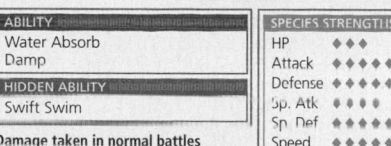

Alola Pokédex	Melemele	Akala	Ula'ula	Poni
151	—	078	070	—

Tadpole Pokémon
WATER FIGHTING
HEIGHT: 4'03"
WEIGHT: 119.0 lbs.

Poliwrath in the Alola region are strong swimmers that use the breaststroke. Many children learn to swim by imitating Poliwrath.

Its percentage of body fat is nearly zero. Its body is entirely muscle, which makes it heavy and forces its swimming prowess to develop.

Same form for male/female

ABILITY
Water Absorb
Damp

HIDDEN ABILITY
Swift Swim

Damage taken in normal battles
NORMAL ×1	FIGHTING ×1	ROCK ×0.5
FIRE ×0.5	POISON ×1	GHOST ×1
WATER ×0.5	GROUND ×1	DRAGON ×1
GRASS ×2	FLYING ×2	DARK ×0.5
ELECTRIC ×2	PSYCHIC ×2	STEEL ×0.5
ICE ×1	BUG ×0.5	FAIRY ×1

SPECIES STRENGTHS
HP ◆◆◆
Attack ◆◆◆◆
Defense ◆◆◆◆◆
Sp. Atk ◆◆◆◆
Sp. Def ◆◆◆◆
Speed ◆◆◆◆

EGG GROUPS
Water 1

ITEM SOMETIMES HELD BY WILD POKÉMON
King's Rock

EVOLUTION
Poliwag → (Lv. 25) → Poliwhirl → (Water Stone) → Poliwrath

MAIN WAY TO REGISTER IN THE POKÉDEX
Catch in SOS battles in the tall grass in Malie Garden when it is raining during the day in your game

❖ LEVEL-UP MOVES
Lv.	Name	Type	Kind	Pow.	Acc.	PP	Range
1	Submission	Fighting	Physical	80	80	20	Normal
1	Circle Throw	Fighting	Physical	60	90	10	Normal
1	Bubble Beam	Water	Special	65	100	20	Normal
1	Hypnosis	Psychic	Status	—	60	20	Normal
1	Double Slap	Normal	Physical	15	85	10	Normal
32	Dynamic Punch	Fighting	Physical	100	50	5	Normal
43	Mind Reader	Normal	Status	—	—	5	Normal
53	Circle Throw	Fighting	Physical	60	90	10	Normal

❖ TM MOVES
No.	Name	Type	Kind	Pow.	Acc.	PP	Range
TM01	Work Up	Normal	Status	—	—	30	Self
TM06	Toxic	Poison	Status	—	90	10	Normal
TM07	Hail	Ice	Status	—	—	10	Both Sides
TM08	Bulk Up	Fighting	Status	—	—	20	Self
TM10	Hidden Power	Normal	Special	60	100	15	Normal
TM13	Ice Beam	Ice	Special	90	100	10	Normal
TM14	Blizzard	Ice	Special	110	70	5	Many Others
TM15	Hyper Beam	Normal	Special	150	90	5	Normal
TM17	Protect	Normal	Status	—	—	10	Self
TM18	Rain Dance	Water	Status	—	—	5	Both Sides
TM21	Frustration	Normal	Physical	—	100	20	Normal
TM26	Earthquake	Ground	Physical	100	100	10	Adjacent
TM27	Return	Normal	Physical	—	100	20	Normal
TM29	Psychic	Psychic	Special	90	100	10	Normal
TM31	Brick Break	Fighting	Physical	75	100	15	Normal
TM32	Double Team	Normal	Status	—	—	15	Self
TM39	Rock Tomb	Rock	Physical	60	95	15	Normal
TM42	Facade	Normal	Physical	70	100	20	Normal
TM44	Rest	Psychic	Status	—	—	10	Self
TM45	Attract	Normal	Status	—	100	15	Normal
TM46	Thief	Dark	Physical	60	100	25	Normal
TM47	Low Sweep	Fighting	Physical	65	100	20	Normal
TM48	Round	Normal	Special	60	100	15	Normal
TM52	Focus Blast	Fighting	Special	120	70	5	Normal
TM55	Scald	Water	Special	80	100	15	Normal
TM56	Fling	Dark	Physical	—	100	10	Normal
TM66	Payback	Dark	Physical	50	100	10	Normal
TM68	Giga Impact	Normal	Physical	150	90	5	Normal
TM78	Bulldoze	Ground	Physical	60	100	20	Adjacent
TM80	Rock Slide	Rock	Physical	75	90	10	Many Others
TM84	Poison Jab	Poison	Physical	80	100	20	Normal
TM87	Swagger	Normal	Status	—	85	15	Normal
TM88	Sleep Talk	Normal	Status	—	—	10	Self
TM90	Substitute	Normal	Status	—	—	10	Self
TM94	Surf	Water	Special	90	100	15	Adjacent
TM98	Waterfall	Water	Physical	80	100	15	Normal
TM100	Confide	Normal	Status	—	—	20	Normal

❖ MOVES TAUGHT BY PEOPLE
Name	Type	Kind	Pow.	Acc.	PP	Range

❖ MOVES LEARNED WHEN EVOLVING
Name	Type	Kind	Pow.	Acc.	PP	Range
Submission	Fighting	Physical	80	80	20	Normal

EGG MOVES
Name	Type	Kind	Pow.	Acc.	PP	Range

❖ EXCLUSIVE Z-MOVE
Name	Base Move	Type	Kind	Pow.	Acc.	Range

POLIWRATH 151

Politoed

Alola Pokédex	Melemele	Akala	Ula'ula	Poni
152	—	079	071	—

Frog Pokémon
WATER
HEIGHT: 3'07"
WEIGHT: 74.7 lbs.

They gather on moonlit nights to form a large chorus. Their cries sound angry and not at all pleasant, but they are certainly distinctive.

It's the leader of Poliwag and Poliwhirl. When Politoed roars, they all cower in fear.

The male has larger vocal sacs on its cheeks.
The female has smaller vocal sacs on its cheeks.

ABILITY
Water Absorb
Damp

HIDDEN ABILITY
Drizzle

Damage taken in normal battles
NORMAL ×1	FIGHTING ×1	ROCK ×1
FIRE ×0.5	POISON ×1	GHOST ×1
WATER ×0.5	GROUND ×1	DRAGON ×1
GRASS ×2	FLYING ×1	DARK ×1
ELECTRIC ×2	PSYCHIC ×1	STEEL ×1
ICE ×0.5	BUG ×1	FAIRY ×1

SPECIES STRENGTHS
HP ◆◆◆
Attack ◆◆◆◆
Defense ◆◆◆◆
Sp. Atk ◆◆◆◆◆
Sp. Def ◆◆◆◆◆◆
Speed ◆◆◆◆

EGG GROUPS
Water 1

ITEM SOMETIMES HELD BY WILD POKÉMON
King's Rock

EVOLUTION
Poliwag → (Lv. 25) → Poliwhirl → (Trade while holding a King's Rock) → Politoed

MAIN WAY TO REGISTER IN THE POKÉDEX
Catch in SOS battles in the tall grass in Malie Garden when it is raining during the night in your game

❖ LEVEL-UP MOVES
Lv.	Name	Type	Kind	Pow.	Acc.	PP	Range
1	Bubble Beam	Water	Special	65	100	20	Normal
1	Hypnosis	Psychic	Status	—	60	20	Normal
1	Double Slap	Normal	Physical	15	85	10	Normal
1	Perish Song	Normal	Status	—	—	5	Adjacent
27	Swagger	Normal	Status	—	85	15	Normal
37	Bounce	Flying	Physical	85	85	5	Normal
48	Hyper Voice	Normal	Special	90	100	10	Many Others

❖ TM MOVES
No.	Name	Type	Kind	Pow.	Acc.	PP	Range
TM06	Toxic	Poison	Status	—	90	10	Normal
TM07	Hail	Ice	Status	—	—	10	Both Sides
TM10	Hidden Power	Normal	Special	60	100	15	Normal
TM13	Ice Beam	Ice	Special	90	100	10	Normal
TM14	Blizzard	Ice	Special	110	70	5	Many Others
TM15	Hyper Beam	Normal	Special	150	90	5	Normal
TM17	Protect	Normal	Status	—	—	10	Self
TM18	Rain Dance	Water	Status	—	—	5	Both Sides
TM21	Frustration	Normal	Physical	—	100	20	Normal
TM26	Earthquake	Ground	Physical	100	100	10	Adjacent
TM27	Return	Normal	Physical	—	100	20	Normal
TM29	Psychic	Psychic	Special	90	100	10	Normal
TM31	Brick Break	Fighting	Physical	75	100	15	Normal
TM32	Double Team	Normal	Status	—	—	15	Self
TM42	Facade	Normal	Physical	70	100	20	Normal
TM44	Rest	Psychic	Status	—	—	10	Self
TM45	Attract	Normal	Status	—	100	15	Normal
TM46	Thief	Dark	Physical	60	100	25	Normal
TM48	Round	Normal	Special	60	100	15	Normal
TM49	Echoed Voice	Normal	Special	40	100	15	Normal
TM52	Focus Blast	Fighting	Special	120	70	5	Normal
TM55	Scald	Water	Special	80	100	15	Normal
TM56	Fling	Dark	Physical	—	100	10	Normal
TM66	Payback	Dark	Physical	50	100	10	Normal
TM68	Giga Impact	Normal	Physical	150	90	5	Normal
TM78	Bulldoze	Ground	Physical	60	100	20	Adjacent
TM87	Swagger	Normal	Status	—	85	15	Normal
TM88	Sleep Talk	Normal	Status	—	—	10	Self
TM90	Substitute	Normal	Status	—	—	10	Self
TM94	Surf	Water	Special	90	100	15	Adjacent
TM98	Waterfall	Water	Physical	80	100	15	Normal
TM100	Confide	Normal	Status	—	—	20	Normal

❖ MOVES TAUGHT BY PEOPLE
Name	Type	Kind	Pow.	Acc.	PP	Range

❖ MOVES LEARNED WHEN EVOLVING
Name	Type	Kind	Pow.	Acc.	PP	Range

EGG MOVES
Name	Type	Kind	Pow.	Acc.	PP	Range

❖ EXCLUSIVE Z-MOVE
Name	Base Move	Type	Kind	Pow.	Acc.	Range

POLITOED 152

Goldeen

Goldfish Pokémon

Alola Pokédex	Melemele	Akala	Ula'ula	Poni
153	—	080	072	—

WATER

HEIGHT: 2'00"
WEIGHT: 33.1 lbs.

When the weather grows warm, they form groups and swim upriver. This sight serves as a poetic reminder that spring has arrived.

Spellbound by the length of its horn and the beauty of its fins, many strange Trainers raise Goldeen and nothing but Goldeen.

ABILITY
Swift Swim
Water Veil

HIDDEN ABILITY
Lightning Rod

Damage taken in normal battles

NORMAL ×1	FIGHTING ×1	ROCK ×1
FIRE ×0.5	POISON ×1	GHOST ×1
WATER ×0.5	GROUND ×1	DRAGON ×1
GRASS ×2	FLYING ×1	DARK ×1
ELECTRIC ×2	PSYCHIC ×1	STEEL ×0.5
ICE ×0.5	BUG ×1	FAIRY ×1

SPECIES STRENGTHS
HP ◆◆
Attack ◆◆◆◆
Defense ◆◆◆
Sp. Atk ◆◆
Sp. Def ◆◆
Speed ◆◆◆◆

EGG GROUPS
Water 2

ITEM SOMETIMES HELD BY WILD POKÉMON
Mystic Water

EVOLUTION

Goldeen → Lv. 33 → Seaking

MAIN WAY TO REGISTER IN THE POKÉDEX
Catch in the fishing spots in Malie Garden

The male has a larger horn. The female has a smaller horn.

❖ LEVEL-UP MOVES

Lv.	Name	Type	Kind	Pow.	Acc.	PP	Range
1	Peck	Flying	Physical	35	100	35	Normal
1	Tail Whip	Normal	Status	—	100	30	Many Others
1	Water Sport	Water	Status	—	—	15	Both Sides
5	Supersonic	Normal	Status	—	55	20	Normal
8	Horn Attack	Normal	Physical	65	100	25	Normal
13	Flail	Normal	Physical	—	100	15	Normal
16	Water Pulse	Water	Special	60	100	20	Normal
21	Aqua Ring	Water	Status	—	—	20	Self
24	Fury Attack	Normal	Physical	15	85	20	Normal
29	Agility	Psychic	Status	—	—	30	Self
32	Waterfall	Water	Physical	80	100	15	Normal
37	Horn Drill	Normal	Physical	—	30	5	Normal
40	Soak	Water	Status	—	100	20	Normal
45	Megahorn	Bug	Physical	120	85	10	Normal

❖ TM MOVES

No.	Name	Type	Kind	Pow.	Acc.	PP	Range
TM06	Toxic	Poison	Status	—	90	10	Normal
TM07	Hail	Ice	Status	—	—	10	Both Sides
TM10	Hidden Power	Normal	Special	60	100	15	Normal
TM13	Ice Beam	Ice	Special	90	100	10	Normal
TM14	Blizzard	Ice	Special	110	70	5	Many Others
TM17	Protect	Normal	Status	—	—	10	Self
TM18	Rain Dance	Water	Status	—	—	5	Both Sides
TM21	Frustration	Normal	Physical	—	100	20	Normal
TM27	Return	Normal	Physical	—	100	20	Normal
TM32	Double Team	Normal	Status	—	—	15	Self
TM42	Facade	Normal	Physical	70	100	20	Normal
TM44	Rest	Psychic	Status	—	—	10	Self
TM45	Attract	Normal	Status	—	100	15	Normal
TM48	Round	Normal	Special	60	100	15	Normal
TM55	Scald	Water	Special	80	100	15	Normal
TM67	Smart Strike	Steel	Physical	70	—	10	Normal
TM84	Poison Jab	Poison	Physical	80	100	20	Normal
TM87	Swagger	Normal	Status	—	85	15	Normal
TM88	Sleep Talk	Normal	Status	—	—	10	Self
TM90	Substitute	Normal	Status	—	—	10	Self
TM94	Surf	Water	Special	90	100	15	Adjacent
TM98	Waterfall	Water	Physical	80	100	15	Normal
TM100	Confide	Normal	Status	—	—	20	Normal

❖ MOVES TAUGHT BY PEOPLE

No.	Name	Type	Kind	Pow.	Acc.	PP	Range

Name	Type	Kind	Pow.	Acc.	PP	Range

❖ MOVES LEARNED WHEN EVOLVING

Name	Type	Kind	Pow.	Acc.	PP	Range

❖ EGG MOVES

Name	Type	Kind	Pow.	Acc.	PP	Range
Psybeam	Psychic	Special	65	100	20	Normal
Haze	Ice	Status	—	—	30	Both Sides
Hydro Pump	Water	Special	110	80	5	Normal
Sleep Talk	Normal	Status	—	—	10	Self
Mud Sport	Ground	Status	—	—	15	Both Sides
Mud-Slap	Ground	Special	20	100	10	Normal
Aqua Tail	Water	Physical	90	90	10	Normal
Body Slam	Normal	Physical	85	100	15	Normal
Mud Shot	Ground	Special	55	95	15	Normal
Skull Bash	Normal	Physical	130	100	10	Normal
Signal Beam	Bug	Special	75	100	15	Normal

❖ EXCLUSIVE Z-MOVE

Name	Base Move	Type	Kind	Pow.	Acc.	Range

Seaking

Goldfish Pokémon

Alola Pokédex	Melemele	Akala	Ula'ula	Poni
154	—	081	073	—

WATER

HEIGHT: 4'03"
WEIGHT: 86.0 lbs.

When the weather grows cold, its whole body flushes a deep red. This sight serves as a poetic reminder that autumn has arrived.

Trainers who are crazy for Seaking are divided into horn enthusiasts and fin enthusiasts. The two groups do not get along well.

ABILITY
Swift Swim
Water Veil

HIDDEN ABILITY
Lightning Rod

Damage taken in normal battles

NORMAL ×1	FIGHTING ×1	ROCK ×1
FIRE ×0.5	POISON ×1	GHOST ×1
WATER ×0.5	GROUND ×1	DRAGON ×1
GRASS ×2	FLYING ×1	DARK ×1
ELECTRIC ×2	PSYCHIC ×1	STEEL ×0.5
ICE ×0.5	BUG ×1	FAIRY ×1

SPECIES STRENGTHS
HP ◆◆◆
Attack ◆◆◆◆◆
Defense ◆◆◆◆
Sp. Atk ◆◆◆◆
Sp. Def ◆◆◆◆◆
Speed ◆◆◆◆

EGG GROUPS
Water 2

ITEM SOMETIMES HELD BY WILD POKÉMON
Mystic Water

EVOLUTION

Goldeen → Lv. 33 → Seaking

MAIN WAY TO REGISTER IN THE POKÉDEX
Catch in SOS battles against Goldeen at the fishing spots in Malie Garden

The male has a larger horn. The female has a smaller horn.

❖ LEVEL-UP MOVES

Lv.	Name	Type	Kind	Pow.	Acc.	PP	Range
1	Megahorn	Bug	Physical	120	85	10	Normal
1	Poison Jab	Poison	Physical	80	100	20	Normal
1	Peck	Flying	Physical	35	100	35	Normal
1	Tail Whip	Normal	Status	—	100	30	Many Others
1	Water Sport	Water	Status	—	—	15	Both Sides
1	Supersonic	Normal	Status	—	55	20	Normal
5	Supersonic	Normal	Status	—	55	20	Normal
8	Horn Attack	Normal	Physical	65	100	25	Normal
13	Flail	Normal	Physical	—	100	15	Normal
16	Water Pulse	Water	Special	60	100	20	Normal
21	Aqua Ring	Water	Status	—	—	20	Self
24	Fury Attack	Normal	Physical	15	85	20	Normal
29	Agility	Psychic	Status	—	—	30	Self
32	Waterfall	Water	Physical	80	100	15	Normal
40	Horn Drill	Normal	Physical	—	30	5	Normal
46	Soak	Water	Status	—	100	20	Normal
54	Megahorn	Bug	Physical	120	85	10	Normal

❖ TM MOVES

No.	Name	Type	Kind	Pow.	Acc.	PP	Range
TM06	Toxic	Poison	Status	—	90	10	Normal
TM07	Hail	Ice	Status	—	—	10	Both Sides
TM10	Hidden Power	Normal	Special	60	100	15	Normal
TM13	Ice Beam	Ice	Special	90	100	10	Normal
TM14	Blizzard	Ice	Special	110	70	5	Many Others
TM15	Hyper Beam	Normal	Special	150	90	5	Normal
TM17	Protect	Normal	Status	—	—	10	Self
TM18	Rain Dance	Water	Status	—	—	5	Both Sides
TM21	Frustration	Normal	Physical	—	100	20	Normal
TM27	Return	Normal	Physical	—	100	20	Normal
TM32	Double Team	Normal	Status	—	—	15	Self
TM42	Facade	Normal	Physical	70	100	20	Normal
TM44	Rest	Psychic	Status	—	—	10	Self
TM45	Attract	Normal	Status	—	100	15	Normal
TM48	Round	Normal	Special	60	100	15	Normal
TM55	Scald	Water	Special	80	100	15	Normal
TM67	Smart Strike	Steel	Physical	70	—	10	Normal
TM68	Giga Impact	Normal	Physical	150	90	5	Normal
TM84	Poison Jab	Poison	Physical	80	100	20	Normal
TM87	Swagger	Normal	Status	—	85	15	Normal
TM88	Sleep Talk	Normal	Status	—	—	10	Self
TM90	Substitute	Normal	Status	—	—	10	Self
TM94	Surf	Water	Special	90	100	15	Adjacent
TM98	Waterfall	Water	Physical	80	100	15	Normal
TM100	Confide	Normal	Status	—	—	20	Normal

❖ MOVES TAUGHT BY PEOPLE

No.	Name	Type	Kind	Pow.	Acc.	PP	Range

Name	Type	Kind	Pow.	Acc.	PP	Range

❖ MOVES LEARNED WHEN EVOLVING

Name	Type	Kind	Pow.	Acc.	PP	Range

❖ EGG MOVES

Name	Type	Kind	Pow.	Acc.	PP	Range

❖ EXCLUSIVE Z-MOVE

Name	Base Move	Type	Kind	Pow.	Acc.	Range

Feebas

Alola Pokédex	Melemele	Akala	Ula'ula	Poni
155	—	082	—	—

Feebas
Fish Pokémon

WATER

HEIGHT: 2'00"
WEIGHT: 16.3 lbs.

A tough Pokémon that is perfectly fine even in dirty water. However, due to its ragged, shabby appearance, it isn't popular.

Although unattractive and unpopular, this Pokémon's marvelous vitality has made it a subject of research.

ABILITY
Swift Swim
Oblivious

HIDDEN ABILITY
Adaptability

Damage taken in normal battles

NORMAL ×1	FIGHTING ×1	ROCK ×1
FIRE ×0.5	POISON ×1	GHOST ×1
WATER ×0.5	GROUND ×1	DRAGON ×1
GRASS ×2	FLYING ×1	DARK ×1
ELECTRIC ×2	PSYCHIC ×1	STEEL ×0.5
ICE ×0.5	BUG ×1	FAIRY ×1

SPECIES STRENGTHS
HP ◆
Attack ◆
Defense ◆
Sp. Atk ◆
Sp. Def ◆◆◆
Speed ◆◆◆◆

EGG GROUPS
Water 1 | Dragon

ITEM SOMETIMES HELD BY WILD POKÉMON
—

EVOLUTION
Feebas → (Trade while holding Prism Scale) → Milotic

MAIN WAY TO REGISTER IN THE POKÉDEX
Catch in the fishing spots on Brooklet Hill

Same form for male/female

◆ LEVEL-UP MOVES

Lv.	Name	Type	Kind	Pow.	Acc.	PP	Range
1	Splash	Normal	Status	—	—	40	Self
15	Tackle	Normal	Physical	40	100	35	Normal
30	Flail	Normal	Physical	—	100	15	Normal

◆ TM MOVES

No.	Name	Type	Kind	Pow.	Acc.	PP	Range
TM06	Toxic	Poison	Status	—	90	10	Normal
TM07	Hail	Ice	Status	—	—	10	Both Sides
TM10	Hidden Power	Normal	Special	60	100	15	Normal
TM13	Ice Beam	Ice	Special	90	100	10	Normal
TM14	Blizzard	Ice	Special	110	70	5	Many Others
TM16	Light Screen	Psychic	Status	—	—	30	Your Side
TM17	Protect	Normal	Status	—	—	10	Self
TM18	Rain Dance	Water	Status	—	—	5	Both Sides
TM21	Frustration	Normal	Physical	—	100	20	Normal
TM27	Return	Normal	Physical	—	100	20	Normal
TM32	Double Team	Normal	Status	—	—	15	Self
TM42	Facade	Normal	Physical	70	100	20	Normal
TM44	Rest	Psychic	Status	—	—	10	Self
TM45	Attract	Normal	Status	—	100	15	Normal
TM48	Round	Normal	Special	60	100	15	Normal
TM55	Scald	Water	Special	80	100	15	Normal
TM87	Swagger	Normal	Status	—	85	15	Normal
TM88	Sleep Talk	Normal	Status	—	—	10	Self
TM90	Substitute	Normal	Status	—	—	10	Self
TM94	Surf	Water	Special	90	100	15	Adjacent
TM98	Waterfall	Water	Physical	80	100	15	Normal
TM100	Confide	Normal	Status	—	—	20	Normal

◆ MOVES TAUGHT BY PEOPLE

Name	Type	Kind	Pow.	Acc.	PP	Range

◆ MOVES LEARNED WHEN EVOLVING

Name	Type	Kind	Pow.	Acc.	PP	Range

◆ EGG MOVES

Name	Type	Kind	Pow.	Acc.	PP	Range
Mirror Coat	Psychic	Special	—	100	20	Varies
Dragon Breath	Dragon	Special	60	100	20	Normal
Mud Sport	Ground	Status	—	—	15	Both Sides
Hypnosis	Psychic	Status	—	60	20	Normal
Confuse Ray	Ghost	Status	—	100	10	Normal
Mist	Ice	Status	—	—	30	Your Side
Haze	Ice	Status	—	—	30	Both Sides
Tickle	Normal	Status	—	100	20	Normal
Brine	Water	Special	65	100	10	Normal
Iron Tail	Steel	Physical	100	75	15	Normal
Dragon Pulse	Dragon	Special	85	100	10	Normal
Captivate	Normal	Status	—	100	20	Many Others

◆ EXCLUSIVE Z-MOVE

Name	Base Move	Type	Kind	Pow.	Acc.	Range

Milotic

Alola Pokédex	Melemele	Akala	Ula'ula	Poni
156	—	083	—	—

Milotic
Tender Pokémon

WATER

HEIGHT: 20'04"
WEIGHT: 357.1 lbs.

Milotic has provided inspiration to many artists. It has even been referred to as the most beautiful Pokémon of all.

It lives at the bottom of clear lakes. In times of war, it shows itself, which soothes people's minds and hearts.

ABILITY
Marvel Scale
Competitive

HIDDEN ABILITY
Cute Charm

Damage taken in normal battles

NORMAL ×1	FIGHTING ×1	ROCK ×1
FIRE ×0.5	POISON ×1	GHOST ×1
WATER ×0.5	GROUND ×1	DRAGON ×1
GRASS ×2	FLYING ×1	DARK ×1
ELECTRIC ×2	PSYCHIC ×1	STEEL ×0.5
ICE ×0.5	BUG ×1	FAIRY ×1

SPECIES STRENGTHS
HP ◆◆◆◆
Attack ◆◆◆
Defense ◆◆◆◆
Sp. Atk ◆◆◆◆◆
Sp. Def ◆◆◆◆◆◆◆
Speed ◆◆◆◆

EGG GROUPS
Water 1 | Dragon

ITEM SOMETIMES HELD BY WILD POKÉMON

EVOLUTION
Feebas → (Trade while holding Prism Scale) → Milotic

MAIN WAY TO REGISTER IN THE POKÉDEX
Receive a Feebas holding a Prism Scale in a trade and it will evolve

The pink fins on its head are shorter on males than on females.

◆ LEVEL-UP MOVES

Lv.	Name	Type	Kind	Pow.	Acc.	PP	Range
1	Water Pulse	Water	Special	60	100	20	Normal
1	Wrap	Normal	Physical	15	90	20	Normal
1	Water Gun	Water	Special	40	100	25	Normal
1	Water Sport	Water	Status	—	—	15	Both Sides
1	Refresh	Normal	Status	—	—	20	Self
4	Water Sport	Water	Status	—	—	15	Both Sides
7	Refresh	Normal	Status	—	—	20	Self
11	Disarming Voice	Fairy	Special	40	—	15	Many Others
14	Twister	Dragon	Special	40	100	20	Many Others
17	Aqua Ring	Water	Status	—	—	20	Self
21	Captivate	Normal	Status	—	100	20	Many Others
24	Dragon Tail	Dragon	Physical	60	90	10	Normal
27	Recover	Normal	Status	—	—	10	Self
31	Aqua Tail	Water	Physical	90	90	10	Normal
34	Attract	Normal	Status	—	100	15	Normal
37	Safeguard	Normal	Status	—	—	25	Your Side
41	Coil	Poison	Status	—	—	20	Self
44	Hydro Pump	Water	Special	110	80	5	Normal
47	Rain Dance	Water	Status	—	—	5	Both Sides

◆ TM MOVES

No.	Name	Type	Kind	Pow.	Acc.	PP	Range
TM06	Toxic	Poison	Status	—	90	10	Normal
TM07	Hail	Ice	Status	—	—	10	Both Sides
TM10	Hidden Power	Normal	Special	60	100	15	Normal
TM13	Ice Beam	Ice	Special	90	100	10	Normal
TM14	Blizzard	Ice	Special	110	70	5	Many Others
TM15	Hyper Beam	Normal	Special	150	90	5	Normal
TM16	Light Screen	Psychic	Status	—	—	30	Your Side
TM17	Protect	Normal	Status	—	—	10	Self
TM18	Rain Dance	Water	Status	—	—	5	Both Sides
TM20	Safeguard	Normal	Status	—	—	25	Your Side
TM21	Frustration	Normal	Physical	—	100	20	Normal
TM27	Return	Normal	Physical	—	100	20	Normal
TM32	Double Team	Normal	Status	—	—	15	Self
TM42	Facade	Normal	Physical	70	100	20	Normal
TM44	Rest	Psychic	Status	—	—	10	Self
TM45	Attract	Normal	Status	—	100	15	Normal
TM48	Round	Normal	Special	60	100	15	Normal
TM55	Scald	Water	Special	80	100	15	Normal
TM59	Brutal Swing	Dark	Physical	60	100	20	Adjacent
TM68	Giga Impact	Normal	Physical	150	90	5	Normal
TM77	Psych Up	Normal	Status	—	—	10	Normal
TM78	Bulldoze	Ground	Physical	60	100	20	Adjacent
TM82	Dragon Tail	Dragon	Physical	60	90	10	Normal
TM87	Swagger	Normal	Status	—	85	15	Normal
TM88	Sleep Talk	Normal	Status	—	—	10	Self
TM90	Substitute	Normal	Status	—	—	10	Self
TM94	Surf	Water	Special	90	100	15	Adjacent
TM98	Waterfall	Water	Physical	80	100	15	Normal

◆ MOVES TAUGHT BY PEOPLE

No.	Name	Type	Kind	Pow.	Acc.	PP	Range
TM100	Confide	Normal	Status	—	—	20	Normal

◆ MOVES LEARNED WHEN EVOLVING

Name	Type	Kind	Pow.	Acc.	PP	Range
Water Pulse	Water	Special	60	100	20	Normal

◆ EGG MOVES

Name	Type	Kind	Pow.	Acc.	PP	Range

◆ EXCLUSIVE Z-MOVE

Name	Base Move	Type	Kind	Pow.	Acc.	Range

Alola Pokédex	Melemele	Akala	Ula'ula	Poni
157	—	084	—	—

☑ Alomomola

Caring Pokémon

WATER

HEIGHT: 3'11"
WEIGHT: 69.7 lbs.

It uses its special mucus to close the wounds of injured Pokémon. The reason for this behavior remains unknown.

They float upon the open sea. Many water Pokémon gather in the area around Alomomola.

ABILITY
Healer
Hydration

HIDDEN ABILITY
Regenerator

Damage taken in normal battles

NORMAL ×1	FIGHTING ×1	ROCK ×1			
FIRE ×0.5	POISON ×1	GHOST ×1			
WATER ×0.5	GROUND ×1	DRAGON ×1			
GRASS ×2	FLYING ×1	DARK ×1			
ELECTRIC ×2	PSYCHIC ×1	STEEL ×0.5			
ICE ×0.5	BUG ×1	FAIRY ×1			

SPECIES STRENGTHS
HP ◆◆◆◆◆◆
Attack ◆◆◆◆
Defense ◆◆◆◆
Sp. Atk ◆◆
Sp. Def ◆◆
Speed ◆◆◆◆

EGG GROUPS
Water 1   Water 2

ITEM SOMETIMES HELD BY WILD POKÉMON
—

EVOLUTION
Does not evolve

MAIN WAY TO REGISTER IN THE POKÉDEX
Catch in the rare fishing spots in Totem's Den on Brooklet Hill

Same form for male/female

❖ LEVEL-UP MOVES

Lv.	Name	Type	Kind	Pow.	Acc.	PP	Range
1	Play Nice	Normal	Status	—	—	20	Normal
1	Hydro Pump	Water	Special	110	80	5	Normal
1	Wide Guard	Rock	Status	—	—	10	Your Side
1	Healing Wish	Psychic	Status	—	—	10	Self
1	Helping Hand	Normal	Status	—	—	20	1 Ally
1	Pound	Normal	Physical	40	100	35	Normal
1	Water Sport	Water	Status	—	—	15	Both Sides
5	Aqua Ring	Water	Status	—	—	20	Self
9	Aqua Jet	Water	Physical	40	100	20	Normal
13	Double Slap	Normal	Physical	15	85	10	Normal
17	Heal Pulse	Psychic	Status	—	—	10	Normal
21	Protect	Normal	Status	—	—	10	Self
25	Water Pulse	Water	Special	60	100	20	Normal
29	Wake-Up Slap	Fighting	Physical	70	100	10	Normal
33	Soak	Water	Status	—	100	20	Normal
37	Wish	Normal	Status	—	—	10	Self
41	Brine	Water	Special	65	100	10	Normal
45	Safeguard	Normal	Status	—	—	25	Your Side
49	Whirlpool	Water	Special	35	85	15	Normal
53	Helping Hand	Normal	Status	—	—	20	1 Ally
57	Healing Wish	Psychic	Status	—	—	10	Self
61	Wide Guard	Rock	Status	—	—	10	Your Side
65	Hydro Pump	Water	Special	110	80	5	Normal

❖ TM MOVES

No.	Name	Type	Kind	Pow.	Acc.	PP	Range
TM04	Calm Mind	Psychic	Status	—	—	20	Self
TM06	Toxic	Poison	Status	—	90	10	Normal
TM07	Hail	Ice	Status	—	—	10	Both Sides
TM10	Hidden Power	Normal	Special	60	100	15	Normal
TM13	Ice Beam	Ice	Special	90	100	10	Normal
TM14	Blizzard	Ice	Special	110	70	5	Many Others
TM16	Light Screen	Psychic	Status	—	—	30	Your Side
TM17	Protect	Normal	Status	—	—	10	Self
TM18	Rain Dance	Water	Status	—	—	5	Both Sides
TM20	Safeguard	Normal	Status	—	—	25	Your Side
TM21	Frustration	Normal	Physical	—	100	20	Normal
TM27	Return	Normal	Physical	—	100	20	Normal
TM29	Psychic	Psychic	Special	90	100	10	Normal
TM30	Shadow Ball	Ghost	Special	80	100	15	Normal
TM32	Double Team	Normal	Status	—	—	15	Self
TM42	Facade	Normal	Physical	70	100	20	Normal
TM44	Rest	Psychic	Status	—	—	10	Self
TM45	Attract	Normal	Status	—	100	15	Normal
TM48	Round	Normal	Special	60	100	15	Normal
TM55	Scald	Water	Special	80	100	15	Normal
TM77	Psych Up	Normal	Status	—	—	10	Normal
TM87	Swagger	Normal	Status	—	85	15	Normal
TM88	Sleep Talk	Normal	Status	—	—	10	Self
TM90	Substitute	Normal	Status	—	—	10	Self
TM94	Surf	Water	Special	90	100	15	Adjacent
TM98	Waterfall	Water	Physical	80	100	15	Normal
TM100	Confide	Normal	Status	—	—	20	Normal

❖ MOVES TAUGHT BY PEOPLE

No.	Name	Type	Kind	Pow.	Acc.	PP	Range

❖ MOVES LEARNED WHEN EVOLVING

Name	Type	Kind	Pow.	Acc.	PP	Range

❖ EGG MOVES

Name	Type	Kind	Pow.	Acc.	PP	Range
Pain Split	Normal	Status	—	—	20	Normal
Refresh	Normal	Status	—	—	20	Self
Tickle	Normal	Status	—	100	20	Normal
Mirror Coat	Psychic	Special	—	100	20	Varies
Mist	Ice	Status	—	—	30	Your Side
Endure	Normal	Status	—	—	10	Self

❖ EXCLUSIVE Z-MOVE

Name	Base Move	Type	Kind	Pow.	Acc.	Range

Reel in Some Real Rare Finds!

During your adventure, you will receive a Fishing Rod on Akala Island. If you see a pile of rocks underwater, that's a spot you can get out your fishing rod and try to catch a Pokémon! These are the only places where you can fish in *Pokémon Sun* and *Pokémon Moon*. You can stand on the shore and fish, or you can fish out in the open seas while riding on the back of Lapras. Press Ⓐ to cast your line when you get close enough to a fishing spot. When you see a "!" symbol appear on the screen, quickly press Ⓐ again to pull up your line. Your chances of getting a hit go way up when the first Pokémon in your party has the Suction Cups or Sticky Hold Ability. (Find out all the Pokémon with these Abilities by checking out the Pokémon Abilities Reverse Lookup tables beginning on page 360).

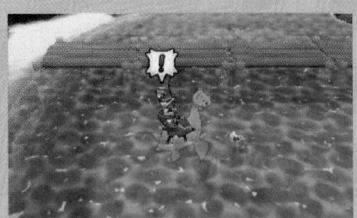

If you approach a rare fishing spot too quickly, though, you may scare off the rare Pokémon that were lurking within it. If you're on land, that means no running or riding on Pokémon as you approach the fishing spot. When you're on the water, you can't be riding Sharpedo or swimming quickly with Lapras (holding down Ⓑ). And when you're on the water, be sure not to get too close to a rare fishing spot. If you pass directly over it, the bubbles will disappear and you'll miss your chance for a rare Pokémon. If you don't get a bite at a rare fishing spot, you can immediately try casting your line out again. As long as you see bubbles, there is still the potential that something rare will be found at that spot. But once you snag an item or catch, defeat, or run away from a battle with a wild Pokémon at a rare fishing spot, you'll find that the bubbles disappear. If you want another shot at the same rare fishing spot, leave the area once and by the time you return, you should find another rare specimen has taken up residence at that fishing spot!

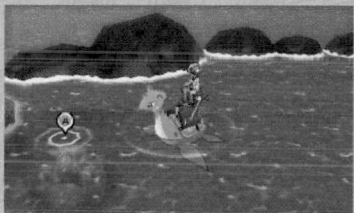

A wild Chinchou appeared!

Chinchou's data will be added to the Pokédex!

Fishing for treasure in Alola

Sometimes you can find items while fishing, too. You'll find that you reel in Pokémon much more often than items, but don't give up too quickly because the items you can find can be worth the trouble. You're most likely to pull up a Pearl, but you may also get lucky and find some very rare items. The rarest items are different for each island, and include valuable Pearl Strings, which can be sold for cash, and Bottle Caps, which can be used for Hyper Training once you've become a Champion (p. 248)!

You obtained a Pearl!

You obtained a Big Pearl!

You obtained a Pearl String!

Island	Normal	Rare	Very Rare
Melemele Island	Pearl	Big Pearl	Pearl String
Akala Island	Pearl	Big Pearl	Heart Scale
Ula'ula Island	Pearl	Big Pearl	Prism Scale
Poni Island	Pearl	Sticky Barb	Bottle Cap

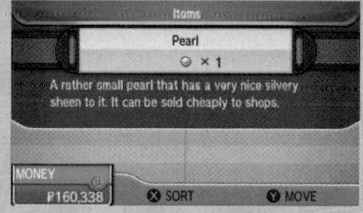

Items
Pearl
◯ × 1
A rather small pearl that has a very nice silvery sheen to it. It can be sold cheaply to shops.
MONEY P160,338 ✕ SORT Ⓨ MOVE

Items
Big Pearl
◯ × 1
A rather large pearl that has a very nice silvery sheen. It can be sold to shops for a high price.
MONEY P160,338 ✕ SORT Ⓨ MOVE

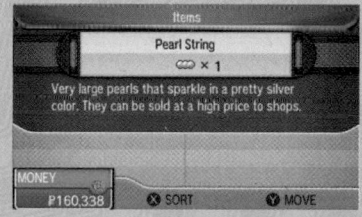

Items
Pearl String
◯ × 1
Very large pearls that sparkle in a pretty silver color. They can be sold at a high price to shops.
MONEY P160,338 ✕ SORT Ⓨ MOVE

Alola Pokédex	Melemele	Akala	Ula'ula	Poni
158	—	085	—	—

Fletchling

Tiny Robin Pokémon

NORMAL **FLYING**

HEIGHT: 1'00"
WEIGHT: 3.7 lbs.

This amiable Pokémon is easy to train. But when battle is joined, it shows its ferocious side.

When it's excited, its temperature can double, spiking hormone production in its body.

ABILITY
Big Pecks

HIDDEN ABILITY
Gale Wings

Damage taken in normal battles

NORMAL ×1	FIGHTING ×1	ROCK ×2			
FIRE ×1	POISON ×1	GHOST ×1			
WATER ×1	GROUND ×0	DRAGON ×1			
GRASS ×0.5	FLYING ×1	DARK ×1			
ELECTRIC ×2	PSYCHIC ×1	STEEL ×1			
ICE ×2	BUG ×0.5	FAIRY ×1			

SPECIES STRENGTHS
HP ◆◆
Attack ◆◆◆
Defense ◆◆
Sp. Atk ◆◆
Sp. Def ◆◆
Speed ◆◆◆

EGG GROUPS
Flying

ITEM SOMETIMES HELD BY WILD POKÉMON
—

MAIN WAY TO REGISTER IN THE POKÉDEX
Catch in the tall grass in Wela Volcano Park

EVOLUTION

Fletchling — Lv. 17 → Fletchinder
Lv. 35 → Talonflame

Same form for male/female

Alola Pokédex	Melemele	Akala	Ula'ula	Poni
159	—	086	—	—

Fletchinder

Ember Pokémon

FIRE **FLYING**

HEIGHT: 2'04"
WEIGHT: 35.3 lbs.

From its beak, it fires embers at its prey. Once it has caught them, it grills them at high heat before feasting upon them.

It will not tolerate other Fletchinder entering its territory, which has a radius of several miles.

ABILITY
Flame Body

HIDDEN ABILITY
Gale Wings

Damage taken in normal battles

NORMAL ×1	FIGHTING ×0.5	ROCK ×4			
FIRE ×0.5	POISON ×1	GHOST ×1			
WATER ×2	GROUND ×0	DRAGON ×1			
GRASS ×0.25	FLYING ×1	DARK ×1			
ELECTRIC ×2	PSYCHIC ×1	STEEL ×0.5			
ICE ×1	BUG ×0.25	FAIRY ×0.5			

SPECIES STRENGTHS
HP ◆◆
Attack ◆◆◆◆
Defense ◆◆◆
Sp. Atk ◆◆◆
Sp. Def ◆◆◆
Speed ◆◆◆◆

EGG GROUPS
Flying

ITEM SOMETIMES HELD BY WILD POKÉMON
—

MAIN WAY TO REGISTER IN THE POKÉDEX
Catch in the tall grass on Route 8

EVOLUTION

Fletchling — Lv. 17 → Fletchinder
Lv. 35 → Talonflame

Same form for male/female

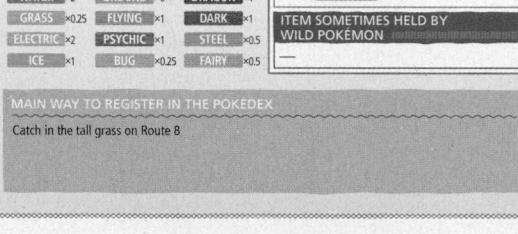

Alola Pokédex	Melemele	Akala	Ula'ula	Poni
160	—	087	—	—

Talonflame

Scorching Pokémon

FIRE **FLYING**

HEIGHT: 3'11"
WEIGHT: 54.0 lbs.

Its favorite foods are Wingull and Pikipek. It attacks with a powerful kick and grasps them firmly in its talons.

It zooms directly at its prey at flight speeds of close to 310 mph, while fiery embers scatter from gaps in its feathers.

ABILITY
Flame Body

HIDDEN ABILITY
Gale Wings

Damage taken in normal battles

NORMAL ×1	FIGHTING ×0.5	ROCK ×4			
FIRE ×0.5	POISON ×1	GHOST ×1			
WATER ×2	GROUND ×0	DRAGON ×1			
GRASS ×0.25	FLYING ×1	DARK ×1			
ELECTRIC ×2	PSYCHIC ×1	STEEL ×0.5			
ICE ×1	BUG ×0.25	FAIRY ×0.5			

SPECIES STRENGTHS
HP ◆◆◆
Attack ◆◆◆◆
Defense ◆◆◆◆
Sp. Atk ◆◆◆◆
Sp. Def ◆◆◆
Speed ◆◆◆◆◆◆◆

EGG GROUPS
Flying

ITEM SOMETIMES HELD BY WILD POKÉMON
—

MAIN WAY TO REGISTER IN THE POKÉDEX
Level up Fletchinder to Lv. 35

EVOLUTION

Fletchling — Lv. 17 → Fletchinder
Lv. 35 → Talonflame

Same form for male/female

FLETCHLING 158

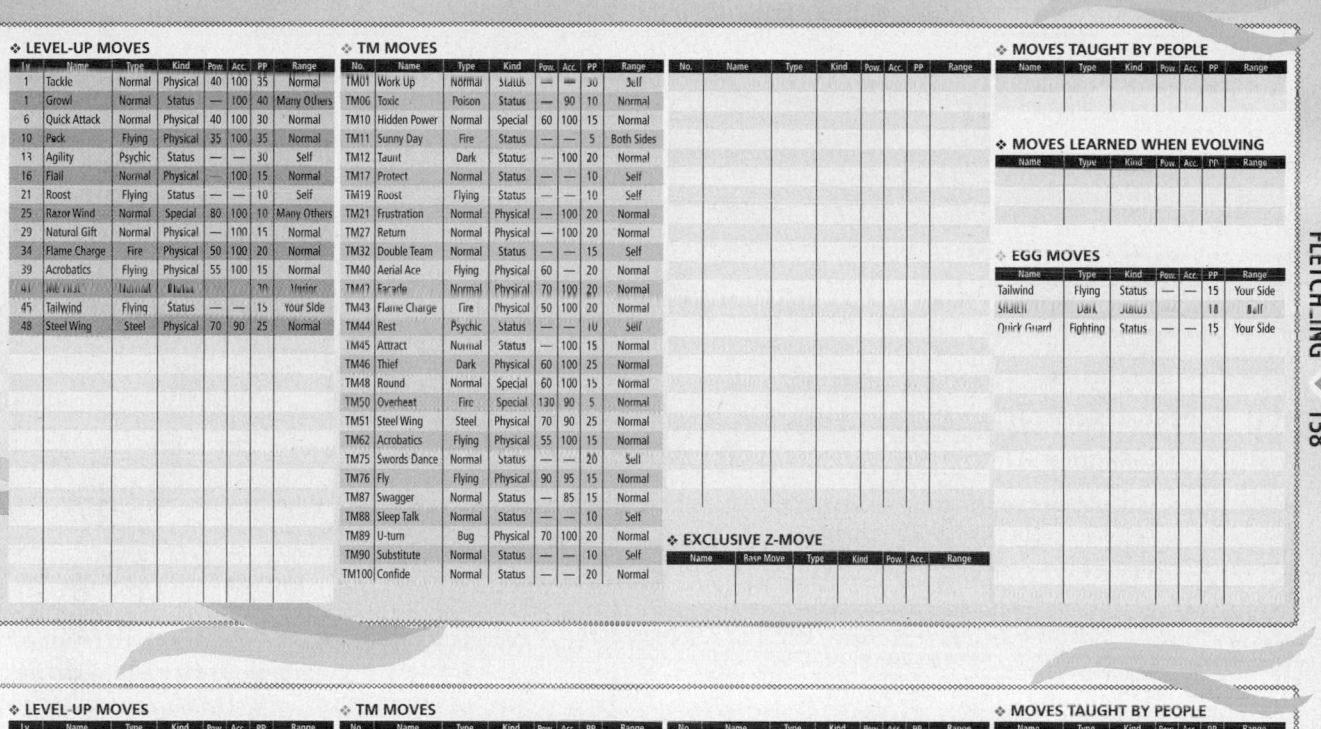

❖ LEVEL-UP MOVES

Lv	Name	Type	Kind	Pow.	Acc.	PP	Range
1	Tackle	Normal	Physical	40	100	35	Normal
1	Growl	Normal	Status	—	100	40	Many Others
6	Quick Attack	Normal	Physical	40	100	30	Normal
10	Peck	Flying	Physical	35	100	35	Normal
13	Agility	Psychic	Status	—	—	30	Self
16	Flail	Normal	Physical	—	100	15	Normal
21	Roost	Flying	Status	—	—	10	Self
25	Razor Wind	Normal	Special	80	100	10	Many Others
29	Natural Gift	Normal	Physical	—	100	15	Normal
34	Flame Charge	Fire	Physical	50	100	20	Normal
39	Acrobatics	Flying	Physical	55	100	15	Normal
41	Me First	Normal	Status	—	—	20	Varies
45	Tailwind	Flying	Status	—	—	15	Your Side
48	Steel Wing	Steel	Physical	70	90	25	Normal

❖ TM MOVES

No.	Name	Type	Kind	Pow.	Acc.	PP	Range
TM01	Work Up	Normal	Status	—	—	30	Self
TM06	Toxic	Poison	Status	—	90	10	Normal
TM10	Hidden Power	Normal	Special	60	100	15	Normal
TM11	Sunny Day	Fire	Status	—	—	5	Both Sides
TM12	Taunt	Dark	Status	—	100	20	Normal
TM17	Protect	Normal	Status	—	—	10	Self
TM19	Roost	Flying	Status	—	—	10	Self
TM21	Frustration	Normal	Physical	—	100	20	Normal
TM27	Return	Normal	Physical	—	100	20	Normal
TM32	Double Team	Normal	Status	—	—	15	Self
TM40	Aerial Ace	Flying	Physical	60	—	20	Normal
TM42	Facade	Normal	Physical	70	100	20	Normal
TM43	Flame Charge	Fire	Physical	50	100	20	Normal
TM44	Rest	Psychic	Status	—	—	10	Self
TM45	Attract	Normal	Status	—	100	15	Normal
TM46	Thief	Dark	Physical	60	100	25	Normal
TM48	Round	Normal	Special	60	100	15	Normal
TM50	Overheat	Fire	Special	130	90	5	Normal
TM51	Steel Wing	Steel	Physical	70	90	25	Normal
TM62	Acrobatics	Flying	Physical	55	100	15	Normal
TM75	Swords Dance	Normal	Status	—	—	20	Self
TM76	Fly	Flying	Physical	90	95	15	Normal
TM87	Swagger	Normal	Status	—	85	15	Normal
TM88	Sleep Talk	Normal	Status	—	—	10	Self
TM89	U-turn	Bug	Physical	70	100	20	Normal
TM90	Substitute	Normal	Status	—	—	10	Self
TM100	Confide	Normal	Status	—	—	20	Normal

❖ MOVES TAUGHT BY PEOPLE

Name	Type	Kind	Pow.	Acc.	PP	Range

❖ MOVES LEARNED WHEN EVOLVING

Name	Type	Kind	Pow.	Acc.	PP	Range

❖ EGG MOVES

Name	Type	Kind	Pow.	Acc.	PP	Range
Tailwind	Flying	Status	—	—	15	Your Side
Snatch	Dark	Status	—	—	10	Self
Quick Guard	Fighting	Status	—	—	15	Your Side

❖ EXCLUSIVE Z-MOVE

Name	Base Move	Type	Kind	Pow.	Acc.	Range

FLETCHINDER 159

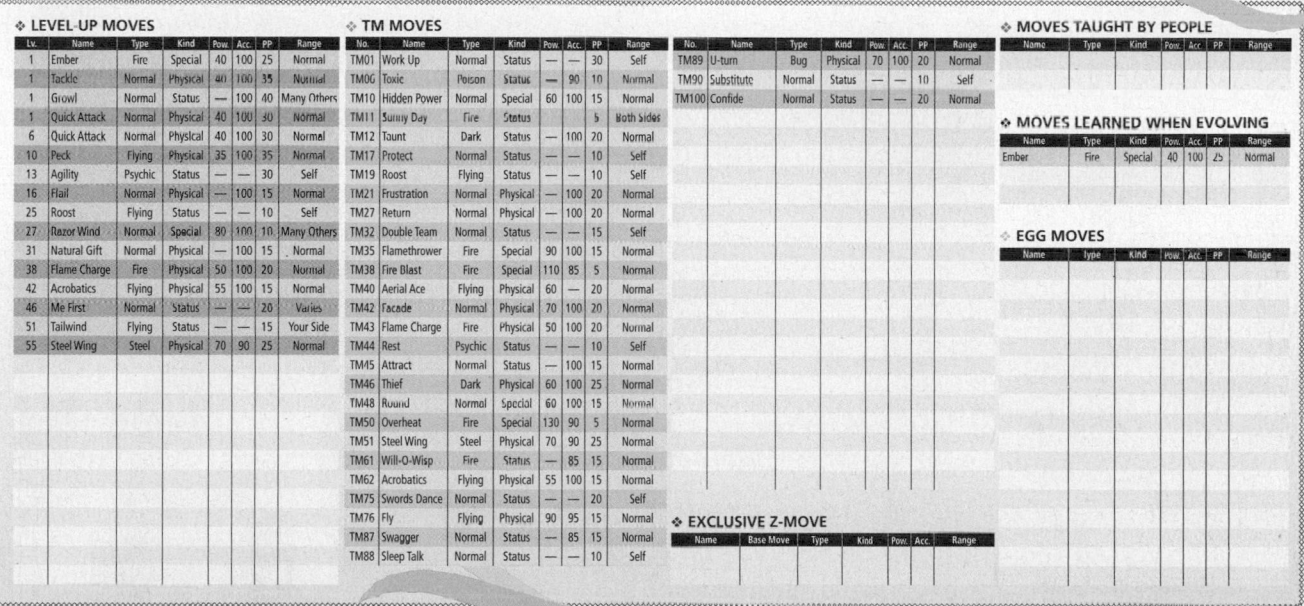

❖ LEVEL-UP MOVES

Lv	Name	Type	Kind	Pow.	Acc.	PP	Range
1	Ember	Fire	Special	40	100	25	Normal
1	Tackle	Normal	Physical	40	100	35	Normal
1	Growl	Normal	Status	—	100	40	Many Others
1	Quick Attack	Normal	Physical	40	100	30	Normal
6	Quick Attack	Normal	Physical	40	100	30	Normal
10	Peck	Flying	Physical	35	100	35	Normal
13	Agility	Psychic	Status	—	—	30	Self
16	Flail	Normal	Physical	—	100	15	Normal
25	Roost	Flying	Status	—	—	10	Self
27	Razor Wind	Normal	Special	80	100	10	Many Others
31	Natural Gift	Normal	Physical	—	100	15	Normal
38	Flame Charge	Fire	Physical	50	100	20	Normal
42	Acrobatics	Flying	Physical	55	100	15	Normal
46	Me First	Normal	Status	—	—	20	Varies
51	Tailwind	Flying	Status	—	—	15	Your Side
55	Steel Wing	Steel	Physical	70	90	25	Normal

❖ TM MOVES

No.	Name	Type	Kind	Pow.	Acc.	PP	Range
TM01	Work Up	Normal	Status	—	—	30	Self
TM06	Toxic	Poison	Status	—	90	10	Normal
TM10	Hidden Power	Normal	Special	60	100	15	Normal
TM11	Sunny Day	Fire	Status	—	—	5	Both Sides
TM12	Taunt	Dark	Status	—	100	20	Normal
TM17	Protect	Normal	Status	—	—	10	Self
TM19	Roost	Flying	Status	—	—	10	Self
TM21	Frustration	Normal	Physical	—	100	20	Normal
TM27	Return	Normal	Physical	—	100	20	Normal
TM32	Double Team	Normal	Status	—	—	15	Self
TM35	Flamethrower	Fire	Special	90	100	15	Normal
TM38	Fire Blast	Fire	Special	110	85	5	Normal
TM40	Aerial Ace	Flying	Physical	60	—	20	Normal
TM42	Facade	Normal	Physical	70	100	20	Normal
TM43	Flame Charge	Fire	Physical	50	100	20	Normal
TM44	Rest	Psychic	Status	—	—	10	Self
TM45	Attract	Normal	Status	—	100	15	Normal
TM46	Thief	Dark	Physical	60	100	25	Normal
TM48	Round	Normal	Special	60	100	15	Normal
TM50	Overheat	Fire	Special	130	90	5	Normal
TM51	Steel Wing	Steel	Physical	70	90	25	Normal
TM61	Will-O-Wisp	Fire	Status	—	85	15	Normal
TM62	Acrobatics	Flying	Physical	55	100	15	Normal
TM75	Swords Dance	Normal	Status	—	—	20	Self
TM76	Fly	Flying	Physical	90	95	15	Normal
TM87	Swagger	Normal	Status	—	85	15	Normal
TM88	Sleep Talk	Normal	Status	—	—	10	Self

❖ MOVES TAUGHT BY PEOPLE

No.	Name	Type	Kind	Pow.	Acc.	PP	Range
TM89	U-turn	Bug	Physical	70	100	20	Normal
TM90	Substitute	Normal	Status	—	—	10	Self
TM100	Confide	Normal	Status	—	—	20	Normal

❖ MOVES LEARNED WHEN EVOLVING

Name	Type	Kind	Pow.	Acc.	PP	Range
Ember	Fire	Special	40	100	25	Normal

❖ EGG MOVES

Name	Type	Kind	Pow.	Acc.	PP	Range

❖ EXCLUSIVE Z-MOVE

Name	Base Move	Type	Kind	Pow.	Acc.	Range

TALONFLAME 160

❖ LEVEL-UP MOVES

Lv	Name	Type	Kind	Pow.	Acc.	PP	Range
1	Ember	Fire	Special	40	100	25	Normal
1	Brave Bird	Flying	Physical	120	100	15	Normal
1	Flare Blitz	Fire	Physical	120	100	15	Normal
1	Tackle	Normal	Physical	40	100	35	Normal
1	Growl	Normal	Status	—	100	40	Many Others
1	Quick Attack	Normal	Physical	40	100	30	Normal
1	Peck	Flying	Physical	35	100	35	Normal
6	Quick Attack	Normal	Physical	40	100	30	Normal
10	Peck	Flying	Physical	35	100	35	Normal
13	Agility	Psychic	Status	—	—	30	Self
16	Flail	Normal	Physical	—	100	15	Normal
25	Roost	Flying	Status	—	—	10	Self
27	Razor Wind	Normal	Special	80	100	10	Many Others
31	Natural Gift	Normal	Physical	—	100	15	Normal
39	Flame Charge	Fire	Physical	50	100	20	Normal
44	Acrobatics	Flying	Physical	55	100	15	Normal
49	Me First	Normal	Status	—	—	20	Varies
55	Tailwind	Flying	Status	—	—	15	Your Side
60	Steel Wing	Steel	Physical	70	90	25	Normal
64	Brave Bird	Flying	Physical	120	100	15	Normal

❖ TM MOVES

No.	Name	Type	Kind	Pow.	Acc.	PP	Range
TM01	Work Up	Normal	Status	—	—	30	Self
TM06	Toxic	Poison	Status	—	90	10	Normal
TM08	Bulk Up	Fighting	Status	—	—	20	Self
TM10	Hidden Power	Normal	Special	60	100	15	Normal
TM11	Sunny Day	Fire	Status	—	—	5	Both Sides
TM12	Taunt	Dark	Status	—	100	20	Normal
TM15	Hyper Beam	Normal	Special	150	90	5	Normal
TM17	Protect	Normal	Status	—	—	10	Self
TM19	Roost	Flying	Status	—	—	10	Self
TM21	Frustration	Normal	Physical	—	100	20	Normal
TM22	Solar Beam	Grass	Special	120	100	10	Normal
TM27	Return	Normal	Physical	—	100	20	Normal
TM32	Double Team	Normal	Status	—	—	15	Self
TM35	Flamethrower	Fire	Special	90	100	15	Normal
TM38	Fire Blast	Fire	Special	110	85	5	Normal
TM40	Aerial Ace	Flying	Physical	60	—	20	Normal
TM42	Facade	Normal	Physical	70	100	20	Normal
TM43	Flame Charge	Fire	Physical	50	100	20	Normal
TM44	Rest	Psychic	Status	—	—	10	Self
TM45	Attract	Normal	Status	—	100	15	Normal
TM46	Thief	Dark	Physical	60	100	25	Normal
TM48	Round	Normal	Special	60	100	15	Normal
TM50	Overheat	Fire	Special	130	90	5	Normal
TM51	Steel Wing	Steel	Physical	70	90	25	Normal
TM61	Will-O-Wisp	Fire	Status	—	85	15	Normal
TM62	Acrobatics	Flying	Physical	55	100	15	Normal
TM68	Giga Impact	Normal	Physical	150	90	5	Normal

❖ MOVES TAUGHT BY PEOPLE

No.	Name	Type	Kind	Pow.	Acc.	PP	Range
TM75	Swords Dance	Normal	Status	—	—	20	Self
TM76	Fly	Flying	Physical	90	95	15	Normal
TM87	Swagger	Normal	Status	—	85	15	Normal
TM88	Sleep Talk	Normal	Status	—	—	10	Self
TM89	U-turn	Bug	Physical	70	100	20	Normal
TM90	Substitute	Normal	Status	—	—	10	Self
TM100	Confide	Normal	Status	—	—	20	Normal

❖ MOVES LEARNED WHEN EVOLVING

Name	Type	Kind	Pow.	Acc.	PP	Range

❖ EGG MOVES

Name	Type	Kind	Pow.	Acc.	PP	Range

❖ EXCLUSIVE Z-MOVE

Name	Base Move	Type	Kind	Pow.	Acc.	Range

Salandit

Alola Pokédex	Melemele	Akala	Ula'ula	Poni
161	—	088		

Toxic Lizard Pokémon

POISON · FIRE

HEIGHT: 2'00"
WEIGHT: 10.6 lbs.

It burns its bodily fluids to create a poisonous gas. When its enemies become disoriented from inhaling the gas, it attacks them.

Volcanoes or dry, craggy places are its home. It emanates a sweet-smelling poisonous gas that attracts bug Pokémon, then attacks them.

ABILITY
Corrosion

HIDDEN ABILITY
Oblivious

SPECIES STRENGTHS
HP	◆◆
Attack	◆◆
Defense	◆◆
Sp. Atk	◆◆◆
Sp. Def	◆◆
Speed	◆◆◆◆

EGG GROUPS
Monster · Dragon

ITEM SOMETIMES HELD BY WILD POKÉMON
Smoke Ball

Damage taken in normal battles

NORMAL ×1	FIGHTING ×0.5	ROCK ×1			
FIRE ×0.5	POISON ×0.5	GHOST ×1			
WATER ×2	GROUND ×4	DRAGON ×1			
GRASS ×0.25	FLYING ×1	DARK ×1			
ELECTRIC ×1	PSYCHIC ×2	STEEL ×0.5			
ICE ×2	BUG ×0.25	FAIRY ×0.25			

EVOLUTION

Salandit → Level up a female Salandit to Lv. 33 → Salazzle

MAIN WAY TO REGISTER IN THE POKÉDEX
Catch in the tall grass in Wela Volcano Park

Same form for male/female

❖ LEVEL-UP MOVES

Lv.	Name	Type	Kind	Pow.	Acc.	PP	Range
1	Scratch	Normal	Physical	40	100	35	Normal
1	Poison Gas	Poison	Status	—	90	40	Many Others
5	Ember	Fire	Special	40	100	25	Normal
8	Sweet Scent	Normal	Status	—	100	20	Many Others
13	Dragon Rage	Dragon	Special	—	100	10	Normal
16	Smog	Poison	Special	30	70	20	Normal
21	Double Slap	Normal	Physical	15	85	10	Normal
24	Flame Burst	Fire	Special	70	100	15	Normal
29	Toxic	Poison	Status	—	90	10	Normal
32	Nasty Plot	Dark	Status	—	—	20	Self
37	Venoshock	Poison	Special	65	100	10	Normal
40	Flamethrower	Fire	Special	90	100	15	Normal
45	Venom Drench	Poison	Status	—	100	20	Many Others
48	Dragon Pulse	Dragon	Special	85	100	10	Normal

❖ TM MOVES

No.	Name	Type	Kind	Pow.	Acc.	PP	Range
TM02	Dragon Claw	Dragon	Physical	80	100	15	Normal
TM06	Toxic	Poison	Status	—	90	10	Normal
TM09	Venoshock	Poison	Special	65	100	10	Normal
TM10	Hidden Power	Normal	Special	60	100	15	Normal
TM12	Taunt	Dark	Status	—	100	20	Normal
TM17	Protect	Normal	Status	—	—	10	Self
TM21	Frustration	Normal	Physical	—	100	20	Normal
TM27	Return	Normal	Physical	—	100	20	Normal
TM28	Leech Life	Bug	Physical	80	100	10	Normal
TM32	Double Team	Normal	Status	—	—	15	Self
TM34	Sludge Wave	Poison	Special	95	100	10	Adjacent
TM35	Flamethrower	Fire	Special	90	100	15	Normal
TM36	Sludge Bomb	Poison	Special	90	100	10	Normal
TM38	Fire Blast	Fire	Special	110	85	5	Normal
TM41	Torment	Dark	Status	—	100	15	Normal
TM42	Facade	Normal	Physical	70	100	20	Normal
TM43	Flame Charge	Fire	Physical	50	100	20	Normal
TM44	Rest	Psychic	Status	—	—	10	Self
TM45	Attract	Normal	Status	—	100	15	Normal
TM46	Thief	Dark	Physical	60	100	25	Normal
TM48	Round	Normal	Special	60	100	15	Normal
TM50	Overheat	Fire	Special	130	90	5	Normal
TM56	Fling	Dark	Physical	—	100	10	Normal
TM61	Will-O-Wisp	Fire	Status	—	85	15	Normal
TM65	Shadow Claw	Ghost	Physical	70	100	15	Normal
TM66	Payback	Dark	Physical	50	100	10	Normal
TM84	Poison Jab	Poison	Physical	80	100	20	Normal
TM87	Swagger	Normal	Status	—	85	15	Normal

❖ MOVES TAUGHT BY PEOPLE

No.	Name	Type	Kind	Pow.	Acc.	PP	Range
TM88	Sleep Talk	Normal	Status	—	—	10	Self
TM90	Substitute	Normal	Status	—	—	10	Self
TM100	Confide	Normal	Status	—	—	20	Normal

❖ MOVES LEARNED WHEN EVOLVING

Name	Type	Kind	Pow.	Acc.	PP	Range

❖ EGG MOVES

Name	Type	Kind	Pow.	Acc.	PP	Range
Belch	Poison	Special	120	90	10	Normal
Knock Off	Dark	Physical	65	100	20	Normal
Sand Attack	Ground	Status	—	100	15	Normal
Snatch	Dark	Status	—	—	10	Self
Fake Out	Normal	Physical	40	100	10	Normal

❖ EXCLUSIVE Z-MOVE

Name	Base Move	Type	Kind	Pow.	Acc.	Range

Salazzle

Alola Pokédex	Melemele	Akala	Ula'ula	Poni
162	—	089		

Toxic Lizard Pokémon

POISON · FIRE

HEIGHT: 3'11"
WEIGHT: 48.9 lbs.

For some reason, only females have been found. It creates a reverse harem of male Salandit that it lives with.

Filled with pheromones, its poisonous gas can be diluted to use in the production of luscious perfumes.

ABILITY
Corrosion

HIDDEN ABILITY
Oblivious

SPECIES STRENGTHS
HP	◆◆◆
Attack	◆◆◆
Defense	◆◆◆
Sp. Atk	◆◆◆◆◆◆
Sp. Def	◆◆◆◆
Speed	◆◆◆◆◆◆◆

EGG GROUPS
Monster · Dragon

ITEM SOMETIMES HELD BY WILD POKÉMON
—

Damage taken in normal battles

NORMAL ×1	FIGHTING ×0.5	ROCK ×1			
FIRE ×0.5	POISON ×0.5	GHOST ×1			
WATER ×2	GROUND ×4	DRAGON ×1			
GRASS ×0.25	FLYING ×1	DARK ×1			
ELECTRIC ×1	PSYCHIC ×2	STEEL ×0.5			
ICE ×0.5	BUG ×0.25	FAIRY ×0.25			

EVOLUTION

Salandit → Level up a female Salandit to Lv. 33 → Salazzle

MAIN WAY TO REGISTER IN THE POKÉDEX
Level up a female Salandit to Lv. 33

Female only

❖ LEVEL-UP MOVES

Lv.	Name	Type	Kind	Pow.	Acc.	PP	Range
1	Captivate	Normal	Status	—	100	20	Many Others
1	Disable	Normal	Status	—	100	20	Normal
1	Encore	Normal	Status	—	100	5	Normal
1	Torment	Dark	Status	—	100	15	Normal
1	Swagger	Normal	Status	—	85	15	Normal
1	Pound	Normal	Physical	40	100	35	Normal
1	Poison Gas	Poison	Status	—	90	40	Many Others
1	Ember	Fire	Special	40	100	25	Normal
1	Sweet Scent	Normal	Status	—	100	20	Many Others
8	Ember	Fire	Special	40	100	25	Normal
8	Sweet Scent	Normal	Status	—	100	20	Many Others
13	Dragon Rage	Dragon	Special	—	100	10	Normal
16	Smog	Poison	Special	30	70	20	Normal
21	Double Slap	Normal	Physical	15	85	10	Normal
24	Flame Burst	Fire	Special	70	100	15	Normal
29	Toxic	Poison	Status	—	90	10	Normal
32	Nasty Plot	Dark	Status	—	—	20	Self
39	Venoshock	Poison	Special	65	100	10	Normal
44	Flamethrower	Fire	Special	90	100	15	Normal
51	Venom Drench	Poison	Status	—	100	20	Many Others
56	Dragon Pulse	Dragon	Special	85	100	10	Normal

❖ TM MOVES

No.	Name	Type	Kind	Pow.	Acc.	PP	Range
TM02	Dragon Claw	Dragon	Physical	80	100	15	Normal
TM06	Toxic	Poison	Status	—	90	10	Normal
TM09	Venoshock	Poison	Special	65	100	10	Normal
TM10	Hidden Power	Normal	Special	60	100	15	Normal
TM12	Taunt	Dark	Status	—	100	20	Normal
TM17	Protect	Normal	Status	—	—	10	Self
TM21	Frustration	Normal	Physical	—	100	20	Normal
TM27	Return	Normal	Physical	—	100	20	Normal
TM28	Leech Life	Bug	Physical	80	100	10	Normal
TM32	Double Team	Normal	Status	—	—	15	Self
TM34	Sludge Wave	Poison	Special	95	100	10	Adjacent
TM35	Flamethrower	Fire	Special	90	100	15	Normal
TM36	Sludge Bomb	Poison	Special	90	100	10	Normal
TM38	Fire Blast	Fire	Special	110	85	5	Normal
TM41	Torment	Dark	Status	—	100	15	Normal
TM42	Facade	Normal	Physical	70	100	20	Normal
TM43	Flame Charge	Fire	Physical	50	100	20	Normal
TM44	Rest	Psychic	Status	—	—	10	Self
TM45	Attract	Normal	Status	—	100	15	Normal
TM46	Thief	Dark	Physical	60	100	25	Normal
TM48	Round	Normal	Special	60	100	15	Normal
TM50	Overheat	Fire	Special	130	90	5	Normal
TM56	Fling	Dark	Physical	—	100	10	Normal
TM61	Will-O-Wisp	Fire	Status	—	85	15	Normal
TM62	Acrobatics	Flying	Physical	55	100	15	Normal
TM65	Shadow Claw	Ghost	Physical	70	100	15	Normal
TM66	Payback	Dark	Physical	50	100	10	Normal
TM82	Dragon Tail	Dragon	Physical	60	90	10	Normal

❖ MOVES TAUGHT BY PEOPLE

No.	Name	Type	Kind	Pow.	Acc.	PP	Range
TM84	Poison Jab	Poison	Physical	80	100	20	Normal
TM87	Swagger	Normal	Status	—	85	15	Normal
TM88	Sleep Talk	Normal	Status	—	—	10	Self
TM90	Substitute	Normal	Status	—	—	10	Self
TM100	Confide	Normal	Status	—	—	20	Normal

❖ MOVES LEARNED WHEN EVOLVING

Name	Type	Kind	Pow.	Acc.	PP	Range
Captivate	Normal	Status	—	100	20	Many Others

❖ EGG MOVES

Name	Type	Kind	Pow.	Acc.	PP	Range

❖ EXCLUSIVE Z-MOVE

Name	Base Move	Type	Kind	Pow.	Acc.	Range

Alola Pokédex	Melemele	Akala	Ula'ula	Poni
163	—	090	—	—

Cubone

Lonely Pokémon

GROUND

HEIGHT: 1'04"
WEIGHT: 14.3 lbs.

When it thinks of its deceased mother, it weeps loudly. Mandibuzz that hear its cries will attack it from the air.

The skull it wears on its head is that of its dead mother. According to some, it will evolve when it comes to terms with the pain of her death.

Same form for male/female

ABILITY
Rock Head
Lightning Rod

HIDDEN ABILITY
Battle Armor

SPECIES STRENGTHS
HP ◆◆
Attack ◆◆◆
Defense ◆◆◆◆◆
Sp. Atk ◆◆
Sp. Def ◆◆◆
Speed ◆◆

EVOLUTION

Damage taken in normal battles

NORMAL	×1	FIGHTING	×1	ROCK	×0.5
FIRE	×1	POISON	×0.5	GHOST	×1
WATER	×2	GROUND	×1	DRAGON	×1
GRASS	×2	FLYING	×1	DARK	×1
ELECTRIC	×0	PSYCHIC	×1	STEEL	×1
ICE	×2	BUG	×1	FAIRY	×1

EGG GROUPS
Monster

ITEM SOMETIMES HELD BY WILD POKÉMON
Thick Club

MAIN WAY TO REGISTER IN THE POKÉDEX
Catch in the tall grass in Wela Volcano Park

❖ LEVEL-UP MOVES

Lv.	Name	Type	Kind	Pow.	Acc.	PP	Range
1	Growl	Normal	Status	—	100	40	Many Others
3	Tail Whip	Normal	Status	—	100	30	Many Others
7	Bone Club	Ground	Physical	65	85	20	Normal
11	Headbutt	Normal	Physical	70	100	15	Normal
13	Leer	Normal	Status	—	100	30	Many Others
17	Focus Energy	Normal	Status	—	—	30	Self
21	Bonemerang	Ground	Physical	50	90	10	Normal
23	Rage	Normal	Physical	20	100	20	Normal
27	False Swipe	Normal	Physical	40	100	40	Normal
31	Thrash	Normal	Physical	120	100	10	1 Random
33	Fling	Dark	Physical	—	100	10	Normal
37	Stomping Tantrum	Ground	Physical	75	100	10	Normal
41	Endeavor	Normal	Physical	—	100	5	Normal
43	Double-Edge	Normal	Physical	120	100	15	Normal
47	Retaliate	Normal	Physical	70	100	5	Normal
51	Bone Rush	Ground	Physical	25	90	10	Normal

❖ TM MOVES

No.	Name	Type	Kind	Pow.	Acc.	PP	Range
TM06	Toxic	Poison	Status		90	10	Normal
TM10	Hidden Power	Normal	Special	60	100	15	Normal
TM11	Sunny Day	Fire	Status	—	—	5	Both Sides
TM13	Ice Beam	Ice	Special	90	100	10	Normal
TM14	Blizzard	Ice	Special	110	70	5	Many Others
TM17	Protect	Normal	Status	—	—	10	Self
TM21	Frustration	Normal	Physical	—	100	20	Normal
TM23	Smack Down	Rock	Physical	50	100	15	Normal
TM26	Earthquake	Ground	Physical	100	100	10	Adjacent
TM27	Return	Normal	Physical	—	100	20	Normal
TM31	Brick Break	Fighting	Physical	75	100	15	Normal
TM32	Double Team	Normal	Status	—	—	15	Self
TM35	Flamethrower	Fire	Special	90	100	15	Normal
TM37	Sandstorm	Rock	Status	—	—	10	Both Sides
TM38	Fire Blast	Fire	Special	110	85	5	Normal
TM39	Rock Tomb	Rock	Physical	60	95	15	Normal
TM40	Aerial Ace	Flying	Physical	60	—	20	Normal
TM42	Facade	Normal	Physical	70	100	20	Normal
TM44	Rest	Psychic	Status	—	—	10	Self
TM45	Attract	Normal	Status	—	100	15	Normal
TM46	Thief	Dark	Physical	60	100	25	Normal
TM48	Round	Normal	Special	60	100	15	Normal
TM49	Echoed Voice	Normal	Special	40	100	15	Normal
TM54	False Swipe	Normal	Physical	40	100	40	Normal
TM56	Fling	Dark	Physical	—	100	10	Normal
TM59	Brutal Swing	Dark	Physical	60	100	20	Adjacent
TM75	Swords Dance	Normal	Status	—	—	20	Self
TM78	Bulldoze	Ground	Physical	60	100	20	Adjacent
TM80	Rock Slide	Rock	Physical	75	90	10	Many Others
TM87	Swagger	Normal	Status	—	85	15	Normal
TM88	Sleep Talk	Normal	Status	—	—	10	Self
TM90	Substitute	Normal	Status	—	—	10	Self
TM100	Confide	Normal	Status	—	—	20	Normal

❖ EXCLUSIVE Z-MOVE

Name	Base Move	Type	Kind	Pow.	Acc.	Range

❖ MOVES TAUGHT BY PEOPLE

Name	Type	Kind	Pow.	Acc.	PP	Range

❖ MOVES LEARNED WHEN EVOLVING

Name	Type	Kind	Pow.	Acc.	PP	Range

❖ EGG MOVES

Name	Type	Kind	Pow.	Acc.	PP	Range
Ancient Power	Rock	Special	60	100	5	Normal
Belly Drum	Normal	Status	—	—	10	Self
Screech	Normal	Status	—	85	40	Normal
Skull Bash	Normal	Physical	130	100	10	Normal
Perish Song	Normal	Status	—	—	5	Adjacent
Double Kick	Fighting	Physical	30	100	30	Normal
Iron Head	Steel	Physical	80	100	15	Normal
Detect	Fighting	Status	—	—	5	Self
Endure	Normal	Status	—	—	10	Self
Chip Away	Normal	Physical	70	100	20	Normal

Alola Pokédex	Melemele	Akala	Ula'ula	Poni
164	—	091	—	—

Marowak

Bone Keeper Pokémon

FIRE GHOST

HEIGHT: 3'03"
WEIGHT: 75.0 lbs.

The bones it possesses were once its mother's. Its mother's regrets have become like a vengeful spirit protecting this Pokémon.

Its custom is to mourn its lost companions. Mounds of dirt by the side of the road mark the graves of the Marowak.

❖ ALOLA FORM ❖

Same form for male/female

ABILITY
Cursed Body
Lightning Rod

HIDDEN ABILITY
Rock Head

SPECIES STRENGTHS
HP ◆◆
Attack ◆◆◆◆
Defense ◆◆◆◆◆◆
Sp. Atk ◆◆◆
Sp. Def ◆◆◆◆◆
Speed ◆◆◆

EVOLUTION

Damage taken in normal battles

NORMAL	×0	FIGHTING	×0	ROCK	×2
FIRE	×0.5	POISON	×0.5	GHOST	×2
WATER	×2	GROUND	×2	DRAGON	×1
GRASS	×0.5	FLYING	×1	DARK	×2
! ELECTRIC	×1	PSYCHIC	×1	STEEL	×0.5
ICE	×0.5	BUG	×0.25	FAIRY	×0.5

EGG GROUPS
Monster

ITEM SOMETIMES HELD BY WILD POKÉMON
—

MAIN WAY TO REGISTER IN THE POKÉDEX
Level up Cubone in the Alola region to Lv. 28 when it is nighttime in your game

❖ LEVEL-UP MOVES

Lv.	Name	Type	Kind	Pow.	Acc.	PP	Range
1	Growl	Normal	Status	—	100	40	Many Others
1	Tail Whip	Normal	Status	—	100	30	Many Others
1	Bone Club	Ground	Physical	65	85	20	Normal
1	Flame Wheel	Fire	Physical	60	100	25	Normal
3	Tail Whip	Normal	Status	—	100	30	Many Others
7	Bone Club	Ground	Physical	65	85	20	Normal
11	Flame Wheel	Fire	Physical	60	100	25	Normal
13	Leer	Normal	Status	—	100	30	Many Others
17	Hex	Ghost	Special	65	100	10	Normal
21	Bonemerang	Ground	Physical	50	90	10	Normal
23	Will-O-Wisp	Fire	Status	—	85	15	Normal
27	Shadow Bone	Ghost	Physical	85	100	10	Normal
33	Thrash	Normal	Physical	120	100	10	1 Random
37	Fling	Dark	Physical	—	100	10	Normal
43	Stomping Tantrum	Ground	Physical	75	100	10	Normal
49	Endeavor	Normal	Physical	—	100	5	Normal
53	Flare Blitz	Fire	Physical	120	100	15	Normal
59	Retaliate	Normal	Physical	70	100	5	Normal
65	Bone Rush	Ground	Physical	25	90	10	Normal

❖ TM MOVES

No.	Name	Type	Kind	Pow.	Acc.	PP	Range
TM06	Toxic	Poison	Status	—	90	10	Normal
TM10	Hidden Power	Normal	Special	60	100	15	Normal
TM11	Sunny Day	Fire	Status	—	—	5	Both Sides
TM13	Ice Beam	Ice	Special	90	100	10	Normal
TM14	Blizzard	Ice	Special	110	70	5	Many Others
TM15	Hyper Beam	Normal	Special	150	90	5	Normal
TM17	Protect	Normal	Status	—	—	10	Self
TM18	Rain Dance	Water	Status	—	—	5	Both Sides
TM21	Frustration	Normal	Physical	—	100	20	Normal
TM23	Smack Down	Rock	Physical	50	100	15	Normal
TM24	Thunderbolt	Electric	Special	90	100	15	Normal
TM25	Thunder	Electric	Special	110	70	10	Normal
TM26	Earthquake	Ground	Physical	100	100	10	Adjacent
TM27	Return	Normal	Physical	—	100	20	Normal
TM30	Shadow Ball	Ghost	Special	80	100	15	Normal
TM31	Brick Break	Fighting	Physical	75	100	15	Normal
TM32	Double Team	Normal	Status	—	—	15	Self
TM35	Flamethrower	Fire	Special	90	100	15	Normal
TM37	Sandstorm	Rock	Status	—	—	10	Both Sides
TM38	Fire Blast	Fire	Special	110	85	5	Normal
TM39	Rock Tomb	Rock	Physical	60	95	15	Normal
TM40	Aerial Ace	Flying	Physical	60	—	20	Normal
TM42	Facade	Normal	Physical	70	100	20	Normal
TM43	Flame Charge	Fire	Physical	50	100	20	Normal
TM44	Rest	Psychic	Status	—	—	10	Self
TM45	Attract	Normal	Status	—	100	15	Normal
TM46	Thief	Dark	Physical	60	100	25	Normal
TM48	Round	Normal	Special	60	100	15	Normal
TM49	Echoed Voice	Normal	Special	40	100	15	Normal
TM52	Focus Blast	Fighting	Special	120	70	5	Normal
TM54	False Swipe	Normal	Physical	40	100	40	Normal
TM56	Fling	Dark	Physical	—	100	10	Normal
TM59	Brutal Swing	Dark	Physical	60	100	20	Adjacent
TM61	Will-O-Wisp	Fire	Status	—	85	15	Normal
TM68	Giga Impact	Normal	Physical	150	90	5	Normal
TM71	Stone Edge	Rock	Physical	100	80	5	Normal
TM75	Swords Dance	Normal	Status	—	—	20	Self
TM78	Bulldoze	Ground	Physical	60	100	20	Adjacent
TM80	Rock Slide	Rock	Physical	75	90	10	Many Others
TM85	Dream Eater	Psychic	Special	100	100	15	Normal
TM87	Swagger	Normal	Status	—	85	15	Normal
TM88	Sleep Talk	Normal	Status	—	—	10	Self
TM90	Substitute	Normal	Status	—	—	10	Self
TM97	Dark Pulse	Dark	Special	80	100	15	Normal
TM100	Confide	Normal	Status	—	—	20	Normal

❖ EXCLUSIVE Z-MOVE

Name	Base Move	Type	Kind	Pow.	Acc.	Range

❖ MOVES TAUGHT BY PEOPLE

Name	Type	Kind	Pow.	Acc.	PP	Range

❖ MOVES LEARNED WHEN EVOLVING

Name	Type	Kind	Pow.	Acc.	PP	Range

❖ EGG MOVES

Name	Type	Kind	Pow.	Acc.	PP	Range

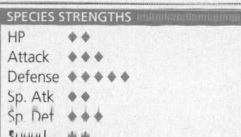

Alola Pokédex	Melemele	Akala	Ula'ula	Poni
165	—	092		

☑ Kangaskhan

Parent Pokémon

NORMAL

HEIGHT: 7'03"
WEIGHT: 176.4 lbs.

Kangaskhan's maternal love is so deep that it will brave death to protect its offspring.

The child in its pouch leaves home after roughly three years. That is the only time the mother is heard to cry wildly.

ABILITY
Early Bird
Scrappy

HIDDEN ABILITY
Inner Focus

SPECIES STRENGTHS
HP ◆◆◆◆
Attack ◆◆◆◆◆
Defense ◆◆◆
Sp. Atk ◆◆
Sp. Def ◆◆◆◆◆
Speed ◆◆◆◆◆◆

EVOLUTION

Does not evolve

EGG GROUPS
Monster

ITEM SOMETIMES HELD BY WILD POKÉMON

MAIN WAY TO REGISTER IN THE POKÉDEX
Catch in the tall grass in Wela Volcano Park

Female only

p. 210

Damage taken in normal battles
NORMAL ×1	FIGHTING ×2	ROCK ×1			
FIRE ×1	POISON ×1	GHOST ×0			
WATER ×1	GROUND ×1	DRAGON ×1			
GRASS ×1	FLYING ×1	DARK ×1			
ELECTRIC ×1	PSYCHIC ×1	STEEL ×1			
ICE ×1	BUG ×1	FAIRY ×1			

❖ LEVEL-UP MOVES
Lv.	Name	Type	Kind	Pow.	Acc.	PP	Range
1	Comet Punch	Normal	Physical	18	85	15	Normal
1	Leer	Normal	Status	—	100	30	Many Others
7	Fake Out	Normal	Physical	40	100	10	Normal
10	Tail Whip	Normal	Status	—	100	30	Many Others
13	Bite	Dark	Physical	60	100	25	Normal
19	Double Hit	Normal	Physical	35	90	10	Normal
22	Rage	Normal	Physical	20	100	20	Normal
25	Mega Punch	Normal	Physical	80	85	20	Normal
31	Chip Away	Normal	Physical	70	100	20	Normal
34	Dizzy Punch	Normal	Physical	70	100	10	Normal
37	Crunch	Dark	Physical	80	100	15	Normal
43	Endure	Normal	Status	—	—	10	Self
46	Outrage	Dragon	Physical	120	100	10	1 Random
49	Sucker Punch	Dark	Physical	70	100	5	Normal
50	Reversal	Fighting	Physical	—	100	15	Normal

❖ TM MOVES
No.	Name	Type	Kind	Pow.	Acc.	PP	Range
TM01	Work Up	Normal	Status	—	—	30	Self
TM05	Roar	Normal	Status	—	—	20	Normal
TM06	Toxic	Poison	Status	—	90	10	Normal
TM07	Hail	Ice	Status	—	—	10	Both Sides
TM10	Hidden Power	Normal	Special	60	100	15	Normal
TM11	Sunny Day	Fire	Status	—	—	5	Both Sides
TM13	Ice Beam	Ice	Special	90	100	10	Normal
TM14	Blizzard	Ice	Special	110	70	5	Many Others
TM15	Hyper Beam	Normal	Special	150	90	5	Normal
TM17	Protect	Normal	Status	—	—	10	Self
TM18	Rain Dance	Water	Status	—	—	5	Both Sides
TM21	Frustration	Normal	Physical	—	100	20	Normal
TM22	Solar Beam	Grass	Special	120	100	10	Normal
TM24	Thunderbolt	Electric	Special	90	100	15	Normal
TM25	Thunder	Electric	Special	110	70	10	Normal
TM26	Earthquake	Ground	Physical	100	100	10	Adjacent
TM27	Return	Normal	Physical	—	100	20	Normal
TM30	Shadow Ball	Ghost	Special	80	100	15	Normal
TM31	Brick Break	Fighting	Physical	75	100	15	Normal
TM32	Double Team	Normal	Status	—	—	15	Self
TM35	Flamethrower	Fire	Special	90	100	15	Normal
TM37	Sandstorm	Rock	Status	—	—	10	Both Sides
TM38	Fire Blast	Fire	Special	110	85	5	Normal
TM39	Rock Tomb	Rock	Physical	60	95	15	Normal
TM40	Aerial Ace	Flying	Physical	60	—	20	Normal
TM42	Facade	Normal	Physical	70	100	20	Normal
TM44	Rest	Psychic	Status	—	—	10	Self
TM45	Attract	Normal	Status	—	100	15	Normal
TM46	Thief	Dark	Physical	60	100	25	Normal
TM48	Round	Normal	Special	60	100	15	Normal
TM52	Focus Blast	Fighting	Special	120	70	5	Normal
TM56	Fling	Dark	Physical	—	100	10	Normal
TM65	Shadow Claw	Ghost	Physical	70	100	15	Normal
TM68	Giga Impact	Normal	Physical	150	90	5	Normal
TM78	Bulldoze	Ground	Physical	60	100	20	Adjacent
TM80	Rock Slide	Rock	Physical	75	90	10	Many Others
TM87	Swagger	Normal	Status	—	85	15	Normal
TM88	Sleep Talk	Normal	Status	—	—	10	Self
TM90	Substitute	Normal	Status	—	—	10	Self
TM94	Surf	Water	Special	90	100	15	Adjacent
TM100	Confide	Normal	Status	—	—	20	Normal

❖ MOVES TAUGHT BY PEOPLE
Name	Type	Kind	Pow.	Acc.	PP	Range

❖ MOVES LEARNED WHEN EVOLVING
Name	Type	Kind	Pow.	Acc.	PP	Range

❖ EGG MOVES
Name	Type	Kind	Pow.	Acc.	PP	Range
Stomp	Normal	Physical	65	100	20	Normal
Foresight	Normal	Status	—	—	40	Normal
Focus Energy	Normal	Status	—	—	30	Self
Disable	Normal	Status	—	100	20	Normal
Counter	Fighting	Physical	—	100	20	Varies
Crush Claw	Normal	Physical	75	95	10	Normal
Double-Edge	Normal	Physical	120	100	15	Normal
Endeavor	Normal	Physical	—	100	5	Normal
Hammer Arm	Fighting	Physical	100	90	10	Normal
Focus Punch	Fighting	Physical	150	100	20	Normal
Trump Card	Normal	Special	—	—	5	Normal
Uproar	Normal	Special	90	100	10	1 Random
Circle Throw	Fighting	Physical	60	90	10	Normal

❖ EXCLUSIVE Z-MOVE
Name	Base Move	Type	Kind	Pow.	Acc.	Range

Mega-Evolved Pokémon

Kangaskhan is a Pokémon that is capable of Mega Evolution, as you can see from the icon near its image above. Mega Evolution is an Evolution beyond all typical Evolutions and has some astounding effects: potentially changing a Pokémon's stats, Ability, and type, as well as its appearance. Once you get the Key Stone from Dexio on the Ancient Poni Path after becoming Champion, you can try it for yourself! To Mega Evolve, a Pokémon must be holding its specific Mega Stone and only certain Pokémon, like Kangaskhan, are capable of Mega Evolution. All of the Mega-Evolved Pokémon to be found in Alola can be found on pages 207 to 214 of this Pokédex.

When Kangaskhan Mega Evolves, its Ability changes to a very unique Ability: Parental Bond. Parental Bond allows Kangaskhan to attack twice in one turn. However, the power of the second attack will be 25% of the first attack, and this Ability does not affect moves that naturally strike multiple times or multiple targets. But another great way to consider using it is to use damaging moves with additional effects, such as lowering the opponent's stats or boosting your Pokémon's stats, because each hit can trigger these additional effects. Consider Mega Evolution when planning out your perfect battle teams!

Magby

Alola Pokédex	Melemele	Akala	Ula'ula	Poni
166	—	093	—	—

Live Coal Pokémon

FIRE

HEIGHT: 2'04"
WEIGHT: 47.2 lbs.

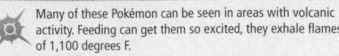

Many of these Pokémon can be seen in areas with volcanic activity. Feeding can get them so excited, they exhale flames of 1,100 degrees F.

A famous potter lives with a Magby. Apparently its soft flames produce fine works.

ABILITY
Flame Body

HIDDEN ABILITY
Vital Spirit

Damage taken in normal battles

NORMAL ×1	FIGHTING ×1	ROCK ×1
FIRE ×0.5	POISON ×1	GHOST ×1
WATER ×2	GROUND ×2	DRAGON ×1
GRASS ×0.5	FLYING ×1	DARK ×1
ELECTRIC ×1	PSYCHIC ×1	STEEL ×0.5
ICE ×0.5	BUG ×0.5	FAIRY ×0.5

SPECIES STRENGTHS
HP	◆◆◆
Attack	◆◆◆◆
Defense	◆◆
Sp. Atk	◆◆◆◆
Sp. Def	◆◆
Speed	◆◆◆◆◆

EGG GROUPS
No Eggs Discovered

ITEM SOMETIMES HELD BY WILD POKÉMON
Magmarizer

MAIN WAY TO REGISTER IN THE POKÉDEX
Catch in the tall grass in Wela Volcano Park

EVOLUTION

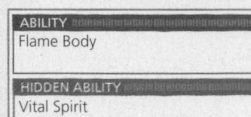

Magby → Lv. 30 → Magmar

Trade Magmar while holding Magmarizer

Magmortar

Same form for male/female

Magmar

Alola Pokédex	Melemele	Akala	Ula'ula	Poni
167	—	094	—	—

Spitfire Pokémon

FIRE

HEIGHT: 4'03"
WEIGHT: 98.1 lbs.

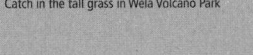

When it's tired, it leaps into the mouth of a volcano and soaks its body in magma to ease its weariness. Its body burns at 2,192 degrees F.

When angered, it spouts brilliant fire from all over its body. It doesn't calm down until its opponent has burned to ash.

ABILITY
Flame Body

HIDDEN ABILITY
Vital Spirit

Damage taken in normal battles

NORMAL ×1	FIGHTING ×1	ROCK ×1
FIRE ×0.5	POISON ×1	GHOST ×1
WATER ×2	GROUND ×2	DRAGON ×1
GRASS ×0.5	FLYING ×1	DARK ×1
ELECTRIC ×1	PSYCHIC ×1	STEEL ×0.5
ICE ×0.5	BUG ×0.5	FAIRY ×0.5

SPECIES STRENGTHS
HP	◆◆◆
Attack	◆◆◆◆◆
Defense	◆◆◆
Sp. Atk	◆◆◆◆◆
Sp. Def	◆◆◆◆◆
Speed	◆◆◆◆◆◆

EGG GROUPS
Human-like

ITEM SOMETIMES HELD BY WILD POKÉMON
Magmarizer

MAIN WAY TO REGISTER IN THE POKÉDEX
Catch in SOS battles against Magby in the tall grass in Wela Volcano Park

EVOLUTION

Magby → Lv. 30 → Magmar

Trade Magmar while holding Magmarizer

Magmortar

Same form for male/female

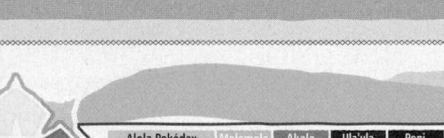

Magmortar

Alola Pokédex	Melemele	Akala	Ula'ula	Poni
168	—	095	—	—

Blast Pokémon

FIRE

HEIGHT: 5'03"
WEIGHT: 149.9 lbs.

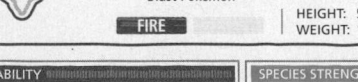

They dwell in volcanic craters. According to what is known, a single pair of male and female Magmortar lives in one volcano.

From its arm, it launches fireballs hotter than 3,500 degrees Fahrenheit. Its arm starts to melt when it fires a whole barrage.

ABILITY
Flame Body

HIDDEN ABILITY
Vital Spirit

Damage taken in normal battles

NORMAL ×1	FIGHTING ×1	ROCK ×2
FIRE ×0.5	POISON ×1	GHOST ×1
WATER ×2	GROUND ×1	DRAGON ×1
GRASS ×0.5	FLYING ×1	DARK ×1
ELECTRIC ×1	PSYCHIC ×1	STEEL ×0.5
ICE ×0.5	BUG ×0.5	FAIRY ×0.5

SPECIES STRENGTHS
HP	◆◆◆
Attack	◆◆◆◆◆
Defense	◆◆◆◆
Sp. Atk	◆◆◆◆◆◆◆
Sp. Def	◆◆◆◆◆◆
Speed	◆◆◆◆◆

EGG GROUPS
Human-like

ITEM SOMETIMES HELD BY WILD POKÉMON
—

MAIN WAY TO REGISTER IN THE POKÉDEX
Receive a Magmar holding a Magmarizer in a trade and it will evolve

EVOLUTION

Magby → Lv. 30 → Magmar

Trade Magmar while holding Magmarizer

Magmortar

Same form for male/female

MAGBY

❖ LEVEL-UP MOVES

Lv.	Name	Type	Kind	Pow.	Acc.	PP	Range
1	Smog	Poison	Special	30	70	20	Normal
1	Leer	Normal	Status	—	100	30	Many Others
5	Ember	Fire	Special	40	100	25	Normal
8	Smokescreen	Normal	Status	—	100	20	Normal
12	Feint Attack	Dark	Physical	60	—	20	Normal
15	Fire Spin	Fire	Special	35	85	15	Normal
19	Clear Smog	Poison	Special	50	—	15	Normal
22	Flame Burst	Fire	Special	70	100	15	Normal
26	Confuse Ray	Ghost	Status	—	100	10	Normal
29	Fire Punch	Fire	Physical	75	100	15	Normal
33	Lava Plume	Fire	Special	80	100	15	Adjacent
36	Sunny Day	Fire	Status	—	—	5	Both Sides
40	Flamethrower	Fire	Special	90	100	15	Normal
43	Fire Blast	Fire	Special	110	85	5	Normal

❖ TM MOVES

No.	Name	Type	Kind	Pow.	Acc.	PP	Range
TM06	Toxic	Poison	Status	—	90	10	Normal
TM10	Hidden Power	Normal	Special	60	100	15	Normal
TM11	Sunny Day	Fire	Status	—	—	5	Both Sides
TM17	Protect	Normal	Status	—	—	10	Self
TM21	Frustration	Normal	Physical	—	100	20	Normal
TM27	Return	Normal	Physical	—	100	20	Normal
TM29	Psychic	Psychic	Special	90	100	10	Normal
TM31	Brick Break	Fighting	Physical	75	100	15	Normal
TM32	Double Team	Normal	Status	—	—	15	Self
TM35	Flamethrower	Fire	Special	90	100	15	Normal
TM38	Fire Blast	Fire	Special	110	85	5	Normal
TM42	Facade	Normal	Physical	70	100	20	Normal
TM43	Flame Charge	Fire	Physical	50	100	20	Normal
TM44	Rest	Psychic	Status	—	—	10	Self
TM45	Attract	Normal	Status	—	100	15	Normal
TM46	Thief	Dark	Physical	60	100	25	Normal
TM48	Round	Normal	Status	60	100	15	Normal
TM50	Overheat	Fire	Special	130	90	5	Normal
TM56	Fling	Dark	Physical	—	100	10	Normal
TM61	Will-O-Wisp	Fire	Status	—	85	15	Normal
TM87	Swagger	Normal	Status	—	85	15	Normal
TM88	Sleep Talk	Normal	Status	—	—	10	Self
TM90	Substitute	Normal	Status	—	—	10	Self
TM100	Confide	Normal	Status	—	—	20	Normal

❖ MOVES TAUGHT BY PEOPLE

Name	Type	Kind	Pow.	Acc.	PP	Range

❖ MOVES LEARNED WHEN EVOLVING

Name	Type	Kind	Pow.	Acc.	PP	Range

❖ EGG MOVES

Name	Type	Kind	Pow.	Acc.	PP	Range
Karate Chop	Fighting	Physical	50	100	25	Normal
Mega Punch	Normal	Physical	80	85	20	Normal
Barrier	Psychic	Status	—	—	20	Self
Screech	Normal	Status	—	85	40	Normal
Cross Chop	Fighting	Physical	100	80	5	Normal
Thunder Punch	Electric	Physical	75	100	15	Normal
Mach Punch	Fighting	Physical	40	100	30	Normal
Dynamic Punch	Fighting	Physical	100	50	5	Normal
Flare Blitz	Fire	Physical	120	100	15	Normal
Belly Drum	Normal	Status	—	—	10	Self
Iron Tail	Steel	Physical	100	75	15	Normal
Focus Energy	Normal	Status	—	—	30	Self
Power Swap	Psychic	Status	—	—	10	Normal
Belch	Poison	Special	120	90	10	Normal

❖ EXCLUSIVE Z-MOVE

Name	Base Move	Type	Kind	Pow.	Acc.	Range

MAGMAR

❖ LEVEL-UP MOVES

Lv.	Name	Type	Kind	Pow.	Acc.	PP	Range
1	Smog	Poison	Special	30	70	20	Normal
1	Leer	Normal	Status	—	100	30	Many Others
1	Ember	Fire	Special	40	100	25	Normal
5	Ember	Fire	Special	40	100	25	Normal
8	Smokescreen	Normal	Status	—	100	20	Normal
12	Feint Attack	Dark	Physical	60	—	20	Normal
15	Fire Spin	Fire	Special	35	85	15	Normal
19	Clear Smog	Poison	Special	50	—	15	Normal
22	Flame Burst	Fire	Special	70	100	15	Normal
26	Confuse Ray	Ghost	Status	—	100	10	Normal
29	Fire Punch	Fire	Physical	75	100	15	Normal
36	Lava Plume	Fire	Special	80	100	15	Adjacent
42	Sunny Day	Fire	Status	—	—	5	Both Sides
49	Flamethrower	Fire	Special	90	100	15	Normal
55	Fire Blast	Fire	Special	110	85	5	Normal

❖ TM MOVES

No.	Name	Type	Kind	Pow.	Acc.	PP	Range
TM06	Toxic	Poison	Status	—	90	10	Normal
TM10	Hidden Power	Normal	Special	60	100	15	Normal
TM11	Sunny Day	Fire	Status	—	—	5	Both Sides
TM15	Hyper Beam	Normal	Special	150	90	5	Normal
TM17	Protect	Normal	Status	—	—	10	Self
TM21	Frustration	Normal	Physical	—	100	20	Normal
TM27	Return	Normal	Physical	—	100	20	Normal
TM29	Psychic	Psychic	Special	90	100	10	Normal
TM31	Brick Break	Fighting	Physical	75	100	15	Normal
TM32	Double Team	Normal	Status	—	—	15	Self
TM35	Flamethrower	Fire	Special	90	100	15	Normal
TM38	Fire Blast	Fire	Special	110	85	5	Normal
TM42	Facade	Normal	Physical	70	100	20	Normal
TM43	Flame Charge	Fire	Physical	50	100	20	Normal
TM44	Rest	Psychic	Status	—	—	10	Self
TM45	Attract	Normal	Status	—	100	15	Normal
TM46	Thief	Dark	Physical	60	100	25	Normal
TM47	Low Sweep	Fighting	Physical	65	100	20	Normal
TM48	Round	Normal	Status	60	100	15	Normal
TM50	Overheat	Fire	Special	130	90	5	Normal
TM52	Focus Blast	Fighting	Special	120	70	5	Normal
TM56	Fling	Dark	Physical	—	100	10	Normal
TM61	Will-O-Wisp	Fire	Status	—	85	15	Normal
TM68	Giga Impact	Normal	Physical	150	90	5	Normal
TM87	Swagger	Normal	Status	—	85	15	Normal
TM88	Sleep Talk	Normal	Status	—	—	10	Self
TM90	Substitute	Normal	Status	—	—	10	Self

❖ MOVES TAUGHT BY PEOPLE

No.	Name	Type	Kind	Pow.	Acc.	PP	Range
TM100	Confide	Normal	Status	—	—	20	Normal

❖ MOVES LEARNED WHEN EVOLVING

Name	Type	Kind	Pow.	Acc.	PP	Range

❖ EGG MOVES

Name	Type	Kind	Pow.	Acc.	PP	Range

❖ EXCLUSIVE Z-MOVE

Name	Base Move	Type	Kind	Pow.	Acc.	Range

MAGMORTAR

❖ LEVEL-UP MOVES

Lv.	Name	Type	Kind	Pow.	Acc.	PP	Range
1	Thunder Punch	Electric	Physical	75	100	15	Normal
1	Smog	Poison	Special	30	70	20	Normal
1	Leer	Normal	Status	—	100	30	Many Others
1	Ember	Fire	Special	40	100	25	Normal
1	Smokescreen	Normal	Status	—	100	20	Normal
5	Ember	Fire	Special	40	100	25	Normal
8	Smokescreen	Normal	Status	—	100	20	Normal
12	Feint Attack	Dark	Physical	60	—	20	Normal
15	Fire Spin	Fire	Special	35	85	15	Normal
19	Clear Smog	Poison	Special	50	—	15	Normal
22	Flame Burst	Fire	Special	70	100	15	Normal
26	Confuse Ray	Ghost	Status	—	100	10	Normal
29	Fire Punch	Fire	Physical	75	100	15	Normal
36	Lava Plume	Fire	Special	80	100	15	Adjacent
42	Sunny Day	Fire	Status	—	—	5	Both Sides
49	Flamethrower	Fire	Special	90	100	15	Normal
55	Fire Blast	Fire	Special	110	85	5	Normal
62	Hyper Beam	Normal	Special	150	90	5	Normal

❖ TM MOVES

No.	Name	Type	Kind	Pow.	Acc.	PP	Range
TM06	Toxic	Poison	Status	—	90	10	Normal
TM10	Hidden Power	Normal	Special	60	100	15	Normal
TM11	Sunny Day	Fire	Status	—	—	5	Both Sides
TM12	Taunt	Dark	Status	—	100	20	Normal
TM15	Hyper Beam	Normal	Special	150	90	5	Normal
TM17	Protect	Normal	Status	—	—	10	Self
TM21	Frustration	Normal	Physical	—	100	20	Normal
TM22	Solar Beam	Grass	Special	120	100	10	Normal
TM24	Thunderbolt	Electric	Special	90	100	15	Normal
TM26	Earthquake	Ground	Physical	100	100	10	Adjacent
TM27	Return	Normal	Physical	—	100	20	Normal
TM29	Psychic	Psychic	Special	90	100	10	Normal
TM31	Brick Break	Fighting	Physical	75	100	15	Normal
TM32	Double Team	Normal	Status	—	—	15	Self
TM35	Flamethrower	Fire	Special	90	100	15	Normal
TM38	Fire Blast	Fire	Special	110	85	5	Normal
TM39	Rock Tomb	Rock	Physical	60	95	15	Normal
TM41	Torment	Dark	Status	—	100	15	Normal
TM42	Facade	Normal	Physical	70	100	20	Normal
TM43	Flame Charge	Fire	Physical	50	100	20	Normal
TM44	Rest	Psychic	Status	—	—	10	Self
TM45	Attract	Normal	Status	—	100	15	Normal
TM46	Thief	Dark	Physical	60	100	25	Normal
TM47	Low Sweep	Fighting	Physical	65	100	20	Normal
TM48	Round	Normal	Status	60	100	15	Normal
TM50	Overheat	Fire	Special	130	90	5	Normal
TM52	Focus Blast	Fighting	Special	120	70	5	Normal

❖ MOVES TAUGHT BY PEOPLE

No.	Name	Type	Kind	Pow.	Acc.	PP	Range
TM56	Fling	Dark	Physical	—	100	10	Normal
TM61	Will-O-Wisp	Fire	Status	—	85	15	Normal
TM68	Giga Impact	Normal	Physical	150	90	5	Normal
TM78	Bulldoze	Ground	Physical	60	100	20	Adjacent
TM80	Rock Slide	Rock	Physical	75	90	10	Many Others
TM87	Swagger	Normal	Status	—	85	15	Normal
TM88	Sleep Talk	Normal	Status	—	—	10	Self
TM90	Substitute	Normal	Status	—	—	10	Self
TM100	Confide	Normal	Status	—	—	20	Normal

❖ MOVES LEARNED WHEN EVOLVING

Name	Type	Kind	Pow.	Acc.	PP	Range

❖ EGG MOVES

Name	Type	Kind	Pow.	Acc.	PP	Range

❖ EXCLUSIVE Z-MOVE

Name	Base Move	Type	Kind	Pow.	Acc.	Range

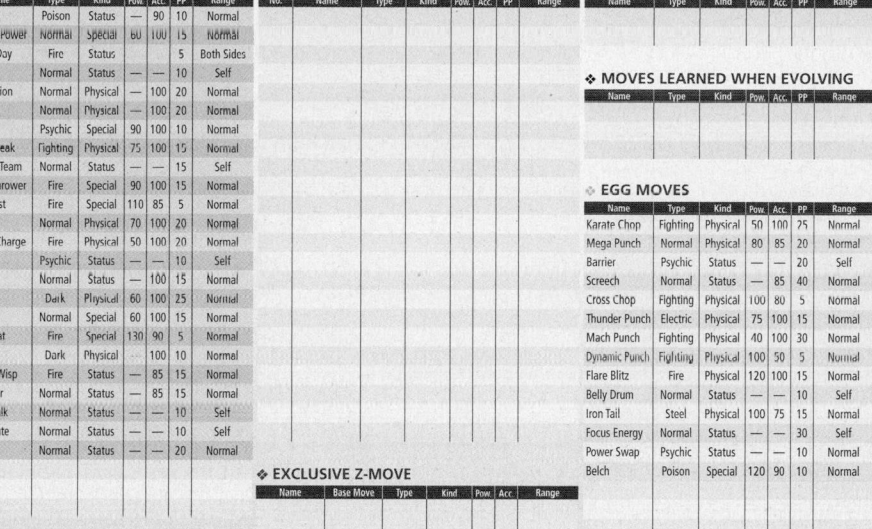
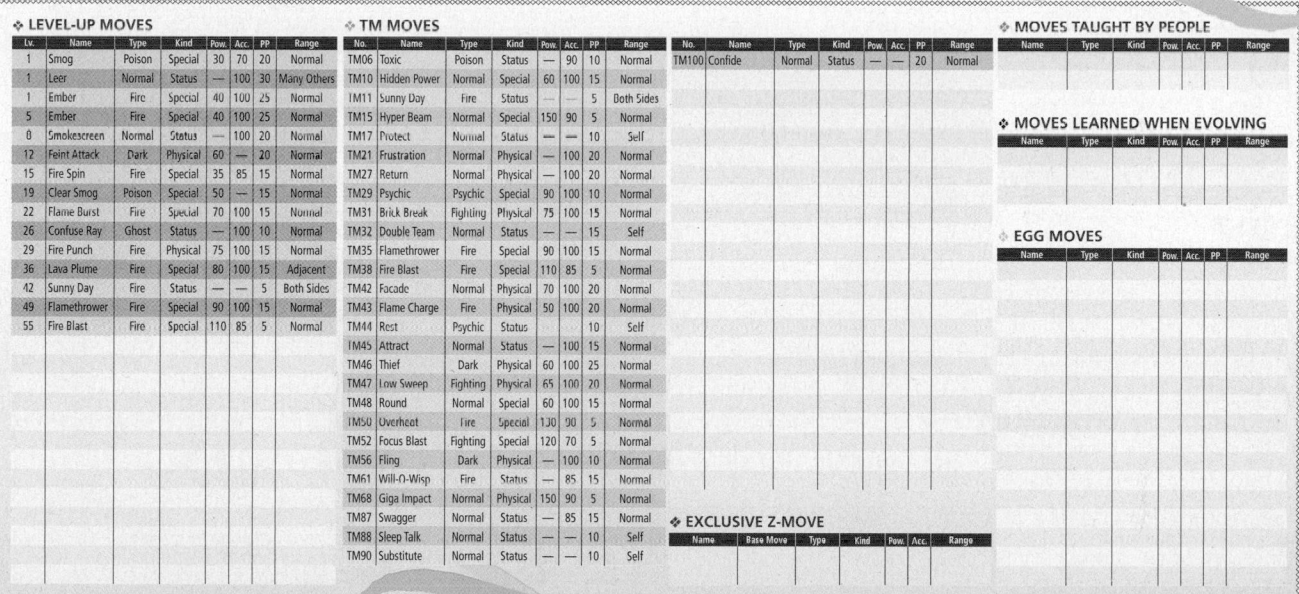

Stufful

Alola Pokédex	Melemele	Akala	Ula'ula	Poni
169	—	096	—	063

Flailing Pokémon

NORMAL FIGHTING

HEIGHT: 1'08"
WEIGHT: 15.0 lbs.

Despite its adorable appearance, when it gets angry and flails about, its arms and legs could knock a pro wrestler sprawling.

A touch from anyone except a known friend sends it into a surging frenzy. It's an incredibly dangerous Pokémon.

ABILITY
Fluffy
Klutz

HIDDEN ABILITY
Cute Charm

SPECIES STRENGTHS
HP ◆◆◆
Attack ◆◆◆◆
Defense ◆◆◆
Sp. Atk ◆◆
Sp. Def ◆◆◆
Speed ◆◆◆

EGG GROUPS
Field

ITEM SOMETIMES HELD BY WILD POKÉMON
—

Damage taken in normal battles
NORMAL	×1	FIGHTING	×2	ROCK	×0.5
FIRE	×1	POISON	×1	GHOST	×0
WATER	×1	GROUND	×1	DRAGON	×1
GRASS	×1	FLYING	×2	DARK	×1
ELECTRIC	×1	PSYCHIC	×2	STEEL	×1
ICE	×1	BUG	×0.5	FAIRY	×2

EVOLUTION
Stufful → Lv. 27 → Bewear

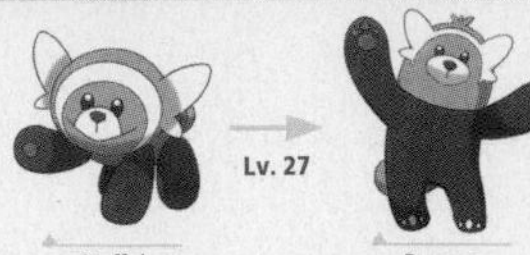

MAIN WAY TO REGISTER IN THE POKÉDEX
Catch in the tall grass in Akala Outskirts

Same form for male/female

❖ LEVEL-UP MOVES
Lv.	Name	Type	Kind	Pow.	Acc.	PP	Range
1	Tackle	Normal	Physical	40	100	35	Normal
1	Leer	Normal	Status	—	100	30	Many Others
5	Bide	Normal	Physical	—	—	10	Self
10	Baby-Doll Eyes	Fairy	Status	—	100	30	Normal
14	Brutal Swing	Dark	Physical	60	100	20	Adjacent
19	Flail	Normal	Physical	—	100	15	Normal
23	Payback	Dark	Physical	50	100	10	Normal
28	Take Down	Normal	Physical	90	85	20	Normal
32	Hammer Arm	Fighting	Physical	100	90	10	Normal
37	Thrash	Normal	Physical	120	100	10	1 Random
41	Pain Split	Normal	Status	—	—	20	Normal
46	Double-Edge	Normal	Physical	120	100	15	Normal
50	Superpower	Fighting	Physical	120	100	5	Normal

❖ TM MOVES
No.	Name	Type	Kind	Pow.	Acc.	PP	Range
TM01	Work Up	Normal	Status	—	—	30	Self
TM05	Roar	Normal	Status	—	—	20	Normal
TM06	Toxic	Poison	Status	—	90	10	Normal
TM08	Bulk Up	Fighting	Status	—	—	20	Self
TM10	Hidden Power	Normal	Special	60	100	15	Normal
TM12	Taunt	Dark	Status	—	100	20	Normal
TM17	Protect	Normal	Status	—	—	10	Self
TM21	Frustration	Normal	Physical	—	100	20	Normal
TM26	Earthquake	Ground	Physical	100	100	10	Adjacent
TM27	Return	Normal	Physical	—	100	20	Normal
TM31	Brick Break	Fighting	Physical	75	100	15	Normal
TM32	Double Team	Normal	Status	—	—	15	Self
TM39	Rock Tomb	Rock	Physical	60	95	15	Normal
TM40	Aerial Ace	Flying	Physical	60	—	20	Normal
TM42	Facade	Normal	Physical	70	100	20	Normal
TM44	Rest	Psychic	Status	—	—	10	Self
TM45	Attract	Normal	Status	—	100	15	Normal
TM47	Low Sweep	Fighting	Physical	65	100	20	Normal
TM48	Round	Normal	Special	60	100	15	Normal
TM52	Focus Blast	Fighting	Special	120	70	5	Normal
TM56	Fling	Dark	Physical	—	100	10	Normal
TM59	Brutal Swing	Dark	Physical	60	100	20	Adjacent
TM66	Payback	Dark	Physical	50	100	10	Normal
TM75	Swords Dance	Normal	Status	—	—	20	Self
TM78	Bulldoze	Ground	Physical	60	100	20	Many Others
TM80	Rock Slide	Rock	Physical	75	90	10	Many Others
TM87	Swagger	Normal	Status	—	85	15	Normal
TM88	Sleep Talk	Normal	Status	—	—	10	Self

❖ MOVES TAUGHT BY PEOPLE
No.	Name	Type	Kind	Pow.	Acc.	PP	Range
TM90	Substitute	Normal	Status	—	—	10	Self
TM100	Confide	Normal	Status	—	—	20	Normal

❖ MOVES LEARNED WHEN EVOLVING
Name	Type	Kind	Pow.	Acc.	PP	Range

❖ EGG MOVES
Name	Type	Kind	Pow.	Acc.	PP	Range
Ice Punch	Ice	Physical	75	100	15	Normal
Thunder Punch	Electric	Physical	75	100	15	Normal
Force Palm	Fighting	Physical	60	100	10	Normal
Endure	Normal	Status	—	—	10	Self
Wide Guard	Rock	Status	—	—	10	Your Side
Mega Kick	Normal	Physical	120	75	5	Normal
Stomping Tantrum	Ground	Physical	75	100	10	Normal

❖ EXCLUSIVE Z-MOVE
Name	Base Move	Type	Kind	Pow.	Acc.	Range

Bewear

Alola Pokédex	Melemele	Akala	Ula'ula	Poni
170	—	097	—	064

Strong Arm Pokémon

NORMAL FIGHTING

HEIGHT: 6'11"
WEIGHT: 297.6 lbs.

This immensely dangerous Pokémon possesses overwhelming physical strength. Its habitat is generally off-limits.

This Pokémon has the habit of hugging its companions. Many Trainers have left this world after their spines were squashed by its hug.

ABILITY
Fluffy
Klutz

HIDDEN ABILITY
Unnerve

SPECIES STRENGTHS
HP ◆◆◆◆◆
Attack ◆◆◆◆◆◆◆
Defense ◆◆◆◆
Sp. Atk ◆◆◆
Sp. Def ◆◆◆
Speed ◆◆◆◆

EGG GROUPS
Field

ITEM SOMETIMES HELD BY WILD POKÉMON
—

Damage taken in normal battles
NORMAL	×1	FIGHTING	×2	ROCK	×0.5
FIRE	×1	POISON	×1	GHOST	×0
WATER	×1	GROUND	×1	DRAGON	×1
GRASS	×1	FLYING	×2	DARK	×0.5
ELECTRIC	×1	PSYCHIC	×2	STEEL	×1
ICE	×1	BUG	×0.5	FAIRY	×2

EVOLUTION
Stufful → Lv. 27 → Bewear

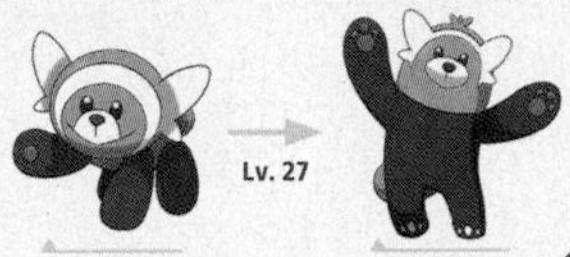

MAIN WAY TO REGISTER IN THE POKÉDEX
Level up Stufful to Lv. 27

Same form for male/female

❖ LEVEL-UP MOVES
Lv.	Name	Type	Kind	Pow.	Acc.	PP	Range
1	Bind	Normal	Physical	15	85	20	Normal
1	Tackle	Normal	Physical	40	100	35	Normal
1	Leer	Normal	Status	—	100	30	Many Others
5	Bide	Normal	Physical	—	—	10	Self
10	Baby-Doll Eyes	Fairy	Status	—	100	30	Normal
14	Brutal Swing	Dark	Physical	60	100	20	Adjacent
19	Flail	Normal	Physical	—	100	15	Normal
23	Payback	Dark	Physical	50	100	10	Normal
30	Take Down	Normal	Physical	90	85	20	Normal
36	Hammer Arm	Fighting	Physical	100	90	10	Normal
43	Thrash	Normal	Physical	120	100	10	1 Random
49	Pain Split	Normal	Status	—	—	20	Normal
56	Double-Edge	Normal	Physical	120	100	15	Normal
62	Superpower	Fighting	Physical	120	100	5	Normal

❖ TM MOVES
No.	Name	Type	Kind	Pow.	Acc.	PP	Range
TM01	Work Up	Normal	Status	—	—	30	Self
TM02	Dragon Claw	Dragon	Physical	80	100	15	Normal
TM05	Roar	Normal	Status	—	—	20	Normal
TM06	Toxic	Poison	Status	—	90	10	Normal
TM08	Bulk Up	Fighting	Status	—	—	20	Self
TM10	Hidden Power	Normal	Special	60	100	15	Normal
TM12	Taunt	Dark	Status	—	100	20	Normal
TM15	Hyper Beam	Normal	Special	150	90	5	Normal
TM17	Protect	Normal	Status	—	—	10	Self
TM21	Frustration	Normal	Physical	—	100	20	Normal
TM26	Earthquake	Ground	Physical	100	100	10	Adjacent
TM27	Return	Normal	Physical	—	100	20	Normal
TM31	Brick Break	Fighting	Physical	75	100	15	Normal
TM32	Double Team	Normal	Status	—	—	15	Self
TM39	Rock Tomb	Rock	Physical	60	95	15	Normal
TM40	Aerial Ace	Flying	Physical	60	—	20	Normal
TM42	Facade	Normal	Physical	70	100	20	Normal
TM44	Rest	Psychic	Status	—	—	10	Self
TM45	Attract	Normal	Status	—	100	15	Normal
TM47	Low Sweep	Fighting	Physical	65	100	20	Normal
TM48	Round	Normal	Special	60	100	15	Normal
TM52	Focus Blast	Fighting	Special	120	70	5	Normal
TM56	Fling	Dark	Physical	—	100	10	Normal
TM59	Brutal Swing	Dark	Physical	60	100	20	Adjacent
TM65	Shadow Claw	Ghost	Physical	70	100	15	Normal
TM66	Payback	Dark	Physical	50	100	10	Normal
TM68	Giga Impact	Normal	Physical	150	90	5	Normal
TM75	Swords Dance	Normal	Status	—	—	20	Self
TM78	Bulldoze	Ground	Physical	60	100	20	Adjacent
TM80	Rock Slide	Rock	Physical	75	90	10	Many Others
TM87	Swagger	Normal	Status	—	85	15	Normal
TM88	Sleep Talk	Normal	Status	—	—	10	Self
TM90	Substitute	Normal	Status	—	—	10	Self
TM100	Confide	Normal	Status	—	—	20	Normal

❖ MOVES TAUGHT BY PEOPLE
Name	Type	Kind	Pow.	Acc.	PP	Range

❖ MOVES LEARNED WHEN EVOLVING
Name	Type	Kind	Pow.	Acc.	PP	Range
Bind	Normal	Physical	15	85	20	Normal

❖ EGG MOVES
Name	Type	Kind	Pow.	Acc.	PP	Range

❖ EXCLUSIVE Z-MOVE
Name	Base Move	Type	Kind	Pow.	Acc.	Range

Pokémon with the Highest Species Strengths in Alola

The six stats are crucial to the combat strength of Pokémon, so you'll want at least a few with high stats in your team, whether you are focusing on physical moves (prioritize Attack and Defense), special moves (prioritize Sp. Atk and Sp. Def), or a mix of both. Here are some of the Pokémon with the highest species strengths available in the Alola region. Mega-Evolved Pokémon can be particularly powerful, and some of the Ultra Beasts also make an appearance!

Pokémon whose HP grows quickly

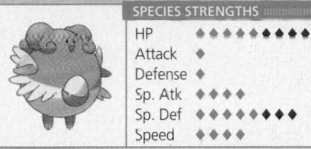

SPECIES STRENGTHS
- HP ◆◆◆◆◆◆◆◆◆◆
- Attack ◆
- Defense ◆
- Sp. Atk ◆◆◆◆
- Sp. Def ◆◆◆◆◆◆◆
- Speed ◆◆◆

Blissey `NORMAL`

SPECIES STRENGTHS
- HP ◆◆◆◆◆◆◆◆
- Attack ◆◆◆◆◆
- Defense ◆◆◆◆◆◆
- Sp. Atk ◆◆◆◆◆
- Sp. Def ◆◆◆◆◆
- Speed ◆◆◆◆◆

Zygarde (Complete Forme) `DRAGON` `GROUND`

SPECIES STRENGTHS
- HP ◆◆◆◆◆◆◆◆
- Attack ◆◆◆◆◆
- Defense ◆◆◆
- Sp. Atk ◆◆◆◆◆
- Sp. Def ◆◆◆
- Speed ◆◆◆

Guzzlord `DARK` `DRAGON`

Pokémon whose Attack grows quickly

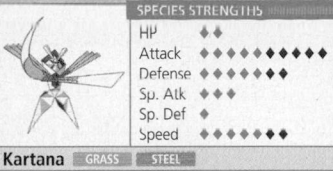

SPECIES STRENGTHS
- HP ◆◆◆
- Attack ◆◆◆◆◆◆◆◆
- Defense ◆◆◆◆◆◆◆
- Sp. Atk ◆◆◆
- Sp. Def ◆◆◆
- Speed ◆◆◆◆◆◆

Kartana `GRASS` `STEEL`

SPECIES STRENGTHS
- HP ◆◆◆◆
- Attack ◆◆◆◆◆◆◆◆
- Defense ◆◆◆
- Sp. Atk ◆◆◆◆
- Sp. Def ◆◆◆
- Speed ◆◆◆◆

Rampardos `ROCK`

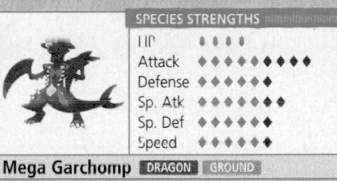

SPECIES STRENGTHS
- HP ◆◆◆◆
- Attack ◆◆◆◆◆◆◆
- Defense ◆◆◆◆◆◆
- Sp. Atk ◆◆◆◆◆◆
- Sp. Def ◆◆◆◆◆
- Speed ◆◆◆◆◆◆

Mega Garchomp `DRAGON` `GROUND`

Pokémon whose Defense grows quickly

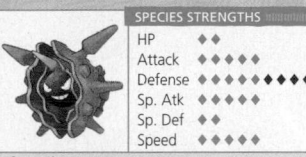

SPECIES STRENGTHS
- HP ◆◆
- Attack ◆◆◆◆
- Defense ◆◆◆◆◆◆◆◆
- Sp. Atk ◆◆◆
- Sp. Def ◆◆
- Speed ◆◆◆◆

Cloyster `WATER` `ICE`

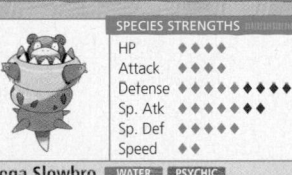

SPECIES STRENGTHS
- HP ◆◆◆◆
- Attack ◆◆◆◆
- Defense ◆◆◆◆◆◆◆◆
- Sp. Atk ◆◆◆◆◆◆◆
- Sp. Def ◆◆◆◆
- Speed ◆◆◆

Mega Slowbro `WATER` `PSYCHIC`

SPECIES STRENGTHS
- HP ◆◆◆
- Attack ◆◆◆
- Defense ◆◆◆◆◆◆◆◆
- Sp. Atk ◆◆◆
- Sp. Def ◆◆◆◆◆◆
- Speed ◆◆

Bastiodon `ROCK` `STEEL`

Pokémon whose Sp. Atk grows quickly

SPECIES STRENGTHS
- HP ◆◆
- Attack ◆◆
- Defense ◆◆◆◆
- Sp. Atk ◆◆◆◆◆◆◆◆
- Sp. Def ◆◆◆◆◆
- Speed ◆◆◆◆◆◆

Mega Alakazam `PSYCHIC`

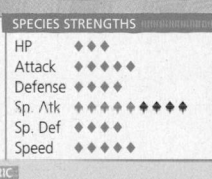

SPECIES STRENGTHS
- HP ◆◆◆
- Attack ◆◆◆◆◆
- Defense ◆◆◆◆◆
- Sp. Atk ◆◆◆◆◆◆◆◆
- Sp. Def ◆◆◆
- Speed ◆◆◆◆◆

Xurkitree `ELECTRIC`

SPECIES STRENGTHS
- HP ◆◆
- Attack ◆◆◆◆
- Defense ◆◆◆◆
- Sp. Atk ◆◆◆◆◆◆◆◆
- Sp. Def ◆◆◆◆◆
- Speed ◆◆◆◆◆◆◆

Mega Gengar `GHOST` `POISON`

Pokémon whose Sp. Def grows quickly

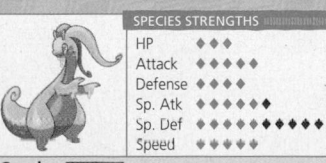

SPECIES STRENGTHS
- HP ◆◆◆
- Attack ◆◆◆◆◆
- Defense ◆◆◆◆
- Sp. Atk ◆◆◆◆◆◆
- Sp. Def ◆◆◆◆◆◆◆◆
- Speed ◆◆◆◆◆

Goodra `DRAGON`

SPECIES STRENGTHS
- HP ◆◆◆
- Attack ◆◆◆
- Defense ◆◆◆◆◆◆◆
- Sp. Atk ◆◆◆◆
- Sp. Def ◆◆◆◆◆◆◆◆
- Speed ◆◆◆

Probopass `ROCK` `STEEL`

SPECIES STRENGTHS
- HP ◆◆
- Attack ◆◆◆
- Defense ◆◆◆◆◆◆◆◆
- Sp. Atk ◆◆◆
- Sp. Def ◆◆◆◆◆◆◆◆
- Speed ◆◆◆

Carbink `ROCK` `FAIRY`

Pokémon whose Speed grows quickly

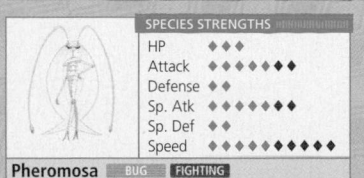

SPECIES STRENGTHS
- HP ◆◆◆
- Attack ◆◆◆◆◆◆◆
- Defense ◆◆
- Sp. Atk ◆◆◆◆◆◆◆
- Sp. Def ◆◆
- Speed ◆◆◆◆◆◆◆◆

Pheromosa `BUG` `FIGHTING`

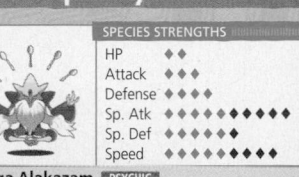

SPECIES STRENGTHS
- HP ◆◆
- Attack ◆◆◆
- Defense ◆◆◆◆
- Sp. Atk ◆◆◆◆◆◆◆◆
- Sp. Def ◆◆◆◆◆
- Speed ◆◆◆◆◆◆◆◆

Mega Alakazam `PSYCHIC`

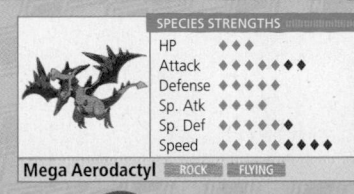

SPECIES STRENGTHS
- HP ◆◆◆
- Attack ◆◆◆◆◆◆◆
- Defense ◆◆◆◆◆
- Sp. Atk ◆◆◆
- Sp. Def ◆◆◆◆◆
- Speed ◆◆◆◆◆◆◆◆

Mega Aerodactyl `ROCK` `FLYING`

Bounsweet

Fruit Pokémon

Alola Pokédex	Melemele	Akala	Ula'ula	Poni
171	—	098	—	—

GRASS

HEIGHT: 1'00"
WEIGHT: 7.1 lbs.

A delectable aroma pours from its body. They are often swallowed whole by Toucannon lured by that wafting deliciousness.

Although it's too sugary for human consumption, Bounsweet's sweat can be watered down into a juice with just the right amount of sweetness.

ABILITY
Leaf Guard
Oblivious

HIDDEN ABILITY
Sweet Veil

Damage taken in normal battles

NORMAL ×1	FIGHTING ×1	ROCK ×1			
FIRE ×2	POISON ×2	GHOST ×1			
WATER ×0.5	GROUND ×0.5	DRAGON ×1			
GRASS ×0.5	FLYING ×2	DARK ×1			
ELECTRIC ×0.5	PSYCHIC ×1	STEEL ×1			
ICE ×2	BUG ×2	FAIRY ×1			

SPECIES STRENGTHS
HP ◆
Attack ◆◆
Defense ◆◆
Sp. Atk ◆◆
Sp. Def ◆◆
Speed ◆◆

EGG GROUPS
Grass

ITEM SOMETIMES HELD BY WILD POKÉMON
Grassy Seed

MAIN WAY TO REGISTER IN THE POKÉDEX
Catch in the tall grass in Lush Jungle

EVOLUTION

Bounsweet → Lv. 18 → Steenee

Level up after learning Stomp

Tsareena

Female only

Steenee

Fruit Pokémon

Alola Pokédex	Melemele	Akala	Ula'ula	Poni
172	—	099	—	—

GRASS

HEIGHT: 2'04"
WEIGHT: 18.1 lbs.

The sepals on its head developed to protect its body. These are quite hard, so even if pecked by bird Pokémon, this Pokémon is totally fine.

This Pokémon is always bouncing around energetically. Other Pokémon are attracted by its lively appearance and pleasant aroma.

ABILITY
Leaf Guard
Oblivious

HIDDEN ABILITY
Sweet Veil

Damage taken in normal battles

NORMAL ×1	FIGHTING ×1	ROCK ×1			
FIRE ×2	POISON ×2	GHOST ×1			
WATER ×0.5	GROUND ×0.5	DRAGON ×1			
GRASS ×0.5	FLYING ×2	DARK ×1			
ELECTRIC ×0.5	PSYCHIC ×1	STEEL ×1			
ICE ×2	BUG ×2	FAIRY ×1			

SPECIES STRENGTHS
HP ◆◆
Attack ◆◆
Defense ◆◆◆
Sp. Atk ◆◆
Sp. Def ◆◆
Speed ◆◆◆◆

EGG GROUPS
Grass

ITEM SOMETIMES HELD BY WILD POKÉMON
—

MAIN WAY TO REGISTER IN THE POKÉDEX
Receive in exchange for a Granbull in Seafolk Village

EVOLUTION

Bounsweet → Lv. 18 → Steenee

Level up after learning Stomp

Tsareena

Female only

Tsareena

Fruit Pokémon

Alola Pokédex	Melemele	Akala	Ula'ula	Poni
173	—	100	—	—

GRASS

HEIGHT: 3'11"
WEIGHT: 47.2 lbs.

Its long, striking legs aren't just for show but to be used to kick with skill. In victory, it shows off by kicking the defeated, laughing boisterously.

A Pokémon known for the beauty of its well-shaped legs, it sometimes appears as a mascot in advertisements for beauty salons.

ABILITY
Leaf Guard
Queenly Majesty

HIDDEN ABILITY
Sweet Veil

Damage taken in normal battles

NORMAL ×1	FIGHTING ×1	ROCK ×1			
FIRE ×2	POISON ×2	GHOST ×1			
WATER ×0.5	GROUND ×0.5	DRAGON ×1			
GRASS ×0.5	FLYING ×2	DARK ×1			
ELECTRIC ×0.5	PSYCHIC ×1	STEEL ×1			
ICE ×2	BUG ×2	FAIRY ×1			

SPECIES STRENGTHS
HP ◆◆◆
Attack ◆◆◆◆◆◆
Defense ◆◆◆◆◆◆
Sp. Atk ◆◆◆
Sp. Def ◆◆◆◆◆◆◆
Speed ◆◆◆◆◆

EGG GROUPS
Grass

ITEM SOMETIMES HELD BY WILD POKÉMON
—

MAIN WAY TO REGISTER IN THE POKÉDEX
Level up Steenee to Lv. 29 and have it learn Stomp, or teach it Stomp later and then level it up again

EVOLUTION

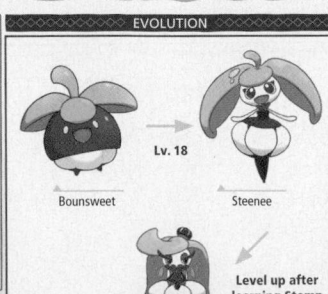

Bounsweet → Lv. 18 → Steenee

Level up after learning Stomp

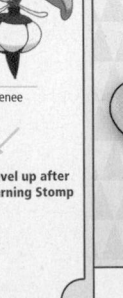

Tsareena

Female only

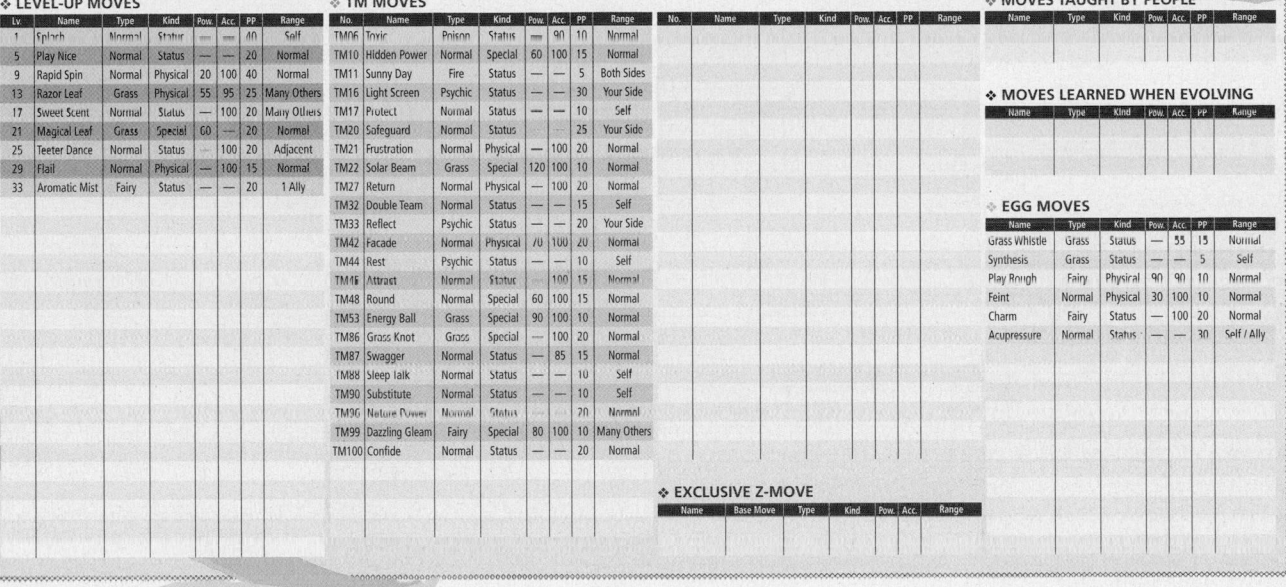

BOUNSWEET

LEVEL-UP MOVES
Lv.	Name	Type	Kind	Pow.	Acc.	PP	Range
1	Splash	Normal	Status	—	—	40	Self
5	Play Nice	Normal	Status	—	—	20	Normal
9	Rapid Spin	Normal	Physical	20	100	40	Normal
13	Razor Leaf	Grass	Physical	55	95	25	Many Others
17	Sweet Scent	Normal	Status	—	100	20	Many Others
21	Magical Leaf	Grass	Special	60	—	20	Normal
25	Teeter Dance	Normal	Status	—	100	20	Adjacent
29	Flail	Normal	Physical	—	100	15	Normal
33	Aromatic Mist	Fairy	Status	—	—	20	1 Ally

TM MOVES
No.	Name	Type	Kind	Pow.	Acc.	PP	Range
TM06	Toxic	Poison	Status	—	90	10	Normal
TM10	Hidden Power	Normal	Special	60	100	15	Normal
TM11	Sunny Day	Fire	Status	—	—	5	Both Sides
TM16	Light Screen	Psychic	Status	—	—	30	Your Side
TM17	Protect	Normal	Status	—	—	10	Self
TM20	Safeguard	Normal	Status	—	—	25	Your Side
TM21	Frustration	Normal	Physical	—	100	20	Normal
TM22	Solar Beam	Grass	Special	120	100	10	Normal
TM27	Return	Normal	Physical	—	100	20	Normal
TM32	Double Team	Normal	Status	—	—	15	Self
TM33	Reflect	Psychic	Status	—	—	20	Your Side
TM42	Facade	Normal	Physical	70	100	20	Normal
TM44	Rest	Psychic	Status	—	—	10	Self
TM45	Attract	Normal	Status	—	100	15	Normal
TM48	Round	Normal	Special	60	100	15	Normal
TM53	Energy Ball	Grass	Special	90	100	10	Normal
TM86	Grass Knot	Grass	Special	—	100	20	Normal
TM87	Swagger	Normal	Status	—	85	15	Normal
TM88	Sleep Talk	Normal	Status	—	—	10	Self
TM90	Substitute	Normal	Status	—	—	10	Self
TM96	Nature Power	Normal	Status	—	—	20	Normal
TM99	Dazzling Gleam	Fairy	Special	80	100	10	Many Others
TM100	Confide	Normal	Status	—	—	20	Normal

MOVES TAUGHT BY PEOPLE
No.	Name	Type	Kind	Pow.	Acc.	PP	Range

MOVES LEARNED WHEN EVOLVING
Name	Type	Kind	Pow.	Acc.	PP	Range

EGG MOVES
Name	Type	Kind	Pow.	Acc.	PP	Range
Grass Whistle	Grass	Status	—	55	15	Normal
Synthesis	Grass	Status	—	—	5	Self
Play Rough	Fairy	Physical	90	90	10	Normal
Feint	Normal	Physical	30	100	10	Normal
Charm	Fairy	Status	—	100	20	Normal
Acupressure	Normal	Status	—	—	30	Self / Ally

EXCLUSIVE Z-MOVE
Name	Base Move	Type	Kind	Pow.	Acc.	Range

STEENEE

LEVEL-UP MOVES
Lv.	Name	Type	Kind	Pow.	Acc.	PP	Range
1	Double Slap	Normal	Physical	15	85	10	Normal
1	Splash	Normal	Status	—	—	40	Self
1	Play Nice	Normal	Status	—	—	20	Normal
1	Rapid Spin	Normal	Physical	20	100	40	Normal
1	Razor Leaf	Grass	Physical	55	95	25	Many Others
5	Play Nice	Normal	Status	—	—	20	Normal
9	Rapid Spin	Normal	Physical	20	100	40	Normal
13	Razor Leaf	Grass	Physical	55	95	25	Many Others
17	Sweet Scent	Normal	Status	—	100	20	Many Others
21	Magical Leaf	Grass	Special	60	—	20	Normal
25	Teeter Dance	Normal	Status	—	100	20	Adjacent
29	Stomp	Normal	Physical	65	100	20	Normal
33	Aromatic Mist	Fairy	Status	—	—	20	1 Ally
37	Captivate	Normal	Status	—	100	20	Many Others
41	Aromatherapy	Grass	Status	—	—	5	Your Party
45	Leaf Storm	Grass	Special	130	90	5	Normal

TM MOVES
No.	Name	Type	Kind	Pow.	Acc.	PP	Range
TM06	Toxic	Poison	Status	—	90	10	Normal
TM10	Hidden Power	Normal	Special	60	100	15	Normal
TM11	Sunny Day	Fire	Status	—	—	5	Both Sides
TM16	Light Screen	Psychic	Status	—	—	30	Your Side
TM17	Protect	Normal	Status	—	—	10	Self
TM20	Safeguard	Normal	Status	—	—	25	Your Side
TM21	Frustration	Normal	Physical	—	100	20	Normal
TM22	Solar Beam	Grass	Special	120	100	10	Normal
TM27	Return	Normal	Physical	—	100	20	Normal
TM32	Double Team	Normal	Status	—	—	15	Self
TM33	Reflect	Psychic	Status	—	—	20	Your Side
TM42	Facade	Normal	Physical	70	100	20	Normal
TM44	Rest	Psychic	Status	—	—	10	Self
TM45	Attract	Normal	Status	—	100	15	Normal
TM47	Low Sweep	Fighting	Physical	65	100	20	Normal
TM48	Round	Normal	Special	60	100	15	Normal
TM53	Energy Ball	Grass	Special	90	100	10	Normal
TM56	Fling	Dark	Physical	—	100	10	Normal
TM66	Payback	Dark	Physical	50	100	10	Normal
TM86	Grass Knot	Grass	Special	—	100	20	Normal
TM87	Swagger	Normal	Status	—	85	15	Normal
TM88	Sleep Talk	Normal	Status	—	—	10	Self
TM90	Substitute	Normal	Status	—	—	10	Self
TM96	Nature Power	Normal	Status	—	—	20	Normal
TM99	Dazzling Gleam	Fairy	Special	80	100	10	Many Others
TM100	Confide	Normal	Status	—	—	20	Normal

MOVES TAUGHT BY PEOPLE
No.	Name	Type	Kind	Pow.	Acc.	PP	Range

MOVES LEARNED WHEN EVOLVING
Name	Type	Kind	Pow.	Acc.	PP	Range
Double Slap	Normal	Physical	15	85	10	Normal

EGG MOVES
Name	Type	Kind	Pow.	Acc.	PP	Range

EXCLUSIVE Z-MOVE
Name	Base Move	Type	Kind	Pow.	Acc.	Range

TSAREENA

LEVEL-UP MOVES
Lv.	Name	Type	Kind	Pow.	Acc.	PP	Range
1	Trop Kick	Grass	Physical	70	100	15	Normal
1	Double Slap	Normal	Physical	15	85	10	Normal
1	Splash	Normal	Status	—	—	40	Self
1	Swagger	Normal	Status	—	85	15	Normal
1	Rapid Spin	Normal	Physical	20	100	40	Normal
1	Razor Leaf	Grass	Physical	55	95	25	Many Others
5	Swagger	Normal	Status	—	85	15	Normal
9	Rapid Spin	Normal	Physical	20	100	40	Normal
13	Razor Leaf	Grass	Physical	55	95	25	Many Others
17	Sweet Scent	Normal	Status	—	100	20	Many Others
21	Magical Leaf	Grass	Special	60	—	20	Normal
25	Teeter Dance	Normal	Status	—	100	20	Adjacent
29	Stomp	Normal	Physical	65	100	20	Normal
33	Aromatic Mist	Fairy	Status	—	—	20	1 Ally
37	Captivate	Normal	Status	—	100	20	Many Others
41	Aromatherapy	Grass	Status	—	—	5	Your Party
45	Leaf Storm	Grass	Special	130	90	5	Normal
49	High Jump Kick	Fighting	Physical	130	90	10	Normal

TM MOVES
No.	Name	Type	Kind	Pow.	Acc.	PP	Range
TM06	Toxic	Poison	Status	—	90	10	Normal
TM10	Hidden Power	Normal	Special	60	100	15	Normal
TM11	Sunny Day	Fire	Status	—	—	5	Both Sides
TM16	Light Screen	Psychic	Status	—	—	30	Your Side
TM17	Protect	Normal	Status	—	—	10	Self
TM20	Safeguard	Normal	Status	—	—	25	Your Side
TM21	Frustration	Normal	Physical	—	100	20	Normal
TM22	Solar Beam	Grass	Special	120	100	10	Normal
TM27	Return	Normal	Physical	—	100	20	Normal
TM32	Double Team	Normal	Status	—	—	15	Self
TM33	Reflect	Psychic	Status	—	—	20	Your Side
TM42	Facade	Normal	Physical	70	100	20	Normal
TM44	Rest	Psychic	Status	—	—	10	Self
TM45	Attract	Normal	Status	—	100	15	Normal
TM47	Low Sweep	Fighting	Physical	65	100	20	Normal
TM48	Round	Normal	Special	60	100	15	Normal
TM53	Energy Ball	Grass	Special	90	100	10	Normal
TM56	Fling	Dark	Physical	—	100	10	Normal
TM62	Acrobatics	Flying	Physical	55	100	15	Normal
TM66	Payback	Dark	Physical	50	100	10	Normal
TM68	Giga Impact	Normal	Physical	150	90	5	Normal
TM86	Grass Knot	Grass	Special	—	100	20	Normal
TM87	Swagger	Normal	Status	—	85	15	Normal
TM88	Sleep Talk	Normal	Status	—	—	10	Self
TM89	U-turn	Bug	Physical	70	100	20	Normal
TM90	Substitute	Normal	Status	—	—	10	Self
TM96	Nature Power	Normal	Status	—	—	20	Normal

MOVES TAUGHT BY PEOPLE
No.	Name	Type	Kind	Pow.	Acc.	PP	Range
TM99	Dazzling Gleam	Fairy	Special	80	100	10	Many Others
TM100	Confide	Normal	Status	—	—	20	Normal

MOVES LEARNED WHEN EVOLVING
Name	Type	Kind	Pow.	Acc.	PP	Range
Trop Kick	Grass	Physical	70	100	15	Normal

EGG MOVES
Name	Type	Kind	Pow.	Acc.	PP	Range

EXCLUSIVE Z-MOVE
Name	Base Move	Type	Kind	Pow.	Acc.	Range

Comfey

Alola Pokédex	Melemele	Akala	Ula'ula	Poni
174	—	101		

Comfey
Posy Picker Pokémon

FAIRY

HEIGHT: 0'04"
WEIGHT: 0.7 lbs.

It attaches flowers to its highly nutritious vine. This revitalizes the flowers, and they give off an aromatic scent.

Baths prepared with the flowers from its vine have a relaxing effect, so this Pokémon is a hit with many people.

ABILITY
Flower Veil
Triage

HIDDEN ABILITY
Natural Cure

SPECIES STRENGTHS
HP	◆◆
Attack	◆◆◆
Defense	◆◆◆◆◆
Sp. Atk	◆◆◆◆
Sp. Def	◆◆◆◆◆◆◆
Speed	◆◆◆◆◆◆

EVOLUTION
Does not evolve

MAIN WAY TO REGISTER IN THE POKÉDEX
Catch in the tall grass in Lush Jungle

Damage taken in normal battles
NORMAL ×1	FIGHTING ×0.5	ROCK ×1			
FIRE ×1	POISON ×2	GHOST ×1			
WATER ×1	GROUND ×1	DRAGON ×0			
GRASS ×1	FLYING ×1	DARK ×1			
ELECTRIC ×1	PSYCHIC ×1	STEEL ×2			
ICE ×1	BUG ×0.5	FAIRY ×1			

EGG GROUPS
Grass

ITEM SOMETIMES HELD BY WILD POKÉMON
Misty Seed

Same form for male/female

❖ LEVEL-UP MOVES
Lv.	Name	Type	Kind	Pow.	Acc.	PP	Range
1	Helping Hand	Normal	Status	—	—	20	1 Ally
1	Vine Whip	Grass	Physical	45	100	25	Normal
1	Flower Shield	Fairy	Status	—	—	10	Varies
4	Leech Seed	Grass	Status	—	90	10	Normal
7	Draining Kiss	Fairy	Special	50	100	10	Normal
10	Magical Leaf	Grass	Special	60	—	20	Normal
13	Growth	Normal	Status	—	—	20	Self
16	Wrap	Normal	Physical	15	90	20	Normal
19	Sweet Kiss	Fairy	Status	—	75	10	Normal
22	Natural Gift	Normal	Physical	—	100	15	Normal
25	Petal Blizzard	Grass	Physical	90	100	15	Adjacent
28	Synthesis	Grass	Status	—	—	5	Self
31	Sweet Scent	Normal	Status	—	100	20	Many Others
34	Grass Knot	Grass	Special	—	100	20	Normal
37	Floral Healing	Fairy	Status	—	—	10	Self
40	Petal Dance	Grass	Special	120	100	10	1 Random
43	Aromatherapy	Grass	Status	—	—	5	Your Party
46	Grassy Terrain	Grass	Status	—	—	10	Both Sides
49	Play Rough	Fairy	Physical	90	90	10	Normal

❖ TM MOVES
No.	Name	Type	Kind	Pow.	Acc.	PP	Range
TM04	Calm Mind	Psychic	Status	—	—	20	Self
TM06	Toxic	Poison	Status	—	90	10	Normal
TM10	Hidden Power	Normal	Special	60	100	15	Normal
TM11	Sunny Day	Fire	Status	—	—	5	Both Sides
TM12	Taunt	Dark	Status	—	100	20	Normal
TM15	Hyper Beam	Normal	Special	150	90	5	Normal
TM16	Light Screen	Psychic	Status	—	—	30	Your Side
TM17	Protect	Normal	Status	—	—	10	Self
TM20	Safeguard	Normal	Status	—	—	25	Your Side
TM21	Frustration	Normal	Physical	—	100	20	Normal
TM22	Solar Beam	Grass	Special	120	100	10	Normal
TM27	Return	Normal	Physical	—	100	20	Normal
TM32	Double Team	Normal	Status	—	—	15	Self
TM42	Facade	Normal	Physical	70	100	20	Normal
TM44	Rest	Psychic	Status	—	—	10	Self
TM45	Attract	Normal	Status	—	100	15	Normal
TM46	Thief	Dark	Physical	60	100	25	Normal
TM48	Round	Normal	Special	60	100	15	Normal
TM49	Echoed Voice	Normal	Special	40	100	15	Normal
TM53	Energy Ball	Grass	Special	90	100	10	Normal
TM56	Fling	Dark	Physical	—	100	10	Normal
TM62	Acrobatics	Flying	Physical	55	100	15	Normal
TM77	Psych Up	Normal	Status	—	—	10	Normal
TM86	Grass Knot	Grass	Special	—	100	20	Normal
TM87	Swagger	Normal	Status	—	85	15	Normal
TM88	Sleep Talk	Normal	Status	—	—	10	Self
TM89	U-turn	Bug	Physical	70	100	20	Normal
TM90	Substitute	Normal	Status	—	—	10	Self

❖ MOVES TAUGHT BY PEOPLE
No.	Name	Type	Kind	Pow.	Acc.	PP	Range
TM92	Trick Room	Psychic	Status	—	—	5	Both Sides
TM96	Nature Power	Normal	Status	—	—	20	Normal
TM99	Dazzling Gleam	Fairy	Special	80	100	10	Many Others
TM100	Confide	Normal	Status	—	—	20	Normal

Name	Type	Kind	Pow.	Acc.	PP	Range

❖ MOVES LEARNED WHEN EVOLVING
Name	Type	Kind	Pow.	Acc.	PP	Range

❖ EGG MOVES
Name	Type	Kind	Pow.	Acc.	PP	Range
Endure	Normal	Status	—	—	10	Self
Amnesia	Psychic	Status	—	—	20	Self
After You	Normal	Status	—	—	15	Normal
Lucky Chant	Normal	Status	—	—	30	Your Side

❖ EXCLUSIVE Z-MOVE
Name	Base Move	Type	Kind	Pow.	Acc.	Range

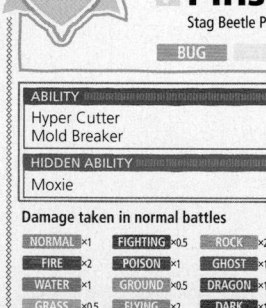

Pinsir

Alola Pokédex	Melemele	Akala	Ula'ula	Poni
175	—	102	—	065

Pinsir
Stag Beetle Pokémon

BUG

HEIGHT: 4'11"
WEIGHT: 121.3 lbs.

It grips its prey in its pincers and splits them apart. Although it is a powerful Pokémon, it can't deal with the cold.

One solid blow from its horns is enough to split apart a large tree. Its greatest rival in Alola is Vikavolt.

ABILITY
Hyper Cutter
Mold Breaker

HIDDEN ABILITY
Moxie

SPECIES STRENGTHS
HP	◆◆◆
Attack	◆◆◆◆◆◆◆
Defense	◆◆◆◆◆◆
Sp. Atk	◆◆◆
Sp. Def	◆◆◆◆
Speed	◆◆◆◆◆

EVOLUTION
Does not evolve

MAIN WAY TO REGISTER IN THE POKÉDEX
Catch in the tall grass in Lush Jungle

Damage taken in normal battles
NORMAL ×1	FIGHTING ×0.5	ROCK ×1			
FIRE ×2	POISON ×1	GHOST ×1			
WATER ×1	GROUND ×0.5	DRAGON ×1			
GRASS ×0.5	FLYING ×2	DARK ×1			
ELECTRIC ×1	PSYCHIC ×1	STEEL ×1			
ICE ×1	BUG ×1	FAIRY ×1			

EGG GROUPS
Bug

ITEM SOMETIMES HELD BY WILD POKÉMON
—

p. 210

Same form for male/female

❖ LEVEL-UP MOVES
Lv.	Name	Type	Kind	Pow.	Acc.	PP	Range
1	Vice Grip	Normal	Physical	55	100	30	Normal
1	Focus Energy	Normal	Status	—	—	30	Self
4	Bind	Normal	Physical	15	85	20	Normal
8	Seismic Toss	Fighting	Physical	—	100	20	Normal
11	Harden	Normal	Status	—	—	30	Self
15	Revenge	Fighting	Physical	60	100	10	Normal
18	Vital Throw	Fighting	Physical	70	—	10	Normal
22	Double Hit	Normal	Physical	35	90	10	Normal
26	Brick Break	Fighting	Physical	75	100	15	Normal
29	X-Scissor	Bug	Physical	80	100	15	Normal
33	Submission	Fighting	Physical	80	80	20	Normal
36	Storm Throw	Fighting	Physical	60	100	10	Normal
40	Swords Dance	Normal	Status	—	—	20	Self
43	Thrash	Normal	Physical	120	100	10	1 Random
47	Superpower	Fighting	Physical	120	100	5	Normal
50	Guillotine	Normal	Physical	—	30	5	Normal

❖ TM MOVES
No.	Name	Type	Kind	Pow.	Acc.	PP	Range
TM06	Toxic	Poison	Status	—	90	10	Normal
TM08	Bulk Up	Fighting	Status	—	—	20	Self
TM10	Hidden Power	Normal	Special	60	100	15	Normal
TM11	Sunny Day	Fire	Status	—	—	5	Both Sides
TM15	Hyper Beam	Normal	Special	150	90	5	Normal
TM17	Protect	Normal	Status	—	—	10	Self
TM18	Rain Dance	Water	Status	—	—	5	Both Sides
TM21	Frustration	Normal	Physical	—	100	20	Normal
TM23	Smack Down	Rock	Physical	50	100	15	Normal
TM26	Earthquake	Ground	Physical	100	100	10	Adjacent
TM27	Return	Normal	Physical	—	100	20	Normal
TM31	Brick Break	Fighting	Physical	75	100	15	Normal
TM32	Double Team	Normal	Status	—	—	15	Self
TM39	Rock Tomb	Rock	Physical	60	95	15	Normal
TM42	Facade	Normal	Physical	70	100	20	Normal
TM44	Rest	Psychic	Status	—	—	10	Self
TM45	Attract	Normal	Status	—	100	15	Normal
TM46	Thief	Dark	Physical	60	100	25	Normal
TM48	Round	Normal	Special	60	100	15	Normal
TM52	Focus Blast	Fighting	Special	120	70	5	Normal
TM54	False Swipe	Normal	Physical	40	100	40	Normal
TM56	Fling	Dark	Physical	—	100	10	Normal
TM59	Brutal Swing	Dark	Physical	60	100	20	Adjacent
TM68	Giga Impact	Normal	Physical	150	90	5	Normal
TM71	Stone Edge	Rock	Physical	100	80	5	Normal
TM75	Swords Dance	Normal	Status	—	—	20	Self
TM78	Bulldoze	Ground	Physical	60	100	20	Adjacent
TM80	Rock Slide	Rock	Physical	75	90	10	Many Others

❖ MOVES TAUGHT BY PEOPLE
No.	Name	Type	Kind	Pow.	Acc.	PP	Range
TM81	X-Scissor	Bug	Physical	80	100	15	Normal
TM87	Swagger	Normal	Status	—	85	15	Normal
TM88	Sleep Talk	Normal	Status	—	—	10	Self
TM90	Substitute	Normal	Status	—	—	10	Self
TM100	Confide	Normal	Status	—	—	20	Normal

❖ MOVES LEARNED WHEN EVOLVING
Name	Type	Kind	Pow.	Acc.	PP	Range

❖ EGG MOVES
Name	Type	Kind	Pow.	Acc.	PP	Range
Fury Attack	Normal	Physical	15	85	20	Normal
Flail	Normal	Physical	—	100	15	Normal
Feint Attack	Dark	Physical	60	—	20	Normal
Quick Attack	Normal	Physical	40	100	30	Normal
Close Combat	Fighting	Physical	120	100	5	Normal
Feint	Normal	Physical	30	100	10	Normal
Me First	Normal	Status	—	—	20	Varies
Bug Bite	Bug	Physical	60	100	20	Normal
Superpower	Fighting	Physical	120	100	5	Normal

❖ EXCLUSIVE Z-MOVE
Name	Base Move	Type	Kind	Pow.	Acc.	Range

Oranguru

Alola Pokédex	Melemele	Akala	Ula'ula	Poni
176	—	103	—	—

Oranguru
Sage Pokémon

NORMAL PSYCHIC

HEIGHT: 4'11"
WEIGHT: 167.6 lbs.

ORANGURU 176

Known for its extreme intelligence, this Pokémon will look down on inexperienced Trainers, so it's best suited to veteran Trainers.

Deep in the jungle, high in the lofty canopy, this Pokémon abides. On rare occasions, it shows up at the beach to match wits with Slowking.

Same form for male/female

ABILITY
Inner Focus
Telepathy

HIDDEN ABILITY
—

Damage taken in normal battles

NORMAL ×1	FIGHTING ×1	ROCK ×1
FIRE ×1	POISON ×1	GHOST ×0
WATER ×1	GROUND ×1	DRAGON ×1
GRASS ×1	FLYING ×1	DARK ×2
ELECTRIC ×1	PSYCHIC ×0.5	STEEL ×1
ICE ×1	BUG ×2	FAIRY ×1

SPECIES STRENGTHS
HP ◆◆◆
Attack ◆◆◆
Defense ◆◆◆◆
Sp. Atk ◆◆◆◆◆
Sp. Def ◆◆◆◆◆◆◆
Speed ◆◆◆◆

EGG GROUPS
Field

ITEM SOMETIMES HELD BY WILD POKÉMON
—

EVOLUTION
Does not evolve

MAIN WAY TO REGISTER IN THE POKÉDEX
Obtain in a trade in *Pokémon Sun* / Catch in the tall grass in Lush Jungle in *Pokémon Moon*

❖ LEVEL-UP MOVES

Lv.	Name	Type	Kind	Pow.	Acc.	PP	Range
1	Confusion	Psychic	Special	50	100	25	Normal
4	After You	Normal	Status	—	100	15	Normal
8	Taunt	Dark	Status	—	100	20	Normal
11	Quash	Dark	Status	—	100	15	Normal
15	Stored Power	Psychic	Special	20	100	10	Normal
18	Psych Up	Normal	Status	—	—	10	Normal
22	Feint Attack	Dark	Physical	60	—	20	Normal
25	Nasty Plot	Dark	Status	—	—	20	Self
29	Zen Headbutt	Psychic	Physical	80	90	15	Normal
32	Rain Dance	Water	Status	—	—	5	Both Sides
36	Foul Play	Dark	Physical	95	100	15	Normal
39	Calm Mind	Psychic	Status	—	—	20	Self
43	Psychic	Psychic	Special	90	100	10	Normal
46	Future Sight	Psychic	Special	120	100	10	Normal
50	Trick Room	Psychic	Status	—	—	5	Both Sides

❖ TM MOVES

No.	Name	Type	Kind	Pow.	Acc.	PP	Range
TM01	Work Up	Normal	Status	—	—	30	Self
TM03	Psyshock	Psychic	Special	80	100	10	Normal
TM04	Calm Mind	Psychic	Status	—	—	20	Self
TM06	Toxic	Poison	Status	—	90	10	Normal
TM10	Hidden Power	Normal	Special	60	100	15	Normal
TM11	Sunny Day	Fire	Status	—	—	5	Both Sides
TM12	Taunt	Dark	Status	—	100	20	Normal
TM16	Light Screen	Psychic	Status	—	—	30	Your Side
TM17	Protect	Normal	Status	—	—	10	Self
TM18	Rain Dance	Water	Status	—	—	5	Both Sides
TM20	Safeguard	Normal	Status	—	—	25	Your Side
TM21	Frustration	Normal	Physical	—	100	20	Normal
TM24	Thunderbolt	Electric	Special	90	100	15	Normal
TM25	Thunder	Electric	Special	110	70	10	Normal
TM26	Earthquake	Ground	Physical	100	100	10	Adjacent
TM27	Return	Normal	Physical	—	100	20	Normal
TM29	Psychic	Psychic	Special	90	100	10	Normal
TM30	Shadow Ball	Ghost	Special	80	100	15	Normal
TM31	Brick Break	Fighting	Physical	75	100	15	Normal
TM32	Double Team	Normal	Status	—	—	15	Self
TM33	Reflect	Psychic	Status	—	—	20	Your Side
TM42	Facade	Normal	Physical	70	100	20	Normal
TM44	Rest	Psychic	Status	—	—	10	Self
TM48	Round	Normal	Special	60	100	15	Normal
TM52	Focus Blast	Fighting	Special	120	70	5	Normal
TM53	Energy Ball	Grass	Special	90	100	10	Normal
TM56	Fling	Dark	Physical	—	100	10	Normal
TM57	Charge Beam	Electric	Special	50	90	10	Normal

No.	Name	Type	Kind	Pow.	Acc.	PP	Range
TM59	Brutal Swing	Dark	Physical	60	100	20	Adjacent
TM60	Quash	Dark	Status	—	100	15	Normal
TM63	Embargo	Dark	Status	—	100	15	Normal
TM66	Payback	Dark	Physical	50	100	10	Normal
TM68	Giga Impact	Normal	Physical	150	90	5	Normal
TM77	Psych Up	Normal	Status	—	—	10	Normal
TM78	Bulldoze	Ground	Physical	60	100	20	Adjacent
TM80	Rock Slide	Rock	Physical	75	90	10	Many Others
TM85	Dream Eater	Psychic	Special	100	100	15	Normal
TM87	Swagger	Normal	Status	—	85	15	Normal
TM88	Sleep Talk	Normal	Status	—	—	10	Self
TM90	Substitute	Normal	Status	—	—	10	Self
TM92	Trick Room	Psychic	Status	—	—	5	Both Sides
TM96	Nature Power	Normal	Status	—	—	20	Normal
TM100	Confide	Normal	Status	—	—	20	Normal

❖ MOVES TAUGHT BY PEOPLE

Name	Type	Kind	Pow.	Acc.	PP	Range

❖ MOVES LEARNED WHEN EVOLVING

Name	Type	Kind	Pow.	Acc.	PP	Range

❖ EGG MOVES

Name	Type	Kind	Pow.	Acc.	PP	Range
Extrasensory	Psychic	Special	80	100	20	Normal
Wonder Room	Psychic	Status	—	—	10	Both Sides
Psychic Terrain	Psychic	Status	—	—	10	Both Sides

❖ EXCLUSIVE Z-MOVE

Name	Base Move	Type	Kind	Pow.	Acc.	Range

Passimian

Alola Pokédex	Melemele	Akala	Ula'ula	Poni
177	—	104	—	—

Passimian
Teamwork Pokémon

FIGHTING

HEIGHT: 6'07"
WEIGHT: 182.5 lbs.

PASSIMIAN 177

They form groups of roughly 20 individuals. Their mutual bond is remarkable—they will never let down a comrade.

They battle with hard berries for weapons. Their techniques are passed from the boss to the group, generation upon generation.

Same form for male/female

ABILITY
Receiver

HIDDEN ABILITY
—

Damage taken in normal battles

NORMAL ×1	FIGHTING ×1	ROCK ×0.5
FIRE ×1	POISON ×1	GHOST ×1
WATER ×1	GROUND ×1	DRAGON ×1
GRASS ×1	FLYING ×2	DARK ×0.5
ELECTRIC ×1	PSYCHIC ×2	STEEL ×1
ICE ×1	BUG ×0.5	FAIRY ×2

SPECIES STRENGTHS
HP ◆◆◆◆
Attack ◆◆◆◆◆◆◆
Defense ◆◆◆◆◆
Sp. Atk ◆◆
Sp. Def ◆◆◆◆
Speed ◆◆◆◆◆

EGG GROUPS
Field

ITEM SOMETIMES HELD BY WILD POKÉMON
—

EVOLUTION
Does not evolve

MAIN WAY TO REGISTER IN THE POKÉDEX
Catch in the tall grass in Lush Jungle in *Pokémon Sun* / Obtain in a trade in *Pokémon Moon*

❖ LEVEL-UP MOVES

Lv.	Name	Type	Kind	Pow.	Acc.	PP	Range
1	Tackle	Normal	Physical	40	100	35	Normal
4	Leer	Normal	Status	—	100	30	Many Others
8	Rock Smash	Fighting	Physical	40	100	15	Normal
11	Focus Energy	Normal	Status	—	—	30	Self
15	Beat Up	Dark	Physical	—	100	10	Normal
18	Scary Face	Normal	Status	—	100	10	Normal
22	Take Down	Normal	Physical	90	85	20	Normal
25	Bestow	Normal	Status	—	—	15	Normal
29	Thrash	Normal	Physical	120	100	10	1 Random
32	Bulk Up	Fighting	Status	—	—	20	Self
36	Double-Edge	Normal	Physical	120	100	15	Normal
39	Fling	Dark	Physical	—	100	10	Normal
43	Close Combat	Fighting	Physical	120	100	5	Normal
46	Reversal	Fighting	Physical	—	100	15	Normal
50	Giga Impact	Normal	Physical	150	90	5	Normal

❖ TM MOVES

No.	Name	Type	Kind	Pow.	Acc.	PP	Range
TM01	Work Up	Normal	Status	—	—	30	Self
TM06	Toxic	Poison	Status	—	90	10	Normal
TM08	Bulk Up	Fighting	Status	—	—	20	Self
TM10	Hidden Power	Normal	Special	60	100	15	Normal
TM11	Sunny Day	Fire	Status	—	—	5	Both Sides
TM12	Taunt	Dark	Status	—	100	20	Normal
TM15	Hyper Beam	Normal	Special	150	90	5	Normal
TM17	Protect	Normal	Status	—	—	10	Self
TM18	Rain Dance	Water	Status	—	—	5	Both Sides
TM21	Frustration	Normal	Physical	—	100	20	Normal
TM23	Smack Down	Rock	Physical	50	100	15	Normal
TM26	Earthquake	Ground	Physical	100	100	10	Adjacent
TM27	Return	Normal	Physical	—	100	20	Normal
TM30	Shadow Ball	Ghost	Special	80	100	15	Normal
TM31	Brick Break	Fighting	Physical	75	100	15	Normal
TM32	Double Team	Normal	Status	—	—	15	Self
TM39	Rock Tomb	Rock	Physical	60	95	15	Normal
TM40	Aerial Ace	Flying	Physical	60	—	20	Normal
TM42	Facade	Normal	Physical	70	100	20	Normal
TM44	Rest	Psychic	Status	—	—	10	Self
TM45	Attract	Normal	Status	—	100	15	Normal
TM46	Thief	Dark	Physical	60	100	25	Normal
TM47	Low Sweep	Fighting	Physical	65	100	20	Normal
TM48	Round	Normal	Special	60	100	15	Normal
TM52	Focus Blast	Fighting	Special	120	70	5	Normal
TM53	Energy Ball	Grass	Special	90	100	10	Normal
TM56	Fling	Dark	Physical	—	100	10	Normal
TM59	Brutal Swing	Dark	Physical	60	100	20	Adjacent

No.	Name	Type	Kind	Pow.	Acc.	PP	Range
TM62	Acrobatics	Flying	Physical	55	100	15	Normal
TM66	Payback	Dark	Physical	50	100	10	Normal
TM68	Giga Impact	Normal	Physical	150	90	5	Normal
TM74	Gyro Ball	Steel	Physical	—	100	5	Normal
TM78	Bulldoze	Ground	Physical	60	100	20	Adjacent
TM80	Rock Slide	Rock	Physical	75	90	10	Many Others
TM86	Grass Knot	Grass	Special	—	100	20	Normal
TM87	Swagger	Normal	Status	—	85	15	Normal
TM88	Sleep Talk	Normal	Status	—	—	10	Self
TM89	U-turn	Bug	Physical	70	100	20	Normal
TM90	Substitute	Normal	Status	—	—	10	Self
TM100	Confide	Normal	Status	—	—	20	Normal

❖ MOVES TAUGHT BY PEOPLE

Name	Type	Kind	Pow.	Acc.	PP	Range

❖ MOVES LEARNED WHEN EVOLVING

Name	Type	Kind	Pow.	Acc.	PP	Range

❖ EGG MOVES

Name	Type	Kind	Pow.	Acc.	PP	Range
Seismic Toss	Fighting	Physical	—	100	20	Normal
Vital Throw	Fighting	Physical	70	—	10	Normal
Quick Guard	Fighting	Status	—	—	15	Your Side
Iron Head	Steel	Physical	80	100	15	Normal
Quick Attack	Normal	Physical	40	100	30	Normal
Feint	Normal	Physical	30	100	10	Normal

❖ EXCLUSIVE Z-MOVE

Name	Base Move	Type	Kind	Pow.	Acc.	Range

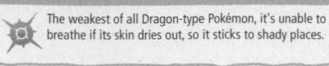

Alola Pokédex	Melemele	Akala	Ula'ula	Poni
178	—	105	074	066

Goomy

Soft Tissue Pokémon

DRAGON

HEIGHT: 1'00"
WEIGHT: 6.2 lbs.

The weakest of all Dragon-type Pokémon, it's unable to breathe if its skin dries out, so it sticks to shady places.

Its source of protection is its slimy, germ-laden mucous membrane. Anyone who touches it needs some thorough hand-washing.

ABILITY
Sap Sipper
Hydration

HIDDEN ABILITY
Gooey

Damage taken in normal battles

NORMAL ×1	FIGHTING ×1	ROCK ×1			
FIRE ×0.5	POISON ×1	GHOST ×1			
WATER ×0.5	GROUND ×1	DRAGON ×2			
GRASS ×0.5	FLYING ×1	DARK ×1			
ELECTRIC ×0.5	PSYCHIC ×1	STEEL ×1			
ICE ×2	BUG ×1	FAIRY ×2			

SPECIES STRENGTHS
HP ◆◆
Attack ◆◆◆
Defense ◆◆
Sp. Atk ◆◆◆
Sp. Def ◆◆◆◆
Speed ◆◆◆

EGG GROUPS
Dragon

ITEM SOMETIMES HELD BY WILD POKÉMON
Shed Shell

MAIN WAY TO REGISTER IN THE POKÉDEX
Catch in SOS battles in the tall grass during rain in Lush Jungle

EVOLUTION

Goomy → Lv. 40 → Sliggoo
Level up to Lv. 50 in the rain
Goodra

Same form for male/female

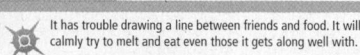

Alola Pokédex	Melemele	Akala	Ula'ula	Poni
179	—	106	075	067

Sliggoo

Soft Tissue Pokémon

DRAGON

HEIGHT: 2'07"
WEIGHT: 38.6 lbs.

It has trouble drawing a line between friends and food. It will calmly try to melt and eat even those it gets along well with.

This Pokémon's mucous can dissolve anything. Toothless, it sprays mucous on its prey. Once they're nicely dissolved, it slurps them up.

ABILITY
Sap Sipper
Hydration

HIDDEN ABILITY
Gooey

Damage taken in normal battles

NORMAL ×1	FIGHTING ×1	ROCK ×1			
FIRE ×0.5	POISON ×1	GHOST ×1			
WATER ×0.5	GROUND ×1	DRAGON ×2			
GRASS ×0.5	FLYING ×1	DARK ×1			
ELECTRIC ×0.5	PSYCHIC ×1	STEEL ×1			
ICE ×2	BUG ×1	FAIRY ×2			

SPECIES STRENGTHS
HP ◆◆◆
Attack ◆◆◆◆
Defense ◆◆◆
Sp. Atk ◆◆◆
Sp. Def ◆◆◆◆◆◆◆◆
Speed ◆◆◆◆

EGG GROUPS
Dragon

ITEM SOMETIMES HELD BY WILD POKÉMON
Shed Shell

MAIN WAY TO REGISTER IN THE POKÉDEX
Catch in SOS battles in the tall grass during rain on Exeggutor Island

EVOLUTION

Goomy → Lv. 40 → Sliggoo
Level up to Lv. 50 in the rain
Goodra

Same form for male/female

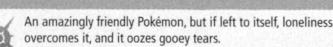

Alola Pokédex	Melemele	Akala	Ula'ula	Poni
180	—	107	076	068

Goodra

Dragon Pokémon

DRAGON

HEIGHT: 6'07"
WEIGHT: 331.8 lbs.

An amazingly friendly Pokémon, but if left to itself, loneliness overcomes it, and it oozes gooey tears.

It gets picked on because it's meek. But then, whoever teased it gets to feel the full force of its horns and a good swatting from its thick tail.

ABILITY
Sap Sipper
Hydration

HIDDEN ABILITY
Gooey

Damage taken in normal battles

NORMAL ×1	FIGHTING ×1	ROCK ×1			
FIRE ×0.5	POISON ×1	GHOST ×1			
WATER ×0.5	GROUND ×1	DRAGON ×2			
GRASS ×0.5	FLYING ×1	DARK ×1			
ELECTRIC ×0.5	PSYCHIC ×1	STEEL ×1			
ICE ×2	BUG ×1	FAIRY ×2			

SPECIES STRENGTHS
HP ◆◆◆
Attack ◆◆◆◆◆
Defense ◆◆◆◆◆
Sp. Atk ◆◆◆◆◆◆
Sp. Def ◆◆◆◆◆◆◆◆◆
Speed ◆◆◆◆◆

EGG GROUPS
Dragon

ITEM SOMETIMES HELD BY WILD POKÉMON
—

MAIN WAY TO REGISTER IN THE POKÉDEX
Level up Sliggoo to Lv. 50 during rain

EVOLUTION

Goomy → Lv. 40 → Sliggoo
Level up to Lv. 50 in the rain
Goodra

Same form for male/female

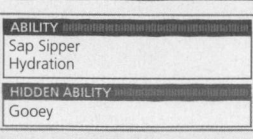
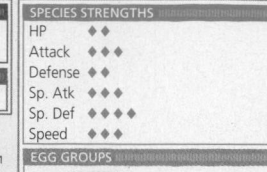
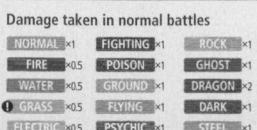
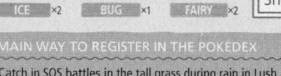
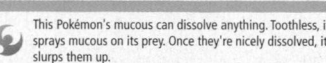
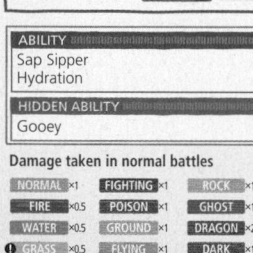
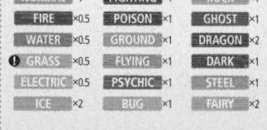

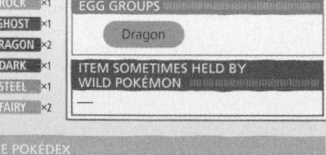

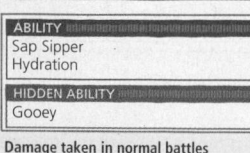

GOOMY 178
SLIGGOO 179
GOODRA 180

GOOMY 178

❖ LEVEL-UP MOVES

Lv.	Name	Type	Kind	Pow.	Acc.	PP	Range
1	Tackle	Normal	Physical	40	100	35	Normal
1	Bubble	Water	Special	40	100	30	Many Others
5	Absorb	Grass	Special	20	100	25	Normal
9	Protect	Normal	Status	—	—	10	Self
13	Bide	Normal	Physical	—	—	10	Self
18	Dragon Breath	Dragon	Special	60	100	20	Normal
25	Rain Dance	Water	Status	—	—	5	Both Sides
28	Flail	Normal	Physical	—	100	15	Normal
32	Body Slam	Normal	Physical	85	100	15	Normal
38	Muddy Water	Water	Special	90	85	10	Many Others
42	Dragon Pulse	Dragon	Special	85	100	10	Normal

❖ TM MOVES

No.	Name	Type	Kind	Pow.	Acc.	PP	Range
TM06	Toxic	Poison	Status	—	90	10	Normal
TM10	Hidden Power	Normal	Special	60	100	15	Normal
TM11	Sunny Day	Fire	Status	—	—	5	Both Sides
TM17	Protect	Normal	Status	—	—	10	Self
TM18	Rain Dance	Water	Status	—	—	5	Both Sides
TM21	Frustration	Normal	Physical	—	100	20	Normal
TM24	Thunderbolt	Electric	Special	90	100	15	Normal
TM27	Return	Normal	Physical	—	100	20	Normal
TM32	Double Team	Normal	Status	—	—	15	Self
TM34	Sludge Wave	Poison	Special	95	100	10	Adjacent
TM36	Sludge Bomb	Poison	Special	90	100	10	Normal
TM42	Facade	Normal	Physical	70	100	20	Normal
TM44	Rest	Psychic	Status	—	—	10	Self
TM45	Attract	Normal	Status	—	100	15	Normal
TM48	Round	Normal	Special	60	100	15	Normal
TM80	Rock Slide	Rock	Physical	75	90	10	Many Others
TM83	Infestation	Bug	Special	20	100	20	Normal
TM87	Swagger	Normal	Status	—	85	15	Normal
TM88	Sleep Talk	Normal	Status	—	—	10	Self
TM90	Substitute	Normal	Status	—	—	10	Self
TM100	Confide	Normal	Status	—	—	20	Normal

❖ MOVES TAUGHT BY PEOPLE

Name	Type	Kind	Pow.	Acc.	PP	Range
Draco Meteor	Dragon	Special	130	90	5	Normal

❖ MOVES LEARNED WHEN EVOLVING

Name	Type	Kind	Pow.	Acc.	PP	Range

❖ EGG MOVES

Name	Type	Kind	Pow.	Acc.	PP	Range
Acid Armor	Poison	Status	—	—	20	Self
Curse	Ghost	Status	—	—	10	Varies
Iron Tail	Steel	Physical	100	75	15	Normal
Poison Tail	Poison	Physical	50	100	25	Normal
Counter	Fighting	Physical	—	100	20	Varies
Endure	Normal	Status	—	—	10	Self

❖ EXCLUSIVE Z-MOVE

Name	Base Move	Type	Kind	Pow.	Acc.	Range

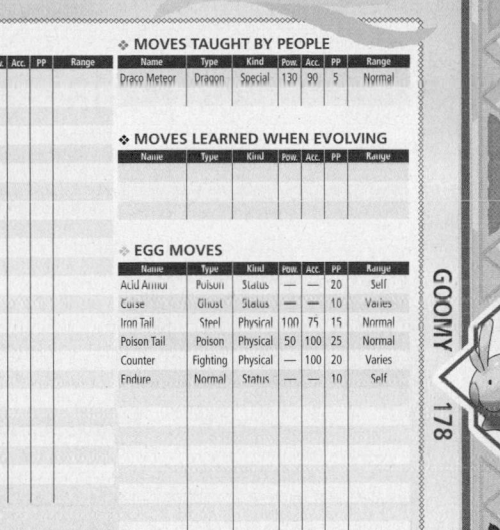

SLIGGOO 179

❖ LEVEL-UP MOVES

Lv.	Name	Type	Kind	Pow.	Acc.	PP	Range
1	Tackle	Normal	Physical	40	100	35	Normal
1	Bubble	Water	Special	40	100	30	Many Others
1	Absorb	Grass	Special	20	100	25	Normal
5	Absorb	Grass	Special	20	100	25	Normal
9	Protect	Normal	Status	—	—	10	Self
13	Bide	Normal	Physical	—	—	10	Self
18	Dragon Breath	Dragon	Special	60	100	20	Normal
25	Rain Dance	Water	Status	—	—	5	Both Sides
28	Flail	Normal	Physical	—	100	15	Normal
32	Body Slam	Normal	Physical	85	100	15	Normal
38	Muddy Water	Water	Special	90	85	10	Many Others
47	Dragon Pulse	Dragon	Special	85	100	10	Normal

❖ TM MOVES

No.	Name	Type	Kind	Pow.	Acc.	PP	Range
TM06	Toxic	Poison	Status	—	90	10	Normal
TM10	Hidden Power	Normal	Special	60	100	15	Normal
TM11	Sunny Day	Fire	Status	—	—	5	Both Sides
TM13	Ice Beam	Ice	Special	90	100	10	Normal
TM14	Blizzard	Ice	Special	110	70	5	Many Others
TM17	Protect	Normal	Status	—	—	10	Self
TM18	Rain Dance	Water	Status	—	—	5	Both Sides
TM21	Frustration	Normal	Physical	—	100	20	Normal
TM24	Thunderbolt	Electric	Special	90	100	15	Normal
TM27	Return	Normal	Physical	—	100	20	Normal
TM32	Double Team	Normal	Status	—	—	15	Self
TM34	Sludge Wave	Poison	Special	95	100	10	Adjacent
TM36	Sludge Bomb	Poison	Special	90	100	10	Normal
TM42	Facade	Normal	Physical	70	100	20	Normal
TM44	Rest	Psychic	Status	—	—	10	Self
TM45	Attract	Normal	Status	—	100	15	Normal
TM48	Round	Normal	Special	60	100	15	Normal
TM80	Rock Slide	Rock	Physical	75	90	10	Many Others
TM83	Infestation	Bug	Special	20	100	20	Normal
TM87	Swagger	Normal	Status	—	85	15	Normal
TM88	Sleep Talk	Normal	Status	—	—	10	Self
TM90	Substitute	Normal	Status	—	—	10	Self
TM100	Confide	Normal	Status	—	—	20	Normal

❖ MOVES TAUGHT BY PEOPLE

Name	Type	Kind	Pow.	Acc.	PP	Range
Draco Meteor	Dragon	Special	130	90	5	Normal

❖ MOVES LEARNED WHEN EVOLVING

Name	Type	Kind	Pow.	Acc.	PP	Range

❖ EGG MOVES

Name	Type	Kind	Pow.	Acc.	PP	Range

❖ EXCLUSIVE Z-MOVE

Name	Base Move	Type	Kind	Pow.	Acc.	Range

GOODRA 180

❖ LEVEL-UP MOVES

Lv.	Name	Type	Kind	Pow.	Acc.	PP	Range
1	Aqua Tail	Water	Physical	90	90	10	Normal
1	Outrage	Dragon	Physical	120	100	10	1 Random
1	Feint	Normal	Physical	30	100	10	Normal
1	Tackle	Normal	Physical	40	100	35	Normal
1	Bubble	Water	Special	40	100	30	Many Others
1	Absorb	Grass	Special	20	100	25	Normal
1	Protect	Normal	Status	—	—	10	Self
5	Absorb	Grass	Special	20	100	25	Normal
9	Protect	Normal	Status	—	—	10	Self
13	Bide	Normal	Physical	—	—	10	Self
18	Dragon Breath	Dragon	Special	60	100	20	Normal
25	Rain Dance	Water	Status	—	—	5	Both Sides
28	Flail	Normal	Physical	—	100	15	Normal
32	Body Slam	Normal	Physical	85	100	15	Normal
38	Muddy Water	Water	Special	90	85	10	Many Others
47	Dragon Pulse	Dragon	Special	85	100	10	Normal
50	Power Whip	Grass	Physical	120	85	10	Normal
55	Outrage	Dragon	Physical	120	100	10	1 Random

❖ TM MOVES

No.	Name	Type	Kind	Pow.	Acc.	PP	Range
TM06	Toxic	Poison	Status	—	90	10	Normal
TM07	Hail	Ice	Status	—	—	10	Both Sides
TM10	Hidden Power	Normal	Special	60	100	15	Normal
TM11	Sunny Day	Fire	Status	—	—	5	Both Sides
TM13	Ice Beam	Ice	Special	90	100	10	Normal
TM14	Blizzard	Ice	Special	110	70	5	Many Others
TM15	Hyper Beam	Normal	Special	150	90	5	Normal
TM17	Protect	Normal	Status	—	—	10	Self
TM18	Rain Dance	Water	Status	—	—	5	Both Sides
TM21	Frustration	Normal	Physical	—	100	20	Normal
TM24	Thunderbolt	Electric	Special	90	100	15	Normal
TM25	Thunder	Electric	Special	110	70	10	Normal
TM26	Earthquake	Ground	Physical	100	100	10	Adjacent
TM27	Return	Normal	Physical	—	100	20	Normal
TM32	Double Team	Normal	Status	—	—	15	Self
TM34	Sludge Wave	Poison	Special	95	100	10	Adjacent
TM35	Flamethrower	Fire	Special	90	100	15	Normal
TM36	Sludge Bomb	Poison	Special	90	100	10	Normal
TM38	Fire Blast	Fire	Special	110	85	5	Normal
TM42	Facade	Normal	Physical	70	100	20	Normal
TM44	Rest	Psychic	Status	—	—	10	Self
TM45	Attract	Normal	Status	—	100	15	Normal
TM48	Round	Normal	Special	60	100	15	Normal
TM52	Focus Blast	Fighting	Special	120	70	5	Normal
TM59	Brutal Swing	Dark	Physical	60	100	20	Adjacent
TM68	Giga Impact	Normal	Physical	150	90	5	Normal
TM78	Bulldoze	Ground	Physical	60	100	20	Adjacent
TM80	Rock Slide	Rock	Physical	75	90	10	Many Others
TM82	Dragon Tail	Dragon	Physical	60	90	10	Normal
TM83	Infestation	Bug	Special	20	100	20	Normal
TM87	Swagger	Normal	Status	—	85	15	Normal
TM88	Sleep Talk	Normal	Status	—	—	10	Self
TM90	Substitute	Normal	Status	—	—	10	Self
TM100	Confide	Normal	Status	—	—	20	Normal

❖ MOVES TAUGHT BY PEOPLE

Name	Type	Kind	Pow.	Acc.	PP	Range
Draco Meteor	Dragon	Special	130	90	5	Normal

❖ MOVES LEARNED WHEN EVOLVING

Name	Type	Kind	Pow.	Acc.	PP	Range
Aqua Tail	Water	Physical	90	90	10	Normal

❖ EGG MOVES

Name	Type	Kind	Pow.	Acc.	PP	Range

❖ EXCLUSIVE Z-MOVE

Name	Base Move	Type	Kind	Pow.	Acc.	Range

Alola Pokédex	Melemele	Akala	Ula'ula	Poni
181	—	108	077	069

☑ Castform
Weather Pokémon

NORMAL

HEIGHT: 1'00"
WEIGHT: 1.8 lbs.

It changes its form depending on the weather. Changes in the temperature or humidity appear to affect its cellular structure.

Its form changes on its own, due to its cells' sensitive reactions to temperature and humidity.

ABILITY
Forecast

HIDDEN ABILITY
—

Damage taken in normal battles
NORMAL ×1	FIGHTING ×2	ROCK ×1
FIRE ×1	POISON ×1	GHOST ×0
WATER ×1	GROUND ×1	DRAGON ×1
GRASS ×1	FLYING ×1	DARK ×1
ELECTRIC ×1	PSYCHIC ×1	STEEL ×1
ICE ×1	BUG ×1	FAIRY ×1

SPECIES STRENGTHS
HP	◆◆◆
Attack	◆◆◆◆
Defense	◆◆◆◆
Sp. Atk	◆◆◆◆
Sp. Def	◆◆◆◆
Speed	◆◆◆◆◆

EGG GROUPS
Fairy   Amorphous

ITEM SOMETIMES HELD BY WILD POKÉMON
Mystic Water

EVOLUTION
Does not evolve

MAIN WAY TO REGISTER IN THE POKÉDEX
Catch in SOS battles in the tall grass during rain in Lush Jungle

Same form for male/female

❖ LEVEL-UP MOVES
Lv.	Name	Type	Kind	Pow.	Acc.	PP	Range
1	Tackle	Normal	Physical	40	100	35	Normal
10	Water Gun	Water	Special	40	100	25	Normal
10	Ember	Fire	Special	40	100	25	Normal
10	Powder Snow	Ice	Special	40	100	25	Many Others
15	Headbutt	Normal	Physical	70	100	15	Normal
20	Rain Dance	Water	Status	—	—	5	Both Sides
20	Sunny Day	Fire	Status	—	—	5	Both Sides
20	Hail	Ice	Status	—	—	10	Both Sides
25	Weather Ball	Normal	Special	50	100	10	Normal
35	Hydro Pump	Water	Special	110	80	5	Normal
35	Fire Blast	Fire	Special	110	85	5	Normal
35	Blizzard	Ice	Special	110	70	5	Many Others
45	Hurricane	Flying	Special	110	70	10	Normal

❖ TM MOVES
No.	Name	Type	Kind	Pow.	Acc.	PP	Range
TM01	Work Up	Normal	Status	—	—	30	Self
TM06	Toxic	Poison	Status	—	90	10	Normal
TM07	Hail	Ice	Status	—	—	10	Both Sides
TM10	Hidden Power	Normal	Special	60	100	15	Normal
TM11	Sunny Day	Fire	Status	—	—	5	Both Sides
TM13	Ice Beam	Ice	Special	90	100	10	Normal
TM14	Blizzard	Ice	Special	110	70	5	Many Others
TM17	Protect	Normal	Status	—	—	10	Self
TM18	Rain Dance	Water	Status	—	—	5	Both Sides
TM21	Frustration	Normal	Physical	—	100	20	Normal
TM22	Solar Beam	Grass	Special	120	100	10	Normal
TM24	Thunderbolt	Electric	Special	90	100	15	Normal
TM25	Thunder	Electric	Special	110	70	10	Normal
TM27	Return	Normal	Physical	—	100	20	Normal
TM30	Shadow Ball	Ghost	Special	80	100	15	Normal
TM32	Double Team	Normal	Status	—	—	15	Self
TM35	Flamethrower	Fire	Special	90	100	15	Normal
TM37	Sandstorm	Rock	Status	—	—	10	Both Sides
TM38	Fire Blast	Fire	Special	110	85	5	Normal
TM42	Facade	Normal	Physical	70	100	20	Normal
TM44	Rest	Psychic	Status	—	—	10	Self
TM45	Attract	Normal	Status	—	100	15	Normal
TM46	Thief	Dark	Physical	60	100	25	Normal
TM48	Round	Normal	Special	60	100	15	Normal
TM53	Energy Ball	Grass	Special	90	100	10	Normal
TM55	Scald	Water	Special	80	100	15	Normal
TM73	Thunder Wave	Electric	Status	—	90	20	Normal
TM77	Psych Up	Normal	Status	—	—	10	Normal

No.	Name	Type	Kind	Pow.	Acc.	PP	Range
TM87	Swagger	Normal	Status	—	85	15	Normal
TM88	Sleep Talk	Normal	Status	—	—	10	Self
TM90	Substitute	Normal	Status	—	—	10	Self
TM100	Confide	Normal	Status	—	—	20	Normal

❖ MOVES TAUGHT BY PEOPLE
Name	Type	Kind	Pow.	Acc.	PP	Range

❖ MOVES LEARNED WHEN EVOLVING
Name	Type	Kind	Pow.	Acc.	PP	Range

❖ EGG MOVES
Name	Type	Kind	Pow.	Acc.	PP	Range
Future Sight	Psychic	Special	120	100	10	Normal
Lucky Chant	Normal	Status	—	—	30	Your Side
Disable	Normal	Status	—	100	20	Normal
Amnesia	Psychic	Status	—	—	20	Self
Ominous Wind	Ghost	Special	60	100	5	Normal
Hex	Ghost	Special	65	100	10	Normal
Clear Smog	Poison	Special	50	—	15	Normal
Reflect Type	Normal	Status	—	—	15	Normal
Guard Swap	Psychic	Status	—	—	10	Normal
Cosmic Power	Psychic	Status	—	—	20	Self

❖ EXCLUSIVE Z-MOVE
Name	Base Move	Type	Kind	Pow.	Acc.	Range

Castform (Sunny Form)

FIRE

This is the form Castform takes on the brightest of days. Its skin is unexpectedly hot to the touch, so approach with care.

This is Castform's form when basking in fair weather. Its body is warm and toasty.

Damage taken in normal battles
NORMAL ×1	FIGHTING ×1	ROCK ×2
FIRE ×0.5	POISON ×1	GHOST ×1
WATER ×2	GROUND ×2	DRAGON ×1
GRASS ×0.5	FLYING ×1	DARK ×1
ELECTRIC ×1	PSYCHIC ×1	STEEL ×0.5
ICE ×0.5	BUG ×0.5	FAIRY ×0.5

MAIN WAY TO REGISTER IN THE POKÉDEX
Castform takes this form when the weather conditions change to harsh sunlight during a battle. It returns to its normal form when the harsh sunlight fades or when the battle ends.

Castform (Rainy Form)

WATER

This is the form Castform takes when soaked with rain. When its body is compressed, water will seep out as if from a sponge.

This is Castform's form during a downpour of rain. Its body retains moisture and gets slippery.

Damage taken in normal battles
NORMAL ×1	FIGHTING ×1	ROCK ×1
FIRE ×0.5	POISON ×1	GHOST ×1
WATER ×0.5	GROUND ×1	DRAGON ×1
GRASS ×2	FLYING ×1	DARK ×1
ELECTRIC ×2	PSYCHIC ×1	STEEL ×0.5
ICE ×0.5	BUG ×1	FAIRY ×1

MAIN WAY TO REGISTER IN THE POKÉDEX
Castform takes this form when the weather conditions change to rain during a battle. It returns to its normal form when the rain lifts or when the battle ends.

Castform (Snowy Form)

ICE

This is the form Castform takes when covered in snow. Its body becomes an ice-like material, with a temperature near 23 degrees Fahrenheit.

This is Castform's form when caught in a hailstorm. Its cold skin is as smooth as ice.

Damage taken in normal battles
NORMAL ×1	FIGHTING ×2	ROCK ×2
FIRE ×2	POISON ×1	GHOST ×1
WATER ×1	GROUND ×1	DRAGON ×1
GRASS ×1	FLYING ×1	DARK ×1
ELECTRIC ×1	PSYCHIC ×1	STEEL ×2
ICE ×0.5	BUG ×1	FAIRY ×1

MAIN WAY TO REGISTER IN THE POKÉDEX
Castform takes this form when the weather conditions change to hail during a battle. It returns to its normal form when the hail stops or when the battle ends.

Wimpod

Turn Tail Pokémon

Alola Pokédex	Melemele	Akala	Ula'ula	Poni
182	—	109	—	070

BUG / WATER

HEIGHT: 1'08"
WEIGHT: 26.5 lbs.

This Pokémon is a coward. As it desperately dashes off, the flailing of its many legs leaves a sparkling clean path in its wake.

Its habitat varies from beaches to seabeds. A natural scavenger, it will gleefully chow down on anything edible, no matter how rotten.

ABILITY
Wimp Out

HIDDEN ABILITY
—

SPECIES STRENGTHS
- HP ◆
- Attack ◆◆
- Defense ◆◆
- Sp. Atk ◆
- Sp. Def ◆
- Speed ◆◆◆◆

EGG GROUPS
Bug / Water 3

ITEM SOMETIMES HELD BY WILD POKÉMON
—

EVOLUTION
Wimpod → Lv. 30 → Golisopod

MAIN WAY TO REGISTER IN THE POKÉDEX
Sneak up on Wimpod when you spot it on Route 8's shore.

Same form for male/female

Damage taken in normal battles
NORMAL ×1	FIGHTING ×0.5	ROCK ×2			
FIRE ×1	POISON ×1	GHOST ×1			
WATER ×0.5	GROUND ×0.5	DRAGON ×1			
GRASS ×1	FLYING ×1	DARK ×1			
ELECTRIC ×2	PSYCHIC ×1	STEEL ×0.5			
ICE ×0.5	BUG ×1	FAIRY ×1			

❖ LEVEL-UP MOVES
Lv.	Name	Type	Kind	Pow.	Acc.	PP	Range
1	Struggle Bug	Bug	Special	50	100	20	Many Others
1	Sand Attack	Ground	Status	—	100	15	Normal

❖ TM MOVES
No.	Name	Type	Kind	Pow.	Acc.	PP	Range
TM06	Toxic	Poison	Status	—	90	10	Normal
TM07	Hail	Ice	Status	—	—	10	Both Sides
TM10	Hidden Power	Normal	Special	60	100	15	Normal
TM12	Taunt	Dark	Status	—	100	20	Normal
TM17	Protect	Normal	Status	—	—	10	Self
TM18	Rain Dance	Water	Status	—	—	5	Both Sides
TM21	Frustration	Normal	Physical	—	100	20	Normal
TM27	Return	Normal	Physical	—	100	20	Normal
TM28	Leech Life	Bug	Physical	80	100	10	Normal
TM32	Double Team	Normal	Status	—	—	15	Self
TM42	Facade	Normal	Physical	70	100	20	Normal
TM44	Rest	Psychic	Status	—	—	10	Self
TM45	Attract	Normal	Status	—	100	15	Normal
TM48	Round	Normal	Special	60	100	15	Normal
TM55	Scald	Water	Special	80	100	15	Normal
TM87	Swagger	Normal	Status	—	85	15	Normal
TM88	Sleep Talk	Normal	Status	—	—	10	Self
TM90	Substitute	Normal	Status	—	—	10	Self
TM94	Surf	Water	Special	90	100	15	Adjacent
TM98	Waterfall	Water	Physical	80	100	15	Normal
TM100	Confide	Normal	Status	—	—	20	Normal

❖ MOVES TAUGHT BY PEOPLE
Name	Type	Kind	Pow.	Acc.	PP	Range

❖ MOVES LEARNED WHEN EVOLVING
Name	Type	Kind	Pow.	Acc.	PP	Range

❖ EGG MOVES
Name	Type	Kind	Pow.	Acc.	PP	Range
Spikes	Ground	Status	—	—	20	Other Side
Metal Claw	Steel	Physical	50	95	35	Normal
Wide Guard	Rock	Status	—	—	10	Your Side
Harden	Normal	Status	—	—	30	Self
Aqua Jet	Water	Physical	40	100	20	Normal

❖ EXCLUSIVE Z-MOVE
Name	Base Move	Type	Kind	Pow.	Acc.	Range

Golisopod

Hard Scale Pokémon

Alola Pokédex	Melemele	Akala	Ula'ula	Poni
183	—	110	—	071

BUG / WATER

HEIGHT: 6'07"
WEIGHT: 238.1 lbs.

With a flashing slash of its giant sharp claws, it cleaves seawater—or even air—right in two.

It battles skillfully with its six arms, but spends most of its time peacefully meditating in caves deep beneath the sea.

ABILITY
Emergency Exit

HIDDEN ABILITY
—

SPECIES STRENGTHS
- HP ◆◆◆
- Attack ◆◆◆◆◆◆
- Defense ◆◆◆◆◆◆◆
- Sp. Atk ◆◆◆
- Sp. Def ◆◆◆◆◆
- Speed ◆◆◆

EGG GROUPS
Bug / Water 3

ITEM SOMETIMES HELD BY WILD POKÉMON
—

EVOLUTION
Wimpod → Lv. 30 → Golisopod

MAIN WAY TO REGISTER IN THE POKÉDEX
Level up Wimpod to Lv. 30

Same form for male/female

Damage taken in normal battles
NORMAL ×1	FIGHTING ×0.5	ROCK ×1			
FIRE ×1	POISON ×1	GHOST ×1			
WATER ×0.5	GROUND ×0.5	DRAGON ×1			
GRASS ×1	FLYING ×1	DARK ×1			
ELECTRIC ×2	PSYCHIC ×1	STEEL ×0.5			
ICE ×0.5	BUG ×1	FAIRY ×1			

❖ LEVEL-UP MOVES
Lv.	Name	Type	Kind	Pow.	Acc.	PP	Range
1	First Impression	Bug	Physical	90	100	10	Normal
1	Struggle Bug	Bug	Special	50	100	20	Many Others
1	Sand Attack	Ground	Status	—	100	15	Normal
1	Fury Cutter	Bug	Physical	40	95	20	Normal
1	Rock Smash	Fighting	Physical	40	100	15	Normal
4	Fury Cutter	Bug	Physical	40	95	20	Normal
7	Rock Smash	Fighting	Physical	40	100	15	Normal
10	Bug Bite	Bug	Physical	60	100	20	Normal
13	Spite	Ghost	Status	—	100	10	Normal
16	Swords Dance	Normal	Status	—	—	20	Self
21	Slash	Normal	Physical	70	100	20	Normal
26	Razor Shell	Water	Physical	75	95	10	Normal
31	Sucker Punch	Dark	Physical	70	100	5	Normal
36	Iron Defense	Steel	Status	—	—	15	Self
41	Pin Missile	Bug	Physical	25	95	20	Normal
48	Liquidation	Water	Physical	85	100	10	Normal

❖ TM MOVES
No.	Name	Type	Kind	Pow.	Acc.	PP	Range
TM06	Toxic	Poison	Status	—	90	10	Normal
TM07	Hail	Ice	Status	—	—	10	Both Sides
TM08	Bulk Up	Fighting	Status	—	—	20	Self
TM09	Venoshock	Poison	Special	65	100	10	Normal
TM10	Hidden Power	Normal	Special	60	100	15	Normal
TM12	Taunt	Dark	Status	—	100	20	Normal
TM13	Ice Beam	Ice	Special	90	100	10	Normal
TM14	Blizzard	Ice	Special	110	70	5	Many Others
TM17	Protect	Normal	Status	—	—	10	Self
TM18	Rain Dance	Water	Status	—	—	5	Both Sides
TM21	Frustration	Normal	Physical	—	100	20	Normal
TM27	Return	Normal	Physical	—	100	20	Normal
TM28	Leech Life	Bug	Physical	80	100	10	Normal
TM31	Brick Break	Fighting	Physical	75	100	15	Normal
TM32	Double Team	Normal	Status	—	—	15	Self
TM34	Sludge Wave	Poison	Special	95	100	10	Adjacent
TM36	Sludge Bomb	Poison	Special	90	100	10	Normal
TM39	Rock Tomb	Rock	Physical	60	95	15	Normal
TM40	Aerial Ace	Flying	Physical	60	—	20	Normal
TM42	Facade	Normal	Physical	70	100	20	Normal
TM44	Rest	Psychic	Status	—	—	10	Self
TM45	Attract	Normal	Status	—	100	15	Normal
TM48	Round	Normal	Special	60	100	15	Normal
TM52	Focus Blast	Fighting	Special	120	70	5	Normal
TM54	False Swipe	Normal	Physical	40	100	40	Normal
TM55	Scald	Water	Special	80	100	15	Normal
TM56	Fling	Dark	Physical	—	100	10	Normal
TM65	Shadow Claw	Ghost	Physical	70	100	15	Normal
TM66	Payback	Dark	Physical	50	100	10	Normal
TM68	Giga Impact	Normal	Physical	150	90	5	Normal
TM75	Swords Dance	Normal	Status	—	—	20	Self
TM77	Psych Up	Normal	Status	—	—	10	Normal
TM79	Frost Breath	Ice	Special	60	90	10	Normal
TM80	Rock Slide	Rock	Physical	75	90	10	Many Others
TM81	X-Scissor	Bug	Physical	80	100	15	Normal
TM84	Poison Jab	Poison	Physical	80	100	20	Normal
TM87	Swagger	Normal	Status	—	85	15	Normal
TM88	Sleep Talk	Normal	Status	—	—	10	Self
TM90	Substitute	Normal	Status	—	—	10	Self
TM94	Surf	Water	Special	90	100	15	Adjacent
TM95	Snarl	Dark	Special	55	95	15	Many Others
TM97	Dark Pulse	Dark	Special	80	100	15	Normal
TM98	Waterfall	Water	Physical	80	100	15	Normal
TM100	Confide	Normal	Status	—	—	20	Normal

❖ MOVES TAUGHT BY PEOPLE
Name	Type	Kind	Pow.	Acc.	PP	Range

❖ MOVES LEARNED WHEN EVOLVING
Name	Type	Kind	Pow.	Acc.	PP	Range
First Impression	Bug	Physical	90	100	10	Normal

❖ EGG MOVES
Name	Type	Kind	Pow.	Acc.	PP	Range

❖ EXCLUSIVE Z-MOVE
Name	Base Move	Type	Kind	Pow.	Acc.	Range

Staryu

Star Shape Pokémon

WATER

Alola Pokédex	Melemele	Akala	Ula'ula	Poni
184	—	111		

HEIGHT: 2'07"
WEIGHT: 76.1 lbs.

Large numbers of these Pokémon make their home at the seaside. At night, a strange red glow radiates from the center of their bodies.

This Pokémon gets nibbled on by Lumineon and others. Thanks to its red core, it regenerates fast, so it's unconcerned by their snack attacks.

ABILITY
Illuminate
Natural Cure

HIDDEN ABILITY
Analytic

SPECIES STRENGTHS
HP ◆
Attack ◆◆◆
Defense ◆◆◆
Sp. Atk ◆◆◆◆
Sp. Def ◆◆◆
Speed ◆◆◆◆◆

EGG GROUPS
Water 3

ITEM SOMETIMES HELD BY WILD POKÉMON
Stardust / Star Piece

Damage taken in normal battles

NORMAL ×1	FIGHTING ×1	ROCK ×1			
FIRE ×0.5	POISON ×1	GHOST ×1			
WATER ×0.5	GROUND ×1	DRAGON ×1			
GRASS ×2	FLYING ×1	DARK ×1			
ELECTRIC ×2	PSYCHIC ×1	STEEL ×0.5			
ICE ×0.5	BUG ×1	FAIRY ×1			

EVOLUTION

Staryu → (Water Stone) → Starmie

MAIN WAY TO REGISTER IN THE POKÉDEX
Catch in the sand clouds on Hano Beach

Gender unknown

❖ LEVEL-UP MOVES

Lv.	Name	Type	Kind	Pow.	Acc.	PP	Range
1	Tackle	Normal	Physical	40	100	35	Normal
1	Harden	Normal	Status	—	—	30	Self
4	Water Gun	Water	Special	40	100	25	Normal
7	Rapid Spin	Normal	Physical	20	100	40	Normal
10	Recover	Normal	Status	—	—	10	Self
13	Psywave	Psychic	Special	—	100	15	Normal
16	Swift	Normal	Special	60	—	20	Many Others
18	Bubble Beam	Water	Special	65	100	20	Normal
22	Camouflage	Normal	Status	—	—	20	Self
24	Gyro Ball	Steel	Physical	—	100	5	Normal
28	Brine	Water	Special	65	100	10	Normal
31	Minimize	Normal	Status	—	—	10	Self
35	Reflect Type	Normal	Status	—	—	15	Normal
37	Power Gem	Rock	Special	80	100	20	Normal
40	Confuse Ray	Ghost	Status	—	100	10	Normal
42	Psychic	Psychic	Special	90	100	10	Normal
46	Light Screen	Psychic	Status	—	—	30	Your Side
49	Cosmic Power	Psychic	Status	—	—	20	Self
53	Hydro Pump	Water	Special	110	80	5	Normal

❖ TM MOVES

No.	Name	Type	Kind	Pow.	Acc.	PP	Range
TM06	Toxic	Poison	Status	—	90	10	Normal
TM07	Hail	Ice	Status	—	—	10	Both Sides
TM10	Hidden Power	Normal	Special	60	100	15	Normal
TM13	Ice Beam	Ice	Special	90	100	10	Normal
TM14	Blizzard	Ice	Special	110	70	5	Many Others
TM16	Light Screen	Psychic	Status	—	—	30	Your Side
TM17	Protect	Normal	Status	—	—	10	Self
TM18	Rain Dance	Water	Status	—	—	5	Both Sides
TM21	Frustration	Normal	Physical	—	100	20	Normal
TM24	Thunderbolt	Electric	Special	90	100	15	Normal
TM25	Thunder	Electric	Special	110	70	10	Normal
TM27	Return	Normal	Physical	—	100	20	Normal
TM29	Psychic	Psychic	Special	90	100	10	Normal
TM32	Double Team	Normal	Status	—	—	15	Self
TM33	Reflect	Psychic	Status	—	—	20	Your Side
TM42	Facade	Normal	Physical	70	100	20	Normal
TM44	Rest	Psychic	Status	—	—	10	Self
TM48	Round	Normal	Special	60	100	15	Normal
TM55	Scald	Water	Special	80	100	15	Normal
TM73	Thunder Wave	Electric	Status	—	90	20	Normal
TM74	Gyro Ball	Steel	Physical	—	100	5	Normal
TM77	Psych Up	Normal	Status	—	—	10	Normal
TM87	Swagger	Normal	Status	—	85	15	Normal
TM88	Sleep Talk	Normal	Status	—	—	10	Self
TM90	Substitute	Normal	Status	—	—	10	Self
TM91	Flash Cannon	Steel	Special	80	100	10	Normal
TM94	Surf	Water	Special	90	100	15	Adjacent
TM98	Waterfall	Water	Physical	80	100	15	Normal

No.	Name	Type	Kind	Pow.	Acc.	PP	Range
TM99	Dazzling Gleam	Fairy	Special	80	100	10	Many Others
TM100	Confide	Normal	Status	—	—	20	Normal

❖ MOVES TAUGHT BY PEOPLE

Name	Type	Kind	Pow.	Acc.	PP	Range

❖ MOVES LEARNED WHEN EVOLVING

Name	Type	Kind	Pow.	Acc.	PP	Range

❖ EGG MOVES

Name	Type	Kind	Pow.	Acc.	PP	Range

❖ EXCLUSIVE Z-MOVE

Name	Base Move	Type	Kind	Pow.	Acc.	Range

Starmie

Mysterious Pokémon

WATER **PSYCHIC**

Alola Pokédex	Melemele	Akala	Ula'ula	Poni
185	—	112		

HEIGHT: 3'07"
WEIGHT: 176.4 lbs.

Its shining core is thought to receive and transmit enigmatic signals. It has been known to cause headaches in those who approach it.

Its unusual body shape, reminiscent of abstract art, led local people to spread rumors that this Pokémon may be an invader from outer space.

ABILITY
Illuminate
Natural Cure

HIDDEN ABILITY
Analytic

SPECIES STRENGTHS
HP ◆◆
Attack ◆◆
Defense ◆◆◆◆
Sp. Atk ◆◆◆◆◆
Sp. Def ◆◆◆◆
Speed ◆◆◆◆◆◆◆

EGG GROUPS
Water 3

ITEM SOMETIMES HELD BY WILD POKÉMON
Stardust / Star Piece

Damage taken in normal battles

NORMAL ×1	FIGHTING ×0.5	ROCK ×1			
FIRE ×0.5	POISON ×1	GHOST ×2			
WATER ×0.5	GROUND ×1	DRAGON ×1			
GRASS ×2	FLYING ×1	DARK ×2			
ELECTRIC ×2	PSYCHIC ×1	STEEL ×0.5			
ICE ×0.5	BUG ×2	FAIRY ×1			

EVOLUTION

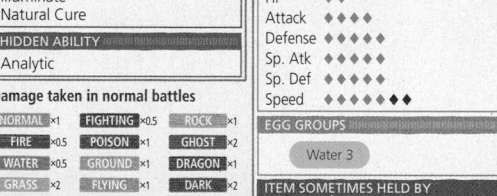

Staryu → (Water Stone) → Starmie

MAIN WAY TO REGISTER IN THE POKÉDEX
Use a Water Stone on Staryu

Gender unknown

❖ LEVEL-UP MOVES

Lv.	Name	Type	Kind	Pow.	Acc.	PP	Range
1	Hydro Pump	Water	Special	110	80	5	Normal
1	Spotlight	Normal	Status	—	—	15	Normal
1	Water Gun	Water	Special	40	100	25	Normal
1	Rapid Spin	Normal	Physical	20	100	40	Normal
1	Recover	Normal	Status	—	—	10	Self
1	Swift	Normal	Special	60	—	20	Many Others
40	Confuse Ray	Ghost	Status	—	100	10	Normal

❖ TM MOVES

No.	Name	Type	Kind	Pow.	Acc.	PP	Range
TM03	Psyshock	Psychic	Special	80	100	10	Normal
TM06	Toxic	Poison	Status	—	90	10	Normal
TM07	Hail	Ice	Status	—	—	10	Both Sides
TM10	Hidden Power	Normal	Special	60	100	15	Normal
TM13	Ice Beam	Ice	Special	90	100	10	Normal
TM14	Blizzard	Ice	Special	110	70	5	Many Others
TM15	Hyper Beam	Normal	Special	150	90	5	Normal
TM16	Light Screen	Psychic	Status	—	—	30	Your Side
TM17	Protect	Normal	Status	—	—	10	Self
TM18	Rain Dance	Water	Status	—	—	5	Both Sides
TM21	Frustration	Normal	Physical	—	100	20	Normal
TM24	Thunderbolt	Electric	Special	90	100	15	Normal
TM25	Thunder	Electric	Special	110	70	10	Normal
TM27	Return	Normal	Physical	—	100	20	Normal
TM29	Psychic	Psychic	Special	90	100	10	Normal
TM32	Double Team	Normal	Status	—	—	15	Self
TM33	Reflect	Psychic	Status	—	—	20	Your Side
TM42	Facade	Normal	Physical	70	100	20	Normal
TM44	Rest	Psychic	Status	—	—	10	Self
TM48	Round	Normal	Special	60	100	15	Normal
TM55	Scald	Water	Special	80	100	15	Normal
TM68	Giga Impact	Normal	Physical	150	90	5	Normal
TM73	Thunder Wave	Electric	Status	—	90	20	Normal
TM74	Gyro Ball	Steel	Physical	—	100	5	Normal
TM77	Psych Up	Normal	Status	—	—	10	Normal
TM85	Dream Eater	Psychic	Special	100	100	15	Normal
TM86	Grass Knot	Grass	Special	—	100	20	Normal
TM87	Swagger	Normal	Status	—	85	15	Normal

No.	Name	Type	Kind	Pow.	Acc.	PP	Range
TM88	Sleep Talk	Normal	Status	—	—	10	Self
TM90	Substitute	Normal	Status	—	—	10	Self
TM91	Flash Cannon	Steel	Special	80	100	10	Normal
TM92	Trick Room	Psychic	Status	—	—	5	Both Sides
TM94	Surf	Water	Special	90	100	15	Adjacent
TM98	Waterfall	Water	Physical	80	100	15	Normal
TM99	Dazzling Gleam	Fairy	Special	80	100	10	Many Others
TM100	Confide	Normal	Status	—	—	20	Normal

❖ MOVES TAUGHT BY PEOPLE

Name	Type	Kind	Pow.	Acc.	PP	Range

❖ MOVES LEARNED WHEN EVOLVING

Name	Type	Kind	Pow.	Acc.	PP	Range

❖ EGG MOVES

Name	Type	Kind	Pow.	Acc.	PP	Range

❖ EXCLUSIVE Z-MOVE

Name	Base Move	Type	Kind	Pow.	Acc.	Range

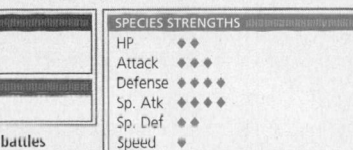

Alola Pokédex	Melemele	Akala	Ula'ula	Poni
186	—	113		

Sandygast
Sand Heap Pokémon

GHOST **GROUND**

HEIGHT: 1'08"
WEIGHT: 154.3 lbs.

Born from a sand mound playfully built by a child, this Pokémon embodies the grudges of the departed.

It takes control of anyone who puts a hand in its mouth. And so it adds to the accumulation of its sand-mound body.

Same form for male/female

ABILITY
Water Compaction

HIDDEN ABILITY
Sand Veil

Damage taken in normal battles

NORMAL	×0	FIGHTING	×0	ROCK	×0.5
FIRE	×1	POISON	×0.25	GHOST	×2
WATER	×2	GROUND	×1	DRAGON	×1
GRASS	×2	FLYING	×1	DARK	×2
ELECTRIC	×0	PSYCHIC	×1	STEEL	×1
ICE	×2	BUG	×0.5	FAIRY	×1

SPECIES STRENGTHS

HP	◆◆
Attack	◆◆◆
Defense	◆◆◆◆
Sp. Atk	◆◆◆◆
Sp. Def	◆◆◆◆
Speed	◆

EGG GROUPS
Amorphous

ITEM SOMETIMES HELD BY WILD POKÉMON
Spell Tag

EVOLUTION

Sandygast → Lv. 42 → Palossand

MAIN WAY TO REGISTER IN THE POKÉDEX
Catch in the sand clouds on Hano Beach

◆ LEVEL-UP MOVES

Lv.	Name	Type	Kind	Pow.	Acc.	PP	Range
1	Harden	Normal	Status	—	—	30	Self
1	Absorb	Grass	Special	20	100	25	Normal
5	Astonish	Ghost	Physical	30	100	15	Normal
9	Sand Attack	Ground	Status	—	100	15	Normal
14	Sand Tomb	Ground	Physical	35	85	15	Normal
18	Mega Drain	Grass	Special	40	100	15	Normal
23	Bulldoze	Ground	Physical	60	100	20	Adjacent
27	Hypnosis	Psychic	Status	—	60	20	Normal
32	Iron Defense	Steel	Status	—	—	15	Self
36	Giga Drain	Grass	Special	75	100	10	Normal
41	Shadow Ball	Ghost	Special	80	100	15	Normal
45	Earth Power	Ground	Special	90	100	10	Normal
50	Shore Up	Ground	Status	—	—	10	Self
54	Sandstorm	Rock	Status	—	—	10	Both Sides

◆ TM MOVES

No.	Name	Type	Kind	Pow.	Acc.	PP	Range
TM06	Toxic	Poison	Status	—	90	10	Normal
TM10	Hidden Power	Normal	Special	60	100	15	Normal
TM17	Protect	Normal	Status	—	—	10	Self
TM21	Frustration	Normal	Physical	—	100	20	Normal
TM26	Earthquake	Ground	Physical	100	100	10	Adjacent
TM27	Return	Normal	Physical	—	100	20	Normal
TM29	Psychic	Psychic	Special	90	100	10	Normal
TM30	Shadow Ball	Ghost	Special	80	100	15	Normal
TM32	Double Team	Normal	Status	—	—	15	Self
TM37	Sandstorm	Rock	Status	—	—	10	Both Sides
TM39	Rock Tomb	Rock	Physical	60	95	15	Normal
TM42	Facade	Normal	Physical	70	100	20	Normal
TM44	Rest	Psychic	Status	—	—	10	Self
TM45	Attract	Normal	Status	—	100	15	Normal
TM48	Round	Normal	Special	60	100	15	Normal
TM53	Energy Ball	Grass	Special	90	100	10	Normal
TM69	Rock Polish	Rock	Status	—	—	20	Self
TM71	Stone Edge	Rock	Physical	100	80	5	Normal
TM78	Bulldoze	Ground	Physical	60	100	20	Adjacent
TM80	Rock Slide	Rock	Physical	75	90	10	Many Others
TM83	Infestation	Bug	Special	20	100	20	Normal
TM87	Swagger	Normal	Status	—	85	15	Normal
TM88	Sleep Talk	Normal	Status	—	—	10	Self
TM90	Substitute	Normal	Status	—	—	10	Self
TM100	Confide	Normal	Status	—	—	20	Normal

◆ MOVES TAUGHT BY PEOPLE

Name	Type	Kind	Pow.	Acc.	PP	Range

◆ MOVES LEARNED WHEN EVOLVING

Name	Type	Kind	Pow.	Acc.	PP	Range

◆ EGG MOVES

Name	Type	Kind	Pow.	Acc.	PP	Range
Amnesia	Psychic	Status	—	—	20	Self
Destiny Bond	Ghost	Status	—	—	5	Self
Ancient Power	Rock	Special	60	100	5	Normal
Stockpile	Normal	Status	—	—	20	Self
Swallow	Normal	Status	—	—	10	Self
Spit Up	Normal	Special	—	100	10	Normal

◆ EXCLUSIVE Z-MOVE

Name	Base Move	Type	Kind	Pow.	Acc.	Range

Alola Pokédex	Melemele	Akala	Ula'ula	Poni
187	—	114		

Palossand
Sand Castle Pokémon

GHOST **GROUND**

HEIGHT: 4'03"
WEIGHT: 551.2 lbs.

Possessed people controlled by this Pokémon transformed its sand mound into a castle. As it evolved, its power to curse grew ever stronger.

Buried beneath the castle are masses of dried-up bones from those whose vitality it has drained.

Same form for male/female

ABILITY
Water Compaction

HIDDEN ABILITY
Sand Veil

Damage taken in normal battles

NORMAL	×0	FIGHTING	×0	ROCK	×0.5
FIRE	×1	POISON	×0.25	GHOST	×2
WATER	×2	GROUND	×1	DRAGON	×1
GRASS	×2	FLYING	×1	DARK	×2
ELECTRIC	×0	PSYCHIC	×1	STEEL	×1
ICE	×2	BUG	×0.5	FAIRY	×1

SPECIES STRENGTHS

HP	◆◆◆
Attack	◆◆◆◆
Defense	◆◆◆◆◆◆◆
Sp. Atk	◆◆◆◆◆
Sp. Def	◆◆◆◆
Speed	◆◆

EGG GROUPS
Amorphous

ITEM SOMETIMES HELD BY WILD POKÉMON
—

EVOLUTION

Sandygast → Lv. 42 → Palossand

MAIN WAY TO REGISTER IN THE POKÉDEX
Level up Sandygast to Lv. 42

◆ LEVEL-UP MOVES

Lv.	Name	Type	Kind	Pow.	Acc.	PP	Range
1	Harden	Normal	Status	—	—	30	Self
1	Absorb	Grass	Special	20	100	25	Normal
1	Astonish	Ghost	Physical	30	100	15	Normal
1	Sand Attack	Ground	Status	—	100	15	Normal
5	Astonish	Ghost	Physical	30	100	15	Normal
9	Sand Attack	Ground	Status	—	100	15	Normal
14	Sand Tomb	Ground	Physical	35	85	15	Normal
18	Mega Drain	Grass	Special	40	100	15	Normal
23	Bulldoze	Ground	Physical	60	100	20	Adjacent
27	Hypnosis	Psychic	Status	—	60	20	Normal
32	Iron Defense	Steel	Status	—	—	15	Self
36	Giga Drain	Grass	Special	75	100	10	Normal
41	Shadow Ball	Ghost	Special	80	100	15	Normal
47	Earth Power	Ground	Special	90	100	10	Normal
54	Shore Up	Ground	Status	—	—	10	Self
60	Sandstorm	Rock	Status	—	—	10	Both Sides

◆ TM MOVES

No.	Name	Type	Kind	Pow.	Acc.	PP	Range
TM06	Toxic	Poison	Status	—	90	10	Normal
TM10	Hidden Power	Normal	Special	60	100	15	Normal
TM17	Protect	Normal	Status	—	—	10	Self
TM21	Frustration	Normal	Physical	—	100	20	Normal
TM26	Earthquake	Ground	Physical	100	100	10	Adjacent
TM27	Return	Normal	Physical	—	100	20	Normal
TM29	Psychic	Psychic	Special	90	100	10	Normal
TM30	Shadow Ball	Ghost	Special	80	100	15	Normal
TM32	Double Team	Normal	Status	—	—	15	Self
TM36	Sludge Bomb	Poison	Special	90	100	10	Normal
TM37	Sandstorm	Rock	Status	—	—	10	Both Sides
TM39	Rock Tomb	Rock	Physical	60	95	15	Normal
TM42	Facade	Normal	Physical	70	100	20	Normal
TM44	Rest	Psychic	Status	—	—	10	Self
TM45	Attract	Normal	Status	—	100	15	Normal
TM48	Round	Normal	Special	60	100	15	Normal
TM53	Energy Ball	Grass	Special	90	100	10	Normal
TM56	Fling	Dark	Physical	—	100	10	Normal
TM60	Quash	Dark	Status	—	100	15	Normal
TM63	Embargo	Dark	Status	—	100	15	Normal
TM68	Giga Impact	Normal	Physical	150	90	5	Normal
TM69	Rock Polish	Rock	Status	—	—	20	Self
TM71	Stone Edge	Rock	Physical	100	80	5	Normal
TM78	Bulldoze	Ground	Physical	60	100	20	Adjacent
TM80	Rock Slide	Rock	Physical	75	90	10	Many Others
TM83	Infestation	Bug	Special	20	100	20	Normal
TM87	Swagger	Normal	Status	—	85	15	Normal
TM88	Sleep Talk	Normal	Status	—	—	10	Self

◆ MOVES TAUGHT BY PEOPLE

No.	Name	Type	Kind	Pow.	Acc.	PP	Range
TM90	Substitute	Normal	Status	—	—	10	Self
TM100	Confide	Normal	Status	—	—	20	Normal

◆ MOVES LEARNED WHEN EVOLVING

Name	Type	Kind	Pow.	Acc.	PP	Range

◆ EGG MOVES

Name	Type	Kind	Pow.	Acc.	PP	Range

◆ EXCLUSIVE Z-MOVE

Name	Base Move	Type	Kind	Pow.	Acc.	Range

Cranidos

Alola Pokédex 188 | Melemele — | Akala — | Ula'ula 115 | Poni —

Head Butt Pokémon

ROCK

HEIGHT: 2'11"
WEIGHT: 69.4 lbs.

It lived in jungles around a hundred million years ago. It used its skillful headbutts to combat Aerodactyl.

In rock layers where Cranidos fossils are found, the fossilized trunks of trees snapped in two are also often found.

ABILITY
Mold Breaker

HIDDEN ABILITY
Sheer Force

Damage taken in normal battles

NORMAL ×0.5	FIGHTING ×2	ROCK ×1
FIRE ×1	POISON ×0.5	GHOST ×1
WATER ×2	GROUND ×2	DRAGON ×1
GRASS ×2	FLYING ×0.5	DARK ×1
ELECTRIC ×1	PSYCHIC ×1	STEEL ×2
ICE ×1	BUG ×1	FAIRY ×1

SPECIES STRENGTHS
- HP ◆◆◆
- Attack ◆◆◆◆◆◆◆
- Defense ◆◆
- Sp. Atk ◆◆
- Sp. Def ◆
- Speed ◆◆◆◆

EGG GROUPS
Monster

ITEM SOMETIMES HELD BY WILD POKÉMON
—

EVOLUTION

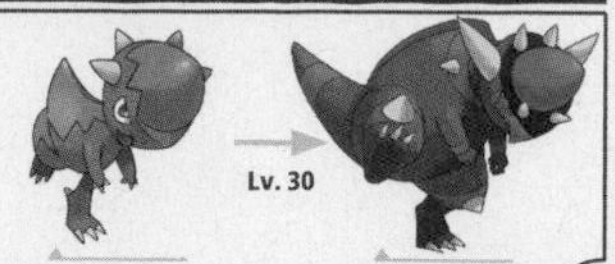

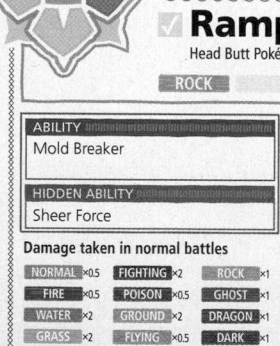

Cranidos → Lv. 30 → Rampardos

MAIN WAY TO REGISTER IN THE POKÉDEX
Have a Skull Fossil restored off Route 8 in *Pokémon Sun* / Obtain in a trade in *Pokémon Moon*

Same form for male/female

❖ LEVEL-UP MOVES

Lv.	Name	Type	Kind	Pow.	Acc.	PP	Range
1	Headbutt	Normal	Physical	70	100	15	Normal
1	Leer	Normal	Status	—	100	30	Many Others
6	Focus Energy	Normal	Status	—	—	30	Self
10	Pursuit	Dark	Physical	40	100	20	Normal
15	Take Down	Normal	Physical	90	85	20	Normal
19	Scary Face	Normal	Status	—	100	10	Normal
24	Assurance	Dark	Physical	60	100	10	Normal
28	Chip Away	Normal	Physical	70	100	20	Normal
33	Ancient Power	Rock	Special	60	100	5	Normal
37	Zen Headbutt	Psychic	Physical	80	90	15	Normal
42	Screech	Normal	Status	—	85	40	Normal
46	Head Smash	Rock	Physical	150	80	5	Normal

❖ TM MOVES

No.	Name	Type	Kind	Pow.	Acc.	PP	Range
TM05	Roar	Normal	Status	—	—	20	Normal
TM06	Toxic	Poison	Status	—	90	10	Normal
TM10	Hidden Power	Normal	Special	60	100	15	Normal
TM11	Sunny Day	Fire	Status	—	—	5	Both Sides
TM13	Ice Beam	Ice	Special	90	100	10	Normal
TM14	Blizzard	Ice	Special	110	70	5	Many Others
TM17	Protect	Normal	Status	—	—	10	Self
TM18	Rain Dance	Water	Status	—	—	5	Both Sides
TM21	Frustration	Normal	Physical	—	100	20	Normal
TM23	Smack Down	Rock	Physical	50	100	15	Normal
TM24	Thunderbolt	Electric	Special	90	100	15	Normal
TM25	Thunder	Electric	Special	110	70	10	Normal
TM26	Earthquake	Ground	Physical	100	100	10	Adjacent
TM27	Return	Normal	Physical	—	100	20	Normal
TM32	Double Team	Normal	Status	—	—	15	Self
TM35	Flamethrower	Fire	Special	90	100	15	Normal
TM37	Sandstorm	Rock	Status	—	—	10	Both Sides
TM38	Fire Blast	Fire	Special	110	85	5	Normal
TM39	Rock Tomb	Rock	Physical	60	95	15	Normal
TM42	Facade	Normal	Physical	70	100	20	Normal
TM44	Rest	Psychic	Status	—	—	10	Self
TM45	Attract	Normal	Status	—	100	15	Normal
TM46	Thief	Dark	Physical	60	100	25	Normal
TM48	Round	Normal	Special	60	100	15	Normal
TM56	Fling	Dark	Physical	—	100	10	Normal
TM66	Payback	Dark	Physical	50	100	10	Normal
TM69	Rock Polish	Rock	Status	—	—	20	Self
TM71	Stone Edge	Rock	Physical	100	80	5	Normal

No.	Name	Type	Kind	Pow.	Acc.	PP	Range
TM75	Swords Dance	Normal	Status	—	—	20	Self
TM78	Bulldoze	Ground	Physical	60	100	20	Adjacent
TM80	Rock Slide	Rock	Physical	75	90	10	Many Others
TM87	Swagger	Normal	Status	—	85	15	Normal
TM88	Sleep Talk	Normal	Status	—	—	10	Self
TM100	Confide	Normal	Status	—	—	20	Normal

❖ MOVES TAUGHT BY PEOPLE

Name	Type	Kind	Pow.	Acc.	PP	Range

❖ MOVES LEARNED WHEN EVOLVING

Name	Type	Kind	Pow.	Acc.	PP	Range

❖ EGG MOVES

Name	Type	Kind	Pow.	Acc.	PP	Range
Crunch	Dark	Physical	80	100	15	Normal
Thrash	Normal	Physical	120	100	10	1 Random
Double-Edge	Normal	Physical	120	100	15	Normal
Leer	Normal	Status	—	100	30	Many Others
Slam	Normal	Physical	80	75	20	Normal
Stomp	Normal	Physical	65	100	20	Normal
Whirlwind	Normal	Status	—	—	20	Normal
Hammer Arm	Fighting	Physical	100	90	10	Normal
Curse	Ghost	Status	—	—	10	Varies
Iron Tail	Steel	Physical	100	75	15	Normal
Iron Head	Steel	Physical	80	100	15	Normal

❖ EXCLUSIVE Z-MOVE

Name	Base Move	Type	Kind	Pow.	Acc.	Range

Rampardos

Alola Pokédex 189 | Melemele — | Akala — | Ula'ula 116 | Poni —

Head Butt Pokémon

ROCK

HEIGHT: 5'03"
WEIGHT: 226.0 lbs.

The result of repeated headbutts is a skull grown thick and hard. However, its brain has shrunk in size compared with Cranidos's.

Records exist of a revived fossil that evolved into Rampardos. It proceeded to escape and then destroy a skyscraper with a headbutt.

ABILITY
Mold Breaker

HIDDEN ABILITY
Sheer Force

Damage taken in normal battles

NORMAL ×0.5	FIGHTING ×2	ROCK ×1
FIRE ×0.5	POISON ×0.5	GHOST ×1
WATER ×2	GROUND ×2	DRAGON ×1
GRASS ×2	FLYING ×0.5	DARK ×1
ELECTRIC ×1	PSYCHIC ×1	STEEL ×2
ICE ×1	BUG ×1	FAIRY ×1

SPECIES STRENGTHS
- HP ◆◆◆◆
- Attack ◆◆◆◆◆◆◆◆
- Defense ◆◆◆
- Sp. Atk ◆◆◆◆
- Sp. Def ◆◆◆
- Speed ◆◆◆◆

EGG GROUPS
Monster

ITEM SOMETIMES HELD BY WILD POKÉMON
—

EVOLUTION

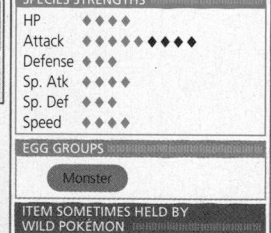

Cranidos → Lv. 30 → Rampardos

MAIN WAY TO REGISTER IN THE POKÉDEX
Level up Cranidos to Lv. 30.

Same form for male/female

❖ LEVEL-UP MOVES

Lv.	Name	Type	Kind	Pow.	Acc.	PP	Range
1	Endeavor	Normal	Physical	—	100	5	Normal
1	Headbutt	Normal	Physical	70	100	15	Normal
1	Leer	Normal	Status	—	100	30	Many Others
1	Focus Energy	Normal	Status	—	—	30	Self
1	Pursuit	Dark	Physical	40	100	20	Normal
6	Focus Energy	Normal	Status	—	—	30	Self
10	Pursuit	Dark	Physical	40	100	20	Normal
15	Take Down	Normal	Physical	90	85	20	Normal
19	Scary Face	Normal	Status	—	100	10	Normal
24	Assurance	Dark	Physical	60	100	10	Normal
28	Chip Away	Normal	Physical	70	100	20	Normal
36	Ancient Power	Rock	Special	60	100	5	Normal
43	Zen Headbutt	Psychic	Physical	80	90	15	Normal
51	Screech	Normal	Status	—	85	40	Normal
58	Head Smash	Rock	Physical	150	80	5	Normal

❖ TM MOVES

No.	Name	Type	Kind	Pow.	Acc.	PP	Range
TM05	Roar	Normal	Status	—	—	20	Normal
TM06	Toxic	Poison	Status	—	90	10	Normal
TM10	Hidden Power	Normal	Special	60	100	15	Normal
TM11	Sunny Day	Fire	Status	—	—	5	Both Sides
TM13	Ice Beam	Ice	Special	90	100	10	Normal
TM14	Blizzard	Ice	Special	110	70	5	Many Others
TM15	Hyper Beam	Normal	Special	150	90	5	Normal
TM17	Protect	Normal	Status	—	—	10	Self
TM18	Rain Dance	Water	Status	—	—	5	Both Sides
TM21	Frustration	Normal	Physical	—	100	20	Normal
TM23	Smack Down	Rock	Physical	50	100	15	Normal
TM24	Thunderbolt	Electric	Special	90	100	15	Normal
TM25	Thunder	Electric	Special	110	70	10	Normal
TM26	Earthquake	Ground	Physical	100	100	10	Adjacent
TM27	Return	Normal	Physical	—	100	20	Normal
TM31	Brick Break	Fighting	Physical	75	100	15	Normal
TM32	Double Team	Normal	Status	—	—	15	Self
TM35	Flamethrower	Fire	Special	90	100	15	Normal
TM37	Sandstorm	Rock	Status	—	—	10	Both Sides
TM38	Fire Blast	Fire	Special	110	85	5	Normal
TM39	Rock Tomb	Rock	Physical	60	95	15	Normal
TM42	Facade	Normal	Physical	70	100	20	Normal
TM44	Rest	Psychic	Status	—	—	10	Self
TM45	Attract	Normal	Status	—	100	15	Normal
TM46	Thief	Dark	Physical	60	100	25	Normal
TM48	Round	Normal	Special	60	100	15	Normal
TM52	Focus Blast	Fighting	Special	120	70	5	Normal
TM56	Fling	Dark	Physical	—	100	10	Normal

No.	Name	Type	Kind	Pow.	Acc.	PP	Range
TM66	Payback	Dark	Physical	50	100	10	Normal
TM68	Giga Impact	Normal	Physical	150	90	5	Normal
TM69	Rock Polish	Rock	Status	—	—	20	Self
TM71	Stone Edge	Rock	Physical	100	80	5	Normal
TM75	Swords Dance	Normal	Status	—	—	20	Self
TM78	Bulldoze	Ground	Physical	60	100	20	Adjacent
TM80	Rock Slide	Rock	Physical	75	90	10	Many Others
TM82	Dragon Tail	Dragon	Physical	60	90	10	Normal
TM87	Swagger	Normal	Status	—	85	15	Normal
TM88	Sleep Talk	Normal	Status	—	—	10	Self
TM90	Substitute	Normal	Status	—	—	10	Self
TM94	Surf	Water	Special	90	100	15	Adjacent
TM100	Confide	Normal	Status	—	—	20	Normal

❖ MOVES TAUGHT BY PEOPLE

Name	Type	Kind	Pow.	Acc.	PP	Range

❖ MOVES LEARNED WHEN EVOLVING

Name	Type	Kind	Pow.	Acc.	PP	Range
Endeavor	Normal	Physical	—	100	5	Normal

❖ EGG MOVES

Name	Type	Kind	Pow.	Acc.	PP	Range

❖ EXCLUSIVE Z-MOVE

Name	Base Move	Type	Kind	Pow.	Acc.	Range

Shieldon

Alola Pokédex	Melemele	Akala	Ula'ula	Poni
190	—	117		

Shieldon
Shield Pokémon

ROCK STEEL

HEIGHT: 1'08"
WEIGHT: 125.7 lbs.

Many fossils of this Pokémon have been found, but almost none have shown signs of damage to the face.

This Pokémon lived in primeval jungles. Few enemies would have been willing to square off against its heavily armored face, so it's thought.

Same form for male/female

ABILITY
Sturdy

HIDDEN ABILITY
Soundproof

Damage taken in normal battles

NORMAL ×0.25	FIGHTING ×4	ROCK ×0.5
FIRE ×1	POISON ×0	GHOST ×1
WATER ×2	GROUND ×4	DRAGON ×1
GRASS ×1	FLYING ×0.25	DARK ×1
ELECTRIC ×1	PSYCHIC ×0.5	STEEL ×1
ICE ×0.5	BUG ×0.5	FAIRY ×0.5

SPECIES STRENGTHS
HP ◆
Attack ◆◆
Defense ◆◆◆◆◆◆
Sp. Atk ◆◆
Sp. Def ◆◆◆◆◆
Speed ◆◆

EGG GROUPS
Monster

ITEM SOMETIMES HELD BY WILD POKÉMON
—

EVOLUTION

Shieldon → Lv. 30 → Bastiodon

MAIN WAY TO REGISTER IN THE POKÉDEX
Obtain in a trade in *Pokémon Sun* / Have an Armor Fossil restored off Route 8 in *Pokémon Moon*

❖ LEVEL-UP MOVES

Lv.	Name	Type	Kind	Pow.	Acc.	PP	Range
1	Tackle	Normal	Physical	40	100	35	Normal
1	Protect	Normal	Status	—	—	10	Self
6	Taunt	Dark	Status	—	100	20	Normal
10	Metal Sound	Steel	Status	—	85	40	Normal
15	Take Down	Normal	Physical	90	85	20	Normal
19	Iron Defense	Steel	Status	—	—	15	Self
24	Swagger	Normal	Status	—	85	15	Normal
28	Ancient Power	Rock	Special	60	100	5	Normal
33	Endure	Normal	Status	—	—	10	Self
37	Metal Burst	Steel	Physical	—	100	10	Varies
42	Iron Head	Steel	Physical	80	100	15	Normal
46	Heavy Slam	Steel	Physical	—	100	10	Normal

❖ TM MOVES

No.	Name	Type	Kind	Pow.	Acc.	PP	Range
TM05	Roar	Normal	Status	—	—	20	Normal
TM06	Toxic	Poison	Status	—	90	10	Normal
TM10	Hidden Power	Normal	Special	60	100	15	Normal
TM11	Sunny Day	Fire	Status	—	—	5	Both Sides
TM12	Taunt	Dark	Status	—	100	20	Normal
TM13	Ice Beam	Ice	Special	90	100	10	Normal
TM14	Blizzard	Ice	Special	110	70	5	Many Others
TM17	Protect	Normal	Status	—	—	10	Self
TM18	Rain Dance	Water	Status	—	—	5	Both Sides
TM21	Frustration	Normal	Physical	—	100	20	Normal
TM23	Smack Down	Rock	Physical	50	100	15	Normal
TM24	Thunderbolt	Electric	Special	90	100	15	Normal
TM25	Thunder	Electric	Special	110	70	10	Normal
TM26	Earthquake	Ground	Physical	100	100	10	Adjacent
TM27	Return	Normal	Physical	—	100	20	Normal
TM32	Double Team	Normal	Status	—	—	15	Self
TM35	Flamethrower	Fire	Special	90	100	15	Normal
TM37	Sandstorm	Rock	Status	—	—	10	Both Sides
TM38	Fire Blast	Fire	Special	110	85	5	Normal
TM39	Rock Tomb	Rock	Physical	60	95	15	Normal
TM41	Torment	Dark	Status	—	100	15	Normal
TM42	Facade	Normal	Physical	70	100	20	Normal
TM44	Rest	Psychic	Status	—	—	10	Self
TM45	Attract	Normal	Status	—	100	15	Normal
TM48	Round	Normal	Special	60	100	15	Normal
TM69	Rock Polish	Rock	Status	—	—	20	Self
TM71	Stone Edge	Rock	Physical	100	80	5	Normal
TM78	Bulldoze	Ground	Physical	60	100	20	Adjacent

No.	Name	Type	Kind	Pow.	Acc.	PP	Range
TM80	Rock Slide	Rock	Physical	75	90	10	Many Others
TM87	Swagger	Normal	Status	—	85	15	Normal
TM88	Sleep Talk	Normal	Status	—	—	10	Self
TM90	Substitute	Normal	Status	—	—	10	Self
TM91	Flash Cannon	Steel	Special	80	100	10	Normal
TM100	Confide	Normal	Status	—	—	20	Normal

❖ MOVES TAUGHT BY PEOPLE

Name	Type	Kind	Pow.	Acc.	PP	Range

❖ MOVES LEARNED WHEN EVOLVING

Name	Type	Kind	Pow.	Acc.	PP	Range

EGG MOVES

Name	Type	Kind	Pow.	Acc.	PP	Range
Headbutt	Normal	Physical	70	100	15	Normal
Scary Face	Normal	Status	—	100	10	Normal
Focus Energy	Normal	Status	—	—	30	Self
Double-Edge	Normal	Physical	120	100	15	Normal
Rock Blast	Rock	Physical	25	90	10	Normal
Body Slam	Normal	Physical	85	100	15	Normal
Screech	Normal	Status	—	85	40	Normal
Curse	Ghost	Status	—	—	10	Varies
Fissure	Ground	Physical	—	30	5	Normal
Counter	Fighting	Physical	—	100	20	Varies
Stealth Rock	Rock	Status	—	—	20	Other Side
Wide Guard	Rock	Status	—	—	10	Your Side
Guard Split	Psychic	Status	—	—	10	Normal

❖ EXCLUSIVE Z-MOVE

Name	Base Move	Type	Kind	Pow.	Acc.	Range

Alola Pokédex	Melemele	Akala	Ula'ula	Poni
191	—	118		

Bastiodon
Shield Pokémon

ROCK STEEL

HEIGHT: 4'03"
WEIGHT: 329.6 lbs.

While it can guard against any sort of attack from the front, it is left without recourse when attacked from behind.

It lived in the same environments as Rampardos. Their fossils have been found together—seemingly from after they'd fought to the finish.

Same form for male/female

ABILITY
Sturdy

HIDDEN ABILITY
Soundproof

Damage taken in normal battles

NORMAL ×0.25	FIGHTING ×4	ROCK ×0.5
FIRE ×1	POISON ×0	GHOST ×1
WATER ×2	GROUND ×4	DRAGON ×0.5
GRASS ×1	FLYING ×0.25	DARK ×1
ELECTRIC ×1	PSYCHIC ×0.5	STEEL ×1
ICE ×0.5	BUG ×0.5	FAIRY ×0.5

SPECIES STRENGTHS
HP ◆◆
Attack ◆◆
Defense ◆◆◆◆◆◆◆◆
Sp. Atk ◆◆◆
Sp. Def ◆◆◆◆◆◆◆◆
Speed ◆◆

EGG GROUPS
Monster

ITEM SOMETIMES HELD BY WILD POKÉMON
—

EVOLUTION

Shieldon → Lv. 30 → Bastiodon

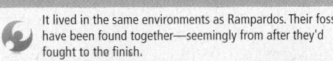

MAIN WAY TO REGISTER IN THE POKÉDEX
Level up Shieldon to Lv. 30

❖ LEVEL-UP MOVES

Lv.	Name	Type	Kind	Pow.	Acc.	PP	Range
1	Block	Normal	Status	—	—	5	Normal
1	Tackle	Normal	Physical	40	100	35	Normal
1	Protect	Normal	Status	—	—	10	Self
1	Taunt	Dark	Status	—	100	20	Normal
1	Metal Sound	Steel	Status	—	85	40	Normal
6	Taunt	Dark	Status	—	100	20	Normal
10	Metal Sound	Steel	Status	—	85	40	Normal
15	Take Down	Normal	Physical	90	85	20	Normal
19	Iron Defense	Steel	Status	—	—	15	Self
24	Swagger	Normal	Status	—	85	15	Normal
28	Ancient Power	Rock	Special	60	100	5	Normal
36	Endure	Normal	Status	—	—	10	Self
43	Metal Burst	Steel	Physical	—	100	10	Varies
51	Iron Head	Steel	Physical	80	100	15	Normal
58	Heavy Slam	Steel	Physical	—	100	10	Normal

❖ TM MOVES

No.	Name	Type	Kind	Pow.	Acc.	PP	Range
TM05	Roar	Normal	Status	—	—	20	Normal
TM06	Toxic	Poison	Status	—	90	10	Normal
TM10	Hidden Power	Normal	Special	60	100	15	Normal
TM11	Sunny Day	Fire	Status	—	—	5	Both Sides
TM12	Taunt	Dark	Status	—	100	20	Normal
TM13	Ice Beam	Ice	Special	90	100	10	Normal
TM14	Blizzard	Ice	Special	110	70	5	Many Others
TM15	Hyper Beam	Normal	Special	150	90	5	Normal
TM17	Protect	Normal	Status	—	—	10	Self
TM18	Rain Dance	Water	Status	—	—	5	Both Sides
TM21	Frustration	Normal	Physical	—	100	20	Normal
TM23	Smack Down	Rock	Physical	50	100	15	Normal
TM24	Thunderbolt	Electric	Special	90	100	15	Normal
TM25	Thunder	Electric	Special	110	70	10	Normal
TM26	Earthquake	Ground	Physical	100	100	10	Adjacent
TM27	Return	Normal	Physical	—	100	20	Normal
TM32	Double Team	Normal	Status	—	—	15	Self
TM35	Flamethrower	Fire	Special	90	100	15	Normal
TM37	Sandstorm	Rock	Status	—	—	10	Both Sides
TM38	Fire Blast	Fire	Special	110	85	5	Normal
TM39	Rock Tomb	Rock	Physical	60	95	15	Normal
TM41	Torment	Dark	Status	—	100	15	Normal
TM42	Facade	Normal	Physical	70	100	20	Normal
TM44	Rest	Psychic	Status	—	—	10	Self
TM45	Attract	Normal	Status	—	100	15	Normal
TM48	Round	Normal	Special	60	100	15	Normal
TM68	Giga Impact	Normal	Physical	150	90	5	Normal
TM69	Rock Polish	Rock	Status	—	—	20	Self

No.	Name	Type	Kind	Pow.	Acc.	PP	Range
TM71	Stone Edge	Rock	Physical	100	80	5	Normal
TM78	Bulldoze	Ground	Physical	60	100	20	Adjacent
TM80	Rock Slide	Rock	Physical	75	90	10	Many Others
TM87	Swagger	Normal	Status	—	85	15	Normal
TM88	Sleep Talk	Normal	Status	—	—	10	Self
TM90	Substitute	Normal	Status	—	—	10	Self
TM91	Flash Cannon	Steel	Special	80	100	10	Normal
TM100	Confide	Normal	Status	—	—	20	Normal

❖ MOVES TAUGHT BY PEOPLE

Name	Type	Kind	Pow.	Acc.	PP	Range

❖ MOVES LEARNED WHEN EVOLVING

Name	Type	Kind	Pow.	Acc.	PP	Range
Block	Normal	Status	—	—	5	Normal

❖ EGG MOVES

Name	Type	Kind	Pow.	Acc.	PP	Range

❖ EXCLUSIVE Z-MOVE

Name	Base Move	Type	Kind	Pow.	Acc.	Range

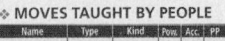

Archen

First Bird Pokémon

ROCK / FLYING

Alola Pokédex	Melemele	Akala	Ula'ula	Poni
	192	—		119

HEIGHT: 1'08"
WEIGHT: 20.9 lbs.

It is the ancestor of all bird Pokémon. Archen itself could not actually fly but moved by hopping from treetop to treetop.

To all appearances flightless, it was able to glide down from tall treetops to snag its prey.

ABILITY
Defeatist

HIDDEN ABILITY
—

SPECIES STRENGTHS
HP	◆◆
Attack	◆◆◆◆◆◆
Defense	◆◆◆
Sp. Atk	◆◆◆◆
Sp. Def	◆◆
Speed	◆◆◆◆◆

Damage taken in normal battles
NORMAL ×0.5	FIGHTING ×1	ROCK ×2	
FIRE ×0.5	POISON ×0.5	GHOST ×1	
WATER ×2	GROUND ×0	DRAGON ×1	
GRASS ×1	FLYING ×0.5	DARK ×1	
ELECTRIC ×2	PSYCHIC ×1	STEEL ×2	
ICE ×2	BUG ×0.5	FAIRY ×1	

EGG GROUPS
Flying, Water 3

ITEM SOMETIMES HELD BY WILD POKÉMON
—

EVOLUTION

Archen → Lv. 37 → Archeops

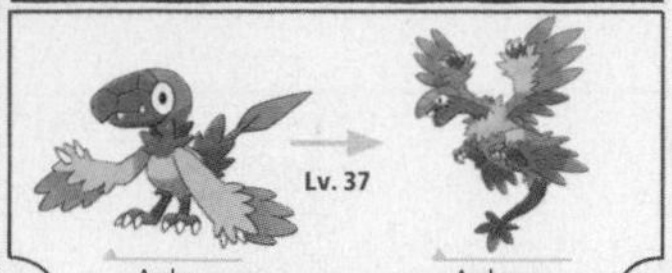

MAIN WAY TO REGISTER IN THE POKÉDEX
Obtain in a trade in *Pokémon Sun* / Have a Plume Fossil restored off Route 8 in *Pokémon Moon*

Same form for male/female

◆ LEVEL-UP MOVES
Lv.	Name	Type	Kind	Pow.	Acc.	PP	Range
1	Quick Attack	Normal	Physical	40	100	30	Normal
1	Leer	Normal	Status	—	100	30	Many Others
1	Wing Attack	Flying	Physical	60	100	35	Normal
5	Rock Throw	Rock	Physical	50	90	15	Normal
8	Double Team	Normal	Status	—	—	15	Self
11	Scary Face	Normal	Status	—	100	10	Normal
15	Pluck	Flying	Physical	60	100	20	Normal
18	Ancient Power	Rock	Special	60	100	5	Normal
21	Agility	Psychic	Status	—	—	30	Self
25	Quick Guard	Fighting	Status	—	—	15	Your Side
28	Acrobatics	Flying	Physical	55	100	15	Normal
31	Dragon Breath	Dragon	Special	60	100	20	Normal
35	Crunch	Dark	Physical	80	100	15	Normal
38	Endeavor	Normal	Physical	—	100	5	Normal
41	U-turn	Bug	Physical	70	100	20	Normal
45	Rock Slide	Rock	Physical	75	90	10	Many Others
48	Dragon Claw	Dragon	Physical	80	100	15	Normal
50	Thrash	Normal	Physical	120	100	10	1 Random

◆ TM MOVES
No.	Name	Type	Kind	Pow.	Acc.	PP	Range
TM02	Dragon Claw	Dragon	Physical	80	100	15	Normal
TM05	Roar	Normal	Status	—	—	20	Normal
TM06	Toxic	Poison	Status	—	90	10	Normal
TM10	Hidden Power	Normal	Special	60	100	15	Normal
TM12	Taunt	Dark	Status	—	100	20	Normal
TM17	Protect	Normal	Status	—	—	10	Self
TM19	Roost	Flying	Status	—	—	10	Self
TM21	Frustration	Normal	Physical	—	100	20	Normal
TM23	Smack Down	Rock	Physical	50	100	15	Normal
TM26	Earthquake	Ground	Physical	100	100	10	Adjacent
TM27	Return	Normal	Physical	—	100	20	Normal
TM32	Double Team	Normal	Status	—	—	15	Self
TM37	Sandstorm	Rock	Status	—	—	10	Both Sides
TM39	Rock Tomb	Rock	Physical	60	95	15	Normal
TM40	Aerial Ace	Flying	Physical	60	—	20	Normal
TM41	Torment	Dark	Status	—	100	15	Normal
TM42	Facade	Normal	Physical	70	100	20	Normal
TM44	Rest	Psychic	Status	—	—	10	Self
TM45	Attract	Normal	Status	—	100	15	Normal
TM48	Round	Normal	Special	60	100	15	Normal
TM51	Steel Wing	Steel	Physical	70	90	25	Normal
TM62	Acrobatics	Flying	Physical	55	100	15	Normal
TM65	Shadow Claw	Ghost	Physical	70	100	15	Normal
TM69	Rock Polish	Rock	Status	—	—	20	Self
TM71	Stone Edge	Rock	Physical	100	80	5	Normal
TM78	Bulldoze	Ground	Physical	60	100	20	Adjacent
TM80	Rock Slide	Rock	Physical	75	90	10	Many Others
TM87	Swagger	Normal	Status	—	85	15	Normal
TM88	Sleep Talk	Normal	Status	—	—	10	Self
TM89	U-turn	Bug	Physical	70	100	20	Normal
TM90	Substitute	Normal	Status	—	—	10	Self
TM100	Confide	Normal	Status	—	—	20	Normal

◆ MOVES TAUGHT BY PEOPLE
Name	Type	Kind	Pow.	Acc.	PP	Range

◆ MOVES LEARNED WHEN EVOLVING
Name	Type	Kind	Pow.	Acc.	PP	Range

◆ EGG MOVES
Name	Type	Kind	Pow.	Acc.	PP	Range
Steel Wing	Steel	Physical	70	90	25	Normal
Defog	Flying	Status	—	—	15	Normal
Dragon Pulse	Dragon	Special	85	100	10	Normal
Head Smash	Rock	Physical	150	80	5	Normal
Knock Off	Dark	Physical	65	100	20	Normal
Earth Power	Ground	Special	90	100	10	Normal
Bite	Dark	Physical	60	100	25	Normal
Ally Switch	Psychic	Status	—	—	15	Self
Switcheroo	Dark	Status	—	100	10	Normal

◆ EXCLUSIVE Z-MOVE
Name	Base Move	Type	Kind	Pow.	Acc.	Range

Archeops

First Bird Pokémon

ROCK / FLYING

Alola Pokédex	Melemele	Akala	Ula'ula	Poni
	193	—		120

HEIGHT: 4'07"
WEIGHT: 70.5 lbs.

Although apparently able to fly, they tended to run along the ground, averaging speeds of roughly 25 mph.

They hunted in flocks. When one Archeops had the prey cornered, another would swoop on it.

ABILITY
Defeatist

HIDDEN ABILITY
—

SPECIES STRENGTHS
HP	◆◆◆
Attack	◆◆◆◆◆◆◆◆
Defense	◆◆◆◆
Sp. Atk	◆◆◆◆◆◆
Sp. Def	◆◆◆◆
Speed	◆◆◆◆◆◆◆◆

Damage taken in normal battles
NORMAL ×0.5	FIGHTING ×1	ROCK ×2	
FIRE ×0.5	POISON ×0.5	GHOST ×1	
WATER ×2	GROUND ×0	DRAGON ×1	
GRASS ×1	FLYING ×0.5	DARK ×1	
ELECTRIC ×2	PSYCHIC ×1	STEEL ×2	
ICE ×2	BUG ×0.5	FAIRY ×1	

EGG GROUPS
Flying, Water 3

ITEM SOMETIMES HELD BY WILD POKÉMON
—

EVOLUTION
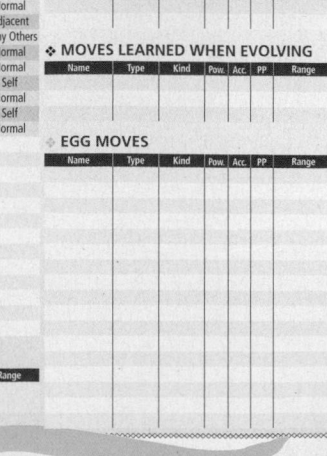
Archen → Lv. 37 → Archeops

MAIN WAY TO REGISTER IN THE POKÉDEX
Level up Archen to Lv. 37

Same form for male/female

◆ LEVEL-UP MOVES
Lv.	Name	Type	Kind	Pow.	Acc.	PP	Range
1	Quick Attack	Normal	Physical	40	100	30	Normal
1	Leer	Normal	Status	—	100	30	Many Others
1	Wing Attack	Flying	Physical	60	100	35	Normal
1	Rock Throw	Rock	Physical	50	90	15	Normal
5	Rock Throw	Rock	Physical	50	90	15	Normal
8	Double Team	Normal	Status	—	—	15	Self
11	Scary Face	Normal	Status	—	100	10	Normal
15	Pluck	Flying	Physical	60	100	20	Normal
18	Ancient Power	Rock	Special	60	100	5	Normal
21	Agility	Psychic	Status	—	—	30	Self
25	Quick Guard	Fighting	Status	—	—	15	Your Side
28	Acrobatics	Flying	Physical	55	100	15	Normal
31	Dragon Breath	Dragon	Special	60	100	20	Normal
35	Crunch	Dark	Physical	80	100	15	Normal
40	Endeavor	Normal	Physical	—	100	5	Normal
45	U-turn	Bug	Physical	70	100	20	Normal
51	Rock Slide	Rock	Physical	75	90	10	Many Others
56	Dragon Claw	Dragon	Physical	80	100	15	Normal
61	Thrash	Normal	Physical	120	100	10	1 Random

◆ TM MOVES
No.	Name	Type	Kind	Pow.	Acc.	PP	Range
TM02	Dragon Claw	Dragon	Physical	80	100	15	Normal
TM05	Roar	Normal	Status	—	—	20	Normal
TM06	Toxic	Poison	Status	—	90	10	Normal
TM10	Hidden Power	Normal	Special	60	100	15	Normal
TM12	Taunt	Dark	Status	—	100	20	Normal
TM15	Hyper Beam	Normal	Special	150	90	5	Normal
TM17	Protect	Normal	Status	—	—	10	Self
TM19	Roost	Flying	Status	—	—	10	Self
TM21	Frustration	Normal	Physical	—	100	20	Normal
TM23	Smack Down	Rock	Physical	50	100	15	Normal
TM26	Earthquake	Ground	Physical	100	100	10	Adjacent
TM27	Return	Normal	Physical	—	100	20	Normal
TM32	Double Team	Normal	Status	—	—	15	Self
TM37	Sandstorm	Rock	Status	—	—	10	Both Sides
TM39	Rock Tomb	Rock	Physical	60	95	15	Normal
TM40	Aerial Ace	Flying	Physical	60	—	20	Normal
TM41	Torment	Dark	Status	—	100	15	Normal
TM42	Facade	Normal	Physical	70	100	20	Normal
TM44	Rest	Psychic	Status	—	—	10	Self
TM45	Attract	Normal	Status	—	100	15	Normal
TM48	Round	Normal	Special	60	100	15	Normal
TM51	Steel Wing	Steel	Physical	70	90	25	Normal
TM52	Focus Blast	Fighting	Special	120	70	5	Normal
TM62	Acrobatics	Flying	Physical	55	100	15	Normal
TM65	Shadow Claw	Ghost	Physical	70	100	15	Normal
TM68	Giga Impact	Normal	Physical	150	90	5	Normal
TM69	Rock Polish	Rock	Status	—	—	20	Self
TM71	Stone Edge	Rock	Physical	100	80	5	Normal
TM76	Fly	Flying	Physical	90	95	15	Normal
TM78	Bulldoze	Ground	Physical	60	100	20	Adjacent
TM80	Rock Slide	Rock	Physical	75	90	10	Many Others
TM82	Dragon Tail	Dragon	Physical	60	90	10	Normal
TM87	Swagger	Normal	Status	—	85	15	Normal
TM88	Sleep Talk	Normal	Status	—	—	10	Self
TM89	U-turn	Bug	Physical	70	100	20	Normal
TM90	Substitute	Normal	Status	—	—	10	Self
TM100	Confide	Normal	Status	—	—	20	Normal

◆ MOVES TAUGHT BY PEOPLE
Name	Type	Kind	Pow.	Acc.	PP	Range

◆ MOVES LEARNED WHEN EVOLVING
Name	Type	Kind	Pow.	Acc.	PP	Range

◆ EGG MOVES
Name	Type	Kind	Pow.	Acc.	PP	Range

◆ EXCLUSIVE Z-MOVE
Name	Base Move	Type	Kind	Pow.	Acc.	Range

Tirtouga
Prototurtle Pokémon

WATER / ROCK

Alola Pokédex	Melemele	Akala	Ula'ula	Poni
194	—	121		

HEIGHT: 2'04"
WEIGHT: 36.4 lbs.

Based on studies of its skeletal structure, it can apparently dive to ocean depths of over half a mile.

Reputed to be the ancestor of most turtle Pokémon, it lived in warm seas approximately a hundred million years ago.

ABILITY
Solid Rock
Sturdy

HIDDEN ABILITY
Swift Swim

SPECIES STRENGTHS
- HP ◆◆
- Attack ◆◆◆
- Defense ◆◆◆◆◆◆◆
- Sp. Atk ◆◆
- Sp. Def ◆◆◆
- Speed ◆◆

EGG GROUPS
Water 1 | Water 3

ITEM SOMETIMES HELD BY WILD POKÉMON
—

EVOLUTION
Tirtouga — Lv. 37 → Carracosta

MAIN WAY TO REGISTER IN THE POKÉDEX
Have a Cover Fossil restored off Route 8 in *Pokémon Sun* / Obtain in a trade in *Pokémon Moon*

Same form for male/female

Damage taken in normal battles
NORMAL ×0.5	FIGHTING ×2	ROCK ×1
FIRE ×0.25	POISON ×0.5	GHOST ×1
WATER ×1	GROUND ×2	DRAGON ×1
GRASS ×4	FLYING ×0.5	DARK ×1
ELECTRIC ×2	PSYCHIC ×1	STEEL ×1
ICE ×0.5	BUG ×1	FAIRY ×1

❖ LEVEL-UP MOVES
Lv.	Name	Type	Kind	Pow.	Acc.	PP	Range
1	Bide	Normal	Physical	—	—	10	Self
1	Withdraw	Water	Status	—	—	40	Self
1	Water Gun	Water	Special	40	100	25	Normal
5	Rollout	Rock	Physical	30	90	20	Normal
8	Bite	Dark	Physical	60	100	25	Normal
11	Protect	Normal	Status	—	—	10	Self
15	Aqua Jet	Water	Physical	40	100	20	Normal
18	Ancient Power	Rock	Special	60	100	5	Normal
21	Crunch	Dark	Physical	80	100	15	Normal
25	Wide Guard	Rock	Status	—	—	10	Your Side
28	Brine	Water	Special	65	100	10	Normal
31	Smack Down	Rock	Physical	50	100	15	Normal
35	Curse	Ghost	Status	—	—	10	Varies
38	Shell Smash	Normal	Status	—	—	15	Self
41	Aqua Tail	Water	Physical	90	90	10	Normal
45	Rock Slide	Rock	Physical	75	90	10	Many Others
48	Rain Dance	Water	Status	—	—	5	Both Sides
50	Hydro Pump	Water	Special	110	80	5	Normal

❖ TM MOVES
No.	Name	Type	Kind	Pow.	Acc.	PP	Range
TM06	Toxic	Poison	Status	—	90	10	Normal
TM10	Hidden Power	Normal	Special	60	100	15	Normal
TM13	Ice Beam	Ice	Special	90	100	10	Normal
TM14	Blizzard	Ice	Special	110	70	5	Many Others
TM17	Protect	Normal	Status	—	—	10	Self
TM18	Rain Dance	Water	Status	—	—	5	Both Sides
TM21	Frustration	Normal	Physical	—	100	20	Normal
TM23	Smack Down	Rock	Physical	50	100	15	Normal
TM26	Earthquake	Ground	Physical	100	100	10	Adjacent
TM27	Return	Normal	Physical	—	100	20	Normal
TM32	Double Team	Normal	Status	—	—	15	Self
TM37	Sandstorm	Rock	Status	—	—	10	Both Sides
TM39	Rock Tomb	Rock	Physical	60	95	15	Normal
TM42	Facade	Normal	Physical	70	100	20	Normal
TM44	Rest	Psychic	Status	—	—	10	Self
TM45	Attract	Normal	Status	—	100	15	Normal
TM48	Round	Normal	Special	60	100	15	Normal
TM55	Scald	Water	Special	80	100	15	Normal
TM69	Rock Polish	Rock	Status	—	—	20	Self
TM71	Stone Edge	Rock	Physical	100	80	5	Normal
TM78	Bulldoze	Ground	Physical	60	100	20	Adjacent
TM80	Rock Slide	Rock	Physical	75	90	10	Many Others
TM87	Swagger	Normal	Status	—	85	15	Normal
TM88	Sleep Talk	Normal	Status	—	—	10	Self
TM90	Substitute	Normal	Status	—	—	10	Self
TM94	Surf	Water	Special	90	100	15	Adjacent
TM98	Waterfall	Water	Physical	80	100	15	Normal
TM100	Confide	Normal	Status	—	—	20	Normal

❖ MOVES TAUGHT BY PEOPLE
Name	Type	Kind	Pow.	Acc.	PP	Range

❖ MOVES LEARNED WHEN EVOLVING
Name	Type	Kind	Pow.	Acc.	PP	Range

❖ EGG MOVES
Name	Type	Kind	Pow.	Acc.	PP	Range
Water Pulse	Water	Special	60	100	20	Normal
Knock Off	Dark	Physical	65	100	20	Normal
Rock Throw	Rock	Physical	50	90	15	Normal
Slam	Normal	Physical	80	75	20	Normal
Iron Defense	Steel	Status	—	—	15	Self
Flail	Normal	Physical	—	100	15	Normal
Whirlpool	Water	Special	35	85	15	Normal
Body Slam	Normal	Physical	85	100	15	Normal
Bide	Normal	Physical	—	—	10	Self
Guard Swap	Psychic	Status	—	—	10	Normal
Liquidation	Water	Physical	85	100	10	Normal

❖ EXCLUSIVE Z-MOVE
Name	Base Move	Type	Kind	Pow.	Acc.	Range

Carracosta
Prototurtle Pokémon

WATER / ROCK

Alola Pokédex	Melemele	Akala	Ula'ula	Poni
195	—	122		

HEIGHT: 3'11"
WEIGHT: 178.6 lbs.

It constructed its sturdy shell by crunching and swallowing the hard shells or bones of its prey.

Active both on land and in the sea, this Pokémon drags its land-based prey into the water to finish it off.

ABILITY
Solid Rock
Sturdy

HIDDEN ABILITY
Swift Swim

SPECIES STRENGTHS
- HP ◆◆◆
- Attack ◆◆◆◆◆◆◆
- Defense ◆◆◆◆◆◆◆◆
- Sp. Atk ◆◆◆◆
- Sp. Def ◆◆◆◆
- Speed ◆◆

EGG GROUPS
Water 1 | Water 3

ITEM SOMETIMES HELD BY WILD POKÉMON
—

EVOLUTION
Tirtouga — Lv. 37 → Carracosta

MAIN WAY TO REGISTER IN THE POKÉDEX
Level up Tirtouga to Lv. 37

Same form for male/female

Damage taken in normal battles
NORMAL ×0.5	FIGHTING ×2	ROCK ×1
FIRE ×0.25	POISON ×0.5	GHOST ×1
WATER ×1	GROUND ×2	DRAGON ×1
GRASS ×4	FLYING ×0.5	DARK ×1
ELECTRIC ×2	PSYCHIC ×1	STEEL ×1
ICE ×0.5	BUG ×1	FAIRY ×1

❖ LEVEL-UP MOVES
Lv.	Name	Type	Kind	Pow.	Acc.	PP	Range
1	Bide	Normal	Physical	—	—	10	Self
1	Withdraw	Water	Status	—	—	40	Self
1	Water Gun	Water	Special	40	100	25	Normal
1	Rollout	Rock	Physical	30	90	20	Normal
5	Rollout	Rock	Physical	30	90	20	Normal
8	Bite	Dark	Physical	60	100	25	Normal
11	Protect	Normal	Status	—	—	10	Self
15	Aqua Jet	Water	Physical	40	100	20	Normal
18	Ancient Power	Rock	Special	60	100	5	Normal
21	Crunch	Dark	Physical	80	100	15	Normal
25	Wide Guard	Rock	Status	—	—	10	Your Side
28	Brine	Water	Special	65	100	10	Normal
31	Smack Down	Rock	Physical	50	100	15	Normal
35	Curse	Ghost	Status	—	—	10	Varies
40	Shell Smash	Normal	Status	—	—	15	Self
45	Aqua Tail	Water	Physical	90	90	10	Normal
51	Rock Slide	Rock	Physical	75	90	10	Many Others
56	Rain Dance	Water	Status	—	—	5	Both Sides
61	Hydro Pump	Water	Special	110	80	5	Normal

❖ TM MOVES
No.	Name	Type	Kind	Pow.	Acc.	PP	Range
TM06	Toxic	Poison	Status	—	90	10	Normal
TM10	Hidden Power	Normal	Special	60	100	15	Normal
TM13	Ice Beam	Ice	Special	90	100	10	Normal
TM14	Blizzard	Ice	Special	110	70	5	Many Others
TM15	Hyper Beam	Normal	Special	150	90	5	Normal
TM17	Protect	Normal	Status	—	—	10	Self
TM18	Rain Dance	Water	Status	—	—	5	Both Sides
TM21	Frustration	Normal	Physical	—	100	20	Normal
TM23	Smack Down	Rock	Physical	50	100	15	Normal
TM26	Earthquake	Ground	Physical	100	100	10	Adjacent
TM27	Return	Normal	Physical	—	100	20	Normal
TM32	Double Team	Normal	Status	—	—	15	Self
TM37	Sandstorm	Rock	Status	—	—	10	Both Sides
TM39	Rock Tomb	Rock	Physical	60	95	15	Normal
TM42	Facade	Normal	Physical	70	100	20	Normal
TM44	Rest	Psychic	Status	—	—	10	Self
TM45	Attract	Normal	Status	—	100	15	Normal
TM48	Round	Normal	Special	60	100	15	Normal
TM52	Focus Blast	Fighting	Special	120	70	5	Normal
TM55	Scald	Water	Special	80	100	15	Normal
TM68	Giga Impact	Normal	Physical	150	90	5	Normal
TM69	Rock Polish	Rock	Status	—	—	20	Self
TM71	Stone Edge	Rock	Physical	100	80	5	Normal
TM78	Bulldoze	Ground	Physical	60	100	20	Adjacent
TM80	Rock Slide	Rock	Physical	75	90	10	Many Others
TM87	Swagger	Normal	Status	—	85	15	Normal
TM88	Sleep Talk	Normal	Status	—	—	10	Self
TM90	Substitute	Normal	Status	—	—	10	Self

❖ MOVES TAUGHT BY PEOPLE
No.	Name	Type	Kind	Pow.	Acc.	PP	Range
TM94	Surf	Water	Special	90	100	15	Adjacent
TM98	Waterfall	Water	Physical	80	100	15	Normal
TM100	Confide	Normal	Status	—	—	20	Normal

❖ MOVES LEARNED WHEN EVOLVING
Name	Type	Kind	Pow.	Acc.	PP	Range

❖ EGG MOVES
Name	Type	Kind	Pow.	Acc.	PP	Range

❖ EXCLUSIVE Z-MOVE
Name	Base Move	Type	Kind	Pow.	Acc.	Range

Phantump

Alola Pokédex	Melemele	Akala	Ula'ula	Poni
196	—	123		

Stump Pokémon

GHOST **GRASS**

HEIGHT: 1'04"
WEIGHT: 15.4 lbs.

These Pokémon are stumps possessed by the spirits of children who died in the forest. Their cries sound like eerie screams.

According to legend, medicine to cure any illness can be made by plucking the green leaves on its head, brewing them, and boiling down the liquid.

Same form for male/female

ABILITY
Natural Cure
Frisk

HIDDEN ABILITY
Harvest

Damage taken in normal battles

NORMAL ×0	FIGHTING ×0	ROCK ×1			
FIRE ×2	POISON ×1	GHOST ×2			
WATER ×0.5	GROUND ×0.5	DRAGON ×1			
GRASS ×0.5	FLYING ×2	DARK ×1			
ELECTRIC ×0.5	PSYCHIC ×1	STEEL ×1			
ICE ×2	BUG ×1	FAIRY ×1			

SPECIES STRENGTHS
HP ◆◆
Attack ◆◆◆◆
Defense ◆◆◆
Sp. Atk ◆◆◆
Sp. Def ◆◆◆
Speed ◆◆◆

EGG GROUPS
Grass   Amorphous

ITEM SOMETIMES HELD BY WILD POKÉMON
—

EVOLUTION

Phantump → Trade Phantump → Trevenant

MAIN WAY TO REGISTER IN THE POKÉDEX
Catch in the tall grass on Memorial Hill

❖ LEVEL-UP MOVES

Lv.	Name	Type	Kind	Pow.	Acc.	PP	Range
1	Tackle	Normal	Physical	40	100	35	Normal
1	Confuse Ray	Ghost	Status	—	100	10	Normal
5	Astonish	Ghost	Physical	30	100	15	Normal
8	Growth	Normal	Status	—	—	20	Self
13	Ingrain	Grass	Status	—	—	20	Self
19	Feint Attack	Dark	Physical	60	—	20	Normal
23	Leech Seed	Grass	Status	—	90	10	Normal
28	Curse	Ghost	Status	—	—	10	Varies
31	Will-O-Wisp	Fire	Status	—	85	15	Normal
35	Forest's Curse	Grass	Status	—	100	20	Normal
39	Destiny Bond	Ghost	Status	—	—	5	Self
45	Phantom Force	Ghost	Physical	90	100	10	Normal
49	Wood Hammer	Grass	Physical	120	100	15	Normal
54	Horn Leech	Grass	Physical	75	100	10	Normal

❖ TM MOVES

No.	Name	Type	Kind	Pow.	Acc.	PP	Range
TM06	Toxic	Poison	Status	—	90	10	Normal
TM10	Hidden Power	Normal	Special	60	100	15	Normal
TM11	Sunny Day	Fire	Status	—	—	5	Both Sides
TM17	Protect	Normal	Status	—	—	10	Self
TM20	Safeguard	Normal	Status	—	—	25	Your Side
TM21	Frustration	Normal	Physical	—	100	20	Normal
TM22	Solar Beam	Grass	Special	120	100	10	Normal
TM27	Return	Normal	Physical	—	100	20	Normal
TM29	Psychic	Psychic	Special	90	100	10	Normal
TM30	Shadow Ball	Ghost	Special	80	100	15	Normal
TM32	Double Team	Normal	Status	—	—	15	Self
TM33	Reflect	Psychic	Status	—	—	20	Your Side
TM42	Facade	Normal	Physical	70	100	20	Normal
TM44	Rest	Psychic	Status	—	—	10	Self
TM45	Attract	Normal	Status	—	100	15	Normal
TM46	Thief	Dark	Physical	60	100	25	Normal
TM48	Round	Normal	Special	60	100	15	Normal
TM53	Energy Ball	Grass	Special	90	100	10	Normal
TM61	Will-O-Wisp	Fire	Status	—	85	15	Normal
TM65	Shadow Claw	Ghost	Physical	70	100	15	Normal
TM78	Bulldoze	Ground	Physical	60	100	20	Adjacent
TM80	Rock Slide	Rock	Physical	75	90	10	Many Others
TM84	Poison Jab	Poison	Physical	80	100	20	Normal
TM85	Dream Eater	Psychic	Special	100	100	15	Normal
TM86	Grass Knot	Grass	Special	—	100	20	Normal
TM87	Swagger	Normal	Status	—	85	15	Normal
TM88	Sleep Talk	Normal	Status	—	—	10	Self
TM90	Substitute	Normal	Status	—	—	10	Self

No.	Name	Type	Kind	Pow.	Acc.	PP	Range
TM92	Trick Room	Psychic	Status	—	—	5	Both Sides
TM96	Nature Power	Normal	Status	—	—	20	Normal
TM97	Dark Pulse	Dark	Special	80	100	15	Normal
TM100	Confide	Normal	Status	—	—	20	Normal

❖ MOVES TAUGHT BY PEOPLE

Name	Type	Kind	Pow.	Acc.	PP	Range

❖ MOVES LEARNED WHEN EVOLVING

Name	Type	Kind	Pow.	Acc.	PP	Range

❖ EGG MOVES

Name	Type	Kind	Pow.	Acc.	PP	Range
Grudge	Ghost	Status	—	—	5	Self
Bestow	Normal	Status	—	—	15	Normal
Imprison	Psychic	Status	—	—	10	Self
Venom Drench	Poison	Status	—	100	20	Many Others

❖ EXCLUSIVE Z-MOVE

Name	Base Move	Type	Kind	Pow.	Acc.	Range

Trevenant

Alola Pokédex	Melemele	Akala	Ula'ula	Poni
197	—	124		

Elder Tree Pokémon

GHOST **GRASS**

HEIGHT: 4'11"
WEIGHT: 156.5 lbs.

This Pokémon is said to devour anyone daring to ravage the forest. To the creatures dwelling in the forest, it offers great kindness.

Through its roots, it exerts control over other trees. A deadly curse falls upon anyone cutting down trees in forests where Trevenant dwell.

Same form for male/female

ABILITY
Natural Cure
Frisk

HIDDEN ABILITY
Harvest

Damage taken in normal battles

NORMAL ×0	FIGHTING ×0	ROCK ×1			
FIRE ×2	POISON ×1	GHOST ×2			
WATER ×0.5	GROUND ×0.5	DRAGON ×1			
GRASS ×0.5	FLYING ×2	DARK ×1			
ELECTRIC ×0.5	PSYCHIC ×1	STEEL ×1			
ICE ×2	BUG ×1	FAIRY ×1			

SPECIES STRENGTHS
HP ◆◆◆
Attack ◆◆◆◆◆◆
Defense ◆◆◆◆
Sp. Atk ◆◆◆◆
Sp. Def ◆◆◆◆
Speed ◆◆◆

EGG GROUPS
Grass   Amorphous

ITEM SOMETIMES HELD BY WILD POKÉMON
—

EVOLUTION

Phantump → Trade Phantump → Trevenant

MAIN WAY TO REGISTER IN THE POKÉDEX
Receive a Phantump in a trade and it will evolve

❖ LEVEL-UP MOVES

Lv.	Name	Type	Kind	Pow.	Acc.	PP	Range
1	Shadow Claw	Ghost	Physical	70	100	15	Normal
1	Horn Leech	Grass	Physical	75	100	10	Normal
1	Tackle	Normal	Physical	40	100	35	Normal
1	Confuse Ray	Ghost	Status	—	100	10	Normal
1	Astonish	Ghost	Physical	30	100	15	Normal
1	Growth	Normal	Status	—	—	20	Self
5	Astonish	Ghost	Physical	30	100	15	Normal
8	Growth	Normal	Status	—	—	20	Self
13	Ingrain	Grass	Status	—	—	20	Self
19	Feint Attack	Dark	Physical	60	—	20	Normal
23	Leech Seed	Grass	Status	—	90	10	Normal
28	Curse	Ghost	Status	—	—	10	Varies
31	Will-O-Wisp	Fire	Status	—	85	15	Normal
35	Forest's Curse	Grass	Status	—	100	20	Normal
39	Destiny Bond	Ghost	Status	—	—	5	Self
45	Phantom Force	Ghost	Physical	90	100	10	Normal
49	Wood Hammer	Grass	Physical	120	100	15	Normal
54	Horn Leech	Grass	Physical	75	100	10	Normal

❖ TM MOVES

No.	Name	Type	Kind	Pow.	Acc.	PP	Range
TM04	Calm Mind	Psychic	Status	—	—	20	Self
TM06	Toxic	Poison	Status	—	90	10	Normal
TM10	Hidden Power	Normal	Special	60	100	15	Normal
TM11	Sunny Day	Fire	Status	—	—	5	Both Sides
TM15	Hyper Beam	Normal	Special	150	90	5	Normal
TM17	Protect	Normal	Status	—	—	10	Self
TM20	Safeguard	Normal	Status	—	—	25	Your Side
TM21	Frustration	Normal	Physical	—	100	20	Normal
TM22	Solar Beam	Grass	Special	120	100	10	Normal
TM26	Earthquake	Ground	Physical	100	100	10	Adjacent
TM27	Return	Normal	Physical	—	100	20	Normal
TM29	Psychic	Psychic	Special	90	100	10	Normal
TM30	Shadow Ball	Ghost	Special	80	100	15	Normal
TM32	Double Team	Normal	Status	—	—	15	Self
TM33	Reflect	Psychic	Status	—	—	20	Your Side
TM42	Facade	Normal	Physical	70	100	20	Normal
TM44	Rest	Psychic	Status	—	—	10	Self
TM45	Attract	Normal	Status	—	100	15	Normal
TM46	Thief	Dark	Physical	60	100	25	Normal
TM48	Round	Normal	Special	60	100	15	Normal
TM52	Focus Blast	Fighting	Special	120	70	5	Normal
TM53	Energy Ball	Grass	Special	90	100	10	Normal
TM59	Brutal Swing	Dark	Physical	60	100	20	Adjacent
TM61	Will-O-Wisp	Fire	Status	—	85	15	Normal
TM65	Shadow Claw	Ghost	Physical	70	100	15	Normal
TM68	Giga Impact	Normal	Physical	150	90	5	Normal
TM78	Bulldoze	Ground	Physical	60	100	20	Adjacent
TM80	Rock Slide	Rock	Physical	75	90	10	Many Others

No.	Name	Type	Kind	Pow.	Acc.	PP	Range
TM81	X-Scissor	Bug	Physical	80	100	15	Normal
TM84	Poison Jab	Poison	Physical	80	100	20	Normal
TM85	Dream Eater	Psychic	Special	100	100	15	Normal
TM86	Grass Knot	Grass	Special	—	100	20	Normal
TM87	Swagger	Normal	Status	—	85	15	Normal
TM88	Sleep Talk	Normal	Status	—	—	10	Self
TM90	Substitute	Normal	Status	—	—	10	Self
TM92	Trick Room	Psychic	Status	—	—	5	Both Sides
TM96	Nature Power	Normal	Status	—	—	20	Normal
TM97	Dark Pulse	Dark	Special	80	100	15	Normal
TM100	Confide	Normal	Status	—	—	20	Normal

❖ MOVES TAUGHT BY PEOPLE

Name	Type	Kind	Pow.	Acc.	PP	Range

❖ MOVES LEARNED WHEN EVOLVING

Name	Type	Kind	Pow.	Acc.	PP	Range
Shadow Claw	Ghost	Physical	70	100	15	Normal

❖ EGG MOVES

Name	Type	Kind	Pow.	Acc.	PP	Range

❖ EXCLUSIVE Z-MOVE

Name	Base Move	Type	Kind	Pow.	Acc.	Range

Alola Pokédex	Melemele	Akala	Ula'ula	Poni
198	—	125		

Nosepass

Compass Pokémon

ROCK

HEIGHT: 3'03"
WEIGHT: 213.8 lbs.

The magnet in Nosepass's nose provides an unerring compass, making it an excellent partner for Trainers going on a journey.

It uses powerful magnetism to drag its prey toward it. It's also been known to pull in metal, which it collects and uses to protect itself.

Same form for male/female

ABILITY
Sturdy
Magnet Pull

HIDDEN ABILITY
Sand Force

SPECIES STRENGTHS
HP ◆
Attack ◆◆◆
Defense ◆◆◆◆◆◆◆
Sp. Atk ◆◆◆
Sp. Def ◆◆◆◆◆
Speed ◆◆

EGG GROUPS
Mineral

ITEM SOMETIMES HELD BY WILD POKÉMON
Magnet

EVOLUTION
Nosepass → **Level up in Vast Poni Canyon** → Probopass

MAIN WAY TO REGISTER IN THE POKÉDEX
Catch in the tall grass in Akala Outskirts

Damage taken in normal battles

NORMAL ×0.5	FIGHTING ×2	ROCK ×1
FIRE ×0.5	POISON ×0.5	GHOST ×1
WATER ×2	GROUND ×2	DRAGON ×1
GRASS ×2	FLYING ×1	DARK ×1
ELECTRIC ×1	PSYCHIC ×1	STEEL ×0.5
ICE ×1	BUG ×1	FAIRY ×1

❖ LEVEL-UP MOVES

Lv.	Name	Type	Kind	Pow.	Acc.	PP	Range
1	Tackle	Normal	Physical	40	100	35	Normal
4	Harden	Normal	Status	—	—	30	Self
7	Block	Normal	Status	—	—	5	Normal
10	Rock Throw	Rock	Physical	50	90	15	Normal
13	Thunder Wave	Electric	Status	—	90	20	Normal
16	Rest	Psychic	Status	—	—	10	Self
19	Spark	Electric	Physical	65	100	20	Normal
22	Rock Slide	Rock	Physical	75	90	10	Many Others
25	Power Gem	Rock	Special	80	100	20	Normal
28	Rock Blast	Rock	Physical	25	90	10	Normal
31	Discharge	Electric	Special	80	100	15	Adjacent
34	Sandstorm	Rock	Status	—	—	10	Both Sides
37	Earth Power	Ground	Special	90	100	10	Normal
40	Stone Edge	Rock	Physical	100	80	5	Normal
43	Lock-On	Normal	Status	—	—	5	Normal
43	Zap Cannon	Electric	Special	120	50	5	Normal

❖ TM MOVES

No.	Name	Type	Kind	Pow.	Acc.	PP	Range
TM06	Toxic	Poison	Status	—	90	10	Normal
TM10	Hidden Power	Normal	Special	60	100	15	Normal
TM11	Sunny Day	Fire	Status	—	—	5	Both Sides
TM12	Taunt	Dark	Status	—	100	20	Normal
TM17	Protect	Normal	Status	—	—	10	Self
TM21	Frustration	Normal	Physical	—	100	20	Normal
TM23	Smack Down	Rock	Physical	50	100	15	Normal
TM24	Thunderbolt	Electric	Special	90	100	15	Normal
TM25	Thunder	Electric	Special	110	70	10	Normal
TM26	Earthquake	Ground	Physical	100	100	10	Adjacent
TM27	Return	Normal	Physical	—	100	20	Normal
TM32	Double Team	Normal	Status	—	—	15	Self
TM37	Sandstorm	Rock	Status	—	—	10	Both Sides
TM39	Rock Tomb	Rock	Physical	60	95	15	Normal
TM41	Torment	Dark	Status	—	100	15	Normal
TM42	Facade	Normal	Physical	70	100	20	Normal
TM44	Rest	Psychic	Status	—	—	10	Self
TM45	Attract	Normal	Status	—	100	15	Normal
TM48	Round	Normal	Special	60	100	15	Normal
TM64	Explosion	Normal	Physical	250	100	5	Adjacent
TM69	Rock Polish	Rock	Status	—	—	20	Self
TM71	Stone Edge	Rock	Physical	100	80	5	Normal
TM72	Volt Switch	Electric	Special	70	100	20	Normal
TM73	Thunder Wave	Electric	Status	—	90	20	Normal
TM78	Bulldoze	Ground	Physical	60	100	20	Adjacent
TM80	Rock Slide	Rock	Physical	75	90	10	Many Others
TM87	Swagger	Normal	Status	—	85	15	Normal
TM88	Sleep Talk	Normal	Status	—	—	10	Self

❖ MOVES TAUGHT BY PEOPLE

Name	Type	Kind	Pow.	Acc.	PP	Range
TM90	Substitute	Normal	Status	—	—	10	Self
TM99	Dazzling Gleam	Fairy	Special	80	100	10	Many Others
TM100	Confide	Normal	Status	—	—	20	Normal

❖ MOVES LEARNED WHEN EVOLVING

Name	Type	Kind	Pow.	Acc.	PP	Range

❖ EGG MOVES

Name	Type	Kind	Pow.	Acc.	PP	Range
Magnitude	Ground	Physical	—	100	30	Adjacent
Rollout	Rock	Physical	30	90	20	Normal
Double-Edge	Normal	Physical	120	100	15	Normal
Block	Normal	Status	—	—	5	Normal
Stealth Rock	Rock	Status	—	—	20	Other Side
Endure	Normal	Status	—	—	10	Self
Wide Guard	Rock	Status	—	—	10	Your Side

❖ EXCLUSIVE Z-MOVE

Name	Base Move	Type	Kind	Pow.	Acc.	Range

Alola Pokédex	Melemele	Akala	Ula'ula	Poni
199	—	126		

Probopass

Compass Pokémon

ROCK **STEEL**

HEIGHT: 4'07"
WEIGHT: 749.6 lbs.

It radiates such a powerful magnetic field that nearby electrical appliances become unusable.

The main body controls three mobile units called Mini-Noses, which it maneuvers to catch prey.

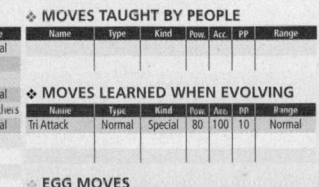
Same form for male/female

ABILITY
Sturdy
Magnet Pull

HIDDEN ABILITY
Sand Force

SPECIES STRENGTHS
HP ◆◆
Attack ◆◆◆
Defense ◆◆◆◆◆◆◆◆
Sp. Atk ◆◆◆◆
Sp. Def ◆◆◆◆◆◆◆◆
Speed ◆◆◆

EGG GROUPS
Mineral

ITEM SOMETIMES HELD BY WILD POKÉMON

EVOLUTION
Nosepass → **Level up in Vast Poni Canyon** → Probopass

MAIN WAY TO REGISTER IN THE POKÉDEX
Level up Nosepass in Vast Poni Canyon

Damage taken in normal battles

NORMAL ×0.25	FIGHTING ×4	ROCK ×0.5
FIRE ×1	POISON ×0	GHOST ×1
WATER ×2	GROUND ×4	DRAGON ×0.5
GRASS ×1	FLYING ×0.25	DARK ×1
ELECTRIC ×1	PSYCHIC ×1	STEEL ×0.5
ICE ×0.5	BUG ×0.5	FAIRY ×0.5

❖ LEVEL-UP MOVES

Lv.	Name	Type	Kind	Pow.	Acc.	PP	Range
1	Tri Attack	Normal	Special	80	100	10	Normal
1	Magnetic Flux	Electric	Status	—	—	20	Your Party
1	Magnet Rise	Electric	Status	—	—	10	Self
1	Gravity	Psychic	Status	—	—	5	Both Sides
1	Wide Guard	Rock	Status	—	—	10	Your Side
1	Tackle	Normal	Physical	40	100	35	Normal
1	Iron Defense	Steel	Status	—	—	15	Self
1	Block	Normal	Status	—	—	5	Normal
1	Magnet Bomb	Steel	Physical	60	—	20	Normal
4	Iron Defense	Steel	Status	—	—	15	Self
7	Block	Normal	Status	—	—	5	Normal
10	Magnet Bomb	Steel	Physical	60	—	20	Normal
13	Thunder Wave	Electric	Status	—	90	20	Normal
16	Rest	Psychic	Status	—	—	10	Self
19	Spark	Electric	Physical	65	100	20	Normal
22	Rock Slide	Rock	Physical	75	90	10	Many Others
25	Power Gem	Rock	Special	80	100	20	Normal
28	Rock Blast	Rock	Physical	25	90	10	Normal
31	Discharge	Electric	Special	80	100	15	Adjacent
34	Sandstorm	Rock	Status	—	—	10	Both Sides
37	Earth Power	Ground	Special	90	100	10	Normal
40	Stone Edge	Rock	Physical	100	80	5	Normal
43	Lock-On	Normal	Status	—	—	5	Normal
43	Zap Cannon	Electric	Special	120	50	5	Normal

❖ TM MOVES

No.	Name	Type	Kind	Pow.	Acc.	PP	Range
TM06	Toxic	Poison	Status	—	90	10	Normal
TM10	Hidden Power	Normal	Special	60	100	15	Normal
TM11	Sunny Day	Fire	Status	—	—	5	Both Sides
TM12	Taunt	Dark	Status	—	100	20	Normal
TM15	Hyper Beam	Normal	Special	150	90	5	Normal
TM17	Protect	Normal	Status	—	—	10	Self
TM21	Frustration	Normal	Physical	—	100	20	Normal
TM23	Smack Down	Rock	Physical	50	100	15	Normal
TM24	Thunderbolt	Electric	Special	90	100	15	Normal
TM25	Thunder	Electric	Special	110	70	10	Normal
TM26	Earthquake	Ground	Physical	100	100	10	Adjacent
TM27	Return	Normal	Physical	—	100	20	Normal
TM32	Double Team	Normal	Status	—	—	15	Self
TM37	Sandstorm	Rock	Status	—	—	10	Both Sides
TM39	Rock Tomb	Rock	Physical	60	95	15	Normal
TM41	Torment	Dark	Status	—	100	15	Normal
TM42	Facade	Normal	Physical	70	100	20	Normal
TM44	Rest	Psychic	Status	—	—	10	Self
TM45	Attract	Normal	Status	—	100	15	Normal
TM48	Round	Normal	Special	60	100	15	Normal
TM64	Explosion	Normal	Physical	250	100	5	Adjacent
TM68	Giga Impact	Normal	Physical	150	90	5	Normal
TM69	Rock Polish	Rock	Status	—	—	20	Self
TM71	Stone Edge	Rock	Physical	100	80	5	Normal
TM72	Volt Switch	Electric	Special	70	100	20	Normal
TM73	Thunder Wave	Electric	Status	—	90	20	Normal
TM78	Bulldoze	Ground	Physical	60	100	20	Adjacent
TM80	Rock Slide	Rock	Physical	75	90	10	Many Others

❖ MOVES TAUGHT BY PEOPLE

No.	Name	Type	Kind	Pow.	Acc.	PP	Range
TM87	Swagger	Normal	Status	—	85	15	Normal
TM88	Sleep Talk	Normal	Status	—	—	10	Self
TM90	Substitute	Normal	Status	—	—	10	Self
TM91	Flash Cannon	Steel	Special	80	100	10	Normal
TM99	Dazzling Gleam	Fairy	Special	80	100	10	Many Others
TM100	Confide	Normal	Status	—	—	20	Normal

❖ MOVES LEARNED WHEN EVOLVING

Name	Type	Kind	Pow.	Acc.	PP	Range
Tri Attack	Normal	Special	80	100	10	Normal

❖ EGG MOVES

Name	Type	Kind	Pow.	Acc.	PP	Range

❖ EXCLUSIVE Z-MOVE

Name	Base Move	Type	Kind	Pow.	Acc.	Range

Alola Pokédex	Melemele	Akala	Ula'ula	Poni
200	—	127	—	—

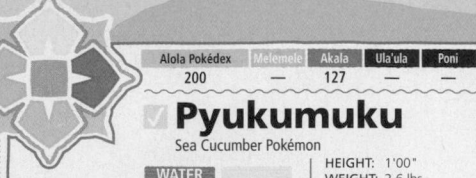

Pyukumuku

Sea Cucumber Pokémon

WATER

HEIGHT: 1'00"
WEIGHT: 2.6 lbs.

It lives in shallow seas, such as areas near a beach. It can eject its internal organs, which it uses to engulf its prey or battle enemies.

These Pokémon line the beaches. The sticky mucous that covers their bodies can be used to soothe sunburned skin. How convenient!

Same form for male/female

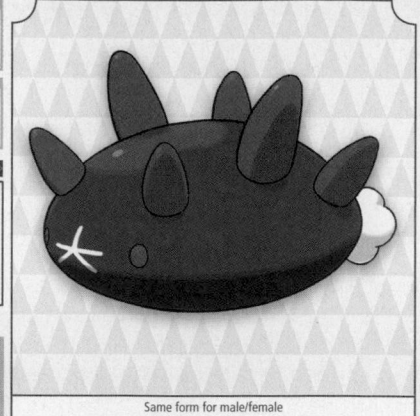

ABILITY
Innards Out

HIDDEN ABILITY
Unaware

Damage taken in normal battles

NORMAL	×1	FIGHTING	×1	ROCK	×1
FIRE	×0.5	POISON	×1	GHOST	×1
WATER	×0.5	GROUND	×1	DRAGON	×1
GRASS	×2	FLYING	×1	DARK	×1
ELECTRIC	×2	PSYCHIC	×1	STEEL	×0.5
ICE	×0.5	BUG	×1	FAIRY	×1

SPECIES STRENGTHS
HP ◆◆
Attack ◆◆◆
Defense ◆◆◆◆◆◆◆
Sp. Atk ◆◆
Sp. Def ◆◆◆◆◆◆◆◆
Speed ◆

EGG GROUPS
Water 1

ITEM SOMETIMES HELD BY WILD POKÉMON
—

EVOLUTION
Does not evolve

MAIN WAY TO REGISTER IN THE POKEDEX
Catch on the water surface on Route 7

❖ LEVEL-UP MOVES

Lv.	Name	Type	Kind	Pow.	Acc.	PP	Range
1	Baton Pass	Normal	Status	—	—	40	Self
1	Water Sport	Water	Status	—	—	15	Both Sides
1	Mud Sport	Ground	Status	—	—	15	Both Sides
1	Harden	Normal	Status	—	—	30	Self
1	Bide	Normal	Physical	—	—	10	Self
5	Helping Hand	Normal	Status	—	—	20	1 Ally
9	Taunt	Dark	Status	—	100	20	Normal
13	Safeguard	Normal	Status	—	—	25	Your Side
17	Counter	Fighting	Physical	—	100	20	Varies
21	Purify	Poison	Status	—	—	20	Normal
25	Curse	Ghost	Status	—	—	10	Varies
29	Gastro Acid	Poison	Status	—	100	10	Normal
33	Pain Split	Normal	Status	—	—	20	Normal
37	Recover	Normal	Status	—	—	10	Self
41	Soak	Water	Status	—	100	20	Normal
45	Toxic	Poison	Status	—	90	10	Normal
49	Memento	Dark	Status	—	100	10	Normal

❖ TM MOVES

No.	Name	Type	Kind	Pow.	Acc.	PP	Range
TM06	Toxic	Poison	Status	—	90	10	Normal
TM07	Hail	Ice	Status	—	—	10	Both Sides
TM12	Taunt	Dark	Status	—	100	20	Normal
TM16	Light Screen	Psychic	Status	—	—	30	Your Side
TM17	Protect	Normal	Status	—	—	10	Self
TM18	Rain Dance	Water	Status	—	—	5	Both Sides
TM20	Safeguard	Normal	Status	—	—	25	Your Side
TM32	Double Team	Normal	Status	—	—	15	Self
TM33	Reflect	Psychic	Status	—	—	20	Your Side
TM44	Rest	Psychic	Status	—	—	10	Self
TM45	Attract	Normal	Status	—	100	15	Normal
TM60	Quash	Dark	Status	—	100	15	Normal
TM77	Psych Up	Normal	Status	—	—	10	Normal
TM87	Swagger	Normal	Status	—	85	15	Normal
TM88	Sleep Talk	Normal	Status	—	—	10	Self
TM90	Substitute	Normal	Status	—	—	10	Self
TM100	Confide	Normal	Status	—	—	20	Normal

No.	Name	Type	Kind	Pow.	Acc.	PP	Range

❖ EXCLUSIVE Z-MOVE

Name	Base Move	Type	Kind	Pow.	Acc.	Range

❖ MOVES TAUGHT BY PEOPLE

Name	Type	Kind	Pow.	Acc.	PP	Range

❖ MOVES LEARNED WHEN EVOLVING

Name	Type	Kind	Pow.	Acc.	PP	Range

❖ EGG MOVES

Name	Type	Kind	Pow.	Acc.	PP	Range
Endure	Normal	Status	—	—	10	Self
Venom Drench	Poison	Status	—	100	20	Many Others
Bestow	Normal	Status	—	—	15	Normal
Tickle	Normal	Status	—	100	20	Normal

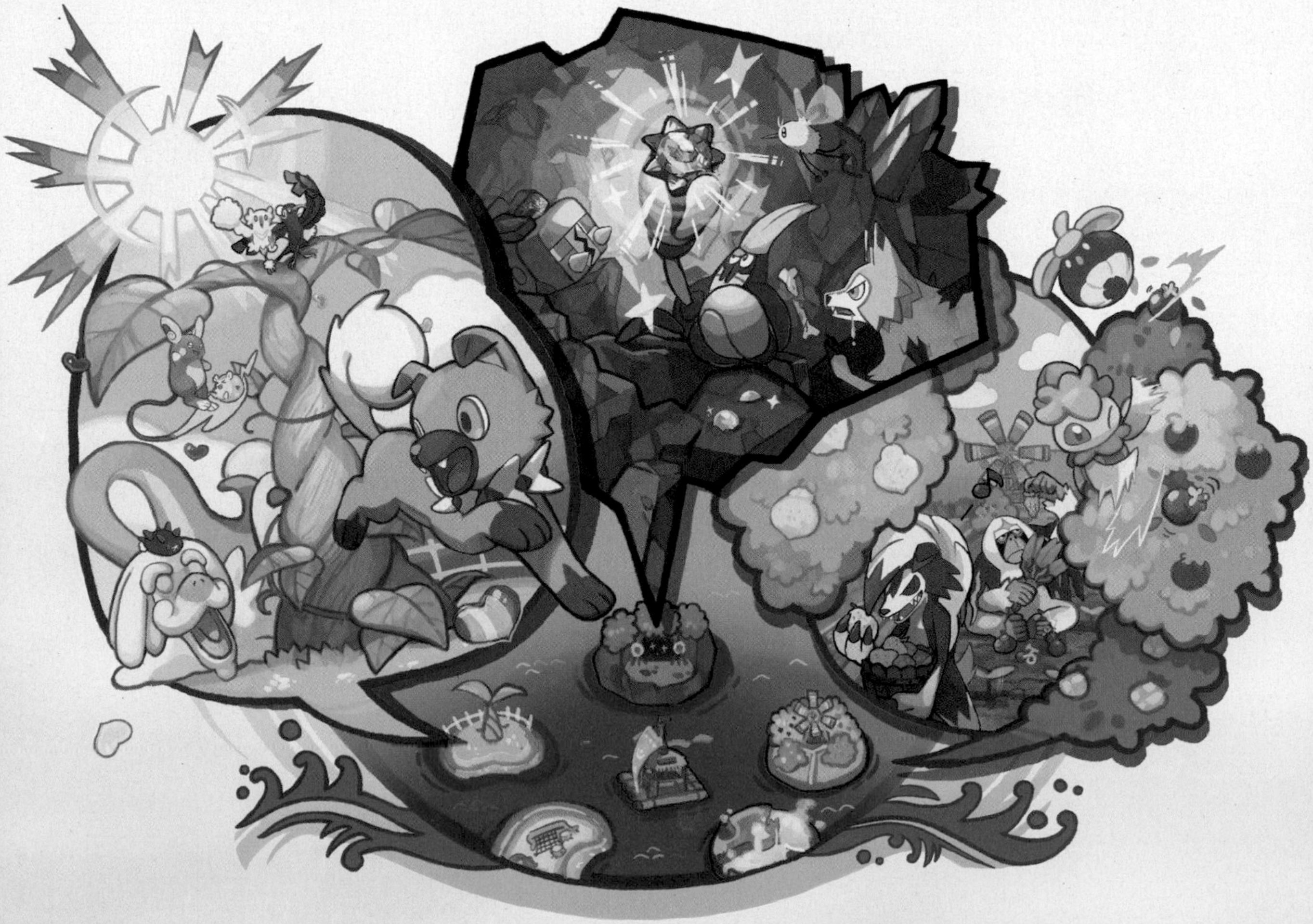

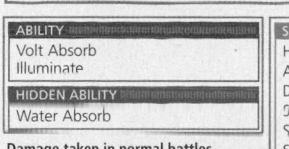

Alola Pokédex	Melemele	Akala	Ula'ula	Poni
201	—	128	—	—

☑ Chinchou

Angler Pokémon

WATER **ELECTRIC**

HEIGHT: 1'08"
WEIGHT: 26.5 lbs.

Its two antennae were originally fins. It discharges electricity to stun its prey before attacking.

It lives in the depths beyond the reach of sunlight. It flashes lights on its antennae to communicate with others of its kind.

ABILITY
Volt Absorb
Illuminate

HIDDEN ABILITY
Water Absorb

SPECIES STRENGTHS
HP	◆◆◆
Attack	◆◆
Defense	◆◆
Sp. Atk	◆◆◆
Sp. Def	◆◆◆
Speed	◆◆◆◆

EGG GROUPS
Water 2

ITEM SOMETIMES HELD BY WILD POKÉMON
Deep Sea Scale

Damage taken in normal battles
NORMAL ×1	FIGHTING ×1	ROCK ×1
FIRE ×0.5	POISON ×1	GHOST ×1
WATER ×0.5	GROUND ×1	DRAGON ×1
GRASS ×2	FLYING ×0.5	DARK ×1
ELECTRIC ×1	PSYCHIC ×1	STEEL ×0.25
ICE ×0.5	BUG ×1	FAIRY ×1

EVOLUTION
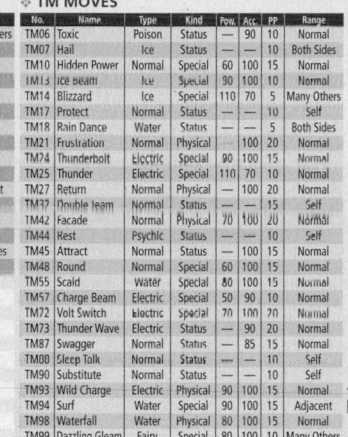
Chinchou → LV. 27 → Lanturn

MAIN WAY TO REGISTER IN THE POKÉDEX
Catch in the rare fishing spot on Route 8

Same form for male/female

❖ LEVEL-UP MOVES
Lv.	Name	Type	Kind	Pow.	Acc.	PP	Range
1	Bubble	Water	Special	40	100	30	Many Others
1	Supersonic	Normal	Status	—	55	20	Normal
6	Thunder Wave	Electric	Status	—	90	20	Normal
9	Electro Ball	Electric	Special	—	100	10	Normal
12	Water Gun	Water	Special	40	100	25	Normal
17	Confuse Ray	Ghost	Status	—	100	10	Normal
20	Bubble Beam	Water	Special	65	100	20	Normal
23	Spark	Electric	Physical	65	100	20	Normal
26	Signal Beam	Bug	Special	75	100	15	Normal
31	Flail	Normal	Physical	—	100	15	Normal
34	Discharge	Electric	Special	80	100	15	Adjacent
39	Take Down	Normal	Physical	90	85	20	Normal
42	Aqua Ring	Water	Status	—	—	20	Self
45	Hydro Pump	Water	Special	110	80	5	Normal
47	Ion Deluge	Electric	Status	—	—	25	Both Sides
50	Charge	Electric	Status	—	—	20	Self

❖ TM MOVES
No.	Name	Type	Kind	Pow.	Acc.	PP	Range
TM06	Toxic	Poison	Status	—	90	10	Normal
TM07	Hail	Ice	Status	—	—	10	Both Sides
TM10	Hidden Power	Normal	Special	60	100	15	Normal
TM13	Ice Beam	Ice	Special	90	100	10	Normal
TM14	Blizzard	Ice	Special	110	70	5	Many Others
TM17	Protect	Normal	Status	—	—	10	Self
TM18	Rain Dance	Water	Status	—	—	5	Both Sides
TM21	Frustration	Normal	Physical	—	100	20	Normal
TM24	Thunderbolt	Electric	Special	90	100	15	Normal
TM25	Thunder	Electric	Special	110	70	10	Normal
TM27	Return	Normal	Physical	—	100	20	Normal
TM32	Double Team	Normal	Status	—	—	15	Self
TM42	Facade	Normal	Physical	70	100	20	Normal
TM44	Rest	Psychic	Status	—	—	10	Self
TM45	Attract	Normal	Status	—	100	15	Normal
TM48	Round	Normal	Special	60	100	15	Normal
TM55	Scald	Water	Special	80	100	15	Normal
TM57	Charge Beam	Electric	Special	50	90	10	Normal
TM72	Volt Switch	Electric	Special	70	100	20	Normal
TM73	Thunder Wave	Electric	Status	—	90	20	Normal
TM87	Swagger	Normal	Status	—	85	15	Normal
TM88	Sleep Talk	Normal	Status	—	—	10	Self
TM90	Substitute	Normal	Status	—	—	10	Self
TM93	Wild Charge	Electric	Physical	90	100	15	Normal
TM94	Surf	Water	Special	90	100	15	Adjacent
TM98	Waterfall	Water	Physical	80	100	15	Normal
TM99	Dazzling Gleam	Fairy	Special	80	100	10	Many Others
TM100	Confide	Normal	Status	—	—	20	Normal

❖ MOVES TAUGHT BY PEOPLE
Name	Type	Kind	Pow.	Acc.	PP	Range

❖ MOVES LEARNED WHEN EVOLVING
Name	Type	Kind	Pow.	Acc.	PP	Range

❖ EGG MOVES
Name	Type	Kind	Pow.	Acc.	PP	Range
Flail	Normal	Physical	—	100	15	Normal
Eerie Impulse	Normal	Status	—	85	40	Normal
Amnesia	Psychic	Status	—	—	20	Self
Psybeam	Psychic	Special	65	100	20	Normal
Whirlpool	Water	Special	35	85	15	Normal
Agility	Psychic	Status	—	—	30	Self
Mist	Ice	Status	—	—	30	Your Side
Shock Wave	Electric	Special	60	—	20	Normal
Brine	Water	Special	65	100	10	Normal
Water Pulse	Water	Special	60	100	20	Normal
Soak	Water	Status	—	100	20	Normal

❖ EXCLUSIVE Z-MOVE
Name	Base Move	Type	Kind	Pow.	Acc.	Range

Alola Pokédex	Melemele	Akala	Ula'ula	Poni
202	—	129	—	—

☑ Lanturn

Light Pokémon

WATER **ELECTRIC**

HEIGHT: 3'11"
WEIGHT: 49.6 lbs.

Should you peer into the ocean at night and see a light shining like the stars, that is Lanturn.

This Pokémon flashes a bright light that blinds its prey. This creates an opening for it to deliver an electrical attack.

ABILITY
Volt Absorb
Illuminate

HIDDEN ABILITY
Water Absorb

SPECIES STRENGTHS
HP	◆◆◆◆◆
Attack	◆◆◆
Defense	◆◆◆
Sp. Atk	◆◆◆◆
Sp. Def	◆◆◆
Speed	◆◆◆◆

EGG GROUPS
Water 2

ITEM SOMETIMES HELD BY WILD POKÉMON
—

Damage taken in normal battles
NORMAL ×1	FIGHTING ×1	ROCK ×1
FIRE ×0.5	POISON ×1	GHOST ×1
WATER ×0.5	GROUND ×1	DRAGON ×1
GRASS ×2	FLYING ×0.5	DARK ×1
ELECTRIC ×1	PSYCHIC ×1	STEEL ×0.25
ICE ×0.5	BUG ×1	FAIRY ×1

EVOLUTION
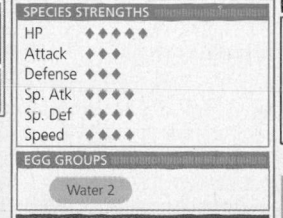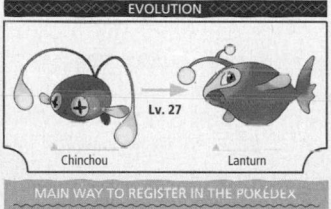
Chinchou → LV. 27 → Lanturn

MAIN WAY TO REGISTER IN THE POKÉDEX
Level up Chinchou to Lv. 27

Same form for male/female

❖ LEVEL-UP MOVES
Lv.	Name	Type	Kind	Pow.	Acc.	PP	Range
1	Stockpile	Normal	Status	—	—	20	Self
1	Swallow	Normal	Status	—	—	10	Self
1	Spit Up	Normal	Special	—	100	10	Normal
1	Eerie Impulse	Normal	Status	—	100	15	Normal
1	Bubble	Water	Special	40	100	30	Many Others
1	Supersonic	Normal	Status	—	55	20	Normal
1	Thunder Wave	Electric	Status	—	90	20	Normal
1	Electro Ball	Electric	Special	—	100	10	Normal
6	Thunder Wave	Electric	Status	—	90	20	Normal
9	Electro Ball	Electric	Special	—	100	10	Normal
12	Water Gun	Water	Special	40	100	25	Normal
17	Confuse Ray	Ghost	Status	—	100	10	Normal
20	Bubble Beam	Water	Special	65	100	20	Normal
23	Spark	Electric	Physical	65	100	20	Normal
29	Signal Beam	Bug	Special	75	100	15	Normal
33	Flail	Normal	Physical	—	100	15	Normal
37	Discharge	Electric	Special	80	100	15	Adjacent
43	Take Down	Normal	Physical	90	85	20	Normal
47	Aqua Ring	Water	Status	—	—	20	Self
51	Hydro Pump	Water	Special	110	80	5	Normal
54	Ion Deluge	Electric	Status	—	—	25	Both Sides
58	Charge	Electric	Status	—	—	20	Self

❖ TM MOVES
No.	Name	Type	Kind	Pow.	Acc.	PP	Range
TM06	Toxic	Poison	Status	—	90	10	Normal
TM07	Hail	Ice	Status	—	—	10	Both Sides
TM10	Hidden Power	Normal	Special	60	100	15	Normal
TM13	Ice Beam	Ice	Special	90	100	10	Normal
TM14	Blizzard	Ice	Special	110	70	5	Many Others
TM15	Hyper Beam	Normal	Special	150	90	5	Normal
TM17	Protect	Normal	Status	—	—	10	Self
TM18	Rain Dance	Water	Status	—	—	5	Both Sides
TM21	Frustration	Normal	Physical	—	100	20	Normal
TM24	Thunderbolt	Electric	Special	90	100	15	Normal
TM25	Thunder	Electric	Special	110	70	10	Normal
TM27	Return	Normal	Physical	—	100	20	Normal
TM32	Double Team	Normal	Status	—	—	15	Self
TM42	Facade	Normal	Physical	70	100	20	Normal
TM44	Rest	Psychic	Status	—	—	10	Self
TM45	Attract	Normal	Status	—	100	15	Normal
TM48	Round	Normal	Special	60	100	15	Normal
TM55	Scald	Water	Special	80	100	15	Normal
TM57	Charge Beam	Electric	Special	50	90	10	Normal
TM68	Giga Impact	Normal	Physical	150	90	5	Normal
TM72	Volt Switch	Electric	Special	70	100	20	Normal
TM73	Thunder Wave	Electric	Status	—	90	20	Normal
TM87	Swagger	Normal	Status	—	85	15	Normal
TM88	Sleep Talk	Normal	Status	—	—	10	Self
TM90	Substitute	Normal	Status	—	—	10	Self
TM93	Wild Charge	Electric	Physical	90	100	15	Normal
TM94	Surf	Water	Special	90	100	15	Adjacent
TM98	Waterfall	Water	Physical	80	100	15	Normal

❖ MOVES TAUGHT BY PEOPLE
No.	Name	Type	Kind	Pow.	Acc.	PP	Range
TM99	Dazzling Gleam	Fairy	Special	80	100	10	Many Others
TM100	Confide	Normal	Status	—	—	20	Normal

❖ MOVES LEARNED WHEN EVOLVING
Name	Type	Kind	Pow.	Acc.	PP	Range
Stockpile	Normal	Status	—	—	20	Self
Swallow	Normal	Status	—	—	10	Self
Spit Up	Normal	Special	—	100	10	Normal

❖ EGG MOVES
Name	Type	Kind	Pow.	Acc.	PP	Range

❖ EXCLUSIVE Z-MOVE
Name	Base Move	Type	Kind	Pow.	Acc.	Range

Type: Null

Alola Pokédex 203 — Melemele — Akala — Ula'ula — Poni

Synthetic Pokémon

NORMAL

HEIGHT: 6'03"
WEIGHT: 265.7 lbs.

The heavy control mask it wears suppresses its intrinsic capabilities. This Pokémon has some hidden special power.

Due to the danger that this synthetic Pokémon may go on a rampage, it wears a control mask to restrain its power.

ABILITY
Battle Armor

HIDDEN ABILITY
—

Damage taken in normal battles

NORMAL ×1	FIGHTING ×2	ROCK ×1
FIRE ×1	POISON ×1	GHOST ×0
WATER ×1	GROUND ×1	DRAGON ×1
GRASS ×1	FLYING ×1	DARK ×1
ELECTRIC ×1	PSYCHIC ×1	STEEL ×1
ICE ×1	BUG ×1	FAIRY ×1

SPECIES STRENGTHS
HP ◆◆◆◆
Attack ◆◆◆◆◆
Defense ◆◆◆◆◆
Sp. Atk ◆◆◆◆◆
Sp. Def ◆◆◆◆◆◆
Speed ◆◆◆◆

EGG GROUPS
No Eggs Discovered

ITEM SOMETIMES HELD BY WILD POKÉMON
—

EVOLUTION
Type: Null → Level up with high friendship → Silvally

MAIN WAY TO REGISTER IN THE POKÉDEX
Receive in Aether Paradise after becoming Champion

Gender unknown

◆ LEVEL-UP MOVES

Lv.	Name	Type	Kind	Pow.	Acc.	PP	Range
1	Tackle	Normal	Physical	40	100	35	Normal
5	Rage	Normal	Physical	20	100	20	Normal
10	Pursuit	Dark	Physical	40	100	20	Normal
15	Imprison	Psychic	Status	—	—	10	Self
20	Aerial Ace	Flying	Physical	60	—	20	Normal
25	Crush Claw	Normal	Physical	75	95	10	Normal
30	Scary Face	Normal	Status	—	100	10	Normal
35	X-Scissor	Bug	Physical	80	100	15	Normal
40	Take Down	Normal	Physical	90	85	20	Normal
45	Metal Sound	Steel	Status	—	85	40	Normal
50	Iron Head	Steel	Physical	80	100	15	Normal
55	Double Hit	Normal	Physical	35	90	10	Normal
60	Air Slash	Flying	Special	75	95	15	Normal
65	Punishment	Dark	Physical	—	100	5	Normal
70	Razor Wind	Normal	Special	80	100	10	Many Others
75	Tri Attack	Normal	Special	80	100	10	Normal
80	Double-Edge	Normal	Physical	120	100	15	Normal
85	Heal Block	Psychic	Status	—	100	15	Many Others

◆ TM MOVES

No.	Name	Type	Kind	Pow.	Acc.	PP	Range
TM01	Work Up	Normal	Status	—	—	30	Self
TM02	Dragon Claw	Dragon	Physical	80	100	15	Normal
TM05	Roar	Normal	Status	—	—	20	Normal
TM06	Toxic	Poison	Status	—	90	10	Normal
TM07	Hail	Ice	Status	—	—	10	Both Sides
TM10	Hidden Power	Normal	Special	60	100	15	Normal
TM11	Sunny Day	Fire	Status	—	—	5	Both Sides
TM17	Protect	Normal	Status	—	—	10	Self
TM18	Rain Dance	Water	Status	—	—	5	Both Sides
TM21	Frustration	Normal	Physical	—	100	20	Normal
TM27	Return	Normal	Physical	—	100	20	Normal
TM32	Double Team	Normal	Status	—	—	15	Self
TM37	Sandstorm	Rock	Status	—	—	10	Both Sides
TM40	Aerial Ace	Flying	Physical	60	—	20	Normal
TM42	Facade	Normal	Physical	70	100	20	Normal
TM43	Flame Charge	Fire	Physical	50	100	20	Normal
TM44	Rest	Psychic	Status	—	—	10	Self
TM48	Round	Normal	Special	60	100	15	Normal
TM65	Shadow Claw	Ghost	Physical	70	100	15	Normal
TM66	Payback	Dark	Physical	50	100	10	Normal
TM68	Giga Impact	Normal	Physical	150	90	5	Normal
TM73	Thunder Wave	Electric	Status	—	90	20	Normal
TM75	Swords Dance	Normal	Status	—	—	20	Self
TM80	Rock Slide	Rock	Physical	75	90	10	Many Others
TM81	X-Scissor	Bug	Physical	80	100	15	Normal
TM87	Swagger	Normal	Status	—	85	15	Normal
TM88	Sleep Talk	Normal	Status	—	—	10	Self
TM89	U-turn	Bug	Physical	70	100	20	Normal

◆ MOVES TAUGHT BY PEOPLE

No.	Name	Type	Kind	Pow.	Acc.	PP	Range
TM90	Substitute	Normal	Status	—	—	10	Self
TM100	Confide	Normal	Status	—	—	20	Normal

◆ MOVES LEARNED WHEN EVOLVING

Name	Type	Kind	Pow.	Acc.	PP	Range

◆ EGG MOVES

Name	Type	Kind	Pow.	Acc.	PP	Range

◆ EXCLUSIVE Z-MOVE

Name	Base Move	Type	Kind	Pow.	Acc.	Range

How to Change Silvally's Forms

Silvally changes forms using a special set of memory drives that Gladion will give you after you become a Champion (p. 248). Give Silvally a memory drive matching the type that you want it to become. It will remain in that form unless you give it a different item.

Type: Fire FIRE
Damage taken in normal battles

NORMAL ×1	FIGHTING ×1	ROCK ×2
FIRE ×0.5	POISON ×1	GHOST ×1
WATER ×2	GROUND ×2	DRAGON ×1
GRASS ×0.5	FLYING ×1	DARK ×1
ELECTRIC ×1	PSYCHIC ×1	STEEL ×0.5
ICE ×0.5	BUG ×0.5	FAIRY ×0.5

Type: Water WATER
Damage taken in normal battles

NORMAL ×1	FIGHTING ×1	ROCK ×1
FIRE ×0.5	POISON ×1	GHOST ×1
WATER ×0.5	GROUND ×1	DRAGON ×1
GRASS ×2	FLYING ×1	DARK ×1
ELECTRIC ×2	PSYCHIC ×1	STEEL ×0.5
ICE ×0.5	BUG ×1	FAIRY ×1

Type: Grass GRASS
Damage taken in normal battles

NORMAL ×1	FIGHTING ×1	ROCK ×1
FIRE ×2	POISON ×2	GHOST ×1
WATER ×0.5	GROUND ×0.5	DRAGON ×1
GRASS ×0.5	FLYING ×2	DARK ×1
ELECTRIC ×0.5	PSYCHIC ×1	STEEL ×1
ICE ×2	BUG ×2	FAIRY ×1

Type: Electric ELECTRIC
Damage taken in normal battles

NORMAL ×1	FIGHTING ×1	ROCK ×1
FIRE ×1	POISON ×1	GHOST ×1
WATER ×1	GROUND ×2	DRAGON ×1
GRASS ×1	FLYING ×0.5	DARK ×1
ELECTRIC ×0.5	PSYCHIC ×1	STEEL ×0.5
ICE ×1	BUG ×1	FAIRY ×1

Type: Ice ICE
Damage taken in normal battles

NORMAL ×1	FIGHTING ×2	ROCK ×2
FIRE ×2	POISON ×1	GHOST ×1
WATER ×1	GROUND ×1	DRAGON ×1
GRASS ×1	FLYING ×1	DARK ×1
ELECTRIC ×1	PSYCHIC ×1	STEEL ×2
ICE ×0.5	BUG ×1	FAIRY ×1

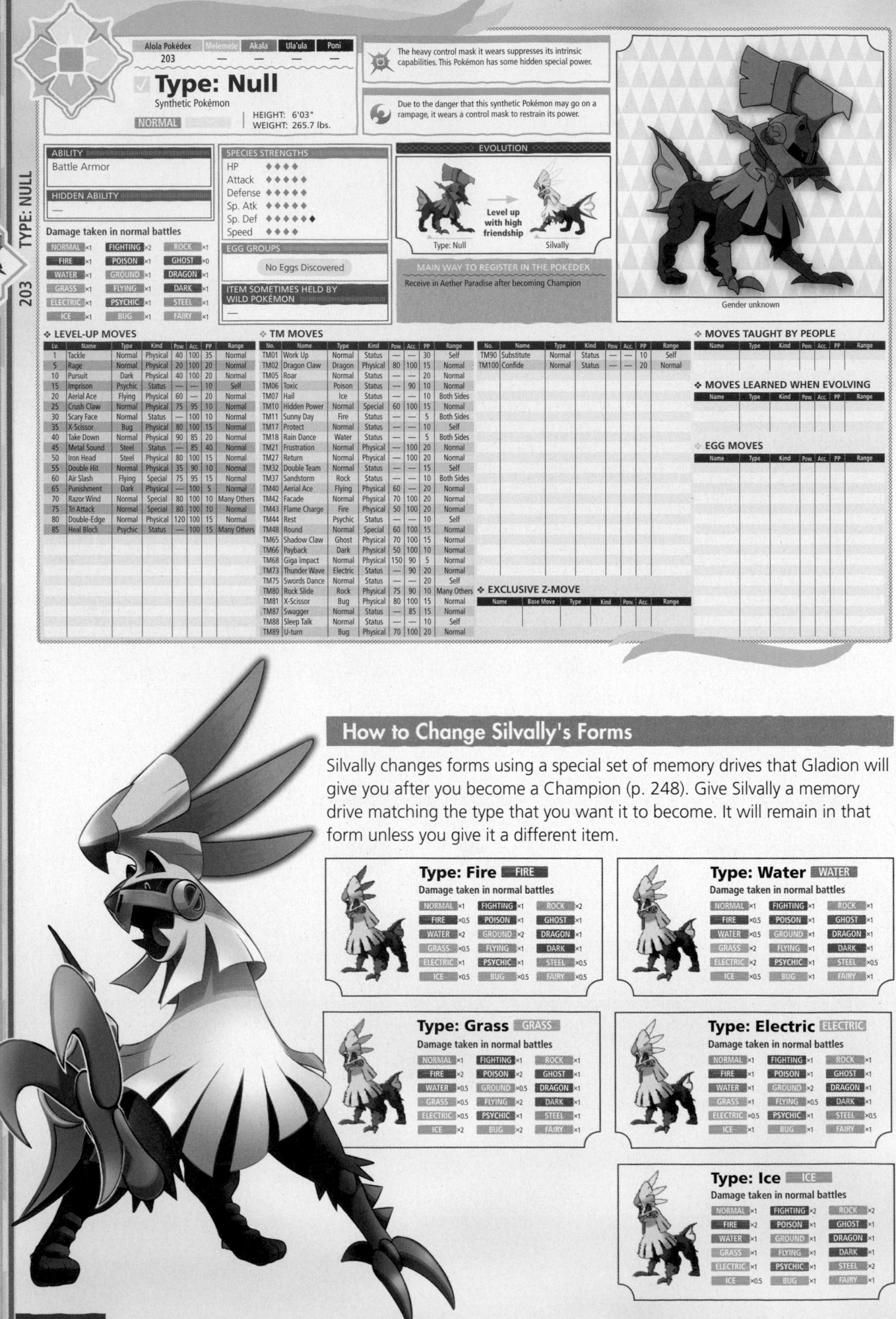

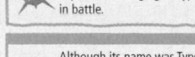

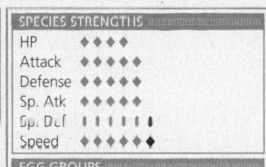

Alola Pokédex	Melemele	Akala	Ula'ula	Poni
204	—	—	—	—

☑ Silvally
Synthetic Pokémon

NORMAL

HEIGHT: 7'07"
WEIGHT: 221.6 lbs.

Its trust in its partner is what awakens it. This Pokémon is capable of changing its type, a flexibility that is well displayed in battle.

Although its name was Type: Null at first, the boy who evolved it into this form gave it the name by which it is now known.

ABILITY
RKS System

HIDDEN ABILITY
—

SPECIES STRENGTHS
HP	◆◆◆◆
Attack	◆◆◆◆◆
Defense	◆◆◆◆◆
Sp. Atk	◆◆◆◆◆
Sp. Def	◆◆◆◆◆
Speed	◆◆◆◆◆◆

EGG GROUPS
No Eggs Discovered

ITEM SOMETIMES HELD BY WILD POKEMON
—

EVOLUTION
Type: Null → Level up with high friendship → Silvally

MAIN WAY TO REGISTER IN THE POKÉDEX
Level up Type: Null with high friendship

TYPE: NORMAL

Gender unknown

Damage taken in normal battles
NORMAL ×1	FIGHTING ×2	ROCK ×1			
FIRE ×1	POISON ×1	GHOST ×0			
WATER ×1	GROUND ×1	DRAGON ×1			
GRASS ×1	FLYING ×1	DARK ×1			
ELECTRIC ×1	PSYCHIC ×1	STEEL ×1			
ICE ×1	BUG ×1	FAIRY ×1			

◆ LEVEL-UP MOVES
Lv.	Name	Type	Kind	Pow.	Acc.	PP	Range
1	Multi-Attack	Normal	Physical	90	100	10	Normal
1	Heal Block	Psychic	Status	—	100	15	Many Others
1	Imprison	Psychic	Status	—	—	10	Self
1	Iron Head	Steel	Physical	80	100	15	Normal
1	Poison Fang	Poison	Physical	50	100	15	Normal
1	Fire Fang	Fire	Physical	65	95	15	Normal
1	Ice Fang	Ice	Physical	65	95	15	Normal
1	Thunder Fang	Electric	Physical	65	95	15	Normal
1	Tackle	Normal	Physical	40	100	35	Normal
5	Rage	Normal	Physical	20	100	20	Normal
10	Pursuit	Dark	Physical	40	100	20	Normal
15	Bite	Dark	Physical	60	100	25	Normal
20	Aerial Ace	Flying	Physical	60	—	20	Normal
25	Crush Claw	Normal	Physical	75	95	10	Normal
30	Scary Face	Normal	Status	—	100	10	Normal
35	X-Scissor	Bug	Physical	80	100	15	Normal
40	Take Down	Normal	Physical	90	85	20	Normal
45	Metal Sound	Steel	Status	—	85	40	Normal
50	Crunch	Dark	Physical	80	100	15	Normal
55	Double Hit	Normal	Physical	35	90	10	Normal
60	Air Slash	Flying	Special	75	95	15	Normal
65	Punishment	Dark	Physical	—	100	5	Normal
70	Razor Wind	Normal	Special	80	100	10	Many Others
75	Tri Attack	Normal	Special	80	100	10	Normal
80	Double-Edge	Normal	Physical	120	100	15	Normal
85	Parting Shot	Dark	Status	—	100	20	Normal

◆ TM MOVES
No.	Name	Type	Kind	Pow.	Acc.	PP	Range
TM01	Work Up	Normal	Status	—	—	30	Self
TM02	Dragon Claw	Dragon	Physical	80	100	15	Normal
TM05	Roar	Normal	Status	—	—	20	Normal
TM06	Toxic	Poison	Status	—	90	10	Normal
TM07	Hail	Ice	Status	—	—	10	Both Sides
TM10	Hidden Power	Normal	Special	60	100	15	Normal
TM11	Sunny Day	Fire	Status	—	—	5	Both Sides
TM13	Ice Beam	Ice	Special	90	100	10	Normal
TM15	Hyper Beam	Normal	Special	150	90	5	Normal
TM17	Protect	Normal	Status	—	—	10	Self
TM18	Rain Dance	Water	Status	—	—	5	Both Sides
TM21	Frustration	Normal	Physical	—	100	20	Normal
TM24	Thunderbolt	Electric	Special	90	100	15	Normal
TM27	Return	Normal	Physical	—	100	20	Normal
TM30	Shadow Ball	Ghost	Special	80	100	15	Normal
TM32	Double Team	Normal	Status	—	—	15	Self
TM35	Flamethrower	Fire	Special	90	100	15	Normal
TM37	Sandstorm	Rock	Status	—	—	10	Both Sides
TM40	Aerial Ace	Flying	Physical	60	—	20	Normal
TM42	Facade	Normal	Physical	70	100	20	Normal
TM43	Flame Charge	Fire	Physical	50	100	20	Normal
TM44	Rest	Psychic	Status	—	—	10	Self
TM48	Round	Normal	Special	60	100	15	Normal
TM51	Steel Wing	Steel	Physical	70	90	25	Normal
TM64	Explosion	Normal	Physical	250	100	5	Adjacent
TM65	Shadow Claw	Ghost	Physical	70	100	15	Normal
TM66	Payback	Dark	Physical	50	100	10	Normal
TM68	Giga Impact	Normal	Physical	150	90	5	Normal
TM73	Thunder Wave	Electric	Status	—	90	20	Normal
TM75	Swords Dance	Normal	Status	—	—	20	Self
TM80	Rock Slide	Rock	Physical	75	90	10	Many Others
TM81	X-Scissor	Bug	Physical	80	100	15	Normal
TM87	Swagger	Normal	Status	—	85	15	Normal
TM88	Sleep Talk	Normal	Status	—	—	10	Self
TM89	U-turn	Bug	Physical	70	100	20	Normal
TM90	Substitute	Normal	Status	—	—	10	Self
TM91	Flash Cannon	Steel	Special	80	100	10	Normal
TM94	Surf	Water	Special	90	100	15	Adjacent
TM95	Snarl	Dark	Special	55	95	15	Many Others
TM100	Confide	Normal	Status	—	—	20	Normal

◆ MOVES TAUGHT BY PEOPLE
Name	Type	Kind	Pow.	Acc.	PP	Range
Draco Meteor	Dragon	Special	130	90	5	Normal

◆ MOVES LEARNED WHEN EVOLVING
Name	Type	Kind	Pow.	Acc.	PP	Range
Multi-Attack	Normal	Physical	90	100	10	Normal

◆ EGG MOVES
Name	Type	Kind	Pow.	Acc.	PP	Range

◆ EXCLUSIVE Z-MOVE
Name	Base Move	Type	Kind	Pow.	Acc.	Range

Type: Fighting FIGHTING
Damage taken in normal battles
NORMAL ×1	FIGHTING ×1	ROCK ×0.5
FIRE ×1	POISON ×1	GHOST ×1
WATER ×1	GROUND ×1	DRAGON ×1
GRASS ×1	FLYING ×2	DARK ×0.5
ELECTRIC ×1	PSYCHIC ×2	STEEL ×1
ICE ×1	BUG ×0.5	FAIRY ×2

Type: Poison POISON
Damage taken in normal battles
NORMAL ×1	FIGHTING ×0.5	ROCK ×1
FIRE ×1	POISON ×0.5	GHOST ×1
WATER ×1	GROUND ×2	DRAGON ×1
GRASS ×0.5	FLYING ×1	DARK ×1
ELECTRIC ×1	PSYCHIC ×2	STEEL ×1
ICE ×1	BUG ×0.5	FAIRY ×0.5

Type: Ground GROUND
Damage taken in normal battles
NORMAL ×1	FIGHTING ×1	ROCK ×0.5
FIRE ×1	POISON ×0.5	GHOST ×1
WATER ×2	GROUND ×1	DRAGON ×1
GRASS ×2	FLYING ×1	DARK ×1
ELECTRIC ×0	PSYCHIC ×1	STEEL ×1
ICE ×2	BUG ×1	FAIRY ×1

Type: Flying FLYING
Damage taken in normal battles
NORMAL ×1	FIGHTING ×0.5	ROCK ×2
FIRE ×1	POISON ×1	GHOST ×1
WATER ×1	GROUND ×0	DRAGON ×1
GRASS ×0.5	FLYING ×1	DARK ×1
ELECTRIC ×2	PSYCHIC ×1	STEEL ×1
ICE ×2	BUG ×0.5	FAIRY ×1

Type: Psychic PSYCHIC
Damage taken in normal battles
NORMAL ×1	FIGHTING ×0.5	ROCK ×1
FIRE ×1	POISON ×1	GHOST ×2
WATER ×1	GROUND ×1	DRAGON ×1
GRASS ×1	FLYING ×1	DARK ×2
ELECTRIC ×1	PSYCHIC ×0.5	STEEL ×1
ICE ×1	BUG ×2	FAIRY ×1

Type: Bug BUG
Damage taken in normal battles
NORMAL ×1	FIGHTING ×0.5	ROCK ×2
FIRE ×2	POISON ×1	GHOST ×1
WATER ×1	GROUND ×0.5	DRAGON ×1
GRASS ×0.5	FLYING ×2	DARK ×1
ELECTRIC ×1	PSYCHIC ×1	STEEL ×1
ICE ×1	BUG ×1	FAIRY ×1

Type: Rock ROCK
Damage taken in normal battles
NORMAL ×0.5	FIGHTING ×2	ROCK ×1
FIRE ×0.5	POISON ×0.5	GHOST ×1
WATER ×2	GROUND ×2	DRAGON ×1
GRASS ×2	FLYING ×0.5	DARK ×1
ELECTRIC ×1	PSYCHIC ×1	STEEL ×2
ICE ×1	BUG ×1	FAIRY ×1

Type: Ghost GHOST
Damage taken in normal battles
NORMAL ×0	FIGHTING ×0	ROCK ×1
FIRE ×1	POISON ×0.5	GHOST ×2
WATER ×1	GROUND ×1	DRAGON ×1
GRASS ×1	FLYING ×1	DARK ×2
ELECTRIC ×1	PSYCHIC ×1	STEEL ×1
ICE ×1	BUG ×0.5	FAIRY ×1

Type: Dragon DRAGON
Damage taken in normal battles
NORMAL ×1	FIGHTING ×1	ROCK ×1
FIRE ×0.5	POISON ×1	GHOST ×1
WATER ×0.5	GROUND ×1	DRAGON ×2
GRASS ×0.5	FLYING ×1	DARK ×1
ELECTRIC ×0.5	PSYCHIC ×1	STEEL ×1
ICE ×2	BUG ×1	FAIRY ×2

Type: Dark DARK
Damage taken in normal battles
NORMAL ×1	FIGHTING ×2	ROCK ×1
FIRE ×1	POISON ×1	GHOST ×0.5
WATER ×1	GROUND ×1	DRAGON ×1
GRASS ×1	FLYING ×1	DARK ×0.5
ELECTRIC ×1	PSYCHIC ×0	STEEL ×1
ICE ×1	BUG ×2	FAIRY ×2

Type: Steel STEEL
Damage taken in normal battles
NORMAL ×0.5	FIGHTING ×2	ROCK ×0.5
FIRE ×2	POISON ×0	GHOST ×1
WATER ×1	GROUND ×2	DRAGON ×0.5
GRASS ×0.5	FLYING ×0.5	DARK ×1
ELECTRIC ×1	PSYCHIC ×0.5	STEEL ×0.5
ICE ×0.5	BUG ×0.5	FAIRY ×0.5

Type: Fairy FAIRY
Damage taken in normal battles
NORMAL ×1	FIGHTING ×0.5	ROCK ×1
FIRE ×1	POISON ×2	GHOST ×1
WATER ×1	GROUND ×1	DRAGON ×0
GRASS ×1	FLYING ×1	DARK ×0.5
ELECTRIC ×1	PSYCHIC ×1	STEEL ×1
ICE ×1	BUG ×0.5	FAIRY ×1

Zygarde
Order Pokémon

Alola Pokédex	Melemele	Akala	Ula'ula	Poni
205	—	—	—	—

DRAGON **GROUND**

HEIGHT: 3'11"
WEIGHT: 73.9 lbs.

Its sharp fangs make short work of finishing off its enemies, but it's unable to maintain this body indefinitely. After a period of time, it falls apart.

This is Zygarde's form when about 10% of its cells have been gathered. It runs across the land at speeds greater than 60 mph.

10% FORME

Gender unknown

ABILITY
Aura Break
Power Construct

HIDDEN ABILITY
—

Damage taken in normal battles

NORMAL	×1	FIGHTING	×1	ROCK	×1
FIRE	×0.5	POISON	×0.5	GHOST	×1
WATER	×1	GROUND	×1	DRAGON	×2
GRASS	×1	FLYING	×1	DARK	×1
ELECTRIC	×0	PSYCHIC	×1	STEEL	×1
ICE	×4	BUG	×1	FAIRY	×2

SPECIES STRENGTHS
HP	◆◆
Attack	◆◆◆◆◆
Defense	◆◆◆◆
Sp. Atk	◆◆◆
Sp. Def	◆◆◆◆◆
Speed	◆◆◆◆◆◆◆

EGG GROUPS
No Eggs Discovered

ITEM SOMETIMES HELD BY WILD POKÉMON
—

EVOLUTION
Does not evolve

MAIN WAY TO REGISTER IN THE POKÉDEX
Assemble a Zygarde in the Aether Base on Route 16 using at least 10 Cells or Cores

◆ LEVEL-UP MOVES

Lv.	Name	Type	Kind	Pow.	Acc.	PP	Range
1	Glare	Normal	Status	—	100	30	Normal
1	Bulldoze	Ground	Physical	60	100	20	Adjacent
1	Dragon Breath	Dragon	Special	60	100	20	Normal
1	Bite	Dark	Physical	60	100	25	Normal
5	Safeguard	Normal	Status	—	—	25	Your Side
10	Dig	Ground	Physical	80	100	10	Normal
18	Bind	Normal	Physical	15	85	20	Normal
26	Land's Wrath	Ground	Physical	90	100	10	Many Others
35	Sandstorm	Rock	Status	—	—	10	Both Sides
44	Haze	Ice	Status	—	—	30	Both Sides
51	Crunch	Dark	Physical	80	100	15	Normal
55	Earthquake	Ground	Physical	100	100	10	Adjacent
59	Camouflage	Normal	Status	—	—	20	Self
63	Dragon Pulse	Dragon	Special	85	100	10	Normal
72	Coil	Poison	Status	—	—	20	Self
80	Outrage	Dragon	Physical	120	100	10	1 Random

◆ TM MOVES

No.	Name	Type	Kind	Pow.	Acc.	PP	Range
TM06	Toxic	Poison	Status	—	90	10	Normal
TM10	Hidden Power	Normal	Special	60	100	15	Normal
TM11	Sunny Day	Fire	Status	—	—	5	Both Sides
TM15	Hyper Beam	Normal	Special	150	90	5	Normal
TM17	Protect	Normal	Status	—	—	10	Self
TM20	Safeguard	Normal	Status	—	—	25	Your Side
TM21	Frustration	Normal	Physical	—	100	20	Normal
TM26	Earthquake	Ground	Physical	100	100	10	Adjacent
TM27	Return	Normal	Physical	—	100	20	Normal
TM31	Brick Break	Fighting	Physical	75	100	15	Normal
TM32	Double Team	Normal	Status	—	—	15	Self
TM34	Sludge Wave	Poison	Special	95	100	10	Adjacent
TM37	Sandstorm	Rock	Status	—	—	10	Both Sides
TM42	Facade	Normal	Physical	70	100	20	Normal
TM44	Rest	Psychic	Status	—	—	10	Self
TM48	Round	Normal	Special	60	100	15	Normal
TM52	Focus Blast	Fighting	Special	120	70	5	Normal
TM68	Giga Impact	Normal	Physical	150	90	5	Normal
TM71	Stone Edge	Rock	Physical	100	80	5	Normal
TM78	Bulldoze	Ground	Physical	60	100	20	Adjacent
TM80	Rock Slide	Rock	Physical	75	90	10	Many Others
TM82	Dragon Tail	Dragon	Physical	60	90	10	Normal
TM86	Grass Knot	Grass	Special	—	100	20	Normal
TM87	Swagger	Normal	Status	—	85	15	Normal
TM88	Sleep Talk	Normal	Status	—	—	10	Self
TM90	Substitute	Normal	Status	—	—	10	Self
TM100	Confide	Normal	Status	—	—	20	Normal

◆ MOVES TAUGHT BY PEOPLE

Name	Type	Kind	Pow.	Acc.	PP	Range
Draco Meteor	Dragon	Special	130	90	5	Normal

◆ MOVES LEARNED WHEN EVOLVING

Name	Type	Kind	Pow.	Acc.	PP	Range

◆ ZYGARDE CORE MOVES

Name	Type	Kind	Pow.	Acc.	PP	Range
Core Enforcer	Dragon	Special	100	100	10	Many Others
Dragon Dance	Dragon	Status	—	—	20	Self
Extreme Speed	Normal	Physical	80	100	5	Normal
Thousand Arrows	Ground	Physical	90	100	10	Many Others
Thousand Waves	Ground	Physical	90	100	10	Many Others

◆ EXCLUSIVE Z-MOVE

Name	Base Move	Type	Kind	Pow.	Acc.	Range

---

205 ZYGARDE

Zygarde
Order Pokémon

Alola Pokédex	Melemele	Akala	Ula'ula	Poni
205	—	—	—	—

DRAGON **GROUND**

HEIGHT: 16'05"
WEIGHT: 672.4 lbs.

This is Zygarde's form when it has gathered 50% of its cells. It wipes out all those who oppose it, showing not a shred of mercy.

It's thought to be monitoring the ecosystem. There are rumors that even greater power lies hidden within it.

50% FORME

Gender unknown

ABILITY
Aura Break
Power Construct

HIDDEN ABILITY
—

Damage taken in normal battles

NORMAL	×1	FIGHTING	×1	ROCK	×0.5
FIRE	×0.5	POISON	×0.5	GHOST	×1
WATER	×1	GROUND	×1	DRAGON	×2
GRASS	×1	FLYING	×1	DARK	×1
ELECTRIC	×0	PSYCHIC	×1	STEEL	×1
ICE	×4	BUG	×1	FAIRY	×2

SPECIES STRENGTHS
HP	◆◆◆◆
Attack	◆◆◆◆◆
Defense	◆◆◆◆◆◆
Sp. Atk	◆◆◆◆
Sp. Def	◆◆◆◆◆◆
Speed	◆◆◆◆◆◆

EGG GROUPS
No Eggs Discovered

ITEM SOMETIMES HELD BY WILD POKÉMON
—

EVOLUTION
Does not evolve

MAIN WAY TO REGISTER IN THE POKÉDEX
Assemble a Zygarde in the Aether Base on Route 16 using at least 50 Cells or Cores

◆ LEVEL-UP MOVES

Lv.	Name	Type	Kind	Pow.	Acc.	PP	Range
1	Glare	Normal	Status	—	100	30	Normal
1	Bulldoze	Ground	Physical	60	100	20	Adjacent
1	Dragon Breath	Dragon	Special	60	100	20	Normal
1	Bite	Dark	Physical	60	100	25	Normal
5	Safeguard	Normal	Status	—	—	25	Your Side
10	Dig	Ground	Physical	80	100	10	Normal
18	Bind	Normal	Physical	15	85	20	Normal
26	Land's Wrath	Ground	Physical	90	100	10	Many Others
35	Sandstorm	Rock	Status	—	—	10	Both Sides
44	Haze	Ice	Status	—	—	30	Both Sides
51	Crunch	Dark	Physical	80	100	15	Normal
55	Earthquake	Ground	Physical	100	100	10	Adjacent
59	Camouflage	Normal	Status	—	—	20	Self
63	Dragon Pulse	Dragon	Special	85	100	10	Normal
72	Coil	Poison	Status	—	—	20	Self
80	Outrage	Dragon	Physical	120	100	10	1 Random

◆ TM MOVES

No.	Name	Type	Kind	Pow.	Acc.	PP	Range
TM06	Toxic	Poison	Status	—	90	10	Normal
TM10	Hidden Power	Normal	Special	60	100	15	Normal
TM11	Sunny Day	Fire	Status	—	—	5	Both Sides
TM15	Hyper Beam	Normal	Special	150	90	5	Normal
TM17	Protect	Normal	Status	—	—	10	Self
TM20	Safeguard	Normal	Status	—	—	25	Your Side
TM21	Frustration	Normal	Physical	—	100	20	Normal
TM26	Earthquake	Ground	Physical	100	100	10	Adjacent
TM27	Return	Normal	Physical	—	100	20	Normal
TM31	Brick Break	Fighting	Physical	75	100	15	Normal
TM32	Double Team	Normal	Status	—	—	15	Self
TM34	Sludge Wave	Poison	Special	95	100	10	Adjacent
TM37	Sandstorm	Rock	Status	—	—	10	Both Sides
TM42	Facade	Normal	Physical	70	100	20	Normal
TM44	Rest	Psychic	Status	—	—	10	Self
TM48	Round	Normal	Special	60	100	15	Normal
TM52	Focus Blast	Fighting	Special	120	70	5	Normal
TM68	Giga Impact	Normal	Physical	150	90	5	Normal
TM71	Stone Edge	Rock	Physical	100	80	5	Normal
TM78	Bulldoze	Ground	Physical	60	100	20	Adjacent
TM80	Rock Slide	Rock	Physical	75	90	10	Many Others
TM82	Dragon Tail	Dragon	Physical	60	90	10	Normal
TM86	Grass Knot	Grass	Special	—	100	20	Normal
TM87	Swagger	Normal	Status	—	85	15	Normal
TM88	Sleep Talk	Normal	Status	—	—	10	Self
TM90	Substitute	Normal	Status	—	—	10	Self
TM100	Confide	Normal	Status	—	—	20	Normal

◆ MOVES TAUGHT BY PEOPLE

Name	Type	Kind	Pow.	Acc.	PP	Range
Draco Meteor	Dragon	Special	130	90	5	Normal

◆ MOVES LEARNED WHEN EVOLVING

Name	Type	Kind	Pow.	Acc.	PP	Range

◆ ZYGARDE CORE MOVES

Name	Type	Kind	Pow.	Acc.	PP	Range
Core Enforcer	Dragon	Special	100	100	10	Many Others
Dragon Dance	Dragon	Status	—	—	20	Self
Extreme Speed	Normal	Physical	80	100	5	Normal
Thousand Arrows	Ground	Physical	90	100	10	Many Others
Thousand Waves	Ground	Physical	90	100	10	Many Others

◆ EXCLUSIVE Z-MOVE

Name	Base Move	Type	Kind	Pow.	Acc.	Range

Zygarde

Alola Pokédex	Melemele	Akala	Ula'ula	Poni
205	—	—	—	—

☑ Zygarde
Order Pokémon

DRAGON **GROUND**

HEIGHT: 14'09"
WEIGHT: 1,344.8 lbs.

This is Zygarde's form at times when it uses its overwhelming power to suppress those who endanger the ecosystem.

This is Zygarde's 100% form. It has enough power to overwhelm even Xerneas or Yveltal.

ABILITY
Power Construct

HIDDEN ABILITY
—

SPECIES STRENGTHS
HP	◆◆◆◆◆◆◆
Attack	◆◆◆◆◆
Defense	◆◆◆◆◆◆
Sp. Atk	◆◆◆◆◆
Sp. Def	◆◆◆◆◆◆
Speed	◆◆◆◆◆

EVOLUTION
Does not evolve

EGG GROUPS
No Eggs Discovered

ITEM SOMETIMES HELD BY WILD POKÉMON
—

MAIN WAY TO REGISTER IN THE POKÉDEX
Assemble a Zygarde with the Power Construct Ability in the Aether Base on Route 16 by using 100 Cells or Cores, and it will change to Complete Forme in battle when its HP drops below half of its maximum

COMPLETE FORME

Gender unknown

Damage taken in normal battles
Type	Mult	Type	Mult	Type	Mult
NORMAL	×1	FIGHTING	×1	ROCK	×0.5
FIRE	×0.5	POISON	×0.5	GHOST	×1
WATER	×1	GROUND	×1	DRAGON	×2
GRASS	×1	FLYING	×1	DARK	×1
ELECTRIC	×1	PSYCHIC	×1	STEEL	×1
ICE	×4	BUG	×1	FAIRY	×2

❖ LEVEL-UP MOVES
Lv.	Name	Type	Kind	Pow.	Acc.	PP	Range
1	Glare	Normal	Status	—	100	30	Normal
1	Bulldoze	Ground	Physical	60	100	20	Adjacent
1	Dragon Breath	Dragon	Special	60	100	20	Normal
1	Bite	Dark	Physical	60	100	25	Normal
5	Safeguard	Normal	Status	—	—	25	Your Side
10	Dig	Ground	Physical	80	100	10	Normal
18	Bind	Normal	Physical	15	85	20	Normal
26	Land's Wrath	Ground	Physical	90	100	10	Many Others
35	Sandstorm	Rock	Status	—	—	10	Both Sides
44	Haze	Ice	Status	—	—	30	Both Sides
51	Crunch	Dark	Physical	80	100	15	Normal
55	Earthquake	Ground	Physical	100	100	10	Adjacent
59	Camouflage	Normal	Status	—	—	20	Self
63	Dragon Pulse	Dragon	Special	85	100	10	Normal
72	Coil	Poison	Status	—	—	20	Self
80	Outrage	Dragon	Physical	120	100	10	1 Random

❖ TM MOVES
No.	Name	Type	Kind	Pow.	Acc.	PP	Range
TM06	Toxic	Poison	Status	—	90	10	Normal
TM10	Hidden Power	Normal	Special	60	100	15	Normal
TM11	Sunny Day	Fire	Status	—	—	5	Both Sides
TM15	Hyper Beam	Normal	Special	150	90	5	Normal
TM17	Protect	Normal	Status	—	—	10	Self
TM20	Safeguard	Normal	Status	—	—	25	Your Side
TM21	Frustration	Normal	Physical	—	100	20	Normal
TM26	Earthquake	Ground	Physical	100	100	10	Adjacent
TM27	Return	Normal	Physical	—	100	20	Normal
TM31	Brick Break	Fighting	Physical	75	100	15	Normal
TM32	Double Team	Normal	Status	—	—	15	Self
TM34	Sludge Wave	Poison	Special	95	100	10	Adjacent
TM37	Sandstorm	Rock	Status	—	—	10	Both Sides
TM42	Facade	Normal	Physical	70	100	20	Normal
TM44	Rest	Psychic	Status	—	—	10	Self
TM48	Round	Normal	Special	60	100	15	Normal
TM52	Focus Blast	Fighting	Special	120	70	5	Normal
TM68	Giga Impact	Normal	Physical	150	90	5	Normal
TM71	Stone Edge	Rock	Physical	100	80	5	Normal
TM78	Bulldoze	Ground	Physical	60	100	20	Adjacent
TM80	Rock Slide	Rock	Physical	75	90	10	Many Others
TM82	Dragon Tail	Dragon	Physical	60	90	10	Normal
TM86	Grass Knot	Grass	Special	—	100	20	Normal
TM87	Swagger	Normal	Status	—	85	15	Normal
TM88	Sleep Talk	Normal	Status	—	—	10	Self
TM90	Substitute	Normal	Status	—	—	10	Self
TM100	Confide	Normal	Status	—	—	20	Normal

❖ MOVES TAUGHT BY PEOPLE
Name	Type	Kind	Pow.	Acc.	PP	Range
Draco Meteor	Dragon	Special	130	90	5	Normal

❖ MOVES LEARNED WHEN EVOLVING
Name	Type	Kind	Pow.	Acc.	PP	Range

❖ ZYGARDE CORE MOVES
Name	Type	Kind	Pow.	Acc.	PP	Range
Core Enforcer	Dragon	Special	100	100	10	Many Others
Dragon Dance	Dragon	Status	—	—	20	Self
Extreme Speed	Normal	Physical	80	100	5	Normal
Thousand Arrows	Ground	Physical	90	100	10	Many Others
Thousand Waves	Ground	Physical	90	100	10	Many Others

❖ EXCLUSIVE Z-MOVE
Name	Base Move	Type	Kind	Pow.	Acc.	Range

Zygarde Cores and Moves

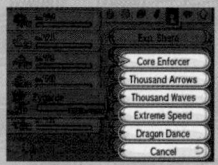

Zygarde is composed of Cells and Cores, which can be found scattered around the Alola region. You can learn more about that on pages 230 to 231, but the important thing to know is that Zygarde Cores are key parts of Zygarde and allow it to remember certain moves that it cannot learn any other way.

Core Location	Move Contained	Move Effects
Your bedroom (Hau'oli Outskirts)	Extreme Speed	Always strikes first. Faster than other moves that strike first, except Fake Out. If two Pokémon use this move, or if the other Pokémon uses the move Feint or First Impression, the one with the higher Speed goes first.
Hala's House (Iki Town)	Thousand Arrows	Will also hit Pokémon with the Levitate Ability or Flying-type Pokémon. Ground-type moves will now hit Pokémon with the Levitate Ability or Flying-type Pokémon. Its power is reduced by 25% when it hits multiple Pokémon in a Double Battle. Its power is reduced by 50% when it hits multiple Pokémon in a Battle Royal.
Olivia's House (Konikoni City)	Dragon Dance	Raises the user's Attack and Speed by 1.
Nanu's Police Station (Route 17)	Thousand Waves	The targets cannot escape. If used during a Trainer battle, the opposing Trainer cannot switch Pokémon. Its power is reduced by 25% when it hits multiple Pokémon in a Double Battle. Its power is reduced by 50% when it hits multiple Pokémon in a Battle Royal.
Hapu's House (Ancient Poni Path)	Core Enforcer	Negates the Abilities of any opponents that have used moves that turn. This effect will disappear if the affected Pokémon is switched out of battle.

Teaching Zygarde moves

To teach Zygarde a move, open your Bag, go to the Key Items Pocket, and select "Zygarde Cube." Select from your team the Zygarde you want to teach a new move to, and then select "Learn Move." Regardless of its Ability, Zygarde can learn all of the five moves contained in Zygarde Cores. You will not see the "Learn Move" menu displayed, however, if you haven't yet found any Cores.

Trubbish

Trash Bag Pokémon

Alola Pokédex	Melemele	Akala	Ula'ula	Poni
206	—	—	078	—

POISON

HEIGHT: 2'00"
WEIGHT: 68.3 lbs.

Unsanitary places are what they like best. They can be spotted in Alola, often with Grimer in hot pursuit.

It gorges on trash until its stomach is full. Then it belches toxic gas. An unlucky whiff of gas will put a person in the hospital.

ABILITY
Stench
Sticky Hold

HIDDEN ABILITY
Aftermath

SPECIES STRENGTHS
HP	◆◆
Attack	◆◆◆
Defense	◆◆◆
Sp. Atk	◆◆
Sp. Def	◆◆◆
Speed	◆◆◆◆

EGG GROUPS
Mineral

ITEM SOMETIMES HELD BY WILD POKÉMON
Silk Scarf

Damage taken in normal battles
NORMAL	×1	FIGHTING	×0.5	ROCK	×1
FIRE	×1	POISON	×0.5	GHOST	×1
WATER	×1	GROUND	×2	DRAGON	×1
GRASS	×0.5	FLYING	×1	DARK	×1
ELECTRIC	×1	PSYCHIC	×1	STEEL	×1
ICE	×1	BUG	×0.5	FAIRY	×0.5

EVOLUTION
Trubbish → Lv. 36 → Garbodor

MAIN WAY TO REGISTER IN THE POKÉDEX
Catch in the tall grass on Outer Cape

Same form for male/female

◆ LEVEL-UP MOVES
Lv.	Name	Type	Kind	Pow.	Acc.	PP	Range
1	Pound	Normal	Physical	40	100	35	Normal
1	Poison Gas	Poison	Status	—	90	40	Many Others
3	Recycle	Normal	Status	—	—	10	Self
7	Toxic Spikes	Poison	Status	—	—	20	Other Side
12	Acid Spray	Poison	Special	40	100	20	Normal
14	Double Slap	Normal	Physical	15	85	10	Normal
18	Sludge	Poison	Special	65	100	20	Normal
23	Stockpile	Normal	Status	—	—	20	Self
23	Swallow	Normal	Status	—	—	10	Self
25	Take Down	Normal	Physical	90	85	20	Normal
29	Sludge Bomb	Poison	Special	90	100	10	Normal
34	Clear Smog	Poison	Special	50	—	15	Normal
36	Toxic	Poison	Status	—	90	10	Normal
40	Amnesia	Psychic	Status	—	—	20	Self
42	Belch	Poison	Special	120	90	10	Normal
45	Gunk Shot	Poison	Physical	120	80	5	Normal
47	Explosion	Normal	Physical	250	100	5	Adjacent

◆ TM MOVES
No.	Name	Type	Kind	Pow.	Acc.	PP	Range
TM06	Toxic	Poison	Status	—	90	10	Normal
TM09	Venoshock	Poison	Special	65	100	10	Normal
TM10	Hidden Power	Normal	Special	60	100	15	Normal
TM11	Sunny Day	Fire	Status	—	—	5	Both Sides
TM17	Protect	Normal	Status	—	—	10	Self
TM18	Rain Dance	Water	Status	—	—	5	Both Sides
TM21	Frustration	Normal	Physical	—	100	20	Normal
TM27	Return	Normal	Physical	—	100	20	Normal
TM32	Double Team	Normal	Status	—	—	15	Self
TM34	Sludge Wave	Poison	Special	95	100	10	Adjacent
TM36	Sludge Bomb	Poison	Special	90	100	10	Normal
TM42	Facade	Normal	Physical	70	100	20	Normal
TM44	Rest	Psychic	Status	—	—	10	Self
TM45	Attract	Normal	Status	—	100	15	Normal
TM46	Thief	Dark	Physical	60	100	25	Normal
TM48	Round	Normal	Special	60	100	15	Normal
TM64	Explosion	Normal	Physical	250	100	5	Adjacent
TM66	Payback	Dark	Physical	50	100	10	Normal
TM83	Infestation	Bug	Special	20	100	20	Normal
TM87	Swagger	Normal	Status	—	85	15	Normal
TM88	Sleep Talk	Normal	Status	—	—	10	Self
TM90	Substitute	Normal	Status	—	—	10	Self
TM97	Dark Pulse	Dark	Special	80	100	15	Normal
TM100	Confide	Normal	Status	—	—	20	Normal

◆ MOVES TAUGHT BY PEOPLE
Name	Type	Kind	Pow.	Acc.	PP	Range

◆ MOVES LEARNED WHEN EVOLVING
Name	Type	Kind	Pow.	Acc.	PP	Range

◆ EGG MOVES
Name	Type	Kind	Pow.	Acc.	PP	Range
Spikes	Ground	Status	—	—	20	Other Side
Rollout	Rock	Physical	30	90	20	Normal
Haze	Ice	Status	—	—	30	Both Sides
Curse	Ghost	Status	—	—	10	Varies
Rock Blast	Rock	Physical	25	90	10	Normal
Sand Attack	Ground	Status	—	100	15	Normal
Mud Sport	Ground	Status	—	—	15	Both Sides
Self-Destruct	Normal	Physical	200	100	5	Adjacent

◆ EXCLUSIVE Z-MOVE
Name	Base Move	Type	Kind	Pow.	Acc.	Range

Garbodor

Trash Heap Pokémon

Alola Pokédex	Melemele	Akala	Ula'ula	Poni
207	—	—	079	—

POISON

HEIGHT: 6'03"
WEIGHT: 236.6 lbs.

Beware the poisonous liquid it shoots from its right arm. If even a little of it gets on you, you'll experience the effects of the unidentified toxin.

For a time, their numbers increased explosively in Alola. Since the arrival of Grimer, their population has decreased dramatically.

ABILITY
Stench
Weak Armor

HIDDEN ABILITY
Aftermath

SPECIES STRENGTHS
HP	◆◆◆
Attack	◆◆◆◆◆
Defense	◆◆◆◆
Sp. Atk	◆◆◆
Sp. Def	◆◆◆◆◆
Speed	◆◆◆◆◆

EGG GROUPS
Mineral

ITEM SOMETIMES HELD BY WILD POKÉMON
Silk Scarf / Black Sludge

Damage taken in normal battles
NORMAL	×1	FIGHTING	×0.5	ROCK	×1
FIRE	×1	POISON	×0.5	GHOST	×1
WATER	×1	GROUND	×2	DRAGON	×1
GRASS	×0.5	FLYING	×1	DARK	×1
ELECTRIC	×1	PSYCHIC	×1	STEEL	×1
ICE	×1	BUG	×0.5	FAIRY	×0.5

EVOLUTION
Trubbish → Lv. 36 → Garbodor

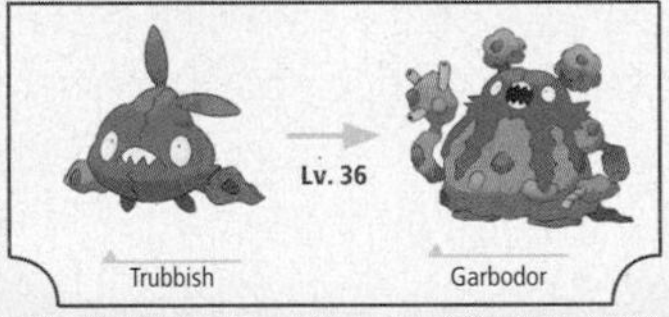

MAIN WAY TO REGISTER IN THE POKÉDEX
Catch in SOS battles against Trubbish in the tall grass on Outer Cape

Same form for male/female

◆ LEVEL-UP MOVES
Lv.	Name	Type	Kind	Pow.	Acc.	PP	Range
1	Pound	Normal	Physical	40	100	35	Normal
1	Poison Gas	Poison	Status	—	90	40	Many Others
1	Recycle	Normal	Status	—	—	10	Self
1	Toxic Spikes	Poison	Status	—	—	20	Other Side
3	Recycle	Normal	Status	—	—	10	Self
7	Toxic Spikes	Poison	Status	—	—	20	Other Side
12	Acid Spray	Poison	Special	40	100	20	Normal
14	Double Slap	Normal	Physical	15	85	10	Normal
18	Sludge	Poison	Special	65	100	20	Normal
23	Stockpile	Normal	Status	—	—	20	Self
23	Swallow	Normal	Status	—	—	10	Self
25	Body Slam	Normal	Physical	85	100	15	Normal
29	Sludge Bomb	Poison	Special	90	100	10	Normal
34	Clear Smog	Poison	Special	50	—	15	Normal
39	Toxic	Poison	Status	—	90	10	Normal
46	Amnesia	Psychic	Status	—	—	20	Self
49	Belch	Poison	Special	120	90	10	Normal
54	Gunk Shot	Poison	Physical	120	80	5	Normal
59	Explosion	Normal	Physical	250	100	5	Adjacent

◆ TM MOVES
No.	Name	Type	Kind	Pow.	Acc.	PP	Range
TM06	Toxic	Poison	Status	—	90	10	Normal
TM09	Venoshock	Poison	Special	65	100	10	Normal
TM10	Hidden Power	Normal	Special	60	100	15	Normal
TM11	Sunny Day	Fire	Status	—	—	5	Both Sides
TM15	Hyper Beam	Normal	Special	150	90	5	Normal
TM17	Protect	Normal	Status	—	—	10	Self
TM18	Rain Dance	Water	Status	—	—	5	Both Sides
TM21	Frustration	Normal	Physical	—	100	20	Normal
TM22	Solar Beam	Grass	Special	120	100	10	Normal
TM23	Smack Down	Rock	Physical	50	100	15	Normal
TM24	Thunderbolt	Electric	Special	90	100	15	Normal
TM27	Return	Normal	Physical	—	100	20	Normal
TM29	Psychic	Psychic	Special	90	100	10	Normal
TM32	Double Team	Normal	Status	—	—	15	Self
TM34	Sludge Wave	Poison	Special	95	100	10	Adjacent
TM36	Sludge Bomb	Poison	Special	90	100	10	Normal
TM42	Facade	Normal	Physical	70	100	20	Normal
TM44	Rest	Psychic	Status	—	—	10	Self
TM45	Attract	Normal	Status	—	100	15	Normal
TM46	Thief	Dark	Physical	60	100	25	Normal
TM48	Round	Normal	Special	60	100	15	Normal
TM52	Focus Blast	Fighting	Special	120	70	5	Normal
TM56	Fling	Dark	Physical	—	100	10	Normal
TM64	Explosion	Normal	Physical	250	100	5	Adjacent
TM66	Payback	Dark	Physical	50	100	10	Normal
TM68	Giga Impact	Normal	Physical	150	90	5	Normal
TM69	Rock Polish	Rock	Status	—	—	20	Self
TM83	Infestation	Bug	Special	20	100	20	Normal

◆ MOVES TAUGHT BY PEOPLE
No.	Name	Type	Kind	Pow.	Acc.	PP	Range
TM87	Swagger	Normal	Status	—	85	15	Normal
TM88	Sleep Talk	Normal	Status	—	—	10	Self
TM90	Substitute	Normal	Status	—	—	10	Self
TM97	Dark Pulse	Dark	Special	80	100	15	Normal
TM100	Confide	Normal	Status	—	—	20	Normal

◆ MOVES LEARNED WHEN EVOLVING
Name	Type	Kind	Pow.	Acc.	PP	Range

◆ EGG MOVES
Name	Type	Kind	Pow.	Acc.	PP	Range

◆ EXCLUSIVE Z-MOVE
Name	Base Move	Type	Kind	Pow.	Acc.	Range

Skarmory

Armor Bird Pokémon

Alola Pokédex	Melemele	Akala	Ula'ula	Poni
208	—	—	080	072

STEEL FLYING

HEIGHT: 5'07"
WEIGHT: 111.3 lbs.

Its feathers, which fall off as it grows, are thin and sharp. In times long past, warriors used them as swords.

Its metal body is sturdy, but it does rust rather easily. So on rainy days, this Pokémon prefers to stay put in its nest.

ABILITY
Keen Eye
Sturdy

HIDDEN ABILITY
Weak Armor

Damage taken in normal battles

NORMAL ×0.5	FIGHTING ×1	ROCK ×1
FIRE ×2	POISON ×0	GHOST ×1
WATER ×1	GROUND ×0	DRAGON ×0.5
GRASS ×0.25	FLYING ×1	DARK ×1
ELECTRIC ×2	PSYCHIC ×0.5	STEEL ×1
ICE ×1	BUG ×0.25	FAIRY ×0.5

SPECIES STRENGTHS
HP ◆◆◆
Attack ◆◆◆◆
Defense ◆◆◆◆◆◆◆
Sp. Atk ◆◆
Sp. Def ◆◆◆◆
Speed ◆◆◆◆◆

EGG GROUPS
Flying

ITEM SOMETIMES HELD BY WILD POKÉMON
Metal Coat

EVOLUTION
Does not evolve

MAIN WAY TO REGISTER IN THE POKÉDEX
Catch from the shaking trees on Route 10

Same form for male/female

LEVEL-UP MOVES

Lv.	Name	Type	Kind	Pow.	Acc.	PP	Range
1	Leer	Normal	Status	—	100	30	Many Others
1	Peck	Flying	Physical	35	100	35	Normal
6	Sand Attack	Ground	Status	—	100	15	Normal
9	Metal Claw	Steel	Physical	50	95	35	Normal
12	Air Cutter	Flying	Special	60	95	25	Many Others
17	Fury Attack	Normal	Physical	15	85	20	Normal
20	Feint	Normal	Physical	30	100	10	Normal
23	Swift	Normal	Special	60	—	20	Many Others
28	Spikes	Ground	Status	—	—	20	Other Side
31	Agility	Psychic	Status	—	—	30	Self
34	Steel Wing	Steel	Physical	70	90	25	Normal
39	Slash	Normal	Physical	70	100	20	Normal
42	Metal Sound	Steel	Status	—	85	40	Normal
45	Air Slash	Flying	Special	75	95	15	Normal
50	Autotomize	Steel	Status	—	—	15	Self
53	Night Slash	Dark	Physical	70	100	15	Normal

TM MOVES

No.	Name	Type	Kind	Pow.	Acc.	PP	Range
TM05	Roar	Normal	Status	—	—	20	Normal
TM06	Toxic	Poison	Status	—	90	10	Normal
TM10	Hidden Power	Normal	Special	60	100	15	Normal
TM11	Sunny Day	Fire	Status	—	—	5	Both Sides
TM12	Taunt	Dark	Status	—	100	20	Normal
TM17	Protect	Normal	Status	—	—	10	Self
TM19	Roost	Flying	Status	—	—	10	Self
TM21	Frustration	Normal	Physical	—	100	20	Normal
TM27	Return	Normal	Physical	—	100	20	Normal
TM32	Double Team	Normal	Status	—	—	15	Self
TM37	Sandstorm	Rock	Status	—	—	10	Both Sides
TM39	Rock Tomb	Rock	Physical	60	95	15	Normal
TM40	Aerial Ace	Flying	Physical	60	—	20	Normal
TM41	Torment	Dark	Status	—	100	15	Normal
TM42	Facade	Normal	Physical	70	100	20	Normal
TM44	Rest	Psychic	Status	—	—	10	Self
TM45	Attract	Normal	Status	—	100	15	Normal
TM46	Thief	Dark	Physical	60	100	25	Normal
TM48	Round	Normal	Special	60	100	15	Normal
TM51	Steel Wing	Steel	Physical	70	90	25	Normal
TM58	Sky Drop	Flying	Physical	60	100	10	Normal
TM66	Payback	Dark	Physical	50	100	10	Normal
TM75	Swords Dance	Normal	Status	—	—	20	Self
TM76	Fly	Flying	Physical	90	95	15	Normal
TM80	Rock Slide	Rock	Physical	75	90	10	Many Others
TM81	X-Scissor	Bug	Physical	80	100	15	Normal
TM87	Swagger	Normal	Status	—	85	15	Normal
TM88	Sleep Talk	Normal	Status	—	—	10	Self
TM90	Substitute	Normal	Status	—	—	10	Self
TM91	Flash Cannon	Steel	Special	80	100	10	Normal
TM97	Dark Pulse	Dark	Special	80	100	15	Normal
TM100	Confide	Normal	Status	—	—	20	Normal

MOVES TAUGHT BY PEOPLE

Name	Type	Kind	Pow.	Acc.	PP	Range

MOVES LEARNED WHEN EVOLVING

Name	Type	Kind	Pow.	Acc.	PP	Range

EGG MOVES

Name	Type	Kind	Pow.	Acc.	PP	Range
Drill Peck	Flying	Physical	80	100	20	Normal
Pursuit	Dark	Physical	40	100	20	Normal
Whirlwind	Normal	Status	—	—	20	Normal
Sky Attack	Flying	Physical	140	90	5	Normal
Curse	Ghost	Status	—	—	10	Varies
Brave Bird	Flying	Physical	120	100	15	Normal
Assurance	Dark	Physical	60	100	10	Normal
Guard Swap	Psychic	Status	—	—	10	Normal
Stealth Rock	Rock	Status	—	—	20	Other Side
Endure	Normal	Status	—	—	10	Self

EXCLUSIVE Z-MOVE

Name	Base Move	Type	Kind	Pow.	Acc.	Range

Ditto

Transform Pokémon

Alola Pokédex	Melemele	Akala	Ula'ula	Poni
209	—	—	081	

NORMAL

HEIGHT: 1'00"
WEIGHT: 8.8 lbs.

It can reorganize its cells to make itself into a duplicate of anything it sees. The quality of the duplicate depends on the individual.

With its astonishing capacity for metamorphosis, it can get along with anything. It does not get along well with its fellow Ditto.

ABILITY
Limber

HIDDEN ABILITY
Imposter

Damage taken in normal battles

NORMAL ×1	FIGHTING ×2	ROCK ×1
FIRE ×1	POISON ×1	GHOST ×0
WATER ×1	GROUND ×1	DRAGON ×1
GRASS ×1	FLYING ×1	DARK ×1
ELECTRIC ×1	PSYCHIC ×1	STEEL ×1
ICE ×1	BUG ×1	FAIRY ×1

SPECIES STRENGTHS
HP ◆◆
Attack ◆◆
Defense ◆◆◆
Sp. Atk ◆◆
Sp. Def ◆◆
Speed ◆◆◆

EGG GROUPS
Ditto

ITEM SOMETIMES HELD BY WILD POKÉMON
Quick Powder / Metal Powder

EVOLUTION
Does not evolve

MAIN WAY TO REGISTER IN THE POKÉDEX
Catch in the tall grass on Mount Hokulani

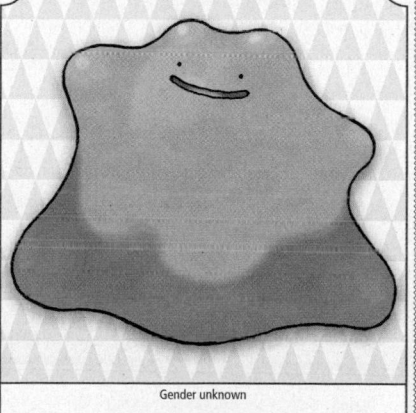

Gender unknown

LEVEL-UP MOVES

Lv.	Name	Type	Kind	Pow.	Acc.	PP	Range
1	Transform	Normal	Status	—	—	10	Normal

TM MOVES

No.	Name	Type	Kind	Pow.	Acc.	PP	Range

MOVES TAUGHT BY PEOPLE

Name	Type	Kind	Pow.	Acc.	PP	Range

MOVES LEARNED WHEN EVOLVING

Name	Type	Kind	Pow.	Acc.	PP	Range

EGG MOVES

Name	Type	Kind	Pow.	Acc.	PP	Range

EXCLUSIVE Z-MOVE

Name	Base Move	Type	Kind	Pow.	Acc.	Range

Cleffa

Star Shape Pokémon

FAIRY

Alola Pokédex	Melemele	Akala	Ula'ula	Poni
210	—	—	082	—

HEIGHT: 1'00"
WEIGHT: 6.6 lbs.

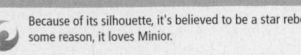 On late nights illuminated by shooting stars, it gazes intently skyward, as if thinking of its home.

Because of its silhouette, it's believed to be a star reborn. For some reason, it loves Minior.

ABILITY
Cute Charm
Magic Guard

HIDDEN ABILITY
Friend Guard

Damage taken in normal battles

NORMAL	×1	FIGHTING	×0.5	ROCK	×1
FIRE	×1	POISON	×2	GHOST	×1
WATER	×1	GROUND	×1	DRAGON	×0
GRASS	×1	FLYING	×1	DARK	×0.5
ELECTRIC	×1	PSYCHIC	×1	STEEL	×2
ICE	×1	BUG	×0.5	FAIRY	×1

SPECIES STRENGTHS
HP	◆◆
Attack	◆◆
Defense	◆◆
Sp. Atk	◆◆
Sp. Def	◆◆◆
Speed	◆

EGG GROUPS
No Eggs Discovered

ITEM SOMETIMES HELD BY WILD POKÉMON
Moon Stone

EVOLUTION

Cleffa → **Level up with high friendship** → Clefairy

Moon Stone

Clefable

MAIN WAY TO REGISTER IN THE POKÉDEX
Catch in the tall grass on Mount Hokulani when it is nighttime in your game

Same form for male/female

Clefairy

Fairy Pokémon

FAIRY

Alola Pokédex	Melemele	Akala	Ula'ula	Poni
211	—	—	083	—

HEIGHT: 2'00"
WEIGHT: 16.5 lbs.

Its adorable behavior and appearance make it popular with men and women, young and old. Its numbers are few, however.

On nights with a full moon, they gather together and dance. The surrounding area is enveloped in an abnormal magnetic field.

ABILITY
Cute Charm
Magic Guard

HIDDEN ABILITY
Friend Guard

Damage taken in normal battles

NORMAL	×1	FIGHTING	×0.5	ROCK	×1
FIRE	×1	POISON	×2	GHOST	×1
WATER	×1	GROUND	×1	DRAGON	×0
GRASS	×1	FLYING	×1	DARK	×0.5
ELECTRIC	×1	PSYCHIC	×1	STEEL	×2
ICE	×1	BUG	×0.5	FAIRY	×1

SPECIES STRENGTHS
HP	◆◆◆
Attack	◆◆◆
Defense	◆◆◆
Sp. Atk	◆◆◆
Sp. Def	◆◆◆◆
Speed	◆◆

EGG GROUPS
Fairy

ITEM SOMETIMES HELD BY WILD POKÉMON
Moon Stone

EVOLUTION

Cleffa → **Level up with high friendship** → Clefairy

Moon Stone

Clefable

MAIN WAY TO REGISTER IN THE POKÉDEX
Catch in SOS battles against Cleffa in the tall grass on Mount Hokulani when it is nighttime in your game

Same form for male/female

Clefable

Fairy Pokémon

FAIRY

Alola Pokédex	Melemele	Akala	Ula'ula	Poni
212	—	—	084	—

HEIGHT: 4'03"
WEIGHT: 88.2 lbs.

They don't like to reveal themselves in front of people. They live quietly in packs deep in the mountains.

According to tradition, people who see a pair of Clefable skipping by can look forward to a happy marriage.

ABILITY
Cute Charm
Magic Guard

HIDDEN ABILITY
Unaware

Damage taken in normal battles

NORMAL	×1	FIGHTING	×0.5	ROCK	×1
FIRE	×1	POISON	×2	GHOST	×1
WATER	×1	GROUND	×1	DRAGON	×0
GRASS	×1	FLYING	×1	DARK	×0.5
ELECTRIC	×1	PSYCHIC	×1	STEEL	×2
ICE	×1	BUG	×0.5	FAIRY	×1

SPECIES STRENGTHS
HP	◆◆◆◆
Attack	◆◆◆◆
Defense	◆◆◆
Sp. Atk	◆◆◆◆◆
Sp. Def	◆◆◆◆◆
Speed	◆◆◆

EGG GROUPS
Fairy

ITEM SOMETIMES HELD BY WILD POKÉMON

EVOLUTION

Cleffa → **Level up with high friendship** → Clefairy

Moon Stone

Clefable

MAIN WAY TO REGISTER IN THE POKÉDEX
Use a Moon Stone on Clefairy

Same form for male/female

CLEFFA 210

❖ LEVEL-UP MOVES

Lv.	Name	Type	Kind	Pow.	Acc.	PP	Range
1	Pound	Normal	Physical	40	100	35	Normal
1	Charm	Fairy	Status	—	100	20	Normal
4	Encore	Normal	Status	—	100	5	Normal
7	Sing	Normal	Status		55	15	Normal
10	Sweet Kiss	Fairy	Status	—	75	10	Normal
13	Copycat	Normal	Status	—	—	20	Self
16	Magical Leaf	Grass	Special	60	—	20	Normal

❖ TM MOVES

No.	Name	Type	Kind	Pow.	Acc.	PP	Range
TM01	Work Up	Normal	Status	—	—	30	Self
TM03	Psyshock	Psychic	Special	80	100	10	Normal
TM06	Toxic	Poison	Status	—	90	10	Normal
TM10	Hidden Power	Normal	Special	60	100	15	Normal
TM11	Sunny Day	Fire	Status	—	—	5	Both Sides
TM16	Light Screen	Psychic	Status	—	—	30	Your Side
TM17	Protect	Normal	Status	—	—	10	Self
TM18	Rain Dance	Water	Status	—	—	5	Both Sides
TM20	Safeguard	Normal	Status	—	—	25	Your Side
TM21	Frustration	Normal	Physical	—	100	20	Normal
TM22	Solar Beam	Grass	Special	120	100	10	Normal
TM27	Return	Normal	Physical	[illegible]	100	20	Normal
TM29	Psychic	Psychic	Special	90	100	10	Normal
TM30	Shadow Ball	Ghost	Special	80	100	15	Normal
TM32	Double Team	Normal	Status	—	—	15	Self
TM33	Reflect	Psychic	Status	—	—	20	Your Side
TM35	Flamethrower	Fire	Special	90	100	15	Normal
TM38	Fire Blast	Fire	Special	110	85	5	Normal
TM42	Facade	Normal	Physical	70	100	20	Normal
TM44	Rest	Psychic	Status	—	—	10	Self
TM45	Attract	Normal	Status	—	100	15	Normal
TM48	Round	Normal	Special	60	100	15	Normal
TM49	Echoed Voice	Normal	Special	40	100	15	Normal
TM56	Fling	Dark	Physical	—	100	10	Normal
TM73	Thunder Wave	Electric	Status	—	90	20	Normal
TM77	Psych Up	Normal	Status	—	—	10	Normal
TM85	Dream Eater	Psychic	Special	100	100	15	Normal
TM86	Grass Knot	Grass	Special	—	100	20	Normal
TM87	Swagger	Normal	Status	—	85	15	Normal
TM88	Sleep Talk	Normal	Status	—	—	10	Self
TM90	Substitute	Normal	Status	—	—	10	Self
TM100	Confide	Normal	Status	—	—	20	Normal

❖ EXCLUSIVE Z-MOVE

Name	Base Move	Type	Kind	Pow.	Acc.	Range

❖ MOVES TAUGHT BY PEOPLE

Name	Type	Kind	Pow.	Acc.	PP	Range

❖ MOVES LEARNED WHEN EVOLVING

Name	Type	Kind	Pow.	Acc.	PP	Range

❖ EGG MOVES

Name	Type	Kind	Pow.	Acc.	PP	Range
Present	Normal	Physical	—	90	15	Normal
Metronome	Normal	Status	—	—	10	Self
Amnesia	Psychic	Status	—	—	20	Self
Belly Drum	Normal	Status	—	—	10	Self
Splash	Normal	Status	—	—	40	Self
Mimic	Normal	Status	—	—	10	Normal
Wish	Normal	Status	—	—	10	Self
Fake Tears	Dark	Status	—	100	20	Normal
Covet	Normal	Physical	60	100	25	Normal
Aromatherapy	Grass	Status	—	—	5	Your Party
Stored Power	Psychic	Special	20	100	10	Normal
Tickle	Normal	Status	—	100	20	Normal
Misty Terrain	Fairy	Status	—	—	10	Both Sides
Heal Pulse	Psychic	Status	—	—	10	Normal

CLEFAIRY 211

❖ LEVEL-UP MOVES

Lv.	Name	Type	Kind	Pow.	Acc.	PP	Range
1	Spotlight	Normal	Status	—	—	15	Normal
1	Disarming Voice	Fairy	Special	40	—	15	Many Others
1	Pound	Normal	Physical	40	100	35	Normal
1	Growl	Normal	Status	—	100	40	Many Others
1	Encore	Normal	Status	—	100	5	Normal
7	Sing	Normal	Status	—	55	15	Normal
10	Double Slap	Normal	Physical	15	85	10	Normal
13	Defense Curl	Normal	Status	—	—	40	Self
16	Follow Me	Normal	Status	—	—	20	Self
19	Bestow	Normal	Status	—	—	15	Normal
22	Wake-Up Slap	Fighting	Physical	70	100	10	Normal
25	Minimize	Normal	Status	—	—	10	Self
28	Stored Power	Psychic	Special	20	100	10	Normal
31	Metronome	Normal	Status	—	—	10	Self
34	Cosmic Power	Psychic	Status	—	—	20	Self
37	Lucky Chant	Normal	Status	—	—	30	Your Side
40	Body Slam	Normal	Physical	85	100	15	Normal
43	Moonlight	Fairy	Status	—	—	5	Self
46	Moonblast	Fairy	Special	95	100	15	Normal
49	Gravity	Psychic	Status	—	—	5	Both Sides
50	Meteor Mash	Steel	Physical	90	90	10	Normal
55	Healing Wish	Psychic	Status	—	—	10	Self
58	After You	Normal	Status	—	—	15	Normal

❖ TM MOVES

No.	Name	Type	Kind	Pow.	Acc.	PP	Range
TM01	Work Up	Normal	Status	—	—	30	Self
TM03	Psyshock	Psychic	Special	80	100	10	Normal
TM04	Calm Mind	Psychic	Status	—	—	20	Self
TM06	Toxic	Poison	Status	—	90	10	Normal
TM10	Hidden Power	Normal	Special	60	100	15	Normal
TM11	Sunny Day	Fire	Status	—	—	5	Both Sides
TM13	Ice Beam	Ice	Special	90	100	10	Normal
TM14	Blizzard	Ice	Special	110	70	5	Many Others
TM16	Light Screen	Psychic	Status	—	—	30	Your Side
TM17	Protect	Normal	Status	—	—	10	Self
TM18	Rain Dance	Water	Status	—	—	5	Both Sides
TM20	Safeguard	Normal	Status	—	—	25	Your Side
TM21	Frustration	Normal	Physical	—	100	20	Normal
TM22	Solar Beam	Grass	Special	120	100	10	Normal
TM24	Thunderbolt	Electric	Special	90	100	15	Normal
TM25	Thunder	Electric	Special	110	70	10	Normal
TM27	Return	Normal	Physical	—	100	20	Normal
TM29	Psychic	Psychic	Special	90	100	10	Normal
TM30	Shadow Ball	Ghost	Special	80	100	15	Normal
TM31	Brick Break	Fighting	Physical	75	100	15	Normal
TM32	Double Team	Normal	Status	—	—	15	Self
TM33	Reflect	Psychic	Status	—	—	20	Your Side
TM35	Flamethrower	Fire	Special	90	100	15	Normal
TM38	Fire Blast	Fire	Special	110	85	5	Normal
TM42	Facade	Normal	Physical	70	100	20	Normal
TM44	Rest	Psychic	Status	—	—	10	Self
TM45	Attract	Normal	Status	—	100	15	Normal
TM48	Round	Normal	Special	60	100	15	Normal
TM49	Echoed Voice	Normal	Special	40	100	15	Normal
TM56	Fling	Dark	Physical	—	100	10	Normal
TM57	Charge Beam	Electric	Special	50	90	10	Normal
TM73	Thunder Wave	Electric	Status	—	90	20	Normal
TM77	Psych Up	Normal	Status	—	—	10	Normal
TM85	Dream Eater	Psychic	Special	100	100	15	Normal
TM86	Grass Knot	Grass	Special	—	100	20	Normal
TM87	Swagger	Normal	Status	—	85	15	Normal
TM88	Sleep Talk	Normal	Status	—	—	10	Self
TM90	Substitute	Normal	Status	—	—	10	Self
TM99	Dazzling Gleam	Fairy	Special	80	100	10	Many Others
TM100	Confide	Normal	Status	—	—	20	Normal

❖ EXCLUSIVE Z-MOVE

Name	Base Move	Type	Kind	Pow.	Acc.	Range

❖ MOVES TAUGHT BY PEOPLE

Name	Type	Kind	Pow.	Acc.	PP	Range

❖ MOVES LEARNED WHEN EVOLVING

Name	Type	Kind	Pow.	Acc.	PP	Range

❖ EGG MOVES

Name	Type	Kind	Pow.	Acc.	PP	Range

CLEFABLE 212

❖ LEVEL-UP MOVES

Lv.	Name	Type	Kind	Pow.	Acc.	PP	Range
1	Spotlight	Normal	Status	—	—	15	Normal
1	Disarming Voice	Fairy	Special	40	—	15	Many Others
1	Sing	Normal	Status	—	55	15	Normal
1	Double Slap	Normal	Physical	15	85	10	Normal
1	Minimize	Normal	Status	—	—	10	Self
1	Metronome	Normal	Status	—	—	10	Self

❖ TM MOVES

No.	Name	Type	Kind	Pow.	Acc.	PP	Range
TM01	Work Up	Normal	Status	—	—	30	Self
TM03	Psyshock	Psychic	Special	80	100	10	Normal
TM04	Calm Mind	Psychic	Status	—	—	20	Self
TM06	Toxic	Poison	Status	—	90	10	Normal
TM10	Hidden Power	Normal	Special	60	100	15	Normal
TM11	Sunny Day	Fire	Status	—	—	5	Both Sides
TM13	Ice Beam	Ice	Special	90	100	10	Normal
TM14	Blizzard	Ice	Special	110	70	5	Many Others
TM15	Hyper Beam	Normal	Special	150	90	5	Normal
TM16	Light Screen	Psychic	Status	—	—	30	Your Side
TM17	Protect	Normal	Status	—	—	10	Self
TM18	Rain Dance	Water	Status	—	—	5	Both Sides
TM20	Safeguard	Normal	Status	—	—	25	Your Side
TM21	Frustration	Normal	Physical	—	100	20	Normal
TM22	Solar Beam	Grass	Special	120	100	10	Normal
TM24	Thunderbolt	Electric	Special	90	100	15	Normal
TM25	Thunder	Electric	Special	110	70	10	Normal
TM27	Return	Normal	Physical	—	100	20	Normal
TM29	Psychic	Psychic	Special	90	100	10	Normal
TM30	Shadow Ball	Ghost	Special	80	100	15	Normal
TM31	Brick Break	Fighting	Physical	75	100	15	Normal
TM32	Double Team	Normal	Status	—	—	15	Self
TM33	Reflect	Psychic	Status	—	—	20	Your Side
TM35	Flamethrower	Fire	Special	90	100	15	Normal
TM38	Fire Blast	Fire	Special	110	85	5	Normal
TM42	Facade	Normal	Physical	70	100	20	Normal
TM44	Rest	Psychic	Status	—	—	10	Self
TM45	Attract	Normal	Status	—	100	15	Normal
TM48	Round	Normal	Special	60	100	15	Normal
TM49	Echoed Voice	Normal	Special	40	100	15	Normal
TM52	Focus Blast	Fighting	Special	120	70	5	Normal
TM56	Fling	Dark	Physical	—	100	10	Normal
TM57	Charge Beam	Electric	Special	50	90	10	Normal
TM68	Giga Impact	Normal	Physical	150	90	5	Normal
TM73	Thunder Wave	Electric	Status	—	90	20	Normal
TM77	Psych Up	Normal	Status	—	—	10	Normal
TM85	Dream Eater	Psychic	Special	100	100	15	Normal
TM86	Grass Knot	Grass	Special	—	100	20	Normal
TM87	Swagger	Normal	Status	—	85	15	Normal
TM88	Sleep Talk	Normal	Status	—	—	10	Self
TM90	Substitute	Normal	Status	—	—	10	Self
TM99	Dazzling Gleam	Fairy	Special	80	100	10	Many Others
TM100	Confide	Normal	Status	—	—	20	Normal

❖ EXCLUSIVE Z-MOVE

Name	Base Move	Type	Kind	Pow.	Acc.	Range

❖ MOVES TAUGHT BY PEOPLE

Name	Type	Kind	Pow.	Acc.	PP	Range

❖ MOVES LEARNED WHEN EVOLVING

Name	Type	Kind	Pow.	Acc.	PP	Range

❖ EGG MOVES

Name	Type	Kind	Pow.	Acc.	PP	Range

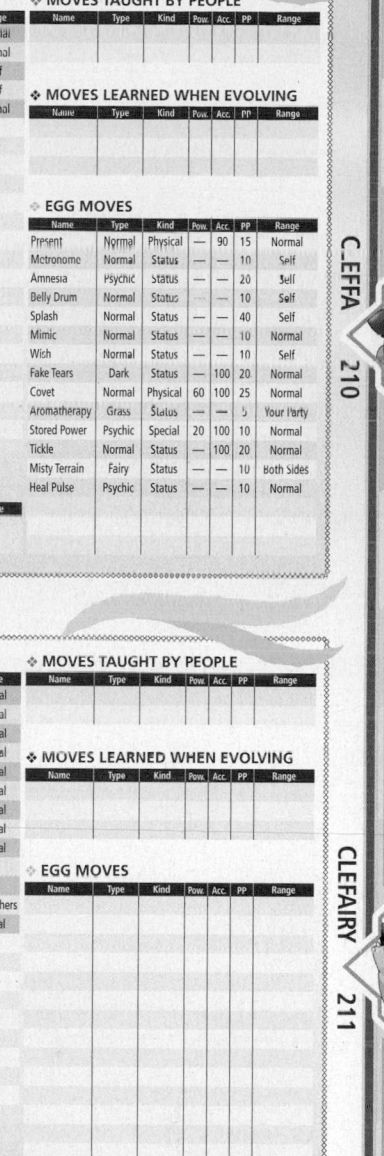

Minior

Alola Pokédex	Melemele	Akala	Ula'ula	Poni
213	—	—	085	—

☑ **Minior**
Meteor Pokémon

ROCK **FLYING**

HEIGHT: 1'00"
WEIGHT: 88.2 lbs.

Originally making its home in the ozone layer, it hurtles to the ground when the shell enclosing its body grows too heavy.

Strong impacts can knock it out of its shell. This Pokémon was born from mutated nanoparticles.

ABILITY
Shields Down

HIDDEN ABILITY
—

Damage taken in normal battles

NORMAL ×0.5	FIGHTING ×1	ROCK ×2	
FIRE ×0.5	POISON ×0.5	GHOST ×1	
WATER ×2	GROUND ×0	DRAGON ×1	
GRASS ×1	FLYING ×0.5	DARK ×1	
ELECTRIC ×2	PSYCHIC ×1	STEEL ×1	
ICE ×2	BUG ×0.5	FAIRY ×1	

SPECIES STRENGTHS
HP ◆◆
Attack ◆◆◆
Defense ◆◆◆◆◆
Sp. Atk ◆◆◆
Sp. Def ◆◆◆◆◆◆
Speed ◆◆◆◆

EGG GROUPS
Mineral

ITEM SOMETIMES HELD BY WILD POKÉMON
Star Piece

EVOLUTION
Does not evolve

MAIN WAY TO REGISTER IN THE POKÉDEX
Catch in the tall grass on Mount Hokulani

METEOR FORM

Gender unknown

❖ LEVEL-UP MOVES

Lv.	Name	Type	Kind	Pow.	Acc.	PP	Range
1	Tackle	Normal	Physical	40	100	35	Normal
3	Defense Curl	Normal	Status	—	—	40	Self
8	Rollout	Rock	Physical	30	90	20	Normal
10	Confuse Ray	Ghost	Status	—	100	10	Normal
15	Swift	Normal	Special	60	—	20	Many Others
17	Ancient Power	Rock	Special	60	100	5	Normal
22	Self-Destruct	Normal	Physical	200	100	5	Adjacent
24	Stealth Rock	Rock	Status	—	—	20	Other Side
29	Take Down	Normal	Physical	90	85	20	Normal
31	Autotomize	Steel	Status	—	—	15	Self
36	Cosmic Power	Psychic	Status	—	—	20	Self
38	Power Gem	Rock	Special	80	100	20	Normal
43	Double-Edge	Normal	Physical	120	100	15	Normal
45	Shell Smash	Normal	Status	—	—	15	Self
50	Explosion	Normal	Physical	250	100	5	Adjacent

❖ TM MOVES

No.	Name	Type	Kind	Pow.	Acc.	PP	Range
TM04	Calm Mind	Psychic	Status	—	—	20	Self
TM06	Toxic	Poison	Status	—	90	10	Normal
TM10	Hidden Power	Normal	Special	60	100	15	Normal
TM15	Hyper Beam	Normal	Special	150	90	5	Normal
TM16	Light Screen	Psychic	Status	—	—	30	Your Side
TM17	Protect	Normal	Status	—	—	10	Self
TM20	Safeguard	Normal	Status	—	—	25	Your Side
TM21	Frustration	Normal	Physical	—	100	20	Normal
TM22	Solar Beam	Grass	Special	120	100	10	Normal
TM26	Earthquake	Ground	Physical	100	100	10	Adjacent
TM27	Return	Normal	Physical	—	100	20	Normal
TM29	Psychic	Psychic	Special	90	100	10	Normal
TM32	Double Team	Normal	Status	—	—	15	Self
TM33	Reflect	Psychic	Status	—	—	20	Your Side
TM37	Sandstorm	Rock	Status	—	—	10	Both Sides
TM39	Rock Tomb	Rock	Physical	60	95	15	Normal
TM42	Facade	Normal	Physical	70	100	20	Normal
TM44	Rest	Psychic	Status	—	—	10	Self
TM45	Attract	Normal	Status	—	100	15	Normal
TM48	Round	Normal	Special	60	100	15	Normal
TM57	Charge Beam	Electric	Special	50	90	10	Normal
TM62	Acrobatics	Flying	Physical	55	100	15	Normal
TM64	Explosion	Normal	Physical	250	100	5	Adjacent
TM68	Giga Impact	Normal	Physical	150	90	5	Normal
TM69	Rock Polish	Rock	Status	—	—	20	Self
TM71	Stone Edge	Rock	Physical	100	80	5	Normal
TM74	Gyro Ball	Steel	Physical	—	100	5	Normal
TM77	Psych Up	Normal	Status	—	—	10	Normal

No.	Name	Type	Kind	Pow.	Acc.	PP	Range
TM78	Bulldoze	Ground	Physical	60	100	20	Adjacent
TM80	Rock Slide	Rock	Physical	75	90	10	Many Others
TM87	Swagger	Normal	Status	—	85	15	Normal
TM88	Sleep Talk	Normal	Status	—	—	10	Self
TM89	U-turn	Bug	Physical	70	100	20	Normal
TM90	Substitute	Normal	Status	—	—	10	Self
TM99	Dazzling Gleam	Fairy	Special	80	100	10	Many Others
TM100	Confide	Normal	Status	—	—	20	Normal

❖ MOVES TAUGHT BY PEOPLE

Name	Type	Kind	Pow.	Acc.	PP	Range

❖ MOVES LEARNED WHEN EVOLVING

Name	Type	Kind	Pow.	Acc.	PP	Range

❖ EGG MOVES

Name	Type	Kind	Pow.	Acc.	PP	Range

❖ EXCLUSIVE Z-MOVE

Name	Base Move	Type	Kind	Pow.	Acc.	Range

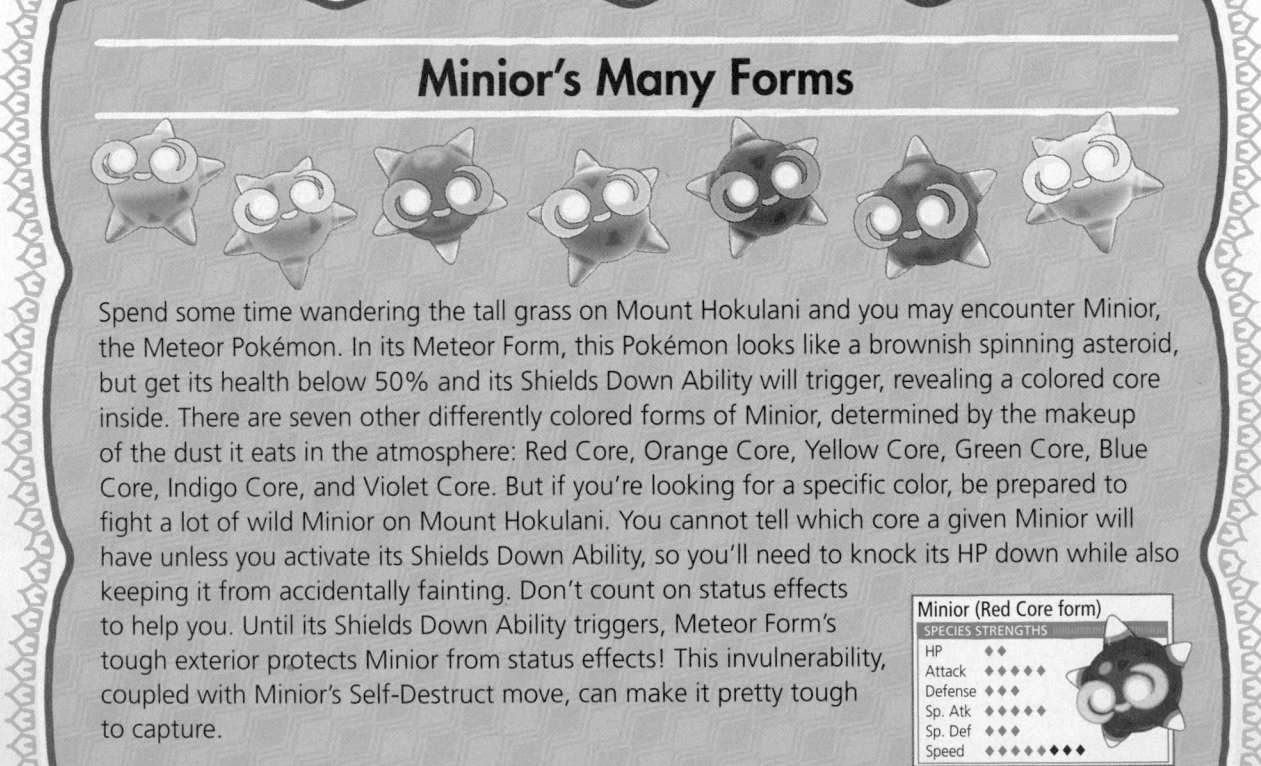

Minior's Many Forms

Spend some time wandering the tall grass on Mount Hokulani and you may encounter Minior, the Meteor Pokémon. In its Meteor Form, this Pokémon looks like a brownish spinning asteroid, but get its health below 50% and its Shields Down Ability will trigger, revealing a colored core inside. There are seven other differently colored forms of Minior, determined by the makeup of the dust it eats in the atmosphere: Red Core, Orange Core, Yellow Core, Green Core, Blue Core, Indigo Core, and Violet Core. But if you're looking for a specific color, be prepared to fight a lot of wild Minior on Mount Hokulani. You cannot tell which core a given Minior will have unless you activate its Shields Down Ability, so you'll need to knock its HP down while also keeping it from accidentally fainting. Don't count on status effects to help you. Until its Shields Down Ability triggers, Meteor Form's tough exterior protects Minior from status effects! This invulnerability, coupled with Minior's Self-Destruct move, can make it pretty tough to capture.

Minior (Red Core form)
SPECIES STRENGTHS
HP ◆◆
Attack ◆◆◆◆◆
Defense ◆◆◆
Sp. Atk ◆◆◆◆◆
Sp. Def ◆◆◆
Speed ◆◆◆◆◆◆◆

Pokémon Can Come in Different Forms

Minior is hardly the only Pokémon that can come in a variety of different forms. Read on to check out the other Pokémon in the Alola region that can take on multiple forms, either in battle or outside of it!

Oricorio

Oricorio has four different styles that it can appear in. Use a Yellow Nectar, Pink Nectar, Red Nectar, or Purple Nectar on Oricorio, and Oricorio will change its style to Pom-Pom Style, Pa'u Style, Baile Style, or Sensu Style, respectively. It will remain in the style you change it to until you use a different type of nectar on it. Each style has a different type, and you can change styles both in and out of battle, so choose whichever one is best for the situation you are in.

Pom-Pom Style
ELECTRIC FLYING

Pa'u Style
PSYCHIC FLYING

Baile Style
FIRE FLYING

Sensu Style
GHOST FLYING

Lycanroc

Lycanroc has two different forms: Midday Form and Midnight Form. You can catch Midday Form during the daytime in your game and Midnight Form during the nighttime. The two forms share one possible Ability, Keen Eye, but the other possible Ability and Hidden Ability are different for each form. The moves learned by each also differ slightly. Lycanroc cannot change forms between Midday Form and Midnight Form, so it will stay in whatever form you first catch, evolve, or receive Lycanroc in.

Midday Form
ROCK

Midnight Form
ROCK

Wishiwashi

During battle, Wishiwashi turns into its School Form as long as it is Lv. 20 or higher and its remaining HP is 1/4 or more. If its remaining HP drops below 1/4 of its max during battle, it will turn into its Solo Form, but it can be returned to its School Form by restoring its HP. Wishiwashi that are lower than Lv. 20 will always appear in their Solo Form.

Solo Form
WATER

School Form
WATER

Castform

Castform is a Pokémon that changes its forms depending on the current weather. When there are no unusual weather conditions affecting the battlefield, it will appear in its Normal Form. When the sunlight is harsh, due to a move like Sunny Day or an Ability like Drought, it will change to its Sunny Form and become Fire type. On the other hand, when it is raining, it will take on its Rainy Form and the Water type. And finally, when hail is falling, it will change to its Snowy Form and the Ice type. It will change forms in battle whenever the weather conditions change.

Normal
NORMAL

Sunny Form
FIRE

Rainy Form
WATER

Snowy Form
ICE

Silvally

Silvally has 17 forms it can take on by holding particular items. Give Silvally a memory drive, such as Grass Memory, Fire Memory, or Water Memory, and its type will change to correspond to that type. It will remain in that form unless you give it a different item to hold.

Type: Grass
GRASS

Type: Fire
FIRE

Type: Water
WATER

And many more! (See pages 140–141 for details.)

Zygarde

Zygarde has three Formes: its 10% Forme, 50% Forme, and Complete Forme. Which Forme it appears in will depend on how many of its Cells and Cores have been gathered together (p. 230–231). It can only change to its Complete Forme during battle and under certain circumstances, but it can change between its 10% Forme and its 50% Forme both in and outside of battle if you meet certain conditions.

10% Forme
DRAGON GROUND

50% Forme
DRAGON GROUND

Complete Forme
DRAGON GROUND

Mimikyu

Mimikyu's Disguise Ability can serve as a decoy and nullifies the first attack from the opponent. Once it is triggered, though, Mimikyu's form changes from its Disguised Form to Busted Form. It will return to its Disguised Form by the time it next enters battle.

Busted Form
GHOST FAIRY

Disguised Form
GHOST FAIRY

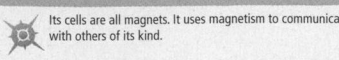

Beldum

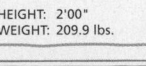

Beldum

Iron Ball Pokémon

STEEL PSYCHIC

HEIGHT: 2'00"
WEIGHT: 209.9 lbs.

Its cells are all magnets. It uses magnetism to communicate with others of its kind.

With magnetic traction, it pulls its opponents in close. When they're in range, it slashes them with its rear claws.

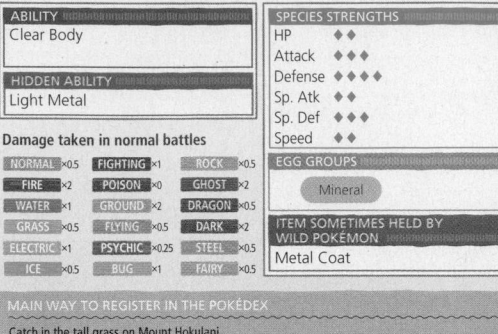

ABILITY
Clear Body

HIDDEN ABILITY
Light Metal

Damage taken in normal battles

NORMAL ×0.5	FIGHTING ×1	ROCK ×1
FIRE ×2	POISON ×0	GHOST ×2
WATER ×1	GROUND ×2	DRAGON ×0.5
GRASS ×0.5	FLYING ×0.5	DARK ×1
ELECTRIC ×1	PSYCHIC ×0.25	STEEL ×0.5
ICE ×0.5	BUG ×1	FAIRY ×0.5

SPECIES STRENGTHS
HP ◆◆
Attack ◆◆◆
Defense ◆◆◆◆
Sp. Atk ◆◆
Sp. Def ◆◆◆
Speed ◆◆

EGG GROUPS
Mineral

ITEM SOMETIMES HELD BY WILD POKÉMON
Metal Coat

MAIN WAY TO REGISTER IN THE POKÉDEX
Catch in the tall grass on Mount Hokulani

EVOLUTION
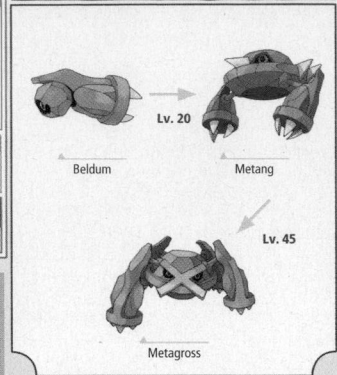

Beldum — Lv. 20 → Metang — Lv. 45 → Metagross

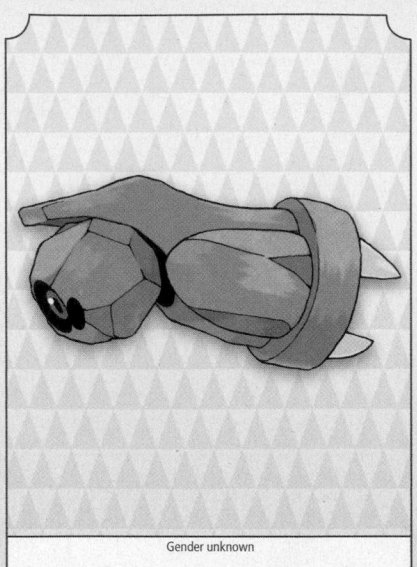

Gender unknown

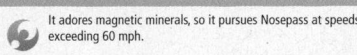

Metang

Metang

Iron Claw Pokémon

STEEL PSYCHIC

HEIGHT: 3'11"
WEIGHT: 446.4 lbs.

When two Beldum link together, their psychic power is doubled. Their intelligence, however, remains unchanged.

It adores magnetic minerals, so it pursues Nosepass at speeds exceeding 60 mph.

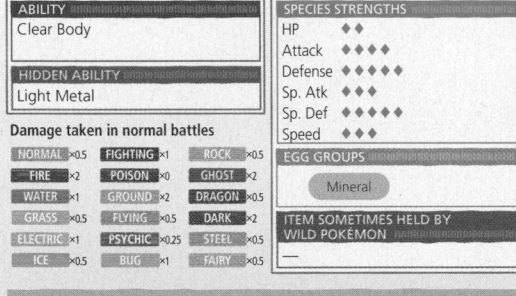

ABILITY
Clear Body

HIDDEN ABILITY
Light Metal

Damage taken in normal battles

NORMAL ×0.5	FIGHTING ×1	ROCK ×1
FIRE ×2	POISON ×0	GHOST ×2
WATER ×1	GROUND ×2	DRAGON ×0.5
GRASS ×0.5	FLYING ×0.5	DARK ×1
ELECTRIC ×1	PSYCHIC ×0.25	STEEL ×0.5
ICE ×0.5	BUG ×1	FAIRY ×0.5

SPECIES STRENGTHS
HP ◆◆
Attack ◆◆◆◆
Defense ◆◆◆◆◆
Sp. Atk ◆◆◆
Sp. Def ◆◆◆◆
Speed ◆◆◆

EGG GROUPS
Mineral

ITEM SOMETIMES HELD BY WILD POKÉMON
—

MAIN WAY TO REGISTER IN THE POKÉDEX
Level up Beldum to Lv. 20

EVOLUTION
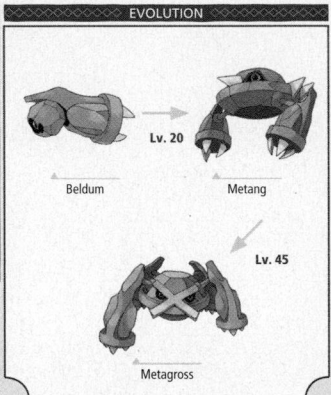

Beldum — Lv. 20 → Metang — Lv. 45 → Metagross

Gender unknown

Metagross

Metagross

Iron Leg Pokémon

STEEL PSYCHIC

HEIGHT: 5'03"
WEIGHT: 1212.5 lbs.

It firmly pins its prey using its four claws and large body. Then the teeth in the mouth on its stomach chew the prey to bits.

A linkage of two Metang, this Pokémon can perform any calculation in a flash by utilizing parallel processing in its four brains.

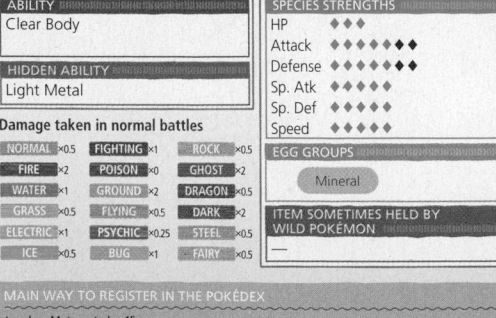

ABILITY
Clear Body

HIDDEN ABILITY
Light Metal

Damage taken in normal battles

NORMAL ×0.5	FIGHTING ×1	ROCK ×1
FIRE ×2	POISON ×0	GHOST ×2
WATER ×1	GROUND ×2	DRAGON ×0.5
GRASS ×0.5	FLYING ×0.5	DARK ×1
ELECTRIC ×1	PSYCHIC ×0.25	STEEL ×0.5
ICE ×0.5	BUG ×1	FAIRY ×0.5

SPECIES STRENGTHS
HP ◆◆◆
Attack ◆◆◆◆◆◆◆
Defense ◆◆◆◆◆◆◆
Sp. Atk ◆◆◆◆
Sp. Def ◆◆◆◆◆
Speed ◆◆◆◆◆

EGG GROUPS
Mineral

ITEM SOMETIMES HELD BY WILD POKÉMON
—

MAIN WAY TO REGISTER IN THE POKÉDEX
Level up Metang to Lv. 45

EVOLUTION
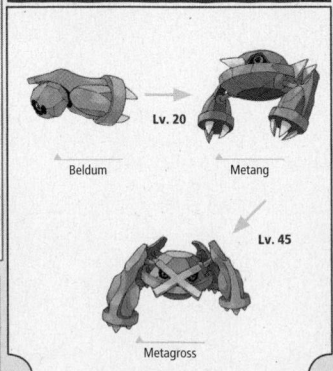

Beldum — Lv. 20 → Metang — Lv. 45 → Metagross

Gender unknown

p. 211

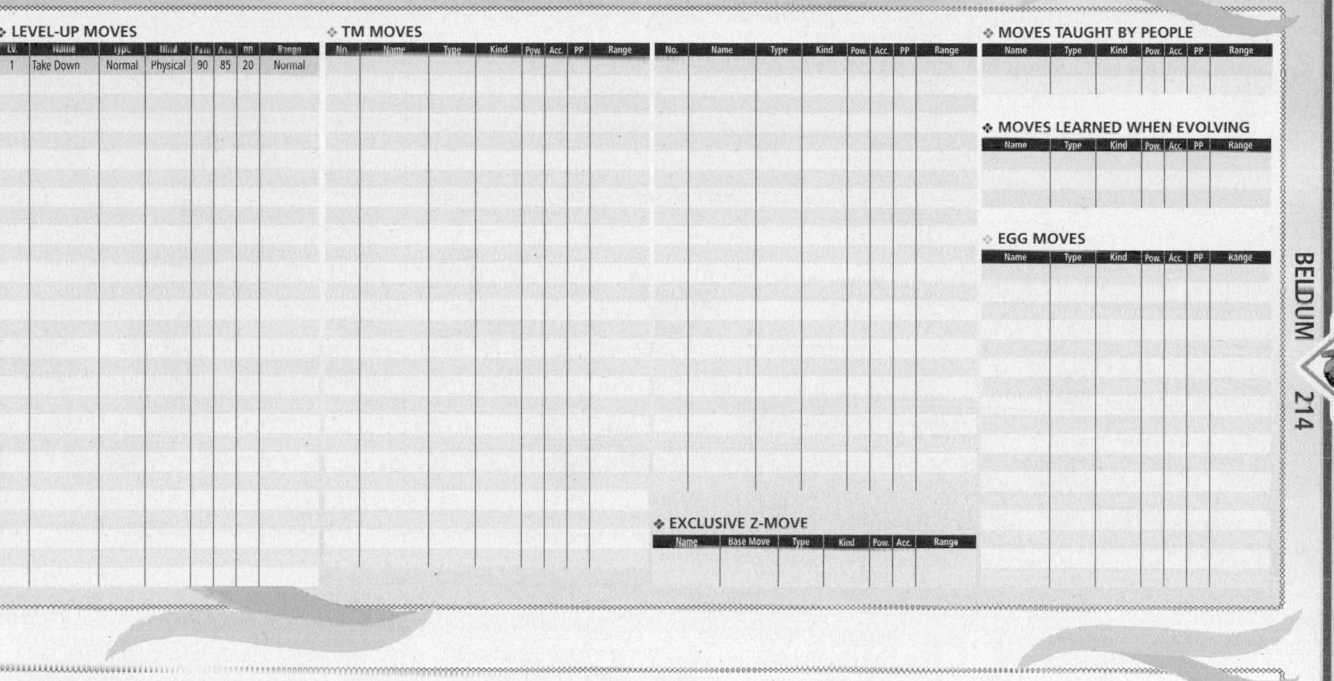

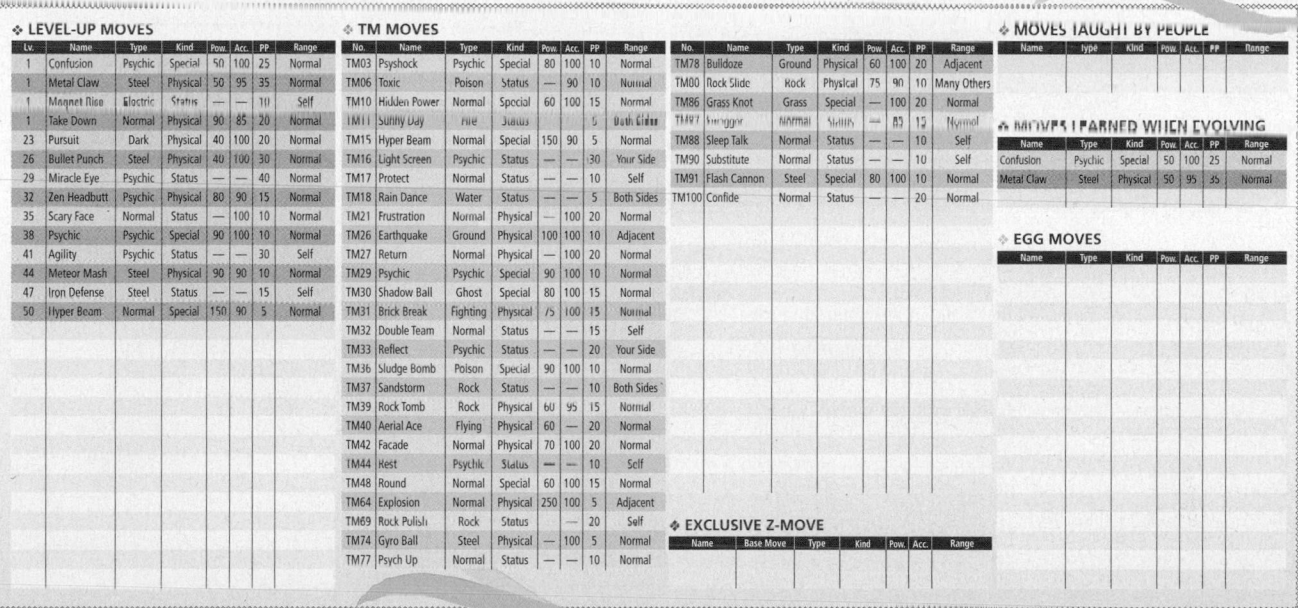

❖ LEVEL-UP MOVES

Lv.	Name	Type	Kind	Pow.	Acc.	PP	Range
1	Take Down	Normal	Physical	90	85	20	Normal

❖ TM MOVES

No.	Name	Type	Kind	Pow.	Acc.	PP	Range

❖ MOVES TAUGHT BY PEOPLE

Name	Type	Kind	Pow.	Acc.	PP	Range

❖ MOVES LEARNED WHEN EVOLVING

Name	Type	Kind	Pow.	Acc.	PP	Range

❖ EGG MOVES

Name	Type	Kind	Pow.	Acc.	PP	Range

❖ EXCLUSIVE Z-MOVE

Name	Base Move	Type	Kind	Pow.	Acc.	Range

❖ LEVEL-UP MOVES

Lv.	Name	Type	Kind	Pow.	Acc.	PP	Range
1	Confusion	Psychic	Special	50	100	25	Normal
1	Metal Claw	Steel	Physical	50	95	35	Normal
1	Magnet Rise	Electric	Status	—	—	10	Self
1	Take Down	Normal	Physical	90	85	20	Normal
23	Pursuit	Dark	Physical	40	100	20	Normal
26	Bullet Punch	Steel	Physical	40	100	30	Normal
29	Miracle Eye	Psychic	Status	—	—	40	Normal
32	Zen Headbutt	Psychic	Physical	80	90	15	Normal
35	Scary Face	Normal	Status	—	100	10	Normal
38	Psychic	Psychic	Special	90	100	10	Normal
41	Agility	Psychic	Status	—	—	30	Self
44	Meteor Mash	Steel	Physical	90	90	10	Normal
47	Iron Defense	Steel	Status	—	—	15	Self
50	Hyper Beam	Normal	Special	150	90	5	Normal

❖ TM MOVES

No.	Name	Type	Kind	Pow.	Acc.	PP	Range
TM03	Psyshock	Psychic	Special	80	100	10	Normal
TM06	Toxic	Poison	Status	—	90	10	Normal
TM10	Hidden Power	Normal	Special	60	100	15	Normal
TM11	Sunny Day	Fire	Status	—	—	5	Both Sides
TM15	Hyper Beam	Normal	Special	150	90	5	Normal
TM16	Light Screen	Psychic	Status	—	—	30	Your Side
TM17	Protect	Normal	Status	—	—	10	Self
TM18	Rain Dance	Water	Status	—	—	5	Both Sides
TM21	Frustration	Normal	Physical	—	100	20	Normal
TM26	Earthquake	Ground	Physical	100	100	10	Adjacent
TM27	Return	Normal	Physical	—	100	20	Normal
TM29	Psychic	Psychic	Special	90	100	10	Normal
TM30	Shadow Ball	Ghost	Special	80	100	15	Normal
TM31	Brick Break	Fighting	Physical	75	100	15	Normal
TM32	Double Team	Normal	Status	—	—	15	Self
TM33	Reflect	Psychic	Status	—	—	20	Your Side
TM36	Sludge Bomb	Poison	Special	90	100	10	Normal
TM37	Sandstorm	Rock	Status	—	—	10	Both Sides
TM39	Rock Tomb	Rock	Physical	60	95	15	Normal
TM40	Aerial Ace	Flying	Physical	60	—	20	Normal
TM42	Facade	Normal	Physical	70	100	20	Normal
TM44	Rest	Psychic	Status	—	—	10	Self
TM48	Round	Normal	Special	60	100	15	Normal
TM64	Explosion	Normal	Physical	250	100	5	Adjacent
TM69	Rock Polish	Rock	Status	—	—	20	Self
TM74	Gyro Ball	Steel	Physical	—	100	5	Normal
TM77	Psych Up	Normal	Status	—	—	10	Normal

No.	Name	Type	Kind	Pow.	Acc.	PP	Range
TM78	Bulldoze	Ground	Physical	60	100	20	Adjacent
TM80	Rock Slide	Rock	Physical	75	90	10	Many Others
TM86	Grass Knot	Grass	Special	—	100	20	Normal
TM87	Swagger	Normal	Status	—	85	15	Normal
TM88	Sleep Talk	Normal	Status	—	—	10	Self
TM90	Substitute	Normal	Status	—	—	10	Self
TM91	Flash Cannon	Steel	Special	80	100	10	Normal
TM100	Confide	Normal	Status	—	—	20	Normal

❖ MOVES TAUGHT BY PEOPLE

Name	Type	Kind	Pow.	Acc.	PP	Range

❖ MOVES LEARNED WHEN EVOLVING

Name	Type	Kind	Pow.	Acc.	PP	Range
Confusion	Psychic	Special	50	100	25	Normal
Metal Claw	Steel	Physical	50	95	35	Normal

❖ EGG MOVES

Name	Type	Kind	Pow.	Acc.	PP	Range

❖ EXCLUSIVE Z-MOVE

Name	Base Move	Type	Kind	Pow.	Acc.	Range

❖ LEVEL-UP MOVES

Lv.	Name	Type	Kind	Pow.	Acc.	PP	Range
1	Hammer Arm	Fighting	Physical	100	90	10	Normal
1	Confusion	Psychic	Special	50	100	25	Normal
1	Metal Claw	Steel	Physical	50	95	35	Normal
1	Magnet Rise	Electric	Status	—	—	10	Self
1	Take Down	Normal	Physical	90	85	20	Normal
23	Pursuit	Dark	Physical	40	100	20	Normal
26	Bullet Punch	Steel	Physical	40	100	30	Normal
29	Miracle Eye	Psychic	Status	—	—	40	Normal
32	Zen Headbutt	Psychic	Physical	80	90	15	Normal
35	Scary Face	Normal	Status	—	100	10	Normal
38	Psychic	Psychic	Special	90	100	10	Normal
41	Agility	Psychic	Status	—	—	30	Self
44	Meteor Mash	Steel	Physical	90	90	10	Normal
52	Iron Defense	Steel	Status	—	—	15	Self
60	Hyper Beam	Normal	Special	150	90	5	Normal

❖ TM MOVES

No.	Name	Type	Kind	Pow.	Acc.	PP	Range
TM03	Psyshock	Psychic	Special	80	100	10	Normal
TM06	Toxic	Poison	Status	—	90	10	Normal
TM10	Hidden Power	Normal	Special	60	100	15	Normal
TM11	Sunny Day	Fire	Status	—	—	5	Both Sides
TM15	Hyper Beam	Normal	Special	150	90	5	Normal
TM16	Light Screen	Psychic	Status	—	—	30	Your Side
TM17	Protect	Normal	Status	—	—	10	Self
TM18	Rain Dance	Water	Status	—	—	5	Both Sides
TM21	Frustration	Normal	Physical	—	100	20	Normal
TM26	Earthquake	Ground	Physical	100	100	10	Adjacent
TM27	Return	Normal	Physical	—	100	20	Normal
TM29	Psychic	Psychic	Special	90	100	10	Normal
TM30	Shadow Ball	Ghost	Special	80	100	15	Normal
TM31	Brick Break	Fighting	Physical	75	100	15	Normal
TM32	Double Team	Normal	Status	—	—	15	Self
TM33	Reflect	Psychic	Status	—	—	20	Your Side
TM36	Sludge Bomb	Poison	Special	90	100	10	Normal
TM37	Sandstorm	Rock	Status	—	—	10	Both Sides
TM39	Rock Tomb	Rock	Physical	60	95	15	Normal
TM40	Aerial Ace	Flying	Physical	60	—	20	Normal
TM42	Facade	Normal	Physical	70	100	20	Normal
TM44	Rest	Psychic	Status	—	—	10	Self
TM48	Round	Normal	Special	60	100	15	Normal
TM64	Explosion	Normal	Physical	250	100	5	Adjacent
TM68	Giga Impact	Normal	Physical	150	90	5	Normal
TM69	Rock Polish	Rock	Status	—	—	20	Self
TM74	Gyro Ball	Steel	Physical	—	100	5	Normal

No.	Name	Type	Kind	Pow.	Acc.	PP	Range
TM77	Psych Up	Normal	Status	—	—	10	Normal
TM78	Bulldoze	Ground	Physical	60	100	20	Adjacent
TM80	Rock Slide	Rock	Physical	75	90	10	Many Others
TM86	Grass Knot	Grass	Special	—	100	20	Normal
TM87	Swagger	Normal	Status	—	85	15	Normal
TM88	Sleep Talk	Normal	Status	—	—	10	Self
TM90	Substitute	Normal	Status	—	—	10	Self
TM91	Flash Cannon	Steel	Special	80	100	10	Normal
TM100	Confide	Normal	Status	—	—	20	Normal

❖ MOVES TAUGHT BY PEOPLE

Name	Type	Kind	Pow.	Acc.	PP	Range

❖ MOVES LEARNED WHEN EVOLVING

Name	Type	Kind	Pow.	Acc.	PP	Range
Hammer Arm	Fighting	Physical	100	90	10	Normal

❖ EGG MOVES

Name	Type	Kind	Pow.	Acc.	PP	Range

❖ EXCLUSIVE Z-MOVE

Name	Base Move	Type	Kind	Pow.	Acc.	Range

Alola Pokédex	Melemele	Akala	Ula'ula	Poni
217	—	—	089	—

Porygon
Virtual Pokémon

NORMAL

HEIGHT: 2'07"
WEIGHT: 80.5 lbs.

 Roughly 20 years ago, it was artificially created, utilizing the latest technology of the time.

 It can convert its body into digital data, which enables it to enter cyberspace.

ABILITY
Trace
Download

HIDDEN ABILITY
Analytic

Damage taken in normal battles

NORMAL	×1	FIGHTING	×2	ROCK	×1
FIRE	×1	POISON	×1	GHOST	×0
WATER	×1	GROUND	×1	DRAGON	×1
GRASS	×1	FLYING	×1	DARK	×1
ELECTRIC	×1	PSYCHIC	×1	STEEL	×1
ICE	×1	BUG	×1	FAIRY	×1

SPECIES STRENGTHS
HP ◆◆◆
Attack ◆◆◆
Defense ◆◆◆◆
Sp. Atk ◆◆◆◆◆
Sp. Def ◆◆◆◆
Speed ◆◆◆

EGG GROUPS
Mineral

ITEM SOMETIMES HELD BY WILD POKÉMON
—

MAIN WAY TO REGISTER IN THE POKÉDEX
Receive from an Aether Employee in the Aether House

EVOLUTION

Porygon → Trade while holding Up-Grade → Porygon2

Trade while holding Dubious Disc → Porygon-Z

Gender unknown

Alola Pokédex	Melemele	Akala	Ula'ula	Poni
218	—	—	090	—

Porygon2
Virtual Pokémon

NORMAL

HEIGHT: 2'00"
WEIGHT: 71.6 lbs.

 For the purposes of planetary development, Porygon was updated with the most cutting-edge technology available.

 Porygon was updated to a new version in readiness for planetary development. But that dream remains unrealized as yet.

ABILITY
Trace
Download

HIDDEN ABILITY
Analytic

Damage taken in normal battles

NORMAL	×1	FIGHTING	×2	ROCK	×1
FIRE	×1	POISON	×1	GHOST	×0
WATER	×1	GROUND	×1	DRAGON	×1
GRASS	×1	FLYING	×1	DARK	×1
ELECTRIC	×1	PSYCHIC	×1	STEEL	×1
ICE	×1	BUG	×1	FAIRY	×1

SPECIES STRENGTHS
HP ◆◆◆
Attack ◆◆◆◆
Defense ◆◆◆◆◆
Sp. Atk ◆◆◆◆◆◆◆
Sp. Def ◆◆◆◆◆◆◆
Speed ◆◆◆◆

EGG GROUPS
Mineral

ITEM SOMETIMES HELD BY WILD POKÉMON
—

MAIN WAY TO REGISTER IN THE POKÉDEX
Receive a Porygon holding an Up-Grade in a trade and it will evolve

EVOLUTION

Porygon → Trade while holding Up-Grade → Porygon2

Trade while holding Dubious Disc → Porygon-Z

Gender unknown

Alola Pokédex	Melemele	Akala	Ula'ula	Poni
219	—	—	091	—

Porygon-Z
Virtual Pokémon

NORMAL

HEIGHT: 2'11"
WEIGHT: 75.0 lbs.

 In order to create a more advanced Pokémon, an additional program was installed, but apparently it contained a defect that makes it move oddly.

Its program was modified to facilitate extra-dimensional activities, but that led to noticeably strange behavior.

ABILITY
Adaptability
Download

HIDDEN ABILITY
Analytic

Damage taken in normal battles

NORMAL	×1	FIGHTING	×2	ROCK	×1
FIRE	×1	POISON	×1	GHOST	×0
WATER	×1	GROUND	×1	DRAGON	×1
GRASS	×1	FLYING	×1	DARK	×1
ELECTRIC	×1	PSYCHIC	×1	STEEL	×1
ICE	×1	BUG	×1	FAIRY	×1

SPECIES STRENGTHS
HP ◆◆◆
Attack ◆◆◆◆
Defense ◆◆◆◆
Sp. Atk ◆◆◆◆◆◆◆
Sp. Def ◆◆◆
Speed ◆◆◆◆◆◆

EGG GROUPS
Mineral

ITEM SOMETIMES HELD BY WILD POKÉMON
—

MAIN WAY TO REGISTER IN THE POKÉDEX
Receive a Porygon2 holding a Dubious Disc in a trade and it will evolve

EVOLUTION

Porygon → Trade while holding Up-Grade → Porygon2

Trade while holding Dubious Disc → Porygon-Z

Gender unknown

PORYGON — 217

LEVEL-UP MOVES

Lv.	Name	Type	Kind	Pow.	Acc.	PP	Range
1	Conversion 2	Normal	Status	—	—	30	Normal
1	Tackle	Normal	Physical	40	100	35	Normal
1	Conversion	Normal	Status	—	—	30	Self
1	Sharpen	Normal	Status	—	—	30	Self
7	Psybeam	Psychic	Special	65	100	20	Normal
12	Agility	Psychic	Status	—	—	30	Self
18	Recover	Normal	Status	—	—	10	Self
23	Magnet Rise	Electric	Status	—	—	10	Self
29	Signal Beam	Bug	Special	75	100	15	Normal
34	Recycle	Normal	Status	—	—	10	Self
40	Discharge	Electric	Special	80	100	15	Adjacent
45	Lock-On	Normal	Status	—	—	5	Normal
50	Tri Attack	Normal	Special	80	100	10	Normal
56	Magic Coat	Psychic	Status	—	—	15	Self
62	Zap Cannon	Electric	Special	120	50	5	Normal

TM MOVES

No.	Name	Type	Kind	Pow.	Acc.	PP	Range
TM03	Psyshock	Psychic	Special	80	100	10	Normal
TM06	Toxic	Poison	Status	—	90	10	Normal
TM10	Hidden Power	Normal	Special	60	100	15	Normal
TM11	Sunny Day	Fire	Status	—	—	5	Both Sides
TM13	Ice Beam	Ice	Special	90	100	10	Normal
TM14	Blizzard	Ice	Special	110	70	5	Many Others
TM15	Hyper Beam	Normal	Special	150	90	5	Normal
TM17	Protect	Normal	Status	—	—	10	Self
TM18	Rain Dance	Water	Status	—	—	5	Both Sides
TM21	Frustration	Normal	Physical	—	100	20	Normal
TM22	Solar Beam	Grass	Special	120	100	10	Normal
TM24	Thunderbolt	Electric	Special	90	100	15	Normal
TM25	Thunder	Electric	Special	110	70	10	Normal
TM27	Return	Normal	Physical	—	100	20	Normal
TM29	Psychic	Psychic	Special	90	100	10	Normal
TM30	Shadow Ball	Ghost	Special	80	100	15	Normal
TM32	Double Team	Normal	Status	—	—	15	Self
TM40	Aerial Ace	Flying	Physical	60	—	20	Normal
TM42	Facade	Normal	Physical	70	100	20	Normal
TM44	Rest	Psychic	Status	—	—	10	Self
TM46	Thief	Dark	Physical	60	100	25	Normal
TM48	Round	Normal	Special	60	100	15	Normal
TM57	Charge Beam	Electric	Special	50	90	10	Normal
TM68	Giga Impact	Normal	Physical	150	90	5	Normal
TM73	Thunder Wave	Electric	Status	—	90	20	Normal
TM77	Psych Up	Normal	Status	—	—	10	Normal
TM85	Dream Eater	Psychic	Special	100	100	15	Normal

MOVES TAUGHT BY PEOPLE

No.	Name	Type	Kind	Pow.	Acc.	PP	Range
TM87	Swagger	Normal	Status	—	85	15	Normal
TM88	Sleep Talk	Normal	Status	—	—	10	Self
TM90	Substitute	Normal	Status	—	—	10	Self
TM92	Trick Room	Psychic	Status	—	—	5	Both Sides
TM100	Confide	Normal	Status	—	—	20	Normal

MOVES LEARNED WHEN EVOLVING

Name	Type	Kind	Pow.	Acc.	PP	Range

EGG MOVES

Name	Type	Kind	Pow.	Acc.	PP	Range

EXCLUSIVE Z-MOVE

Name	Base Move	Type	Kind	Pow.	Acc.	Range

PORYGON2 — 218

LEVEL-UP MOVES

Lv.	Name	Type	Kind	Pow.	Acc.	PP	Range
1	Zap Cannon	Electric	Special	120	50	5	Normal
1	Magic Coat	Psychic	Status	—	—	15	Self
1	Conversion 2	Normal	Status	—	—	30	Normal
1	Tackle	Normal	Physical	40	100	35	Normal
1	Conversion	Normal	Status	—	—	30	Self
1	Defense Curl	Normal	Status	—	—	40	Self
7	Psybeam	Psychic	Special	65	100	20	Normal
12	Agility	Psychic	Status	—	—	30	Self
18	Recover	Normal	Status	—	—	10	Self
23	Magnet Rise	Electric	Status	—	—	10	Self
29	Signal Beam	Bug	Special	75	100	15	Normal
34	Recycle	Normal	Status	—	—	10	Self
40	Discharge	Electric	Special	80	100	15	Adjacent
45	Lock-On	Normal	Status	—	—	5	Normal
50	Tri Attack	Normal	Special	80	100	10	Normal
56	Magic Coat	Psychic	Status	—	—	15	Self
62	Zap Cannon	Electric	Special	120	50	5	Normal
67	Hyper Beam	Normal	Special	150	90	5	Normal

TM MOVES

No.	Name	Type	Kind	Pow.	Acc.	PP	Range
TM03	Psyshock	Psychic	Special	80	100	10	Normal
TM06	Toxic	Poison	Status	—	90	10	Normal
TM10	Hidden Power	Normal	Special	60	100	15	Normal
TM11	Sunny Day	Fire	Status	—	—	5	Both Sides
TM13	Ice Beam	Ice	Special	90	100	10	Normal
TM14	Blizzard	Ice	Special	110	70	5	Many Others
TM15	Hyper Beam	Normal	Special	150	90	5	Normal
TM17	Protect	Normal	Status	—	—	10	Self
TM18	Rain Dance	Water	Status	—	—	5	Both Sides
TM21	Frustration	Normal	Physical	—	100	20	Normal
TM22	Solar Beam	Grass	Special	120	100	10	Normal
TM24	Thunderbolt	Electric	Special	90	100	15	Normal
TM25	Thunder	Electric	Special	110	70	10	Normal
TM27	Return	Normal	Physical	—	100	20	Normal
TM29	Psychic	Psychic	Special	90	100	10	Normal
TM30	Shadow Ball	Ghost	Special	80	100	15	Normal
TM32	Double Team	Normal	Status	—	—	15	Self
TM40	Aerial Ace	Flying	Physical	60	—	20	Normal
TM42	Facade	Normal	Physical	70	100	20	Normal
TM44	Rest	Psychic	Status	—	—	10	Self
TM46	Thief	Dark	Physical	60	100	25	Normal
TM48	Round	Normal	Special	60	100	15	Normal
TM57	Charge Beam	Electric	Special	50	90	10	Normal
TM68	Giga Impact	Normal	Physical	150	90	5	Normal
TM73	Thunder Wave	Electric	Status	—	90	20	Normal
TM77	Psych Up	Normal	Status	—	—	10	Normal
TM85	Dream Eater	Psychic	Special	100	100	15	Normal

MOVES TAUGHT BY PEOPLE

No.	Name	Type	Kind	Pow.	Acc.	PP	Range
TM87	Swagger	Normal	Status	—	85	15	Normal
TM88	Sleep Talk	Normal	Status	—	—	10	Self
TM90	Substitute	Normal	Status	—	—	10	Self
TM92	Trick Room	Psychic	Status	—	—	5	Both Sides
TM100	Confide	Normal	Status	—	—	20	Normal

MOVES LEARNED WHEN EVOLVING

Name	Type	Kind	Pow.	Acc.	PP	Range

EGG MOVES

Name	Type	Kind	Pow.	Acc.	PP	Range

EXCLUSIVE Z-MOVE

Name	Base Move	Type	Kind	Pow.	Acc.	Range

PORYGON-Z — 219

LEVEL-UP MOVES

Lv.	Name	Type	Kind	Pow.	Acc.	PP	Range
1	Trick Room	Psychic	Status	—	—	5	Both Sides
1	Zap Cannon	Electric	Special	120	50	5	Normal
1	Magic Coat	Psychic	Status	—	—	15	Self
1	Conversion 2	Normal	Status	—	—	30	Normal
1	Tackle	Normal	Physical	40	100	35	Normal
1	Conversion	Normal	Status	—	—	30	Self
1	Nasty Plot	Dark	Status	—	—	20	Self
7	Psybeam	Psychic	Special	65	100	20	Normal
12	Agility	Psychic	Status	—	—	30	Self
18	Recover	Normal	Status	—	—	10	Self
23	Magnet Rise	Electric	Status	—	—	10	Self
29	Signal Beam	Bug	Special	75	100	15	Normal
34	Embargo	Dark	Status	—	100	15	Normal
40	Discharge	Electric	Special	80	100	15	Adjacent
45	Lock-On	Normal	Status	—	—	5	Normal
50	Tri Attack	Normal	Special	80	100	10	Normal
56	Magic Coat	Psychic	Status	—	—	15	Self
62	Zap Cannon	Electric	Special	120	50	5	Normal
67	Hyper Beam	Normal	Special	150	90	5	Normal

TM MOVES

No.	Name	Type	Kind	Pow.	Acc.	PP	Range
TM03	Psyshock	Psychic	Special	80	100	10	Normal
TM06	Toxic	Poison	Status	—	90	10	Normal
TM10	Hidden Power	Normal	Special	60	100	15	Normal
TM11	Sunny Day	Fire	Status	—	—	5	Both Sides
TM13	Ice Beam	Ice	Special	90	100	10	Normal
TM14	Blizzard	Ice	Special	110	70	5	Many Others
TM15	Hyper Beam	Normal	Special	150	90	5	Normal
TM17	Protect	Normal	Status	—	—	10	Self
TM18	Rain Dance	Water	Status	—	—	5	Both Sides
TM21	Frustration	Normal	Physical	—	100	20	Normal
TM22	Solar Beam	Grass	Special	120	100	10	Normal
TM24	Thunderbolt	Electric	Special	90	100	15	Normal
TM25	Thunder	Electric	Special	110	70	10	Normal
TM27	Return	Normal	Physical	—	100	20	Normal
TM29	Psychic	Psychic	Special	90	100	10	Normal
TM30	Shadow Ball	Ghost	Special	80	100	15	Normal
TM32	Double Team	Normal	Status	—	—	15	Self
TM40	Aerial Ace	Flying	Physical	60	—	20	Normal
TM42	Facade	Normal	Physical	70	100	20	Normal
TM44	Rest	Psychic	Status	—	—	10	Self
TM46	Thief	Dark	Physical	60	100	25	Normal
TM48	Round	Normal	Special	60	100	15	Normal
TM57	Charge Beam	Electric	Special	50	90	10	Normal
TM63	Embargo	Dark	Status	—	100	15	Normal
TM68	Giga Impact	Normal	Physical	150	90	5	Normal
TM73	Thunder Wave	Electric	Status	—	90	20	Normal
TM77	Psych Up	Normal	Status	—	—	10	Normal

MOVES TAUGHT BY PEOPLE

No.	Name	Type	Kind	Pow.	Acc.	PP	Range
TM85	Dream Eater	Psychic	Special	100	100	15	Normal
TM87	Swagger	Normal	Status	—	85	15	Normal
TM88	Sleep Talk	Normal	Status	—	—	10	Self
TM90	Substitute	Normal	Status	—	—	10	Self
TM92	Trick Room	Psychic	Status	—	—	5	Both Sides
TM97	Dark Pulse	Dark	Special	80	100	15	Normal
TM100	Confide	Normal	Status	—	—	20	Normal

MOVES LEARNED WHEN EVOLVING

Name	Type	Kind	Pow.	Acc.	PP	Range

EGG MOVES

Name	Type	Kind	Pow.	Acc.	PP	Range

EXCLUSIVE Z-MOVE

Name	Base Move	Type	Kind	Pow.	Acc.	Range

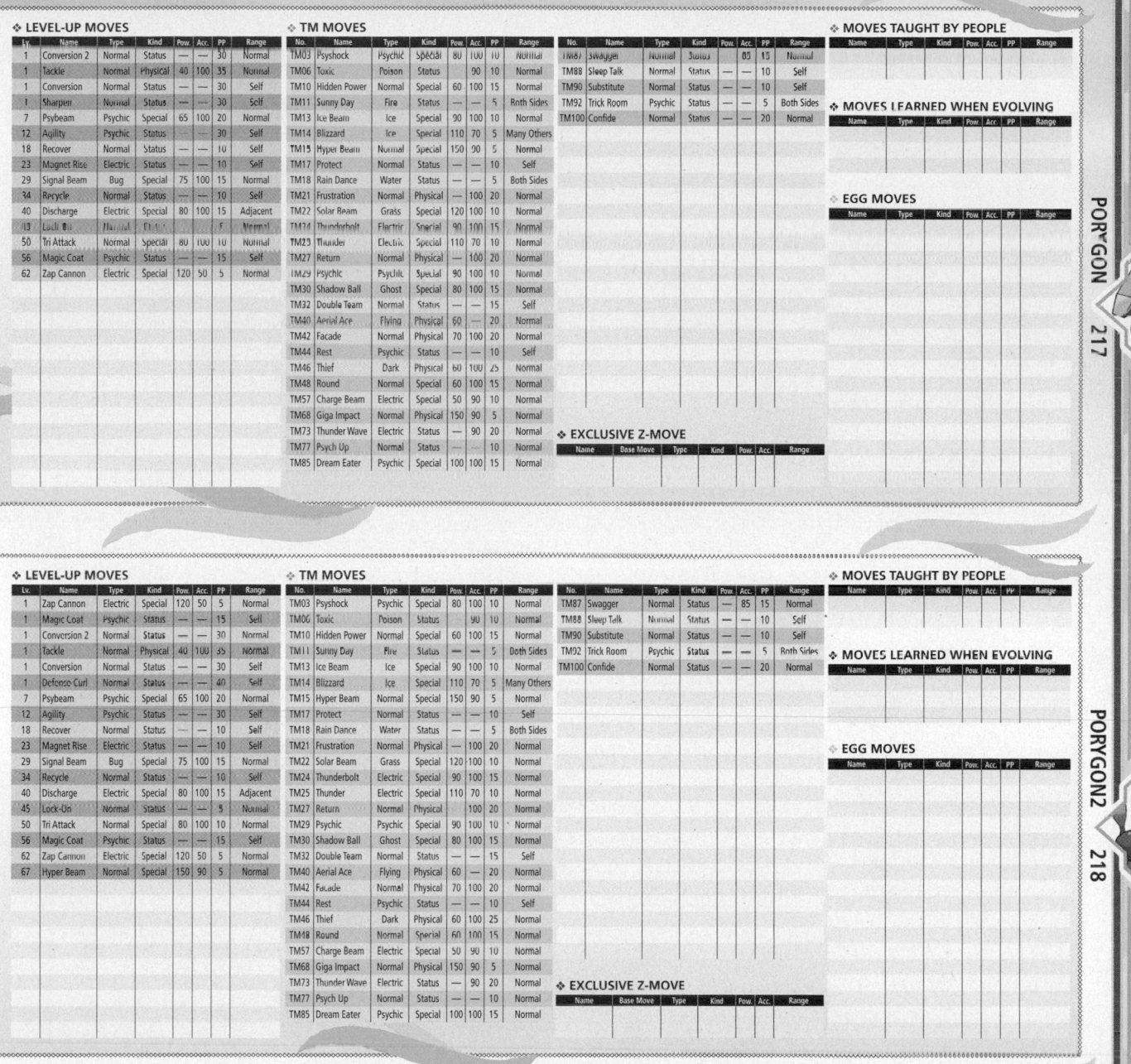

Trading to Evolve

You may know that some Pokémon are version exclusives, meaning that they can only be caught in either *Pokémon Sun* or *Pokémon Moon*. This makes trading essential to collecting all of the Pokémon found in the Alola Pokédex—but it is not the only reason you should get familiar with Pokémon trading. Some Pokémon also only evolve when they are traded, and some of them will even need to be holding a particular item when they are traded away to be able to evolve. If you have a friend to trade with nearby, you can easily trade by using the Quick Link option that appears on the lower screen when you press ⊗ to open the X menu. You can also find fellow Trainers to trade with by setting up a Link Trade on Festival Plaza or by using the GTS (p. 31).

Pokémon Name	Evolves Into	How to Evolve
Boldore	Gigalith	Trade a Boldore to make it evolve
Electabuzz	Electivire	Trade an Electabuzz that is holding an Electirizer to make it evolve
Feebas	Milotic	Trade a Feebas that is holding a Prism Scale to make it evolve
Alolan Graveler	Alolan Golem	Trade an Alolan Graveler to make it evolve
Haunter	Gengar	Trade a Haunter to make it evolve
Kadabra	Alakazam	Trade a Kadabra to make it evolve
Machoke	Machamp	Trade a Machoke to make it evolve
Magmar	Magmortar	Trade a Magmar that is holding a Magmarizer to make it evolve
Phantump	Trevenant	Trade a Phantump to make it evolve
Poliwhirl	Politoed	Trade a Poliwhirl that is holding a King's Rock to make it evolve
Porygon	Porygon2	Trade a Porygon that is holding an Up-Grade to make it evolve
Porgyon2	Porygon-Z	Trade a Porygon2 that is holding a Dubious Disc to make it evolve
Scyther	Scizor	Trade a Scyther that is holding a Metal Coat to make it evolve
Slowpoke	Slowking	Trade a Slowpoke that is holding a King's Rock to make it evolve

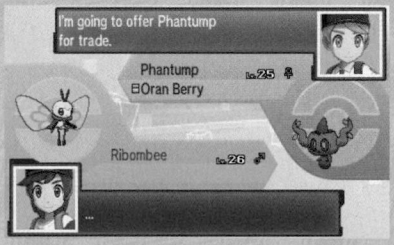

Since these Pokémon evolve thanks to being traded, they will evolve after arriving in the recipient's game. If you are the one sending any of these Pokémon out in a trade, you unfortunately won't register their Evolutions in your game's Pokédex that way. For example, you'll want to also ask for a Kadabra in a trade in order to get Alakazam for yourself, or send your Kadabra to a good friend who will send it back to you after it evolves. And remember that Pokémon received in trades get more Exp. Points from battles than Pokémon you've caught in your own game—especially if they come from another region—so head to Festival Plaza and get trading at once!

Alola Pokédex	Melemele	Akala	Ula'ula	Poni
220	—	—	092	—

Pancham

Playful Pokémon

FIGHTING

HEIGHT: 2'00"
WEIGHT: 17.6 lbs.

It grows up imitating the behavior of Pangoro, which it looks up to as a leader.

There's no point to the leaf in its mouth, aside from an effort to look cool. It's mischievous, so it's not well suited to inexperienced Trainers.

Same form for male/female

ABILITY
Iron Fist
Mold Breaker

HIDDEN ABILITY
Scrappy

SPECIES STRENGTHS
HP ♦♦♦
Attack ♦♦♦♦
Defense ♦♦♦
Sp. Atk ♦♦
Sp. Def ♦♦
Speed ♦♦♦

EVOLUTION

Level up to Lv. 32 with a Dark-type Pokémon in your party
Pancham
Pangoro

Damage taken in normal battles

NORMAL	×1	FIGHTING	×1	ROCK	×0.5
FIRE	×1	POISON	×1	GHOST	×1
WATER	×1	GROUND	×1	DRAGON	×1
GRASS	×1	FLYING	×2	DARK	×0.5
ELECTRIC	×1	PSYCHIC	×2	STEEL	×1
ICE	×1	BUG	×0.5	FAIRY	×2

EGG GROUPS
Field
Human-like

ITEM SOMETIMES HELD BY WILD POKÉMON
Mental Herb

MAIN WAY TO REGISTER IN THE POKÉDEX
Catch in the tall grass on Route 11

❖ LEVEL-UP MOVES

Lv.	Name	Type	Kind	Pow.	Acc.	PP	Range
1	Tackle	Normal	Physical	40	100	35	Normal
1	Leer	Normal	Status	—	100	30	Many Others
7	Arm Thrust	Fighting	Physical	15	100	20	Normal
10	Work Up	Normal	Status	—	—	30	Self
12	Karate Chop	Fighting	Physical	50	100	25	Normal
15	Comet Punch	Normal	Physical	18	85	15	Normal
20	Slash	Normal	Physical	70	100	20	Normal
25	Circle Throw	Fighting	Physical	60	90	10	Normal
27	Vital Throw	Fighting	Physical	70	—	10	Normal
33	Body Slam	Normal	Physical	85	100	15	Normal
39	Crunch	Dark	Physical	80	100	15	Normal
42	Entrainment	Normal	Status	—	100	15	Normal
45	Parting Shot	Dark	Status	—	100	20	Normal
48	Sky Uppercut	Fighting	Physical	85	90	15	Normal

❖ TM MOVES

No.	Name	Type	Kind	Pow.	Acc.	PP	Range
TM01	Work Up	Normal	Status	—	—	30	Self
TM05	Roar	Normal	Status	—	—	20	Normal
TM06	Toxic	Poison	Status	—	90	10	Normal
TM08	Bulk Up	Fighting	Status	—	—	20	Self
TM10	Hidden Power	Normal	Special	60	100	15	Normal
TM11	Sunny Day	Fire	Status	—	—	5	Both Sides
TM17	Protect	Normal	Status	—	—	10	Self
TM18	Rain Dance	Water	Status	—	—	5	Both Sides
TM21	Frustration	Normal	Physical	—	100	20	Normal
TM27	Return	Normal	Physical	—	100	20	Normal
TM31	Brick Break	Fighting	Physical	75	100	15	Normal
TM32	Double Team	Normal	Status	—	—	15	Self
TM36	Sludge Bomb	Poison	Special	90	100	10	Normal
TM39	Rock Tomb	Rock	Physical	60	95	15	Normal
TM40	Aerial Ace	Flying	Physical	60	—	20	Normal
TM41	Torment	Dark	Status	—	100	15	Normal
TM42	Facade	Normal	Physical	70	100	20	Normal
TM44	Rest	Psychic	Status	—	—	10	Self
TM45	Attract	Normal	Status	—	100	15	Normal
TM47	Low Sweep	Fighting	Physical	65	100	20	Normal
TM48	Round	Normal	Special	60	100	15	Normal
TM49	Echoed Voice	Normal	Special	40	100	15	Normal
TM54	False Swipe	Normal	Physical	40	100	40	Normal
TM56	Fling	Dark	Physical	—	100	10	Normal
TM65	Shadow Claw	Ghost	Physical	70	100	15	Normal
TM66	Payback	Dark	Physical	50	100	10	Normal
TM71	Stone Edge	Rock	Physical	100	80	5	Normal
TM75	Swords Dance	Normal	Status	—	—	20	Self
TM78	Bulldoze	Ground	Physical	60	100	20	Adjacent
TM80	Rock Slide	Rock	Physical	75	90	10	Many Others
TM86	Grass Knot	Grass	Special	—	100	20	Normal
TM87	Swagger	Normal	Status	—	85	15	Normal
TM88	Sleep Talk	Normal	Status	—	—	10	Self
TM90	Substitute	Normal	Status	—	—	10	Self
TM94	Surf	Water	Special	90	100	15	Adjacent
TM97	Dark Pulse	Dark	Special	80	100	15	Normal
TM100	Confide	Normal	Status	—	—	20	Normal

❖ EXCLUSIVE Z-MOVE

Name	Base Move	Type	Kind	Pow.	Acc.	Range

❖ MOVES TAUGHT BY PEOPLE

Name	Type	Kind	Pow.	Acc.	PP	Range

❖ MOVES LEARNED WHEN EVOLVING

Name	Type	Kind	Pow.	Acc.	PP	Range

❖ EGG MOVES

Name	Type	Kind	Pow.	Acc.	PP	Range
Quash	Dark	Status	—	100	15	Normal
Me First	Normal	Status	—	—	20	Varies
Quick Guard	Fighting	Status	—	—	15	Your Side
Foul Play	Dark	Physical	95	100	15	Normal
Storm Throw	Fighting	Physical	60	100	10	Normal
Power Trip	Dark	Physical	20	100	10	Normal

Alola Pokédex	Melemele	Akala	Ula'ula	Poni
221	—	—	093	—

Pangoro

Daunting Pokémon

FIGHTING DARK

HEIGHT: 6'11"
WEIGHT: 299.8 lbs.

It boasts superb physical strength. Those who wish to become Pangoro's Trainer have no choice but to converse with their fists.

From the slight twitches of its bamboo leaf, it deduces its opponent's movements. It's eager to tussle but kindhearted toward its companions.

Same form for male/female

ABILITY
Iron Fist
Mold Breaker

HIDDEN ABILITY
Scrappy

SPECIES STRENGTHS
HP ♦♦♦♦
Attack ♦♦♦♦♦♦♦
Defense ♦♦♦♦
Sp. Atk ♦♦♦♦
Sp. Def ♦♦♦♦
Speed ♦♦♦♦

EVOLUTION

Level up to Lv. 32 with a Dark-type Pokémon in your party
Pancham
Pangoro

Damage taken in normal battles

NORMAL	×1	FIGHTING	×2	ROCK	×0.5
FIRE	×1	POISON	×1	GHOST	×0.5
WATER	×1	GROUND	×1	DRAGON	×1
GRASS	×1	FLYING	×2	DARK	×0.25
ELECTRIC	×1	PSYCHIC	×0	STEEL	×1
ICE	×1	BUG	×1	FAIRY	×4

EGG GROUPS
Field
Human-like

ITEM SOMETIMES HELD BY WILD POKÉMON
Mental Herb

MAIN WAY TO REGISTER IN THE POKÉDEX
Catch in SOS battles against Pancham in the tall grass on Route 11

❖ LEVEL-UP MOVES

Lv.	Name	Type	Kind	Pow.	Acc.	PP	Range
1	Bullet Punch	Steel	Physical	40	100	30	Normal
1	Hammer Arm	Fighting	Physical	100	90	10	Normal
1	Low Sweep	Fighting	Physical	65	100	20	Normal
1	Entrainment	Normal	Status	—	100	15	Normal
1	Tackle	Normal	Physical	40	100	35	Normal
1	Leer	Normal	Status	—	100	30	Many Others
1	Arm Thrust	Fighting	Physical	15	100	20	Normal
1	Work Up	Normal	Status	—	—	30	Self
7	Arm Thrust	Fighting	Physical	15	100	20	Normal
10	Work Up	Normal	Status	—	—	30	Self
12	Karate Chop	Fighting	Physical	50	100	25	Normal
15	Comet Punch	Normal	Physical	18	85	15	Normal
20	Slash	Normal	Physical	70	100	20	Normal
25	Circle Throw	Fighting	Physical	60	90	10	Normal
27	Vital Throw	Fighting	Physical	70	—	10	Normal
35	Body Slam	Normal	Physical	85	100	15	Normal
42	Crunch	Dark	Physical	80	100	15	Normal
45	Entrainment	Normal	Status	—	100	15	Normal
48	Parting Shot	Dark	Status	—	100	20	Normal
52	Sky Uppercut	Fighting	Physical	85	90	15	Normal
57	Low Sweep	Fighting	Physical	65	100	20	Normal
65	Taunt	Dark	Status	—	100	20	Normal
70	Hammer Arm	Fighting	Physical	100	90	10	Normal

❖ TM MOVES

No.	Name	Type	Kind	Pow.	Acc.	PP	Range
TM01	Work Up	Normal	Status	—	—	30	Self
TM02	Dragon Claw	Dragon	Physical	80	100	15	Normal
TM05	Roar	Normal	Status	—	—	20	Normal
TM06	Toxic	Poison	Status	—	90	10	Normal
TM08	Bulk Up	Fighting	Status	—	—	20	Self
TM10	Hidden Power	Normal	Special	60	100	15	Normal
TM11	Sunny Day	Fire	Status	—	—	5	Both Sides
TM12	Taunt	Dark	Status	—	100	20	Normal
TM15	Hyper Beam	Normal	Special	150	90	5	Normal
TM17	Protect	Normal	Status	—	—	10	Self
TM18	Rain Dance	Water	Status	—	—	5	Both Sides
TM21	Frustration	Normal	Physical	—	100	20	Normal
TM26	Earthquake	Ground	Physical	100	100	10	Adjacent
TM27	Return	Normal	Physical	—	100	20	Normal
TM31	Brick Break	Fighting	Physical	75	100	15	Normal
TM32	Double Team	Normal	Status	—	—	15	Self
TM36	Sludge Bomb	Poison	Special	90	100	10	Normal
TM39	Rock Tomb	Rock	Physical	60	95	15	Normal
TM40	Aerial Ace	Flying	Physical	60	—	20	Normal
TM41	Torment	Dark	Status	—	100	15	Normal
TM42	Facade	Normal	Physical	70	100	20	Normal
TM44	Rest	Psychic	Status	—	—	10	Self
TM45	Attract	Normal	Status	—	100	15	Normal
TM46	Thief	Dark	Physical	60	100	25	Normal
TM47	Low Sweep	Fighting	Physical	65	100	20	Normal
TM48	Round	Normal	Special	60	100	15	Normal
TM49	Echoed Voice	Normal	Special	40	100	15	Normal
TM52	Focus Blast	Fighting	Special	120	70	5	Normal
TM54	False Swipe	Normal	Physical	40	100	40	Normal
TM56	Fling	Dark	Physical	—	100	10	Normal
TM60	Quash	Dark	Status	—	100	15	Normal
TM63	Embargo	Dark	Status	—	100	15	Normal
TM65	Shadow Claw	Ghost	Physical	70	100	15	Normal
TM66	Payback	Dark	Physical	50	100	10	Normal
TM68	Giga Impact	Normal	Physical	150	90	5	Normal
TM71	Stone Edge	Rock	Physical	100	80	5	Normal
TM75	Swords Dance	Normal	Status	—	—	20	Self
TM78	Bulldoze	Ground	Physical	60	100	20	Adjacent
TM80	Rock Slide	Rock	Physical	75	90	10	Many Others
TM81	X-Scissor	Bug	Physical	80	100	15	Normal
TM83	Infestation	Bug	Special	20	100	20	Normal
TM84	Poison Jab	Poison	Physical	80	100	20	Normal
TM86	Grass Knot	Grass	Special	—	100	20	Normal
TM87	Swagger	Normal	Status	—	85	15	Normal
TM88	Sleep Talk	Normal	Status	—	—	10	Self
TM90	Substitute	Normal	Status	—	—	10	Self
TM94	Surf	Water	Special	90	100	15	Adjacent
TM95	Snarl	Dark	Special	55	95	15	Many Others
TM97	Dark Pulse	Dark	Special	80	100	15	Normal
TM100	Confide	Normal	Status	—	—	20	Normal

❖ EXCLUSIVE Z-MOVE

Name	Base Move	Type	Kind	Pow.	Acc.	Range

❖ MOVES TAUGHT BY PEOPLE

Name	Type	Kind	Pow.	Acc.	PP	Range

❖ MOVES LEARNED WHEN EVOLVING

Name	Type	Kind	Pow.	Acc.	PP	Range
Bullet Punch	Steel	Physical	40	100	30	Normal

❖ EGG MOVES

Name	Type	Kind	Pow.	Acc.	PP	Range

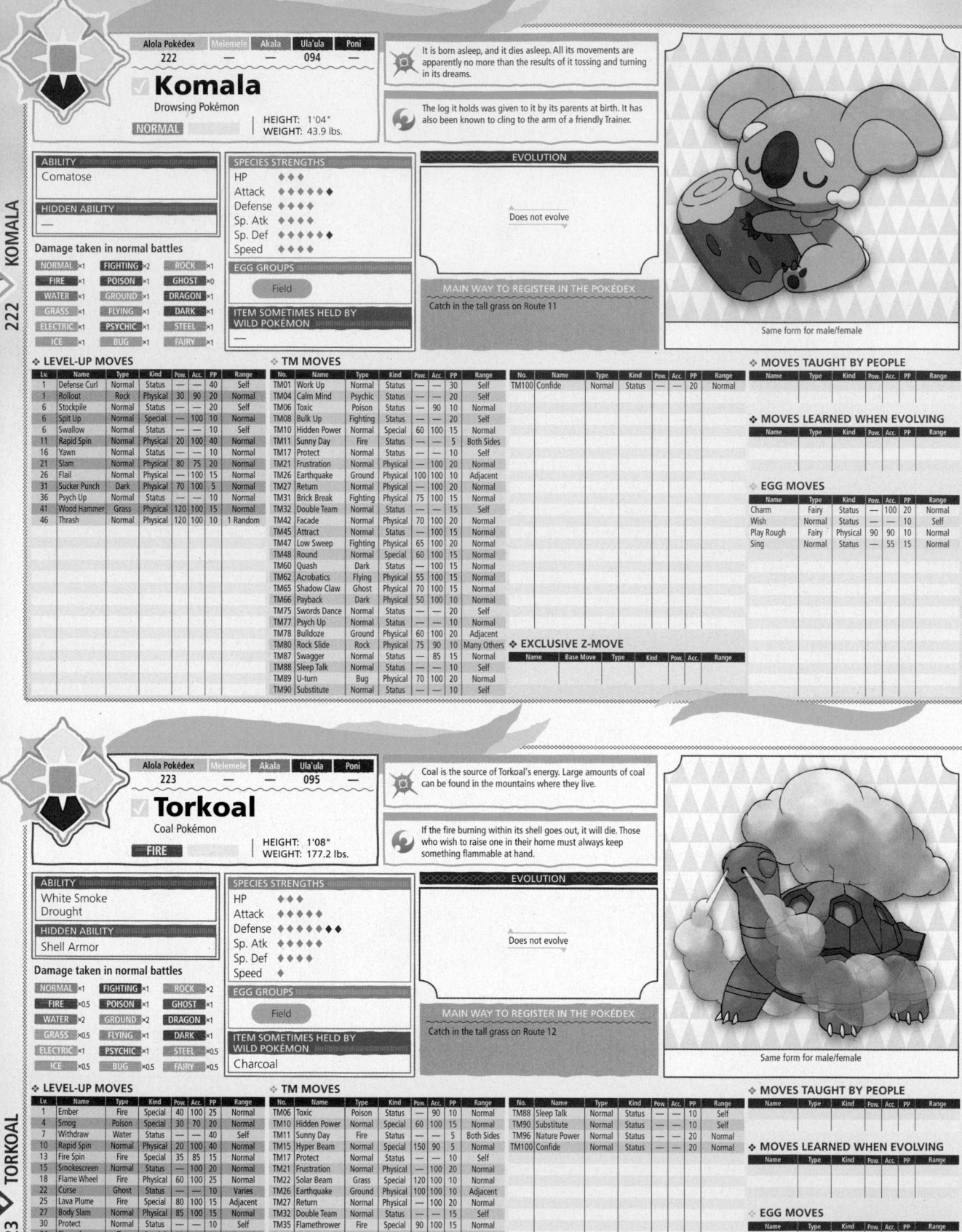

Komala

Alola Pokédex 222 | Melemele — | Akala — | Ula'ula 094 | Poni —

Drowsing Pokémon

NORMAL

HEIGHT: 1'04"
WEIGHT: 43.9 lbs.

It is born asleep, and it dies asleep. All its movements are apparently no more than the results of it tossing and turning in its dreams.

The log it holds was given to it by its parents at birth. It has also been known to cling to the arm of a friendly Trainer.

ABILITY
Comatose

HIDDEN ABILITY
—

SPECIES STRENGTHS
HP ◆◆◆
Attack ◆◆◆◆◆◆
Defense ◆◆◆◆
Sp. Atk ◆◆◆◆
Sp. Def ◆◆◆◆◆◆
Speed ◆◆◆◆

EGG GROUPS
Field

ITEM SOMETIMES HELD BY WILD POKÉMON
—

EVOLUTION
Does not evolve

MAIN WAY TO REGISTER IN THE POKÉDEX
Catch in the tall grass on Route 11

Same form for male/female

Damage taken in normal battles
NORMAL ×1	FIGHTING ×2	ROCK ×1
FIRE ×1	POISON ×1	GHOST ×0
WATER ×1	GROUND ×1	DRAGON ×1
GRASS ×1	FLYING ×1	DARK ×1
ELECTRIC ×1	PSYCHIC ×1	STEEL ×1
ICE ×1	BUG ×1	FAIRY ×1

❖ LEVEL-UP MOVES
Lv.	Name	Type	Kind	Pow.	Acc.	PP	Range
1	Defense Curl	Normal	Status	—	—	40	Self
1	Rollout	Rock	Physical	30	90	20	Normal
6	Stockpile	Normal	Status	—	—	20	Self
6	Spit Up	Normal	Special	—	100	10	Normal
6	Swallow	Normal	Status	—	—	10	Self
11	Rapid Spin	Normal	Physical	20	100	40	Normal
16	Yawn	Normal	Status	—	—	10	Normal
21	Slam	Normal	Physical	80	75	20	Normal
26	Flail	Normal	Physical	—	100	15	Normal
31	Sucker Punch	Dark	Physical	70	100	5	Normal
36	Psych Up	Normal	Status	—	—	10	Normal
41	Wood Hammer	Grass	Physical	120	100	15	Normal
46	Thrash	Normal	Physical	120	100	10	1 Random

❖ TM MOVES
No.	Name	Type	Kind	Pow.	Acc.	PP	Range
TM01	Work Up	Normal	Status	—	—	30	Self
TM04	Calm Mind	Psychic	Status	—	—	20	Self
TM06	Toxic	Poison	Status	—	90	10	Normal
TM08	Bulk Up	Fighting	Status	—	—	20	Self
TM10	Hidden Power	Normal	Special	60	100	15	Normal
TM11	Sunny Day	Fire	Status	—	—	5	Both Sides
TM17	Protect	Normal	Status	—	—	10	Self
TM21	Frustration	Normal	Physical	—	100	20	Normal
TM26	Earthquake	Ground	Physical	100	100	10	Adjacent
TM27	Return	Normal	Physical	—	100	20	Normal
TM31	Brick Break	Fighting	Physical	75	100	15	Normal
TM32	Double Team	Normal	Status	—	—	15	Self
TM42	Facade	Normal	Physical	70	100	20	Normal
TM45	Attract	Normal	Status	—	100	15	Normal
TM47	Low Sweep	Fighting	Physical	65	100	20	Normal
TM48	Round	Normal	Special	60	100	15	Normal
TM60	Quash	Dark	Status	—	100	15	Normal
TM62	Acrobatics	Flying	Physical	55	100	15	Normal
TM65	Shadow Claw	Ghost	Physical	70	100	15	Normal
TM66	Payback	Dark	Physical	50	100	10	Normal
TM75	Swords Dance	Normal	Status	—	—	20	Self
TM77	Psych Up	Normal	Status	—	—	10	Normal
TM78	Bulldoze	Ground	Physical	60	100	20	Adjacent
TM80	Rock Slide	Rock	Physical	75	90	10	Many Others
TM87	Swagger	Normal	Status	—	85	15	Normal
TM88	Sleep Talk	Normal	Status	—	—	10	Self
TM89	U-turn	Bug	Physical	70	100	20	Normal
TM90	Substitute	Normal	Status	—	—	10	Self

No.	Name	Type	Kind	Pow.	Acc.	PP	Range
TM100	Confide	Normal	Status	—	—	20	Normal

❖ MOVES TAUGHT BY PEOPLE
Name	Type	Kind	Pow.	Acc.	PP	Range

❖ MOVES LEARNED WHEN EVOLVING
Name	Type	Kind	Pow.	Acc.	PP	Range

❖ EGG MOVES
Name	Type	Kind	Pow.	Acc.	PP	Range
Charm	Fairy	Status	—	100	20	Normal
Wish	Normal	Status	—	—	10	Self
Play Rough	Fairy	Physical	90	90	10	Normal
Sing	Normal	Status	—	55	15	Normal

❖ EXCLUSIVE Z-MOVE
Name	Base Move	Type	Kind	Pow.	Acc.	Range

Torkoal

Alola Pokédex 223 | Melemele — | Akala — | Ula'ula 095 | Poni —

Coal Pokémon

FIRE

HEIGHT: 1'08"
WEIGHT: 177.2 lbs.

Coal is the source of Torkoal's energy. Large amounts of coal can be found in the mountains where they live.

If the fire burning within its shell goes out, it will die. Those who wish to raise one in their home must always keep something flammable at hand.

ABILITY
White Smoke
Drought

HIDDEN ABILITY
Shell Armor

SPECIES STRENGTHS
HP ◆◆◆
Attack ◆◆◆◆◆
Defense ◆◆◆◆◆◆◆
Sp. Atk ◆◆◆◆◆
Sp. Def ◆◆◆
Speed ◆

EGG GROUPS
Field

ITEM SOMETIMES HELD BY WILD POKÉMON
Charcoal

EVOLUTION
Does not evolve

MAIN WAY TO REGISTER IN THE POKÉDEX
Catch in the tall grass on Route 12

Same form for male/female

Damage taken in normal battles
NORMAL ×1	FIGHTING ×1	ROCK ×2
FIRE ×0.5	POISON ×1	GHOST ×1
WATER ×2	GROUND ×2	DRAGON ×1
GRASS ×0.5	FLYING ×1	DARK ×1
ELECTRIC ×1	PSYCHIC ×1	STEEL ×0.5
ICE ×0.5	BUG ×0.5	FAIRY ×0.5

❖ LEVEL-UP MOVES
Lv.	Name	Type	Kind	Pow.	Acc.	PP	Range
1	Ember	Fire	Special	40	100	25	Normal
4	Smog	Poison	Special	30	70	20	Normal
7	Withdraw	Water	Status	—	—	40	Self
10	Rapid Spin	Normal	Physical	20	100	40	Normal
13	Fire Spin	Fire	Special	35	85	15	Normal
15	Smokescreen	Normal	Status	—	100	20	Normal
18	Flame Wheel	Fire	Physical	60	100	25	Normal
22	Curse	Ghost	Status	—	—	10	Varies
25	Lava Plume	Fire	Special	80	100	15	Adjacent
27	Body Slam	Normal	Physical	85	100	15	Normal
30	Protect	Normal	Status	—	—	10	Self
34	Flamethrower	Fire	Special	90	100	15	Normal
38	Iron Defense	Steel	Status	—	—	15	Self
40	Amnesia	Psychic	Status	—	—	20	Self
42	Flail	Normal	Physical	—	100	15	Normal
45	Heat Wave	Fire	Special	95	90	10	Many Others
47	Shell Smash	Normal	Status	—	—	15	Self
50	Inferno	Fire	Special	100	50	5	Normal

❖ TM MOVES
No.	Name	Type	Kind	Pow.	Acc.	PP	Range
TM06	Toxic	Poison	Status	—	90	10	Normal
TM10	Hidden Power	Normal	Special	60	100	15	Normal
TM11	Sunny Day	Fire	Status	—	—	5	Both Sides
TM15	Hyper Beam	Normal	Special	150	90	5	Normal
TM17	Protect	Normal	Status	—	—	10	Self
TM21	Frustration	Normal	Physical	—	100	20	Normal
TM22	Solar Beam	Grass	Special	120	100	10	Normal
TM26	Earthquake	Ground	Physical	100	100	10	Adjacent
TM27	Return	Normal	Physical	—	100	20	Normal
TM32	Double Team	Normal	Status	—	—	15	Self
TM35	Flamethrower	Fire	Special	90	100	15	Normal
TM36	Sludge Bomb	Poison	Special	90	100	10	Normal
TM38	Fire Blast	Fire	Special	110	85	5	Normal
TM39	Rock Tomb	Rock	Physical	60	95	15	Normal
TM42	Facade	Normal	Physical	70	100	20	Normal
TM43	Flame Charge	Fire	Physical	50	100	20	Normal
TM44	Rest	Psychic	Status	—	—	10	Self
TM45	Attract	Normal	Status	—	100	15	Normal
TM48	Round	Normal	Special	60	100	15	Normal
TM50	Overheat	Fire	Special	130	90	5	Normal
TM61	Will-O-Wisp	Fire	Status	—	85	15	Normal
TM64	Explosion	Normal	Physical	250	100	5	Adjacent
TM68	Giga Impact	Normal	Physical	150	90	5	Normal
TM71	Stone Edge	Rock	Physical	100	80	5	Normal
TM74	Gyro Ball	Steel	Physical	—	100	5	Normal
TM78	Bulldoze	Ground	Physical	60	100	20	Adjacent
TM80	Rock Slide	Rock	Physical	75	90	10	Many Others
TM87	Swagger	Normal	Status	—	85	15	Normal

No.	Name	Type	Kind	Pow.	Acc.	PP	Range
TM88	Sleep Talk	Normal	Status	—	—	10	Self
TM90	Substitute	Normal	Status	—	—	10	Self
TM96	Nature Power	Normal	Status	—	—	20	Normal
TM100	Confide	Normal	Status	—	—	20	Normal

❖ MOVES TAUGHT BY PEOPLE
Name	Type	Kind	Pow.	Acc.	PP	Range

❖ MOVES LEARNED WHEN EVOLVING
Name	Type	Kind	Pow.	Acc.	PP	Range

❖ EGG MOVES
Name	Type	Kind	Pow.	Acc.	PP	Range
Eruption	Fire	Special	150	100	5	Many Others
Endure	Normal	Status	—	—	10	Self
Sleep Talk	Normal	Status	—	—	10	Self
Yawn	Normal	Status	—	—	10	Normal
Fissure	Ground	Physical	—	30	5	Normal
Skull Bash	Normal	Physical	130	100	10	Normal
Flame Burst	Fire	Special	70	100	15	Normal
Clear Smog	Poison	Special	50	—	15	Normal
Superpower	Fighting	Physical	120	100	5	Normal

❖ EXCLUSIVE Z-MOVE
Name	Base Move	Type	Kind	Pow.	Acc.	Range

KOMALA 222

TORKOAL 223

Turtonator

Alola Pokédex	Melemele	Akala	Ula'ula	Poni
224	—	—	096	—

Turtonator
Blast Turtle Pokémon
FIRE DRAGON
HEIGHT: 6'07"
WEIGHT: 467.4 lbs.

Same form for male/female

The shell on its back is chemically unstable and explodes violently if struck. The hole in its stomach is its weak point.

It gushes fire and poisonous gases from its nostrils. Its dung is an explosive substance and can be put to various uses.

ABILITY
Shell Armor

HIDDEN ABILITY
—

SPECIES STRENGTHS
HP ◆◆
Attack ◆◆◆◆
Defense ◆◆◆◆◆◆◆◆
Sp. Atk ◆◆◆◆◆
Sp. Def ◆◆◆◆◆
Speed ◆◆

EGG GROUPS
Monster   Dragon

ITEM SOMETIMES HELD BY WILD POKÉMON
Charcoal

EVOLUTION
Does not evolve

MAIN WAY TO REGISTER IN THE POKÉDEX
Catch in the tall grass on Blush Mountain in *Pokémon Sun* / Obtain in a trade in *Pokémon Moon*

Damage taken in normal battles

NORMAL ×1	FIGHTING ×1	ROCK ×2	
FIRE ×0.25	POISON ×1	GHOST ×1	
WATER ×1	GROUND ×2	DRAGON ×1	
GRASS ×0.25	FLYING ×1	DARK ×1	
ELECTRIC ×0.5	PSYCHIC ×1	STEEL ×0.5	
ICE ×1	BUG ×0.5	FAIRY ×1	

❖ LEVEL-UP MOVES

Lv.	Name	Type	Kind	Pow.	Acc.	PP	Range
1	Ember	Fire	Special	40	100	25	Normal
1	Tackle	Normal	Physical	40	100	35	Normal
5	Smog	Poison	Special	30	70	20	Normal
9	Protect	Normal	Status	—	—	10	Self
13	Incinerate	Fire	Special	60	100	15	Many Others
17	Flail	Normal	Physical	—	100	15	Normal
21	Endure	Normal	Status	—	—	10	Self
25	Iron Defense	Steel	Status	—	—	15	Self
29	Flamethrower	Fire	Special	90	100	15	Normal
33	Body Slam	Normal	Physical	85	100	15	Normal
37	Shell Smash	Normal	Status	—	—	15	Self
41	Dragon Pulse	Dragon	Special	85	100	10	Normal
45	Shell Trap	Fire	Special	150	100	5	Many Others
49	Overheat	Fire	Special	130	90	5	Normal
53	Explosion	Normal	Physical	250	100	5	Adjacent

❖ TM MOVES

No.	Name	Type	Kind	Pow.	Acc.	PP	Range
TM01	Work Up	Normal	Status	—	—	30	Self
TM02	Dragon Claw	Dragon	Physical	80	100	15	Normal
TM05	Roar	Normal	Status	—	—	20	Normal
TM06	Toxic	Poison	Status	—	90	10	Normal
TM08	Bulk Up	Fighting	Status	—	—	20	Self
TM09	Venoshock	Poison	Special	65	100	10	Normal
TM10	Hidden Power	Normal	Special	60	100	15	Normal
TM11	Sunny Day	Fire	Status	—	—	5	Both Sides
TM12	Taunt	Dark	Status	—	100	20	Normal
TM15	Hyper Beam	Normal	Special	150	90	5	Normal
TM17	Protect	Normal	Status	—	—	10	Self
TM21	Frustration	Normal	Physical	—	100	20	Normal
TM22	Solar Beam	Grass	Special	120	100	10	Normal
TM23	Smack Down	Rock	Physical	50	100	15	Normal
TM26	Earthquake	Ground	Physical	100	100	10	Adjacent
TM27	Return	Normal	Physical	—	100	20	Normal
TM32	Double Team	Normal	Status	—	—	15	Self
TM35	Flamethrower	Fire	Special	90	100	15	Normal
TM38	Fire Blast	Fire	Special	110	85	5	Normal
TM39	Rock Tomb	Rock	Physical	60	95	15	Normal
TM42	Facade	Normal	Physical	70	100	20	Normal
TM43	Flame Charge	Fire	Physical	50	100	20	Normal
TM44	Rest	Psychic	Status	—	—	10	Self
TM45	Attract	Normal	Status	—	100	15	Normal
TM48	Round	Normal	Special	60	100	15	Normal
TM50	Overheat	Fire	Special	130	90	5	Normal
TM52	Focus Blast	Fighting	Special	120	70	5	Normal
TM56	Fling	Dark	Physical	—	100	10	Normal
TM57	Charge Beam	Electric	Special	50	90	10	Normal
TM59	Brutal Swing	Dark	Physical	60	100	20	Adjacent
TM61	Will-O-Wisp	Fire	Status	—	85	15	Normal
TM64	Explosion	Normal	Physical	250	100	5	Adjacent
TM66	Payback	Dark	Physical	50	100	10	Normal
TM68	Giga Impact	Normal	Physical	150	90	5	Normal
TM71	Stone Edge	Rock	Physical	100	80	5	Normal
TM78	Bulldoze	Ground	Physical	60	100	20	Adjacent
TM82	Dragon Tail	Dragon	Physical	60	90	10	Normal
TM87	Swagger	Normal	Status	—	85	15	Normal
TM88	Sleep Talk	Normal	Status	—	—	10	Self
TM90	Substitute	Normal	Status	—	—	10	Self
TM91	Flash Cannon	Steel	Special	80	100	10	Normal
TM100	Confide	Normal	Status	—	—	20	Normal

❖ MOVES TAUGHT BY PEOPLE

Name	Type	Kind	Pow.	Acc.	PP	Range
Draco Meteor	Dragon	Special	130	90	5	Normal

❖ MOVES LEARNED WHEN EVOLVING

Name	Type	Kind	Pow.	Acc.	PP	Range

❖ EGG MOVES

Name	Type	Kind	Pow.	Acc.	PP	Range
Wide Guard	Rock	Status	—	—	10	Your Side
Revenge	Fighting	Physical	60	100	10	Normal
Head Smash	Rock	Physical	150	80	5	Normal
Fire Spin	Fire	Special	35	85	15	Normal

❖ EXCLUSIVE Z-MOVE

Name	Base Move	Type	Kind	Pow.	Acc.	Range

Togedemaru

Alola Pokédex	Melemele	Akala	Ula'ula	Poni
225	—	—	097	—

Togedemaru
Roly-Poly Pokémon
ELECTRIC STEEL
HEIGHT: 1'00"
WEIGHT: 7.3 lbs.

Same form for male/female

The spiny fur on its back is normally at rest. When this Pokémon becomes agitated, its fur stands on end and stabs into its attackers.

The long hairs on its back act as lightning rods. The bolts of lightning it attracts are stored as energy in its electric sac.

ABILITY
Iron Barbs
Lightning Rod

HIDDEN ABILITY
Sturdy

SPECIES STRENGTHS
HP ◆◆◆
Attack ◆◆◆◆◆
Defense ◆◆◆
Sp. Atk ◆◆
Sp. Def ◆◆◆
Speed ◆◆◆◆◆◆

EGG GROUPS
Field   Fairy

ITEM SOMETIMES HELD BY WILD POKÉMON
Electric Seed

EVOLUTION
Does not evolve

MAIN WAY TO REGISTER IN THE POKÉDEX
Catch in the tall grass on Blush Mountain

Damage taken in normal battles

NORMAL ×0.5	FIGHTING ×2	ROCK ×0.5	
FIRE ×2	POISON ×0	GHOST ×1	
WATER ×1	GROUND ×4	DRAGON ×1	
GRASS ×0.5	FLYING ×0.25	DARK ×1	
ELECTRIC ×0.5	PSYCHIC ×0.5	STEEL ×0.25	
ICE ×0.5	BUG ×0.5	FAIRY ×1	

❖ LEVEL-UP MOVES

Lv.	Name	Type	Kind	Pow.	Acc.	PP	Range
1	Tackle	Normal	Physical	40	100	35	Normal
1	Thunder Shock	Electric	Special	40	100	30	Normal
5	Defense Curl	Normal	Status	—	—	40	Self
9	Rollout	Rock	Physical	30	90	20	Normal
13	Charge	Electric	Status	—	—	20	Self
17	Spark	Electric	Physical	65	100	20	Normal
21	Nuzzle	Electric	Physical	20	100	20	Normal
25	Magnet Rise	Electric	Status	—	—	10	Self
29	Discharge	Electric	Special	80	100	15	Adjacent
33	Zing Zap	Electric	Physical	80	100	10	Normal
37	Electric Terrain	Electric	Status	—	—	10	Both Sides
41	Wild Charge	Electric	Physical	90	100	15	Normal
45	Pin Missile	Bug	Physical	25	95	20	Normal
49	Spiky Shield	Grass	Status	—	—	10	Self
53	Fell Stinger	Bug	Physical	50	100	25	Normal

❖ TM MOVES

No.	Name	Type	Kind	Pow.	Acc.	PP	Range
TM01	Work Up	Normal	Status	—	—	30	Self
TM06	Toxic	Poison	Status	—	90	10	Normal
TM10	Hidden Power	Normal	Special	60	100	15	Normal
TM17	Protect	Normal	Status	—	—	10	Self
TM21	Frustration	Normal	Physical	—	100	20	Normal
TM24	Thunderbolt	Electric	Special	90	100	15	Normal
TM25	Thunder	Electric	Special	110	70	10	Normal
TM27	Return	Normal	Physical	—	100	20	Normal
TM32	Double Team	Normal	Status	—	—	15	Self
TM33	Reflect	Psychic	Status	—	—	20	Your Side
TM42	Facade	Normal	Physical	70	100	20	Normal
TM44	Rest	Psychic	Status	—	—	10	Self
TM45	Attract	Normal	Status	—	100	15	Normal
TM46	Thief	Dark	Physical	60	100	25	Normal
TM48	Round	Normal	Special	60	100	15	Normal
TM56	Fling	Dark	Physical	—	100	10	Normal
TM57	Charge Beam	Electric	Special	50	90	10	Normal
TM66	Payback	Dark	Physical	50	100	10	Normal
TM68	Giga Impact	Normal	Physical	150	90	5	Normal
TM72	Volt Switch	Electric	Special	70	100	20	Normal
TM73	Thunder Wave	Electric	Status	—	90	20	Normal
TM74	Gyro Ball	Steel	Physical	—	100	5	Normal
TM84	Poison Jab	Poison	Physical	80	100	20	Normal
TM86	Grass Knot	Grass	Special	—	100	20	Normal
TM87	Swagger	Normal	Status	—	85	15	Normal
TM88	Sleep Talk	Normal	Status	—	—	10	Self
TM89	U-turn	Bug	Physical	70	100	20	Normal
TM90	Substitute	Normal	Status	—	—	10	Self
TM93	Wild Charge	Electric	Physical	90	100	15	Normal
TM100	Confide	Normal	Status	—	—	20	Normal

❖ MOVES TAUGHT BY PEOPLE

Name	Type	Kind	Pow.	Acc.	PP	Range

❖ MOVES LEARNED WHEN EVOLVING

Name	Type	Kind	Pow.	Acc.	PP	Range

❖ EGG MOVES

Name	Type	Kind	Pow.	Acc.	PP	Range
Reversal	Fighting	Physical	—	100	15	Normal
Present	Normal	Physical	—	90	15	Normal
Encore	Normal	Status	—	100	5	Normal
Twineedle	Bug	Physical	25	100	20	Normal
Wish	Normal	Status	—	—	10	Self
Fake Out	Normal	Physical	40	100	10	Normal
Tickle	Normal	Status	—	100	20	Normal
Flail	Normal	Physical	—	100	15	Normal
Disarming Voice	Fairy	Special	40	—	15	Many Others

❖ EXCLUSIVE Z-MOVE

Name	Base Move	Type	Kind	Pow.	Acc.	Range

Elekid

Alola Pokédex	Melemele	Akala	Ula'ula	Poni
226	—	—	098	—

Elekid

Electric Pokémon

ELECTRIC

HEIGHT: 2'00"
WEIGHT: 51.8 lbs.

When it's in a house, electrical outlets serve as its baby bottles. It sucks down electricity.

This Pokémon is constantly fighting with Togedemaru that try to steal its electricity. It's a pretty even match.

ABILITY
Static

HIDDEN ABILITY
Vital Spirit

Damage taken in normal battles

NORMAL ×1	FIGHTING ×1	ROCK ×1			
FIRE ×1	POISON ×1	GHOST ×1			
WATER ×1	GROUND ×2	DRAGON ×1			
GRASS ×1	FLYING ×0.5	DARK ×1			
ELECTRIC ×0.5	PSYCHIC ×1	STEEL ×0.5			
ICE ×1	BUG ×1	FAIRY ×1			

SPECIES STRENGTHS
HP ◆◆
Attack ◆◆◆
Defense ◆◆
Sp. Atk ◆◆◆◆
Sp. Def ◆◆
Speed ◆◆◆◆◆◆

EGG GROUPS
No Eggs Discovered

ITEM SOMETIMES HELD BY WILD POKÉMON
Electirizer

EVOLUTION

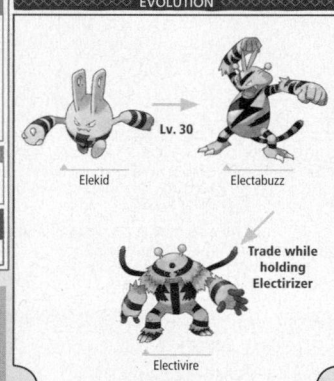

Elekid → Lv. 30 → Electabuzz

Trade while holding Electirizer

Electivire

MAIN WAY TO REGISTER IN THE POKÉDEX
Catch in the tall grass on Route 12

Same form for male/female

Alola Pokédex	Melemele	Akala	Ula'ula	Poni
227	—	—	099	—

Electabuzz

Electric Pokémon

ELECTRIC

HEIGHT: 3'07"
WEIGHT: 66.1 lbs.

Half of all sudden blackouts are caused by Electabuzz gathering at electric power plants and gobbling up electricity.

Electricity leaks from it in amounts far greater than the amount of electricity it eats.

ABILITY
Static

HIDDEN ABILITY
Vital Spirit

Damage taken in normal battles

NORMAL ×1	FIGHTING ×1	ROCK ×1			
FIRE ×1	POISON ×1	GHOST ×1			
WATER ×1	GROUND ×2	DRAGON ×1			
GRASS ×1	FLYING ×0.5	DARK ×1			
ELECTRIC ×0.5	PSYCHIC ×1	STEEL ×0.5			
ICE ×1	BUG ×1	FAIRY ×1			

SPECIES STRENGTHS
HP ◆◆◆
Attack ◆◆◆◆
Defense ◆◆◆
Sp. Atk ◆◆◆◆
Sp. Def ◆◆◆◆◆
Speed ◆◆◆◆◆◆◆

EGG GROUPS
Human-like

ITEM SOMETIMES HELD BY WILD POKÉMON
Electirizer

EVOLUTION

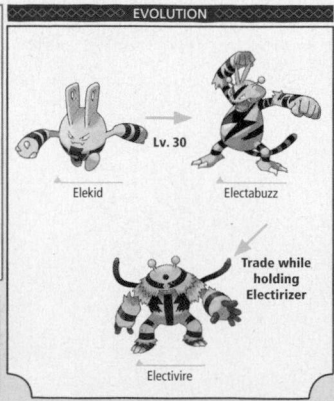

Elekid → Lv. 30 → Electabuzz

Trade while holding Electirizer

Electivire

MAIN WAY TO REGISTER IN THE POKÉDEX
Catch in SOS battles against Elekid in the tall grass on Route 12

Same form for male/female

Alola Pokédex	Melemele	Akala	Ula'ula	Poni
228	—	—	100	—

Electivire

Thunderbolt Pokémon

ELECTRIC

HEIGHT: 5'11"
WEIGHT: 305.6 lbs.

It pushes the tips of its tails against its foes and then lets loose a high-voltage current. Its foes are burned to a crisp in an instant.

When it gets excited, it thumps its chest. With every thud, thunder roars and electric sparks shower all around.

ABILITY
Motor Drive

HIDDEN ABILITY
Vital Spirit

Damage taken in normal battles

NORMAL ×1	FIGHTING ×1	ROCK ×1			
FIRE ×1	POISON ×1	GHOST ×1			
WATER ×1	GROUND ×2	DRAGON ×1			
GRASS ×1	FLYING ×0.5	DARK ×1			
ELECTRIC ×0.5	PSYCHIC ×1	STEEL ×0.5			
ICE ×1	BUG ×1	FAIRY ×1			

SPECIES STRENGTHS
HP ◆◆◆
Attack ◆◆◆◆◆◆◆
Defense ◆◆◆◆
Sp. Atk ◆◆◆◆
Sp. Def ◆◆◆◆◆
Speed ◆◆◆◆◆◆

EGG GROUPS
Human-like

ITEM SOMETIMES HELD BY WILD POKÉMON
—

EVOLUTION

Elekid → Lv. 30 → Electabuzz

Trade while holding Electirizer

Electivire

MAIN WAY TO REGISTER IN THE POKÉDEX
Receive an Electabuzz holding an Electirizer in a trade and it will evolve

Same form for male/female

ELEKID 226

❖ LEVEL-UP MOVES

Lv.	Name	Type	Kind	Pow.	Acc.	PP	Range
1	Quick Attack	Normal	Physical	40	100	30	Normal
1	Leer	Normal	Status	—	100	30	Many Others
5	Thunder Shock	Electric	Special	40	100	30	Normal
8	Low Kick	Fighting	Physical	—	100	20	Normal
12	Swift	Normal	Special	60	—	20	Many Others
15	Shock Wave	Electric	Special	60	—	20	Normal
19	Thunder Wave	Electric	Status	—	90	20	Normal
22	Electro Ball	Electric	Special	—	100	10	Normal
26	Light Screen	Psychic	Status	—	—	30	Your Side
29	Thunder Punch	Electric	Physical	75	100	15	Normal
33	Discharge	Electric	Special	80	100	15	Adjacent
36	Screech	Normal	Status	—	85	40	Normal
40	Thunderbolt	Electric	Special	90	100	15	Normal
43	Thunder	Electric	Special	110	70	10	Normal

❖ TM MOVES

No.	Name	Type	Kind	Pow.	Acc.	PP	Range
TM06	Toxic	Poison	Status	—	90	10	Normal
TM10	Hidden Power	Normal	Special	60	100	15	Normal
TM16	Light Screen	Psychic	Status	—	—	30	Your Side
TM17	Protect	Normal	Status	—	—	10	Self
TM18	Rain Dance	Water	Status	—	—	5	Both Sides
TM21	Frustration	Normal	Physical	—	100	20	Normal
TM24	Thunderbolt	Electric	Special	90	100	15	Normal
TM25	Thunder	Electric	Special	110	70	10	Normal
TM27	Return	Normal	Physical	—	100	20	Normal
TM29	Psychic	Psychic	Special	90	100	10	Normal
TM31	Brick Break	Fighting	Physical	75	100	15	Normal
TM32	Double Team	Normal	Status	—	—	15	Self
TM42	Facade	Normal	Physical	70	100	20	Normal
TM44	Rest	Psychic	Status	—	—	10	Self
TM45	Attract	Normal	Status	—	100	15	Normal
TM46	Thief	Dark	Physical	60	100	25	Normal
TM48	Round	Normal	Special	60	100	15	Normal
TM56	Fling	Dark	Physical	—	100	10	Normal
TM57	Charge Beam	Electric	Special	50	90	10	Normal
TM72	Volt Switch	Electric	Special	70	100	20	Normal
TM73	Thunder Wave	Electric	Status	—	90	20	Normal
TM87	Swagger	Normal	Status	—	85	15	Normal
TM88	Sleep Talk	Normal	Status	—	—	10	Self
TM90	Substitute	Normal	Status	—	—	10	Self
TM93	Wild Charge	Electric	Physical	90	100	15	Normal
TM100	Confide	Normal	Status	—	—	20	Normal

❖ EXCLUSIVE Z-MOVE

Name	Base Move	Type	Kind	Pow.	Acc.	Range

❖ MOVES TAUGHT BY PEOPLE

Name	Type	Kind	Pow.	Acc.	PP	Range

❖ MOVES LEARNED WHEN EVOLVING

Name	Type	Kind	Pow.	Acc.	PP	Range

❖ EGG MOVES

Name	Type	Kind	Pow.	Acc.	PP	Range
Karate Chop	Fighting	Physical	50	100	25	Normal
Barrier	Psychic	Status	—	—	20	Self
Rolling Kick	Fighting	Physical	60	85	15	Normal
Meditate	Psychic	Status	—	—	40	Self
Cross Chop	Fighting	Physical	100	80	5	Normal
Fire Punch	Fire	Physical	75	100	15	Normal
Ice Punch	Ice	Physical	75	100	15	Normal
Dynamic Punch	Fighting	Physical	100	50	5	Normal
Feint	Normal	Physical	30	100	10	Normal
Hammer Arm	Fighting	Physical	100	90	10	Normal
Focus Punch	Fighting	Physical	150	100	20	Normal

ELECTABUZZ 227

❖ LEVEL-UP MOVES

Lv.	Name	Type	Kind	Pow.	Acc.	PP	Range
1	Quick Attack	Normal	Physical	40	100	30	Normal
1	Leer	Normal	Status	—	100	30	Many Others
1	Thunder Shock	Electric	Special	40	100	30	Normal
5	Thunder Shock	Electric	Special	40	100	30	Normal
8	Low Kick	Fighting	Physical	—	100	20	Normal
12	Swift	Normal	Special	60	—	20	Many Others
15	Shock Wave	Electric	Special	60	—	20	Normal
19	Thunder Wave	Electric	Status	—	90	20	Normal
22	Electro Ball	Electric	Special	—	100	10	Normal
26	Light Screen	Psychic	Status	—	—	30	Your Side
29	Thunder Punch	Electric	Physical	75	100	15	Normal
36	Discharge	Electric	Special	80	100	15	Adjacent
42	Screech	Normal	Status	—	85	40	Normal
49	Thunderbolt	Electric	Special	90	100	15	Normal
55	Thunder	Electric	Special	110	70	10	Normal

❖ TM MOVES

No.	Name	Type	Kind	Pow.	Acc.	PP	Range
TM06	Toxic	Poison	Status	—	90	10	Normal
TM10	Hidden Power	Normal	Special	60	100	15	Normal
TM15	Hyper Beam	Normal	Special	150	90	5	Normal
TM16	Light Screen	Psychic	Status	—	—	30	Your Side
TM17	Protect	Normal	Status	—	—	10	Self
TM18	Rain Dance	Water	Status	—	—	5	Both Sides
TM21	Frustration	Normal	Physical	—	100	20	Normal
TM24	Thunderbolt	Electric	Special	90	100	15	Normal
TM25	Thunder	Electric	Special	110	70	10	Normal
TM27	Return	Normal	Physical	—	100	20	Normal
TM29	Psychic	Psychic	Special	90	100	10	Normal
TM31	Brick Break	Fighting	Physical	75	100	15	Normal
TM32	Double Team	Normal	Status	—	—	15	Self
TM42	Facade	Normal	Physical	70	100	20	Normal
TM44	Rest	Psychic	Status	—	—	10	Self
TM45	Attract	Normal	Status	—	100	15	Normal
TM46	Thief	Dark	Physical	60	100	25	Normal
TM47	Low Sweep	Fighting	Physical	65	100	20	Normal
TM48	Round	Normal	Special	60	100	15	Normal
TM52	Focus Blast	Fighting	Special	120	70	5	Normal
TM56	Fling	Dark	Physical	—	100	10	Normal
TM57	Charge Beam	Electric	Special	50	90	10	Normal
TM68	Giga Impact	Normal	Physical	150	90	5	Normal
TM72	Volt Switch	Electric	Special	70	100	20	Normal
TM73	Thunder Wave	Electric	Status	—	90	20	Normal
TM87	Swagger	Normal	Status	—	85	15	Normal
TM88	Sleep Talk	Normal	Status	—	—	10	Self
TM90	Substitute	Normal	Status	—	—	10	Self
TM93	Wild Charge	Electric	Physical	90	100	15	Normal
TM100	Confide	Normal	Status	—	—	20	Normal

❖ EXCLUSIVE Z-MOVE

Name	Base Move	Type	Kind	Pow.	Acc.	Range

❖ MOVES TAUGHT BY PEOPLE

Name	Type	Kind	Pow.	Acc.	PP	Range

❖ MOVES LEARNED WHEN EVOLVING

Name	Type	Kind	Pow.	Acc.	PP	Range

❖ EGG MOVES

Name	Type	Kind	Pow.	Acc.	PP	Range

ELECTIVIRE 228

❖ LEVEL-UP MOVES

Lv.	Name	Type	Kind	Pow.	Acc.	PP	Range
1	Electric Terrain	Electric	Status	—	—	10	Both Sides
1	Ion Deluge	Electric	Status	—	—	25	Both Sides
1	Fire Punch	Fire	Physical	75	100	15	Normal
1	Quick Attack	Normal	Physical	40	100	30	Normal
1	Leer	Normal	Status	—	100	30	Many Others
1	Thunder Shock	Electric	Special	40	100	30	Normal
1	Low Kick	Fighting	Physical	—	100	20	Normal
5	Thunder Shock	Electric	Special	40	100	30	Normal
8	Low Kick	Fighting	Physical	—	100	20	Normal
12	Swift	Normal	Special	60	—	20	Many Others
15	Shock Wave	Electric	Special	60	—	20	Normal
19	Thunder Wave	Electric	Status	—	90	20	Normal
22	Electro Ball	Electric	Special	—	100	10	Normal
26	Light Screen	Psychic	Status	—	—	30	Your Side
29	Thunder Punch	Electric	Physical	75	100	15	Normal
36	Discharge	Electric	Special	80	100	15	Adjacent
42	Screech	Normal	Status	—	85	40	Normal
49	Thunderbolt	Electric	Special	90	100	15	Normal
55	Thunder	Electric	Special	110	70	10	Normal
62	Giga Impact	Normal	Physical	150	90	5	Normal
65	Electric Terrain	Electric	Status	—	—	10	Both Sides

❖ TM MOVES

No.	Name	Type	Kind	Pow.	Acc.	PP	Range
TM06	Toxic	Poison	Status	—	90	10	Normal
TM10	Hidden Power	Normal	Special	60	100	15	Normal
TM12	Taunt	Dark	Status	—	100	20	Normal
TM15	Hyper Beam	Normal	Special	150	90	5	Normal
TM16	Light Screen	Psychic	Status	—	—	30	Your Side
TM17	Protect	Normal	Status	—	—	10	Self
TM18	Rain Dance	Water	Status	—	—	5	Both Sides
TM21	Frustration	Normal	Physical	—	100	20	Normal
TM24	Thunderbolt	Electric	Special	90	100	15	Normal
TM25	Thunder	Electric	Special	110	70	10	Normal
TM26	Earthquake	Ground	Physical	100	100	10	Adjacent
TM27	Return	Normal	Physical	—	100	20	Normal
TM29	Psychic	Psychic	Special	90	100	10	Normal
TM31	Brick Break	Fighting	Physical	75	100	15	Normal
TM32	Double Team	Normal	Status	—	—	15	Self
TM35	Flamethrower	Fire	Special	90	100	15	Normal
TM39	Rock Tomb	Rock	Physical	60	95	15	Normal
TM41	Torment	Dark	Status	—	100	15	Normal
TM42	Facade	Normal	Physical	70	100	20	Normal
TM44	Rest	Psychic	Status	—	—	10	Self
TM45	Attract	Normal	Status	—	100	15	Normal
TM46	Thief	Dark	Physical	60	100	25	Normal
TM47	Low Sweep	Fighting	Physical	65	100	20	Normal
TM48	Round	Normal	Special	60	100	15	Normal
TM52	Focus Blast	Fighting	Special	120	70	5	Normal
TM56	Fling	Dark	Physical	—	100	10	Normal
TM57	Charge Beam	Electric	Special	50	90	10	Normal
TM68	Giga Impact	Normal	Physical	150	90	5	Normal
TM72	Volt Switch	Electric	Special	70	100	20	Normal
TM73	Thunder Wave	Electric	Status	—	90	20	Normal
TM78	Bulldoze	Ground	Physical	60	100	20	Adjacent
TM80	Rock Slide	Rock	Physical	75	90	10	Many Others
TM87	Swagger	Normal	Status	—	85	15	Normal
TM88	Sleep Talk	Normal	Status	—	—	10	Self
TM90	Substitute	Normal	Status	—	—	10	Self
TM93	Wild Charge	Electric	Physical	90	100	15	Normal
TM100	Confide	Normal	Status	—	—	20	Normal

❖ EXCLUSIVE Z-MOVE

Name	Base Move	Type	Kind	Pow.	Acc.	Range

❖ MOVES TAUGHT BY PEOPLE

Name	Type	Kind	Pow.	Acc.	PP	Range

❖ MOVES LEARNED WHEN EVOLVING

Name	Type	Kind	Pow.	Acc.	PP	Range

❖ EGG MOVES

Name	Type	Kind	Pow.	Acc.	PP	Range

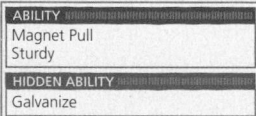

229 GEODUDE

Alola Pokédex	Melemele	Akala	Ula'ula	Poni
229	—	—	101	—

Geodude
Rock Pokémon

`ROCK` `ELECTRIC` | HEIGHT: 1'04" | WEIGHT: 44.8 lbs.

Its body is a magnetic stone. Iron sand attaches firmly to the portions of its body that are particularly magnetic.

If you accidentally step on a Geodude sleeping on the ground, you'll hear a crunching sound and feel a shock ripple through your entire body.

ABILITY
Magnet Pull
Sturdy

HIDDEN ABILITY
Galvanize

Damage taken in normal battles

NORMAL	×0.5	FIGHTING	×2	ROCK	×1
FIRE	×0.5	POISON	×0.5	GHOST	×1
WATER	×2	GROUND	×4	DRAGON	×1
GRASS	×2	FLYING	×0.25	DARK	×1
ELECTRIC	×0.5	PSYCHIC	×1	STEEL	×1
ICE	×1	BUG	×1	FAIRY	×1

SPECIES STRENGTHS
HP ◆◆
Attack ◆◆◆◆
Defense ◆◆◆◆◆
Sp. Atk ◆◆
Sp. Def ◆◆
Speed ◆

EGG GROUPS
Mineral

ITEM SOMETIMES HELD BY WILD POKÉMON
Cell Battery

MAIN WAY TO REGISTER IN THE POKÉDEX
Catch in the tall grass on Route 12

EVOLUTION

Alolan Geodude → Lv. 25 → Alolan Graveler

Trade Alolan Graveler

Alolan Golem

❖ ALOLA FORM ❖

Same form for male/female

---

230 GRAVELER

Alola Pokédex	Melemele	Akala	Ula'ula	Poni
230	—	—	102	—

Graveler
Rock Pokémon

`ROCK` `ELECTRIC` | HEIGHT: 3'03" | WEIGHT: 242.5 lbs.

Its preferred food is dravite. After it has eaten this mineral, crystals form inside the Pokémon, rising to the surface of part of its body.

They eat rocks and often get into a scrap over them. The shock of Graveler smashing together causes a flash of light and a booming noise.

ABILITY
Magnet Pull
Sturdy

HIDDEN ABILITY
Galvanize

Damage taken in normal battles

NORMAL	×0.5	FIGHTING	×2	ROCK	×1
FIRE	×0.5	POISON	×0.5	GHOST	×1
WATER	×2	GROUND	×4	DRAGON	×1
GRASS	×2	FLYING	×0.25	DARK	×1
ELECTRIC	×0.5	PSYCHIC	×1	STEEL	×1
ICE	×1	BUG	×1	FAIRY	×1

SPECIES STRENGTHS
HP ◆◆
Attack ◆◆◆◆◆
Defense ◆◆◆◆◆◆
Sp. Atk ◆◆
Sp. Def ◆◆
Speed ◆◆

EGG GROUPS
Mineral

ITEM SOMETIMES HELD BY WILD POKÉMON
Cell Battery

MAIN WAY TO REGISTER IN THE POKÉDEX
Catch in the brown tall grass on Route 17

EVOLUTION

Alolan Geodude → Lv. 25 → Alolan Graveler

Trade Alolan Graveler

Alolan Golem

❖ ALOLA FORM ❖

Same form for male/female

231 GOLEM

Alola Pokédex	Melemele	Akala	Ula'ula	Poni
231	—	—	103	—

Golem
Megaton Pokémon

`ROCK` `ELECTRIC` | HEIGHT: 5'07" | WEIGHT: 696.7 lbs.

It fires rocks charged with electricity. Even if the rock isn't fired that accurately, just grazing an opponent will cause numbness and fainting.

Because it can't fire boulders at a rapid pace, it's been known to seize nearby Geodude and fire them from its back.

ABILITY
Magnet Pull
Sturdy

HIDDEN ABILITY
Galvanize

Damage taken in normal battles

NORMAL	×0.5	FIGHTING	×2	ROCK	×1
FIRE	×0.5	POISON	×0.5	GHOST	×1
WATER	×2	GROUND	×4	DRAGON	×1
GRASS	×2	FLYING	×0.25	DARK	×1
ELECTRIC	×0.5	PSYCHIC	×1	STEEL	×1
ICE	×1	BUG	×1	FAIRY	×1

SPECIES STRENGTHS
HP ◆◆◆
Attack ◆◆◆◆◆◆
Defense ◆◆◆◆◆◆◆
Sp. Atk ◆◆◆
Sp. Def ◆◆◆◆
Speed ◆◆◆

EGG GROUPS
Mineral

ITEM SOMETIMES HELD BY WILD POKÉMON

MAIN WAY TO REGISTER IN THE POKÉDEX
Trade a Haunter to a man at the Pokémon Center in Tapu Village to receive an Alolan Graveler and it will evolve

EVOLUTION

Alolan Geodude → Lv. 25 → Alolan Graveler

Trade Alolan Graveler

Alolan Golem

❖ ALOLA FORM ❖

Same form for male/female

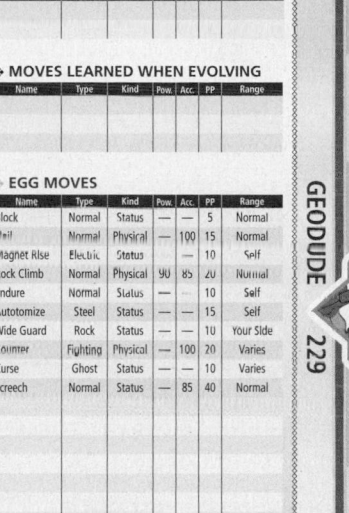

GEODUDE 229

❖ LEVEL-UP MOVES

Lv.	Name	Type	Kind	Pow.	Acc.	PP	Range
1	Tackle	Normal	Physical	40	100	35	Normal
1	Defense Curl	Normal	Status	—	—	40	Self
4	Charge	Electric	Status	—	—	20	Self
6	Rock Polish	Rock	Status	—	—	20	Self
10	Rollout	Rock	Physical	30	90	20	Normal
12	Spark	Electric	Physical	65	100	20	Normal
16	Rock Throw	Rock	Physical	50	90	15	Normal
18	Smack Down	Rock	Physical	50	100	15	Normal
22	Thunder Punch	Electric	Physical	75	100	15	Normal
24	Self-Destruct	Normal	Physical	200	100	5	Adjacent
28	Stealth Rock	Rock	Status	—	—	20	Other Side
30	Rock Blast	Rock	Physical	25	90	10	Normal
34	Discharge	Electric	Special	80	100	15	Adjacent
36	Explosion	Normal	Physical	250	100	5	Adjacent
40	Double-Edge	Normal	Physical	120	100	15	Normal
42	Stone Edge	Rock	Physical	100	80	5	Normal

❖ TM MOVES

No.	Name	Type	Kind	Pow.	Acc.	PP	Range
TM06	Toxic	Poison	Status	—	90	10	Normal
TM10	Hidden Power	Normal	Special	60	100	15	Normal
TM11	Sunny Day	Fire	Status	—	—	5	Both Sides
TM17	Protect	Normal	Status	—	—	10	Self
TM21	Frustration	Normal	Physical	—	100	20	Normal
TM23	Smack Down	Rock	Physical	50	100	15	Normal
TM24	Thunderbolt	Electric	Special	90	100	15	Normal
TM25	Thunder	Electric	Special	110	70	10	Normal
TM26	Earthquake	Ground	Physical	100	100	10	Adjacent
TM27	Return	Normal	Physical	—	100	20	Normal
TM31	Brick Break	Fighting	Physical	75	100	15	Normal
TM32	Double Team	Normal	Status	—	—	15	Self
TM35	Flamethrower	Fire	Special	90	100	15	Normal
TM37	Sandstorm	Rock	Status	—	—	10	Both Sides
TM38	Fire Blast	Fire	Special	110	85	5	Normal
TM39	Rock Tomb	Rock	Physical	60	95	15	Normal
TM42	Facade	Normal	Physical	70	100	20	Normal
TM44	Rest	Psychic	Status	—	—	10	Self
TM45	Attract	Normal	Status	—	100	15	Normal
TM48	Round	Normal	Special	60	100	15	Normal
TM56	Fling	Dark	Physical	—	100	10	Normal
TM57	Charge Beam	Electric	Special	50	90	10	Normal
TM59	Brutal Swing	Dark	Physical	60	100	20	Adjacent
TM64	Explosion	Normal	Physical	250	100	5	Adjacent
TM69	Rock Polish	Rock	Status	—	—	20	Self
TM71	Stone Edge	Rock	Physical	100	80	5	Normal
TM72	Volt Switch	Electric	Special	70	100	20	Normal
TM74	Gyro Ball	Steel	Physical	—	100	5	Normal
TM78	Bulldoze	Ground	Physical	60	100	20	Adjacent
TM80	Rock Slide	Rock	Physical	75	90	10	Many Others
TM87	Swagger	Normal	Status	—	85	15	Normal
TM88	Sleep Talk	Normal	Status	—	—	10	Self
TM90	Substitute	Normal	Status	—	—	10	Self
TM96	Nature Power	Normal	Status	—	—	20	Normal
TM100	Confide	Normal	Status	—	—	20	Normal

❖ EXCLUSIVE Z-MOVE

Name	Base Move	Type	Kind	Pow.	Acc.	Range

❖ MOVES TAUGHT BY PEOPLE

Name	Type	Kind	Pow.	Acc.	PP	Range

❖ MOVES LEARNED WHEN EVOLVING

Name	Type	Kind	Pow.	Acc.	PP	Range

❖ EGG MOVES

Name	Type	Kind	Pow.	Acc.	PP	Range
Block	Normal	Status	—	—	5	Normal
Flail	Normal	Physical	—	100	15	Normal
Magnet Rise	Electric	Status	—	—	10	Self
Rock Climb	Normal	Physical	90	85	20	Normal
Endure	Normal	Status	—	—	10	Self
Autotomize	Steel	Status	—	—	15	Self
Wide Guard	Rock	Status	—	—	10	Your Side
Counter	Fighting	Physical	—	100	20	Varies
Curse	Ghost	Status	—	—	10	Varies
Screech	Normal	Status	—	85	40	Normal

GRAVELER 230

❖ LEVEL-UP MOVES

Lv.	Name	Type	Kind	Pow.	Acc.	PP	Range
1	Tackle	Normal	Physical	40	100	35	Normal
1	Defense Curl	Normal	Status	—	—	40	Self
1	Charge	Electric	Status	—	—	20	Self
1	Rock Polish	Rock	Status	—	—	20	Self
4	Charge	Electric	Status	—	—	20	Self
6	Rock Polish	Rock	Status	—	—	20	Self
10	Rollout	Rock	Physical	30	90	20	Normal
12	Spark	Electric	Physical	65	100	20	Normal
16	Rock Throw	Rock	Physical	50	90	15	Normal
18	Smack Down	Rock	Physical	50	100	15	Normal
22	Thunder Punch	Electric	Physical	75	100	15	Normal
24	Self-Destruct	Normal	Physical	200	100	5	Adjacent
30	Stealth Rock	Rock	Status	—	—	20	Other Side
34	Rock Blast	Rock	Physical	25	90	10	Normal
40	Discharge	Electric	Special	80	100	15	Adjacent
44	Explosion	Normal	Physical	250	100	5	Adjacent
50	Double-Edge	Normal	Physical	120	100	15	Normal
54	Stone Edge	Rock	Physical	100	80	5	Normal

❖ TM MOVES

No.	Name	Type	Kind	Pow.	Acc.	PP	Range
TM06	Toxic	Poison	Status	—	90	10	Normal
TM10	Hidden Power	Normal	Special	60	100	15	Normal
TM11	Sunny Day	Fire	Status	—	—	5	Both Sides
TM17	Protect	Normal	Status	—	—	10	Self
TM21	Frustration	Normal	Physical	—	100	20	Normal
TM23	Smack Down	Rock	Physical	50	100	15	Normal
TM24	Thunderbolt	Electric	Special	90	100	15	Normal
TM25	Thunder	Electric	Special	110	70	10	Normal
TM26	Earthquake	Ground	Physical	100	100	10	Adjacent
TM27	Return	Normal	Physical	—	100	20	Normal
TM31	Brick Break	Fighting	Physical	75	100	15	Normal
TM32	Double Team	Normal	Status	—	—	15	Self
TM35	Flamethrower	Fire	Special	90	100	15	Normal
TM37	Sandstorm	Rock	Status	—	—	10	Both Sides
TM38	Fire Blast	Fire	Special	110	85	5	Normal
TM39	Rock Tomb	Rock	Physical	60	95	15	Normal
TM42	Facade	Normal	Physical	70	100	20	Normal
TM44	Rest	Psychic	Status	—	—	10	Self
TM45	Attract	Normal	Status	—	100	15	Normal
TM48	Round	Normal	Special	60	100	15	Normal
TM56	Fling	Dark	Physical	—	100	10	Normal
TM57	Charge Beam	Electric	Special	50	90	10	Normal
TM59	Brutal Swing	Dark	Physical	60	100	20	Adjacent
TM64	Explosion	Normal	Physical	250	100	5	Adjacent
TM69	Rock Polish	Rock	Status	—	—	20	Self
TM71	Stone Edge	Rock	Physical	100	80	5	Normal
TM72	Volt Switch	Electric	Special	70	100	20	Normal
TM74	Gyro Ball	Steel	Physical	—	100	5	Normal
TM78	Bulldoze	Ground	Physical	60	100	20	Adjacent
TM80	Rock Slide	Rock	Physical	75	90	10	Many Others
TM87	Swagger	Normal	Status	—	85	15	Normal
TM88	Sleep Talk	Normal	Status	—	—	10	Self
TM90	Substitute	Normal	Status	—	—	10	Self
TM96	Nature Power	Normal	Status	—	—	20	Normal
TM100	Confide	Normal	Status	—	—	20	Normal

❖ EXCLUSIVE Z-MOVE

Name	Base Move	Type	Kind	Pow.	Acc.	Range

❖ MOVES TAUGHT BY PEOPLE

Name	Type	Kind	Pow.	Acc.	PP	Range

❖ MOVES LEARNED WHEN EVOLVING

Name	Type	Kind	Pow.	Acc.	PP	Range

❖ EGG MOVES

Name	Type	Kind	Pow.	Acc.	PP	Range

GOLEM 231

❖ LEVEL-UP MOVES

Lv.	Name	Type	Kind	Pow.	Acc.	PP	Range
1	Heavy Slam	Steel	Physical	—	100	10	Normal
1	Tackle	Normal	Physical	40	100	35	Normal
1	Defense Curl	Normal	Status	—	—	40	Self
1	Charge	Electric	Status	—	—	20	Self
1	Rock Polish	Rock	Status	—	—	20	Self
4	Charge	Electric	Status	—	—	20	Self
6	Rock Polish	Rock	Status	—	—	20	Self
10	Steamroller	Bug	Physical	65	100	20	Normal
12	Spark	Electric	Physical	65	100	20	Normal
16	Rock Throw	Rock	Physical	50	90	15	Normal
18	Smack Down	Rock	Physical	50	100	15	Normal
22	Thunder Punch	Electric	Physical	75	100	15	Normal
24	Self-Destruct	Normal	Physical	200	100	5	Adjacent
30	Stealth Rock	Rock	Status	—	—	20	Other Side
34	Rock Blast	Rock	Physical	25	90	10	Normal
40	Discharge	Electric	Special	80	100	15	Adjacent
44	Explosion	Normal	Physical	250	100	5	Adjacent
50	Double-Edge	Normal	Physical	120	100	15	Normal
54	Stone Edge	Rock	Physical	100	80	5	Normal
60	Heavy Slam	Steel	Physical	—	100	10	Normal

❖ TM MOVES

No.	Name	Type	Kind	Pow.	Acc.	PP	Range
TM05	Roar	Normal	Status	—	—	20	Normal
TM06	Toxic	Poison	Status	—	90	10	Normal
TM10	Hidden Power	Normal	Special	60	100	15	Normal
TM11	Sunny Day	Fire	Status	—	—	5	Both Sides
TM15	Hyper Beam	Normal	Special	150	90	5	Normal
TM17	Protect	Normal	Status	—	—	10	Self
TM21	Frustration	Normal	Physical	—	100	20	Normal
TM23	Smack Down	Rock	Physical	50	100	15	Normal
TM24	Thunderbolt	Electric	Special	90	100	15	Normal
TM25	Thunder	Electric	Special	110	70	10	Normal
TM26	Earthquake	Ground	Physical	100	100	10	Adjacent
TM27	Return	Normal	Physical	—	100	20	Normal
TM31	Brick Break	Fighting	Physical	75	100	15	Normal
TM32	Double Team	Normal	Status	—	—	15	Self
TM35	Flamethrower	Fire	Special	90	100	15	Normal
TM37	Sandstorm	Rock	Status	—	—	10	Both Sides
TM38	Fire Blast	Fire	Special	110	85	5	Normal
TM39	Rock Tomb	Rock	Physical	60	95	15	Normal
TM42	Facade	Normal	Physical	70	100	20	Normal
TM44	Rest	Psychic	Status	—	—	10	Self
TM45	Attract	Normal	Status	—	100	15	Normal
TM48	Round	Normal	Special	60	100	15	Normal
TM49	Echoed Voice	Normal	Special	40	100	15	Normal
TM52	Focus Blast	Fighting	Special	120	70	5	Normal
TM56	Fling	Dark	Physical	—	100	10	Normal
TM57	Charge Beam	Electric	Special	50	90	10	Normal
TM59	Brutal Swing	Dark	Physical	60	100	20	Adjacent
TM64	Explosion	Normal	Physical	250	100	5	Adjacent
TM68	Giga Impact	Normal	Physical	150	90	5	Normal
TM69	Rock Polish	Rock	Status	—	—	20	Self
TM71	Stone Edge	Rock	Physical	100	80	5	Normal
TM72	Volt Switch	Electric	Special	70	100	20	Normal
TM74	Gyro Ball	Steel	Physical	—	100	5	Normal
TM78	Bulldoze	Ground	Physical	60	100	20	Adjacent
TM80	Rock Slide	Rock	Physical	75	90	10	Many Others
TM87	Swagger	Normal	Status	—	85	15	Normal
TM88	Sleep Talk	Normal	Status	—	—	10	Self
TM90	Substitute	Normal	Status	—	—	10	Self
TM93	Wild Charge	Electric	Physical	90	100	15	Normal
TM96	Nature Power	Normal	Status	—	—	20	Normal
TM100	Confide	Normal	Status	—	—	20	Normal

❖ EXCLUSIVE Z-MOVE

Name	Base Move	Type	Kind	Pow.	Acc.	Range

❖ MOVES TAUGHT BY PEOPLE

Name	Type	Kind	Pow.	Acc.	PP	Range

❖ MOVES LEARNED WHEN EVOLVING

Name	Type	Kind	Pow.	Acc.	PP	Range

❖ EGG MOVES

Name	Type	Kind	Pow.	Acc.	PP	Range

Sandile

Alola Pokédex	Melemele	Akala	Ula'ula	Poni
232	—	—	104	—

Desert Croc Pokémon

GROUND　DARK

HEIGHT: 2'04"
WEIGHT: 33.5 lbs.

It submerges itself in sand and moves as if swimming. This wise behavior keeps its enemies from finding it and maintains its temperature.

It conceals itself in the sand and chomps down on the legs of any prey that unwarily walk over it. Its favorite food is Trapinch.

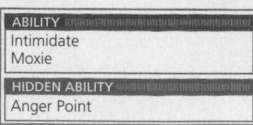

ABILITY
Intimidate
Moxie

HIDDEN ABILITY
Anger Point

SPECIES STRENGTHS
HP ◆◆
Attack ◆◆◆◆
Defense ◆◆
Sp. Atk ◆◆
Sp. Def ◆◆
Speed ◆◆◆◆

Damage taken in normal battles

NORMAL	×1	FIGHTING	×2	ROCK	×1
FIRE	×1	POISON	×0.5	GHOST	×0.5
WATER	×2	GROUND	×1	DRAGON	×1
GRASS	×2	FLYING	×1	DARK	×0.5
ELECTRIC	×0	PSYCHIC	×0	STEEL	×1
ICE	×2	BUG	×2	FAIRY	×2

EGG GROUPS
Field

ITEM SOMETIMES HELD BY WILD POKÉMON
Black Glasses

MAIN WAY TO REGISTER IN THE POKÉDEX
Catch in Haina Desert

EVOLUTION

Sandile　→ Lv. 29　Krokorok
Lv. 40
Krookodile

Same form for male/female

Krokorok

Alola Pokédex	Melemele	Akala	Ula'ula	Poni
233	—	—	105	—

Desert Croc Pokémon

GROUND　DARK

HEIGHT: 3'03"
WEIGHT: 73.6 lbs.

They move in groups of a few individuals. A female is often the leader of the group, and the males will gather food.

Thanks to the special membrane covering its eyes, it can see its surroundings clearly, even in the middle of the night.

ABILITY
Intimidate
Moxie

HIDDEN ABILITY
Anger Point

SPECIES STRENGTHS
HP ◆◆
Attack ◆◆◆◆
Defense ◆◆◆
Sp. Atk ◆◆
Sp. Def ◆◆
Speed ◆◆◆◆◆

Damage taken in normal battles

NORMAL	×1	FIGHTING	×2	ROCK	×0.5
FIRE	×1	POISON	×0.5	GHOST	×0.5
WATER	×2	GROUND	×1	DRAGON	×1
GRASS	×2	FLYING	×1	DARK	×0.5
ELECTRIC	×0	PSYCHIC	×0	STEEL	×1
ICE	×2	BUG	×2	FAIRY	×2

EGG GROUPS
Field

ITEM SOMETIMES HELD BY WILD POKÉMON
—

MAIN WAY TO REGISTER IN THE POKÉDEX
Level up Sandile to Lv. 29

EVOLUTION

Sandile　→ Lv. 29　Krokorok
Lv. 40
Krookodile

Same form for male/female

Krookodile

Alola Pokédex	Melemele	Akala	Ula'ula	Poni
234	—	—	106	—

Intimidation Pokémon

GROUND　DARK

HEIGHT: 4'11"
WEIGHT: 212.3 lbs.

Its unique faculty of sight can detect small prey more than 30 miles away, even in the midst of a sandstorm.

After clamping down with its powerful jaws, it twists its body around to rip its prey in half.

ABILITY
Intimidate
Moxie

HIDDEN ABILITY
Anger Point

SPECIES STRENGTHS
HP ◆◆◆◆
Attack ◆◆◆◆◆◆
Defense ◆◆◆◆
Sp. Atk ◆◆◆
Sp. Def ◆◆◆◆
Speed ◆◆◆◆◆◆

Damage taken in normal battles

NORMAL	×1	FIGHTING	×2	ROCK	×0.5
FIRE	×1	POISON	×0.5	GHOST	×0.5
WATER	×2	GROUND	×1	DRAGON	×1
GRASS	×2	FLYING	×1	DARK	×0.5
ELECTRIC	×0	PSYCHIC	×0	STEEL	×1
ICE	×2	BUG	×2	FAIRY	×2

EGG GROUPS
Field

ITEM SOMETIMES HELD BY WILD POKÉMON
—

MAIN WAY TO REGISTER IN THE POKÉDEX
Level up Krokorok to Lv. 40

EVOLUTION
Sandile　→ Lv. 29　Krokorok
Lv. 40
Krookodile

Same form for male/female

SANDILE 232

❖ LEVEL-UP MOVES

Lv.	Name	Type	Kind	Pow.	Acc.	PP	Range
1	Leer	Normal	Status	—	100	30	Many Others
1	Rage	Normal	Physical	20	100	20	Normal
4	Bite	Dark	Physical	60	100	25	Normal
7	Sand Attack	Ground	Status	—	100	15	Normal
10	Torment	Dark	Status	—	100	15	Normal
13	Sand Tomb	Ground	Physical	35	85	15	Normal
16	Assurance	Dark	Physical	60	100	10	Normal
19	Mud-Slap	Ground	Special	20	100	10	Normal
22	Embargo	Dark	Status	—	100	15	Normal
25	Swagger	Normal	Status	—	85	15	Normal
28	Crunch	Dark	Physical	80	100	15	Normal
31	Dig	Ground	Physical	80	100	10	Normal
34	Scary Face	Normal	Status	—	100	10	Normal
37	Foul Play	Dark	Physical	95	100	15	Normal
40	Sandstorm	Rock	Status	—	—	10	Both Sides
43	Earthquake	Ground	Physical	100	100	10	Adjacent
46	Thrash	Normal	Physical	120	100	10	1 Random

❖ TM MOVES

No.	Name	Type	Kind	Pow.	Acc.	PP	Range
TM05	Roar	Normal	Status	—	—	20	Normal
TM06	Toxic	Poison	Status	—	90	10	Normal
TM10	Hidden Power	Normal	Special	60	100	15	Normal
TM12	Taunt	Dark	Status	—	100	20	Normal
TM17	Protect	Normal	Status	—	—	10	Self
TM21	Frustration	Normal	Physical	—	100	20	Normal
TM26	Earthquake	Ground	Physical	100	100	10	Adjacent
TM27	Return	Normal	Physical	—	100	20	Normal
TM32	Double Team	Normal	Status	—	—	15	Self
TM36	Sludge Bomb	Poison	Special	90	100	10	Normal
TM37	Sandstorm	Rock	Status	—	—	10	Both Sides
TM39	Rock Tomb	Rock	Physical	60	95	15	Normal
TM41	Torment	Dark	Status	—	100	15	Normal
TM42	Facade	Normal	Physical	70	100	20	Normal
TM44	Rest	Psychic	Status	—	—	10	Self
TM45	Attract	Normal	Status	—	100	15	Normal
TM46	Thief	Dark	Physical	60	100	25	Normal
TM48	Round	Normal	Special	60	100	15	Normal
TM63	Embargo	Dark	Status	—	100	15	Normal
TM66	Payback	Dark	Physical	50	100	10	Normal
TM71	Stone Edge	Rock	Physical	100	80	5	Normal
TM78	Bulldoze	Ground	Physical	60	100	20	Adjacent
TM80	Rock Slide	Rock	Physical	75	90	10	Many Others
TM87	Swagger	Normal	Status	—	85	15	Normal
TM88	Sleep Talk	Normal	Status	—	—	10	Self
TM90	Substitute	Normal	Status	—	—	10	Self
TM95	Snarl	Dark	Special	55	95	15	Many Others
TM97	Dark Pulse	Dark	Special	80	100	15	Normal
TM100	Confide	Normal	Status	—	—	20	Normal

❖ EXCLUSIVE Z-MOVE

Name	Base Move	Type	Kind	Pow.	Acc.	Range

❖ MOVES TAUGHT BY PEOPLE

Name	Type	Kind	Pow.	Acc.	PP	Range

❖ MOVES LEARNED WHEN EVOLVING

Name	Type	Kind	Pow.	Acc.	PP	Range

❖ EGG MOVES

Name	Type	Kind	Pow.	Acc.	PP	Range
Double-Edge	Normal	Physical	120	100	15	Normal
Rock Climb	Normal	Physical	90	85	20	Normal
Pursuit	Dark	Physical	40	100	20	Normal
Uproar	Normal	Special	90	100	10	1 Random
Fire Fang	Fire	Physical	65	95	15	Normal
Thunder Fang	Electric	Physical	65	95	15	Normal
Beat Up	Dark	Physical	—	100	10	Normal
Focus Energy	Normal	Status	—	—	30	Self
Counter	Fighting	Physical	—	100	20	Varies
Mean Look	Normal	Status	—	—	5	Normal
Me First	Normal	Status	—	—	20	Varies
Power Trip	Dark	Physical	20	100	10	Normal

KROKOROK 233

❖ LEVEL-UP MOVES

Lv.	Name	Type	Kind	Pow.	Acc.	PP	Range
1	Leer	Normal	Status	—	100	30	Many Others
1	Rage	Normal	Physical	20	100	20	Normal
1	Bite	Dark	Physical	60	100	25	Normal
1	Sand Attack	Ground	Status	—	100	15	Normal
4	Bite	Dark	Physical	60	100	25	Normal
7	Sand Attack	Ground	Status	—	100	15	Normal
10	Torment	Dark	Status	—	100	15	Normal
13	Sand Tomb	Ground	Physical	35	85	15	Normal
16	Assurance	Dark	Physical	60	100	10	Normal
19	Mud-Slap	Ground	Special	20	100	10	Normal
22	Embargo	Dark	Status	—	100	15	Normal
25	Swagger	Normal	Status	—	85	15	Normal
28	Crunch	Dark	Physical	80	100	15	Normal
32	Dig	Ground	Physical	80	100	10	Normal
36	Scary Face	Normal	Status	—	100	10	Normal
40	Foul Play	Dark	Physical	95	100	15	Normal
44	Sandstorm	Rock	Status	—	—	10	Both Sides
48	Earthquake	Ground	Physical	100	100	10	Adjacent
52	Thrash	Normal	Physical	120	100	10	1 Random

❖ TM MOVES

No.	Name	Type	Kind	Pow.	Acc.	PP	Range
TM05	Roar	Normal	Status	—	—	20	Normal
TM06	Toxic	Poison	Status	—	90	10	Normal
TM10	Hidden Power	Normal	Special	60	100	15	Normal
TM12	Taunt	Dark	Status	—	100	20	Normal
TM17	Protect	Normal	Status	—	—	10	Self
TM21	Frustration	Normal	Physical	—	100	20	Normal
TM26	Earthquake	Ground	Physical	100	100	10	Adjacent
TM27	Return	Normal	Physical	—	100	20	Normal
TM31	Brick Break	Fighting	Physical	75	100	15	Normal
TM32	Double Team	Normal	Status	—	—	15	Self
TM36	Sludge Bomb	Poison	Special	90	100	10	Normal
TM37	Sandstorm	Rock	Status	—	—	10	Both Sides
TM39	Rock Tomb	Rock	Physical	60	95	15	Normal
TM41	Torment	Dark	Status	—	100	15	Normal
TM42	Facade	Normal	Physical	70	100	20	Normal
TM44	Rest	Psychic	Status	—	—	10	Self
TM45	Attract	Normal	Status	—	100	15	Normal
TM46	Thief	Dark	Physical	60	100	25	Normal
TM47	Low Sweep	Fighting	Physical	65	100	20	Normal
TM48	Round	Normal	Special	60	100	15	Normal
TM56	Fling	Dark	Physical	—	100	10	Normal
TM59	Brutal Swing	Dark	Physical	60	100	20	Adjacent
TM63	Embargo	Dark	Status	—	100	15	Normal
TM65	Shadow Claw	Ghost	Physical	70	100	15	Normal
TM66	Payback	Dark	Physical	50	100	10	Normal
TM71	Stone Edge	Rock	Physical	100	80	5	Normal
TM78	Bulldoze	Ground	Physical	60	100	20	Adjacent
TM80	Rock Slide	Rock	Physical	75	90	10	Many Others
TM86	Grass Knot	Grass	Special	—	100	20	Normal
TM87	Swagger	Normal	Status	—	85	15	Normal
TM88	Sleep Talk	Normal	Status	—	—	10	Self
TM90	Substitute	Normal	Status	—	—	10	Self
TM95	Snarl	Dark	Special	55	95	15	Many Others
TM97	Dark Pulse	Dark	Special	80	100	15	Normal
TM100	Confide	Normal	Status	—	—	20	Normal

❖ EXCLUSIVE Z-MOVE

Name	Base Move	Type	Kind	Pow.	Acc.	Range

❖ MOVES TAUGHT BY PEOPLE

Name	Type	Kind	Pow.	Acc.	PP	Range

❖ MOVES LEARNED WHEN EVOLVING

Name	Type	Kind	Pow.	Acc.	PP	Range

❖ EGG MOVES

Name	Type	Kind	Pow.	Acc.	PP	Range

KROOKODILE 234

❖ LEVEL-UP MOVES

Lv.	Name	Type	Kind	Pow.	Acc.	PP	Range
1	Power Trip	Dark	Physical	20	100	10	Normal
1	Leer	Normal	Status	—	100	30	Many Others
1	Rage	Normal	Physical	20	100	20	Normal
1	Bite	Dark	Physical	60	100	25	Normal
1	Sand Attack	Ground	Status	—	100	15	Normal
4	Bite	Dark	Physical	60	100	25	Normal
7	Sand Attack	Ground	Status	—	100	15	Normal
10	Torment	Dark	Status	—	100	15	Normal
13	Sand Tomb	Ground	Physical	35	85	15	Normal
16	Assurance	Dark	Physical	60	100	10	Normal
19	Mud-Slap	Ground	Special	20	100	10	Normal
22	Embargo	Dark	Status	—	100	15	Normal
25	Swagger	Normal	Status	—	85	15	Normal
28	Crunch	Dark	Physical	80	100	15	Normal
32	Dig	Ground	Physical	80	100	10	Normal
36	Scary Face	Normal	Status	—	100	10	Normal
42	Foul Play	Dark	Physical	95	100	15	Normal
48	Sandstorm	Rock	Status	—	—	10	Both Sides
54	Earthquake	Ground	Physical	100	100	10	Adjacent
60	Outrage	Dragon	Physical	120	100	10	1 Random

❖ TM MOVES

No.	Name	Type	Kind	Pow.	Acc.	PP	Range
TM02	Dragon Claw	Dragon	Physical	80	100	15	Normal
TM05	Roar	Normal	Status	—	—	20	Normal
TM06	Toxic	Poison	Status	—	90	10	Normal
TM08	Bulk Up	Fighting	Status	—	—	20	Self
TM10	Hidden Power	Normal	Special	60	100	15	Normal
TM12	Taunt	Dark	Status	—	100	20	Normal
TM15	Hyper Beam	Normal	Special	150	90	5	Normal
TM17	Protect	Normal	Status	—	—	10	Self
TM21	Frustration	Normal	Physical	—	100	20	Normal
TM23	Smack Down	Rock	Physical	50	100	15	Normal
TM26	Earthquake	Ground	Physical	100	100	10	Adjacent
TM27	Return	Normal	Physical	—	100	20	Normal
TM31	Brick Break	Fighting	Physical	75	100	15	Normal
TM32	Double Team	Normal	Status	—	—	15	Self
TM36	Sludge Bomb	Poison	Special	90	100	10	Normal
TM37	Sandstorm	Rock	Status	—	—	10	Both Sides
TM39	Rock Tomb	Rock	Physical	60	95	15	Normal
TM40	Aerial Ace	Flying	Physical	60	—	20	Normal
TM41	Torment	Dark	Status	—	100	15	Normal
TM42	Facade	Normal	Physical	70	100	20	Normal
TM44	Rest	Psychic	Status	—	—	10	Self
TM45	Attract	Normal	Status	—	100	15	Normal
TM46	Thief	Dark	Physical	60	100	25	Normal
TM47	Low Sweep	Fighting	Physical	65	100	20	Normal
TM48	Round	Normal	Special	60	100	15	Normal
TM52	Focus Blast	Fighting	Special	120	70	5	Normal
TM56	Fling	Dark	Physical	—	100	10	Normal
TM59	Brutal Swing	Dark	Physical	60	100	20	Adjacent
TM63	Embargo	Dark	Status	—	100	15	Normal
TM65	Shadow Claw	Ghost	Physical	70	100	15	Normal
TM66	Payback	Dark	Physical	50	100	10	Normal
TM68	Giga Impact	Normal	Physical	150	90	5	Normal
TM71	Stone Edge	Rock	Physical	100	80	5	Normal
TM78	Bulldoze	Ground	Physical	60	100	20	Adjacent
TM80	Rock Slide	Rock	Physical	75	90	10	Many Others
TM82	Dragon Tail	Dragon	Physical	60	90	10	Normal
TM86	Grass Knot	Grass	Special	—	100	20	Normal
TM87	Swagger	Normal	Status	—	85	15	Normal
TM88	Sleep Talk	Normal	Status	—	—	10	Self
TM90	Substitute	Normal	Status	—	—	10	Self
TM95	Snarl	Dark	Special	55	95	15	Many Others
TM97	Dark Pulse	Dark	Special	80	100	15	Normal
TM100	Confide	Normal	Status	—	—	20	Normal

❖ EXCLUSIVE Z-MOVE

Name	Base Move	Type	Kind	Pow.	Acc.	Range

❖ MOVES TAUGHT BY PEOPLE

Name	Type	Kind	Pow.	Acc.	PP	Range

❖ MOVES LEARNED WHEN EVOLVING

Name	Type	Kind	Pow.	Acc.	PP	Range

❖ EGG MOVES

Name	Type	Kind	Pow.	Acc.	PP	Range

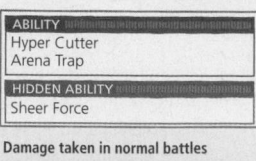

Alola Pokédex	Melemele	Akala	Ula'ula	Poni
235	—	—	107	—

☑ Trapinch

Ant Pit Pokémon

GROUND

HEIGHT: 2'04"
WEIGHT: 33.1 lbs.

It can live for a week without eating a thing. It waits patiently at the bottom of its nest for prey to appear.

As it digs through the sand, its giant jaws crush any rocks that obstruct its path. It builds a funnel-shaped nest.

ABILITY
Hyper Cutter
Arena Trap

HIDDEN ABILITY
Sheer Force

Damage taken in normal battles

NORMAL	×1	FIGHTING	×1	ROCK	×0.5
FIRE	×1	POISON	×0.5	GHOST	×1
WATER	×2	GROUND	×1	DRAGON	×1
GRASS	×2	FLYING	×1	DARK	×1
ELECTRIC	×0	PSYCHIC	×1	STEEL	×1
ICE	×2	BUG	×1	FAIRY	×1

SPECIES STRENGTHS
HP ◆◆
Attack ◆◆◆◆◆
Defense ◆◆◆
Sp. Atk ◆◆
Sp. Def ◆◆
Speed ◆

EGG GROUPS
Bug

ITEM SOMETIMES HELD BY WILD POKÉMON
Soft Sand

MAIN WAY TO REGISTER IN THE POKÉDEX
Catch in sand clouds in Haina Desert

EVOLUTION

Trapinch → Lv. 35 → Vibrava → Lv. 45 → Flygon

Same form for male/female

Alola Pokédex	Melemele	Akala	Ula'ula	Poni
236	—	—	108	—

☑ Vibrava

Vibration Pokémon

GROUND DRAGON

HEIGHT: 3'07"
WEIGHT: 33.7 lbs.

Rather than using its underdeveloped wings for flight, it rubs them together, producing ultrasonic waves to attack its enemies.

To help make its wings grow, it dissolves quantities of prey in its digestive juices and guzzles them down every day.

ABILITY
Levitate

HIDDEN ABILITY
—

Damage taken in normal battles

NORMAL	×1	FIGHTING	×1	ROCK	×0.5
FIRE	×0.5	POISON	×0.5	GHOST	×1
WATER	×1	! GROUND	×1	DRAGON	×1
GRASS	×1	FLYING	×1	DARK	×1
ELECTRIC	×0	PSYCHIC	×1	STEEL	×1
ICE	×4	BUG	×1	FAIRY	×2

SPECIES STRENGTHS
HP ◆◆
Attack ◆◆◆◆
Defense ◆◆◆
Sp. Atk ◆◆◆
Sp. Def ◆◆◆
Speed ◆◆◆◆◆

EGG GROUPS
Bug

ITEM SOMETIMES HELD BY WILD POKÉMON
—

MAIN WAY TO REGISTER IN THE POKÉDEX
Level up Trapinch to Lv. 35

EVOLUTION

Trapinch → Lv. 35 → Vibrava → Lv. 45 → Flygon

Same form for male/female

Alola Pokédex	Melemele	Akala	Ula'ula	Poni
237	—	—	109	—

☑ Flygon

Mystic Pokémon

GROUND DRAGON

HEIGHT: 6'07"
WEIGHT: 180.8 lbs.

The flapping of its wings sounds something like singing. Those lured by the sound are enveloped in a sandstorm, becoming Flygon's prey.

This Pokémon hides in the heart of sandstorms it creates and seldom appears where people can see it.

ABILITY
Levitate

HIDDEN ABILITY
—

Damage taken in normal battles

NORMAL	×1	FIGHTING	×1	ROCK	×0.5
FIRE	×0.5	POISON	×0.5	GHOST	×1
WATER	×1	! GROUND	×1	DRAGON	×2
GRASS	×1	FLYING	×1	DARK	×1
ELECTRIC	×0	PSYCHIC	×1	STEEL	×1
ICE	×4	BUG	×1	FAIRY	×2

SPECIES STRENGTHS
HP ◆◆◆
Attack ◆◆◆◆
Defense ◆◆◆◆
Sp. Atk ◆◆◆◆
Sp. Def ◆◆◆◆◆
Speed ◆◆◆◆◆◆

EGG GROUPS
Bug

ITEM SOMETIMES HELD BY WILD POKÉMON
—

MAIN WAY TO REGISTER IN THE POKÉDEX
Level up Vibrava to Lv. 45

EVOLUTION

Trapinch → Lv. 35 → Vibrava → Lv. 45 → Flygon

Same form for male/female

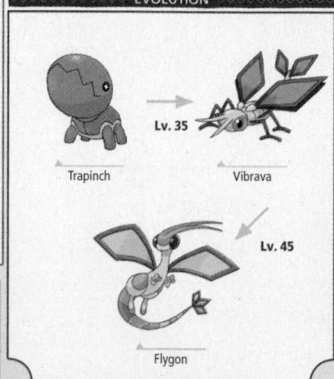

TRAPINCH — 235

LEVEL-UP MOVES

Lv.	Name	Type	Kind	Pow.	Acc.	PP	Range
1	Sand Attack	Ground	Status	—	100	15	Normal
1	Bite	Dark	Physical	60	100	25	Normal
1	Feint Attack	Dark	Physical	60	—	20	Normal
1	Bide	Normal	Physical	—	—	10	Self
5	Mud-Slap	Ground	Special	20	100	10	Normal
8	Bulldoze	Ground	Physical	60	100	20	Adjacent
12	Sand Tomb	Ground	Physical	35	85	15	Normal
15	Rock Slide	Rock	Physical	75	90	10	Many Others
19	Dig	Ground	Physical	80	100	10	Normal
22	Crunch	Dark	Physical	80	100	15	Normal
26	Earth Power	Ground	Special	90	100	10	Normal
29	Feint	Normal	Physical	30	100	10	Normal
33	Earthquake	Ground	Physical	100	100	10	Adjacent
36	Sandstorm	Rock	Status	—	—	10	Both Sides
40	Superpower	Fighting	Physical	120	100	5	Normal
43	Hyper Beam	Normal	Special	150	90	5	Normal
47	Fissure	Ground	Physical	—	30	5	Normal

TM MOVES

No.	Name	Type	Kind	Pow.	Acc.	PP	Range
TM06	Toxic	Poison	Status	—	90	10	Normal
TM10	Hidden Power	Normal	Special	60	100	15	Normal
TM11	Sunny Day	Fire	Status	—	—	5	Both Sides
TM15	Hyper Beam	Normal	Special	150	90	5	Normal
TM17	Protect	Normal	Status	—	—	10	Self
TM21	Frustration	Normal	Physical	—	100	20	Normal
TM22	Solar Beam	Grass	Special	120	100	10	Normal
TM26	Earthquake	Ground	Physical	100	100	10	Adjacent
TM27	Return	Normal	Physical	—	100	20	Normal
TM32	Double Team	Normal	Status	—	—	15	Self
TM37	Sandstorm	Rock	Status	—	—	10	Both Sides
TM39	Rock Tomb	Rock	Physical	60	95	15	Normal
TM42	Facade	Normal	Physical	70	100	20	Normal
TM44	Rest	Psychic	Status	—	—	10	Self
TM45	Attract	Normal	Status	—	100	15	Normal
TM48	Round	Normal	Special	60	100	15	Normal
TM78	Bulldoze	Ground	Physical	60	100	20	Adjacent
TM80	Rock Slide	Rock	Physical	75	90	10	Many Others
TM87	Swagger	Normal	Status	—	85	15	Normal
TM88	Sleep Talk	Normal	Status	—	—	10	Self
TM90	Substitute	Normal	Status	—	—	10	Self
TM100	Confide	Normal	Status	—	—	20	Normal

MOVES TAUGHT BY PEOPLE

(none)

MOVES LEARNED WHEN EVOLVING

(none)

EGG MOVES

Name	Type	Kind	Pow.	Acc.	PP	Range
Focus Energy	Normal	Status	—	—	30	Self
Quick Attack	Normal	Physical	40	100	30	Normal
Gust	Flying	Special	40	100	35	Normal
Flail	Normal	Physical	—	100	15	Normal
Fury Cutter	Bug	Physical	40	95	20	Normal
Mud Shot	Ground	Special	55	95	15	Normal
Endure	Normal	Status	—	—	10	Self
Earth Power	Ground	Special	90	100	10	Normal
Bug Bite	Bug	Physical	60	100	20	Normal
Signal Beam	Bug	Special	75	100	15	Normal

EXCLUSIVE Z-MOVE

(none)

VIBRAVA — 236

LEVEL-UP MOVES

Lv.	Name	Type	Kind	Pow.	Acc.	PP	Range
1	Dragon Breath	Dragon	Special	60	100	20	Normal
1	Sand Attack	Ground	Status	—	100	15	Normal
1	Sonic Boom	Normal	Special	—	90	20	Normal
1	Feint Attack	Dark	Physical	60	—	20	Normal
1	Bide	Normal	Physical	—	—	10	Self
5	Mud-Slap	Ground	Special	20	100	10	Normal
8	Bulldoze	Ground	Physical	60	100	20	Adjacent
12	Sand Tomb	Ground	Physical	35	85	15	Normal
15	Rock Slide	Rock	Physical	75	90	10	Many Others
19	Supersonic	Normal	Status	—	55	20	Normal
22	Screech	Normal	Status	—	85	40	Normal
26	Earth Power	Ground	Special	90	100	10	Normal
29	Bug Buzz	Bug	Special	90	100	10	Normal
33	Earthquake	Ground	Physical	100	100	10	Adjacent
36	Sandstorm	Rock	Status	—	—	10	Both Sides
40	Uproar	Normal	Special	90	100	10	1 Random
43	Hyper Beam	Normal	Special	150	90	5	Normal
47	Boomburst	Normal	Special	140	100	10	Adjacent

TM MOVES

No.	Name	Type	Kind	Pow.	Acc.	PP	Range
TM06	Toxic	Poison	Status	—	90	10	Normal
TM10	Hidden Power	Normal	Special	60	100	15	Normal
TM11	Sunny Day	Fire	Status	—	—	5	Both Sides
TM15	Hyper Beam	Normal	Special	150	90	5	Normal
TM17	Protect	Normal	Status	—	—	10	Self
TM19	Roost	Flying	Status	—	—	10	Self
TM21	Frustration	Normal	Physical	—	100	20	Normal
TM22	Solar Beam	Grass	Special	120	100	10	Normal
TM26	Earthquake	Ground	Physical	100	100	10	Adjacent
TM27	Return	Normal	Physical	—	100	20	Normal
TM32	Double Team	Normal	Status	—	—	15	Self
TM37	Sandstorm	Rock	Status	—	—	10	Both Sides
TM39	Rock Tomb	Rock	Physical	60	95	15	Normal
TM42	Facade	Normal	Physical	70	100	20	Normal
TM44	Rest	Psychic	Status	—	—	10	Self
TM45	Attract	Normal	Status	—	100	15	Normal
TM48	Round	Normal	Special	60	100	15	Normal
TM51	Steel Wing	Steel	Physical	70	90	25	Normal
TM76	Fly	Flying	Physical	90	95	15	Normal
TM78	Bulldoze	Ground	Physical	60	100	20	Adjacent
TM80	Rock Slide	Rock	Physical	75	90	10	Many Others
TM87	Swagger	Normal	Status	—	85	15	Normal
TM88	Sleep Talk	Normal	Status	—	—	10	Self
TM89	U-turn	Bug	Physical	70	100	20	Normal
TM90	Substitute	Normal	Status	—	—	10	Self
TM100	Confide	Normal	Status	—	—	20	Normal

MOVES TAUGHT BY PEOPLE

Name	Type	Kind	Pow.	Acc.	PP	Range
Draco Meteor	Dragon	Special	130	90	5	Normal

MOVES LEARNED WHEN EVOLVING

Name	Type	Kind	Pow.	Acc.	PP	Range
Dragon Breath	Dragon	Special	60	100	20	Normal

EGG MOVES

(none)

EXCLUSIVE Z-MOVE

(none)

FLYGON — 237

LEVEL-UP MOVES

Lv.	Name	Type	Kind	Pow.	Acc.	PP	Range
1	Dragon Claw	Dragon	Physical	80	100	15	Normal
1	Dragon Breath	Dragon	Special	60	100	20	Normal
1	Dragon Dance	Dragon	Status	—	—	20	Self
1	Sand Attack	Ground	Status	—	100	15	Normal
1	Sonic Boom	Normal	Special	—	90	20	Normal
1	Feint Attack	Dark	Physical	60	—	20	Normal
1	Bide	Normal	Physical	—	—	10	Self
5	Mud-Slap	Ground	Special	20	100	10	Normal
8	Bulldoze	Ground	Physical	60	100	20	Adjacent
12	Sand Tomb	Ground	Physical	35	85	15	Normal
15	Rock Slide	Rock	Physical	75	90	10	Many Others
19	Supersonic	Normal	Status	—	55	20	Normal
22	Screech	Normal	Status	—	85	40	Normal
26	Earth Power	Ground	Special	90	100	10	Normal
29	Dragon Tail	Dragon	Physical	60	90	10	Normal
33	Earthquake	Ground	Physical	100	100	10	Adjacent
36	Sandstorm	Rock	Status	—	—	10	Both Sides
40	Uproar	Normal	Special	90	100	10	1 Random
43	Hyper Beam	Normal	Special	150	90	5	Normal
47	Dragon Rush	Dragon	Physical	100	75	10	Normal

TM MOVES

No.	Name	Type	Kind	Pow.	Acc.	PP	Range
TM02	Dragon Claw	Dragon	Physical	80	100	15	Normal
TM06	Toxic	Poison	Status	—	90	10	Normal
TM10	Hidden Power	Normal	Special	60	100	15	Normal
TM11	Sunny Day	Fire	Status	—	—	5	Both Sides
TM15	Hyper Beam	Normal	Special	150	90	5	Normal
TM17	Protect	Normal	Status	—	—	10	Self
TM19	Roost	Flying	Status	—	—	10	Self
TM21	Frustration	Normal	Physical	—	100	20	Normal
TM22	Solar Beam	Grass	Special	120	100	10	Normal
TM26	Earthquake	Ground	Physical	100	100	10	Adjacent
TM27	Return	Normal	Physical	—	100	20	Normal
TM32	Double Team	Normal	Status	—	—	15	Self
TM35	Flamethrower	Fire	Special	90	100	15	Normal
TM37	Sandstorm	Rock	Status	—	—	10	Both Sides
TM38	Fire Blast	Fire	Special	110	85	5	Normal
TM39	Rock Tomb	Rock	Physical	60	95	15	Normal
TM40	Aerial Ace	Flying	Physical	60	—	20	Normal
TM42	Facade	Normal	Physical	70	100	20	Normal
TM44	Rest	Psychic	Status	—	—	10	Self
TM45	Attract	Normal	Status	—	100	15	Normal
TM48	Round	Normal	Special	60	100	15	Normal
TM51	Steel Wing	Steel	Physical	70	90	25	Normal
TM59	Brutal Swing	Dark	Physical	60	100	20	Adjacent
TM68	Giga Impact	Normal	Physical	150	90	5	Normal
TM71	Stone Edge	Rock	Physical	100	80	5	Normal
TM76	Fly	Flying	Physical	90	95	15	Normal
TM78	Bulldoze	Ground	Physical	60	100	20	Adjacent
TM80	Rock Slide	Rock	Physical	75	90	10	Many Others
TM82	Dragon Tail	Dragon	Physical	60	90	10	Normal
TM87	Swagger	Normal	Status	—	85	15	Normal
TM88	Sleep Talk	Normal	Status	—	—	10	Self
TM89	U-turn	Bug	Physical	70	100	20	Normal
TM90	Substitute	Normal	Status	—	—	10	Self
TM100	Confide	Normal	Status	—	—	20	Normal

MOVES TAUGHT BY PEOPLE

Name	Type	Kind	Pow.	Acc.	PP	Range
Draco Meteor	Dragon	Special	130	90	5	Normal

MOVES LEARNED WHEN EVOLVING

Name	Type	Kind	Pow.	Acc.	PP	Range
Dragon Claw	Dragon	Physical	80	100	15	Normal

EGG MOVES

(none)

EXCLUSIVE Z-MOVE

(none)

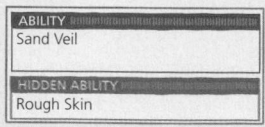

Alola Pokédex	Melemele	Akala	Ula'ula	Poni
238	—	—	110	—

☑ Gible

Land Shark Pokémon

DRAGON **GROUND**

HEIGHT: 2'04"
WEIGHT: 45.2 lbs.

It lives in caves warmed by geothermal heat. Even so, when the weather gets cold, it will huddle close with others of its kind.

It skulks in caves, and when prey or an enemy passes by, it leaps out and chomps them. The force of its attack sometimes chips its teeth.

ABILITY
Sand Veil

HIDDEN ABILITY
Rough Skin

Damage taken in normal battles

NORMAL	×1	FIGHTING	×1	ROCK	×1
FIRE	×0.5	POISON	×0.5	GHOST	×1
WATER	×1	GROUND	×1	DRAGON	×1
GRASS	×1	FLYING	×1	DARK	×1
ELECTRIC	×0	PSYCHIC	×1	STEEL	×1
ICE	×4	BUG	×1	FAIRY	×2

SPECIES STRENGTHS
HP ◆◆
Attack ◆◆◆◆
Defense ◆◆◆
Sp. Atk ◆◆
Sp. Def ◆◆
Speed ◆◆◆

EGG GROUPS
Monster   Dragon

ITEM SOMETIMES HELD BY WILD POKÉMON
—

EVOLUTION

Gible → Lv. 24 → Gabite → Lv. 48 → Garchomp

MAIN WAY TO REGISTER IN THE POKÉDEX
Leave a female Gabite or Garchomp at the Pokémon Nursery with another Pokémon, then hatch the Egg that is found

The male has a notch in its back fin.
The female has no notch in its back fin.

GIBLE 238

Alola Pokédex	Melemele	Akala	Ula'ula	Poni
239	—	—	111	—

☑ Gabite

Cave Pokémon

DRAGON **GROUND**

HEIGHT: 4'07"
WEIGHT: 123.5 lbs.

In rare cases, it molts and sheds its scales. Medicine containing its scales as an ingredient will make a weary body feel invigorated.

Shiny objects are its passion. It can be found in its cave, scarcely moving, its gaze fixed on the jewels it's amassed or Carbink it has caught.

ABILITY
Sand Veil

HIDDEN ABILITY
Rough Skin

Damage taken in normal battles

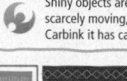

NORMAL	×1	FIGHTING	×1	ROCK	×0.5
FIRE	×0.5	POISON	×0.5	GHOST	×1
WATER	×1	GROUND	×1	DRAGON	×1
GRASS	×1	FLYING	×1	DARK	×1
ELECTRIC	×0	PSYCHIC	×1	STEEL	×1
ICE	×4	BUG	×1	FAIRY	×2

SPECIES STRENGTHS
HP ◆◆◆
Attack ◆◆◆◆◆
Defense ◆◆◆◆
Sp. Atk ◆◆◆
Sp. Def ◆◆◆
Speed ◆◆◆◆◆

EGG GROUPS
Monster   Dragon

ITEM SOMETIMES HELD BY WILD POKÉMON
—

EVOLUTION

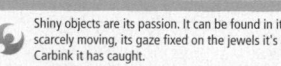

Gible → Lv. 24 → Gabite → Lv. 48 → Garchomp

MAIN WAY TO REGISTER IN THE POKÉDEX
Catch in SOS battles during sandstorms in Haina Desert

The male has a notch in its back fin.
The female has no notch in its back fin.

GABITE 239

Alola Pokédex	Melemele	Akala	Ula'ula	Poni
240	—	—	112	—

☑ Garchomp

Mach Pokémon

DRAGON **GROUND**

HEIGHT: 6'03"
WEIGHT: 209.4 lbs.

It can fly at speeds rivaling jet planes. It dives into flocks of bird Pokémon and gulps the entire flock down whole.

The protuberances on its head serve as sensors. It can even detect distant prey.

ABILITY
Sand Veil

HIDDEN ABILITY
Rough Skin

Damage taken in normal battles

NORMAL	×1	FIGHTING	×1	ROCK	×0.5
FIRE	×0.5	POISON	×0.5	GHOST	×1
WATER	×1	GROUND	×1	DRAGON	×1
GRASS	×1	FLYING	×1	DARK	×1
ELECTRIC	×0	PSYCHIC	×1	STEEL	×1
ICE	×4	BUG	×1	FAIRY	×2

SPECIES STRENGTHS
HP ◆◆◆◆
Attack ◆◆◆◆◆◆
Defense ◆◆◆◆
Sp. Atk ◆◆◆
Sp. Def ◆◆◆◆◆
Speed ◆◆◆◆◆◆

EGG GROUPS
Monster   Dragon

ITEM SOMETIMES HELD BY WILD POKÉMON
—

EVOLUTION

Gible → Lv. 24 → Gabite → Lv. 48 → Garchomp

MAIN WAY TO REGISTER IN THE POKÉDEX
Level up Gabite to Lv. 48

The male has a notch in its back fin.
The female has no notch in its back fin.

GARCHOMP 240

GIBLE 238

LEVEL-UP MOVES

Lv.	Name	Type	Kind	Pow.	Acc.	PP	Range
1	Tackle	Normal	Physical	40	100	35	Normal
3	Sand Attack	Ground	Status	—	100	15	Normal
7	Dragon Rage	Dragon	Special	—	100	10	Normal
13	Sandstorm	Rock	Status	—	—	10	Both Sides
15	Take Down	Normal	Physical	90	85	20	Normal
19	Sand Tomb	Ground	Physical	35	85	15	Normal
25	Slash	Normal	Physical	70	100	20	Normal
27	Dragon Claw	Dragon	Physical	80	100	15	Normal
31	Dig	Ground	Physical	80	100	10	Normal
37	Dragon Rush	Dragon	Physical	100	75	10	Normal

TM MOVES

No.	Name	Type	Kind	Pow.	Acc.	PP	Range
TM02	Dragon Claw	Dragon	Physical	80	100	15	Normal
TM05	Roar	Normal	Status	—	—	20	Normal
TM06	Toxic	Poison	Status	—	90	10	Normal
TM10	Hidden Power	Normal	Special	60	100	15	Normal
TM11	Sunny Day	Fire	Status	—	—	5	Both Sides
TM17	Protect	Normal	Status	—	—	10	Self
TM18	Rain Dance	Water	Status	—	—	5	Both Sides
TM21	Frustration	Normal	Physical	—	100	20	Normal
TM26	Earthquake	Ground	Physical	100	100	10	Adjacent
TM27	Return	Normal	Physical	—	100	20	Normal
TM32	Double Team	Normal	Status	—	—	15	Self
TM35	Flamethrower	Fire	Special	90	100	15	Normal
TM37	Sandstorm	Rock	Status	—	—	10	Both Sides
TM38	Fire Blast	Fire	Special	110	85	5	Normal
TM39	Rock Tomb	Rock	Physical	60	95	15	Normal
TM40	Aerial Ace	Flying	Physical	60	—	20	Normal
TM42	Facade	Normal	Physical	70	100	20	Normal
TM44	Rest	Psychic	Status	—	—	10	Self
TM45	Attract	Normal	Status	—	100	15	Normal
TM48	Round	Normal	Special	60	100	15	Normal
TM65	Shadow Claw	Ghost	Physical	70	100	15	Normal
TM71	Stone Edge	Rock	Physical	100	80	5	Normal
TM78	Bulldoze	Ground	Physical	60	100	20	Adjacent
TM80	Rock Slide	Rock	Physical	75	90	10	Many Others
TM87	Swagger	Normal	Status	—	85	15	Normal
TM88	Sleep Talk	Normal	Status	—	—	10	Self
TM90	Substitute	Normal	Status	—	—	10	Self

No.	Name	Type	Kind	Pow.	Acc.	PP	Range
TM100	Confide	Normal	Status	—	—	20	Normal

MOVES TAUGHT BY PEOPLE

Name	Type	Kind	Pow.	Acc.	PP	Range
Draco Meteor	Dragon	Special	130	90	5	Normal

MOVES LEARNED WHEN EVOLVING

Name	Type	Kind	Pow.	Acc.	PP	Range

EGG MOVES

Name	Type	Kind	Pow.	Acc.	PP	Range
Dragon Breath	Dragon	Special	60	100	20	Normal
Outrage	Dragon	Physical	120	100	10	1 Random
Twister	Dragon	Special	40	100	20	Many Others
Scary Face	Normal	Status	—	100	10	Normal
Double-Edge	Normal	Physical	120	100	15	Normal
Thrash	Normal	Physical	120	100	10	1 Random
Metal Claw	Steel	Physical	50	95	35	Normal
Sand Tomb	Ground	Physical	35	85	15	Normal
Body Slam	Normal	Physical	85	100	15	Normal
Iron Head	Steel	Physical	80	100	15	Normal
Mud Shot	Ground	Special	55	95	15	Normal
Rock Climb	Normal	Physical	90	85	20	Normal
Iron Tail	Steel	Physical	100	75	15	Normal

EXCLUSIVE Z-MOVE

Name	Base Move	Type	Kind	Pow.	Acc.	Range

GABITE 239

LEVEL-UP MOVES

Lv.	Name	Type	Kind	Pow.	Acc.	PP	Range
1	Dual Chop	Dragon	Physical	40	90	15	Normal
1	Tackle	Normal	Physical	40	100	35	Normal
1	Sand Attack	Ground	Status	—	100	15	Normal
1	Dragon Rage	Dragon	Special	—	100	10	Normal
3	Sand Attack	Ground	Status	—	100	15	Normal
7	Dragon Rage	Dragon	Special	—	100	10	Normal
13	Sandstorm	Rock	Status	—	—	10	Both Sides
15	Take Down	Normal	Physical	90	85	20	Normal
19	Sand Tomb	Ground	Physical	35	85	15	Normal
28	Slash	Normal	Physical	70	100	20	Normal
33	Dragon Claw	Dragon	Physical	80	100	15	Normal
40	Dig	Ground	Physical	80	100	10	Normal
49	Dragon Rush	Dragon	Physical	100	75	10	Normal

TM MOVES

No.	Name	Type	Kind	Pow.	Acc.	PP	Range
TM02	Dragon Claw	Dragon	Physical	80	100	15	Normal
TM05	Roar	Normal	Status	—	—	20	Normal
TM06	Toxic	Poison	Status	—	90	10	Normal
TM10	Hidden Power	Normal	Special	60	100	15	Normal
TM11	Sunny Day	Fire	Status	—	—	5	Both Sides
TM17	Protect	Normal	Status	—	—	10	Self
TM18	Rain Dance	Water	Status	—	—	5	Both Sides
TM21	Frustration	Normal	Physical	—	100	20	Normal
TM26	Earthquake	Ground	Physical	100	100	10	Adjacent
TM27	Return	Normal	Physical	—	100	20	Normal
TM32	Double Team	Normal	Status	—	—	15	Self
TM35	Flamethrower	Fire	Special	90	100	15	Normal
TM37	Sandstorm	Rock	Status	—	—	10	Both Sides
TM38	Fire Blast	Fire	Special	110	85	5	Normal
TM39	Rock Tomb	Rock	Physical	60	95	15	Normal
TM40	Aerial Ace	Flying	Physical	60	—	20	Normal
TM42	Facade	Normal	Physical	70	100	20	Normal
TM44	Rest	Psychic	Status	—	—	10	Self
TM45	Attract	Normal	Status	—	100	15	Normal
TM48	Round	Normal	Special	60	100	15	Normal
TM65	Shadow Claw	Ghost	Physical	70	100	15	Normal
TM71	Stone Edge	Rock	Physical	100	80	5	Normal
TM78	Bulldoze	Ground	Physical	60	100	20	Adjacent
TM80	Rock Slide	Rock	Physical	75	90	10	Many Others
TM87	Swagger	Normal	Status	—	85	15	Normal
TM88	Sleep Talk	Normal	Status	—	—	10	Self
TM90	Substitute	Normal	Status	—	—	10	Self

No.	Name	Type	Kind	Pow.	Acc.	PP	Range
TM100	Confide	Normal	Status	—	—	20	Normal

MOVES TAUGHT BY PEOPLE

Name	Type	Kind	Pow.	Acc.	PP	Range
Draco Meteor	Dragon	Special	130	90	5	Normal

MOVES LEARNED WHEN EVOLVING

Name	Type	Kind	Pow.	Acc.	PP	Range
Dual Chop	Dragon	Physical	40	90	15	Normal

EGG MOVES

Name	Type	Kind	Pow.	Acc.	PP	Range

EXCLUSIVE Z-MOVE

Name	Base Move	Type	Kind	Pow.	Acc.	Range

GARCHOMP 240

LEVEL-UP MOVES

Lv.	Name	Type	Kind	Pow.	Acc.	PP	Range
1	Crunch	Dark	Physical	80	100	15	Normal
1	Dual Chop	Dragon	Physical	40	90	15	Normal
1	Fire Fang	Fire	Physical	65	95	15	Normal
1	Tackle	Normal	Physical	40	100	35	Normal
1	Sand Attack	Ground	Status	—	100	15	Normal
1	Dragon Rage	Dragon	Special	—	100	10	Normal
1	Sandstorm	Rock	Status	—	—	10	Both Sides
3	Sand Attack	Ground	Status	—	100	15	Normal
7	Dragon Rage	Dragon	Special	—	100	10	Normal
13	Sandstorm	Rock	Status	—	—	10	Both Sides
15	Take Down	Normal	Physical	90	85	20	Normal
19	Sand Tomb	Ground	Physical	35	85	15	Normal
28	Slash	Normal	Physical	70	100	20	Normal
33	Dragon Claw	Dragon	Physical	80	100	15	Normal
40	Dig	Ground	Physical	80	100	10	Normal
55	Dragon Rush	Dragon	Physical	100	75	10	Normal

TM MOVES

No.	Name	Type	Kind	Pow.	Acc.	PP	Range
TM02	Dragon Claw	Dragon	Physical	80	100	15	Normal
TM05	Roar	Normal	Status	—	—	20	Normal
TM06	Toxic	Poison	Status	—	90	10	Normal
TM10	Hidden Power	Normal	Special	60	100	15	Normal
TM11	Sunny Day	Fire	Status	—	—	5	Both Sides
TM15	Hyper Beam	Normal	Special	150	90	5	Normal
TM17	Protect	Normal	Status	—	—	10	Self
TM18	Rain Dance	Water	Status	—	—	5	Both Sides
TM21	Frustration	Normal	Physical	—	100	20	Normal
TM26	Earthquake	Ground	Physical	100	100	10	Adjacent
TM27	Return	Normal	Physical	—	100	20	Normal
TM31	Brick Break	Fighting	Physical	75	100	15	Normal
TM32	Double Team	Normal	Status	—	—	15	Self
TM35	Flamethrower	Fire	Special	90	100	15	Normal
TM37	Sandstorm	Rock	Status	—	—	10	Both Sides
TM38	Fire Blast	Fire	Special	110	85	5	Normal
TM39	Rock Tomb	Rock	Physical	60	95	15	Normal
TM40	Aerial Ace	Flying	Physical	60	—	20	Normal
TM42	Facade	Normal	Physical	70	100	20	Normal
TM44	Rest	Psychic	Status	—	—	10	Self
TM45	Attract	Normal	Status	—	100	15	Normal
TM48	Round	Normal	Special	60	100	15	Normal
TM54	False Swipe	Normal	Physical	40	100	40	Normal
TM56	Fling	Dark	Physical	—	100	10	Normal
TM59	Brutal Swing	Dark	Physical	60	100	20	Adjacent
TM65	Shadow Claw	Ghost	Physical	70	100	15	Normal
TM68	Giga Impact	Normal	Physical	150	90	5	Normal

No.	Name	Type	Kind	Pow.	Acc.	PP	Range
TM71	Stone Edge	Rock	Physical	100	80	5	Normal
TM75	Swords Dance	Normal	Status	—	—	20	Self
TM78	Bulldoze	Ground	Physical	60	100	20	Adjacent
TM80	Rock Slide	Rock	Physical	75	90	10	Many Others
TM82	Dragon Tail	Dragon	Physical	60	90	10	Normal
TM84	Poison Jab	Poison	Physical	80	100	20	Normal
TM87	Swagger	Normal	Status	—	85	15	Normal
TM88	Sleep Talk	Normal	Status	—	—	10	Self
TM90	Substitute	Normal	Status	—	—	10	Self
TM94	Surf	Water	Special	90	100	15	Adjacent
TM100	Confide	Normal	Status	—	—	20	Normal

MOVES TAUGHT BY PEOPLE

Name	Type	Kind	Pow.	Acc.	PP	Range
Draco Meteor	Dragon	Special	130	90	5	Normal

MOVES LEARNED WHEN EVOLVING

Name	Type	Kind	Pow.	Acc.	PP	Range
Crunch	Dark	Physical	80	100	15	Normal

EGG MOVES

Name	Type	Kind	Pow.	Acc.	PP	Range

EXCLUSIVE Z-MOVE

Name	Base Move	Type	Kind	Pow.	Acc.	Range

Klefki

Key Ring Pokémon

Alola Pokédex	Melemele	Akala	Ula'ula	Poni
241	—	—	113	—

STEEL · FAIRY

HEIGHT: 0'08"
WEIGHT: 6.6 lbs.

This even-tempered Pokémon has a habit of collecting keys. It will sneak into people's homes to steal their keys.

It inserts its horn into chinks in metal, absorbing metal ions. For some reason, it collects keys.

ABILITY
Prankster

HIDDEN ABILITY
Magician

SPECIES STRENGTHS
HP	◆◆
Attack	◆◆◆◆
Defense	◆◆◆◆◆
Sp. Atk	◆◆◆◆
Sp. Def	◆◆◆◆◆
Speed	◆◆◆◆◆

EVOLUTION

Does not evolve

Same form for male/female

Damage taken in normal battles

NORMAL ×0.5	FIGHTING ×1	ROCK ×0.5
FIRE ×2	POISON ×0	GHOST ×1
WATER ×0.5	GROUND ×2	DRAGON ×0
GRASS ×0.5	FLYING ×0.5	DARK ×1
ELECTRIC ×1	PSYCHIC ×0.5	STEEL ×1
ICE ×1	BUG ×0.25	FAIRY ×0.5

EGG GROUPS
Mineral

ITEM SOMETIMES HELD BY WILD POKÉMON
—

MAIN WAY TO REGISTER IN THE POKÉDEX
Catch in the abandoned Thrifty Megamart off Route 14

◆ LEVEL-UP MOVES

Lv.	Name	Type	Kind	Pow.	Acc.	PP	Range
1	Fairy Lock	Fairy	Status	—	—	10	Both Sides
1	Tackle	Normal	Physical	40	100	35	Normal
5	Fairy Wind	Fairy	Special	40	100	30	Normal
8	Astonish	Ghost	Physical	30	100	15	Normal
12	Metal Sound	Steel	Status	—	85	40	Normal
15	Spikes	Ground	Status	—	—	20	Other Side
18	Draining Kiss	Fairy	Special	50	100	10	Normal
23	Crafty Shield	Fairy	Status	—	—	10	Your Side
27	Foul Play	Dark	Physical	95	100	15	Normal
32	Torment	Dark	Status	—	100	15	Normal
34	Mirror Shot	Steel	Special	65	85	10	Normal
36	Imprison	Psychic	Status	—	—	10	Self
40	Recycle	Normal	Status	—	—	10	Self
43	Play Rough	Fairy	Physical	90	90	10	Normal
44	Magic Room	Psychic	Status	—	—	10	Both Sides
50	Heal Block	Psychic	Status	—	100	15	Many Others

◆ TM MOVES

No.	Name	Type	Kind	Pow.	Acc.	PP	Range
TM03	Psyshock	Psychic	Special	80	100	10	Normal
TM04	Calm Mind	Psychic	Status	—	—	20	Self
TM06	Toxic	Poison	Status	—	90	10	Normal
TM10	Hidden Power	Normal	Special	60	100	15	Normal
TM11	Sunny Day	Fire	Status	—	—	5	Both Sides
TM15	Hyper Beam	Normal	Special	150	90	5	Normal
TM16	Light Screen	Psychic	Status	—	—	30	Your Side
TM17	Protect	Normal	Status	—	—	10	Self
TM18	Rain Dance	Water	Status	—	—	5	Both Sides
TM20	Safeguard	Normal	Status	—	—	25	Your Side
TM21	Frustration	Normal	Physical	—	100	20	Normal
TM27	Return	Normal	Physical	—	100	20	Normal
TM29	Psychic	Psychic	Special	90	100	10	Normal
TM32	Double Team	Normal	Status	—	—	15	Self
TM33	Reflect	Psychic	Status	—	—	20	Your Side
TM41	Torment	Dark	Status	—	100	15	Normal
TM42	Facade	Normal	Physical	70	100	20	Normal
TM44	Rest	Psychic	Status	—	—	10	Self
TM45	Attract	Normal	Status	—	100	15	Normal
TM46	Thief	Dark	Physical	60	100	25	Normal
TM48	Round	Normal	Special	60	100	15	Normal
TM68	Giga Impact	Normal	Physical	150	90	5	Normal
TM73	Thunder Wave	Electric	Status	—	90	20	Normal
TM77	Psych Up	Normal	Status	—	—	10	Normal
TM87	Swagger	Normal	Status	—	85	15	Normal
TM88	Sleep Talk	Normal	Status	—	—	10	Self
TM90	Substitute	Normal	Status	—	—	10	Self
TM91	Flash Cannon	Steel	Special	80	100	10	Normal

◆ MOVES TAUGHT BY PEOPLE

No.	Name	Type	Kind	Pow.	Acc.	PP	Range
TM99	Dazzling Gleam	Fairy	Special	80	100	10	Many Others
TM100	Confide	Normal	Status	—	—	20	Normal

◆ MOVES LEARNED WHEN EVOLVING

Name	Type	Kind	Pow.	Acc.	PP	Range

◆ EGG MOVES

Name	Type	Kind	Pow.	Acc.	PP	Range
Switcheroo	Dark	Status	—	100	10	Normal
Thief	Dark	Physical	60	100	25	Normal
Lock-On	Normal	Status	—	—	5	Normal
Iron Defense	Steel	Status	—	—	15	Self

◆ EXCLUSIVE Z-MOVE

Name	Base Move	Type	Kind	Pow.	Acc.	Range

Mimikyu

Disguise Pokémon

Alola Pokédex	Melemele	Akala	Ula'ula	Poni
242	—	—	114	—

GHOST · FAIRY

HEIGHT: 0'08"
WEIGHT: 1.5 lbs.

Its actual appearance is unknown. A scholar who saw what was under its rag was overwhelmed by terror and died from the shock.

A lonely Pokémon, it conceals its terrifying appearance beneath an old rag so it can get closer to people and other Pokémon.

ABILITY
Disguise

HIDDEN ABILITY
—

SPECIES STRENGTHS
HP	◆◆
Attack	◆◆◆◆◆
Defense	◆◆◆◆
Sp. Atk	◆◆◆
Sp. Def	◆◆◆◆◆◆
Speed	◆◆◆◆◆◆

EVOLUTION

Does not evolve

Same form for male/female

Damage taken in normal battles

NORMAL ×0	FIGHTING ×1	ROCK ×1
FIRE ×1	POISON ×1	GHOST ×2
WATER ×1	GROUND ×1	DRAGON ×0
GRASS ×1	FLYING ×1	DARK ×1
ELECTRIC ×1	PSYCHIC ×1	STEEL ×1
ICE ×1	BUG ×0.25	FAIRY ×1

EGG GROUPS
Amorphous

ITEM SOMETIMES HELD BY WILD POKÉMON
Chesto Berry

MAIN WAY TO REGISTER IN THE POKÉDEX
Catch in the abandoned Thrifty Megamart off Route 14

◆ LEVEL-UP MOVES

Lv.	Name	Type	Kind	Pow.	Acc.	PP	Range
1	Wood Hammer	Grass	Physical	120	100	15	Normal
1	Splash	Normal	Status	—	—	40	Self
1	Scratch	Normal	Physical	40	100	35	Normal
1	Astonish	Ghost	Physical	30	100	15	Normal
1	Copycat	Normal	Status	—	—	20	Self
5	Double Team	Normal	Status	—	—	15	Self
10	Baby-Doll Eyes	Fairy	Status	—	100	30	Normal
14	Shadow Sneak	Ghost	Physical	40	100	30	Normal
19	Mimic	Normal	Status	—	—	10	Normal
23	Feint Attack	Dark	Physical	60	—	20	Normal
28	Charm	Fairy	Status	—	100	20	Normal
32	Slash	Normal	Physical	70	100	20	Normal
37	Shadow Claw	Ghost	Physical	70	100	15	Normal
41	Hone Claws	Dark	Status	—	—	15	Self
46	Play Rough	Fairy	Physical	90	90	10	Normal
50	Pain Split	Normal	Status	—	—	20	Normal

◆ TM MOVES

No.	Name	Type	Kind	Pow.	Acc.	PP	Range
TM01	Work Up	Normal	Status	—	—	30	Self
TM06	Toxic	Poison	Status	—	90	10	Normal
TM08	Bulk Up	Fighting	Status	—	—	20	Self
TM10	Hidden Power	Normal	Special	60	100	15	Normal
TM12	Taunt	Dark	Status	—	100	20	Normal
TM15	Hyper Beam	Normal	Special	150	90	5	Normal
TM16	Light Screen	Psychic	Status	—	—	30	Your Side
TM17	Protect	Normal	Status	—	—	10	Self
TM20	Safeguard	Normal	Status	—	—	25	Your Side
TM21	Frustration	Normal	Physical	—	100	20	Normal
TM24	Thunderbolt	Electric	Special	90	100	15	Normal
TM25	Thunder	Electric	Special	110	70	10	Normal
TM27	Return	Normal	Physical	—	100	20	Normal
TM28	Leech Life	Bug	Physical	80	100	10	Normal
TM29	Psychic	Psychic	Special	90	100	10	Normal
TM30	Shadow Ball	Ghost	Special	80	100	15	Normal
TM32	Double Team	Normal	Status	—	—	15	Self
TM42	Facade	Normal	Physical	70	100	20	Normal
TM44	Rest	Psychic	Status	—	—	10	Self
TM45	Attract	Normal	Status	—	100	15	Normal
TM46	Thief	Dark	Physical	60	100	25	Normal
TM48	Round	Normal	Special	60	100	15	Normal
TM56	Fling	Dark	Physical	—	100	10	Normal
TM57	Charge Beam	Electric	Special	50	90	10	Normal
TM61	Will-O-Wisp	Fire	Status	—	85	15	Normal
TM63	Embargo	Dark	Status	—	100	15	Normal
TM65	Shadow Claw	Ghost	Physical	70	100	15	Normal
TM66	Payback	Dark	Physical	50	100	10	Normal

◆ MOVES TAUGHT BY PEOPLE

No.	Name	Type	Kind	Pow.	Acc.	PP	Range
TM73	Thunder Wave	Electric	Status	—	90	20	Normal
TM75	Swords Dance	Normal	Status	—	—	20	Self
TM77	Psych Up	Normal	Status	—	—	10	Normal
TM81	X-Scissor	Bug	Physical	80	100	15	Normal
TM83	Infestation	Bug	Special	20	100	20	Normal
TM85	Dream Eater	Psychic	Special	100	100	15	Normal
TM87	Swagger	Normal	Status	—	85	15	Normal
TM88	Sleep Talk	Normal	Status	—	—	10	Self
TM90	Substitute	Normal	Status	—	—	10	Self
TM92	Trick Room	Psychic	Status	—	—	5	Both Sides
TM97	Dark Pulse	Dark	Special	80	100	15	Normal
TM99	Dazzling Gleam	Fairy	Special	80	100	10	Many Others
TM100	Confide	Normal	Status	—	—	20	Normal

◆ MOVES LEARNED WHEN EVOLVING

Name	Type	Kind	Pow.	Acc.	PP	Range

◆ EGG MOVES

Name	Type	Kind	Pow.	Acc.	PP	Range
Grudge	Ghost	Status	—	—	5	Self
Destiny Bond	Ghost	Status	—	—	5	Self
Curse	Ghost	Status	—	—	10	Varies
Nightmare	Ghost	Status	—	100	15	Normal

◆ EXCLUSIVE Z-MOVE

Name	Base Move	Type	Kind	Pow.	Acc.	Range

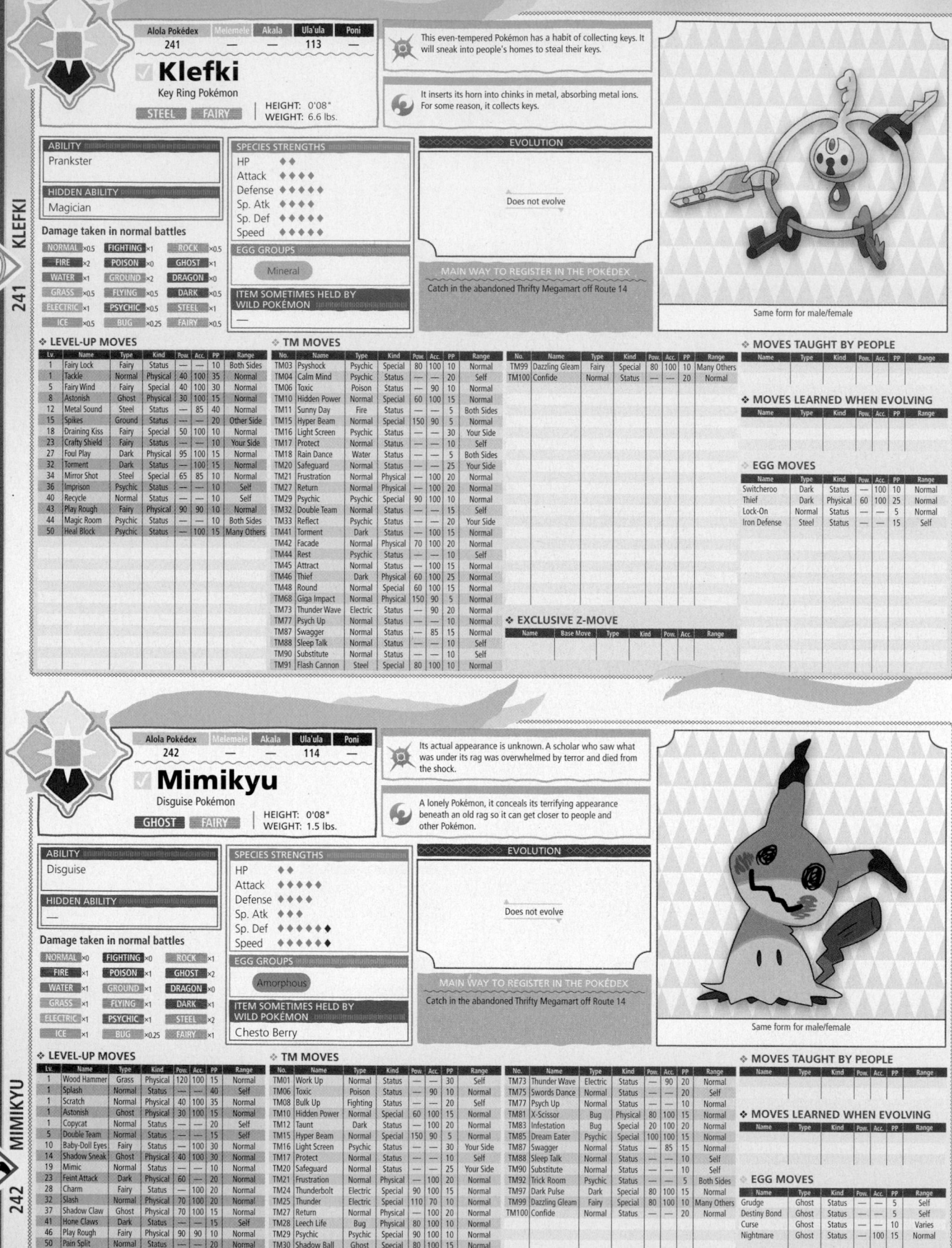

Pokémon Ghost Stories

Mimikyu's history may sound sad, but it is hardly the only Pokémon to have a dark backstory. A surprising number of Pokémon have origins shrouded in mystery and misery. If you're not the type to get easily spooked, read on for a selection of some of the scariest and saddest Pokémon found in Alola!

Mimikyu

Mimikyu lives its life completely covered by its cloth and is always hidden. People believe that anybody who sees its true form beneath the cloth will have something dire happen to them. People in the Alola region are convinced that you must never try to peek beneath its covering. Mimikyu's health fails when it's bathed in the rays of the sun, so it prefers to stick to dark places. It's rumored that the reason it covers itself with a cloth is to avoid sunlight. The rising popularity of Pikachu-styled merchandise around 20 years ago is the reason that Mimikyu makes itself look like Pikachu. In fact, this Pokémon is dreadfully lonely, and it thought it would be able to make friends with humans if only it looked like Pikachu.

Mimikyu's Busted Form

Mimikyu's Disguise Ability prevents it from taking damage from the first attack to strike it. But once it is hit, its disguise will get busted and it will thereafter be as vulnerable as any other Pokémon. More importantly, perhaps, it will also be rather downtrodden to see its precious disguise damaged.

The wild Mimikyu's disguise was busted!

 It had gone to all the effort of disguising itself, but its neck broke. Whatever is inside is probably unharmed, but it is still sad.

 If its neck is broken or its rag is torn during an attack, it works through the night to patch it.

Minior

Minior is the Meteor Pokémon. It emerges from mutated nanoparticles and usually lives in the atmosphere, feeding on dust and detritus. As it feeds and grows, the shell surrounding a Minior grows thicker and thicker until it grows too heavy, upon which time the Minior will fall helplessly to the planet's surface. A strong impact will cause Minior's shell to break, which makes it lighter and faster, but a Minior cannot survive long once its core is exposed. It faces impending destruction unless it is safely encapsulated in a Poké Ball by a quick-thinking Trainer.

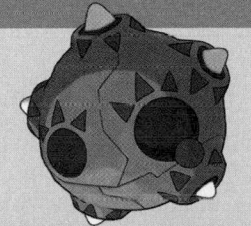

Palossand

Palossand controls human adults, making them build a sand castle that provides camouflage and also raises its defensive abilities. Unlike Sandygast, if Palossand loses some of the sand from its body, it can restore itself on its own. When moving about in search of prey, the shovel on top of Palossand's head revolves. It's said that the shovel could be serving as some kind of radar. Palossand loves the vitality of Pokémon and drags small Pokémon into its body so it can steal their life force. Its sandy vortex swallows them up in a heartbeat! Pokémon dragged into Palossand leave traces of their ill will behind. It's thought that this negative energy may be the starting point of new Sandygast...

Alolan Marowak

Alolan Marowak is a Fire- and Ghost-type Pokémon, and it is said that the burning bone it carries once belonged to its mother. Marowak is thought to be protected by the spirit of its lost mother, whose regrets have transformed it into something like a vengeful spirit. Alolan Marowak care deeply for one another and they live in close union with their partners, mourning for any lost companions. If you find mounds of dirt by the side of the road, then know that you have stumbled upon the graves of fallen Marowak.

Bruxish

Alola Pokédex	Melemele	Akala	Ula'ula	Poni
243	—		115	

Bruxish
Gnash Teeth Pokémon

WATER | PSYCHIC

HEIGHT: 2'11"
WEIGHT: 41.9 lbs.

When it unleashes its psychic power from the protuberance on its head, the grating sound of grinding teeth echoes through the area.

It stuns its prey with psychokinesis and then grinds them to mush with its strong teeth. Even Shellder's shell is no match for it.

Same form for male/female

ABILITY
Dazzling
Strong Jaw

HIDDEN ABILITY
Wonder Skin

SPECIES STRENGTHS
HP ◆◆◆
Attack ◆◆◆◆◆◆
Defense ◆◆◆◆
Sp. Atk ◆◆◆
Sp. Def ◆◆◆◆
Speed ◆◆◆◆◆◆

EGG GROUPS
Water 2

ITEM SOMETIMES HELD BY WILD POKÉMON
Razor Fang

EVOLUTION
Does not evolve

MAIN WAY TO REGISTER IN THE POKÉDEX
Catch in the rare fishing spot on the Secluded Shore off Route 12

Damage taken in normal battles

NORMAL ×1	FIGHTING ×0.5	ROCK ×1			
FIRE ×0.5	POISON ×1	GHOST ×1			
WATER ×0.5	GROUND ×1	DRAGON ×1			
GRASS ×2	FLYING ×1	DARK ×1			
ELECTRIC ×2	PSYCHIC ×0.5	STEEL ×0.5			
ICE ×1	BUG ×2	FAIRY ×1			

❖ LEVEL-UP MOVES

Lv.	Name	Type	Kind	Pow.	Acc.	PP	Range
1	Water Gun	Water	Special	40	100	25	Normal
4	Astonish	Ghost	Physical	30	100	15	Normal
9	Confusion	Psychic	Special	50	100	25	Normal
12	Bite	Dark	Physical	60	100	25	Normal
17	Aqua Jet	Water	Physical	40	100	20	Normal
20	Disable	Normal	Status	—	100	20	Normal
25	Psywave	Psychic	Special	—	100	15	Normal
28	Crunch	Dark	Physical	80	100	15	Normal
33	Aqua Tail	Water	Physical	90	90	10	Normal
36	Screech	Normal	Status	—	85	40	Normal
41	Psychic Fangs	Psychic	Physical	85	100	10	Normal
44	Synchronoise	Psychic	Special	120	100	10	Adjacent

❖ TM MOVES

No.	Name	Type	Kind	Pow.	Acc.	PP	Range
TM04	Calm Mind	Psychic	Status	—	—	20	Self
TM06	Toxic	Poison	Status	—	90	10	Normal
TM08	Bulk Up	Fighting	Status	—	—	20	Self
TM09	Venoshock	Poison	Special	65	100	10	Normal
TM10	Hidden Power	Normal	Special	60	100	15	Normal
TM12	Taunt	Dark	Status	—	100	20	Normal
TM13	Ice Beam	Ice	Special	90	100	10	Normal
TM14	Blizzard	Ice	Special	110	70	5	Many Others
TM16	Light Screen	Psychic	Status	—	—	30	Your Side
TM17	Protect	Normal	Status	—	—	10	Self
TM18	Rain Dance	Water	Status	—	—	5	Both Sides
TM20	Safeguard	Normal	Status	—	—	25	Your Side
TM21	Frustration	Normal	Physical	—	100	20	Normal
TM27	Return	Normal	Physical	—	100	20	Normal
TM29	Psychic	Psychic	Special	90	100	10	Normal
TM32	Double Team	Normal	Status	—	—	15	Self
TM33	Reflect	Psychic	Status	—	—	20	Your Side
TM40	Aerial Ace	Flying	Physical	60	—	20	Normal
TM41	Torment	Dark	Status	—	100	15	Normal
TM42	Facade	Normal	Physical	70	100	20	Normal
TM44	Rest	Psychic	Status	—	—	10	Self
TM45	Attract	Normal	Status	—	100	15	Normal
TM48	Round	Normal	Special	60	100	15	Normal
TM55	Scald	Water	Special	80	100	15	Normal
TM56	Fling	Dark	Physical	—	100	10	Normal
TM63	Embargo	Dark	Status	—	100	15	Normal
TM66	Payback	Dark	Physical	50	100	10	Normal
TM68	Giga Impact	Normal	Physical	150	90	5	Normal

No.	Name	Type	Kind	Pow.	Acc.	PP	Range
TM75	Swords Dance	Normal	Status	—	—	20	Self
TM79	Frost Breath	Ice	Special	60	90	10	Normal
TM85	Dream Eater	Psychic	Special	100	100	15	Normal
TM87	Swagger	Normal	Status	—	85	15	Normal
TM88	Sleep Talk	Normal	Status	—	—	10	Self
TM90	Substitute	Normal	Status	—	—	10	Self
TM92	Trick Room	Psychic	Status	—	—	5	Both Sides
TM94	Surf	Water	Special	90	100	15	Adjacent
TM98	Waterfall	Water	Physical	80	100	15	Normal
TM100	Confide	Normal	Status	—	—	20	Normal

❖ MOVES TAUGHT BY PEOPLE

Name	Type	Kind	Pow.	Acc.	PP	Range

❖ MOVES LEARNED WHEN EVOLVING

Name	Type	Kind	Pow.	Acc.	PP	Range

EGG MOVES

Name	Type	Kind	Pow.	Acc.	PP	Range
Water Pulse	Water	Special	60	100	20	Normal
Poison Fang	Poison	Physical	50	100	15	Normal
Ice Fang	Ice	Physical	65	95	15	Normal
Rage	Normal	Physical	20	100	20	Normal

❖ EXCLUSIVE Z-MOVE

Name	Base Move	Type	Kind	Pow.	Acc.	Range

Drampa

Alola Pokédex	Melemele	Akala	Ula'ula	Poni
244	—	—		116

Drampa
Placid Pokémon

NORMAL | DRAGON

HEIGHT: 9'10"
WEIGHT: 407.9 lbs.

It has a compassionate personality, but if it is angered, it completely destroys its surroundings with its intense breath.

This Pokémon is friendly to people and loves children most of all. It comes from deep in the mountains to play with children it likes in town.

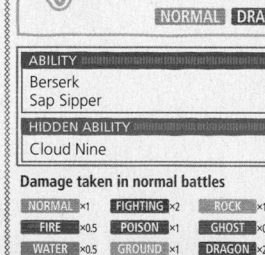

Same form for male/female

ABILITY
Berserk
Sap Sipper

HIDDEN ABILITY
Cloud Nine

SPECIES STRENGTHS
HP ◆◆◆
Attack ◆◆◆
Defense ◆◆◆◆◆
Sp. Atk ◆◆◆◆◆◆◆
Sp. Def ◆◆◆◆
Speed ◆◆

EGG GROUPS
Monster | Dragon

ITEM SOMETIMES HELD BY WILD POKÉMON
Persim Berry

EVOLUTION
Does not evolve

MAIN WAY TO REGISTER IN THE POKÉDEX
Obtain in a trade in *Pokémon Sun* / Catch in the cave on Mount Lanakila in *Pokémon Moon*

Damage taken in normal battles

NORMAL ×1	FIGHTING ×2	ROCK ×1			
FIRE ×0.5	POISON ×1	GHOST ×0			
WATER ×0.5	GROUND ×1	DRAGON ×2			
GRASS ×0.5	FLYING ×1	DARK ×1			
ELECTRIC ×0.5	PSYCHIC ×1	STEEL ×1			
ICE ×2	BUG ×1	FAIRY ×2			

❖ LEVEL-UP MOVES

Lv.	Name	Type	Kind	Pow.	Acc.	PP	Range
1	Play Nice	Normal	Status	—	—	20	Normal
1	Echoed Voice	Normal	Special	40	100	15	Normal
5	Twister	Dragon	Special	40	100	20	Many Others
9	Protect	Normal	Status	—	—	10	Self
13	Glare	Normal	Status	—	100	30	Normal
17	Light Screen	Psychic	Status	—	—	30	Your Side
21	Dragon Rage	Dragon	Special	—	100	10	Normal
25	Natural Gift	Normal	Physical	—	100	15	Normal
29	Dragon Breath	Dragon	Special	60	100	20	Normal
33	Safeguard	Normal	Status	—	—	25	Your Side
37	Extrasensory	Psychic	Special	80	100	20	Normal
41	Dragon Pulse	Dragon	Special	85	100	10	Normal
45	Fly	Flying	Physical	90	95	15	Normal
49	Hyper Voice	Normal	Special	90	100	10	Many Others
53	Outrage	Dragon	Physical	120	100	10	1 Random

❖ TM MOVES

No.	Name	Type	Kind	Pow.	Acc.	PP	Range
TM01	Work Up	Normal	Status	—	—	30	Self
TM02	Dragon Claw	Dragon	Physical	80	100	15	Normal
TM04	Calm Mind	Psychic	Status	—	—	20	Self
TM05	Roar	Normal	Status	—	—	20	Normal
TM06	Toxic	Poison	Status	—	90	10	Normal
TM10	Hidden Power	Normal	Special	60	100	15	Normal
TM11	Sunny Day	Fire	Status	—	—	5	Both Sides
TM13	Ice Beam	Ice	Special	90	100	10	Normal
TM14	Blizzard	Ice	Special	110	70	5	Many Others
TM15	Hyper Beam	Normal	Special	150	90	5	Normal
TM16	Light Screen	Psychic	Status	—	—	30	Your Side
TM17	Protect	Normal	Status	—	—	10	Self
TM18	Rain Dance	Water	Status	—	—	5	Both Sides
TM19	Roost	Flying	Status	—	—	10	Self
TM20	Safeguard	Normal	Status	—	—	25	Your Side
TM21	Frustration	Normal	Physical	—	100	20	Normal
TM22	Solar Beam	Grass	Special	120	100	10	Normal
TM24	Thunderbolt	Electric	Special	90	100	15	Normal
TM25	Thunder	Electric	Special	110	70	10	Normal
TM26	Earthquake	Ground	Physical	100	100	10	Adjacent
TM27	Return	Normal	Physical	—	100	20	Normal
TM30	Shadow Ball	Ghost	Special	80	100	15	Normal
TM32	Double Team	Normal	Status	—	—	15	Self
TM35	Flamethrower	Fire	Special	90	100	15	Normal
TM38	Fire Blast	Fire	Special	110	85	5	Normal
TM42	Facade	Normal	Physical	70	100	20	Normal
TM44	Rest	Psychic	Status	—	—	10	Self
TM45	Attract	Normal	Status	—	100	15	Normal

No.	Name	Type	Kind	Pow.	Acc.	PP	Range
TM48	Round	Normal	Special	60	100	15	Normal
TM49	Echoed Voice	Normal	Special	40	100	15	Normal
TM51	Steel Wing	Steel	Physical	70	90	25	Normal
TM52	Focus Blast	Fighting	Special	120	70	5	Normal
TM53	Energy Ball	Grass	Special	90	100	10	Normal
TM56	Fling	Dark	Physical	—	100	10	Normal
TM65	Shadow Claw	Ghost	Physical	70	100	15	Normal
TM68	Giga Impact	Normal	Physical	150	90	5	Normal
TM73	Thunder Wave	Electric	Status	—	90	20	Normal
TM76	Fly	Flying	Physical	90	95	15	Normal
TM77	Psych Up	Normal	Status	—	—	10	Normal
TM78	Bulldoze	Ground	Physical	60	100	20	Adjacent
TM80	Rock Slide	Rock	Physical	75	90	10	Many Others
TM82	Dragon Tail	Dragon	Physical	60	90	10	Normal
TM86	Grass Knot	Grass	Special	—	100	20	Normal
TM88	Sleep Talk	Normal	Status	—	—	10	Self
TM90	Substitute	Normal	Status	—	—	10	Self
TM94	Surf	Water	Special	90	100	15	Adjacent
TM95	Snarl	Dark	Special	55	95	15	Many Others
TM96	Nature Power	Normal	Status	—	—	20	Normal
TM100	Confide	Normal	Status	—	—	20	Normal

❖ MOVES TAUGHT BY PEOPLE

Name	Type	Kind	Pow.	Acc.	PP	Range
Draco Meteor	Dragon	Special	130	90	5	Normal

❖ MOVES LEARNED WHEN EVOLVING

Name	Type	Kind	Pow.	Acc.	PP	Range

EGG MOVES

Name	Type	Kind	Pow.	Acc.	PP	Range
Hurricane	Flying	Special	110	70	10	Normal
Dragon Rush	Dragon	Physical	100	75	10	Normal
Razor Wind	Normal	Special	80	100	10	Many Others
Mist	Ice	Status	—	—	30	Your Side
Play Rough	Fairy	Physical	90	90	10	Normal

❖ EXCLUSIVE Z-MOVE

Name	Base Move	Type	Kind	Pow.	Acc.	Range

Absol
Disaster Pokémon

DARK

Alola Pokédex			
245	—	—	117
Melemele	Akala	Ula'ula	Poni

HEIGHT: 3'11"
WEIGHT: 103.6 lbs.

Long ago, superstitions were spread about it, saying it brought disaster. This fed a hatred of it, and it was driven deep into the mountains.

Although it's said to bring disaster, in actuality, this Pokémon possesses a calm disposition and warns people of any crises that loom.

Same form for male/female
n. 712

ABILITY
Pressure
Super Luck

HIDDEN ABILITY
Justified

SPECIES STRENGTHS
HP	◆◆◆
Attack	◆◆◆◆◆◆◆
Defense	◆◆◆
Sp. Atk	◆◆◆◆
Sp. Def	◆◆◆
Speed	◆◆◆◆◆

EVOLUTION
Does not evolve

Damage taken in normal battles
NORMAL	×1	FIGHTING	×2	ROCK	×1
FIRE	×1	POISON	×1	GHOST	×0.5
WATER	×1	GROUND	×1	DRAGON	×1
GRASS	×1	FLYING	×1	DARK	×0.5
ELECTRIC	×1	PSYCHIC	×0	STEEL	×1
ICE	×1	BUG	×2	FAIRY	×2

EGG GROUPS
Field

ITEM SOMETIMES HELD BY WILD POKÉMON
—

MAIN WAY TO REGISTER IN THE POKÉDEX
Catch in the tall grass or the cave on Mount Lanakila.

❖ LEVEL-UP MOVES
Lv.	Name	Type	Kind	Pow.	Acc.	PP	Range
1	Perish Song	Normal	Status	—	—	5	Adjacent
1	Future Sight	Psychic	Special	120	100	10	Normal
1	Scratch	Normal	Physical	40	100	35	Normal
1	Feint	Normal	Physical	30	100	10	Normal
1	Leer	Normal	Status	—	100	30	Many Others
1	Quick Attack	Normal	Physical	40	100	30	Normal
4	Leer	Normal	Status	—	100	30	Many Others
7	Quick Attack	Normal	Physical	40	100	30	Normal
10	Pursuit	Dark	Physical	40	100	20	Normal
13	Taunt	Dark	Status	—	100	20	Normal
16	Bite	Dark	Physical	60	100	25	Normal
19	Double Team	Normal	Status	—	—	15	Self
22	Slash	Normal	Physical	70	100	20	Normal
25	Swords Dance	Normal	Status	—	—	20	Self
29	Night Slash	Dark	Physical	70	100	15	Normal
33	Detect	Fighting	Status	—	—	5	Self
37	Psycho Cut	Psychic	Physical	70	100	20	Normal
41	Me First	Normal	Status	—	—	20	Varies
45	Sucker Punch	Dark	Physical	70	100	5	Normal
49	Razor Wind	Normal	Special	80	100	10	Many Others
53	Future Sight	Psychic	Special	120	100	10	Normal
57	Perish Song	Normal	Status	—	—	5	Adjacent

❖ TM MOVES
No.	Name	Type	Kind	Pow.	Acc.	PP	Range
TM04	Calm Mind	Psychic	Status	—	—	20	Self
TM06	Toxic	Poison	Status	—	90	10	Normal
TM07	Hail	Ice	Status	—	—	10	Both Sides
TM10	Hidden Power	Normal	Special	60	100	15	Normal
TM11	Sunny Day	Fire	Status	—	—	5	Both Sides
TM12	Taunt	Dark	Status	—	100	20	Normal
TM13	Ice Beam	Ice	Special	90	100	10	Normal
TM14	Blizzard	Ice	Special	110	70	5	Many Others
TM15	Hyper Beam	Normal	Special	150	90	5	Normal
TM17	Protect	Normal	Status	—	—	10	Self
TM18	Rain Dance	Water	Status	—	—	5	Both Sides
TM21	Frustration	Normal	Physical	—	100	20	Normal
TM24	Thunderbolt	Electric	Special	90	100	15	Normal
TM25	Thunder	Electric	Special	110	70	10	Normal
TM27	Return	Normal	Physical	—	100	20	Normal
TM30	Shadow Ball	Ghost	Special	80	100	15	Normal
TM32	Double Team	Normal	Status	—	—	15	Self
TM35	Flamethrower	Fire	Special	90	100	15	Normal
TM37	Sandstorm	Rock	Status	—	—	10	Both Sides
TM38	Fire Blast	Fire	Special	110	85	5	Normal
TM39	Rock Tomb	Rock	Physical	60	95	15	Normal
TM40	Aerial Ace	Flying	Physical	60	—	20	Normal
TM41	Torment	Dark	Status	—	100	15	Normal
TM42	Facade	Normal	Physical	70	100	20	Normal
TM44	Rest	Psychic	Status	—	—	10	Self
TM45	Attract	Normal	Status	—	100	15	Normal
TM46	Thief	Dark	Physical	60	100	25	Normal
TM48	Round	Normal	Special	60	100	15	Normal
TM49	Echoed Voice	Normal	Special	40	100	15	Normal
TM54	False Swipe	Normal	Physical	40	100	40	Normal
TM57	Charge Beam	Electric	Special	50	90	10	Normal
TM59	Brutal Swing	Dark	Physical	60	100	20	Adjacent
TM61	Will-O-Wisp	Fire	Status	—	85	15	Normal
TM65	Shadow Claw	Ghost	Physical	70	100	15	Normal
TM66	Payback	Dark	Physical	50	100	10	Normal
TM68	Giga Impact	Normal	Physical	150	90	5	Normal
TM71	Stone Edge	Rock	Physical	100	80	5	Normal
TM73	Thunder Wave	Electric	Status	—	90	20	Normal
TM75	Swords Dance	Normal	Status	—	—	20	Self
TM77	Psych Up	Normal	Status	—	—	10	Normal
TM81	X-Scissor	Bug	Physical	80	100	15	Normal
TM85	Dream Eater	Psychic	Special	100	100	15	Normal
TM87	Swagger	Normal	Status	—	85	15	Normal
TM88	Sleep Talk	Normal	Status	—	—	10	Self
TM90	Substitute	Normal	Status	—	—	10	Self
TM95	Snarl	Dark	Special	55	95	15	Many Others
TM99	Dark Pulse	Dark	Special	80	100	15	Normal
TM100	Confide	Normal	Status	—	—	20	Normal

❖ EXCLUSIVE Z-MOVE
Name	Base Move	Type	Kind	Pow.	Acc.	Range

❖ MOVES TAUGHT BY PEOPLE
Name	Type	Kind	Pow.	Acc.	PP	Range

❖ MOVES LEARNED WHEN EVOLVING
Name	Type	Kind	Pow.	Acc.	PP	Range

❖ EGG MOVES
Name	Type	Kind	Pow.	Acc.	PP	Range
Baton Pass	Normal	Status	—	—	40	Self
Feint Attack	Dark	Physical	60	—	20	Normal
Double-Edge	Normal	Physical	120	100	15	Normal
Magic Coat	Psychic	Status	—	—	15	Self
Curse	Ghost	Status	—	—	10	Varies
Mean Look	Normal	Status	—	—	5	Normal
Zen Headbutt	Psychic	Physical	80	90	15	Normal
Punishment	Dark	Physical	—	100	5	Normal
Sucker Punch	Dark	Physical	70	100	5	Normal
Assurance	Dark	Physical	60	100	10	Normal
Me First	Normal	Status	—	—	20	Varies
Megahorn	Bug	Physical	120	85	10	Normal
Hex	Ghost	Special	65	100	10	Normal
Perish Song	Normal	Status	—	—	5	Adjacent
Play Rough	Fairy	Physical	90	90	10	Normal

Snorunt

Snow Hat Pokémon

Alola Pokédex	Melemele	Akala	Ula'ula	Poni
246	—	—	118	—

ICE

HEIGHT: 2'04"
WEIGHT: 37.0 lbs.

Their numbers seem to have rapidly increased in Alola. Custom has it that houses where Snorunt live will be prosperous for generations to come.

It can only survive in cold areas. It bounces happily around, even in environments as cold as -150 degrees Fahrenheit.

ABILITY
Inner Focus
Ice Body

HIDDEN ABILITY
Moody

Damage taken in normal battles

NORMAL ×1	FIGHTING ×2	ROCK ×2
FIRE ×2	POISON ×1	GHOST ×1
WATER ×1	GROUND ×1	DRAGON ×1
GRASS ×1	FLYING ×1	DARK ×1
ELECTRIC ×1	PSYCHIC ×1	STEEL ×1
ICE ×0.5	BUG ×1	FAIRY ×1

SPECIES STRENGTHS
HP ◆◆
Attack ◆◆
Defense ◆◆◆
Sp. Atk ◆◆◆
Sp. Def ◆◆◆
Speed ◆◆

EGG GROUPS
Fairy   Mineral

ITEM SOMETIMES HELD BY WILD POKÉMON
Snowball

MAIN WAY TO REGISTER IN THE POKÉDEX
Catch in the tall grass or the cave on Mount Lanakila

EVOLUTION

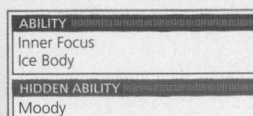

Snorunt → Lv. 42 → Glalie

Use a Dawn Stone on a female Snorunt

Froslass

Same form for male/female

Glalie

Face Pokémon

Alola Pokédex	Melemele	Akala	Ula'ula	Poni
247	—	—	119	—

ICE

HEIGHT: 4'11"
WEIGHT: 565.5 lbs.

Legend says a boulder on an icy mountain absorbed the distress and regrets of a stranded mountaineer, giving rise to Glalie.

Its prey is instantaneously frozen stiff by the cold air it exhales from its huge mouth. While they're in that frozen state, it gobbles them up.

ABILITY
Inner Focus
Ice Body

HIDDEN ABILITY
Moody

Damage taken in normal battles

NORMAL ×1	FIGHTING ×2	ROCK ×2
FIRE ×2	POISON ×1	GHOST ×1
WATER ×1	GROUND ×1	DRAGON ×1
GRASS ×1	FLYING ×1	DARK ×1
ELECTRIC ×1	PSYCHIC ×1	STEEL ×1
ICE ×0.5	BUG ×1	FAIRY ×1

SPECIES STRENGTHS
HP ◆◆◆
Attack ◆◆◆◆
Defense ◆◆◆◆
Sp. Atk ◆◆◆◆
Sp. Def ◆◆◆◆
Speed ◆◆◆◆◆

EGG GROUPS
Fairy   Mineral

ITEM SOMETIMES HELD BY WILD POKÉMON
—

MAIN WAY TO REGISTER IN THE POKÉDEX
Catch in SOS battles in the tall grass or the cave on Mount Lanakila

EVOLUTION

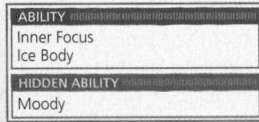

Snorunt → Lv. 42 → Glalie

p. 212

Same form for male/female

Froslass

Snow Land Pokémon

Alola Pokédex	Melemele	Akala	Ula'ula	Poni
248	—	—	120	—

ICE   GHOST

HEIGHT: 4'03"
WEIGHT: 58.6 lbs.

When it finds humans or Pokémon it likes, it freezes them and takes them to its chilly den, where they become decorations.

The soul of a woman lost on a snowy mountain possessed an icicle, becoming this Pokémon. The food it most relishes is the souls of men.

ABILITY
Snow Cloak

HIDDEN ABILITY
Cursed Body

Damage taken in normal battles

NORMAL ×0	FIGHTING ×0	ROCK ×2
FIRE ×2	POISON ×0.5	GHOST ×2
WATER ×1	GROUND ×1	DRAGON ×1
GRASS ×1	FLYING ×1	DARK ×1
ELECTRIC ×1	PSYCHIC ×1	STEEL ×1
ICE ×0.5	BUG ×0.5	FAIRY ×1

SPECIES STRENGTHS
HP ◆◆◆
Attack ◆◆◆◆
Defense ◆◆◆◆
Sp. Atk ◆◆◆◆
Sp. Def ◆◆◆◆
Speed ◆◆◆◆◆◆◆

EGG GROUPS
Fairy   Mineral

ITEM SOMETIMES HELD BY WILD POKÉMON
—

MAIN WAY TO REGISTER IN THE POKÉDEX
Use a Dawn Stone on a female Snorunt

EVOLUTION

Snorunt → Use a Dawn Stone on a female Snorunt → Froslass

Female only

SNORUNT

LEVEL-UP MOVES

Lv.	Name	Type	Kind	Pow.	Acc.	PP	Range
1	Powder Snow	Ice	Special	40	100	25	Many Others
1	Leer	Normal	Status	—	100	30	Many Others
5	Double Team	Normal	Status	—	—	15	Self
10	Ice Shard	Ice	Physical	40	100	30	Normal
14	Icy Wind	Ice	Special	55	95	15	Many Others
19	Bite	Dark	Physical	60	100	25	Normal
23	Ice Fang	Ice	Physical	65	95	15	Normal
28	Headbutt	Normal	Physical	70	100	15	Normal
32	Protect	Normal	Status	—	—	10	Self
37	Frost Breath	Ice	Special	60	90	15	Normal
41	Crunch	Dark	Physical	80	100	15	Normal
46	Blizzard	Ice	Special	110	70	5	Many Others
50	Hail	Ice	Status	—	—	10	Both Sides

TM MOVES

No.	Name	Type	Kind	Pow.	Acc.	PP	Range
TM06	Toxic	Poison	Status	—	90	10	Normal
TM07	Hail	Ice	Status	—	—	10	Both Sides
TM10	Hidden Power	Normal	Special	60	100	15	Normal
TM13	Ice Beam	Ice	Special	90	100	10	Normal
TM14	Blizzard	Ice	Special	110	70	5	Many Others
TM16	Light Screen	Psychic	Status	—	—	30	Your Side
TM17	Protect	Normal	Status	—	—	10	Self
TM18	Rain Dance	Water	Status	—	—	5	Both Sides
TM20	Safeguard	Normal	Status	—	—	25	Your Side
TM21	Frustration	Normal	Physical	—	100	20	Normal
TM27	Return	Normal	Physical	—	100	20	Normal
TM30	Shadow Ball	Ghost	Special	80	100	15	Normal
TM32	Double Team	Normal	Status	—	—	15	Self
TM42	Facade	Normal	Physical	70	100	20	Normal
TM44	Rest	Psychic	Status	—	—	10	Self
TM45	Attract	Normal	Status	—	100	15	Normal
TM48	Round	Normal	Special	60	100	15	Normal
TM79	Frost Breath	Ice	Special	60	90	10	Normal
TM87	Swagger	Normal	Status	—	85	15	Normal
TM88	Sleep Talk	Normal	Status	—	—	10	Self
TM90	Substitute	Normal	Status	—	—	10	Self
TM100	Confide	Normal	Status	—	—	20	Normal

MOVES TAUGHT BY PEOPLE

Name	Type	Kind	Pow.	Acc.	PP	Range

MOVES LEARNED WHEN EVOLVING

Name	Type	Kind	Pow.	Acc.	PP	Range

EGG MOVES

Name	Type	Kind	Pow.	Acc.	PP	Range
Block	Normal	Status	—	—	5	Normal
Spikes	Ground	Status	—	—	20	Other Side
Rollout	Rock	Physical	30	90	20	Normal
Disable	Normal	Status	—	100	20	Normal
Bide	Normal	Physical	—	—	10	Self
Weather Ball	Normal	Special	50	100	10	Normal
Avalanche	Ice	Physical	60	100	10	Normal
Hex	Ghost	Special	65	100	10	Normal
Fake Tears	Dark	Status	—	100	20	Normal
Switcheroo	Dark	Status	—	100	10	Normal

EXCLUSIVE Z-MOVE

Name	Base Move	Type	Kind	Pow.	Acc.	Range

GLALIE

LEVEL-UP MOVES

Lv.	Name	Type	Kind	Pow.	Acc.	PP	Range
1	Freeze-Dry	Ice	Special	70	100	20	Normal
1	Sheer Cold	Ice	Special	—	30	5	Normal
1	Powder Snow	Ice	Special	40	100	25	Many Others
1	Leer	Normal	Status	—	100	30	Many Others
1	Double Team	Normal	Status	—	—	15	Self
1	Ice Shard	Ice	Physical	40	100	30	Normal
5	Double Team	Normal	Status	—	—	15	Self
10	Ice Shard	Ice	Physical	40	100	30	Normal
14	Icy Wind	Ice	Special	55	95	15	Many Others
19	Bite	Dark	Physical	60	100	25	Normal
23	Ice Fang	Ice	Physical	65	95	15	Normal
28	Headbutt	Normal	Physical	70	100	15	Normal
32	Protect	Normal	Status	—	—	10	Self
37	Frost Breath	Ice	Special	60	90	10	Normal
41	Crunch	Dark	Physical	80	100	15	Normal
48	Blizzard	Ice	Special	110	70	5	Many Others
54	Hail	Ice	Status	—	—	10	Both Sides
61	Sheer Cold	Ice	Special	—	30	5	Normal

TM MOVES

No.	Name	Type	Kind	Pow.	Acc.	PP	Range
TM06	Toxic	Poison	Status	—	90	10	Normal
TM07	Hail	Ice	Status	—	—	10	Both Sides
TM10	Hidden Power	Normal	Special	60	100	15	Normal
TM12	Taunt	Dark	Status	—	100	20	Normal
TM13	Ice Beam	Ice	Special	90	100	10	Normal
TM14	Blizzard	Ice	Special	110	70	5	Many Others
TM15	Hyper Beam	Normal	Special	150	90	5	Normal
TM16	Light Screen	Psychic	Status	—	—	30	Your Side
TM17	Protect	Normal	Status	—	—	10	Self
TM18	Rain Dance	Water	Status	—	—	5	Both Sides
TM20	Safeguard	Normal	Status	—	—	25	Your Side
TM21	Frustration	Normal	Physical	—	100	20	Normal
TM26	Earthquake	Ground	Physical	100	100	10	Adjacent
TM27	Return	Normal	Physical	—	100	20	Normal
TM30	Shadow Ball	Ghost	Special	80	100	15	Normal
TM32	Double Team	Normal	Status	—	—	15	Self
TM41	Torment	Dark	Status	—	100	15	Normal
TM42	Facade	Normal	Physical	70	100	20	Normal
TM44	Rest	Psychic	Status	—	—	10	Self
TM45	Attract	Normal	Status	—	100	15	Normal
TM48	Round	Normal	Special	60	100	15	Normal
TM64	Explosion	Normal	Physical	250	100	5	Adjacent
TM66	Payback	Dark	Physical	50	100	10	Normal
TM68	Giga Impact	Normal	Physical	150	90	5	Normal
TM74	Gyro Ball	Steel	Physical	—	100	5	Normal
TM78	Bulldoze	Ground	Physical	60	100	20	Adjacent
TM79	Frost Breath	Ice	Special	60	90	10	Normal
TM87	Swagger	Normal	Status	—	85	15	Normal
TM88	Sleep Talk	Normal	Status	—	—	10	Self
TM90	Substitute	Normal	Status	—	—	10	Self
TM97	Dark Pulse	Dark	Special	80	100	15	Normal
TM100	Confide	Normal	Status	—	—	20	Normal

MOVES TAUGHT BY PEOPLE

Name	Type	Kind	Pow.	Acc.	PP	Range

MOVES LEARNED WHEN EVOLVING

Name	Type	Kind	Pow.	Acc.	PP	Range
Freeze-Dry	Ice	Special	70	100	20	Normal

EGG MOVES

Name	Type	Kind	Pow.	Acc.	PP	Range

EXCLUSIVE Z-MOVE

Name	Base Move	Type	Kind	Pow.	Acc.	Range

FROSLASS

LEVEL-UP MOVES

Lv.	Name	Type	Kind	Pow.	Acc.	PP	Range
1	Ominous Wind	Ghost	Special	60	100	5	Normal
1	Destiny Bond	Ghost	Status	—	—	5	Self
1	Powder Snow	Ice	Special	40	100	25	Many Others
1	Leer	Normal	Status	—	100	30	Many Others
1	Double Team	Normal	Status	—	—	15	Self
1	Ice Shard	Ice	Physical	40	100	30	Normal
5	Double Team	Normal	Status	—	—	15	Self
10	Ice Shard	Ice	Physical	40	100	30	Normal
14	Icy Wind	Ice	Special	55	95	15	Many Others
19	Astonish	Ghost	Physical	30	100	15	Normal
23	Draining Kiss	Fairy	Special	50	100	10	Normal
28	Will-O-Wisp	Fire	Status	—	85	15	Normal
32	Confuse Ray	Ghost	Status	—	100	10	Normal
37	Wake-Up Slap	Fighting	Physical	70	100	10	Normal
41	Captivate	Normal	Status	—	100	20	Many Others
42	Shadow Ball	Ghost	Special	80	100	15	Normal
48	Blizzard	Ice	Special	110	70	5	Many Others
54	Hail	Ice	Status	—	—	10	Both Sides
61	Destiny Bond	Ghost	Status	—	—	5	Self

TM MOVES

No.	Name	Type	Kind	Pow.	Acc.	PP	Range
TM06	Toxic	Poison	Status	—	90	10	Normal
TM07	Hail	Ice	Status	—	—	10	Both Sides
TM10	Hidden Power	Normal	Special	60	100	15	Normal
TM12	Taunt	Dark	Status	—	100	20	Normal
TM13	Ice Beam	Ice	Special	90	100	10	Normal
TM14	Blizzard	Ice	Special	110	70	5	Many Others
TM15	Hyper Beam	Normal	Special	150	90	5	Normal
TM16	Light Screen	Psychic	Status	—	—	30	Your Side
TM17	Protect	Normal	Status	—	—	10	Self
TM18	Rain Dance	Water	Status	—	—	5	Both Sides
TM20	Safeguard	Normal	Status	—	—	25	Your Side
TM21	Frustration	Normal	Physical	—	100	20	Normal
TM24	Thunderbolt	Electric	Special	90	100	15	Normal
TM25	Thunder	Electric	Special	110	70	10	Normal
TM27	Return	Normal	Physical	—	100	20	Normal
TM29	Psychic	Psychic	Special	90	100	10	Normal
TM30	Shadow Ball	Ghost	Special	80	100	15	Normal
TM32	Double Team	Normal	Status	—	—	15	Self
TM41	Torment	Dark	Status	—	100	15	Normal
TM42	Facade	Normal	Physical	70	100	20	Normal
TM44	Rest	Psychic	Status	—	—	10	Self
TM45	Attract	Normal	Status	—	100	15	Normal
TM48	Round	Normal	Special	60	100	15	Normal
TM56	Fling	Dark	Physical	—	100	10	Normal
TM61	Will-O-Wisp	Fire	Status	—	85	15	Normal
TM63	Embargo	Dark	Status	—	100	15	Normal
TM66	Payback	Dark	Physical	50	100	10	Normal
TM68	Giga Impact	Normal	Physical	150	90	5	Normal
TM70	Aurora Veil	Ice	Status	—	—	20	Your Side
TM73	Thunder Wave	Electric	Status	—	90	20	Normal
TM77	Psych Up	Normal	Status	—	—	10	Normal
TM79	Frost Breath	Ice	Special	60	90	10	Normal
TM85	Dream Eater	Psychic	Special	100	100	15	Normal
TM87	Swagger	Normal	Status	—	85	15	Normal
TM88	Sleep Talk	Normal	Status	—	—	10	Self
TM90	Substitute	Normal	Status	—	—	10	Self
TM100	Confide	Normal	Status	—	—	20	Normal

MOVES TAUGHT BY PEOPLE

Name	Type	Kind	Pow.	Acc.	PP	Range

MOVES LEARNED WHEN EVOLVING

Name	Type	Kind	Pow.	Acc.	PP	Range
Ominous Wind	Ghost	Special	60	100	5	Normal

EGG MOVES

Name	Type	Kind	Pow.	Acc.	PP	Range

EXCLUSIVE Z-MOVE

Name	Base Move	Type	Kind	Pow.	Acc.	Range

Sneasel

Alola Pokédex	Melemele	Akala	Ula'ula	Poni
249	—	—	121	

Sneasel
Sharp Claw Pokémon

DARK **ICE**

HEIGHT: 2'11"
WEIGHT: 61.7 lbs.

It has a cunning yet savage disposition. It waits for parents to leave their nests, and then it sneaks in to steal their eggs.

It uses its claws to poke holes in eggs so it can slurp out the insides. Breeders consider it a scourge and will drive it away or eradicate it.

ABILITY
Inner Focus
Keen Eye

HIDDEN ABILITY
Pickpocket

SPECIES STRENGTHS
HP	◆◆
Attack	◆◆◆◆◆
Defense	◆◆◆
Sp. Atk	◆◆◆
Sp. Def	◆◆◆◆
Speed	◆◆◆◆◆◆◆

Damage taken in normal battles
NORMAL ×1	FIGHTING ×4	ROCK ×2
FIRE ×2	POISON ×1	GHOST ×0.5
WATER ×1	GROUND ×1	DRAGON ×1
GRASS ×1	FLYING ×2	DARK ×1
ELECTRIC ×1	PSYCHIC ×0	STEEL ×2
ICE ×0.5	BUG ×2	FAIRY ×2

EGG GROUPS
Field

ITEM SOMETIMES HELD BY WILD POKÉMON
Quick Claw

EVOLUTION
Sneasel → Level up at night while holding a Razor Claw → Weavile

MAIN WAY TO REGISTER IN THE POKÉDEX
Catch in the tall grass or the cave on Mount Lanakila

The male has larger ears. The female has smaller ears.

◆ LEVEL-UP MOVES
Lv.	Name	Type	Kind	Pow.	Acc.	PP	Range
1	Scratch	Normal	Physical	40	100	35	Normal
1	Leer	Normal	Status	—	100	30	Many Others
1	Taunt	Dark	Status	—	100	20	Normal
8	Quick Attack	Normal	Physical	40	100	30	Normal
10	Feint Attack	Dark	Physical	60	—	20	Normal
14	Icy Wind	Ice	Special	55	95	15	Many Others
16	Fury Swipes	Normal	Physical	18	80	15	Normal
20	Agility	Psychic	Status	—	—	30	Self
22	Metal Claw	Steel	Physical	50	95	35	Normal
25	Hone Claws	Dark	Status	—	—	15	Self
28	Beat Up	Dark	Physical	—	100	10	Normal
32	Screech	Normal	Status	—	85	40	Normal
35	Slash	Normal	Physical	70	100	20	Normal
40	Snatch	Dark	Status	—	—	10	Self
44	Punishment	Dark	Physical	—	100	5	Normal
47	Ice Shard	Ice	Physical	40	100	30	Normal

◆ TM MOVES
No.	Name	Type	Kind	Pow.	Acc.	PP	Range
TM04	Calm Mind	Psychic	Status	—	—	20	Self
TM06	Toxic	Poison	Status	—	90	10	Normal
TM07	Hail	Ice	Status	—	—	10	Both Sides
TM10	Hidden Power	Normal	Special	60	100	15	Normal
TM11	Sunny Day	Fire	Status	—	—	5	Both Sides
TM12	Taunt	Dark	Status	—	100	20	Normal
TM13	Ice Beam	Ice	Special	90	100	10	Normal
TM14	Blizzard	Ice	Special	110	70	5	Many Others
TM17	Protect	Normal	Status	—	—	10	Self
TM18	Rain Dance	Water	Status	—	—	5	Both Sides
TM21	Frustration	Normal	Physical	—	100	20	Normal
TM27	Return	Normal	Physical	—	100	20	Normal
TM30	Shadow Ball	Ghost	Special	80	100	15	Normal
TM31	Brick Break	Fighting	Physical	75	100	15	Normal
TM32	Double Team	Normal	Status	—	—	15	Self
TM33	Reflect	Psychic	Status	—	—	20	Your Side
TM40	Aerial Ace	Flying	Physical	60	—	20	Normal
TM41	Torment	Dark	Status	—	100	15	Normal
TM42	Facade	Normal	Physical	70	100	20	Normal
TM44	Rest	Psychic	Status	—	—	10	Self
TM45	Attract	Normal	Status	—	100	15	Normal
TM46	Thief	Dark	Physical	60	100	25	Normal
TM47	Low Sweep	Fighting	Physical	65	100	20	Normal
TM48	Round	Normal	Special	60	100	15	Normal
TM54	False Swipe	Normal	Physical	40	100	40	Normal
TM56	Fling	Dark	Physical	—	100	10	Normal
TM63	Embargo	Dark	Status	—	100	15	Normal
TM65	Shadow Claw	Ghost	Physical	70	100	15	Normal
TM66	Payback	Dark	Physical	50	100	10	Normal
TM75	Swords Dance	Normal	Status	—	—	20	Self
TM77	Psych Up	Normal	Status	—	—	10	Normal
TM81	X-Scissor	Bug	Physical	80	100	15	Normal
TM84	Poison Jab	Poison	Physical	80	100	20	Normal
TM85	Dream Eater	Psychic	Special	100	100	15	Normal
TM87	Swagger	Normal	Status	—	85	15	Normal
TM88	Sleep Talk	Normal	Status	—	—	10	Self
TM90	Substitute	Normal	Status	—	—	10	Self
TM94	Surf	Water	Special	90	100	15	Adjacent
TM95	Snarl	Dark	Special	55	95	15	Many Others
TM97	Dark Pulse	Dark	Special	80	100	15	Normal
TM100	Confide	Normal	Status	—	—	20	Normal

◆ MOVES TAUGHT BY PEOPLE
Name	Type	Kind	Pow.	Acc.	PP	Range

◆ MOVES LEARNED WHEN EVOLVING
Name	Type	Kind	Pow.	Acc.	PP	Range

◆ EGG MOVES
Name	Type	Kind	Pow.	Acc.	PP	Range
Counter	Fighting	Physical	—	100	20	Varies
Spite	Ghost	Status	—	100	10	Normal
Foresight	Normal	Status	—	—	40	Normal
Bite	Dark	Physical	60	100	25	Normal
Crush Claw	Normal	Physical	75	95	10	Normal
Fake Out	Normal	Physical	40	100	10	Normal
Double Hit	Normal	Physical	35	90	10	Normal
Punishment	Dark	Physical	—	100	5	Normal
Pursuit	Dark	Physical	40	100	20	Normal
Ice Shard	Ice	Physical	40	100	30	Normal
Ice Punch	Ice	Physical	75	100	15	Normal
Assist	Normal	Status	—	—	20	Self
Avalanche	Ice	Physical	60	100	10	Normal
Feint	Normal	Physical	30	100	10	Normal
Icicle Crash	Ice	Physical	85	90	10	Normal
Throat Chop	Dark	Physical	80	100	15	Normal

◆ EXCLUSIVE Z-MOVE
Name	Base Move	Type	Kind	Pow.	Acc.	Range

Weavile

Alola Pokédex	Melemele	Akala	Ula'ula	Poni
250	—	—	122	

Weavile
Sharp Claw Pokémon

DARK **ICE**

HEIGHT: 3'07"
WEIGHT: 75.0 lbs.

They travel in groups of four or five, leaving signs for one another on trees and rocks. They bring down their prey with coordinated attacks.

They dwell in cold places. This Pokémon's main food source in Alola is Vulpix and Sandshrew, which they carefully divide among their group.

ABILITY
Pressure

HIDDEN ABILITY
Pickpocket

SPECIES STRENGTHS
HP	◆◆◆
Attack	◆◆◆◆◆◆◆
Defense	◆◆◆
Sp. Atk	◆◆
Sp. Def	◆◆◆◆◆
Speed	◆◆◆◆◆◆◆

Damage taken in normal battles
NORMAL ×1	FIGHTING ×4	ROCK ×2
FIRE ×2	POISON ×1	GHOST ×0.5
WATER ×1	GROUND ×1	DRAGON ×1
GRASS ×1	FLYING ×2	DARK ×1
ELECTRIC ×1	PSYCHIC ×0	STEEL ×2
ICE ×0.5	BUG ×2	FAIRY ×2

EGG GROUPS
Field

ITEM SOMETIMES HELD BY WILD POKÉMON

EVOLUTION
Sneasel → Level up at night while holding a Razor Claw → Weavile

MAIN WAY TO REGISTER IN THE POKÉDEX
Level up Sneasel while it is holding a Razor Claw when it is nighttime in your game

The male has larger ears. The female has smaller ears.

◆ LEVEL-UP MOVES
Lv.	Name	Type	Kind	Pow.	Acc.	PP	Range
1	Embargo	Dark	Status	—	100	15	Normal
1	Revenge	Fighting	Physical	60	100	10	Normal
1	Assurance	Dark	Physical	60	100	10	Normal
1	Scratch	Normal	Physical	40	100	35	Normal
1	Leer	Normal	Status	—	100	30	Many Others
1	Taunt	Dark	Status	—	100	20	Normal
1	Quick Attack	Normal	Physical	40	100	30	Normal
8	Quick Attack	Normal	Physical	40	100	30	Normal
10	Feint Attack	Dark	Physical	60	—	20	Normal
14	Icy Wind	Ice	Special	55	95	15	Many Others
16	Fury Swipes	Normal	Physical	18	80	15	Normal
20	Nasty Plot	Dark	Status	—	—	20	Self
22	Metal Claw	Steel	Physical	50	95	35	Normal
25	Hone Claws	Dark	Status	—	—	15	Self
28	Fling	Dark	Physical	—	100	10	Normal
32	Screech	Normal	Status	—	85	40	Normal
35	Night Slash	Dark	Physical	70	100	15	Normal
40	Snatch	Dark	Status	—	—	10	Self
44	Punishment	Dark	Physical	—	100	5	Normal
47	Dark Pulse	Dark	Special	80	100	15	Normal

◆ TM MOVES
No.	Name	Type	Kind	Pow.	Acc.	PP	Range
TM04	Calm Mind	Psychic	Status	—	—	20	Self
TM06	Toxic	Poison	Status	—	90	10	Normal
TM07	Hail	Ice	Status	—	—	10	Both Sides
TM10	Hidden Power	Normal	Special	60	100	15	Normal
TM11	Sunny Day	Fire	Status	—	—	5	Both Sides
TM12	Taunt	Dark	Status	—	100	20	Normal
TM13	Ice Beam	Ice	Special	90	100	10	Normal
TM14	Blizzard	Ice	Special	110	70	5	Many Others
TM15	Hyper Beam	Normal	Special	150	90	5	Normal
TM17	Protect	Normal	Status	—	—	10	Self
TM18	Rain Dance	Water	Status	—	—	5	Both Sides
TM21	Frustration	Normal	Physical	—	100	20	Normal
TM27	Return	Normal	Physical	—	100	20	Normal
TM30	Shadow Ball	Ghost	Special	80	100	15	Normal
TM31	Brick Break	Fighting	Physical	75	100	15	Normal
TM32	Double Team	Normal	Status	—	—	15	Self
TM33	Reflect	Psychic	Status	—	—	20	Your Side
TM40	Aerial Ace	Flying	Physical	60	—	20	Normal
TM41	Torment	Dark	Status	—	100	15	Normal
TM42	Facade	Normal	Physical	70	100	20	Normal
TM44	Rest	Psychic	Status	—	—	10	Self
TM45	Attract	Normal	Status	—	100	15	Normal
TM46	Thief	Dark	Physical	60	100	25	Normal
TM47	Low Sweep	Fighting	Physical	65	100	20	Normal
TM48	Round	Normal	Special	60	100	15	Normal
TM52	Focus Blast	Fighting	Special	120	70	5	Normal
TM54	False Swipe	Normal	Physical	40	100	40	Normal
TM56	Fling	Dark	Physical	—	100	10	Normal
TM63	Embargo	Dark	Status	—	100	15	Normal
TM65	Shadow Claw	Ghost	Physical	70	100	15	Normal
TM66	Payback	Dark	Physical	50	100	10	Normal
TM68	Giga Impact	Normal	Physical	150	90	5	Normal
TM75	Swords Dance	Normal	Status	—	—	20	Self
TM77	Psych Up	Normal	Status	—	—	10	Normal
TM81	X-Scissor	Bug	Physical	80	100	15	Normal
TM84	Poison Jab	Poison	Physical	80	100	20	Normal
TM85	Dream Eater	Psychic	Special	100	100	15	Normal
TM87	Swagger	Normal	Status	—	85	15	Normal
TM88	Sleep Talk	Normal	Status	—	—	10	Self
TM90	Substitute	Normal	Status	—	—	10	Self
TM94	Surf	Water	Special	90	100	15	Adjacent
TM95	Snarl	Dark	Special	55	95	15	Many Others
TM97	Dark Pulse	Dark	Special	80	100	15	Normal
TM100	Confide	Normal	Status	—	—	20	Normal

◆ MOVES TAUGHT BY PEOPLE
Name	Type	Kind	Pow.	Acc.	PP	Range

◆ MOVES LEARNED WHEN EVOLVING
Name	Type	Kind	Pow.	Acc.	PP	Range

◆ EGG MOVES
Name	Type	Kind	Pow.	Acc.	PP	Range

◆ EXCLUSIVE Z-MOVE
Name	Base Move	Type	Kind	Pow.	Acc.	Range

Ice Your Opponents!

Alolan Vulpix and Alolan Sandshrew may be some of the more high-profile Ice types in the game, but they aren't the only Ice types in Alola. Check out the chart below for info on some of the frostier residents of Alola, and some ideas for how you can use them.

Pokémon Name	Type 1	Type 2	Key Feature	Notes
Delibird	ICE	FLYING	Ability: Hustle	Delibird has the potential to deliver when it comes to combos. The Hustle Ability boosts a Pokémon's Attack stat but lowers its accuracy. You can bypass this drawback by teaching your Delibird Aerial Ace, which bypasses accuracy checks, to deal some pretty hefty damage.
Glaceon	ICE		High Sp. Atk + Defense	Glaceon can fill a vital role in your team as a durable yet strong special attacker.
Castform (Snowy Form)	ICE		Ability: Forecast changes its type based on the weather.	Pair Castform with an Alolan Ninetales that has the Snow Warning Ability to dish out some good Ice-type damage right from the get-go, without having to set up the weather first by using a move like Hail.
Mega Glalie	ICE		Ability: Refrigerate	This Ability turns Glalie's normal moves into Ice-type moves, which will give them a power boost thanks to the same-type attack bonus. Have your Glalie learn Hyper Beam or Giga Impact to dish out massive damage when it becomes a Mega-Evolved Pokémon.
Froslass	ICE	GHOST	Ability: Snow Cloak	Froslass have good species strength for Speed and they can learn some strong moves—but a Froslass isn't exactly a defensive powerhouse. You can mitigate this by pairing a Snow Cloak Froslass with some timely hail to reduce the accuracy of the moves your opponent uses against your Froslass.
Alolan Sandslash	ICE	STEEL	Hidden Ability: Slush Rush	Alolan Sandslash has some surprising combo potential if you're being hit by hail. Its Hidden Ability Slush Rush will boost its Speed when it's hailing!
Alolan Ninetales	ICE	FAIRY	Hidden Ability: Snow Warning	Alolan Ninetales has lots of combo potential, especially for Double Battles, if you can catch one with its Hidden Ability Snow Warning! This Ability makes it begin hailing as soon as the Pokémon enters battle.
Vanilluxe	ICE		Ability: Ice Body	Vanilluxe forms another good combo with a Snow Warning Alolan Ninetales. Ice Body will heal your Vanilluxe when it is hailing, and Alolan Ninetales's Snow Warning Ability will automatically make it hail when it appears in battle!
Crabominable	FIGHTING	ICE	Ability: Iron Fist	Crabominable has a good species strength for Attack, and its Iron Fist Ability increases the power of punch moves, like Ice Punch and Dynamic Punch. You can deal surprising amounts of damage with this combo!
Cloyster	WATER	ICE	Ability: Skill Link	This Ability ensures that moves that normally hit 2–5 times will always hit the full 5 times. If you're a Pokémon Egg inheritance expert, work to get a Cloyster that knows Icicle Spear and Skill Link to make this defensive dynamo dish out some serious damage.
Weavile	DARK	ICE	High Attack + Speed	Teach this Pokémon strong physical moves like Giga Impact to knock out your opponent's Pokémon before they even have a chance to attack you.
Lapras	WATER	ICE	Ability: Water Absorb	Turn this Pokémon into a terror in Double Battles by having its partner use moves like Surf that hit all Pokémon, allowing Lapras to heal itself thanks to its Water Absorb Ability.

Sandshrew

Mouse Pokémon

Alola Pokédex

	Melemele	Akala	Ula'ula	Poni
251	—	—	123	—

ICE STEEL

HEIGHT: 2'04"
WEIGHT: 88.2 lbs.

It lives on snowy mountains. Its steel shell is very hard—so much so, it can't roll its body up into a ball.

An ancient tradition of Alolan festivals, still carried on to this day, is a competition to slide Sandshrew across ice as far as one can.

ABILITY
Snow Cloak

HIDDEN ABILITY
Slush Rush

Damage taken in normal battles

NORMAL ×0.5	FIGHTING ×4	ROCK ×1			
FIRE ×4	POISON ×0	GHOST ×1			
WATER ×1	GROUND ×2	DRAGON ×0.5			
GRASS ×0.5	FLYING ×0.5	DARK ×1			
ELECTRIC ×1	PSYCHIC ×0.5	STEEL ×1			
ICE ×0.25	BUG ×0.5	FAIRY ×0.5			

SPECIES STRENGTHS
- HP ◆◆
- Attack ◆◆◆◆
- Defense ◆◆◆◆◆
- Sp. Atk ◆◆
- Sp. Def ◆◆
- Speed ◆◆◆

EGG GROUPS
Field

ITEM SOMETIMES HELD BY WILD POKÉMON
Grip Claw

EVOLUTION

Alolan Sandshrew → (Ice Stone) → Alolan Sandslash

MAIN WAY TO REGISTER IN THE POKÉDEX
Obtain in a trade in *Pokémon Sun* / Catch in the tall grass on Mount Lanakila in *Pokémon Moon*

❖ ALOLA FORM ❖
Same form for male/female

❖ LEVEL-UP MOVES

Lv.	Name	Type	Kind	Pow.	Acc.	PP	Range
1	Scratch	Normal	Physical	40	100	35	Normal
1	Defense Curl	Normal	Status	—	—	40	Self
3	Bide	Normal	Physical	—	—	10	Self
5	Powder Snow	Ice	Special	40	100	25	Many Others
7	Ice Ball	Ice	Physical	30	90	20	Normal
9	Rapid Spin	Normal	Physical	20	100	40	Normal
11	Fury Cutter	Bug	Physical	40	95	20	Normal
14	Metal Claw	Steel	Physical	50	95	35	Normal
17	Swift	Normal	Special	60	—	20	Many Others
20	Fury Swipes	Normal	Physical	18	80	15	Normal
23	Iron Defense	Steel	Status	—	—	15	Self
26	Slash	Normal	Physical	70	100	20	Normal
30	Iron Head	Steel	Physical	80	100	15	Normal
34	Gyro Ball	Steel	Physical	—	100	5	Normal
38	Swords Dance	Normal	Status	—	—	20	Self
42	Hail	Ice	Status	—	—	10	Both Sides
46	Blizzard	Ice	Special	110	70	5	Many Others

❖ TM MOVES

No.	Name	Type	Kind	Pow.	Acc.	PP	Range
TM01	Work Up	Normal	Status	—	—	30	Self
TM06	Toxic	Poison	Status	—	90	10	Normal
TM07	Hail	Ice	Status	—	—	10	Both Sides
TM10	Hidden Power	Normal	Special	60	100	15	Normal
TM11	Sunny Day	Fire	Status	—	—	5	Both Sides
TM14	Blizzard	Ice	Special	110	70	5	Many Others
TM17	Protect	Normal	Status	—	—	10	Self
TM20	Safeguard	Normal	Status	—	—	25	Your Side
TM21	Frustration	Normal	Physical	—	100	20	Normal
TM26	Earthquake	Ground	Physical	100	100	10	Adjacent
TM27	Return	Normal	Physical	—	100	20	Normal
TM28	Leech Life	Bug	Physical	80	100	10	Normal
TM31	Brick Break	Fighting	Physical	75	100	15	Normal
TM32	Double Team	Normal	Status	—	—	15	Self
TM40	Aerial Ace	Flying	Physical	60	—	20	Normal
TM42	Facade	Normal	Physical	70	100	20	Normal
TM44	Rest	Psychic	Status	—	—	10	Self
TM45	Attract	Normal	Status	—	100	15	Normal
TM46	Thief	Dark	Physical	60	100	25	Normal
TM48	Round	Normal	Special	60	100	15	Normal
TM56	Fling	Dark	Physical	—	100	10	Normal
TM65	Shadow Claw	Ghost	Physical	70	100	15	Normal
TM70	Aurora Veil	Ice	Status	—	—	20	Your Side
TM74	Gyro Ball	Steel	Physical	—	100	5	Normal
TM75	Swords Dance	Normal	Status	—	—	20	Self
TM78	Bulldoze	Ground	Physical	60	100	20	Adjacent
TM79	Frost Breath	Ice	Special	60	90	10	Normal
TM80	Rock Slide	Rock	Physical	75	90	10	Many Others
TM81	X-Scissor	Bug	Physical	80	100	15	Normal
TM84	Poison Jab	Poison	Physical	80	100	20	Normal
TM87	Swagger	Normal	Status	—	85	15	Normal
TM88	Sleep Talk	Normal	Status	—	—	10	Self
TM90	Substitute	Normal	Status	—	—	10	Self
TM100	Confide	Normal	Status	—	—	20	Normal

❖ MOVES TAUGHT BY PEOPLE

Name	Type	Kind	Pow.	Acc.	PP	Range

❖ MOVES LEARNED WHEN EVOLVING

Name	Type	Kind	Pow.	Acc.	PP	Range

❖ EGG MOVES

Name	Type	Kind	Pow.	Acc.	PP	Range
Flail	Normal	Physical	—	100	15	Normal
Counter	Fighting	Physical	—	100	20	Varies
Icicle Spear	Ice	Physical	25	100	30	Normal
Metal Claw	Steel	Physical	50	95	35	Normal
Crush Claw	Normal	Physical	75	95	10	Normal
Night Slash	Dark	Physical	70	100	15	Normal
Icicle Crash	Ice	Physical	85	90	10	Normal
Endure	Normal	Status	—	—	10	Self
Chip Away	Normal	Physical	70	100	20	Normal
Curse	Ghost	Status	—	—	10	Varies
Amnesia	Psychic	Status	—	—	20	Self

❖ EXCLUSIVE Z-MOVE

Name	Base Move	Type	Kind	Pow.	Acc.	Range

Sandslash

Mouse Pokémon

Alola Pokédex

	Melemele	Akala	Ula'ula	Poni
252	—	—	124	—

ICE STEEL

HEIGHT: 3'11"
WEIGHT: 121.3 lbs.

Fleeing a volcanic eruption, it settled on a snowy mountain. As it races through the snowfields, it sends up a spray of snow.

This Pokémon's steel spikes are sheathed in ice. Stabs from these spikes cause deep wounds and severe frostbite as well.

ABILITY
Snow Cloak

HIDDEN ABILITY
Slush Rush

Damage taken in normal battles

NORMAL ×0.5	FIGHTING ×4	ROCK ×1			
FIRE ×4	POISON ×0	GHOST ×1			
WATER ×1	GROUND ×2	DRAGON ×0.5			
GRASS ×0.5	FLYING ×0.5	DARK ×1			
ELECTRIC ×1	PSYCHIC ×0.5	STEEL ×1			
ICE ×0.25	BUG ×0.5	FAIRY ×0.5			

SPECIES STRENGTHS
- HP ◆◆◆
- Attack ◆◆◆◆◆
- Defense ◆◆◆◆◆◆◆
- Sp. Atk ◆
- Sp. Def ◆◆◆◆
- Speed ◆◆◆◆

EGG GROUPS
Field

ITEM SOMETIMES HELD BY WILD POKÉMON
—

EVOLUTION

Alolan Sandshrew → (Ice Stone) → Alolan Sandslash

MAIN WAY TO REGISTER IN THE POKÉDEX
Use an Ice Stone on an Alolan Sandshrew

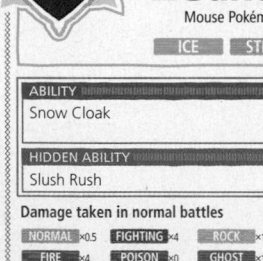

❖ ALOLA FORM ❖
Same form for male/female

❖ LEVEL-UP MOVES

Lv.	Name	Type	Kind	Pow.	Acc.	PP	Range
1	Icicle Spear	Ice	Physical	25	100	30	Normal
1	Metal Burst	Steel	Physical	—	100	10	Varies
1	Icicle Crash	Ice	Physical	85	90	10	Normal
1	Slash	Normal	Physical	70	100	20	Normal
1	Defense Curl	Normal	Status	—	—	40	Self
1	Ice Ball	Ice	Physical	30	90	20	Normal
1	Metal Claw	Steel	Physical	50	95	35	Normal

❖ TM MOVES

No.	Name	Type	Kind	Pow.	Acc.	PP	Range
TM01	Work Up	Normal	Status	—	—	30	Self
TM06	Toxic	Poison	Status	—	90	10	Normal
TM07	Hail	Ice	Status	—	—	10	Both Sides
TM10	Hidden Power	Normal	Special	60	100	15	Normal
TM11	Sunny Day	Fire	Status	—	—	5	Both Sides
TM14	Blizzard	Ice	Special	110	70	5	Many Others
TM15	Hyper Beam	Normal	Special	150	90	5	Normal
TM17	Protect	Normal	Status	—	—	10	Self
TM20	Safeguard	Normal	Status	—	—	25	Your Side
TM21	Frustration	Normal	Physical	—	100	20	Normal
TM26	Earthquake	Ground	Physical	100	100	10	Adjacent
TM27	Return	Normal	Physical	—	100	20	Normal
TM28	Leech Life	Bug	Physical	80	100	10	Normal
TM31	Brick Break	Fighting	Physical	75	100	15	Normal
TM32	Double Team	Normal	Status	—	—	15	Self
TM40	Aerial Ace	Flying	Physical	60	—	20	Normal
TM42	Facade	Normal	Physical	70	100	20	Normal
TM44	Rest	Psychic	Status	—	—	10	Self
TM45	Attract	Normal	Status	—	100	15	Normal
TM46	Thief	Dark	Physical	60	100	25	Normal
TM48	Round	Normal	Special	60	100	15	Normal
TM52	Focus Blast	Fighting	Special	120	70	5	Normal
TM56	Fling	Dark	Physical	—	100	10	Normal
TM65	Shadow Claw	Ghost	Physical	70	100	15	Normal
TM68	Giga Impact	Normal	Physical	150	90	5	Normal
TM70	Aurora Veil	Ice	Status	—	—	20	Your Side
TM74	Gyro Ball	Steel	Physical	—	100	5	Normal
TM75	Swords Dance	Normal	Status	—	—	20	Self
TM78	Bulldoze	Ground	Physical	60	100	20	Adjacent
TM79	Frost Breath	Ice	Special	60	90	10	Normal
TM80	Rock Slide	Rock	Physical	75	90	10	Many Others
TM81	X-Scissor	Bug	Physical	80	100	15	Normal
TM84	Poison Jab	Poison	Physical	80	100	20	Normal
TM87	Swagger	Normal	Status	—	85	15	Normal
TM88	Sleep Talk	Normal	Status	—	—	10	Self
TM90	Substitute	Normal	Status	—	—	10	Self
TM100	Confide	Normal	Status	—	—	20	Normal

❖ MOVES TAUGHT BY PEOPLE

Name	Type	Kind	Pow.	Acc.	PP	Range

❖ MOVES LEARNED WHEN EVOLVING

Name	Type	Kind	Pow.	Acc.	PP	Range
Icicle Spear	Ice	Physical	25	100	30	Normal

❖ EGG MOVES

Name	Type	Kind	Pow.	Acc.	PP	Range

❖ EXCLUSIVE Z-MOVE

Name	Base Move	Type	Kind	Pow.	Acc.	Range

Vulpix

Alola Pokédex	Melemele	Akala	Ula'ula	Poni
253	—	—	125	

Fox Pokémon

ICE

HEIGHT: 2'00"
WEIGHT: 21.8 lbs.

It exhales air colder than -58 degrees Fahrenheit. Elderly people in Alola call this Pokémon by an older name—Keokeo.

In hot weather, this Pokémon makes ice shards with its six tails and sprays them around to cool itself off.

❖ ALOLA FORM ❖

Same form for male/female

ABILITY
Snow Cloak

HIDDEN ABILITY
Snow Warning

SPECIES STRENGTHS
HP ◆◆
Attack ◆◆
Defense ◆◆
Sp. Atk ◆◆◆
Sp. Def ◆◆◆◆
Speed ◆◆◆◆

EGG GROUPS
Field

ITEM SOMETIMES HELD BY WILD POKÉMON
Snowball

EVOLUTION
 → Ice Stone →
Alolan Vulpix   Alolan Ninetales

MAIN WAY TO REGISTER IN THE POKÉDEX
Catch in the tall grass on Mount Lanakila in *Pokémon Sun* / Obtain in a trade in *Pokémon Moon*

Damage taken in normal battles
NORMAL ×1	FIGHTING ×2	ROCK ×1
FIRE ×2	POISON ×1	GHOST ×1
WATER ×1	GROUND ×1	DRAGON ×1
GRASS ×1	FLYING ×1	DARK ×1
ELECTRIC ×1	PSYCHIC ×1	STEEL ×2
ICE ×0.5	BUG ×1	FAIRY ×1

❖ LEVEL-UP MOVES
Lv.	Name	Type	Kind	Pow.	Acc.	PP	Range
1	Powder Snow	Ice	Special	40	100	25	Many Others
4	Tail Whip	Normal	Status	—	100	30	Many Others
7	Roar	Normal	Status	—	—	20	Normal
9	Baby-Doll Eyes	Fairy	Status	—	100	30	Normal
10	Ice Shard	Ice	Physical	40	100	30	Normal
12	Confuse Ray	Ghost	Status	—	100	10	Normal
15	Icy Wind	Ice	Special	55	95	15	Many Others
18	Payback	Dark	Physical	50	100	10	Normal
20	Mist	Ice	Status	—	—	30	Your Side
23	Feint Attack	Dark	Physical	60	—	20	Normal
26	Hex	Ghost	Special	65	100	10	Normal
28	Aurora Beam	Ice	Special	65	100	20	Normal
31	Extrasensory	Psychic	Special	80	100	20	Normal
34	Safeguard	Normal	Status	—	—	25	Your Side
36	Ice Beam	Ice	Special	90	100	10	Normal
39	Imprison	Psychic	Status	—	—	10	Self
42	Blizzard	Ice	Special	110	70	5	Many Others
44	Grudge	Ghost	Status	—	—	5	Self
47	Captivate	Normal	Status	—	100	20	Many Others
50	Sheer Cold	Ice	Special	—	30	5	Normal

♦ TM MOVES
No.	Name	Type	Kind	Pow.	Acc.	PP	Range
TM05	Roar	Normal	Status	—	—	20	Normal
TM06	Toxic	Poison	Status	—	90	10	Normal
TM07	Hail	Ice	Status	—	—	10	Both Sides
TM10	Hidden Power	Normal	Special	60	100	15	Normal
TM13	Ice Beam	Ice	Special	90	100	10	Normal
TM14	Blizzard	Ice	Special	110	70	5	Many Others
TM17	Protect	Normal	Status	—	—	10	Self
TM18	Rain Dance	Water	Status	—	—	5	Both Sides
TM20	Safeguard	Normal	Status	—	—	25	Your Side
TM21	Frustration	Normal	Physical	—	100	20	Normal
TM27	Return	Normal	Physical	—	100	20	Normal
TM32	Double Team	Normal	Status	—	—	15	Self
TM42	Facade	Normal	Physical	70	100	20	Normal
TM44	Rest	Psychic	Status	—	—	10	Self
TM45	Attract	Normal	Status	—	100	15	Normal
TM48	Round	Normal	Special	60	100	15	Normal
TM66	Payback	Dark	Physical	50	100	10	Normal
TM70	Aurora Veil	Ice	Status	—	—	20	Your Side
TM77	Psych Up	Normal	Status	—	—	10	Normal
TM79	Frost Breath	Ice	Special	60	90	10	Normal
TM87	Swagger	Normal	Status	—	85	15	Normal
TM88	Sleep Talk	Normal	Status	—	—	10	Self
TM90	Substitute	Normal	Status	—	—	10	Self
TM97	Dark Pulse	Dark	Special	80	100	15	Normal
TM100	Confide	Normal	Status	—	—	20	Normal

♦ MOVES TAUGHT BY PEOPLE
(none)

❖ MOVES LEARNED WHEN EVOLVING
(none)

❖ EGG MOVES
Name	Type	Kind	Pow.	Acc.	PP	Range
Freeze-Dry	Ice	Special	70	100	20	Normal
Hypnosis	Psychic	Status	—	60	20	Normal
Hail	Normal	Physical	—	100	15	Normal
Spite	Ghost	Status	—	100	10	Normal
Disable	Normal	Status	—	100	20	Normal
Howl	Normal	Status	—	—	40	Self
Agility	Psychic	Status	—	—	30	Self
Encore	Normal	Status	—	100	5	Normal
Moonblast	Fairy	Special	95	100	15	Normal
Power Swap	Psychic	Status	—	—	10	Normal
Secret Power	Normal	Physical	70	100	20	Normal
Charm	Fairy	Status	—	100	20	Normal
Tail Slap	Normal	Physical	25	85	10	Normal
Extrasensory	Psychic	Special	80	100	20	Normal

❖ EXCLUSIVE Z-MOVE
(none)

VULPIX 253

Ninetales

Alola Pokédex	Melemele	Akala	Ula'ula	Poni
254	—	—	126	

Fox Pokémon

ICE | FAIRY

HEIGHT: 3'07"
WEIGHT: 43.9 lbs.

It creates drops of ice in its coat and showers them over its enemies. Anyone who angers it will be frozen stiff in an instant.

Possessing a calm demeanor, this Pokémon was revered as a deity incarnate before it was identified as a regional variant of Ninetales.

❖ ALOLA FORM ❖

Same form for male/female

ABILITY
Snow Cloak

HIDDEN ABILITY
Snow Warning

SPECIES STRENGTHS
HP ◆◆◆
Attack ◆◆◆◆
Defense ◆◆◆◆
Sp. Atk ◆◆◆◆
Sp. Def ◆◆◆◆◆◆
Speed ◆◆◆◆◆◆◆

EGG GROUPS
Field

ITEM SOMETIMES HELD BY WILD POKÉMON
—

EVOLUTION
 → Ice Stone →
Alolan Vulpix   Alolan Ninetales

MAIN WAY TO REGISTER IN THE POKÉDEX
Use an Ice Stone on an Alolan Vulpix.

Damage taken in normal battles
NORMAL ×1	FIGHTING ×1	ROCK ×2
FIRE ×2	POISON ×2	GHOST ×1
WATER ×1	GROUND ×1	DRAGON ×0
GRASS ×1	FLYING ×1	DARK ×0.5
ELECTRIC ×1	PSYCHIC ×1	STEEL ×1
ICE ×0.5	BUG ×0.5	FAIRY ×1

❖ LEVEL-UP MOVES
Lv.	Name	Type	Kind	Pow.	Acc.	PP	Range
1	Dazzling Gleam	Fairy	Special	80	100	10	Many Others
1	Imprison	Psychic	Status	—	—	10	Self
1	Nasty Plot	Dark	Status	—	—	20	Self
1	Ice Beam	Ice	Special	90	100	10	Normal
1	Ice Shard	Ice	Physical	40	100	30	Normal
1	Confuse Ray	Ghost	Status	—	100	10	Normal
1	Safeguard	Normal	Status	—	—	25	Your Side

♦ TM MOVES
No.	Name	Type	Kind	Pow.	Acc.	PP	Range
TM03	Psyshock	Psychic	Special	80	100	10	Normal
TM04	Calm Mind	Psychic	Status	—	—	20	Self
TM05	Roar	Normal	Status	—	—	20	Normal
TM06	Toxic	Poison	Status	—	90	10	Normal
TM07	Hail	Ice	Status	—	—	10	Both Sides
TM10	Hidden Power	Normal	Special	60	100	15	Normal
TM13	Ice Beam	Ice	Special	90	100	10	Normal
TM14	Blizzard	Ice	Special	110	70	5	Many Others
TM15	Hyper Beam	Normal	Special	150	90	5	Normal
TM17	Protect	Normal	Status	—	—	10	Self
TM18	Rain Dance	Water	Status	—	—	5	Both Sides
TM20	Safeguard	Normal	Status	—	—	25	Your Side
TM21	Frustration	Normal	Physical	—	100	20	Normal
TM27	Return	Normal	Physical	—	100	20	Normal
TM32	Double Team	Normal	Status	—	—	15	Self
TM42	Facade	Normal	Physical	70	100	20	Normal
TM44	Rest	Psychic	Status	—	—	10	Self
TM45	Attract	Normal	Status	—	100	15	Normal
TM48	Round	Normal	Special	60	100	15	Normal
TM66	Payback	Dark	Physical	50	100	10	Normal
TM68	Giga Impact	Normal	Physical	150	90	5	Normal
TM70	Aurora Veil	Ice	Status	—	—	20	Your Side
TM77	Psych Up	Normal	Status	—	—	10	Normal
TM85	Dream Eater	Psychic	Special	100	100	15	Normal
TM87	Swagger	Normal	Status	—	85	15	Normal
TM88	Sleep Talk	Normal	Status	—	—	10	Self
TM90	Substitute	Normal	Status	—	—	10	Self

❖ MOVES TAUGHT BY PEOPLE
No.	Name	Type	Kind	Pow.	Acc.	PP	Range
TM97	Dark Pulse	Dark	Special	80	100	15	Normal
TM99	Dazzling Gleam	Fairy	Special	80	100	10	Many Others
TM100	Confide	Normal	Status	—	—	20	Normal

❖ MOVES LEARNED WHEN EVOLVING
Name	Type	Kind	Pow.	Acc.	PP	Range
Dazzling Gleam	Fairy	Special	80	100	10	Many Others

❖ EGG MOVES
(none)

❖ EXCLUSIVE Z-MOVE
(none)

NINETALES 254

Vanillite

Fresh Snow Pokémon

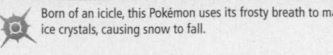

Alola Pokédex	Melemele	Akala	Ula'ula	Poni
255	—	—	127	—

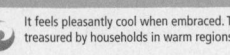

ICE

HEIGHT: 1'04"
WEIGHT: 12.6 lbs.

Born of an icicle, this Pokémon uses its frosty breath to make ice crystals, causing snow to fall.

It feels pleasantly cool when embraced. This Pokémon is treasured by households in warm regions.

ABILITY
Ice Body
Snow Cloak

HIDDEN ABILITY
Weak Armor

Damage taken in normal battles

NORMAL ×1	FIGHTING ×2	ROCK ×1
FIRE ×2	POISON ×1	GHOST ×1
WATER ×1	GROUND ×1	DRAGON ×1
GRASS ×1	FLYING ×1	DARK ×1
ELECTRIC ×1	PSYCHIC ×1	STEEL ×1
ICE ×0.5	BUG ×1	FAIRY ×1

SPECIES STRENGTHS
HP	◆
Attack	◆◆◆
Defense	◆◆◆
Sp. Atk	◆◆◆◆
Sp. Def	◆◆◆
Speed	◆◆◆

EGG GROUPS
Mineral

ITEM SOMETIMES HELD BY WILD POKÉMON
Never-Melt Ice

MAIN WAY TO REGISTER IN THE POKÉDEX
Catch in SOS battles in the tall grass during hail in Tapu Village

EVOLUTION

Vanillite → Lv. 35 → Vanillish

Lv. 47 → Vanilluxe

Same form for male/female

Vanillish

Icy Snow Pokémon

Alola Pokédex	Melemele	Akala	Ula'ula	Poni
256	—	—	128	—

ICE

HEIGHT: 3'07"
WEIGHT: 90.4 lbs.

Hot days cause its body to melt. It can be restored by refreezing it, but the process leaves its body slightly warped.

This Pokémon has existed since the Ice Age. It controls particles of ice, freezes its opponents, and then shatters them with a headbutt.

ABILITY
Ice Body
Snow Cloak

HIDDEN ABILITY
Weak Armor

Damage taken in normal battles

NORMAL ×1	FIGHTING ×2	ROCK ×1
FIRE ×2	POISON ×1	GHOST ×1
WATER ×1	GROUND ×1	DRAGON ×1
GRASS ×1	FLYING ×1	DARK ×1
ELECTRIC ×1	PSYCHIC ×1	STEEL ×1
ICE ×0.5	BUG ×1	FAIRY ×1

SPECIES STRENGTHS
HP	◆◆
Attack	◆◆◆◆
Defense	◆◆◆◆
Sp. Atk	◆◆◆◆
Sp. Def	◆◆◆◆
Speed	◆◆◆◆

EGG GROUPS
Mineral

ITEM SOMETIMES HELD BY WILD POKÉMON
Never-Melt Ice

EVOLUTION
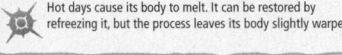

Vanillite → Lv. 35 → Vanillish

Lv. 47 → Vanilluxe

MAIN WAY TO REGISTER IN THE POKÉDEX
Catch in SOS battles in the tall grass during hail on Mount Lanakila

Same form for male/female

Vanilluxe

Snowstorm Pokémon

Alola Pokédex	Melemele	Akala	Ula'ula	Poni
257	—	—	129	—

ICE

HEIGHT: 4'03"
WEIGHT: 126.8 lbs.

Each of its two heads has a brain, and when they are in agreement, it attacks its enemies by exhaling a violent blizzard.

Even if it loses one of its heads, it can live relatively problem-free. It makes snow clouds inside its body.

ABILITY
Ice Body
Snow Warning

HIDDEN ABILITY
Weak Armor

Damage taken in normal battles

NORMAL ×1	FIGHTING ×2	ROCK ×1
FIRE ×2	POISON ×1	GHOST ×1
WATER ×1	GROUND ×1	DRAGON ×1
GRASS ×1	FLYING ×1	DARK ×1
ELECTRIC ×1	PSYCHIC ×1	STEEL ×1
ICE ×0.5	BUG ×1	FAIRY ×1

SPECIES STRENGTHS
HP	◆◆◆
Attack	◆◆◆◆◆
Defense	◆◆◆◆◆◆
Sp. Atk	◆◆◆◆◆◆
Sp. Def	◆◆◆◆◆◆
Speed	◆◆◆◆◆

EGG GROUPS
Mineral

ITEM SOMETIMES HELD BY WILD POKÉMON
—

EVOLUTION

Vanillite → Lv. 35 → Vanillish

Lv. 47 → Vanilluxe

MAIN WAY TO REGISTER IN THE POKÉDEX
Level up Vanillish to Lv. 47.

Same form for male/female

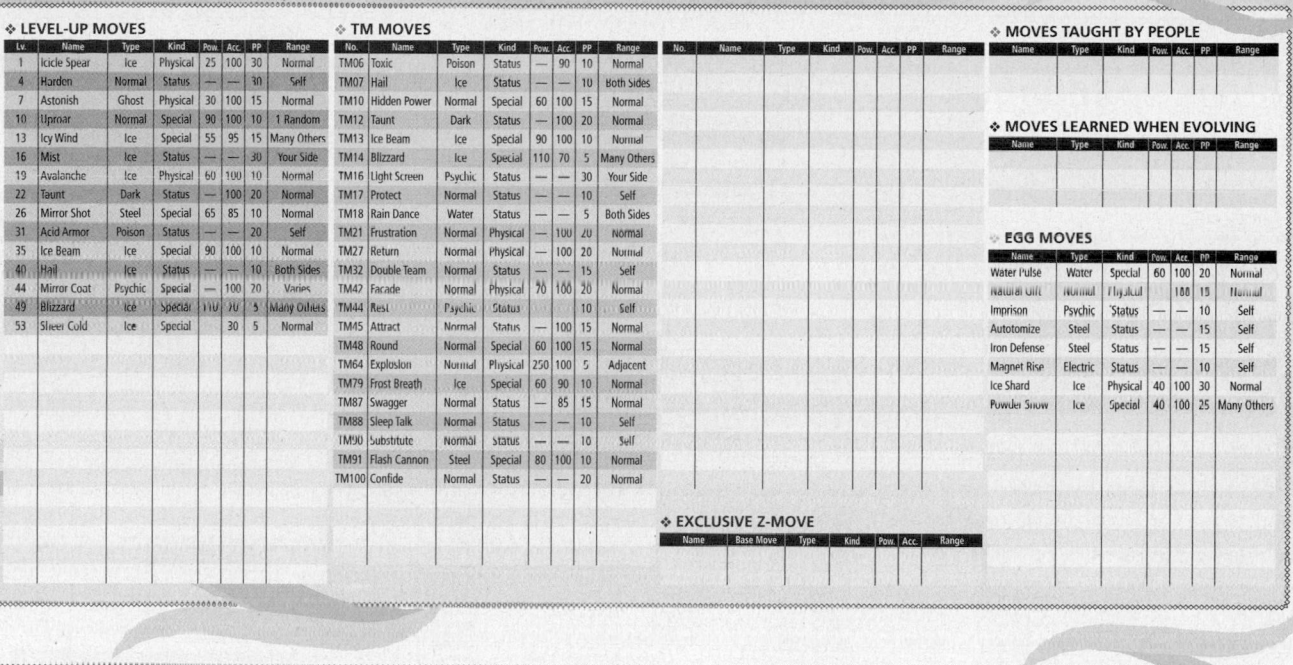

❖ LEVEL-UP MOVES

Lv.	Name	Type	Kind	Pow.	Acc.	PP	Range
1	Icicle Spear	Ice	Physical	25	100	30	Normal
4	Harden	Normal	Status	—	—	30	Self
7	Astonish	Ghost	Physical	30	100	15	Normal
10	Uproar	Normal	Special	90	100	10	1 Random
13	Icy Wind	Ice	Special	55	95	15	Many Others
16	Mist	Ice	Status	—	—	30	Your Side
19	Avalanche	Ice	Physical	60	100	10	Normal
22	Taunt	Dark	Status	—	100	20	Normal
26	Mirror Shot	Steel	Special	65	85	10	Normal
31	Acid Armor	Poison	Status	—	—	20	Self
35	Ice Beam	Ice	Special	90	100	10	Normal
40	Hail	Ice	Status	—	—	10	Both Sides
44	Mirror Coat	Psychic		—	100	20	Varies
49	Blizzard	Ice	Special	110	70	5	Many Others
53	Sheer Cold	Ice	Special	—	30	5	Normal

❖ TM MOVES

No.	Name	Type	Kind	Pow.	Acc.	PP	Range
TM06	Toxic	Poison	Status	—	90	10	Normal
TM07	Hail	Ice	Status	—	—	10	Both Sides
TM10	Hidden Power	Normal	Special	60	100	15	Normal
TM12	Taunt	Dark	Status	—	100	20	Normal
TM13	Ice Beam	Ice	Special	90	100	10	Normal
TM14	Blizzard	Ice	Special	110	70	5	Many Others
TM16	Light Screen	Psychic	Status	—	—	30	Your Side
TM17	Protect	Normal	Status	—	—	10	Self
TM18	Rain Dance	Water	Status	—	—	5	Both Sides
TM21	Frustration	Normal	Physical	—	100	20	Normal
TM27	Return	Normal	Physical	—	100	20	Normal
TM32	Double Team	Normal	Status	—	—	15	Self
TM42	Facade	Normal	Physical	70	100	20	Normal
TM44	Rest	Psychic	Status	—	—	10	Self
TM45	Attract	Normal	Status	—	100	15	Normal
TM48	Round	Normal	Special	60	100	15	Normal
TM64	Explosion	Normal	Physical	250	100	5	Adjacent
TM79	Frost Breath	Ice	Special	60	90	10	Normal
TM87	Swagger	Normal	Status	—	85	15	Normal
TM88	Sleep Talk	Normal	Status	—	—	10	Self
TM90	Substitute	Normal	Status	—	—	10	Self
TM91	Flash Cannon	Steel	Special	80	100	10	Normal
TM100	Confide	Normal	Status	—	—	20	Normal

❖ MOVES TAUGHT BY PEOPLE

Name	Type	Kind	Pow.	Acc.	PP	Range

❖ MOVES LEARNED WHEN EVOLVING

Name	Type	Kind	Pow.	Acc.	PP	Range

❖ EGG MOVES

Name	Type	Kind	Pow.	Acc.	PP	Range
Water Pulse	Water	Special	60	100	20	Normal
Natural Gift	Normal	Physical	—	100	15	Normal
Imprison	Psychic	Status	—	—	10	Self
Autotomize	Steel	Status	—	—	15	Self
Iron Defense	Steel	Status	—	—	15	Self
Magnet Rise	Electric	Status	—	—	10	Self
Ice Shard	Ice	Physical	40	100	30	Normal
Powder Snow	Ice	Special	40	100	25	Many Others

❖ EXCLUSIVE Z-MOVE

Name	Base Move	Type	Kind	Pow.	Acc.	Range

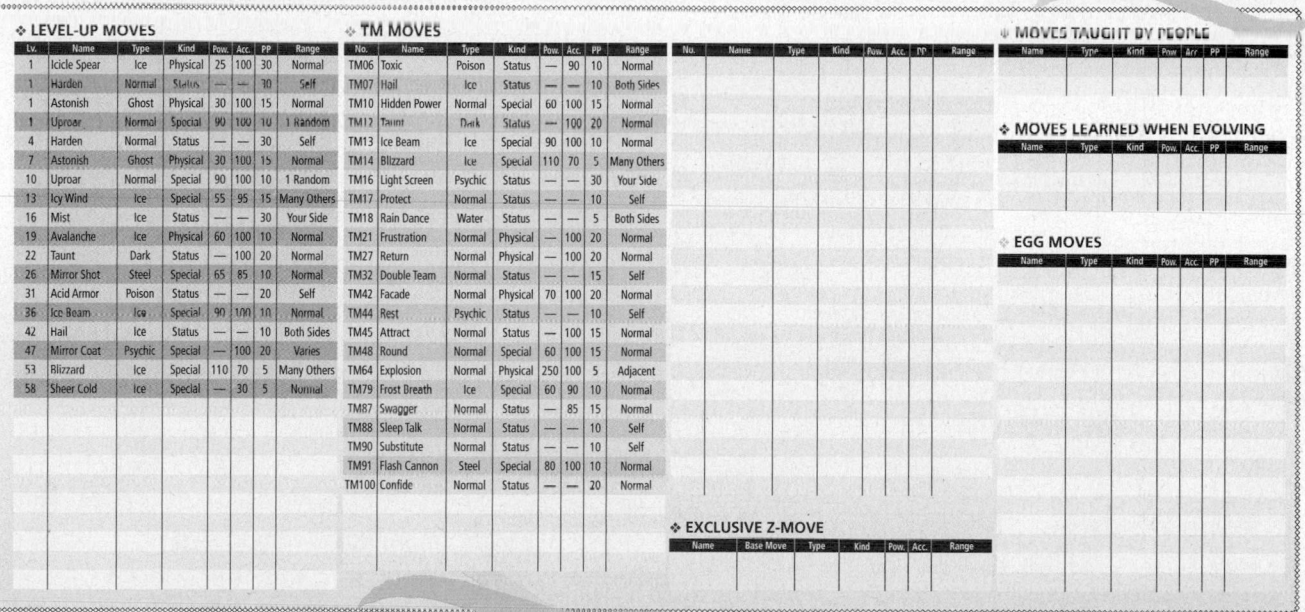

❖ LEVEL-UP MOVES

Lv.	Name	Type	Kind	Pow.	Acc.	PP	Range
1	Icicle Spear	Ice	Physical	25	100	30	Normal
1	Harden	Normal	Status	—	—	30	Self
1	Astonish	Ghost	Physical	30	100	15	Normal
1	Uproar	Normal	Special	90	100	10	1 Random
4	Harden	Normal	Status	—	—	30	Self
7	Astonish	Ghost	Physical	30	100	15	Normal
10	Uproar	Normal	Special	90	100	10	1 Random
13	Icy Wind	Ice	Special	55	95	15	Many Others
16	Mist	Ice	Status	—	—	30	Your Side
19	Avalanche	Ice	Physical	60	100	10	Normal
22	Taunt	Dark	Status	—	100	20	Normal
26	Mirror Shot	Steel	Special	65	85	10	Normal
31	Acid Armor	Poison	Status	—	—	20	Self
36	Ice Beam	Ice	Special	90	100	10	Normal
42	Hail	Ice	Status	—	—	10	Both Sides
47	Mirror Coat	Psychic	Special	—	100	20	Varies
53	Blizzard	Ice	Special	110	70	5	Many Others
58	Sheer Cold	Ice	Special	—	30	5	Normal

❖ TM MOVES

No.	Name	Type	Kind	Pow.	Acc.	PP	Range
TM06	Toxic	Poison	Status	—	90	10	Normal
TM07	Hail	Ice	Status	—	—	10	Both Sides
TM10	Hidden Power	Normal	Special	60	100	15	Normal
TM12	Taunt	Dark	Status	—	100	20	Normal
TM13	Ice Beam	Ice	Special	90	100	10	Normal
TM14	Blizzard	Ice	Special	110	70	5	Many Others
TM16	Light Screen	Psychic	Status	—	—	30	Your Side
TM17	Protect	Normal	Status	—	—	10	Self
TM18	Rain Dance	Water	Status	—	—	5	Both Sides
TM21	Frustration	Normal	Physical	—	100	20	Normal
TM27	Return	Normal	Physical	—	100	20	Normal
TM32	Double Team	Normal	Status	—	—	15	Self
TM42	Facade	Normal	Physical	70	100	20	Normal
TM44	Rest	Psychic	Status	—	—	10	Self
TM45	Attract	Normal	Status	—	100	15	Normal
TM48	Round	Normal	Special	60	100	15	Normal
TM64	Explosion	Normal	Physical	250	100	5	Adjacent
TM79	Frost Breath	Ice	Special	60	90	10	Normal
TM87	Swagger	Normal	Status	—	85	15	Normal
TM88	Sleep Talk	Normal	Status	—	—	10	Self
TM90	Substitute	Normal	Status	—	—	10	Self
TM91	Flash Cannon	Steel	Special	80	100	10	Normal
TM100	Confide	Normal	Status	—	—	20	Normal

❖ MOVES TAUGHT BY PEOPLE

No.	Name	Type	Kind	Pow.	Acc.	PP	Range

❖ MOVES LEARNED WHEN EVOLVING

Name	Type	Kind	Pow.	Acc.	PP	Range

❖ EGG MOVES

Name	Type	Kind	Pow.	Acc.	PP	Range

❖ EXCLUSIVE Z-MOVE

Name	Base Move	Type	Kind	Pow.	Acc.	Range

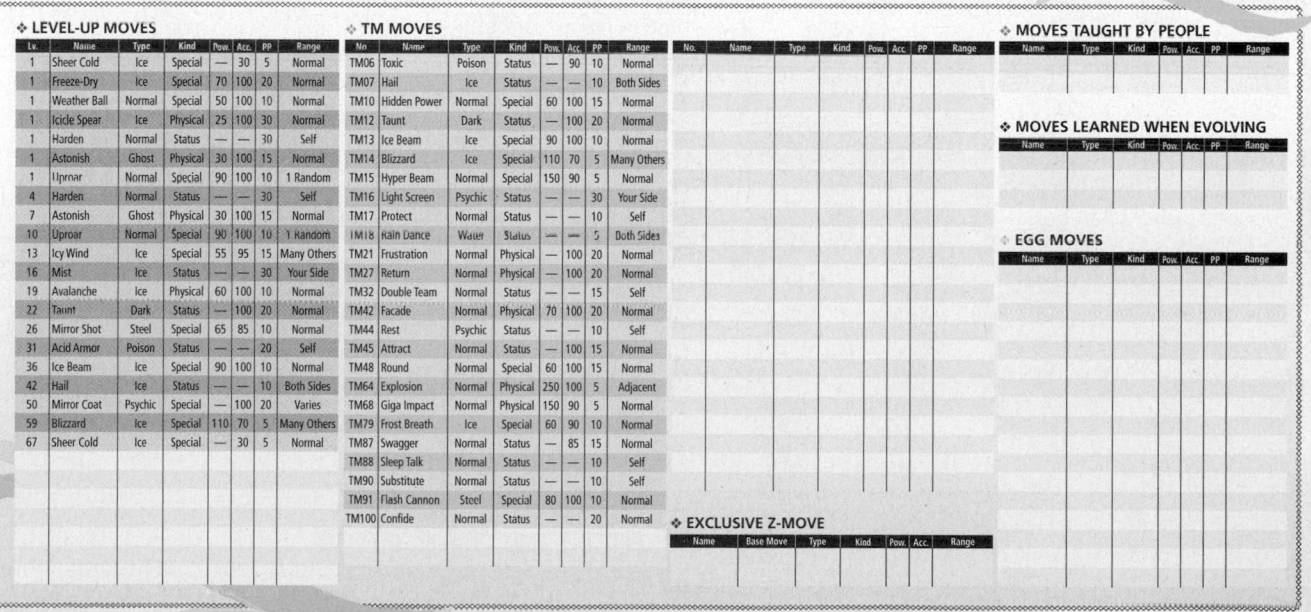

❖ LEVEL-UP MOVES

Lv.	Name	Type	Kind	Pow.	Acc.	PP	Range
1	Sheer Cold	Ice	Special	—	30	5	Normal
1	Freeze-Dry	Ice	Special	70	100	20	Normal
1	Weather Ball	Normal	Special	50	100	10	Normal
1	Icicle Spear	Ice	Physical	25	100	30	Normal
1	Harden	Normal	Status	—	—	30	Self
1	Astonish	Ghost	Physical	30	100	15	Normal
1	Uproar	Normal	Special	90	100	10	1 Random
4	Harden	Normal	Status	—	—	30	Self
7	Astonish	Ghost	Physical	30	100	15	Normal
10	Uproar	Normal	Special	90	100	10	1 Random
13	Icy Wind	Ice	Special	55	95	15	Many Others
16	Mist	Ice	Status	—	—	30	Your Side
19	Avalanche	Ice	Physical	60	100	10	Normal
22	Taunt	Dark	Status	—	100	20	Normal
26	Mirror Shot	Steel	Special	65	85	10	Normal
31	Acid Armor	Poison	Status	—	—	20	Self
36	Ice Beam	Ice	Special	90	100	10	Normal
42	Hail	Ice	Status	—	—	10	Both Sides
50	Mirror Coat	Psychic		—	100	20	Varies
59	Blizzard	Ice	Special	110	70	5	Many Others
67	Sheer Cold	Ice	Special	—	30	5	Normal

❖ TM MOVES

No.	Name	Type	Kind	Pow.	Acc.	PP	Range
TM06	Toxic	Poison	Status	—	90	10	Normal
TM07	Hail	Ice	Status	—	—	10	Both Sides
TM10	Hidden Power	Normal	Special	60	100	15	Normal
TM12	Taunt	Dark	Status	—	100	20	Normal
TM13	Ice Beam	Ice	Special	90	100	10	Normal
TM14	Blizzard	Ice	Special	110	70	5	Many Others
TM15	Hyper Beam	Normal	Special	150	90	5	Normal
TM16	Light Screen	Psychic	Status	—	—	30	Your Side
TM17	Protect	Normal	Status	—	—	10	Self
TM18	Rain Dance	Water	Status	—	—	5	Both Sides
TM21	Frustration	Normal	Physical	—	100	20	Normal
TM27	Return	Normal	Physical	—	100	20	Normal
TM32	Double Team	Normal	Status	—	—	15	Self
TM42	Facade	Normal	Physical	70	100	20	Normal
TM44	Rest	Psychic	Status	—	—	10	Self
TM45	Attract	Normal	Status	—	100	15	Normal
TM48	Round	Normal	Special	60	100	15	Normal
TM64	Explosion	Normal	Physical	250	100	5	Adjacent
TM68	Giga Impact	Normal	Physical	150	90	5	Normal
TM79	Frost Breath	Ice	Special	60	90	10	Normal
TM87	Swagger	Normal	Status	—	85	15	Normal
TM88	Sleep Talk	Normal	Status	—	—	10	Self
TM90	Substitute	Normal	Status	—	—	10	Self
TM91	Flash Cannon	Steel	Special	80	100	10	Normal
TM100	Confide	Normal	Status	—	—	20	Normal

❖ MOVES TAUGHT BY PEOPLE

No.	Name	Type	Kind	Pow.	Acc.	PP	Range

❖ MOVES LEARNED WHEN EVOLVING

Name	Type	Kind	Pow.	Acc.	PP	Range

❖ EGG MOVES

Name	Type	Kind	Pow.	Acc.	PP	Range

❖ EXCLUSIVE Z-MOVE

Name	Base Move	Type	Kind	Pow.	Acc.	Range

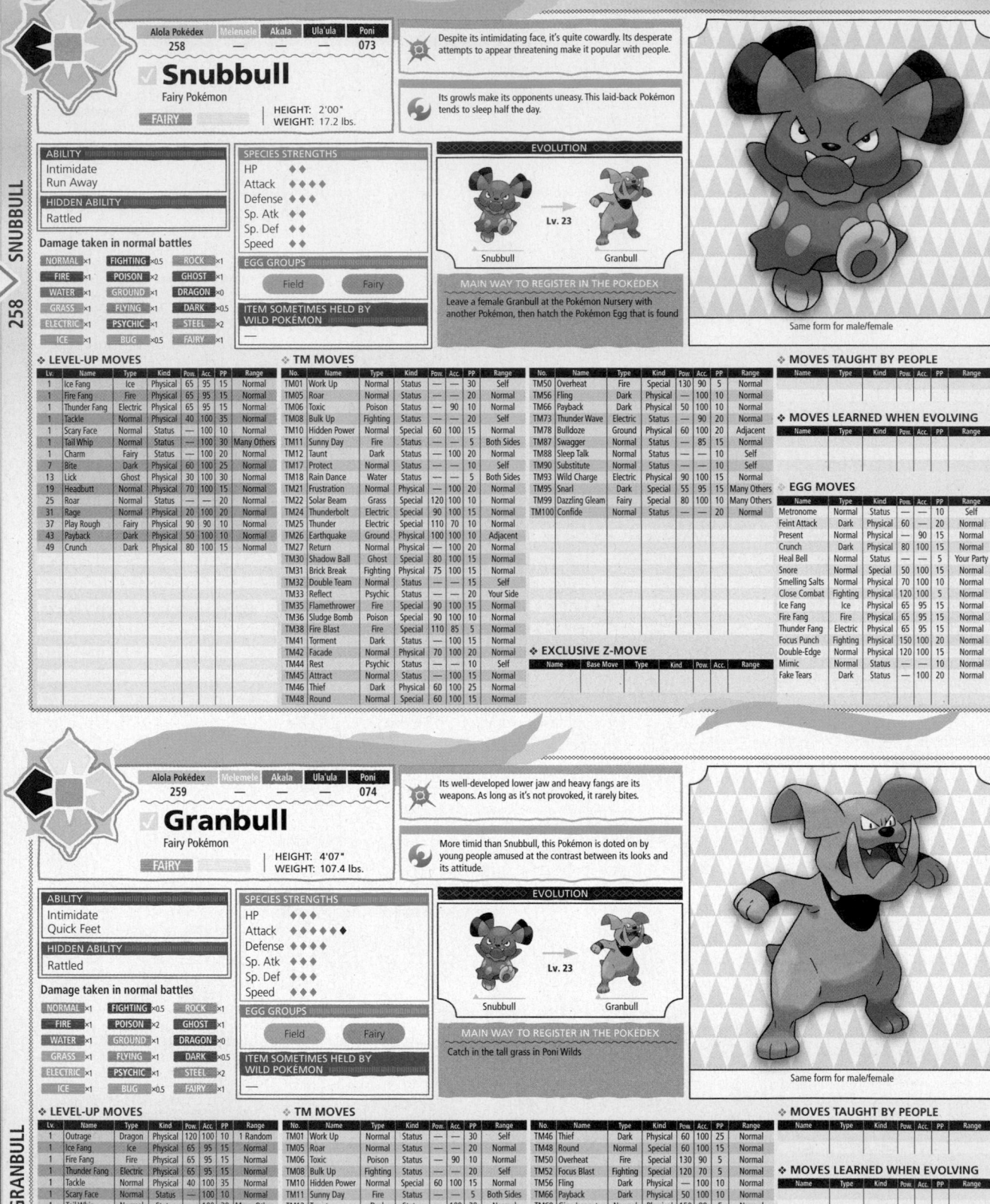

Snubbull

Alola Pokédex	Melemele	Akala	Ula'ula	Poni
	258	—	—	073

Snubbull
Fairy Pokémon
FAIRY
HEIGHT: 2'00"
WEIGHT: 17.2 lbs.

Despite its intimidating face, it's quite cowardly. Its desperate attempts to appear threatening make it popular with people.

Its growls make its opponents uneasy. This laid-back Pokémon tends to sleep half the day.

ABILITY
Intimidate
Run Away

HIDDEN ABILITY
Rattled

Damage taken in normal battles

NORMAL ×1	FIGHTING ×0.5	ROCK ×1
FIRE ×1	POISON ×2	GHOST ×1
WATER ×1	GROUND ×1	DRAGON ×0
GRASS ×1	FLYING ×1	DARK ×1
ELECTRIC ×1	PSYCHIC ×1	STEEL ×2
ICE ×1	BUG ×0.5	FAIRY ×1

SPECIES STRENGTHS
HP ◆◆
Attack ◆◆◆
Defense ◆◆◆
Sp. Atk ◆◆
Sp. Def ◆◆
Speed ◆◆

EGG GROUPS
Field
Fairy

ITEM SOMETIMES HELD BY WILD POKÉMON
—

EVOLUTION
Snubbull → Lv. 23 → Granbull

MAIN WAY TO REGISTER IN THE POKÉDEX
Leave a female Granbull at the Pokémon Nursery with another Pokémon, then hatch the Pokémon Egg that is found

Same form for male/female

LEVEL-UP MOVES

Lv.	Name	Type	Kind	Pow.	Acc.	PP	Range
1	Ice Fang	Ice	Physical	65	95	15	Normal
1	Fire Fang	Fire	Physical	65	95	15	Normal
1	Thunder Fang	Electric	Physical	65	95	15	Normal
1	Tackle	Normal	Physical	40	100	35	Normal
1	Scary Face	Normal	Status	—	100	10	Normal
1	Tail Whip	Normal	Status	—	100	30	Many Others
1	Charm	Fairy	Status	—	100	20	Normal
7	Bite	Dark	Physical	60	100	25	Normal
13	Lick	Ghost	Physical	30	100	30	Normal
19	Headbutt	Normal	Physical	70	100	15	Normal
25	Roar	Normal	Status	—	—	20	Normal
31	Rage	Normal	Physical	20	100	20	Normal
37	Play Rough	Fairy	Physical	90	90	10	Normal
43	Payback	Dark	Physical	50	100	10	Normal
49	Crunch	Dark	Physical	80	100	15	Normal

TM MOVES

No.	Name	Type	Kind	Pow.	Acc.	PP	Range
TM01	Work Up	Normal	Status	—	—	30	Self
TM05	Roar	Normal	Status	—	—	20	Normal
TM06	Toxic	Poison	Status	—	90	10	Normal
TM08	Bulk Up	Fighting	Status	—	—	20	Self
TM10	Hidden Power	Normal	Special	60	100	15	Normal
TM11	Sunny Day	Fire	Status	—	—	5	Both Sides
TM12	Taunt	Dark	Status	—	100	20	Normal
TM17	Protect	Normal	Status	—	—	10	Self
TM18	Rain Dance	Water	Status	—	—	5	Both Sides
TM21	Frustration	Normal	Physical	—	100	20	Normal
TM22	Solar Beam	Grass	Special	120	100	10	Normal
TM24	Thunderbolt	Electric	Special	90	100	15	Normal
TM25	Thunder	Electric	Special	110	70	10	Normal
TM26	Earthquake	Ground	Physical	100	100	10	Adjacent
TM27	Return	Normal	Physical	—	100	20	Normal
TM30	Shadow Ball	Ghost	Special	80	100	15	Normal
TM31	Brick Break	Fighting	Physical	75	100	15	Normal
TM32	Double Team	Normal	Status	—	—	15	Self
TM33	Reflect	Psychic	Status	—	—	20	Your Side
TM35	Flamethrower	Fire	Special	90	100	15	Normal
TM36	Sludge Bomb	Poison	Special	90	100	10	Normal
TM38	Fire Blast	Fire	Special	110	85	5	Normal
TM41	Torment	Dark	Status	—	100	15	Normal
TM42	Facade	Normal	Physical	70	100	20	Normal
TM44	Rest	Psychic	Status	—	—	10	Self
TM45	Attract	Normal	Status	—	100	15	Normal
TM46	Thief	Dark	Physical	60	100	25	Normal
TM48	Round	Normal	Special	60	100	15	Normal
TM50	Overheat	Fire	Special	130	90	5	Normal
TM56	Fling	Dark	Physical	—	100	10	Normal
TM66	Payback	Dark	Physical	50	100	10	Normal
TM73	Thunder Wave	Electric	Status	—	90	20	Normal
TM78	Bulldoze	Ground	Physical	60	100	20	Adjacent
TM87	Swagger	Normal	Status	—	85	15	Normal
TM88	Sleep Talk	Normal	Status	—	—	10	Self
TM90	Substitute	Normal	Status	—	—	10	Self
TM93	Wild Charge	Electric	Physical	90	100	15	Normal
TM95	Snarl	Dark	Special	55	95	15	Many Others
TM99	Dazzling Gleam	Fairy	Special	80	100	10	Many Others
TM100	Confide	Normal	Status	—	—	20	Normal

MOVES TAUGHT BY PEOPLE

Name	Type	Kind	Pow.	Acc.	PP	Range

MOVES LEARNED WHEN EVOLVING

Name	Type	Kind	Pow.	Acc.	PP	Range

EGG MOVES

Name	Type	Kind	Pow.	Acc.	PP	Range
Metronome	Normal	Status	—	—	10	Self
Feint Attack	Dark	Physical	60	—	20	Normal
Present	Normal	Physical	—	90	15	Normal
Crunch	Dark	Physical	80	100	15	Normal
Heal Bell	Normal	Status	—	—	5	Your Party
Snore	Normal	Special	50	100	15	Normal
Smelling Salts	Normal	Physical	70	100	10	Normal
Close Combat	Fighting	Physical	120	100	5	Normal
Ice Fang	Ice	Physical	65	95	15	Normal
Fire Fang	Fire	Physical	65	95	15	Normal
Thunder Fang	Electric	Physical	65	95	15	Normal
Focus Punch	Fighting	Physical	150	100	20	Normal
Double-Edge	Normal	Physical	120	100	15	Normal
Mimic	Normal	Status	—	—	10	Normal
Fake Tears	Dark	Status	—	100	20	Normal

EXCLUSIVE Z-MOVE

Name	Base Move	Type	Kind	Pow.	Acc.	Range

Granbull

Alola Pokédex	Melemele	Akala	Ula'ula	Poni
	259	—	—	074

Granbull
Fairy Pokémon
FAIRY
HEIGHT: 4'07"
WEIGHT: 107.4 lbs.

Its well-developed lower jaw and heavy fangs are its weapons. As long as it's not provoked, it rarely bites.

More timid than Snubbull, this Pokémon is doted on by young people amused at the contrast between its looks and its attitude.

ABILITY
Intimidate
Quick Feet

HIDDEN ABILITY
Rattled

Damage taken in normal battles

NORMAL ×1	FIGHTING ×0.5	ROCK ×1
FIRE ×1	POISON ×2	GHOST ×1
WATER ×1	GROUND ×1	DRAGON ×0
GRASS ×1	FLYING ×1	DARK ×1
ELECTRIC ×1	PSYCHIC ×1	STEEL ×2
ICE ×1	BUG ×0.5	FAIRY ×1

SPECIES STRENGTHS
HP ◆◆◆
Attack ◆◆◆◆◆◆
Defense ◆◆◆
Sp. Atk ◆◆◆
Sp. Def ◆◆◆
Speed ◆◆◆

EGG GROUPS
Field
Fairy

ITEM SOMETIMES HELD BY WILD POKÉMON
—

EVOLUTION
Snubbull → Lv. 23 → Granbull

MAIN WAY TO REGISTER IN THE POKÉDEX
Catch in the tall grass in Poni Wilds

Same form for male/female

LEVEL-UP MOVES

Lv.	Name	Type	Kind	Pow.	Acc.	PP	Range
1	Outrage	Dragon	Physical	120	100	10	1 Random
1	Ice Fang	Ice	Physical	65	95	15	Normal
1	Fire Fang	Fire	Physical	65	95	15	Normal
1	Thunder Fang	Electric	Physical	65	95	15	Normal
1	Tackle	Normal	Physical	40	100	35	Normal
1	Scary Face	Normal	Status	—	100	10	Normal
1	Tail Whip	Normal	Status	—	100	30	Many Others
1	Charm	Fairy	Status	—	100	20	Normal
7	Bite	Dark	Physical	60	100	25	Normal
13	Lick	Ghost	Physical	30	100	30	Normal
19	Headbutt	Normal	Physical	70	100	15	Normal
27	Roar	Normal	Status	—	—	20	Normal
35	Rage	Normal	Physical	20	100	20	Normal
43	Play Rough	Fairy	Physical	90	90	10	Normal
51	Payback	Dark	Physical	50	100	10	Normal
59	Crunch	Dark	Physical	80	100	15	Normal
67	Outrage	Dragon	Physical	120	100	10	1 Random

TM MOVES

No.	Name	Type	Kind	Pow.	Acc.	PP	Range
TM01	Work Up	Normal	Status	—	—	30	Self
TM05	Roar	Normal	Status	—	—	20	Normal
TM06	Toxic	Poison	Status	—	90	10	Normal
TM08	Bulk Up	Fighting	Status	—	—	20	Self
TM10	Hidden Power	Normal	Special	60	100	15	Normal
TM11	Sunny Day	Fire	Status	—	—	5	Both Sides
TM12	Taunt	Dark	Status	—	100	20	Normal
TM15	Hyper Beam	Normal	Special	150	90	5	Normal
TM17	Protect	Normal	Status	—	—	10	Self
TM18	Rain Dance	Water	Status	—	—	5	Both Sides
TM21	Frustration	Normal	Physical	—	100	20	Normal
TM22	Solar Beam	Grass	Special	120	100	10	Normal
TM24	Thunderbolt	Electric	Special	90	100	15	Normal
TM25	Thunder	Electric	Special	110	70	10	Normal
TM26	Earthquake	Ground	Physical	100	100	10	Adjacent
TM27	Return	Normal	Physical	—	100	20	Normal
TM30	Shadow Ball	Ghost	Special	80	100	15	Normal
TM31	Brick Break	Fighting	Physical	75	100	15	Normal
TM32	Double Team	Normal	Status	—	—	15	Self
TM33	Reflect	Psychic	Status	—	—	20	Your Side
TM35	Flamethrower	Fire	Special	90	100	15	Normal
TM36	Sludge Bomb	Poison	Special	90	100	10	Normal
TM38	Fire Blast	Fire	Special	110	85	5	Normal
TM39	Rock Tomb	Rock	Physical	60	95	15	Normal
TM41	Torment	Dark	Status	—	100	15	Normal
TM42	Facade	Normal	Physical	70	100	20	Normal
TM44	Rest	Psychic	Status	—	—	10	Self
TM45	Attract	Normal	Status	—	100	15	Normal

No.	Name	Type	Kind	Pow.	Acc.	PP	Range
TM46	Thief	Dark	Physical	60	100	25	Normal
TM48	Round	Normal	Special	60	100	15	Normal
TM50	Overheat	Fire	Special	130	90	5	Normal
TM52	Focus Blast	Fighting	Special	120	70	5	Normal
TM56	Fling	Dark	Physical	—	100	10	Normal
TM66	Payback	Dark	Physical	50	100	10	Normal
TM68	Giga Impact	Normal	Physical	150	90	5	Normal
TM71	Stone Edge	Rock	Physical	100	80	5	Normal
TM73	Thunder Wave	Electric	Status	—	90	20	Normal
TM78	Bulldoze	Ground	Physical	60	100	20	Adjacent
TM80	Rock Slide	Rock	Physical	75	90	10	Many Others
TM87	Swagger	Normal	Status	—	85	15	Normal
TM88	Sleep Talk	Normal	Status	—	—	10	Self
TM90	Substitute	Normal	Status	—	—	10	Self
TM93	Wild Charge	Electric	Physical	90	100	15	Normal
TM95	Snarl	Dark	Special	55	95	15	Many Others
TM99	Dazzling Gleam	Fairy	Special	80	100	10	Many Others
TM100	Confide	Normal	Status	—	—	20	Normal

MOVES TAUGHT BY PEOPLE

Name	Type	Kind	Pow.	Acc.	PP	Range

MOVES LEARNED WHEN EVOLVING

Name	Type	Kind	Pow.	Acc.	PP	Range

EGG MOVES

Name	Type	Kind	Pow.	Acc.	PP	Range

EXCLUSIVE Z-MOVE

Name	Base Move	Type	Kind	Pow.	Acc.	Range

Shellos

Alola Pokédex	Melemele	Akala	Ula'ula	Poni
260	—	—	—	075

Sea Slug Pokémon

WATER

HEIGHT: 1'00"
WEIGHT: 13.9 lbs.

Shellos lives in the sea and feasts on plankton. The lovelier the ocean where Shellos resides, the more vibrant its color becomes.

The difference in color from one Shellos to another seems to be a result of their diet. No large changes can be seen in their capabilities.

ABILITY
Sticky Hold
Storm Drain

HIDDEN ABILITY
Sand Force

SPECIES STRENGTHS
HP	◆◆◆
Attack	◆◆◆
Defense	◆◆◆
Sp. Atk	◆◆
Sp. Def	◆◆◆
Speed	◆◆

EGG GROUPS
Water 1 — Amorphous

ITEM SOMETIMES HELD BY WILD POKÉMON
—

EVOLUTION

Shellos → Lvl 30 → Gastrodon

MAIN WAY TO REGISTER IN THE POKÉDEX
Leave a female Gastrodon at the Pokémon Nursery with another Pokémon, then hatch the Pokémon Egg that is found

EAST SEA

Same form for male/female

Damage taken in normal battles
NORMAL ×1	FIGHTING ×1	ROCK ×1
FIRE ×0.5	POISON ×1	GHOST ×1
WATER ×0.5	GROUND ×1	DRAGON ×1
GRASS ×2	FLYING ×1	DARK ×1
ELECTRIC ×2	PSYCHIC ×1	STEEL ×0.5
ICE ×0.5	BUG ×1	FAIRY ×1

◆ LEVEL-UP MOVES
Lv.	Name	Type	Kind	Pow.	Acc.	PP	Range
1	Mud-Slap	Ground	Special	20	100	10	Normal
2	Mud Sport	Ground	Status	—	—	15	Both Sides
4	Harden	Normal	Status	—	—	30	Self
7	Water Pulse	Water	Special	60	100	20	Normal
11	Mud Bomb	Ground	Special	65	85	10	Normal
16	Hidden Power	Normal	Special	60	100	15	Normal
22	Rain Dance	Water	Status	—	—	5	Both Sides
29	Body Slam	Normal	Physical	85	100	15	Normal
37	Muddy Water	Water	Special	90	85	10	Many Others
46	Recover	Normal	Status	—	—	10	Self

◆ TM MOVES
No.	Name	Type	Kind	Pow.	Acc.	PP	Range
TM06	Toxic	Poison	Status	—	90	10	Normal
TM07	Hail	Ice	Status	—	—	10	Both Sides
TM10	Hidden Power	Normal	Special	60	100	15	Normal
TM13	Ice Beam	Ice	Special	90	100	10	Normal
TM14	Blizzard	Ice	Special	110	70	5	Many Others
TM17	Protect	Normal	Status	—	—	10	Self
TM18	Rain Dance	Water	Status	—	—	5	Both Sides
TM21	Frustration	Normal	Physical	—	100	20	Normal
TM27	Return	Normal	Physical	—	100	20	Normal
TM32	Double Team	Normal	Status	—	—	15	Self
TM42	Facade	Normal	Physical	70	100	20	Normal
TM44	Rest	Psychic	Status	—	—	10	Self
TM45	Attract	Normal	Status	—	100	15	Normal
TM48	Round	Normal	Special	60	100	15	Normal
TM55	Scald	Water	Special	80	100	15	Normal
TM83	Infestation	Bug	Special	20	100	20	Normal
TM87	Swagger	Normal	Status	—	85	15	Normal
TM88	Sleep Talk	Normal	Status	—	—	10	Self
TM90	Substitute	Normal	Status	—	—	10	Self
TM94	Surf	Water	Special	90	100	15	Adjacent
TM100	Confide	Normal	Status	—	—	20	Normal

◆ EXCLUSIVE Z-MOVE
Name	Base Move	Type	Kind	Pow.	Acc.	Range

◆ MOVES TAUGHT BY PEOPLE
Name	Type	Kind	Pow.	Acc.	PP	Range

◆ MOVES LEARNED WHEN EVOLVING
Name	Type	Kind	Pow.	Acc.	PP	Range

◆ EGG MOVES
Name	Type	Kind	Pow.	Acc.	PP	Range
Counter	Fighting	Physical	—	100	20	Varies
Mirror Coat	Psychic	Special	—	100	20	Varies
Stockpile	Normal	Status	—	—	20	Self
Swallow	Normal	Status	—	—	10	Self
Spit Up	Normal	Special	—	100	10	Normal
Yawn	Normal	Status	—	—	10	Normal
Memento	Dark	Status	—	100	10	Normal
Curse	Ghost	Status	—	—	10	Varies
Amnesia	Psychic	Status	—	—	20	Self
Fissure	Ground	Physical	—	30	5	Normal
Trump Card	Normal	Special	—	—	5	Normal
Sludge	Poison	Special	65	100	20	Normal
Clear Smog	Poison	Special	50	—	15	Normal
Brine	Water	Special	65	100	10	Normal
Mist	Ice	Status	—	—	30	Your Side
Acid Armor	Poison	Status	—	—	20	Self

Gastrodon

Alola Pokédex	Melemele	Akala	Ula'ula	Poni
261	—	—	—	076

Sea Slug Pokémon

WATER **GROUND**

HEIGHT: 2'11"
WEIGHT: 65.9 lbs.

A team of researchers is scouring the oceans of the world in search of a Gastrodon in a color never seen before.

Experiments are being conducted to discover what happens when a Gastrodon is raised in a location other than the sea where it was born.

ABILITY
Sticky Hold
Storm Drain

HIDDEN ABILITY
Sand Force

SPECIES STRENGTHS
HP	◆◆◆◆
Attack	◆◆◆◆
Defense	◆◆◆◆
Sp. Atk	◆◆◆◆◆
Sp. Def	◆◆◆◆
Speed	◆◆◆

EGG GROUPS
Water 1 — Amorphous

ITEM SOMETIMES HELD BY WILD POKÉMON
—

EVOLUTION
Shellos → LV. 30 → Gastrodon

MAIN WAY TO REGISTER IN THE POKÉDEX
Catch on the water surface in Poni Wilds

EAST SEA
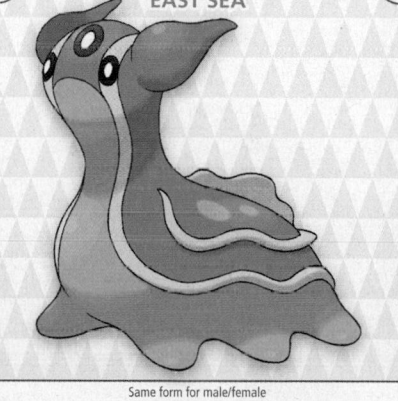
Same form for male/female

Damage taken in normal battles
NORMAL ×1	FIGHTING ×1	ROCK ×0.5
FIRE ×0.5	POISON ×0.5	GHOST ×1
WATER ×1	GROUND ×1	DRAGON ×1
GRASS ×4	FLYING ×1	DARK ×1
ELECTRIC ×0	PSYCHIC ×1	STEEL ×0.5
ICE ×1	BUG ×1	FAIRY ×1

◆ LEVEL-UP MOVES
Lv.	Name	Type	Kind	Pow.	Acc.	PP	Range
1	Mud-Slap	Ground	Special	20	100	10	Normal
1	Mud Sport	Ground	Status	—	—	15	Both Sides
1	Harden	Normal	Status	—	—	30	Self
1	Water Pulse	Water	Special	60	100	20	Normal
2	Mud Sport	Ground	Status	—	—	15	Both Sides
4	Harden	Normal	Status	—	—	30	Self
7	Water Pulse	Water	Special	60	100	20	Normal
11	Mud Bomb	Ground	Special	65	85	10	Normal
16	Hidden Power	Normal	Special	60	100	15	Normal
22	Rain Dance	Water	Status	—	—	5	Both Sides
29	Body Slam	Normal	Physical	85	100	15	Normal
41	Muddy Water	Water	Special	90	85	10	Many Others
54	Recover	Normal	Status	—	—	10	Self

◆ TM MOVES
No.	Name	Type	Kind	Pow.	Acc.	PP	Range
TM06	Toxic	Poison	Status	—	90	10	Normal
TM07	Hail	Ice	Status	—	—	10	Both Sides
TM10	Hidden Power	Normal	Special	60	100	15	Normal
TM13	Ice Beam	Ice	Special	90	100	10	Normal
TM14	Blizzard	Ice	Special	110	70	5	Many Others
TM15	Hyper Beam	Normal	Special	150	90	5	Normal
TM17	Protect	Normal	Status	—	—	10	Self
TM18	Rain Dance	Water	Status	—	—	5	Both Sides
TM21	Frustration	Normal	Physical	—	100	20	Normal
TM26	Earthquake	Ground	Physical	100	100	10	Adjacent
TM27	Return	Normal	Physical	—	100	20	Normal
TM32	Double Team	Normal	Status	—	—	15	Self
TM34	Sludge Wave	Poison	Special	95	100	10	Adjacent
TM36	Sludge Bomb	Poison	Special	90	100	10	Normal
TM37	Sandstorm	Rock	Status	—	—	10	Both Sides
TM39	Rock Tomb	Rock	Physical	60	95	15	Normal
TM42	Facade	Normal	Physical	70	100	20	Normal
TM44	Rest	Psychic	Status	—	—	10	Self
TM45	Attract	Normal	Status	—	100	15	Normal
TM48	Round	Normal	Special	60	100	15	Normal
TM55	Scald	Water	Special	80	100	15	Normal
TM68	Giga Impact	Normal	Physical	150	90	5	Normal
TM71	Stone Edge	Rock	Physical	100	80	5	Normal
TM78	Bulldoze	Ground	Physical	60	100	20	Adjacent
TM80	Rock Slide	Rock	Physical	75	90	10	Many Others
TM83	Infestation	Bug	Special	20	100	20	Normal
TM87	Swagger	Normal	Status	—	85	15	Normal
TM88	Sleep Talk	Normal	Status	—	—	10	Self
TM90	Substitute	Normal	Status	—	—	10	Self
TM94	Surf	Water	Special	90	100	15	Adjacent
TM98	Waterfall	Water	Physical	80	100	15	Normal
TM100	Confide	Normal	Status	—	—	20	Normal

◆ EXCLUSIVE Z-MOVE
Name	Base Move	Type	Kind	Pow.	Acc.	Range

◆ MOVES TAUGHT BY PEOPLE
Name	Type	Kind	Pow.	Acc.	PP	Range

◆ MOVES LEARNED WHEN EVOLVING
Name	Type	Kind	Pow.	Acc.	PP	Range

◆ EGG MOVES
Name	Type	Kind	Pow.	Acc.	PP	Range

Relicanth

Longevity Pokémon

Alola Pokédex	Melemele	Akala	Ula'ula	Poni
262	—	—	—	077

WATER **ROCK**

HEIGHT: 3'03"
WEIGHT: 51.6 lbs.

Its form has remained the same for one hundred million years. Its body is filled with fat, so it can withstand the water pressure of the deep sea.

It was fortuitously discovered during a deep sea expedition. Its teeth have atrophied, so it now survives on microscopic organisms it sucks up.

ABILITY
Swift Swim
Rock Head

HIDDEN ABILITY
Sturdy

Damage taken in normal battles

NORMAL ×0.5	FIGHTING ×2	ROCK ×1	
FIRE ×0.25	POISON ×0.5	GHOST ×1	
WATER ×1	GROUND ×2	DRAGON ×1	
GRASS ×4	FLYING ×0.5	DARK ×1	
ELECTRIC ×2	PSYCHIC ×1	STEEL ×1	
ICE ×0.5	BUG ×1	FAIRY ×1	

SPECIES STRENGTHS
HP ◆◆◆◆
Attack ◆◆◆◆◆
Defense ◆◆◆◆◆◆◆
Sp. Atk ◆◆◆◆
Sp. Def ◆◆◆◆
Speed ◆◆◆◆

EGG GROUPS
Water 1   Water 2

ITEM SOMETIMES HELD BY WILD POKÉMON
Deep Sea Scale

EVOLUTION
Does not evolve

MAIN WAY TO REGISTER IN THE POKÉDEX
Catch in the rare fishing spot in Poni Wilds

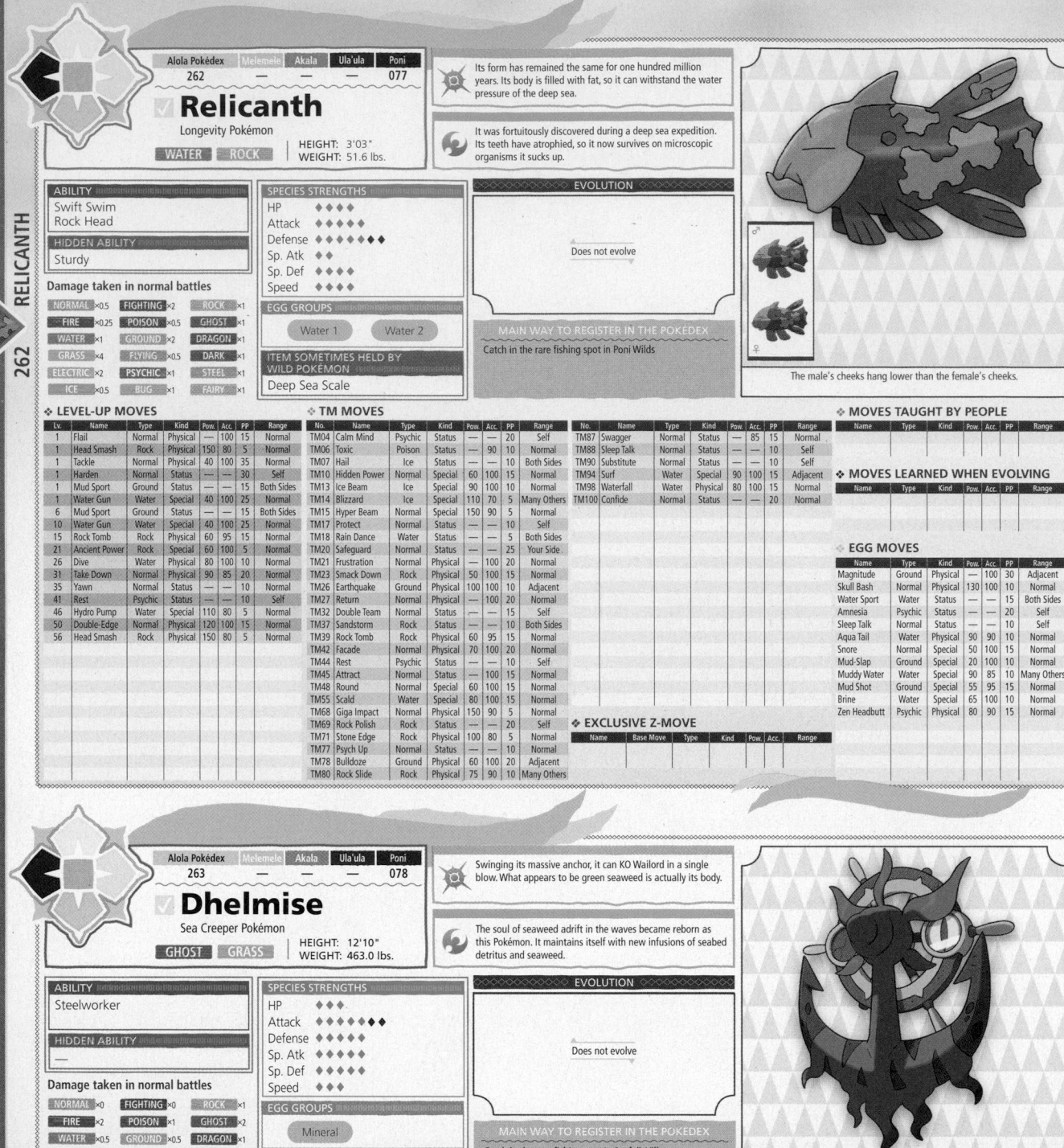

The male's cheeks hang lower than the female's cheeks.

❖ LEVEL-UP MOVES

Lv.	Name	Type	Kind	Pow.	Acc.	PP	Range
1	Flail	Normal	Physical	—	100	15	Normal
1	Head Smash	Rock	Physical	150	80	5	Normal
1	Tackle	Normal	Physical	40	100	35	Normal
1	Harden	Normal	Status	—	—	30	Self
1	Mud Sport	Ground	Status	—	—	15	Both Sides
1	Water Gun	Water	Special	40	100	25	Normal
6	Mud Sport	Ground	Status	—	—	15	Both Sides
10	Water Gun	Water	Special	40	100	25	Normal
10	Protect	Normal	Status	—	—	10	Self
15	Rock Tomb	Rock	Physical	60	95	15	Normal
21	Ancient Power	Rock	Special	60	100	5	Normal
26	Dive	Water	Physical	80	100	10	Normal
31	Take Down	Normal	Physical	90	85	20	Normal
35	Yawn	Normal	Status	—	—	10	Normal
41	Rest	Psychic	Status	—	—	10	Self
46	Hydro Pump	Water	Special	110	80	5	Normal
50	Double-Edge	Normal	Physical	120	100	15	Normal
56	Head Smash	Rock	Physical	150	80	5	Normal

❖ TM MOVES

No.	Name	Type	Kind	Pow.	Acc.	PP	Range
TM04	Calm Mind	Psychic	Status	—	—	20	Self
TM06	Toxic	Poison	Status	—	90	10	Normal
TM07	Hail	Ice	Status	—	—	10	Both Sides
TM10	Hidden Power	Normal	Special	60	100	15	Normal
TM13	Ice Beam	Ice	Special	90	100	10	Normal
TM14	Blizzard	Ice	Special	110	70	5	Many Others
TM15	Hyper Beam	Normal	Special	150	90	5	Normal
TM17	Protect	Normal	Status	—	—	10	Self
TM18	Rain Dance	Water	Status	—	—	5	Both Sides
TM20	Safeguard	Normal	Status	—	—	25	Your Side
TM21	Frustration	Normal	Physical	—	100	20	Normal
TM23	Smack Down	Rock	Physical	50	100	15	Normal
TM26	Earthquake	Ground	Physical	100	100	10	Adjacent
TM27	Return	Normal	Physical	—	100	20	Normal
TM32	Double Team	Normal	Status	—	—	15	Self
TM37	Sandstorm	Rock	Status	—	—	10	Both Sides
TM39	Rock Tomb	Rock	Physical	60	95	15	Normal
TM42	Facade	Normal	Physical	70	100	20	Normal
TM44	Rest	Psychic	Status	—	—	10	Self
TM45	Attract	Normal	Status	—	100	15	Normal
TM48	Round	Normal	Special	60	100	15	Normal
TM55	Scald	Water	Special	80	100	15	Normal
TM68	Giga Impact	Normal	Physical	150	90	5	Normal
TM69	Rock Polish	Rock	Status	—	—	20	Self
TM71	Stone Edge	Rock	Physical	100	80	5	Normal
TM77	Psych Up	Normal	Status	—	—	10	Normal
TM78	Bulldoze	Ground	Physical	60	100	20	Adjacent
TM80	Rock Slide	Rock	Physical	75	90	10	Many Others

No.	Name	Type	Kind	Pow.	Acc.	PP	Range
TM87	Swagger	Normal	Status	—	85	15	Normal
TM88	Sleep Talk	Normal	Status	—	—	10	Self
TM90	Substitute	Normal	Status	—	—	10	Self
TM94	Surf	Water	Special	90	100	15	Adjacent
TM98	Waterfall	Water	Physical	80	100	15	Normal
TM100	Confide	Normal	Status	—	—	20	Normal

❖ MOVES TAUGHT BY PEOPLE

Name	Type	Kind	Pow.	Acc.	PP	Range

❖ MOVES LEARNED WHEN EVOLVING

Name	Type	Kind	Pow.	Acc.	PP	Range

❖ EGG MOVES

Name	Type	Kind	Pow.	Acc.	PP	Range
Magnitude	Ground	Physical	—	100	30	Adjacent
Skull Bash	Normal	Physical	130	100	10	Normal
Water Sport	Water	Status	—	—	15	Both Sides
Amnesia	Psychic	Status	—	—	20	Self
Sleep Talk	Normal	Status	—	—	10	Self
Aqua Tail	Water	Physical	90	90	10	Normal
Snore	Normal	Special	50	100	15	Normal
Mud-Slap	Ground	Special	20	100	10	Normal
Muddy Water	Water	Special	90	85	10	Many Others
Mud Shot	Ground	Special	55	95	15	Normal
Brine	Water	Special	65	100	10	Normal
Zen Headbutt	Psychic	Physical	80	90	15	Normal

❖ EXCLUSIVE Z-MOVE

Name	Base Move	Type	Kind	Pow.	Acc.	Range

Dhelmise

Sea Creeper Pokémon

Alola Pokédex	Melemele	Akala	Ula'ula	Poni
263	—	—	—	078

GHOST **GRASS**

HEIGHT: 12'10"
WEIGHT: 463.0 lbs.

Swinging its massive anchor, it can KO Wailord in a single blow. What appears to be green seaweed is actually its body.

The soul of seaweed adrift in the waves became reborn as this Pokémon. It maintains itself with new infusions of seabed detritus and seaweed.

ABILITY
Steelworker

HIDDEN ABILITY
—

Damage taken in normal battles

NORMAL ×0	FIGHTING ×0	ROCK ×1	
FIRE ×2	POISON ×1	GHOST ×1	
WATER ×0.5	GROUND ×0.5	DRAGON ×1	
GRASS ×1	FLYING ×1	DARK ×1	
ELECTRIC ×0.5	PSYCHIC ×1	STEEL ×1	
ICE ×2	BUG ×1	FAIRY ×1	

SPECIES STRENGTHS
HP ◆◆◆
Attack ◆◆◆◆◆◆◆◆
Defense ◆◆◆◆◆
Sp. Atk ◆◆◆◆◆
Sp. Def ◆◆◆◆◆
Speed ◆◆◆

EGG GROUPS
Mineral

ITEM SOMETIMES HELD BY WILD POKÉMON
—

EVOLUTION
Does not evolve

MAIN WAY TO REGISTER IN THE POKÉDEX
Catch in the rare fishing spot in Seafolk Village

Gender unknown

❖ LEVEL-UP MOVES

Lv.	Name	Type	Kind	Pow.	Acc.	PP	Range
1	Switcheroo	Dark	Status	—	100	10	Normal
1	Absorb	Grass	Special	20	100	25	Normal
1	Growth	Normal	Status	—	—	20	Self
1	Rapid Spin	Normal	Physical	20	100	40	Normal
1	Astonish	Ghost	Physical	30	100	15	Normal
5	Mega Drain	Grass	Special	40	100	15	Normal
9	Wrap	Normal	Physical	15	90	20	Normal
14	Gyro Ball	Steel	Physical	—	100	5	Normal
18	Metal Sound	Steel	Status	—	85	40	Normal
23	Giga Drain	Grass	Special	75	100	10	Normal
27	Whirlpool	Water	Special	35	85	15	Normal
32	Anchor Shot	Steel	Physical	80	100	20	Normal
36	Shadow Ball	Ghost	Special	80	100	15	Normal
41	Energy Ball	Grass	Special	90	100	10	Normal
45	Slam	Normal	Physical	80	75	20	Normal
50	Heavy Slam	Steel	Physical	—	100	10	Normal
54	Phantom Force	Ghost	Physical	90	100	10	Normal
59	Power Whip	Grass	Physical	120	85	10	Normal

❖ TM MOVES

No.	Name	Type	Kind	Pow.	Acc.	PP	Range
TM06	Toxic	Poison	Status	—	90	10	Normal
TM10	Hidden Power	Normal	Special	60	100	15	Normal
TM11	Sunny Day	Fire	Status	—	—	5	Both Sides
TM15	Hyper Beam	Normal	Special	150	90	5	Normal
TM17	Protect	Normal	Status	—	—	10	Self
TM18	Rain Dance	Water	Status	—	—	5	Both Sides
TM21	Frustration	Normal	Physical	—	100	20	Normal
TM22	Solar Beam	Grass	Special	120	100	10	Normal
TM26	Earthquake	Ground	Physical	100	100	10	Adjacent
TM27	Return	Normal	Physical	—	100	20	Normal
TM30	Shadow Ball	Ghost	Special	80	100	15	Normal
TM31	Brick Break	Fighting	Physical	75	100	15	Normal
TM32	Double Team	Normal	Status	—	—	15	Self
TM34	Sludge Wave	Poison	Special	95	100	10	Adjacent
TM40	Aerial Ace	Flying	Physical	60	—	20	Normal
TM42	Facade	Normal	Physical	70	100	20	Normal
TM44	Rest	Psychic	Status	—	—	10	Self
TM45	Attract	Normal	Status	—	100	15	Normal
TM46	Thief	Dark	Physical	60	100	25	Normal
TM48	Round	Normal	Special	60	100	15	Normal
TM53	Energy Ball	Grass	Special	90	100	10	Normal
TM59	Brutal Swing	Dark	Physical	60	100	20	Adjacent
TM63	Embargo	Dark	Status	—	100	15	Normal
TM65	Shadow Claw	Ghost	Physical	70	100	15	Normal
TM66	Payback	Dark	Physical	50	100	10	Normal
TM68	Giga Impact	Normal	Physical	150	90	5	Normal
TM74	Gyro Ball	Steel	Physical	—	100	5	Normal
TM75	Swords Dance	Normal	Status	—	—	20	Self

No.	Name	Type	Kind	Pow.	Acc.	PP	Range
TM78	Bulldoze	Ground	Physical	60	100	20	Adjacent
TM80	Rock Slide	Rock	Physical	75	90	10	Many Others
TM86	Grass Knot	Grass	Special	—	100	20	Normal
TM87	Swagger	Normal	Status	—	85	15	Normal
TM88	Sleep Talk	Normal	Status	—	—	10	Self
TM90	Substitute	Normal	Status	—	—	10	Self
TM91	Flash Cannon	Steel	Special	80	100	10	Normal
TM94	Surf	Water	Special	90	100	15	Adjacent
TM100	Confide	Normal	Status	—	—	20	Normal

❖ MOVES TAUGHT BY PEOPLE

Name	Type	Kind	Pow.	Acc.	PP	Range

❖ MOVES LEARNED WHEN EVOLVING

Name	Type	Kind	Pow.	Acc.	PP	Range

❖ EGG MOVES

Name	Type	Kind	Pow.	Acc.	PP	Range

❖ EXCLUSIVE Z-MOVE

Name	Base Move	Type	Kind	Pow.	Acc.	Range

Carvanha

Savage Pokémon

Alola Pokédex	Melemele	Akala	Ula'ula	Poni
264	—	—	—	079

WATER · DARK

HEIGHT: 2'07"
WEIGHT: 45.9 lbs.

Each school has its own territory. Any intruders are mercilessly attacked with fangs bared.

If they scent the faintest trace of blood, they rush to attack en masse. When alone, they're rather cowardly.

ABILITY
Rough Skin

HIDDEN ABILITY
Speed Boost

Damage taken in normal battles

NORMAL ×1	FIGHTING ×2	ROCK ×1
FIRE ×0.5	POISON ×1	GHOST ×0.5
WATER ×0.5	GROUND ×1	DRAGON ×1
GRASS ×2	FLYING ×1	DARK ×0.5
ELECTRIC ×2	PSYCHIC ×0	STEEL ×0.5
ICE ×0.5	BUG ×2	FAIRY ×1

SPECIES STRENGTHS
- HP ◆◆
- Attack ◆◆◆◆
- Defense ◆
- Sp. Atk ◆◆◆◆
- Sp. Def ◆
- Speed ◆◆◆

EGG GROUPS
Water 2

ITEM SOMETIMES HELD BY WILD POKÉMON
Deep Sea Tooth

EVOLUTION
Carvanha → Lv. 30 → Sharpedo

MAIN WAY TO REGISTER IN THE POKÉDEX
Leave a female Sharpedo at the Pokémon Nursery with another Pokémon, then hatch the Egg that is found

Same form for male/female

❖ LEVEL-UP MOVES

Lv.	Name	Type	Kind	Pow.	Acc.	PP	Range
1	Leer	Normal	Status	—	100	30	Many Others
1	Bite	Dark	Physical	60	100	25	Normal
4	Rage	Normal	Physical	20	100	20	Normal
8	Focus Energy	Normal	Status	—	—	30	Self
11	Aqua Jet	Water	Physical	40	100	20	Normal
15	Assurance	Dark	Physical	60	100	10	Normal
18	Screech	Normal	Status	—	85	40	Normal
22	Swagger	Normal	Status	—	85	15	Normal
25	Ice Fang	Ice	Physical	65	95	15	Normal
29	Scary Face	Normal	Status	—	100	10	Normal
32	Poison Fang	Poison	Physical	50	100	15	Normal
36	Crunch	Dark	Physical	80	100	15	Normal
39	Agility	Psychic	Status	—	—	20	Self
43	Take Down	Normal	Physical	90	85	20	Normal

❖ TM MOVES

No.	Name	Type	Kind	Pow.	Acc.	PP	Range
TM06	Toxic	Poison	Status	—	90	10	Normal
TM07	Hail	Ice	Status	—	—	10	Both Sides
TM10	Hidden Power	Normal	Special	60	100	15	Normal
TM12	Taunt	Dark	Status	—	100	20	Normal
TM13	Ice Beam	Ice	Special	90	100	10	Normal
TM14	Blizzard	Ice	Special	110	70	5	Many Others
TM17	Protect	Normal	Status	—	—	10	Self
TM18	Rain Dance	Water	Status	—	—	5	Both Sides
TM21	Frustration	Normal	Physical	—	100	20	Normal
TM27	Return	Normal	Physical	—	100	20	Normal
TM32	Double Team	Normal	Status	—	—	15	Self
TM41	Torment	Dark	Status	—	100	15	Normal
TM43	Facade	Normal	Physical	70	100	20	Self
TM44	Rest	Psychic	Status	—	—	10	Self
TM45	Attract	Normal	Status	—	100	15	Normal
TM46	Thief	Dark	Physical	60	100	25	Normal
TM48	Round	Normal	Special	60	100	15	Normal
TM55	Scald	Water	Special	80	100	15	Normal
TM66	Payback	Dark	Physical	50	100	10	Normal
TM87	Swagger	Normal	Status	—	85	15	Normal
TM88	Sleep Talk	Normal	Status	—	—	10	Self
TM90	Substitute	Normal	Status	—	—	10	Self
TM94	Surf	Water	Special	90	100	15	Adjacent
TM95	Snarl	Dark	Special	55	95	15	Many Others
TM97	Dark Pulse	Dark	Special	80	100	15	Normal
TM98	Waterfall	Water	Physical	80	100	15	Normal
TM100	Confide	Normal	Status	—	—	20	Normal

❖ MOVES TAUGHT BY PEOPLE

Name	Type	Kind	Pow.	Acc.	PP	Range

❖ MOVES LEARNED WHEN EVOLVING

Name	Type	Kind	Pow.	Acc.	PP	Range

❖ EGG MOVES

Name	Type	Kind	Pow.	Acc.	PP	Range
Hydro Pump	Water	Special	110	80	5	Normal
Double Edge	Normal	Physical	120	100	15	Normal
Thrash	Normal	Physical	120	100	10	1 Random
Ancient Power	Rock	Special	60	100	5	Normal
Swift	Normal	Special	60	—	20	Many Others
Brine	Water	Special	65	100	10	Normal
Destiny Bond	Ghost	Status	—	—	5	Self
Psychic Fangs	Psychic	Physical	85	100	10	Normal

❖ EXCLUSIVE Z-MOVE

Name	Base Move	Type	Kind	Pow.	Acc.	Range

Sharpedo

Brutal Pokémon

Alola Pokédex	Melemele	Akala	Ula'ula	Poni
265	—	—	—	080

WATER · DARK

HEIGHT: 5'11"
WEIGHT: 195.8 lbs.

It pursues its prey at speeds of 75 mph and finishes them off with fangs that can crush iron. It is known as the bully of the sea.

It has a sad history. In the past, its dorsal fin was a treasured foodstuff, so this Pokémon became a victim of overfishing.

ABILITY
Rough Skin

HIDDEN ABILITY
Speed Boost

Damage taken in normal battles

NORMAL ×1	FIGHTING ×2	ROCK ×1
FIRE ×0.5	POISON ×1	GHOST ×0.5
WATER ×0.5	GROUND ×1	DRAGON ×1
GRASS ×2	FLYING ×1	DARK ×0.5
ELECTRIC ×2	PSYCHIC ×0	STEEL ×0.5
ICE ×0.5	BUG ×2	FAIRY ×1

SPECIES STRENGTHS
- HP ◆◆◆
- Attack ◆◆◆◆◆◆
- Defense ◆◆
- Sp. Atk ◆◆◆◆◆
- Sp. Def ◆◆
- Speed ◆◆◆◆◆◆

EGG GROUPS
Water 2

ITEM SOMETIMES HELD BY WILD POKÉMON
Deep Sea Tooth

EVOLUTION
Carvanha → Lv. 30 → Sharpedo

MAIN WAY TO REGISTER IN THE POKÉDEX
Catch in the rare fishing spot on Poni Breaker Coast

p. 213

Same form for male/female

❖ LEVEL-UP MOVES

Lv.	Name	Type	Kind	Pow.	Acc.	PP	Range
1	Slash	Normal	Physical	70	100	20	Normal
1	Night Slash	Dark	Physical	70	100	15	Normal
1	Feint	Normal	Physical	30	100	10	Normal
1	Leer	Normal	Status	—	100	30	Many Others
1	Bite	Dark	Physical	60	100	25	Normal
1	Rage	Normal	Physical	20	100	20	Normal
1	Focus Energy	Normal	Status	—	—	30	Self
4	Rage	Normal	Physical	20	100	20	Normal
8	Focus Energy	Normal	Status	—	—	30	Self
11	Aqua Jet	Water	Physical	40	100	20	Normal
15	Assurance	Dark	Physical	60	100	10	Normal
18	Screech	Normal	Status	—	85	40	Normal
22	Swagger	Normal	Status	—	85	15	Normal
25	Ice Fang	Ice	Physical	65	95	15	Normal
29	Scary Face	Normal	Status	—	100	10	Normal
34	Poison Fang	Poison	Physical	50	100	15	Normal
40	Crunch	Dark	Physical	80	100	15	Normal
45	Agility	Psychic	Status	—	—	30	Self
51	Skull Bash	Normal	Physical	130	100	10	Normal
56	Taunt	Dark	Status	—	100	20	Normal
62	Night Slash	Dark	Physical	70	100	15	Normal

❖ TM MOVES

No.	Name	Type	Kind	Pow.	Acc.	PP	Range
TM05	Roar	Normal	Status	—	—	20	Normal
TM06	Toxic	Poison	Status	—	90	10	Normal
TM07	Hail	Ice	Status	—	—	10	Both Sides
TM10	Hidden Power	Normal	Special	60	100	15	Normal
TM12	Taunt	Dark	Status	—	100	20	Normal
TM13	Ice Beam	Ice	Special	90	100	10	Normal
TM14	Blizzard	Ice	Special	110	70	5	Many Others
TM15	Hyper Beam	Normal	Special	150	90	5	Normal
TM17	Protect	Normal	Status	—	—	10	Self
TM18	Rain Dance	Water	Status	—	—	5	Both Sides
TM21	Frustration	Normal	Physical	—	100	20	Normal
TM26	Earthquake	Ground	Physical	100	100	10	Adjacent
TM27	Return	Normal	Physical	—	100	20	Normal
TM32	Double Team	Normal	Status	—	—	15	Self
TM39	Rock Tomb	Rock	Physical	60	95	15	Normal
TM41	Torment	Dark	Status	—	100	15	Normal
TM42	Facade	Normal	Physical	70	100	20	Normal
TM44	Rest	Psychic	Status	—	—	10	Self
TM45	Attract	Normal	Status	—	100	15	Normal
TM46	Thief	Dark	Physical	60	100	25	Normal
TM48	Round	Normal	Special	60	100	15	Normal
TM55	Scald	Water	Special	80	100	15	Normal
TM66	Payback	Dark	Physical	50	100	10	Normal
TM68	Giga Impact	Normal	Physical	150	90	5	Normal
TM78	Bulldoze	Ground	Physical	60	100	20	Adjacent
TM84	Poison Jab	Poison	Physical	80	100	20	Normal
TM87	Swagger	Normal	Status	—	85	15	Normal
TM88	Sleep Talk	Normal	Status	—	—	10	Self

❖ MOVES TAUGHT BY PEOPLE

No.	Name	Type	Kind	Pow.	Acc.	PP	Range
TM90	Substitute	Normal	Status	—	—	10	Self
TM94	Surf	Water	Special	90	100	15	Adjacent
TM95	Snarl	Dark	Special	55	95	15	Many Others
TM97	Dark Pulse	Dark	Special	80	100	15	Normal
TM98	Waterfall	Water	Physical	80	100	15	Normal
TM100	Confide	Normal	Status	—	—	20	Normal

❖ MOVES LEARNED WHEN EVOLVING

Name	Type	Kind	Pow.	Acc.	PP	Range
Slash	Normal	Physical	70	100	20	Normal

❖ EGG MOVES

Name	Type	Kind	Pow.	Acc.	PP	Range

❖ EXCLUSIVE Z-MOVE

Name	Base Move	Type	Kind	Pow.	Acc.	Range

Wailmer

Ball Whale Pokémon

WATER

Alola Pokédex	Melemele	Akala	Ula'ula	Poni
266	—	—	—	081

HEIGHT: 6'07"
WEIGHT: 286.6 lbs.

It loves to startle people. It fills itself up with seawater and plays by bouncing around like a ball.

It shows off by spraying jets of seawater from the nostrils above its eyes. It eats a solid ton of Wishiwashi every day.

ABILITY
Water Veil
Oblivious

HIDDEN ABILITY
Pressure

SPECIES STRENGTHS
HP	◆◆◆◆◆
Attack	◆◆◆
Defense	◆◆
Sp. Atk	◆◆◆
Sp. Def	◆◆
Speed	◆◆◆◆

EGG GROUPS
Field / Water 2

ITEM SOMETIMES HELD BY WILD POKÉMON
—

Damage taken in normal battles
NORMAL ×1	FIGHTING ×1	ROCK ×1			
FIRE ×0.5	POISON ×1	GHOST ×1			
WATER ×0.5	GROUND ×0.5	DRAGON ×1			
GRASS ×2	FLYING ×1	DARK ×1			
ELECTRIC ×2	PSYCHIC ×1	STEEL ×0.5			
ICE ×0.5	BUG ×1	FAIRY ×1			

EVOLUTION
Wailmer — Lv. 40 → Wailord

Same form for male/female

MAIN WAY TO REGISTER IN THE POKÉDEX
Catch in the rare fishing spot in Seafolk Village

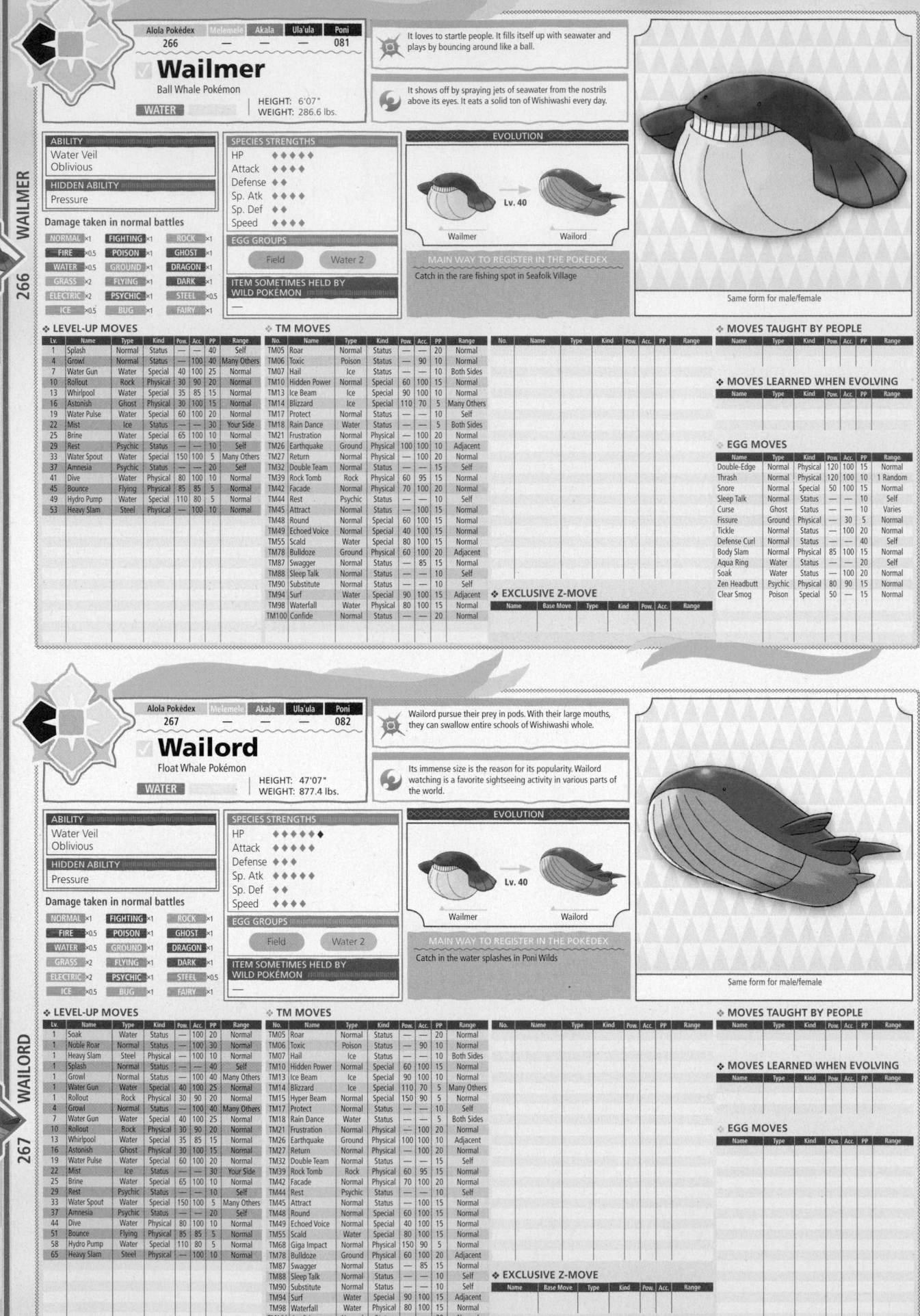

❖ LEVEL-UP MOVES
Lv.	Name	Type	Kind	Pow.	Acc.	PP	Range
1	Splash	Normal	Status	—	—	40	Self
4	Growl	Normal	Status	—	100	40	Many Others
7	Water Gun	Water	Special	40	100	25	Normal
10	Rollout	Rock	Physical	30	90	20	Normal
13	Whirlpool	Water	Special	35	85	15	Normal
16	Astonish	Ghost	Physical	30	100	15	Normal
19	Water Pulse	Water	Special	60	100	20	Normal
22	Mist	Ice	Status	—	—	30	Your Side
25	Brine	Water	Special	65	100	10	Normal
29	Rest	Psychic	Status	—	—	10	Self
33	Water Spout	Water	Special	150	100	5	Many Others
37	Amnesia	Psychic	Status	—	—	20	Self
41	Dive	Water	Physical	80	100	10	Normal
45	Bounce	Flying	Physical	85	85	5	Normal
49	Hydro Pump	Water	Special	110	80	5	Normal
53	Heavy Slam	Steel	Physical	—	100	10	Normal

❖ TM MOVES
No.	Name	Type	Kind	Pow.	Acc.	PP	Range
TM05	Roar	Normal	Status	—	—	20	Normal
TM06	Toxic	Poison	Status	—	90	10	Normal
TM07	Hail	Ice	Status	—	—	10	Both Sides
TM10	Hidden Power	Normal	Special	60	100	15	Normal
TM13	Ice Beam	Ice	Special	90	100	10	Normal
TM14	Blizzard	Ice	Special	110	70	5	Many Others
TM17	Protect	Normal	Status	—	—	10	Self
TM18	Rain Dance	Water	Status	—	—	5	Both Sides
TM21	Frustration	Normal	Physical	—	100	20	Normal
TM26	Earthquake	Ground	Physical	100	100	10	Adjacent
TM27	Return	Normal	Physical	—	100	20	Normal
TM32	Double Team	Normal	Status	—	—	15	Self
TM39	Rock Tomb	Rock	Physical	60	95	15	Normal
TM42	Facade	Normal	Physical	70	100	20	Normal
TM44	Rest	Psychic	Status	—	—	10	Self
TM45	Attract	Normal	Status	—	100	15	Normal
TM48	Round	Normal	Special	60	100	15	Normal
TM49	Echoed Voice	Normal	Special	40	100	15	Normal
TM55	Scald	Water	Special	80	100	15	Normal
TM78	Bulldoze	Ground	Physical	60	100	20	Adjacent
TM87	Swagger	Normal	Status	—	85	15	Normal
TM88	Sleep Talk	Normal	Status	—	—	10	Self
TM90	Substitute	Normal	Status	—	—	10	Self
TM94	Surf	Water	Special	90	100	15	Adjacent
TM98	Waterfall	Water	Physical	80	100	15	Normal
TM100	Confide	Normal	Status	—	—	20	Normal

❖ MOVES TAUGHT BY PEOPLE
Name	Type	Kind	Pow.	Acc.	PP	Range

❖ MOVES LEARNED WHEN EVOLVING
Name	Type	Kind	Pow.	Acc.	PP	Range

❖ EGG MOVES
Name	Type	Kind	Pow.	Acc.	PP	Range
Double-Edge	Normal	Physical	120	100	15	Normal
Thrash	Normal	Physical	120	100	10	1 Random
Snore	Normal	Special	50	100	15	Normal
Sleep Talk	Normal	Status	—	—	10	Self
Curse	Ghost	Status	—	—	10	Varies
Fissure	Ground	Physical	—	30	5	Normal
Tickle	Normal	Status	—	100	20	Normal
Defense Curl	Normal	Status	—	—	40	Self
Body Slam	Normal	Physical	85	100	15	Normal
Aqua Ring	Water	Status	—	—	20	Self
Soak	Water	Status	—	100	20	Normal
Zen Headbutt	Psychic	Physical	80	90	15	Normal
Clear Smog	Poison	Special	50	—	15	Normal

❖ EXCLUSIVE Z-MOVE
Name	Base Move	Type	Kind	Pow.	Acc.	Range

Wailord

Float Whale Pokémon

WATER

Alola Pokédex	Melemele	Akala	Ula'ula	Poni
267	—	—	—	082

HEIGHT: 47'07"
WEIGHT: 877.4 lbs.

Wailord pursue their prey in pods. With their large mouths, they can swallow entire schools of Wishiwashi whole.

Its immense size is the reason for its popularity. Wailord watching is a favorite sightseeing activity in various parts of the world.

ABILITY
Water Veil
Oblivious

HIDDEN ABILITY
Pressure

SPECIES STRENGTHS
HP	◆◆◆◆◆◆
Attack	◆◆◆◆◆
Defense	◆◆◆
Sp. Atk	◆◆◆◆◆
Sp. Def	◆◆
Speed	◆◆◆◆

EGG GROUPS
Field / Water 2

ITEM SOMETIMES HELD BY WILD POKÉMON
—

Damage taken in normal battles
NORMAL ×1	FIGHTING ×1	ROCK ×1			
FIRE ×0.5	POISON ×1	GHOST ×1			
WATER ×0.5	GROUND ×0.5	DRAGON ×1			
GRASS ×2	FLYING ×1	DARK ×1			
ELECTRIC ×2	PSYCHIC ×1	STEEL ×0.5			
ICE ×0.5	BUG ×1	FAIRY ×1			

EVOLUTION
Wailmer — Lv. 40 → Wailord

Same form for male/female

MAIN WAY TO REGISTER IN THE POKÉDEX
Catch in the water splashes in Poni Wilds

❖ LEVEL-UP MOVES
Lv.	Name	Type	Kind	Pow.	Acc.	PP	Range
1	Soak	Water	Status	—	100	20	Normal
1	Noble Roar	Normal	Status	—	100	30	Normal
1	Heavy Slam	Steel	Physical	—	100	10	Normal
1	Splash	Normal	Status	—	—	40	Self
1	Growl	Normal	Status	—	100	40	Many Others
1	Water Gun	Water	Special	40	100	25	Normal
1	Rollout	Rock	Physical	30	90	20	Normal
4	Growl	Normal	Status	—	100	40	Many Others
7	Water Gun	Water	Special	40	100	25	Normal
10	Rollout	Rock	Physical	30	90	20	Normal
13	Whirlpool	Water	Special	35	85	15	Normal
16	Astonish	Ghost	Physical	30	100	15	Normal
19	Water Pulse	Water	Special	60	100	20	Normal
22	Mist	Ice	Status	—	—	30	Your Side
25	Brine	Water	Special	65	100	10	Normal
29	Rest	Psychic	Status	—	—	10	Self
33	Water Spout	Water	Special	150	100	5	Many Others
37	Amnesia	Psychic	Status	—	—	20	Self
44	Dive	Water	Physical	80	100	10	Normal
51	Bounce	Flying	Physical	85	85	5	Normal
58	Hydro Pump	Water	Special	110	80	5	Normal
65	Heavy Slam	Steel	Physical	—	100	10	Normal

❖ TM MOVES
No.	Name	Type	Kind	Pow.	Acc.	PP	Range
TM05	Roar	Normal	Status	—	—	20	Normal
TM06	Toxic	Poison	Status	—	90	10	Normal
TM07	Hail	Ice	Status	—	—	10	Both Sides
TM10	Hidden Power	Normal	Special	60	100	15	Normal
TM13	Ice Beam	Ice	Special	90	100	10	Normal
TM14	Blizzard	Ice	Special	110	70	5	Many Others
TM15	Hyper Beam	Normal	Special	150	90	5	Normal
TM17	Protect	Normal	Status	—	—	10	Self
TM18	Rain Dance	Water	Status	—	—	5	Both Sides
TM21	Frustration	Normal	Physical	—	100	20	Normal
TM26	Earthquake	Ground	Physical	100	100	10	Adjacent
TM27	Return	Normal	Physical	—	100	20	Normal
TM32	Double Team	Normal	Status	—	—	15	Self
TM39	Rock Tomb	Rock	Physical	60	95	15	Normal
TM42	Facade	Normal	Physical	70	100	20	Normal
TM44	Rest	Psychic	Status	—	—	10	Self
TM45	Attract	Normal	Status	—	100	15	Normal
TM48	Round	Normal	Special	60	100	15	Normal
TM49	Echoed Voice	Normal	Special	40	100	15	Normal
TM55	Scald	Water	Special	80	100	15	Normal
TM68	Giga Impact	Normal	Physical	150	90	5	Normal
TM78	Bulldoze	Ground	Physical	60	100	20	Adjacent
TM87	Swagger	Normal	Status	—	85	15	Normal
TM88	Sleep Talk	Normal	Status	—	—	10	Self
TM90	Substitute	Normal	Status	—	—	10	Self
TM94	Surf	Water	Special	90	100	15	Adjacent
TM98	Waterfall	Water	Physical	80	100	15	Normal
TM100	Confide	Normal	Status	—	—	20	Normal

❖ MOVES TAUGHT BY PEOPLE
Name	Type	Kind	Pow.	Acc.	PP	Range

❖ MOVES LEARNED WHEN EVOLVING
Name	Type	Kind	Pow.	Acc.	PP	Range

❖ EGG MOVES
Name	Type	Kind	Pow.	Acc.	PP	Range

❖ EXCLUSIVE Z-MOVE
Name	Base Move	Type	Kind	Pow.	Acc.	Range

Alola Pokédex	Melemele	Akala	Ula'ula	Poni
268				093

Lapras
Transport Pokémon

WATER **ICE**

HEIGHT: 8'02"
WEIGHT: 485.0 lbs.

Its high intelligence enables it to comprehend human speech. When it's in a good mood, it sings in its beautiful voice.

These Pokémon were once near extinction due to poaching. Following protective regulations, there is now an overabundance of them.

Same form for male/female

ABILITY
Water Absorb
Shell Armor

HIDDEN ABILITY
Hydration

SPECIES STRENGTHS
HP	◆◆◆◆
Attack	◆◆◆◆◆
Defense	◆◆◆◆
Sp. Atk	◆◆◆◆◆
Sp. Def	◆◆◆◆◆ ◆
Speed	◆◆◆◆

EGG GROUPS
Monster | Water 1

ITEM SOMETIMES HELD BY WILD POKÉMON
Mystic Water

EVOLUTION
Does not evolve

MAIN WAY TO REGISTER IN THE POKÉDEX
Catch on the water surface in Poni Wilds

Damage taken in normal battles
NORMAL ×1	FIGHTING ×2	ROCK ×1
FIRE ×1	POISON ×1	GHOST ×1
WATER ×0.5	GROUND ×1	DRAGON ×1
GRASS ×2	FLYING ×1	DARK ×1
ELECTRIC ×2	PSYCHIC ×1	STEEL ×1
ICE ×0.25	BUG ×1	FAIRY ×1

❖ LEVEL-UP MOVES
Lv.	Name	Type	Kind	Pow.	Acc.	PP	Range
1	Sing	Normal	Status	—	55	15	Normal
1	Growl	Normal	Status	—	100	40	Many Others
1	Water Gun	Water	Special	40	100	25	Normal
4	Mist	Ice	Status	—	—	30	Your Side
7	Confuse Ray	Ghost	Status	—	100	10	Normal
10	Ice Shard	Ice	Physical	40	100	30	Normal
14	Water Pulse	Water	Special	60	100	20	Normal
18	Body Slam	Normal	Physical	85	100	15	Normal
22	Rain Dance	Water	Status	—	—	5	Both Sides
27	Perish Song	Normal	Status	—	—	5	Adjacent
33	Ice Beam	Ice	Special	90	100	10	Normal
37	Brine	Water	Special	65	100	10	Normal
43	Safeguard	Normal	Status	—	—	25	Your Side
47	Hydro Pump	Water	Special	110	80	5	Normal
50	Sheer Cold	Ice	Special	—	30	5	Normal

❖ TM MOVES
No.	Name	Type	Kind	Pow.	Acc.	PP	Range
TM05	Roar	Normal	Status	—	—	20	Normal
TM06	Toxic	Poison	Status	—	90	10	Normal
TM07	Hail	Ice	Status	—	—	10	Both Sides
TM10	Hidden Power	Normal	Special	60	100	15	Normal
TM13	Ice Beam	Ice	Special	90	100	10	Normal
TM14	Blizzard	Ice	Special	110	70	5	Many Others
TM15	Hyper Beam	Normal	Special	150	90	5	Normal
TM17	Protect	Normal	Status	—	—	10	Self
TM18	Rain Dance	Water	Status	—	—	5	Both Sides
TM20	Safeguard	Normal	Status	—	—	25	Your Side
TM21	Frustration	Normal	Physical	—	100	20	Normal
TM24	Thunderbolt	Electric	Special	90	100	15	Normal
TM25	Thunder	Electric	Special	110	70	10	Normal
TM27	Return	Normal	Physical	—	100	20	Normal
TM29	Psychic	Psychic	Special	90	100	10	Normal
TM32	Double Team	Normal	Status	—	—	15	Self
TM42	Facade	Normal	Physical	70	100	20	Normal
TM44	Rest	Psychic	Status	—	—	10	Self
TM45	Attract	Normal	Status	—	100	15	Normal
TM48	Round	Normal	Special	60	100	15	Normal
TM49	Echoed Voice	Normal	Special	40	100	15	Normal
TM67	Smart Strike	Steel	Physical	70	—	10	Normal
TM68	Giga Impact	Normal	Physical	150	90	5	Normal
TM78	Bulldoze	Ground	Physical	60	100	20	Adjacent
TM79	Frost Breath	Ice	Special	60	90	10	Normal
TM85	Dream Eater	Psychic	Special	100	100	15	Normal
TM87	Swagger	Normal	Status	—	85	15	Normal
TM88	Sleep Talk	Normal	Status	—	—	10	Self
TM90	Substitute	Normal	Status	—	—	10	Self
TM94	Surf	Water	Special	90	100	15	Adjacent
TM98	Waterfall	Water	Physical	80	100	15	Normal
TM100	Confide	Normal	Status	—	—	20	Normal

❖ MOVES TAUGHT BY PEOPLE
Name	Type	Kind	Pow.	Acc.	PP	Range

❖ MOVES LEARNED WHEN EVOLVING
Name	Type	Kind	Pow.	Acc.	PP	Range

EGG MOVES
Name	Type	Kind	Pow.	Acc.	PP	Range
Foresight	Normal	Status	—	—	40	Normal
Tickle	Normal	Status	—	—	20	Normal
Refresh	Normal	Status	—	—	20	Self
Dragon Dance	Dragon	Status	—	—	20	Self
Curse	Ghost	Status	—	—	10	Varies
Sleep Talk	Normal	Status	—	—	10	Self
Horn Drill	Normal	Physical	—	30	5	Normal
Ancient Power	Rock	Special	60	100	5	Normal
Whirlpool	Water	Special	35	85	15	Normal
Fissure	Ground	Physical	—	30	5	Normal
Dragon Pulse	Dragon	Special	85	100	10	Normal
Avalanche	Ice	Physical	60	100	10	Normal
Future Sight	Psychic	Special	120	100	10	Normal
Freeze-Dry	Ice	Special	70	100	20	Normal

❖ EXCLUSIVE Z-MOVE
Name	Base Move	Type	Kind	Pow.	Acc.	Range

Let's Go for a Ride!

You will get access to all of the Ride Pokémon in the Alola region during the course of your adventure, and that allows you to call on them anytime that you need a bit of help getting around the landscape. But what if you want all of these great Pokémon on your battle team? Almost all of them can be found and caught in Alola, so you're in luck!

Tauros (#137) NORMAL

Ability: Intimidate / Anger Point / Sheer Force
Catch one in the tall grass in Poni Plains

Stoutland (#122) NORMAL

Ability: Intimidate / Sand Rush / Scrappy
Catch a Lillipup on Route 4 and evolve it into Herdier and then Stoutland

Lapras (#268) WATER ICE
Ability: Water Absorb / Shell Armor / Hydration
Catch one on the surface of the water in the Poni Wilds

Mudsdale (#133) GROUND

Ability: Own Tempo / Stamina / Inner Focus
Catch one in the patches of tall grass in the northwest areas of the Poni Plains

Sharpedo (#265) WATER DARK

Ability: Rough Skin / Speed Boost
Catch one in the rare fishing spot on Poni Breaker Coast

Machamp (#97) FIGHTING

Ability: Guts / No Guard / Steadfast
Receive a Machoke in a trade and it will evolve into Machamp

Charizard (—) FIRE FLYING
Ability: Blaze / Solar Power
Charizard could be obtained in *Pokémon X* or *Pokémon Y*, if you chose to receive a Charmander from the professor in those games and then evolved it fully. You could also choose Charmander in the virtual console games *Pokémon Red* and *Pokémon Blue*. You can transfer Pokémon from all of these games to *Pokémon Sun* and *Pokémon Moon* using *Pokémon Bank* (p. 31). If you don't have a copy of any of these games, though, or you didn't choose Charmander in any of them, then try to obtain Charizard in a trade via the GTS (p. 31) or another trade method. And remember that you can get Charizardite X and Charizardite Y, two Mega Stones that can be used to Mega Evolve your Charizard in battle, by defeating Red in the Battle Tree (p. 271–273)!

Exeggcute
Egg Pokémon

Alola Pokédex	Melemele	Akala	Ula'ula	Poni
769	—	—	—	084

GRASS | PSYCHIC

HEIGHT: 1'04"
WEIGHT: 5.5 lbs.

Its six eggs use telepathy to communicate among themselves. It is believed to carry plant genes and the genes of other species.

Six of them together form a full-fledged Pokémon. It's often hunted by Crabrawler, but uses psychokinesis to drive it off.

ABILITY
Chlorophyll

HIDDEN ABILITY
Harvest

Damage taken in normal battles

NORMAL ×1	FIGHTING ×0.5	ROCK ×2			
FIRE ×2	POISON ×1	GHOST ×2			
WATER ×0.5	GROUND ×1	DRAGON ×1			
GRASS ×0.5	FLYING ×2	DARK ×1			
ELECTRIC ×0.5	PSYCHIC ×0.5	STEEL ×1			
ICE ×2	BUG ×4	FAIRY ×1			

SPECIES STRENGTHS
HP ◆◆
Attack ◆◆
Defense ◆◆◆◆
Sp. Atk ◆◆
Sp. Def ◆◆
Speed ◆◆◆

EGG GROUPS
Grass

ITEM SOMETIMES HELD BY WILD POKÉMON
Psychic Seed

EVOLUTION

Exeggcute → (Leaf Stone) → Alolan Exeggutor

MAIN WAY TO REGISTER IN THE POKÉDEX
Catch in the tall grass on Exeggutor Island

Same form for male/female

LEVEL-UP MOVES

Lv.	Name	Type	Kind	Pow.	Acc.	PP	Range
1	Barrage	Normal	Physical	15	85	20	Normal
1	Uproar	Normal	Special	90	100	10	1 Random
1	Hypnosis	Psychic	Status	—	60	20	Normal
7	Reflect	Psychic	Status	—	—	20	Your Side
11	Leech Seed	Grass	Status	—	90	10	Normal
17	Bullet Seed	Grass	Physical	25	100	30	Normal
19	Stun Spore	Grass	Status	—	75	30	Normal
21	Poison Powder	Poison	Status	—	75	35	Normal
23	Sleep Powder	Grass	Status	—	75	15	Normal
27	Confusion	Psychic	Special	50	100	25	Normal
33	Worry Seed	Grass	Status	—	100	10	Normal
37	Natural Gift	Normal	Physical	—	100	15	Normal
43	Solar Beam	Grass	Special	120	100	10	Normal
47	Extrasensory	Psychic	Special	80	100	20	Normal
50	Bestow	Normal	Status	—	—	15	Normal

TM MOVES

No.	Name	Type	Kind	Pow.	Acc.	PP	Range
TM06	Toxic	Poison	Status	—	90	10	Normal
TM10	Hidden Power	Normal	Special	60	100	15	Normal
TM11	Sunny Day	Fire	Status	—	—	5	Both Sides
TM16	Light Screen	Psychic	Status	—	—	30	Your Side
TM17	Protect	Normal	Status	—	—	10	Self
TM21	Frustration	Normal	Physical	—	100	20	Normal
TM22	Solar Beam	Grass	Special	120	100	10	Normal
TM27	Return	Normal	Physical	—	100	20	Normal
TM29	Psychic	Psychic	Special	90	100	10	Normal
TM32	Double Team	Normal	Status	—	—	15	Self
TM33	Reflect	Psychic	Status	—	—	20	Your Side
TM36	Sludge Bomb	Poison	Special	90	100	10	Normal
TM42	Facade	Normal	Physical	70	100	20	Normal
TM44	Rest	Psychic	Status	—	—	10	Self
TM45	Attract	Normal	Status	—	100	15	Normal
TM46	Thief	Dark	Physical	60	100	25	Normal
TM48	Round	Normal	Special	60	100	15	Normal
TM53	Energy Ball	Grass	Special	90	100	10	Normal
TM64	Explosion	Normal	Physical	250	100	5	Adjacent
TM75	Swords Dance	Normal	Status	—	—	20	Self
TM77	Psych Up	Normal	Status	—	—	10	Normal
TM83	Infestation	Bug	Special	20	100	20	Normal
TM85	Dream Eater	Psychic	Special	100	100	15	Normal
TM86	Grass Knot	Grass	Special	—	100	20	Normal
TM87	Swagger	Normal	Status	—	85	15	Normal
TM88	Sleep Talk	Normal	Status	—	—	10	Self
TM90	Substitute	Normal	Status	—	—	10	Self
TM92	Trick Room	Psychic	Status	—	—	5	Both Sides

No.	Name	Type	Kind	Pow.	Acc.	PP	Range
TM96	Nature Power	Normal	Status	—	—	20	Normal
TM100	Confide	Normal	Status	—	—	20	Normal

EXCLUSIVE Z-MOVE

Name	Base Move	Type	Kind	Pow.	Acc.	Range

MOVES TAUGHT BY PEOPLE

Name	Type	Kind	Pow.	Acc.	PP	Range

MOVES LEARNED WHEN EVOLVING

Name	Type	Kind	Pow.	Acc.	PP	Range

EGG MOVES

Name	Type	Kind	Pow.	Acc.	PP	Range
Synthesis	Grass	Status	—	—	5	Self
Moonlight	Fairy	Status	—	—	5	Self
Ancient Power	Rock	Special	60	100	5	Normal
Ingrain	Grass	Status	—	—	20	Self
Curse	Ghost	Status	—	—	10	Varies
Nature Power	Normal	Status	—	—	20	Normal
Lucky Chant	Normal	Status	—	—	30	Your Side
Leaf Storm	Grass	Special	130	90	5	Normal
Power Swap	Psychic	Status	—	—	10	Normal
Giga Drain	Grass	Special	75	100	10	Normal
Skill Swap	Psychic	Status	—	—	10	Normal
Natural Gift	Normal	Physical	—	100	15	Normal
Block	Normal	Status	—	—	5	Normal
Grassy Terrain	Grass	Status	—	—	10	Both Sides

Exeggutor
Coconut Pokémon

Alola Pokédex	Melemele	Akala	Ula'ula	Poni
270	—	—	—	085

GRASS | DRAGON

HEIGHT: 35'09"
WEIGHT: 916.2 lbs.

Alola is the best environment for this Pokémon. Local people take pride in its appearance, saying this is how Exeggutor ought to look.

As it grew taller and taller, it outgrew its reliance on psychic powers, while within it awakened the power of the sleeping dragon.

ABILITY
Frisk

HIDDEN ABILITY
Harvest

Damage taken in normal battles

NORMAL ×1	FIGHTING ×1	ROCK ×1			
FIRE ×1	POISON ×2	GHOST ×1			
WATER ×0.25	GROUND ×0.5	DRAGON ×2			
GRASS ×0.25	FLYING ×2	DARK ×1			
ELECTRIC ×0.25	PSYCHIC ×1	STEEL ×1			
ICE ×4	BUG ×2	FAIRY ×1			

SPECIES STRENGTHS
HP ◆◆◆◆
Attack ◆◆◆◆◆◆
Defense ◆◆◆◆◆◆
Sp. Atk ◆◆◆◆◆◆◆◆
Sp. Def ◆◆◆◆
Speed ◆◆◆

EGG GROUPS
Grass

ITEM SOMETIMES HELD BY WILD POKÉMON
—

EVOLUTION

Exeggcute → (Leaf Stone) → Alolan Exeggutor

MAIN WAY TO REGISTER IN THE POKÉDEX
Catch in the tall grass on Exeggutor Island

✦ ALOLA FORM ✦

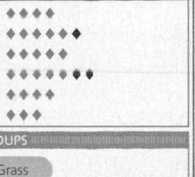

Same form for male/female

LEVEL-UP MOVES

Lv.	Name	Type	Kind	Pow.	Acc.	PP	Range
1	Dragon Hammer	Dragon	Physical	90	100	15	Normal
1	Seed Bomb	Grass	Physical	80	100	15	Normal
1	Barrage	Normal	Physical	15	85	20	Normal
1	Hypnosis	Psychic	Status	—	60	20	Normal
1	Confusion	Psychic	Special	50	100	25	Normal
17	Psyshock	Psychic	Special	80	100	10	Normal
27	Egg Bomb	Normal	Physical	100	75	10	Normal
37	Wood Hammer	Grass	Physical	120	100	15	Normal
47	Leaf Storm	Grass	Special	130	90	5	Normal

TM MOVES

No.	Name	Type	Kind	Pow.	Acc.	PP	Range
TM03	Psyshock	Psychic	Special	80	100	10	Normal
TM06	Toxic	Poison	Status	—	90	10	Normal
TM10	Hidden Power	Normal	Special	60	100	15	Normal
TM11	Sunny Day	Fire	Status	—	—	5	Both Sides
TM15	Hyper Beam	Normal	Special	150	90	5	Normal
TM16	Light Screen	Psychic	Status	—	—	30	Your Side
TM17	Protect	Normal	Status	—	—	10	Self
TM21	Frustration	Normal	Physical	—	100	20	Normal
TM22	Solar Beam	Grass	Special	120	100	10	Normal
TM26	Earthquake	Ground	Physical	100	100	10	Adjacent
TM27	Return	Normal	Physical	—	100	20	Normal
TM29	Psychic	Psychic	Special	90	100	10	Normal
TM31	Brick Break	Fighting	Physical	75	100	15	Normal
TM32	Double Team	Normal	Status	—	—	15	Self
TM33	Reflect	Psychic	Status	—	—	20	Your Side
TM35	Flamethrower	Fire	Special	90	100	15	Normal
TM36	Sludge Bomb	Poison	Special	90	100	10	Normal
TM42	Facade	Normal	Physical	70	100	20	Normal
TM44	Rest	Psychic	Status	—	—	10	Self
TM45	Attract	Normal	Status	—	100	15	Normal
TM46	Thief	Dark	Physical	60	100	25	Normal
TM48	Round	Normal	Special	60	100	15	Normal
TM53	Energy Ball	Grass	Special	90	100	10	Normal
TM59	Brutal Swing	Dark	Physical	60	100	20	Adjacent
TM64	Explosion	Normal	Physical	250	100	5	Adjacent
TM68	Giga Impact	Normal	Physical	150	90	5	Normal
TM75	Swords Dance	Normal	Status	—	—	20	Self
TM77	Psych Up	Normal	Status	—	—	10	Normal

No.	Name	Type	Kind	Pow.	Acc.	PP	Range
TM78	Bulldoze	Ground	Physical	60	100	20	Adjacent
TM82	Dragon Tail	Dragon	Physical	60	90	10	Normal
TM83	Infestation	Bug	Special	20	100	20	Normal
TM85	Dream Eater	Psychic	Special	100	100	15	Normal
TM86	Grass Knot	Grass	Special	—	100	20	Normal
TM87	Swagger	Normal	Status	—	85	15	Normal
TM88	Sleep Talk	Normal	Status	—	—	10	Self
TM90	Substitute	Normal	Status	—	—	10	Self
TM92	Trick Room	Psychic	Status	—	—	5	Both Sides
TM96	Nature Power	Normal	Status	—	—	20	Normal
TM100	Confide	Normal	Status	—	—	20	Normal

MOVES TAUGHT BY PEOPLE

Name	Type	Kind	Pow.	Acc.	PP	Range
Draco Meteor	Dragon	Special	130	90	5	Normal

MOVES LEARNED WHEN EVOLVING

Name	Type	Kind	Pow.	Acc.	PP	Range
Dragon Hammer	Dragon	Physical	90	100	15	Normal

EGG MOVES

Name	Type	Kind	Pow.	Acc.	PP	Range

✦ EXCLUSIVE Z-MOVE

Name	Base Move	Type	Kind	Pow.	Acc.	Range

Jangmo-o

Alola Pokédex	Melemele	Akala	Ula'ula	Poni
271	—	—	—	086

☑ **Jangmo-o**
Scaly Pokémon

DRAGON

HEIGHT: 2'00"
WEIGHT: 65.5 lbs.

It expresses its feelings by smacking its scales. Metallic sounds echo through the tall mountains where Jangmo-o lives.

They live in mountains where no trace of humans can be detected. Jangmo-o grow little by little as they battle one another.

ABILITY
Bulletproof
Soundproof

HIDDEN ABILITY
Overcoat

Damage taken in normal battles

NORMAL ×1	FIGHTING ×1	ROCK			
FIRE ×0.5	POISON ×1	GHOST			
WATER ×0.5	GROUND ×1	DRAGON ×2			
GRASS ×0.5	FLYING ×1	DARK			
ELECTRIC ×0.5	PSYCHIC ×1	STEEL			
ICE ×2	BUG ×1	FAIRY ×2			

SPECIES STRENGTHS
HP ◆◆
Attack ◆◆◆
Defense ◆◆◆◆
Sp. Atk ◆◆
Sp. Def ◆◆
Speed ◆◆◆

EGG GROUPS
Dragon

ITEM SOMETIMES HELD BY WILD POKÉMON
Razor Claw

MAIN WAY TO REGISTER IN THE POKÉDEX
Catch in the tall grass in Vast Poni Canyon

EVOLUTION

Jangmo-o → **Lv. 35** → Hakamo-o
Lv. 45 → Kommo-o

Same form for male/female

Hakamo-o

Alola Pokédex	Melemele	Akala	Ula'ula	Poni
272	—	—	—	087

☑ **Hakamo-o**
Scaly Pokémon

DRAGON **FIGHTING**

HEIGHT: 3'11"
WEIGHT: 103.6 lbs.

It leaps at its prey with a courageous shout. Its scaly punches tear its opponents to shreds.

It sheds and regrows its scales on a continuous basis. The scales become harder and sharper each time they're regrown.

ABILITY
Bulletproof
Soundproof

HIDDEN ABILITY
Overcoat

Damage taken in normal battles

NORMAL ×1	FIGHTING ×1	ROCK ×0.5	
FIRE ×0.5	POISON ×1	GHOST ×1	
WATER ×0.5	GROUND ×1	DRAGON ×2	
GRASS ×0.5	FLYING ×2	DARK ×0.5	
ELECTRIC ×0.5	PSYCHIC ×2	STEEL ×1	
ICE ×2	BUG ×0.5	FAIRY ×4	

SPECIES STRENGTHS
HP ◆◆
Attack ◆◆◆◆
Defense ◆◆◆◆◆
Sp. Atk ◆◆◆
Sp. Def ◆◆◆◆
Speed ◆◆◆◆

EGG GROUPS
Dragon

ITEM SOMETIMES HELD BY WILD POKÉMON
Razor Claw

MAIN WAY TO REGISTER IN THE POKÉDEX
Catch in SOS battles against Jangmo-o in the tall grass in Vast Poni Canyon

EVOLUTION

Jangmo-o → **Lv. 35** → Hakamo-o
Lv. 45 → Kommo-o

Same form for male/female

Kommo-o

Alola Pokédex	Melemele	Akala	Ula'ula	Poni
273	—	—	—	088

☑ **Kommo-o**
Scaly Pokémon

DRAGON **FIGHTING**

HEIGHT: 5'03"
WEIGHT: 172.4 lbs.

When it spots enemies, it threatens them by jingling the scales on its tail. Weak opponents will crack and flee in panic.

Its rigid scales function as offense and defense. In the past, its scales were processed and used to make weapons and other commodities.

ABILITY
Bulletproof
Soundproof

HIDDEN ABILITY
Overcoat

Damage taken in normal battles

NORMAL ×1	FIGHTING ×1	ROCK ×0.5	
FIRE ×0.5	POISON ×1	GHOST ×1	
WATER ×0.5	GROUND ×1	DRAGON ×2	
GRASS ×0.5	FLYING ×2	DARK ×0.5	
ELECTRIC ×0.5	PSYCHIC ×2	STEEL ×1	
ICE ×2	BUG ×0.5	FAIRY ×4	

SPECIES STRENGTHS
HP ◆◆◆
Attack ◆◆◆◆◆◆
Defense ◆◆◆◆◆◆◆
Sp. Atk ◆◆◆◆◆
Sp. Def ◆◆◆◆◆◆
Speed ◆◆◆◆◆

EGG GROUPS
Dragon

ITEM SOMETIMES HELD BY WILD POKÉMON
Razor Claw

MAIN WAY TO REGISTER IN THE POKÉDEX
Catch in SOS battles against Jangmo-o in the tall grass in Vast Poni Canyon

EVOLUTION
Jangmo-o → **Lv. 35** → Hakamo-o
Lv. 45 → Kommo-o

Same form for male/female

JANGMO-O 271

❖ LEVEL-UP MOVES

Lv.	Name	Type	Kind	Pow.	Acc.	PP	Range
1	Tackle	Normal	Physical	40	100	35	Normal
5	Leer	Normal	Status	—	100	30	Many Others
9	Bide	Normal	Physical	—	—	10	Self
13	Protect	Normal	Status	—	—	10	Self
17	Dragon Tail	Dragon	Physical	60	90	10	Normal
21	Scary Face	Normal	Status	—	100	10	Normal
25	Headbutt	Normal	Physical	70	100	15	Normal
29	Work Up	Normal	Status	—	—	30	Self
33	Screech	Normal	Status	—	85	40	Normal
37	Iron Defense	Steel	Status	—	—	15	Self
41	Dragon Claw	Dragon	Physical	80	100	15	Normal
45	Noble Roar	Normal	Status	—	100	30	Normal
49	Dragon Dance	Dragon	Status	—	—	20	Self
53	Outrage	Dragon	Physical	120	100	10	1 Random

❖ TM MOVES

No.	Name	Type	Kind	Pow.	Acc.	PP	Range
TM01	Work Up	Normal	Status	—	—	30	Self
TM02	Dragon Claw	Dragon	Physical	80	100	15	Normal
TM05	Roar	Normal	Status	—	—	20	Normal
TM06	Toxic	Poison	Status	—	90	10	Normal
TM08	Bulk Up	Fighting	Status	—	—	20	Self
TM10	Hidden Power	Normal	Special	60	100	15	Normal
TM12	Taunt	Dark	Status	—	100	20	Normal
TM17	Protect	Normal	Status	—	—	10	Self
TM20	Safeguard	Normal	Status	—	—	25	Your Side
TM21	Frustration	Normal	Physical	—	100	20	Normal
TM26	Earthquake	Ground	Physical	100	100	10	Adjacent
TM27	Return	Normal	Physical	—	100	20	Normal
TM31	Brick Break	Fighting	Physical	75	100	15	Normal
TM32	Double Team	Normal	Status	—	—	15	Self
TM37	Sandstorm	Rock	Status	—	—	10	Both Sides
TM39	Rock Tomb	Rock	Physical	60	95	15	Normal
TM40	Aerial Ace	Flying	Physical	60	—	20	Normal
TM42	Facade	Normal	Physical	70	100	20	Normal
TM44	Rest	Psychic	Status	—	—	10	Self
TM45	Attract	Normal	Status	—	100	15	Normal
TM48	Round	Normal	Special	60	100	15	Normal
TM49	Echoed Voice	Normal	Special	40	100	15	Normal
TM52	Focus Blast	Fighting	Special	120	70	5	Normal
TM54	False Swipe	Normal	Physical	40	100	40	Normal
TM65	Shadow Claw	Ghost	Physical	70	100	15	Normal
TM66	Payback	Dark	Physical	50	100	10	Normal
TM75	Swords Dance	Normal	Status	—	—	20	Self
TM78	Bulldoze	Ground	Physical	60	100	20	Adjacent
TM80	Rock Slide	Rock	Physical	75	90	10	Many Others
TM81	X-Scissor	Bug	Physical	80	100	15	Normal
TM82	Dragon Tail	Dragon	Physical	60	90	10	Normal
TM87	Swagger	Normal	Status	—	85	15	Normal
TM88	Sleep Talk	Normal	Status	—	—	10	Self
TM90	Substitute	Normal	Status	—	—	10	Self
TM100	Confide	Normal	Status	—	—	20	Normal

❖ EXCLUSIVE Z-MOVE

Name	Base Move	Type	Kind	Pow.	Acc.	Range

❖ MOVES TAUGHT BY PEOPLE

Name	Type	Kind	Pow.	Acc.	PP	Range
Draco Meteor	Dragon	Special	130	90	5	Normal

❖ MOVES LEARNED WHEN EVOLVING

Name	Type	Kind	Pow.	Acc.	PP	Range

❖ EGG MOVES

Name	Type	Kind	Pow.	Acc.	PP	Range
Counter	Fighting	Physical	—	100	20	Varies
Reversal	Fighting	Physical	—	100	15	Normal
Dragon Breath	Dragon	Special	60	100	20	Normal

HAKAMO-O 272

❖ LEVEL-UP MOVES

Lv.	Name	Type	Kind	Pow.	Acc.	PP	Range
1	Sky Uppercut	Fighting	Physical	85	90	15	Normal
1	Autotomize	Steel	Status	—	—	15	Self
1	Tackle	Normal	Physical	40	100	35	Normal
1	Leer	Normal	Status	—	100	30	Many Others
1	Bide	Normal	Physical	—	—	10	Self
1	Protect	Normal	Status	—	—	10	Self
5	Leer	Normal	Status	—	100	30	Many Others
9	Bide	Normal	Physical	—	—	10	Self
13	Protect	Normal	Status	—	—	10	Self
17	Dragon Tail	Dragon	Physical	60	90	10	Normal
21	Scary Face	Normal	Status	—	100	10	Normal
25	Headbutt	Normal	Physical	70	100	15	Normal
29	Work Up	Normal	Status	—	—	30	Self
33	Screech	Normal	Status	—	85	40	Normal
38	Iron Defense	Steel	Status	—	—	15	Self
43	Dragon Claw	Dragon	Physical	80	100	15	Normal
48	Noble Roar	Normal	Status	—	100	30	Normal
53	Dragon Dance	Dragon	Status	—	—	20	Self
58	Outrage	Dragon	Physical	120	100	10	1 Random

❖ TM MOVES

No.	Name	Type	Kind	Pow.	Acc.	PP	Range
TM01	Work Up	Normal	Status	—	—	30	Self
TM02	Dragon Claw	Dragon	Physical	80	100	15	Normal
TM05	Roar	Normal	Status	—	—	20	Normal
TM06	Toxic	Poison	Status	—	90	10	Normal
TM08	Bulk Up	Fighting	Status	—	—	20	Self
TM10	Hidden Power	Normal	Special	60	100	15	Normal
TM12	Taunt	Dark	Status	—	100	20	Normal
TM17	Protect	Normal	Status	—	—	10	Self
TM20	Safeguard	Normal	Status	—	—	25	Your Side
TM21	Frustration	Normal	Physical	—	100	20	Normal
TM26	Earthquake	Ground	Physical	100	100	10	Adjacent
TM27	Return	Normal	Physical	—	100	20	Normal
TM31	Brick Break	Fighting	Physical	75	100	15	Normal
TM32	Double Team	Normal	Status	—	—	15	Self
TM37	Sandstorm	Rock	Status	—	—	10	Both Sides
TM39	Rock Tomb	Rock	Physical	60	95	15	Normal
TM40	Aerial Ace	Flying	Physical	60	—	20	Normal
TM42	Facade	Normal	Physical	70	100	20	Normal
TM44	Rest	Psychic	Status	—	—	10	Self
TM45	Attract	Normal	Status	—	100	15	Normal
TM48	Round	Normal	Special	60	100	15	Normal
TM49	Echoed Voice	Normal	Special	40	100	15	Normal
TM52	Focus Blast	Fighting	Special	120	70	5	Normal
TM54	False Swipe	Normal	Physical	40	100	40	Normal
TM56	Fling	Dark	Physical	—	100	10	Normal
TM59	Brutal Swing	Dark	Physical	60	100	20	Adjacent
TM65	Shadow Claw	Ghost	Physical	70	100	15	Normal
TM66	Payback	Dark	Physical	50	100	10	Normal
TM75	Swords Dance	Normal	Status	—	—	20	Self
TM78	Bulldoze	Ground	Physical	60	100	20	Adjacent
TM80	Rock Slide	Rock	Physical	75	90	10	Many Others
TM81	X-Scissor	Bug	Physical	80	100	15	Normal
TM82	Dragon Tail	Dragon	Physical	60	90	10	Normal
TM87	Swagger	Normal	Status	—	85	15	Normal
TM88	Sleep Talk	Normal	Status	—	—	10	Self
TM90	Substitute	Normal	Status	—	—	10	Self
TM100	Confide	Normal	Status	—	—	20	Normal

❖ EXCLUSIVE Z-MOVE

Name	Base Move	Type	Kind	Pow.	Acc.	Range

❖ MOVES TAUGHT BY PEOPLE

Name	Type	Kind	Pow.	Acc.	PP	Range
Draco Meteor	Dragon	Special	130	90	5	Normal

❖ MOVES LEARNED WHEN EVOLVING

Name	Type	Kind	Pow.	Acc.	PP	Range
Sky Uppercut	Fighting	Physical	85	90	15	Normal

❖ EGG MOVES

Name	Type	Kind	Pow.	Acc.	PP	Range

KOMMO-O 273

❖ LEVEL-UP MOVES

Lv.	Name	Type	Kind	Pow.	Acc.	PP	Range
1	Clanging Scales	Dragon	Special	110	100	5	Many Others
1	Sky Uppercut	Fighting	Physical	85	90	15	Normal
1	Belly Drum	Normal	Status	—	—	10	Self
1	Autotomize	Steel	Status	—	—	15	Self
1	Tackle	Normal	Physical	40	100	35	Normal
1	Leer	Normal	Status	—	100	30	Many Others
1	Bide	Normal	Physical	—	—	10	Self
1	Protect	Normal	Status	—	—	10	Self
5	Leer	Normal	Status	—	100	30	Many Others
9	Bide	Normal	Physical	—	—	10	Self
13	Protect	Normal	Status	—	—	10	Self
17	Dragon Tail	Dragon	Physical	60	90	10	Normal
21	Scary Face	Normal	Status	—	100	10	Normal
25	Headbutt	Normal	Physical	70	100	15	Normal
29	Work Up	Normal	Status	—	—	30	Self
33	Screech	Normal	Status	—	85	40	Normal
38	Iron Defense	Steel	Status	—	—	15	Self
43	Dragon Claw	Dragon	Physical	80	100	15	Normal
51	Noble Roar	Normal	Status	—	100	30	Normal
59	Dragon Dance	Dragon	Status	—	—	20	Self
67	Outrage	Dragon	Physical	120	100	10	1 Random

❖ TM MOVES

No.	Name	Type	Kind	Pow.	Acc.	PP	Range
TM01	Work Up	Normal	Status	—	—	30	Self
TM02	Dragon Claw	Dragon	Physical	80	100	15	Normal
TM05	Roar	Normal	Status	—	—	20	Normal
TM06	Toxic	Poison	Status	—	90	10	Normal
TM08	Bulk Up	Fighting	Status	—	—	20	Self
TM10	Hidden Power	Normal	Special	60	100	15	Normal
TM12	Taunt	Dark	Status	—	100	20	Normal
TM15	Hyper Beam	Normal	Special	150	90	5	Normal
TM17	Protect	Normal	Status	—	—	10	Self
TM20	Safeguard	Normal	Status	—	—	25	Your Side
TM21	Frustration	Normal	Physical	—	100	20	Normal
TM26	Earthquake	Ground	Physical	100	100	10	Adjacent
TM27	Return	Normal	Physical	—	100	20	Normal
TM31	Brick Break	Fighting	Physical	75	100	15	Normal
TM32	Double Team	Normal	Status	—	—	15	Self
TM35	Flamethrower	Fire	Special	90	100	15	Normal
TM37	Sandstorm	Rock	Status	—	—	10	Both Sides
TM39	Rock Tomb	Rock	Physical	60	95	15	Normal
TM40	Aerial Ace	Flying	Physical	60	—	20	Normal
TM42	Facade	Normal	Physical	70	100	20	Normal
TM44	Rest	Psychic	Status	—	—	10	Self
TM45	Attract	Normal	Status	—	100	15	Normal
TM48	Round	Normal	Special	60	100	15	Normal
TM49	Echoed Voice	Normal	Special	40	100	15	Normal
TM52	Focus Blast	Fighting	Special	120	70	5	Normal
TM54	False Swipe	Normal	Physical	40	100	40	Normal
TM56	Fling	Dark	Physical	—	100	10	Normal
TM59	Brutal Swing	Dark	Physical	60	100	20	Adjacent
TM65	Shadow Claw	Ghost	Physical	70	100	15	Normal
TM66	Payback	Dark	Physical	50	100	10	Normal
TM68	Giga Impact	Normal	Physical	150	90	5	Normal
TM69	Rock Polish	Rock	Status	—	—	20	Self
TM75	Swords Dance	Normal	Status	—	—	20	Self
TM78	Bulldoze	Ground	Physical	60	100	20	Adjacent
TM80	Rock Slide	Rock	Physical	75	90	10	Many Others
TM81	X-Scissor	Bug	Physical	80	100	15	Normal
TM82	Dragon Tail	Dragon	Physical	60	90	10	Normal
TM84	Poison Jab	Poison	Physical	80	100	20	Normal
TM87	Swagger	Normal	Status	—	85	15	Normal
TM88	Sleep Talk	Normal	Status	—	—	10	Self
TM90	Substitute	Normal	Status	—	—	10	Self
TM91	Flash Cannon	Steel	Special	80	100	10	Normal
TM100	Confide	Normal	Status	—	—	20	Normal

❖ EXCLUSIVE Z-MOVE

Name	Base Move	Type	Kind	Pow.	Acc.	Range

❖ MOVES TAUGHT BY PEOPLE

Name	Type	Kind	Pow.	Acc.	PP	Range
Draco Meteor	Dragon	Special	130	90	5	Normal

❖ MOVES LEARNED WHEN EVOLVING

Name	Type	Kind	Pow.	Acc.	PP	Range
Clanging Scales	Dragon	Special	110	100	5	Many Others

❖ EGG MOVES

Name	Type	Kind	Pow.	Acc.	PP	Range

Alola Pokédex	Melemele	Akala	Ula'ula	Poni
274	—	—	—	089

Emolga
Sky Squirrel Pokémon

ELECTRIC **FLYING**

HEIGHT: 1'04"
WEIGHT: 11.0 lbs.

It glides using its cape-like membrane. Electrical energy scatters from it, shocking its friends and foes alike.

It grills berries and bug Pokémon with electric shocks and makes a meal of them. It usually nests in the holes gouged in trees by Pikipek.

ABILITY
Static

HIDDEN ABILITY
Motor Drive

Damage taken in normal battles

NORMAL ×1	FIGHTING ×0.5	ROCK ×2	
FIRE ×1	POISON ×1	GHOST ×1	
WATER ×1	GROUND ×0	DRAGON ×1	
GRASS ×0.5	FLYING ×0.5	DARK ×1	
ELECTRIC ×1	PSYCHIC ×1	STEEL ×0.5	
ICE ×2	BUG ×1	FAIRY ×1	

SPECIES STRENGTHS
HP ◆◆
Attack ◆◆◆◆
Defense ◆◆◆
Sp. Atk ◆◆◆◆
Sp. Def ◆◆◆
Speed ◆◆◆◆◆◆◆◆◆

EGG GROUPS
Field

ITEM SOMETIMES HELD BY WILD POKÉMON

EVOLUTION
Does not evolve

MAIN WAY TO REGISTER IN THE POKÉDEX
Catch from the shaking trees in Poni Plains

Same form for male/female

❖ LEVEL-UP MOVES

Lv.	Name	Type	Kind	Pow.	Acc.	PP	Range
1	Thunder Shock	Electric	Special	40	100	30	Normal
4	Quick Attack	Normal	Physical	40	100	30	Normal
7	Tail Whip	Normal	Status	—	100	30	Many Others
10	Charge	Electric	Status	—	—	20	Self
13	Spark	Electric	Physical	65	100	20	Normal
15	Nuzzle	Electric	Physical	20	100	20	Normal
16	Pursuit	Dark	Physical	40	100	20	Normal
19	Double Team	Normal	Status	—	—	15	Self
22	Shock Wave	Electric	Special	60	—	20	Normal
26	Electro Ball	Electric	Special	—	100	10	Normal
30	Acrobatics	Flying	Physical	55	100	15	Normal
34	Light Screen	Psychic	Status	—	—	30	Your Side
38	Encore	Normal	Status	—	100	5	Normal
42	Volt Switch	Electric	Special	70	100	20	Normal
46	Agility	Psychic	Status	—	—	30	Self
50	Discharge	Electric	Special	80	100	15	Adjacent

❖ TM MOVES

No.	Name	Type	Kind	Pow.	Acc.	PP	Range
TM06	Toxic	Poison	Status	—	90	10	Normal
TM10	Hidden Power	Normal	Special	60	100	15	Normal
TM12	Taunt	Dark	Status	—	100	20	Normal
TM16	Light Screen	Psychic	Status	—	—	30	Your Side
TM17	Protect	Normal	Status	—	—	10	Self
TM18	Rain Dance	Water	Status	—	—	5	Both Sides
TM19	Roost	Flying	Status	—	—	10	Self
TM21	Frustration	Normal	Physical	—	100	20	Normal
TM24	Thunderbolt	Electric	Special	90	100	15	Normal
TM25	Thunder	Electric	Special	110	70	10	Normal
TM27	Return	Normal	Physical	—	100	20	Normal
TM32	Double Team	Normal	Status	—	—	15	Self
TM40	Aerial Ace	Flying	Physical	60	—	20	Normal
TM42	Facade	Normal	Physical	70	100	20	Normal
TM44	Rest	Psychic	Status	—	—	10	Self
TM45	Attract	Normal	Status	—	100	15	Normal
TM48	Round	Normal	Special	60	100	15	Normal
TM56	Fling	Dark	Physical	—	100	10	Normal
TM57	Charge Beam	Electric	Special	50	90	10	Normal
TM62	Acrobatics	Flying	Physical	55	100	15	Normal
TM72	Volt Switch	Electric	Special	70	100	20	Normal
TM73	Thunder Wave	Electric	Status	—	90	20	Normal
TM87	Swagger	Normal	Status	—	85	15	Normal
TM88	Sleep Talk	Normal	Status	—	—	10	Self
TM89	U-turn	Bug	Physical	70	100	20	Normal
TM90	Substitute	Normal	Status	—	—	10	Self
TM93	Wild Charge	Electric	Physical	90	100	15	Normal
TM100	Confide	Normal	Status	—	—	20	Normal

❖ MOVES TAUGHT BY PEOPLE

Name	Type	Kind	Pow.	Acc.	PP	Range

❖ MOVES LEARNED WHEN EVOLVING

Name	Type	Kind	Pow.	Acc.	PP	Range

❖ EGG MOVES

Name	Type	Kind	Pow.	Acc.	PP	Range
Roost	Flying	Status	—	—	10	Self
Iron Tail	Steel	Physical	100	75	15	Normal
Astonish	Ghost	Physical	30	100	15	Normal
Air Slash	Flying	Special	75	95	15	Normal
Shock Wave	Electric	Special	60	—	20	Normal
Charm	Fairy	Status	—	100	20	Normal
Covet	Normal	Physical	60	100	25	Normal
Tickle	Normal	Status	—	100	20	Normal
Baton Pass	Normal	Status	—	—	40	Self
Ion Deluge	Electric	Status	—	—	25	Both Sides
Speed Swap	Psychic	Status	—	—	10	Normal

❖ EXCLUSIVE Z-MOVE

Name	Base Move	Type	Kind	Pow.	Acc.	Range

Rare Type Combinations

The 18 known Pokémon types can be combined into an astounding 171 possible combinations—but Pokémon have not yet been discovered for all of these possible combinations, and some combinations remain incredibly rare. Here are some of the rare combinations that you can find in the Alola region to try to baffle opponents!

Alolan Rattata (#015)
DARK **NORMAL**

Alolan Raichu (#026)
ELECTRIC **PSYCHIC**

Cutiefly (#083)
BUG **FAIRY**

Surskit (#139)
BUG **WATER**

Salandit (#161)
POISON **FIRE**

Alolan Geodude (#229)
ROCK **ELECTRIC**

Mimikyu (#242)
GHOST **FAIRY**

Drampa (#244)
NORMAL **DRAGON**

Froslass (#248)
ICE **GHOST**

Weavile (#250)
DARK **ICE**

Alolan Sandshrew (#251)
ICE **STEEL**

Alolan Ninetales (#254)
ICE **FAIRY**

Hakamo-o (#272)
DRAGON **FIGHTING**

Scyther

Alola Pokédex	Melemele	Akala	Ula'ula	Poni
275	—	—		090

Mantis Pokémon

BUG **FLYING**

HEIGHT: 4'11"
WEIGHT: 123.5 lbs.

It confuses its prey with its quick, ninja-like movements. Then, in an instant, it cleaves them with its scythes.

While young, they live together deep in the mountains, training themselves in how to fight with their scythes and move at high speeds.

ABILITY
Swarm
Technician

HIDDEN ABILITY
Steadfast

Damage taken in normal battles

NORMAL	×1	FIGHTING	×0.25	ROCK	×4
FIRE	×2	POISON	×1	GHOST	×1
WATER	×1	GROUND	×0	DRAGON	×1
GRASS	×0.25	FLYING	×2	DARK	×1
ELECTRIC	×2	PSYCHIC	×1	STEEL	×1
ICE	×2	BUG	×0.5	FAIRY	×1

SPECIES STRENGTHS
HP	◆◆◆
Attack	◆◆◆◆◆◆
Defense	◆◆◆◆
Sp. Atk	◆◆◆
Sp. Def	◆◆◆◆◆
Speed	◆◆◆◆◆◆◆

EGG GROUPS
Bug

ITEM SOMETIMES HELD BY WILD POKÉMON
—

EVOLUTION

Scyther → Trade while holding **Metal Coat** → Scizor

MAIN WAY TO REGISTER IN THE POKÉDEX
Catch from the shaking bushes in Poni Plains

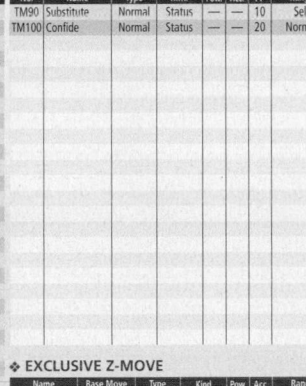 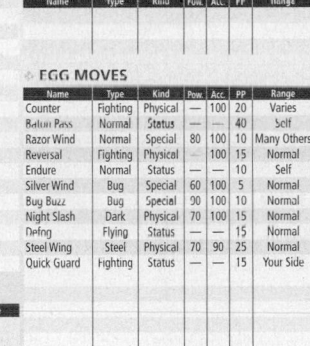

• The male has a shorter abdomen. The female has a longer abdomen.

❖ LEVEL-UP MOVES

Lv.	Name	Type	Kind	Pow.	Acc.	PP	Range
1	Vacuum Wave	Fighting	Special	40	100	30	Normal
1	Quick Attack	Normal	Physical	40	100	30	Normal
1	Leer	Normal	Status	—	100	30	Many Others
5	Focus Energy	Normal	Status	—	—	30	Self
9	Pursuit	Dark	Physical	40	100	20	Normal
13	False Swipe	Normal	Physical	40	100	40	Normal
17	Agility	Psychic	Status	—	—	30	Self
21	Wing Attack	Flying	Physical	60	100	35	Normal
25	Fury Cutter	Bug	Physical	40	95	20	Normal
29	Slash	Normal	Physical	70	100	20	Normal
33	Razor Wind	Normal	Special	80	100	10	Many Others
37	Double Team	Normal	Status	—	—	15	Self
41	X-Scissor	Bug	Physical	80	100	15	Normal
45	Night Slash	Dark	Physical	70	100	15	Normal
49	Double Hit	Normal	Physical	35	90	10	Normal
50	Air Slash	Flying	Special	75	95	15	Normal
57	Swords Dance	Normal	Status	—	—	20	Self
61	Feint	Normal	Physical	30	100	10	Normal

❖ TM MOVES

No.	Name	Type	Kind	Pow.	Acc.	PP	Range
TM06	Toxic	Poison	Status	—	90	10	Normal
TM10	Hidden Power	Normal	Special	60	100	15	Normal
TM11	Sunny Day	Fire	Status	—	—	5	Both Sides
TM15	Hyper Beam	Normal	Special	150	90	5	Normal
TM16	Light Screen	Psychic	Status	—	—	30	Your Side
TM17	Protect	Normal	Status	—	—	10	Self
TM18	Rain Dance	Water	Status	—	—	5	Both Sides
TM19	Roost	Flying	Status	—	—	10	Self
TM20	Safeguard	Normal	Status	—	—	25	Your Side
TM21	Frustration	Normal	Physical	—	100	20	Normal
TM27	Return	Normal	Physical	—	100	20	Normal
TM31	Brick Break	Fighting	Physical	75	100	15	Normal
TM32	Double Team	Normal	Status	—	—	15	Self
TM40	Aerial Ace	Flying	Physical	60	—	20	Normal
TM42	Facade	Normal	Physical	70	100	20	Normal
TM44	Rest	Psychic	Status	—	—	10	Self
TM45	Attract	Normal	Status	—	100	15	Normal
TM46	Thief	Dark	Physical	60	100	25	Normal
TM48	Round	Normal	Special	60	100	15	Normal
TM51	Steel Wing	Steel	Physical	70	90	25	Normal
TM54	False Swipe	Normal	Physical	40	100	40	Normal
TM59	Brutal Swing	Dark	Physical	60	100	20	Adjacent
TM68	Giga Impact	Normal	Physical	150	90	5	Normal
TM75	Swords Dance	Normal	Status	—	—	20	Self
TM81	X-Scissor	Bug	Physical	80	100	15	Normal
TM87	Swagger	Normal	Status	—	85	15	Normal
TM88	Sleep Talk	Normal	Status	—	—	10	Self
TM89	U-turn	Bug	Physical	70	100	20	Normal

❖ MOVES TAUGHT BY PEOPLE

No.	Name	Type	Kind	Pow.	Acc.	PP	Range
TM90	Substitute	Normal	Status	—	—	10	Self
TM100	Confide	Normal	Status	—	—	20	Normal

❖ MOVES LEARNED WHEN EVOLVING

Name	Type	Kind	Pow.	Acc.	PP	Range

❖ EGG MOVES

Name	Type	Kind	Pow.	Acc.	PP	Range
Counter	Fighting	Physical	—	100	20	Varies
Baton Pass	Normal	Status	—	—	40	Self
Razor Wind	Normal	Special	80	100	10	Many Others
Reversal	Fighting	Physical	—	100	15	Normal
Endure	Normal	Status	—	—	10	Self
Silver Wind	Bug	Special	60	100	5	Normal
Bug Buzz	Bug	Special	90	100	10	Normal
Night Slash	Dark	Physical	70	100	15	Normal
Defog	Flying	Status	—	—	15	Normal
Steel Wing	Steel	Physical	70	90	25	Normal
Quick Guard	Fighting	Status	—	—	15	Your Side

❖ EXCLUSIVE Z-MOVE

Name	Base Move	Type	Kind	Pow.	Acc.	Range

Scizor

Alola Pokédex	Melemele	Akala	Ula'ula	Poni
276	—	—	—	091

Pincer Pokémon

BUG **STEEL**

HEIGHT: 5'11"
WEIGHT: 260.1 lbs.

It uses its wings to adjust its body temperature. Otherwise, its metal body would become too hot and melt in the heat of battle.

Once it has identified an enemy, this Pokémon smashes it mercilessly with pincers hard as steel.

ABILITY
Swarm
Technician

HIDDEN ABILITY
Light Metal

Damage taken in normal battles

NORMAL	×0.5	FIGHTING	×1	ROCK	×1
FIRE	×4	POISON	×0	GHOST	×1
WATER	×1	GROUND	×1	DRAGON	×0.5
GRASS	×0.25	FLYING	×1	DARK	×1
ELECTRIC	×1	PSYCHIC	×0.5	STEEL	×0.5
ICE	×0.5	BUG	×0.5	FAIRY	×0.5

SPECIES STRENGTHS
HP	◆◆◆
Attack	◆◆◆◆◆◆◆◆
Defense	◆◆◆◆◆◆
Sp. Atk	◆◆◆
Sp. Def	◆◆◆◆◆
Speed	◆◆◆◆

EGG GROUPS
Bug

ITEM SOMETIMES HELD BY WILD POKÉMON
—

EVOLUTION
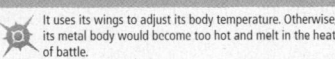

Scyther → Trade while holding **Metal Coat** → Scizor

MAIN WAY TO REGISTER IN THE POKÉDEX
Receive a Scyther holding a Metal Coat in a trade and it will evolve

p. 713

The male has a shorter abdomen. The female has a longer abdomen.

❖ LEVEL-UP MOVES

Lv.	Name	Type	Kind	Pow.	Acc.	PP	Range
1	Feint	Normal	Physical	30	100	10	Normal
1	Bullet Punch	Steel	Physical	40	100	30	Normal
1	Quick Attack	Normal	Physical	40	100	30	Normal
1	Leer	Normal	Status	—	100	30	Many Others
5	Focus Energy	Normal	Status	—	—	30	Self
9	Pursuit	Dark	Physical	40	100	20	Normal
13	False Swipe	Normal	Physical	40	100	40	Normal
17	Agility	Psychic	Status	—	—	30	Self
21	Metal Claw	Steel	Physical	50	95	35	Normal
25	Fury Cutter	Bug	Physical	40	95	20	Normal
29	Slash	Normal	Physical	70	100	20	Normal
33	Razor Wind	Normal	Special	80	100	10	Many Others
37	Iron Defense	Steel	Status	—	—	15	Self
41	X-Scissor	Bug	Physical	80	100	15	Normal
45	Night Slash	Dark	Physical	70	100	15	Normal
49	Double Hit	Normal	Physical	35	90	10	Normal
50	Iron Head	Steel	Physical	80	100	15	Normal
57	Swords Dance	Normal	Status	—	—	20	Self
61	Feint	Normal	Physical	30	100	10	Normal

❖ TM MOVES

No.	Name	Type	Kind	Pow.	Acc.	PP	Range
TM06	Toxic	Poison	Status	—	90	10	Normal
TM09	Venoshock	Poison	Special	65	100	10	Normal
TM10	Hidden Power	Normal	Special	60	100	15	Normal
TM11	Sunny Day	Fire	Status	—	—	5	Both Sides
TM15	Hyper Beam	Normal	Special	150	90	5	Normal
TM16	Light Screen	Psychic	Status	—	—	30	Your Side
TM17	Protect	Normal	Status	—	—	10	Self
TM18	Rain Dance	Water	Status	—	—	5	Both Sides
TM19	Roost	Flying	Status	—	—	10	Self
TM20	Safeguard	Normal	Status	—	—	25	Your Side
TM21	Frustration	Normal	Physical	—	100	20	Normal
TM27	Return	Normal	Physical	—	100	20	Normal
TM31	Brick Break	Fighting	Physical	75	100	15	Normal
TM32	Double Team	Normal	Status	—	—	15	Self
TM37	Sandstorm	Rock	Status	—	—	10	Both Sides
TM40	Aerial Ace	Flying	Physical	60	—	20	Normal
TM42	Facade	Normal	Physical	70	100	20	Normal
TM44	Rest	Psychic	Status	—	—	10	Self
TM45	Attract	Normal	Status	—	100	15	Normal
TM46	Thief	Dark	Physical	60	100	25	Normal
TM48	Round	Normal	Special	60	100	15	Normal
TM51	Steel Wing	Steel	Physical	70	90	25	Normal
TM54	False Swipe	Normal	Physical	40	100	40	Normal
TM56	Fling	Dark	Physical	—	100	10	Normal
TM59	Brutal Swing	Dark	Physical	60	100	20	Adjacent
TM62	Acrobatics	Flying	Physical	55	100	15	Normal
TM68	Giga Impact	Normal	Physical	150	90	5	Normal
TM75	Swords Dance	Normal	Status	—	—	20	Self
TM81	X-Scissor	Bug	Physical	80	100	15	Normal
TM87	Swagger	Normal	Status	—	85	15	Normal
TM88	Sleep Talk	Normal	Status	—	—	10	Self
TM89	U-turn	Bug	Physical	70	100	20	Normal
TM90	Substitute	Normal	Status	—	—	10	Self
TM91	Flash Cannon	Steel	Special	80	100	10	Normal
TM100	Confide	Normal	Status	—	—	20	Normal

❖ MOVES TAUGHT BY PEOPLE

Name	Type	Kind	Pow.	Acc.	PP	Range

❖ MOVES LEARNED WHEN EVOLVING

Name	Type	Kind	Pow.	Acc.	PP	Range

❖ EGG MOVES

Name	Type	Kind	Pow.	Acc.	PP	Range

❖ EXCLUSIVE Z-MOVE

Name	Base Move	Type	Kind	Pow.	Acc.	Range

Murkrow
Darkness Pokémon

Alola Pokédex				
	Melemele	Akala	Ula'ula	Poni
277	—	—	—	092

DARK FLYING

HEIGHT: 1'08"
WEIGHT: 4.6 lbs.

☀ They awaken at dusk and take wing in the twilight, leading to the expression, "Get home before the Murkrow fly."

☾ Seen as a symbol of bad luck, it's generally disliked. Yet it gives presents—objects that sparkle or shine—to Trainers it's close to.

ABILITY
Insomnia
Super Luck

HIDDEN ABILITY
Prankster

SPECIES STRENGTHS
HP ◆◆
Attack ◆◆◆◆◆
Defense ◆◆
Sp. Atk ◆◆◆◆◆
Sp. Def ◆◆
Speed ◆◆◆◆◆◆

EGG GROUPS
Flying

ITEM SOMETIMES HELD BY WILD POKÉMON

EVOLUTION
Murkrow → (Dusk Stone) → Honchkrow

MAIN WAY TO REGISTER IN THE POKÉDEX
Catch in the tall grass in Vast Poni Canyon

The male has a larger crest. The female has a smaller crest.

Damage taken in normal battles

NORMAL	×1	FIGHTING	×1	ROCK	×1
FIRE	×1	POISON	×1	GHOST	×0
WATER	×1	GROUND	×0	DRAGON	×1
GRASS	×0.5	FLYING	×1	DARK	×0.5
ELECTRIC	×2	PSYCHIC	×0	STEEL	×1
ICE	×2	BUG	×1	FAIRY	×2

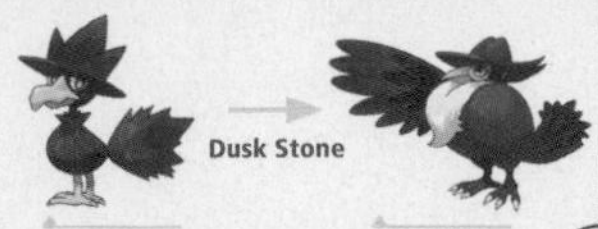

❖ LEVEL-UP MOVES

Lv.	Name	Type	Kind	Pow.	Acc.	PP	Range
1	Peck	Flying	Physical	35	100	35	Normal
1	Astonish	Ghost	Physical	30	100	15	Normal
5	Pursuit	Dark	Physical	40	100	20	Normal
11	Haze	Ice	Status	—	—	30	Both Sides
15	Wing Attack	Flying	Physical	60	100	35	Normal
21	Night Shade	Ghost	Special	—	100	15	Normal
25	Assurance	Dark	Physical	60	100	10	Normal
31	Taunt	Dark	Status	—	100	20	Normal
35	Feint Attack	Dark	Physical	60	—	20	Normal
41	Mean Look	Normal	Status	—	—	5	Normal
45	Foul Play	Dark	Physical	95	100	15	Normal
50	Tailwind	Flying	Status	—	—	15	Your Side
55	Sucker Punch	Dark	Physical	70	100	5	Normal
61	Torment	Dark	Status	—	100	15	Normal
65	Quash	Dark	Status	—	100	15	Normal

❖ TM MOVES

No.	Name	Type	Kind	Pow.	Acc.	PP	Range
TM04	Calm Mind	Psychic	Status	—	—	20	Self
TM06	Toxic	Poison	Status	—	90	10	Normal
TM10	Hidden Power	Normal	Special	60	100	15	Normal
TM11	Sunny Day	Fire	Status	—	—	5	Both Sides
TM12	Taunt	Dark	Status	—	100	20	Normal
TM17	Protect	Normal	Status	—	—	10	Self
TM18	Rain Dance	Water	Status	—	—	5	Both Sides
TM19	Roost	Flying	Status	—	—	10	Self
TM21	Frustration	Normal	Physical	—	100	20	Normal
TM27	Return	Normal	Physical	—	100	20	Normal
TM29	Psychic	Psychic	Special	90	100	10	Normal
TM30	Shadow Ball	Ghost	Special	80	100	15	Normal
TM32	Double Team	Normal	Status	—	—	15	Self
TM40	Aerial Ace	Flying	Physical	60	—	20	Normal
TM41	Torment	Dark	Status	—	100	15	Normal
TM42	Facade	Normal	Physical	70	100	20	Normal
TM44	Rest	Psychic	Status	—	—	10	Self
TM45	Attract	Normal	Status	—	100	15	Normal
TM46	Thief	Dark	Physical	60	100	25	Normal
TM48	Round	Normal	Special	60	100	15	Normal
TM51	Steel Wing	Steel	Physical	70	90	25	Normal
TM60	Quash	Dark	Status	—	100	15	Normal
TM63	Embargo	Dark	Status	—	100	15	Normal
TM66	Payback	Dark	Physical	50	100	10	Normal
TM73	Thunder Wave	Electric	Status	—	90	20	Normal
TM76	Fly	Flying	Physical	90	95	15	Normal
TM77	Psych Up	Normal	Status	—	—	10	Normal
TM85	Dream Eater	Psychic	Special	100	100	15	Normal
TM87	Swagger	Normal	Status	—	85	15	Normal
TM88	Sleep Talk	Normal	Status	—	—	10	Self
TM90	Substitute	Normal	Status	—	—	10	Self
TM95	Snarl	Dark	Special	55	95	15	Many Others
TM97	Dark Pulse	Dark	Special	80	100	15	Normal
TM100	Confide	Normal	Status	—	—	20	Normal

❖ MOVES TAUGHT BY PEOPLE

Name	Type	Kind	Pow.	Acc.	PP	Range

❖ MOVES LEARNED WHEN EVOLVING

Name	Type	Kind	Pow.	Acc.	PP	Range

❖ EGG MOVES

Name	Type	Kind	Pow.	Acc.	PP	Range
Whirlwind	Normal	Status	—	—	20	Normal
Drill Peck	Flying	Physical	80	100	20	Normal
Mirror Move	Flying	Status	—	—	20	Normal
Wing Attack	Flying	Physical	60	100	35	Normal
Sky Attack	Flying	Physical	140	90	5	Normal
Confuse Ray	Ghost	Status	—	100	10	Normal
Feather Dance	Flying	Status	—	100	15	Normal
Perish Song	Normal	Status	—	—	5	Adjacent
Psycho Shift	Psychic	Status	—	100	10	Normal
Screech	Normal	Status	—	85	40	Normal
Feint Attack	Dark	Physical	60	—	20	Normal
Brave Bird	Flying	Physical	120	100	15	Normal
Roost	Flying	Status	—	—	10	Self
Assurance	Dark	Physical	60	100	10	Normal
Flatter	Dark	Status	—	100	15	Normal

❖ EXCLUSIVE Z-MOVE

Name	Base Move	Type	Kind	Pow.	Acc.	Range

Honchkrow
Big Boss Pokémon

Alola Pokédex				
	Melemele	Akala	Ula'ula	Poni
278	—	—	—	093

DARK FLYING

HEIGHT: 2'11"
WEIGHT: 60.2 lbs.

☀ A single cry from this nocturnal Pokémon, and more than a hundred of its Murkrow cronies will assemble.

☾ If its Murkrow cronies fail to catch food for it, or if it feels they have betrayed it, it will hunt them down wherever they are and punish them.

ABILITY
Insomnia
Super Luck

HIDDEN ABILITY
Moxie

SPECIES STRENGTHS
HP ◆◆◆◆
Attack ◆◆◆◆◆◆◆
Defense ◆◆◆
Sp. Atk ◆◆◆◆◆◆
Sp. Def ◆◆◆
Speed ◆◆◆◆◆

EGG GROUPS
Flying

ITEM SOMETIMES HELD BY WILD POKÉMON

EVOLUTION
Murkrow → (Dusk Stone) → Honchkrow

MAIN WAY TO REGISTER IN THE POKÉDEX
Use a Dusk Stone on Murkrow

Same form for male/female

Damage taken in normal battles

NORMAL	×1	FIGHTING	×1	ROCK	×2
FIRE	×1	POISON	×1	GHOST	×0.5
WATER	×1	GROUND	×0	DRAGON	×1
GRASS	×0.5	FLYING	×1	DARK	×0.5
ELECTRIC	×2	PSYCHIC	×0	STEEL	×1
ICE	×2	BUG	×1	FAIRY	×2

❖ LEVEL-UP MOVES

Lv.	Name	Type	Kind	Pow.	Acc.	PP	Range
1	Night Slash	Dark	Physical	70	100	15	Normal
1	Sucker Punch	Dark	Physical	70	100	5	Normal
1	Astonish	Ghost	Physical	30	100	15	Normal
1	Pursuit	Dark	Physical	40	100	20	Normal
1	Haze	Ice	Status	—	—	30	Both Sides
1	Wing Attack	Flying	Physical	60	100	35	Normal
25	Swagger	Normal	Status	—	85	15	Normal
35	Nasty Plot	Dark	Status	—	—	20	Self
45	Foul Play	Dark	Physical	95	100	15	Normal
55	Night Slash	Dark	Physical	70	100	15	Normal
65	Quash	Dark	Status	—	100	15	Normal
75	Dark Pulse	Dark	Special	80	100	15	Normal

❖ TM MOVES

No.	Name	Type	Kind	Pow.	Acc.	PP	Range
TM04	Calm Mind	Psychic	Status	—	—	20	Self
TM06	Toxic	Poison	Status	—	90	10	Normal
TM10	Hidden Power	Normal	Special	60	100	15	Normal
TM11	Sunny Day	Fire	Status	—	—	5	Both Sides
TM12	Taunt	Dark	Status	—	100	20	Normal
TM15	Hyper Beam	Normal	Special	150	90	5	Normal
TM17	Protect	Normal	Status	—	—	10	Self
TM18	Rain Dance	Water	Status	—	—	5	Both Sides
TM19	Roost	Flying	Status	—	—	10	Self
TM21	Frustration	Normal	Physical	—	100	20	Normal
TM27	Return	Normal	Physical	—	100	20	Normal
TM29	Psychic	Psychic	Special	90	100	10	Normal
TM30	Shadow Ball	Ghost	Special	80	100	15	Normal
TM32	Double Team	Normal	Status	—	—	15	Self
TM40	Aerial Ace	Flying	Physical	60	—	20	Normal
TM41	Torment	Dark	Status	—	100	15	Normal
TM42	Facade	Normal	Physical	70	100	20	Normal
TM44	Rest	Psychic	Status	—	—	10	Self
TM45	Attract	Normal	Status	—	100	15	Normal
TM46	Thief	Dark	Physical	60	100	25	Normal
TM48	Round	Normal	Special	60	100	15	Normal
TM51	Steel Wing	Steel	Physical	70	90	25	Normal
TM60	Quash	Dark	Status	—	100	15	Normal
TM63	Embargo	Dark	Status	—	100	15	Normal
TM66	Payback	Dark	Physical	50	100	10	Normal
TM68	Giga Impact	Normal	Physical	150	90	5	Normal
TM73	Thunder Wave	Electric	Status	—	90	20	Normal
TM76	Fly	Flying	Physical	90	95	15	Normal
TM77	Psych Up	Normal	Status	—	—	10	Normal
TM85	Dream Eater	Psychic	Special	100	100	15	Normal
TM87	Swagger	Normal	Status	—	85	15	Normal
TM88	Sleep Talk	Normal	Status	—	—	10	Self
TM90	Substitute	Normal	Status	—	—	10	Self
TM95	Snarl	Dark	Special	55	95	15	Many Others
TM97	Dark Pulse	Dark	Special	80	100	15	Normal
TM100	Confide	Normal	Status	—	—	20	Normal

❖ MOVES TAUGHT BY PEOPLE

Name	Type	Kind	Pow.	Acc.	PP	Range

❖ MOVES LEARNED WHEN EVOLVING

Name	Type	Kind	Pow.	Acc.	PP	Range

❖ EGG MOVES

Name	Type	Kind	Pow.	Acc.	PP	Range

❖ EXCLUSIVE Z-MOVE

Name	Base Move	Type	Kind	Pow.	Acc.	Range

Alola Pokédex	Melemele	Akala	Ula'ula	Poni
279	—	—	—	094

Riolu

Emanation Pokémon

FIGHTING

HEIGHT: 2'04"
WEIGHT: 44.5 lbs.

It can discern the physical and emotional states of people, Pokémon, and other natural things from the shape of their aura waves.

It's tough enough to run right through the night, and it's also a hard worker, but it's still just a youngster.

Same form for male/female

ABILITY
Steadfast
Inner Focus

HIDDEN ABILITY
Prankster

Damage taken in normal battles

NORMAL	×1	FIGHTING	×1	ROCK	×0.5
FIRE	×1	POISON	×1	GHOST	×1
WATER	×1	GROUND	×1	DRAGON	×1
GRASS	×1	FLYING	×2	DARK	×0.5
ELECTRIC	×1	PSYCHIC	×2	STEEL	×1
ICE	×1	BUG	×0.5	FAIRY	×2

SPECIES STRENGTHS
HP ◆◆
Attack ◆◆◆◆
Defense ◆◆
Sp. Atk ◆◆
Sp. Def ◆◆
Speed ◆◆◆◆

EGG GROUPS
No Eggs Discovered

ITEM SOMETIMES HELD BY WILD POKÉMON
—

EVOLUTION

Level up with high friendship during the day

Riolu → Lucario

MAIN WAY TO REGISTER IN THE POKÉDEX
Catch in the tall grass in Poni Grove

❖ LEVEL-UP MOVES

Lv.	Name	Type	Kind	Pow.	Acc.	PP	Range
1	Foresight	Normal	Status	—	—	40	Normal
1	Quick Attack	Normal	Physical	40	100	30	Normal
1	Endure	Normal	Status	—	—	10	Self
6	Counter	Fighting	Physical	—	100	20	Varies
11	Feint	Normal	Physical	30	100	10	Normal
15	Force Palm	Fighting	Physical	60	100	10	Normal
19	Copycat	Normal	Status	—	—	20	Self
24	Screech	Normal	Status	—	85	40	Normal
29	Reversal	Fighting	Physical	—	100	15	Normal
47	Nasty Plot	Dark	Status	—	—	20	Self
50	Final Gambit	Fighting	Special	—	100	5	Normal

❖ TM MOVES

No.	Name	Type	Kind	Pow.	Acc.	PP	Range
TM01	Work Up	Normal	Status	—	—	30	Self
TM05	Roar	Normal	Status	—	—	20	Normal
TM06	Toxic	Poison	Status	—	90	10	Normal
TM08	Bulk Up	Fighting	Status	—	—	20	Self
TM10	Hidden Power	Normal	Special	60	100	15	Normal
TM11	Sunny Day	Fire	Status	—	—	5	Both Sides
TM17	Protect	Normal	Status	—	—	10	Self
TM18	Rain Dance	Water	Status	—	—	5	Both Sides
TM21	Frustration	Normal	Physical	—	100	20	Normal
TM26	Earthquake	Ground	Physical	100	100	10	Adjacent
TM27	Return	Normal	Physical	—	100	20	Normal
TM31	Brick Break	Fighting	Physical	75	100	15	Normal
TM32	Double Team	Normal	Status	—	—	15	Self
TM39	Rock Tomb	Rock	Physical	60	95	15	Normal
TM42	Facade	Normal	Physical	70	100	20	Normal
TM44	Rest	Psychic	Status	—	—	10	Self
TM45	Attract	Normal	Status	—	100	15	Normal
TM47	Low Sweep	Fighting	Physical	65	100	20	Normal
TM48	Round	Normal	Special	60	100	15	Normal
TM52	Focus Blast	Fighting	Special	120	70	5	Normal
TM56	Fling	Dark	Physical	—	100	10	Normal
TM65	Shadow Claw	Ghost	Physical	70	100	15	Normal
TM66	Payback	Dark	Physical	50	100	10	Normal
TM75	Swords Dance	Normal	Status	—	—	20	Self
TM78	Bulldoze	Ground	Physical	60	100	20	Adjacent
TM80	Rock Slide	Rock	Physical	75	90	10	Many Others
TM84	Poison Jab	Poison	Physical	80	100	20	Normal
TM87	Swagger	Normal	Status	—	85	15	Normal
TM88	Sleep Talk	Normal	Status	—	—	10	Self
TM90	Substitute	Normal	Status	—	—	10	Self
TM100	Confide	Normal	Status	—	—	20	Normal

❖ EXCLUSIVE Z-MOVE

Name	Base Move	Type	Kind	Pow.	Acc.	Range

❖ MOVES TAUGHT BY PEOPLE

Name	Type	Kind	Pow.	Acc.	PP	Range

❖ MOVES LEARNED WHEN EVOLVING

Name	Type	Kind	Pow.	Acc.	PP	Range

❖ EGG MOVES

Name	Type	Kind	Pow.	Acc.	PP	Range
Cross Chop	Fighting	Physical	100	80	5	Normal
Detect	Fighting	Status	—	—	5	Self
Bite	Dark	Physical	60	100	25	Normal
Mind Reader	Normal	Status	—	—	5	Normal
Sky Uppercut	Fighting	Physical	85	90	15	Normal
High Jump Kick	Fighting	Physical	130	90	10	Normal
Agility	Psychic	Status	—	—	30	Self
Vacuum Wave	Fighting	Special	40	100	30	Normal
Crunch	Dark	Physical	80	100	15	Normal
Low Kick	Fighting	Physical	—	100	20	Normal
Iron Defense	Steel	Status	—	—	15	Self
Blaze Kick	Fire	Physical	85	90	10	Normal
Bullet Punch	Steel	Physical	40	100	30	Normal
Follow Me	Normal	Status	—	—	20	Self
Circle Throw	Fighting	Physical	60	90	10	Normal

Alola Pokédex	Melemele	Akala	Ula'ula	Poni
280	—	—	—	095

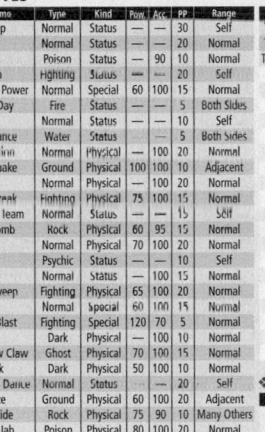

Lucario

Aura Pokémon

FIGHTING STEEL

HEIGHT: 3'11"
WEIGHT: 119.0 lbs.

Not only does it perceive auras, but it has also gained the power to control them. It employs them in battle.

They can detect the species of a living being— and its emotions—from over half a mile away. They control auras and hunt their prey in packs.

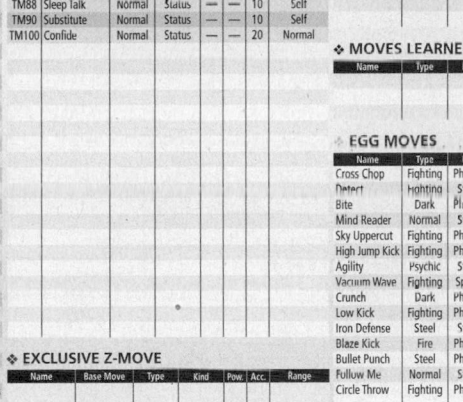

p. 214

Same form for male/female

ABILITY
Steadfast
Inner Focus

HIDDEN ABILITY
Justified

Damage taken in normal battles

NORMAL	×0.5	FIGHTING	×2	ROCK	×0.25
FIRE	×2	POISON	×0	GHOST	×1
WATER	×1	GROUND	×2	DRAGON	×0.5
GRASS	×0.5	FLYING	×1	DARK	×0.5
ELECTRIC	×1	PSYCHIC	×1	STEEL	×0.5
ICE	×0.5	BUG	×0.25	FAIRY	×1

SPECIES STRENGTHS
HP ◆◆◆
Attack ◆◆◆◆◆◆
Defense ◆◆◆◆
Sp. Atk ◆◆◆◆◆◆
Sp. Def ◆◆◆◆
Speed ◆◆◆◆◆◆

EGG GROUPS
Field
Human-like

ITEM SOMETIMES HELD BY WILD POKÉMON
—

EVOLUTION

Level up with high friendship during the day

Riolu → Lucario

MAIN WAY TO REGISTER IN THE POKÉDEX
Level up Riolu with high friendship when it is daytime in your game

❖ LEVEL-UP MOVES

Lv.	Name	Type	Kind	Pow.	Acc.	PP	Range
1	Aura Sphere	Fighting	Special	80	—	20	Normal
1	Laser Focus	Normal	Status	—	—	30	Self
1	Foresight	Normal	Status	—	—	40	Normal
1	Quick Attack	Normal	Physical	40	100	30	Normal
1	Detect	Fighting	Status	—	—	5	Self
1	Metal Claw	Steel	Physical	50	95	35	Normal
6	Counter	Fighting	Physical	—	100	20	Varies
11	Feint	Normal	Physical	30	100	10	Normal
15	Power-Up Punch	Fighting	Physical	40	100	20	Normal
19	Swords Dance	Normal	Status	—	—	20	Self
24	Metal Sound	Steel	Status	—	85	40	Normal
29	Bone Rush	Ground	Physical	25	90	10	Normal
33	Quick Guard	Fighting	Status	—	—	15	Your Side
37	Me First	Normal	Status	—	—	20	Varies
42	Work Up	Normal	Status	—	—	30	Self
47	Calm Mind	Psychic	Status	—	—	20	Self
51	Heal Pulse	Psychic	Status	—	—	10	Normal
55	Close Combat	Fighting	Physical	120	100	5	Normal
60	Dragon Pulse	Dragon	Special	85	100	10	Normal
65	Extreme Speed	Normal	Physical	80	100	5	Normal

❖ TM MOVES

No.	Name	Type	Kind	Pow.	Acc.	PP	Range
TM01	Work Up	Normal	Status	—	—	30	Self
TM04	Calm Mind	Psychic	Status	—	—	20	Self
TM05	Roar	Normal	Status	—	—	20	Normal
TM06	Toxic	Poison	Status	—	90	10	Normal
TM08	Bulk Up	Fighting	Status	—	—	20	Self
TM10	Hidden Power	Normal	Special	60	100	15	Normal
TM11	Sunny Day	Fire	Status	—	—	5	Both Sides
TM15	Hyper Beam	Normal	Special	150	90	5	Normal
TM17	Protect	Normal	Status	—	—	10	Self
TM18	Rain Dance	Water	Status	—	—	5	Both Sides
TM21	Frustration	Normal	Physical	—	100	20	Normal
TM26	Earthquake	Ground	Physical	100	100	10	Adjacent
TM27	Return	Normal	Physical	—	100	20	Normal
TM29	Psychic	Psychic	Special	90	100	10	Normal
TM30	Shadow Ball	Ghost	Special	80	100	15	Normal
TM31	Brick Break	Fighting	Physical	75	100	15	Normal
TM32	Double Team	Normal	Status	—	—	15	Self
TM39	Rock Tomb	Rock	Physical	60	95	15	Normal
TM42	Facade	Normal	Physical	70	100	20	Normal
TM44	Rest	Psychic	Status	—	—	10	Self
TM45	Attract	Normal	Status	—	100	15	Normal
TM47	Low Sweep	Fighting	Physical	65	100	20	Normal
TM48	Round	Normal	Special	60	100	15	Normal
TM52	Focus Blast	Fighting	Special	120	70	5	Normal
TM56	Fling	Dark	Physical	—	100	10	Normal
TM65	Shadow Claw	Ghost	Physical	70	100	15	Normal
TM66	Payback	Dark	Physical	50	100	10	Normal
TM68	Giga Impact	Normal	Physical	150	90	5	Normal
TM71	Stone Edge	Rock	Physical	100	80	5	Normal
TM75	Swords Dance	Normal	Status	—	—	20	Self
TM78	Bulldoze	Ground	Physical	60	100	20	Adjacent
TM80	Rock Slide	Rock	Physical	75	90	10	Many Others
TM84	Poison Jab	Poison	Physical	80	100	20	Normal
TM87	Swagger	Normal	Status	—	85	15	Normal
TM88	Sleep Talk	Normal	Status	—	—	10	Self
TM90	Substitute	Normal	Status	—	—	10	Self
TM91	Flash Cannon	Steel	Special	80	100	10	Normal
TM97	Dark Pulse	Dark	Special	80	100	15	Normal
TM100	Confide	Normal	Status	—	—	20	Normal

❖ EXCLUSIVE Z-MOVE

Name	Base Move	Type	Kind	Pow.	Acc.	Range

❖ MOVES TAUGHT BY PEOPLE

Name	Type	Kind	Pow.	Acc.	PP	Range

❖ MOVES LEARNED WHEN EVOLVING

Name	Type	Kind	Pow.	Acc.	PP	Range
Aura Sphere	Fighting	Special	80	—	20	Normal

❖ EGG MOVES

Name	Type	Kind	Pow.	Acc.	PP	Range

Dratini

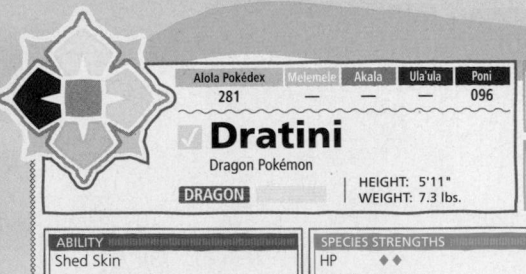
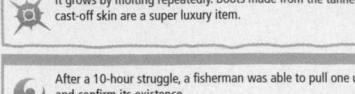
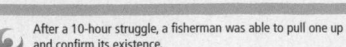

Alola Pokédex	Melemele	Akala	Ula'ula	Poni
281	—	—	—	096

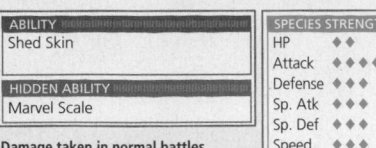

☑ **Dratini**
Dragon Pokémon
DRAGON

HEIGHT: 5'11"
WEIGHT: 7.3 lbs.

It grows by molting repeatedly. Boots made from the tanned cast-off skin are a super luxury item.

After a 10-hour struggle, a fisherman was able to pull one up and confirm its existence.

ABILITY
Shed Skin

HIDDEN ABILITY
Marvel Scale

Damage taken in normal battles

NORMAL ×1	FIGHTING ×1	ROCK ×1
FIRE ×0.5	POISON ×1	GHOST ×1
WATER ×0.5	GROUND ×1	DRAGON ×2
GRASS ×0.5	FLYING ×1	DARK ×1
ELECTRIC ×0.5	PSYCHIC ×1	STEEL ×1
ICE ×2	BUG ×1	FAIRY ×1

SPECIES STRENGTHS
HP ◆◆
Attack ◆◆◆◆
Defense ◆◆◆
Sp. Atk ◆◆◆
Sp. Def ◆◆◆
Speed ◆◆◆

EGG GROUPS
Water 1 · Dragon

ITEM SOMETIMES HELD BY WILD POKÉMON
Dragon Scale

MAIN WAY TO REGISTER IN THE POKÉDEX
Catch in the rare fishing spot in Vast Poni Canyon

EVOLUTION

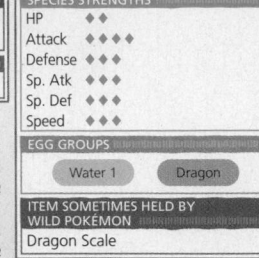

Dratini → Lv. 30 → Dragonair → Lv. 55 → Dragonite

Same form for male/female

Dragonair

Alola Pokédex	Melemele	Akala	Ula'ula	Poni
282	—	—	—	097

☑ **Dragonair**
Dragon Pokémon
DRAGON

HEIGHT: 13'01"
WEIGHT: 36.4 lbs.

It has long been thought that its crystalline orbs are imbued with the power to control the weather.

From time immemorial, it has been venerated by agricultural peoples as an entity able to control the weather.

ABILITY
Shed Skin

HIDDEN ABILITY
Marvel Scale

Damage taken in normal battles

NORMAL ×1	FIGHTING ×1	ROCK ×1
FIRE ×0.5	POISON ×1	GHOST ×1
WATER ×0.5	GROUND ×1	DRAGON ×2
GRASS ×0.5	FLYING ×1	DARK ×1
ELECTRIC ×0.5	PSYCHIC ×1	STEEL ×1
ICE ×2	BUG ×1	FAIRY ×1

SPECIES STRENGTHS
HP ◆◆
Attack ◆◆◆◆◆
Defense ◆◆◆◆
Sp. Atk ◆◆◆◆
Sp. Def ◆◆◆◆
Speed ◆◆◆◆◆

EGG GROUPS
Water 1 · Dragon

ITEM SOMETIMES HELD BY WILD POKÉMON
Dragon Scale

MAIN WAY TO REGISTER IN THE POKÉDEX
Level up Dratini to Lv. 30

EVOLUTION

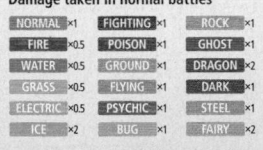

Dratini → Lv. 30 → Dragonair → Lv. 55 → Dragonite

Same form for male/female

Dragonite

Alola Pokédex	Melemele	Akala	Ula'ula	Poni
283	—	—	—	098

☑ **Dragonite**
Dragon Pokémon
DRAGON **FLYING**

HEIGHT: 7'03"
WEIGHT: 463.0 lbs.

This Pokémon saved a shipwrecked man, taking him to a remote island—a paradise occupied solely by Dragonite.

Incur the wrath of this normally calm Pokémon at your peril, because it will smash everything to smithereens before it's satisfied.

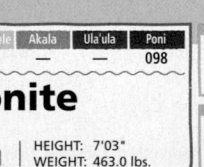

ABILITY
Inner Focus

HIDDEN ABILITY
Multiscale

Damage taken in normal battles

NORMAL ×1	FIGHTING ×0.5	ROCK ×1
FIRE ×0.5	POISON ×1	GHOST ×1
WATER ×0.5	GROUND ×0	DRAGON ×1
GRASS ×0.25	FLYING ×1	DARK ×1
ELECTRIC ×1	PSYCHIC ×1	STEEL ×1
ICE ×4	BUG ×0.5	FAIRY ×1

SPECIES STRENGTHS
HP ◆◆◆
Attack ◆◆◆◆◆◆◆◆
Defense ◆◆◆◆◆
Sp. Atk ◆◆◆◆◆
Sp. Def ◆◆◆◆◆◆
Speed ◆◆◆◆◆

EGG GROUPS
Water 1 · Dragon

ITEM SOMETIMES HELD BY WILD POKÉMON
Dragon Scale

MAIN WAY TO REGISTER IN THE POKÉDEX
Level up Dragonair to Lv. 55

EVOLUTION

Dratini → Lv. 30 → Dragonair → Lv. 55 → Dragonite

Same form for male/female

❖ LEVEL-UP MOVES

Lv.	Name	Type	Kind	Pow.	Acc.	PP	Range
1	Wrap	Normal	Physical	15	90	20	Normal
1	Leer	Normal	Status	—	100	30	Many Others
5	Thunder Wave	Electric	Status	—	90	20	Normal
11	Twister	Dragon	Special	40	100	20	Many Others
15	Dragon Rage	Dragon	Special	—	100	10	Normal
21	Slam	Normal	Physical	80	75	20	Normal
25	Agility	Psychic	Status	—	—	30	Self
31	Dragon Tail	Dragon	Physical	60	90	10	Normal
35	Aqua Tail	Water	Physical	90	90	10	Normal
41	Dragon Rush	Dragon	Physical	100	75	10	Normal
45	Safeguard	Normal	Status	—	—	25	Your Side
51	Dragon Dance	Dragon	Status	—	—	20	Self
55	Outrage	Dragon	Physical	120	100	10	1 Random
61	Hyper Beam	Normal	Special	150	90	5	Normal

❖ TM MOVES

No.	Name	Type	Kind	Pow.	Acc.	PP	Range
TM06	Toxic	Poison	Status		90	10	Normal
TM07	Hail	Ice	Status	—	—	10	Both Sides
TM10	Hidden Power	Normal	Special	60	100	15	Normal
TM11	Sunny Day	Fire	Status	—	—	5	Both Sides
TM13	Ice Beam	Ice	Special	90	100	10	Normal
TM14	Blizzard	Ice	Special	110	70	5	Many Others
TM15	Hyper Beam	Normal	Special	150	90	5	Normal
TM16	Light Screen	Psychic	Status	—	—	30	Your Side
TM17	Protect	Normal	Status	—	—	10	Self
TM18	Rain Dance	Water	Status	—	—	5	Both Sides
TM20	Safeguard	Normal	Status	—	—	25	Your Side
TM21	Frustration	Normal	Physical	—	100	20	Normal
TM24	Thunderbolt	Electric	Special	90	100	15	Normal
TM25	Thunder	Electric	Special	110	70	10	Normal
TM27	Return	Normal	Physical	—	100	20	Normal
TM32	Double Team	Normal	Status	—	—	15	Self
TM35	Flamethrower	Fire	Special	90	100	15	Normal
TM38	Fire Blast	Fire	Special	110	85	5	Normal
TM42	Facade	Normal	Physical	70	100	20	Normal
TM44	Rest	Psychic	Status	—	—	10	Self
TM45	Attract	Normal	Status	—	100	15	Normal
TM48	Round	Normal	Special	60	100	15	Normal
TM59	Brutal Swing	Dark	Physical	60	100	20	Adjacent
TM73	Thunder Wave	Electric	Status	—	90	20	Normal
TM82	Dragon Tail	Dragon	Physical	60	90	10	Normal
TM87	Swagger	Normal	Status	—	85	15	Normal
TM88	Sleep Talk	Normal	Status	—	—	10	Self
TM90	Substitute	Normal	Status	—	—	10	Self
TM94	Surf	Water	Special	90	100	15	Adjacent
TM98	Waterfall	Water	Physical	80	100	15	Normal
TM100	Confide	Normal	Status	—	—	20	Normal

❖ EXCLUSIVE Z-MOVE

Name	Base Move	Type	Kind	Pow.	Acc.	Range

❖ MOVES TAUGHT BY PEOPLE

Name	Type	Kind	Pow.	Acc.	PP	Range
Draco Meteor	Dragon	Special	130	90	5	Normal

❖ MOVES LEARNED WHEN EVOLVING

Name	Type	Kind	Pow.	Acc.	PP	Range

❖ EGG MOVES

Name	Type	Kind	Pow.	Acc.	PP	Range
Mist	Ice	Status	—	—	30	Your Side
Haze	Ice	Status	—	—	30	Both Sides
Supersonic	Normal	Status		55	20	Normal
Dragon Breath	Dragon	Special	60	100	20	Normal
Dragon Dance	Dragon	Status	—	—	20	Self
Dragon Rush	Dragon	Physical	100	75	10	Normal
Extreme Speed	Normal	Physical	80	100	5	Normal
Water Pulse	Water	Special	60	100	20	Normal
Aqua Jet	Water	Physical	40	100	20	Normal
Dragon Pulse	Dragon	Special	85	100	10	Normal
Iron Tail	Steel	Physical	100	75	15	Normal

DRATINI

281

❖ LEVEL-UP MOVES

Lv.	Name	Type	Kind	Pow.	Acc.	PP	Range
1	Wrap	Normal	Physical	15	90	20	Normal
1	Leer	Normal	Status	—	100	30	Many Others
1	Thunder Wave	Electric	Status	—	90	20	Normal
1	Twister	Dragon	Special	40	100	20	Many Others
5	Thunder Wave	Electric	Status	—	90	20	Normal
11	Twister	Dragon	Special	40	100	20	Many Others
15	Dragon Rage	Dragon	Special	—	100	10	Normal
21	Slam	Normal	Physical	80	75	20	Normal
25	Agility	Psychic	Status	—	—	30	Self
33	Dragon Tail	Dragon	Physical	60	90	10	Normal
39	Aqua Tail	Water	Physical	90	90	10	Normal
47	Dragon Rush	Dragon	Physical	100	75	10	Normal
53	Safeguard	Normal	Status	—	—	25	Your Side
61	Dragon Dance	Dragon	Status	—	—	20	Self
67	Outrage	Dragon	Physical	120	100	10	1 Random
75	Hyper Beam	Normal	Special	150	90	5	Normal

❖ TM MOVES

No.	Name	Type	Kind	Pow.	Acc.	PP	Range
TM06	Toxic	Poison	Status	—	90	10	Normal
TM07	Hail	Ice	Status	—	—	10	Both Sides
TM10	Hidden Power	Normal	Special	60	100	15	Normal
TM11	Sunny Day	Fire	Status	—	—	5	Both Sides
TM13	Ice Beam	Ice	Special	90	100	10	Normal
TM14	Blizzard	Ice	Special	110	70	5	Many Others
TM15	Hyper Beam	Normal	Special	150	90	5	Normal
TM16	Light Screen	Psychic	Status	—	—	30	Your Side
TM17	Protect	Normal	Status	—	—	10	Self
TM18	Rain Dance	Water	Status	—	—	5	Both Sides
TM20	Safeguard	Normal	Status	—	—	25	Your Side
TM21	Frustration	Normal	Physical	—	100	20	Normal
TM24	Thunderbolt	Electric	Special	90	100	15	Normal
TM25	Thunder	Electric	Special	110	70	10	Normal
TM27	Return	Normal	Physical	—	100	20	Normal
TM32	Double Team	Normal	Status	—	—	15	Self
TM35	Flamethrower	Fire	Special	90	100	15	Normal
TM38	Fire Blast	Fire	Special	110	85	5	Normal
TM42	Facade	Normal	Physical	70	100	20	Normal
TM44	Rest	Psychic	Status	—	—	10	Self
TM45	Attract	Normal	Status	—	100	15	Normal
TM48	Round	Normal	Special	60	100	15	Normal
TM59	Brutal Swing	Dark	Physical	60	100	20	Adjacent
TM73	Thunder Wave	Electric	Status	—	90	20	Normal
TM82	Dragon Tail	Dragon	Physical	60	90	10	Normal
TM87	Swagger	Normal	Status	—	85	15	Normal
TM88	Sleep Talk	Normal	Status	—	—	10	Self
TM90	Substitute	Normal	Status	—	—	10	Self
TM94	Surf	Water	Special	90	100	15	Adjacent
TM98	Waterfall	Water	Physical	80	100	15	Normal
TM100	Confide	Normal	Status	—		20	Normal

❖ EXCLUSIVE Z-MOVE

Name	Base Move	Type	Kind	Pow.	Acc.	Range

❖ MOVES TAUGHT BY PEOPLE

Name	Type	Kind	Pow.	Acc.	PP	Range
Draco Meteor	Dragon	Special	130	90	5	Normal

❖ MOVES LEARNED WHEN EVOLVING

Name	Type	Kind	Pow.	Acc.	PP	Range

❖ EGG MOVES

Name	Type	Kind	Pow.	Acc.	PP	Range

DRAGONAIR

282

❖ LEVEL-UP MOVES

Lv.	Name	Type	Kind	Pow.	Acc.	PP	Range
1	Wing Attack	Flying	Physical	60	100	35	Normal
1	Hurricane	Flying	Special	110	70	10	Normal
1	Fire Punch	Fire	Physical	75	100	15	Normal
1	Thunder Punch	Electric	Physical	75	100	15	Normal
1	Roost	Flying	Status	—	—	10	Self
1	Wrap	Normal	Physical	15	90	20	Normal
1	Leer	Normal	Status	—	100	30	Many Others
1	Thunder Wave	Electric	Status	—	90	20	Normal
1	Twister	Dragon	Special	40	100	20	Many Others
5	Thunder Wave	Electric	Status	—	90	20	Normal
11	Twister	Dragon	Special	40	100	20	Many Others
15	Dragon Rage	Dragon	Special	—	100	10	Normal
21	Slam	Normal	Physical	80	75	20	Normal
25	Agility	Psychic	Status	—	—	30	Self
33	Dragon Tail	Dragon	Physical	60	90	10	Normal
39	Aqua Tail	Water	Physical	90	90	10	Normal
47	Dragon Rush	Dragon	Physical	100	75	10	Normal
53	Safeguard	Normal	Status	—	—	25	Your Side
61	Dragon Dance	Dragon	Status	—	—	20	Self
67	Outrage	Dragon	Physical	120	100	10	1 Random
75	Hyper Beam	Normal	Special	150	90	5	Normal
81	Hurricane	Flying	Special	110	70	10	Normal

❖ TM MOVES

No.	Name	Type	Kind	Pow.	Acc.	PP	Range
TM02	Dragon Claw	Dragon	Physical	80	100	15	Normal
TM05	Roar	Normal	Status	—	—	20	Normal
TM06	Toxic	Poison	Status	—	90	10	Normal
TM07	Hail	Ice	Status	—	—	10	Both Sides
TM10	Hidden Power	Normal	Special	60	100	15	Normal
TM11	Sunny Day	Fire	Status	—	—	5	Both Sides
TM13	Ice Beam	Ice	Special	90	100	10	Normal
TM14	Blizzard	Ice	Special	110	70	5	Many Others
TM15	Hyper Beam	Normal	Special	150	90	5	Normal
TM16	Light Screen	Psychic	Status	—	—	30	Your Side
TM17	Protect	Normal	Status	—	—	10	Self
TM18	Rain Dance	Water	Status	—	—	5	Both Sides
TM19	Roost	Flying	Status	—	—	10	Self
TM20	Safeguard	Normal	Status	—	—	25	Your Side
TM21	Frustration	Normal	Physical	—	100	20	Normal
TM24	Thunderbolt	Electric	Special	90	100	15	Normal
TM25	Thunder	Electric	Special	110	70	10	Normal
TM26	Earthquake	Ground	Physical	100	100	10	Adjacent
TM27	Return	Normal	Physical	—	100	20	Normal
TM31	Brick Break	Fighting	Physical	75	100	15	Normal
TM32	Double Team	Normal	Status	—	—	15	Self
TM35	Flamethrower	Fire	Special	90	100	15	Normal
TM37	Sandstorm	Rock	Status	—	—	10	Both Sides
TM38	Fire Blast	Fire	Special	110	85	5	Normal
TM39	Rock Tomb	Rock	Physical	60	95	15	Normal
TM40	Aerial Ace	Flying	Physical	60	—	20	Normal
TM42	Facade	Normal	Physical	70	100	20	Normal
TM44	Rest	Psychic	Status	—	—	10	Self
TM45	Attract	Normal	Status	—	100	15	Normal
TM48	Round	Normal	Special	60	100	15	Normal
TM51	Steel Wing	Steel	Physical	70	90	25	Normal
TM52	Focus Blast	Fighting	Special	120	70	5	Normal
TM56	Fling	Dark	Physical	—	100	10	Normal
TM58	Sky Drop	Flying	Physical	60	100	10	Normal
TM59	Brutal Swing	Dark	Physical	60	100	20	Adjacent
TM68	Giga Impact	Normal	Physical	150	90	5	Normal
TM71	Stone Edge	Rock	Physical	100	80	5	Normal
TM73	Thunder Wave	Electric	Status	—	90	20	Normal
TM76	Fly	Flying	Physical	90	95	15	Normal
TM78	Bulldoze	Ground	Physical	60	100	20	Adjacent
TM80	Rock Slide	Rock	Physical	75	90	10	Many Others
TM82	Dragon Tail	Dragon	Physical	60	90	10	Normal
TM87	Swagger	Normal	Status	—	85	15	Normal
TM88	Sleep Talk	Normal	Status	—	—	10	Self
TM90	Substitute	Normal	Status	—	—	10	Self
TM94	Surf	Water	Special	90	100	15	Adjacent
TM98	Waterfall	Water	Physical	80	100	15	Normal
TM100	Confide	Normal	Status	—	—	20	Normal

❖ EXCLUSIVE Z-MOVE

Name	Base Move	Type	Kind	Pow.	Acc.	Range

❖ MOVES TAUGHT BY PEOPLE

Name	Type	Kind	Pow.	Acc.	PP	Range
Draco Meteor	Dragon	Special	130	90	5	Normal

❖ MOVES LEARNED WHEN EVOLVING

Name	Type	Kind	Pow.	Acc.	PP	Range
Wing Attack	Flying	Physical	60	100	35	Normal

❖ EGG MOVES

Name	Type	Kind	Pow.	Acc.	PP	Range

DRAGONITE

283

Alola Pokédex	Melemele	Akala	Ula'ula	Poni
284	—	—	—	099

☑ Aerodactyl
Fossil Pokémon

ROCK | FLYING

HEIGHT: 5'11"
WEIGHT: 130.1 lbs.

A Pokémon from the age of the dinosaurs. It used its sawlike fangs to shred its prey before eating them.

In ancient times, it ruled the skies. A widely accepted theory is that it went extinct due to a large meteor impact.

ABILITY
Rock Head
Pressure

HIDDEN ABILITY
Unnerve

SPECIES STRENGTHS
HP	◆◆◆
Attack	◆◆◆◆◆◆
Defense	◆◆◆◆
Sp. Atk	◆◆◆
Sp. Def	◆◆◆◆
Speed	◆◆◆◆◆◆◆

EVOLUTION
Does not evolve

Same form for male/female

p. 214

Damage taken in normal battles
NORMAL ×0.5	FIGHTING ×1		ROCK ×2
FIRE ×0.5	POISON ×0.5		GHOST ×1
WATER ×2	GROUND ×0		DRAGON ×1
GRASS ×1	FLYING ×0.5		DARK ×1
ELECTRIC ×2	PSYCHIC ×1		STEEL ×1
ICE ×2	BUG ×1		FAIRY ×1

EGG GROUPS
Flying

ITEM SOMETIMES HELD BY WILD POKÉMON

MAIN WAY TO REGISTER IN THE POKÉDEX
Receive from a female Ace Trainer in the shop boat in Seafolk Village

❖ LEVEL-UP MOVES
Lv.	Name	Type	Kind	Pow.	Acc.	PP	Range
1	Iron Head	Steel	Physical	80	100	15	Normal
1	Ice Fang	Ice	Physical	65	95	15	Normal
1	Fire Fang	Fire	Physical	65	95	15	Normal
1	Thunder Fang	Electric	Physical	65	95	15	Normal
1	Wing Attack	Flying	Physical	60	100	35	Normal
1	Supersonic	Normal	Status	—	55	20	Normal
1	Bite	Dark	Physical	60	100	25	Normal
1	Scary Face	Normal	Status	—	100	10	Normal
9	Roar	Normal	Status	—	—	20	Normal
17	Agility	Psychic	Status	—	—	30	Self
25	Ancient Power	Rock	Special	60	100	5	Normal
33	Crunch	Dark	Physical	80	100	15	Normal
41	Take Down	Normal	Physical	90	85	20	Normal
49	Sky Drop	Flying	Physical	60	100	10	Normal
57	Iron Head	Steel	Physical	80	100	15	Normal
65	Hyper Beam	Normal	Special	150	90	5	Normal
73	Rock Slide	Rock	Physical	75	90	10	Many Others
81	Giga Impact	Normal	Physical	150	90	5	Normal

❖ TM MOVES
No.	Name	Type	Kind	Pow.	Acc.	PP	Range
TM02	Dragon Claw	Dragon	Physical	80	100	15	Normal
TM05	Roar	Normal	Status	—	—	20	Normal
TM06	Toxic	Poison	Status	—	90	10	Normal
TM10	Hidden Power	Normal	Special	60	100	15	Normal
TM11	Sunny Day	Fire	Status	—	—	5	Both Sides
TM12	Taunt	Dark	Status	—	100	20	Normal
TM15	Hyper Beam	Normal	Special	150	90	5	Normal
TM17	Protect	Normal	Status	—	—	10	Self
TM18	Rain Dance	Water	Status	—	—	5	Both Sides
TM19	Roost	Flying	Status	—	—	10	Self
TM21	Frustration	Normal	Physical	—	100	20	Normal
TM23	Smack Down	Rock	Physical	50	100	15	Normal
TM26	Earthquake	Ground	Physical	100	100	10	Adjacent
TM27	Return	Normal	Physical	—	100	20	Normal
TM32	Double Team	Normal	Status	—	—	15	Self
TM35	Flamethrower	Fire	Special	90	100	15	Normal
TM37	Sandstorm	Rock	Status	—	—	10	Both Sides
TM38	Fire Blast	Fire	Special	110	85	5	Normal
TM39	Rock Tomb	Rock	Physical	60	95	15	Normal
TM40	Aerial Ace	Flying	Physical	60	—	20	Normal
TM41	Torment	Dark	Status	—	100	15	Normal
TM42	Facade	Normal	Physical	70	100	20	Normal
TM44	Rest	Psychic	Status	—	—	10	Self
TM45	Attract	Normal	Status	—	100	15	Normal
TM46	Thief	Dark	Physical	60	100	25	Normal
TM48	Round	Normal	Special	60	100	15	Normal
TM51	Steel Wing	Steel	Physical	70	90	25	Normal
TM58	Sky Drop	Flying	Physical	60	100	10	Normal

No.	Name	Type	Kind	Pow.	Acc.	PP	Range
TM59	Brutal Swing	Dark	Physical	60	100	20	Adjacent
TM66	Payback	Dark	Physical	50	100	10	Normal
TM68	Giga Impact	Normal	Physical	150	90	5	Normal
TM69	Rock Polish	Rock	Status	—	—	20	Self
TM71	Stone Edge	Rock	Physical	100	80	5	Normal
TM76	Fly	Flying	Physical	90	95	15	Normal
TM78	Bulldoze	Ground	Physical	60	100	20	Adjacent
TM80	Rock Slide	Rock	Physical	75	90	10	Many Others
TM87	Swagger	Normal	Status	—	85	15	Normal
TM88	Sleep Talk	Normal	Status	—	—	10	Self
TM90	Substitute	Normal	Status	—	—	10	Self
TM100	Confide	Normal	Status	—	—	20	Normal

❖ MOVES TAUGHT BY PEOPLE
Name	Type	Kind	Pow.	Acc.	PP	Range

❖ MOVES LEARNED WHEN EVOLVING
Name	Type	Kind	Pow.	Acc.	PP	Range

❖ EGG MOVES
Name	Type	Kind	Pow.	Acc.	PP	Range
Whirlwind	Normal	Status	—	—	20	Normal
Pursuit	Dark	Physical	40	100	20	Normal
Foresight	Normal	Status	—	—	40	Normal
Steel Wing	Steel	Physical	70	90	25	Normal
Dragon Breath	Dragon	Special	60	100	20	Normal
Curse	Ghost	Status	—	—	10	Varies
Assurance	Dark	Physical	60	100	10	Normal
Roost	Flying	Status	—	—	10	Self
Tailwind	Flying	Status	—	—	15	Your Side
Wide Guard	Rock	Status	—	—	10	Your Side

❖ EXCLUSIVE Z-MOVE
Name	Base Move	Type	Kind	Pow.	Acc.	Range

Fossil Pokémon from Other Regions

While there are four Fossils available in these games—Skull Fossil and Cover Fossil in *Pokémon Sun* and Armor Fossil and Plume Fossil in *Pokémon Moon*—the Pokémon that they can be restored to are not the only ancient Pokémon that can be brought back to life from age-old Fossils! Other Fossils have been found in different regions of the Pokémon world, and you may be able to find the Pokémon they are restored to via the GTS (p. 31) or a Link Trade. If you're very lucky, perhaps you might even receive one in a Wonder Trade someday! Check out some other ancient Pokémon that can be restored from Fossils below—and if you get them for yourself, train them well to see what they evolve into, too!

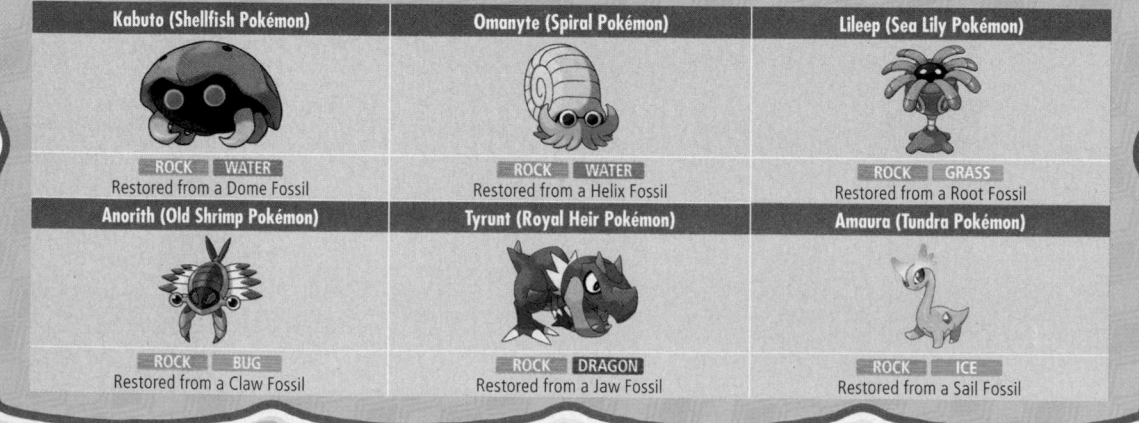

Kabuto (Shellfish Pokémon)
ROCK | WATER
Restored from a Dome Fossil

Omanyte (Spiral Pokémon)
ROCK | WATER
Restored from a Helix Fossil

Lileep (Sea Lily Pokémon)
ROCK | GRASS
Restored from a Root Fossil

Anorith (Old Shrimp Pokémon)
ROCK | BUG
Restored from a Claw Fossil

Tyrunt (Royal Heir Pokémon)
ROCK | DRAGON
Restored from a Jaw Fossil

Amaura (Tundra Pokémon)
ROCK | ICE
Restored from a Sail Fossil

Alola Pokédex	Melemele	Akala	Ula'ula	Poni
285	120	—	—	—

Tapu Koko

Land Spirit Pokémon

ELECTRIC FAIRY

HEIGHT: 5'11"
WEIGHT: 45.2 lbs.

This guardian deity of Melemele is brimming with curiosity. It summons thunderclouds and stores their lightning inside its body.

It confuses its enemies by flying too quickly for the eye to follow. It has a hair-trigger temper but forgets what made it angry an instant later.

Gender unknown

ABILITY
Electric Surge

HIDDEN ABILITY
—

Damage taken in normal battles

NORMAL	×1	FIGHTING	×0.5	ROCK	×1
FIRE	×1	POISON	×2	GHOST	×1
WATER	×1	GROUND	×2	DRAGON	×0
GRASS	×1	FLYING	×0.5	DARK	×0.5
ELECTRIC	×0.5	PSYCHIC	×1	STEEL	×1
ICE	×1	BUG	×0.5	FAIRY	×1

SPECIES STRENGTHS
HP ◆◆◆
Attack ◆◆◆◆◆◆
Defense ◆◆◆◆◆
Sp. Atk ◆◆◆◆◆
Sp. Def ◆◆◆◆
Speed ◆◆◆◆◆◆◆◆◆

EGG GROUPS
No Eggs Discovered

ITEM SOMETIMES HELD BY WILD POKEMON
—

EVOLUTION
Does not evolve

MAIN WAY TO REGISTER IN THE POKÉDEX
Catch in the Ruins of Conflict after becoming Champion

❖ LEVEL-UP MOVES

Lv.	Name	Type	Kind	Pow.	Acc.	PP	Range
1	Electric Terrain	Electric	Status	—	—	10	Both Sides
1	Brave Bird	Flying	Physical	120	100	15	Normal
1	Power Swap	Psychic	Status	—	—	10	Normal
1	Mean Look	Normal	Status	—	—	5	Normal
1	Quick Attack	Normal	Physical	40	100	30	Normal
1	False Swipe	Normal	Physical	40	100	40	Normal
1	Withdraw	Water	Status	—	—	40	Self
1	Thunder Shock	Electric	Special	40	100	30	Normal
8	Spark	Electric	Physical	65	100	20	Normal
14	Shock Wave	Electric	Special	60		20	Normal
20	Screech	Normal	Status	—	85	40	Normal
26	Charge	Electric	Status	—	—	20	Self
32	Wild Charge	Electric	Physical	90	100	15	Normal
38	Mirror Move	Flying	Status	—	—	20	Normal
43	Nature's Madness	Fairy	Special	—	90	10	Normal
48	Discharge	Electric	Special	80	100	15	Adjacent
53	Agility	Psychic	Status	—	—	30	Self
58	Electro Ball	Electric	Special	—	100	10	Normal

❖ TM MOVES

No.	Name	Type	Kind	Pow.	Acc.	PP	Range
TM01	Work Up	Normal	Status	—	—	30	Self
TM04	Calm Mind	Psychic	Status	—	—	20	Self
TM05	Roar	Normal	Status	—	—	20	Normal
TM06	Toxic	Poison	Status	—	90	10	Normal
TM10	Hidden Power	Normal	Special	60	100	15	Normal
TM12	Taunt	Dark	Status	—	100	20	Normal
TM15	Hyper Beam	Normal	Special	150	90	5	Normal
TM16	Light Screen	Psychic	Status	—	—	30	Your Side
TM17	Protect	Normal	Status	—	—	10	Self
TM18	Rain Dance	Water	Status	—	—	5	Both Sides
TM19	Roost	Flying	Status	—	—	10	Self
TM20	Safeguard	Normal	Status	—	—	25	Your Side
TM21	Frustration	Normal	Physical	—	100	20	Normal
TM24	Thunderbolt	Electric	Special	90	100	15	Normal
TM25	Thunder	Electric	Special	110	70	10	Normal
TM27	Return	Normal	Physical	—	100	20	Normal
TM32	Double Team	Normal	Status	—	—	15	Self
TM33	Reflect	Psychic	Status	—	—	20	Your Side
TM40	Aerial Ace	Flying	Physical	60	—	20	Normal
TM41	Torment	Dark	Status		100	15	Normal
TM42	Facade	Normal	Physical	70	100	20	Normal
TM46	Thief	Dark	Physical	60	100	25	Normal
TM48	Round	Normal	Special	60	100	15	Normal
TM49	Echoed Voice	Normal	Special	40	100	15	Normal
TM51	Steel Wing	Steel	Physical	70	90	25	Normal
TM54	False Swipe	Normal	Physical	40	100	40	Normal
TM58	Sky Drop	Flying	Physical	60	100	10	Normal
TM62	Acrobatics	Flying	Physical	55	100	15	Normal
TM68	Giga Impact	Normal	Physical	150	90	5	Normal
TM72	Volt Switch	Electric	Special	70	100	20	Normal
TM73	Thunder Wave	Electric	Status	—	90	20	Normal
TM76	Fly	Flying	Physical	90	95	15	Normal
TM77	Psych Up	Normal	Status	—	—	10	Normal
TM86	Grass Knot	Grass	Special	—	100	20	Normal
TM87	Swagger	Normal	Status	—	85	15	Normal
TM88	Sleep Talk	Normal	Status	—	—	10	Self
TM89	U-turn	Bug	Physical	70	100	20	Normal
TM90	Substitute	Normal	Status	—	—	10	Self
TM93	Wild Charge	Electric	Physical	90	100	15	Normal
TM96	Nature Power	Normal	Status	—	—	20	Normal
TM99	Dazzling Gleam	Fairy	Special	80	100	10	Many Others
TM100	Confide	Normal	Status	—	—	20	Normal

❖ EXCLUSIVE Z-MOVE

Name	Base Move	Type	Kind	Pow.	Acc.	Range
Guardian of Alola	Nature's Madness	Fairy	Special	—	—	Normal

❖ MOVES TAUGHT BY PEOPLE

Name	Type	Kind	Pow.	Acc.	PP	Range

❖ MOVES LEARNED WHEN EVOLVING

Name	Type	Kind	Pow.	Acc.	PP	Range

❖ EGG MOVES

Name	Type	Kind	Pow.	Acc.	PP	Range

Alola Pokédex	Melemele	Akala	Ula'ula	Poni
286	—	130	—	—

Tapu Lele

Land Spirit Pokémon

PSYCHIC FAIRY

HEIGHT: 3'11"
WEIGHT: 41.0 lbs.

This guardian deity of Akala is guilelessly cruel. The fragrant aroma of flowers is the source of its energy.

As it flutters about, it scatters its strangely glowing scales. Touching them is said to restore good health on the spot.

Gender unknown

ABILITY
Psychic Surge

HIDDEN ABILITY
—

Damage taken in normal battles

NORMAL	×1	FIGHTING	×0.25	ROCK	×1
FIRE	×1	POISON	×2	GHOST	×2
WATER	×1	GROUND	×1	DRAGON	×0
GRASS	×1	FLYING	×1	DARK	×1
ELECTRIC	×1	PSYCHIC	×0.5	STEEL	×2
ICE	×1	BUG	×1	FAIRY	×1

SPECIES STRENGTHS
HP ◆◆◆
Attack ◆◆◆◆◆
Defense ◆◆◆◆
Sp. Atk ◆◆◆◆◆◆◆◆
Sp. Def ◆◆◆◆◆◆◆◆
Speed ◆◆◆◆◆◆

EGG GROUPS
No Eggs Discovered

ITEM SOMETIMES HELD BY WILD POKÉMON
—

EVOLUTION
Does not evolve

MAIN WAY TO REGISTER IN THE POKÉDEX
Catch in the Ruins of Life after becoming Champion

❖ LEVEL-UP MOVES

Lv.	Name	Type	Kind	Pow.	Acc.	PP	Range
1	Psychic Terrain	Psychic	Status	—	—	10	Both Sides
1	Aromatic Mist	Fairy	Status	—	—	20	1 Ally
1	Aromatherapy	Grass	Status	—	—	5	Your Party
1	Mean Look	Normal	Status	—	—	5	Normal
1	Draining Kiss	Fairy	Special	50	100	10	Normal
1	Astonish	Ghost	Physical	30	100	15	Normal
1	Withdraw	Water	Status	—	—	40	Self
1	Confusion	Psychic	Special	50	100	25	Normal
8	Psywave	Psychic	Special	—	100	15	Normal
14	Psybeam	Psychic	Special	65	100	20	Normal
20	Sweet Scent	Normal	Status	—	100	20	Many Others
26	Skill Swap	Psychic	Status	—	—	10	Normal
32	Psyshock	Psychic	Special	80	100	10	Normal
38	Tickle	Normal	Status	—	100	20	Normal
43	Nature's Madness	Fairy	Special	—	90	10	Normal
48	Extrasensory	Psychic	Special	80	100	20	Normal
53	Flatter	Dark	Status	—	100	15	Normal
58	Moonblast	Fairy	Special	95	100	15	Normal

❖ TM MOVES

No.	Name	Type	Kind	Pow.	Acc.	PP	Range
TM03	Psyshock	Psychic	Special	80	100	10	Normal
TM04	Calm Mind	Psychic	Status	—	—	20	Self
TM06	Toxic	Poison	Status	—	90	10	Normal
TM10	Hidden Power	Normal	Special	60	100	15	Normal
TM11	Sunny Day	Fire	Status	—	—	5	Both Sides
TM12	Taunt	Dark	Status	—	100	20	Normal
TM15	Hyper Beam	Normal	Special	150	90	5	Normal
TM16	Light Screen	Psychic	Status	—	—	30	Your Side
TM17	Protect	Normal	Status	—	—	10	Self
TM20	Safeguard	Normal	Status	—	—	25	Your Side
TM21	Frustration	Normal	Physical	—	100	20	Normal
TM24	Thunderbolt	Electric	Special	90	100	15	Normal
TM25	Thunder	Electric	Special	110	70	10	Normal
TM27	Return	Normal	Physical	—	100	20	Normal
TM29	Psychic	Psychic	Special	90	100	10	Normal
TM30	Shadow Ball	Ghost	Special	80	100	15	Normal
TM32	Double Team	Normal	Status	—	—	15	Self
TM33	Reflect	Psychic	Status	—	—	20	Your Side
TM41	Torment	Dark	Status	—	100	15	Normal
TM42	Facade	Normal	Physical	70	100	20	Normal
TM46	Thief	Dark	Physical	60	100	25	Normal
TM48	Round	Normal	Special	60	100	15	Normal
TM49	Echoed Voice	Normal	Special	40	100	15	Normal
TM52	Focus Blast	Fighting	Special	120	70	5	Normal
TM53	Energy Ball	Grass	Special	90	100	10	Normal
TM56	Fling	Dark	Physical	—	100	10	Normal
TM57	Charge Beam	Electric	Special	50	90	10	Normal
TM68	Giga Impact	Normal	Physical	150	90	5	Normal
TM77	Psych Up	Normal	Status	—	—	10	Normal
TM86	Grass Knot	Grass	Special	—	100	20	Normal
TM87	Swagger	Normal	Status	—	85	15	Normal
TM88	Sleep Talk	Normal	Status	—	—	10	Self
TM90	Substitute	Normal	Status	—	—	10	Self
TM96	Nature Power	Normal	Status	—	—	20	Normal
TM99	Dazzling Gleam	Fairy	Special	80	100	10	Many Others
TM100	Confide	Normal	Status	—	—	20	Normal

❖ EXCLUSIVE Z-MOVE

Name	Base Move	Type	Kind	Pow.	Acc.	Range
Guardian of Alola	Nature's Madness	Fairy	Special	—	—	Normal

❖ MOVES TAUGHT BY PEOPLE

Name	Type	Kind	Pow.	Acc.	PP	Range

❖ MOVES LEARNED WHEN EVOLVING

Name	Type	Kind	Pow.	Acc.	PP	Range

❖ EGG MOVES

Name	Type	Kind	Pow.	Acc.	PP	Range

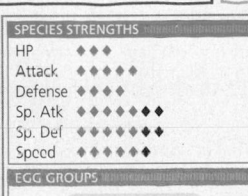

Tapu Bulu

Land Spirit Pokémon

Alola Pokédex	Melemele	Akala	Ula'ula	Poni
287	—	—	130	—

GRASS FAIRY

HEIGHT: 6'03"
WEIGHT: 100.3 lbs.

It pulls large trees up by the roots and swings them around. It causes vegetation to grow, and then it absorbs energy from the growth.

The guardian deity of Ula'ula is a lazy Pokémon. It commands plants to immobilize its foes and then deals them a savage blow with its horns.

ABILITY
Grassy Surge

HIDDEN ABILITY
—

SPECIES STRENGTHS
HP	◆◆◆
Attack	◆◆◆◆◆◆◆◆
Defense	◆◆◆◆◆◆
Sp. Atk	◆◆◆◆◆
Sp. Def	◆◆◆◆◆◆◆
Speed	◆◆◆◆◆

Damage taken in normal battles
NORMAL ×1	FIGHTING ×0.5	ROCK ×1
FIRE ×2	POISON ×4	GHOST ×1
WATER ×0.5	GROUND ×0.5	DRAGON ×0
GRASS ×0.5	FLYING ×2	DARK ×0.5
ELECTRIC ×0.5	PSYCHIC ×1	STEEL ×1
ICE ×2	BUG ×1	FAIRY ×1

EGG GROUPS
No Eggs Discovered

ITEM SOMETIMES HELD BY WILD POKÉMON
—

EVOLUTION
Does not evolve

MAIN WAY TO REGISTER IN THE POKÉDEX
Catch in the Ruins of Abundance after becoming Champion

Gender unknown

❖ LEVEL-UP MOVES
Lv.	Name	Type	Kind	Pow.	Acc.	PP	Range
1	Grassy Terrain	Grass	Status	—	—	10	Both Sides
1	Wood Hammer	Grass	Physical	120	100	15	Normal
1	Superpower	Fighting	Physical	120	100	5	Normal
1	Mean Look	Normal	Status	—	—	5	Normal
1	Disable	Normal	Status	—	100	20	Normal
1	Bulk Up	Fighting	Status	—	—	20	Self
1	Whirlwind	Normal	Status	—	—	20	Normal
1	Withdraw	Water	Status	—	—	40	Self
1	Leafage	Grass	Physical	40	100	40	Normal
8	Horn Attack	Normal	Physical	65	100	25	Normal
14	Giga Drain	Grass	Special	75	100	10	Normal
20	Scary Face	Normal	Status	—	100	10	Normal
26	Leech Seed	Grass	Status	—	90	10	Normal
32	Horn Leech	Grass	Physical	75	100	10	Normal
38	Rototiller	Ground	Status	—	—	10	Adjacent
43	Nature's Madness	Fairy	Special	—	90	10	Normal
48	Zen Headbutt	Psychic	Physical	80	90	15	Normal
53	Megahorn	Bug	Physical	120	85	10	Normal
58	Skull Bash	Normal	Physical	130	100	10	Normal

❖ TM MOVES
No.	Name	Type	Kind	Pow.	Acc.	PP	Range
TM01	Work Up	Normal	Status	—	—	30	Self
TM04	Calm Mind	Psychic	Status	—	—	20	Self
TM05	Roar	Normal	Status	—	—	20	Normal
TM06	Toxic	Poison	Status	—	90	10	Normal
TM08	Bulk Up	Fighting	Status	—	—	20	Self
TM10	Hidden Power	Normal	Special	60	100	15	Normal
TM11	Sunny Day	Fire	Status	—	—	5	Both Sides
TM12	Taunt	Dark	Status	—	100	20	Normal
TM15	Hyper Beam	Normal	Special	150	90	5	Normal
TM16	Light Screen	Psychic	Status	—	—	30	Your Side
TM17	Protect	Normal	Status	—	—	10	Self
TM20	Safeguard	Normal	Status	—	—	25	Your Side
TM21	Frustration	Normal	Physical	—	100	20	Normal
TM22	Solar Beam	Grass	Special	120	100	10	Normal
TM27	Return	Normal	Physical	—	100	20	Normal
TM31	Brick Break	Fighting	Physical	75	100	15	Normal
TM33	Reflect	Psychic	Status	—	—	20	Your Side
TM39	Rock Tomb	Rock	Physical	60	95	15	Normal
TM41	Torment	Dark	Status	—	100	15	Normal
TM42	Facade	Normal	Physical	70	100	20	Normal
TM48	Round	Normal	Special	60	100	15	Normal
TM49	Echoed Voice	Normal	Special	40	100	15	Normal
TM52	Focus Blast	Fighting	Special	120	70	5	Normal
TM53	Energy Ball	Grass	Special	90	100	10	Normal
TM54	False Swipe	Normal	Physical	40	100	40	Normal
TM56	Fling	Dark	Physical	—	100	10	Normal
TM59	Brutal Swing	Dark	Physical	60	100	20	Adjacent
TM66	Payback	Dark	Physical	50	100	10	Normal
TM67	Smart Strike	Steel	Physical	70	—	10	Normal
TM68	Giga Impact	Normal	Physical	150	90	5	Normal
TM71	Stone Edge	Rock	Physical	100	80	5	Normal
TM75	Swords Dance	Normal	Status	—	—	20	Self
TM77	Psych Up	Normal	Status	—	—	10	Normal
TM80	Rock Slide	Rock	Physical	75	90	10	Many Others
TM86	Grass Knot	Grass	Special	—	100	20	Normal
TM87	Swagger	Normal	Status	—	85	15	Normal
TM88	Sleep Talk	Normal	Status	—	—	10	Self
TM90	Substitute	Normal	Status	—	—	10	Self
TM95	Snarl	Dark	Special	55	95	15	Many Others
TM96	Nature Power	Normal	Status	—	—	20	Normal
TM99	Dazzling Gleam	Fairy	Special	80	100	10	Many Others
TM100	Confide	Normal	Status	—	—	20	Normal

❖ MOVES TAUGHT BY PEOPLE
Name	Type	Kind	Pow.	Acc.	PP	Range

❖ MOVES LEARNED WHEN EVOLVING
Name	Type	Kind	Pow.	Acc.	PP	Range

❖ EGG MOVES
Name	Type	Kind	Pow.	Acc.	PP	Range

❖ EXCLUSIVE Z-MOVE
Name	Base Move	Type	Kind	Pow.	Acc.	Range
Guardian of Alola	Nature's Madness	Fairy	Special	—	—	Normal

Tapu Fini

Land Spirit Pokémon

Alola Pokédex	Melemele	Akala	Ula'ula	Poni
288	—	—	—	100

WATER FAIRY

HEIGHT: 4'03"
WEIGHT: 46.7 lbs.

The dense fog it creates brings the downfall and destruction of its confused enemies. Ocean currents are the source of its energy.

The guardian deity of Poni, it can control water. People say it can create pure water that will wash away any uncleanness.

ABILITY
Misty Surge

HIDDEN ABILITY
—

SPECIES STRENGTHS
HP	◆◆◆
Attack	◆◆◆◆
Defense	◆◆◆◆◆◆
Sp. Atk	◆◆◆◆◆
Sp. Def	◆◆◆◆◆◆◆◆
Speed	◆◆◆◆◆

Damage taken in normal battles
NORMAL ×1	FIGHTING ×0.5	ROCK ×1
FIRE ×0.5	POISON ×2	GHOST ×1
WATER ×0.5	GROUND ×1	DRAGON ×0
GRASS ×2	FLYING ×1	DARK ×0.5
ELECTRIC ×2	PSYCHIC ×1	STEEL ×1
ICE ×0.5	BUG ×0.5	FAIRY ×1

EGG GROUPS
No Eggs Discovered

ITEM SOMETIMES HELD BY WILD POKÉMON
—

EVOLUTION
Does not evolve

MAIN WAY TO REGISTER IN THE POKÉDEX
Catch in the Ruins of Hope after becoming Champion

Gender unknown

❖ LEVEL-UP MOVES
Lv.	Name	Type	Kind	Pow.	Acc.	PP	Range
1	Misty Terrain	Fairy	Status	—	—	10	Both Sides
1	Moonblast	Fairy	Special	95	100	15	Normal
1	Heal Pulse	Psychic	Status	—	—	10	Normal
1	Mean Look	Normal	Status	—	—	5	Normal
1	Haze	Ice	Status	—	—	30	Both Sides
1	Mist	Ice	Status	—	—	30	Your Side
1	Withdraw	Water	Status	—	—	40	Self
1	Water Gun	Water	Special	40	100	25	Normal
8	Water Pulse	Water	Special	60	100	20	Normal
14	Whirlpool	Water	Special	35	85	15	Normal
20	Soak	Water	Status	—	100	20	Normal
26	Refresh	Normal	Status	—	—	20	Self
32	Brine	Water	Special	65	100	10	Normal
38	Defog	Flying	Status	—	—	15	Normal
43	Nature's Madness	Fairy	Special	—	90	10	Normal
48	Muddy Water	Water	Special	90	85	10	Many Others
53	Aqua Ring	Water	Status	—	—	20	Self
58	Hydro Pump	Water	Special	110	80	5	Normal

❖ TM MOVES
No.	Name	Type	Kind	Pow.	Acc.	PP	Range
TM04	Calm Mind	Psychic	Status	—	—	20	Self
TM06	Toxic	Poison	Status	—	90	10	Normal
TM10	Hidden Power	Normal	Special	60	100	15	Normal
TM12	Taunt	Dark	Status	—	100	20	Normal
TM13	Ice Beam	Ice	Special	90	100	10	Normal
TM14	Blizzard	Ice	Special	110	70	5	Many Others
TM15	Hyper Beam	Normal	Special	150	90	5	Normal
TM16	Light Screen	Psychic	Status	—	—	30	Your Side
TM17	Protect	Normal	Status	—	—	10	Self
TM18	Rain Dance	Water	Status	—	—	5	Both Sides
TM20	Safeguard	Normal	Status	—	—	25	Your Side
TM21	Frustration	Normal	Physical	—	100	20	Normal
TM27	Return	Normal	Physical	—	100	20	Normal
TM30	Shadow Ball	Ghost	Special	80	100	15	Normal
TM32	Double Team	Normal	Status	—	—	15	Self
TM33	Reflect	Psychic	Status	—	—	20	Your Side
TM41	Torment	Dark	Status	—	100	15	Normal
TM42	Facade	Normal	Physical	70	100	20	Normal
TM48	Round	Normal	Special	60	100	15	Normal
TM49	Echoed Voice	Normal	Special	40	100	15	Normal
TM55	Scald	Water	Special	80	100	15	Normal
TM56	Fling	Dark	Physical	—	100	10	Normal
TM67	Smart Strike	Steel	Physical	70	—	10	Normal
TM68	Giga Impact	Normal	Physical	150	90	5	Normal
TM77	Psych Up	Normal	Status	—	—	10	Normal
TM86	Grass Knot	Grass	Special	—	100	20	Normal
TM87	Swagger	Normal	Status	—	85	15	Normal
TM88	Sleep Talk	Normal	Status	—	—	10	Self
TM90	Substitute	Normal	Status	—	—	10	Self
TM94	Surf	Water	Special	90	100	15	Adjacent
TM96	Nature Power	Normal	Status	—	—	20	Normal
TM98	Waterfall	Water	Physical	80	100	15	Normal
TM99	Dazzling Gleam	Fairy	Special	80	100	10	Many Others
TM100	Confide	Normal	Status	—	—	20	Normal

❖ MOVES TAUGHT BY PEOPLE
Name	Type	Kind	Pow.	Acc.	PP	Range

❖ MOVES LEARNED WHEN EVOLVING
Name	Type	Kind	Pow.	Acc.	PP	Range

❖ EGG MOVES
Name	Type	Kind	Pow.	Acc.	PP	Range

❖ EXCLUSIVE Z-MOVE
Name	Base Move	Type	Kind	Pow.	Acc.	Range
Guardian of Alola	Nature's Madness	Fairy	Special	—	—	Normal

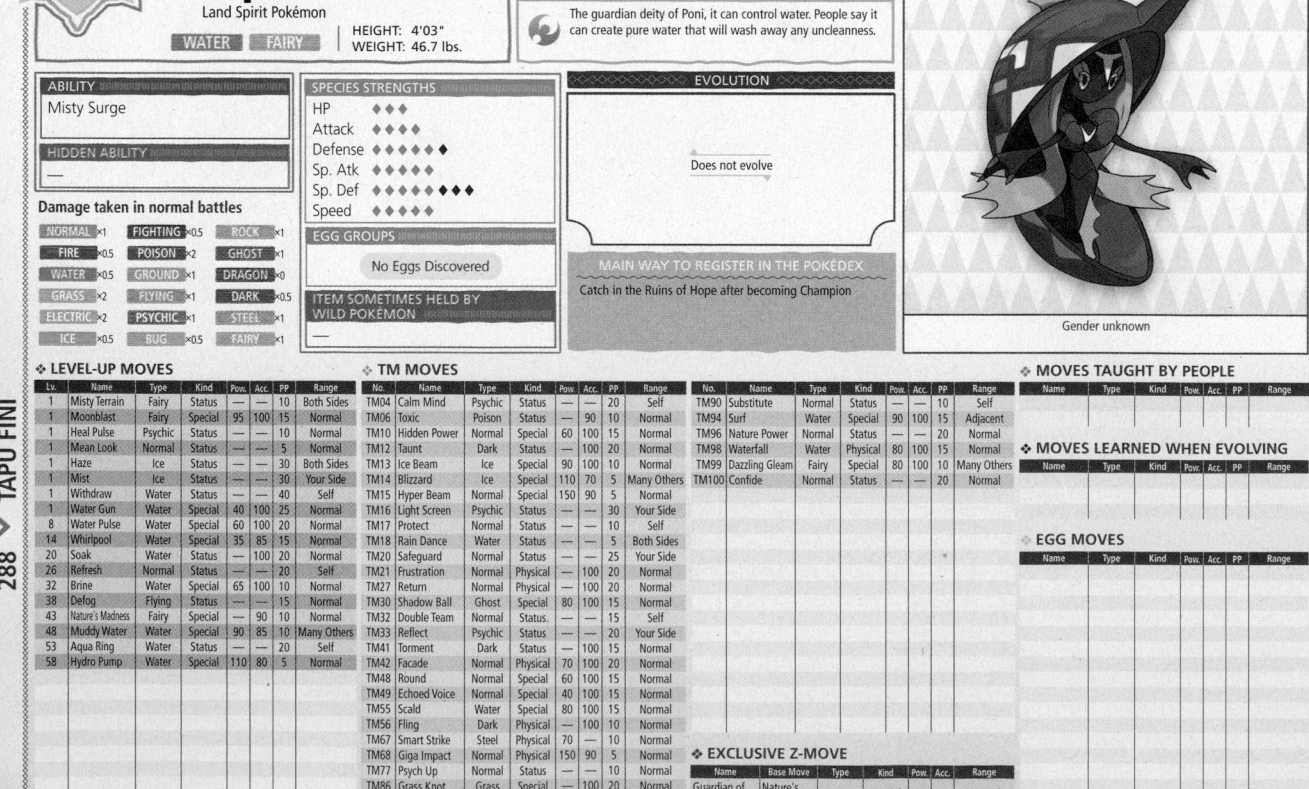

Cosmog

Alola Pokédex	Melemele	Akala	Ula'ula	Poni
289	—	—	—	—

Nebula Pokémon

PSYCHIC

HEIGHT: 0'08"
WEIGHT: 0.2 lbs.

Its body is gaseous and frail. It slowly grows as it collects dust from the atmosphere.

In ages past, it was called the child of the stars. It's said to be a Pokémon from another world, but no specific details are known.

ABILITY
Unaware

HIDDEN ABILITY
—

SPECIES STRENGTHS
HP	◆◆
Attack	◆◆
Defense	◆◆
Sp. Atk	◆◆
Sp. Def	◆
Speed	◆◆

EGG GROUPS
No Eggs Discovered

ITEM SOMETIMES HELD BY WILD POKÉMON
—

Damage taken in normal battles
NORMAL ×1	FIGHTING ×0.5	ROCK ×1
FIRE ×1	POISON ×1	GHOST ×1
WATER ×1	GROUND ×1	DRAGON ×1
GRASS ×1	FLYING ×1	DARK ×2
ELECTRIC ×1	PSYCHIC ×0.5	STEEL ×1
ICE ×1	BUG ×1	FAIRY ×1

EVOLUTION
Cosmog → Lv. 43 → Cosmoem → Lv. 53 → Solgaleo / Lv. 53 → Lunala

MAIN WAY TO REGISTER IN THE POKÉDEX
Visit a parallel world with Solgaleo or Lunala (p. 257)

Gender unknown

❖ LEVEL-UP MOVES
Lv.	Name	Type	Kind	Pow.	Acc.	PP	Range
1	Splash	Normal	Status	—	—	40	Self
23	Teleport	Psychic	Status	—	—	20	Self

❖ TM MOVES
No.	Name	Type	Kind	Pow.	Acc.	PP	Range	No.	Name	Type	Kind	Pow.	Acc.	PP	Range

❖ MOVES TAUGHT BY PEOPLE
Name	Type	Kind	Pow.	Acc.	PP	Range

❖ MOVES LEARNED WHEN EVOLVING
Name	Type	Kind	Pow.	Acc.	PP	Range

❖ EGG MOVES
Name	Type	Kind	Pow.	Acc.	PP	Range

❖ EXCLUSIVE Z-MOVE
Name	Base Move	Type	Kind	Pow.	Acc.	Range

Cosmoem

Alola Pokédex	Melemele	Akala	Ula'ula	Poni
290	—	—	—	—

Protostar Pokémon

PSYCHIC

HEIGHT: 0'04"
WEIGHT: 2204.4 lbs.

Motionless as if dead, its body is faintly warm to the touch. In the distant past, it was called the cocoon of the stars.

There's something accumulating around the black core within its hard shell. People think this Pokémon may come from another world.

ABILITY
Sturdy

HIDDEN ABILITY
—

SPECIES STRENGTHS
HP	◆◆
Attack	◆◆
Defense	◆◆◆◆◆◆◆
Sp. Atk	◆◆
Sp. Def	◆◆◆◆◆◆◆
Speed	◆◆

EGG GROUPS
No Eggs Discovered

ITEM SOMETIMES HELD BY WILD POKÉMON
—

Damage taken in normal battles
NORMAL ×1	FIGHTING ×0.5	ROCK ×1
FIRE ×1	POISON ×1	GHOST ×2
WATER ×1	GROUND ×1	DRAGON ×1
GRASS ×1	FLYING ×1	DARK ×2
ELECTRIC ×1	PSYCHIC ×0.5	STEEL ×1
ICE ×1	BUG ×2	FAIRY ×1

EVOLUTION
Cosmog → Lv. 43 → Cosmoem → Lv. 53 → Solgaleo / Lv. 53 → Lunala

MAIN WAY TO REGISTER IN THE POKÉDEX
Level up Cosmog to Lv. 43

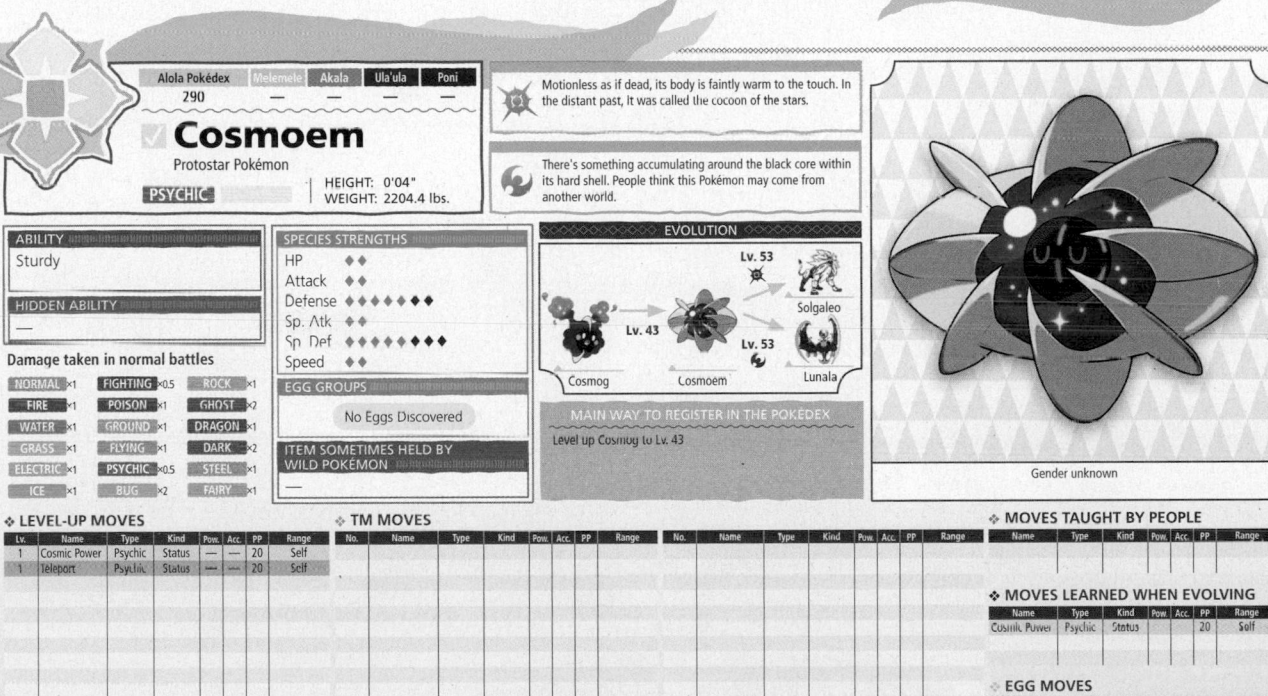

Gender unknown

❖ LEVEL-UP MOVES
Lv.	Name	Type	Kind	Pow.	Acc.	PP	Range
1	Cosmic Power	Psychic	Status	—	—	20	Self
1	Teleport	Psychic	Status	—	—	20	Self

❖ TM MOVES
No.	Name	Type	Kind	Pow.	Acc.	PP	Range	No.	Name	Type	Kind	Pow.	Acc.	PP	Range

❖ MOVES TAUGHT BY PEOPLE
Name	Type	Kind	Pow.	Acc.	PP	Range

❖ MOVES LEARNED WHEN EVOLVING
Name	Type	Kind	Pow.	Acc.	PP	Range
Cosmic Power	Psychic	Status			20	Self

❖ EGG MOVES
Name	Type	Kind	Pow.	Acc.	PP	Range

❖ EXCLUSIVE Z-MOVE
Name	Base Move	Type	Kind	Pow.	Acc.	Range

Alola Pokédex	Melemele	Akala	Ula'ula	Poni
291	—	—	—	—

☑ **Solgaleo**

Sunne Pokémon

PSYCHIC **STEEL**

HEIGHT: 11'02"
WEIGHT: 507.1 lbs.

It is said to live in another world. The intense light it radiates from the surface of its body can make the darkest of nights light up like midday.

This Pokémon is said to be a male evolution of Cosmog. At the activation of its third eye, it departs for another world.

Gender unknown

ABILITY
Full Metal Body

HIDDEN ABILITY
—

Damage taken in normal battles

NORMAL ×0.5	FIGHTING ×1	ROCK ×0.5	
FIRE ×2	POISON ×0	GHOST ×1	
WATER ×1	GROUND ×2	DRAGON ×1	
GRASS ×0.5	FLYING ×0.5	DARK ×1	
ELECTRIC ×1	PSYCHIC ×0.25	STEEL ×0.5	
ICE ×0.5	BUG ×1	FAIRY ×0.5	

SPECIES STRENGTHS
HP	◆◆◆◆◆
Attack	◆◆◆◆◆◆◆
Defense	◆◆◆◆◆◆◆
Sp. Atk	◆◆◆◆◆◆◆
Sp. Def	◆◆◆◆◆
Speed	◆◆◆◆◆◆

EGG GROUPS
No Eggs Discovered

ITEM SOMETIMES HELD BY WILD POKÉMON
—

EVOLUTION

Cosmog — Lv. 43 → Cosmoem — Lv. 53 → Solgaleo

MAIN WAY TO REGISTER IN THE POKÉDEX
Catch after battling it in *Pokémon Sun* / Obtain in a trade in *Pokémon Moon*

❖ LEVEL-UP MOVES

Lv.	Name	Type	Kind	Pow.	Acc.	PP	Range
1	Sunsteel Strike	Steel	Physical	100	100	5	Normal
1	Cosmic Power	Psychic	Status	—	—	20	Self
1	Wake-Up Slap	Fighting	Physical	70	100	10	Normal
1	Teleport	Psychic	Status	—	—	20	Self
1	Metal Claw	Steel	Physical	50	95	35	Normal
7	Iron Head	Steel	Physical	80	100	15	Normal
13	Metal Sound	Steel	Status	—	85	40	Normal
19	Zen Headbutt	Psychic	Physical	80	90	15	Normal
23	Flash Cannon	Steel	Special	80	100	10	Normal
31	Morning Sun	Normal	Status	—	—	5	Self
37	Crunch	Dark	Physical	80	100	15	Normal
43	Metal Burst	Steel	Physical	—	100	10	Varies
47	Solar Beam	Grass	Special	120	100	10	Normal
59	Noble Roar	Normal	Status	—	100	30	Normal
61	Flare Blitz	Fire	Physical	120	100	15	Normal
67	Wide Guard	Rock	Status	—	—	10	Your Side
73	Giga Impact	Normal	Physical	150	90	5	Normal

❖ TM MOVES

No.	Name	Type	Kind	Pow.	Acc.	PP	Range
TM01	Work Up	Normal	Status	—	—	30	Self
TM03	Psyshock	Psychic	Special	80	100	10	Normal
TM04	Calm Mind	Psychic	Status	—	—	20	Self
TM05	Roar	Normal	Status	—	—	20	Normal
TM06	Toxic	Poison	Status	—	90	10	Normal
TM10	Hidden Power	Normal	Special	60	100	15	Normal
TM11	Sunny Day	Fire	Status	—	—	5	Both Sides
TM15	Hyper Beam	Normal	Special	150	90	5	Normal
TM16	Light Screen	Psychic	Status	—	—	30	Your Side
TM17	Protect	Normal	Status	—	—	10	Self
TM20	Safeguard	Normal	Status	—	—	25	Your Side
TM21	Frustration	Normal	Physical	—	100	20	Normal
TM22	Solar Beam	Grass	Special	120	100	10	Normal
TM24	Thunderbolt	Electric	Special	90	100	15	Normal
TM25	Thunder	Electric	Special	110	70	10	Normal
TM26	Earthquake	Ground	Physical	100	100	10	Adjacent
TM27	Return	Normal	Physical	—	100	20	Normal
TM29	Psychic	Psychic	Special	90	100	10	Normal
TM32	Double Team	Normal	Status	—	—	15	Self
TM33	Reflect	Psychic	Status	—	—	20	Your Side
TM35	Flamethrower	Fire	Special	90	100	15	Normal
TM38	Fire Blast	Fire	Special	110	85	5	Normal
TM39	Rock Tomb	Rock	Physical	60	95	15	Normal
TM42	Facade	Normal	Physical	70	100	20	Normal
TM43	Flame Charge	Fire	Physical	50	100	20	Normal
TM44	Rest	Psychic	Status	—	—	10	Self
TM48	Round	Normal	Special	60	100	15	Normal
TM52	Focus Blast	Fighting	Special	120	70	5	Normal

No.	Name	Type	Kind	Pow.	Acc.	PP	Range
TM68	Giga Impact	Normal	Physical	150	90	5	Normal
TM71	Stone Edge	Rock	Physical	100	80	5	Normal
TM73	Thunder Wave	Electric	Status	—	90	20	Normal
TM74	Gyro Ball	Steel	Physical	—	100	5	Normal
TM77	Psych Up	Normal	Status	—	—	10	Normal
TM78	Bulldoze	Ground	Physical	60	100	20	Adjacent
TM80	Rock Slide	Rock	Physical	75	90	10	Many Others
TM87	Swagger	Normal	Status	—	85	15	Normal
TM88	Sleep Talk	Normal	Status	—	—	10	Self
TM90	Substitute	Normal	Status	—	—	10	Self
TM91	Flash Cannon	Steel	Special	80	100	10	Normal
TM92	Trick Room	Psychic	Status	—	—	5	Both Sides
TM93	Wild Charge	Electric	Physical	90	100	15	Normal
TM95	Snarl	Dark	Special	55	95	15	Many Others
TM100	Confide	Normal	Status	—	—	20	Normal

❖ MOVES TAUGHT BY PEOPLE

Name	Type	Kind	Pow.	Acc.	PP	Range

❖ MOVES LEARNED WHEN EVOLVING

Name	Type	Kind	Pow.	Acc.	PP	Range
Sunsteel Strike	Steel	Physical	100	100	5	Normal

❖ EGG MOVES

Name	Type	Kind	Pow.	Acc.	PP	Range

❖ EXCLUSIVE Z-MOVE

Name	Base Move	Type	Kind	Pow.	Acc.	Range

Radiant Sun Phase

Alola Pokédex	Melemele	Akala	Ula'ula	Poni
292	—	—	—	—

Lunala

Moone Pokémon

PSYCHIC **GHOST**

HEIGHT: 13'01"
WEIGHT: 264.6 lbs.

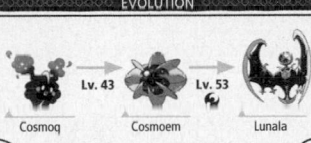

It is said to be a female evolution of Cosmog. When its third eye activates, away it flies to another world.

Said to live in another world, this Pokémon devours light, drawing the moonless dark veil of night over the brightness of day.

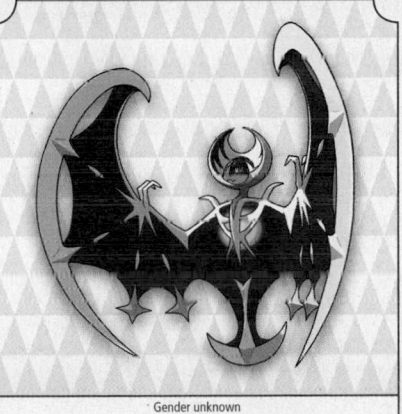

ABILITY
Shadow Shield

HIDDEN ABILITY
—

SPECIES STRENGTHS
HP	◆◆◆◆◆
Attack	◆◆◆◆◆
Defense	◆◆◆◆◆
Sp. Atk	◆◆◆◆◆◆◆
Sp. Def	◆◆◆◆◆◆
Speed	◆◆◆◆◆◆

EVOLUTION

Cosmog — Lv. 43 → Cosmoem — Lv. 53 → Lunala

MAIN WAY TO REGISTER IN THE POKEDEX
Obtain in a trade in *Pokémon Sun* / Catch after battling it in *Pokémon Moon*

Gender unknown

Damage taken in normal battles

NORMAL ×0	FIGHTING ×0	ROCK ×1	
FIRE ×1	POISON ×0.5	GHOST ×4	
WATER ×1	GROUND ×1	DRAGON ×1	
GRASS ×1	FLYING ×1	DARK ×4	
ELECTRIC ×1	PSYCHIC ×0.5	STEEL ×1	
ICE ×1	BUG ×1	FAIRY ×1	

EGG GROUPS
No Eggs Discovered

ITEM SOMETIMES HELD BY WILD POKEMON
—

❖ LEVEL-UP MOVES

Lv.	Name	Type	Kind	Pow.	Acc.	PP	Range
1	Moongeist Beam	Ghost	Special	100	100	5	Normal
1	Cosmic Power	Psychic	Status	—	—	20	Self
1	Hypnosis	Psychic	Status	—	60	20	Normal
1	Teleport	Psychic	Status	—	—	20	Self
1	Confusion	Psychic	Special	50	100	25	Normal
7	Night Shade	Ghost	Special	—	100	15	Normal
13	Confuse Ray	Ghost	Status	—	100	10	Normal
19	Air Slash	Flying	Special	75	95	15	Normal
23	Shadow Ball	Ghost	Special	80	100	15	Normal
31	Moonlight	Fairy	Status	—	—	5	Self
37	Night Daze	Dark	Special	85	95	10	Normal
43	Magic Coat	Psychic	Status	—	—	15	Self
47	Moonblast	Fairy	Special	95	100	15	Normal
59	Dream Eater	Psychic	Special	100	100	15	Normal
61	Phantom Force	Ghost	Physical	90	100	10	Normal
67	Wide Guard	Rock	Status	—	—	10	Your Side
73	Hyper Beam	Normal	Special	150	90	5	Normal

❖ TM MOVES

No.	Name	Type	Kind	Pow.	Acc.	PP	Range
TM01	Work Up	Normal	Status	—	—	30	Self
TM03	Psyshock	Psychic	Special	80	100	10	Normal
TM04	Calm Mind	Psychic	Status	—	—	20	Self
TM05	Roar	Normal	Status	—	—	20	Normal
TM06	Toxic	Poison	Status	—	90	10	Normal
TM10	Hidden Power	Normal	Special	60	100	15	Normal
TM11	Sunny Day	Fire	Status	—	—	5	Both Sides
TM13	Ice Beam	Ice	Special	90	100	10	Normal
TM14	Blizzard	Ice	Special	110	70	5	Many Others
TM15	Hyper Beam	Normal	Special	150	90	5	Normal
TM16	Light Screen	Psychic	Status	—	—	30	Your Side
TM17	Protect	Normal	Status	—	—	10	Self
TM19	Roost	Flying	Status	—	—	10	Self
TM20	Safeguard	Normal	Status	—	—	25	Your Side
TM21	Frustration	Normal	Physical	—	100	20	Normal
TM22	Solar Beam	Grass	Special	120	100	10	Normal
TM24	Thunderbolt	Electric	Special	90	100	15	Normal
TM25	Thunder	Electric	Special	110	70	10	Normal
TM27	Return	Normal	Physical	—	100	20	Normal
TM29	Psychic	Psychic	Special	90	100	10	Normal
TM30	Shadow Ball	Ghost	Special	80	100	15	Normal
TM32	Double Team	Normal	Status	—	—	15	Self
TM33	Reflect	Psychic	Status	—	—	20	Your Side
TM40	Aerial Ace	Flying	Physical	60	—	20	Normal
TM42	Facade	Normal	Physical	70	100	20	Normal
TM44	Rest	Psychic	Status	—	—	10	Self
TM48	Round	Normal	Special	60	100	15	Normal
TM52	Focus Blast	Fighting	Special	120	70	5	Normal

No.	Name	Type	Kind	Pow.	Acc.	PP	Range
TM57	Charge Beam	Electric	Special	50	90	10	Normal
TM58	Sky Drop	Flying	Physical	60	100	10	Normal
TM61	Will-O-Wisp	Fire	Status	—	85	15	Normal
TM62	Acrobatics	Flying	Physical	55	100	15	Normal
TM65	Shadow Claw	Ghost	Physical	70	100	15	Normal
TM68	Giga Impact	Normal	Physical	150	90	5	Normal
TM73	Thunder Wave	Electric	Status	—	90	20	Normal
TM76	Fly	Flying	Physical	90	95	15	Normal
TM77	Psych Up	Normal	Status	—	—	10	Normal
TM85	Dream Eater	Psychic	Special	100	100	15	Normal
TM87	Swagger	Normal	Status	—	85	15	Normal
TM88	Sleep Talk	Normal	Status	—	—	10	Self
TM90	Substitute	Normal	Status	—	—	10	Self
TM92	Trick Room	Psychic	Status	—	—	5	Both Sides
TM99	Dazzling Gleam	Fairy	Special	80	100	10	Many Others
TM100	Confide	Normal	Status	—	—	20	Normal

❖ MOVES TAUGHT BY PEOPLE

Name	Type	Kind	Pow.	Acc.	PP	Range

❖ MOVES LEARNED WHEN EVOLVING

Name	Type	Kind	Pow.	Acc.	PP	Range
Moongeist Beam	Ghost	Special	100	100	5	Normal

❖ EGG MOVES

Name	Type	Kind	Pow.	Acc.	PP	Range

❖ EXCLUSIVE Z-MOVE

Name	Base Move	Type	Kind	Pow.	Acc.	Range

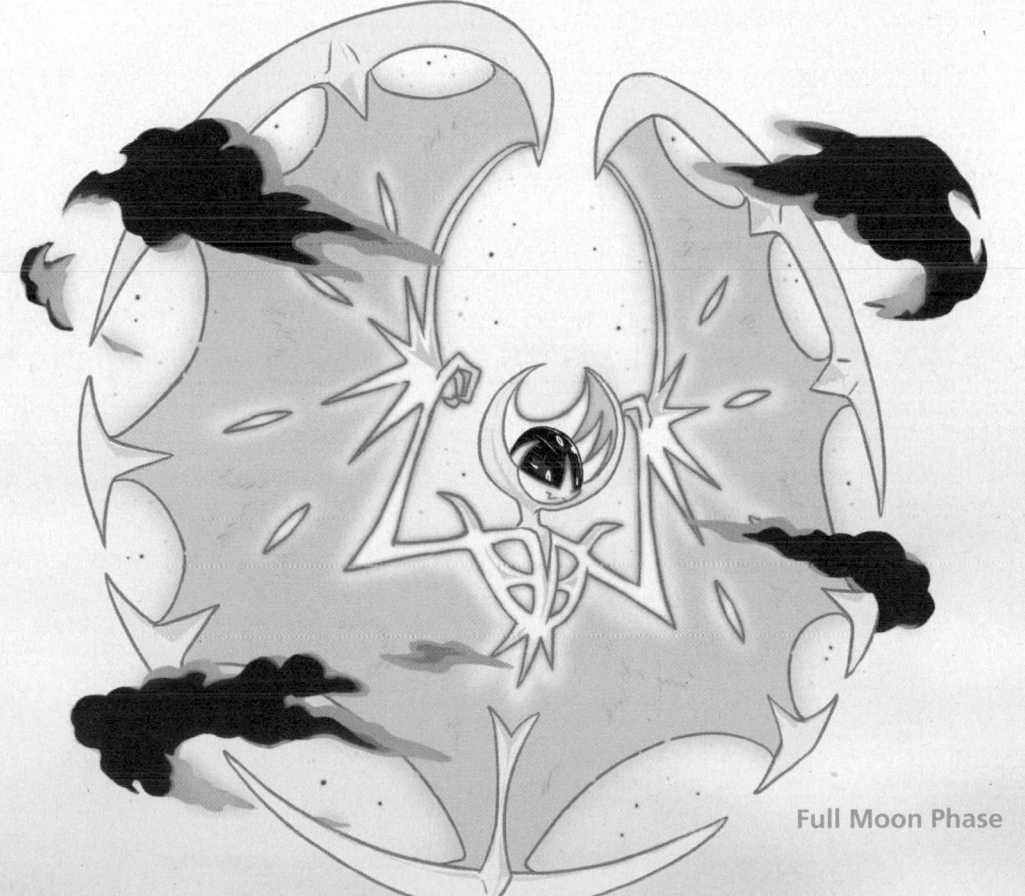

Full Moon Phase

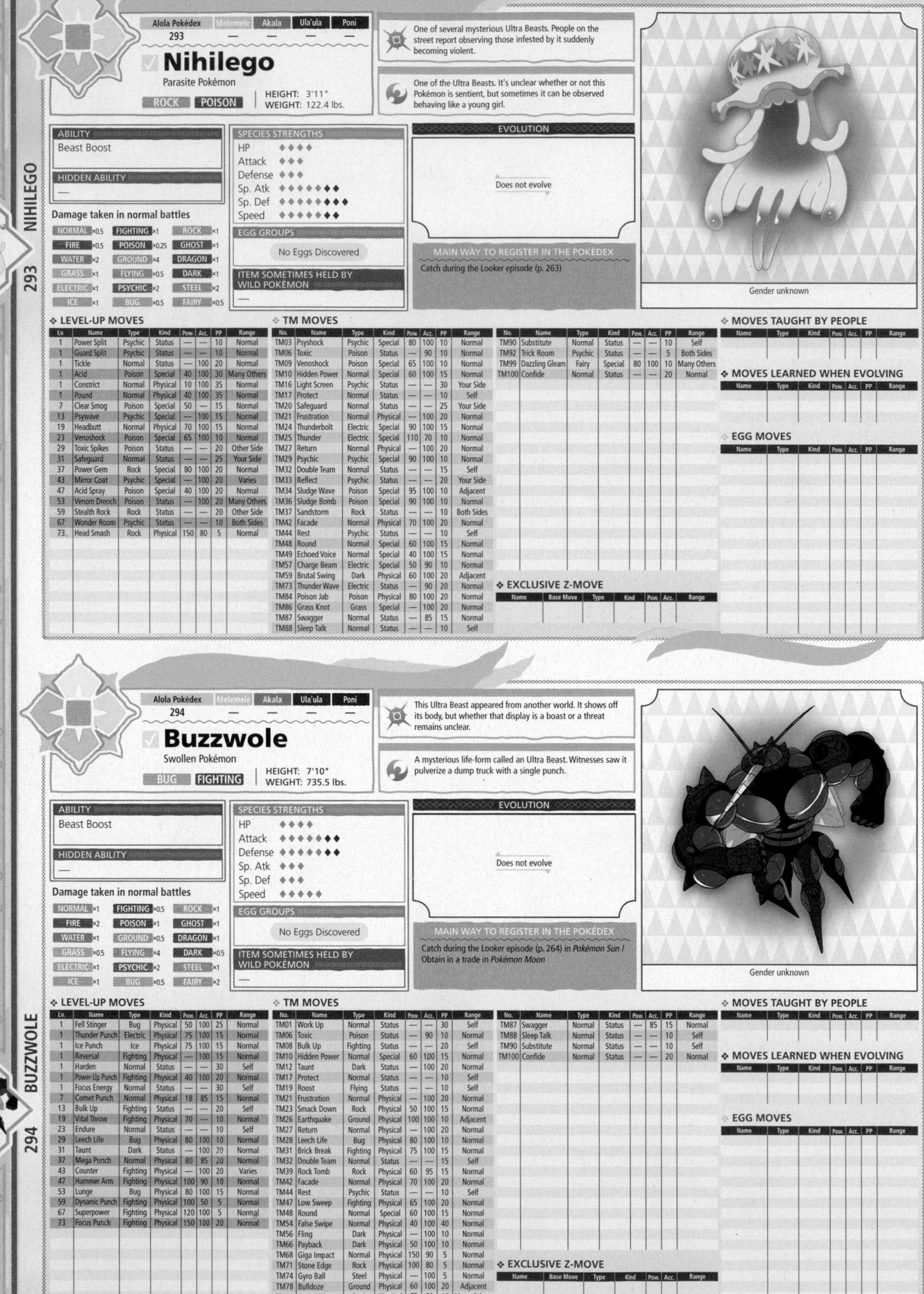

Nihilego

Parasite Pokémon

Alola Pokédex	Melemele	Akala	Ula'ula	Poni
293	—	—	—	—

ROCK **POISON**

HEIGHT: 3'11"
WEIGHT: 122.4 lbs.

One of several mysterious Ultra Beasts. People on the street report observing those infested by it suddenly becoming violent.

One of the Ultra Beasts. It's unclear whether or not this Pokémon is sentient, but sometimes it can be observed behaving like a young girl.

ABILITY
Beast Boost

HIDDEN ABILITY
—

Damage taken in normal battles

NORMAL ×0.5	FIGHTING ×1	ROCK ×1
FIRE ×1	POISON ×0.25	GHOST ×1
WATER ×2	GROUND ×1	DRAGON ×1
GRASS ×1	FLYING ×0.5	DARK ×1
ELECTRIC ×1	PSYCHIC ×2	STEEL ×1
ICE ×1	BUG ×0.5	FAIRY ×0.5

SPECIES STRENGTHS
HP ◆◆◆
Attack ◆◆◆
Defense ◆◆◆
Sp. Atk ◆◆◆◆◆◆
Sp. Def ◆◆◆◆◆◆◆
Speed ◆◆◆◆◆◆◆

EGG GROUPS
No Eggs Discovered

ITEM SOMETIMES HELD BY WILD POKÉMON
—

EVOLUTION
Does not evolve

MAIN WAY TO REGISTER IN THE POKÉDEX
Catch during the Looker episode (p. 263)

Gender unknown

❖ LEVEL-UP MOVES

Lv.	Name	Type	Kind	Pow.	Acc.	PP	Range
1	Power Split	Psychic	Status	—	—	10	Normal
1	Guard Split	Psychic	Status	—	—	10	Normal
1	Tickle	Normal	Status	—	100	20	Normal
1	Acid	Poison	Special	40	100	30	Many Others
1	Constrict	Normal	Physical	10	100	35	Normal
1	Pound	Normal	Physical	40	100	35	Normal
7	Clear Smog	Poison	Special	50	—	15	Normal
13	Psywave	Psychic	Special	—	100	15	Normal
19	Headbutt	Normal	Physical	70	100	15	Normal
23	Venoshock	Poison	Special	65	100	10	Normal
29	Toxic Spikes	Poison	Status	—	—	20	Other Side
31	Safeguard	Normal	Status	—	—	25	Your Side
37	Power Gem	Rock	Special	80	100	20	Normal
43	Mirror Coat	Psychic	Special	—	100	20	Varies
47	Acid Spray	Poison	Special	40	100	20	Normal
53	Venom Drench	Poison	Status	—	100	20	Many Others
59	Stealth Rock	Rock	Status	—	—	20	Other Side
67	Wonder Room	Psychic	Status	—	—	10	Both Sides
73	Head Smash	Rock	Physical	150	80	5	Normal

❖ TM MOVES

No.	Name	Type	Kind	Pow.	Acc.	PP	Range
TM03	Psyshock	Psychic	Special	80	100	10	Normal
TM06	Toxic	Poison	Status	—	90	10	Normal
TM09	Venoshock	Poison	Special	65	100	10	Normal
TM10	Hidden Power	Normal	Special	60	100	15	Normal
TM16	Light Screen	Psychic	Status	—	—	30	Your Side
TM17	Protect	Normal	Status	—	—	10	Self
TM20	Safeguard	Normal	Status	—	—	25	Your Side
TM21	Frustration	Normal	Physical	—	100	20	Normal
TM24	Thunderbolt	Electric	Special	90	100	15	Normal
TM25	Thunder	Electric	Special	110	70	10	Normal
TM27	Return	Normal	Physical	—	100	20	Normal
TM29	Psychic	Psychic	Special	90	100	10	Normal
TM32	Double Team	Normal	Status	—	—	15	Self
TM33	Reflect	Psychic	Status	—	—	20	Your Side
TM34	Sludge Wave	Poison	Special	95	100	10	Adjacent
TM36	Sludge Bomb	Poison	Special	90	100	10	Normal
TM37	Sandstorm	Rock	Status	—	—	10	Both Sides
TM42	Facade	Normal	Physical	70	100	20	Normal
TM44	Rest	Psychic	Status	—	—	10	Self
TM48	Round	Normal	Special	60	100	15	Normal
TM49	Echoed Voice	Normal	Special	40	100	15	Normal
TM57	Charge Beam	Electric	Special	50	90	10	Normal
TM59	Brutal Swing	Dark	Physical	60	100	20	Adjacent
TM73	Thunder Wave	Electric	Status	—	90	20	Normal
TM84	Poison Jab	Poison	Physical	80	100	20	Normal
TM86	Grass Knot	Grass	Special	—	100	20	Normal
TM87	Swagger	Normal	Status	—	85	15	Normal
TM88	Sleep Talk	Normal	Status	—	—	10	Self

❖ MOVES TAUGHT BY PEOPLE

No.	Name	Type	Kind	Pow.	Acc.	PP	Range
TM90	Substitute	Normal	Status	—	—	10	Self
TM92	Trick Room	Psychic	Status	—	—	5	Both Sides
TM99	Dazzling Gleam	Fairy	Special	80	100	10	Many Others
TM100	Confide	Normal	Status	—	—	20	Normal

❖ MOVES LEARNED WHEN EVOLVING

Name	Type	Kind	Pow.	Acc.	PP	Range

❖ EGG MOVES

Name	Type	Kind	Pow.	Acc.	PP	Range

❖ EXCLUSIVE Z-MOVE

Name	Base Move	Type	Kind	Pow.	Acc.	Range

Buzzwole

Swollen Pokémon

Alola Pokédex	Melemele	Akala	Ula'ula	Poni
294	—	—	—	—

BUG **FIGHTING**

HEIGHT: 7'10"
WEIGHT: 735.5 lbs.

This Ultra Beast appeared from another world. It shows off its body, but whether that display is a boast or a threat remains unclear.

A mysterious life-form called an Ultra Beast. Witnesses saw it pulverize a dump truck with a single punch.

ABILITY
Beast Boost

HIDDEN ABILITY
—

Damage taken in normal battles

NORMAL ×1	FIGHTING ×0.5	ROCK ×1
FIRE ×2	POISON ×1	GHOST ×1
WATER ×1	GROUND ×0.5	DRAGON ×1
GRASS ×0.5	FLYING ×4	DARK ×0.5
ELECTRIC ×1	PSYCHIC ×2	STEEL ×1
ICE ×1	BUG ×0.5	FAIRY ×2

SPECIES STRENGTHS
HP ◆◆◆◆
Attack ◆◆◆◆◆◆◆
Defense ◆◆◆◆◆◆◆
Sp. Atk ◆◆◆
Sp. Def ◆◆◆
Speed ◆◆◆◆◆

EGG GROUPS
No Eggs Discovered

ITEM SOMETIMES HELD BY WILD POKÉMON
—

EVOLUTION
Does not evolve

MAIN WAY TO REGISTER IN THE POKÉDEX
Catch during the Looker episode (p. 264) in *Pokémon Sun* /
Obtain in a trade in *Pokémon Moon*

Gender unknown

❖ LEVEL-UP MOVES

Lv.	Name	Type	Kind	Pow.	Acc.	PP	Range
1	Fell Stinger	Bug	Physical	50	100	25	Normal
1	Thunder Punch	Electric	Physical	75	100	15	Normal
1	Ice Punch	Ice	Physical	75	100	15	Normal
1	Reversal	Fighting	Physical	—	100	15	Normal
1	Harden	Normal	Status	—	—	30	Self
1	Power-Up Punch	Fighting	Physical	40	100	20	Normal
1	Focus Energy	Normal	Status	—	—	30	Self
7	Comet Punch	Normal	Physical	18	85	15	Normal
13	Bulk Up	Fighting	Status	—	—	20	Self
19	Vital Throw	Fighting	Physical	70	—	10	Normal
23	Endure	Normal	Status	—	—	10	Self
29	Leech Life	Bug	Physical	80	100	10	Normal
31	Taunt	Dark	Status	—	100	20	Normal
37	Mega Punch	Normal	Physical	80	85	20	Normal
43	Counter	Fighting	Physical	—	100	20	Varies
47	Hammer Arm	Fighting	Physical	100	90	10	Normal
53	Lunge	Bug	Physical	80	100	15	Normal
59	Dynamic Punch	Fighting	Physical	100	50	5	Normal
67	Superpower	Fighting	Physical	120	100	5	Normal
73	Focus Punch	Fighting	Physical	150	100	20	Normal

❖ TM MOVES

No.	Name	Type	Kind	Pow.	Acc.	PP	Range
TM01	Work Up	Normal	Status	—	—	30	Self
TM06	Toxic	Poison	Status	—	90	10	Normal
TM08	Bulk Up	Fighting	Status	—	—	20	Self
TM10	Hidden Power	Normal	Special	60	100	15	Normal
TM12	Taunt	Dark	Status	—	100	20	Normal
TM17	Protect	Normal	Status	—	—	10	Self
TM19	Roost	Flying	Status	—	—	10	Self
TM21	Frustration	Normal	Physical	—	100	20	Normal
TM23	Smack Down	Rock	Physical	50	100	15	Normal
TM26	Earthquake	Ground	Physical	100	100	10	Adjacent
TM27	Return	Normal	Physical	—	100	20	Normal
TM28	Leech Life	Bug	Physical	80	100	10	Normal
TM31	Brick Break	Fighting	Physical	75	100	15	Normal
TM32	Double Team	Normal	Status	—	—	15	Self
TM39	Rock Tomb	Rock	Physical	60	95	15	Normal
TM42	Facade	Normal	Physical	70	100	20	Normal
TM44	Rest	Psychic	Status	—	—	10	Self
TM47	Low Sweep	Fighting	Physical	65	100	20	Normal
TM48	Round	Normal	Special	60	100	15	Normal
TM54	False Swipe	Normal	Physical	40	100	40	Normal
TM56	Fling	Dark	Physical	—	100	10	Normal
TM66	Payback	Dark	Physical	50	100	10	Normal
TM68	Giga Impact	Normal	Physical	150	90	5	Normal
TM71	Stone Edge	Rock	Physical	100	80	5	Normal
TM74	Gyro Ball	Steel	Physical	—	100	5	Normal
TM78	Bulldoze	Ground	Physical	60	100	20	Adjacent
TM80	Rock Slide	Rock	Physical	75	90	10	Many Others
TM84	Poison Jab	Poison	Physical	80	100	20	Normal

❖ MOVES TAUGHT BY PEOPLE

No.	Name	Type	Kind	Pow.	Acc.	PP	Range
TM87	Swagger	Normal	Status	—	85	15	Normal
TM88	Sleep Talk	Normal	Status	—	—	10	Self
TM90	Substitute	Normal	Status	—	—	10	Self
TM100	Confide	Normal	Status	—	—	20	Normal

❖ MOVES LEARNED WHEN EVOLVING

Name	Type	Kind	Pow.	Acc.	PP	Range

❖ EGG MOVES

Name	Type	Kind	Pow.	Acc.	PP	Range

❖ EXCLUSIVE Z-MOVE

Name	Base Move	Type	Kind	Pow.	Acc.	Range

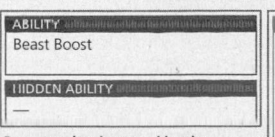

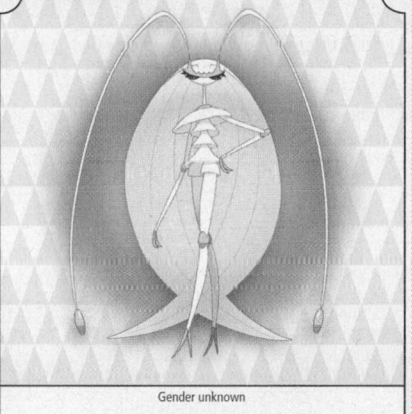

Alola Pokédex

295

Melemele	Akala	Ula'ula	Poni
—	—	—	—

Pheromosa

Lissome Pokémon

BUG **FIGHTING**

HEIGHT: 5'11"
WEIGHT: 55.1 lbs.

One of the dangerous Ultra Beasts, it has been spotted running across the land at terrific speeds.

One of the Ultra Beasts. It refuses to touch anything, perhaps because it senses some uncleanness in this world.

ABILITY
Beast Boost

HIDDEN ABILITY
—

Damage taken in normal battles

NORMAL ×1	FIGHTING ×0.5	ROCK ×1
FIRE ×2	POISON ×1	GHOST ×1
WATER ×1	GROUND ×0.5	DRAGON ×1
GRASS ×0.5	FLYING ×4	DARK ×0.5
ELECTRIC ×1	PSYCHIC ×2	STEEL ×1
ICE ×1	BUG ×0.5	FAIRY ×2

SPECIES STRENGTHS
HP ◆◆◆
Attack ◆◆◆◆◆◆
Defense ◆◆
Sp. Atk ◆◆◆◆◆◆◆
Sp. Def ◆◆
Speed ◆◆◆◆◆◆◆◆◆

EGG GROUPS
No Eggs Discovered

ITEM SOMETIMES HELD BY WILD POKÉMON
—

EVOLUTION
Does not evolve

MAIN WAY TO REGISTER IN THE POKÉDEX
Obtain in a trade in *Pokémon Sun* / Catch during the Looker episode (p. 264) in *Pokémon Moon*

Gender unknown

❖ LEVEL-UP MOVES

Lv.	Name	Type	Kind	Pow.	Acc.	PP	Range
1	Quiver Dance	Bug	Status	—	—	20	Self
1	Quick Guard	Fighting	Status	—	—	15	Your Side
1	Low Kick	Fighting	Physical	—	100	20	Normal
1	Rapid Spin	Normal	Physical	20	100	40	Normal
1	Leer	Normal	Status	—	100	30	Many Others
1	Double Kick	Fighting	Physical	30	100	30	Normal
7	Swift	Normal	Special	60	—	20	Many Others
13	Stomp	Normal	Physical	65	100	20	Normal
19	Feint	Normal	Physical	30	100	10	Normal
23	Silver Wind	Bug	Special	60	100	5	Normal
29	Bounce	Flying	Physical	85	85	5	Normal
31	Jump Kick	Fighting	Physical	100	95	10	Normal
37	Agility	Psychic	Status	—	—	30	Self
43	Triple Kick	Fighting	Physical	10	90	10	Normal
47	Lunge	Bug	Physical	80	100	15	Normal
53	Bug Buzz	Bug	Special	90	100	10	Normal
59	Me First	Normal	Status	—	—	20	Varies
67	High Jump Kick	Fighting	Physical	130	90	10	Normal
73	Speed Swap	Psychic	Status	—	—	10	Normal

❖ TM MOVES

No.	Name	Type	Kind	Pow.	Acc.	PP	Range
TM06	Toxic	Poison	Status	—	90	10	Normal
TM10	Hidden Power	Normal	Special	60	100	15	Normal
TM12	Taunt	Dark	Status	—	100	20	Normal
TM13	Ice Beam	Ice	Special	90	100	10	Normal
TM14	Blizzard	Ice	Special	110	70	5	Many Others
TM15	Hyper Beam	Normal	Special	150	90	5	Normal
TM17	Protect	Normal	Status	—	—	10	Self
TM19	Roost	Flying	Status	—	—	10	Self
TM21	Frustration	Normal	Physical	—	100	20	Normal
TM27	Return	Normal	Physical	—	100	20	Normal
TM31	Brick Break	Fighting	Physical	75	100	15	Normal
TM32	Double Team	Normal	Status	—	—	15	Self
TM41	Torment	Dark	Status	—	100	15	Normal
TM42	Facade	Normal	Physical	70	100	20	Normal
TM44	Rest	Psychic	Status	—	—	10	Self
TM47	Low Sweep	Fighting	Physical	65	100	20	Normal
TM48	Round	Normal	Special	60	100	15	Normal
TM49	Echoed Voice	Normal	Special	40	100	15	Normal
TM52	Focus Blast	Fighting	Special	120	70	5	Normal
TM54	False Swipe	Normal	Physical	40	100	40	Normal
TM56	Fling	Dark	Physical	—	100	10	Normal
TM68	Giga Impact	Normal	Physical	150	90	5	Normal
TM84	Poison Jab	Poison	Physical	80	100	20	Normal
TM87	Swagger	Normal	Status	—	85	15	Normal
TM88	Sleep Talk	Normal	Status	—	—	10	Self
TM89	U-turn	Bug	Physical	70	100	20	Normal
TM90	Substitute	Normal	Status	—	—	10	Self
TM100	Confide	Normal	Status	—	—	20	Normal

❖ MOVES TAUGHT BY PEOPLE

No.	Name	Type	Kind	Pow.	Acc.	PP	Range

❖ MOVES LEARNED WHEN EVOLVING

Name	Type	Kind	Pow.	Acc.	PP	Range

❖ EGG MOVES

Name	Type	Kind	Pow.	Acc.	PP	Range

❖ EXCLUSIVE Z-MOVE

Name	Base Move	Type	Kind	Pow.	Acc.	Range

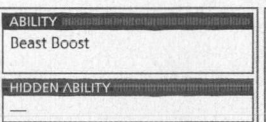

Alola Pokédex

296

Melemele	Akala	Ula'ula	Poni
—	—	—	—

Xurkitree

Glowing Pokémon

ELECTRIC

HEIGHT: 12'06"
WEIGHT: 220.5 lbs.

One of the mysterious life-forms known as Ultra Beasts. Astonishing electric shocks emanate from its entire body, according to witnesses.

It appeared from the Ultra Wormhole. It raided a power plant, so people think it energizes itself with electricity.

ABILITY
Beast Boost

HIDDEN ABILITY
—

Damage taken in normal battles

NORMAL ×1	FIGHTING ×1	ROCK ×1
FIRE ×1	POISON ×1	GHOST ×1
WATER ×1	GROUND ×2	DRAGON ×1
GRASS ×1	FLYING ×0.5	DARK ×1
ELECTRIC ×0.5	PSYCHIC ×1	STEEL ×0.5
ICE ×1	BUG ×1	FAIRY ×1

SPECIES STRENGTHS
HP ◆◆◆
Attack ◆◆◆◆
Defense ◆◆◆◆
Sp. Atk ◆◆◆◆◆◆◆◆
Sp. Def ◆◆◆◆
Speed ◆◆◆◆

EGG GROUPS
No Eggs Discovered

ITEM SOMETIMES HELD BY WILD POKÉMON
—

EVOLUTION
Does not evolve

MAIN WAY TO REGISTER IN THE POKÉDEX
Catch during the Looker episode (p. 265)

Gender unknown

❖ LEVEL-UP MOVES

Lv.	Name	Type	Kind	Pow.	Acc.	PP	Range
1	Tail Glow	Bug	Status	—	—	20	Self
1	Spark	Electric	Physical	65	100	20	Normal
1	Charge	Electric	Status	—	—	20	Self
1	Wrap	Normal	Physical	15	90	20	Normal
1	Thunder Shock	Electric	Special	40	100	30	Normal
7	Thunder Wave	Electric	Status	—	90	20	Normal
13	Shock Wave	Electric	Special	60	—	20	Normal
19	Ingrain	Grass	Status	—	—	20	Self
23	Thunder Punch	Electric	Physical	75	100	15	Normal
29	Eerie Impulse	Electric	Status	—	100	15	Normal
31	Signal Beam	Bug	Special	75	100	15	Normal
37	Thunderbolt	Electric	Special	90	100	15	Normal
43	Hypnosis	Psychic	Status	—	60	20	Normal
47	Discharge	Electric	Special	80	100	15	Adjacent
53	Electric Terrain	Electric	Status	—	—	10	Both Sides
59	Power Whip	Grass	Physical	120	85	10	Normal
67	Ion Deluge	Electric	Status	—	—	25	Both Sides
73	Zap Cannon	Electric	Special	120	50	5	Normal

❖ TM MOVES

No.	Name	Type	Kind	Pow.	Acc.	PP	Range
TM04	Calm Mind	Psychic	Status	—	—	20	Self
TM06	Toxic	Poison	Status	—	90	10	Normal
TM10	Hidden Power	Normal	Special	60	100	15	Normal
TM11	Sunny Day	Fire	Status	—	—	5	Both Sides
TM15	Hyper Beam	Normal	Special	150	90	5	Normal
TM16	Light Screen	Psychic	Status	—	—	30	Your Side
TM17	Protect	Normal	Status	—	—	10	Self
TM18	Rain Dance	Water	Status	—	—	5	Both Sides
TM21	Frustration	Normal	Physical	—	100	20	Normal
TM22	Solar Beam	Grass	Special	120	100	10	Normal
TM24	Thunderbolt	Electric	Special	90	100	15	Normal
TM25	Thunder	Electric	Special	110	70	10	Normal
TM27	Return	Normal	Physical	—	100	20	Normal
TM32	Double Team	Normal	Status	—	—	15	Self
TM33	Reflect	Psychic	Status	—	—	20	Your Side
TM42	Facade	Normal	Physical	70	100	20	Normal
TM44	Rest	Psychic	Status	—	—	10	Self
TM48	Round	Normal	Special	60	100	15	Normal
TM53	Energy Ball	Grass	Special	90	100	10	Normal
TM56	Fling	Dark	Physical	—	100	10	Normal
TM57	Charge Beam	Electric	Special	50	90	10	Normal
TM59	Brutal Swing	Dark	Physical	60	100	20	Adjacent
TM68	Giga Impact	Normal	Physical	150	90	5	Normal
TM72	Volt Switch	Electric	Special	70	100	20	Normal
TM73	Thunder Wave	Electric	Status	—	90	20	Normal
TM86	Grass Knot	Grass	Special	—	100	20	Normal
TM87	Swagger	Normal	Status	—	85	15	Normal
TM88	Sleep Talk	Normal	Status	—	—	10	Self

❖ MOVES TAUGHT BY PEOPLE

No.	Name	Type	Kind	Pow.	Acc.	PP	Range
TM90	Substitute	Normal	Status	—	—	10	Self
TM93	Wild Charge	Electric	Physical	90	100	15	Normal
TM96	Nature Power	Normal	Status	—	—	20	Normal
TM99	Dazzling Gleam	Fairy	Special	80	100	10	Many Others
TM100	Confide	Normal	Status	—	—	20	Normal

❖ MOVES LEARNED WHEN EVOLVING

Name	Type	Kind	Pow.	Acc.	PP	Range

❖ EGG MOVES

Name	Type	Kind	Pow.	Acc.	PP	Range

❖ EXCLUSIVE Z-MOVE

Name	Base Move	Type	Kind	Pow.	Acc.	Range

PHEROMOSA 295

XURKITREE 296

203

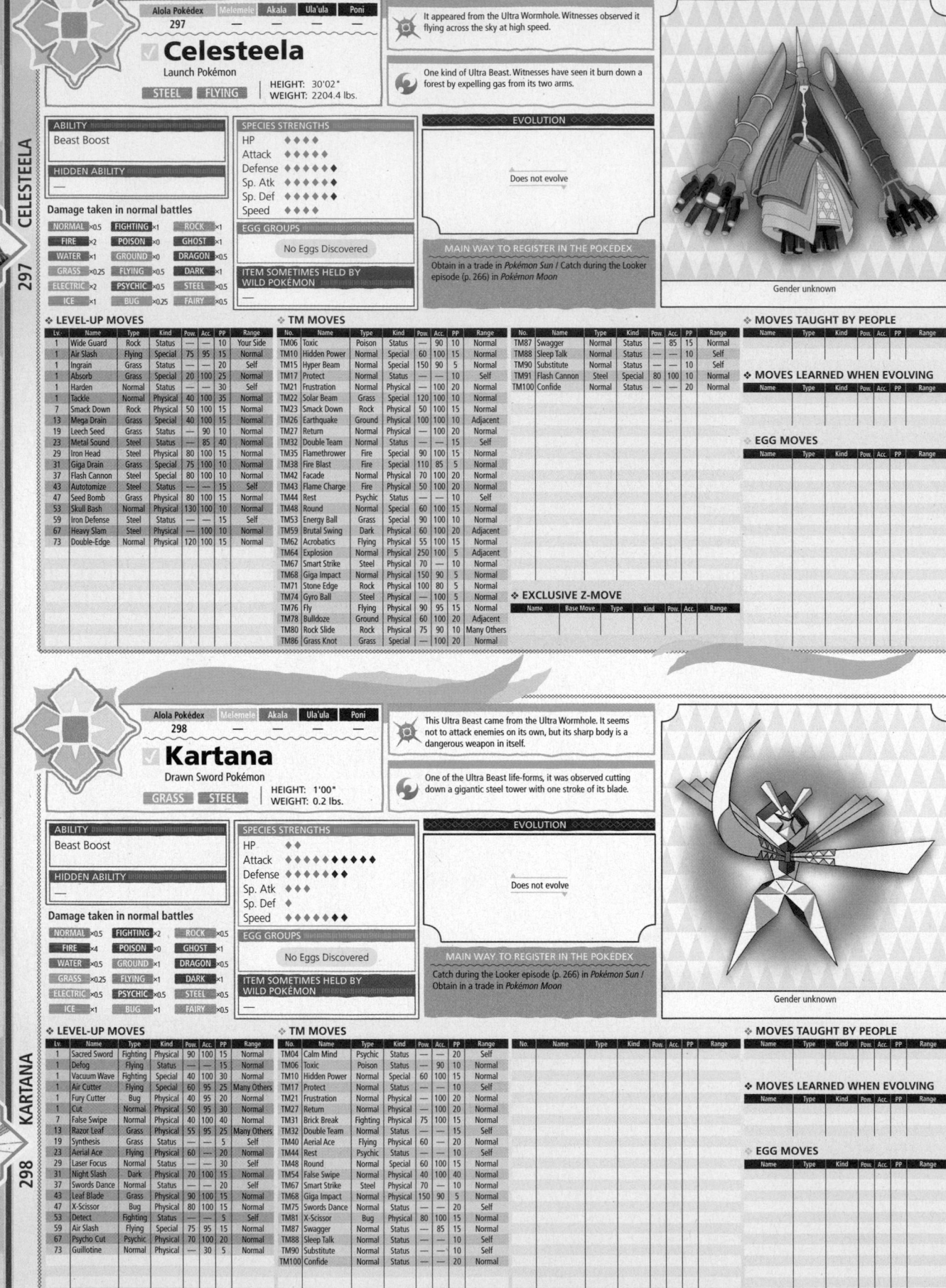

Celesteela

Alola Pokédex
297

Melemele	Akala	Ula'ula	Poni
—	—	—	—

Launch Pokémon

STEEL · FLYING

HEIGHT: 30'02"
WEIGHT: 2204.4 lbs.

☀ It appeared from the Ultra Wormhole. Witnesses observed it flying across the sky at high speed.

🌙 One kind of Ultra Beast. Witnesses have seen it burn down a forest by expelling gas from its two arms.

ABILITY
Beast Boost

HIDDEN ABILITY
—

SPECIES STRENGTHS
- HP ◆◆◆◆
- Attack ◆◆◆◆◆
- Defense ◆◆◆◆◆◆
- Sp. Atk ◆◆◆◆◆◆
- Sp. Def ◆◆◆◆◆◆
- Speed ◆◆◆◆

EGG GROUPS
No Eggs Discovered

ITEM SOMETIMES HELD BY WILD POKÉMON
—

EVOLUTION
Does not evolve

MAIN WAY TO REGISTER IN THE POKÉDEX
Obtain in a trade in *Pokémon Sun* / Catch during the Looker episode (p. 266) in *Pokémon Moon*

Gender unknown

Damage taken in normal battles
NORMAL ×0.5	FIGHTING ×1	ROCK ×1	
FIRE ×2	POISON ×0	GHOST ×1	
WATER ×1	GROUND ×0	DRAGON ×0.5	
GRASS ×0.25	FLYING ×0.5	DARK ×1	
ELECTRIC ×2	PSYCHIC ×0.5	STEEL ×0.5	
ICE ×1	BUG ×0.25	FAIRY ×0.5	

❖ LEVEL-UP MOVES
Lv.	Name	Type	Kind	Pow.	Acc.	PP	Range
1	Wide Guard	Rock	Status	—	—	10	Your Side
1	Air Slash	Flying	Special	75	95	15	Normal
1	Ingrain	Grass	Status	—	—	20	Self
1	Absorb	Grass	Special	20	100	25	Normal
1	Harden	Normal	Status	—	—	30	Self
1	Tackle	Normal	Physical	40	100	35	Normal
7	Smack Down	Rock	Physical	50	100	15	Normal
13	Mega Drain	Grass	Special	40	100	15	Normal
19	Leech Seed	Grass	Status	—	90	10	Normal
23	Metal Sound	Steel	Status	—	85	40	Normal
29	Iron Head	Steel	Physical	80	100	15	Normal
31	Giga Drain	Grass	Special	75	100	10	Normal
37	Flash Cannon	Steel	Special	80	100	10	Normal
43	Autotomize	Steel	Status	—	—	15	Self
47	Seed Bomb	Grass	Physical	80	100	15	Normal
53	Skull Bash	Normal	Physical	130	100	15	Normal
59	Iron Defense	Steel	Status	—	—	15	Self
67	Heavy Slam	Steel	Physical	—	100	10	Normal
73	Double-Edge	Normal	Physical	120	100	15	Normal

❖ TM MOVES
No.	Name	Type	Kind	Pow.	Acc.	PP	Range
TM06	Toxic	Poison	Status	—	90	10	Normal
TM10	Hidden Power	Normal	Special	60	100	15	Normal
TM15	Hyper Beam	Normal	Special	150	90	5	Normal
TM17	Protect	Normal	Status	—	—	10	Self
TM21	Frustration	Normal	Physical	—	100	20	Normal
TM22	Solar Beam	Grass	Special	120	100	10	Normal
TM23	Smack Down	Rock	Physical	50	100	15	Normal
TM26	Earthquake	Ground	Physical	100	100	10	Adjacent
TM27	Return	Normal	Physical	—	100	20	Normal
TM32	Double Team	Normal	Status	—	—	15	Self
TM35	Flamethrower	Fire	Special	90	100	15	Normal
TM38	Fire Blast	Fire	Special	110	85	5	Normal
TM42	Facade	Normal	Physical	70	100	20	Normal
TM43	Flame Charge	Fire	Physical	50	100	20	Normal
TM44	Rest	Psychic	Status	—	—	10	Self
TM48	Round	Normal	Special	60	100	15	Normal
TM53	Energy Ball	Grass	Special	90	100	10	Normal
TM59	Brutal Swing	Dark	Physical	60	100	20	Adjacent
TM62	Acrobatics	Flying	Physical	55	100	15	Normal
TM64	Explosion	Normal	Physical	250	100	5	Adjacent
TM67	Smart Strike	Steel	Physical	70	—	10	Normal
TM68	Giga Impact	Normal	Physical	150	90	5	Normal
TM71	Stone Edge	Rock	Physical	100	80	5	Normal
TM74	Gyro Ball	Steel	Physical	—	100	5	Normal
TM76	Fly	Flying	Physical	90	95	15	Normal
TM78	Bulldoze	Ground	Physical	60	100	20	Adjacent
TM80	Rock Slide	Rock	Physical	75	90	10	Many Others
TM86	Grass Knot	Grass	Special	—	100	20	Normal

❖ MOVES TAUGHT BY PEOPLE
No.	Name	Type	Kind	Pow.	Acc.	PP	Range
TM87	Swagger	Normal	Status	—	85	15	Normal
TM88	Sleep Talk	Normal	Status	—	—	10	Self
TM90	Substitute	Normal	Status	—	—	10	Self
TM91	Flash Cannon	Steel	Special	80	100	10	Normal
TM100	Confide	Normal	Status	—	—	20	Normal

❖ MOVES LEARNED WHEN EVOLVING
Name	Type	Kind	Pow.	Acc.	PP	Range

❖ EGG MOVES
Name	Type	Kind	Pow.	Acc.	PP	Range

❖ EXCLUSIVE Z-MOVE
Name	Base Move	Type	Kind	Pow.	Acc.	Range

Kartana

Alola Pokédex
298

Melemele	Akala	Ula'ula	Poni
—	—	—	—

Drawn Sword Pokémon

GRASS · STEEL

HEIGHT: 1'00"
WEIGHT: 0.2 lbs.

☀ This Ultra Beast came from the Ultra Wormhole. It seems not to attack enemies on its own, but its sharp body is a dangerous weapon in itself.

🌙 One of the Ultra Beast life-forms, it was observed cutting down a gigantic steel tower with one stroke of its blade.

ABILITY
Beast Boost

HIDDEN ABILITY
—

SPECIES STRENGTHS
- HP ◆◆
- Attack ◆◆◆◆◆◆◆◆◆◆
- Defense ◆◆◆◆◆◆◆◆
- Sp. Atk ◆◆◆
- Sp. Def ◆
- Speed ◆◆◆◆◆◆◆◆

EGG GROUPS
No Eggs Discovered

ITEM SOMETIMES HELD BY WILD POKÉMON
—

EVOLUTION
Does not evolve

MAIN WAY TO REGISTER IN THE POKÉDEX
Catch during the Looker episode (p. 266) in *Pokémon Sun* / Obtain in a trade in *Pokémon Moon*

Gender unknown

Damage taken in normal battles
NORMAL ×0.5	FIGHTING ×2	ROCK ×0.5	
FIRE ×4	POISON ×0	GHOST ×1	
WATER ×0.5	GROUND ×1	DRAGON ×0.5	
GRASS ×0.25	FLYING ×1	DARK ×1	
ELECTRIC ×1	PSYCHIC ×0.5	STEEL ×0.5	
ICE ×1	BUG ×1	FAIRY ×0.5	

❖ LEVEL-UP MOVES
Lv.	Name	Type	Kind	Pow.	Acc.	PP	Range
1	Sacred Sword	Fighting	Physical	90	100	15	Normal
1	Defog	Flying	Status	—	—	15	Normal
1	Vacuum Wave	Fighting	Special	40	100	30	Normal
1	Air Cutter	Flying	Special	60	95	25	Many Others
1	Fury Cutter	Bug	Physical	40	95	20	Normal
1	Cut	Normal	Physical	50	95	30	Normal
7	False Swipe	Normal	Physical	40	100	40	Normal
13	Razor Leaf	Grass	Physical	55	95	25	Many Others
19	Synthesis	Grass	Status	—	—	5	Self
23	Aerial Ace	Flying	Physical	60	—	20	Normal
29	Laser Focus	Normal	Status	—	—	30	Self
31	Night Slash	Dark	Physical	70	100	15	Normal
37	Swords Dance	Normal	Status	—	—	20	Self
43	Leaf Blade	Grass	Physical	90	100	15	Normal
47	X-Scissor	Bug	Physical	80	100	15	Normal
53	Detect	Fighting	Status	—	—	5	Self
59	Air Slash	Flying	Special	75	95	15	Normal
67	Psycho Cut	Psychic	Physical	70	100	20	Normal
73	Guillotine	Normal	Physical	—	30	5	Normal

❖ TM MOVES
No.	Name	Type	Kind	Pow.	Acc.	PP	Range
TM04	Calm Mind	Psychic	Status	—	—	20	Self
TM06	Toxic	Poison	Status	—	90	10	Normal
TM10	Hidden Power	Normal	Special	60	100	15	Normal
TM17	Protect	Normal	Status	—	—	10	Self
TM21	Frustration	Normal	Physical	—	100	20	Normal
TM27	Return	Normal	Physical	—	100	20	Normal
TM31	Brick Break	Fighting	Physical	75	100	15	Normal
TM32	Double Team	Normal	Status	—	—	15	Self
TM40	Aerial Ace	Flying	Physical	60	—	20	Normal
TM44	Rest	Psychic	Status	—	—	10	Self
TM48	Round	Normal	Special	60	100	15	Normal
TM54	False Swipe	Normal	Physical	40	100	40	Normal
TM67	Smart Strike	Steel	Physical	70	—	10	Normal
TM68	Giga Impact	Normal	Physical	150	90	5	Normal
TM75	Swords Dance	Normal	Status	—	—	20	Self
TM81	X-Scissor	Bug	Physical	80	100	15	Normal
TM87	Swagger	Normal	Status	—	85	15	Normal
TM88	Sleep Talk	Normal	Status	—	—	10	Self
TM90	Substitute	Normal	Status	—	—	10	Self
TM100	Confide	Normal	Status	—	—	20	Normal

❖ MOVES TAUGHT BY PEOPLE
No.	Name	Type	Kind	Pow.	Acc.	PP	Range

❖ MOVES LEARNED WHEN EVOLVING
Name	Type	Kind	Pow.	Acc.	PP	Range

❖ EGG MOVES
Name	Type	Kind	Pow.	Acc.	PP	Range

❖ EXCLUSIVE Z-MOVE
Name	Base Move	Type	Kind	Pow.	Acc.	Range

Guzzlord

Alola Pokédex	Melemele	Akala	Ula'ula	Poni
299	—	—	—	—

Guzzlord
Junkivore Pokémon

DARK **DRAGON**

HEIGHT: 18'01"
WEIGHT: 1957.7 lbs.

It has gobbled mountains and swallowed whole buildings, according to reports. It's one of the Ultra Beasts.

A dangerous Ultra Beast, it appears to be eating constantly, but for some reason its droppings have never been found.

ABILITY
Beast Boost

HIDDEN ABILITY
—

SPECIES STRENGTHS
HP	◆◆◆◆◆◆◆◆
Attack	◆◆◆◆◆
Defense	◆◆◆
Sp. Atk	◆◆◆◆◆
Sp. Def	◆◆◆
Speed	◆◆◆

EGG GROUPS
No Eggs Discovered

ITEM SOMETIMES HELD BY WILD POKÉMON
—

EVOLUTION
Does not evolve

MAIN WAY TO REGISTER IN THE POKÉDEX
Catch during the Looker episode (p. 267)

Gender unknown

Damage taken in normal battles
NORMAL ×1	FIGHTING ×2	ROCK ×1
FIRE ×0.5	POISON ×1	GHOST ×0.5
WATER ×0.5	GROUND ×1	DRAGON ×2
GRASS ×0.5	FLYING ×1	DARK ×0.5
ELECTRIC ×0.5	PSYCHIC ×0	STEEL ×1
ICE ×2	BUG ×2	FAIRY ×4

❖ LEVEL-UP MOVES
Lv.	Name	Type	Kind	Pow.	Acc.	PP	Range
1	Belch	Poison	Special	120	90	10	Normal
1	Wide Guard	Rock	Status	—	—	10	Your Side
1	Swallow	Normal	Status	—	—	10	Self
1	Stockpile	Normal	Status	—	—	20	Self
1	Dragon Rage	Dragon	Special	—	100	10	Normal
1	Bite	Dark	Physical	60	100	25	Normal
7	Stomp	Normal	Physical	65	100	20	Normal
13	Brutal Swing	Dark	Physical	60	100	20	Adjacent
19	Steamroller	Bug	Physical	65	100	20	Normal
23	Dragon Tail	Dragon	Physical	60	90	10	Normal
29	Iron Tail	Steel	Physical	100	75	15	Normal
31	Stomping Tantrum	Ground	Physical	75	100	10	Normal
37	Crunch	Dark	Physical	80	100	15	Normal
43	Hammer Arm	Fighting	Physical	100	90	10	Normal
47	Thrash	Normal	Physical	120	100	10	1 Random
53	Gastro Acid	Poison	Status	—	100	10	Normal
59	Heavy Slam	Steel	Physical	—	100	10	Normal
67	Wring Out	Normal	Special	—	100	5	Normal
73	Dragon Rush	Dragon	Physical	100	75	10	Normal

❖ TM MOVES
No.	Name	Type	Kind	Pow.	Acc.	PP	Range
TM02	Dragon Claw	Dragon	Physical	80	100	15	Normal
TM06	Toxic	Poison	Status	—	90	10	Normal
TM10	Hidden Power	Normal	Special	60	100	15	Normal
TM15	Hyper Beam	Normal	Special	150	90	5	Normal
TM17	Protect	Normal	Status	—	—	10	Self
TM21	Frustration	Normal	Physical	—	100	20	Normal
TM23	Smack Down	Rock	Physical	50	100	15	Normal
TM26	Earthquake	Ground	Physical	100	100	10	Adjacent
TM27	Return	Normal	Physical	—	100	20	Normal
TM31	Brick Break	Fighting	Physical	75	100	15	Normal
TM32	Double Team	Normal	Status	—	—	15	Self
TM34	Sludge Wave	Poison	Special	95	100	10	Adjacent
TM35	Flamethrower	Fire	Special	90	100	15	Normal
TM36	Sludge Bomb	Poison	Special	90	100	10	Normal
TM38	Fire Blast	Fire	Special	110	85	5	Normal
TM39	Rock Tomb	Rock	Physical	60	95	15	Normal
TM42	Facade	Normal	Physical	70	100	20	Normal
TM44	Rest	Psychic	Status	—	—	10	Self
TM46	Thief	Dark	Physical	60	100	25	Normal
TM48	Round	Normal	Special	60	100	15	Normal
TM56	Fling	Dark	Physical	—	100	10	Normal
TM59	Brutal Swing	Dark	Physical	60	100	20	Adjacent
TM65	Shadow Claw	Ghost	Physical	70	100	15	Normal
TM66	Payback	Dark	Physical	50	100	10	Normal
TM68	Giga Impact	Normal	Physical	150	90	5	Normal
TM71	Stone Edge	Rock	Physical	100	80	5	Normal
TM74	Gyro Ball	Steel	Physical	—	100	5	Normal
TM78	Bulldoze	Ground	Physical	60	100	20	Adjacent
TM80	Rock Slide	Rock	Physical	75	90	10	Many Others
TM82	Dragon Tail	Dragon	Physical	60	90	10	Normal
TM84	Poison Jab	Poison	Physical	80	100	20	Normal
TM88	Sleep Talk	Normal	Status	—	—	10	Self
TM90	Substitute	Normal	Status	—	—	10	Self
TM95	Snarl	Dark	Special	55	95	15	Many Others
TM97	Dark Pulse	Dark	Special	80	100	15	Normal

❖ MOVES TAUGHT BY PEOPLE
Name	Type	Kind	Pow.	Acc.	PP	Range
Draco Meteor	Dragon	Special	130	90	5	Normal

❖ MOVES LEARNED WHEN EVOLVING
Name	Type	Kind	Pow.	Acc.	PP	Range

❖ EGG MOVES
Name	Type	Kind	Pow.	Acc.	PP	Range

❖ EXCLUSIVE Z-MOVE
Name	Base Move	Type	Kind	Pow.	Acc.	Range

Necrozma

Alola Pokédex	Melemele	Akala	Ula'ula	Poni
300	—	—	—	—

Necrozma
Prism Pokémon

PSYCHIC

HEIGHT: 7'10"
WEIGHT: 507.1 lbs.

Reminiscent of the Ultra Beasts, this life-form, apparently asleep underground, is thought to have come from another world in ancient times.

Light is apparently the source of its energy. It has an extraordinarily vicious disposition and is constantly firing off laser beams.

ABILITY
Prism Armor

HIDDEN ABILITY
—

SPECIES STRENGTHS
HP	◆◆◆◆
Attack	◆◆◆◆◆◆◆
Defense	◆◆◆◆◆
Sp. Atk	◆◆◆◆◆◆◆
Sp. Def	◆◆◆◆◆
Speed	◆◆◆◆◆

EGG GROUPS
No Eggs Discovered

ITEM SOMETIMES HELD BY WILD POKÉMON
—

EVOLUTION
Does not evolve

MAIN WAY TO REGISTER IN THE POKÉDEX
Catch when it appears on Ten Carat Hill after completing the Looker episode (p. 268)

Gender unknown

Damage taken in normal battles
NORMAL ×1	FIGHTING ×0.5	ROCK ×1
FIRE ×1	POISON ×1	GHOST ×2
WATER ×1	GROUND ×1	DRAGON ×1
GRASS ×1	FLYING ×1	DARK ×2
ELECTRIC ×1	PSYCHIC ×0.5	STEEL ×1
ICE ×1	BUG ×2	FAIRY ×1

❖ LEVEL-UP MOVES
Lv.	Name	Type	Kind	Pow.	Acc.	PP	Range
1	Moonlight	Fairy	Status	—	—	5	Self
1	Morning Sun	Normal	Status	—	—	5	Self
1	Charge Beam	Electric	Special	50	90	10	Normal
1	Mirror Shot	Steel	Special	65	85	10	Normal
1	Metal Claw	Steel	Physical	50	95	35	Normal
1	Confusion	Psychic	Special	50	100	25	Normal
7	Slash	Normal	Physical	70	100	20	Normal
13	Stored Power	Psychic	Special	20	100	10	Normal
19	Rock Blast	Rock	Physical	25	90	10	Normal
23	Night Slash	Dark	Physical	70	100	15	Normal
31	Gravity	Psychic	Status	—	—	5	Both Sides
37	Psycho Cut	Psychic	Physical	70	100	20	Normal
43	Power Gem	Rock	Special	80	100	20	Normal
47	Autotomize	Steel	Status	—	—	15	Self
53	Stealth Rock	Rock	Status	—	—	20	Other Side
59	Iron Defense	Steel	Status	—	—	15	Self
67	Wring Out	Normal	Special	—	100	5	Normal
73	Prismatic Laser	Psychic	Special	160	100	10	Normal

❖ TM MOVES
No.	Name	Type	Kind	Pow.	Acc.	PP	Range
TM03	Psyshock	Psychic	Special	80	100	10	Normal
TM04	Calm Mind	Psychic	Status	—	—	20	Self
TM06	Toxic	Poison	Status	—	90	10	Normal
TM10	Hidden Power	Normal	Special	60	100	15	Normal
TM15	Hyper Beam	Normal	Special	150	90	5	Normal
TM16	Light Screen	Psychic	Status	—	—	30	Your Side
TM17	Protect	Normal	Status	—	—	10	Self
TM21	Frustration	Normal	Physical	—	100	20	Normal
TM22	Solar Beam	Grass	Special	120	100	10	Normal
TM26	Earthquake	Ground	Physical	100	100	10	Adjacent
TM27	Return	Normal	Physical	—	100	20	Normal
TM29	Psychic	Psychic	Special	90	100	10	Normal
TM31	Brick Break	Fighting	Physical	75	100	15	Normal
TM32	Double Team	Normal	Status	—	—	15	Self
TM33	Reflect	Psychic	Status	—	—	20	Your Side
TM39	Rock Tomb	Rock	Physical	60	95	15	Normal
TM40	Aerial Ace	Flying	Physical	60	—	20	Normal
TM42	Facade	Normal	Physical	70	100	20	Normal
TM44	Rest	Psychic	Status	—	—	10	Self
TM46	Thief	Dark	Physical	60	100	25	Normal
TM48	Round	Normal	Special	60	100	15	Normal
TM56	Fling	Dark	Physical	—	100	10	Normal
TM57	Charge Beam	Electric	Special	50	90	10	Normal
TM59	Brutal Swing	Dark	Physical	60	100	20	Adjacent
TM63	Embargo	Dark	Status	—	100	15	Normal
TM65	Shadow Claw	Ghost	Physical	70	100	15	Normal
TM67	Smart Strike	Steel	Physical	70	—	10	Normal
TM68	Giga Impact	Normal	Physical	150	90	5	Normal
TM69	Rock Polish	Rock	Status	—	—	20	Self
TM71	Stone Edge	Rock	Physical	100	80	5	Normal
TM73	Thunder Wave	Electric	Status	—	90	20	Normal
TM74	Gyro Ball	Steel	Physical	—	100	5	Normal
TM75	Swords Dance	Normal	Status	—	—	20	Self
TM78	Bulldoze	Ground	Physical	60	100	20	Adjacent
TM80	Rock Slide	Rock	Physical	75	90	10	Many Others
TM81	X-Scissor	Bug	Physical	80	100	15	Normal
TM87	Swagger	Normal	Status	—	85	15	Normal
TM90	Substitute	Normal	Status	—	—	10	Self
TM91	Flash Cannon	Steel	Special	80	100	10	Normal
TM92	Trick Room	Psychic	Status	—	—	5	Both Sides
TM97	Dark Pulse	Dark	Special	80	100	15	Normal
TM100	Confide	Normal	Status	—	—	20	Normal

❖ MOVES TAUGHT BY PEOPLE
Name	Type	Kind	Pow.	Acc.	PP	Range

❖ MOVES LEARNED WHEN EVOLVING
Name	Type	Kind	Pow.	Acc.	PP	Range

❖ EGG MOVES
Name	Type	Kind	Pow.	Acc.	PP	Range

❖ EXCLUSIVE Z-MOVE
Name	Base Move	Type	Kind	Pow.	Acc.	Range

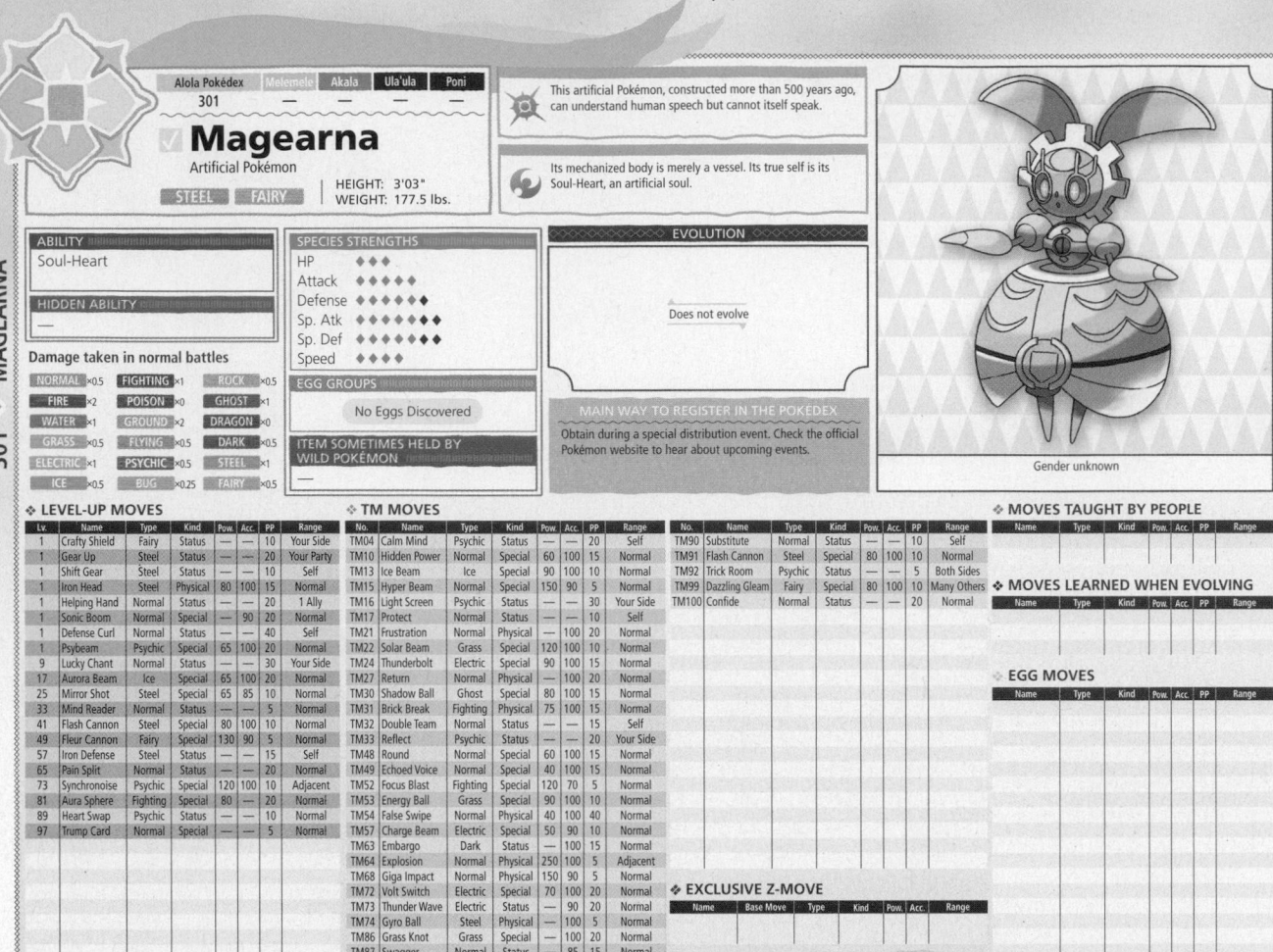

Magearna
Artificial Pokémon

STEEL · FAIRY

HEIGHT: 3'03"
WEIGHT: 177.5 lbs.

This artificial Pokémon, constructed more than 500 years ago, can understand human speech but cannot itself speak.

Its mechanized body is merely a vessel. Its true self is its Soul-Heart, an artificial soul.

ABILITY
Soul-Heart

HIDDEN ABILITY
—

SPECIES STRENGTHS
HP	◆◆◆
Attack	◆◆◆◆◆
Defense	◆◆◆◆◆◆
Sp. Atk	◆◆◆◆◆◆◆
Sp. Def	◆◆◆◆◆◆◆
Speed	◆◆◆◆

EGG GROUPS
No Eggs Discovered

ITEM SOMETIMES HELD BY WILD POKÉMON
—

EVOLUTION
Does not evolve

MAIN WAY TO REGISTER IN THE POKÉDEX
Obtain during a special distribution event. Check the official Pokémon website to hear about upcoming events.

Gender unknown

Damage taken in normal battles
NORMAL ×0.5	FIGHTING ×1	ROCK ×0.5			
FIRE ×2	POISON ×0	GHOST ×1			
WATER ×1	GROUND ×1	DRAGON ×0			
GRASS ×0.5	FLYING ×0.5	DARK ×1			
ELECTRIC ×1	PSYCHIC ×0.5	STEEL ×1			
ICE ×1	BUG ×0.25	FAIRY ×0.5			

❖ LEVEL-UP MOVES
Lv.	Name	Type	Kind	Pow.	Acc.	PP	Range
1	Crafty Shield	Fairy	Status	—	—	10	Your Side
1	Gear Up	Steel	Status	—	—	20	Your Party
1	Shift Gear	Steel	Status	—	—	10	Self
1	Iron Head	Steel	Physical	80	100	15	Normal
1	Helping Hand	Normal	Status	—	—	20	1 Ally
1	Sonic Boom	Normal	Special	—	90	20	Normal
1	Defense Curl	Normal	Status	—	—	40	Self
1	Psybeam	Psychic	Special	65	100	20	Normal
9	Lucky Chant	Normal	Status	—	—	30	Your Side
17	Aurora Beam	Ice	Special	65	100	20	Normal
25	Mirror Shot	Steel	Special	65	85	10	Normal
33	Mind Reader	Normal	Status	—	—	5	Normal
41	Flash Cannon	Steel	Special	80	100	10	Normal
49	Fleur Cannon	Fairy	Special	130	90	5	Normal
57	Iron Defense	Steel	Status	—	—	15	Self
65	Pain Split	Normal	Status	—	—	20	Normal
73	Synchronoise	Psychic	Special	120	100	10	Adjacent
81	Aura Sphere	Fighting	Special	80	—	20	Normal
89	Heart Swap	Psychic	Status	—	—	10	Normal
97	Trump Card	Normal	Special	—	—	5	Normal

❖ TM MOVES
No.	Name	Type	Kind	Pow.	Acc.	PP	Range
TM04	Calm Mind	Psychic	Status	—	—	20	Self
TM10	Hidden Power	Normal	Special	60	100	15	Normal
TM13	Ice Beam	Ice	Special	90	100	10	Normal
TM15	Hyper Beam	Normal	Special	150	90	5	Normal
TM16	Light Screen	Psychic	Status	—	—	30	Your Side
TM17	Protect	Normal	Status	—	—	10	Self
TM21	Frustration	Normal	Physical	—	100	20	Normal
TM22	Solar Beam	Grass	Special	120	100	10	Normal
TM24	Thunderbolt	Electric	Special	90	100	15	Normal
TM27	Return	Normal	Physical	—	100	20	Normal
TM30	Shadow Ball	Ghost	Special	80	100	15	Normal
TM31	Brick Break	Fighting	Physical	75	100	15	Normal
TM32	Double Team	Normal	Status	—	—	15	Self
TM33	Reflect	Psychic	Status	—	—	20	Your Side
TM48	Round	Normal	Special	60	100	15	Normal
TM49	Echoed Voice	Normal	Special	40	100	15	Normal
TM52	Focus Blast	Fighting	Special	120	70	5	Normal
TM53	Energy Ball	Grass	Special	90	100	10	Normal
TM54	False Swipe	Normal	Physical	40	100	40	Normal
TM57	Charge Beam	Electric	Special	50	90	10	Normal
TM63	Embargo	Dark	Status	—	100	15	Normal
TM64	Explosion	Normal	Physical	250	100	5	Adjacent
TM68	Giga Impact	Normal	Physical	150	90	5	Normal
TM72	Volt Switch	Electric	Special	70	100	20	Normal
TM73	Thunder Wave	Electric	Status	—	90	20	Normal
TM74	Gyro Ball	Steel	Physical	—	100	5	Normal
TM86	Grass Knot	Grass	Special	—	100	20	Normal
TM87	Swagger	Normal	Status	—	85	15	Normal

No.	Name	Type	Kind	Pow.	Acc.	PP	Range
TM90	Substitute	Normal	Status	—	—	10	Self
TM91	Flash Cannon	Steel	Special	80	100	10	Normal
TM92	Trick Room	Psychic	Status	—	—	5	Both Sides
TM99	Dazzling Gleam	Fairy	Special	80	100	10	Many Others
TM100	Confide	Normal	Status	—	—	20	Normal

❖ MOVES TAUGHT BY PEOPLE
Name	Type	Kind	Pow.	Acc.	PP	Range

❖ MOVES LEARNED WHEN EVOLVING
Name	Type	Kind	Pow.	Acc.	PP	Range

❖ EGG MOVES
Name	Type	Kind	Pow.	Acc.	PP	Range

❖ EXCLUSIVE Z-MOVE
Name	Base Move	Type	Kind	Pow.	Acc.	Range

Mythical Pokémon, Mega-Evolved Pokémon, and More

From Single Battle to Battle Royal, there are many ways to battle in the game. There is also variety in which Pokémon you will be able to use at the various battling venues. Generally, you will be able to use whichever Pokémon you'd like when battling within the game, but "Special Pokémon" are banned at the Battle Tree and may be banned in some of the modes available at the Battle Spot. Magearna is one of these special Pokémon, as it is a Mythical Pokémon only available during special events. The Mega-Evolved Pokémon that are covered on the following pages may also be banned from some competitive tournaments, so be sure to read the rules and regulations for competitions when constructing your perfect team.

In general, most special Pokémon are Legendary Pokémon, such as those that appear in game box art, or Mythical Pokémon, which are not normally catchable within a Pokémon game. Here is a list of special Pokémon identified to date:

Special Pokémon

Mewtwo	Kyogre	Giratina	Victini	Genesect	Volcanion
Mew	Rayquaza	Phione	Reshiram	Xerneas	Cosmog
Lugia	Jirachi	Manaphy	Zekrom	Yveltal	Cosmoem
Ho-Oh	Deoxys	Darkrai	Kyurem	Zygarde	Solgaleo
Celebi	Dialga	Shaymin	Keldeo	Diancie	Lunala
Groudon	Palkia	Arceus	Meloetta	Hoopa	Magearna

...and perhaps more that are yet to be discovered!

Mega Slowbro

Hermit Crab Pokémon

WATER **PSYCHIC**

HEIGHT: 6'07"
WEIGHT: 264.6 lbs.

All the energy from Mega Evolution poured into the Shellder on its tail, leaving Slowpoke to be swallowed whole.

When bathed in the energy of Mega Evolution, Shellder converts into impregnable armor. There is virtually no change in Slowpoke.

Same form for male/female		

ABILITY
Shell Armor

SPECIES STRENGTHS

HP	◆◆◆◆
Attack	◆◆◆◆
Defense	◆◆◆◆◆◆◆◆◆
Sp. Atk	◆◆◆◆◆◆◆
Sp. Def	◆◆◆◆◆
Speed	◆◆

Damage taken in normal battles

NORMAL	×1	FIGHTING	×0.5	ROCK	×1
FIRE	×0.5	POISON	×1	GHOST	×2
WATER	×0.5	GROUND	×1	DRAGON	×1
GRASS	×2	FLYING	×1	DARK	×2
ELECTRIC	×2	PSYCHIC	×0.5	STEEL	×0.5
ICE	×0.5	BUG	×2	FAIRY	×1

MEGA EVOLUTION

Slowbro → Mega Slowbro

Have Slowbro hold Slowbronite and Mega Evolve in battle

For more information on Slowbro, turn back to page 36.

REQUIRED MEGA STONE

 **Slowbronite**
Get it in exchange for 64 BP at the Battle Tree (p. 271)

Mega Alakazam

Psi Pokémon

PSYCHIC

HEIGHT: 3'11"
WEIGHT: 105.0 lbs.

As a result of Mega Evolution, its power has been entirely converted into psychic energy, and it has lost all strength in its muscles.

Its hidden psychic power has been unleashed. A glance at someone gives it knowledge of the course of that person's life, from birth to death.

Same form for male/female		

ABILITY
Trace

SPECIES STRENGTHS

HP	◆◆
Attack	◆◆◆
Defense	◆◆◆◆
Sp. Atk	◆◆◆◆◆◆◆◆◆
Sp. Def	◆◆◆◆◆◆◆
Speed	◆◆◆◆◆◆◆◆

Damage taken in normal battles

NORMAL	×1	FIGHTING	×0.5	ROCK	×1
FIRE	×1	POISON	×1	GHOST	×2
WATER	×1	GROUND	×1	DRAGON	×1
GRASS	×1	FLYING	×1	DARK	×2
ELECTRIC	×1	PSYCHIC	×0.5	STEEL	×1
ICE	×1	BUG	×2	FAIRY	×1

MEGA EVOLUTION

Alakazam → Mega Alakazam

Have Alakazam hold Alakazite and Mega Evolve in battle

For more information on Alakazam, turn back to page 40.

REQUIRED MEGA STONE

 **Alakazite**
Receive from Dexio on Poni Ancient Path in exchange for a battle after becoming Champion (p. 254), or get it in exchange for 64 BP at the Battle Tree (p. 271)

Mega Gengar

Shadow Pokémon

| GHOST | POISON |

HEIGHT: 4'07"
WEIGHT: 89.3 lbs.

Gengar's relationships are warped. It has no interest in opponents unless it perceives them as prey.

The energy of Mega Evolution awakened it. It sinks into another dimension, where it keeps a patient watch for its chance to attack.

Same form for male/female

ABILITY
Shadow Tag

SPECIES STRENGTHS
HP	◆◆
Attack	◆◆◆◆
Defense	◆◆◆◆
Sp. Atk	◆◆◆◆◆◆◆◆
Sp. Def	◆◆◆◆◆
Speed	◆◆◆◆◆◆◆

Damage taken in normal battles
NORMAL	×0	FIGHTING	×0	ROCK	×1
FIRE	×1	POISON	×0.25	GHOST	×2
WATER	×1	GROUND	×2	DRAGON	×1
GRASS	×0.5	FLYING	×1	DARK	×2
ELECTRIC	×1	PSYCHIC	×2	STEEL	×1
ICE	×1	BUG	×0.25	FAIRY	×0.5

MEGA EVOLUTION

Gengar → Mega Gengar

Have Gengar hold Gengarite and Mega Evolve in battle

For more information on Gengar, turn back to page 52.

REQUIRED MEGA STONE
Gengarite
Get it in exchange for 64 BP at the Battle Tree (p. 271)

Mega Gyarados

Atrocious Pokémon

| WATER | DARK |

HEIGHT: 21'04"
WEIGHT: 672.4 lbs.

Mega Evolution also affects its brain, leaving no other function except its destructive instinct to burn everything to cinders.

It jets water from the orifices on its sides, streaking above the water surface at supersonic speed.

Same form for male/female

ABILITY
Mold Breaker

SPECIES STRENGTHS
HP	◆◆◆◆
Attack	◆◆◆◆◆◆◆
Defense	◆◆◆◆◆◆
Sp. Atk	◆◆◆◆
Sp. Def	◆◆◆◆◆◆◆
Speed	◆◆◆◆◆

Damage taken in normal battles
NORMAL	×1	FIGHTING	×2	ROCK	×1
FIRE	×0.5	POISON	×1	GHOST	×0.5
WATER	×0.5	GROUND	×1	DRAGON	×1
GRASS	×2	FLYING	×1	DARK	×0.5
ELECTRIC	×2	PSYCHIC	×0	STEEL	×0.5
ICE	×0.5	BUG	×2	FAIRY	×2

MEGA EVOLUTION

Gyarados → Mega Gyarados

Have Gyarados hold Gyaradosite and Mega Evolve in battle

For more information on Gyarados, turn back to page 70.

REQUIRED MEGA STONE
Gyaradosite
Get it in exchange for 64 BP at the Battle Tree (p. 271)

Mega Sableye

Darkness Pokémon

| DARK | GHOST |

HEIGHT: 1'08"
WEIGHT: 364.9 lbs.

The jewel from its chest, which has grown gigantic due to the effects of Mega Evolution, can turn back any attack.

Supporting a giant heavy jewel, it can't change direction very nimbly and is vulnerable to attack from behind.

Same form for male/female

ABILITY
Magic Bounce

SPECIES STRENGTHS

HP ◆◆
Attack ◆◆◆◆◆
Defense ◆◆◆◆◆◆◆
Sp. Atk ◆◆◆◆◆
Sp. Def ◆◆◆◆◆◆◆
Speed ◆

Damage taken in normal battles

NORMAL ×0	FIGHTING ×0	ROCK ×1
FIRE ×1	POISON ×0.5	GHOST ×1
WATER ×1	GROUND ×1	DRAGON ×1
GRASS ×1	FLYING ×1	DARK ×1
ELECTRIC ×1	PSYCHIC ×0	STEEL ×1
ICE ×1	BUG ×1	FAIRY ×2

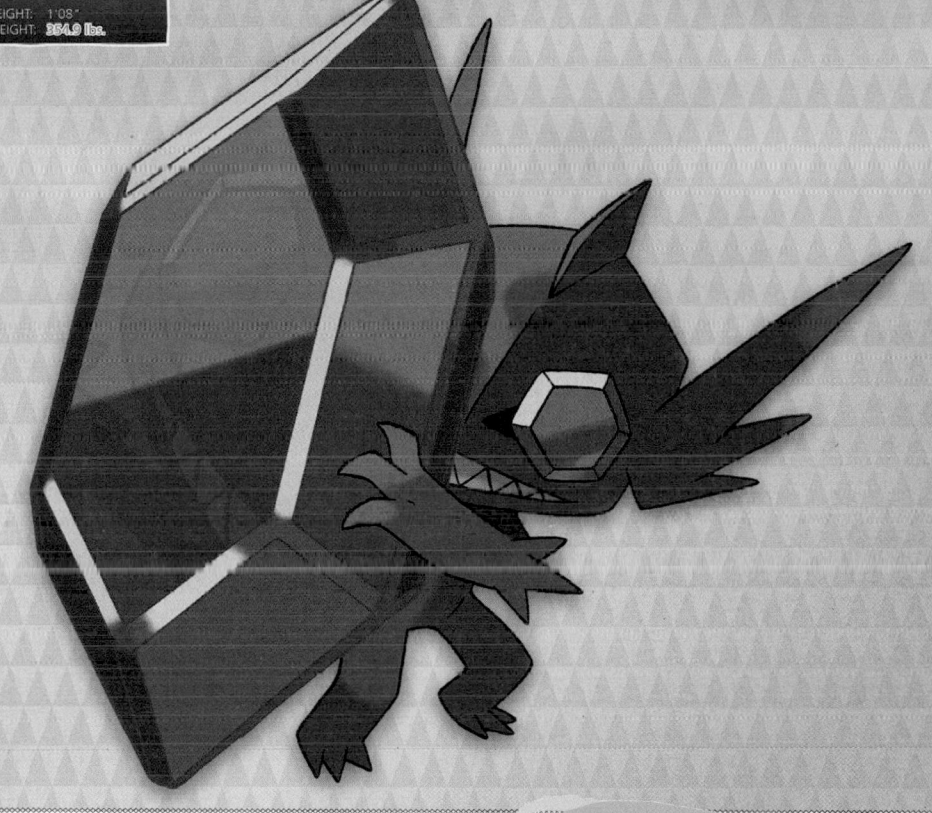

MEGA EVOLUTION

Sableye → Have Sableye hold Sablenite and Mega Evolve in battle → Mega Sableye

For more information on Sableye, turn back to page 76.

REQUIRED MEGA STONE

Sablenite
Get it in exchange for 64 BP at the Battle Tree (p. 271)

Mega Salamence

Dragon Pokémon

| DRAGON | FLYING |

HEIGHT: 5'11"
WEIGHT: 248.2 lbs.

Anyone standing in its path gets sliced right in two, while this Pokémon continues its flight without interruption.

Mega Evolution fuels its brutality, and it may even turn on the Trainer who raised it. It's been dubbed "the blood-soaked crescent."

Same form for male/female

ABILITY
Aerilate

SPECIES STRENGTHS

HP ◆◆◆◆
Attack ◆◆◆◆◆◆◆◆
Defense ◆◆◆◆◆◆◆
Sp. Atk ◆◆◆◆◆◆◆
Sp. Def ◆◆◆◆◆
Speed ◆◆◆◆◆◆◆◆

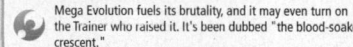

Damage taken in normal battles

NORMAL ×1	FIGHTING ×0.5	ROCK ×2
FIRE ×0.5	POISON ×1	GHOST ×1
WATER ×0.5	GROUND ×0	DRAGON ×2
GRASS ×0.25	FLYING ×1	DARK ×1
ELECTRIC ×1	PSYCHIC ×1	STEEL ×1
ICE ×4	BUG ×0.5	FAIRY ×2

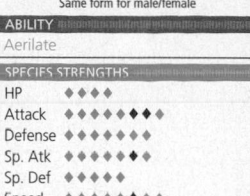

MEGA EVOLUTION

Salamence → Have Salamence hold Salamencite and Mega Evolve in battle → Mega Salamence

For more information on Salamence, turn back to page 88.

REQUIRED MEGA STONE

Salamencite
Get it in exchange for 64 BP at the Battle Tree (p. 271)

Mega Kangaskhan

Parent Pokémon

NORMAL

HEIGHT: 7'03"
WEIGHT: 220.5 lbs.

Mega Kangaskhan's strength derives from the mother's happiness about her child's growth. Watching it grow up keeps her spirits high.

Thanks to Mega Evolution, its child grows. But as the child is good only at fighting and nothing else, its mother feels uneasy about its future.

Female only

ABILITY
Parental Bond

SPECIES STRENGTHS

HP	◆◆◆◆
Attack	◆◆◆◆◆◆◆
Defense	◆◆◆◆◆
Sp. Atk	◆◆◆
Sp. Def	◆◆◆◆
Speed	◆◆◆◆◆◆

Damage taken in normal battles

NORMAL	×1	FIGHTING	×2	ROCK	×1
FIRE	×1	POISON	×1	GHOST	×0
WATER	×1	GROUND	×1	DRAGON	×1
GRASS	×1	FLYING	×1	DARK	×1
ELECTRIC	×1	PSYCHIC	×1	STEEL	×1
ICE	×1	BUG	×1	FAIRY	×1

MEGA EVOLUTION

Kangaskhan → **Have Kangaskhan hold Kangaskhanite and Mega Evolve in battle** → Mega Kangaskhan

For more information on Kangaskhan, turn back to page 116.

REQUIRED MEGA STONE

Kangaskhanite
Get it in exchange for 64 BP at the Battle Tree (p. 271)

Mega Pinsir

Stag Beetle Pokémon

BUG FLYING

HEIGHT: 5'07"
WEIGHT: 130.1 lbs.

The influence of Mega Evolution leaves it in a state of constant excitement. It pierces enemies with its two large horns before shredding them.

Bathed in the energy of Mega Evolution, its wings become unusually developed. It flies at speeds of approximately 30 mph.

Same form for male/female

ABILITY
Aerilate

SPECIES STRENGTHS

HP	◆◆◆
Attack	◆◆◆◆◆◆◆◆
Defense	◆◆◆◆◆◆
Sp. Atk	◆◆◆◆
Sp. Def	◆◆◆◆◆
Speed	◆◆◆◆◆◆

Damage taken in normal battles

NORMAL	×1	FIGHTING	×0.25	ROCK	×4
FIRE	×2	POISON	×1	GHOST	×1
WATER	×1	GROUND	×1	DRAGON	×1
GRASS	×0.25	FLYING	×2	DARK	×1
ELECTRIC	×2	PSYCHIC	×1	STEEL	×1
ICE	×2	BUG	×0.5	FAIRY	×1

MEGA EVOLUTION

Pinsir → **Have Pinsir hold Pinsirite and Mega Evolve in battle** → Mega Pinsir

For more information on Pinsir, turn back to page 124.

REQUIRED MEGA STONE

Pinsirite
Get it in exchange for 64 BP at the Battle Tree (p. 271)

Mega Metagross

Iron Leg Pokémon

STEEL **PSYCHIC**

HEIGHT: 8'02"
WEIGHT: 2078.7 lbs.

MEGA METAGROSS

This form results from one Metagross, one Metang, and two Beldum linking up.

Mega Evolution stimulated its brain. It emerged as a ruthless Pokémon that will clutch at any means of ensuring its victories.

Gender unknown

ABILITY
Tough Claws

SPECIES STRENGTHS

HP	◆◆◆
Attack	◆◆◆◆◆◆◆
Defense	◆◆◆◆◆◆◆
Sp. Atk	◆◆◆◆◆◆
Sp. Def	◆◆◆◆◆◆◆
Speed	◆◆◆◆◆◆◆

Damage taken in normal battles

NORMAL ×0.5	FIGHTING ×1	ROCK ×0.5
FIRE ×2	POISON ×0	GHOST ×2
WATER ×1	GROUND ×2	DRAGON ×0.5
GRASS ×0.5	FLYING ×0.5	DARK ×1
ELECTRIC ×1	PSYCHIC ×0.25	STEEL ×0.5
ICE ×0.5	BUG ×1	FAIRY ×0.5

MEGA EVOLUTION

Metagross

Have Metagross hold Metagrossite and Mega Evolve in battle

Mega Metagross

For more information on Metagross, turn back to page 150.

REQUIRED MEGA STONE

Metagrossite
Get it in exchange for 64 BP at the Battle Tree (p. 271)

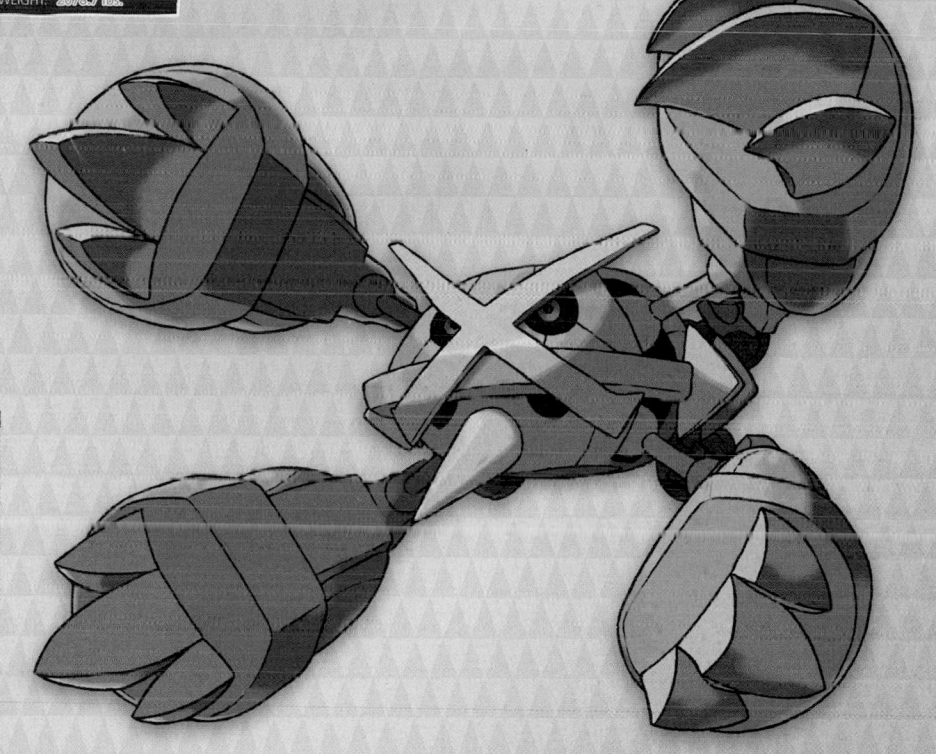

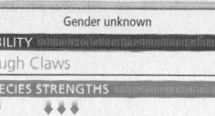

Mega Garchomp

Mach Pokémon

DRAGON **GROUND**

HEIGHT: 6'03"
WEIGHT: 209.4 lbs.

MEGA GARCHOMP

Excess energy melted its arms and wings, transforming them into giant scythes.

Its vaunted wings become scythes, sending it mad with rage. It swings its scythes wildly and slices the ground to pieces.

Same form for male/female

ABILITY
Sand Force

SPECIES STRENGTHS

HP	◆◆◆◆
Attack	◆◆◆◆◆◆◆
Defense	◆◆◆◆◆
Sp. Atk	◆◆◆◆◆◆
Sp. Def	◆◆◆◆◆
Speed	◆◆◆◆◆◆

Damage taken in normal battles

NORMAL ×1	FIGHTING ×1	ROCK ×0.5
FIRE ×0.5	POISON ×0.5	GHOST ×1
WATER ×1	GROUND ×1	DRAGON ×1
GRASS ×1	FLYING ×1	DARK ×1
ELECTRIC ×0	PSYCHIC ×1	STEEL ×1
ICE ×4	BUG ×1	FAIRY ×2

MEGA EVOLUTION

Garchomp

Have Garchomp hold Garchompite and Mega Evolve in battle

Mega Garchomp

For more information on Garchomp, turn back to page 166.

REQUIRED MEGA STONE

Garchompite
Get it in exchange for 64 BP at the Battle Tree (p. 271)

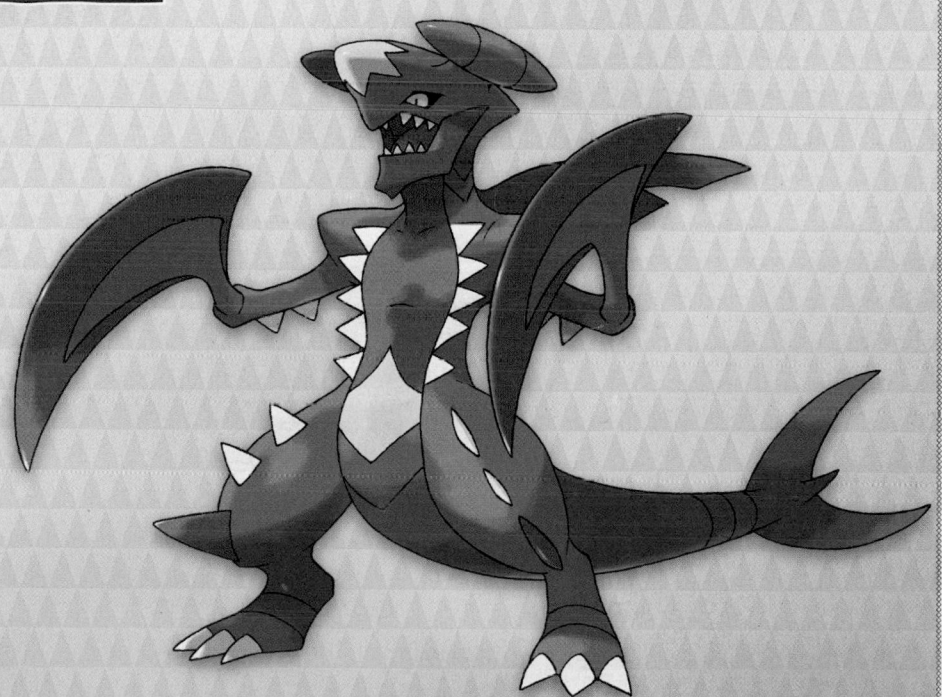

Mega Absol

Disaster Pokémon

DARK

HEIGHT: 3'11"
WEIGHT: 108 lbs.

When this Pokémon whips the winglike fur on its back as though beating its wings, it sends an intimidating aura flying at its opponents.

As the energy of Mega Evolution fills it, its fur bristles. What you see on its back are not true wings, and this Pokémon isn't able to fly.

Same form for male/female

ABILITY
Magic Bounce

SPECIES STRENGTHS

HP	◆◆◆
Attack	◆◆◆◆◆◆◆
Defense	◆◆◆
Sp. Atk	◆◆◆◆◆◆
Sp. Def	◆◆◆
Speed	◆◆◆◆◆◆◆

Damage taken in normal battles

NORMAL	×1	FIGHTING	×2	ROCK	×1
FIRE	×1	POISON	×1	GHOST	×0.5
WATER	×1	GROUND	×1	DRAGON	×1
GRASS	×1	FLYING	×1	DARK	×0.5
ELECTRIC	×1	PSYCHIC	×0	STEEL	×1
ICE	×1	BUG	×2	FAIRY	×2

⬡⬡⬡⬡⬡ MEGA EVOLUTION ⬡⬡⬡⬡⬡

Absol → **Have Absol hold Absolite and Mega Evolve in battle** → Mega Absol

For more information on Absol, turn back to page 171.

REQUIRED MEGA STONE

Absolite
Get it in exchange for 64 BP at the Battle Tree (p. 271)

Mega Glalie

Face Pokémon

ICE

HEIGHT: 6'11"
WEIGHT: 772.1 lbs.

The excess energy from Mega Evolution spilled over from its mouth, breaking its jaw. It spews endless blizzards.

It envelops prey in its mouth, freezing them instantly. But its jaw is dislocated, so it's unable to eat them.

Same form for male/female

ABILITY
Refrigerate

SPECIES STRENGTHS

HP	◆◆◆
Attack	◆◆◆◆◆◆
Defense	◆◆◆◆
Sp. Atk	◆◆◆◆◆◆◆
Sp. Def	◆◆◆◆◆
Speed	◆◆◆◆◆◆

Damage taken in normal battles

NORMAL	×1	FIGHTING	×1	ROCK	×2
FIRE	×2	POISON	×1	GHOST	×1
WATER	×1	GROUND	×1	DRAGON	×1
GRASS	×1	FLYING	×1	DARK	×1
ELECTRIC	×1	PSYCHIC	×1	STEEL	×2
ICE	×0.5	BUG	×1	FAIRY	×1

⬡⬡⬡⬡⬡ MEGA EVOLUTION ⬡⬡⬡⬡⬡

Glalie → **Have Glalie hold Glalitite and Mega Evolve in battle** → Mega Glalie

For more information on Glalie, turn back to page 172.

REQUIRED MEGA STONE

Glalitite
Get it in exchange for 64 BP at the Battle Tree (p. 271)

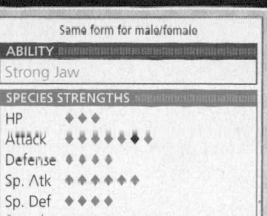

Mega Sharpedo

Brutal Pokémon

| WATER | DARK |

HEIGHT: 6'02"
WEIGHT: 287.3 lbs.

The spines sprouting from its head are transformed fangs. If they're injured or broken off, the spines will regenerate countless times.

As a consequence of Mega Evolution, its combative instincts exploded. The yellow marks it bears are scars from a long history of battles.

Same form for male/female

ABILITY
Strong Jaw

SPECIES STRENGTHS

HP	◆◆◆
Attack	◆◆◆◆◆◆◆
Defense	◆◆◆◆
Sp. Atk	◆◆◆◆◆◆
Sp. Def	◆◆◆◆
Speed	◆◆◆◆◆◆◆

Damage taken in normal battles

NORMAL	×1	FIGHTING	×2	ROCK	×1
FIRE	×0.5	POISON	×1	GHOST	×0.5
WATER	×0.5	GROUND	×1	DRAGON	×1
GRASS	×2	FLYING	×1	DARK	×0.5
ELECTRIC	×2	PSYCHIC	×0	STEEL	×0.5
ICE	×0.5	BUG	×2	FAIRY	×2

MEGA EVOLUTION

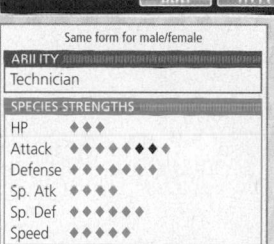

Sharpedo → Have Sharpedo hold Sharpedonite and Mega Evolve in battle → Mega Sharpedo

For more information on Sharpedo, turn back to page 183.

REQUIRED MEGA STONE

Sharpedonite
Get it in exchange for 64 BP at the Battle Tree (p. 271)

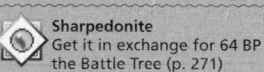

Mega Scizor

Pincer Pokémon

| BUG | STEEL |

HEIGHT: 6'07"
WEIGHT: 275.6 lbs.

The excess energy that bathes this Pokémon keeps it in constant danger of overflow. It can't sustain a battle over long periods of time.

Due to the effects of Mega Evolution, its pincers have taken on a more diabolical form, ripping anything they pinch to shreds.

Same form for male/female

ABILITY
Technician

SPECIES STRENGTHS

HP	◆◆◆
Attack	◆◆◆◆◆◆◆
Defense	◆◆◆◆◆◆
Sp. Atk	◆◆◆
Sp. Def	◆◆◆◆◆◆
Speed	◆◆◆◆◆

Damage taken in normal battles

NORMAL	×0.5	FIGHTING	×1	ROCK	×1
FIRE	×4	POISON	×0	GHOST	×1
WATER	×1	GROUND	×1	DRAGON	×0.5
GRASS	×0.25	FLYING	×1	DARK	×1
ELECTRIC	×1	PSYCHIC	×0.5	STEEL	×0.5
ICE	×0.5	BUG	×0.5	FAIRY	×0.5

MEGA EVOLUTION

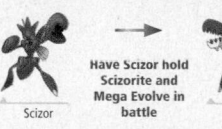

Scizor → Have Scizor hold Scizorite and Mega Evolve in battle → Mega Scizor

For more information on Scizor, turn back to page 191.

REQUIRED MEGA STONE

Scizorite
Get it in exchange for 64 BP at the Battle Tree (p. 271)

Mega Lucario

Aura Pokémon

FIGHTING **STEEL**

HEIGHT: 4'03"
WEIGHT: 126.8 lbs.

Black streaks all over its body show where its auras and the energy of Mega Evolution intermingled and raced through it.

It readies itself to face its enemies by focusing its mental energies. Its fighting style can be summed up in a single word: heartless.

Same form for male/female

ABILITY
Adaptability

SPECIES STRENGTHS

HP	◆◆◆
Attack	◆◆◆◆◆
Defense	◆◆◆◆◆
Sp. Atk	◆◆◆◆◆◆
Sp. Def	◆◆◆◆
Speed	◆◆◆◆◆

Damage taken in normal battles

NORMAL	×0.5	FIGHTING	×2	ROCK	×0.25
FIRE	×2	POISON	×0	GHOST	×1
WATER	×1	GROUND	×2	DRAGON	×0.5
GRASS	×0.5	FLYING	×1	DARK	×0.5
ELECTRIC	×1	PSYCHIC	×1	STEEL	×0.5
ICE	×0.5	BUG	×0.25	FAIRY	×1

MEGA EVOLUTION

Lucario → Mega Lucario

Have Lucario hold Lucarionite and Mega Evolve in battle

For more information on Lucario, turn back to page 193.

REQUIRED MEGA STONE

Lucarionite
Get it in exchange for 64 BP at the Battle Tree (p. 271)

Mega Aerodactyl

Fossil Pokémon

ROCK **FLYING**

HEIGHT: 6'11"
WEIGHT: 174.2 lbs.

Part of its body has become stone. Some scholars claim that this is Aerodactyl's true appearance.

When it Mega Evolves, it becomes more vicious than ever before. Some say that's because its excess of power is causing it pain.

Same form for male/female

ABILITY
Tough Claws

SPECIES STRENGTHS

HP	◆◆◆
Attack	◆◆◆◆◆◆◆
Defense	◆◆◆◆
Sp. Atk	◆◆◆
Sp. Def	◆◆◆◆◆
Speed	◆◆◆◆◆◆◆

Damage taken in normal battles

NORMAL	×0.5	FIGHTING	×1	ROCK	×2
FIRE	×0.5	POISON	×0.5	GHOST	×1
WATER	×2	GROUND	×0	DRAGON	×1
GRASS	×1	FLYING	×0.5	DARK	×1
ELECTRIC	×2	PSYCHIC	×1	STEEL	×2
ICE	×2	BUG	×0.5	FAIRY	×1

MEGA EVOLUTION

Aerodactyl → Mega Aerodactyl

Have Aerodactyl hold Aerodactylite and Mega Evolve in battle

For more information on Aerodactyl, turn back to page 196.

REQUIRED MEGA STONE

Aerodactylite
Get it in exchange for 64 BP at the Battle Tree (p. 271)

How to Complete
the Alola Pokédex

Complete the Alola Pokédex

In the Alola Pokédex, you can register the over 300 Pokémon that can be obtained in the Alola region. There are many Pokémon that have unique forms and lifestyles, thanks to living in the unique environment of this region. As you complete your island challenge, or even after you've become a Champion, why not give completing the Alola Pokédex a try? If you hope to achieve this lofty goal, you'll need the help of family members or friends. Trade Pokémon with one another to try to aim for a complete Pokédex!

POKÉDEX 30%

Try to complete your Pokédex up to 100%!

Key to Symbols
Registered in Pokédex ● Seen ? Not yet seen

Obtain a Pokémon to complete its page in the Alola Pokédex

The Alola Pokédex is a high-tech tool that fills in its pages and automatically displays information about any Pokémon you see or catch. When you obtain a Pokémon for yourself, you'll be able to see detailed information about its ecology and can even observe its unique movements and cries.
Be sure to check it out during your adventures as you complete your island challenge!

❖ Obtain a Pokémon to complete its page in the Alola Pokédex

1 Before seeing the Pokémon, you will only see ?
For Pokémon that you haven't yet seen in Alola, you will only be able to see the Pokédex number.

2 Once you've seen a Pokémon, you can see its name and habitat
Once you have seen a Pokémon, its name and types will be displayed, as well as actual data on the habitats where it can be found.

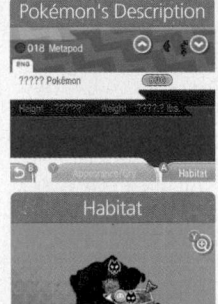

Pokémon's Description

Habitat

3 Obtain a Pokémon and all of its data will be displayed
All of the Pokémon's data is displayed at this point. The upper screen will show information like the Pokémon's Evolutions.

Pokémon's Description

Pokémon's Evolutions

Receive special rewards for completing the Alola Pokédex

As you complete your Pokédexes, you can receive rewards from the game director in the GAME FREAK office in Akala Island's Heahea City. Once you've completed a Pokédex, be sure to go visit him.

I'm the game director. Now let me see that Pokédex of yours...

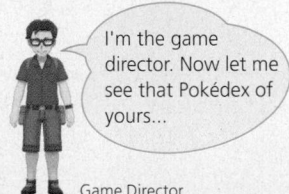

I'm the game director. Now let me see that Pokédex of yours...

Game Director

❖ Stamps you receive from the game director for completing the Island Pokédexes and the Alola Pokédex

Melemele Pokédex Completion

Akala Pokédex Completion

Ula'ula Pokédex Completion

Poni Pokédex Completion

Alola Pokédex Completion (when playing *Pokémon Sun*)

Alola Pokédex Completion (when playing *Pokémon Moon*)

❖ Items you receive for completing the Alola Pokédex

Shiny Charm

When you complete the Alola Pokédex, you can receive a Shiny Charm from the game director. This item makes it easier to encounter rare Shiny Pokémon, which are differently colored than usual. It is said that your chance of finding one is usually only around 1 in 4,000!

Normal Rockruff

Shiny Rockruff

Have the Rotom Dex evaluate your progress

If you tap "Pokédex Evaluation" on your Rotom Dex, you will hear from Rotom about how you are doing on completing each Island Pokédex and may also receive some advice on how to complete each one.

Pokédex Evaluation

Alola Pokédex	153	234
Melemele Pokédex	62	92
Akala Pokédex	66	104
Ula'ula Pokédex	67	103
Poni Pokédex	46	71

Pokédex Evaluation

Rotom's Feedback

50%

Whole meadowzzzz of flowers are pretty rare in Alola... Maybe there are some rare Pokémon in them, too!

Know All the Ways Pokémon Appcar in the Alola Region

Alola's Environment 1 — Which Pokémon appear can differ from one patch of grass to the next

In the Alola region, which Pokémon appear can sometimes differ from one patch of grass to the next, even in the same area. Take Route 1, for example, where Pichu can be found living in some patches of grass while Munchlax is found in others.

Route 1 (Near Iki Town)

A wild Pichu appeared!

Route 1 (West)

A wild Munchlax appeared!

Alola's Environment 2 — Which Pokémon appear can differ between day and night

As time passes in the Alola region, you will find that each day is divided into a period of daytime and nighttime. There are some wild Pokémon that only appear during one of these periods. When you're trying to catch a wild Pokémon, check whether it appears during particular times!

Daytime

A wild Yungoos appeared!

Nighttime

A wild Rattata appeared!

❖ Daytime and nighttime differ in *Pokémon Sun* and *Pokémon Moon*

Time periods in *Pokémon Sun* (simplified)

TIME OF DAY IN THE GAME	NIGHTTIME						DAYTIME												NIGHTTIME					
Time set on your Nintendo 3DS	12 AM	1 AM	2 AM	3 AM	4 AM	5 AM	6 AM	7 AM	8 AM	9 AM	10 AM	11 AM	12 PM	1 PM	2 PM	3 PM	4 PM	5 PM	6 PM	7 PM	8 PM	9 PM	10 PM	11 PM

Time periods in *Pokémon Moon* (simplified)

TIME OF DAY IN THE GAME	DAYTIME						NIGHTTIME												DAYTIME					
Time set on your Nintendo 3DS	12 AM	1 AM	2 AM	3 AM	4 AM	5 AM	6 AM	7 AM	8 AM	9 AM	10 AM	11 AM	12 PM	1 PM	2 PM	3 PM	4 PM	5 PM	6 PM	7 PM	8 PM	9 PM	10 PM	11 PM

Alola's Environment 3 — Some Pokémon have regional variants

In the Alola region, there are Pokémon that have regional variants—forms that have evolved differently here than they have in other regions. These Pokémon appear in their "Alola Form" and are only found here in Alola.

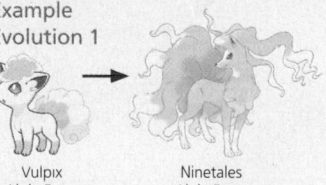

Example Evolution 1

Vulpix Alola Form → Ninetales Alola Form

Example Evolution 2

Pikachu → Raichu Alola Form

Complete Your Island Pokédexes

The Alola Pokédex is made up of four Island Pokédexes. These are the Melemele Pokédex, the Akala Pokédex, the Ula'ula Pokédex, and the Poni Pokédex. If you're hoping to complete the Alola Pokédex, you should aim for completing each of these Island Pokédexes first. Each Island Pokédex requires between 100 and 130 Pokémon to be completed. The conditions for completing each Pokédex are simple enough, and if you catch Pokémon in the aim of completing your Island Pokédexes, you'll find yourself gradually getting closer and closer to completing your Alola Pokédex.

The habitat of the Pokémon you've selected is displayed here.

Check out the Pokémon that you've seen or caught here.

Island Pokédexes are designed to be easy to complete

The Island Pokédexes are designed to be easy to complete. This is because the same Pokémon may appear in multiple Island Pokédexes. For example, Zubat is in all four Pokédexes, so catching one allows you to fill in a bit of your Melemele Pokédex, Akala Pokédex, Ula'ula Pokédex, and Poni Pokédex simultaneously.

❖ Example Pokémon that can be registered in multiple Island Pokédexes

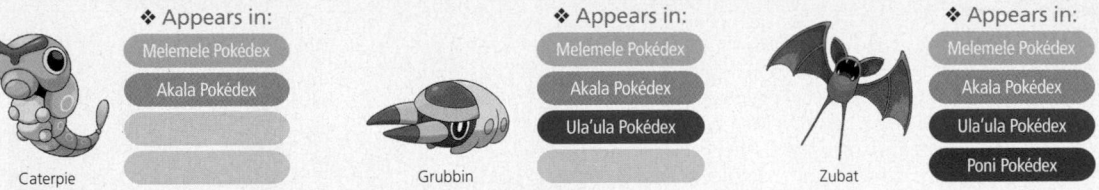

❖ Appears in:
- Melemele Pokédex
- Akala Pokédex

Caterpie

❖ Appears in:
- Melemele Pokédex
- Akala Pokédex
- Ula'ula Pokédex

Grubbin

❖ Appears in:
- Melemele Pokédex
- Akala Pokédex
- Ula'ula Pokédex
- Poni Pokédex

Zubat

Special Pokémon that do not appear in the Island Pokédexes

Certain Pokémon that are particularly hard to obtain do not appear in the four Island Pokédexes. Even if you don't obtain the Pokémon known as Mythical Pokémon or the Ultra Beasts or Legendary Pokémon, you can still complete each Island Pokédex. So give it a go, and try to have fun completing your Island Pokédexes!

Type: Null · Silvally · Zygarde · Cosmog · Cosmoem · Solgaleo · Lunala · Nihilego

Buzzwole · Pheromosa · Xurkitree · Celesteela · Kartana · Guzzlord · Necrozma · Magearna

Island Pokédex lists

The following pages list up all of the Pokémon in the four Island Pokédexes. Use them as a reference when you want to see which of the four Island Pokédexes—the Melemele Pokédex, Akala Pokédex, Ula'ula Pokédex, or Poni Pokédex—a Pokémon in the Alola region belongs to. The Poké Ball icon in one of the columns below indicates that a Pokémon appears in that particular Island Pokédex.

POKÉMON	ALOLA POKÉDEX NO.	MELEMELE POKÉDEX	AKALA POKÉDEX	ULA'ULA POKÉDEX	PONI POKÉDEX
Rowlet	001	●			
Dartrix	002	●			
Decidueye	003	●			
Litten	004	●			
Torracat	005	●			
Incineroar	006	●			

POKÉMON	ALOLA POKÉDEX NO.	MELEMELE POKÉDEX	AKALA POKÉDEX	ULA'ULA POKÉDEX	PONI POKÉDEX
Popplio	007	●			
Brionne	008	●			
Primarina	009	●			
Pikipek	010	●	●	●	●
Trumbeak	011	●	●	●	●
Toucannon	012	●	●	●	●
Yungoos	013	●	●	●	●
Gumshoos	014	●	●	●	●
Rattata	015	●	●	●	●

POKÉMON	ALOLA POKÉDEX NO.	MELEMELE POKÉDEX	AKALA POKÉDEX	ULA'ULA POKÉDEX	PONI POKÉDEX
Raticate	016	●	●	●	●
Caterpie	017	●	●		
Metapod	018	●	●		
Butterfree	019	●	●		
Ledyba	020	●		●	
Ledian	021	●		●	
Spinarak	022	●		●	
Ariados	023	●		●	
Pichu	024	●			

Pokémon	No.	1	2	3	4
Pikachu	025	●			
Raichu	026	●			
Grubbin	027	●	●	●	
Charjabug	028	●	●	●	
Vikavolt	029	●	●		
Bonsly	030	●	●		
Sudowoodo	031	●	●		
Happiny	032	●	●	●	●
Chansey	033	●	●	●	●
Blissey	034	↑	↑	↑	↑
Munchlax	035	●			
Snorlax	036	●			
Slowpoke	037	●		●	
Slowbro	038	●		●	
Slowking	039	●		●	
Wingull	040	●	●	●	●
Pelipper	041	↑	↑	↑	↑
Abra	042	●			
Kadabra	043	●			
Alakazam	044	●			
Meowth	045	●		●	
Persian	046	●		●	
Magnemite	047	●		●	
Magneton	048	●		●	
Magnezone	049	●		●	
Grimer	050	●		●	
Muk	051	●		●	
Growlithe	052	●			
Arcanine	053	●			
Drowzee	054				●
Hypno	055	●			●
Makuhita	056	●			●
Hariyama	057	●			●
Smeargle	058	●			
Crabrawler	059	●	●	●	●
Crabominable	060	●	●	●	●
Gastly	061	●	●	●	
Haunter	062	●	●	●	
Gengar	063	●	●	●	
Drifloon	064	●			
Drifblim	065	●			
Misdreavus	066	●			
Mismagius	067	●			
Zubat	068	●	●	●	●
Golbat	069	●	●	●	●
Crobat	070	●	●	●	●
Diglett	071	●	●	●	●
Dugtrio	072	●		●	●
Spearow	073	●		●	●
Fearow	074			●	●
Rufflet	075	●			●
Braviary	076	●			●
Vullaby	077	●			●
Mandibuzz	078	●			●
Mankey	079	●			●

Pokémon	No.	1	2	3	4
Primeape	080	●			●
Delibird	081	●			
Oricorio	082	↑	↑	↑	↑
Cutiefly	083	●		●	
Ribombee	084	●		●	
Petilil	085	●		●	
Lilligant	086	●		●	
Cottonee	087	●		●	
Whimsicott	088	●		●	
Psyduck	089	●	●	●	
Golduck	090	●	●	●	
Magikarp	091	●	●	●	
Gyarados	092	●	●	●	
Barboach	093	●	●	●	
Whiscash	094	●	●	●	
Machop	095	●			●
Machoke	096	●			●
Machamp	097	●			●
Roggenrola	098	●		●	
Boldore	099	●		●	
Gigalith	100	●		●	
Carbink	101	●		●	
Sableye	102	●		●	
Rockruff	103	●		●	
Lycanroc	104	●			●
Spinda	105	●			
Tentacool	106	●	●	●	●
Tentacruel	107	●	●	●	●
Finneon	108	●	●	●	●
Lumineon	109	●	●	●	●
Wishiwashi	110	●	●	●	
Luvdisc	111	●	●	●	
Corsola	112	●		●	
Mareanie	113	●		●	
Toxapex	114	●	●		
Shellder	115	●			
Cloyster	116	↑			
Bagon	117	●			
Shelgon	118	●			
Salamence	119	●			
Lillipup	120		●		
Herdier	121		●		
Stoutland	122		●		
Eevee	123		●		
Vaporeon	124		●		
Jolteon	125		●		
Flareon	126		●		
Espeon	127		●		
Umbreon	128		●		
Leafeon	129		●		
Glaceon	130		●		
Sylveon	131		●		
Mudbray	132		●	●	●
Mudsdale	133		●	●	●
Igglybuff	134		●		

Pokémon	No.	1	2	3	4
Jigglypuff	135	●			
Wigglytuff	136	●			
Tauros	137	↑			↑
Miltank	138	●			●
Surskit	139	●	●		
Masquerain	140	●	●		
Dewpider	141	●	●		
Araquanid	142	●	●		
Fomantis	143	●			
Lurantis	144	●			
Morelull	145	●	●		
Shiinotic	146	●	●		
Paras	147	●	●		
Parasect	148	●	●		
Poliwag	149	●	●		
Poliwhirl	150	●	●		
Poliwrath	151	●	●		
Politoed	152	●	●		
Goldeen	153	●	●		
Seaking	154	●	●		
Feebas	155	●			
Milotic	156	●			
Alomomola	157	●			
Fletchling	158	●			
Fletchinder	159	●			
Talonflame	160	●			
Salandit	161	●			
Salazzle	162	●			
Cubone	163	●			
Marowak	164	●			
Kangaskhan	165	●			
Magby	166	●			
Magmar	167	●			
Magmortar	168	●			
Stufful	169	●			●
Bewear	170	●			●
Bounsweet	171	●			
Steenee	172	●			
Tsareena	173	●			
Comfey	174	●			
Pinsir	175	●			●
Oranguru	176	●			
Passimian	177	●			
Goomy	178	●	●	●	
Sliggoo	179	●	●	●	
Goodra	180	●	●	●	
Castform	181	●	●	●	
Wimpod	182	●			●
Golisopod	183	●			●
Staryu	184	●			
Starmie	185	●			
Sandygast	186	●			
Palossand	187	●			
Cranidos	188	●			
Rampardos	189	●			

POKÉMON	ALOLA POKÉDEX NO.	MELEMELE POKÉDEX	AKALA POKÉDEX	ULA'ULA POKÉDEX	PONI POKÉDEX
Shieldon	190		●		
Bastiodon	191		●		
Archen	192		●		
Archeops	193		●		
Tirtouga	194		●		
Carracosta	195		●		
Phantump	196		●		
Trevenant	197		●		
Nosepass	198		●		
Probopass	199		●		
Pyukumuku	200		●		
Chinchou	201		●		
Lanturn	202		●		
Trubbish	206			●	
Garbodor	207			●	
Skarmory	208			●	●
Ditto	209			●	
Cleffa	210			●	
Clefairy	211			●	
Clefable	212			●	
Minior	213			●	
Beldum	214			●	
Metang	215			●	
Metagross	216			●	
Porygon	217			●	
Porygon2	218			●	
Porygon-Z	219			●	
Pancham	220			●	
Pangoro	221			●	
Komala	222		●		
Torkoal	223			●	
Turtonator	224			●	
Togedemaru	225			●	
Elekid	226			●	
Electabuzz	227			●	
Electivire	228			●	
Geodude	229			●	
Graveler	230			●	
Golem	231			●	
Sandile	232			●	
Krokorok	233			●	
Krookodile	234			●	
Trapinch	235			●	
Vibrava	236			●	
Flygon	237			●	
Gible	238			●	
Gabite	239			●	
Garchomp	240			●	
Klefki	241			●	
Mimikyu	242			●	
Bruxish	243			●	
Drampa	244			●	
Absol	245			●	
Snorunt	246			●	
Glalie	247			●	
Froslass	248			●	
Sneasel	249			●	
Weavile	250			●	
Sandshrew	251			●	
Sandslash	252			●	
Vulpix	253			●	
Ninetales	254			●	
Vanillite	255			●	
Vanillish	256			●	
Vanilluxe	257			●	
Snubbull	258				●
Granbull	259				●
Shellos	260				●
Gastrodon	261				●
Relicanth	262				●
Dhelmise	263				●
Carvanha	264				●
Sharpedo	265				●
Wailmer	266				●
Wailord	267				●
Lapras	268				●
Exeggcute	269				●
Exeggutor	270				●
Jangmo-o	271				●
Hakamo-o	272				●
Kommo-o	273				●
Emolga	274				●
Scyther	275				●
Scizor	276				●
Murkrow	277				●
Honchkrow	278				●
Riolu	279				●
Lucario	280				●
Dratini	281				●
Dragonair	282				●
Dragonite	283				●
Aerodactyl	284				●
Tapu Koko	285	●			
Tapu Lele	286		●		
Tapu Bulu	287			●	
Tapu Fini	288				●

Learn the Techniques for Catching Wild Pokémon

You catch wild Pokémon by throwing Poké Balls at them. This is the most basic method required for completing your Pokédex. But before you try to take on the challenge of completing the Alola Pokédex, you should learn the more advanced techniques that will make it easier to catch the Pokémon you want. If you use these techniques, it should become significantly easier to catch wild Pokémon.

❖ Techniques to know for catching Pokémon

Basic Technique 1 — Reduce the wild Pokémon's HP as much as possible

Throwing a Poké Ball at a wild Pokémon is no guarantee that you'll catch it—it may still escape from the ball! That's because the Pokémon is still bursting with fight and spirit. Use moves to attack the Pokémon and lower its HP, and you'll find that your chances of catching it go up quite a lot once it's been weakened.

Reduce the Pokémon's HP until it's in the red

Basic Technique 2 — Use status conditions on wild Pokémon

Some Pokémon moves can inflict status conditions on a target. If you inflict the Pokémon you're hoping to catch with a status condition, it can make it easier to catch. The Asleep status condition is especially effective in this way. Try lowering your opponent's HP down to the bare minimum, then dish out a status condition on top!

Putting targets to sleep is the way to go!

Practical Technique 1 — Throw out a Quick Ball first

A Quick Ball has the unique effect of being more likely to catch a Pokémon if it is used on the very first turn in a battle. You might even catch a Legendary Pokémon in a single try! When you run into a Pokémon that you want to catch, start by throwing out a Quick Ball and giving this technique a shot.

Practical Technique 2 — Use the right kind of Poké Ball for the kind of Pokémon you want to catch

When you're throwing out Ultra Ball after Ultra Ball and yet you just can't seem to catch the Pokémon you want, then it may be time to use other Poké Balls. Try using a Dusk Ball if you're in a cave, or maybe a Dive Ball if you're on the water surface. Choosing the right kind of Poké Ball to use will also boost your chances of catching Pokémon.

Become an expert in the features of the different Poké Balls

Many different kinds of Poké Balls appear in *Pokémon Sun* and *Pokémon Moon*. The ones that you can buy at any Poké Mart can be considered the "basic" varieties. Each different kind of Poké Ball has its own unique characteristics, though. Learn how they function differently, and use the right ball for each Pokémon and location.

❖ Basic Poké Balls

Poké Ball

A basic ball that can be used for catching Pokémon.

- Available at Poké Marts once:
You start the game

Great Ball

A ball that makes it even easier to catch Pokémon than a Poké Ball does.

- Available at Poké Marts once:
You clear Ilima's trial on Melemele Island

Ultra Ball

A ball that makes it even easier to catch Pokémon than a Great Ball does.

- Available at Poké Marts once:
You clear Mallow's trial on Akala Island

Master Ball

The ultimate ball, which allows you to catch any Pokémon without fail.

- How to obtain:
Receive one from Gladion after you defeat Aether President Lusamine in battle at Aether Paradise

Premier Ball

A ball that functions like a normal Poké Ball. It is given out to commemorate some special event.

- How to obtain:
Receive one if you buy 10 or more Poké Balls at a time

❖ Poké Balls that function in unique ways

Quick Ball

A ball that is more effective at catching Pokémon when it is used as soon as battle begins.

- Available at the following Poké Mart:
In the Pokémon Center on Route 8 (Akala Island)

Timer Ball

A ball that becomes more effective at catching Pokémon the more turns have passed in battle.

- Available at the following Poké Mart:
In the Pokémon Center in Paniola Town (Akala Island)

Heal Ball

A ball that will restore max HP and remove any status conditions for the Pokémon caught with it.

- Available at the following Poké Mart:
In the Pokémon Center on Route 2 (Melemele Island)

Dusk Ball

A ball that is more effective at catching Pokémon at nighttime and in dark places like caves.

- Available at the following Poké Mart:
In the Pokémon Center on Route 8 (Akala Island)

Net Ball

A ball that makes it even easier to catch Bug- or Water-type Pokémon.

- Available at the following Poké Mart:
In the Pokémon Center in Paniola Town (Akala Island)

Dive Ball

A ball that makes it easier to catch Pokémon that live in the water.

- Available at the following Poké Mart:
In the Pokémon Center on Route 8 (Akala Island)

Nest Ball

A ball that is more effective at catching a target Pokémon the lower its level is.

- Available at the following Poké Mart:
In the Pokémon Center on Route 2 (Melemele Island)

Luxury Ball

A ball that makes the Pokémon you catch with it grow friendly toward you more quickly.

- Available at the following Poké Mart:
In the Pokémon Center on Route 2 (Melemele Island)

Repeat Ball

A ball that makes it easier to catch a Pokémon from a species that you have caught before.

- Available at the following Poké Mart:
In the Pokémon Center in Paniola Town (Akala Island)

Beast Ball

A special ball that was developed to catch Ultra Beasts.

- How to obtain:
During the Looker Episode after entering the Hall of Fame (p. 262)

Tip — Catch lots of Pokémon if you want to get a critical capture!

As you catch more and more wild Pokémon, you increase the likelihood that you will be able to catch Pokémon. This is because you are increasing the chances that you will trigger a critical capture, a special phenomena in which you throw a Poké Ball and it shakes just once before catching a Pokémon.

Raise Pokémon That Are Good for Catching Others

When you are trying to catch wild Pokémon, it is important to add Pokémon to your party that are well-suited to Pokémon catching. Try raising some Pokémon that reduce a wild Pokémon's HP to 1 and even inflict status conditions, through the right combination of moves and Abilities. This is an essential technique for completing the Alola Pokédex.

❖ Example Pokémon from the Alola Pokédex that are great for catching

Evolve Paras into Parasect and have it learn these moves

> **Evolution Conditions**
> Level up Paras to Lv. 24

| MOVE | Spore | GRASS |
| MOVE | False Swipe | NORMAL |

Use the move Spore first to make the target Asleep. Once you've done that, use False Swipe to reduce its HP to 1 and then throw that Poké Ball!

HOW TO OBTAIN PARASECT

Catch a Paras in the patches of tall grass near the entrance in Akala Island's Brooklet Hill during the day, and level it up to Lv. 24.

Have Absol learn these moves

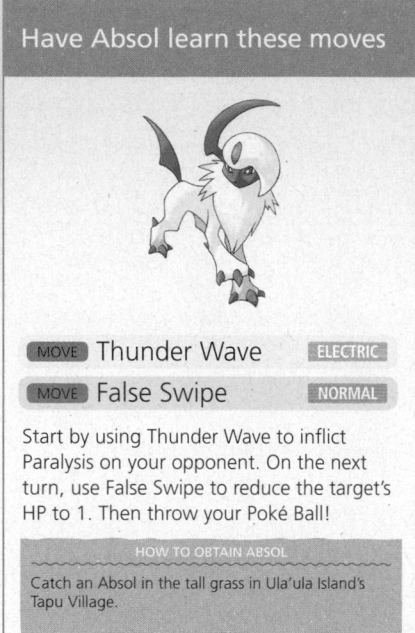

| MOVE | Thunder Wave | ELECTRIC |
| MOVE | False Swipe | NORMAL |

Start by using Thunder Wave to inflict Paralysis on your opponent. On the next turn, use False Swipe to reduce the target's HP to 1. Then throw your Poké Ball!

HOW TO OBTAIN ABSOL

Catch an Absol in the tall grass in Ula'ula Island's Tapu Village.

Evolve Yungoos into Gumshoos and have it learn these moves

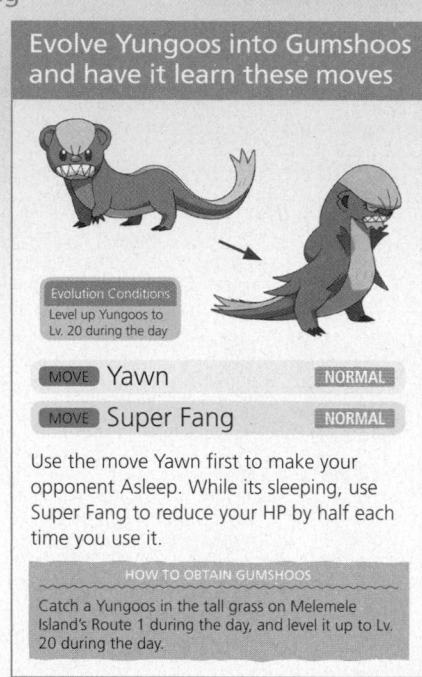

> **Evolution Conditions**
> Level up Yungoos to Lv. 20 during the day

| MOVE | Yawn | NORMAL |
| MOVE | Super Fang | NORMAL |

Use the move Yawn first to make your opponent Asleep. While its sleeping, use Super Fang to reduce your HP by half each time you use it.

HOW TO OBTAIN GUMSHOOS

Catch a Yungoos in the tall grass on Melemele Island's Route 1 during the day, and level it up to Lv. 20 during the day.

Go to Another World to Move Between Day and Night

When you want to catch a Pokémon that only appears during a set time period, why not just travel in time? After you fulfill certain conditions, visit the Altar of the Sunne in *Pokémon Sun* or the Altar of the Moone in *Pokémon Moon* to move through time and space! For more details, turn to page 257.

In *Pokémon Sun*

In *Pokémon Moon*

❖ How to move from nighttime to daytime in *Pokémon Sun*

1	Enter the Hall of Fame
2	Have Solgaleo in your party
3	Go to the Altar of the Sunne on Poni Island when it is nighttime
4	Examine the distortion to move to an alternate world where it is daytime

❖ How to move from daytime to nighttime in *Pokémon Moon*

1	Enter the Hall of Fame
2	Have Lunala in your party
3	Go to the Altar of the Moone on Poni Island when it is daytime
4	Examine the distortion to move to an alternate world where it is nighttime

Turn back to page 217 for more about the time periods in these games. ▷

Tip

Get Cosmog in an alternate world!

After you travel to the alternate world, visit the lake on Ula'ula Island and you will see both Solgaleo and Lunala appear together for a moment, before both disappear somewhere. After they disappear, a Cosmog will appear and you can claim it for your team. Read more on page 257.

Catch Pokémon That Appear in the Tall Grass and More

In order to find Pokémon you haven't yet caught, you'll need to know where those Pokémon live and how to meet them. Refer to the list below to familiarize yourself with where you can find particular Pokémon. Once you obtain each of the Pokémon you're looking for, you can check it off in the box beside its name.

A wild Stufful appeared!

❖ Examples of the environs where wild Pokémon appear

Tall Grass	Caves	Deserts
Even in the same area or route, which Pokémon will appear can differ from one patch of grass to the next. 	You can encounter wild Pokémon anywhere that you go while walking through a cave. 	You can encounter wild Pokémon anywhere that you go while walking in a desert. 

For more details about which Pokémon appear in which patches of grass or fishing spots, please see *Pokémon Sun & Pokémon Moon: The Official Alola Region Strategy Guide.* ▶

❖ Wild Pokémon in the Alola Pokédex that appear in tall grass, caves, and deserts

Alola Pokédex 010
☑ Pikipek
Catch in the tall grass on the east side of Route 1 (Melemele Island)

Alola Pokédex 011
☑ Trumbeak
Catch in the tall grass on Route 8 (Akala Island)

Alola Pokédex 013
☑ Yungoos
Catch in the tall grass on the east side of Route 1 (Melemele Island) during the day

Alola Pokédex 014
☑ Gumshoos
Catch in the tall grass in the Akala Outskirts (Akala Island) during the day

Alola Pokédex 015
☑ Rattata (Alola Form)
Catch in the tall grass on the east side of Route 1 (Melemele Island) at night

Alola Pokédex 016
☑ Raticate (Alola Form)
Catch in the tall grass in the Akala Outskirts (Akala Island) at night

Alola Pokédex 017
☑ Caterpie
Catch in the tall grass on the east side of Route 1 (Melemele Island)

Alola Pokédex 018
☑ Metapod
Catch in the tall grass on the west side of Route 1 (Melemele Island)

Alola Pokédex 019
☑ Butterfree
Catch among the yellow flowers in Melemele Meadow (Melemele Island)

Alola Pokédex 020
☑ Ledyba
Catch in the tall grass on the east side of Route 1 (Melemele Island) during the day

Alola Pokédex 021
☑ Ledian
Catch in the tall grass in Malie Garden (Ula'ula Island) during the day

Alola Pokédex 022
☑ Spinarak
Catch in the tall grass on the east side of Route 1 (Melemele Island) at night

Alola Pokédex 023
☑ Ariados
Catch in the tall grass in Malie Garden (Ula'ula Island) at night

Alola Pokédex 024
☑ Pichu
Catch in the tall grass near Iki Town on Route 1 (Melemele Island)

Alola Pokédex 027
☑ Grubbin
Catch in the tall grass near Iki Town on Route 1 (Melemele Island)

Alola Pokédex 028
☑ Charjabug
Catch in the tall grass on Blush Mountain (Ula'ula Island)

Alola Pokédex 030
☑ Bonsly
Catch in the tall grass on the west side of Route 1 (Melemele Island)

Alola Pokédex 035
☑ Munchlax
Catch in the tall grass on the west side of Route 1 (Melemele Island)

Alola Pokédex 037
☑ Slowpoke
Catch in the tall grass in the Hau'oli Outskirts (Melemele Island)

Alola Pokédex 040
☑ Wingull
Catch in the tall grass in the Hau'oli Outskirts (Melemele Island)

Alola Pokédex 041
☑ Pelipper
Catch in the tall grass in Tapu Village (Ula'ula Island)

Alola Pokédex 042
☑ Abra
Catch in the tall grass in Hau'oli City (Melemele Island)

Alola Pokédex 045
☑ Meowth (Alola Form)
Catch in the tall grass around the Trainers' School (Melemele Island)

Alola Pokédex 047
☑ Magnemite
Catch in the tall grass around the Trainers' School (Melemele Island)

Alola Pokédex 050
☑ Grimer (Alola Form)
Catch in the tall grass around the Trainers' School (Melemele Island)

Alola Pokédex 052
☑ Growlithe
Catch in the tall grass on the north side of Route 2 (Melemele Island)

Alola Pokédex 054
☑ Drowzee
Catch in the tall grass on the south side of Route 2 (Melemele Island)

Alola Pokédex 055
☑ Hypno
Catch in the starred patches of tall grass in the Poni Plains (Poni Island)

Alola Pokédex 058
☑ Smeargle
Catch in the tall grass on the south side of Route 2 (Melemele Island)

Alola Pokédex 061
☑ Gastly
Catch in the tall grass in Hau'oli Cemetery (Melemele Island)

Alola Pokédex 062
☑ Haunter
Catch at the abandoned site of the Thrifty Megamart on Route 14 (Ula'ula Island)

Alola Pokédex 064
☑ Drifloon
Catch in the tall grass in Hau'oli Cemetery (Melemele Island) during the day

Alola Pokédex 066
☑ Misdreavus
Catch in the tall grass in Hau'oli Cemetery (Melemele Island) at night

Alola Pokédex 068
☑ Zubat
Catch in the tall grass in Hau'oli Cemetery (Melemele Island)

Alola Pokédex 069
☑ Golbat
Catch at the abandoned site of the Thrifty Megamart on Route 14 (Ula'ula Island)

Alola Pokédex 071
☑ Diglett (Alola Form)
Catch inside Verdant Cavern (Melemele Island)

Alola Pokédex 072
☑ Dugtrio (Alola Form)
Catch in Haina Desert (Ula'ula Island)

Alola Pokédex 073
☑ Spearow
Catch in the tall grass on the north side of Route 2 (Melemele Island)

Alola Pokédex 074
☑ Fearow
Catch in the tall grass on Route 10 (Ula'ula Island)

Alola Pokédex 079
☑ Mankey
Catch in the tall grass on Route 3 (Melemele Island)

Alola Pokédex 081
☑ Delibird
Catch in the tall grass on the north side of Route 3 (Melemele Island)

Alola Pokédex 082
☑ Oricorio (Pom-Pom Style)
Catch among the yellow flowers in Melemele Meadow (Melemele Island)

Alola Pokédex 082
☑ Oricorio (Pa'u Style)
Catch in the tall grass on the south side of Route 6 (Akala Island)

Alola Pokédex 082
☑ Oricorio (Baile Style)
Catch among the red flowers in Ula'ula Meadow (Ula'ula Island)

Alola Pokédex 082
☑ Oricorio (Sensu Style)
Catch in the tall grass in Poni Meadow (Poni Island)

Alola Pokédex 083
☑ Cutiefly
Catch in the tall grass on the north side of Route 2 (Melemele Island)

Alola Pokédex 084
☑ Ribombee
Catch among the red flowers or in the tall grass in Ula'ula Meadow (Ula'ula Island)

Alola Pokédex 085
☑ Petilil
Catch among the yellow flowers in Melemele Meadow (Melemele Island) (*Pokémon Moon* only)

Alola Pokédex 087
☑ Cottonee
Catch among the yellow flowers in Melemele Meadow (Melemele Island) (*Pokémon Sun* only)

Alola Pokédex 089
☑ Psyduck
Catch in the patches of tall grass on Brooklet Hill (Akala Island)

Alola Pokédex 090
☑ Golduck
Catch in the tall grass in the Poni Gauntlet (Poni Island)

Alola Pokédex 095
☑ Machop
Catch in the tall grass in Ten Carat Hill's Farthest Hollow (Melemele Island)

Alola Pokédex 096
☑ Machoke
Catch in the tall grass outside of Vast Poni Canyon's caves (Poni Island)

Alola Pokédex 098
☑ Roggenrola
Catch in the caves of Ten Carat Hill (Melemele Island)

Alola Pokédex 099
☑ Boldore
Catch in the tall grass outside of Vast Poni Canyon's caves (Poni Island)

Alola Pokédex 101
☑ Carbink
Catch in the caves of Ten Carat Hill (Melemele Island)

Alola Pokédex 103
☑ Rockruff
Catch in the tall grass in Ten Carat Hill's Farthest Hollow (Melemele Island)

Alola Pokédex 104
☑ Lycanroc (Midday Form)
Catch in the tall grass outside of Vast Poni Canyon's caves (Poni Island) during the day

Alola Pokédex 104
☑ Lycanroc (Midnight Form)
Catch in the tall grass outside of Vast Poni Canyon's caves (Poni Island) at night

Alola Pokédex 105
☑ Spinda
Catch in the tall grass in Ten Carat Hill's Farthest Hollow (Melemele Island)

Alola Pokédex 117 — **Bagon** — Catch in the tall grass on the south side of Route 3 (Melemele Island)	Alola Pokédex 120 — Lillipup — Catch in the tall grass on Route 4 (Akala Island)	Alola Pokédex 123 — Eevee — Catch in the tall grass on Route 4 (Akala Island)	Alola Pokédex 132 — Mudbray — Catch in the tall grass on Route 4 (Akala Island)	Alola Pokédex 133 — Mudsdale — Catch in the northwest patches of tall grass in the Poni Plains (Poni Island)
Alola Pokédex 134 — Igglybuff — Catch in the tall grass on Route 4 (Akala Island) during the day	Alola Pokédex 137 — Tauros — Catch in the tall grass in Paniola Ranch (Akala Island)	Alola Pokédex 138 — Miltank — Catch in the tall grass in Paniola Ranch (Akala Island)	Alola Pokédex 139 — Surskit — Catch in the patches of tall grass near the entrance of Brooklet Hill (Akala Island) at night	Alola Pokédex 140 — Masquerain — Catch in the tall grass in Malie Garden (Ula'ula Island) at night
Alola Pokédex 141 — Dewpider — Catch in the patches of tall grass on the southside of Brooklet Hill (Akala Island) during the day	Alola Pokédex 142 — Araquanid — Catch in the tall grass in Malie Garden (Ula'ula Island) during the day	Alola Pokédex 143 — Fomantis — Catch in the tall grass on Route 5 (Akala Island)	Alola Pokédex 145 — Morelull — Catch in the patches of tall grass near the entrance of Brooklet Hill (Akala Island) at night	Alola Pokédex 147 — Paras — Catch in the patches of tall grass near the entrance of Brooklet Hill (Akala Island) during the day
Alola Pokédex 149 — Poliwag — Catch in the patches of tall grass on the southside of Brooklet Hill (Akala Island)	Alola Pokédex 158 — Fletchling — Catch in the tall grass in Wela Volcano Park (Akala Island)	Alola Pokédex 159 — **Fletchinder** — Catch in the tall grass on Route 8 (Akala Island)	Alola Pokédex 161 — **Salandit** — Catch in the tall grass in Wela Volcano Park (Akala Island)	Alola Pokédex 163 — Cubone — Catch in the tall grass in Wela Volcano Park (Akala Island)
Alola Pokédex 165 — Kangaskhan — Catch in the tall grass in Wela Volcano Park (Akala Island)	Alola Pokédex 166 — **Magby** — Catch in the tall grass in Wela Volcano Park (Akala Island)	Alola Pokédex 169 — Stufful — Catch in the tall grass on Route 8 (Akala Island)	Alola Pokédex 170 — Bewear — Catch in the tall grass in the Poni Gauntlet (Poni Island)	Alola Pokédex 171 — Bounsweet — Catch in the tall grass on west side of Lush Jungle (Akala Island)
Alola Pokédex 174 — Comfey — Catch in the tall grass in Lush Jungle (Akala Island)	Alola Pokédex 175 — Pinsir — Catch in the tall grass in the north end of Lush Jungle (Akala Island)	Alola Pokédex 176 — Oranguru — Catch in the tall grass in Lush Jungle (Akala Island) (*Pokémon Moon only*)	Alola Pokédex 177 — **Passimian** — Catch in the tall grass in Lush Jungle (Akala Island) (*Pokémon Sun only*)	Alola Pokédex 196 — **Phantump** — Catch in the tall grass in Memorial Hill (Akala Island)
Alola Pokédex 198 — Nosepass — Catch in the tall grass in the Akala Outskirts (Akala Island)	Alola Pokédex 206 — **Trubbish** — Catch in the tall grass in Malie City's Outer Cape (Ula'ula Island)	Alola Pokédex 208 — Skarmory — Catch in the tall grass on Route 10 (Ula'ula Island)	Alola Pokédex 209 — Ditto — Catch in the tall grass on Mount Hokulani (Ula'ula Island)	Alola Pokédex 210 — Cleffa — Catch in the tall grass on Mount Hokulani (Ula'ula Island) at night
Alola Pokédex 213 — Minior — Catch in the tall grass on Mount Hokulani (Ula'ula Island)	Alola Pokédex 214 — Beldum — Catch in the tall grass on Mount Hokulani (Ula'ula Island)	Alola Pokédex 220 — **Pancham** — Catch in the tall grass on Route 10 (Ula'ula Island)	Alola Pokédex 222 — Komala — Catch in the tall grass on Route 11 (Ula'ula Island)	Alola Pokédex 223 — **Torkoal** — Catch in the tall grass on Route 12 (Ula'ula Island)
Alola Pokédex 224 — **Turtonator** — Catch in the tall grass on Blush Mountain (Ula'ula Island) (*Pokémon Sun only*)	Alola Pokédex 225 — Togedemaru — Catch in the tall grass on Blush Mountain (Ula'ula Island)	Alola Pokédex 226 — Elekid — Catch in the tall grass on Route 12 (Ula'ula Island)	Alola Pokédex 229 — Geodude (Alola Form) — Catch in the tall grass on Route 12 (Ula'ula Island)	Alola Pokédex 230 — Graveler (Alola Form) — Catch in the brown tall grass on Route 17 (Ula'ula Island)
Alola Pokédex 232 — Sandile — Catch in Haina Desert (Ula'ula Island)	Alola Pokédex 241 — Klefki — Catch at the abandoned site of the Thrifty Megamart on Route 14 (Ula'ula Island)	Alola Pokédex 242 — **Mimikyu** — Catch at the abandoned site of the Thrifty Megamart on Route 14 (Ula'ula Island)	Alola Pokédex 244 — Drampa — Catch in the cave inside Mount Lanakila (Ula'ula Island) (*Pokémon Moon only*)	Alola Pokédex 245 — **Absol** — Catch in the tall grass in Tapu Village (Ula'ula Island)
Alola Pokédex 246 — Snorunt — Catch in the tall grass in Tapu Village (Ula'ula Island)	Alola Pokédex 249 — **Sneasel** — Catch in the tall grass on Mount Lanakila (Ula'ula Island)	Alola Pokédex 251 — Sandshrew (Alola Form) — Catch in the tall grass in Tapu Village (Ula'ula Island) (*Pokémon Moon only*)	Alola Pokédex 253 — Vulpix (Alola Form) — Catch in the tall grass in Tapu Village (Ula'ula Island) (*Pokémon Sun only*)	Alola Pokédex 259 — Granbull — Catch in the tall grass in the Poni Wilds (Poni Island)
Alola Pokédex 261 — Gastrodon (East Sea) — Catch in the tall grass in the Poni Wilds (Poni Island)	Alola Pokédex 269 — Exeggcute — Catch in the tall grass on Exeggutor Island (Poni Island)	Alola Pokédex 270 — Exeggutor (Alola Form) — Catch in the tall grass on Exeggutor Island (Poni Island)	Alola Pokédex 271 — **Jangmo-o** — Catch in the tall grass outside of Vast Poni Canyon's caves (Poni Island)	Alola Pokédex 277 — Murkrow — Catch in the tall grass outside of Vast Poni Canyon's caves (Poni Island)
Alola Pokédex 279 — **Riolu** — Catch in the tall grass in Poni Grove (Poni Island)				

Catch Pokémon That Appear as Allies in SOS Battles

The wild Pokémon of the Alola region have a tendency to call on allies during battle. The Pokémon that they call on are most often of the same species, but not always. There are some Pokémon in fact that only reveal themselves in the wild when they are called upon as an ally in an SOS battle.

❖ Things that increase the likelihood that a Pokémon will call for allies

Adrenaline Orb

1	Reducing the wild Pokémon's HP
2	Using an Adrenaline Orb during the battle
3	Having a Pokémon with the Ability Intimidate, Pressure, or Unnerve at the head of your party
4	If the wild Pokémon tried to call an ally on the last turn but none appeared
5	If an ally was hit with a supereffective move on the same turn that it first appeared in

❖ **Wild Pokémon in the Alola Pokédex that only appear as allies in SOS battles**

Alola Pokédex 025	Alola Pokédex 031	Alola Pokédex 033	Alola Pokédex 036	Alola Pokédex 038
Pikachu	**Sudowoodo**	**Chansey**	**Snorlax**	**Slowbro**
Catch when it appears as an ally in a battle against the Pichu that appear in the tall grass near Iki Town on Route 1 (Melemele Island)	Catch when it appears as an ally in a battle against the Bonsly that appear in the tall grass on the west side of Route 1 (Melemele Island)	Catch when it appears as an ally in a battle against the Elekid that appear in the tall grass on Route 12 (Ula'ula Island)	Catch when it appears as an ally against the Munchlax that appear in the tall grass on the west side of Route 1 (Melemele Island)	Catch when it appears as an ally in a battle against the Slowpoke that appear in the tall grass on Kala'e Bay (Melemele Island)

Alola Pokédex 063	Alola Pokédex 070	Alola Pokédex 092	Alola Pokédex 094	Alola Pokédex 102
Gengar	**Crobat**	**Gyarados**	**Whiscash**	**Sableye**
Catch when it appears as an ally in a battle against the Haunter that appear in the abandoned site of the Thrifty Megamart on Route 14 (Ula'ula Island)	Catch when it appears as an ally in a battle against the Golbat that appear in the interior of Resolution Cave (Poni Island)	Catch when it appears as an ally in a battle against the Magikarp you can fish up at the fishing spots in Brooklet Hill (Akala Island)	Catch when it appears as an ally in a battle against the Barboach you can fish up at the fishing spots in Seaward Cave (Melemele Island)	Catch when it appears as an ally in a battle against the Carbink that appear in the caves of Ten Carat Hill (Melemele Island)

Alola Pokédex 113	Alola Pokédex 118	Alola Pokédex 119	Alola Pokédex 127	Alola Pokédex 128
Mareanie	**Shelgon**	**Salamence**	**Espeon**	**Umbreon**
Catch when it appears as an ally in a battle against the Corsola you can fish up at the fishing spot on Route 9 (Akala Island)	Catch when it appears as an ally in a battle against the Bagon that appear in the tall grass on Kala'e Bay (Melemele Island)	Catch when it appears as an ally in a battle against the Bagon that appear in the tall grass on the south side of Route 3 (Melemele Island)	Catch when it appears as an ally in a battle held during the day against the Eevee that appear in the tall grass on Route 4 (Akala Island)	Catch when it appears as an ally in a battle held at night against the Eevee that appear in the tall grass on Route 4 (Akala Island)

Alola Pokédex 135	Alola Pokédex 154	Alola Pokédex 167	Alola Pokédex 185	Alola Pokédex 207
Jigglypuff	**Seaking**	**Magmar**	**Starmie**	**Garbodor**
Catch when it appears as an ally in a battle against the Igglybuff that appear in the tall grass on Route 4 (Akala Island) during the day	Catch when it appears as an ally in a battle against the Goldeen you can fish up at the fishing spots in Brooklet Hill (Akala Island)	Catch when it appears as an ally in a battle against the Magby that appear in the tall grass in Wela Volcano Park (Akala Island)	Catch when it appears as an ally in a battle against the Staryu you can fish up at the fishing spots on Route 7 (Akala Island)	Catch when it appears as an ally in a battle against the Trubbish that appear in the tall grass in Malie City's Outer Cape (Ula'ula Island)

Alola Pokédex 211	Alola Pokédex 221	Alola Pokédex 227	Alola Pokédex 247	Alola Pokédex 272
Clefairy	**Pangoro**	**Electabuzz**	**Glalie**	**Hakamo-o**
Catch when it appears as an ally in a battle against the Cleffa that appear in the tall grass on Mount Hokulani (Ula'ula Island) at night	Catch when it appears as an ally in a battle against the Pancham that appear in the tall grass on Route 10 (Ula'ula Island)	Catch when it appears as an ally in a battle against the Elekid that appear in the tall grass on Route 12 (Ula'ula Island)	Catch when it appears as an ally in a battle against the Snorunt that appear in the tall grass on Mount Lanakila (Ula'ula Island)	Catch when it appears as an ally in a battle against the Jangmo-o that appear in the tall grass outside of Vast Poni Canyon's caves (Poni Island)

Alola Pokédex 273	Alola Pokédex 280	Alola Pokédex 282	Alola Pokédex 283	
Kommo-o	**Lucario**	**Dragonair**	**Dragonite**	
Catch when it appears as an ally in a battle against the Jangmo-o that appear in the tall grass outside of Vast Poni Canyon's caves (Poni Island)	Catch when it appears as an ally in a battle against the Riolu that appear in the tall grass in Poni Grove (Poni Island)	Catch when it appears as an ally in a battle against the Dratini you can fish up at the fishing spots in Vast Poni Canyon's third cave (Poni Island)	Catch when it appears as an ally in a battle against the Dratini you can fish up at the fishing spots along the Poni Gauntlet (Poni Island)	

Catch SOS Ally Pokémon in Special Weather Conditions

In some locations, you may find that the ally Pokémon that appear in SOS battles differ depending on the current weather conditions. If there is a Pokémon that you're hoping to catch, use moves like Rain Dance, Hail, and Sandstorm to change the weather. The Pokémon covered below do not appear in the wild under any other conditions, so if you want to catch them, you'll want to use this method!

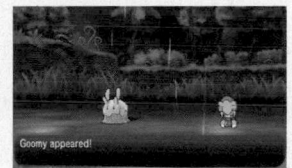

Goomy appeared!

❖ **Wild Pokémon in the Alola Pokédex that only appear as allies during certain weather conditions**

Alola Pokédex 150	Alola Pokédex 151	Alola Pokédex 152	Alola Pokédex 178	Alola Pokédex 179
Poliwhirl	**Poliwrath**	**Politoed**	**Goomy**	**Sliggoo**
Catch when it appears as an ally while it is raining during a battle against the Pokémon that appear in the tall grass in Malie Garden (Ula'ula Island)	Catch when it appears as an ally while it is raining during the day in a battle against the Pokémon that appear in the tall grass in Malie Garden (Ula'ula Island)	Catch when it appears as an ally while it is raining at night during a battle against the Pokémon that appear in the tall grass in Malie Garden (Ula'ula Island)	Catch when it appears as an ally while it is raining during a battle against the Pokémon that appear in the tall grass near Route 5 in Lush Jungle (Akala Island)	Catch when it appears as an ally while it is raining during a battle against the Pokémon that appear in the tall grass on Exeggutor Island (Poni Island)

Alola Pokédex 181	Alola Pokédex 239	Alola Pokédex 255	Alola Pokédex 256	
Castform	**Gabite**	**Vanillite**	**Vanillish**	
Catch when it appears as an ally while it is raining, hailing, or if there is a sandstorm raging during a battle against the Pokémon that appear in the tall grass near Route 5 in Lush Jungle (Akala Island)	Catch when it appears as an ally while a sandstorm is raging during a battle against the Pokémon that appear in Haina Desert (Ula'ula Island)	Catch when it appears as an ally while it is hailing during a battle against the Pokémon that appear in the tall grass in Tapu Village (Ula'ula Island)	Catch when it appears as an ally while it is raining during a battle against the Pokémon that appear in the tall grass on Mount Lanakila (Ula'ula Island)	

Catch Pokémon That Appear on the Water Surface

When you travel across the surface of a body of water using Lapras Paddle and Sharpedo Jet, you may encounter some of the wild Pokémon that live in the water. These Pokémon can differ from the Pokémon that you may fish up with a Fishing Rod. When you run into one, try catching it with a Dive Ball or Net Ball.

❖ Wild Pokémon in the Alola Pokédex that appear on the water surface

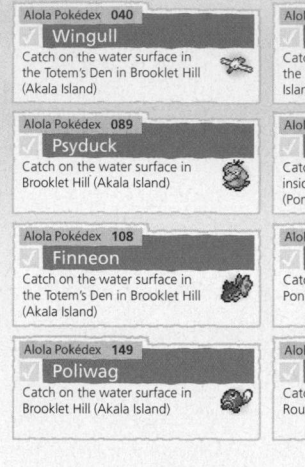
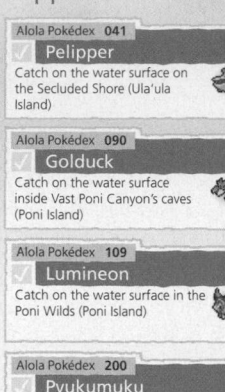

Alola Pokédex 040	Alola Pokédex 041	Alola Pokédex 068	Alola Pokédex 069
☑ Wingull	☑ Pelipper	☑ Zubat	☑ Golbat
Catch on the water surface in the Totem's Den in Brooklet Hill (Akala Island)	Catch on the water surface on the Secluded Shore (Ula'ula Island)	Catch on the water surface in Seaward Cave (Melemele Island)	Catch on the water surface inside Vast Poni Canyon's caves (Poni Island)

Alola Pokédex 089	Alola Pokédex 090	Alola Pokédex 106	Alola Pokédex 107
☑ Psyduck	☑ Golduck	☑ Tentacool	☑ Tentacruel
Catch on the water surface in Brooklet Hill (Akala Island)	Catch on the water surface inside Vast Poni Canyon's caves (Poni Island)	Catch on the water surface in the Totem's Den in Brooklet Hill (Akala Island)	Catch on the water surface in the Poni Wilds (Poni Island)

Alola Pokédex 108	Alola Pokédex 109	Alola Pokédex 139	Alola Pokédex 141
☑ Finneon	☑ Lumineon	☑ Surskit	☑ Dewpider
Catch on the water surface in the Totem's Den in Brooklet Hill (Akala Island)	Catch on the water surface in the Poni Wilds (Poni Island)	Catch on the water surface in Brooklet Hill (Akala Island) at night	Catch on the water surface in Brooklet Hill (Akala Island) during the day

Alola Pokédex 149	Alola Pokédex 200	Alola Pokédex 261	Alola Pokédex 268
☑ Poliwag	☑ Pyukumuku	☑ Gastrodon (East Sea)	☑ Lapras
Catch on the water surface in Brooklet Hill (Akala Island)	Catch on the water surface on Route 7 (Akala Island)	Catch on the water surface in the Poni Wilds (Poni Island)	Catch on the water surface in the Poni Wilds (Poni Island)

Catch Wild Pokémon Using Your Fishing Rod

If you go to a fishing spot and use your Fishing Rod, you can encounter Pokémon that live in the water. Among such fishing spots, though, you'll find that some have bubble erupting from them—these are rare fishing spots. You are more likely to find rare wild Pokémon that are difficult to encounter outside these rare fishing spots.

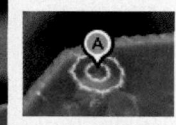

A bubbling rare fishing spot

❖ Actions that will cause rare fishing spots to disappear

1	Running as you approach a rare fishing spot
2	Approaching a rare fishing spot that is reached on land while riding on a Ride Pokémon
3	Approaching a rare fishing spot in the water while having Lapras swim at its top speed
4	Swimming over a rare fishing spot while riding on Lapras's back

Note: You cannot use your Fishing Rod while traveling across the water riding on Sharpedo.

❖ Wild Pokémon in the Alola Pokédex that appear at fishing spots

Alola Pokédex 091	Alola Pokédex 093	Alola Pokédex 110	Alola Pokédex 111	Alola Pokédex 112
☑ Magikarp	☑ Barboach	☑ Wishiwashi (Solo Form)	☑ Luvdisc	☑ Corsola
Catch by fishing it up at the fishing spots in Brooklet Hill (Akala Island)	Catch by fishing it up at the fishing spots in Seaward Cave (Melemele Island)	Catch by fishing it up at the fishing spots in the Totem's Den in Brooklet Hill (Akala Island)	Catch by fishing it up at the fishing spot on Route 9 (Akala Island)	Catch by fishing it up at the fishing spot on Route 9 (Akala Island)

Alola Pokédex 115	Alola Pokédex 153	Alola Pokédex 155	Alola Pokédex 157	Alola Pokédex 184
☑ Shellder	☑ Goldeen	☑ Feebas	☑ Alomomola	☑ Staryu
Catch by fishing it up at the fishing spots in Kala'e Bay (Melemele Island)	Catch by fishing it up at the fishing spots in Brooklet Hill (Akala Island)	Catch by fishing it up at the fishing spots in Brooklet Hill (Akala Island)	Catch by fishing it up at the fishing spots in the Totem's Den in Brooklet Hill (Akala Island)	Catch by fishing it up at the fishing spot on Route 7 (Akala Island)

Alola Pokédex 201	Alola Pokédex 243	Alola Pokédex 262	Alola Pokédex 263	Alola Pokédex 265
☑ Chinchou	☑ Bruxish	☑ Relicanth	☑ Dhelmise	☑ Sharpedo
Catch by fishing it up at the fishing spot on Route 8 (Akala Island)	Catch by fishing it up at the fishing spot on Secluded Shore (Ula'ula Island)	Catch by fishing it up at the fishing spots in the Poni Wilds (Poni Island)	Catch by fishing it up at the fishing spot in Seafolk Village (Poni Island)	Catch by fishing it up at the fishing spots on Poni Breaker Coast (Poni Island)

Alola Pokédex 266	Alola Pokédex 281
☑ Wailmer	☑ Dratini
Catch by fishing it up at the fishing spot in Seafolk Village (Poni Island)	Catch by fishing it up at the fishing spots in Vast Poni Canyon's caves (Poni Island)

Catch Wild Pokémon That Appear in Special Conditions

Some of the Pokémon in the Alola region are quite fiesty, and they may leap out to approach a passing Trainer on their own! You might be surprised by their gung-ho spirit at first, but you should know that many of the Pokémon that appear in this way are also very rare species. Don't miss your chance to catch them when they appear.

❖ Pokémon that appear in ambushes

Moving shadows in the grass

When walking through the tall grass, a shadow may appear and rush toward you. Catch the Pokémon that attacks!

Piles of Berries

If you examine the piles of Berries that can be found at the base of Berry trees, you may find that a Crabrawler appears from the pile to attack you!

Shadows cast from above

You may find shadows cast on the ground in places. These shadows are cast by Pokémon flying overhead. If you pass beneath one of these shadows, the Pokémon will attack.

Shadows that leap out of trees

When you approach some of the lush trees in Alola, shadows may leap out at you from their branches. Catch the Pokémon that attacks!

Shadows that leap out of bushes

Shadows sometimes leap out at you from low bushes you pass by. Catch the Pokémon that attacks!

Splashes on the water surface

When traveling across the water surface, you may hear and see splashes approaching you in the water. If you run into the splashes, a Pokémon will attack!

Moving sand clouds

On beaches and in the desert, you may see clouds of sand or dust moving about. If you run into one, the Pokémon that was causing the cloud will attack!

Tip

Wimpod can be found in places like Akala Island's Route 8 or Poni Island's Poni Wilds. If you get close to one, it will zip right off back into its hidey-hole. If you want to catch one, you may find that using Tauros Charge is effective. If you can make contact with a Wimpod before it runs away, it will be drawn into battle.

❖ Wild Pokémon in the Alola Pokédex that are encountered in special ways

Alola Pokédex 013 ☑ Yungoos	Alola Pokédex 014 ☑ Gumshoos	Alola Pokédex 015 ☑ Rattata (Alola Form)	Alola Pokédex 016 ☑ Raticate (Alola Form)	Alola Pokédex 056 ☑ Makuhita
Catch when you run into a moving shadow that appears among the tall grass on Route 2 (Melemele Island) during the day	Catch when you run into a moving shadow that appears among the tall grass in the Poni Plains (Poni Island) during the day	Catch when you run into a moving shadow that appears among the tall grass on Route 2 (Melemele Island) at night	Catch when you run into a moving shadow that appears among the tall grass in the Poni Plains (Poni Island) at night	Catch when you run into a moving shadow that appears among the tall grass on Route 2 (Melemele Island)
Alola Pokédex 057 ☑ Hariyama	**Alola Pokédex 059** ☑ Crabrawler	**Alola Pokédex 071** ☑ Diglett (Alola Form)	**Alola Pokédex 072** ☑ Dugtrio (Alola Form)	**Alola Pokédex 073** ☑ Spearow
Catch when you run into a moving shadow that appears among the tall grass in the Poni Plains (Poni Island)	Catch when one attacks you after you examine a pile of Berries at the base of a Berry tree.	Catch when you run into a dust cloud moving around on Route 5 (Akala Island)	Catch when you run into a sand cloud moving around in Haina Desert (Ula'ula Island)	Catch when you run into a shadow cast from above on Route 3 (Melemele Island)
Alola Pokédex 074 ☑ Fearow	**Alola Pokédex 075** ☑ Rufflet	**Alola Pokédex 076** ☑ Braviary	**Alola Pokédex 077** ☑ Vullaby	**Alola Pokédex 078** ☑ Mandibuzz
Catch from a shadow leaps that out at you from the shaking trees on Route 10 (Ula'ula Island)	Catch when you run into a shadow cast from above on Route 3 (Melemele Island) (*Pokémon Sun* only)	Catch when you run into a shadow cast from above in the Poni Plains (Poni Island) (*Pokémon Sun* only)	Catch when you run into a shadow cast from above on Route 3 (Melemele Island) (*Pokémon Moon* only)	Catch when you run into a shadow cast from above in the Poni Plains (Poni Island) (*Pokémon Moon* only)
Alola Pokédex 080 ☑ Primeape	**Alola Pokédex 085** ☑ Petilil	**Alola Pokédex 087** ☑ Cottonee	**Alola Pokédex 106** ☑ Tentacool	**Alola Pokédex 143** ☑ Fomantis
Catch from a shadow that leaps out at you from the shaking trees in the Poni Plains (Poni Island)	Catch from a shadow that leaps out at you from the shaking bushes in the Poni Plains (Poni Island) (*Pokémon Moon* only)	Catch a shadow that leaps out at you from the shaking bushes in the Poni Plains (Poni Island) (*Pokémon Sun* only)	Catch when you encounter splashing on the water surface off of Hano Beach (Akala Island)	Catch from a shadow that leaps out at you from the shaking tree on the west side of Lush Jungle (Akala Island)

Alola Pokédex 182	Alola Pokédex 184	Alola Pokédex 186	Alola Pokédex 208	Alola Pokédex 232
Wimpod	Staryu	Sandygast	Skarmory	Sandile
Catch when you run into a Wimpod that appears on Route 8 (Akala Island)	Catch when you run into a sand cloud moving around on Hano Beach (Akala Island)	Catch when you run into a sand cloud moving around on Hano Beach (Akala Island)	Catch from a shadow leaps that out at you from the shaking trees on Route 10 (Ula'ula Island)	Catch when you run into a sand cloud moving around in Haina Desert (Ula'ula Island)

Alola Pokédex 235	Alola Pokédex 266	Alola Pokédex 267	Alola Pokédex 274	Alola Pokédex 275
Trapinch	Wailmer	Wailord	Emolga	Scyther
Catch when you run into a sand cloud moving around in Haina Desert (Ula'ula Island)	Catch when you encounter splashing on the water surface in the Poni Wilds (Poni Island)	Catch when you encounter splashing on the water surface in the Poni Wilds (Poni Island)	Catch from a shadow that leaps out at you from the shaking trees in the Poni Plains (Poni Island)	Catch from a shadow that leaps out at you from the shaking bushes in the Poni Plains (Poni Island)

Obtain Ancient Pokémon Restored from Fossils

At Olivia's jewelry shop in Akala Island's Konikoni City, you can purchase Pokémon Fossils. The kinds of Fossils that you can buy differ between *Pokémon Sun* and *Pokémon Moon*. You should also know that you can only buy one of each particular kind of Fossil. Fossils can be restored into living Pokémon if you bring them to the Fossil Restoration Center found just off Route 8 on Akala Island.

Do you have any Fossils on you? Do you wanna turn 'em back into Pokémon?

❖ Pokémon in the Alola Pokédex that can be obtained by restoring Fossils

Alola Pokédex 188	Alola Pokédex 190	Alola Pokédex 192	Alola Pokédex 194
Cranidos	Shieldon	Archen	Tirtouga
Buy a Skull Fossil in Konikoni City, and have it restored at the Fossil Restoration Center off of Akala Island's Route 8 (*Pokémon Sun* only)	Buy an Armor Fossil in Konikoni City, and have it restored at the Fossil Restoration Center off of Akala Island's Route 8 (*Pokémon Moon* only)	Buy a Plume Fossil in Konikoni City, and have it restored at the Fossil Restoration Center off of Akala Island's Route 8 (*Pokémon Moon* only)	Buy a Cover Fossil in Konikoni City, and have it restored at the Fossil Restoration Center off of Akala Island's Route 8 (*Pokémon Sun* only)

Obtain Rare Pokémon during Your Adventures

There are a great many rare Pokémon that don't appear in the wild but are waiting to meeting you during your adventures in Alola. Some of these Pokémon may be given to you by other people, while others may be hatched from Pokémon Eggs. As you progress through the story, you will even get to meet the Legendary Pokémon. There are also Pokémon like Rowlet, Litten, and Popplio, which you will only be able to obtain one of in your copy of the games. Trade with friends or use the GTS (p. 31) to get these Pokémon for yourself!

Tip

How to obtain two Solgaleo or Lunala

Solgaleo is the Legendary Pokémon in *Pokémon Sun*, and Lunala is the Legendary Pokémon in *Pokémon Moon*—and you can obtain two of the Legendary Pokémon that appears in your version of the game! The first you can catch during the climax of the main story. The second is obtained by evolving the Cosmog that you can obtain by traveling to an alternate world (p. 257).

❖ Rare Pokémon in the Alola Pokédex you may be given or encounter during your adventures

Alola Pokédex 001	Alola Pokédex 004	Alola Pokédex 007	Alola Pokédex 123	Alola Pokédex 203
Rowlet	Litten	Popplio	Eevee	Type: Null
Receive from Hala in Iki Town (Melemele Island)	Receive from Hala in Iki Town (Melemele Island)	Receive from Hala in Iki Town (Melemele Island)	Hatch from the Pokémon Egg that you receive at the Pokémon Nursery in Paniola Ranch (Akala Island)	Receive from Gladion in Aether Paradise (2F) after entering the Hall of Fame

Alola Pokédex 217	Alola Pokédex 284	Alola Pokédex 285	Alola Pokédex 286	Alola Pokédex 287
Porygon	Aerodactyl	Tapu Koko	Tapu Lele	Tapu Bulu
Receive from an Aether Foundation member at the Aether House on Route 15 (Ula'ula Island) after entering the Hall of Fame	Receive from a woman in Seafolk Village (Poni Island)	Catch it within the Ruins of Conflict (Melemele Island) after defeating Professor Kukui at the Pokémon League	Catch it when you examine the statue within the Ruins of Life (Akala Island) after entering the Hall of Fame	Catch it when you examine the statue within the Ruins of Abundance (Ula'ula Island) after entering the Hall of Fame

Alola Pokédex 288	Alola Pokédex 289	Alola Pokédex 290	Alola Pokédex 291	Alola Pokédex 292
Tapu Fini	Cosmog	Cosmoem	Solgaleo	Lunala
Catch it when you examine the statue within the Ruins of Hope (Poni Island) after entering the Hall of Fame	See page 257 for details on how to obtain Cosmog	Level up Cosmog to Lv. 43	Catch it at the Altar of the Sunne in Vast Poni Canyon after visiting Ultra Space (*Pokémon Sun* only)	Catch it at the Altar of the Moone in Vast Poni Canyon after visiting Ultra Space (*Pokémon Moon* only)

Alola Pokédex 300
Necrozma
See page 268 for details on how to obtain Necrozma

Catch Ultra Beasts by Assisting the International Police

After you enter the Hall of fame, you will receive a request from the International Police. They want you to help with capturing certain Ultra Beasts (or UBs). Catching these Ultra Beasts is also necessary if you hope to complete your Alola Pokédex. Catch them using the special Beast Balls.

??? appeared!

Anabel   Looker   Beast Ball

❖ Techniques for catching Ultra Beasts

1	Put a Pokémon with a slightly lower level than the Ultra Beast at the head of your party
2	Use a Max Repel or another repellent when you enter the area where the Ultra Beast should appear
3	Only throw Beast Balls when you encounter an Ultra Beast

❖ The Ultra Beasts the International Police will ask you to capture

Alola Pokédex 293 — Nihilego
Work with the International Police after entering the Hall of Fame (p. 263), and catch it when it appears at Lv. 55 in either Wela Volcano Park or Diglett's Tunnel (Akala Island)

Alola Pokédex 294 — Buzzwole
Work with the International Police after entering the Hall of Fame (p. 264), and catch it when it appears at Lv. 65 within Melemele Meadow (Melemele Island) (*Pokémon Sun only*)

Alola Pokédex 295 — Pheromosa
Work with the International Police after entering the Hall of Fame (p. 264), and catch it when it appears at Lv. 60 in Verdant Cavern (Melemele Island) (*Pokémon Moon only*)

Alola Pokédex 296 — Xurkitree
Work with the International Police after entering the Hall of Fame (p. 265), and catch it when it appears at Lv. 65 in either Lush Jungle or Memorial Hill (Akala Island)

Alola Pokédex 297 — Celesteela
Work with the International Police after entering the Hall of Fame (p. 266), and catch it when it appears at Lv. 60 within Haina Desert or Malie Garden (Ula'ula Island) (*Pokémon Moon only*)

Alola Pokédex 298 — Kartana
Work with the International Police after entering the Hall of Fame (p. 266), and catch it when it appears at Lv. 60 on Route 17 or in Malie Garden (Ula'ula Island) (*Pokémon Sun only*)

Alola Pokédex 299 — Guzzlord
Work with the International Police after entering the Hall of Fame (p. 267), and catch it when it appears at Lv. 70 within the deepest part of Resolution Cave (Poni Island)

Collect Zygarde Cores and Zygarde Cells

After you obtain the Zygarde Cube on Akala Island, you will find that 5 Zygarde Cores appear around the Alola region, and a further 95 Zygarde Cells as well. These Cores and Cells seem to make up Zygarde's body and brain. By finding them and putting them back together, you'll be able to get a powerful Zygarde on your side.

❖ Recognizing Zygarde Cores and Cells

Zygarde Cores

Cores appear to make up Zygarde's brain or something like it. By collecting them, you can have Zygarde remember rare moves.

Zygarde Cells

Cells appear to make up the Zygarde's body. Some can only be found during the day, while others are only seen at night.

Assemble Cells and Cores at the Aether Base on Ula'ula Island's Route 16

Go to the Aether Base on Ula'ula Island's Route 16 when you've gathered enough Zygarde Cores and Cells to assemble them. If you choose "Assembly" on the Reassembly Unit, you can assemble the Cells and Cores into a Zygarde. Choosing "Separation" will let you separate Zygarde back out into its component Cells and Cores. When you assemble a Zygarde, the Forme that it will take will depend on the number of Cells and Cores that you used.

❖ How to assemble a Zygarde using Cores, Cells, and the Reassembly Unit

1 Go to the Aether Base	2 Assemble Cores and Cells	3 Create a Zygarde
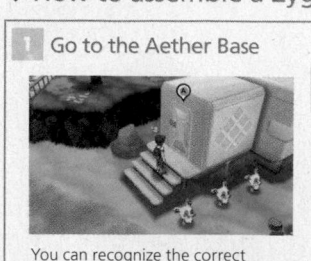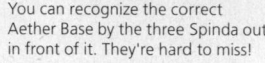	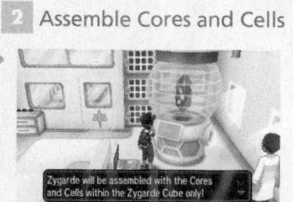	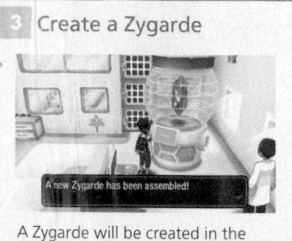
You can recognize the correct Aether Base by the three Spinda out in front of it. They're hard to miss!	Use the Reassembly Unit to assemble the Cores and Cells you have gathered into a Zygarde.	A Zygarde will be created in the Forme corresponding to the number of Cells and Cores used.

Consider bringing a Zygarde from *Pokémon X* or *Pokémon Y* using *Pokémon Bank*

If you bring a Zygarde from either *Pokémon X* or *Pokémon Y* using *Pokémon Bank* (p. 31), you can separate it out into 50 Cells. If you add these 50 Cells to a further 50 Cells that you collect around the Alola region, you can create a Zygarde that can take on its Complete Forme.

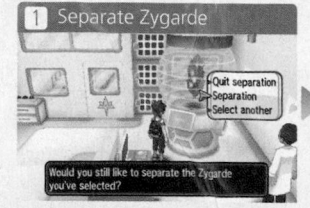

Hints for collecting Zygarde Cores and Cells

The location of every last Zygarde Core and Cell was included in *Pokémon Sun & Pokémon Moon: The Official Alola Region Strategy Guide*, and below you will find a simplified list that provides hints about locations where you can find Zygarde Cores and Cells as well. Zygarde can learn unique moves that can only be learned by using its Zygarde Cores (on next page), so be sure to get them all. You can change the Forme of your assembled Zygarde (between 10% Forme or 50% Forme) and have it learn moves using the Zygarde Cube.

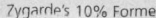

Zygarde's 10% Forme

Zygarde's 50% Forme

Zygarde's Complete Forme

❖ Hints on where to find Zygarde Cores and Cells around Alola

LOCATIONS	DAY ONLY	DAY OR NIGHT	NIGHT ONLY	TOTAL	CONDITIONS OR NOTES
Melemele Island — Hau'oli Outskirts	—	2	1	3	After obtaining Zygarde Cube / One is a Core that teaches Extreme Speed
Melemele Island — Route 1	2	—	—	2	After obtaining Zygarde Cube
Melemele Island — Iki Town	—	1	1	2	After obtaining Zygarde Cube / One is a Core that teaches Thousand Arrows
Melemele Island — Hau'oli City	—	1	1	2	After obtaining Zygarde Cube
Melemele Island — Route 2	—	1	—	1	After obtaining Zygarde Cube
Melemele Island — Hau'oli Cemetery	—	1	—	1	After obtaining Zygarde Cube
Melemele Island — Verdant Cavern	—	1	—	1	After obtaining Zygarde Cube
Melemele Island — Route 3	1	1	—	2	After obtaining Zygarde Cube
Melemele Island — Kala'e Bay	—	1	—	1	After obtaining Zygarde Cube
Akala Island — Heahea City	—	1	1	2	—
Akala Island — Route 4	—	1	—	1	—
Akala Island — Paniola Ranch	1	—	1	2	—
Akala Island — Royal Avenue	1	—	1	2	—
Akala Island — Route 7	—	1	—	1	—
Akala Island — Wela Volcano Park	—	1	—	1	—
Akala Island — Route 8	1	1	—	2	—
Akala Island — Route 5	—	1	—	1	After clearing Kiawe's trial
Akala Island — Lush Jungle	—	1	—	1	Requires Machamp Shove
Akala Island — Diglett's Tunnel	—	1	—	1	—
Akala Island — Konikoni City	—	1	1	2	One is a Core that teaches Dragon Dance
Akala Island — Akala Outskirts	—	1	—	1	—
Akala Island — Hano Beach	1	1	—	2	—
Ula'ula Island — Malie City	1	—	1	2	—
Ula'ula Island — Malie Garden	—	1	—	1	—
Ula'ula Island — Malie City's Outer Cape	1	—	—	1	—
Ula'ula Island — Route 10	1	—	—	1	—
Ula'ula Island — Hokulani Observatory (Mount Hokulani)	—	—	1	1	—
Ula'ula Island — Route 11	—	—	1	1	—
Ula'ula Island — Route 12	—	2	—	2	—
Ula'ula Island — Blush Mountain	—	1	—	1	—
Ula'ula Island — Secluded Shore	1	—	1	2	—
Ula'ula Island — Route 13	—	1	1	2	—
Ula'ula Island — Tapu Village	—	1	—	1	—
Ula'ula Island — Route 15	1	—	1	2	—
Ula'ula Island — Route 14	—	1	1	2	—
Ula'ula Island — Haina Desert	—	1	—	1	—
Ula'ula Island — Ruins of Abundance	—	1	—	1	—
Ula'ula Island — Route 16	1	—	—	1	—
Ula'ula Island — Ula'ula Meadow	—	2	—	2	—
Ula'ula Island — Route 17	—	3	—	3	One is a Core that teaches Thousand Waves
Ula'ula Island — Po Town	1	—	1	2	—
Aether Paradise	1	3	1	5	After clearing the Poni Island Grand Trial
Poni Island — Seafolk Village	—	2	—	2	—
Poni Island — Poni Wilds	1	1	1	3	—
Poni Island — Ancient Poni Path	1	2	1	4	One is a Core that teaches Core Enforcer
Poni Island — Poni Breaker Coast	1	—	1	2	—
Poni Island — Ruins of Hope	—	1	—	1	—
Poni Island — Vast Poni Canyon	—	4	—	4	—
Ula'ula Island — Mount Lanakila	—	2	—	2	—
Melemele Island — Ruins of Conflict	—	1	—	1	After entering the Hall of Fame
Poni Island — Poni Grove	—	2	—	2	After entering the Hall of Fame
Poni Island — Poni Plains	1	1	1	3	After entering the Hall of Fame
Poni Island — Poni Meadow	—	1	—	1	After entering the Hall of Fame
Poni Island — Resolution Cave	1	1	1	3	After entering the Hall of Fame
Poni Island — Poni Coast	—	2	—	2	After entering the Hall of Fame
Poni Island — Poni Gauntlet	—	2	—	2	After entering the Hall of Fame

Obtain Pokémon through Leveling Up and Evolving

Some species of Pokémon cannot be encountered in the wild. Many of them can be obtained by having an earlier Evolution take part in battles to level up until it evolves. In *Pokémon Sun* and *Pokémon Moon*, there are many ways you can help your Pokémon level up. Use them to your advantage, and help your Pokémon evolve!

❖ Evolution example: Pikipek to Toucannon

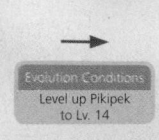
Evolution Conditions
Level up Pikipek to Lv. 14

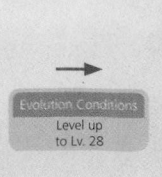
Evolution Conditions
Level up to Lv. 28

Pikipek — Trumbeak — Toucannon

❖ Ways to quickly help Pokémon gain Exp. Points and evolve

1 Make them more affectionate with Pokémon Refresh

Take good care of your Pokémon in Pokémon Refresh and once their Affection level has reached two hearts, the number of Exp. Points it earns from battles will be boosted by 20%.

2 Have your Pokémon play at Poké Pelago

At Isle Evelup, your Pokémon can gain Exp. Points if you give it a Level Boost Drink to drink while it's playing on the equipment.

3 Have the Pokémon hold a Lucky Egg

If you have a Pokémon hold a Lucky Egg, the number of Exp. Points it earns from battles will be boosted by 50%.

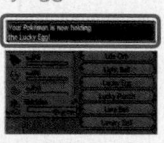 

Lucky Egg

4 Use the food stalls in Festival Plaza

The food stalls in Festival Plaza offer menu items that can raise a Pokémon's level if you order them.

❖ Pokémon in the Alola Pokédex that evolve by leveling up

Alola Pokédex 002 Dartrix	Alola Pokédex 003 Decidueye	Alola Pokédex 005 Torracat	Alola Pokédex 006 Incineroar	Alola Pokédex 008 Brionne
Level up Rowlet to Lv. 17	Level up Dartrix to Lv. 34	Level up Litten to Lv. 17	Level up Torracat to Lv. 34	Level up Popplio to Lv. 17
Alola Pokédex 009 Primarina	Alola Pokédex 011 Trumbeak	Alola Pokédex 012 Toucannon	Alola Pokédex 018 Metapod	Alola Pokédex 019 Butterfree
Level up Brionne to Lv. 34.	Level up Pikipek to Lv. 14	Level up Trumbeak to Lv. 28	Level up Caterpie to Lv. 7	Level up Metapod to Lv. 10
Alola Pokédex 021 Ledian	Alola Pokédex 023 Ariados	Alola Pokédex 028 Charjabug	Alola Pokédex 038 Slowbro	Alola Pokédex 041 Pelipper
Level up Ledyba to Lv. 18	Level up Spinarak to Lv. 22	Level up Grubbin to Lv. 20	Level up Slowpoke to Lv. 37	Level up Wingull to Lv. 25
Alola Pokédex 043 Kadabra	Alola Pokédex 048 Magneton	Alola Pokédex 051 Muk (Alola Form)	Alola Pokédex 055 Hypno	Alola Pokédex 057 Hariyama
Level up Abra to Lv. 16	Level up Magnemite to Lv. 30	Level up Grimer (Alola Form) to Lv. 38	Level up Drowzee to Lv. 26	Level up Makuhita to Lv. 24
Alola Pokédex 062 Haunter	Alola Pokédex 065 Drifblim	Alola Pokédex 069 Golbat	Alola Pokédex 072 Dugtrio (Alola Form)	Alola Pokédex 074 Fearow
Level up Gastly to Lv. 25	Level up Drifloon to Lv. 28	Level up Zubat to Lv. 22	Level up Diglett (Alola Form) to Lv. 26	Level up Spearow to Lv. 20
Alola Pokédex 076 Braviary	Alola Pokédex 078 Mandibuzz	Alola Pokédex 080 Primeape	Alola Pokédex 084 Ribombee	Alola Pokédex 090 Golduck
Level up Rufflet to Lv. 54	Level up Vullaby to Lv. 54	Level up Mankey to Lv. 28	Level up Cutiefly to Lv. 25	Level up Psyduck to Lv. 33
Alola Pokédex 092 Gyarados	Alola Pokédex 094 Whiscash	Alola Pokédex 096 Machoke	Alola Pokédex 099 Boldore	Alola Pokédex 107 Tentacruel
Level up Magikarp to Lv. 20	Level up Barboach to Lv. 30	Level up Machop to Lv. 28	Level up Roggenrola to Lv. 25	Level up Tentacool to lv. 30
Alola Pokédex 109 Lumineon	Alola Pokédex 114 Toxapex	Alola Pokédex 118 Shelgon	Alola Pokédex 119 Salamence	Alola Pokédex 121 Herdier
Level up Finneon to Lv. 31	Level up Mareanie to Lv. 38	Level up Bagon to Lv. 30	Level up Shelgon to Lv. 50	Level up Lillipup to Lv. 16

Alola Pokédex 122	Alola Pokédex 133	Alola Pokédex 140	Alola Pokédex 142	Alola Pokédex 146
☑ Stoutland	☑ Mudsdale	☑ Masquerain	☑ Araquanid	☑ Shiinotic
Level up Herdier to Lv. 32	Level up Mudbray to Lv. 30	Level up Surskit to Lv. 22	Level up Dewpider to Lv. 22	Level up Morelull to Lv. 24

Alola Pokédex 148	Alola Pokédex 150	Alola Pokédex 154	Alola Pokédex 159	Alola Pokédex 160
☑ Parasect	☑ Poliwhirl	☑ Seaking	☑ Fletchinder	☑ Talonflame
Level up Paras to Lv. 24	Level up Poliwag to Lv. 25	Level up Goldeen to Lv. 33	Level up Fletchling to Lv. 17	Level up Fletchinder to Lv. 35

Alola Pokédex 162	Alola Pokédex 167	Alola Pokédex 170	Alola Pokédex 172	Alola Pokédex 179
☑ Salazzle	☑ Magmar	☑ Bewear	☑ Steenee	☑ Sliggoo
Level up a female Salandit to Lv. 33	Level up Magby to Lv. 30	Level up Stufful to Lv. 27	Level up Bounsweet to Lv. 18	Level up Goomy to Lv. 40

Alola Pokédex 183	Alola Pokédex 187	Alola Pokédex 189	Alola Pokédex 191	Alola Pokédex 193
☑ Golisopod	☑ Palossand	☑ Rampardos	☑ Bastiodon	☑ Archeops
Level up Wimpod to Lv. 30	Level up Sandygast to Lv. 42	Level up Cranidos to Lv. 30	Level up to Shieldon to Lv. 30	Level up Archen to Lv. 37

Alola Pokédex 195	Alola Pokédex 202	Alola Pokédex 207	Alola Pokédex 215	Alola Pokédex 216
☑ Carracosta	☑ Lanturn	☑ Garbodor	☑ Metang	☑ Metagross
Level to Tirtouga to Lv. 37	Level up Chinchou to Lv. 27	Level up Trubbish to Lv. 36	Level up Beldum to Lv. 20	Level up Metang to Lv. 45

Alola Pokédex 227	Alola Pokédex 230	Alola Pokédex 233	Alola Pokédex 234	Alola Pokédex 236
☑ Electabuzz	☑ Graveler (Alola Form)	☑ Krokorok	☑ Krookodile	☑ Vibrava
Level up Elekid to Lv. 30	Level up Geodude (Alola Form) to Lv. 25	Level up Sandile to Lv. 29	Level up Krokorok to Lv. 40	Level up Trapinch to Lv. 35

Alola Pokédex 237	Alola Pokédex 239	Alola Pokédex 240	Alola Pokédex 247	Alola Pokédex 256
☑ Flygon	☑ Gabite	☑ Garchomp	☑ Glalie	☑ Vanillish
Level up Vibrava to Lv. 45	Level up Gible to Lv. 24	Level up Gabite to Lv. 48	Level up Snorunt to Lv. 42	Level up Vanillite to Lv. 35

Alola Pokédex 257	Alola Pokédex 259	Alola Pokédex 261	Alola Pokédex 265	Alola Pokédex 267
☑ Vanilluxe	☑ Granbull	☑ Gastrodon (East Sea)	☑ Sharpedo	☑ Wailord
Level up Vanillish to Lv. 47	Level up Snubbull to Lv. 23	Level up Shellos (East Sea) to Lv. 30	Level up Carvanha to Lv. 30	Level up Wailmer to Lv. 40

Alola Pokédex 272	Alola Pokédex 273	Alola Pokédex 282	Alola Pokédex 283	Alola Pokédex 290
☑ Hakamo-o	☑ Kommo-o	☑ Dragonair	☑ Dragonite	☑ Cosmoem
Level up Jangmo-o to Lv. 35	Level up Hakamo-o to Lv. 45	Level up Dratini to Lv. 30	Level up Dragonair to Lv. 55	Level up Cosmog to Lv. 43

Alola Pokédex 291	Alola Pokédex 292
☑ Solgaleo	☑ Lunala
Level up Cosmoem to Lv. 53 (*Pokémon Sun* only)	Level up Cosmoem to Lv. 53 (*Pokémon Moon* only)

Obtain Pokémon That Only Evolve at Particular Times

Among the many Pokémon species, you will find some that evolve only when leveled up during a particular time of day. As time passes in the Alola region, you can roughly divide it into two periods: daytime and nighttime. If you're trying to evolve a particular Pokémon, pay attention to what time of day it is and then take them into battle to try to help them level up. Some of these Pokémon must also be friendly toward you to evolve. Turn to page 234 to learn more about how to make your Pokémon friendly toward you.

❖ Pokémon in the Alola Pokédex that evolve when leveled up during particular times

Alola Pokédex 014	Alola Pokédex 016	Alola Pokédex 033	Alola Pokédex 104	Alola Pokédex 104
☑ Gumshoos	☑ Raticate (Alola Form)	☑ Chansey	☑ Lycanroc (Midday Form)	☑ Lycanroc (Midnight Form)
Level up Yungoos to Lv. 20 when it is daytime in your game	Level up Rattata (Alola Form) to Lv. 20 at night in your game	Have Happiny hold an Oval Stone and level it up when it is daytime in your game	Level up Rockruff to Lv. 25 when it is daytime in your game (*Pokémon Sun* only)	Level up Rockruff to Lv. 25 at night in your game (*Pokémon Moon* only)

Alola Pokédex 127	Alola Pokédex 128	Alola Pokédex 144	Alola Pokédex 164	Alola Pokédex 250
☑ Espeon	☑ Umbreon	☑ Lurantis	☑ Marowak (Alola Form)	☑ Weavile
Level up Eevee when it is daytime in your game and when it is friendly toward you	Level up Eevee at nighttime in your game and when it is friendly toward you	Level up Fomantis to Lv. 34 when it is daytime in your game	Level up Cubone to Lv. 28 when it is nighttime in your game	Have Sneasel hold a Razor Claw and level it up at night in your game

Alola Pokédex 280
☑ Lucario
Level up Riolu when it is daytime in your game and when it is friendly toward you

Turn back to page 217 for more about how night and day are divided in the Alola region ▶

❖ Obtain the items needed for these Pokémon to evolve

Oval Stone	Often held by Happiny in the wild	Razor Claw	Sometimes held by Jangmo-o and Hakamo-o in the wild

Obtain Pokémon That Only Evolve When Friendly

Pokémon come to trust their Trainers and become friendly toward them with time. There are some Pokémon that evolve when they level up after they have grown sufficiently friendly toward you. Friendship increases when Pokémon feel happy. But if you do things that make your Pokémon unhappy, like causing them to faint in battle, then they will feel less friendly toward you.

❖ Main ways to make Pokémon friendly toward you

1 Have them take part in battles against powerful Trainers, like captains and kahunas

2 Use items to raise their base stats, like HP Ups, Proteins, or Irons

3 Use items on them during battles, like X Attacks, X Speeds, or Dire Hits

4 Give them Berries that increase friendship, like Pomeg Berries or Kelpsy Berries

5 Treat them to a lomi-lomi massage in Konikoni City (Akala Island)

6 Have them hold a Soothe Bell

7 Catch them in Luxury Balls

8 Catch them in a Friend Ball (which maximizes their friendship once they are caught)

9 Put them in the hot springs on Poké Pelago's Isle Avue

10 Use the Friendship Café or Friendship Parlor food stalls in Festival Plaza

❖ Pokémon in the Alola Pokédex that evolve when they are friendly

Alola Pokédex 025
✓ Pikachu
Level up Pichu when it is friendly toward you

Alola Pokédex 034
✓ Blissey
Level up Chansey when it is friendly toward you

Alola Pokédex 036
✓ Snorlax
Level up Munchlax when it is friendly toward you

Alola Pokédex 046
✓ Persian (Alola Form)
Level up Meowth (Alola Form) when it is friendly toward you

Alola Pokédex 070
✓ Crobat
Level up Golbat when it is friendly toward you

Alola Pokédex 127
✓ Espeon
Level up Eevee when it is daytime in your game and when it is friendly toward you

Alola Pokédex 128
✓ Umbreon
Level up Eevee at night in your game and when it is friendly toward you

Alola Pokédex 135
✓ Jigglypuff
Level up Igglybuff when it is friendly toward you

Alola Pokédex 204
✓ Silvally
Level up Type: Null when it is friendly toward you

Alola Pokédex 211
✓ Clefairy
Level up Cleffa when it is friendly toward you

Alola Pokédex 280
✓ Lucario
Level up Riolu when it is daytime in your game and when it is friendly toward you

Obtain Pokémon That Only Evolve in Special Places

Among the many Pokémon species, you will also find some that evolve only when leveled up in a specific location. Put these Pokémon in your party and visit the locations listed below, then have them level up and they will evolve. You can have your Pokémon level up by battling or catching wild Pokémon in these locations.

❖ Pokémon in the Alola Pokédex that evolve when leveled up in particular locations

Alola Pokédex 029
✓ Vikavolt
Level up Charjabug in the Vast Poni Canyon (Poni Island)

Alola Pokédex 049
✓ Magnezone
Level up Magneton in the Vast Poni Canyon (Poni Island)

Alola Pokédex 060
✓ Crabominable
Level up Crabrawler on Mount Lanakila (Ula'ula Island)

Alola Pokédex 129
✓ Leafeon
Level up Eevee near the moss-covered stone in Lush Jungle (Akala Island)

Alola Pokédex 130
✓ Glaceon
Level up Eevee near the ice-covered stone inside Mount Lanakila's cave (Ula'ula Island)

Alola Pokédex 199
✓ Probopass
Level up Nosepass in the Vast Poni Canyon (Poni Island)

Obtain Pokémon That Only Evolve with Certain Moves

Some Pokémon species only evolve if you have them level up and then learn a particular move, or if you teach them that move first and then add them to your party to have them level up.

❖ Main ways to teach Pokémon the moves they need to know

1 Put the Pokémon in your party and have them level up to learn new moves

2 Have Madam Memorial in the Mount Lanakila Pokémon Center (Ula'ula Island) teach them the move they need

Madam Memorial can remind your Pokémon of moves they have forgotten or haven't learned in exchange for a Heart Scale

❖ Pokémon in the Alola Pokédex that evolve when they know certain moves

Alola Pokédex 031	Alola Pokédex 131	Alola Pokédex 173
✓ **Sudowoodo**	✓ **Sylveon**	✓ **Tsareena**
Raise Bonsly to Lv. 15 and have it learn Mimic (or have it learn Mimic first and then level it up)	Make Eevee affectionate toward you through Pokémon Refresh or other means, then level it up and have it learn a Fairy-type move (or have an affectionate Eevee learn a Fairy-type move first and then level it up)	Raise Steenee to Lv. 29 and have it learn Stomp (or have it learn Stomp first and then level it up)

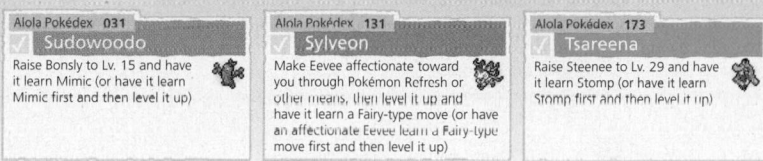

Obtain Pokémon That Only Evolve with Special Stones

There are Pokémon that evolve when you use particular stones on them, thanks to the mysterious power within those stones. There had been nine such stones discovered in the past, but in the Alola region you can also find the Ice Stone—meaning that there are now 10 known Evolution stones! You can pick some of these stones up when walking around in Alola, but if that is all you do, you won't have enough of them to complete the Alola Pokédex. But there are a number of ways to obtain more of these stones than you can simply find in the field. Use all of the methods available to you to get as many stones as you need (p. 236).

❖ Pokémon in the Alola Pokédex that evolve when you use stones on them

Alola Pokédex 026	Alola Pokédex 053	Alola Pokédex 067	Alola Pokédex 086	Alola Pokédex 088
✓ **Raichu** (Alola Form)	✓ **Arcanine**	✓ **Mismagius**	✓ **Lilligant**	✓ **Whimsicott**
Use a Thunder Stone on Pikachu	Use a Fire Stone on Growlithe	Use a Dusk Stone on Misdreavus	Use a Sun Stone on Petilil	Use a Sun Stone on Cottonee
Alola Pokédex 116	Alola Pokédex 124	Alola Pokédex 125	Alola Pokédex 126	Alola Pokédex 136
✓ **Cloyster**	✓ **Vaporeon**	✓ **Jolteon**	✓ **Flareon**	✓ **Wigglytuff**
Use a Water Stone on Shellder	Use a Water Stone on Eevee	Use a Thunder Stone on Eevee	Use a Fire Stone on Eevee	Use a Moon Stone on Jigglypuff
Alola Pokédex 151	Alola Pokédex 185	Alola Pokédex 212	Alola Pokédex 248	Alola Pokédex 252
✓ **Poliwrath**	✓ **Starmie**	✓ **Clefable**	✓ **Froslass**	✓ **Sandslash** (Alola Form)
Use a Water Stone on Poliwhirl	Use a Water Stone on Staryu	Use a Moon Stone on Clefairy	Use a Dawn Stone on a female Snorunt	Use an Ice Stone on Sandshrew (Alola Form)
Alola Pokédex 254	Alola Pokédex 270	Alola Pokédex 278		
✓ **Ninetales** (Alola Form)	✓ **Exeggutor** (Alola Form)	✓ **Honchkrow**		
Use an Ice Stone on Vulpix (Alola Form)	Use a Leaf Stone on Exeggcute	Use a Dusk Stone on Murkrow		

Get all the Evolution stones you need

There are 10 varieties of stones that can help Pokémon evolve. To complete the Alola Pokédex, you will need nine of them—all but a Shiny Stone. Obtain them during your adventures and use them when you want to evolve your Pokémon. And note that some of the Pokémon listed on page 235 can also be encountered and caught in the wild.

❖ Stones that help Pokémon evolve

Fire Stone	You will need two to evolve both Eevee and Growlithe	
Thunder Stone	You will need two to evolve both Pikachu and Eevee	
Ice Stone	You will need two to evolve both Sandshrew (Alola Form) and Vulpix (Alola Form)	
Moon Stone	You will need two to evolve both Jigglypuff and Clefairy	
Dusk Stone	You will need two to evolve both Misdreavus and Murkrow	

Water Stone	You will need four to evolve Shellder, Poliwhirl, and others
Leaf Stone	You will need one to evolve Exeggcute into into Exeggutor (Alola Form)
Sun Stone	You will need two to evolve both Petilil and Cottonee
Shiny Stone	There are no Pokémon in the Alola Pokédex that require a Shiny Stone to evolve
Dawn Stone	You will need one to evolve a female Snorunt into Froslass

Get plenty of stones to evolve your Pokémon

In *Pokémon Sun* and *Pokémon Moon*, Evolution stones are easier to get than ever, including four of them being available to buy at shops. But the best way to get evolution stones is probably the Isle Aphun in Poké Pelago. If you send your Pokémon to explore the caves there, they can discover and bring back Evolution stones with you.

❖ Various ways to obtain Evolution stones

How to Obtain 1 — Find them during your adventures

During your adventures in the Alola region, you can find some Evolution stones that have been dropped on the ground in the field. You can obtain one of each of the following stones in this way: Fire Stone, Water Stone, Ice Stone, Sun Stone, Moon Stone, Shiny Stone, and Dusk Stone. The Leaf Stone, Thunder Stone, and Dawn Stone are the only Evolution stones you will not find in the field.

How to Obtain 2 — Buy stones at Olivia's jewelry shop in Konikoni City (Akala Island)

Evolution stones are offered up for sale at Olivia's jewelry shop in Konikoni City (Akala Island). You can buy Fire Stones, Thunder Stones, Water Stones, and Leaf Stones here for ₽3,000 each. We recommend that you buy up plenty of Water Stones, as they are the Evolution stone you will need the most of.

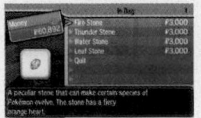

How to Obtain 3 — Have Pokémon find stones on Poké Pelago's Isle Aphun

At the Isle Aphun in Poké Pelago, Pokémon can explore caves to find treasures. If you develop Isle Aphun to Phase 2 or 3, your Pokémon will be able to explore the Path for Brilliant-Stone Hunting, where they will then be able to find any of the 10 varieties of Evolution stones.

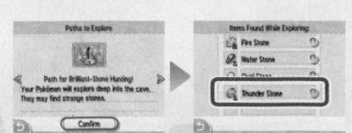

Obtain Pokémon That Only Evolve through Other Means

Pokémon truly are mysterious. They don't just evolve when you help them level up or use certain stones on them—there are some species that evolve only in very special conditions that you might not ever imagine. That doesn't mean that these conditions are hard to meet, though! Prime examples in the Alola Pokédex are Pokémon like Sylveon, Goodra, or Pangoro. Read on for the lowdown on the surprising ways you evolve these Pokémon.

❖ Special methods for helping some Pokémon evolve

Raise Eevee's affection in Pokémon Refresh	Use Pokémon moves or Abilities to make it rain	Have a Dark-type Pokémon in your party
		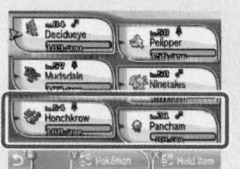
To evolve an Eevee into Sylveon, you have to first raise Eevee's affection using something like Pokémon Refresh. Then you need to level Eevee up and have it learn a Fairy-type move, or have it already know a Fairy type move before it levels up, and it will evolve!	To evolve Sliggoo into Goodra, you have to level it up to Lv. 50 when it is raining. If you want to easily find some rain in the Alola region, try Route 17 on Ula'ula Island. You can also make it rain with the move Rain Dance.	To evolve Pancham into Pangoro, you will need to have a Dark-type Pokémon in your team. Some examples of the Dark-type Pokémon you can find in the Alola Pokédex are Rattata's Alola Form, Meowth's Alola Form, Honchkrow, or Absol.

❖ Pokémon in the Alola Pokédex that evolve through special means

Alola Pokédex 131 — Sylveon	Alola Pokédex 180 — Goodra	Alola Pokédex 221 — Pangoro
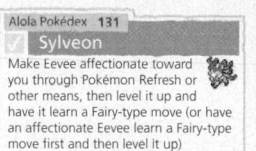 Make Eevee affectionate toward you through Pokémon Refresh or other means, then level it up and have it learn a Fairy-type move (or have an affectionate Eevee learn a Fairy-type move first and then level it up)	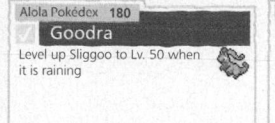 Level up Sliggoo to Lv. 50 when it is raining	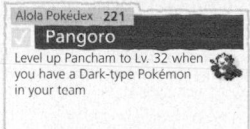 Level up Pancham to Lv. 32 when you have a Dark-type Pokémon in your team

Obtain Pokémon by Trading with People in Alola

During your travel around the islands of Alola, you will sometimes meet people who tell you that they want to trade Pokémon. Most of the time, the Pokémon that they want to receive can be found living nearby. If you don't have one already, go out and catch one. You can sometimes obtain rare Pokémon by trading with such people in towns. For example, when you trade one person for a Graveler (Alola Form), it will evolve into an Golem (Alola Form) and allow you to register two Pokémon in your Pokédex at once!

❖ Trading Pokémon with people in towns

1 Agree to a Pokémon trade	2 Choose a Pokémon to trade	3 Complete the trade

People who want to trade Pokémon can be found in Pokémon Centers and other places. If they tell you that they want to trade Pokémon, be sure to agree!	If you have the Pokémon that the other person wants, it will appear brighter than all of the others in your Boxes so it is easy to see.	Once you've completed the trade, check out your new Pokémon's nickname! It's always fun to see what kind of name other Trainers come up with for their Pokémon.

❖ Pokémon in the Alola Pokédex you can receive in trades

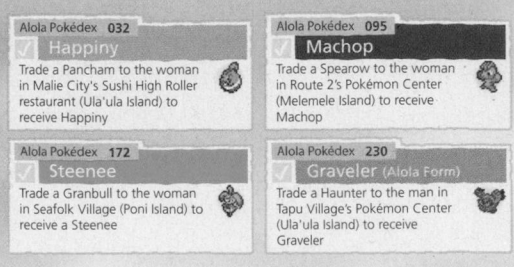

Alola Pokédex 032 Happiny	Alola Pokédex 095 Machop	Alola Pokédex 150 Poliwhirl	Alola Pokédex 160 Talonflame	Alola Pokédex 171 Bounsweet
Trade a Pancham to the woman in Malie City's Sushi High Roller restaurant (Ula'ula Island) to receive Happiny	Trade a Spearow to the woman in Route 2's Pokémon Center (Melemele Island) to receive Machop	Trade a Zubat to the girl in Konikoni City's Pokémon Center (Akala Island) to receive Poliwhirl	Trade a Bewear to the man in the Poni Gauntlet (Poni Island) to receive Talonflame	Trade a Lillipup to the man in Route 5's Pokémon Center (Akala Island) to receive Bounsweet

Alola Pokédex 172 Steenee	Alola Pokédex 230 Graveler (Alola Form)
Trade a Granbull to the woman in Seafolk Village (Poni Island) to receive a Steenee	Trade a Haunter to the man in Tapu Village's Pokémon Center (Ula'ula Island) to receive Graveler

Obtain Pokémon by Hatching Eggs

If you leave one male and one female Pokémon together at the Pokémon Nursery in Paniola Ranch (Akala Island), you may come back in time to discover a Pokémon Egg. If you put that Egg in your party and carry it around with you on your adventure, it will hatch into a Pokémon. There are some Pokémon that can only be obtained in this way.

❖ How to find a Pokémon Egg at the Pokémon Nursery in Paniola Ranch (Akala Island)

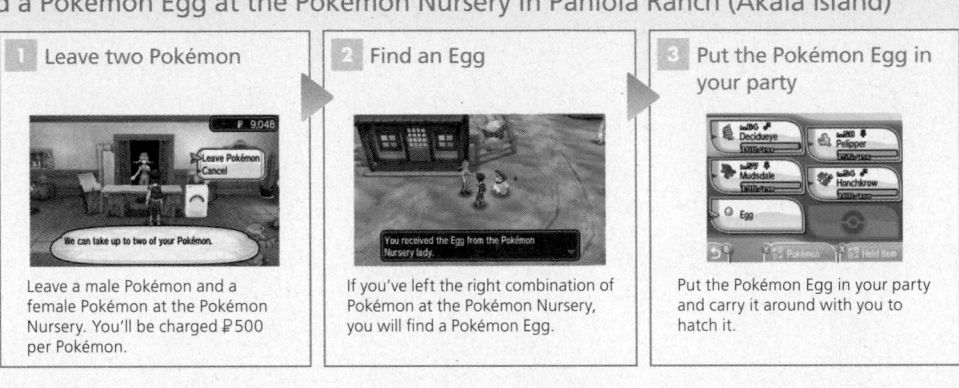

1 Leave two Pokémon

Leave a male Pokémon and a female Pokémon at the Pokémon Nursery. You'll be charged ₱500 per Pokémon.

2 Find an Egg

If you've left the right combination of Pokémon at the Pokémon Nursery, you will find a Pokémon Egg.

3 Put the Pokémon Egg in your party

Put the Pokémon Egg in your party and carry it around with you to hatch it.

The Pokémon Nursery worker gives hints to help you find Pokémon Eggs

If you talk to the Pokémon Nursery worker standing outside the Pokémon Nursery, you can hear how your two Pokémon are getting along. How she describes their relationship will give you a hint of how likely you are to find a Pokémon Egg.

Pokémon Nursery worker

❖ Pokémon Nursery worker's messages

"They really seem to like hanging out!"	More likely to find an Egg
"They seem to get along all right."	
"They don't seem to like each other very much, though."	Less likely to find an Egg
"They don't seem to like playing together, though."	Will not find an Egg

❖ Pokémon that can only be registered in the Alola Pokédex by hatching Pokémon Eggs

Alola Pokédex 238 Gible	Alola Pokédex 258 Snubbull
Leave a Gabite or Garchomp at the Pokémon Nursery, and hatch the Pokémon Egg that is found	Leave a Granbull at the Pokémon Nursery, and hatch the Pokémon Egg that is found

Alola Pokédex 260 Shellos (East Sea)	Alola Pokédex 264 Carvanha
Leave a Gastrodon (East Sea) at the Pokémon Nursery, and hatch the Pokémon Egg that is found	Leave a Sharpedo at the Pokémon Nursery, and hatch the Pokémon Egg that is found

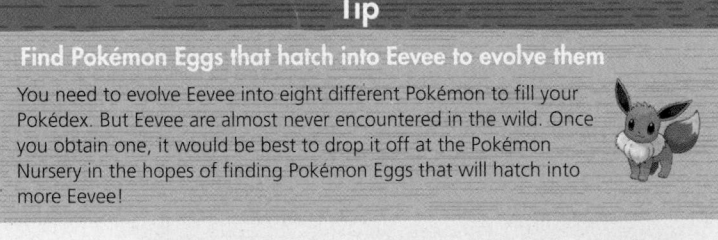

Tip

Find Pokémon Eggs that hatch into Eevee to evolve them

You need to evolve Eevee into eight different Pokémon to fill your Pokédex. But Eevee are almost never encountered in the wild. Once you obtain one, it would be best to drop it off at the Pokémon Nursery in the hopes of finding Pokémon Eggs that will hatch into more Eevee!

Use these tips to become a Pokémon Egg expert

If you put a Pokémon Egg in your party and carry it around with you on your adventure, it will eventually hatch into a Pokémon. Depending on the kind of Pokémon Egg that it is, though, it might take quite a lot of time. That's why you may want to use the following tricks to help your Pokémon Eggs hatch more quickly in *Pokémon Sun* and *Pokémon Moon*.

Technique 1 — Get the Oval Charm by defeating Morimoto after entering the Hall of Fame

After you enter the Hall of Fame, visit the GAME FREAK office in Heahea City on Akala Island. Morimoto can be found there, and he is all too happy to battle you. If you can defeat Morimoto, he will give you an Oval Charm. This precious item makes you more likely to find Pokémon Eggs just by having it in your possession.

Morimoto   Oval Charm

Technique 2 — Use Tauros Charge to run around with your Pokémon Eggs in your party

Pokémon Eggs hatch when you put them in your party and carry them around with you. Use this fact wisely by covering more distance in a shorter amount of time. You can do this by using Tauros Charge to run around the roads of Alola. Route 6 is your best bet as it's a straight path that lies just to the side of the Pokémon Nursery.

Tauros

Technique 3 — Have Pokémon with the Flame Body Ability in your party

There are some Pokémon Abilities that can help you hatch Eggs more quickly. The Flame Body Ability is one of these. Put a Pokémon with this Ability, such as Talonflame or Magmar, in your party to hatch your Pokémon Eggs in a hurry.

Talonflame   Magmar

Technique 4 — Put Pokémon Eggs in the hot springs on Poké Pelago's Isle Avue

You can drop off Pokémon Eggs at the hot springs on Poké Pelago's Isle Avue. If you do, it will reduce the amount of time that it will take them to hatch. Sometimes the Pokémon Eggs will hatch just as soon as you pull them out of the hot springs! If you develop Isle Avue to Lv. 3, you can leave up to 18 Pokémon Eggs in the hot springs at a time.

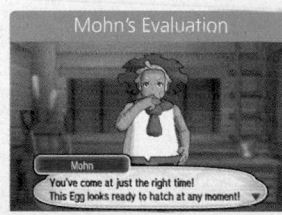

Mohn's Evaluation

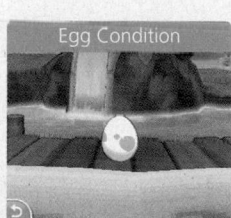

Egg Condition

There are many rules which dictate the kind of Pokémon Eggs you can find at the Pokémon Nursery, including how the Pokémon that hatch from them might inherit moves, Abilities, and more from the Pokémon that were dropped off there. The details are covered in *Pokémon Sun & Pokémon Moon: The Official Alola Region Strategy Guide*. But the two most important rules that you'll need to know are these two below. Use these basic rules and the Egg Group tables found on the following pages to try your hand at discovering Pokémon Eggs. Note that the Egg Group tables include Pokémon that cannot normally be caught in Alola; if you want to use one of them to find Eggs, try to obtain one through the GTS or by other means. You can tell which Pokémon are not found in Alola because they will not have an Alola Pokédex number to the left of their names.

Egg Rule 1   **Drop off a male and female Pokémon, and you may find a Pokémon Egg**

The easiest way to find a Pokémon Egg is to leave a male Pokémon and a female Pokémon of the same species at the Pokémon Nursery. This is the most basic method you can use. But each Pokémon also belongs to something called an Egg Group. Egg Groups are key to finding Pokémon Eggs and you can find a list of the Egg Groups for Alola region Pokémon on the following pages. Even if the male and female Pokémon do not belong to the same species, you can still find an Pokémon Egg if they both belong to the same Egg Group. Komala and Mudsdale to the right are an example of this: even though their species are different, they both belong to the Field Group. You can find a Pokémon Egg from such a combination, and it will hatch into the first Pokémon in an Evolution line.

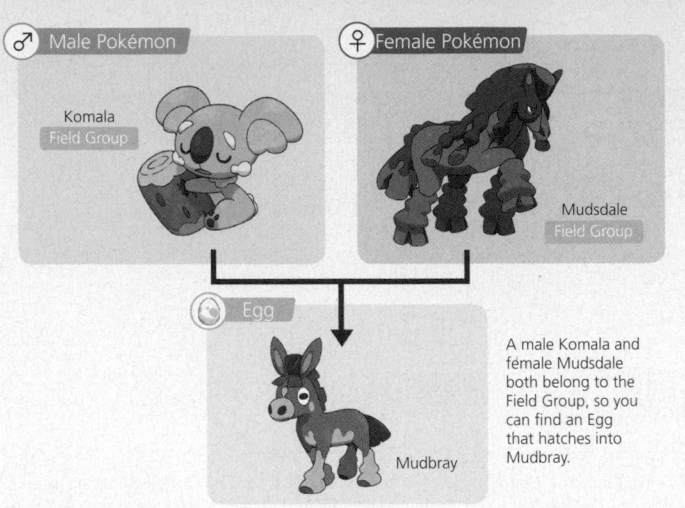

A male Komala and fémale Mudsdale both belong to the Field Group, so you can find an Egg that hatches into Mudbray.

❖ **Basic rules for finding Pokémon Eggs**

1   You can find a Pokémon Egg if you leave a male Pokémon and a female Pokémon from the same Egg Group together

2   The Pokémon Egg will hatch into the same species as the female Pokémon left at the Nursery, or an earlier Evolution in its Evolution line

3   As a general rule, Eggs will almost always hatch into the first Pokémon in an Evolution line

4   You will not find any Pokémon Eggs from a Pokémon that belongs to the "No Eggs Discovered" Group

Egg Rule 2   **You can find almost any Pokémon Egg if you leave a Ditto at the Nursery**

Some Pokémon only have male specimens, and others have unknown genders. Since Pokémon Eggs hatch in a species based on the female Pokémon left at the Pokémon Nursery, it seems impossible to ever find Pokémon Eggs for such Pokémon. But if you leave one of them with a Ditto, you can discover a Pokémon Egg that hatches into these tricky Pokémon! Ditto appears in the tall grass on Mount Hokulani (Ula'ula Island).

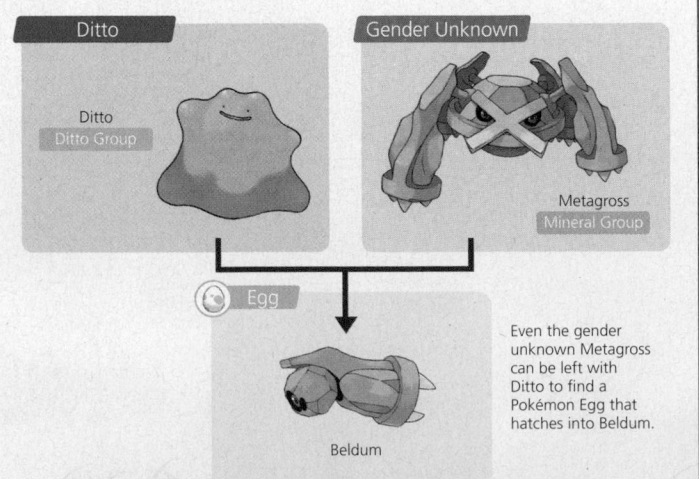

Even the gender unknown Metagross can be left with Ditto to find a Pokémon Egg that hatches into Beldum.

❖ **Basic rule for finding Pokémon Eggs with Ditto**

1   You can find a Pokémon Egg even for male Pokémon or gender unknown Pokémon if you leave one with a Ditto

AMORPHOUS GROUP

Amorphous Group Only
- Banette ♂/♀
- Chandelure ♂/♀
- Chimecho ♂/♀
- 65 Drifblim ♂/♀
- 64 Drifloon ♂/♀
- Duosion ♂/♀
- Dusclops ♂/♀
- Dusknoir ♂/♀
- Duskull ♂/♀
- Eelektrik ♂/♀
- Eelektross ♂/♀
- Frillish ♂/♀
- Gallade ♂
- Gardevoir ♂/♀
- 61 Gastly ♂/♀
- 63 Gengar ♂/♀
- Gourgeist ♂/♀
- 50 Grimer ♂/♀
- Gulpin ♂/♀
- 62 Haunter ♂/♀
- Jellicent ♂/♀
- Kirlia ♂/♀
- Koffing ♂/♀
- Lampent ♂/♀
- Litwick ♂/♀
- Magcargo ♂/♀
- 242 Mimikyu ♂/♀
- 66 Misdreavus ♂/♀
- 67 Mismagius ♂/♀
- 51 Muk ♂/♀
- 187 Palossand ♂/♀
- Pumpkaboo ♂/♀
- Ralts ♂/♀
- Reuniclus ♂/♀
- Rotom Unknown
- 186 Sandygast ♂/♀
- Shuppet ♂/♀
- Slugma ♂/♀
- Solosis ♂/♀
- Spiritomb ♂/♀
- Swalot ♂/♀
- Tynamo ♂/♀
- Weezing ♂/♀
- Wobbuffet ♂/♀

Amorphous Group and Fairy Group
- 181 Castform ♂/♀

Amorphous Group and Grass Group
- 196 Phantump ♂/♀
- 197 Trevenant ♂/♀

Amorphous Group and Mineral Group
- Cofagrigus ♂/♀
- Yamask ♂/♀

Amorphous Group and Water Group 1
- 261 Gastrodon ♂/♀
- 260 Shellos ♂/♀
- Stunfisk ♂/♀

BUG GROUP

Bug Group Only
- Accelgor ♂/♀
- 23 Ariados ♂/♀
- Beautifly ♂/♀
- Beedrill ♂/♀
- Burmy ♂/♀
- 19 Butterfree ♂/♀
- Cascoon ♂/♀
- 17 Caterpie ♂/♀
- 28 Charjabug ♂/♀
- Combee ♂/♀
- Durant ♂/♀
- Dustox ♂/♀
- Escavalier ♂/♀
- 237 Flygon ♂/♀
- Forretress ♂/♀
- Galvantula ♂/♀
- Gligar ♂/♀
- Gliscor ♂/♀
- 27 Grubbin ♂/♀
- Heracross ♂/♀
- Joltik ♂/♀
- Kakuna ♂/♀
- Karrablast ♂/♀
- Kricketot ♂/♀
- Kricketune ♂/♀
- Larvesta ♂/♀
- Leavanny ♂/♀
- 71 Ledian ♂/♀
- 20 Ledyba ♂/♀
- 18 Metapod ♂/♀
- Mothim ♂
- Nincada ♂/♀
- Ninjask ♂/♀
- Pineco ♂/♀
- 175 Pinsir ♂/♀
- Scatterbug ♂/♀
- 276 Scizor ♂/♀
- Scolipede ♂/♀
- 275 Scyther ♂/♀
- Sewaddle ♂/♀
- Shelmet ♂/♀
- Shuckle ♂/♀
- Silcoon ♂/♀
- Spewpa ♂/♀
- 22 Spinarak ♂/♀
- Swadloon ♂/♀
- 235 Trapinch ♂/♀
- Venipede ♂/♀
- Venomoth ♂/♀
- Venonat ♂/♀
- Vespiquen ♀
- 236 Vibrava ♂/♀
- 29 Vikavolt ♂/♀
- Vivillon ♂/♀
- Volcarona ♂/♀
- Weedle ♂/♀
- Whirlipede ♂/♀
- Wormadam ♀
- Wurmple ♂/♀
- Yanma ♂/♀
- Yanmega ♂/♀

Bug Group and Fairy Group
- 83 Cutiefly ♂/♀
- 84 Ribombee ♂/♀

Bug Group and Grass Group
- 147 Paras ♂/♀
- 148 Parasect ♂/♀

Bug Group and Human-Like Group
- Illumise ♀
- Volbeat ♂

Bug Group and Mineral Group
- Crustle ♂/♀
- Dwebble ♂/♀

Bug Group and Water Group 1
- 142 Araquanid ♂/♀
- 141 Dewpider ♂/♀
- 140 Masquerain ♂/♀
- 139 Surskit ♂/♀

Bug Group and Water Group 3
- Drapion ♂/♀
- 183 Golisopod ♂/♀
- Skorupi ♂/♀
- 182 Wimpod ♂/♀

DITTO GROUP
- 209 Ditto Unknown

DRAGON GROUP

Dragon Group Only
- 117 Bagon ♂/♀
- Deino ♂/♀
- 180 Goodra ♂/♀
- 178 Goomy ♂/♀
- 272 Hakamo-o ♂/♀
- Hydreigon ♂/♀
- 271 Jangmo-o ♂/♀
- 273 Kommo-o ♂/♀
- 119 Salamence ♂/♀
- 118 Shelgon ♂/♀
- 179 Sliggoo ♂/♀
- Zweilous ♂/♀

Dragon Group and Field Group
- Arbok ♂/♀
- Ekans ♂/♀
- Scrafty ♂/♀
- Scraggy ♂/♀
- Seviper ♂/♀

Dragon Group and Flying Group
- Swablu ♂/♀
- Altaria ♂/♀

Dragon Group and Monster Group
- Axew ♂/♀
- Charizard ♂/♀
- Charmander ♂/♀
- Charmeleon ♂/♀
- 244 Drampa ♂/♀
- Druddigon ♂/♀
- 239 Gabite ♂/♀
- 240 Garchomp ♂/♀
- 238 Gible ♂/♀
- Grovyle ♂/♀
- Haxorus ♂/♀
- Heliolisk ♂/♀
- Helioptile ♂/♀
- 161 Salandit ♂/♀
- 162 Salazzle ♀
- Sceptile ♂/♀
- Treecko ♂/♀
- 224 Turtonator ♂/♀
- Tyrantrum ♂/♀
- Tyrunt ♂/♀

Dragon Group and Water Group 1
- Horsea ♂/♀
- Seadra ♂/♀
- Kingdra ♂/♀
- 155 Feebas ♂/♀
- 156 Milotic ♂/♀
- Skrelp ♂/♀
- Dragalge ♂/♀
- 281 Dratini ♂/♀
- 282 Dragonair ♂/♀
- 283 Dragonite ♂/♀

Dragon Group and Water Group 2
- 91 Magikarp ♂/♀
- 92 Gyarados ♂/♀

FAIRY GROUP

Fairy Group Only
- Aromatisse ♂/♀
- Audino ♂/♀
- 34 Blissey ♀
- 33 Chansey ♀
- 212 Clefable ♂/♀
- 211 Clefairy ♂/♀
- Flabébé ♀
- Floette ♀
- Florges ♀
- 135 Jigglypuff ♂/♀
- Minun ♂/♀
- Plusle ♂/♀
- Slurpuff ♂/♀
- Spritzee ♂/♀
- Swirlix ♂/♀
- 136 Wigglytuff ♂/♀

Fairy Group and Amorphous Group
- 181 Castform ♂/♀

Fairy Group and Bug Group
- 83 Cutiefly ♂/♀
- 84 Ribombee ♂/♀

Fairy Group and Field Group
- Dedenne ♂/♀
- Delcatty ♂/♀
- 259 Granbull ♂/♀
- Mawile ♂/♀
- Pachirisu ♂/♀
- 25 Pikachu ♂/♀
- 26 Raichu ♂/♀
- Skitty ♂/♀
- 258 Snubbull ♂/♀
- 225 Togedemaru ♂/♀

Fairy Group and Flying Group
- Togetic ♂/♀
- Togekiss ♂/♀

Fairy Group and Grass Group
- Breloom ♂/♀
- Cherrim ♂/♀
- Cherubi ♂/♀
- 87 Cottonee ♂/♀
- Hoppip ♂/♀
- Jumpluff ♂/♀
- Roselia ♂/♀
- Roserade ♂/♀
- Shroomish ♂/♀
- Skiploom ♂/♀
- 88 Whimsicott ♂/♀

Fairy Group and Mineral Group
- 101 Carbink Unknown
- 248 Froslass ♀
- 247 Glalie ♂/♀
- 246 Snorunt ♂/♀

Fairy Group and Water Group 1
- Azumarill ♂/♀
- Manaphy Unknown
- Marill ♂/♀
- Phione Unknown

FIELD GROUP

Field Group Only
- 245 Absol ♂/♀
- Aipom ♂/♀
- Ambipom ♂/♀
- 53 Arcanine ♂/♀
- Beartic ♂/♀
- 170 Bewear ♂/♀
- Blaziken ♂/♀
- Blitzle ♂/♀
- Bouffalant ♂/♀
- Braixen ♂/♀
- Bunnelby ♂/♀
- Camerupt ♂/♀
- Chesnaught ♂/♀
- Chespin ♂/♀
- Cinccino ♂/♀
- Combusken ♂/♀
- Cubchoo ♂/♀
- Cyndaquil ♂/♀
- Darmanitan ♂/♀
- Darumaka ♂/♀
- Deerling ♂/♀
- Delphox ♂/♀
- Dewott ♂/♀
- Diggersby ♂/♀
- 71 Diglett ♂/♀
- Donphan ♂/♀
- Drilbur ♂/♀
- 72 Dugtrio ♂/♀
- Dunsparce ♂/♀
- 123 Eevee ♂/♀
- Electrike ♂/♀
- Emboar ♂/♀
- 274 Emolga ♂/♀
- 127 Espeon ♂/♀
- Espurr ♂/♀
- Excadrill ♂/♀
- Fennekin ♂/♀
- 126 Flareon ♂/♀
- Furfrou ♂/♀
- Furret ♂/♀
- Girafarig ♂/♀
- 130 Glaceon ♂/♀
- Glameow ♂/♀
- Gogoat ♂/♀
- 52 Growlithe ♂/♀
- Grumpig ♂/♀
- 14 Gumshoos ♂/♀
- Heatmor ♂/♀
- 121 Herdier ♂/♀
- Hippopotas ♂/♀
- Hippowdon ♂/♀
- Houndoom ♂/♀
- Houndour ♂/♀
- 6 Incineroar ♂/♀
- 125 Jolteon ♂/♀
- Kecleon ♂/♀
- 222 Komala ♂/♀
- 233 Krokorok ♂/♀
- 234 Krookodile ♂/♀
- 129 Leafeon ♂/♀
- Liepard ♂/♀
- 120 Lillipup ♂/♀
- Linoone ♂/♀
- Litleo ♂/♀
- 4 Litten ♂/♀
- Luxio ♂/♀
- Luxray ♂/♀
- 104 Lycanroc ♂/♀
- Mamoswine ♂/♀
- Manectric ♂/♀
- 79 Mankey ♂/♀
- Meowstic ♂/♀
- 45 Meowth ♂/♀
- Mightyena ♂/♀
- 138 Miltank ♀
- Minccino ♂/♀
- 132 Mudbray ♂/♀
- 133 Mudsdale ♂/♀
- Munna ♂/♀
- Musharna ♂/♀
- 254 Ninetales ♂/♀
- Numel ♂/♀
- 176 Oranguru ♂/♀
- Oshawott ♂/♀
- Panpour ♂/♀
- Pansage ♂/♀
- Pansear ♂/♀

FIELD GROUP

Field Group Only

No.	Name	Gender
177	Passimian	♂/♀
	Patrat	♂/♀
46	Persian	♂/♀
	Phanpy	♂/♀
	Pignite	♂/♀
	Piloswine	♂/♀
	Ponyta	♂/♀
	Poochyena	♂/♀
80	Primeape	♂/♀
	Purrloin	♂/♀
	Purugly	♂/♀
	Pyroar	♂/♀
	Quilava	♂/♀
	Quilladin	♂/♀
	Rapidash	♂/♀
16	Raticate	♂/♀
15	Rattata	♂/♀
103	Rockruff	♂/♀
	Samurott	♂/♀
232	Sandile	♂/♀
251	Sandshrew	♂/♀
252	Sandslash	♂/♀
	Sawsbuck	♂/♀
	Sentret	♂/♀
	Shinx	♂/♀
	Simipour	♂/♀
	Simisage	♂/♀
	Simisear	♂/♀
	Skiddo	♂/♀
	Skuntank	♂/♀
	Slaking	♂/♀
	Slakoth	♂/♀
58	Smeargle	♂/♀
249	Sneasel	♂/♀
	Spoink	♂/♀
	Stantler	♂/♀
122	Stoutland	♂/♀
169	Stufful	♂/♀
	Stunky	♂/♀
	Swinub	♂/♀
131	Sylveon	♂/♀
137	Tauros	♂
	Teddiursa	♂/♀
	Tepig	♂/♀
	Torchic	♂/♀
223	Torkoal	♂/♀
5	Torracat	♂/♀
	Typhlosion	♂/♀
128	Umbreon	♂/♀
	Ursaring	♂/♀
124	Vaporeon	♂/♀
	Vigoroth	♂/♀
253	Vulpix	♂/♀
	Watchog	♂/♀
250	Weavile	♂/♀
13	Yungoos	♂/♀
	Zangoose	♂/♀
	Zebstrika	♂/♀
	Zigzagoon	♂/♀
	Zoroark	♂/♀
	Zorua	♂/♀

Field Group and Dragon Group

No.	Name	Gender
	Arbok	♂/♀
	Ekans	♂/♀
	Scrafty	♂/♀
	Scraggy	♂/♀
	Seviper	♂/♀

Field Group and Fairy Group

No.	Name	Gender
	Dedenne	♂/♀
	Delcatty	♂/♀
259	Granbull	♂/♀
	Mawile	♂/♀
	Pachirisu	♂/♀
25	Pikachu	♂/♀
26	Raichu	♂/♀
	Skitty	♂/♀
258	Snubbull	♂/♀
225	Togedemaru	♂/♀

Field Group and Flying Group

No.	Name	Gender
	Farfetch'd	♂/♀
	Swoobat	♂/♀
	Woobat	♂/♀

Field Group and Grass Group

No.	Name	Gender
	Nuzleaf	♂/♀
	Seedot	♂/♀
	Serperior	♂/♀
	Servine	♂/♀
	Shiftry	♂/♀
	Snivy	♂/♀

Field Group and Human-Like Group

No.	Name	Gender
	Buneary	♂/♀
	Chimchar	♂/♀
	Infernape	♂/♀
	Lopunny	♂/♀
280	Lucario	♂/♀
	Mienfoo	♂/♀
	Mienshao	♂/♀
	Monferno	♂/♀
220	Pancham	♂/♀
221	Pangoro	♂/♀
105	Spinda	♂/♀

Field Group and Monster Group

No.	Name	Gender
	Ampharos	♂/♀
	Exploud	♂/♀
	Flaaffy	♂/♀
	Loudred	♂/♀
	Mareep	♂/♀
	Nidoking	♂
	Nidoran♀	♀
	Nidoran♂	♂
	Nidorino	♂
	Rhydon	♂/♀
	Rhyhorn	♂/♀
	Rhyperior	♂/♀
	Whismur	♂/♀

Field Group and Water Group 1

No.	Name	Gender
	Bibarel	♂/♀
	Bidoof	♂/♀
8	Brionne	♂/♀
	Buizel	♂/♀
81	Delibird	♂/♀
	Dewgong	♂/♀
	Empoleon	♂/♀
	Floatzel	♂/♀
90	Golduck	♂/♀
	Piplup	♂/♀
7	Popplio	♂/♀
9	Primarina	♂/♀
	Prinplup	♂/♀
89	Psyduck	♂/♀
	Quagsire	♂/♀
	Sealeo	♂/♀
	Seel	♂/♀
	Spheal	♂/♀
	Walrein	♂/♀
	Wooper	♂/♀

Field Group and Water Group 2

No.	Name	Gender
266	Wailmer	♂/♀
267	Wailord	♂/♀

FLYING GROUP

Flying Group Only

No.	Name	Gender
284	Aerodactyl	♂/♀
76	Braviary	♂
	Chatot	♂/♀
70	Crobat	♂/♀
2	Dartrix	♂/♀
3	Decidueye	♂/♀
	Dodrio	♂/♀
	Doduo	♂/♀
74	Fearow	♂/♀
159	Fletchinder	♂/♀
158	Fletchling	♂/♀
69	Golbat	♂/♀
278	Honchkrow	♂/♀
	Hoothoot	♂/♀
78	Mandibuzz	♀
277	Murkrow	♂/♀
	Natu	♂/♀
	Noctowl	♂/♀
	Noibat	♂/♀
	Noivern	♂/♀
82	Oricorio	♂/♀
	Pidgeot	♂/♀
	Pidgeotto	♂/♀
	Pidgey	♂/♀
	Pidove	♂/♀
10	Pikipek	♂/♀
1	Rowlet	♂/♀
75	Rufflet	♂
	Sigilyph	♂/♀
208	Skarmory	♂/♀
73	Spearow	♂/♀
	Staraptor	♂/♀
	Staravia	♂/♀
	Starly	♂/♀
	Swellow	♂/♀
	Taillow	♂/♀
160	Talonflame	♂/♀
12	Toucannon	♂/♀
	Tranquill	♂/♀
11	Trumbeak	♂/♀
	Unfezant	♂/♀
77	Vullaby	♀
	Xatu	♂/♀
68	Zubat	♂/♀

Flying Group and Dragon Group

No.	Name	Gender
	Altaria	♂/♀
	Swablu	♂/♀

Flying Group and Fairy Group

No.	Name	Gender
	Togetic	♂/♀
	Togekiss	♂/♀

Flying Group and Field Group

No.	Name	Gender
	Farfetch'd	♂/♀
	Swoobat	♂/♀
	Woobat	♂/♀

Flying Group and Water Group 1

No.	Name	Gender
	Ducklett	♂/♀
41	Pelipper	♂/♀
	Swanna	♂/♀
40	Wingull	♂/♀

Flying Group and Water Group 3

No.	Name	Gender
192	Archen	♂/♀
193	Archeops	♂/♀

GRASS GROUP

Grass Group Only

No.	Name	Gender
	Amoonguss	♂/♀
	Bellossom	♂/♀
	Bellsprout	♂/♀
171	Bounsweet	♀
	Carnivine	♂/♀
174	Comfey	♀
269	Exeggcute	♂/♀
270	Exeggutor	♂/♀
143	Fomantis	♀
	Foongus	♂/♀
	Gloom	♂/♀
86	Lilligant	♀
144	Lurantis	♂/♀
	Maractus	♂/♀
145	Morelull	♂/♀
	Oddish	♂/♀
85	Petilil	♀
146	Shiinotic	♂/♀
172	Steenee	♀
	Sunflora	♂/♀
	Sunkern	♂/♀
	Tangela	♂/♀
	Tangrowth	♂/♀
173	Tsareena	♀
	Victreebel	♂/♀
	Vileplume	♂/♀
	Weepinbell	♂/♀

Grass Group and Amorphous Group

No.	Name	Gender
196	Phantump	♂/♀
197	Trevenant	♂/♀

Grass Group and Bug Group

No.	Name	Gender
147	Paras	♂/♀
148	Parasect	♂/♀

Grass Group and Fairy Group

No.	Name	Gender
	Breloom	♂/♀
	Cherrim	♂/♀
	Cherubi	♂/♀
87	Cottonee	♂/♀
	Hoppip	♂/♀
	Jumpluff	♂/♀
	Roselia	♂/♀
	Roserade	♂/♀
	Shroomish	♂/♀
	Skiploom	♂/♀
88	Whimsicott	♂/♀

Grass Group and Field Group

No.	Name	Gender
	Nuzleaf	♂/♀
	Seedot	♂/♀
	Serperior	♂/♀
	Servine	♂/♀
	Shiftry	♂/♀
	Snivy	♂/♀

Grass Group and Human-Like Group

No.	Name	Gender
	Cacnea	♂/♀
	Cacturne	♂/♀

Grass Group and Mineral Group

No.	Name	Gender
	Ferroseed	♂/♀
	Ferrothorn	♂/♀

Grass Group and Monster Group

No.	Name	Gender
	Abomasnow	♂/♀
	Bayleef	♂/♀
	Bulbasaur	♂/♀
	Chikorita	♂/♀
	Grotle	♂/♀
	Ivysaur	♂/♀
	Meganium	♂/♀
	Snover	♂/♀
	Torterra	♂/♀
	Tropius	♂/♀
	Turtwig	♂/♀
	Venusaur	♂/♀

Grass Group and Water Group 1

No.	Name	Gender
	Lombre	♂/♀
	Lotad	♂/♀
	Ludicolo	♂/♀

HUMAN-LIKE GROUP

Human-Like Group Only

No.	Name	Gender
42	Abra	♂/♀
44	Alakazam	♂/♀
	Beheeyem	♂/♀
	Bisharp	♂/♀
	Conkeldurr	♂/♀
	Croagunk	♂/♀
54	Drowzee	♂/♀
227	Electabuzz	♂/♀
228	Electivire	♂/♀
	Elgyem	♂/♀
	Gothita	♂/♀
	Gothitelle	♂/♀
	Gothorita	♂/♀
	Gurdurr	♂/♀
57	Hariyama	♂/♀
	Hawlucha	♂/♀
	Hitmonchan	♂
	Hitmonlee	♂
	Hitmontop	♂
55	Hypno	♂/♀
	Jynx	♀
43	Kadabra	♂/♀
97	Machamp	♂/♀
96	Machoke	♂/♀
95	Machop	♂/♀
167	Magmar	♂/♀
168	Magmortar	♂/♀
56	Makuhita	♂/♀
	Medicham	♂/♀
	Meditite	♂/♀
	Mr. Mime	♂/♀
	Pawniard	♂/♀
102	Sableye	♂/♀
	Sawk	♂
	Throh	♂
	Timburr	♂/♀
	Toxicroak	♂/♀

Human-Like Group and Bug Group

No.	Name	Gender
	Volbeat	♂
	Illumise	♀

Human-Like Group and Field Group

No.	Name	Gender
105	Spinda	♂/♀
	Chimchar	♂/♀
	Monferno	♂/♀
	Infernape	♂/♀
	Buneary	♂/♀
	Lopunny	♂/♀
	Mienfoo	♂/♀
	Mienshao	♂/♀
220	Pancham	♂/♀
221	Pangoro	♂/♀
280	Lucario	♂/♀

Human-Like Group and Grass Group

No.	Name	Gender
	Cacnea	♂/♀
	Cacturne	♂/♀

MINERAL GROUP

Mineral Group Only

No.	Name	Gender
	Aegislash	♂/♀
	Baltoy	Unknown
214	Beldum	Unknown
99	Boldore	♂/♀
	Bronzong	Unknown
	Bronzor	Unknown
	Claydol	Unknown
	Cryogonal	Unknown
263	Dhelmise	Unknown
	Doublade	♂/♀
	Electrode	Unknown
207	Garbodor	♂/♀
229	Geodude	♂/♀
100	Gigalith	♂/♀
231	Golem	♂/♀
	Golett	Unknown
	Golurk	Unknown
230	Graveler	♂/♀

MINERAL GROUP

Mineral Group Only

No.	Name	Gender
	Honedge	♂/♀
	Klang	Unknown
241	Klefki	♂/♀
	Klink	Unknown
	Klinklang	Unknown
	Lunatone	Unknown
47	Magnemite	Unknown
48	Magneton	Unknown
49	Magnezone	Unknown
216	Metagross	Unknown
215	Metang	Unknown
213	Minior	Unknown
198	Nosepass	♂/♀
	Onix	♂/♀
217	Porygon	Unknown
218	Porygon2	Unknown
219	Porygon-Z	Unknown
199	Probopass	♂/♀
98	Roggenrola	♂/♀
	Shedinja	Unknown
	Solrock	Unknown
	Steelix	♂/♀
31	Sudowoodo	♂/♀
206	Trubbish	♂/♀
256	Vanillish	♂/♀
255	Vanillite	♂/♀
257	Vanilluxe	♂/♀
	Voltorb	Unknown

Mineral Group and Amorphous Group

No.	Name	Gender
	Cofagrigus	♂/♀
	Yamask	♂/♀

Mineral Group and Bug Group

No.	Name	Gender
	Crustle	♂/♀
	Dwebble	♂/♀

Mineral Group and Fairy Group

No.	Name	Gender
101	Carbink	Unknown
248	Froslass	♀
247	Glalie	♂/♀
246	Snorunt	♂/♀

Mineral Group and Grass Group

No.	Name	Gender
	Ferroseed	♂/♀
	Ferrothorn	♂/♀

MONSTER GROUP

Monster Group Only

No.	Name	Gender
	Aggron	♂/♀
	Amaura	♂/♀
	Aron	♂/♀
	Aurorus	♂/♀
	Avalugg	♂/♀
191	Bastiodon	♂/♀
	Bergmite	♂/♀
188	Cranidos	♂/♀
163	Cubone	♂/♀
165	Kangaskhan	♀
	Lairon	♂/♀
	Larvitar	♂/♀
	Lickilicky	♂/♀
	Lickitung	♂/♀
164	Marowak	♂/♀
	Pupitar	♂/♀
189	Rampardos	♂/♀
190	Shieldon	♂/♀
36	Snorlax	♂/♀
	Tyranitar	♂/♀

Monster Group and Dragon Group

No.	Name	Gender
	Axew	♂/♀
	Charizard	♂/♀
	Charmander	♂/♀
	Charmeleon	♂/♀
244	Drampa	♂/♀
	Druddigon	♂/♀
	Fraxure	♂/♀
239	Gabite	♂/♀
240	Garchomp	♂/♀
238	Gible	♂/♀
	Grovyle	♂/♀
	Haxorus	♂/♀
	Heliolisk	♂/♀
	Helioptile	♂/♀
161	Salandit	♂/♀
162	Salazzle	♀
	Sceptile	♂/♀
	Treecko	♂/♀
224	Turtonator	♂/♀
	Tyrantrum	♂/♀
	Tyrunt	♂/♀

Monster Group and Field Group

No.	Name	Gender
	Ampharos	♂/♀
	Exploud	♂/♀
	Flaaffy	♂/♀
	Loudred	♂/♀
	Mareep	♂/♀
	Nidoking	♂
	Nidoran♀	♀
	Nidoran♂	♂
	Nidorino	♂
	Rhydon	♂/♀
	Rhyhorn	♂/♀
	Rhyperior	♂/♀
	Whismur	♂/♀

Monster Group and Grass Group

No.	Name	Gender
	Abomasnow	♂/♀
	Bayleef	♂/♀
	Bulbasaur	♂/♀
	Chikorita	♂/♀
	Grotle	♂/♀
	Ivysaur	♂/♀
	Meganium	♂/♀
	Snover	♂/♀
	Torterra	♂/♀
	Tropius	♂/♀
	Turtwig	♂/♀
	Venusaur	♂/♀

Monster Group and Water Group 1

No.	Name	Gender
	Blastoise	♂/♀
	Croconaw	♂/♀
	Feraligatr	♂/♀
268	Lapras	♂/♀
	Marshtomp	♂/♀
	Mudkip	♂/♀
38	Slowbro	♂/♀
39	Slowking	♂/♀
37	Slowpoke	♂/♀
	Squirtle	♂/♀
	Swampert	♂/♀
	Totodile	♂/♀
	Wartortle	♂/♀

WATER GROUP 1

Water Group 1 Only

No.	Name	Gender
	Clamperl	♂/♀
	Froakie	♂/♀
	Frogadier	♂/♀
	Gorebyss	♂/♀
	Greninja	♂/♀
	Huntail	♂/♀
	Mantine	♂/♀
113	Mareanie	♂/♀
	Palpitoad	♂/♀
152	Politoed	♂/♀
149	Poliwag	♂/♀
150	Poliwhirl	♂/♀
151	Poliwrath	♂/♀
200	Pyukumuku	♂/♀
	Seismitoad	♂/♀
114	Toxapex	♂/♀
	Tympole	♂/♀

Water Group 1 and Amorphous Group

No.	Name	Gender
261	Gastrodon	♂/♀
260	Shellos	♂/♀
	Stunfisk	♂/♀

Water Group 1 and Bug Group

No.	Name	Gender
142	Araquanid	♂/♀
141	Dewpider	♂/♀
140	Masquerain	♂/♀
139	Surskit	♂/♀

Water Group 1 and Dragon Group

No.	Name	Gender
	Dragalge	♂/♀
282	Dragonair	♂/♀
283	Dragonite	♂/♀
281	Dratini	♂/♀
155	Feebas	♂/♀
	Horsea	♂/♀
	Kingdra	♂/♀
156	Milotic	♂/♀
	Seadra	♂/♀
	Skrelp	♂/♀

Water Group 1 and Fairy Group

No.	Name	Gender
	Azumarill	♂/♀
	Manaphy	Unknown
	Marill	♂/♀
	Phione	Unknown

Water Group 1 and Field Group

No.	Name	Gender
	Bibarel	♂/♀
	Bidoof	♂/♀
8	Brionne	♂/♀
	Buizel	♂/♀
81	Delibird	♂/♀
	Dewgong	♂/♀
	Empoleon	♂/♀
	Floatzel	♂/♀
90	Golduck	♂/♀
	Piplup	♂/♀
7	Popplio	♂/♀
9	Primarina	♂/♀
	Prinplup	♂/♀
89	Psyduck	♂/♀
	Quagsire	♂/♀
	Sealeo	♂/♀
	Seel	♂/♀
	Spheal	♂/♀
	Walrein	♂/♀
	Wooper	♂/♀

Water Group 1 and Flying Group

No.	Name	Gender
	Ducklett	♂/♀
41	Pelipper	♂/♀
	Swanna	♂/♀
40	Wingull	♂/♀

Water Group 1 and Grass Group

No.	Name	Gender
	Lombre	♂/♀
	Lotad	♂/♀
	Ludicolo	♂/♀

Water Group 1 and Monster Group

No.	Name	Gender
	Blastoise	♂/♀
	Croconaw	♂/♀
	Feraligatr	♂/♀
268	Lapras	♂/♀
	Marshtomp	♂/♀
	Mudkip	♂/♀
38	Slowbro	♂/♀
39	Slowking	♂/♀
37	Slowpoke	♂/♀
	Squirtle	♂/♀
	Swampert	♂/♀
	Totodile	♂/♀
	Wartortle	♂/♀

Water Group 1 and Water Group 2

No.	Name	Gender
157	Alomomola	♂/♀
	Inkay	♂/♀
	Malamar	♂/♀
	Octillery	♂/♀
262	Relicanth	♂/♀
	Remoraid	♂/♀

Water Group 1 and Water Group 3

No.	Name	Gender
195	Carracosta	♂/♀
	Clauncher	♂/♀
	Clawitzer	♂/♀
	Corphish	♂/♀
112	Corsola	♂/♀
	Crawdaunt	♂/♀
	Kabuto	♂/♀
	Kabutops	♂/♀
	Omanyte	♂/♀
	Omastar	♂/♀
194	Tirtouga	♂/♀

WATER GROUP 2

Water Group 2 Only

No.	Name	Gender
93	Barboach	♂/♀
	Basculin	♂/♀
243	Bruxish	♂/♀
264	Carvanha	♂/♀
201	Chinchou	♂/♀
108	Finneon	♂/♀
153	Goldeen	♂/♀
202	Lanturn	♂/♀
109	Lumineon	♂/♀
111	Luvdisc	♂/♀
	Qwilfish	♂/♀
154	Seaking	♂/♀
265	Sharpedo	♂/♀
94	Whiscash	♂/♀
110	Wishiwashi	♂/♀

Water Group 2 and Dragon Group

No.	Name	Gender
92	Gyarados	♂/♀
91	Magikarp	♂/♀

Water Group 2 and Field Group

No.	Name	Gender
266	Wailmer	♂/♀
267	Wailord	♂/♀

Water Group 2 and Water Group 1

No.	Name	Gender
157	Alomomola	♂/♀
	Inkay	♂/♀
	Malamar	♂/♀
	Octillery	♂/♀
262	Relicanth	♂/♀
	Remoraid	♂/♀

WATER GROUP 3

Water Group 3 Only

No.	Name	Gender
	Anorith	♂/♀
	Armaldo	♂/♀
	Barbaracle	♂/♀
	Binacle	♂/♀
116	Cloyster	♂/♀
60	Crabominable	♂/♀
59	Crabrawler	♂/♀
	Cradily	♂/♀
	Kingler	♂/♀
	Krabby	♂/♀
	Lileep	♂/♀
115	Shellder	♂/♀
185	Starmie	Unknown
184	Staryu	Unknown
106	Tentacool	♂/♀
107	Tentacruel	♂/♀

Water Group 3 and Bug Group

No.	Name	Gender
	Drapion	♂/♀
183	Golisopod	♂/♀
	Skorupi	♂/♀
182	Wimpod	♂/♀

Water Group 3 and Flying Group

No.	Name	Gender
192	Archen	♂/♀
193	Archeops	♂/♀

Water Group 3 and Water Group 1

No.	Name	Gender
195	Carracosta	♂/♀
	Clauncher	♂/♀
	Clawitzer	♂/♀
	Corphish	♂/♀
112	Corsola	♂/♀
	Crawdaunt	♂/♀
	Kabuto	♂/♀
	Kabutops	♂/♀
	Omanyte	♂/♀
	Omastar	♂/♀
194	Tirtouga	♂/♀

Tip

Notice that some Pokémon are not listed in any of these tables. This means that no one has ever successfully found a Pokémon Egg after leaving them at the Pokémon Nursery. Many special Pokémon, like Legendary Pokémon, fall into this "No Eggs Discovered" group.

Despite their similar names, Water Group 1, Water Group 2, and Water Group 3 are in fact separate Egg Groups. Don't assume that leaving a Pokémon from Water Group 1 and Water Group 3, for example, will make you able to find a Pokémon Egg. The Pokémon still need to share a common group between them!

Make Friends with Wild Pokémon at Poké Pelago

Pokémon you've deposited in your PC Boxes freely play at the Isle Abeens. Sometimes wild Pokémon come to the Isle Abeens to play. Tap a wild Pokémon and wait a while, and it may go into a Poké Ball on its own and be registered in your Alola Pokédex.

❖ The process of adding a wild Pokémon that has come to play to your team

1 Tap Pokémon with ?

Tap a Pokémon with "?" over its head. You'll see that they like this place.

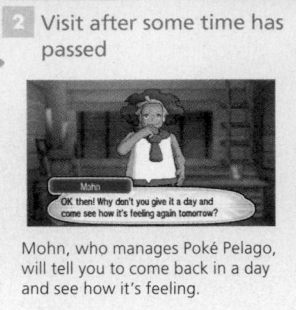

2 Visit after some time has passed

Mohn, who manages Poké Pelago, will tell you to come back in a day and see how it's feeling.

3 Pokémon join you on its own

A Pokémon that likes this place will have a heart over its head. Tap the Pokémon, and it will go into a Poké Ball on its own.

❖ Pokémon in the Alola Pokédex that come to the Isle Abeens to play

Alola Pokédex 010 Pikipek	Alola Pokédex 040 Wingull	Alola Pokédex 043 Kadabra	Alola Pokédex 047 Magnemite	Alola Pokédex 061 Gastly
Alola Pokédex 065 Drifblim	Alola Pokédex 067 Mismagius	Alola Pokédex 068 Zubat	Alola Pokédex 073 Spearow	Alola Pokédex 075 Rufflet
Alola Pokédex 077 Vullaby	Alola Pokédex 101 Carbink	Alola Pokédex 115 Shellder	Alola Pokédex 149 Poliwag	Alola Pokédex 158 Fletchling
Alola Pokédex 175 Pinsir	Alola Pokédex 184 Staryu	Alola Pokédex 197 Trevenant	Alola Pokédex 200 Pyukumuku	Alola Pokédex 208 Skarmory
Alola Pokédex 215 Metang	Alola Pokédex 241 Klefki	Alola Pokédex 268 Lapras	Alola Pokédex 274 Emolga	Alola Pokédex 275 Scyther
Alola Pokédex 277 Murkrow				

☀ *Pokémon Sun only*
☽ *Pokémon Moon only*

Put Poké Beans into the Poké Bean crate, and wild Pokémon come to play more often

The more islands you land on, the more Pokémon species show up on the Isle Abeens. Once you enter the Hall of Fame, as many as 26 species of Pokémon come to the Isle Abeens! Also, the more Poké Beans you put into the Pokémon Bean crate, the better the odds of wild Pokémon appearing.

Pikipek went into a Poké Ball!

❖ Likelihood of wild Pokémon coming to the Isle Abeens to play

Pokémon	After landing on Poké Pelago	After landing on Ula'ula Island	After landing on Poni Island	After entering the Hall of Fame
Pikipek	Often	Often	Often	Often
Wingull	Often	Often	Often	Often
Kadabra	Sometimes	Sometimes	Sometimes	Sometimes
Magnemite	Very often	Often	Often	Often
Gastly	Very often	Often	Often	Often
Drifblim	Sometimes	Sometimes	Sometimes	Sometimes
Mismagius	—	—	—	Sometimes
Zubat	Often	Often	Often	Often
Spearow	Often	Often	Often	Often
Rufflet ☀	Sometimes	Sometimes	Sometimes	Sometimes
Vullaby ☽	Sometimes	Sometimes	Sometimes	Sometimes
Carbink	Very often	Often	Often	Often
Shellder	Often	Often	Often	Often

Pokémon	After landing on Poké Pelago	After landing on Ula'ula Island	After landing on Poni Island	After entering the Hall of Fame
Poliwag	—	Very often	Often	Often
Fletchling	—	Very often	Often	Often
Pinsir	—	Very often	Often	Often
Staryu	—	Very often	Often	Often
Trevenant	—	Sometimes	Sometimes	Sometimes
Pyukumuku	—	Very often	Often	Often
Skarmory	—	—	Very often	Often
Metang	—	—	Sometimes	Sometimes
Klefki	—	—	Very often	Often
Lapras	—	—	—	Very often
Emolga	—	—	—	Very often
Scyther	—	—	—	Very often
Murkrow	Sometimes	Sometimes	Sometimes	Sometimes

☀ *Pokémon Sun only*   ☽ *Pokémon Moon only*

Obtain Pokémon via Trade

Trade is necessary to complete the Alola Pokédex. There are many ways to trade, such as Quick Link, which allows you to trade Pokémon with a person nearby, and GTS and Wonder Trade at Festival Plaza. People you'll be connected with via the Internet may be strangers, but you share the same desire to complete your Alola Pokédex. Give trading a try!

❖ Trading options available in *Pokémon Sun* and *Pokémon Moon*

 **Quick Link** **1** Trade Pokémon with a person nearby

Tap "Quick Link" on the lower screen, and you can trade Pokémon with a person nearby. As you can communicate with your trading partner about which Pokémon you want, you can fill your Alola Pokédex very efficiently.

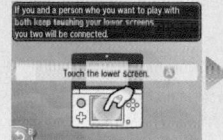
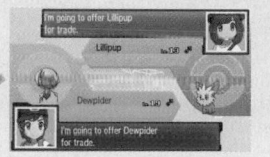

Link Trade **2** Trade Pokémon with people all over the world at Festival Plaza

Tap "Festival Plaza" on the lower screen, and you can trade Pokémon with people who visit your Festival Plaza from all over the world. If you trade Pokémon with people from other countries, not only can you fill your Pokédex, but also you can unlock their language pages in your Alola Pokédex.

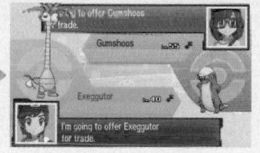

Wonder Trade **3** Trade Pokémon and be surprised by which Pokémon you get

Go to Festival Plaza, tap "Trade" on the lower screen, and select "Wonder Trade." Offer one Pokémon for trade, and you'll get another player's Pokémon in return. It's fun because you don't know which Pokémon you'll get!

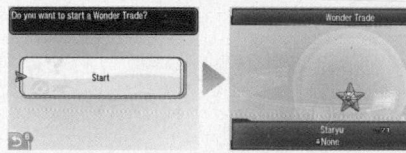

GTS **4** Trade Pokémon with people all over the world efficiently

The GTS (Global Trade Station) is a feature in which you trade Pokémon by setting conditions. Go to Festival Plaza, tap "Trade" on the lower screen, and select "GTS." Then choose "Seek Pokémon" or "Deposit Pokémon."

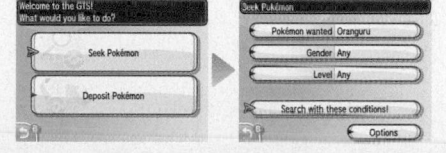

Obtain rare Pokémon via trade

There are Pokémon that exist only in *Pokémon Sun* or *Pokémon Moon*. Also, there is a time when you can pick only one Pokémon among multiple Pokémon. To register Pokémon that are not obtainable in your game, you need to trade Pokémon. Communicate and trade with people around the world, and complete your Alola Pokédex!

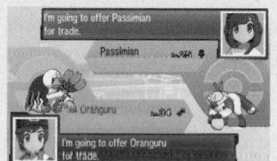

❖ Pokémon in the Alola Pokédex that appear only in *Pokémon Sun*

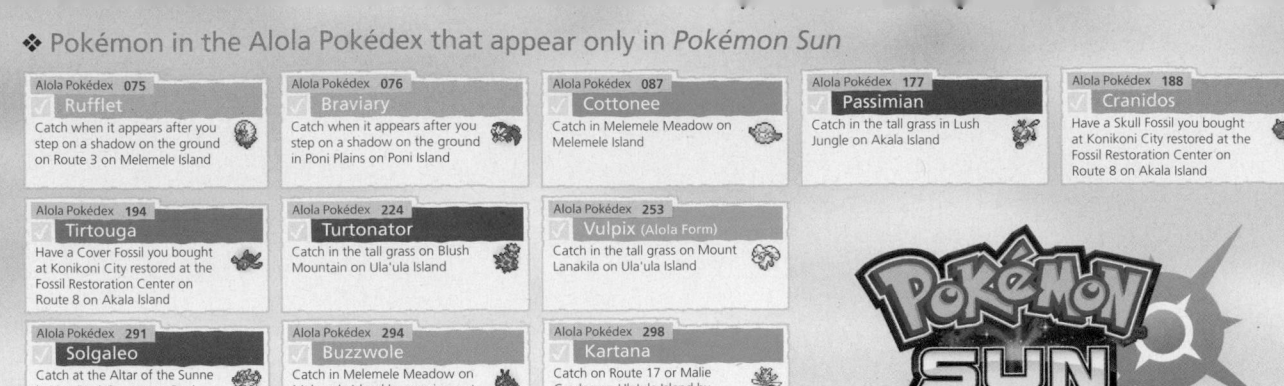

Alola Pokédex 075 Rufflet	Alola Pokédex 076 Braviary	Alola Pokédex 087 Cottonee	Alola Pokédex 177 Passimian	Alola Pokédex 188 Cranidos
Catch when it appears after you step on a shadow on the ground on Route 3 on Melemele Island	Catch when it appears after you step on a shadow on the ground in Poni Plains on Poni Island	Catch in Melemele Meadow on Melemele Island	Catch in the tall grass in Lush Jungle on Akala Island	Have a Skull Fossil you bought at Konikoni City restored at the Fossil Restoration Center on Route 8 on Akala Island

Alola Pokédex 194 Tirtouga	Alola Pokédex 224 Turtonator	Alola Pokédex 253 Vulpix (Alola Form)
Have a Cover Fossil you bought at Konikoni City restored at the Fossil Restoration Center on Route 8 on Akala Island	Catch in the tall grass on Blush Mountain on Ula'ula Island	Catch in the tall grass on Mount Lanakila on Ula'ula Island

Alola Pokédex 291 Solgaleo	Alola Pokédex 294 Buzzwole	Alola Pokédex 298 Kartana
Catch at the Altar of the Sunne in Vast Poni Canyon on Poni Island after visiting Ultra Space	Catch in Melemele Meadow on Melemele Island by carrying out missions to catch UBs requested by the International Police after entering the Hall of Fame	Catch on Route 17 or Malie Garden on Ula'ula Island by carrying out missions to catch UBs requested by the International Police after entering the Hall of Fame

❖ Pokémon in the Alola Pokédex that appear only in *Pokémon Moon*

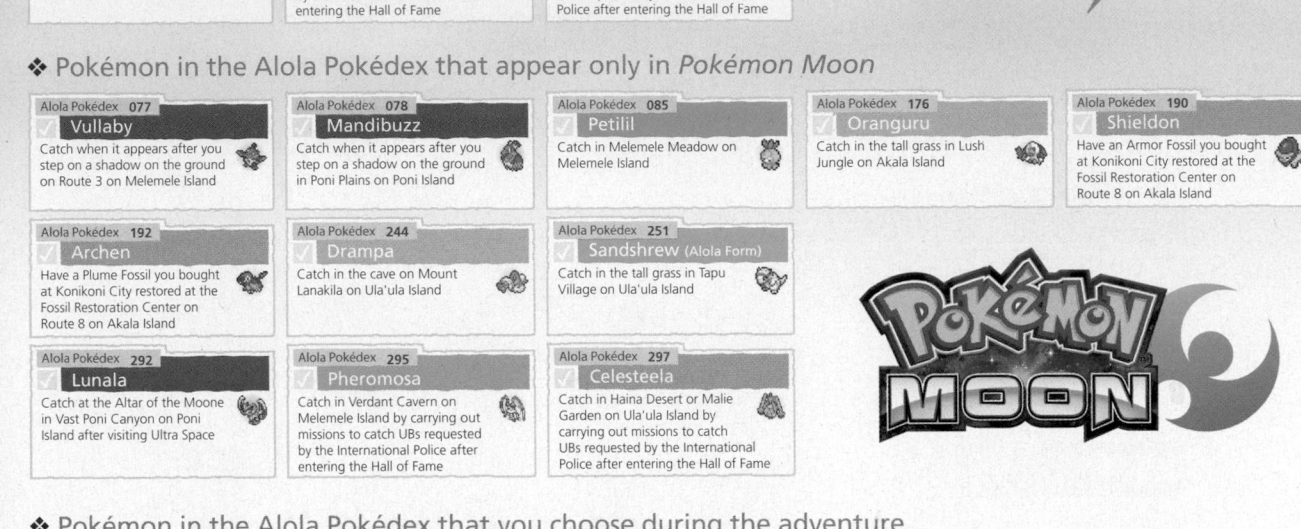

Alola Pokédex 077 Vullaby	Alola Pokédex 078 Mandibuzz	Alola Pokédex 085 Petilil	Alola Pokédex 176 Oranguru	Alola Pokédex 190 Shieldon
Catch when it appears after you step on a shadow on the ground on Route 3 on Melemele Island	Catch when it appears after you step on a shadow on the ground in Poni Plains on Poni Island	Catch in Melemele Meadow on Melemele Island	Catch in the tall grass in Lush Jungle on Akala Island	Have an Armor Fossil you bought at Konikoni City restored at the Fossil Restoration Center on Route 8 on Akala Island

Alola Pokédex 192 Archen	Alola Pokédex 244 Drampa	Alola Pokédex 251 Sandshrew (Alola Form)
Have a Plume Fossil you bought at Konikoni City restored at the Fossil Restoration Center on Route 8 on Akala Island	Catch in the cave on Mount Lanakila on Ula'ula Island	Catch in the tall grass in Tapu Village on Ula'ula Island

Alola Pokédex 292 Lunala	Alola Pokédex 295 Pheromosa	Alola Pokédex 297 Celesteela
Catch at the Altar of the Moone in Vast Poni Canyon on Poni Island after visiting Ultra Space	Catch in Verdant Cavern on Melemele Island by carrying out missions to catch UBs requested by the International Police after entering the Hall of Fame	Catch in Haina Desert or Malie Garden on Ula'ula Island by carrying out missions to catch UBs requested by the International Police after entering the Hall of Fame

❖ Pokémon in the Alola Pokédex that you choose during the adventure

Alola Pokédex 001 Rowlet	Alola Pokédex 004 Litten	Alola Pokédex 007 Popplio
Receive from Hala in Iki Town on Melemele Island	Receive from Hala in Iki Town on Melemele Island	Receive from Hala in Iki Town on Melemele Island

Make Pokémon evolve by trading

Some Pokémon evolve by trading. Get these Pokémon by trading with other players. Some Pokémon that evolve through trade also need special items. The recommended method for trading is to choose "Deposit Pokémon" at the GTS.

❖ Pokémon in the Alola Pokédex that evolve through trade

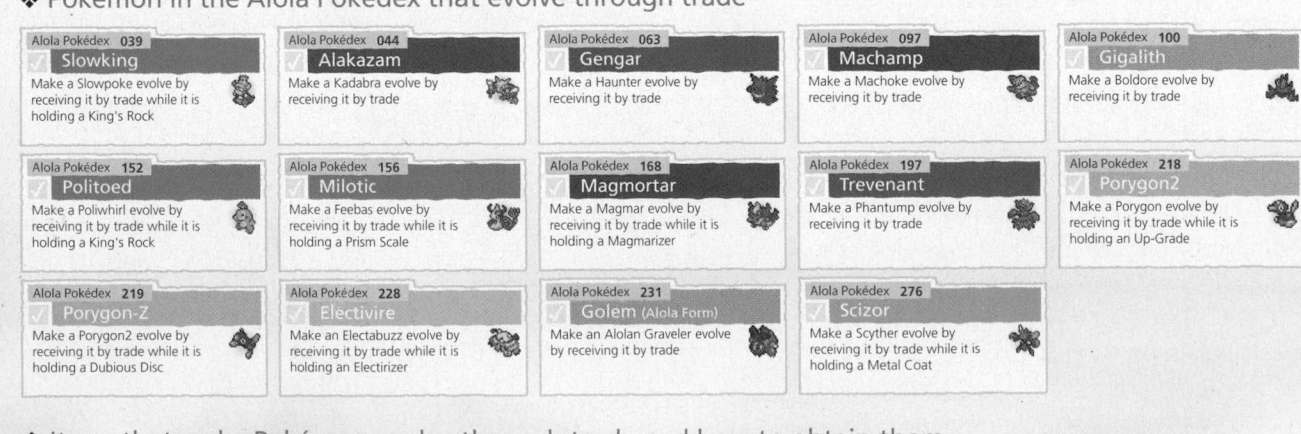

Alola Pokédex 039 Slowking	Alola Pokédex 044 Alakazam	Alola Pokédex 063 Gengar	Alola Pokédex 097 Machamp	Alola Pokédex 100 Gigalith
Make a Slowpoke evolve by receiving it by trade while it is holding a King's Rock	Make a Kadabra evolve by receiving it by trade	Make a Haunter evolve by receiving it by trade	Make a Machoke evolve by receiving it by trade	Make a Boldore evolve by receiving it by trade

Alola Pokédex 152 Politoed	Alola Pokédex 156 Milotic	Alola Pokédex 168 Magmortar	Alola Pokédex 197 Trevenant	Alola Pokédex 218 Porygon2
Make a Poliwhirl evolve by receiving it by trade while it is holding a King's Rock	Make a Feebas evolve by receiving it by trade while it is holding a Prism Scale	Make a Magmar evolve by receiving it by trade while it is holding a Magmarizer	Make a Phantump evolve by receiving it by trade	Make a Porygon evolve by receiving it by trade while it is holding an Up-Grade

Alola Pokédex 219 Porygon-Z	Alola Pokédex 228 Electivire	Alola Pokédex 231 Golem (Alola Form)	Alola Pokédex 276 Scizor
Make a Porygon2 evolve by receiving it by trade while it is holding a Dubious Disc	Make an Electabuzz evolve by receiving it by trade while it is holding an Electirizer	Make an Alolan Graveler evolve by receiving it by trade	Make a Scyther evolve by receiving it by trade while it is holding a Metal Coat

❖ Items that make Pokémon evolve through trade and how to obtain them

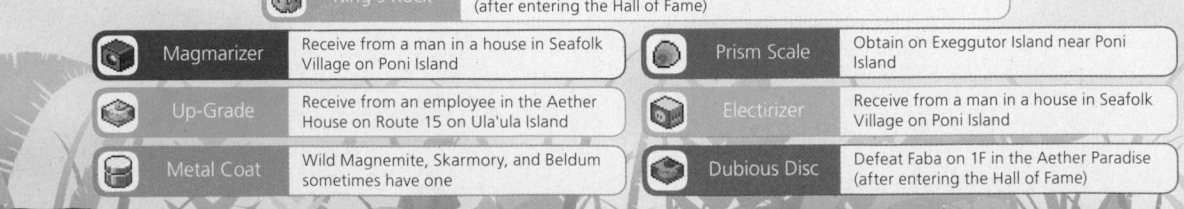

King's Rock	Defeat the principal on 3F in the Trainers' School on Melemele Island (after entering the Hall of Fame)

Magmarizer	Receive from a man in a house in Seafolk Village on Poni Island	Prism Scale	Obtain on Exeggutor Island near Poni Island
Up-Grade	Receive from an employee in the Aether House on Route 15 on Ula'ula Island	Electirizer	Receive from a man in a house in Seafolk Village on Poni Island
Metal Coat	Wild Magnemite, Skarmory, and Beldum sometimes have one	Dubious Disc	Defeat Faba on 1F in the Aether Paradise (after entering the Hall of Fame)

Champion's Guide to Alola

Champion's Guide to Alola

Even if you've completed your island challenge and etched your name into Alola's history books as the region's first-ever Pokémon League Champion, your time in this wondrous tropical region doesn't have to be over yet! Many new adventures are available to you as Alola's Champion. Read on to discover all of the exciting escapades that await!

Melemele Island—Champion Activities

1 | Meet a mysterious stranger

After you first clear the game, a mysterious man standing outside your home hands you a card that instructs you to visit the Roadside Motel on Route 8. Going there will begin an adventure involving a certain member of the International Police and those mind-boggling Ultra Beasts! (Turn to page 262 if you'd like to get started right away.)

Reward: Enigmatic Card

2 | Claim a TM from Kukui

Head south from your home and pop into the nearby Pokémon Research Lab. Catch up with Professor Kukui, who hands you TM90 Substitute just for dropping by. If you go up to the loft where Lillie used to stay, you can even get a peek at her secret diary.

Reward: TM90 Substitute

3 | Get another gift from Kukui

If you've been working on filling your Pokédex, Professor Kukui will also give you a special reward: a Lucky Egg! Give this item to a Pokémon to hold, and it will earn extra Exp. Points in battle. Note that you may need to leave the Pokémon Lab and return to get both goodies.

Reward: Lucky Egg

4 | Report to the principal's office

Head toward Hau'oli City next and stop by the old Trainers' School. Go up to the top floor, where a burly Black Belt is blocking off a room. Beat him in battle to make him step aside, then enter the room he was guarding to battle against the principal! Make the grade, and a King's Rock will be your reward.

Reward: King's Rock

Principal Asuka's Pokémon

Principal Asuka certainly knows her stuff. Her Pokémon have no common weaknesses, so you'll want to switch yours out as needed to gain the advantage. Give her a private lesson in just how powerful Alola's first-ever Champion has become!

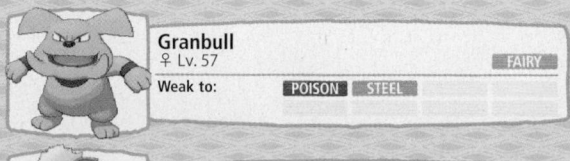

Granbull
♀ Lv. 57   FAIRY
Weak to: POISON   STEEL

Arcanine
♀ Lv. 57   FIRE
Weak to: WATER   GROUND   ROCK

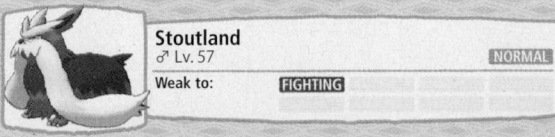

Stoutland
♂ Lv. 57   NORMAL
Weak to: FIGHTING

5 | Do some Hyper Training

You can now find Mr. Hyper standing between the two Move Tutors in the Hau'oli City shopping mall. If you've found any Bottle Caps, he can help your Pokémon max out their individual strengths through Hyper Training! The details of Hyper Training and individual strengths were explained in *Pokémon Sun & Pokémon Moon: The Official Alola Region Strategy Guide*.

6 | Settle the score with Guzma

Visit Guzma's family home (the one with the swing) on Route 2, and Guzma will tell you to meet him at the Hau'oli City Beachfront. Go to the beach if you're ready to have it out with a serious Guzma—and potentially win a Dawn Stone. Also pick up TM87 from his mom, if you haven't already.

Reward: TM87 Swagger, Dawn Stone

Guzma's Pokémon

Guzma gives you everything he's got this time around, so be prepared for a grueling battle against his barrage of Bug types. You've faced Guzma several times before, and while his team has grown stronger since your last clash at Aether Paradise, he doesn't throw too many new tricks at you. Fill your team with Fire-, Flying-, and Rock-type Pokémon to squash Guzma with supereffective attacks, but beware that Guzma's gang can really dish out the damage. Moving first is vital, so feed your Pokémon some Carbos to help improve their Speed stats, and give your best battler a Quick Claw to increase its chances of moving first each turn.

Golisopod ♂ Lv. 63 — BUG | WATER
Weak to: ELECTRIC | FLYING | ROCK

Ariados ♂ Lv. 63 — BUG | POISON
Weak to: FIRE | FLYING | PSYCHIC | ROCK

Pinsir ♂ Lv. 63 — BUG
Weak to: FIRE | FLYING | ROCK

Masquerain ♂ Lv. 63 — BUG | FLYING
Weak to: 4x ROCK | FIRE | ELECTRIC | ICE | FLYING

Scizor ♂ Lv. 63 — BUG | STEEL
Weak to: 4x FIRE

In case you missed it...

These optional jaunts around Melemele Island were available to you before becoming Champion, but here's a quick rundown in case you missed them:

- Explore all of the Seaward Cave and Kala'e Bay
- Search Melemele Sea on the backs of Lapras and Sharpedo
- Delve into the depths of Ten Carat Hill
- Master the Battle Buffet and meet the Battle Buffet Queen
- Put your Poké Finder to use at Melemele's photo spots: Hau'oli City Beachfront, Hau'oli City Shopping District, Hau'oli Cemetery, Kala'e Bay, and Melemele Meadow
- Make off with every last Zygarde Cell and Core around Melemele (p. 231)
- Catch Tapu Koko if you failed the first time and pick up an Electric Seed near the repaired Plank Bridge

Akala Island—Champion Activities

1 Challenge GAME FREAK's Morimoto

Head to Heahea City and visit GAME FREAK's office, which is located between the Pokémon Center and the Dimensional Research Lab. Now that you've become Champion, you can challenge Morimoto from GAME FREAK! It won't be easy, but the reward is well worth the effort.

Reward: Oval Charm

GAME FREAK Morimoto's Pokémon

Battling Morimoto? Now that's something only a true Champion would try! Be ready with plenty of medicines, for Morimoto's team likes to pound your Pokémon with moves that can cause confusion. His Kangaskhan lets loose with Dizzy Punch, while Machamp mixes you up with Dynamic Punch. His Flareon, Vaporeon, and Dragonite can also inflict status conditions, so come prepared with plenty of Full Restores to heal your Pokémon and remove these unwanted conditions.

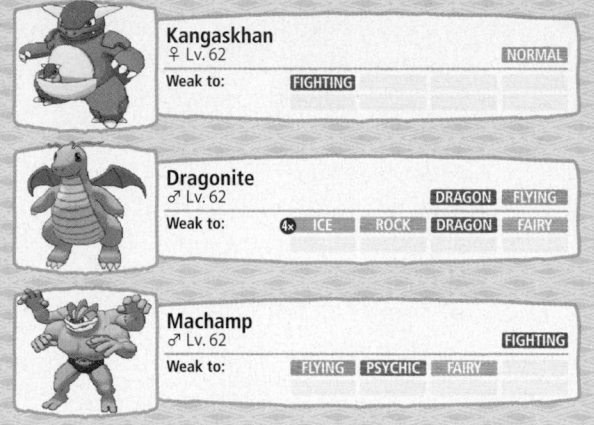

Kangaskhan ♀ Lv. 62	NORMAL
Weak to: FIGHTING	

Dragonite ♂ Lv. 62	DRAGON FLYING
Weak to: 4× ICE ROCK DRAGON FAIRY	

Machamp ♂ Lv. 62	FIGHTING
Weak to: FLYING PSYCHIC FAIRY	

Jolteon ♂ Lv. 62	ELECTRIC
Weak to: GROUND	

Flareon ♂ Lv. 62	FIRE
Weak to: WATER GROUND ROCK	

Vaporeon ♂ Lv. 62	WATER
Weak to: GRASS ELECTRIC	

2 Pad your Trainer Passport with Pokédex stamps

Have you been catching lots of Pokémon? Get out there and complete an Island Pokédex, then return to GAME FREAK's office and talk to the game director. He'll mark your Trainer Passport with a special stamp for each Island Pokédex you complete!

Reward: Trainer Passport stamps

3 Get a tricky TM at Hano Grand Resort

Head east into Hano Grand Resort to find Kahili hanging out in the hotel lobby. She's here to work on her golf game, and harbors no hard feelings from your battle at the Pokémon League. In fact, she hands you TM92 Trick Room in the hopes that you'll find it useful!

Reward: TM92 Trick Room

4 Get a bit of protection

If you swing by Paniola Town, you can talk with Kiawe's father in their family home. He will be glad to see that his boy is making friends and will reward you with a Protector! A Protector is needed to make the Pokémon Rhydon evolve into Rhyperior, if you happen to ever acquire one in a trade.

Reward: Protector

5 | Catch up with Colress on Route 8

Fly to Route 8, then head east to find the scientist Colress standing near the Aether Base. This time, he gives you drives that allow a Pokémon called Genesect to fire off different types of attacks. Genesect was available as part of special events in the past. Perhaps it will appear again in another event someday!

Reward: Douse Drive, Shock Drive, Burn Drive, Chill Drive

Tip

Want a little glimpse into Gladion's past? Stop by the Roadside Motel on Route 8 and talk to the manager in the office.

6 | Get some gifts at Mallow's family restaurant

Fly to Konikoni City next and pop by Mallow's family restaurant. Talk to the Punk Girl inside to get a few special gifts from Mallow. They're items that will help certain Pokémon evolve! Head upstairs afterward and talk to the Cook on the couch to claim a Dragon Fang. What a haul!

Reward: Whipped Dream, Sachet, Dragon Fang

7 | Track down the Eevee Evolution users!

Remember the clerk at the Thrifty Megamart who said he might have a challenge for you? Return to the shop as a Champion, and he will ask you to track down eight Trainers that he knew in his youth. Defeat them all, then return to claim your reward: a Z-Crystal that allows Eevee to use its signature Z-Move—Extreme Evoboost!

Reward: Eevium Z

Finding the Eevee Evolution Users

There are eight Trainers that Kagetora knew in his youth, and he wants you to help him check in on them. You'll have to fly all around the region to meet them all. If you're having trouble finding any of them, here are their exact locations. Each uses only the Pokémon that they've long specialized in (so Vaporeon User Polly sends out a Vaporeon), making these battles no problem to prepare for if you're a real Champion.

Trainer	Location	Island
Vaporeon User Polly	Trainers' School in Hau'oli Outskirts	Melemele Island
Flareon User Chad	Tide Song Hotel in Heahea City	Akala Island
Jolteon User Jane	Malie Community Center in Malie City	Ula'ula Island
Espeon User Ishaan	Geothermal Power Plant on Blush Mountain	Ula'ula Island
Umbreon User Braiden	Hau'oli Cemetery off Route 2	Melemele Island
Glaceon User Rea	Iki Town	Melemele Island
Leafeon User Linnea	Hano Beach	Akala Island
Sylveon User Sakura	Seafolk Village	Poni Island

8 | Catch Tapu Lele!

Fly to the Ruins of Life and maneuver through with Machamp to reach the shrine chamber, then touch the statue and try to catch Tapu Lele! It's a good idea to save your game before the battle, just in case things don't go your way.

Pokémon: Tapu Lele

Tapu Lele

Tape Lele has the Psychic Surge Ability, which creates the Psychic Terrain battle condition as it enters battle. This condition protects Pokémon on the ground from priority moves used against them for five turns. Psychic Terrain also boosts the power of Psychic-type moves for its duration, making Tapu Lele's Extrasensory move very dangerous. Although Dark-type Pokémon are immune to Psychic-type moves, keep your Dark types away from the fray, because Tapu Lele also lashes out with Nature's Madness and Moonblast: two Fairy-type moves that will do big damage against Dark-type Pokémon. Tapu Lele also uses Flatter to confuse your Pokémon and raise their Sp. Atk, so be ready to counter with curatives such as Big Malasadas, Full Heals, and Full Restores.

Tapu Lele
Lv. 60   PSYCHIC FAIRY
Weak to: POISON GHOST STEEL

In case you missed it...

These optional excursions around Akala Island were available to you before becoming Champion, but here's a quick listing in case you missed them.

- Become a Battle Royal master at the Battle Royal Dome on Royal Avenue
- Take your Poké Finder for a spin at Akala's photo spots: Brooklet Hill, Wela Volcano Park, Lush Jungle, Royal Avenue, Paniola Ranch, and Route 8
- Acquire all of Akala's Zygarde Cells and Cores (p. 231)

Ula'ula Island—Champion Activities

1 | Score a special stone in Haina Desert

Return to Haina Desert and track down an old man who now appears in Area 3. Fly to Route 13, enter the desert from its main entrance, go north and then east to find him. Once you've found the old fellow, show him Solrock ☀ or Lunatone ☾ to receive a Sun Stone ☀ / Moon Stone ☾! Note that these two Pokémon can't be found in Alola, so you'll need to obtain them through *Pokémon Bank* (p. 31) or trade (p. 245).

Reward: Sun Stone ☀ / Moon Stone ☾

2 | Swing by Po Town and support Team Skull

Times haven't been kind to Team Skull. Pop by Po Town's Pokémon Center, and you'll find the Grunts there are now eager to flee the scene. Everyone deserves a fresh start, so support their cause by dropping ₽10,000 on one of their trademark Skull Tank shirts.

3 | Acquire a Pokémon and an item from the Aether House

Fly to Tapu Village, and head west and then north to reach Route 15. Head for the Aether House, where two grateful Aether employees hand you a Porygon and its useful Up-Grade for helping to dispel the shadow that hung over their charitable foundation.

Pokémon: Porygon   **Reward: Up-Grade**

4 | Defend your seat as Champion

You've worked hard to become Alola's first every Champion—now you get to defend your title! Fly back to the Pokémon League and defeat the Elite Four once more and when you return to the Champion's room to sit upon your throne, a challenger will appear to try to claim it! Turn to pages 269–270 to see who might appear.

5 | Catch Tapu Bulu!

Make your way through Haina Desert to reach the Ruins of Abundance, or simply fly there if you've been there before. Shove the stone boulders with Machamp to reach the shrine chamber, then touch the statue and try to catch Tapu Bulu! You may want to save your game before the battle in case things don't play out as expected.

Pokémon: Tapu Bulu

Tapu Bulu

Tapu Bulu has the Grassy Surge Ability, which creates the Grassy Terrain battle condition as it enters battle. This condition causes Pokémon on the ground to recover a little HP each turn for five turns. Grassy Terrain also

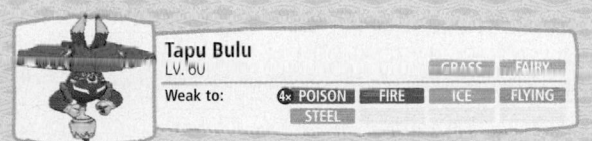

boosts the power of Grass-type moves for its duration. Like its fellow guardian deities, Tapu Bulu uses Nature's Madness to halve your Pokémon's HP. It also uses Skull Bash, a two-turn Normal-type move that increases Tapu Bulu's Defense on the first turn, and then causes Tapu Bulu to lash out for damage on the second. And it also uses Zen Headbutt, a strong Psychic-type move with a chance to make your Pokémon flinch and fail to act.

In case you missed it...

These optional asides around Ula'ula Island were available to you before becoming Champion, but here's a quick rundown in case you missed them.

- Explore all of Haina Desert
- Master all of the battle styles that Gester can teach you near the Recycling Plant in Malie City's Outer Cape
- Stop by the Aether Base on Route 16 and use the Reassembly Unit to assemble Zygarde (p. 230)
- Fire up your Poké Finder at Ula'ula's photo spots: Route 13, Mount Hokulani, Mount Lanakila, Ula'ula Meadow, the abandoned Thrifty Megamart, and Blush Mountain
- Collect all of Ula'ula's Zygarde Cells and Cores (p. 231)

Poni Island—Champion Activities

1 | Nab some Nuggets

Visit Seafolk Village's Pokémon Center and talk to the Sightseer near the café—but be ready for battle! He sends out a Shiny Exeggcute, which should be short work for your team. After the battle, he graciously hands you a half-dozen Nuggets!

Reward: Nugget ×6

2 | Battle Dexio on Ancient Poni Path

Fly to the Ancient Poni Path, then run south and then east to meet those traveling researchers, Sina and Dexio. After reminding you to make use of the Reassembly Unit in the Aether Base on Route 16, Dexio challenges you to a battle. Beat him to unlock the power of Mega Evolution!

Reward: Key Stone, Alakazite

Dexio's Pokémon

Dexio favors Psychic-type Pokémon, but don't expect to topple his team solely by sending out Dark types—many of his Pokémon can unleash unexpected moves that are super effective against Dark-type Pokémon. For example, Metagross can use Brick Break, a Fighting-type move that will smash any Dark types you send out. If you try to rely on Bug-type Pokémon, be aware that Slowking uses Power Gem—a Rock-type move that will squash any Bug types you employ. His Alolan Raichu makes things interesting with Reflect, which effectively halves your team's physical damage output for five turns. Dexio's biggest threat by far is Alakazam because it can Mega Evolve into Mega Alakazam. This Psychic-type Pokémon's high Speed stat often lets it move first, and it will devastate any Dark-type Pokémon you send out with its furious Focus Blast. Try to wipe out Alakazam with a Z-Move, or surprise it with Sucker Punch—a Dark-type move that always strikes first if the opponent is readying an attack move of its own.

Espeon
♂ Lv. 61 — PSYCHIC
Weak to: BUG GHOST DARK

Alolan Raichu
♀ Lv. 61 — ELECTRIC PSYCHIC
Weak to: GROUND BUG GHOST DARK

Slowking
♂ Lv. 61 — WATER PSYCHIC
Weak to: GRASS ELECTRIC BUG GHOST DARK

Metagross
Lv. 61 — STEEL PSYCHIC
Weak to: FIRE GROUND GHOST DARK

Mega Alakazam
♂ Lv. 61 — PSYCHIC
Weak to: BUG GHOST DARK

3 | Defeat the Hidden Maidens!

A pair of Swimmers on Poni Breaker Coast are visiting from another region, hoping to strike it big here in Alola. Help them out with a battle for their promotional video and they'll reward you with two TMs for the moves Surf and Waterfall!

Reward: TM94 Surf, TM98 Waterfall

Mega Evolution

Mega Evolution is an Evolution beyond all typical Evolutions! It happens only during battle and has some astounding effects. Mega Evolution can change a Pokémon's stats, Ability, and type, as well as its appearance, making it far more formidable. Only certain Pokémon are capable of undergoing this incredible transformation

Key Stone and Mega Stone

A few conditions must be met before your Pokémon can Mega Evolve. First, you need a Key Stone, which Dexio gives you after you've become Champion and battled him on the Ancient Poni Path Key Stones are commonly embedded in accessories, like necklaces and bracelets worn by Trainers—such as your Z-Ring.

A Mega Stone is needed for each Pokémon that wishes to take advantage of Mega Evolution. Mega Stones are a type of held item that allow Pokémon that are capable of Mega Evolution to Mega Evolve. Note that each Pokémon capable of Mega Evolution has its own unique Mega Stone—Alakazam needs to hold Alakazite in order to Mega Evolve, for example. Dexio also gives you an Alakazite when he hands you the Key Stone, giving you the power to Mega Evolve Alakazam right away. Most other Mega Stones available in Alola can be purchased by talking to the right attendant at the BP shop at the Battle Tree.

Once you have everything you need, you'll be ready to unleash Mega Evolution. Unlike other Evolutions, Mega Evolution is triggered during battle, and the effect wears off when the battle ends. Choose the "Fight" option, and then tap the "Mega Evolution" icon on the Touch Screen before selecting a move. Your Pokémon will then Mega Evolve before your eyes and unleash the move you've chosen.

Tip

You can only Mega Evolve one Pokémon per battle, even if you have more than one Pokémon in your team capable of Mega Evolution. Mega-Evolved Pokémon can be switched in and out of battle without undoing their transformation, but if a Mega-Evolved Pokémon faints during battle, it will revert to its normal form.

Mega Stones found in *Pokémon Sun* and *Pokémon Moon*

Mega Stone	How to Obtain
Absolite	Purchase at the BP shop at the Battle Tree
Aerodactylite	Purchase at the BP shop at the Battle Tree
Alakazite	Get one for defeating Dexio, or purchase at the BP shop at the Battle Tree
Blastoisinite	Defeat Red at the Battle Tree
Charizardite X	Defeat Red at the Battle Tree
Charizardite Y	Defeat Red at the Battle Tree
Garchompite	Purchase at the BP shop at the Battle Tree
Gengarite	Purchase at the BP shop at the Battle Tree
Glalitite	Purchase at the BP shop at the Battle Tree
Gyaradosite	Purchase at the BP shop at the Battle Tree
Kangaskhanite	Purchase at the BP shop at the Battle Tree
Lucarionite	Purchase at the BP shop at the Battle Tree
Metagrossite	Purchase at the BP shop at the Battle Tree
Pinsirite	Purchase at the BP shop at the Battle Tree
Sablenite	Purchase at the BP shop at the Battle Tree
Salamencite	Purchase at the BP shop at the Battle Tree
Scizorite	Purchase at the BP shop at the Battle Tree
Sharpedonite	Purchase at the BP shop at the Battle Tree
Slowbronite	Purchase at the BP shop at the Battle Tree
Venusaurite	Defeat Red at the Battle Tree

Rayquaza and Primal Reversion

An ancient Legendary Pokémon from the Hoenn region, Rayquaza, is capable of undergoing Mega Evolution without the need for a Mega Stone—all it needs is to know the move Dragon Ascent. If you have obtained Rayquaza from another game, speak with the old man in Seafolk Village's Pokémon Center to teach Rayquaza Dragon Ascent, and once you've gained access to Mega Evolution, Rayquaza will be able to Mega Evolve during battle.

Two other ancient Legendary Pokémon from the Hoenn region, Groudon and Kyogre, can also undergo a powerful transformation that's akin to Mega Evolution. Their transformation is known as Primal Reversion—but rather than requiring Mega Stones, Groudon must be given a Red Orb to hold, while Kyogre must hold a Blue Orb. Both of these items can be purchased at Antiquities of the Ages in the Hau'oli City shopping mall.

---

4 | Explore Poni Island's eastern reaches

Your quest to become Champion never took you to the east side of Poni Island. In fact, you couldn't have visited these areas before now! Take the Ancient Poni Path's northeast trail to reach Poni Grove and the sprawling plains that lie beyond. (Turn to pages 259–261 to see what's in store!)

---

5 | Upgrade your PC Boxes at the Battle Tree

At the Battle Tree (p. 271), you can have an Ace Trainer upgrade your PC Boxes to have the Judge feature as long as you've been busy hatching at least 20 Pokémon Eggs found at the Pokémon Nursery. The Battle Tree lies beyond the grueling Poni Gauntlet (p. 261).

---

6 | Catch Tapu Fini!

Fly back to the Ruins of Hope, which you visited when Hapu was appointed kahuna of Poni Island. Walk right into the shrine chamber once more, and touch the statue to try to catch Tapu Fini! Save your game before the battle so you can easily try again if you fail to catch it.

Pokémon: Tapu Fini

Tapu Fini

Tapu Fini has the Misty Surge Ability, which creates the Misty Terrain battle condition as it enters battle. While this condition is active, Pokémon on the ground won't get any status conditions for five turns. Misty Terrain also halves the damage from Dragon-type moves for its

Tapu Fini
Lv. 60   WATER FAIRY
Weak to: GRASS ELECTRIC POISON

duration, but Tapu Fini is immune to Dragon-type moves, so this shouldn't be much of a factor for you. Tapu Fini can cut your Pokémon's HP in half with Nature's Madness, and wash them away with Muddy Water, a strong Water-type move that can reduce your Pokémon's accuracy. Tapu Fini also uses Aqua Ring to recover HP each turn. Play a largely defensive battle until Misty Terrain wears off, then look to inflict status conditions on Tapu Fini and catch it once its HP is low.

In case you missed it...

These optional asides around Poni Island were available to you before becoming Champion, but here's a quick listing in case you missed them:

- Take your Poké Finder for a spin in these photo spots: Vast Poni Canyon, Poni Meadow, and Poni Coast
- Procure all of Poni's Zygarde Cells and Cores (p. 231)

Journey to Another World!

After you've caught Solgaleo ☀ or Lunala ☽ and become Alola's first-ever Champion, visit the Altar of the Sunne ☀ / Altar of the Moone ☽ with Solgaleo or Lunala in your team. Go there at night if you're playing *Pokémon Sun*, or during the day if you're playing *Pokémon Moon*.

At the top of the altar, you'll find a strange distortion. When you examine it, you'll be asked if you'd like to go to another world that lies beyond it. Say yes to transport yourself to the Altar of the Moone ☀ / Altar of the Sunne ☽. You are now in a different world, one where time runs opposite to the Alola that you came from! Fly over to Ula'ula Island, make your way to Ula'ula Meadow, and take the path out of it at the northeast corner. This will lead you to the Lake of the Sunne ☀ / Lake of the Moone ☽.

When you reach the top of the platform in the middle of the lake, your Solgaleo/Lunala will suddenly roar at the sky. If you're playing *Pokémon Sun*, Lunala will appear and stare down your Solgaleo. If you're playing *Pokémon Moon*, Solgaleo will appear and stare down your Lunala. Then your Legendary Pokémon will return to its Poké Ball, its counterpart will disappear, and a Cosmog will appear before you. Examine it and you'll be able to take it with you! Return to the Altar of the Moone / Altar of the Sunne to go back to the world from which you originally came.

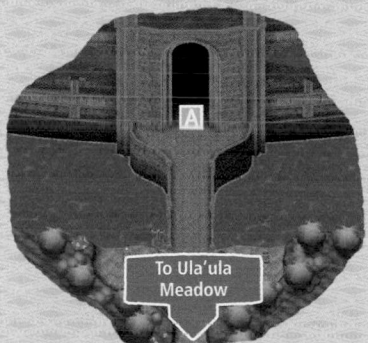

**Lake of the Moone /
Lake of the Sunne (Exterior)**

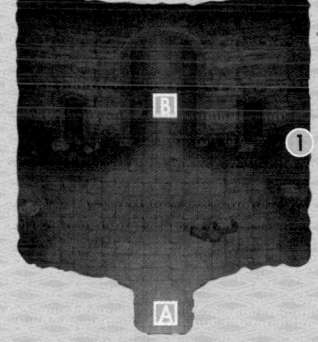

**Lake of the Moone /
Lake of the Sunne (Interior)**

**Lake of the Moone /
Lake of the Sunne (Hallway)**

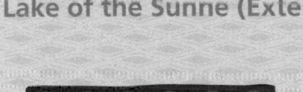

Items

☐	1	TM03 Psyshock

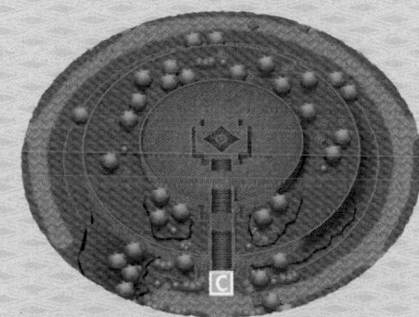

Lake of the Sunne (Altar)

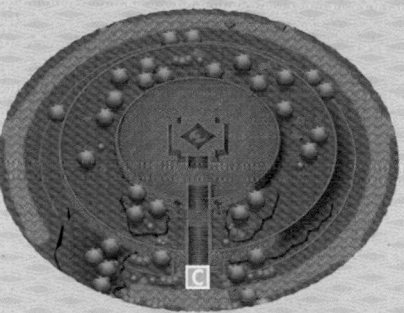

Lake of the Moone (Altar)

Tip

Visiting this parallel world is also a good way to catch Pokémon that only appear at night or during the day, if you are having a hard time playing at those times in your game. Time will be reversed, allowing you to explore and see Alola in a new light!

ALOLA REGION
40KER EX

HOW TO COMPLETE
THE ALOLA POKÉDEX

CHAMPION'S
GUIDE TO ALOLA

ADVENTURE
DATA

Aether Paradise—Champion Activities

1 | Battle against Aether Foundation Faba

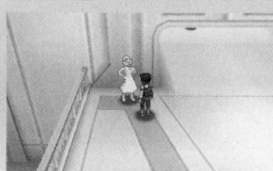

Fly to Aether Paradise and enter the main building. Run north, past the elevator, to find Faba standing on the left side of the tunnel that leads out to the mansion's courtyard. Faba's turned over a new leaf since your last visit and he asks if you wouldn't mind a friendly battle.

Reward: Dubious Disc

Aether Foundation Faba's Pokémon

Faba's team of Psychic-type Pokémon is both fast and crafty. Many of them will move first each turn unless your Pokémon are equally speedy, and in addition to dishing out damage with strong moves like Psychic, they can also use sneaky status moves to gain unexpected advantages. Alakazam, for instance, can use Disable to prevent your Pokémon from using the move they just used for four turns, while Slowbro can use Yawn to make your Pokémon fall Asleep. Fortunately, Faba's team is riddled with common weaknesses, so capitalize with Pokémon that can punish them with supereffective damage.

Slowbro ♂ Lv. 61 — WATER | PSYCHIC
Weak to: GRASS | ELECTRIC | BUG | GHOST | DARK

Bruxish ♂ Lv. 61 — WATER | PSYCHIC
Weak to: GRASS | ELECTRIC | BUG | GHOST | DARK

Alolan Raichu ♂ Lv. 61 — ELECTRIC | PSYCHIC
Weak to: GROUND | BUG | GHOST | DARK

Alakazam ♂ Lv. 61 — PSYCHIC
Weak to: BUG | GHOST | DARK

Hypno ♂ Lv. 61 — PSYCHIC
Weak to: BUG | GHOST | DARK

2 | Get a bunch of gifts from Gladion

Take the elevator up to 2F after your battle with Faba and head north to find Gladion. He can't make up for his mother's offenses, but he gives you a familiar Pokémon and a whole stack of memory drives in the hopes that they will serve you well.

Pokémon: Type: Null　　**Reward: Memory Drive ×17**

Type: Null and Silvally

You got your very own Type: Null! Gladion also handed you all the memory that its Evolution, Silvally, can use. When Type: Null becomes friendly enough toward you, it will evolve to Silvally. Silvally's RKS System Ability lets it change type depending on the memory it's holding. If you give it a Ground Memory to hold, it will become a Ground-type Pokémon. A Poison Memory will make it a Poison-type Pokémon, and so on. Silvally's signature move, Multi-Attack, will also change types depending on the memory it's holding.

3 | Receive a message from Lillie

Ride down to B2F to find Wicke. She'll fill you in on the latest from Lillie, then give you two Big Malasadas. Pop by Secret Lab A next to pick up some items that will help power up some rare Pokémon.

Reward: Big Malasada ×2, DNA Splicers, Prison Bottle, Soul Dew

Poni Grove / Poni Plains

Ride Pokémon Needed

Nestled near the Ancient Poni Path's northeast corner, Poni Grove serves as the gateway to Poni Island's eastern lands. Located on the east side of Poni Island, Poni Plains are home to a wide variety of wild Pokémon.

Team Recommendations

ELECTRIC	ICE	FIGHTING
POISON	FLYING	ROCK

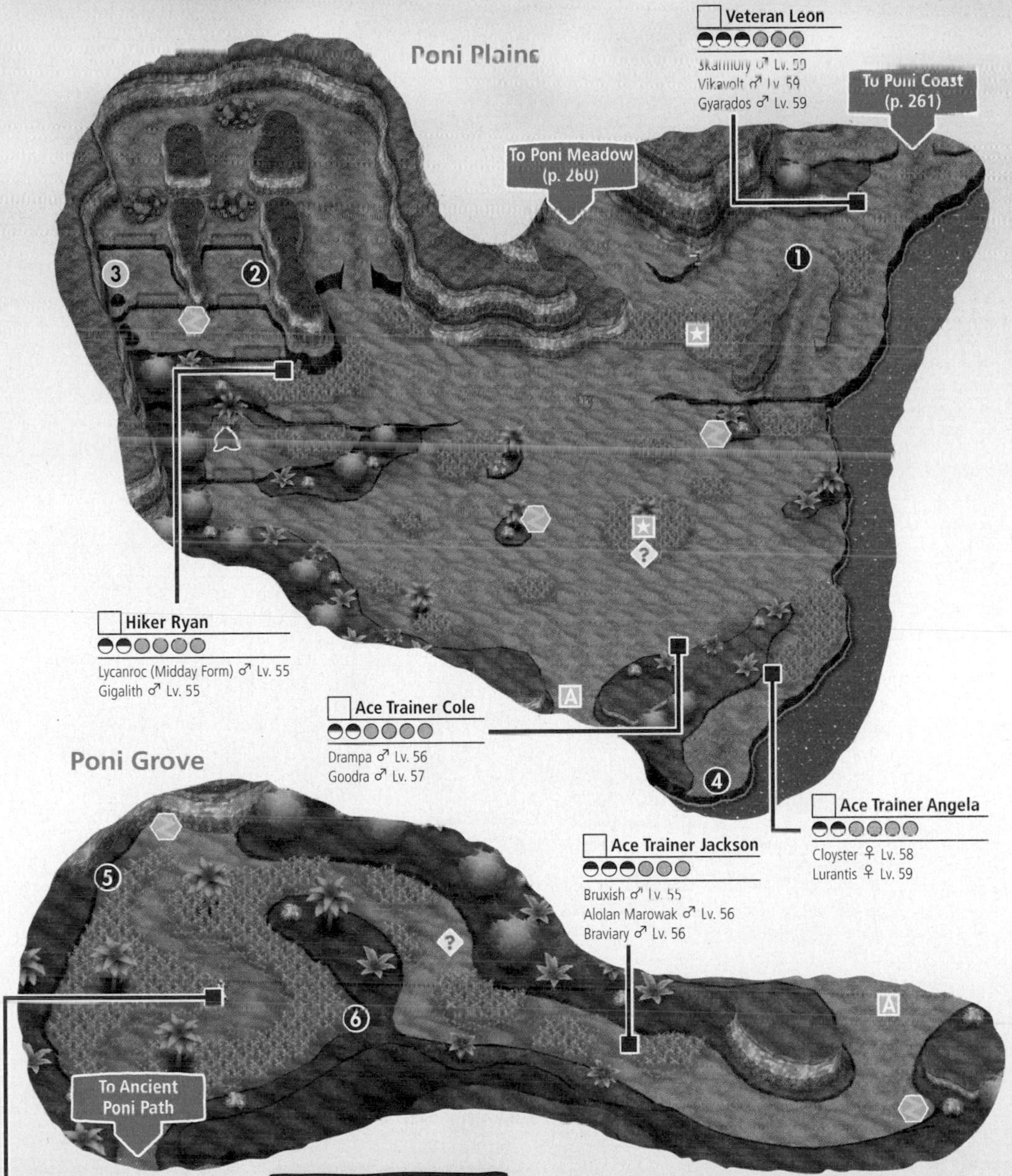

Poni Plains

Veteran Leon
◯◯◯◯◯◯
Skarmory ♂ Lv. 59
Vikavolt ♂ Lv. 59
Gyarados ♂ Lv. 59

To Poni Coast (p. 261)

To Poni Meadow (p. 260)

③ ② **①**

Hiker Ryan
◯◯◯◯◯◯
Lycanroc (Midday Form) ♂ Lv. 55
Gigalith ♂ Lv. 55

Poni Grove

⑤

⑥

To Ancient Poni Path

Black Belt Roy
◯◯◯◯◯◯
Crabominable ♂ Lv. 56

Ace Trainer Cole
◯◯◯◯◯◯
Drampa ♂ Lv. 56
Goodra ♂ Lv. 57

Ace Trainer Jackson
◯◯◯◯◯◯
Bruxish ♂ Lv. 55
Alolan Marowak ♂ Lv. 56
Braviary ♂ Lv. 56

Ace Trainer Angela
◯◯◯◯◯◯
Cloyster ♀ Lv. 58
Lurantis ♀ Lv. 59

④

Ⓐ

Ⓐ

Tall Grass

Poni Plains (Northwest)

Cottonee	☀	◯
Fearow		◯
Gumshoos	◯	△
Miltank		△
Mudsdale		◡
Petilil	☾	◯
Alolan Raticate	☽	△
Tauros		△
Trumbeak		△

Poni Plains (Central)

Cottonee	☀	◡
Gumshoos	◡	◯
Miltank		△
Petilil	☾	◯
Alolan Raticate	☽	◯
Tauros		△
Trumbeak		◡

Poni Plains (East)

Cottonee	☀	◯
Gumshoos	◯	◯
Miltank		△
Pelipper		◯
Petilil	☾	◯
Alolan Raticate	☽	◯
Tauros		△
Trumbeak		△

Poni Plains ✦

Cottonee	☀	◯
Gumshoos	◯	◯
Hypno		◯
Miltank		△
Petilil	☾	◯
Alolan Raticate	☽	◯
Tauros		△
Trumbeak		△

Poni Grove

Granbull		◯
Gumshoos	◯	◯
Pinsir		△
Alolan Raticate	☽	◯
Riolu		△
Trumbeak		◯

Rustling Grass

Gumshoos	◯	◎
Hariyama		◯
Alolan Raticate	☽	◎

Shaking Bush

Cottonee	☀	◎
Petilil	☾	◎
Scyther		◯

Shaking Trees

Emolga		◯
Primeape		◎

Pokémon Shadows

Braviary	☀	◎
Fearow		◎
Mandibuzz	☾	◯

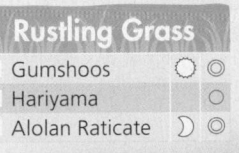
◯ frequent ◯ average
△ rare ▲ almost never
◯ day only ☽ night only
☀ Pokémon Sun ☾ Pokémon Moon

Items

Poni Plains

1	X Defense
2	Star Piece
3	TM24 Thunderbolt
4	Carbos

Poni Grove

5	X Sp. Atk
6	Max Potion

Hidden Items

Poni Plains
PP Max

Poni Grove
Max Ether

Map Icons

❶ Item
❓ Hidden Item
⑴ TM
⬡ Zygarde Core/Cell

◎ Photo Spot
🎣 Fishing spot
🎣 Rare fishing spot
🍒 Berry pile

1 Battle a Tough Trainer

Defeat every Trainer around Poni Plains for a chance to battle against Ace Trainer Cole, who stands near the area's south end. The battle won't be easy, but victory comes with a great reward!

Reward: TM60 Quash

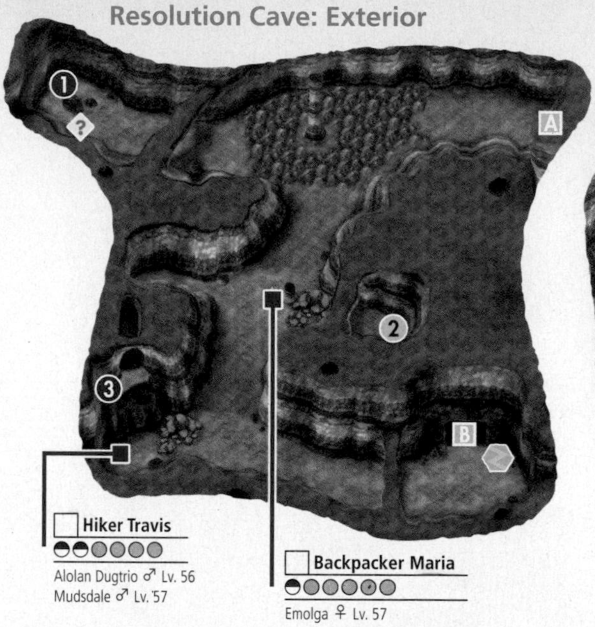

Poni Meadow / Resolution Cave

Ride Pokémon Needed

Poni Plains' northwest path leads to this secluded haven, where the trees grow so large that their roots can be crossed like bridges. The colorful flowers of these same trees produce Purple Nectar that falls to the ground. Beyond Poni Meadow lies the mysterious cave. Many valuable items await discovery here, and the cave's unique "X" shape seems oddly familiar.

Team Recommendations

FIRE	GRASS	ELECTRIC
ICE	PSYCHIC	POISON

Resolution Cave: Exterior

Poni Meadow

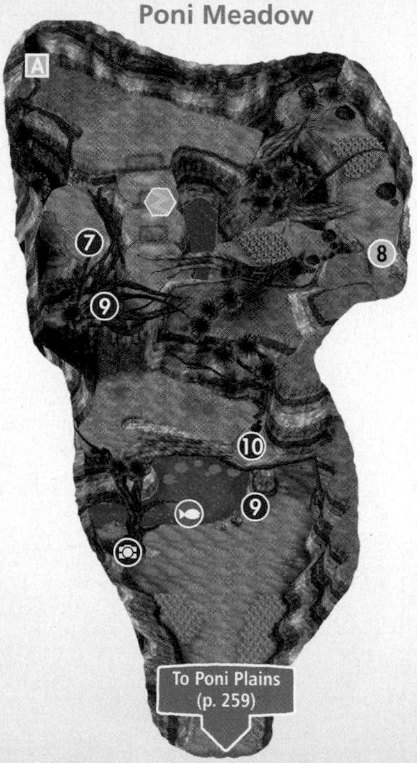

Hiker Travis
Alolan Dugtrio ♂ Lv. 56
Mudsdale ♂ Lv. 57

Backpacker Maria
Emolga ♀ Lv. 57

Resolution Cave: Interior

To Poni Plains (p. 259)

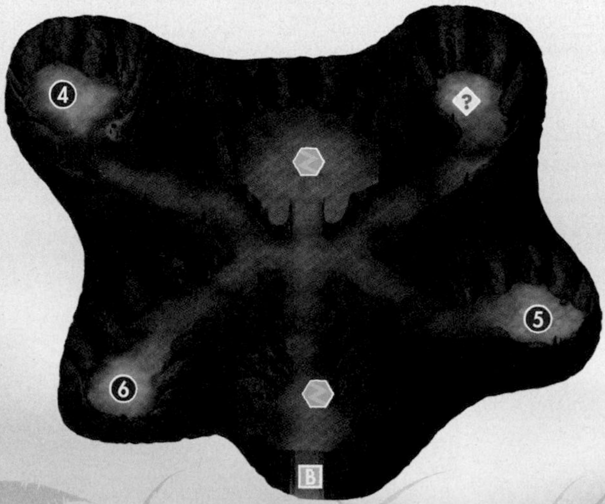

Items

Resolution Cave
- 1 Elixir
- 2 TM26 Earthquake
- 3 Terrain Extender
- 4 Adrenaline Orb
- 5 Life Orb
- 6 Light Ball

Poni Meadow
- 7 Power Herb
- 8 TM50 Overheat
- 9 Purple Nectar ×2
- 10 Honey

Tall Grass

Cottonee	☀	◎
Oricorio*		◯
Petilil	🌙	◎
Ribombee		◯

Fishing Spots

Barboach	◎
Dratini	▲
Magikarp	◎

Rare Fishing Spots

Barboach	◎
Dratini	△
Magikarp	◎

Hidden Items

Resolution Cave: Exterior
- HP Up

Resolution Cave: Interior
- Big Nugget

Cave

Alolan Dugtrio	◯
Golbat	◎

◎ frequent ◯ average
△ rare ▲ almost never
☀ day only 🌙 night only
☀ Pokémon Sun 🌙 Pokémon Moon

*The form of Oricorio found in Poni Meadow is the purple Oricorio (Sensu Style).

CHAMPION'S GUIDE TO ALOLA

HOW TO COMPLETE THE ALOLA POKÉDEX

ALOLA REGION POKÉDEX

ADVENTURE DATA

Poni Coast / Poni Gauntlet

Stretching north of the Poni Plains, this rough and rocky coastline leads to the grueling Poni Gauntlet. Though it features no beach, Poni Coast's crystal-clear waters nonetheless make it a popular spot for adventurous sightseers. Filled with powerful Trainers, the picturesque path must be trekked in order to reach the Battle Tree. Travelers are advised to assemble their best Pokémon before attempting to pass through.

Poni Gauntlet

To Battle Tree (p. 271)

Team Recommendations
| FIRE | GRASS | ELECTRIC |
| FIGHTING | POISON | STEEL |

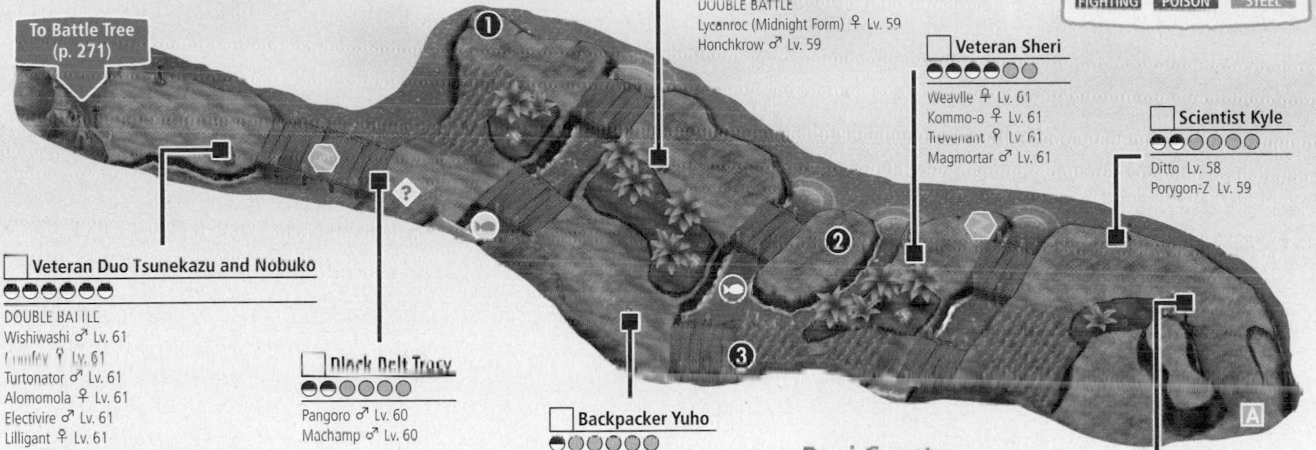

Punk Pair Marie and Troy
◉◉◉○○○

DOUBLE BATTLE
Lycanroc (Midnight Form) ♀ Lv. 59
Honchkrow ♂ Lv. 59

Veteran Sheri
◉◉◉◉○○

Weavile ♀ Lv. 61
Kommo-o ♀ Lv. 61
Trevenant ♀ Lv. 61
Magmortar ♂ Lv. 61

Scientist Kyle
◉◉○○○○

Ditto Lv. 58
Porygon-Z Lv. 59

Veteran Duo Tsunekazu and Nobuko
◉◉◉◉◉◉

DOUBLE BATTLE
Wishiwashi ♂ Lv. 61
Comfey ♀ Lv. 61
Turtonator ♂ Lv. 61
Alomomola ♀ Lv. 61
Electivire ♂ Lv. 61
Lilligant ♀ Lv. 61

Black Belt Tracy
◉◉◉○○○

Pangoro ♂ Lv. 60
Machamp ♂ Lv. 60

Backpacker Yuho
◉◉○○○○

Mimikyu ♀ Lv. 59

Poni Coast

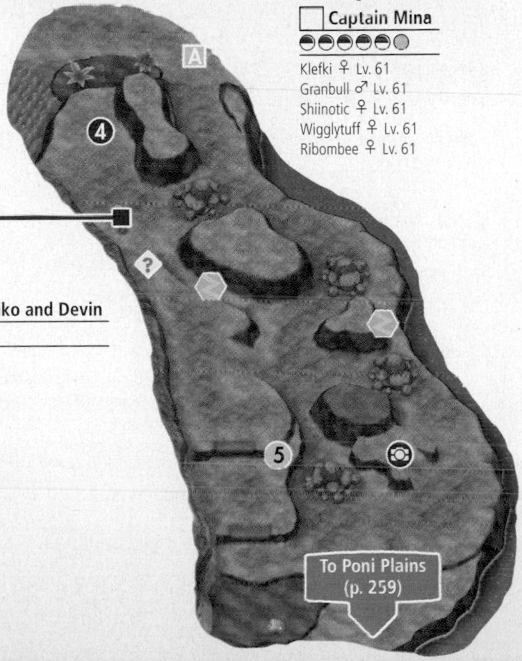

Captain Mina
◉◉◉◉◉◉

Klefki ♀ Lv. 61
Granbull ♂ Lv. 61
Shiinotic ♀ Lv. 61
Wigglytuff ♀ Lv. 61
Ribombee ♀ Lv. 61

Honeymooners Noriko and Devin
◉◉◉○○○

DOUBLE BATTLE
Ninetales ♀ Lv. 58
Sandslash ♂ Lv. 58
Exeggutor ♀ Lv. 59
Golem ♂ Lv. 59

To Poni Plains (p. 259)

Items
	Poni Gauntlet	
1	Misty Seed	
2	Big Pearl	
3	Guard Spec.	
	Poni Coast	
4	Comet Shard	
5	TM97 Dark Pulse	

Hidden Items
Poni Gauntlet
Max Elixir
Poni Coast
Max Revive

◎ frequent ○ average
△ rare ▲ almost never
○ day only ☾ night only
☀ Pokémon Sun 🌙 Pokémon Moon

Fishing Spots
Barboach	◎
Dratini	▲
Magikarp	◎

Rare Fishing Spots
Barboach	
Dratini	△
Magikarp	◎

Dust Clouds
Alolan Dugtrio	◎

Tall Grass
Bewear	▲
Golduck	△
Granbull	○
Gumshoos	☀○
Pelipper	○
Alolan Raticate	☾○

1 Trade for Talonflame

The Punk Guy near the Battle Tree's entrance would like to trade you his Talonflame in exchange for your Bewear. Try to catch a Bewear here in Poni Gauntlet, then talk to the Punk Guy to make the trade!

Pokémon: Talonflame

2 Battle Captain Mina!

Mina, the artsy girl you met on the bridge in Vast Poni Canyon, stands near the Poni Gauntlet's entrance. Beat every other Trainer in the area, and you can battle her team of Fairy-type Pokémon.

Reward: Bottle Cap

Tip

A place known as the Battle Tree lies just beyond the Poni Gauntlet. If you haven't yet quenched your thirst for battle, turn to page 271 to learn all about this competitive arena.

ALOLA REGION POKÉDEX · HOW TO COMPLETE THE ALOLA POKÉDEX · CHAMPION'S GUIDE TO ALOLA · ADVENTURE DATA

Looker Episode

Remember the strange old man you met near your house the day after the festival? He handed you an Enigmatic Card. Check it in your Bag for a curious message: "Your presence is requested at the Roadside Motel on Route 8." Going there kicks off a series of adventures involving a certain member of the International Police, some familiar old faces, and those amazing Ultra Beasts!

1 | Visit the Roadside Motel on Route 8

Fly to Route 8 on Akala Island and enter the Roadside Motel's guest room. There, you meet two members of the International Police—a hardboiled detective named Looker, and his no-nonsense boss, Anabel. The pair reveals that the Ultra Beast you battled back at Aether Paradise wasn't the only one that Lusamine released by opening the Ultra Wormhole. As part of the special UB Task Force, Looker and Anabel request your help in dealing with the Ultra Beasts, but first you must prove your power by battling against Anabel!

Anabel's Pokémon

Anabel is a strong Trainer, so you'd better be ready before battling her team. Include a Fighting-type Pokémon to counter Weavile and Snorlax, and tuck a few Awakenings into your Bag to rouse any Pokémon that Snorlax makes Asleep with Yawn. Beware of Alakazam's Focus Blast—it's a Fighting-type move that will punish any Dark-type Pokémon you put in harm's way. Weavile also has a Fighting-type move, Brick Break, which can wallop any Rock or Steel types you send against it. Salamence is perhaps Anabel's biggest threat, because it's fast and powerful and can unleash a variety of strong attacks that can inflict your Pokémon with Paralysis or cause it to be painfully Burned. Send out a tough Pokémon that can soak up plenty of damage, or try to wipe out Salamence with supereffective Ice-type moves.

Alakazam
♂ Lv. 61 — PSYCHIC
Weak to: BUG GHOST DARK

Weavile
♀ Lv. 61 — DARK ICE
Weak to: 4× FIGHTING FIRE BUG ROCK STEEL FAIRY

Mismagius
♀ Lv. 61 — GHOST
Weak to: GHOST DARK

Salamence
♂ Lv. 61 — DRAGON FLYING
Weak to: 4× ICE ROCK DRAGON FAIRY

Snorlax
♂ Lv. 61 — NORMAL
Weak to: FIGHTING

2 | Meet Ms. Wicke at Aether Paradise

Impressed with your skill, Anabel wastes no time in handing down your first order: you are to meet the vice-chief Ms. Wicke at the Aether Paradise labs! Fly to Aether Paradise without delay, enter the main building, and take the elevator down to the B2F: Lab area. Enter the room at the end of the hall to reach Secret Lab B, where Wicke awaits. After handing you 10 prototype Poké Balls that are specially designed to catch Ultra Beasts, Wicke suggests that you return to Anabel and Looker for further instructions.

Reward: Beast Ball ×10

Tip

If this is your first visit to Aether Paradise since becoming Champion, check out all the new activities you can explore on page 258.

3 | Return to the motel and report in

Now that you're brimming with Beast Balls, return to the Roadside Motel for your next assignment. Looker isn't there at first, but he suddenly barges in with news of an Ultra Beast sighting. It seems that UB-01 Symbiont has been sighted right here on Akala Island! Your mission is to find and battle Symbiont in an effort to catch it. Knowing the UB's potential for mayhem, Anabel heads out in advance to protect the populace.

Tip

Talk to Looker after Anabel leaves for more intel on the Ultra Beast you're after.

4 | Track down and catch UB-01 Symbiont!

Symbiont moves between Wela Volcano Park and Diglett's Tunnel, so you may need to explore both locations to find it. Keep searching until the Ultra Beast suddenly appears before you in a random encounter! A furious battle erupts once you've tracked down Symbiont, so save your game in advance. Wear down the raging Ultra Beast, inflict it with status conditions if you can, and then throw one of your newly acquired Beast Balls to catch it!

UB-01 Symbiont: Nihilego

Codenamed Symbiont, this mysterious Ultra Beast's true identity is Nihilego. It's the same UB you battled during your first visit to Aether Paradise, only this time it won't be fleeing after a few turns. Avoid using supereffective moves if you're hoping to catch Nihilego—the chance of defeating it is too great a risk. Wear it down slowly but surely instead. Potentially use TM54 False Swipe to teach your Pokémon a move that won't inflict much damage or leave Nihilego with less than 1 HP. Beware Nihilego's onslaught of Rock-type attacks, and when the time is right, throw a Beast Ball to seal the Ultra Beast safely away.

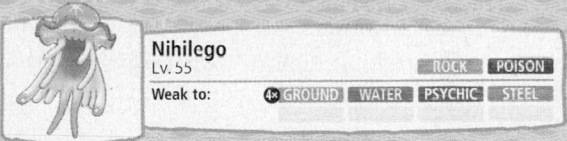

Nihilego
Lv. 55 — `ROCK` `POISON`
Weak to: `4x GROUND` `WATER` `PSYCHIC` `STEEL`

5 | Report back to the UB Task Force

After you've caught Nihilego, return to the Roadside Motel and update Looker and Anabel. Your celebratory feast is put on the back burner when Looker returns with news of another Ultra Beast sighting—this time on Melemele Island! Anabel heads out to set up a new base of operations at Melemele's motel. Fly to Route 2 and join her there to receive more intel.

6 | Catch two UB-02 Absorption ☀ / four UB-02 Beauty 🌙

A surprise guest shows up at Melemele's motel: it's Nanu and he has news of the Ultra Beast you're after! It turns out there are several Ultra Beasts for you to catch this time, and they're running amok in the same area. Make your way to Melemele Meadow ☀ / Verdant Cavern 🌙, where the UB sightings have peaked. Remember: you're looking for several Ultra Beasts this time! Find them, battle them, and catch them to complete your mission. The extra Beast Balls that Looker gives you should come in handy.

Reward: Beast Ball ×10

UB-02 Absorption: Buzzwole ☀

Whoa, those are some jacked Ultra Beasts! They must work out. Buzzwole use the Fighting-type move Dynamic Punch to confuse your Pokémon, so be prepared to heal them with items like Big Malasadas, Full Heals, and Full Restores. They can also bash your Pokémon with Hammer Arm, another strong Fighting-type move that reduces the Buzzwole's Speed stat after each use. The Buzzwole's aura raises their Defense, so don't shy away from using supereffective physical moves at first. Weaken the Buzzwole and try to inflict them with a status condition to make them easier to catch in a Beast Ball.

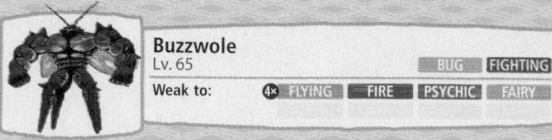

Buzzwole
Lv. 65   BUG FIGHTING
Weak to: 4× FLYING FIRE PSYCHIC FAIRY

UB-02 Beauty: Pheromosa 🌑

If you're playing *Pokémon Moon*, your targets will instead be Pheromosa. Don't be addled by these alluring Ultra Beasts, because they're far stronger than they appear. Unlike the Buzzwole, the Pheromosa's aura sharply raises their Speed stat, so expect them to act first unless you've got some great priority moves to try out. They lash out with Bug Buzz, a powerful Bug-type move, and they also have another Bug-type move in store for you: Lunge, which lowers your Pokémon's Attack each time it lands. Avoid sending out Psychic-type Pokémon, as Lunge can really light them up. Flying-type moves will likely defeat the Pheromosa, so target their other weaknesses instead.

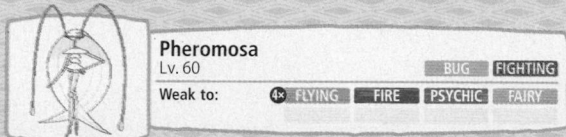

Pheromosa
Lv. 60   BUG FIGHTING
Weak to: 4× FLYING FIRE PSYCHIC FAIRY

7 | Inform Looker of your success

After you've caught your targets, report back to Looker at the motel on Route 2. It's not long before disaster strikes again, and Anabel urges you to regroup at your previous base of operations on Akala Island. Fly there without delay, pausing only to rest at Route 8's Pokémon Center before rushing over to the Roadside Motel.

8 | Battle Mina, then catch two UB-03 Lighting

Back at the Roadside Motel, Looker introduces you to his latest informant: Captain Mina! They already know where the next Ultra Beast lurks, but Mina insists on testing your strength in battle beforehand. Defeat Mina, pocket the Beast Balls that Looker gives you, and then hurry off to search Memorial Hill and Lush Jungle for two UB-03 Lighting, which can appear in either area as random encounters.

Reward: Beast Ball ×10

Captain Mina's Pokémon

This may or may not be your first battle against Mina, depending on whether or not you've fully explored Poni Gauntlet. Her Klefki sets the stage with Light Screen and Reflect, two defensive moves that halve the damage Mina's team receives from special and physical attacks, respectively, for five turns. Her Granbull shakes up your Steel-type Pokémon with Earthquake and also uses Stone Edge to punish any Flying- or Bug-type Pokémon you send out to counter this powerful Ground-type move. Try to spend turns on Klefki, working to wear out its Light Screen and Reflect before Granbull takes to the fray. Shiinotic uses Spore to make your Pokémon fall Asleep, then attacks them with Dream Eater, a Psychic-type move that damages sleeping Pokémon and restores Shiinotic's HP. Rouse your drowsy Pokémon with Awakenings and other curatives, and try to wipe out Shiinotic with a supereffective Poison-type attack as fast as possible. Wigglytuff uses Flamethrower to surprise any Steel-type Pokémon you send out, so use that same Poison-type move you chose again to deal it supereffective damage with less risk of counter.

Klefki
♀ Lv. 61 — STEEL | FAIRY
Weak to: FIRE | GROUND

Granbull
♂ Lv. 61 — FAIRY
Weak to: POISON | STEEL

Shiinotic
♀ Lv. 61 — GRASS | FAIRY
Weak to: 4× POISON | FIRE | FLYING | STEEL

Wigglytuff
♀ Lv. 61 — NORMAL | FAIRY
Weak to: POISON | STEEL

Ribombee
♀ Lv. 61 — BUG | FAIRY
Weak to: FIRE | POISON | FLYING | ROCK | STEEL

UB-03 Lighting: Xurkitree

This unique-looking Ultra Beast is all charged up. It enters battle with an aura that sharply raises its Sp. Atk, and it's quick to use Electric Terrain, which boosts the power of Electric-type moves for five turns. You could

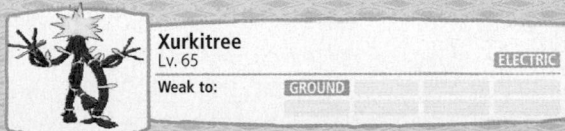

Xurkitree
Lv. 65 — ELECTRIC
Weak to: GROUND

be in for a shockingly fast defeat if you don't send out a strong Ground-type Pokémon to nullify the brunt of Xurkitree's high-voltage offense. Even still, Xurkitree can jolt you with its Power Whip, a strong Grass-type move that's super effective against Ground-type Pokémon. Grass-type moves are weak against Steel-type Pokémon, however, so Alolan Dugtrio won't suffer as much harm from Power Whip as other Ground-type Pokémon you might employ.

9 | Report to the UB Task Force

After catching both Xurkitree, return to the Roadside Motel and report your success to Looker. You've done great work, but there's no time to celebrate, for Nanu soon appears with news of another UB sighting on Ula'ula Island! It seems that Nanu and Looker have a rocky history, but it's not clear exactly what the issue is. Regardless, Ula'ula is your next stop! Fly to Tapu Village and head east to reach the motel on Route 13.

Enter the motel on Route 13 to meet up with Looker and Anabel at your new base of operations. The pair soon hands you your next mission: catch four UB-04 Blade ☀ / two UB-04 Blaster ☾, which may appear as random encounters in either Route 17 ☀ / Haina Desert ☾ or Malie Garden. After receiving your supply of Beast Balls, rush off to either location to begin your search. Catch the requested amount of UBs to complete your assignment!

Reward: Beast Ball ×10

UB-04 Blade: Kartana ☀

Don't be fooled by these Ultra Beasts' small size, because they can slice through your team in seconds. Their aura sharply raises their Attack, causing them to hit extremely hard with Leaf Blade, a Grass-type physical move that has a high chance to score critical hits. Its Attack can be further raised by its Beast Boost Ability, which activates each time it knocks out one of your Pokémon. Try not to let this happen, and consider fleeing if it does. Kartana will likely be wiped out by Fire-type moves, so hit it with a stiff Fighting-type move instead. Find a Fighting-type move that leaves Kartana with very little HP after one blow, then throw a Beast Ball to catch the UB before it does too much damage.

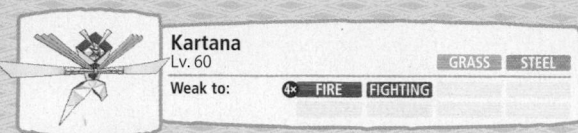

Kartana
Lv. 60 GRASS STEEL
Weak to: 4× FIRE FIGHTING

UB-04 Blaster: Celesteela ☾

If you're playing *Pokémon Moon*, your targets will instead be Celesteela. These Ultra Beasts' aura raise their Defense sharply, so hit them with supereffective moves to chop down their HP as fast as you can. They attack with Skull Bash, a two-turn move in which the Celesteela tuck in their heads and raise their Defense on the first turn, then lash out to damage your Pokémon on the next turn. The Defense boost the Celesteela get from Skull Bash is permanent, so again, rely on supereffective moves to reduce Celesteela's HP as quickly as possible. The Celesteela also use Autotomize to sharply raise their Speed stat, so don't get too comfortable during this battle, even if your Pokémon are initially moving first.

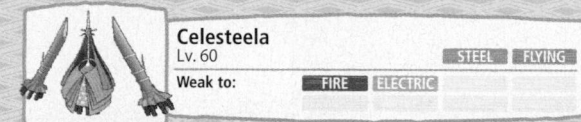

Celesteela
Lv. 60 STEEL FLYING
Weak to: FIRE ELECTRIC

With these UBs safely contained, head back to the motel on Route 13 and inform Looker of your success. Nanu soon arrives, and you finally learn why he and Looker share so much tension. It's a sad tale, but there's no time for emotion to get the better of you, for the final UB has been sighted on Poni Island! The team agrees to meet up at the floating restaurant in Seafolk Village to fill their bellies and discuss the next move.

Fly to Seafolk Village and enter the floating restaurant to meet up with Nanu and Looker. The two reveal even more details about their troubled past, as well as how they came to know Anabel. Humor Nanu with a battle after hearing out their tale, then claim your Beast Balls from Looker before heading off to catch UB-05 Glutton. It lurks deep within the Resolution Cave (p. 260), far beyond the Ancient Poni Path, past Poni Plains and Poni Meadow.

Reward: Beast Ball ×10

Island Kahuna Nanu's Pokémon

Nanu's crew of crafty Dark-type Pokémon are prepared to counter any Fighting, Bug, or Fairy types you send out, so expect a challenging battle. His Sableye uses Toxic to make your Pokémon Poisoned, so pack your Bag full of Antidotes and Full Restores. His Absol and Honchkrow unleash Aerial Ace to assail any Fighting- or Bug-type Pokémon you employ, and Honchkrow also uses Psychic to punish your Fighting-type Pokémon even more. His Alolan Persian has the move Power Gem to crush your Bug types, so target a different weakness if need be.

Sableye
♀ Lv. 63 — DARK GHOST
Weak to: FAIRY

Absol
♂ Lv. 63 — DARK
Weak to: FIGHTING BUG FAIRY

Honchkrow
♂ Lv. 63 — DARK FLYING
Weak to: ELECTRIC ICE ROCK FAIRY

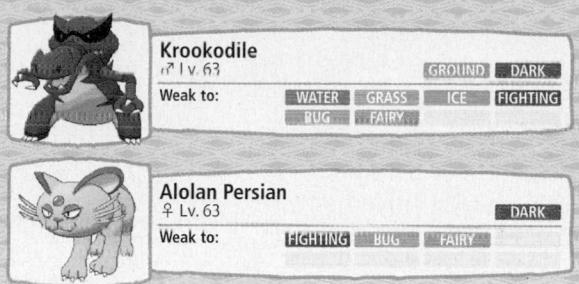

Krookodile
♂ Lv. 63 — GROUND DARK
Weak to: WATER GRASS ICE FIGHTING BUG FAIRY

Alolan Persian
♀ Lv. 63 — DARK
Weak to: FIGHTING BUG FAIRY

UB-05 Glutton: Guzzlord

Like the previous UB, Guzzlord's aura sharply raises its Attack, as does its Beast Boost Ability, which triggers each time one of your Pokémon faint. It can use Gastro Acid to suppress your Pokémon's Ability, and it lashes out with Thrash: a Normal-type move that causes Guzzlord to attack furiously two to three times in a row,

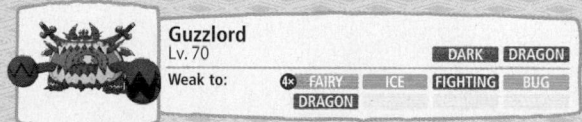

Guzzlord
Lv. 70 — DARK DRAGON
Weak to: 4× FAIRY ICE FIGHTING BUG DRAGON

becoming confused afterward due to fatigue. This actually makes Guzzlord a bit easier to capture, provided your team lasts through its Thrash onslaught. Work at chopping down Guzzlord's HP while its Thrash is active, then throw a Beast Ball the moment it becomes confused. Catching Guzzlord is vital at this point, because it may end up hurting and defeating itself due to its confusion!

13 | Return to the restaurant and report in

With the final Ultra Beast stored cozily in a Beast Ball, fly back to Seafolk Village to inform Looker of your great success. He and Anabel couldn't be happier to have the UB situation under control. You couldn't have done it without the Beast Balls bestowed to you by vice-chief Wicke, and Looker and Anabel invite you to join them in personally thanking Wicke for her support.

14 | Thank Wicke at Aether Paradise

Fly to Aether Paradise, enter the main building, and take the elevator down to the B2F: Lab area. Wicke awaits in Secret Lab B, the last door at the end of the hall. After a heartfelt display of gratitude, Looker suddenly bursts in with troubling news: he's spotted a strange black creature flying over Melemele Island! If you think there's anything to Looker's tale, consider exploring around Melemele, especially Ten Carat Hill. You may encounter the elusive and mysterious Necrozma! Regardless, you've completed your final mission for the International Police, and the IP always pay their debts!

Reward: ₽1,000,000

Necrozma

What is this creature? Is it an Ultra Beast that the International Police missed—or something else entirely? It seems reminiscent of the Ultra Beasts, but Beast Balls do not appear to be very effective for catching it. Instead opt for high-performance Poké Balls, like Ultra Balls or even Timer Balls if the battle is really dragging on. And while it appears to have three weaknesses—Bug-, Ghost-, and Dark-type moves—due to it being a Psychic type, you will find these moves less effective than you might hope. Necrozma's Ability, Prism Armor, reduces the damage taken by normally supereffective moves by 25%. But as long as you can keep your Pokémon from fainting, that may be a good thing. You don't want to risk knocking Necrozma out because it will not appear again easily. Save your game before stepping into Ten Carat Hill to be on the safe side. Consider bringing along Dark-type Pokémon for this battle because they will negate Necrozma's Prismatic Laser attack. And watch out for Wring Out, a powerful Normal-type move that does more damage the more HP your Pokémon has left!

Necrozma
Lv. 75   PSYCHIC
Weak to: BUG   GHOST   DARK

Congratulations!

You have completed the Looker Episode and caught all of the Ultra Beasts that found their way into the Alola region when Lusamine's plans went awry! You should have caught multiple specimens of the beasts that are exclusive to one version of the game or the other, so head to the GTS or find a friend to trade version exclusives with so that you can complete your Alola Pokédex and get every last one of these formidable beasts for yourself!

Defending Your Champion Title

You've worked hard to become Alola's first-ever Champion—now you get to defend your title! Fly back to the Pokémon League on Ula'ula Island and defeat the Elite Four once more. Then return to the Champion's chamber and claim your throne once you are ready to face your first challenger: Hau! Every time you beat the Pokémon League, one of the following Trainers will challenge you and they all come ready to fight. Save your game as you progress through the Pokémon League in case things don't go your way!

If you chose Rowlet		If you chose Litten		If you chose Popplio	

Primarina ♂ Lv. 63 WATER FAIRY	**Flareon** ♂ Lv. 63 FIRE	**Decidueye** ♂ Lv. 63 GRASS GHOST	**Vaporeon** ♂ Lv. 63 WATER	**Incineroar** ♂ Lv. 63 FIRE DARK	**Leafeon** ♂ Lv. 63 GRASS

The rest of Hau's team

Alolan Raichu ♂ Lv. 63 ELECTRIC PSYCHIC	**Crabominable** ♂ Lv. 63 FIGHTING ICE	**Komala** ♀ Lv. 63 NORMAL	Hau is the first challenger you face when defending your Champion title. His team should be very familiar to you by now, and as always, two of his Pokémon will vary depending on the first partner Pokémon you chose back at Iki Town.

Potential Challenger: Molayne

Skarmory ♂ Lv. 61 STEEL FLYING	**Alolan Sandslash** ♂ Lv. 61 ICE STEEL	**Alolan Dugtrio** ♂ Lv. 61 GROUND STEEL	**Metagross** Lv. 61 STEEL PSYCHIC	**Magnezone** Lv. 61 ELECTRIC STEEL	

You've battled Molayne once before, just prior to taking on Sophocles's trial. He still favors Steel-type Pokémon, setting the stage for you to shine with supereffective Fire-, Fighting-, and Ground-type moves.

Potential Challenger: Plumeria

Gengar ♂ Lv. 61 GHOST POISON	**Salazzle** ♀ Lv. 61 POISON FIRE	**Toxapex** ♂ Lv. 61 POISON WATER	**Alolan Muk** ♀ Lv. 61 POISON DARK	**Crobat** ♀ Lv. 61 POISON FLYING	

It's been quite a while since you last battled Plumeria back near the Ruins of Life. The Team Skull Admin's Poison-type team has grown quite powerful since then, but you'll still find them highly susceptible to Ground- and Psychic-type moves.

Potential Challenger: Pokémon Professor Kukui

If you chose Rowlet	If you chose Litten	If you chose Popplio

Incineroar ♂ Lv. 65 FIRE DARK	**Primarina** ♀ Lv. 65 WATER FAIRY	**Decidueye** ♂ Lv. 65 GRASS GHOST

The rest of Pokémon Professor Kukui's team

Lycanroc (Midday Form) ♂ Lv. 65 ROCK	**Magnezone** Lv. 65 ELECTRIC STEEL	**Braviary** ♂ Lv. 65 FLYING NORMAL	**Alolan Ninetales** ♀ Lv. 65 ICE FAIRY	**Snorlax** ♂ Lv. 65 NORMAL

Boasting a well-balanced team, Professor Kukui seeks to realize his dream of becoming Alola's Champion. Strive to take advantage of his Pokémon's weaknesses whenever possible, but beware that many of his Pokémon possess moves that are super effective against their weaknesses.

Potential Challenger: Ryuki

Garchomp	**Turtonator**	**Kommo-o**	**Dragonite**	**Drampa**
♂ Lv. 61	♂ Lv. 61	♂ Lv. 61	♂ Lv. 61	♂ Lv. 61
DRAGON GROUND	FIRE DRAGON	DRAGON FIGHTING	DRAGON FLYING	NORMAL DRAGON

A Dragon-type Pokémon user, Ryuki churns out furious amounts of damage and is a real threat to your Champion title. Exposing your Dragon-type Pokémon to Ryuki's horde is unwise unless you're confident you'll move first each turn. Look to tame Ryuki's team with fast-acting Fairy-type Pokémon instead.

Potential Challenger: Gladion

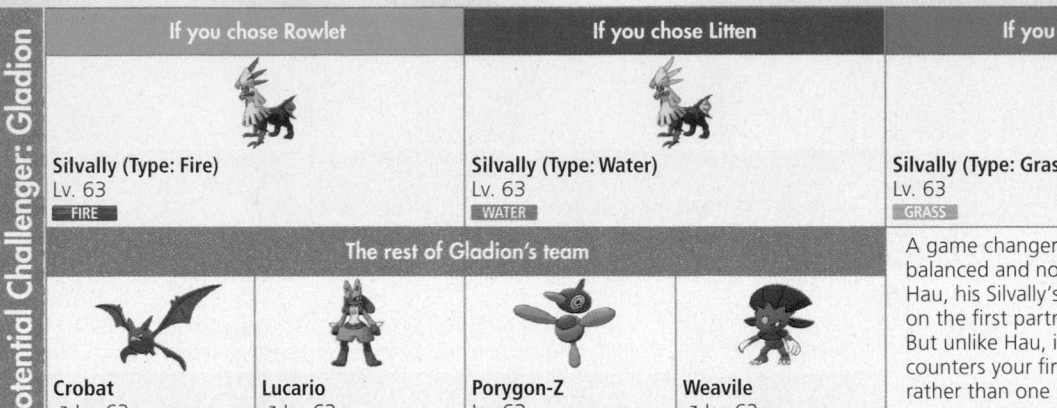

If you chose Rowlet	If you chose Litten	If you chose Popplio
Silvally (Type: Fire)	**Silvally (Type: Water)**	**Silvally (Type: Grass)**
Lv. 63	Lv. 63	Lv. 63
FIRE	WATER	GRASS

The rest of Gladion's team				
Crobat	**Lucario**	**Porygon-Z**	**Weavile**	A game changer, Gladion's team is well balanced and not easily beaten. Like Hau, his Silvally's type varies depending on the first partner Pokémon you chose. But unlike Hau, its type will be one that counters your first partner Pokémon, rather than one it is weak to.
♂ Lv. 63	♂ Lv. 63	Lv. 63	♂ Lv. 63	
POISON FLYING	FIGHTING STEEL	NORMAL	DARK ICE	

Potential Challenger: Captain Sophocles

Togedemaru	**Alolan Golem**	**Magnezone**	**Vikavolt**	**Electivire**
♀ Lv. 61	♂ Lv. 61	Lv. 61	♂ Lv. 61	♂ Lv. 61
ELECTRIC STEEL	ROCK ELECTRIC	ELECTRIC STEEL	BUG ELECTRIC	ELECTRIC

Young and ambitious, Sophocles seeks to supplant you as Alola's Champion. His Electric-type team is prepared to counter your Ground-type Pokémon, so be ready to exploit their other common weaknesses, of which there are many.

Potential Challenger: Island Kahuna Hapu

Alolan Dugtrio	**Krookodile**	**Flygon**	**Mudsdale**	**Gastrodon**
♀ Lv. 63	♂ Lv. 63	♂ Lv. 63	♂ Lv. 63	♀ Lv. 63
GROUND STEEL	GROUND DARK	GROUND DRAGON	GROUND	WATER GROUND

Not satisfied with her status as Poni Island's new kahuna, Hapu has her sights set on your Champion crown. Her tough team of Ground-type Pokémon are good at downing Flying-type Pokémon, so don't think you can take her out simply by taking to the skies.

Potential Challenger: Youngster Tristan

Emolga	**Magmortar**	**Sharpedo**	**Tauros**	**Alolan Exeggutor**
♂ Lv. 59	♂ Lv. 59	♂ Lv. 59	♂ Lv. 59	♂ Lv. 59
ELECTRIC FLYING	FIRE	WATER DARK	NORMAL	GRASS DRAGON

Though his Pokémon's levels are a bit lower than other potential challengers, Youngster Tristan nonetheless grasps the value of a well-rounded team. Switch out your Pokémon as needed to stay one step ahead of him.

Potential Challenger: Aether Branch Chief Faba

Slowbro	**Hypno**	**Alolan Raichu**	**Alakazam**	**Bruxish**
♂ Lv. 61	♂ Lv. 61	♂ Lv. 61	♂ Lv. 61	♂ Lv. 61
WATER PSYCHIC	PSYCHIC	ELECTRIC PSYCHIC	PSYCHIC	WATER PSYCHIC

Unlike other potential challengers, Faba is somewhat predictable, as he always appears on the first day of each month. He may have turned over a new leaf since Lusamine's defeat, but Faba's fondness for Psychic-type Pokémon will never change.

Battle Tree

Located just beyond the Poni Gauntlet (p. 261), the Battle Tree is a special place where powerful Trainers gather to put their skills to the ultimate test. Fans of the Pokémon video game series will find the Battle Tree similar to the Battle Tower, Battle Subway, and Battle Maison features in previous titles.

Your goal at the Battle Tree is simple: win as many battles as you can in a row without losing. It may sound easy, but the more wins you rack up, the tougher your opponents will become!

Rules and restrictions

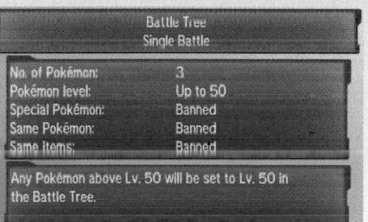

Battle Tree Single Battle	
No. of Pokémon:	3
Pokémon level:	Up to 50
Special Pokémon:	Banned
Same Pokémon:	Banned
Same items:	Banned
Any Pokémon above Lv. 50 will be set to Lv. 50 in the Battle Tree.	

Before we get to the good stuff, let's quickly go over the basics. First, know that any Pokémon above Lv. 50 will be set to Lv. 50 at the Battle Tree. If your team features Pokémon that are above Lv. 50, those Pokémon will be temporarily lowered to Lv. 50 during your time there.

In addition, your Pokémon must all differ from one another in species and held items at the Battle Tree. Legendary and Mythical Pokémon are not eligible to participate at the Battle Tree, and you cannot use any items from your Bag during these battles.

Battle formats

Three battle formats are featured at the Battle Tree: Single Battles, Double Battles, and Multi Battles.

Single Battle

In the Single Battle format, you and your opponent each battle with a team of three Pokémon. Pokémon are sent out one at a time to battle against one of the opposing Trainer's Pokémon. The battle ends after all three of one Trainer's Pokémon have fainted, with the other player claiming victory. This format includes the Single Battle and Super Single Battle modes.

Double Battle

In the Double Battle format, you and your opponent each battle with a team of four Pokémon. Two Pokémon are sent out by each Trainer at the start, battling side by side to defeat the opposing Trainer's team. Battle continues until all four of one Trainer's Pokémon have fainted, at which point the other Trainer is deemed the winner. This format includes the Double Battle and Super Double Battle modes.

Multi Battle

In the Multi Battle and Super Multi Battle format, you battle with a partner— either an NPC Trainer you've scouted or a friend playing with you via wireless communication. Each Trainer brings two Pokémon and together you face off against two NPC opponents, each with two Pokémon themselves, until all four of the Pokémon on one team have fainted. If you want to play this mode with a friend instead of an NPC Trainer, simply speak with the receptionist at the Battle Tree, and she'll set everything up for you.

Battle ranks

Each of the aforementioned battle formats features two ranks: Normal Rank and Super Rank. Win 19 battles in a row in the Normal Rank for Single, Double, or Multi Battles, and you'll face off against a boss (or a team of two bosses, in the case of Multi Battles) who you may remember. Defeat these Battle Legends in your 20th Normal Rank battle to unlock the Super Rank for these modes!

Tip

Manage 49 wins in a row at Super Rank, and then beat the boss (or bosses, in the case of Multi Battles), and you'll get a special stamp for your Trainer Passport! There are three such stamps to strive for: one for Single Battles, one for Double Battles, and one for Multi Battles. In Single Battles, you'll have to take on Red, while Double Battles will pit you against Blue. And Multi Battles force you to battle them both! The first time you defeat Red, you'll also be rewarded with some rare Mega Stones (p. 255)!

Battle Points

Unlike the battles you've experienced out in the wild, your Pokémon don't receive Exp. Points when they battle at the Battle Tree. Instead, you earn Battle Points (BP) each time you win a battle. BP can be exchanged for prizes at the counter to the west of the Battle Tree, or at the counter found at the Battle Royal Dome on Royal Avenue. BP can also be spent to scout Trainers you've defeated at the Battle Tree, allowing you to battle alongside them as teammates in Multi Battles. As your win streak increases, so too does the amount of BP you receive with each win.

Battle Points Earned		
Win streak	**Normal**	**Super**
1–10	1	2
11–19	2	3
20 (vs. Battle Legend)	20	3
21–30	—	4
31–40	—	5
41–49	—	6
50 (vs. Battle Legend)	—	50
51+	—	7

Scouting Multi Battle teammates

After winning a Single or Double Battle, you'll have the option to "scout" the Trainer you've just beaten for 10 BP. Once scouted, you can team up with that Trainer in future Multi Battles! Reach Super Rank by achieving 20 straight wins in Normal Rank battles, and you'll start to encounter familiar Trainers from *Pokémon Sun* and *Pokémon Moon* and past Pokémon games every 10 battles. With the exception of a few notable "Battle Legends," these Trainers can also be registered via the scout system, so consider saving some of your hard-earned BP to scout these special allies! You can register up to 50 teammates that you've scouted using this system, so no need to be shy about asking great Trainers to join your roster.

Tip

Each Trainer you scout has two Pokémon to offer. Browse through your options and pick a team that best complements your own!

Checking your win streak

Maintaining a win streak is your primary goal at the Battle Tree. Once you lose a battle, your win streak falls back to zero, forcing you to start over again from scratch. Speak to the woman to the east of the Battle Tree if you'd like to check your current win streak. She can also recount your best win streaks in each battle mode.

Taking a break

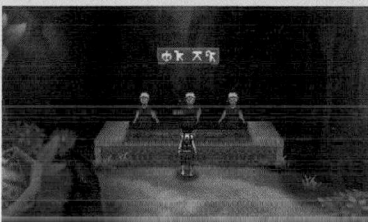

The Battle Tree is an intense place, and you'll probably need a break from all the action at some point. After each battle, you have the option to put your Battle Tree challenge on hold, save your progress, and then return later and resume your win streak right where you left off. Tackling the Battle Tree is tough enough—be sure you aren't battling fatigue at the same time!

 Your win streak ends if you turn off your Nintendo 3DS system at the Battle Tree without saving. Always save before you take a break!

Battle Tree prizes

In addition to scouting Trainers, the Battle Points you earn at the Battle Tree can be spent on a variety of special prizes. Step up to the counter to the west of the Battle Tree and speak to the staff to view the items you can spend your hard-earned BP on.

Left attendant		Middle attendant		Right attendant	
King's Rock	32 BP	Toxic Orb	16 BP	Gengarite	64 BP
Deep Sea Tooth	32 BP	Flame Orb	16 BP	Scizorite	64 BP
Deep Sea Scale	32 BP	Iron Ball	16 BP	Pinsirite	64 BP
Dragon Scale	32 BP	Ring Target	16 BP	Aerodactylite	64 BP
Up-Grade	32 BP	White Herb	24 BP	Lucarionite	64 BP
Dubious Disc	32 BP	Mental Herb	24 BP	Kangaskhanite	64 BP
Protector	32 BP	Power Herb	24 BP	Gyaradosite	64 BP
Electirizer	32 BP	Focus Sash	32 BP	Absolite	64 BP
Magmarizer	32 BP	Air Balloon	32 BP	Alakazite	64 BP
Reaper Cloth	32 BP	Red Card	32 BP	Garchompite	64 BP
Whipped Dream	32 BP	Eject Button	32 BP	Sablenite	64 BP
Sachet	32 BP	Weakness Policy	32 BP	Metagrossite	64 BP
		Choice Band	48 BP	Sharpedonite	64 BP
		Choice Specs	48 BP	Slowbronite	64 BP
		Choice Scarf	48 BP	Glalitite	64 BP
		Life Orb	48 BP	Salamencite	64 BP
		Rocky Helmet	48 BP		
		Assault Vest	48 BP		
		Safety Goggles	48 BP		
		Terrain Extender	48 BP		
		Protective Pads	48 BP		

Win streak prizes

Visit the Battle Tree each day, because you may get prizes based on your best win streak from the previous day. Talk to the receptionist each day and see what your previous day's work has earned you!

Win Streak	Prize
5 straight wins	Moomoo Milk
10 straight wins	PP Up
20 straight wins	Rare Candy
30 straight wins	Bottle Cap
40 straight wins	PP Max
50 straight wins	Ability Capsule
100 straight wins	Lansat Berry
200 straight wins	Starf Berry

Things to Do Daily

Your adventure never truly ends in *Pokémon Sun* and *Pokémon Moon*. Each new day brings a variety of activities that you can enjoy on a regular basis.

Melemele Activities

Play the loto
Visit the tourist bureau in Hau'oli City and talk to the receptionist to draw a Loto Ticket once each day. It's free to play, and you might win something neat!

Fill up on battle
Satisfy your hunger for battle at the Battle Buffet in the Hau'oli City shopping mall. You can battle there once per day.

Akala Activities

Challenge Morimoto
Once you're Champion, you can visit GAME FREAK's office in Heahea City and take on Morimoto once per day.

Get a massage
Talk to the lady next to the incense vendor in Konikoni City, and she'll give your Pokémon a free lomi lomi massage once each day, making it more friendly.

Earn some cash
Work as a Pyukumuku chucker on Hano Beach anytime you need to line your pockets. You can complete this job once a day.

Poni Activities

Reap rewards from the Battle Tree
Earn daily rewards from the Battle Tree based on your performance from the previous day. String together wins, then return the next day to reap your rewards!

Poké Pelago Activities

Give and receive Beans
Send out a Bean Bottle each day, hope to get one in return, and shake loose some Poké Beans on Isle Abeens.

Festival Plaza Activities

Get your tickets
Chat with the woman in front of the castle to receive three free Festival Tickets each day for hosting missions.

Anywhere Activities

Visit a café
Order a drink at a Pokémon Center's Café and the barista will give you a special treat and some Poké Beans once per day.

Grab a malasada
Buy a Big Malasada once per day at each of the malasada shops on Melemele, Akala, and Ula'ula Islands.

Bag some Berries
Fresh Berries can be harvested from the base of Berry trees (p. 311–312) all around Alola each day. And you can get a Berry a day at the Thrifty Megamart on Royal Avenue.

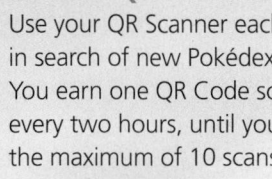

Use the QR Scanner
Use your QR Scanner each day in search of new Pokédex data. You earn one QR Code scan every two hours, until you reach the maximum of 10 scans.

Adventure Data

Explanations of the Move List

Move	The move's name
Type	The move's type
Kind	Physical moves deal more damage when a Pokémon's Attack is high. Special moves deal more damage when a Pokémon's Sp. Atk is high. Status moves cause effects, such as status conditions.
Pow.	The move's attack power
Acc.	The move's accuracy
PP	How many times the move can be used
Range	The number and types of targets the move affects
DA	Moves that make direct contact with the target
Z-Move Pow./ Effects	The boosted power or additional effects that this move will have when powered up by Z-Power and used as a Z-Move

Range Guide

Normal: The move affects the selected target.

Self: The move affects only the user.

1 Ally: The move affects an adjacent ally in Double and Multi Battles.

Self/Ally: The move affects the user or one of its allies.

Your Party: The move affects your entire party, including party Pokémon that are still in their Poké Balls.

1 Random: The move affects one of the opposing Pokémon at random.

Many Others: The move affects multiple Pokémon at the same time.

Adjacent: The move affects the surrounding Pokémon at the same time.

Your Side: The move affects the side of the field where your Pokémon are.

Other Side: The move affects the opponent's side of the field.

Both Sides: The move affects the entire playing field without regard to opposing and ally Pokémon.

Varies: The move is influenced by things like the opposing Pokémon's move or the user's type, so the effect and range are not fixed.

Moves

Move	Type	Kind	Pow.	Acc.	PP	Range	DA	Z-Move Pow./ Effects	Battle Effects
Absorb	Grass	Special	20	100	25	Normal	—	100	Restores HP by up to half of the damage dealt to the target.
Accelerock	Rock	Physical	40	100	20	Normal	◯	100	Always strikes first. The user with the higher Speed goes first if similar moves are used.
Acid	Poison	Special	40	100	30	Many Others	—	100	A 10% chance of lowering the targets' Sp. Def by 1. Its power is reduced by 25% when it hits multiple Pokémon in a Double Battle. Its power is reduced by 50% when it hits multiple Pokémon in a Battle Royal.
Acid Armor	Poison	Status	—	—	20	Self	—	Resets negative stat changes	Raises the user's Defense by 2.
Acid Spray	Poison	Special	40	100	20	Normal	—	100	Lowers the target's Sp. Def by 2.
Acrobatics	Flying	Physical	55	100	15	Normal	◯	100	This move's power is doubled if the user isn't holding an item.
Acupressure	Normal	Status	—	—	30	Self / Ally	—	Critical hits land more easily	Raises a random stat by 2.
Aerial Ace	Flying	Physical	60	—	20	Normal	◯	120	A sure hit.
Aeroblast	Flying	Special	100	95	5	Normal	—	180	Critical hits land more easily.
After You	Normal	Status	—	—	15	Normal	—	Raises the user's Speed	The user helps the target and makes it use its move right after the user, regardless of its Speed. It fails if the target was going to use its move right after anyway, or if the target has already used its move this turn.
Agility	Psychic	Status	—	—	30	Self	—	Resets negative stat changes	Raises the user's Speed by 2.
Air Cutter	Flying	Special	60	95	25	Many Others	—	120	Critical hits land more easily. Its power is reduced by 25% when it hits multiple Pokémon in a Double Battle. Its power is reduced by 50% when it hits multiple Pokémon in a Battle Royal.
Air Slash	Flying	Special	75	95	15	Normal	—	140	A 30% chance of making the target flinch (unable to use moves on that turn).
Ally Switch	Psychic	Status	—	—	15	Self	—	Raises the user's Speed by 2	This move goes first. The user switches places with an ally.
Amnesia	Psychic	Status	—	—	20	Self	—	Resets negative stat changes	Raises the user's Sp. Def by 2.
Anchor Shot	Steel	Physical	80	100	20	Normal	◯	160	The target cannot escape. If used during a Trainer battle, the opposing Trainer cannot switch Pokémon. When used on a Ghost type, no additional effect takes place.
Ancient Power	Rock	Special	60	100	5	Normal	—	120	A 10% chance of raising the user's Attack, Defense, Speed, Sp. Atk, and Sp. Def stats by 1.
Aqua Jet	Water	Physical	40	100	20	Normal	◯	100	Always strikes first. The user with the higher Speed goes first if similar moves are used.
Aqua Ring	Water	Status	—	—	20	Self	—	Raises the user's Defense	Restores 1/16 of max HP every turn.
Aqua Tail	Water	Physical	90	90	10	Normal	◯	175	A regular attack.
Arm Thrust	Fighting	Physical	15	100	20	Normal	◯	100	Attacks 2–5 times in a row in a single turn.
Aromatherapy	Grass	Status	—	—	5	Your Party	—	Restores the user's HP	Heals status conditions of all your Pokémon, including those in your party.
Aromatic Mist	Fairy	Status	—	—	20	1 Ally	—	Raises the user's Sp. Def by 2	Raises one ally's Sp. Def by 1.
Assist	Normal	Status	—	—	20	Self	—	None	Uses a random move from one of the Pokémon in your party that is not in battle.

Move	Type	Kind	Pow.	Acc.	PP	Range	DA	Z-Move Pow./Effects	Battle Effects
Assurance	Dark	Physical	60	100	10	Normal	◯	120	Move's power is doubled if the target has already taken some damage in the same turn.
Astonish	Ghost	Physical	30	100	15	Normal	◯	100	A 30% chance of making the target flinch (unable to use moves on that turn).
Attack Order	Bug	Physical	90	100	15	Normal	—	175	Critical hits land more easily.
Attract	Normal	Status	—	100	15	Normal	Resets negative stat changes		Leaves the target unable to attack 50% of the time. Only works if the user and the target are of different genders.
Aura Sphere	Fighting	Special	80	—	20	Normal	160		A sure hit.
Aurora Beam	Ice	Special	65	100	20	Normal	120		A 10% chance of lowering the target's Attack by 1.
Aurora Veil	Ice	Status	—	—	20	Your Side	—	Raises the user's Speed	Damage from opponents' physical and special attacks is halved for 5 turns. This move can only be used when the weather condition is hail. Effect lasts 5 turns even if the user is switched out. Effect is weaker in Double Battles and Battle Royal.
Autotomize	Steel	Status	—	—	15	Self	—	Resets negative stat changes	Raises the user's Speed by 2 and lowers its weight by 220 lbs.
Avalanche	Ice	Physical	60	100	10	Normal	◯	120	Always strikes last. This move's power is doubled if the user has taken damage from the target that turn.
Baby-Doll Eyes	Fairy	Status	—	100	30	Normal	Raises the user's Defense		Always strikes first. Lowers the target's Attack by 1.
Baneful Bunker	Poison	Status	—	—	10	Self	—	Raises the user's Defense	The user takes no damage in the same turn this move is used. If an opposing Pokémon uses a move that makes direct contact, the attacker will be inflicted with the Poison status condition. Fails more easily when used repeatedly.
Barrage	Normal	Physical	15	85	20	Normal	100		Attacks 2–5 times in a row in a single turn.
Barrier	Psychic	Status	—	—	20	Self	Resets negative stat changes		Raises the user's Defense by 2
Baton Pass	Normal	Status	—	—	40	Self	—	Resets negative stat changes	User swaps out with an ally Pokémon and passes along any stat changes.
Beak Blast	Flying	Physical	100	100	15	Normal	180		Charges up and attacks on the same turn. If an opposing Pokémon uses a move that makes direct contact while the user is charging up, this move inflicts the Burned status condition on the attacker.
Beat Up	Dark	Physical	—	100	10	Normal	—	100	Attacks once for each Pokémon in your party, including the user. But won't count Pokémon that have fainted or have status conditions.
Belch	Poison	Special	120	90	10	Normal	—	190	Cannot be used without first eating a Berry.
Belly Drum	Normal	Status	—	—	10	Self	Restores the user's HP		The user loses half of its maximum HP but raises its Attack to the maximum.
Bestow	Normal	Status	—	—	15	Normal	Raises the user's Speed by 2		If the target is not holding an item and the user is, the user can give that item to the target. Fails if the user is not holding an item or the target is holding an item.
Bide	Normal	Physical	—	—	10	Self	100		Inflicts twice the damage received during the next 2 turns. Cannot choose moves during those 2 turns.
Bind	Normal	Physical	15	85	20	Normal	◯	100	Inflicts damage equal to 1/8 the target's max HP for 4–5 turns. The target cannot flee during that time.
Bite	Dark	Physical	60	100	25	Normal	◯	120	A 30% chance of making the target flinch (unable to use moves on that turn).
Blast Burn	Fire	Special	150	90	5	Normal	—	200	The user can't move during the next turn. If the target is Frozen, it will be thawed.
Blaze Kick	Fire	Physical	85	90	10	Normal	◯	160	A 10% chance of inflicting the Burned status condition on the target. Critical hits land more easily. If the target is Frozen, it will be thawed.
Blizzard	Ice	Special	110	70	5	Many Others	—	185	A 10% chance of inflicting the Frozen status condition on the targets. Is 100% accurate in the hail weather condition. Its power is reduced by 25% when it hits multiple Pokémon in a Double Battle. Its power is reduced by 50% when it hits multiple Pokémon in a Battle Royal.
Block	Normal	Status	—	—	5	Normal	Raises the user's Defense		The target cannot escape. If used during a Trainer battle, the opposing Trainer cannot switch Pokémon. Has no effect on Ghost-type Pokémon.
Blue Flare	Fire	Special	130	85	5	Normal	—	195	A 20% chance of inflicting the Burned status condition on the target. If the target is Frozen, it will be thawed.
Body Slam	Normal	Physical	85	100	15	Normal	◯	160	A 30% chance of inflicting the Paralysis status condition on the target. If the target has used Minimize, this move will be a sure hit and its power will be doubled.
Bolt Strike	Electric	Physical	130	85	5	Normal	◯	195	A 20% chance of inflicting the Paralysis status condition on the targets.
Bone Club	Ground	Physical	65	85	20	Normal	—	120	A 10% chance of making the target flinch (unable to use moves on that turn).
Bone Rush	Ground	Physical	25	90	10	Normal	—	140	Attacks 2–5 times in a row in a single turn.
Bonemerang	Ground	Physical	50	90	10	Normal	—	100	Attacks twice in a row in a single turn.
Boomburst	Normal	Special	140	100	10	Adjacent	—	200	Its power is reduced by 25% when it hits multiple Pokémon in a Double Battle. Its power is reduced by 50% when it hits multiple Pokémon in a Battle Royal. Strikes the target even if it is using Substitute.
Bounce	Flying	Physical	85	85	5	Normal	◯	160	The user flies into the air on the first turn and attacks on the second. A 30% chance of inflicting the Paralysis status condition on the target.
Brave Bird	Flying	Physical	120	100	15	Normal	◯	190	The user takes 1/3 of the damage inflicted.
Brick Break	Fighting	Physical	75	100	15	Normal	◯	140	This move is not affected by Aurora Veil or Reflect. It removes the effect of Aurora Veil, Light Screen, and Reflect.
Brine	Water	Special	65	100	10	Normal	—	120	This move's power is doubled if the target's HP is at half or below.
Brutal Swing	Dark	Physical	60	100	20	Adjacent	◯	120	A regular attack. Its power is reduced by 25% when it hits multiple Pokémon in a Double Battle. Its power is reduced by 50% when it hits multiple Pokémon in a Battle Royal.
Bubble	Water	Special	40	100	30	Many Others	—	100	A 10% chance of lowering the targets' Speed by 1. Its power is reduced by 25% when it hits multiple Pokémon in a Double Battle. Its power is reduced by 50% when it hits multiple Pokémon in a Battle Royal.
Bubble Beam	Water	Special	65	100	20	Normal	—	120	A 10% chance of lowering the target's Speed by 1.
Bug Bite	Bug	Physical	60	100	20	Normal	◯	120	If the target is holding a Berry, the user eats that Berry and uses its battle effect if it has one.
Bug Buzz	Bug	Special	90	100	10	Normal	—	175	A 10% chance of lowering the target's Sp. Def by 1. Strikes the target even if it is using Substitute.

Move	Type	Kind	Pow.	Acc.	PP	Range	DA	Z-Move Pow./ Effects	Battle Effects
Bulk Up	Fighting	Status	—	—	20	Self	—	Raises the user's Attack	Raises the user's Attack and Defense by 1.
Bulldoze	Ground	Physical	60	100	20	Adjacent	—	120	Lowers the target's Speed by 1. Its power is reduced by 25% when it hits multiple Pokémon in a Double Battle. Its power is reduced by 50% when it hits multiple Pokémon in a Battle Royal.
Bullet Punch	Steel	Physical	40	100	30	Normal	○	100	Always strikes first. The user with the higher Speed goes first if similar moves are used.
Bullet Seed	Grass	Physical	25	100	30	Normal	—	140	Attacks 2–5 times in a row in a single turn.
Burn Up	Fire	Special	130	100	5	Normal	—	195	After attacking, the user is no longer Fire type.
Calm Mind	Psychic	Status	—	—	20	Self	—	Resets negative stat changes	Raises the user's Sp. Atk and Sp. Def by 1.
Camouflage	Normal	Status	—	—	20	Self	—	Raises the user's evasion	Changes the user's type to match the environment: Cave: Rock type. Dirt / Sand: Ground type. Electric Terrain: Electric type. Grass / Grassy Terrain: Grass type. Indoors / Link Battle: Normal type. Misty Terrain: Fairy type. Psychic Terrain / Ultra Space: Psychic type. Snow/Ice: Ice type. Volcano: Fire type. Water Surface / Puddle / Shoal: Water type.
Captivate	Normal	Status	—	100	20	Many Others	—	Raises the user's Sp. Def by 2	Lowers the targets' Sp. Atk by 2. Only works if the user and the targets are of different genders.
Celebrate	Normal	Status	—	—	40	Self	—	Raises all of the user's stats	No effect.
Charge	Electric	Status	—	—	20	Self	—	Raises the user's Sp. Def	Doubles the attack power of an Electric-type move used the next turn. Raises the user's Sp. Def by 1.
Charge Beam	Electric	Special	50	90	10	Normal	—	100	A 70% chance of raising the user's Sp. Atk by 1.
Charm	Fairy	Status	—	100	20	Normal	—	Raises the user's Defense	Lowers the target's Attack by 2.
Chatter	Flying	Special	65	100	20	Normal	—	120	When the user is Chatot, this move also makes the target confused. Strikes the target even if it is using Substitute.
Chip Away	Normal	Physical	70	100	20	Normal	○	140	Damage dealt is not affected by the opposing Pokémon's stat changes.
Circle Throw	Fighting	Physical	60	90	10	Normal	○	120	Always strikes last. Ends wild Pokémon battles after attacking. When battling multiple wild Pokémon or if the wild Pokémon's level is higher than the user's, no additional effect takes place. In a battle with a Trainer, this move forces another Pokémon to switch in. If there is no Pokémon to switch in, no additional effect takes place.
Clamp	Water	Physical	35	85	15	Normal	○	100	Inflicts damage equal to 1/8 the target's max HP for 4–5 turns. The target cannot flee during that time.
Clanging Scales	Dragon	Special	110	100	5	Many Others	—	185	As an additional effect, lowers the user's Defense by 1. Its power is reduced by 25% when it hits multiple Pokémon in a Double Battle. Its power is reduced by 50% when it hits multiple Pokémon in a Battle Royal.
Clear Smog	Poison	Special	50	—	15	Normal	—	100	Eliminates every stat change of the target.
Close Combat	Fighting	Physical	120	100	5	Normal	○	190	Lowers the user's Defense and Sp. Def by 1.
Coil	Poison	Status	—	—	20	Self	—	Resets negative stat changes	Raises the user's Attack, Defense, and accuracy by 1.
Comet Punch	Normal	Physical	18	85	15	Normal	—	100	Attacks 2–5 times in a row in a single turn.
Confide	Normal	Status	—	—	20	Normal	—	Raises the user's Sp. Def	A sure hit. Lowers the target's Sp. Atk by 1. Strikes the target even if it is using Baneful Bunker, Detect, King's Shield, Mat Block, Protect, Spiky Shield, or Substitute.
Confuse Ray	Ghost	Status	—	100	10	Normal	—	Raises the user's Sp. Atk	Makes the target confused.
Confusion	Psychic	Special	50	100	25	Normal	—	100	A 10% chance of making the target confused.
Constrict	Normal	Physical	10	100	35	Normal	○	100	A 10% chance of lowering the target's Speed by 1.
Conversion	Normal	Status	—	—	30	Self	—	Raises all of the user's stats	Changes the user's type to that of one of its moves.
Conversion 2	Normal	Status	—	—	30	Normal	—	Restores the user's HP	Changes the user's type to one that is strong against the last move the target used.
Copycat	Normal	Status	—	—	20	Self	—	Increases the user's accuracy	Uses the last move used.
Core Enforcer	Dragon	Special	100	100	10	Many Others	—	140	Nullifies Abilities of targets that used a move on the same turn. Fails with certain Abilities, however.
Cosmic Power	Psychic	Status	—	—	20	Self	—	Raises the user's Sp. Def	Raises the user's Defense and Sp. Def by 1.
Cotton Guard	Grass	Status	—	—	10	Self	—	Resets negative stat changes	Raises the user's Defense by 3.
Cotton Spore	Grass	Status	—	100	40	Many Others	—	Resets negative stat changes	Lowers the targets' Speed by 2. Has no effect on Grass-type Pokémon.
Counter	Fighting	Physical	—	100	20	Varies	○	100	If the user is attacked physically, this move inflicts twice the damage done to the user. Always strikes last.
Covet	Normal	Physical	60	100	25	Normal	○	120	When the target is holding an item and the user is not, the user can steal that item. A regular attack if the target is not holding an item.
Crabhammer	Water	Physical	100	90	10	Normal	○	180	Critical hits land more easily.
Crafty Shield	Fairy	Status	—	—	10	Your Side	—	Raises the user's Sp. Def	Protects the user and allies from status moves used in the same turn. Does not protect against damage-dealing moves.
Cross Chop	Fighting	Physical	100	80	5	Normal	○	180	Critical hits land more easily.
Cross Poison	Poison	Physical	70	100	20	Normal	○	140	Critical hits land more easily. A 10% chance of inflicting the Poison status condition on the target.
Crunch	Dark	Physical	80	100	15	Normal	○	160	A 20% chance of lowering the target's Defense by 1.
Crush Claw	Normal	Physical	75	95	10	Normal	○	140	A 50% chance of lowering the target's Defense by 1.
Crush Grip	Normal	Physical	—	100	5	Normal	○	190	The more HP the target has left, the greater the move's power becomes (max 120).
Curse	Ghost	Status	—	—	10	Varies	—	Ghost type: restores all of the user's HP. Other types: raises the user's Attack.	Lowers the user's Speed by 1 and raises its Attack and Defense by 1. If used by a Ghost-type Pokémon, the user loses half of its maximum HP, but the move lowers the target's HP by 1/4 of its maximum every turn.

Move	Type	Kind	Pow.	Acc.	PP	Range	DA	Z-Move Pow./Effects	Battle Effects
Cut	Normal	Physical	50	95	30	Normal	○	100	A regular attack.
Dark Pulse	Dark	Special	80	100	15	Normal	—	160	Has a 20% chance of making the target flinch (unable to use moves on that turn).
Dark Void	Dark	Status	—	50	10	Many Others	—	Resets negative stat changes	Inflicts the Asleep status condition on the targets.
Darkest Lariat	Dark	Physical	85	100	10	Normal	○	160	Damage dealt is not affected by the opposing Pokémon's stat changes.
Dazzling Gleam	Fairy	Special	80	100	10	Many Others	—	160	Its power is reduced by 25% when it hits multiple Pokémon in a Double Battle. Its power is reduced by 50% when it hits multiple Pokémon in a Battle Royal.
Defend Order	Bug	Status	—	—	10	Self	—	Raises the user's Defense	Raises the user's Defense and Sp. Def by 1.
Defense Curl	Normal	Status	—	—	40	Self	—	Increases the user's accuracy	Raises the user's Defense by 1.
Defog	Flying	Status	—	—	15	Normal	—	Increases the user's accuracy	Lowers the target's evasion by 1. Nullifies the effects of Aurora Veil, Light Screen, Reflect, Safeguard, Mist, Spikes, Toxic Spikes, and Stealth Rock on the target's side.
Destiny Bond	Ghost	Status	—	—	5	Self	—	Follow Me	If the user faints due to damage from a Pokémon, that Pokémon faints as well. Fails when used in succession.
Detect	Fighting	Status	—	—	5	Self	—	Raises the user's evasion	The user evades all moves that turn. If used in succession, its chance of failing rises.
Diamond Storm	Rock	Physical	100	95	5	Many Others	—	180	A 50% chance of raising the user's Defense by 2. Its power is reduced by 25% when it hits multiple Pokémon in a Double Battle. Its power is reduced by 50% when it hits multiple Pokémon in a Battle Royal.
Dig	Ground	Physical	80	100	10	Normal	○	160	The user burrows underground on the first turn and attacks on the second.
Disable	Normal	Status	—	100	20	Normal	—	Resets negative stat changes	The target can't use the move it just used for 4 turns.
Disarming Voice	Fairy	Special	40	—	15	Many Others	—	100	A sure hit. Strikes the targets even if they are using Substitute. Its power is reduced by 25% when it hits multiple Pokémon in a Double Battle. Its power is reduced by 50% when it hits multiple Pokémon in a Battle Royal.
Discharge	Electric	Special	80	100	15	Adjacent	—	160	A 30% chance of inflicting the Paralysis status condition on the target. Its power is reduced by 25% when it hits multiple Pokémon in a Double Battle. Its power is reduced by 50% when it hits multiple Pokémon in a Battle Royal.
Dive	Water	Physical	80	100	10	Normal	○	160	The user dives deep on the first turn and attacks on the second.
Dizzy Punch	Normal	Physical	70	100	10	Normal	○	140	A 20% chance of making the target confused.
Doom Desire	Steel	Special	140	100	5	Normal	—	200	Attacks the target after 2 turns. This move is affected by the target's type.
Double Hit	Normal	Physical	35	90	10	Normal	○	140	Attacks twice in a row in a single turn.
Double Kick	Fighting	Physical	30	100	30	Normal	○	100	Attacks twice in a row in a single turn.
Double Slap	Normal	Physical	15	85	10	Normal	○	100	Attacks 2–5 times in a row in a single turn.
Double Team	Normal	Status	—	—	15	Self	—	Resets negative stat changes	Raises the user's evasion by 1.
Double-Edge	Normal	Physical	120	100	15	Normal	○	190	The user takes 1/3 of the damage inflicted.
Draco Meteor	Dragon	Special	130	90	5	Normal	—	195	Lowers the user's Sp. Atk by 2.
Dragon Ascent	Flying	Physical	120	100	5	Normal	○	190	Lowers the user's Defense and Sp. Def by 1.
Dragon Breath	Dragon	Special	60	100	20	Normal	—	120	A 30% chance of inflicting the Paralysis status condition on the target.
Dragon Claw	Dragon	Physical	80	100	15	Normal	○	160	A regular attack.
Dragon Dance	Dragon	Status	—	—	20	Self	—	Resets negative stat changes	Raises the user's Attack and Speed by 1.
Dragon Hammer	Dragon	Physical	90	100	15	Normal	○	175	A regular attack.
Dragon Pulse	Dragon	Special	85	100	10	Normal	—	160	A regular attack.
Dragon Rage	Dragon	Special	—	100	10	Normal	—	100	Deals a fixed 40 points of damage.
Dragon Rush	Dragon	Physical	100	75	10	Normal	○	180	A 20% chance of making the target flinch (unable to use moves on that turn). If the target has used Minimize, this move will be a sure hit and its power will be doubled.
Dragon Tail	Dragon	Physical	60	90	10	Normal	○	120	Attacks last. Ends wild Pokémon battles after attacking. When battling multiple wild Pokémon or if the wild Pokémon's level is higher than the user's, no additional effect takes place. In a battle with a Trainer, this move forces another Pokémon to switch in. If there is no Pokémon to switch in, no additional effect takes place.
Drain Punch	Fighting	Physical	75	100	10	Normal	○	140	Restores HP by up to half of the damage dealt to the target.
Draining Kiss	Fairy	Special	50	100	10	Normal	○	100	Restores HP by up to 3/4 of the damage dealt to the target.
Dream Eater	Psychic	Special	100	100	15	Normal	—	180	Only works when the target is Asleep. Restores HP by up to half of the damage dealt to the target.
Drill Peck	Flying	Physical	80	100	20	Normal	○	160	A regular attack.
Drill Run	Ground	Physical	80	95	10	Normal	○	160	Critical hits land more easily.
Dual Chop	Dragon	Physical	40	90	15	Normal	○	100	Attacks twice in a row in a single turn.
Dynamic Punch	Fighting	Physical	100	50	5	Normal	○	180	Makes the target confused.
Earth Power	Ground	Special	90	100	10	Normal	—	175	A 10% chance of lowering the target's Sp. Def by 1.
Earthquake	Ground	Physical	100	100	10	Adjacent	—	180	Does twice the damage if targets are underground due to using Dig. Its power is reduced by 25% when it hits multiple Pokémon in a Double Battle. Its power is reduced by 50% when it hits multiple Pokémon in a Battle Royal.
Echoed Voice	Normal	Special	40	100	15	Normal	—	100	If this move is used every turn, no matter which Pokémon uses it, its power increases (max 200). If no Pokémon uses it in a turn, the power returns to normal. Strikes the target even if it is using Substitute.
Eerie Impulse	Electric	Status	—	100	15	Normal	—	Raises the user's Sp. Def	Lowers the target's Sp. Atk by 2.
Egg Bomb	Normal	Physical	100	75	10	Normal	—	180	A regular attack.
Electric Terrain	Electric	Status	—	—	10	Both Sides	—	Raises the user's Speed	Electrifies the field for 5 turns. During that time, Pokémon on the ground will be able to do 50% more damage with Electric-type moves and cannot fall Asleep.
Electrify	Electric	Status	—	—	20	Normal	—	Raises the user's Sp. Atk	Changes any attack used by the target in the same turn into an Electric-type move.
Electro Ball	Electric	Special	—	100	10	Normal	—	160	The faster the user is than the target, the greater the move's power (max 150).

Move	Type	Kind	Pow.	Acc.	PP	Range	DA	Z-Move Pow./ Effects	Battle Effects
Electroweb	Electric	Special	55	95	15	Many Others	—	100	Lowers the targets' Speed by 1. Its power is reduced by 25% when it hits multiple Pokémon in a Double Battle. Its power is reduced by 50% when it hits multiple Pokémon in a Battle Royal.
Embargo	Dark	Status	—	100	15	Normal	—	Raises the user's Sp. Atk	The target can't use items for 5 turns. The Trainer also can't use items on that Pokémon.
Ember	Fire	Special	40	100	25	Normal	—	100	A 10% chance of inflicting the Burned status condition on the target. If the target is Frozen, it will be thawed.
Encore	Normal	Status	—	100	5	Normal	—	Raises the user's Speed	The target is forced to keep using the last move it used. This effect lasts 3 turns.
Endeavor	Normal	Physical	—	100	5	Normal	◯	160	Inflicts damage equal to the target's HP minus the user's HP.
Endure	Normal	Status	—	—	10	Self	—	Resets negative stat changes	Leaves the user with 1 HP when hit by a move that would knock it out. If used in succession, its chance of failing rises.
Energy Ball	Grass	Special	90	100	10	Normal	—	175	A 10% chance of lowering the target's Sp. Def by 1.
Entrainment	Normal	Status	—	100	15	Normal	—	Raises the user's Sp. Def	Makes the target's Ability the same as the user's. Fails with certain Abilities, however.
Eruption	Fire	Special	150	100	5	Many Others	—	200	If the user's HP is low, this move has lower power. If the targets are Frozen, they will be thawed. Its power is reduced by 25% when it hits multiple Pokémon in a Double Battle. Its power is reduced by 50% when it hits multiple Pokémon in a Battle Royal.
Explosion	Normal	Physical	250	100	5	Adjacent	—	200	The user faints after using it. Its power is reduced by 25% when it hits multiple Pokémon in a Double Battle. Its power is reduced by 50% when it hits multiple Pokémon in a Battle Royal.
Extrasensory	Psychic	Special	80	100	20	Normal	—	160	A 10% chance of making the target flinch (unable to use moves on that turn).
Extreme Speed	Normal	Physical	80	100	5	Normal	◯	160	Always strikes first. Faster than other moves that strike first, except Fake Out. If two Pokémon use this move, or if the other Pokémon uses the move Feint or First Impression, the one with the higher Speed goes first.
Facade	Normal	Physical	70	100	20	Normal	◯	140	This move's power is doubled if the user has a Paralysis, Poisoned, or Burned status condition.
Fairy Lock	Fairy	Status	—	—	10	Both Sides	—	Raises the user's Defense	The target cannot escape during the next turn. If used during a Trainer battle, the opposing Trainer cannot switch Pokémon. Has no effect on Ghost-type Pokémon.
Fairy Wind	Fairy	Special	40	100	30	Normal	—	100	A regular attack.
Fake Out	Normal	Physical	40	100	10	Normal	◯	100	Always strikes first and makes the target flinch (unable to use moves on that turn). Only works on the first turn after the user is sent out. Faster than other moves that strike first.
Fake Tears	Dark	Status	—	100	20	Normal	—	Raises the user's Sp. Atk	Lowers the target's Sp. Def by 2.
False Swipe	Normal	Physical	40	100	40	Normal	◯	100	Always leaves 1 HP, even if the damage would have made the target faint.
Feather Dance	Flying	Status	—	100	15	Normal	—	Raises the user's Defense	Lowers the target's Attack by 2.
Feint	Normal	Physical	30	100	10	Normal	—	100	Always strikes first. Faster than other moves that strike first, except Fake Out. If two Pokémon use this move, or if the other Pokémon uses the move Extreme Speed or First Impression, the one with the higher Speed goes first. Strikes the target even if it is using Baneful Bunker, Detect, King's Shield, Mat Block, Protect, Quick Guard, Spiky Shield, or Wide Guard, and eliminates the effects of those moves.
Feint Attack	Dark	Physical	60	—	20	Normal	◯	120	A sure hit.
Fell Stinger	Bug	Physical	50	100	25	Normal	◯	100	When the Pokémon knocks out an opponent with this move, its Attack goes up 3.
Fiery Dance	Fire	Special	80	100	10	Normal	—	160	A 50% chance of raising the user's Sp. Atk by 1. If the target is Frozen, it will be thawed.
Final Gambit	Fighting	Special	—	100	5	Normal	—	180	Does damage to the target equal to the user's remaining HP. If the move lands, the user faints. If the move does not land, the user will not faint.
Fire Blast	Fire	Special	110	85	5	Normal	—	185	A 10% chance of inflicting the Burned status condition on the target. If the target is Frozen, it will be thawed.
Fire Fang	Fire	Physical	65	95	15	Normal	◯	120	A 10% chance of inflicting the Burned status condition or making the target flinch (unable to use moves on that turn). If the target is Frozen, it will be thawed.
Fire Lash	Fire	Physical	80	100	15	Normal	◯	160	Lowers the target's Defense by 1.
Fire Pledge	Fire	Special	80	100	10	Normal	—	160	When combined with Water Pledge or Grass Pledge, the power and effect change. If combined with Water Pledge, the power is 150 and it becomes a Water-type move. This makes it more likely that your team's moves will have additional effects for 4 turns. If combined with Grass Pledge, the power is 150 and it remains a Fire-type move. This damages opposing Pokémon, except Fire types, for 4 turns. If the target is Frozen, it will be thawed.
Fire Punch	Fire	Physical	75	100	15	Normal	◯	140	A 10% chance of inflicting the Burned status condition on the target. If the target is Frozen, it will be thawed.
Fire Spin	Fire	Special	35	85	15	Normal	—	100	Inflicts damage equal to 1/8 the target's max HP for 4–5 turns. The target cannot flee during that time. If the target is Frozen, it will be thawed.
First Impression	Bug	Physical	90	100	10	Normal	◯	175	Always strikes first. Only works on the first turn after the user is sent out. Faster than other moves that strike first, except Fake Out. If two Pokémon use this move, or if the other Pokémon uses the move Extreme Speed or Feint, the one with the higher Speed goes first.
Fissure	Ground	Physical	—	30	5	Normal	—	180	The target faints with one hit if the user's level is equal to or greater than the target's level. The higher the user's level is compared to the target's, the more accurate the move is.
Flail	Normal	Physical	—	100	15	Normal	◯	160	The lower the user's HP is, the greater the move's power becomes (max 200).
Flame Burst	Fire	Special	70	100	15	Normal	—	140	It deals damage equal to 1/16 of the max HP of opposing Pokémon next to the target during Double Battles or Battle Royals. If the target is Frozen, it will be thawed.
Flame Charge	Fire	Physical	50	100	20	Normal	—	100	Raises the user's Speed by 1. If the target is Frozen, it will be thawed.
Flame Wheel	Fire	Physical	60	100	25	Normal	◯	120	A 10% chance of inflicting the Burned status condition on the target. If the target is Frozen, it will be thawed. This move can be used even if the user is Frozen. If the user is Frozen, this also thaws the user.
Flamethrower	Fire	Special	90	100	15	Normal	—	175	A 10% chance of inflicting the Burned status condition on the target. If the target is Frozen, it will be thawed.
Flare Blitz	Fire	Physical	120	100	15	Normal	◯	190	User takes 1/3 of the damage done to the target. A 10% chance of inflicting the Burned status condition on the target. If the target is Frozen, it will be thawed. This move can be used even if the user is Frozen. If the user is Frozen, this also thaws the user.

Move	Type	Kind	Pow.	Acc.	PP	Range	DA	Z-Move Pow./Effects	Battle Effects
Flash	Normal	Status	—	100	20	Normal	—	Raises the user's evasion	Lowers the target's accuracy by 1.
Flash Cannon	Steel	Special	80	100	10	Normal	—	160	A 10% chance of lowering the target's Sp. Def by 1.
Flatter	Dark	Status	—	100	15	Normal	—	Raises the user's Sp. Def	Makes the target confused, but also raises its Sp. Atk by 1.
Fleur Cannon	Fairy	Special	130	90	5	Normal	—	195	Lowers the user's Sp. Atk by 2.
Fling	Dark	Physical	—	100	10	Normal	—	100	The user attacks by throwing its held item at the target. Power and effect vary depending on the item.
Floral Healing	Fairy	Status	—	—	10	Normal	—	Resets negative stat changes	Restores a target other than the user's HP by up to half of its maximum HP. If Grassy Terrain is in effect, it recovers 2/3 of the target's maximum HP.
Flower Shield	Fairy	Status	—	—	10	Varies	—	Raises the user's Defense	Raises the Defense of any Grass-type Pokémon by 1.
Fly	Flying	Physical	90	95	15	Normal	○	175	The user flies into the air on the first turn and attacks on the second.
Flying Press	Fighting	Physical	100	95	10	Normal	○	170	This move is both Fighting type and Flying type. If the target has used Minimize, it will be a sure hit and its power will be doubled.
Focus Blast	Fighting	Special	120	70	5	Normal	—	190	A 10% chance of lowering the target's Sp. Def by 1.
Focus Energy	Normal	Status	—	—	30	Self	—	Increases the user's accuracy	Heightens the critical-hit ratio of the user's subsequent moves.
Focus Punch	Fighting	Physical	150	100	20	Normal	○	200	Always strikes last. The move misses if the user is hit before this move lands.
Follow Me	Normal	Status	—	—	20	Self	—	Resets negative stat changes	This move goes first. Opposing Pokémon aim only at the user.
Force Palm	Fighting	Physical	60	100	10	Normal	○	120	A 30% chance of inflicting the Paralysis status condition on the target.
Foresight	Normal	Status	—	—	40	Normal	—	Critical hits land more easily	Attacks land easily regardless of the target's evasion. Makes Ghost-type Pokémon vulnerable to Normal- and Fighting-type moves.
Forest's Curse	Grass	Status	—	100	20	Normal	—	Raises all of the user's stats	Gives the target the Grass type
Foul Play	Dark	Physical	95	100	15	Normal	○	175	The user turns the target's power against it. Damage varies depending on the target's Attack and Defense.
Freeze Shock	Ice	Physical	140	90	5	Normal	—	200	Builds power on the first turn and attacks on the second. A 30% chance of inflicting the Paralysis status condition on the target.
Freeze-Dry	Ice	Special	70	100	20	Normal	—	140	Super effective even against Water-type Pokémon. A 10% chance of inflicting the Frozen status condition.
Frenzy Plant	Grass	Special	150	90	5	Normal	—	200	The user can't move during the next turn.
Frost Breath	Ice	Special	60	90	10	Normal	—	120	Always delivers a critical hit.
Frustration	Normal	Physical	—	100	20	Normal	○	160	The lower the user's friendship, the greater this move's power (max 102).
Fury Attack	Normal	Physical	15	85	20	Normal	○	100	Attacks 2–5 times in a row in a single turn.
Fury Cutter	Bug	Physical	40	95	20	Normal	○	100	This move doubles in power with every successful hit (max 160). Power returns to normal once it misses.
Fury Swipes	Normal	Physical	18	80	15	Normal	○	100	Attacks 2–5 times in a row in a single turn.
Fusion Bolt	Electric	Physical	100	100	5	Normal	—	180	Attack's power is doubled if used immediately after Fusion Flare.
Fusion Flare	Fire	Special	100	100	5	Normal	—	180	Attack's power is doubled if used immediately after Fusion Bolt. If the target is Frozen, it will be thawed. This move can be used even if the user is Frozen. If the user is Frozen, this also thaws the user.
Future Sight	Psychic	Special	120	100	10	Normal	—	190	Attacks the target after 2 turns. This move is affected by the target's type.
Gastro Acid	Poison	Status	—	100	10	Normal	—	Raises the user's Speed	Disables the target's Ability. Fails with certain Abilities, however.
Gear Grind	Steel	Physical	50	85	15	Normal	○	180	Attacks twice in a row in a single turn.
Gear Up	Steel	Status	—	—	20	Your Party	—	Raises the user's Sp. Atk	Raises the Attack and Sp. Atk of allies with either the Plus or Minus Abilities.
Geomancy	Fairy	Status	—	—	10	Self	—	Raises all of the user's stats	Builds power on the first turn and increases the user's Sp. Atk, Sp. Def, and Speed by 2 on the second.
Giga Drain	Grass	Special	75	100	10	Normal	—	140	Restores HP by up to half of the damage dealt to the target.
Giga Impact	Normal	Physical	150	90	5	Normal	○	200	The user can't move during the next turn.
Glaciate	Ice	Special	65	95	10	Many Others	—	120	Lowers the targets' Speed by 1. Its power is reduced by 25% when it hits multiple Pokémon in a Double Battle. Its power is reduced by 50% when it hits multiple Pokémon in a Battle Royal.
Glare	Normal	Status	—	100	30	Normal	—	Raises the user's Sp. Def	Inflicts the Paralysis status condition on the target.
Grass Knot	Grass	Special	—	100	20	Normal	○	160	The heavier the target is compared to the user, the greater the move's power becomes (max 120).
Grass Pledge	Grass	Special	80	100	10	Normal	—	160	When combined with Water Pledge or Fire Pledge, the power and effect change. If combined with Water Pledge, the power is 150 and it remains a Grass-type move. This lowers the Speed of opposing Pokémon for 4 turns. If combined with Fire Pledge, the power is 150 and it becomes a Fire-type move. This damages all non-Fire types for 4 turns. If the target is Frozen, it will be thawed.
Grass Whistle	Grass	Status	—	55	15	Normal	—	Raises the user's Speed	Inflicts the Asleep status condition on the target. Strikes the target even if it is using Substitute.
Grassy Terrain	Grass	Status	—	—	10	Both Sides	—	Raises the user's Defense	Covers the field with grass for 5 turns. During that time, Pokémon on the ground will be able to do 50% more damage with Grass-type moves and will recover 1/16 of the Pokémon's maximum HP each turn. Damage done to Pokémon on the ground by Earthquake, Bulldoze, or Magnitude is halved.
Gravity	Psychic	Status	—	—	5	Both Sides	—	Raises the user's Sp. Atk	Raises the accuracy of all Pokémon in battle for 5 turns. Ground-type moves will now hit a Pokémon with the Levitate Ability or a Flying-type Pokémon. Prevents the use of Bounce, Fly, High Jump Kick, Jump Kick, Magnet Rise, Sky Drop, Splash, and Telekinesis. Pulls any airborne Pokémon to the ground.
Growl	Normal	Status	—	100	40	Many Others	—	Raises the user's Defense	Lowers the targets' Attack by 1. Strikes the targets even if they are using Substitute.

Move	Type	Kind	Pow.	Acc.	PP	Range	DA	Z-Move Pow./ Effects	Battle Effects
Growth	Normal	Status	—	—	20	Self	—	Raises the user's Sp. Atk	Raises the user's Attack and Sp. Atk by 1. Raises them by 2 when the weather condition is sunny or extremely harsh sunlight.
Grudge	Ghost	Status	—	—	5	Self	—	Adds effects of Follow Me	Any move that causes the user to faint will have its PP dropped to 0.
Guard Split	Psychic	Status	—	—	10	Normal	—	Raises the user's Speed	The user and the target's Defense and Sp. Def are added, then divided equally between them.
Guard Swap	Psychic	Status	—	—	10	Normal	—	Raises the user's Speed	Swaps Defense and Sp. Def changes between the user and the target.
Guillotine	Normal	Physical	—	30	5	Normal	○	180	The target faints with one hit if the user's level is equal to or greater than the target's level. The higher the user's level is compared to the target's, the more accurate the move is.
Gunk Shot	Poison	Physical	120	80	5	Normal	○	190	A 30% chance of inflicting the Poisoned status condition on the target.
Gust	Flying	Special	40	100	35	Normal	—	100	It even hits Pokémon that are in the sky due to using moves such as Fly and Bounce, dealing them twice the usual damage.
Gyro Ball	Steel	Physical	—	100	5	Normal	○	160	The slower the user is than the target, the greater the move's power becomes (max 150).
Hail	Ice	Status	—	—	10	Both Sides	—	Raises the user's Speed	Changes the weather condition to hail for 5 turns, dealing damage every turn equal to 1/16 of its max HP to each Pokémon in the field that is not an Ice type.
Hammer Arm	Fighting	Physical	100	90	10	Normal	○	180	Lowers the user's Speed by 1.
Happy Hour	Normal	Status	—	—	30	Your Side	—	Raises all of the user's stats	Doubles the amount of prize money received after battle.
Harden	Normal	Status	—	—	30	Self	—	Raises the user's Defense	Raises the user's Defense by 1.
Haze	Ice	Status	—	—	30	Both Sides	—	Restores the user's HP	Eliminates every stat change of the targets.
Head Charge	Normal	Physical	120	100	15	Normal	○	190	The user takes 1/4 of the damage inflicted.
Head Smash	Rock	Physical	150	80	5	Normal	○	200	The user takes 1/2 of the damage inflicted.
Headbutt	Normal	Physical	70	100	15	Normal	○	140	A 30% chance of making the target flinch (unable to use moves on that turn).
Heal Bell	Normal	Status	—	—	5	Your Party	—	Restores the user's HP	Heals status conditions of all your Pokémon, including those in your party. Affects the target even if it is using Substitute.
Heal Block	Psychic	Status	—	100	15	Many Others	—	Raises the user's Sp. Atk by 2	Targets cannot have HP restored by moves, Abilities, or held items for 5 turns.
Heal Order	Bug	Status	—	—	10	Self	—	Resets negative stat changes	Restores HP by up to half of the user's maximum HP.
Heal Pulse	Psychic	Status	—	—	10	Normal	—	Resets negative stat changes	Restores the target's HP by up to half of its maximum HP.
Healing Wish	Psychic	Status	—	—	10	Self	—	None	The user faints, but fully heals the next Pokémon's HP and status conditions.
Heart Stamp	Psychic	Physical	60	100	25	Normal	○	120	A 30% chance of making the target flinch (unable to use moves on that turn).
Heart Swap	Psychic	Status	—	—	10	Normal	—	Critical hits land more easily	Swaps all stat changes between the user and the target.
Heat Crash	Fire	Physical	—	100	10	Normal	○	160	The heavier the user is compared to the target, the greater the move's power becomes (max 120). If the target is Frozen, it will be thawed. If the target has used Minimize, this move will be a sure hit and its power will be doubled.
Heat Wave	Fire	Special	95	90	10	Many Others	—	175	A 10% chance of inflicting the Burned status condition on the targets. If the targets are Frozen, they will be thawed. Its power is reduced by 25% when it hits multiple Pokémon in a Double Battle. Its power is reduced by 50% when it hits multiple Pokémon in a Battle Royal.
Heavy Slam	Steel	Physical	—	100	10	Normal	○	160	The heavier the user is compared to the target, the greater the move's power becomes (max 120).
Helping Hand	Normal	Status	—	—	20	1 Ally	—	Resets negative stat changes	Always strikes first. Strengthens the attack power of one ally's moves by 50%.
Hex	Ghost	Special	65	100	10	Normal	—	160	Deals twice the usual damage to a target affected by status conditions.
Hidden Power	Normal	Special	60	100	15	Normal	—	120	Type changes depending on the user.
High Horsepower	Ground	Physical	95	95	10	Normal	○	175	A regular attack.
High Jump Kick	Fighting	Physical	130	90	10	Normal	○	195	If this move misses, the user loses half of its maximum HP.
Hold Back	Normal	Physical	40	100	40	Normal	○	100	Always leaves 1 HP, even if the damage would have made the target faint.
Hold Hands	Normal	Status	—	—	40	1 Ally	—	Raises all of the user's stats	No effect.
Hone Claws	Dark	Status	—	—	15	Self	—	Raises the user's Attack	Raises Attack and accuracy by 1.
Horn Attack	Normal	Physical	65	100	25	Normal	—	120	A regular attack.
Horn Drill	Normal	Physical	—	30	5	Normal	○	180	The target faints with one hit if the user's level is equal to or greater than the target's level. The higher the user's level is compared to the target's, the more accurate the move is.
Horn Leech	Grass	Physical	75	100	10	Normal	○	140	Restores HP by up to half of the damage dealt to the target.
Howl	Normal	Status	—	—	40	Self	—	Raises the user's Attack	Raises the user's Attack by 1.
Hurricane	Flying	Special	110	70	10	Normal	—	185	A 30% chance of making the target confused. Is 100% accurate in the rain / heavy rain weather conditions and 50% accurate in the sunny / extremely harsh sunlight weather conditions. It can hit Pokémon that are in the sky due to using moves such as Fly and Bounce.
Hydro Cannon	Water	Special	150	90	5	Normal	—	200	The user can't move during the next turn.
Hydro Pump	Water	Special	110	80	5	Normal	—	185	A regular attack.
Hyper Beam	Normal	Special	150	90	5	Normal	—	200	The user can't move during the next turn.
Hyper Fang	Normal	Physical	80	90	15	Normal	○	160	A 10% chance of making the target flinch (unable to use moves on that turn).
Hyper Voice	Normal	Special	90	100	10	Many Others	—	175	Strikes the targets even if they are using Substitute. Its power is reduced by 25% when it hits multiple Pokémon in a Double Battle. Its power is reduced by 50% when it hits multiple Pokémon in a Battle Royal.

Move	Type	Kind	Pow.	Acc.	PP	Range	DA	Z-Move Pow./Effects	Battle Effects
Hyperspace Fury	Dark	Physical	100	—	5	Normal	—	180	A sure hit. Strikes the target even if it is using Baneful Bunker, Detect, King's Shield, Mat Block, Protect, or Spiky Shield. Fails when used by Hoopa Confined. Can only be used by Hoopa Unbound.
Hyperspace Hole	Psychic	Special	80	—	5	Normal	—	160	A sure hit. Strikes the target even if it is using Baneful Bunker, Detect, King's Shield, Mat Block, Protect, or Spiky Shield.
Hypnosis	Psychic	Status	—	60	20	Normal	—	Raises the user's Speed	Inflicts the Asleep status condition on the target.
Ice Ball	Ice	Physical	30	90	20	Normal	◯	100	Attacks consecutively over 5 turns or until it misses. Cannot choose other moves during this time. Damage dealt doubles with each successful hit (max 480). Its power is doubled if used after Defense Curl.
Ice Beam	Ice	Special	90	100	10	Normal	—	175	A 10% chance of inflicting the Frozen status condition on the target.
Ice Burn	Ice	Special	140	90	5	Normal	—	200	Builds power on the first turn and attacks on the second. A 30% chance of inflicting the Burned status condition on the targets.
Ice Fang	Ice	Physical	65	95	15	Normal	◯	120	A 10% chance of inflicting the Frozen status condition or making the target flinch (unable to use moves on that turn).
Ice Hammer	Ice	Physical	100	90	10	Normal	◯	180	Lowers the user's Speed by 1.
Ice Punch	Ice	Physical	75	100	15	Normal	◯	140	A 10% chance of inflicting the Frozen status condition on the target.
Ice Shard	Ice	Physical	40	100	30	Normal	—	100	Always strikes first. The user with the higher Speed goes first if similar moves are used.
Icicle Crash	Ice	Physical	85	90	10	Normal	—	160	A 30% chance of making the target flinch (unable to use moves on that turn).
Icicle Spear	Ice	Physical	25	100	30	Normal	◯	140	Attacks 2–5 times in a row in a single turn.
Icy Wind	Ice	Special	55	95	15	Many Others	—	100	Lowers the targets' Speed by 1. Its power is reduced by 25% when it hits multiple Pokémon in a Double Battle. Its power is reduced by 50% when it hits multiple Pokémon in a Battle Royal.
Imprison	Psychic	Status	—	—	10	Self	—	Raises the user's Sp. Def by 2	Opposing Pokémon cannot use a move if the user knows that move as well.
Incinerate	Fire	Special	60	100	15	Many Others	—	120	Burns up the Berry or Gem being held by the targets, which makes them unusable. If the targets are Frozen, they will be thawed. Its power is reduced by 25% when it hits multiple Pokémon in a Double Battle. Its power is reduced by 50% when it hits multiple Pokémon in a Battle Royal.
Inferno	Fire	Special	100	50	5	Normal	—	180	Inflicts the Burned status condition on the target. If the target is Frozen, it will be thawed.
Infestation	Bug	Special	20	100	20	Normal	◯	100	Inflicts damage equal to 1/8 the target's max HP for 4–5 turns. The target cannot flee during that time.
Ingrain	Grass	Status	—	—	20	Self	—	Raises the user's Sp. Def	Restores 1/16 of max HP every turn. The user cannot be switched out after using this move. Ground-type moves will now hit the user even if it is a Flying-type Pokémon or has the Levitate Ability.
Instruct	Psychic	Status	—	—	15	Normal	—	Raises the user's Sp. Atk	The target is forced to use the same move it just used.
Ion Deluge	Electric	Status	—	—	25	Both Sides	—	Raises the user's Sp. Atk	Attacks first. Changes any Normal-type moves used in the same turn into Electric-type moves.
Iron Defense	Steel	Status	—	—	15	Self	—	Resets negative stat changes	Raises the user's Defense by 2.
Iron Head	Steel	Physical	80	100	15	Normal	◯	160	A 30% chance of making the target flinch (unable to use moves on that turn).
Iron Tail	Steel	Physical	100	75	15	Normal	◯	180	A 30% chance of lowering the target's Defense by 1.
Judgment	Normal	Special	100	100	10	Normal	—	180	A regular attack. This move's type changes according to the plate that Arceus is holding.
Jump Kick	Fighting	Physical	100	95	10	Normal	◯	180	If this move misses, the user loses half of its maximum HP.
Karate Chop	Fighting	Physical	50	100	25	Normal	◯	100	Critical hits land more easily.
Kinesis	Psychic	Status	—	80	15	Normal	—	Raises the user's evasion	Lowers the target's accuracy by 1.
King's Shield	Steel	Status	—	—	10	Self	—	Resets negative stat changes	The user evades all attacks that turn. If an opposing Pokémon uses a move that makes direct contact, its Attack will be lowered by 2. Fails more easily when used repeatedly.
Knock Off	Dark	Physical	65	100	20	Normal	◯	120	The target drops its held item. It gets the item back after the battle. This move does 50% more damage to opponents holding items.
Land's Wrath	Ground	Physical	90	100	10	Many Others	—	185	Its power is reduced by 25% when it hits multiple Pokémon in a Double Battle. Its power is reduced by 50% when it hits multiple Pokémon in a Battle Royal.
Laser Focus	Normal	Status	—	—	30	Self	—	Raises the user's Attack	The user's next move will always be a critical hit.
Last Resort	Normal	Physical	140	100	5	Normal	◯	200	Fails unless the user has used each of its other moves at least once.
Lava Plume	Fire	Special	80	100	15	Adjacent	—	160	A 30% chance of inflicting the Burned status condition on the target. If the targets are Frozen, they will be thawed. Its power is reduced by 25% when it hits multiple Pokémon in a Double Battle. Its power is reduced by 50% when it hits multiple Pokémon in a Battle Royal.
Leaf Blade	Grass	Physical	90	100	15	Normal	◯	175	Critical hits land more easily.
Leaf Storm	Grass	Special	130	90	5	Normal	—	195	Lowers the user's Sp. Atk by 2.
Leaf Tornado	Grass	Special	65	90	10	Normal	—	120	A 50% chance of lowering the target's accuracy by 1.
Leafage	Grass	Physical	40	100	40	Normal	—	100	A regular attack.
Leech Life	Bug	Physical	80	100	10	Normal	◯	160	Restores HP by up to half of the damage dealt to the target.
Leech Seed	Grass	Status	—	90	10	Normal	—	Resets negative stat changes	Steals 1/8 of the target's max HP every turn and absorbs it to restore the user. Keeps working even after the user switches out. Does not work on Grass types.
Leer	Normal	Status	—	100	30	Many Others	—	Raises the user's Attack	Lowers the targets' Defense by 1.
Lick	Ghost	Physical	30	100	30	Normal	—	100	A 30% chance of inflicting the Paralysis status condition on the target.
Light Screen	Psychic	Status	—	—	30	Your Side	—	Raises the user's Sp. Def	Halves the damage to the Pokémon on your side from special moves. Effect lasts 5 turns even if the user is switched out. Effect is weaker in Double Battles and Battle Royal.
Liquidation	Water	Physical	85	100	10	Normal	◯	160	A 20% chance of lowering the target's Defense by 1.
Lock-On	Normal	Status	—	—	5	Normal	—	Raises the user's Speed	The user's next move will be a sure hit.

Move	Type	Kind	Pow.	Acc.	PP	Range	DA	Z-Move Pow./ Effects	Battle Effects
Lovely Kiss	Normal	Status	—	75	10	Normal	—	Raises the user's Speed	Inflicts the Asleep status condition on the target.
Low Kick	Fighting	Physical	—	100	20	Normal	○	160	The heavier the target is compared to the user, the greater the move's power becomes (max 120).
Low Sweep	Fighting	Physical	65	100	20	Normal	○	120	Lowers the target's Speed by 1.
Lucky Chant	Normal	Status	—	—	30	Your Side	—	Raises the user's evasion	The Pokémon on your side take no critical hits for 5 turns.
Lunar Dance	Psychic	Status	—	—	10	Self	—	None	The user faints, but fully heals the next Pokémon's HP, PP, and status conditions.
Lunge	Bug	Physical	80	100	15	Normal	○	160	Lowers the target's Attack by 1.
Luster Purge	Psychic	Special	70	100	5	Normal	—	140	Has a 50% chance of lowering the target's Sp. Def by 1.
Mach Punch	Fighting	Physical	40	100	30	Normal	○	100	Always strikes first. The user with the higher Speed goes first if similar moves are used.
Magic Coat	Psychic	Status	—	—	15	Self	—	Raises the user's Sp. Def by 2	Always strikes first. Reflects moves with effects like Leech Seed or those that inflict status conditions such as Asleep, Paralysis, or Poisoned.
Magic Room	Psychic	Status	—	—	10	Both Sides	—	Raises the user's Sp. Def	Always strikes last. No held items will have any effect for 5 turns. Fling cannot be used to throw items while Magic Room is in effect. The effect ends if the move is used again.
Magical Leaf	Grass	Special	60	—	20	Normal	—	120	A sure hit.
Magma Storm	Fire	Special	100	75	5	Normal	—	180	Inflicts damage over 4–5 turns. The target cannot flee during that time. If the targets are Frozen, they will be thawed.
Magnet Bomb	Steel	Physical	60	—	20	Normal	—	120	A sure hit.
Magnet Rise	Electric	Status	—	—	10	Self	—	Raises the user's evasion	Nullifies Ground-type moves for 5 turns.
Magnetic Flux	Electric	Status	—	—	20	Your Party	—	Raises the user's Sp. Def	Raises the Defense and Sp. Def of allies with either the Plus or Minus Abilities.
Magnitude	Ground	Physical	—	100	30	Adjacent	—	140	This move's power varies among 10, 30, 50, 70, 90, 110, and 150. Does twice the damage if targets are underground due to using Dig. Its power is reduced by 25% when it hits multiple Pokémon in a Double Battle. Its power is reduced by 50% when it hits multiple Pokémon in a Battle Royal.
Mat Block	Fighting	Status	—	—	10	Your Side	—	Raises the user's Defense	Protects the user and allies from damage-dealing moves used in the same turn. Only works on the first turn after the user is sent out. Does not protect against status moves.
Me First	Normal	Status	—	—	20	Varies	—	Raises the user's Speed by 2	Copies the target's chosen move and uses it with 50% greater power. Fails if it does not strike first.
Mean Look	Normal	Status	—	—	5	Normal	—	Raises the user's Sp. Def	The target cannot escape. If used during a Trainer battle, the opposing Trainer cannot switch Pokémon. Has no effect on Ghost-type Pokémon.
Meditate	Psychic	Status	—	—	40	Self	—	Raises the user's Attack	Raises the user's Attack by 1.
Mega Drain	Grass	Special	40	100	15	Normal	—	120	Restores HP by up to half of the damage dealt to the target.
Mega Kick	Normal	Physical	120	75	5	Normal	○	190	A regular attack.
Mega Punch	Normal	Physical	80	85	20	Normal	○	160	A regular attack.
Megahorn	Bug	Physical	120	85	10	Normal	○	190	A regular attack.
Memento	Dark	Status	—	100	10	Normal	—	Restores the HP of the next ally that enters the field	The user faints, but the target's Attack and Sp. Atk are lowered by 2.
Metal Burst	Steel	Physical	—	100	10	Varies	—	100	Targets the Pokémon that most recently damaged the user with a move. Inflicts 1.5 times the damage taken.
Metal Claw	Steel	Physical	50	95	35	Normal	○	100	A 10% chance of raising the user's Attack by 1.
Metal Sound	Steel	Status	—	85	40	Normal	—	Raises the user's Sp. Atk	Lowers the target's Sp. Def by 2. Strikes the target even if it is using Substitute.
Meteor Mash	Steel	Physical	90	90	10	Normal	○	175	Has a 20% chance of raising the user's Attack by 1.
Metronome	Normal	Status	—	—	10	Self	—	None	Uses one move randomly chosen from all possible moves.
Milk Drink	Normal	Status	—	—	10	Self	—	Resets negative stat changes	Restores HP by up to half of the user's maximum HP.
Mimic	Normal	Status	—	—	10	Normal	—	Increases the user's accuracy	Copies the target's last-used move (copied move has a PP of 5). Fails if used before the opposing Pokémon uses a move.
Mind Reader	Normal	Status	—	—	5	Normal	—	Raises the user's Sp. Atk	The user's next move will be a sure hit.
Minimize	Normal	Status	—	—	10	Self	—	Resets negative stat changes	Raises the user's evasion by 2.
Miracle Eye	Psychic	Status	—	—	40	Normal	—	Raises the user's Sp. Atk	Attacks land easily regardless of the target's evasion. Makes Dark-type Pokémon vulnerable to Psychic-type moves.
Mirror Coat	Psychic	Special	—	100	20	Varies	—	100	If the user is attacked with a special move, this move inflicts twice the damage done to the user. Always strikes last.
Mirror Move	Flying	Status	—	—	20	Normal	—	Raises the user's Attack by 2	Uses the last move that the target used.
Mirror Shot	Steel	Special	65	85	10	Normal	—	120	A 30% chance of lowering the target's accuracy by 1.
Mist	Ice	Status	—	—	30	Your Side	—	Restores the user's HP	Protects against stat-lowering moves and additional effects for 5 turns.
Mist Ball	Psychic	Special	70	100	5	Normal	—	140	Has a 50% chance of reducing the target's Sp. Atk by 1.
Misty Terrain	Fairy	Status	—	—	10	Both Sides	—	Raises the user's Sp. Def	Covers the field with mist for 5 turns. During that time, Pokémon on the ground take half damage from Dragon-type moves and cannot be afflicted with new status conditions or confusion.
Moonblast	Fairy	Special	95	100	15	Normal	—	175	A 30% chance of lowering the target's Sp. Atk by 1.
Moongeist Beam	Ghost	Special	100	100	5	Normal	—	180	Ignores the effects of the target's Ability.
Moonlight	Fairy	Status	—	—	5	Self	—	Resets negative stat changes	Recovers 1/2 of the user's maximum HP in normal weather conditions. Recovers 2/3 of the user's maximum HP in sunny or extremely harsh sunlight weather conditions. Recovers 1/4 of the user's maximum HP in rain/heavy rain/sandstorm/hail weather conditions.

Move	Type	Kind	Pow.	Acc.	PP	Range	DA	Z-Move Pow./Effects	Battle Effects
Morning Sun	Normal	Status	—	—	5	Self	—	Resets negative stat changes	Recovers 1/2 of the user's maximum HP in normal weather conditions. Recovers 2/3 of the user's maximum HP in sunny or extremely harsh sunlight weather conditions. Recovers 1/4 of the user's maximum HP in rain/heavy rain/sandstorm/hail weather conditions.
Mud Bomb	Ground	Special	65	85	10	Normal	—	120	A 30% chance of lowering the target's accuracy by 1.
Mud Shot	Ground	Special	55	95	15	Normal	—	100	Lowers the target's Speed by 1.
Mud Sport	Ground	Status	—	—	15	Both Sides	—	Raises the user's Sp. Def	Lowers the power of Electric-type moves to 1/3 of normal for 5 turns.
Mud-Slap	Ground	Special	20	100	10	Normal	—	100	Lowers the target's accuracy by 1.
Muddy Water	Water	Special	90	85	10	Many Others	—	175	A 30% chance of lowering the targets' accuracy by 1. Its power is reduced by 25% when it hits multiple Pokémon in a Double Battle. Its power is reduced by 50% when it hits multiple Pokémon in a Battle Royal.
Multi-Attack	Normal	Physical	90	100	10	Normal	◯	185	A regular attack. This move's type changes according to the memory disc that Silvally is holding.
Mystical Fire	Fire	Special	75	100	10	Normal	—	140	Lowers the target's Sp. Atk by 1.
Nasty Plot	Dark	Status	—	—	20	Self	—	Resets negative stat changes	Raises the user's Sp. Atk by 2.
Natural Gift	Normal	Physical	—	100	15	Normal	—	160	This move's type and power change according to the Berry held by the user. The Berry is consumed when this move is used. This move fails if the user is not holding a Berry.
Nature Power	Normal	Status	—	—	20	Normal	—	—	This move varies depending on the environment: Cave: Power Gem. Dirt/Sand: Earth Power. Grass / Grassy Terrain: Energy Ball. Electric Terrain: Thunderbolt. Ice: Ice Beam. Indoors / Link Battle: Tri Attack. Misty Terrain: Moonblast. Psychic Terrain / Ultra Space: Psychic. Snow: Frost Breath. Volcano: Lava Plume. Water Surface / Puddles / Shoals: Hydro Pump.
Nature's Madness	Fairy	Special	—	90	10	Normal	—	100	Halves the target's HP.
Needle Arm	Grass	Physical	60	100	15	Normal	◯	120	A 30% chance of making the target flinch (unable to use moves on that turn).
Night Daze	Dark	Special	85	95	10	Normal	—	160	A 40% chance of lowering the target's accuracy by 1
Night Shade	Ghost	Special	—	100	15	Normal	—	100	Deals a fixed amount of damage equal to the user's level.
Night Slash	Dark	Physical	70	100	15	Normal	◯	140	Critical hits land more easily.
Nightmare	Ghost	Status	—	100	15	Normal	—	Raises the user's Sp. Atk	Lowers the target's HP by 1/4 of maximum after each turn. Fails if the target is not Asleep.
Noble Roar	Normal	Status	—	100	30	Normal	—	Raises the user's Defense	Lowers the target's Attack and Sp. Atk by 1. Strikes the target even if it is using Substitute.
Nuzzle	Electric	Physical	20	100	20	Normal	◯	100	Inflicts the Paralysis status condition on the target.
Oblivion Wing	Flying	Special	80	100	10	Normal	—	160	Restores HP by up to 3/4 of the damage dealt to the target.
Octazooka	Water	Special	65	85	10	Normal	—	120	A 50% chance of lowering the target's accuracy by 1.
Odor Sleuth	Normal	Status	—	—	40	Normal	—	Raises the user's Attack	Attacks land easily regardless of the target's evasion. Makes Ghost-type Pokémon vulnerable to Normal- and Fighting-type moves.
Ominous Wind	Ghost	Special	60	100	5	Normal	—	120	A 10% chance of raising the user's Attack, Defense, Speed, Sp. Atk, and Sp. Def stats by 1.
Origin Pulse	Water	Special	110	85	10	Many Others	—	185	Its power is reduced by 25% when it hits multiple Pokémon in a Double Battle. Its power is reduced by 50% when it hits multiple Pokémon in a Battle Royal.
Outrage	Dragon	Physical	120	100	10	1 Random	◯	190	Attacks consecutively over 2–3 turns. Cannot choose other moves during this time. The user becomes Confused after using this move.
Overheat	Fire	Special	130	90	5	Normal	—	195	Lowers the user's Sp. Atk by 2. If the target is Frozen, it will be thawed.
Pain Split	Normal	Status	—	—	20	Normal	—	Raises the user's Defense	The user and target's HP are added, then divided equally between them.
Parabolic Charge	Electric	Special	65	100	20	Adjacent	—	120	Restores HP by up to half of the damage dealt to the target. Its power is reduced by 25% when it hits multiple Pokémon in a Double Battle. Its power is reduced by 50% when it hits multiple Pokémon in a Battle Royal.
Parting Shot	Dark	Status	—	100	20	Normal	—	Restores the HP of the next ally that enters the field	Lowers the target's Attack and Sp. Atk by 1. After attacking, user switches out with another Pokémon in the party. Strikes the target even if it is using Substitute.
Pay Day	Normal	Physical	40	100	20	Normal	—	100	Increases the amount of prize money received after battle (the user's level, multiplied by the number of attacks, multiplied by 5).
Payback	Dark	Physical	50	100	10	Normal	◯	100	This move's power is doubled if the user strikes after the target.
Peck	Flying	Physical	35	100	35	Normal	◯	100	A regular attack.
Perish Song	Normal	Status	—	—	5	Adjacent	—	Resets negative stat changes	All adjacent Pokémon in battle will faint after 3 turns, unless switched out. Strikes the target even if it is using Substitute.
Petal Blizzard	Grass	Physical	90	100	15	Adjacent	—	175	Its power is reduced by 25% when it hits multiple Pokémon in a Double Battle. Its power is reduced by 50% when it hits multiple Pokémon in a Battle Royal.
Petal Dance	Grass	Special	120	100	10	1 Random	◯	190	Attacks consecutively over 2–3 turns. Cannot choose other moves during this time. The user becomes confused after using this move.
Phantom Force	Ghost	Physical	90	100	10	Normal	◯	175	User disappears on the first turn and attacks on the second. Strikes the target even if it is using Baneful Bunker, Detect, King's Shield, Mat Block, Protect, Spiky Shield, or Substitute. If the target has used Minimize, it will be a sure hit and its power will be doubled.
Pin Missile	Bug	Physical	25	95	20	Normal	—	140	Attacks 2–5 times in a row in a single turn.
Play Nice	Normal	Status	—	—	20	Normal	—	Raises the user's Defense	A sure hit. Lowers the target's Attack by 1. Strikes the target even if it is using Baneful Bunker, Detect, King's Shield, Mat Block, Protect, Spiky Shield, or Substitute.
Play Rough	Fairy	Physical	90	90	10	Normal	◯	175	A 10% chance of lowering the target's Attack by 1.
Pluck	Flying	Physical	60	100	20	Normal	—	120	If the target is holding a Berry, the user eats that Berry and uses its battle effect if it has one.
Poison Fang	Poison	Physical	50	100	15	Normal	◯	100	A 50% chance of inflicting the Badly Poisoned status condition on the target. Damage from being Badly Poisoned increases with every turn.
Poison Gas	Poison	Status	—	90	40	Many Others	—	Raises the user's Defense	Inflicts the Poisoned status condition on the targets.

Move	Type	Kind	Pow.	Acc.	PP	Range	DA	Z-Move Pow./Effects	Battle Effects
Poison Jab	Poison	Physical	80	100	20	Normal	○	160	A 30% chance of inflicting the Poisoned status condition on the target.
Poison Powder	Poison	Status	—	75	35	Normal	—	Raises the user's Defense	Inflicts the Poisoned status condition on the targets. Has no effect on Grass-type Pokémon.
Poison Sting	Poison	Physical	15	100	35	Normal	—	100	A 30% chance of inflicting the Poisoned status condition on the target.
Poison Tail	Poison	Physical	50	100	25	Normal	○	100	A 10% chance of inflicting the Poisoned status condition on the target. Critical hits land more easily.
Pollen Puff	Bug	Special	90	100	15	Normal	—	175	When targeting an ally, it restores HP by up to half of the target's maximum HP.
Pound	Normal	Physical	40	100	35	Normal	○	100	A regular attack.
Powder	Bug	Status	—	100	20	Normal	—	Raises the user's Sp. Def by 2	Always attacks first. Has no effect on Grass-type Pokémon. Deals damage equal to 1/4 of max HP if the target uses a Fire-type move in the same turn.
Powder Snow	Ice	Special	40	100	25	Many Others	—	100	A 10% chance of inflicting the Frozen status condition on the targets. Its power is reduced by 25% when it hits multiple Pokémon in a Double Battle. Its power is reduced by 50% when it hits multiple Pokémon in a Battle Royal.
Power Gem	Rock	Special	80	100	20	Normal	—	160	A regular attack.
Power Split	Psychic	Status	—	—	10	Normal	—	Raises the user's Speed	The user and the target's Attack and Sp. Atk are added, then divided equally between them.
Power Swap	Psychic	Status	—	—	10	Normal	—	Raises the user's Speed	Swaps Attack and Sp. Atk changes between the user and the target.
Power Trick	Psychic	Status	—	—	10	Self	—	Raises the user's Attack	Swaps original Attack and Defense stats (does not swap stat changes).
Power Trip	Dark	Physical	20	100	10	Normal	○	160	With each level that the user's stats increase, the move's power increases by 20 (max 860).
Power Whip	Grass	Physical	120	85	10	Normal	○	190	A regular attack.
Power-Up Punch	Fighting	Physical	40	100	20	Normal	○	100	Raises the user's Attack by 1.
Precipice Blades	Ground	Physical	120	85	10	Many Others	—	190	Its power is reduced by 25% when it hits multiple Pokémon in a Double Battle. Its power is reduced by 50% when it hits multiple Pokémon in a Battle Royal.
Present	Normal	Physical	—	90	15	Normal	—	100	This move's power varies among 40 (40% chance), 80 (30% chance), and 120 (10% chance). It also has a 20% chance of healing the target by 1/4 of its maximum HP.
Prismatic Laser	Psychic	Special	160	100	10	Normal	—	200	The user can't move during the next turn.
Protect	Normal	Status	—	—	10	Self	—	Resets negative stat changes	The user evades all moves that turn. If used in succession, its chance of failing rises.
Psybeam	Psychic	Special	65	100	20	Normal	—	120	A 10% chance of making the target confused.
Psych Up	Normal	Status	—	—	10	Normal	—	Restores the user's HP	Copies the target's stat changes to the user.
Psychic	Psychic	Special	90	100	10	Normal	—	175	A 10% chance of lowering the target's Sp. Def by 1.
Psychic Fangs	Psychic	Physical	85	100	10	Normal	○	160	This move is not affected by Aurora Veil or Reflect. It removes the effect of Aurora Veil, Light Screen, and Reflect.
Psychic Terrain	Psychic	Status	—	—	10	Both Sides	—	Raises the user's Sp. Atk	Covers the field with psychic energy for 5 turns. During that time, Pokémon on the ground will be able to do 50% more damage with Psychic-type moves and will evade first-strike moves.
Psycho Boost	Psychic	Special	140	90	5	Normal	—	200	Lowers the user's Sp. Atk by 2.
Psycho Cut	Psychic	Physical	70	100	20	Normal	—	140	Critical hits land more easily.
Psycho Shift	Psychic	Status	—	100	10	Normal	—	Raises the user's Sp. Atk by 2	Shifts the user's Paralysis, Poisoned, Badly Poisoned, Burned, or Asleep status conditions to the target and heals the user.
Psyshock	Psychic	Special	80	100	10	Normal	—	160	Damage depends on the user's Sp. Atk and the target's Defense.
Psystrike	Psychic	Special	100	100	10	Normal	—	180	Damage depends on the user's Sp. Atk and the target's Defense.
Psywave	Psychic	Special	—	100	15	Normal	—	100	Inflicts damage equal to the user's level multiplied by a random value between 0.5 and 1.5.
Punishment	Dark	Physical	—	100	5	Normal	○	160	With each level that the target's stats increase, the move's power becomes greater (max 200).
Purify	Poison	Status	—	—	20	Normal	—	Raises all of the user's stats	Heals the target's status conditions. After healing the target's status conditions, it restores the user's HP by up to half of the user's maximum HP.
Pursuit	Dark	Physical	40	100	20	Normal	○	100	Does twice the usual damage if the target is switching out.
Quash	Dark	Status	—	100	15	Normal	—	Raises the user's Speed	The user suppresses the target and makes it move last that turn. Fails if the target has already used its move that turn.
Quick Attack	Normal	Physical	40	100	30	Normal	○	100	Always strikes first. The user with the higher Speed goes first if similar moves are used.
Quick Guard	Fighting	Status	—	—	15	Your Side	—	Raises the user's Defense	Protects the user and its allies from first-strike moves.
Quiver Dance	Bug	Status	—	—	20	Self	—	Resets negative stat changes	Raises the user's Sp. Atk, Sp. Def, and Speed by 1.
Rage	Normal	Physical	20	100	20	Normal	○	100	Attack rises by 1 with each hit the user takes.
Rage Powder	Bug	Status	—	—	20	Self	—	Resets negative stat changes	This move goes first. Opposing Pokémon aim only at the user. Has no effect on Grass-type Pokémon.
Rain Dance	Water	Status	—	—	5	Both Sides	—	Raises the user's Speed	Changes the weather condition to rain for 5 turns, strengthening Water-type moves by 50% and reducing the power of Fire-type moves by 50%.
Rapid Spin	Normal	Physical	20	100	40	Normal	○	100	Releases the user from moves such as Bind, Leech Seed, Spikes, and Wrap.
Razor Leaf	Grass	Physical	55	95	25	Many Others	—	100	Critical hits land more easily. Its power is reduced by 25% when it hits multiple Pokémon in a Double Battle. Its power is reduced by 50% when it hits multiple Pokémon in a Battle Royal.
Razor Shell	Water	Physical	75	95	10	Normal	○	140	A 50% chance of lowering the target's Defense by 1.
Razor Wind	Normal	Special	80	100	10	Many Others	—	160	The user stores power on the first turn and attacks on the second. Critical hits land more easily. Its power is reduced by 25% when it hits multiple Pokémon in a Double Battle. Its power is reduced by 50% when it hits multiple Pokémon in a Battle Royal.

Move	Type	Kind	Pow.	Acc.	PP	Range	DA	Z-Move Pow./ Effects	Battle Effects
Recover	Normal	Status	—	—	10	Self	—	Resets negative stat changes	Restores HP by up to half of the user's maximum HP.
Recycle	Normal	Status	—	—	10	Self	—	Raises the user's Speed by 2	A held item that has been used can be used again.
Reflect	Psychic	Status	—	—	20	Your Side	—	Raises the user's Defense	Halves the damage to the Pokémon on your side from physical moves. Effect lasts 5 turns even if the user is switched out. Effect is weaker in Double Battles and Battle Royal.
Reflect Type	Normal	Status	—	—	15	Normal	—	Raises the user's Sp. Atk	The user becomes the same type as the target.
Refresh	Normal	Status	—	—	20	Self	—	Restores the user's HP	Heals Poisoned, Badly Poisoned, Paralysis, and Burned conditions.
Relic Song	Normal	Special	75	100	10	Many Others	—	140	10% chance of inflicting the Asleep status condition on the targets. Its power is reduced by 25% when it hits multiple Pokémon in a Double Battle. Its power is reduced by 50% when it hits multiple Pokémon in a Battle Royal. After using the move, Meloetta undergoes a Forme Change. Strikes the targets even if they are using Substitute.
Rest	Psychic	Status	—	—	10	Self	—	Resets negative stat changes	Fully restores HP, but makes the user Asleep for 2 turns.
Retaliate	Normal	Physical	70	100	5	Normal	( )	140	This move's power is doubled if an ally fainted in the previous turn.
Return	Normal	Physical	—	100	20	Normal	◯	160	This move's power is affected by friendship. The higher the user's friendship, the greater the move's power (max 102).
Revelation Dance	Normal	Special	90	100	15	Normal	—	175	This move's type becomes the same as the user's first type.
Revenge	Fighting	Physical	60	100	10	Normal	◯	120	Attacks last. This move's power is doubled if the user has taken damage from the target that turn.
Reversal	Fighting	Physical	—	100	15	Normal	◯	160	The lower the user's HP is, the greater the move's power becomes (max 200).
Roar	Normal	Status	—	—	20	Normal	—	Raises the user's Defense	Ends wild Pokémon battles. In a battle with a Trainer, this move forces the opposing Trainer to switch Pokémon. When there are no Pokémon to switch in, this move fails. Attacks last. If the opposing Pokémon's level is higher than the user's, this move fails. In a battle with more than one wild Pokémon, this move fails. Strikes the target even if it is using Substitute. Strikes the target even if it is using Baneful Bunker, Detect, King's Shield, Mat Block, Protect, Spiky Shield, or Substitute.
Roar of Time	Dragon	Special	150	90	5	Normal	—	200	The user can't move during the next turn.
Rock Blast	Rock	Physical	25	90	10	Normal	—	140	Attacks 2–5 times in a row in a single turn.
Rock Climb	Normal	Physical	90	85	20	Normal	◯	175	A 20% chance of making the target confused.
Rock Polish	Rock	Status	—	—	20	Self	—	Resets negative stat changes	Raises the user's Speed by 2.
Rock Slide	Rock	Physical	75	90	10	Many Others	—	140	A 30% chance of making the targets flinch (unable to use moves on that turn). Its power is reduced by 25% when it hits multiple Pokémon in a Double Battle. Its power is reduced by 50% when it hits multiple Pokémon in a Battle Royal.
Rock Smash	Fighting	Physical	40	100	15	Normal	◯	100	A 50% chance of lowering the target's Defense by 1.
Rock Throw	Rock	Physical	50	90	15	Normal	—	100	A regular attack.
Rock Tomb	Rock	Physical	60	95	15	Normal	—	120	Lowers the target's Speed by 1.
Rock Wrecker	Rock	Physical	150	90	5	Normal	—	200	The user can't move during the next turn.
Role Play	Psychic	Status	—	—	10	Normal	—	Raises the user's Speed	Copies the target's Ability. Fails with certain Abilities, however.
Rolling Kick	Fighting	Physical	60	85	15	Normal	◯	120	A 30% chance of making the target flinch (unable to use moves on that turn).
Rollout	Rock	Physical	30	90	20	Normal	◯	100	Attacks consecutively over 5 turns or until it misses. Cannot choose other moves during this time. Damage dealt doubles with every successful hit (max 480). Does twice the damage if used after Defense Curl.
Roost	Flying	Status	—	—	10	Self	—	Resets negative stat changes	Restores HP by up to half of the user's maximum HP, but takes away the Flying type from the user for that turn.
Rototiller	Ground	Status	—	—	10	Adjacent	—	Raises the user's Attack	Raises the Attack and Sp. Atk of Grass-type Pokémon by 1.
Round	Normal	Special	60	100	15	Normal	—	120	When multiple Pokémon use this move in a turn, the first one to use it is followed immediately by the others. Attack's power is doubled when following another Pokémon using the same move. Strikes the target even if it is using Substitute.
Sacred Fire	Fire	Physical	100	95	5	Normal	—	180	A 50% chance of inflicting the Burned status condition on the target. If the target is Frozen, it will be thawed. This move can be used even if the user is Frozen. If the user is Frozen, this also thaws the user.
Sacred Sword	Fighting	Physical	90	100	15	Normal	◯	175	Ignores the stat changes of the opposing Pokémon.
Safeguard	Normal	Status	—	—	25	Your Side	—	Raises the user's Speed	Protects the Pokémon on your side from status conditions and confusion for 5 turns. Effects last even if the user switches out.
Sand Attack	Ground	Status	—	100	15	Normal	—	Raises the user's evasion	Lowers the target's accuracy by 1.
Sand Tomb	Ground	Physical	35	85	15	Normal	—	100	Inflicts damage equal to 1/8 the target's max HP for 4–5 turns. The target cannot flee during that time.
Sandstorm	Rock	Status	—	—	10	Both Sides	—	Raises the user's Speed	Changes the weather condition to sandstorm for 5 turns. Raises the Sp. Def of Rock-type Pokémon by 50% for the length of the sandstorm. All Pokémon other than Rock, Steel, and Ground types take damage each turn equal to 1/16 of their max HP.
Scald	Water	Special	80	100	15	Normal	—	160	A 30% chance of inflicting the Burned status condition on the target. This move can be used even when the user is Frozen. Using this move will thaw the user, relieving the Frozen status condition.
Scary Face	Normal	Status	—	100	10	Normal	—	Raises the user's Speed	Lowers the target's speed by 2.
Scratch	Normal	Physical	40	100	35	Normal	◯	100	A regular attack.
Screech	Normal	Status	—	85	40	Normal	—	Raises the user's Attack	Lowers the target's Defense by 2. Strikes the target even if it is using Substitute.

Move	Type	Kind	Pow.	Acc.	PP	Range	DA	Z-Move Pow./Effects	Battle Effects
Searing Shot	Fire	Special	100	100	5	Adjacent	—	180	A 30% chance of inflicting the Burned status condition on the targets. If the targets are Frozen, they will be thawed. Its power is reduced by 25% when it hits multiple Pokémon in a Double Battle. Its power is reduced by 50% when it hits multiple Pokémon in a Battle Royal.
Secret Power	Normal	Physical	70	100	20	Normal	—	140	A 30% chance of one of the following additional effects, depending on the environment: Cave: Target flinches. Dirt/Sand: Lowers accuracy by 1. Grass / Grassy Terrain / Link Battle: Inflicts Asleep status condition. Indoors / Electric Terrain / Link Battle: Inflicts Paralysis status condition. Misty Terrain: Lowers Sp. Atk by 1. Psychic Terrain / Ultra Space: Lowers Defense by 1. Snow/Ice: Inflicts Frozen status condition. Swamp: Lowers Speed by 1. Volcano: Burned status condition. Water Surface / Puddles / Shoals: Lowers Attack by 1.
Secret Sword	Fighting	Special	85	100	10	Normal	—	160	Damage depends on the user's Sp. Atk and the target's Defense.
Seed Bomb	Grass	Physical	80	100	15	Normal	—	160	A regular attack.
Seed Flare	Grass	Special	120	85	5	Normal	—	190	A 40% chance of lowering the target's Sp. Def by 2.
Seismic Toss	Fighting	Physical	—	100	20	Normal	○	100	Deals a fixed amount of damage equal to the user's level.
Self-Destruct	Normal	Physical	200	100	5	Adjacent	—	200	The user faints after using it. Its power is reduced by 25% when it hits multiple Pokémon in a Double Battle. Its power is reduced by 50% when it hits multiple Pokémon in a Battle Royal.
Shadow Ball	Ghost	Special	80	100	15	Normal	—	160	A 20% chance of lowering the target's Sp. Def by 1.
Shadow Bone	Ghost	Physical	85	100	10	Normal	—	160	A 20% chance of lowering the target's Defense by 1.
Shadow Claw	Ghost	Physical	70	100	15	Normal	○	140	Critical hits land more easily.
Shadow Force	Ghost	Physical	120	100	5	Normal	○	190	Makes the user invisible on the first turn and attacks on the second. Strikes the target even if it is using Baneful Bunker, Detect, King's Shield, Mat Block, Protect, Spiky Shield, or Substitute. If the target has used Minimize, this move will be a sure hit and its power will be doubled.
Shadow Punch	Ghost	Physical	60	—	20	Normal	○	120	A sure hit.
Shadow Sneak	Ghost	Physical	40	100	30	Normal	○	100	Always strikes first. The user with the higher Speed goes first if similar moves are used.
Sharpen	Normal	Status	—	—	30	Self	—	Raises the user's Attack	Raises the user's Attack by 1.
Sheer Cold	Ice	Special	—	30	5	Normal	—	180	The target faints with one hit if the user's level is equal to or greater than the target's level. The higher the user's level is compared to the target's, the more accurate the move is. Accuracy is lowered when a Pokémon that is not an Ice type uses it. Does not hit Ice-type Pokémon.
Shell Smash	Normal	Status	—	—	15	Self	—	Resets negative stat changes	Lowers the user's Defense and Sp. Def by 1 and raises the user's Attack, Sp. Atk, and Speed by 2.
Shell Trap	Fire	Special	150	100	5	Many Others	—	200	Sets a trap at the start of the turn. When the user is hit by a physical attack during that turn, the trap explodes and deals damage.
Shift Gear	Steel	Status	—	—	10	Self	—	Resets negative stat changes	Raises the user's Speed by 2 and Attack by 1.
Shock Wave	Electric	Special	60	—	20	Normal	—	120	A sure hit.
Shore Up	Ground	Status	—	—	10	Self	—	Resets negative stat changes	Restores HP by up to half of the user's maximum HP. Recovers 2/3 of the user's maximum HP in the sandstorm weather condition.
Signal Beam	Bug	Special	75	100	15	Normal	—	140	A 10% chance of making the target confused.
Silver Wind	Bug	Special	60	100	5	Normal	—	120	A 10% chance of raising the user's Attack, Defense, Speed, Sp. Atk, and Sp. Def stats by 1.
Simple Beam	Normal	Status	—	—	15	Normal	—	Raises the user's Sp. Atk	Changes the target's Ability to Simple. Fails with certain Abilities, however.
Sing	Normal	Status	—	55	15	Normal	—	Raises the user's Speed	Inflicts the Asleep status condition on the target. Strikes the target even if it is using Substitute.
Sketch	Normal	Status	—	—	1	Normal	—	Raises all of the user's stats	Copies the last move used by the target. The user then forgets Sketch and learns the new move.
Skill Swap	Psychic	Status	—	—	10	Normal	—	Raises the user's Speed	Swaps Abilities between the user and target. Fails with certain Abilities, however.
Skull Bash	Normal	Physical	130	100	10	Normal	○	195	Builds power on the first turn and attacks on the second. It raises the user's Defense stat by 1 on the first turn.
Sky Attack	Flying	Physical	140	90	5	Normal	—	200	Builds power on the first turn and attacks on the second. Critical hits land more easily. A 30% chance of making the target flinch (unable to use moves on that turn).
Sky Drop	Flying	Physical	60	100	10	Normal	○	120	The user takes the target into the sky, and then damages it by dropping it during the next turn. Does not damage Flying-type Pokémon. Pokémon weighing over 440.9 lbs. cannot be lifted.
Sky Uppercut	Fighting	Physical	85	90	15	Normal	○	160	It even hits Pokémon that are in the sky due to having used moves such as Fly and Bounce.
Slack Off	Normal	Status	—	—	10	Self	—	Resets negative stat changes	Restores HP by up to half of the user's maximum HP.
Slam	Normal	Physical	80	75	20	Normal	○	160	A regular attack.
Slash	Normal	Physical	70	100	20	Normal	○	140	Critical hits land more easily.
Sleep Powder	Grass	Status	—	75	15	Normal	—	Raises the user's Speed	Inflicts the Asleep status condition on the target. Has no effect on Grass-type Pokémon.
Sleep Talk	Normal	Status	—	—	10	Self	—	Critical hits land more easily	Only works when the user is Asleep. Randomly uses one of the user's moves.
Sludge	Poison	Special	65	100	20	Normal	—	120	A 30% chance of inflicting the Poisoned status condition on the target.
Sludge Bomb	Poison	Special	90	100	10	Normal	—	175	A 30% chance of inflicting the Poisoned status condition on the target.
Sludge Wave	Poison	Special	95	100	10	Adjacent	—	175	A 10% chance of inflicting the Poisoned status condition on the target. Its power is reduced by 25% when it hits multiple Pokémon in a Double Battle. Its power is reduced by 50% when it hits multiple Pokémon in a Battle Royal.
Smack Down	Rock	Physical	50	100	15	Normal	—	100	Ground-type moves will now hit a Pokémon with the Levitate Ability or a Flying-type Pokémon. They will also hit a Pokémon that is in the sky due to using a move such as Fly or Bounce.
Smart Strike	Steel	Physical	70	—	10	Normal	○	140	A sure hit.

Move	Type	Kind	Pow.	Acc.	PP	Range	DA	Z-Move Pow./Effects	Battle Effects
Smelling Salts	Normal	Physical	70	100	10	Normal	◯	140	Deals twice the usual damage to targets with Paralysis, but heals that status condition.
Smog	Poison	Special	30	70	20	Normal	—	100	A 40% chance of inflicting the Poisoned status condition on the target.
Smokescreen	Normal	Status	—	100	20	Normal	—	Raises the user's evasion	Lowers the target's accuracy by 1.
Snarl	Dark	Special	55	95	15	Many Others	—	100	Lowers the targets' Sp. Atk by 1. Its power is reduced by 25% when it hits multiple Pokémon in a Double Battle. Its power is reduced by 50% when it hits multiple Pokémon in a Battle Royal. Strikes the targets even if they are using Substitute.
Snatch	Dark	Status	—	—	10	Self	—	Raises the user's Speed by 2	Steals the effects of recovery or stat-changing moves used by the target on that turn and applies them to the user.
Snore	Normal	Special	50	100	15	Normal	—	100	Only works when the user is Asleep. A 30% chance of making the target flinch (unable to use moves on that turn). Strikes the target even if it is using Substitute.
Soak	Water	Status	—	100	20	Normal	—	Raises the user's Sp. Atk	Changes the target's type to Water.
Soft-Boiled	Normal	Status	—	—	10	Self	—	Resets negative stat changes	Restores HP by up to half of the user's maximum HP.
Solar Beam	Grass	Special	120	100	10	Normal	—	190	Builds power on the first turn and attacks on the second. In sunny or extremely harsh sunlight weather conditions, attacks on the first turn. In rain/heavy rain/sandstorm/hail weather conditions, the power is halved.
Solar Blade	Grass	Physical	125	100	10	Normal	◯	190	Builds power on the first turn and attacks on the second. In sunny or extremely harsh sunlight weather conditions, attacks on the first turn. In rain / heavy rain / sandstorm / hail weather conditions, the power is halved.
Sonic Boom	Normal	Special	—	90	20	Normal	—	100	Deals a fixed 20 points of damage.
Spacial Rend	Dragon	Special	100	95	5	Normal	—	180	Critical hits land more easily.
Spark	Electric	Physical	65	100	20	Normal	◯	120	A 30% chance of inflicting the Paralysis status condition on the target.
Sparkling Aria	Water	Special	90	100	10	Adjacent	—	175	Heals the Burned status condition from its targets. Its power is reduced by 25% when it hits multiple Pokémon in a Double Battle. Its power is reduced by 50% when it hits multiple Pokémon in a Battle Royal.
Speed Swap	Psychic	Status	—	—	10	Normal	—	Raises the user's Speed	Switches the user's Speed with the target's Speed.
Spider Web	Bug	Status	—	—	10	Normal	—	Raises the user's Defense	The target cannot escape. If used during a Trainer battle, the opposing Trainer cannot switch Pokémon. Has no effect on Ghost-type Pokémon.
Spike Cannon	Normal	Physical	20	100	15	Normal	—	100	Attacks 2–5 times in a row in a single turn.
Spikes	Ground	Status	—	—	20	Other Side	—	Raises the user's Defense	Damages Pokémon as they are sent out to the opposing side. Power rises with each use, up to 3 times (1st time: 1/8 of maximum HP, 2nd time: 1/6 of maximum HP, and 3rd time: 1/4 of maximum HP). Ineffective against Flying-type Pokémon and Pokémon with the Levitate Ability.
Spiky Shield	Grass	Status	—	—	10	Self	—	Raises the user's Defense	The user takes no damage in the same turn this move is used. If an opposing Pokémon uses a move that makes direct contact, the attacker will be damaged for 1/8 of its maximum HP. Fails more easily when used repeatedly.
Spirit Shackle	Ghost	Physical	80	100	10	Normal	—	160	The target cannot escape. If used during a Trainer battle, the opposing Trainer cannot switch Pokémon. When used on a Ghost type, no additional effect takes place.
Spit Up	Normal	Special	—	100	10	Normal	—	100	The more times the user has used Stockpile, the greater the move's power becomes (max 300). Fails if the user has not used Stockpile first. Nullifies Defense and Sp. Def stat increases caused by Stockpile.
Spite	Ghost	Status	—	100	10	Normal	—	Restores the user's HP	Takes 4 points from the PP of the target's last used move.
Splash	Normal	Status	—	—	40	Self	—	Raises the user's Attack by 3	No effect.
Spore	Grass	Status	—	100	15	Normal	—	Resets negative stat changes	Inflicts the Asleep status condition on the target. Has no effect on Grass-type Pokémon.
Spotlight	Normal	Status	—	—	15	Normal	—	Raises the user's Sp. Def	Designates which Pokémon will be attacked.
Stealth Rock	Rock	Status	—	—	20	Other Side	—	Raises the user's Defense	Damages Pokémon as they are sent out to the opposing side. Damage is subject to type matchups.
Steam Eruption	Water	Special	110	95	5	Normal	—	185	A 10% chance of inflicting the Burned status condition on the target. If the target is Frozen, it will be thawed.
Steamroller	Bug	Physical	65	100	20	Normal	◯	120	A 30% chance of making the targets flinch (unable to use moves on that turn). If the target has used Minimize, this move will be a sure hit and its power will be doubled.
Steel Wing	Steel	Physical	70	90	25	Normal	◯	140	A 10% chance of raising the user's Defense by 1.
Sticky Web	Bug	Status	—	—	20	Other Side	—	Raises the user's Speed	Lowers the Speed of any Pokémon sent out to the opposing side by 1.
Stockpile	Normal	Status	—	—	20	Self	—	Restores the user's HP	Raises the user's Defense and Sp. Def by 1. Can be used up to 3 times.
Stomp	Normal	Physical	65	100	20	Normal	◯	120	A 30% chance of making the targets flinch (unable to use moves on that turn). If the target has used Minimize, this move will be a sure hit and its power will be doubled.
Stomping Tantrum	Ground	Physical	75	100	10	Normal	◯	140	If the user's attack missed during the previous turn, this move's power is doubled.
Stone Edge	Rock	Physical	100	80	5	Normal	—	180	Critical hits land more easily.
Stored Power	Psychic	Special	20	100	10	Normal	—	160	With each level that the user's stats increase, the move's power increases by 20 (max 860).
Storm Throw	Fighting	Physical	60	100	10	Normal	◯	120	Always delivers a critical hit.
Strength	Normal	Physical	80	100	15	Normal	◯	160	A regular attack.
Strength Sap	Grass	Status	—	100	10	Normal	—	Raises the user's Defense	Lowers the target's Attack by 1. Restores the user's HP by an amount equal to the target's Attack.
String Shot	Bug	Status	—	95	40	Many Others	—	Raises the user's Speed	Lowers the targets' Speed by 2.
Struggle	Normal	Physical	50	—	1	Normal	◯	—	This move becomes available when all other moves are out of PP. The user takes damage equal to 1/4 of its maximum HP. Inflicts damage regardless of type matchup.

Move	Type	Kind	Pow.	Acc.	PP	Range	DA	Z-Move Pow./Effects	Battle Effects
Struggle Bug	Bug	Special	50	100	20	Many Others	—	100	Lowers the targets' Sp. Atk by 1. Its power is reduced by 25% when it hits multiple Pokémon in a Double Battle. Its power is reduced by 50% when it hits multiple Pokémon in a Battle Royal.
Stun Spore	Grass	Status	—	75	30	Normal	—	Raises the user's Sp. Def	Inflicts the Paralysis status condition on the target. Has no effect on Grass-type Pokémon.
Submission	Fighting	Physical	80	80	20	Normal	◯	160	The user takes 1/4 of the damage inflicted.
Substitute	Normal	Status	—	—	10	Self	—	Resets negative stat changes	Uses 1/4 of maximum HP to create a copy of the user.
Sucker Punch	Dark	Physical	70	100	5	Normal	◯	140	This move attacks first and deals damage only if the target's chosen move is an attack move.
Sunny Day	Fire	Status	—	—	5	Both Sides	—	Raises the user's Speed	Changes the weather condition to sunny for 5 turns, strengthening Fire-type moves by 50% and reducing the power of Water-type moves by 50%.
Sunsteel Strike	Steel	Physical	100	100	5	Normal	◯	180	Ignores the effects of the target's Ability.
Super Fang	Normal	Physical	—	90	10	Normal	◯	100	Halves the target's HP.
Superpower	Fighting	Physical	120	100	5	Normal	◯	190	Lowers the user's Attack and Defense by 1.
Supersonic	Normal	Status	—	55	20	Normal	—	Raises the user's Speed	Makes the target confused. Strikes the target even if it is using Substitute.
Surf	Water	Special	90	100	15	Adjacent	—	175	Does twice the damage if the target is using Dive when attacked. Its power is reduced by 25% when it hits multiple Pokémon in a Double Battle. Its power is reduced by 50% when it hits multiple Pokémon in a Battle Royal.
Swagger	Normal	Status	—	85	15	Normal	—	Resets negative stat changes	Makes the target confused, but also raises its Attack by 2.
Swallow	Normal	Status	—	—	10	Self	—	Resets negative stat changes	Restores HP, the amount of which is determined by how many times the user has used Stockpile. Fails if the user has not used Stockpile first. Nullifies Defense and Sp. Def stat increases caused by Stockpile.
Sweet Kiss	Fairy	Status	—	75	10	Normal	—	Raises the user's Sp. Atk	Makes the target confused.
Sweet Scent	Normal	Status	—	100	20	Many Others	—	Increases the user's accuracy	Lowers the targets' evasion by 2.
Swift	Normal	Special	60	—	20	Many Others	—	120	A sure hit. Its power is reduced by 25% when it hits multiple Pokémon in a Double Battle. Its power is reduced by 50% when it hits multiple Pokémon in a Battle Royal.
Switcheroo	Dark	Status	—	100	10	Normal	—	Raises the user's Speed by 2	Swaps items between the user and the target.
Swords Dance	Normal	Status	—	—	20	Self	—	Resets negative stat changes	Raises the user's Attack by 2.
Synchronoise	Psychic	Special	120	100	10	Adjacent	—	190	Inflicts damage on any Pokémon of the same type as the user. Its power is reduced by 25% when it hits multiple Pokémon in a Double Battle. Its power is reduced by 50% when it hits multiple Pokémon in a Battle Royal.
Synthesis	Grass	Status	—	—	5	Self	—	Resets negative stat changes	Recovers 1/2 of the user's maximum HP in normal weather conditions. Recovers 2/3 of the user's maximum HP in sunny or extremely harsh sunlight weather conditions. Recovers 1/4 of the user's maximum HP in rain/heavy rain/sandstorm/hail weather conditions.
Tackle	Normal	Physical	40	100	35	Normal	◯	100	A regular attack.
Tail Glow	Bug	Status	—	—	20	Self	—	Resets negative stat changes	Raises the user's Sp. Atk by 3.
Tail Slap	Normal	Physical	25	85	10	Normal	◯	140	Attacks 2–5 times in a row in a single turn.
Tail Whip	Normal	Status	—	100	30	Many Others	—	Raises the user's Attack	Lowers the targets' Defense by 1.
Tailwind	Flying	Status	—	—	15	Your Side	—	Critical hits land more easily	Doubles the Speed of the Pokémon on your side for 4 turns.
Take Down	Normal	Physical	90	85	20	Normal	◯	175	The user takes 1/4 of the damage inflicted.
Taunt	Dark	Status	—	100	20	Normal	—	Raises the user's Attack	Prevents the target from using anything other than attack moves for 3 turns.
Tearful Look	Normal	Status	—	—	20	Normal	—	Raises the user's Defense	Lowers the target's Attack and Sp. Atk. Strikes the target even if it is using Baneful Bunker, Detect, King's Shield, Mat Block, Protect, or Spiky Shield.
Techno Blast	Normal	Special	120	100	5	Normal	—	190	A regular attack. This move's type changes according to the drive that Genesect is holding.
Teeter Dance	Normal	Status	—	100	20	Adjacent	—	Raises the user's Sp. Atk	Makes the target confused.
Telekinesis	Psychic	Status	—	—	15	Normal	—	Raises the user's Sp. Atk	Makes the target float for 3 turns. All moves land regardless of their accuracy except for Ground-type moves and one-hit knock-out moves such as Fissure, Guillotine, Horn Drill, and Sheer Cold.
Teleport	Psychic	Status	—	—	20	Self	—	Restores the user's HP	Ends wild Pokémon battles.
Thief	Dark	Physical	60	100	25	Normal	◯	120	When the target is holding an item and the user is not, the user can steal that item. When the target is not holding an item, this move will function as a normal attack.
Thousand Arrows	Ground	Physical	90	100	10	Many Others	—	180	Flying-type Pokémon or Pokémon with the Levitate Ability that are hit by this attack will now be hit by Ground-type moves. Its power is reduced by 25% when it hits multiple Pokémon in a Double Battle. Its power is reduced by 50% when it hits multiple Pokémon in a Battle Royal.
Thousand Waves	Ground	Physical	90	100	10	Many Others	—	175	The targets cannot escape. If used during a Trainer battle, the opposing Trainer cannot switch Pokémon. Its power is reduced by 25% when it hits multiple Pokémon in a Double Battle. Its power is reduced by 50% when it hits multiple Pokémon in a Battle Royal.
Thrash	Normal	Physical	120	100	10	1 Random	◯	190	Attacks consecutively over 2–3 turns. Cannot choose other moves during this time. The user becomes confused after using this move.
Throat Chop	Dark	Physical	80	100	15	Normal	◯	160	The target will not be able to use sound moves for 2 turns.
Thunder	Electric	Special	110	70	10	Normal	—	185	A 30% chance of inflicting the Paralysis status condition on the target. Is 100% accurate in the rain or heavy rain weather condition and 50% accurate in the sunny or extremely harsh sunlight weather condition. It hits even Pokémon that are in the sky due to using moves such as Fly and Bounce.

Move	Type	Kind	Pow.	Acc.	PP	Range	DA	Z-Move Pow./ Effects	Battle Effects
Thunder Fang	Electric	Physical	65	95	15	Normal	◯	120	A 10% chance of inflicting the Paralysis status condition or making the target flinch (unable to use moves on that turn).
Thunder Punch	Electric	Physical	75	100	15	Normal	◯	140	A 10% chance of inflicting the Paralysis status condition on the target.
Thunder Shock	Electric	Special	40	100	30	Normal	—	100	A 10% chance of inflicting the Paralysis status condition on the target.
Thunder Wave	Electric	Status	—	90	20	Normal	—	Raises the user's Sp. Def.	Inflicts the Paralysis status condition on the target. Does not work on Ground types.
Thunderbolt	Electric	Special	90	100	15	Normal	—	175	A 10% chance of inflicting the Paralysis status condition on the target.
Tickle	Normal	Status	—	100	20	Normal	—	Raises the user's Defense.	Lowers the target's Attack and Defense by 1.
Topsy-Turvy	Dark	Status	—	—	20	Normal	—	Raises the user's Attack.	Reverses the effects of any stat changes affecting the target.
Torment	Dark	Status	—	100	15	Normal	—	Raises the user's Defense.	Makes the target unable to use the same move twice in a row.
Toxic	Poison	Status	—	90	10	Normal	—	Raises the user's Defense.	Inflicts the Badly Poisoned status condition on the target. Damage from being Badly Poisoned increases with every turn. It never misses if used by a Poison type Pokémon.
Toxic Spikes	Poison	Status	—	—	20	Other Side	—	Raises the user's Defense.	Lays a trap of poison spikes on the opposing side that inflict the Poisoned status condition on Pokémon that switch into battle. Using Toxic Spikes twice inflicts the Badly Poisoned condition. The damage from the Badly Poisoned condition increases every turn. Toxic Spikes' effects end when a Poison-type Pokémon switches into battle. Ineffective against Flying-type Pokémon and Pokémon with the Levitate Ability.
Toxic Thread	Poison	Status	—	100	20	Normal	—	Raises the user's Speed.	Inflicts the Poisoned status condition on the target and lowers its Speed by 1.
Transform	Normal	Status	—	—	10	Normal	—	Restores the user's HP.	The user transforms into the target. The user has the same moves and Ability as the target (all moves have 5 PP).
Tri Attack	Normal	Special	80	100	10	Normal	—	160	A 20% chance of inflicting the Paralysis, Burned, or Frozen status condition on the target.
Trick	Psychic	Status	—	100	10	Normal	—	Raises the user's Speed by 2.	Swaps items between the user and the target.
Trick Room	Psychic	Status	—	—	5	Both Sides	—	Increases the user's accuracy.	Always strikes last. For 5 turns, Pokémon with lower Speed go first. First-strike moves still go first. Self-canceling if used again while Trick Room is still in effect.
Trick-or-Treat	Ghost	Status	—	100	20	Normal	—	Raises all of the user's stats.	Gives the target the Ghost type in addition to its original type(s).
Triple Kick	Fighting	Physical	10	90	10	Normal	◯	120	Attacks 3 times in a row in a single turn. Power raises from 10 to 20 to 30 as long as it continues to hit.
Trop Kick	Grass	Physical	70	100	15	Normal	◯	140	Lowers the target's Attack by 1.
Trump Card	Normal	Special	—	—	5	Normal	◯	160	A sure hit. The lower the user's PP is, the greater the move's power becomes (max 200).
Twineedle	Bug	Physical	25	100	20	Normal	—	100	Attacks twice in a row in a single turn. A 20% chance of inflicting the Poisoned status condition on the target.
Twister	Dragon	Special	40	100	20	Many Others	—	100	A 20% chance of making the targets flinch (unable to use moves on that turn). It even hits Pokémon that are in the sky due to using moves such as Fly and Bounce, dealing them twice the usual damage. Its power is reduced by 25% when it hits multiple Pokémon in a Double Battle. Its power is reduced by 50% when it hits multiple Pokémon in a Battle Royal.
U-turn	Bug	Physical	70	100	20	Normal	◯	140	After attacking, the user switches out with another Pokémon in the party.
Uproar	Normal	Special	90	100	10	1 Random	—	175	The user makes an uproar for 3 turns. During that time, no Pokémon can fall Asleep. Strikes the target even if it is using Substitute.
V-create	Fire	Physical	180	95	5	Normal	◯	220	Lowers the user's Defense, Sp. Def, and Speed by 1. If the target is Frozen, it will be thawed.
Vacuum Wave	Fighting	Special	40	100	30	Normal	—	100	Always strikes first. The user with the higher Speed goes first if similar moves are used.
Venom Drench	Poison	Status	—	100	20	Many Others	—	Raises the user's Defense.	Lowers the Attack, Sp. Atk, and Speed of opposing Pokémon afflicted with Poison or Badly Poisoned status conditions by 1.
Venoshock	Poison	Special	65	100	10	Normal	—	120	Does twice the damage to a target that has the Poison or Badly Poisoned status condition.
Vice Grip	Normal	Physical	55	100	30	Normal	◯	100	A regular attack.
Vine Whip	Grass	Physical	45	100	25	Normal	◯	100	A regular attack.
Vital Throw	Fighting	Physical	70	—	10	Normal	◯	140	Always strikes later than normal, but has perfect accuracy.
Volt Switch	Electric	Special	70	100	20	Normal	◯	140	After attacking, the user switches out with another Pokémon in the party.
Volt Tackle	Electric	Physical	120	100	15	Normal	◯	190	The user takes 1/3 of the damage inflicted. A 10% chance of inflicting the Paralysis status condition on the target.
Wake-Up Slap	Fighting	Physical	70	100	10	Normal	◯	140	Does twice the usual damage to a target that is Asleep, but heals that status condition.
Water Gun	Water	Special	40	100	25	Normal	—	100	A regular attack.
Water Pledge	Water	Special	80	100	10	Normal	—	160	When combined with Fire Pledge or Grass Pledge, the power and effect change. If combined with Fire Pledge, the power is 150 and it remains a Water-type move. This makes it more likely that your team's moves will have additional effects for 4 turns. If combined with Grass Pledge, the power is 150 and it becomes a Grass-type move. This lowers the Speed of opposing Pokémon for 4 turns.
Water Pulse	Water	Special	60	100	20	Normal	—	120	A 20% chance of making the target confused.
Water Shuriken	Water	Special	15	100	20	Normal	—	100	Always strikes first. The user with the higher Speed goes first if similar moves are used. Attacks 2–5 times in a row in a single turn. When used by Ash-Greninja that has undergone a form change due to its Battle Bond, the move's power is raised to 20 and it attacks 3 times in a row in a single turn.
Water Sport	Water	Status	—	—	15	Both Sides	—	Raises the user's Sp. Def.	Lowers the power of Fire-type moves to 1/3 of normal for 5 turns.
Water Spout	Water	Special	150	100	5	Many Others	—	200	If the user's HP is low, this move has lower power. Its power is reduced by 25% when it hits multiple Pokémon in a Double Battle. Its power is reduced by 50% when it hits multiple Pokémon in a Battle Royal.
Waterfall	Water	Physical	80	100	15	Normal	◯	160	A 20% chance of making the target flinch (unable to use moves on that turn).

Move	Type	Kind	Pow.	Acc.	PP	Range	DA	Z-Move Pow./ Effects	Battle Effects
Weather Ball	Normal	Special	50	100	10	Normal	—	160	In special weather conditions, this move's type changes and its attack power doubles. Sunny / extremely harsh sunlight weather condition: Fire type. Rain / heavy rain weather condition: Water type. Hail weather condition: Ice type. Sandstorm weather condition: Rock type.
Whirlpool	Water	Special	35	85	15	Normal	—	100	Inflicts damage equal to 1/8 the target's max HP for 4–5 turns. The target cannot flee during that time. Does twice the damage if the target is using Dive when attacked.
Whirlwind	Normal	Status	—	—	20	Normal	—	Raises the user's Sp. Def.	Ends wild Pokémon battles. In a battle with a Trainer, this move forces the opposing Trainer to switch Pokémon. When there are no Pokémon to switch in, this move fails. Attacks last. If the opposing Pokémon's level is higher than the user's, this move fails. In a battle with more than one wild Pokémon, this move fails. Strikes the target even if it is using Baneful Bunker, Detect, King's Shield, Mat Block, Protect, Spiky Shield, or Substitute.
Wide Guard	Rock	Status	—	—	10	Your Side	—	Raises the user's Defense.	Protects your side from the effects of any moves used that turn that target multiple Pokémon.
Wild Charge	Electric	Physical	90	100	15	Normal	◯	175	The user takes 1/4 of the damage inflicted.
Will-O-Wisp	Fire	Status	—	85	15	Normal	—	Raises the user's Attack.	Inflicts the Burned status condition on the target.
Wing Attack	Flying	Physical	60	100	35	Normal	◯	120	A regular attack.
Wish	Normal	Status	—	—	10	Self	—	Raises the user's Sp. Def.	Restores 1/2 of maximum HP at the end of the next turn. Works even if the user has switched out.
Withdraw	Water	Status	—	—	40	Self	—	Raises the user's Defense.	Raises the user's Defense by 1.
Wonder Room	Psychic	Status	—	—	10	Both Sides	—	Raises the user's Sp. Def.	Always strikes last. Each Pokémon's Defense and Sp. Def stats are swapped for 5 turns. The effect ends if the move is used again.
Wood Hammer	Grass	Physical	120	100	15	Normal	◯	190	The user takes 1/3 of the damage inflicted.
Work Up	Normal	Status	—	—	30	Self	—	Raises the user's Attack.	Raises the user's Attack and Sp. Atk by 1.
Worry Seed	Grass	Status	—	100	10	Normal	—	Raises the user's Speed.	Changes the target's Ability to Insomnia. Fails with certain Abilities, however.
Wrap	Normal	Physical	15	90	20	Normal	◯	100	Inflicts damage equal to 1/8 the target's max HP for 4–5 turns. The target cannot flee during that time.
Wring Out	Normal	Special	—	100	5	Normal	◯	190	The more HP the target has left, the greater the move's power becomes (max 120).
X-Scissor	Bug	Physical	80	100	15	Normal	◯	160	A regular attack.
Yawn	Normal	Status	—	—	10	Normal	—	Raises the user's Speed.	Inflicts the Asleep status condition on the target at the end of the next turn unless the target switches out.
Zap Cannon	Electric	Special	120	50	5	Normal	—	190	Inflicts the Paralysis status condition on the target.
Zen Headbutt	Psychic	Physical	80	90	15	Normal	◯	160	A 20% chance of making the target flinch (unable to use moves on that turn).
Zing Zap	Electric	Physical	80	100	10	Normal	◯	160	A 30% chance of making the target flinch (unable to use moves on that turn).

How to Obtain TMs

No.	Move	Type	How to Obtain	Price
TM01	Work Up	Normal	Get from a Rising Star in the Trainers' School	—
TM02	Dragon Claw	Dragon	Find at the trial site in the Vast Poni Canyon	—
TM03	Psyshock	Psychic	Find at the Lake of the Moone ☽ / Lake of the Sunne ☀	—
TM04	Calm Mind	Psychic	Buy at the Seafolk Village Poké Mart	₽10,000
TM05	Roar	Normal	Find in Kala'e Bay	—
TM06	Toxic	Poison	Find at the dock in Aether Paradise	—
TM07	Hail	Ice	Buy at the Royal Avenue Poké Mart	₽50,000
TM08	Bulk Up	Fighting	Buy at the TM shop in Konikoni City	₽10,000
TM09	Venoshock	Poison	Buy at the TM shop in Konikoni City	₽10,000
TM10	Hidden Power	Normal	Get from a Pokémon Breeder at the Pokémon Nursery	—
TM11	Sunny Day	Fire	Buy at the Royal Avenue Poké Mart	₽50,000
TM12	Taunt	Dark	Get from a man in a trailer on Route 13	—
TM13	Ice Beam	Ice	Find on Mount Lanakila	—
TM14	Blizzard	Ice	Buy at the Seafolk Village Poké Mart	₽30,000
TM15	Hyper Beam	Normal	Buy at the Seafolk Village Poké Mart	₽50,000
TM16	Light Screen	Psychic	Buy at the Heahea City Poké Mart	₽10,000
TM17	Protect	Normal	Buy at the Heahea City Poké Mart	₽10,000
TM18	Rain Dance	Water	Buy at the Royal Avenue Poké Mart	₽50,000
TM19	Roost	Flying	Buy at the Malie City Poké Mart	₽10,000
TM20	Safeguard	Normal	Buy at the Heahea City Poké Mart	₽10,000
TM21	Frustration	Normal	Get from an Oranguru in the malasada shop in Malie City ☽	—
TM22	Solar Beam	Grass	Buy at the Seafolk Village Poké Mart	₽10,000
TM23	Smack Down	Rock	Buy at the Malie City Poké Mart	₽10,000
TM24	Thunderbolt	Electric	Find in Poni Plains*	—
TM25	Thunder	Electric	Buy at the Seafolk Village Poké Mart	₽30,000
TM26	Earthquake	Ground	Find at Resolution Cave entrance*	—
TM27	Return	Normal	Get from a Police Officer in the malasada shop in Malie City ☽	—
TM28	Leech Life	Bug	Find in Akala Outskirts	—
TM29	Psychic	Psychic	Get from Wicke in Aether Paradise	—
TM30	Shadow Ball	Ghost	Find on Route 14	—
TM31	Brick Break	Fighting	Find in Verdant Cavern	—
TM32	Double Team	Normal	Buy at the TM shop in Konikoni City	₽10,000
TM33	Reflect	Psychic	Buy at the Heahea City Poké Mart	₽10,000
TM34	Sludge Wave	Poison	Buy at the Seafolk Village Poké Mart	₽10,000
TM35	Flamethrower	Fire	Find in the third cave in the Vast Poni Canyon	—
TM36	Sludge Bomb	Poison	Find in the Shady House	—
TM37	Sandstorm	Rock	Buy at the Royal Avenue Poké Mart	₽50,000
TM38	Fire Blast	Fire	Buy at the Seafolk Village Poké Mart	₽30,000
TM39	Rock Tomb	Rock	Find in Wela Volcano Park	—
TM40	Aerial Ace	Flying	Buy at the Malie City Poké Mart	₽10,000
TM41	Torment	Dark	Find on Route 5 (south)	—
TM42	Facade	Normal	Buy at the Malie City Poké Mart	₽10,000
TM43	Flame Charge	Fire	Get from Colress on Route 8	—
TM44	Rest	Psychic	Get from Hypno in Thrifty Megamart	—
TM45	Attract	Normal	Get from Machamp caddy in Hano Grand Hotel	—
TM46	Thief	Dark	Find in Verdant Cavern	—
TM47	Low Sweep	Fighting	Buy at the TM shop in Konikoni City	₽10,000
TM48	Round	Normal	Get from a Janitor as a reward for cleaning the mall at the shopping mall ☽	—
TM49	Echoed Voice	Normal	Find in Hau'oli City Shopping District	—
TM50	Overheat	Fire	Find in Poni Meadow*	—
TM51	Steel Wing	Steel	Buy at the Malie City Poké Mart	₽10,000
TM52	Focus Blast	Fighting	Buy at the Seafolk Village Poké Mart	₽30,000

No.	Move	Type	How to Obtain	Price
TM53	Energy Ball	Grass	Find on Route 8	—
TM54	False Swipe	Normal	Get from Kukui after Hala's grand trial	—
TM55	Scald	Water	Find in Brooklet Hill	—
TM56	Fling	Dark	Get from a mourning woman at the Hau'oli Cemetery ☽	—
TM57	Charge Beam	Electric	Find on Route 5 (south)	—
TM58	Sky Drop	Flying	Get from an Ace Trainer after defeating all Trainers on Route 8	—
TM59	Brutal Swing	Dark	Find on Route 5 (north)	—
TM60	Quash	Dark	Get from an Ace Trainer after defeating all Trainers around Poni Plains*	—
TM61	Will-O-Wisp	Fire	Find in Konikoni City	—
TM62	Acrobatics	Flying	Find in the Farthest Hollow in Ten Carat Hill	—
TM63	Embargo	Dark	Get from a Scientist in the Geothermal Power Plant ○	—
TM64	Explosion	Normal	Find in Ten Carat Hill	—
TM65	Shadow Claw	Ghost	Buy at the TM shop in Konikoni City	₽10,000
TM66	Payback	Dark	Buy at the Malie City Poké Mart	₽10,000
TM67	Smart Strike	Steel	Get from Kukui after Mallow's trial	—
TM68	Giga Impact	Normal	Buy at the Seafolk Village Poké Mart	₽50,000
TM69	Rock Polish	Rock	Buy at the Malie City Poké Mart	₽10,000
TM70	Aurora Veil	Ice	Buy at the Heahea City Poké Mart	₽30,000
TM71	Stone Edge	Rock	Buy at the Seafolk Village Poké Mart	₽30,000
TM72	Volt Switch	Electric	Find on Mount Hokulani	—
TM73	Thunder Wave	Electric	Find on Route 7	—
TM74	Gyro Ball	Steel	Find on Route 11	—
TM75	Swords Dance	Normal	Buy at the Malie City Poké Mart	₽10,000
TM76	Fly	Flying	Get from a woman in Malie Library	—
TM77	Psych Up	Normal	Get from a Collector after defeating all Trainers on Route 12	—
TM78	Bulldoze	Ground	Buy at the Malie City Poké Mart	₽10,000
TM79	Frost Breath	Ice	Find on the Ancient Poni Path	—
TM80	Rock Slide	Rock	Find in Melemele Sea	—
TM81	X-Scissor	Bug	Find on Route 16	—
TM82	Dragon Tail	Dragon	Buy at the TM shop in Konikoni City	₽10,000
TM83	Infestation	Bug	Find on Route 3	—
TM84	Poison Jab	Poison	Find on Route 17	—
TM85	Dream Eater	Psychic	Find in Haina Desert (Area 4)	—
TM86	Grass Knot	Grass	Find in Lush Jungle	—
TM87	Swagger	Normal	Get from Guzma's mom in his house on Route 2	—
TM88	Sleep Talk	Normal	Find in Paniola Town	—
TM89	U-turn	Bug	Buy at the Malie City Poké Mart	₽10,000
TM90	Substitute	Normal	Get from Professor Kukui in the Pokémon Research Lab*	—
TM91	Flash Cannon	Steel	Find in Seafolk Village	—
TM92	Trick Room	Psychic	Get from Kahili at Hano Grand Resort*	—
TM93	Wild Charge	Electric	Find on Route 15	—
TM94	Surf	Water	Get from Swimmer Girls on Poni Breaker Coast*	—
TM95	Snarl	Dark	Get from a Veteran after defeating all Trainers on Mount Hokulani	—
TM96	Nature Power	Normal	Get from a Trial Guide after defeating all Trainers on Route 5	—
TM97	Dark Pulse	Dark	Find on Poni Coast*	—
TM98	Waterfall	Water	Get from Swimmer Girls on Poni Breaker Coast*	—
TM99	Dazzling Gleam	Fairy	Find in the Vast Poni Canyon	—
TM100	Confide	Normal	Find in the Hau'oli Cemetery	—

Note: TMs marked with an asterisk can only be obtained after entering the Hall of Fame.

Z-Moves & Moves Taught by People

Z-Moves

Name	Type	Kind	Pow.	Acc.	Range	DA	Battle effects	Base move
Breakneck Blitz	Normal	Physical/Special	Varies	—	Normal	—	A regular attack	Any damage-dealing Normal-type move
All-Out Pummeling	Fighting	Physical/Special	Varies	—	Normal	—	A regular attack	Any damage-dealing Fighting-type move
Supersonic Skystrike	Flying	Physical/Special	Varies	—	Normal	—	A regular attack	Any damage-dealing Flying-type move
Acid Downpour	Poison	Physical/Special	Varies	—	Normal	—	A regular attack	Any damage-dealing Poison-type move
Tectonic Rage	Ground	Physical/Special	Varies	—	Normal	—	A regular attack	Any damage-dealing Ground-type move
Continental Crush	Rock	Physical/Special	Varies	—	Normal	—	A regular attack	Any damage-dealing Rock-type move
Savage Spin-Out	Bug	Physical/Special	Varies	—	Normal	—	A regular attack	Any damage-dealing Bug-type move
Never-Ending Nightmare	Ghost	Physical/Special	Varies	—	Normal	—	A regular attack	Any damage-dealing Ghost-type move
Corkscrew Crash	Steel	Physical/Special	Varies	—	Normal	—	A regular attack	Any damage-dealing Steel-type move
Inferno Overdrive	Fire	Physical/Special	Varies	—	Normal	—	A regular attack	Any damage-dealing Fire-type move
Hydro Vortex	Water	Physical/Special	Varies	—	Normal	—	A regular attack	Any damage-dealing Water-type move
Bloom Doom	Grass	Physical/Special	Varies	—	Normal	—	A regular attack	Any damage-dealing Grass-type move
Gigavolt Havoc	Electric	Physical/Special	Varies	—	Normal	—	A regular attack	Any damage-dealing Electric-type move
Shattered Psyche	Psychic	Physical/Special	Varies	—	Normal	—	A regular attack	Any damage-dealing Psychic-type move
Subzero Slammer	Ice	Physical/Special	Varies	—	Normal	—	A regular attack	Any damage-dealing Ice-type move
Devastating Drake	Dragon	Physical/Special	Varies	—	Normal	—	A regular attack	Any damage-dealing Dragon-type move
Black Hole Eclipse	Dark	Physical/Special	Varies	—	Normal	—	A regular attack	Any damage-dealing Dark-type move
Twinkle Tackle	Fairy	Physical/Special	Varies	—	Normal	—	A regular attack	Any damage-dealing Fairy-type move
Catastropika	Electric	Physical	210	—	Normal	○	A regular attack	Volt Tackle
Sinister Arrow Raid	Ghost	Physical	180	—	Normal	—	A regular attack	Spirit Shackle
Malicious Moonsault	Dark	Physical	180	—	Normal	○	A regular attack	Darkest Lariat
Oceanic Operetta	Water	Special	195	—	Normal	—	A regular attack	Sparkling Aria
Guardian of Alola	Fairy	Special	—	—	Normal	—	Deals damage equal to 3/4 of the target's current HP	Nature's Madness
Stoked Sparksurfer	Electric	Special	175	—	Normal	—	Inflicts the Paralysis status condition on the target	Thunderbolt
Pulverizing Pancake	Normal	Physical	210	—	Normal	○	A regular attack	Giga Impact
Extreme Evoboost	Normal	Status	—	—	Self	—	Raises the user's Attack, Defense, Sp. Atk, Sp. Def, and Speed by 2 each	Last Resort

Move Tutors found around Alola

Tutor location	Move name	Pokémon that can learn it	Special conditions
Hau'oli City Shopping Mall	Frenzy Plant	Venusaur, Meganium, Sceptile, Torterra, Serperior, Chesnaught, Decidueye	Must have max friendship
Hau'oli City Shopping Mall	Blast Burn	Charizard, Typhlosion, Blaziken, Infernape, Emboar, Delphox, Incineroar	Must have max friendship
Hau'oli City Shopping Mall	Hydro Cannon	Blastoise, Feraligatr, Swampert, Empoleon, Samurott, Greninja, Primarina	Must have max friendship
Hau'oli City Shopping Mall	Grass Pledge	Bulbasaur, Ivysaur, Venusaur, Chikorita, Bayleef, Meganium, Treecko, Grovyle, Sceptile, Turtwig, Grotle, Torterra, Snivy, Servine, Serperior, Pansage, Simisage, Chespin, Quilladin, Chesnaught, Rowlet, Dartrix, Decidueye	—
Hau'oli City Shopping Mall	Fire Pledge	Charmander, Charmeleon, Charizard, Cyndaquil, Quilava, Typhlosion, Torchic, Combusken, Blaziken, Chimchar, Monferno, Infernape, Tepig, Pignite, Emboar, Pansear, Simisear, Fennekin, Braixen, Delphox, Litten, Torracat, Incineroar	—
Hau'oli City Shopping Mall	Water Pledge	Squirtle, Wartortle, Blastoise, Totodile, Croconaw, Feraligatr, Mudkip, Marshtomp, Swampert, Piplup, Prinplup, Empoleon, Oshawott, Dewott, Samurott, Panpour, Simipour, Froakie, Frogadier, Greninja, Popplio, Brionne, Primarina	—
Hano Grand Resort	Secret Sword	Keldeo	—
Hano Grand Resort	Relic Song	Meloetta	—
Seafolk Village	Draco Meteor	Any Dragon-type Pokémon	Must have high friendship
Seafolk Village	Dragon Ascent	Rayquaza	—

Move Deleter & Move Reminder

Who	Where	What
Move Deleter	Pokémon Center in Hau'oli City on Melemele Island	Can delete any move from your Pokémon, allowing them to know fewer than four moves at a time.
Move Reminder	Pokémon Center on Mount Lanakila on Ula'ula Island	Can remind your Pokémon of any move they could usually learn by leveling up, as well as any Egg Moves they previously knew but forgot.

Abilities

Ability	Effect in battle	Effect when the Pokémon is the lead in your party
Adaptability	The power boost received by using a move of the same type as the Pokémon will be 100% instead of 50%.	—
Aerilate	Changes Normal-type moves to Flying type and increases their power by 20%.	—
Aftermath	Knocks off 1/4 of the attacking Pokémon's maximum HP when a direct attack causes the Pokémon to faint.	—
Air Lock	Eliminates effects of weather on Pokémon.	—
Analytic	The power of its move is increased by 30% when the Pokémon moves last.	—
Anger Point	Raises the Pokémon's Attack to the maximum when hit by a critical hit.	—
Anticipation	Warns if your opponent's Pokémon has supereffective moves or one-hit knock out moves when the Pokémon enters battle.	—
Arena Trap	Prevents the opponent's Pokémon from fleeing or switching out. Ineffective against Flying- or Ghost-type Pokémon and Pokémon with the Levitate Ability.	Makes it easier to encounter wild Pokémon
Aroma Veil	Protects the team from Attract, Disable, Encore, Heal Block, Taunt, and Torment.	—
Aura Break	Reverses the effects of the Fairy Aura Ability and lowers the power of Fairy-type moves by 25%. Reverses the Dark Aura Ability and lowers the power of Dark-type moves by 25%.	—
Bad Dreams	Lowers the HP of any opposing Pokémon that are Asleep by 1/8 of their maximum HP every turn.	—
Battery	Raises the power of an ally's special moves by 30%.	—
Battle Armor	Opposing Pokémon's moves will not hit critically.	—
Battle Bond	The Pokémon changes form when it defeats a Pokémon.	—
Beast Boost	When the Pokémon knocks out another Pokémon with a move, its most prominent stat goes up 1.	—
Berserk	Raises Sp. Atk by 1 when the Pokémon takes a hit that causes its HP to become 1/2 or less.	—
Big Pecks	Prevents Defense from being lowered.	—
Blaze	Raises the power of Fire-type moves by 50% when the Pokémon's HP drops to 1/3 or less.	—
Bulletproof	Protects against Acid Spray, Aura Sphere, Barrage, Bullet Seed, Egg Bomb, Electro Ball, Energy Ball, Focus Blast, Gyro Ball, Ice Ball, Magnet Bomb, Mist Ball, Mud Bomb, Octazooka, Rock Wrecker, Searing Shot, Seed Bomb, Shadow Ball, Sludge Bomb, Weather Ball, and Zap Cannon.	—
Cheek Pouch	Eating a Berry not only grants its usual benefits, but also restores 1/3 of the Pokémon's maximum HP.	—
Chlorophyll	Doubles Speed in the sunny or extremely harsh sunlight weather conditions.	—
Clear Body	Protects against stat-lowering moves and Abilities.	—
Cloud Nine	Eliminates effects of weather on Pokémon.	—
Color Change	Changes the Pokémon's type into the type of the move that just hit it.	—
Comatose	The Pokémon is permanently affected by the Asleep status condition. It can use moves while Asleep.	—
Competitive	When an opponent's move or Ability lowers the Pokémon's stats, the Pokémon's Sp. Atk rises by 2.	—
Compound Eyes	Raises accuracy by 30%.	Raises encounter rate with wild Pokémon holding items
Contrary	Makes stat changes have an opposite effect (increase instead of decrease and vice versa).	—
Corrosion	Makes the Pokémon able to inflict the Poisoned status condition on Steel types and Poison types.	—
Cursed Body	Provides a 30% chance of inflicting Disable on the move the opponent used to hit the Pokémon. (Cannot use that move for three turns.)	—
Cute Charm	Provides a 30% chance of causing infatuation when hit with a direct attack.	Raises encounter rate of wild Pokémon of the opposite gender
Damp	Prevents Pokémon on either side from using Explosion or Self-Destruct. Nullifies the Aftermath Ability.	—
Dancer	The Pokémon immediately follows and uses the same move when another Pokémon in battle uses a dance move.	—
Dark Aura	Raises the power of Dark-type moves by 1/3. Affects all Pokémon in the field.	—
Dazzling	Prevents the opposing Pokémon from using priority attacking moves.	—
Defeatist	The Pokémon's Attack and Sp. Atk gets halved when HP becomes 1/2 or less.	—
Defiant	When an opponent's move or Ability lowers the Pokémon's stats, the Pokémon's Attack rises by 2.	—
Delta Stream	Makes the weather strong winds when the Pokémon enters battle. This weather makes Flying-type Pokémon receive half the damage from supereffective moves against them.	—
Desolate Land	Makes the weather extremely harsh sunlight when the Pokémon enters battle. This weather raises the power of Fire-type moves by 50%, reduces that of Water-type moves to zero, and prevents the Frozen status condition.	—
Disguise	Once per battle, this Ability prevents damage when hit by a move. Then the Pokémon's form changes.	—

Ability	Effect in battle	Effect when the Pokémon is the lead in your party
Download	When the Pokémon enters battle, this Ability raises its Attack by 1 if the opposing Pokémon's Defense is lower than its Sp. Def, and raises its Sp. Atk by 1 if the opposing Pokémon's Sp. Def is lower than its Defense. If the opponent's Defense and Sp. Def are the same, this Ability raises its Sp. Atk by 1.	—
Drizzle	Makes the weather rain for five turns when the Pokémon enters battle. Does nothing when the weather is extremely harsh sunlight, heavy rain, or strong winds.	—
Drought	Makes the weather sunny for five turns when the Pokémon enters battle. Does nothing when the weather is extremely harsh sunlight, heavy rain, or strong winds.	—
Dry Skin	Restores HP by 1/4 of the Pokémon's maximum HP when the Pokémon is hit by a Water-type move. Restores HP by 1/8 of its maximum HP at the end of every turn in the rain or heavy rain weather condition. However, the damage the Pokémon receives from Fire-type moves increases by 25%. Takes damage of 1/8 of its maximum HP at the end of every turn in the sunny or extremely harsh sunlight weather condition.	—
Early Bird	Causes the Pokémon to wake quickly from the Asleep status condition.	—
Effect Spore	Provides a 30% chance of inflicting the Poisoned, Paralysis, or Asleep status conditions when hit with a direct attack. Grass-type Pokémon are immune to this effect.	—
Electric Surge	Turns the field into Electric Terrain for five turns when the Pokémon enters battle.	—
Emergency Exit	The Pokémon switches places with a party Pokémon automatically when its HP drops to 1/2 or less.	—
Fairy Aura	Raises the power of Fairy-type moves by 1/3. Affects all Pokémon in the field.	—
Filter	Decreases the damage received from supereffective moves by 25%.	—
Flame Body	Provides a 30% chance of inflicting the Burned status condition when hit with a direct attack.	Facilitates hatching Pokémon Eggs in your party
Flare Boost	Increases the power of special moves by 50% when Burned.	—
Flash Fire	When the Pokémon is hit by a Fire-type move, rather than taking damage, its Fire-type moves increase power by 50%.	—
Flower Gift	Raises Attack and Sp. Def of the Pokémon and its allies by 50% in the sunny or extremely harsh sunlight weather condition.	—
Flower Veil	Grass-type allies cannot have their stats lowered, and they are protected from being inflicted with status conditions.	—
Fluffy	Halves the damage taken from moves that make direct contact. Doubles the damage taken from Fire-type moves.	—
Forecast	Changes Castform's form and type. Sunny or extremely harsh sunlight weather conditions: changes to Fire type. Rain or heavy rain weather conditions: changes to Water type. Hail weather condition: changes to Ice type.	—
Forewarn	Reveals a move an opponent knows when the Pokémon enters battle. Damaging moves with high power are prioritized.	—
Friend Guard	Reduces damage done to allies by 25%.	—
Frisk	Checks an opponent's held item when the Pokémon enters battle.	—
Full Metal Body	Protects against stat-lowering moves and Abilities.	—
Fur Coat	Halves the damage taken from physical moves.	—
Gale Wings	Gives priority to Flying-type moves when HP is full.	—
Galvanize	Changes Normal-type moves to Electric type and increases their power by 20%.	—
Gluttony	Allows the Pokémon to use its held Berry sooner when it has low HP.	—
Gooey	Lowers the Speed of an attacker that makes direct contact by 1.	—
Grass Pelt	Raises Defense by 50% when the field is affected by Grassy Terrain.	—
Grassy Surge	Turns the field into Grassy Terrain for five turns when the Pokémon enters battle.	—
Guts	Attack stat rises by 50% when the Pokémon is affected by a status condition.	—
Harvest	At the end of every turn, provides a 50% chance of restoring the Berry the Pokémon used, and a 100% chance when the weather condition is sunny or extremely harsh sunlight.	—
Healer	At the end of every turn, it provides a 33% chance that an ally Pokémon's status condition will be healed.	—
Heatproof	Halves damage from Fire-type moves and from the Burned status condition.	—
Heavy Metal	Doubles the Pokémon's weight.	—
Honey Gather	If the Pokémon isn't holding an item, it will sometimes be left holding Honey after a battle (even if it didn't participate). Its chance of finding Honey increases with its level.	—
Huge Power	Doubles Attack.	—
Hustle	Raises Attack by 50%, but lowers the accuracy of the Pokémon's physical moves by 20%.	Makes it easier to encounter high-level wild Pokémon
Hydration	Cures status conditions at the end of each turn during the rain or heavy rain weather conditions.	—
Hyper Cutter	Prevents Attack from being lowered.	—
Ice Body	Restores HP by 1/16 of the Pokémon's maximum HP at the end of every turn in the hail weather condition rather than taking damage.	—
Illuminate	No effect.	Makes it easier to encounter wild Pokémon
Illusion	Appears in battle disguised as the last Pokémon in the party.	—
Immunity	Protects against the Poisoned status condition.	—
Imposter	Transforms itself into the Pokémon it is facing as it enters battle.	—
Infiltrator	Moves can hit ignoring the effects of Aurora Veil, Light Screen, Mist, Reflect, Safeguard, or Substitute.	—
Innards Out	Upon fainting, the Pokémon does damage to the attacker equal to its last remaining HP.	—
Inner Focus	The Pokémon doesn't flinch as an additional effect of a move.	—
Insomnia	Protects against the Asleep status condition.	—
Intimidate	When this Pokémon enters battle, it lowers the opposing Pokémon's Attack by 1.	Lowers encounter rate with low-level wild Pokémon

Ability	Effect in battle	Effect when the Pokémon is the lead in your party
Iron Barbs	Reduces the HP of an opponent that hits the Pokémon with a direct attack by 1/8 of its maximum HP.	—
Iron Fist	Increases the power of Bullet Punch, Comet Punch, Dizzy Punch, Drain Punch, Dynamic Punch, Fire Punch, Focus Punch, Hammer Arm, Ice Punch, Mach Punch, Mega Punch, Meteor Mash, Power-Up Punch, Shadow Punch, Sky Uppercut, and Thunder Punch by 20%.	—
Justified	When the Pokémon is hit by a Dark-type move, Attack goes up by 1.	—
Keen Eye	Prevents accuracy from being lowered. Ignores evasiveness-raising moves.	Lowers encounter rate with low-level wild Pokémon
Klutz	The Pokémon can't use held items.	—
Leaf Guard	Protects the Pokémon from status conditions when in the sunny or extremely harsh sunlight weather conditions.	—
Levitate	Gives full immunity from all Ground-type moves.	—
Light Metal	Halves the Pokémon's weight.	—
Lightning Rod	Draws all Electric-type moves to the Pokémon. When the Pokémon is hit by an Electric-type move, rather than taking damage, its Sp. Atk goes up by 1.	—
Limber	Protects against the Paralysis status condition.	—
Liquid Ooze	When an opposing Pokémon uses an HP-draining move, it damages the user instead.	—
Magic Bounce	Reflects status moves that lower stats or inflict status conditions.	—
Magic Guard	The Pokémon will not take damage from anything other than direct damage. Nullifies the Aftermath, Bad Dreams, Innards Out, Iron Barbs, Liquid Ooze, and Rough Skin Abilities, the hail and sandstorm weather conditions, and the Burned, Poisoned, and Badly Poisoned status conditions. The effects of Bind, Clamp, Curse, Fire Pledge, Fire Spin, Flame Burst, Infestation, Leech Seed, Magma Storm, Nightmare, Sand Tomb, Spikes, Stealth Rock, Whirlpool, and Wrap are negated, as are the item effects from Black Sludge, Life Orb, Rocky Helmet, and Sticky Barb. The Pokémon also receives no recoil or move-failure damage from attacks. Receives no damage from attacking a Pokémon that has used the Spiky Shield move or damage from using a Fire-type move after the Powder move has been used.	—
Magician	The Pokémon seizes the item of an opponent it hits with a move. Fails if the Pokémon is already holding an item.	—
Magma Armor	Prevents the Frozen status condition.	Facilitates hatching Pokémon Eggs in your party
Magnet Pull	Prevents Steel-type opponents from fleeing or switching out.	Raises encounter rate with wild Steel-type Pokémon
Marvel Scale	Defense stat increases by 50% when the Pokémon is affected by a status condition.	—
Mega Launcher	Raises the power of Aura Sphere, Dark Pulse, Dragon Pulse, Origin Pulse, and Water Pulse by 50%. Heal Pulse will restore 75% of the target's maximum HP.	—
Merciless	The Pokémon delivers critical hits as long as the target has the Poisoned status condition.	—
Minus	Raises Sp. Atk by 50% when another ally has the Ability Plus or Minus.	—
Misty Surge	Turns the field into Misty Terrain for five turns when the Pokémon enters battle.	—
Mold Breaker	Allows the Pokémon to use moves on targets regardless of their Abilities. Does not nullify Abilities that have effects after an attack. For example, the Pokémon can score a critical hit against a target with Battle Armor, but it will still take damage from Rough Skin.	—
Moody	Raises one stat by 2 and lowers another by 1 at the end of every turn.	—
Motor Drive	When the Pokémon is hit by an Electric-type move, its Speed goes up by 1 and damage and effects of the move are nullified.	—
Moxie	When the Pokémon knocks out another Pokémon with a move, its Attack goes up 1.	—
Multiscale	Halves damage when HP is full.	—
Multitype	Type changes according to the plate or Z-Crystal Arceus is holding.	—
Mummy	Changes the Ability of the opponent that hits the Pokémon with a direct attack to Mummy.	—
Natural Cure	Cures the Pokémon's status conditions when it switches out.	—
No Guard	Moves used by or against the Pokémon always strike their targets.	Makes it easier to encounter wild Pokémon
Normalize	Changes all of the Pokémon's moves to Normal type and increases their power by 20%.	—
Oblivious	Protects against infatuation. Immune to Captivate and Taunt.	—
Overcoat	Protects the Pokémon from weather damage, such as hail and sandstorm. Protects it from Cotton Spore, Poison Powder, Powder, Rage Powder, Sleep Powder, Spore, and Stun Spore. Immune to the Effect Spore Ability.	—
Overgrow	Raises the power of Grass-type moves by 50% when the Pokémon's HP drops to 1/3 or less.	—
Own Tempo	Protects against confusion.	—
Parental Bond	Causes attacks to strike twice, with the second hit dealing only one fourth the normal damage. Does not affect moves that naturally strike multiple times or moves that strike multiple targets.	—
Pickpocket	Steals an item when hit with a direct attack. It fails if the Pokémon is already holding an item.	—
Pickup	At the end of every turn, the Pokémon picks up the item that the opposing Pokémon used that turn. Fails if the Pokémon is already holding an item.	If the Pokémon has no held item, it sometimes picks one up after battle (even if it didn't participate). It picks up different items depending on its level.
Pixilate	Changes Normal-type moves to Fairy type and increases their power by 20%.	—
Plus	Raises Sp. Atk by 50% when another ally has the Ability Plus or Minus.	—
Poison Heal	Restores 1/8 of the Pokémon's maximum HP at the end of every turn if the Pokémon has the Poisoned or Badly Poisoned status condition rather than taking damage.	—
Poison Point	Provides a 30% chance of inflicting the Poisoned status condition when the Pokémon is hit by a direct attack.	—
Poison Touch	Provides a 30% chance of inflicting the Poisoned status condition when the Pokémon uses a direct attack.	—
Power Construct	The Pokémon changes its form to Complete Form when the Pokémon's HP drops to 1/2 or less.	—

Ability	Effect in battle	Effect when the Pokémon is the lead in your party
Power of Alchemy	Copies the Ability of a defeated ally.	—
Prankster	Gives priority to status moves. Fails if the target is a Dark type.	—
Pressure	When the Pokémon is hit by an opponent's move, it depletes 1 additional PP from that move.	Makes it easier to encounter high-level wild Pokémon
Primordial Sea	Makes the weather heavy rain when the Pokémon enters battle. This weather raises the power of Water-type moves by 50% and reduces that of Fire-type moves to zero.	—
Prism Armor	Decreases the damage received from supereffective moves by 25%.	—
Protean	Changes the Pokémon's type to the same type as the move it is about to use.	—
Psychic Surge	Turns the field into Psychic Terrain for five turns when the Pokémon enters battle.	—
Pure Power	Doubles its Attack stat.	—
Queenly Majesty	Prevents the opposing Pokémon from using priority attacking moves.	—
Quick Feet	Increases Speed by 50% when the Pokémon is affected by status conditions.	Lowers wild Pokémon encounter rate
Rain Dish	Restores HP by 1/16 of the Pokémon's maximum HP at the end of every turn in the rain or heavy rain weather conditions.	—
Rattled	When the Pokémon is hit by a Ghost-, Dark-, or Bug-type move, Speed goes up by 1.	—
Receiver	Copies the Ability of a defeated ally.	—
Reckless	Raises the power of moves by 20% with recoil damage.	—
Refrigerate	Changes Normal-type moves to Ice type and increases their power by 20%.	—
Regenerator	Restores 1/3 its maximum HP when withdrawn from battle.	—
Rivalry	If the target is the same gender, the Pokémon's Attack goes up by 25%. If the target is of the opposite gender, its Attack goes down by 25%. No effect when the gender is unknown.	—
RKS System	Type changes according to the memory disc the Pokémon is holding.	—
Rock Head	No recoil damage from moves like Take Down and Double-Edge.	—
Rough Skin	Knocks off 1/8 of the attacking Pokémon's maximum HP when the Pokémon makes a direct attack.	—
Run Away	Allows the Pokémon to always escape from a battle with a wild Pokémon.	—
Sand Force	Raises the power of Ground-, Rock-, and Steel-type moves by 30% in the sandstorm weather condition. Sandstorm does not damage the Pokémon.	—
Sand Rush	Doubles Speed in the sandstorm weather condition. Sandstorm does not damage the Pokémon.	—
Sand Stream	Makes the weather sandstorm for five turns when the Pokémon enters battle. Rock-type Pokémon's Sp. Def increases by 50% and Pokémon other than Rock, Steel, and Ground types take damage of 1/16 of the Pokémon's maximum HP during the weather sandstorm. Does nothing when the weather is extremely harsh sunlight, heavy rain, or strong winds.	—
Sand Veil	The accuracy of the opposing Pokémon's move decreases by 20% in the sandstorm weather condition. Sandstorm does not damage the Pokémon with this Ability.	Lowers encounter rate with wild Pokémon in the sandstorm weather condition
Sap Sipper	When the Pokémon is hit by a Grass-type move, rather than taking damage, its Attack goes up by 1.	—
Schooling	If the Pokémon's level is 20 or above, it takes another form. It changes back to its previous form when its HP drops to 1/4 or less.	—
Scrappy	Allows the Pokémon to hit Ghost-type Pokémon with Normal- and Fighting-type moves. (The type matchup changes from "It doesn't affect..." to normal.)	—
Serene Grace	Doubles chances of moves inflicting additional effects.	—
Shadow Shield	Halves damage when HP is full.	—
Shadow Tag	Prevents the opposing Pokémon from fleeing or switching out. If both your and the opposing Pokémon have this Ability, the effect is canceled. Does not affect Ghost types.	—
Shed Skin	At the end of every turn, provides a 33% chance of curing the Pokémon's status conditions.	—
Sheer Force	When moves with an additional effect are used, power increases by 30%, but the additional effect is lost.	—
Shell Armor	Opposing Pokémon's moves will not hit critically.	—
Shield Dust	Protects the Pokémon from additional effects of moves.	—
Shields Down	The Pokémon changes its form from a defensive one to an offensive one when its HP drops to half or less.	—
Simple	Doubles the effects of stat changes.	—
Skill Link	Moves that strike successively strike the maximum number of times (2-5 times means it always strikes 5 times).	—
Slow Start	Halves Attack and Speed for 5 turns after the Pokémon enters battle.	—
Slush Rush	Doubles Speed in the hail weather condition. Hail does not damage the Pokémon.	—
Sniper	Moves that deliver a critical hit deal 125% more damage.	—
Snow Cloak	The accuracy of the opposing Pokémon's move decreases by 20% in the hail weather condition. Hail does not damage Pokémon with this Ability.	Lowers encounter rate with wild Pokémon in the hail weather condition
Snow Warning	Makes the weather hail for five turns when the Pokémon enters battle. Pokémon other than Ice types take damage of 1/16 of the Pokémon's maximum HP during the weather hail. Does nothing when the weather is extremely harsh sunlight, heavy rain, or strong winds.	—
Solar Power	Raises Sp. Atk by 50%, but takes damage of 1/8 of the Pokémon's maximum HP at the end of every turn in the sunny or extremely harsh sunlight weather conditions.	—
Solid Rock	Decreases the damage received from supereffective moves by 25%.	—
Soul-Heart	Raises Sp. Atk by 1 every time another Pokémon faints.	—
Soundproof	Protects the Pokémon from sound-based moves: Boomburst, Bug Buzz, Chatter, Clanging Scales, Confide, Disarming Voice, Echoed Voice, Grass Whistle, Growl, Heal Bell, Hyper Voice, Metal Sound, Noble Roar, Parting Shot, Perish Song, Roar, Round, Screech, Sing, Snarl, Snore, Sparkling Aria, Supersonic, and Uproar.	—
Speed Boost	Raises Speed by 1 at the end of every turn.	—

Ability	Effect in battle	Effect when the Pokémon is the lead in your party
Stakeout	The Pokémon deals double the damage to the new target if the original target is replaced by another of its party.	—
Stall	The Pokémon's moves are used last in the turn.	—
Stamina	Raises Defense by 1 every time the Pokémon takes move damage.	—
Stance Change	Changes from Shield Forme to Blade Forme when an attack move is used. Changes from Blade Forme to Shield Forme when King's Shield is used.	—
Static	A 30% chance of inflicting the Paralysis status condition when hit with a direct attack.	Raises encounter rate with wild Electric-type Pokémon
Steadfast	Raises Speed by 1 every time the Pokémon flinches.	—
Steelworker	Increases the power of Steel-type moves by 50%.	—
Stench	Has a 10% chance of making the target flinch when the Pokémon uses a move to deal damage.	Lowers wild Pokémon encounter rate
Sticky Hold	Prevents the Pokémon's held item from being stolen.	Makes Pokémon bite more often when fishing
Storm Drain	Draws all Water-type moves to the Pokémon. When the Pokémon is hit by a Water-type move, rather than taking damage, Sp. Atk goes up by 1.	—
Strong Jaw	Raises the power of Bite, Crunch, Fire Fang, Hyper Fang, Ice Fang, Poison Fang, and Thunder Fang by 50%.	—
Sturdy	Protects the Pokémon against one-hit KO moves like Horn Drill and Sheer Cold. Leaves the Pokémon with 1 HP if hit by a move that would knock it out when its HP is full.	—
Suction Cups	Nullifies moves like Dragon Tail, Roar, and Whirlwind, and items like a Red Card, which would force Pokémon to switch out.	Makes Pokémon bite more often when fishing
Super Luck	Heightens the critical-hit ratio of the Pokémon's moves.	—
Surge Surfer	Doubles Speed when the field is affected by Electric Terrain.	—
Swarm	Raises the power of Bug-type moves by 50% when the Pokémon's HP drops to 1/3 or less.	—
Sweet Veil	Protects the team against the Asleep status condition.	—
Swift Swim	Doubles Speed in the rain or heavy rain weather conditions.	—
Symbiosis	When an ally uses its item, the Pokémon gives its own item to that ally.	—
Synchronize	When the Pokémon receives the Poisoned, Paralysis, or Burned status condition, this inflicts the same condition.	Raises encounter rate with wild Pokémon with the same Nature
Tangled Feet	Raises evasion when the Pokémon is confused.	—
Tangling Hair	Lowers by 1 the Speed of an attacker that makes direct contact.	—
Technician	If the move's power is 60 or less, its power will increase by 50%. Also takes effect if a move's power is altered by itself or by another move.	—
Telepathy	Prevents damage from allies.	—
Teravolt	Use moves on targets regardless of their Abilities. Does not nullify Abilities that have effects after an attack. For example, the Pokémon can score a critical hit against the target with Battle Armor, but it will still take damage from Rough Skin.	—
Thick Fat	Halves damage from Fire- and Ice-type moves.	—
Tinted Lens	Nullifies the type disadvantage of the Pokémon's not-very-effective moves: 1/2 damage turns into regular damage, 1/4 damage turns into 1/2 damage.	—
Torrent	Raises the power of Water-type moves by 50% when the Pokémon's HP drops to 1/3 or less.	—
Tough Claws	Raises the power of direct attacks by 30%.	—
Toxic Boost	Increases the power of physical moves by 50% when it has the Poisoned or Badly Poisoned status condition.	—
Trace	Makes the Pokémon's Ability the same as the opponent's, except for certain Abilities like Trace.	—
Triage	Gives priority to healing moves.	—
Truant	Allows the Pokémon to use a move only once every other turn.	—
Turboblaze	Use moves on targets regardless of their Abilities. Does not nullify Abilities that have effects after an attack. For example, the Pokémon can score a critical hit against the target with Battle Armor, but it will still take damage from Rough Skin.	—
Unaware	Ignores the stat changes of the opposing Pokémon, except Speed.	—
Unburden	Doubles Speed if the Pokémon loses or consumes a held item. Its Speed returns to normal if the Pokémon holds another item. No effect if the Pokémon starts out with no held item.	—
Unnerve	Prevent the opposing Pokémon from eating Berries.	—
Victory Star	The accuracy of the Pokémon and its allies is 10% higher.	—
Vital Spirit	Protects against the Asleep status condition.	Makes it easier to encounter high-level wild Pokémon
Volt Absorb	When the Pokémon is hit by an Electric-type move, HP is restored by 25% of its maximum HP rather than taking damage.	—
Water Absorb	When the Pokémon is hit by a Water-type move, HP is restored by 25% of its maximum HP rather than taking damage.	—
Water Bubble	Halves damage from Fire-type moves. Prevents the Burned status condition.	—
Water Compaction	Raises Defense by 2 every time the Pokémon is hit by a Water-type move.	—
Water Veil	Prevents the Burned status condition.	—
Weak Armor	When the Pokémon is hit by a physical attack, Defense goes down by 1, but Speed goes up by 1.	—
White Smoke	Protects against stat-lowering moves and Abilities.	Lowers wild Pokémon encounter rate.
Wimp Out	The Pokémon switches places with a party Pokémon automatically when its HP drops to half or less during a Trainer battle. If a wild Pokémon has this Ability, it will flee battle when its HP drops to half or less.	—
Wonder Guard	Protects the Pokémon against all moves except supereffective ones.	—
Wonder Skin	Makes status moves more likely to miss.	—
Zen Mode	When over half its HP is lost, the Pokémon changes form.	—

Items Picked Up with the Pickup Ability

Pokémon with the Pickup Ability sometimes pick up items after a battle. The Pokémon will not be able to pick up a new item, however, if it is already holding another item. The kinds of item that may be picked up vary depending on the level of the Pokémon with the Pickup Ability.

	Low Lv. →										→ High Lv.
Potion	☆										
Antidote	◎	☆									
Super Potion	◎	◎	☆								
Great Ball	◎	◎	◎	☆							
Repel	◎	◎	◎	◎	☆						
Escape Rope	◎	◎	◎	◎	◎	☆					
Full Heal	◎	◎	◎	◎	◎	◎	☆				
Hyper Potion	△	△	△	◎	◎	◎	◎	☆			
Ultra Ball	△	△	△	△	◎	◎	◎	◎	☆		
Revive		▲	▲	△	△	○	◎	◎	◎	◎	☆
Ether				▲	▲	▲					
Elixir							△	△			
Max Elixir										▲	△
Rare Candy			△	△	△	○	○	○	○	○	○
Heart Scale						▲	△	◎	◎	◎	◎
Full Restore			▲	▲	▲	△	△	△	△	◎	◎
Max Revive									▲	◎	◎
PP Up										▲	△
Prism Scale		△	△	△	△	△	△	△	△	△	△
Sun Stone		△	△	△	◎	◎	◎	◎	◎	◎	◎
Moon Stone		△	△	△	◎	◎	◎	◎	◎	◎	◎
Nugget	△	△									
Balm Mushroom		▲	△								
Pearl String			▲	△							
Big Nugget				▲	△	△	△	△	△	△	△
Destiny Knot	▲	▲	▲	▲	▲	▲	▲	▲	▲	▲	▲
Leftovers	▲	▲	▲	▲	▲	▲	▲	▲	▲	▲	▲

☆ Frequently picked up ◎ Commonly picked up ○ Sometimes picked up △ Rarely picked up ▲ Almost never picked up

Pokémon Natures

Each individual Pokémon has a Nature, which affects how its stats grow when it levels up. Most Natures will cause one stat to increase more quickly and one stat to increase more slowly than others. A few Natures, however, provide no benefit and no liability. Your Pokémon's Nature will also affect which flavors it likes and dislikes when it comes to malasadas and certain Berries.

Nature	Increased stat	Decreased stat	Favorite flavor	Disliked flavor
Adamant	ATK	SP. ATK	Spicy	Dry
Bashful	—	—	—	—
Bold	DEF	ATK	Sour	Spicy
Brave	ATK	SPD	Spicy	Sweet
Calm	SP. DEF	ATK	Bitter	Spicy
Careful	SP. DEF	SP. ATK	Bitter	Dry
Docile	—	—	—	—
Gentle	SP. DEF	DEF	Bitter	Sour
Hardy	—	—	—	—
Hasty	SPD	DEF	Sweet	Sour
Impish	DEF	SP. ATK	Sour	Dry
Jolly	SPD	SP. ATK	Sweet	Dry
Lax	DEF	SP. DEF	Sour	Bitter
Lonely	ATK	DEF	Spicy	Sour
Mild	SP. ATK	DEF	Dry	Sour
Modest	SP. ATK	ATK	Dry	Spicy
Naive	SPD	SP. DEF	Sweet	Bitter
Naughty	ATK	SP. DEF	Spicy	Bitter
Quiet	SP. ATK	SPD	Dry	Sweet
Quirky	—	—	—	—
Rash	SP. ATK	SP. DEF	Dry	Bitter
Relaxed	DEF	SPD	Sour	Sweet
Sassy	SP. DEF	SPD	Bitter	Sweet
Serious	—	—	—	—
Timid	SPD	ATK	Sweet	Spicy

Pokémon Characteristics

On top of having a Nature, each individual Pokémon has a Characteristic. This also affects how the Pokémon's stats grow when it levels up. Characteristics give a hint of which of the Pokémon's stats likely has the highest individual strength.

Stat that grows easily	Characteristic
HP	Loves to eat
	Takes plenty of siestas
	Nods off a lot
	Scatters things often
	Likes to relax
ATTACK	Proud of its power
	Likes to thrash about
	A little quick tempered
	Likes to fight
	Quick tempered
DEFENSE	Sturdy body
	Capable of taking hits
	Highly persistent
	Good endurance
	Good perseverance
SP. ATK	Highly curious
	Mischievous
	Thoroughly cunning
	Often lost in thought
	Very finicky
SP. DEF	Strong willed
	Somewhat vain
	Strongly defiant
	Hates to lose
	Somewhat stubborn
SPEED	Likes to run
	Alert to sounds
	Impetuous and silly
	Somewhat of a clown
	Quick to flee

Base Points Received for Defeating Wild Pokémon in Alola

Alola Pokédex No.	Melemele Pokédex No.	Akala Pokédex No.	Ula'ula Pokédex No.	Poni Pokédex No.	Pokémon Name	HP	ATTACK	DEFENSE	SPEED	SP. ATK	SP. DEF
10	10	1	1	1	Pikipek		○				
11	11	2	2	2	Trumbeak		○				
13	13	4	4	4	Yungoos		○				
14	14	5	5	5	Gumshoos		○				
15	15	6	6	6	Rattata				○		
16	16	7	7	7	Raticate				○		
17	17	8			Caterpie	○					
18	18	9			Metapod			○			
19	19	10			Butterfree					○	○
20	20	8			Ledyba						○
21	21	9			Ledian						○
22	22	10			Spinarak		○				

Alola Pokédex No.	Melemele Pokédex No.	Akala Pokédex No.	Ula'ula Pokédex No.	Poni Pokédex No.	Pokémon Name	HP	ATTACK	DEFENSE	SPEED	SP. ATK	SP. DEF
23	23		11		Ariados		○				
24	24				Pichu					○	
25	25				Pikachu					○	
27	27	11	12		Grubbin		○				
28	28	12	13		Charjabug			○			
30	30	14			Bonsly			○			
31	31	15			Sudowoodo			○			
32	32	16	15	8	Happiny	○					
33	33	17	16	9	Chansey	○					
35	35				Munchlax	○					
36	36				Snorlax	○					
37	37		18		Slowpoke	○					

Alola Pokédex No.	Melemele Pokédex No.	Akala Pokédex No.	Ula'ula Pokédex No.	Poni Pokédex No.	Pokémon Name	HP	ATTACK	DEFENSE	SPEED	SP. ATK	SP. DEF
38	38		19		Slowbro			○			
40	40	19	21	11	Wingull				○		
41	41	20	22	12	Pelipper			○			
42	42				Abra					○	
45	45		23		Meowth				○		
47	47		25		Magnemite					○	
50	50		28		Grimer	○					
52	52				Growlithe		○				
54	54			13	Drowzee						○
55	55			14	Hypno						○
56	56			15	Makuhita	○					
57	57			16	Hariyama	○					
58	58				Smeargle				○		
59	59	21	30	17	Crabrawler		○				
61	61	23	32		Gastly					○	
62	62	24	33		Haunter					○	
63	63	25	34		Gengar					○	
64	64				Drifloon	○					
66	66				Misdreavus						○
68	68	26	35	19	Zubat				○		
69	69	27	36	20	Golbat				○		
70	70	28	37	21	Crobat				○		
71	71	29	38	22	Diglett				○		
72	72	30	39	23	Dugtrio		○				
73	73		40	24	Spearow				○		
74	74		41	25	Fearow				○		
75	75			26	Rufflet		○				
76	76			27	Braviary		○				
77	77			28	Vullaby			○			
78	78			29	Mandibuzz					○	
79	79			30	Mankey		○				
80	80			31	Primeape		○				
81	81				Delibird				○		
82	82	31	42	32	Oricorio					○	
83	83		43	33	Cutiefly				○		
84	84		44	34	Ribombee				○		
85	85		45	35	Petilil					○	
87	87		47	37	Cottonee				○		
89	89	32	49	39	Psyduck					○	
90	90	33	50	40	Golduck					○	
91	91	34	51	41	Magikarp				○		
92	92	35	52	42	Gyarados		○				
93	93	36		43	Barboach	○					
94	94	37		44	Whiscash	○					
95	95			45	Machop		○				
96	96			46	Machoke		○				
98	98			48	Roggenrola			○			
99	99			49	Boldore		○	○			
101	101			51	Carbink			○			○
102	102			52	Sableye		○	○			
103	103			53	Rockruff		○				
104	104			54	Lycanroc		○				
105	105				Spinda					○	
106	106	38	53	55	Tentacool						○
107	107	39	54	56	Tentacruel						○
108	108	40	55	57	Finneon				○		
109	109	41	56	58	Lumineon				○		
110	110	42	57		Wishiwashi	○					
111	111	43			Luvdisc				○		
112	112	44			Corsola			○			○
113	113	45			Mareanie			○			
115	115				Shellder			○			
117	117				Bagon		○				
118	118				Shelgon			○			
119	119				Salamence		○				
120		47			Lillipup		○				
123		50			Eevee						○
127		54			Espeon					○	
128		55			Umbreon						○
132		59	58	59	Mudbray		○				
133		60	59	60	Mudsdale		○				
134		61			Igglybuff	○					
135		62			Jigglypuff	○					
137		64		61	Tauros		○		○		
138		65		62	Miltank			○			
139		66	60		Surskit				○		
140		67	61		Masquerain					○	○
141		68	62		Dewpider						○
142		69	63		Araquanid						○
143		70			Fomantis		○				
145		72	64		Morelull						○
147		74	66		Paras		○				
149		76	68		Poliwag				○		
150		77	69		Poliwhirl				○		
152		79	71		Politoed						○
153		80	72		Goldeen		○				
154		81	73		Seaking		○				
155		82			Feebas				○		
157		84			Alomomola	○					
158		85			Fletchling				○		
159		86			Fletchinder				○		
161		88			Salandit				○		
163		90			Cubone			○			
165		92			Kangaskhan	○					
166		93			Magby				○		
167		94			Magmar					○	
169		96		63	Stufful		○				
170		97		64	Bewear		○				
171		98			Bounsweet	○					
174		101			Comfey						○
175		102	65		Pinsir		○				
176		103			Oranguru						○

Alola Pokédex No.	Melemele Pokédex No.	Akala Pokédex No.	Ula'ula Pokédex No.	Poni Pokédex No.	Pokémon Name	HP	ATTACK	DEFENSE	SPEED	SP. ATK	SP. DEF
177	104				Passimian		○				
178	105	74	66		Goomy						○
179	106	75	67		Sliggoo						○
181	108	77	69		Castform	○					
182	109		70		Wimpod				○		
184	111				Staryu				○		
185	112				Starmie				○		
186	113				Sandygast			○			
196	123				Phantump		○				
198	125				Nosepass			○			
200	127				Pyukumuku						○
201	128				Chinchou	○					
206		78			Trubbish				○		
207		79			Garbodor		○				
208		80	72		Skarmory			○			
209		81			Ditto	○					
210		82			Cleffa						○
211		83			Clefairy	○					
213		85			Minior				○		○
214		86			Beldum		○				
220		92			Pancham		○				
221		93			Pangoro		○				
222		94			Komala		○				
223		95			Torkoal			○			
224		96			Turtonator			○			
225		97			Togedemaru		○				
226		98			Elekid				○		
227		99			Electabuzz				○		
229		101			Geodude			○			
230		102			Graveler			○			
232		104			Sandile		○				
235		107			Trapinch		○				
239		111			Gabite		○				

Alola Pokédex No.	Melemele Pokédex No.	Akala Pokédex No.	Ula'ula Pokédex No.	Poni Pokédex No.	Pokémon Name	HP	ATTACK	DEFENSE	SPEED	SP. ATK	SP. DEF
241		113			Klefki			○			
242		114			Mimikyu						○
243		115			Bruxish		○				
244		116			Drampa					○	
245		117			Absol		○				
246		118			Snorunt	○					
247		119			Glalie	○					
248		121			Sneasel				○		
251		123			Sandshrew			○			
253		125			Vulpix						○
255		127			Vanillite					○	
256		128			Vanillish					○	
259			74		Granbull		○				
261			76		Gastrodon	○					
262			77		Relicanth	○		○			
263			78		Whiscash		○				
265			80		Sharpedo		○				
266			81		Wailmer	○					
267			82		Wailord	○					
268			83		Lapras	○					
269			84		Exeggcute			○			
270			85		Exeggutor					○	
271			86		Jangmo-o			○			
272			87		Hakamo-o			○			
273			88		Kommo-o			○			
274			89		Emolga				○		
275			90		Scyther		○				
277			92		Murkrow				○		
279			94		Riolu		○				
280			95		Lucario		○			○	
281			96		Dratini		○				
282			97		Dragonair		○				
283			98		Dragonite		○				

Items

Item	Description	Main way to obtain	Price
Ability Capsule	Allows a Pokémon with two Abilities (excluding Hidden Abilities) to switch between these Abilities.	Win 50 straight battles at the Battle Tree	—
Absolite	When held, it allows Absol to Mega Evolve into Mega Absol during battle.	Get for 64 BP at the Battle Tree	64 BP
Absorb Bulb	Raises the holder's Sp. Atk by 1 when it is hit by a Water-type move. It goes away after use.	Sometimes held by wild Petilil or Cottonee	—
Adamant Orb	When held by Dialga, it boosts the power of Dragon-and Steel-type moves by 20%.	Buy at Antiquities of the Ages in Hau'oli shopping mall	₽10,000
Adrenaline Orb	Using it makes wild Pokémon more likely to call for help. If held by a Pokémon, it boosts Speed when intimidated. It can only be used once.	Route 4 / Ula'ula Meadow / Ancient Poni Path	₽300
Aerodactylite	When held, it allows Aerodactyl to Mega Evolve into Mega Aerodactyl during battle.	Get for 64 BP at the Battle Tree	64 BP
Air Balloon	The holder floats and Ground-type moves will no longer hit the holder. The balloon pops when the holder is hit by an attack.	Receive from a girl in Malie Garden during the day (after completing the Ula'ula grand trial)	—
Alakazite	When held, it allows Alakazam to Mega Evolve into Mega Alakazam during battle.	Get for 64 BP at the Battle Tree	64 BP
Amulet Coin	Doubles the prize money from a battle if the Pokémon holding it joins in.	Paniola Ranch	—
Antidote	Cures the Poisoned status condition.	Buy at any Poké Mart (from the start)	₽200

Item	Description	Main way to obtain	Price
Armor Fossil	A Pokémon Fossil. When restored, it becomes Shieldon.	Buy at Olivia's shop in Konikoni City ⟲	₽7,000
Assault Vest	Raises Sp. Def when held by 50%, but prevents the use of status moves.	Get for 48 BP at the Battle Tree	48 BP
Awakening	Cures the Asleep status condition.	Buy at any Poké Mart (from the start)	₽100
Balm Mushroom	A fragrant mushroom. It can be sold at shops for a high price.	Sometimes picked up by a Pokémon with the Pickup Ability	—
Berry Juice	Restores the HP of one Pokémon by 20 points.	Receive at a lottery shop as a prize in Festival Plaza	—
Big Malasada	The Alola region's local specialty—fried bread. It can be used once to heal all the status conditions and confusion of a Pokémon.	Buy at Malasada Shops around Alola	₽350
Big Mushroom	A big mushroom. It can be sold at shops for a high price.	Hau'oli Cemetery / Berry Fields / Heahea City / Malie Garden	—
Big Nugget	A big nugget of pure gold. It can be sold at shops for a high price.	Defeat five Trainers at a bridge in Malie Garden (after defeating Team Skull Boss)	—
Big Pearl	A big pearl. It can be sold at shops for a high price.	Route 8 / Poni Gauntlet / Fishing spots (except Poni Island)	—
Big Root	When the holder uses an HP-draining move, it increases the amount of HP recovered by 30%.	Lush Jungle	—
Binding Band	When held, the damage done to a target by moves like Bind or Wrap will be 1/6 of the target's maximum HP every turn.	Get for 48 BP at the Battle Royal Dome	48 BP
Black Belt	When held by a Pokémon, it boosts the power of Fighting-type moves by 20%.	Sometimes held by wild Makuhita	—
Black Glasses	When held by a Pokémon, it boosts the power of Dark-type moves by 20%.	Hano Beach / Often held by wild Krookodile	—
Black Sludge	If the holder is a Poison-type Pokémon, it restores 1/16 of its maximum HP every turn. If the holder is any other type, it loses 1/8 of its maximum HP every turn.	Sometimes held by wild Grimer or Garbodor	—
Blastoisinite	When held, it allows Blastoise to Mega Evolve into Mega Blastoise during battle.	Defeat Red at the Battle Tree	—
Blue Orb	A shiny blue orb that is said to have a legend tied to it. It's known to have a deep connection with the Hoenn region.	Buy at Antiquities of the Ages in Hau'oli shopping mall	₽10,000
Blue Shard	Can be exchanged for Bottle Caps in Festival Plaza.	Sometimes found by your Pokémon on Isle Aphun in Poké Pelago	—
Bottle Cap	A beautiful bottle cap that gives off a silver gleam. Some people are happy to receive one.	Fishing spots on Poni Island	—
Bright Powder	Lowers the opponent's accuracy.	Get for 48 BP at the Battle Royal Dome	48 BP
Bug Memory	When held by Silvally, its type changes to Bug type.	Receive from Gladion (after becoming Champion)	—
Burn Drive	When held by Genesect, it changes Genesect's Techno Blast move so it becomes Fire type.	Receive from Colress on Route 8 (after becoming Champion)	—
Burn Heal	Cures the Burned status condition.	Buy at any Poké Mart (from the start)	₽300
Calcium	Raises the base Sp. Atk stat of a Pokémon.	Buy at the Poké Mart on Mount Hokulani	₽10,000
Carbos	Raises the base Speed stat of a Pokémon.	Poni Plains / Buy at the Poké Mart on Mount Hokulani	₽10,000
Casteliacone	Heals all the status problems and confusion of a single Pokémon.	Buy a drink at the Pokémon Center café on a Wednesday	—
Cell Battery	Increases Attack by 1 when the holder is hit with Electric-type moves. It goes away after use.	Sometimes held by wild Charjabug	—
Charcoal	When held by a Pokémon, it boosts the power of Fire-type moves by 20%.	Wela Volcano Park	—
Charizardite X	When held, it allows Charizard to Mega Evolve into Mega Charizard X during battle.	Defeat Red at the Battle Tree	—
Charizardite Y	When held, it allows Charizard to Mega Evolve into Mega Charizard Y during battle.	Defeat Red at the Battle Tree	—
Chill Drive	When held by Genesect, it changes Genesect's Techno Blast move so it becomes Ice type.	Receive from Colress on Route 8 (after becoming Champion)	—
Choice Band	The holder can use only one of its moves, but the power of physical moves increases by 50%.	Get for 48 BP at the Battle Tree	48 BP
Choice Scarf	The holder can use only one of its moves, but Speed increases by 50%.	Get for 48 BP at the Battle Tree	48 BP
Choice Specs	The holder can use only one of its moves, but the power of special moves increases by 50%.	Get for 48 BP at the Battle Tree	48 BP
Cleanse Tag	Helps keep wild Pokémon away if the holder is the first one in the party.	Memorial Hill	—
Clever Wing	Slightly increases the base Sp. Def stat of a single Pokémon. It can be used until the max of base stats.	Sometimes dropped on Ula'ula Island by Skarmory	—
Comet Shard	A shard that fell to the ground when a comet approached. It can be sold at shops for a high price.	Poni Coast / Haina Desert	—
Cover Fossil	A Pokémon Fossil. When restored, it becomes Tirtouga.	Buy at Olivia's shop in Konikoni City ✦	₽7,000
Damp Rock	Extends the duration of the rainy weather by three turns when held.	Receive from a woman after taking a quiz at the community center in Malie City	—
Dark Memory	When held by Silvally, its type changes to Dark type.	Receive from Gladion (after becoming Champion)	—
Dawn Stone	It can evolve male Kirlia and female Snorunt.	Sometimes found by your Pokémon on Isle Aphun in Poké Pelago	—
Deep Sea Scale	When held by Clamperl, it doubles Sp. Def. Link Trade Clamperl while it holds the Deep Sea Scale to evolve it into Gorebyss.	Sometimes held by wild Chinchou or Relicanth	—
Deep Sea Tooth	When held by Clamperl, it doubles Sp. Atk. Link Trade Clamperl while it holds the Deep Sea Tooth to evolve it into Huntail.	Sometimes held by wild Carvanha or Sharpedo	—
Destiny Knot	When a Pokémon holding it is inflicted with Infatuation, the Pokémon shares the condition with its attacker.	Get for 48 BP at the Battle Royal Dome	48 BP
Dire Hit	Significantly raises the critical-hit ratio of the Pokémon on which it is used. It can be used only once and wears off if the Pokémon is withdrawn.	Buy at the Poké Mart in Hau'oli City	₽1,000

Item	Description	Main way to obtain	Price
DNA Splicers	A pair of splicers that fuse Kyurem and Zekrom or Reshiram.	Receive from an Aether Employee in Aether Paradise (after becoming Champion)	—
Douse Drive	When held by Genesect, it changes Genesect's Techno Blast move so it becomes Water type.	Receive from Colress on Route 8 (after becoming Champion)	—
Draco Plate	When held by a Pokémon, it boosts the power of Dragon-type moves by 20%. (When held by Arceus, it shifts Arceus's type to Dragon type.)	Hau'oli City Shopping District	—
Dragon Fang	When held by a Pokémon, it boosts the power of Dragon-type moves by 20%.	Sometimes held by Bagon, Shelgon, or Salamence	—
Dragon Memory	When held by Silvally, its type changes to Dragon type.	Receive from Gladion (after becoming Champion)	—
Dragon Scale	Link Trade Seadra while it holds the Dragon Scale to evolve it into Kingdra.	Sometimes held by wild Dratini, Dragonair, or Dragonite	—
Dread Plate	When held by a Pokémon, it boosts the power of Dark-type moves by 20%. (When held by Arceus, it shifts Arceus's type to Dark type.)	Buy at Antiquities of the Ages in Hau'oli shopping mall	₽10,000
Dubious Disc	Link Trade Porygon2 while it holds the Dubious Disc to evolve it into Porygon-Z.	Receive from Faba after defeating him at Aether Paradise (after becoming Champion)	—
Dusk Stone	It can evolve Doublade, Lampent, Misdreavus, and Murkrow.	Poni Wilds	—
Earth Plate	When held by a Pokémon, it boosts the power of Ground-type moves by 20%. (When held by Arceus, it shifts Arceus's type to Ground type.)	Hau'oli Outskirts	—
Eject Button	If the holder is hit by an attack, it switches places with a party Pokémon. It goes away after use.	Get for 32 BP at the Battle Tree	32 BP
Electirizer	Link Trade Electabuzz while it holds the Electirizer to evolve it into Electivire.	Receive from the guy in the southwest houseboat in Seafolk Village	—
Electric Memory	When held by Silvally, its type changes to Electric type.	Receive from Gladion (after becoming Champion)	—
Electric Seed	It boosts Defense of a Pokémon on Electric Terrain by 1 during battle. It can only be used once.	Sometimes held by wild Togedemaru	—
Elixir	Restores the PP of all of a Pokémon's moves by 10 points.	Route 12 / Vast Poni Canyon / Resolution Cave	—
Energy Powder	Restores the HP of one Pokémon by 60 points. Very bitter (lowers a Pokémon's friendship).	Buy at the herb vendor in Konikoni City	₽500
Energy Root	Restores the HP of one Pokémon by 120 points. Very bitter (lowers a Pokémon's friendship).	Buy at the herb vendor in Konikoni City	₽1,200
Escape Rope	Use it to escape instantly from a cave or a dungeon.	Buy at any Poké Mart (from the start)	₽1,000
Ether	Restores the PP of a Pokémon's move by 10 points.	Hau'oli City Shopping District / Route 5 / Paniola Ranch	—
Everstone	Prevents the Pokémon that holds it from evolving.	Visit Ilima's house and defeat him (after completing the Melemele grand trial)	—
Eviolite	Raises Defense and Sp. Def by 50% when held by a Pokémon that can still evolve.	Konikoni City	—
Expert Belt	Raises the power of supereffective moves by 20%.	Seaward Cave	—
Fairy Memory	When held by Silvally, its type changes to Fairy type.	Receive from Gladion (after becoming Champion)	—
Festival Ticket	A ticket that allows you to host a mission in Festival Plaza.	Receive daily from the woman in Festival Plaza (after reaching Rank 4)	—
Fighting Memory	When held by Silvally, its type changes to Fighting type.	Receive from Gladion (after becoming Champion)	—
Fire Memory	When held by Silvally, its type changes to Fire type.	Receive from Gladion (after becoming Champion)	—
Fire Stone	It can evolve Eevee, Growlithe, Pansear, and Vulpix.	Buy at Olivia's jewelry shop in Konikoni City	₽3,000
Fist Plate	When held by a Pokémon, it boosts the power of Fighting-type moves by 20%. (When held by Arceus, it shifts Arceus's type to Fighting type.)	Buy at Antiquities of the Ages in Hau'oli shopping mall	₽10,000
Flame Orb	Inflicts the Burned status condition on the holder during battle.	Defeat all the Trainers in Ula'ula Meadow	—
Flame Plate	When held by a Pokémon, it boosts the power of Fire-type moves by 20%. (When held by Arceus, it shifts Arceus's type to Fire type.)	Trainers' School	—
Float Stone	Halves the holder's weight.	Get for 48 BP at the Battle Royal Dome	48 BP
Flying Memory	When held by Silvally, its type changes to Flying type.	Receive from Gladion (after becoming Champion)	—
Focus Band	Has a 10% chance of leaving the holder with 1 HP when it receives damage that would cause it to faint.	Receive from a Police Officer in Route 9 Police Station (after completing the Akala grand trial)	—
Focus Sash	A holder with full HP is left with 1 HP when it is hit by a move that would cause it to faint. Then the item disappears.	Defeat all the Trainers in the Poni Wilds	—
Fresh Water	Restores the HP of one Pokémon by 30 points.	Buy at a vending machine	Varies
Full Heal	Cures all status conditions and confusion.	Buy at any Poké Mart (after completing 5 trials)	₽400
Full Incense	When held by a Pokémon, it makes the holder move later.	Buy at the incense vendor in Konikoni City	₽5,000
Full Restore	Restore the HP of a Pokémon and cures status conditions and confusion.	Buy at any Poké Mart (after completing 7 trials)	₽3,000
Garchompite	When held, it allows Garchomp to Mega Evolve into Mega Garchomp during battle.	Get for 64 BP at the Battle Tree	64 BP
Gengarite	When held, it allows Gengar to Mega Evolve into Mega Gengar during battle.	Get for 64 BP at the Battle Tree	64 BP
Genius Wing	Slightly increases the base Sp. Atk stat of a single Pokémon. It can be used until the base stat reaches its maximum value.	Sometimes dropped on Poni Island by Braviary and Mandibuzz	—
Ghost Memory	When held by Silvally, its type changes to Ghost type.	Receive from Gladion (after becoming Champion)	—
Glalitite	When held, it allows Glalie to Mega Evolve into Mega Glalie during battle.	Get for 64 BP at the Battle Tree	64 BP
Gold Bottle Cap	A beautiful bottle cap that gives off a golden gleam. Some people are happy to receive one.	Sometimes found by your Pokémon on Isle Aphun in Poké Pelago	—
Gracidea	A flower to convey gratitude. Shaymin will change its Forme if Gracidea is used on it (except at night).	Receive from a clerk in the Gracidea apparel shop in Hau'oli shopping mall	—
Grass Memory	When held by Silvally, its type changes to Grass type.	Receive from Gladion (after becoming Champion)	—

Item	Description	Main way to obtain	Price
Grassy Seed	It boosts Defense of a Pokémon on Grassy Terrain by 1 during battle. It can only be used once.	Malie Garden / Sometimes held by wild Bounsweet	—
Green Shard	Can be exchanged for Bottle Caps in Festival Plaza.	Sometimes found by your Pokémon on Isle Aphun in Poké Pelago	—
Grip Claw	Extends the duration of moves like Bind and Wrap to seven turns.	Sometimes held by wild Alolan Sandshrew	—
Griseous Orb	When held by Giratina, it changes it into its Origin Forme, and boosts the power of Dragon- and Ghost-type moves by 20%.	Buy at Antiquities of the Ages in Hau'oli shopping mall	₽10,000
Ground Memory	When held by Silvally, its type changes to Ground type.	Receive from Gladion (after becoming Champion)	—
Guard Spec.	Prevents stat reduction among the Trainer's party Pokémon for five turns. It can be used only once.	Buy at the Poké Mart in Hau'oli City	₽1,500
Gyaradosite	When held, it allows Gyarados to Mega Evolve into Mega Gyarados during battle.	Get for 64 BP at the Battle Tree	64 BP
Hard Stone	When held by a Pokémon, it boosts the power of Rock-type moves by 20%.	Ten Carat Hill / Sometimes held by wild Roggenrola or Boldore	—
Heal Powder	Cures all status conditions and confusion. Very bitter (lowers a Pokémon's friendship).	Buy at the herb vendor in Konikoni City	₽300
Health Wing	Slightly increases the base HP of a single Pokémon. It can be used until the max of base stats.	Sometimes dropped on Ula'ula and Poni Islands by Fearow	—
Heart Scale	A pretty, heart-shaped scale that is extremely rare. Highly sought-after by certain people.	Seafolk Village's floating restaurant / Fishing spots on Akala Island / Often held by wild Luvdisc	—
Heat Rock	When held by a Pokémon, it extends the duration of the sunny weather by three turns.	Receive from a woman after taking a quiz at the community center in Malie City	—
Honey	Attracts wild Pokémon where wild Pokémon can appear.	Buy at any Poké Mart (after completing 2 trials)	₽300
HP Up	Raises the base HP of a Pokémon.	Royal Avenue / Buy at the Poké Mart on Mount Hokulani	₽10,000
Hyper Potion	Restores the HP of one Pokémon by 120 points.	Buy at any Poké Mart (after completing 4 trials)	₽1,500
Ice Heal	Cures the Frozen status condition.	Buy at any Poké Mart (from the start)	₽100
Ice Memory	When held by Silvally, its type changes to Ice type.	Receive from Gladion (after becoming Champion)	—
Ice Stone	It can evolve Alolan Vulpix and Alolan Sandshrew.	Po Town	—
Icicle Plate	When held by a Pokémon, it boosts the power of Ice-type moves by 20%. (When held by Arceus, it shifts Arceus's type to Ice type.)	Hau'oli City Beachfront	—
Icy Rock	Extends the duration of the hail by three turns when held.	Receive from a woman after taking a quiz at the community center in Malie City	—
Insect Plate	When held by a Pokémon, it boosts the power of Bug-type moves by 20%. (When held by Arceus, it shifts Arceus's type to Bug type.)	Hau'oli City Shopping District	—
Iron	Raises the base Defense stat of a Pokémon.	Shady House / Buy at the Poké Mart on Mount Hokulani	₽10,000
Iron Ball	Halves the holder's Speed. If the holder has the Levitate Ability or is a Flying-type Pokémon, Ground-type moves can hit it.	Get for 16 BP at the Battle Tree	16 BP
Iron Plate	When held by a Pokémon, it boosts the power of Steel-type moves by 20%. (When held by Arceus, it shifts Arceus's type to Steel type.)	Buy at Antiquities of the Ages in Hau'oli shopping mall	₽10,000
Kangaskhanite	When held, it allows Kangaskhan to Mega Evolve into Mega Kangaskhan during battle.	Get for 64 BP at the Battle Tree	64 BP
Key Stone	A stone filled with an unexplained power. It makes Pokémon that battle with a Mega Stone Mega Evolve.	Receive from Dexio (after becoming Champion)	—
King's Rock	When the holder successfully inflicts damage, the target may also flinch. Link Trade Poliwhirl or Slowpoke while they hold a King's Rock to evolve them.	Sometimes held by wild Slowbro, Hariyama, Poliwhirl, or Politoed	—
Lagging Tail	When held by a Pokémon, it makes it move later.	Sometimes held by wild Slowpoke	—
Lava Cookie	Lavaridge Town's famous specialty. Cures all status conditions and confusion.	Buy a drink at the Pokémon Center café on a Saturday	—
Lax Incense	Boosts the holder's evasion.	Buy at the incense vendor in Konikoni City	₽5,000
Leaf Stone	It can evolve Exeggcute, Gloom, Nuzleaf, Pansage, and Weepinbell.	Buy at Olivia's jewelry shop in Konikoni City	₽3,000
Leftovers	It restores 1/16 of the holder's maximum HP every turn.	Often held by wild Munchlax or Snorlax	—
Lemonade	Restores the HP of one Pokémon by 70 points.	Buy at a vending machine	Varies
Life Orb	Lowers the holder's HP each time it attacks, but raises the power of moves by 30%.	Resolution Cave	—
Light Ball	Doubles the power of both physical and special moves when held by Pikachu.	Resolution Cave / Sometimes held by wild Pikachu	—
Light Clay	Extends the duration of moves like Reflect, Light Screen, and Aurora Veil by three turns.	Sometimes held by wild Mudbray or Mudsdale	—
Lucarionite	When held, it allows Lucario to Mega Evolve into Mega Lucario during battle.	Get for 64 BP at the Battle Tree	64 BP
Luck Incense	Doubles prize money from a battle if the holding Pokémon joins in.	Buy at the incense vendor in Konikoni City	₽11,000
Lucky Egg	Increases the number of Experience Points received from battle by 50%.	Receive from Professor Kukui when your Pokédex is filled by a few dozen Pokémon (after becoming Champion)	—
Lucky Punch	It is a pair of gloves that boosts Chansey's critical-hit ratio.	Receive from a Rising Star in the northeast houseboat in Seafolk Village	—
Luminous Moss	Increases Sp. Def by 1 when the holder is hit with Water-type moves. It goes away after use.	Sometimes held by wild Corsola	—
Lumiose Galette	A popular pastry sold in Lumiose City. Cures all status conditions and confusion for one Pokémon.	Buy a drink at the Pokémon Center café on a Monday	—
Lustrous Orb	When held by Palkia, it boosts the power of Dragon- and Water-type moves by 20%.	Buy at Antiquities of the Ages in Hau'oli shopping mall	₽10,000
Magmarizer	Link Trade Magmar while it holds the Magmarizer to evolve it into Magmortar.	Receive from the guy in the southwest houseboat in Seafolk Village	—

Item	Description	Main way to obtain	Price
Magnet	When held by a Pokémon, it boosts the power of Electric-type moves by 20%.	Sometimes held by wild Nosepass	—
Max Elixir	Completely restores the PP of all of a Pokémon's moves.	Sometimes picked up by a Pokémon with the Pickup Ability	—
Max Ether	Completely restores the PP of a Pokémon's move.	Receive from Hau in Diglett's Tunnel	—
Max Potion	Completely restores the HP of a single Pokémon.	Buy at any Poké Mart (after completing 6 trials)	₽2,500
Max Repel	Prevents weak wild Pokémon from appearing for a long while after its use.	Buy at any Poké Mart (after completing 5 trials)	₽900
Max Revive	Revives a fainted Pokémon and fully restores its HP.	Seaward Cave / Lush Jungle / Shady House	—
Meadow Plate	When held by a Pokémon, it boosts the power of Grass-type moves by 20%. (When held by Arceus, it shifts Arceus's type to Grass type.)	Hau'oli City Shopping District	—
Mental Herb	The holder shakes off the effects of Attract, Disable, Encore, Heal Block, Taunt, and Torment. It goes away after use.	Sometimes held by wild Pancham	—
Metagrossite	When held, it allows Metagross to Mega Evolve into Mega Metagross during battle.	Get for 64 BP at the Battle Tree	64 BP
Metal Coat	When held by a Pokémon, it boosts the power of Steel-type moves by 20%. Link trade Onix or Scyther while they hold a Metal Coat to evolve them.	Sometimes held by wild Magnemite, Skarmory, or Beldum	—
Metal Powder	When held by Ditto, Defense doubles.	Sometimes held by wild Ditto	—
Metronome	When held, it raises the power of a move used consecutively by that Pokémon (up to a maximum increase of 100%).	Receive from the Veteran in Grand Hano Resort	—
Mind Plate	When held by a Pokémon, it boosts the power of Psychic-type moves by 20%. (When held by Arceus, it shifts Arceus's type to Psychic type.)	Hau'oli Outskirts	—
Miracle Seed	When held by a Pokémon, it boosts the power of Grass-type moves by 20%.	Route 8 / Sometimes held by wild Fomantis	—
Misty Seed	It boosts Sp. Def of a Pokémon on Misty Terrain by 1 during battle. It can only be used once.	Poni Gauntlet / Sometimes held by wild Comfey	—
Moomoo Milk	Restores the HP of one Pokémon by 100 points.	Often held by wild Miltank	—
Moon Stone	It can evolve Clefairy, Jigglypuff, Munna, Nidorina, Nidorino, and Skitty.	Route 13	—
Muscle Band	When held by a Pokémon, it boosts the power of physical moves by 10%.	Visit Lana's house in Konikoni City and defeat Lana and her little sisters (after completing the Akala grand trial)	—
Muscle Wing	Slightly increases the base Attack stat of a single Pokémon. It can be used until the max of base stats.	Sometimes dropped on Poni Island by Braviary and Mandibuzz	—
Mystic Water	When held by a Pokémon, it boosts the power of Water-type moves by 20%.	Sometimes held by wild Dewpider, Araquanid, or Goldeen	—
Never-Melt Ice	When held by a Pokémon, it boosts the power of Ice-type moves by 20%.	Seaward Cave	—
Normal Gem	It boosts the power of a Normal-type move by 30% one time. It goes away after use.	Route 15	—
Nugget	A nugget of pure gold. It can be sold at shops for a high price.	Route 1 / Ten Carat Hill / Malie City Outer Cape	—
Odd Incense	When held by a Pokémon, it boosts the power of Psychic-type moves by 20%.	Buy at the incense vendor in Konikoni City	₽2,000
Old Gateau	The Old Chateau's hidden specialty. It can heal all the status conditions and confusion.	Buy a drink at the Pokémon Center café on a Thursday	—
Oval Charm	An oval charm said to increase the chance of Pokémon Eggs being found at the Nursery.	Receive from Morimoto at GAME FREAK's office in Heahea City after defeating him (after becoming Champion)	—
Oval Stone	Level up Happiny between 4 a.m. and 7:59 p.m. while it holds the Oval Stone to evolve it into Chansey.	Often held by wild Happiny	—
Paralyze Heal	Cures the Paralysis status condition.	Buy at any Poké Mart (from the start)	₽300
Pearl	A pretty pearl. It can be sold at shops for a low price.	Fishing spots / often held by wild Shellder	—
Pearl String	Very large pearls that sparkle in a pretty silver collar. It can be sold at shops for a high price.	Hano Beach / Poni Wilds / Fishing spots on Melemele Island	—
Pink Nectar	It changes the form of Oricorio.	Sparkling spots near the flowering shrubs in the middle of Royal Avenue	—
Pinsirite	When held, it allows Pinsir to Mega Evolve into Mega Pinsir during battle.	Get for 64 BP at the Battle Tree	64 BP
Pixie Plate	When held by a Pokémon, it boosts the power of Fairy-type moves by 20%. (When held by Arceus, it shifts Arceus's type to Fairy type.)	Buy at Antiquities of the Ages in Hau'oli shopping mall	₽10,000
Plume Fossil	A Pokémon Fossil. When restored, it becomes Archen.	Buy at Olivia's shop in Konikoni City 🌀	₽7,000
Poison Barb	When held by a Pokémon, it boosts the power of Poison-type moves by 20%.	Melemele Meadow	—
Poison Memory	When held by Silvally, its type changes to Poison type.	Receive from Gladion (after becoming Champion)	—
Poké Doll	Ensures that the holder can successfully run from a wild Pokémon encounter.	Receive from Lillie in Hau'oli City's Marina (after becoming Champion)	—
Poké Toy	Ensures that the holder can successfully run from a wild Pokémon encounter.	Buy a Toy Set at a goody shop in Festival Plaza	—
Potion	Restores the HP of one Pokémon by 20 points.	Buy at any Poké Mart (from the start)	₽200
Power Anklet	Halves the holder's Speed, but makes the Speed base stat easier to raise.	Get for 16 BP at the Battle Royal Dome	16 BP
Power Band	Halves the holder's Speed, but makes the Sp. Def base stat easier to raise.	Get for 16 BP at the Battle Royal Dome	16 BP
Power Belt	Halves the holder's Speed, but makes the Defense base stat easier to raise.	Get for 16 BP at the Battle Royal Dome	16 BP
Power Bracer	Halves the holder's Speed, but makes the Attack base stat easier to raise.	Get for 16 BP at the Battle Royal Dome	16 BP
Power Herb	The holder can immediately use a move that requires a one-turn charge. It goes away after use.	Poni Meadow	—
Power Lens	Halves the holder's Speed, but makes the Sp. Atk base stat easier to raise.	Get for 16 BP at the Battle Royal Dome	16 BP
Power Weight	Halves the holder's Speed, but makes the HP base stat easier to raise.	Get for 16 BP at the Battle Royal Dome	16 BP
PP Max	Increases the max number of PP as high as it will go.	Defeat all the Trainers on Route 15	—
PP Up	Increases the max number of PP by one level.	Route 16	—

Item	Description	Main way to obtain	Price
Pretty Wing	A beautiful feather. It can be sold at shops for a low price.	Sometimes dropped by Pokémon flying overhead on Route 3	—
Prism Scale	Link Trade Feebas while it holds the Prism Scale to evolve it into Milotic.	Exeggutor Island / Fishing spots on Ula'ula Island	—
Prison Bottle	A bottle believed to have been used to seal away the power of a certain Pokémon long, long ago.	Receive from an Aether Employee in Aether Paradise (after becoming Champion)	—
Protective Pads	These pads protect the holder from effects caused by making direct contact with the target.	Get for 48 BP at the Battle Tree	48 BP
Protector	Link Trade Rhydon while it holds the Protector to evolve it into Rhyperior.	Receive from Kiawe's father in his house in Paniola Town (after becoming Champion)	—
Protein	Raises the base Attack stat of a Pokémon.	Buy at the Poké Mart on Mount Hokulani	₽10,000
Psychic Memory	When held by Silvally, its type changes to Psychic type.	Receive from Gladion (after becoming Champion)	—
Psychic Seed	It boosts Sp. Def of a Pokémon on Psychic Terrain by 1 during battle. It can only be used once.	Sometimes held by wild Exeggcute	—
Pure Incense	Helps keep wild Pokémon away if the holder is the first one in the party.	Buy at the incense vendor in Konikoni City	₽6,000
Purple Nectar	It changes the form of Oricorio.	Sparkling spots in Poni Meadow	—
Quick Claw	Allows the holder to strike first sometimes.	Receive from a woman in the Trainers' School	—
Quick Powder	When held by Ditto, Speed doubles.	Often held by wild Ditto	—
Rage Candy Bar	Mahogany Town's famous snack. Heals all the status conditions and confusion of a Pokémon.	Buy a drink at the Pokémon Center café on a Tuesday	—
Rare Bone	A rare bone. It can be sold at shops for a high price.	Sometimes found by your Pokémon on Isle Aphun in Poké Pelago	—
Rare Candy	Raises a Pokémon's level by 1.	Brooklet Hill / Route 6 / Aether Paradise / Po Town	—
Razor Claw	Boosts the holder's critical-hit ratio.	Often held by wild Kommo-o	—
Razor Fang	When the holder hits a target with an attack, there is a 10% chance the target will flinch.	Sometimes held by wild Bruxish	—
Reaper Cloth	Link Trade Dusclops while it holds the Reaper Cloth to evolve it into Dusknoir.	Receive from the little girl in the Malie City Pokémon Center (after completing the Ula'ula grand trial)	—
Red Card	If the holder is hit by an attack that makes direct contact, the opposing Trainer is forced to switch out the attacking Pokémon. It goes away after use.	Defeat all the Trainers on Route 3	—
Red Nectar	It changes the form of Oricorio.	Sparkling spots in Ula'ula Meadow	—
Red Orb	A shiny red orb that is said to have a legend tied to it. It's known to have a deep connection with the Hoenn region.	Buy at Antiquities of the Ages in Hau'oli shopping mall	₽10,000
Red Shard	Can be exchanged for Bottle Caps in Festival Plaza.	Sometimes found by your Pokémon on Isle Aphun in Poké Pelago	—
Repel	Prevents weak wild Pokémon from appearing for a while after its use.	Buy at any Poké Mart (from the start)	₽400
Resist Wing	Slightly increases the base Defense stat of a single Pokémon. It can be used until the max of base stats.	Sometimes dropped on Ula'ula Island by Skarmory	—
Reveal Glass	A looking glass necessary to change Tornadus, Thundurus, and Landorus from Incarnate Forme into Therian Forme.	Receive from Professor Burnet at the Dimensional Research Lab (after completing the Akala grand trial)	—
Revival Herb	Revives a fainted Pokémon. Very bitter (lowers a Pokémon's friendship).	Buy at the herb vendor in Konikoni City	₽2,800
Revive	Revives a fainted Pokémon and restores half of its HP.	Buy at any Poké Mart (after completing 2 trials)	₽2,000
Ring Target	Moves that would otherwise have no effect will hit the holder.	Get for 16 BP at the Battle Tree	16 BP
Rock Incense	When held by a Pokémon, it boosts the power of Rock-type moves by 20%.	Buy at the incense vendor in Konikoni City	₽2,000
Rock Memory	When held by Silvally, its type changes to Rock type.	Receive from Gladion (after becoming Champion)	—
Rocky Helmet	When the bearer is hit with an attack that makes direct contact, it damages the attacker for 1/6 of its maximum HP.	Get for 48 BP at the Battle Tree	48 BP
Rose Incense	When held by a Pokémon, it boosts the power of Grass-type moves by 20%.	Buy at the incense vendor in Konikoni City	₽2,000
Sablenite	When held, it allows Sableye to Mega Evolve into Mega Sableye during battle.	Get for 64 BP at the Battle Tree	64 BP
Sachet	Link Trade Spritzee while it holds the Sachet to evolve it into Aromatisse.	Receive from the Punk Girl at Mallow's restaurant in Konikoni City (after becoming Champion)	—
Sacred Ash	Revives fainted Pokémon in a party and fully restores their HP.	Sometimes picked up by your Pokémon at a haunted house in Festival Plaza	—
Safety Goggles	Protect the holder from weather-related damage, from certain moves (Cotton Spore, Poison Powder, Powder, Rage Powder, Sleep Powder, Spore, and Stun Spore), and from the Effect Spore Ability.	Receive from the Hiker in Haina Desert at night (after completing the Ula'ula grand trial)	—
Salamencite	When held, it allows Salamence to Mega Evolve into Mega Salamence during battle.	Get for 64 BP at the Battle Tree	64 BP
Scizorite	When held, it allows Scizor to Mega Evolve into Mega Scizor during battle.	Get for 64 BP at the Battle Tree	64 BP
Scope Lens	Boosts the holder's critical-hit ratio.	Receive from a man after defeating his Tauros in Paniola Ranch	—
Sea Incense	When held by a Pokémon, it boosts the power of Water-type moves by 20%.	Buy at the incense vendor in Konikoni City	₽2,000
Shalour Sable	Shalour City's famous shortbread. It can be used once to heal all the status conditions and confusion of a Pokémon.	Buy a drink at the Pokémon Center café on a Friday	—
Sharp Beak	When held by a Pokémon, it boosts the power of Flying-type moves by 20%.	Route 3 / Sometimes held by wild Spearow or Fearow	—
Sharpedonite	When held, it allows Sharpedo to Mega Evolve into Mega Sharpedo during battle.	Get for 64 BP at the Battle Tree	64 BP
Shed Shell	Always allows the holder to be switched out.	Sometimes held by wild Goomy or Sliggoo	—
Shell Bell	Restores the holder's HP by up to 1/8th of the damage dealt to the target.	Receive from Delibird in the city hall in Hau'oli City (after completing the Melemele grand trial)	—
Shiny Charm	A shiny charm said to increase the change of finding a Shiny Pokémon in the wild.	Receive from the game director after completing the Alola Pokédex and showing it to him at GAME FREAK's office in Heahea City	—

Item	Description	Main way to obtain	Price
Shiny Stone	It can evolve Floette, Minccino, Togetic, and Roselia.	Ancient Poni Path	—
Shock Drive	When held by Genesect, it changes Genesect's Techno Blast move so it becomes Electric type.	Receive from Colress on Route 8 (after becoming Champion)	—
Silk Scarf	When held by a Pokémon, it boosts the power of Normal-type moves by 20%.	Receive from the woman outside the apparel shop in Hau'oli City	—
Silver Powder	When held by a Pokémon, it boosts the power of Bug-type moves by 20%.	Berry Fields	—
Skull Fossil	A Pokémon Fossil. When restored, it becomes Cranidos.	Buy at Olivia's shop in Konikoni City ☀	₽7,000
Sky Plate	When held by a Pokémon, it boosts the power of Flying-type moves by 20%. (When held by Arceus, it shifts Arceus's type to Flying type.)	Buy at Antiquities of the Ages in Hau'oli shopping mall	₽10,000
Slowbronite	When held, it allows Slowbro to Mega Evolve into Mega Slowbro during battle.	Get for 64 BP at the Battle Tree	64 BP
Smoke Ball	Allows the holder to successfully run away from wild Pokémon.	Po Town / Sometimes held by wild Salandit	—
Smooth Rock	Extends the duration of the sandstorm weather by three turns when held.	Receive from a woman after taking a quiz at the community center in Malie City	—
Snowball	Increases Attack by 1 when the holder is hit with Ice-type moves. It goes away after use.	Sometimes held by wild Snorunt or Vulpix	—
Soda Pop	Restores the HP of one Pokémon by 50 points.	Buy at a vending machine	Varies
Soft Sand	When held by a Pokémon, it boosts the power of Ground-type moves by 20%.	Melemele Sea / Sometimes held by wild Diglett or Dugtrio	—
Soothe Bell	The holder's friendship improves more quickly.	Receive from the Pokémon Breeder on Route 3	—
Soul Dew	When held by Latios or Latias, it boosts the power of Dragon- and Psychic-type moves by 20%.	Receive from an Aether Employee in Aether Paradise (after becoming Champion)	—
Spell Tag	When held by a Pokémon, it boosts the power of Ghost-type moves by 20%.	Memorial Hill / Sometimes held by wild Sandygast or Palossand	—
Splash Plate	When held by a Pokémon, it boosts the power of Water-type moves by 20%. (When held by Arceus, it shifts Arceus's type to Water type.)	Buy at Antiquities of the Ages in Hau'oli shopping mall	₽10,000
Spooky Plate	When held by a Pokémon, it boosts the power of Ghost-type moves by 20%. (When held by Arceus, it shifts Arceus's type to Ghost type.)	Hau'oli Cemetery	—
Star Piece	A red gem. It can be sold at shops for a high price.	Route 2 / Poni Plains	—
Stardust	Lovely, red-colored sand. It can be sold at shops for a low price.	Often held by wild Staryu or Starmie	—
Steel Memory	When held by Silvally, its type changes to Steel type.	Receive from Gladion (after becoming Champion)	—
Stick	When held by Farfetch'd, it raises the critical-hit ratio of its moves.	Receive from an Aether Employee in Aether Paradise	—
Sticky Barb	Damages the holder by 1/8 of its maximum HP every turn. It latches on to the attacker that touches the holder if the attacker doesn't have an item.	Fishing spots on Poni Island	—
Stone Plate	When held by a Pokémon, it boosts the power of Rock-type moves by 20%. (When held by Arceus, it shifts Arceus's type to Rock type.)	Buy at Antiquities of the Ages in Hau'oli shopping mall	₽10,000
Strange Souvenir	An ornament depicting a mysterious Pokémon that has been venerated as a guardian deity for an extremely long time in the Alola region.	Receive from the Gentleman in the community center in Malie City	—
Sun Stone	It can evolve Cottonee, Gloom, Helioptile, Petilil, and Sunkern.	Blush Mountain	—
Super Potion	Restores the HP of one Pokémon by 60 points.	Buy at any Poké Mart (after completing 1 trial)	₽700
Super Repel	Prevents weak wild Pokémon from appearing for a long while after its use.	Buy at any Poké Mart (after completing 3 trials)	₽700
Sweet Heart	Restores the HP of one Pokémon by 20 points.	Buy a drink at the Pokémon Center café on a Sunday	—
Swift Wing	Slightly increases the base Speed stat of a single Pokémon. It can be used until the max of base stats.	Sometimes dropped on Ula'ula and Poni Islands by Fearow	—
Terrain Extender	An item to be held by a Pokémon. It extends the effects of terrain by three turns.	Resolution Cave	—
Thick Club	When held by Cubone or Marowak, the power of Physical Moves is doubled.	Sometimes held by wild Cubone	—
Thunder Stone	It can evolve Eelektrik, Eevee, and Pikachu.	Buy at Olivia's jewelry shop in Konikoni City	₽3,000
Tiny Mushroom	A tiny mushroom. It can be sold at shops for a low price.	Route 11 / Hau'oli City Shopping District	—
Toxic Orb	Inflicts the Badly Poisoned status condition on the holder during battle.	Get for 16 BP at the Battle Tree	16 BP
Toxic Plate	When held by a Pokémon, it boosts the power of Poison-type moves by 20%. (When held by Arceus, it shifts Arceus's type to Poison type.)	Hau'oli City Shopping District	—
Twisted Spoon	When held by a Pokémon, it boosts the power of Psychic-type moves by 20%.	Receive from the Janitor after defeating him and his son in Malie City Outer Cape	—
Up-Grade	Link Trade Porygon while it holds the Up-Grade to evolve it into Porygon2.	Receive from an Aether Employee in Aether House (after completing the Ula'ula Grand Trial)	—
Venusaurite	When held, it allows Venusaur to Mega Evolve into Mega Venusaur during battle.	Defeat Red at the Battle Tree	—
Water Memory	When held by Silvally, its type changes to Water type.	Receive from Gladion (after becoming Champion)	—
Water Stone	It can evolve Eevee, Lombre, Panpour, Poliwhirl, Shellder, and Staryu.	Buy at Olivia's jewelry shop in Konikoni City	₽3,000
Wave Incense	When held by a Pokémon, it boosts the power of Water-type moves by 20%.	Buy at the incense vendor in Konikoni City	₽2,000
Weakness Policy	Increases Attack and Sp. Atk by 2 if the holder is hit with a move that it's weak to.	Get for 32 BP at the Battle Tree	32 BP
Whipped Dream	Link Trade Swirlix while it holds a Whipped Dream to evolve it into Slurpuff.	Receive from the Punk Girl at Mallow's restaurant in Konikoni City (after becoming Champion)	—
White Herb	Restores lowered stats. It goes away after use.	Get for 24 BP at the Battle Tree	24 BP
Wide Lens	Raises the holder's accuracy by 10%.	Talk to a Corsola in front of the Pokémon Research Lab (after obtaining a Fishing Rod)	—
Wise Glasses	When held by a Pokémon, it boosts the power of special moves by 10%.	Get for 48 BP at the Battle Royal Dome	48 BP
X Accuracy	Raises the accuracy of a Pokémon by 2 during battle.	Buy at the Poké Mart in Hau'oli City	₽1,000
X Attack	Raises the Attack stat of a Pokémon by 2 during battle.	Buy at the Poké Mart in Hau'oli City	₽1,000

HOW TO COMPLETE THE ALOLA POKÉDEX

CHAMPION'S GUIDE TO ALOLA

Item	Description	Main way to obtain	Price
X Defense	Raises the Defense stat of a Pokémon by 2 during battle.	Buy at the Poké Mart in Hau'oli City	₽2,000
X Sp. Atk	Raises the Sp. Atk stat of a Pokémon by 2 during battle.	Buy at the Poké Mart in Hau'oli City	₽1,000
X Sp. Def	Raises the Sp. Def stat of a Pokémon by 2 during battle.	Buy at the Poké Mart in Hau'oli City	₽2,000
X Speed	Raises the Speed of a Pokémon by 2 during battle.	Buy at the Poké Mart in Hau'oli City	₽1,000
Yellow Nectar	It changes the form of Oricorio.	Sparkling spots in Melemele Meadow	—
Yellow Shard	Can be exchanged for Bottle Caps in Festival Plaza.	Sometimes found by your Pokémon on Isle Aphun in Poké Pelago	—
Zap Plate	When held by a Pokémon, it boosts the power of Electric-type moves by 20%. (When held by Arceus, it shifts Arceus's type to Electric type.)	Buy at Antiquities of the Ages in Hau'oli shopping mall	₽10,000
Zinc	Raises the base Sp. Def stat of a Pokémon.	Buy at the Poké Mart on Mount Hokulani	₽10,000
Zoom Lens	Raises the holder's accuracy by 20% when it moves after the opposing Pokémon.	Get for 48 BP at the Battle Royal Dome	48 BP

Note: For a list of TMs and how to obtain them, turn to page 293. (A list of Z-Crystals and where to find them can be found in *Pokémon Sun* & *Pokémon Moon*: The Official Alola Region Strategy Guide.)

Poké Balls Available in Alola

Name	Description	Main Way to Obtain in Alola	Effect in Battle	Price
Poké Ball	Standard Poké Ball with a decent success rate	Buy it at the Thrifty Megamart on Royal Avenue or at any Poké Mart		₽100/200
Great Ball	High-performance Poké Ball with a high success rate	Buy it at the Thrifty Megamart on Royal Avenue or at any Poké Mart (after completing 1 trial)		₽300/600
Ultra Ball	Ultra high-performance Poké Ball with a very high success rate	Buy it at any Poké Mart (after completing 4 trials)		₽800
Master Ball	Guaranteed to catch any Pokémon	Receive one from Gladion		—
Luxury Ball	Quickly makes the caught Pokémon feel friendly toward you	Buy it at the Route 2 Poké Mart		₽1,000
Heal Ball	Restores HP and removes status conditions for the caught Pokémon	Buy it at the Thrifty Megamart on Royal Avenue or at the Route 2 Poké Mart		₽150/300
Nest Ball	Best for catching low-level Pokémon	Buy it at the Thrifty Megamart on Royal Avenue or at the Route 2 Poké Mart		₽500/1,000
Repeat Ball	Best for catching a Pokémon species you've caught before	Buy it at the Paniola Town Poké Mart		₽1,000
Net Ball	Best for catching Water- or Bug-type Pokémon	Buy it at the Paniola Town Poké Mart		₽1,000
Dive Ball	Best for catching Pokémon that live underwater	Buy it at the Route 8 Poké Mart		₽1,000
Dusk Ball	Best for catching Pokémon at night or in dark places like caves	Buy it at the Route 8 Poké Mart		₽1,000

Name	Description	Main Way to Obtain in Alola	Effect in Battle	Price
Quick Ball	Best for using at the very outset of a battle	Buy it at the Route 8 Poké Mart		₽1,000
Timer Ball	Best for using when a battle has lasted many turns	Buy it at the Thrifty Megamart on Royal Avenue or at the Paniola Town Poké Mart		₽500/1,000
Premier Ball	Rare Poké Ball made to celebrate an event of some sort	Buy 10 or more Poké Balls at a time		—
Fast Ball	Best for catching Pokémon that normally run away	Find one on Mount Hokulani		—
Level Ball	Best for catching Pokémon with a lower level than your Pokémon	Find one on Mount Hokulani		—
Lure Ball	Best for catching Pokémon found through fishing	Receive one from Samson Oak		—
Heavy Ball	Best for catching Pokémon that weigh a lot	Find one on Mount Hokulani		—
Love Ball	Best for catching Pokémon of the opposite gender to your Pokémon	Receive one from Samson Oak		—
Friend Ball	Immediately makes the caught Pokémon feel friendly toward you	Receive one from Samson Oak		—
Moon Ball	Best for catching Pokémon that evolve with a Moon Stone	Receive one from Samson Oak		—
Beast Ball	Best for catching Ultra Beasts	Receive from Wicke when assisting Looker after becoming Champion		—

Note: There are other Poké Balls that cannot be obtained in *Pokémon Sun* or *Pokémon Moon*. But if you obtain a Pokémon via a trade, special event, or other means, check out the special effects of other unique balls like Cherish Balls or Sport Balls when your Pokémon pop into battle!

Berries

	Name	Pokémon Effects	Dye Color	Avg. Hours to Grow	Typical Harvest	Main Way to Obtain in Alola
	Aguav Berry	Restores some HP when in a pinch, but confuses Pokémon that don't like bitter flavors	Dark Green	24	3-9	Berry tree on Route 4
	Apicot Berry	Raises the holder's Sp. Def when in a pinch	Pastel Navy Blue	72	2-8	Berry tree on Secluded Shore
	Aspear Berry	Allows a Pokémon to recover from being Frozen during battle	Dark Yellow	24	4-12	Berry tree on Secluded Shore
	Babiri Berry	Lessens the damage from one supereffective Steel-type attack when held	—	48	2-6	Central Berry tree in Poni Wilds
	Bluk Berry	An unusual Berry not normally found in the Alola region	—	24	4-12	Thrifty Megamart
	Charti Berry	Lessens the damage from one supereffective Rock-type attack when held	Dark Orange	48	2-6	Northwest Berry tree in Poni Wilds
	Cheri Berry	Allows a Pokémon to cure its own Paralysis during battle	Pastel Red	24	4-12	Berry tree on Route 3
	Chesto Berry	Allows a Pokémon to wake itself from being Asleep during battle	Pastel Navy Blue / Pastel Purple	24	4-12	Berry tree on Route 2
	Chilan Berry	Lessens the damage from one supereffective Normal-type attack when held	—	48	2-6	Northwest Berry tree in Poni Wilds
	Chople Berry	Lessens the damage from one supereffective Fighting-type attack when held	Dark Orange	48	2-6	Northwest Berry tree in Poni Wilds
	Coba Berry	Lessens the damage from one supereffective Flying-type attack when held	Dark Blue / Dark Navy Blue	48	2-6	Northeast Berry tree in Poni Wilds
	Colbur Berry	Lessens the damage from one supereffective Dark-type attack when held	Dark Purple	48	2-6	Northwest Berry tree in Poni Wilds
	Figy Berry	Restores some HP when in a pinch, but confuses Pokémon that don't like spicy flavors	Dark Red	24	3-9	Berry tree on Route 4
	Ganlon Berry	Raises the holder's Defense when in a pinch	Pastel Purple	72	2-8	Berry tree on Route 17
	Grepa Berry	Increases a Pokémon's friendship and lowers its base Sp. Def	Pastel Yellow	48	5-14	Berry tree on Route 10
	Haban Berry	Lessens the damage from one supereffective Dragon-type attack when held	—	48	2-6	Northeast Berry tree in Poni Wilds
	Hondew Berry	Increases a Pokémon's friendship and lowers its base Sp. Atk	Pastel Green	48	5-14	Berry tree on Route 10
	Iapapa Berry	Restores some HP when in a pinch, but confuses Pokémon that don't like sour flavors	Dark Yellow	24	3-9	Berry tree on Route 4
	Kasib Berry	Lessens the damage from one supereffective Ghost-type attack when held	Dark Purple	48	2-6	Northeast Berry tree in Poni Wilds
	Kebia Berry	Lessens the damage from one supereffective Poison-type attack when held	—	48	2-6	Northeast Berry tree in Poni Wilds
	Kee Berry	Increases the holder's Defense if hit with a physical move	Pastel Orange	72	2-8	Berry tree on Route 10
	Kelpsy Berry	Increases a Pokémon's friendship and lowers its base Attack	Pastel Blue / Pastel Navy Blue	48	5-14	Berry tree on Route 10
	Lansat Berry	Raises the holder's critical-hit ratio when in a pinch	—	72	2-4	Win 100 times in a row at the Battle Tree
	Leppa Berry	Allows a Pokémon to restore 10 PP to a move during battle	Pastel Orange	24	4-12	Berry tree on Route 2
	Liechi Berry	Raises the holder's Attack when in a pinch	Dark Red	72	2-8	Northeast Berry tree in Poni Wilds
	Lum Berry	Allows a Pokémon to recover from any status condition or confusion during battle	Pastel Green	48	4-10	Berry tree on Route 4
	Mago Berry	Restores some HP when in a pinch but confuses Pokémon that don't like sweet flavors	Pastel Pink / Dark Pink	24	3-9	Berry tree on Route 4 / Thrifty Megamart
	Maranga Berry	Increases the holder's Sp. Def if hit with a special move	Pastel Blue	72	2-8	Berry tree in Poni Plains
	Occa Berry	Lessens the damage from one supereffective Fire-type attack when held	Dark Red	48	2-6	Northwest Berry tree in Poni Wilds
	Oran Berry	Allows a Pokémon to recover 10 HP during battle	Pastel Blue	24	4-12	Berry tree in the Berry Fields / Thrifty Megamart
	Passho Berry	Lessens the damage from one supereffective Water-type attack when held	Dark Blue / Dark Navy Blue	48	2-6	Central Berry tree in Poni Wilds
	Payapa Berry	Lessens the damage from one supereffective Psychic-type attack when held	Dark Navy Blue / Dark Purple	48	2-6	Central Berry tree in Poni Wilds
	Pecha Berry	Allows a Pokémon to cure its own Poisoned condition during battle	Pastel Pink	24	4-12	Berry tree on Route 3
	Persim Berry	Allows a Pokémon to cure its own confusion during battle	Pastel Pink	24	4-12	Berry tree in the Berry Fields
	Petaya Berry	Raises the holder's Sp. Atk when in a pinch	Dark Pink	72	2-8	Central Berry tree in Poni Wilds
	Pinap Berry	An unusual Berry not normally found in the Alola region	—	24	4-12	Thrifty Megamart
	Pomeg Berry	Increases a Pokémon's friendship and lowers its base HP	Pastel Red	48	5-14	Berry tree on Route 10
	Qualot Berry	Increases a Pokémon's friendship and lowers its base Defense	Pastel Yellow	48	5-14	Berry tree on Route 10

	Name	Pokémon Effects	Dye Color	Avg. Hours to Grow	Typical Harvest	Main Way to Obtain in Alola
	Rawst Berry	Allows a Pokémon to cure its own Burned condition during battle	Pastel Green	24	4-12	Berry tree on Route 5 / Thrifty Megamart
	Rindo Berry	Lessens the damage from one supereffective Grass-type attack when held	Dark Green	48	2-6	Northeast Berry tree in Poni Wilds
	Roseli Berry	Lessens the damage from one supereffective Fairy-type attack when held	Dark Pink	48	2-6	Central Berry tree in Poni Wilds
	Salac Berry	Raises the holder's Speed when in a pinch	Dark Green	72	2-8	Northwest Berry tree in Poni Wilds
	Shuca Berry	Lessens the damage from one supereffective Ground-type attack when held	Dark Orange	48	2-6	Northwest Berry tree in Poni Wilds
	Sitrus Berry	Allows a Pokémon to recover a percentage of its max HP during battle	Pastel Yellow / Pastel Orange	48	5-15	Berry tree on Route 16 / Thrifty Megamart
	Starf Berry	Raises one of the holder's stats when in a pinch	—	72	2-4	Win 200 times in a row at the Battle Tree
	Tamato Berry	Increases a Pokémon's friendship and lowers its base Speed	Pastel Red	48	5-14	Thrifty Megamart
	Tanga Berry	Lessens the damage from one supereffective Bug-type attack when held	—	48	2-6	Northeast Berry tree in Poni Wilds
	Wacan Berry	Lessens the damage from one supereffective Electric-type attack when held	Dark Yellow	48	2-6	Central Berry tree in Poni Wilds
	Wiki Berry	Restores some HP when in a pinch, but confuses Pokémon that don't like dry flavors	Pastel Purple	24	3-9	Berry tree on Route 4
	Yache Berry	Lessens the damage from one supereffective Ice-type attack when held	Dark Blue	48	2-6	Central Berry tree in Poni Wilds

Berry Tree Locations

Island	Berries you can find there	Location		Crabrawler Encounters
Melemele	Oran, Persim	Berry Fields off of Route 2		—
Melemele	Oran, Chesto, Leppa, Persim, Sitrus	North of Pokémon Center on Route 2		△
Melemele	Chesto, Pecha, Cheri, Leppa, Sitrus	East end of Route 3		△
Akala	Pecha, Lum, Mago, Figy, Wiki, Aguav, Iapapa	North end of Route 4		△
Akala	Pecha, Cheri, Rawst, Persim, Lum	West side of Route 5		△
Akala	Oran, Chesto, Cheri, Pecha, Lum, Persim, Sitrus	Middle of Route 8		△
Ula'ula	Pomeg, Kelpsy, Qualot, Hondew, Grepa, Tamato, Kee	Middle of Route 10	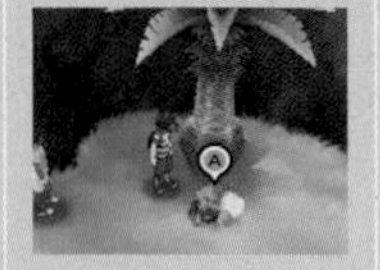	◎

Island	Berries you can find there	Location		Crabrawler Encounters
Ula'ula	Aspear, Cheri, Chesto, Leppa, Apicot	Off of Route 12		△
Ula'ula	Oran, Sitrus, Aspear, Pecha, Persim, Lum	West side of Route 16		△
Ula'ula	Sitrus, Leppa, Pecha, Rawst, Lum, Ganlon	North end of Route 17		△
Poni	Salac, Shuca, Chilan, Chople, Colbur, Charti, Occa	Northwest corner of Poni Wilds		△
Poni	Passho, Roseli, Yache, Wacan, Payapa, Babiri, Petaya	Center of Poni Wilds		△
Poni	Rindo, Kasib, Coba, Kebia, Tanga, Haban, Liechi	Northeast corner of Poni Wilds		△
Poni	Occa, Passho, Rindo, Wacan, Shuca, Yache, Maranga	Northwest corner of Poni Plains		◎

◎ frequent △ rare — never

Items Held by Wild Pokémon in Alola

Alola Pokédex No.	Pokémon Name	Often Holding	Sometimes Holding
10	Pikipek		Oran Berry
11	Trumbeak		Sitrus Berry
13	Yungoos		Pecha Berry
14	Gumshoos		Pecha Berry
15	Rattata		Pecha Berry
16	Raticate		Pecha Berry
19	Butterfree		Silver Powder
25	Pikachu		Light Ball
28	Charjabug		Cell Battery
32	Happiny	Oval Stone	
33	Chansey	Lucky Punch	
35	Munchlax	Leftovers	
36	Snorlax	Leftovers	
37	Slowpoke		Lagging Tail
38	Slowbro		King's Rock
40	Wingull	Pretty Wing	
41	Pelipper	Pretty Wing	
42	Abra		Twisted Spoon
45	Meowth		Quick Claw
47	Magnemite		Metal Coat
50	Grimer		Black Sludge
56	Makuhita		Black Belt
57	Hariyama		King's Rock
71	Diglett		Soft Sand
72	Dugtrio		Soft Sand
73	Spearow		Sharp Beak
74	Fearow		Sharp Beak
82	Oricorio		Honey
83	Cutiefly		Honey
84	Ribombee		Honey
85	Petilil		Absorb Bulb
87	Cottonee		Absorb Bulb
95	Machop		Focus Band
96	Machoke		Focus Band
98	Roggenrola	Everstone	Hard Stone
99	Boldore	Everstone	Hard Stone
102	Sableye		Wide Lens
106	Tentacool		Poison Barb
107	Tentacruel		Poison Barb
111	Luvdisc	Heart Scale	
112	Corsola		Luminous Moss
113	Mareanie		Poison Barb
115	Shellder	Pearl	Big Pearl
117	Bagon		Dragon Fang
118	Shelgon		Dragon Fang
119	Salamence		Dragon Fang
132	Mudbray		Light Clay
133	Mudsdale		Light Clay

Alola Pokédex No.	Pokémon Name	Often Holding	Sometimes Holding
135	Jigglypuff		Moon Stone
138	Miltank	Moomoo Milk	
140	Masquerain		Silver Powder
141	Dewpider		Mystic Water
142	Araquanid		Mystic Water
143	Fomantis		Miracle Seed
145	Morelull	Tiny Mushroom	Big Mushroom
147	Paras	Tiny Mushroom	Big Mushroom
150	Poliwhirl		King's Rock
152	Politoed		King's Rock
153	Goldeen		Mystic Water
154	Seaking		Mystic Water
161	Salandit		Smoke Ball
163	Cubone		Thick Club
166	Magby		Magmarizer
167	Magmar		Magmarizer
171	Bounsweet		Grassy Seed
174	Comfey		Misty Seed
178	Goomy		Shed Shell
179	Sliggoo		Shed Shell
181	Castform	Mystic Water	
184	Staryu	Stardust	Star Piece
185	Starmie	Stardust	Star Piece
186	Sandygast		Spell Tag
198	Nosepass		Magnet
201	Chinchou		Deep Sea Scale
206	Trubbish		Silk Scarf
207	Garbodor	Silk Scarf	Black Sludge
208	Skarmory		Metal Coat
209	Ditto	Quick Powder	Metal Powder
210	Cleffa		Moon Stone
211	Clefairy		Moon Stone
213	Minior		Star Piece
214	Beldum		Metal Coat
220	Pancham		Mental Herb
221	Pangoro		Mental Herb
223	Torkoal		Charcoal
224	Turtonator		Charcoal
225	Togedemaru		Electric Seed

Alola Pokédex No.	Pokémon Name	Often Holding	Sometimes Holding
226	Elekid		Electirizer
227	Electabuzz		Electirizer
229	Geodude		Cell Battery
230	Graveler		Cell Battery
232	Sandile		Black Glasses
235	Trapinch		Soft Sand
242	Mimikyu		Chesto Berry
243	Bruxish		Razor Fang
244	Drampa		Persim Berry
246	Snorunt		Snowball
249	Sneasel		Quick Claw
251	Sandshrew		Grip Claw
253	Vulpix		Snowball
255	Vanillite		Never-Melt Ice
256	Vanillish		Never-Melt Ice
262	Relicanth		Deep Sea Scale
264	Carvanha		Deep Sea Tooth
265	Sharpedo		Deep Sea Tooth
268	Lapras	Mystic Water	
269	Exeggcute		Psychic Seed
271	Jangmo-o		Razor Claw
272	Hakamo-o		Razor Claw
273	Kommo-o	Razor Claw	
281	Dratini		Dragon Scale
282	Dragonair		Dragon Scale
283	Dragonite		Dragon Scale

Pokémon Moves Reverse Lookup

The tables on the following pages allow you to look up which Pokémon can learn each of the moves available in the Alola region. Pokémon are listed in alphabetical order and prefaced by their Alola Pokédex number, so you can easily find them in the Pokédex pages found on pages 9 through 206 of this book. In the brackets following each Pokémon's name, you can quickly see how the Pokémon can learn a specific move. If you find a number, that means the Pokémon can learn the move when it reaches that level. You may also see a number of letters. TM means the Pokémon can learn the move from a Technical Machine, EV means the Pokémon can learn it by evolving, E means the Pokémon can learn it as an Egg Move, and T means that someone in the Alola region can teach the move to the Pokémon. Finally, you may see ZC after Zygarde—this indicates a move that Zygarde can learn from a Zygarde Core (p. 231).

Type	Move Name	Pokémon					
Grass	Absorb	023 Ariados [1, 5]	297 Celesteela [1]	087 Cottonee [1]	070 Crobat [1]	083 Cutiefly [1]	263 Dhelmise [1]
		069 Golbat [1]	180 Goodra [1, 5]	178 Goomy [5]	145 Morelull [1]	187 Palossand [1]	147 Paras [11]
		148 Parasect [1, 11]	085 Petilil [1]	084 Ribombee [1]	186 Sandygast [1]	146 Shiinotic [1]	179 Sliggoo [1, 5]
		022 Spinarak [5]	068 Zubat [1]				
Rock	Accelerock	104 Lycanroc (Midday Form) [1, EV]					
Poison	Acid	293 Nihilego [1]	106 Tentacool [10]	107 Tentacruel [1, 10]			
	Acid Armor	050 Alolan Grimer [43]	051 Alolan Muk [46]	178 Goomy [E]	260 Shellos [E]	256 Vanillish [31]	255 Vanillite [31]
		257 Vanilluxe [31]	124 Vaporeon [29]				
	Acid Spray	050 Alolan Grimer [15]	051 Alolan Muk [15]	207 Garbodor [12]	293 Nihilego [47]	106 Tentacool [22]	107 Tentacruel [22]
		206 Trubbish [12]					
Flying	Acrobatics (TM62)	192 Archen [28, TM]	193 Archeops [28, TM]	008 Brionne [TM]	019 Butterfree [TM]	297 Celesteela [TM]	028 Charjabug [19, TM]
		174 Comfey [TM]	070 Crobat [TM]	083 Cutiefly [TM]	003 Decidueye [TM]	065 Drifblim [TM]	064 Drifloon [TM]
		274 Emolga [30, TM]	159 Fletchinder [42, TM]	158 Fletchling [39, TM]	069 Golbat [TM]	027 Grubbin [19, TM]	006 Incineroar [TM]
		222 Komala [TM]	021 Ledian [TM]	020 Ledyba [TM]	004 Litten [TM]	292 Lunala [TM]	079 Mankey [TM]
		213 Minior [TM]	082 Oricorio [TM]	177 Passimian [TM]	007 Popplio [TM]	009 Primarina [TM]	080 Primeape [TM]
		084 Ribombee [TM]	162 Salazzle [TM]	276 Scizor [TM]	160 Talonflame [44, TM]	285 Tapu Koko [TM]	005 Torracat [TM]
		173 Tsareena [TM]	029 Vikavolt [19, TM]	068 Zubat [TM]			
Normal	Acupressure	171 Bounsweet [E]	106 Tentacool [E]				
Flying	Aerial Ace (TM40)	245 Absol [TM]	284 Aerodactyl [TM]	071 Alolan Diglett [TM]	072 Alolan Dugtrio [TM]	164 Alolan Marowak [TM]	045 Alolan Meowth [TM]
		046 Alolan Persian [TM]	251 Alolan Sandshrew [TM]	252 Alolan Sandslash [TM]	053 Arcanine [TM]	192 Archen [TM]	193 Archeops [TM]
		117 Bagon [TM]	170 Bewear [TM]	076 Braviary [23, TM]	243 Bruxish [TM]	019 Butterfree [TM]	070 Crobat [TM]
		163 Cubone [TM]	083 Cutiefly [TM]	081 Delibird [TM]	263 Dhelmise [TM]	283 Dragonite [TM]	274 Emolga [TM]
		074 Fearow [15, TM]	159 Fletchinder [TM]	158 Fletchling [TM]	237 Flygon [TM]	239 Gabite [TM]	240 Garchomp [TM]
		238 Gible [TM]	069 Golbat [TM]	090 Golduck [TM]	183 Golisopod [TM]	052 Growlithe [TM]	272 Hakamo-o [TM]
		121 Herdier [TM]	278 Honchkrow [TM]	271 Jangmo-o [TM]	165 Kangaskhan [TM]	298 Kartana [23, TM]	273 Kommo-o [TM]
		234 Krookodile [TM]	129 Leafeon [TM]	021 Ledian [TM]	020 Ledyba [TM]	120 Lillipup [TM]	292 Lunala [TM]
		144 Lurantis [TM]	078 Mandibuzz [TM]	079 Mankey [TM]	140 Masquerain [TM]	216 Metagross [TM]	215 Metang [TM]
		066 Misdreavus [TM]	067 Mismagius [TM]	277 Murkrow [TM]	300 Necrozma [TM]	082 Oricorio [TM]	220 Pancham [TM]
		221 Pangoro [TM]	147 Paras [TM]	148 Parasect [TM]	177 Passimian [TM]	041 Pelipper [TM]	010 Pikipek [TM]
		217 Porygon [TM]	218 Porygon2 [TM]	219 Porygon-Z [TM]	080 Primeape [TM]	089 Psyduck [TM]	084 Ribombee [TM]
		075 Rufflet [23, TM]	102 Sableye [TM]	119 Salamence [TM]	276 Scizor [TM]	275 Scyther [TM]	118 Shelgon [TM]
		204 Silvally [20, TM]	208 Skarmory [TM]	038 Slowbro [TM]	249 Sneasel [TM]	073 Spearow [15, TM]	122 Stoutland [TM]
		169 Stufful [TM]	160 Talonflame [TM]	285 Tapu Koko [TM]	012 Toucannon [TM]	011 Trumbeak [TM]	203 Type: Null [20, TM]
		077 Vullaby [TM]	250 Weavile [TM]	040 Wingull [29, TM]	068 Zubat [TM]		
Normal	After You	211 Clefairy [58]	174 Comfey [E]	120 Lillipup [E]	035 Munchlax [E]	176 Oranguru [4]	085 Petilil [44]
		036 Snorlax [E]					
Psychic	Agility	284 Aerodactyl [17]	253 Alolan Vulpix [E]	192 Archen [21]	193 Archeops [21]	023 Ariados [37]	264 Carvanha [39]
		201 Chinchou [E]	282 Dragonair [25]	283 Dragonite [25]	281 Dratini [25]	274 Emolga [46]	074 Fearow [27]
		108 Finneon [E]	159 Fletchinder [13]	158 Fletchling [13]	153 Goldeen [29]	052 Growlithe [30]	125 Jolteon [29]
		021 Ledian [33]	020 Ledyba [29]	111 Luvdisc [7]	216 Metagross [41]	215 Metang [41]	082 Oricorio [46]
		147 Paras [E]	295 Pheromosa [37]	025 Pikachu [45]	217 Porygon [12]	218 Porygon2 [12]	219 Porygon-Z [12]
		279 Riolu [E]	276 Scizor [17]	275 Scyther [17]	154 Seaking [29]	265 Sharpedo [45]	208 Skarmory [31]
		249 Sneasel [20]	073 Spearow [25]	022 Spinarak [33]	139 Surskit [22]	160 Talonflame [13]	285 Tapu Koko [53]
		029 Vikavolt [49]	040 Wingull [36, E]				
Flying	Air Cutter	070 Crobat [19]	069 Golbat [19]	298 Kartana [1]	140 Masquerain [22]	082 Oricorio [13]	208 Skarmory [12]
		040 Wingull [22]	068 Zubat [19]				

Type	Move Name	Pokémon					
Flying	Air Slash	076 Braviary [41]	019 Butterfree [43]	297 Celesteela [1]	070 Crobat [48]	274 Emolga [E]	069 Golbat [48]
		298 Kartana [59]	021 Ledian [42]	020 Ledyba [36]	292 Lunala [19]	078 Mandibuzz [41]	140 Masquerain [38]
		082 Oricorio [36]	075 Rufflet [41]	275 Scyther [50]	204 Silvally [60]	208 Skarmory [45]	203 Type: Null [60]
		029 Vikavolt [1]	077 Vullaby [41]	040 Wingull [40]	068 Zubat [41]		
	Ally Switch	042 Abra [E]	044 Alakazam [36]	192 Archen [E]	043 Kadabra [36]		
Psychic	Amnesia	045 Alolan Meowth [E]	251 Alolan Sandshrew [E]	093 Barboach [15]	181 Castform [E]	201 Chinchou [E]	210 Cleffa [E]
		174 Comfey [E]	112 Corsola [E]	059 Crabrawler [E]	065 Drifblim [46]	064 Drifloon [40]	207 Garbodor [46]
		090 Golduck [41]	145 Morelull [E]	035 Munchlax [9]	007 Popplio [E]	089 Psyduck [37]	262 Relicanth [E]
		186 Sandygast [E]	260 Shellos [E]	038 Slowbro [43]	037 Slowpoke [41]	036 Snorlax [9]	223 Torkoal [40]
		206 Trubbish [40]	266 Wailmer [37]	267 Wailord [37]	094 Whiscash [15]		
Steel	Anchor Shot	263 Dhelmise [32]					
Rock	Ancient Power	284 Aerodactyl [25]	071 Alolan Diglett [E]	192 Archen [18]	193 Archeops [18]	191 Bastiodon [28]	101 Carbink [31]
		195 Carracosta [18]	264 Carvanha [E]	112 Corsola [17]	188 Cranidos [33]	163 Cubone [E]	269 Exeggcute [E]
		268 Lapras [E]	213 Minior [17]	189 Rampardos [36]	262 Relicanth [21]	186 Sandygast [E]	190 Shieldon [28]
		194 Tirtouga [18]					
Water	Aqua Jet	157 Alomomola [9]	008 Brionne [15]	243 Bruxish [17]	195 Carracosta [15]	264 Carvanha [11]	281 Dratini [E]
		090 Golduck [1]	111 Luvdisc [E]	007 Popplio [15]	009 Primarina [15]	265 Sharpedo [11]	139 Surskit [30, E]
		194 Tirtouga [15]	182 Wimpod [E]				
	Aqua Ring	157 Alomomola [5]	142 Araquanid [26]	201 Chinchou [42]	112 Corsola [38, E]	141 Dewpider [24]	108 Finneon [33]
		153 Goldeen [21]	202 Lanturn [47]	109 Lumineon [35]	111 Luvdisc [40, E]	156 Milotic [17]	007 Popplio [E]
		154 Seaking [21]	115 Shellder [E]	288 Tapu Fini [53]	106 Tentacool [E]	134 Vaporeon [25]	266 Wailmer [E]
		040 Wingull [E]	110 Wishiwashi [17]				
	Aqua Tail	093 Barboach [28]	243 Bruxish [33]	195 Carracosta [45]	282 Dragonair [39]	283 Dragonite [39]	281 Dratini [35]
		108 Finneon [E]	153 Goldeen [E]	090 Golduck [28]	180 Goodra [1, EV]	092 Gyarados [30]	156 Milotic [31]
		089 Psyduck [28]	262 Relicanth [E]	194 Tirtouga [41]	094 Whiscash [28]	110 Wishiwashi [38]	
Fighting	Arm Thrust	057 Hariyama [1, 7]	056 Makuhita [7]	220 Pancham [7]	221 Pangoro [1, 7]		
Grass	Aromatherapy	033 Chansey [E]	210 Cleffa [E]	174 Comfey [43]	083 Cutiefly [36]	143 Fomantis [E]	032 Happiny [E]
		147 Paras [43]	148 Parasect [51]	085 Petilil [28]	084 Ribombee [42]	172 Steenee [41]	286 Tapu Lele [1]
		173 Tsareena [41]					
Fairy	Aromatic Mist	171 Bounsweet [33]	007 Popplio [E]	172 Steenee [33]	286 Tapu Lele [1]	173 Tsareena [33]	
Normal	Assist	045 Alolan Meowth [E]	054 Drowzee [E]	249 Sneasel [E]	105 Spinda [E]		
Dark	Assurance	245 Absol [E]	284 Aerodactyl [E]	050 Alolan Grimer [E]	045 Alolan Meowth [41]	046 Alolan Persian [49]	016 Alolan Raticate [19]
		015 Alolan Rattata [19]	264 Carvanha [15]	188 Cranidos [24]	074 Fearow [23]	233 Krokorok [16]	234 Krookodile [16]
		079 Mankey [26]	277 Murkrow [25, E]	080 Primeape [26]	189 Rampardos [24]	232 Sandile [16]	265 Sharpedo [15]
		208 Skarmory [E]	073 Spearow [22]	128 Umbreon [25]	250 Weavile [1]		
Ghost	Astonish	071 Alolan Diglett [7]	072 Alolan Dugtrio [7]	243 Bruxish [4]	070 Crobat [1, 7]	002 Dartrix [11]	003 Decidueye [11]
		263 Dhelmise [1]	065 Drifblim [1, 4]	064 Drifloon [4]	274 Emolga [E]	248 Froslass [19]	061 Gastly [E]
		069 Golbat [1, 7]	278 Honchkrow [1]	241 Klefki [8]	242 Mimikyu [1]	066 Misdreavus [10]	067 Mismagius [1]
		145 Morelull [4]	277 Murkrow [1]	187 Palossand [1, 5]	196 Phantump [5]	001 Rowlet [11]	102 Sableye [9]
		186 Sandygast [5]	146 Shiinotic [1, 4]	073 Spearow [E]	286 Tapu Lele [1]	197 Trevenant [1, 5]	256 Vanillish [1, 7]
		255 Vanillite [7]	257 Vanilluxe [1, 7]	266 Wailmer [16]	267 Wailord [16]	068 Zubat [7]	
Normal	Attract (TM45)	042 Abra [TM]	245 Absol [TM]	284 Aerodactyl [TM]	044 Alakazam [TM]	071 Alolan Diglett [TM]	072 Alolan Dugtrio [TM]
		270 Alolan Exeggutor [TM]	229 Alolan Geodude [TM]	231 Alolan Golem [TM]	230 Alolan Graveler [TM]	050 Alolan Grimer [TM]	164 Alolan Marowak [TM]
		045 Alolan Meowth [TM]	051 Alolan Muk [TM]	254 Alolan Ninetales [TM]	046 Alolan Persian [TM]	026 Alolan Raichu [TM]	016 Alolan Raticate [TM]
		015 Alolan Rattata [TM]	251 Alolan Sandshrew [TM]	252 Alolan Sandslash [TM]	253 Alolan Vulpix [TM]	157 Alomomola [TM]	142 Araquanid [TM]
		053 Arcanine [TM]	192 Archen [TM]	193 Archeops [TM]	023 Ariados [TM]	117 Bagon [TM]	093 Barboach [TM]
		191 Bastiodon [TM]	170 Bewear [TM]	034 Blissey [TM]	099 Boldore [TM]	030 Bonsly [TM]	171 Bounsweet [TM]
		076 Braviary [TM]	008 Brionne [TM]	243 Bruxish [TM]	019 Butterfree [TM]	195 Carracosta [TM]	264 Carvanha [TM]
		181 Castform [TM]	033 Chansey [TM]	028 Charjabug [TM]	201 Chinchou [TM]	212 Clefable [TM]	211 Clefairy [TM]
		210 Cleffa [TM]	116 Cloyster [TM]	174 Comfey [TM]	112 Corsola [TM]	087 Cottonee [TM]	060 Crabominable [TM]
		059 Crabrawler [TM]	188 Cranidos [TM]	070 Crobat [TM]	163 Cubone [TM]	083 Cutiefly [TM]	002 Dartrix [TM]
		003 Decidueye [TM]	081 Delibird [TM]	141 Dewpider [TM]	263 Dhelmise [TM]	282 Dragonair [TM]	283 Dragonite [TM]
		244 Drampa [TM]	281 Dratini [TM]	065 Drifblim [TM]	064 Drifloon [TM]	054 Drowzee [TM]	123 Eevee [TM]
		227 Electabuzz [TM]	228 Electivire [TM]	226 Elekid [TM]	274 Emolga [TM]	127 Espeon [TM]	269 Exeggcute [TM]
		074 Fearow [TM]	155 Feebas [TM]	108 Finneon [10, TM]	126 Flareon [TM]	159 Fletchinder [TM]	158 Fletchling [TM]
		237 Flygon [TM]	143 Fomantis [TM]	248 Froslass [TM]	239 Gabite [TM]	207 Garbodor [TM]	240 Garchomp [TM]
		061 Gastly [TM]	261 Gastrodon [TM]	063 Gengar [TM]	238 Gible [TM]	100 Gigalith [TM]	130 Glaceon [TM]
		247 Glalie [TM]	069 Golbat [TM]	153 Goldeen [TM]	090 Golduck [TM]	183 Golisopod [TM]	180 Goodra [TM]
		178 Goomy [TM]	259 Granbull [TM]	052 Growlithe [TM]	027 Grubbin [TM]	014 Gumshoos [TM]	092 Gyarados [TM]
		272 Hakamo-o [TM]	032 Happiny [TM]	057 Hariyama [TM]	062 Haunter [TM]	121 Herdier [TM]	278 Honchkrow [TM]
		055 Hypno [TM]	134 Igglybuff [TM]	006 Incineroar [TM]	271 Jangmo-o [TM]	135 Jigglypuff [TM]	125 Jolteon [TM]

Type	Move Name	Pokémon					
Normal	Attract (TM45)	043 Kadabra [TM]	165 Kangaskhan [TM]	241 Klefki [TM]	222 Komala [TM]	273 Kommo-o [TM]	233 Krokorok [TM]
		234 Krookodile [TM]	202 Lanturn [TM]	268 Lapras [TM]	129 Leafeon [TM]	021 Ledian [TM]	020 Ledyba [TM]
		086 Lilligant [TM]	120 Lillipup [TM]	004 Litten [TM]	280 Lucario [TM]	109 Lumineon [1, 10, TM]	144 Lurantis [TM]
		111 Luvdisc [20, TM]	104 Lycanroc (Midday Form) [TM]	104 Lycanroc (Midnight Form) [TM]	097 Machamp [TM]	096 Machoke [TM]	095 Machop [TM]
		166 Magby [TM]	167 Magmar [TM]	168 Magmortar [TM]	056 Makuhita [TM]	078 Mandibuzz [TM]	079 Mankey [TM]
		113 Mareanie [TM]	140 Masquerain [TM]	156 Milotic [34, TM]	138 Miltank [TM]	242 Mimikyu [TM]	213 Minior [TM]
		066 Misdreavus [TM]	067 Mismagius [TM]	145 Morelull [TM]	132 Mudbray [TM]	133 Mudsdale [TM]	035 Munchlax [TM]
		277 Murkrow [TM]	198 Nosepass [TM]	082 Oricorio [TM]	187 Palossand [TM]	220 Pancham [TM]	221 Pangoro [TM]
		147 Paras [TM]	148 Parasect [TM]	177 Passimian [TM]	041 Pelipper [TM]	085 Petilil [TM]	196 Phantump [TM]
		024 Pichu [TM]	025 Pikachu [TM]	010 Pikipek [TM]	175 Pinsir [TM]	152 Politoed [TM]	149 Poliwag [TM]
		150 Poliwhirl [TM]	151 Poliwrath [TM]	007 Popplio [TM]	009 Primarina [TM]	080 Primeape [TM]	199 Probopass [TM]
		089 Psyduck [TM]	200 Pyukumuku [TM]	189 Rampardos [TM]	262 Relicanth [TM]	084 Ribombee [TM]	279 Riolu [TM]
		103 Rockruff [TM]	098 Roggenrola [TM]	001 Rowlet [TM]	075 Rufflet [TM]	102 Sableye [TM]	119 Salamence [TM]
		161 Salandit [TM]	162 Salazzle [TM]	232 Sandile [TM]	186 Sandygast [TM]	276 Scizor [TM]	275 Scyther [TM]
		154 Seaking [TM]	265 Sharpedo [TM]	118 Shelgon [TM]	115 Shellder [TM]	260 Shellos [TM]	190 Shieldon [TM]
		146 Shiinotic [TM]	208 Skarmory [TM]	179 Sliggoo [TM]	038 Slowbro [TM]	039 Slowking [TM]	037 Slowpoke [TM]
		249 Sneasel [TM]	036 Snorlax [TM]	246 Snorunt [TM]	258 Snubbull [TM]	073 Spearow [TM]	022 Spinarak [TM]
		105 Spinda [TM]	172 Steenee [TM]	122 Stoutland [TM]	169 Stufful [TM]	031 Sudowoodo [TM]	139 Surskit [TM]
		131 Sylveon [TM]	160 Talonflame [TM]	137 Tauros [TM]	106 Tentacool [TM]	107 Tentacruel [TM]	194 Tirtouga [TM]
		225 Togedemaru [TM]	223 Torkoal [TM]	005 Torracat [TM]	012 Toucannon [TM]	114 Toxapex [TM]	235 Trapinch [TM]
		197 Trevenant [TM]	206 Trubbish [TM]	011 Trumbeak [TM]	173 Tsareena [TM]	224 Turtonator [TM]	128 Umbreon [TM]
		256 Vanillish [TM]	255 Vanillite [TM]	257 Vanilluxe [TM]	124 Vaporeon [TM]	236 Vibrava [TM]	029 Vikavolt [TM]
		077 Vullaby [TM]	266 Wailmer [TM]	267 Wailord [TM]	250 Weavile [TM]	088 Whimsicott [TM]	094 Whiscash [TM]
		136 Wigglytuff [TM]	182 Wimpod [TM]	040 Wingull [TM]	110 Wishiwashi [TM]	013 Yungoos [TM]	068 Zubat [TM]
Fighting	Aura Sphere	280 Lucario [1, EV]	301 Magearna [81]				
Ice	Aurora Beam	253 Alolan Vulpix [28]	116 Cloyster [1]	081 Delibird [E]	141 Dewpider [E]	108 Finneon [E]	301 Magearna [17]
		115 Shellder [37]	106 Tentacool [E]	124 Vaporeon [20]			
	Aurora Veil (TM70)	254 Alolan Ninetales [TM]	251 Alolan Sandshrew [TM]	252 Alolan Sandslash [TM]	253 Alolan Vulpix [TM]	081 Delibird [TM]	248 Froslass [TM]
		130 Glaceon [TM]					
Steel	Autotomize	229 Alolan Geodude [E]	297 Celesteela [43]	272 Hakamo-o [1]	273 Kommo-o [1]	213 Minior [31]	300 Necrozma [47]
		098 Roggenrola [E]	208 Skarmory [50]	255 Vanillite [E]			
Ice	Avalanche	060 Crabominable [29]	268 Lapras [E]	115 Shellder [E]	249 Sneasel [E]	246 Snorunt [E]	256 Vanillish [19]
		255 Vanillite [19]	257 Vanilluxe [19]				
Fairy	Baby-Doll Eyes	253 Alolan Vulpix [9]	170 Bewear [10]	008 Brionne [11]	123 Eevee [9]	127 Espeon [9]	126 Flareon [9]
		130 Glaceon [9]	125 Jolteon [9]	129 Leafeon [9]	120 Lillipup [10]	242 Mimikyu [10]	007 Popplio [11]
		009 Primarina [11]	169 Stufful [10]	131 Sylveon [9]	128 Umbreon [9]	124 Vaporeon [9]	
Poison	Baneful Bunker	114 Toxapex [1, EV]					
Normal	Barrage	270 Alolan Exeggutor [1]	269 Exeggcute [1]				
Psychic	Barrier	042 Abra [E]	112 Corsola [E]	054 Drowzee [E]	226 Elekid [E]	130 Glaceon [29]	166 Magby [E]
		049 Magnezone [1]	115 Shellder [E]	106 Tentacool [28]	107 Tentacruel [28]		
Normal	Baton Pass	245 Absol [E]	083 Cutiefly [E]	065 Drifblim [52]	064 Drifloon [44]	123 Eevee [33]	274 Emolga [E]
		021 Ledian [29]	020 Ledyba [26]	082 Oricorio [16]	200 Pyukumuku [1]	001 Rowlet [E]	275 Scyther [E]
		022 Spinarak [E]	105 Spinda [E]	139 Surskit [35]			
Flying	Beak Blast	012 Toucannon [1, EV]					
Dark	Beat Up	071 Alolan Diglett [E]	087 Cottonee [E]	079 Mankey [E]	177 Passimian [15]	232 Sandile [E]	249 Sneasel [28]
		110 Wishiwashi [33]					
Poison	Belch	050 Alolan Grimer [46]	051 Alolan Muk [52]	207 Garbodor [49]	299 Guzzlord [1]	166 Magby [E]	138 Miltank [E]
		035 Munchlax [E]	161 Salandit [E]	037 Slowpoke [E]	036 Snorlax [E]	206 Trubbish [42]	094 Whiscash [1]
	Belly Drum	210 Cleffa [E]	163 Cubone [E]	057 Hariyama [26]	273 Kommo-o [1]	166 Magby [E]	056 Makuhita [25]
		035 Munchlax [44]	149 Poliwag [31]	150 Poliwhirl [37]	037 Slowpoke [E]	036 Snorlax [44]	
	Bestow	034 Blissey [20]	033 Chansey [20]	211 Clefairy [19]	083 Cutiefly [E]	081 Delibird [E]	269 Exeggcute [50]
		177 Passimian [25]	196 Phantump [E]	024 Pichu [E]	200 Pyukumuku [E]		
Normal	Bide	251 Alolan Sandshrew [3]	170 Bewear [5]	195 Carracosta [1]	112 Corsola [E]	237 Flygon [1]	180 Goodra [13]
		178 Goomy [13]	014 Gumshoos [16]	272 Hakamo-o [1, 9]	271 Jangmo-o [9]	273 Kommo-o [1, 9]	020 Ledyba [E]
		138 Miltank [15]	132 Mudbray [22]	133 Mudsdale [22]	085 Petilil [E]	024 Pichu [E]	200 Pyukumuku [1]
		179 Sliggoo [13]	246 Snorunt [E]	169 Stufful [5]	194 Tirtouga [1, E]	235 Trapinch [1]	236 Vibrava [1]
		013 Yungoos [16]					
	Bind	170 Bewear [EV]	175 Pinsir [4]	205 Zygarde [18]			
Dark	Bite	245 Absol [16]	284 Aerodactyl [1]	050 Alolan Grimer [7]	045 Alolan Meowth [6]	051 Alolan Muk [1, 7]	046 Alolan Persian [1, 6]
		016 Alolan Raticate [10]	015 Alolan Rattata [10]	142 Araquanid [21]	053 Arcanine [1]	192 Archen [E]	117 Bagon [10]
		243 Bruxish [12]	195 Carracosta [8]	264 Carvanha [1]	028 Charjabug [1, 10]	070 Crobat [1, 11]	141 Dewpider [21]

ALOLA REGION POKÉDEX

HOW TO COMPLETE THE ALOLA POKÉDEX

CHAMPION'S GUIDE TO ALOLA

ADVENTURE DATA

Type	Move Name	Pokémon					
Dark	Bite	123 Eevee [17]	126 Flareon [17]	130 Glaceon [17]	247 Glalie [19]	069 Golbat [1, 11]	259 Granbull [7]
		052 Growlithe [1]	027 Grubbin [10]	014 Gumshoos [19]	299 Guzzlord [1]	092 Gyarados [1, EV]	121 Herdier [1, 8]
		006 Incineroar [24]	165 Kangaskhan [13]	233 Krokorok [1, 4]	234 Krookodile [1, 4]	120 Lillipup [8]	004 Litten [22]
		104 Lycanroc (Midday Form) [1, 7]	104 Lycanroc (Midnight Form) [1, 7]	113 Mareanie [9]	279 Riolu [E]	103 Rockruff [7]	119 Salamence [1, 10]
		232 Sandile [4]	265 Sharpedo [1]	118 Shelgon [1, 10]	204 Silvally [15]	249 Sneasel [E]	246 Snorunt [19]
		258 Snubbull [7]	122 Stoutland [1, 8]	194 Tirtouga [8]	005 Torracat [24]	114 Toxapex [1, 9]	235 Trapinch [1]
		029 Vikavolt [1, 10]	013 Yungoos [19]	068 Zubat [11]	205 Zygarde [1]		
Fire	Blast Burn	006 Incineroar [T]					
Fire	Blaze Kick	279 Riolu [E]					
Ice	Blizzard (TM14)	245 Absol [TM]	164 Alolan Marowak [TM]	254 Alolan Ninetales [TM]	016 Alolan Raticate [TM]	015 Alolan Rattata [TM]	251 Alolan Sandshrew [46, TM]
		252 Alolan Sandslash [TM]	253 Alolan Vulpix [42, TM]	157 Alomomola [TM]	142 Araquanid [TM]	093 Barboach [TM]	191 Bastiodon [TM]
		034 Blissey [TM]	008 Brionne [TM]	243 Bruxish [TM]	195 Carracosta [TM]	264 Carvanha [TM]	181 Castform [35, TM]
		033 Chansey [TM]	201 Chinchou [TM]	212 Clefable [TM]	211 Clefairy [TM]	116 Cloyster [TM]	112 Corsola [TM]
		060 Crabominable [TM]	188 Cranidos [TM]	163 Cubone [TM]	081 Delibird [TM]	141 Dewpider [TM]	282 Dragonair [TM]
		283 Dragonite [TM]	244 Drampa [TM]	281 Dratini [TM]	155 Feebas [TM]	108 Finneon [TM]	248 Froslass [48, TM]
		261 Gastrodon [TM]	130 Glaceon [45, TM]	247 Glalie [48, TM]	153 Goldeen [TM]	090 Golduck [TM]	183 Golisopod [TM]
		180 Goodra [TM]	092 Gyarados [TM]	135 Jigglypuff [TM]	165 Kangaskhan [TM]	202 Lanturn [TM]	268 Lapras [TM]
		109 Lumineon [TM]	292 Lunala [TM]	111 Luvdisc [TM]	113 Mareanie [TM]	140 Masquerain [TM]	156 Milotic [TM]
		138 Miltank [TM]	035 Munchlax [TM]	041 Pelipper [TM]	295 Pheromosa [TM]	152 Politoed [TM]	149 Poliwag [TM]
		150 Poliwhirl [TM]	151 Poliwrath [TM]	007 Popplio [TM]	217 Porygon [TM]	218 Porygon2 [TM]	219 Porygon-Z [TM]
		009 Primarina [TM]	089 Psyduck [TM]	189 Rampardos [TM]	262 Relicanth [TM]	154 Seaking [TM]	265 Sharpedo [TM]
		115 Shellder [TM]	260 Shellos [TM]	190 Shieldon [TM]	179 Sliggoo [TM]	038 Slowbro [TM]	039 Slowking [TM]
		037 Slowpoke [TM]	249 Sneasel [TM]	036 Snorlax [TM]	246 Snorunt [46, TM]	185 Starmie [TM]	184 Staryu [TM]
		139 Surskit [TM]	288 Tapu Fini [TM]	137 Tauros [TM]	106 Tentacool [TM]	107 Tentacruel [TM]	194 Tirtouga [TM]
		114 Toxapex [TM]	256 Vanillish [53, TM]	255 Vanillite [49, TM]	257 Vanilluxe [59, TM]	124 Vaporeon [TM]	266 Wailmer [TM]
		267 Wailord [TM]	250 Weavile [TM]	094 Whiscash [TM]	136 Wigglytuff [TM]	040 Wingull [TM]	
Normal	Block	229 Alolan Geodude [E]	191 Bastiodon [1, EV]	030 Bonsly [29]	269 Exeggcute [E]	198 Nosepass [7, E]	199 Probopass [1, 7]
		037 Slowpoke [E]	036 Snorlax [41]	246 Snorunt [E]	031 Sudowoodo [29]		
Normal	Body Slam	211 Clefairy [40]	064 Drifloon [E]	207 Garbodor [25]	261 Gastrodon [29]	238 Gible [E]	153 Goldeen [E]
		180 Goodra [32]	178 Goomy [32]	052 Growlithe [E]	135 Jigglypuff [32]	268 Lapras [18]	004 Litten [E]
		138 Miltank [24]	132 Mudbray [E]	035 Munchlax [25]	220 Pancham [33]	221 Pangoro [35]	149 Poliwag [21]
		150 Poliwhirl [21]	260 Shellos [29]	190 Shieldon [E]	179 Sliggoo [32]	036 Snorlax [25]	194 Tirtouga [E]
		223 Torkoal [27]	224 Turtonator [33]	266 Wailmer [E]			
Ground	Bone Club	164 Alolan Marowak [1, 7]	163 Cubone [7]				
Ground	Bone Rush	164 Alolan Marowak [65]	163 Cubone [51]	280 Lucario [29]	078 Mandibuzz [1, EV]		
Ground	Bonemerang	164 Alolan Marowak [21]	163 Cubone [21]				
Normal	Boomburst	010 Pikipek [E]	236 Vibrava [47]				
Flying	Bounce	108 Finneon [45]	109 Lumineon [53]	295 Pheromosa [29]	152 Politoed [37]	266 Wailmer [45]	267 Wailord [51]
Flying	Brave Bird	076 Braviary [1, 63]	002 Dartrix [51]	003 Decidueye [55]	078 Mandibuzz [1, 63]	277 Murkrow [E]	010 Pikipek [E]
		001 Rowlet [43]	075 Rufflet [59]	208 Skarmory [E]	160 Talonflame [1, 64]	285 Tapu Koko [1]	077 Vullaby [59]
		068 Zubat [E]					
Fighting	Brick Break (TM31)	270 Alolan Exeggutor [TM]	229 Alolan Geodude [TM]	231 Alolan Golem [TM]	230 Alolan Graveler [TM]	164 Alolan Marowak [TM]	051 Alolan Muk [TM]
		026 Alolan Raichu [TM]	251 Alolan Sandshrew [TM]	252 Alolan Sandslash [TM]	117 Bagon [TM]	170 Bewear [TM]	034 Blissey [TM]
		030 Bonsly [TM]	294 Buzzwole [TM]	033 Chansey [TM]	212 Clefable [TM]	211 Clefairy [TM]	060 Crabominable [TM]
		059 Crabrawler [TM]	163 Cubone [TM]	081 Delibird [TM]	263 Dhelmise [TM]	283 Dragonite [TM]	054 Drowzee [TM]
		227 Electabuzz [TM]	228 Electivire [TM]	226 Elekid [TM]	240 Garchomp [TM]	063 Gengar [TM]	090 Golduck [TM]
		183 Golisopod [TM]	259 Granbull [TM]	299 Guzzlord [TM]	272 Hakamo-o [TM]	057 Hariyama [TM]	055 Hypno [TM]
		006 Incineroar [TM]	271 Jangmo-o [TM]	135 Jigglypuff [TM]	165 Kangaskhan [TM]	298 Kartana [TM]	222 Komala [TM]
		273 Kommo-o [TM]	233 Krokorok [TM]	234 Krookodile [TM]	021 Ledian [TM]	020 Ledyba [TM]	280 Lucario [TM]
		144 Lurantis [TM]	104 Lycanroc (Midday Form) [TM]	104 Lycanroc (Midnight Form) [TM]	097 Machamp [TM]	096 Machoke [TM]	095 Machop [TM]
		166 Magby [TM]	301 Magearna [TM]	167 Magmar [TM]	168 Magmortar [TM]	056 Makuhita [TM]	079 Mankey [TM]
		216 Metagross [TM]	215 Metang [TM]	138 Miltank [TM]	035 Munchlax [TM]	300 Necrozma [TM]	176 Oranguru [TM]
		220 Pancham [TM]	221 Pangoro [TM]	147 Paras [TM]	148 Parasect [TM]	177 Passimian [TM]	295 Pheromosa [TM]
		025 Pikachu [TM]	010 Pikipek [TM]	175 Pinsir [26, TM]	152 Politoed [TM]	150 Poliwhirl [TM]	151 Poliwrath [TM]
		080 Primeape [TM]	089 Psyduck [TM]	189 Rampardos [TM]	279 Riolu [TM]	102 Sableye [TM]	119 Salamence [TM]
		276 Scizor [TM]	275 Scyther [TM]	118 Shelgon [TM]	038 Slowbro [TM]	039 Slowking [TM]	249 Sneasel [TM]
		036 Snorlax [TM]	258 Snubbull [TM]	105 Spinda [TM]	169 Stufful [TM]	031 Sudowoodo [TM]	287 Tapu Bulu [TM]
		012 Toucannon [TM]	011 Trumbeak [TM]	250 Weavile [TM]	136 Wigglytuff [TM]	205 Zygarde [TM]	

Type	Move Name	Pokémon					
Water	Brine	157 Alomomola [41]	195 Carracosta [28]	264 Carvanha [E]	201 Chinchou [E]	112 Corsola [27]	155 Feebas [E]
		108 Finneon [E]	057 Hariyama [1]	268 Lapras [37]	111 Luvdisc [E]	041 Pelipper [22]	262 Relicanth [E]
		115 Shellder [44]	260 Shellos [E]	184 Staryu [28]	288 Tapu Fini [32]	106 Tentacool [34]	107 Tentacruel [36]
		194 Tirtouga [28]	266 Wailmer [25]	267 Wailord [25]	040 Wingull [E]	110 Wishiwashi [14]	
Dark	Brutal Swing (TM59)	245 Absol [TM]	284 Aerodactyl [TM]	270 Alolan Exeggutor [TM]	229 Alolan Geodude [TM]	231 Alolan Golem [TM]	230 Alolan Graveler [TM]
		050 Alolan Grimer [TM]	164 Alolan Marowak [TM]	051 Alolan Muk [TM]	170 Bewear [14, TM]	297 Celesteela [TM]	060 Crabominable [TM]
		059 Crabrawler [TM]	163 Cubone [TM]	081 Delibird [TM]	263 Dhelmise [TM]	282 Dragonair [TM]	283 Dragonite [TM]
		281 Dratini [TM]	237 Flygon [TM]	240 Garchomp [TM]	180 Goodra [TM]	299 Guzzlord [13, TM]	092 Gyarados [TM]
		272 Hakamo-o [TM]	006 Incineroar [TM]	273 Kommo-o [TM]	233 Krokorok [TM]	234 Krookodile [TM]	156 Milotic [TM]
		300 Necrozma [TM]	293 Nihilego [TM]	176 Oranguru [TM]	177 Passimian [TM]	175 Pinsir [TM]	119 Salamence [TM]
		276 Scizor [TM]	275 Scyther [TM]	169 Stufful [14, TM]	287 Tapu Bulu [TM]	197 Trevenant [TM]	224 Turtonator [TM]
		296 Xurkitree [TM]					
Water	Bubble	142 Araquanid [1]	201 Chinchou [1]	112 Corsola [4]	060 Crabominable [1]	059 Crabrawler [1]	141 Dewpider [1]
		180 Goodra [1]	178 Goomy [1]	202 Lanturn [1]	140 Masquerain [1]	149 Poliwag [11]	150 Poliwhirl [11]
		179 Sliggoo [1]	139 Surskit [1]	106 Tentacool [E]			
	Bubble Beam	142 Araquanid [16]	008 Brionne [24]	201 Chinchou [20]	112 Corsola [10]	060 Crabominable [17]	059 Crabrawler [17]
		141 Dewpider [16]	202 Lanturn [20]	152 Politoed [1]	149 Poliwag [25, E]	150 Poliwhirl [27]	151 Poliwrath [1]
		007 Popplio [22]	009 Primarina [24]	115 Shellder [E]	184 Staryu [18]	139 Surskit [17]	106 Tentacool [25]
		107 Tentacruel [25]					
Bug	Bug Bite	142 Araquanid [1, 13]	023 Ariados [1]	017 Caterpie [9]	028 Charjabug [13]	141 Dewpider [13]	183 Golisopod [10]
		027 Grubbin [13]	020 Ledyba [E]	147 Paras [E]	175 Pinsir [E]	139 Surskit [E]	235 Trapinch [E]
		029 Vikavolt [13]					
	Bug Buzz	019 Butterfree [31]	083 Cutiefly [26]	021 Ledian [38]	020 Ledyba [33, E]	140 Masquerain [1, 42]	295 Pheromosa [53]
		084 Ribombee [28]	275 Scyther [E]	236 Vibrava [29]	029 Vikavolt [31]		
Fighting	Bulk Up (TM08)	016 Alolan Raticate [TM]	170 Bewear [TM]	076 Braviary [TM]	243 Bruxish [TM]	294 Buzzwole [13, TM]	060 Crabominable [TM]
		059 Crabrawler [TM]	183 Golisopod [TM]	259 Granbull [TM]	272 Hakamo-o [TM]	057 Hariyama [TM]	006 Incineroar [1, TM]
		271 Jangmo-o [TM]	222 Komala [TM]	273 Kommo-o [TM]	234 Krookodile [TM]	004 Litten [TM]	280 Lucario [TM]
		104 Lycanroc (Midday Form) [TM]	104 Lycanroc (Midnight Form) [TM]	097 Machamp [43, TM]	096 Machoke [43, TM]	095 Machop [37, TM]	056 Makuhita [TM]
		079 Mankey [TM]	242 Mimikyu [TM]	220 Pancham [TM]	221 Pangoro [TM]	177 Passimian [32, TM]	175 Pinsir [TM]
		151 Poliwrath [TM]	080 Primeape [TM]	279 Riolu [TM]	075 Rufflet [TM]	258 Snubbull [TM]	169 Stufful [TM]
		160 Talonflame [TM]	287 Tapu Bulu [TM]	005 Torracat [TM]	224 Turtonator [TM]		
Ground	Bulldoze (TM78)	284 Aerodactyl [TM]	071 Alolan Diglett [18, TM]	072 Alolan Dugtrio [18, TM]	270 Alolan Exeggutor [TM]	229 Alolan Geodude [TM]	231 Alolan Golem [TM]
		230 Alolan Graveler [TM]	164 Alolan Marowak [TM]	251 Alolan Sandshrew [TM]	252 Alolan Sandslash [TM]	053 Arcanine [TM]	192 Archen [TM]
		193 Archeops [TM]	093 Barboach [TM]	191 Bastiodon [TM]	170 Bewear [TM]	034 Blissey [TM]	099 Boldore [TM]
		294 Buzzwole [TM]	195 Carracosta [TM]	297 Celesteela [TM]	033 Chansey [TM]	112 Corsola [TM]	060 Crabominable [TM]
		059 Crabrawler [TM]	188 Cranidos [TM]	163 Cubone [TM]	263 Dhelmise [TM]	283 Dragonite [TM]	244 Drampa [TM]
		228 Electivire [TM]	237 Flygon [8, TM]	239 Gabite [TM]	240 Garchomp [TM]	261 Gastrodon [TM]	238 Gible [TM]
		100 Gigalith [TM]	247 Glalie [TM]	180 Goodra [TM]	259 Granbull [TM]	014 Gumshoos [TM]	299 Guzzlord [TM]
		092 Gyarados [TM]	272 Hakamo-o [TM]	057 Hariyama [TM]	006 Incineroar [TM]	271 Jangmo-o [TM]	165 Kangaskhan [TM]
		222 Komala [TM]	273 Kommo-o [TM]	233 Krokorok [TM]	234 Krookodile [TM]	268 Lapras [TM]	280 Lucario [TM]
		097 Machamp [TM]	096 Machoke [TM]	095 Machop [TM]	168 Magmortar [TM]	056 Makuhita [TM]	079 Mankey [TM]
		216 Metagross [TM]	215 Metang [TM]	156 Milotic [TM]	138 Miltank [TM]	213 Minior [TM]	132 Mudbray [10, TM]
		133 Mudsdale [1, 10, TM]	035 Munchlax [TM]	300 Necrozma [TM]	198 Nosepass [TM]	176 Oranguru [TM]	187 Palossand [23, TM]
		220 Pancham [TM]	221 Pangoro [TM]	177 Passimian [TM]	196 Phantump [TM]	175 Pinsir [TM]	152 Politoed [TM]
		150 Poliwhirl [TM]	151 Poliwrath [TM]	080 Primeape [TM]	199 Probopass [TM]	189 Rampardos [TM]	262 Relicanth [TM]
		279 Riolu [TM]	098 Roggenrola [TM]	119 Salamence [TM]	232 Sandile [TM]	186 Sandygast [23, TM]	265 Sharpedo [TM]
		190 Shieldon [TM]	038 Slowbro [TM]	039 Slowking [TM]	037 Slowpoke [TM]	036 Snorlax [TM]	258 Snubbull [TM]
		291 Solgaleo [TM]	169 Stufful [TM]	031 Sudowoodo [TM]	137 Tauros [TM]	194 Tirtouga [TM]	223 Torkoal [TM]
		235 Trapinch [8, TM]	197 Trevenant [TM]	224 Turtonator [TM]	236 Vibrava [8, TM]	266 Wailmer [TM]	267 Wailord [TM]
		094 Whiscash [TM]	110 Wishiwashi [TM]	205 Zygarde [1, TM]			
Steel	Bullet Punch	095 Machop [E]	056 Makuhita [E]	216 Metagross [26]	215 Metang [26]	221 Pangoro [1, EV]	279 Riolu [E]
		276 Scizor [1]					
Grass	Bullet Seed	269 Exeggcute [17]	010 Pikipek [31]	012 Toucannon [40]	011 Trumbeak [37]		
Fire	Burn Up	052 Growlithe [E]					
Psychic	Calm Mind (TM04)	042 Abra [TM]	245 Absol [TM]	044 Alakazam [41, TM]	254 Alolan Ninetales [TM]	026 Alolan Raichu [TM]	157 Alomomola [TM]
		034 Blissey [TM]	030 Bonsly [TM]	243 Bruxish [TM]	101 Carbink [TM]	033 Chansey [TM]	212 Clefable [TM]
		211 Clefairy [TM]	174 Comfey [TM]	112 Corsola [TM]	083 Cutiefly [TM]	244 Drampa [TM]	065 Drifblim [TM]
		064 Drifloon [TM]	054 Drowzee [TM]	127 Espeon [TM]	090 Golduck [TM]	278 Honchkrow [TM]	055 Hypno [TM]
		043 Kadabra [4]	298 Kartana [TM]	241 Klefki [TM]	222 Komala [E]	280 Lucario [47, TM]	292 Lunala [E]
		301 Magearna [TM]	213 Minior [TM]	066 Misdreavus [TM]	067 Mismagius [TM]	277 Murkrow [TM]	300 Necrozma [TM]

Type	Move Name	Pokémon					
Psychic	Calm Mind (TM04)	176 Oranguru [39, TM]	082 Oricorio [TM]	089 Psyduck [TM]	262 Relicanth [TM]	084 Ribombee [TM]	102 Sableye [TM]
		038 Slowbro [TM]	039 Slowking [TM]	037 Slowpoke [TM]	249 Sneasel [TM]	291 Solgaleo [TM]	105 Spinda [TM]
		031 Sudowoodo [TM]	131 Sylveon [TM]	287 Tapu Bulu [TM]	288 Tapu Fini [TM]	285 Tapu Koko [TM]	286 Tapu Lele [TM]
		197 Trevenant [TM]	250 Weavile [TM]	296 Xurkitree [TM]			
Normal	Camouflage	112 Corsola [E]	184 Staryu [22]	205 Zygarde [59]			
Normal	Captivate	045 Alolan Meowth [46]	046 Alolan Persian [56]	253 Alolan Vulpix [47]	008 Brionne [46]	019 Butterfree [37]	087 Cottonee [E]
		123 Eevee [E]	155 Feebas [E]	108 Finneon [26]	248 Froslass [41]	134 Igglybuff [E]	109 Lumineon [26]
		111 Luvdisc [37, E]	156 Milotic [21]	138 Miltank [35]	082 Oricorio [33, E]	007 Popplio [39]	009 Primarina [49]
		102 Sableye [E]	162 Salazzle [1, EV]	172 Steenee [37]	173 Tsareena [37]		
Electric	Charge	229 Alolan Geodude [4]	231 Alolan Golem [1, 4]	230 Alolan Graveler [1, 4]	028 Charjabug [1, EV]	201 Chinchou [50]	274 Emolga [10]
		202 Lanturn [58]	024 Pichu [E]	285 Tapu Koko [26]	225 Togedemaru [13]	029 Vikavolt [1]	296 Xurkitree [1]
Electric	Charge Beam (TM57)	042 Abra [TM]	245 Absol [TM]	044 Alakazam [TM]	229 Alolan Geodude [TM]	231 Alolan Golem [TM]	230 Alolan Graveler [TM]
		026 Alolan Raichu [TM]	034 Blissey [TM]	033 Chansey [TM]	028 Charjabug [TM]	201 Chinchou [TM]	212 Clefable [TM]
		211 Clefairy [TM]	065 Drifblim [TM]	064 Drifloon [TM]	227 Electabuzz [TM]	228 Electivire [TM]	226 Elekid [TM]
		274 Emolga [TM]	027 Grubbin [TM]	135 Jigglypuff [TM]	125 Jolteon [TM]	043 Kadabra [TM]	202 Lanturn [TM]
		292 Lunala [TM]	301 Magearna [TM]	047 Magnemite [TM]	048 Magneton [TM]	049 Magnezone [TM]	242 Mimikyu [TM]
		213 Minior [TM]	066 Misdreavus [TM]	067 Mismagius [TM]	300 Necrozma [1, TM]	293 Nihilego [TM]	176 Oranguru [TM]
		024 Pichu [TM]	025 Pikachu [TM]	217 Porygon [TM]	218 Porygon2 [TM]	219 Porygon-Z [TM]	146 Shiinotic [TM]
		286 Tapu Lele [TM]	225 Togedemaru [TM]	224 Turtonator [TM]	029 Vikavolt [TM]	136 Wigglytuff [TM]	296 Xurkitree [TM]
Fairy	Charm	045 Alolan Meowth [E]	253 Alolan Vulpix [E]	171 Bounsweet [E]	210 Cleffa [1]	087 Cottonee [28]	123 Eevee [29, E]
		274 Emolga [E]	108 Finneon [E]	259 Granbull [1]	032 Happiny [1]	134 Igglybuff [1]	222 Komala [1]
		120 Lillipup [E]	111 Luvdisc [1]	242 Mimikyu [28]	035 Munchlax [E]	085 Petilil [E]	024 Pichu [1]
		007 Popplio [E]	036 Snorlax [E]	258 Snubbull [1]			
Normal	Chip Away	251 Alolan Sandshrew [E]	188 Cranidos [28]	163 Cubone [E]	165 Kangaskhan [31]	056 Makuhita [E]	035 Munchlax [17]
		189 Rampardos [28]	036 Snorlax [17]				
Fighting	Circle Throw	165 Kangaskhan [E]	220 Pancham [25]	221 Pangoro [25]	151 Poliwrath [1, 53]	279 Riolu [E]	
Water	Clamp	115 Shellder [25]					
Dragon	Clanging Scales	273 Kommo-o [1, EV]					
Poison	Clear Smog	050 Alolan Grimer [E]	181 Castform [E]	064 Drifloon [E]	207 Garbodor [34]	061 Gastly [E]	166 Magby [19]
		167 Magmar [19]	168 Magmortar [19]	293 Nihilego [7]	089 Psyduck [E]	260 Shellos [E]	223 Torkoal [E]
		206 Trubbish [34]	266 Wailmer [E]				
Fighting	Close Combat	060 Crabominable [49]	059 Crabrawler [49]	052 Growlithe [E]	057 Hariyama [46]	280 Lucario [55]	095 Machop [E]
		056 Makuhita [40]	079 Mankey [36, E]	132 Mudbray [E]	177 Passimian [43]	175 Pinsir [E]	080 Primeape [39]
		258 Snubbull [E]					
Poison	Coil	156 Milotic [41]	205 Zygarde [72]				
Normal	Comet Punch	294 Buzzwole [7]	165 Kangaskhan [1]	021 Ledian [24]	020 Ledyba [22]	220 Pancham [15]	221 Pangoro [15]
Normal	Confide (TM100)	042 Abra [TM]	245 Absol [TM]	284 Aerodactyl [TM]	044 Alakazam [TM]	071 Alolan Diglett [TM]	072 Alolan Dugtrio [TM]
		270 Alolan Exeggutor [TM]	229 Alolan Geodude [TM]	231 Alolan Golem [TM]	230 Alolan Graveler [TM]	050 Alolan Grimer [TM]	164 Alolan Marowak [TM]
		045 Alolan Meowth [TM]	051 Alolan Muk [TM]	254 Alolan Ninetales [TM]	046 Alolan Persian [TM]	026 Alolan Raichu [TM]	016 Alolan Raticate [TM]
		015 Alolan Rattata [TM]	251 Alolan Sandshrew [TM]	252 Alolan Sandslash [TM]	253 Alolan Vulpix [TM]	157 Alomomola [TM]	142 Araquanid [TM]
		053 Arcanine [TM]	192 Archen [TM]	193 Archeops [TM]	023 Ariados [TM]	117 Bagon [TM]	093 Barboach [TM]
		191 Bastiodon [TM]	170 Bewear [TM]	034 Blissey [TM]	099 Boldore [TM]	030 Bonsly [TM]	171 Bounsweet [TM]
		076 Braviary [TM]	008 Brionne [TM]	243 Bruxish [TM]	019 Butterfree [TM]	294 Buzzwole [TM]	101 Carbink [TM]
		195 Carracosta [TM]	264 Carvanha [TM]	181 Castform [TM]	297 Celesteela [TM]	033 Chansey [TM]	028 Charjabug [TM]
		201 Chinchou [TM]	212 Clefable [TM]	211 Clefairy [TM]	210 Cleffa [TM]	116 Cloyster [TM]	174 Comfey [TM]
		112 Corsola [TM]	087 Cottonee [TM]	060 Crabominable [TM]	059 Crabrawler [TM]	188 Cranidos [TM]	070 Crobat [TM]
		163 Cubone [TM]	083 Cutiefly [TM]	002 Dartrix [TM]	003 Decidueye [TM]	081 Delibird [TM]	141 Dewpider [TM]
		263 Dhelmise [TM]	282 Dragonair [TM]	283 Dragonite [TM]	244 Drampa [TM]	281 Dratini [TM]	065 Drifblim [TM]
		064 Drifloon [TM]	054 Drowzee [TM]	123 Eevee [TM]	227 Electabuzz [TM]	228 Electivire [TM]	226 Elekid [TM]
		274 Emolga [TM]	127 Espeon [TM]	269 Exeggcute [TM]	074 Fearow [TM]	155 Feebas [TM]	108 Finneon [TM]
		126 Flareon [TM]	159 Fletchinder [TM]	158 Fletchling [TM]	237 Flygon [TM]	143 Fomantis [TM]	248 Froslass [TM]
		239 Gabite [TM]	207 Garbodor [TM]	240 Garchomp [TM]	061 Gastly [TM]	261 Gastrodon [TM]	063 Gengar [TM]
		238 Gible [TM]	100 Gigalith [TM]	130 Glaceon [TM]	247 Glalie [TM]	069 Golbat [TM]	153 Goldeen [TM]
		090 Golduck [TM]	183 Golisopod [TM]	180 Goodra [TM]	178 Goomy [TM]	259 Granbull [TM]	052 Growlithe [TM]
		027 Grubbin [TM]	014 Gumshoos [TM]	092 Gyarados [TM]	272 Hakamo-o [TM]	032 Happiny [TM]	057 Hariyama [TM]
		062 Haunter [TM]	121 Herdier [TM]	278 Honchkrow [TM]	055 Hypno [TM]	134 Igglybuff [TM]	006 Incineroar [TM]
		271 Jangmo-o [TM]	135 Jigglypuff [TM]	125 Jolteon [TM]	043 Kadabra [TM]	165 Kangaskhan [TM]	298 Kartana [TM]
		241 Klefki [TM]	222 Komala [TM]	273 Kommo-o [TM]	233 Krokorok [TM]	234 Krookodile [TM]	202 Lanturn [TM]
		268 Lapras [TM]	129 Leafeon [TM]	021 Ledian [TM]	020 Ledyba [TM]	086 Lilligant [TM]	120 Lillipup [TM]
		004 Litten [TM]	280 Lucario [TM]	109 Lumineon [TM]	292 Lunala [TM]	144 Lurantis [TM]	111 Luvdisc [TM]

Type	Move Name	Pokémon					
Normal	Confide (TM100)	104 Lycanroc (Midday Form) [TM]	104 Lycanroc (Midnight Form) [TM]	097 Machamp [TM]	096 Machoke [TM]	095 Machop [TM]	166 Magby [TM]
		301 Magearna [TM]	167 Magmar [TM]	168 Magmortar [TM]	047 Magnemite [TM]	048 Magneton [TM]	049 Magnezone [TM]
		056 Makuhita [TM]	078 Mandibuzz [TM]	079 Mankey [TM]	113 Mareanie [TM]	140 Masquerain [TM]	216 Metagross [TM]
		215 Metang [TM]	156 Milotic [TM]	138 Miltank [TM]	242 Mimikyu [TM]	213 Minior [TM]	066 Misdreavus [TM]
		067 Mismagius [TM]	145 Morelull [TM]	132 Mudbray [TM]	133 Mudsdale [TM]	035 Munchlax [TM]	277 Murkrow [TM]
		300 Necrozma [TM]	293 Nihilego [TM]	198 Nosepass [TM]	176 Oranguru [TM]	082 Oricorio [TM]	187 Palossand [TM]
		220 Pancham [TM]	221 Pangoro [TM]	147 Paras [TM]	148 Parasect [TM]	177 Passimian [TM]	041 Pelipper [TM]
		085 Petilil [TM]	196 Phantump [TM]	295 Pheromosa [TM]	024 Pichu [TM]	025 Pikachu [TM]	010 Pikipek [TM]
		175 Pinsir [TM]	152 Politoed [TM]	149 Poliwag [TM]	150 Poliwhirl [TM]	151 Poliwrath [TM]	007 Popplio [TM]
		217 Porygon [TM]	218 Porygon2 [TM]	219 Porygon-Z [TM]	009 Primarina [TM]	080 Primeape [TM]	199 Probopass [TM]
		089 Psyduck [TM]	200 Pyukumuku [TM]	189 Rampardos [TM]	262 Relicanth [TM]	084 Ribombee [TM]	279 Riolu [TM]
		103 Rockruff [TM]	098 Roggenrola [TM]	001 Rowlet [TM]	075 Rufflet [TM]	102 Sableye [TM]	119 Salamence [TM]
		161 Salandit [TM]	162 Salazzle [TM]	232 Sandile [TM]	186 Sandygast [TM]	276 Scizor [TM]	275 Scyther [TM]
		154 Seaking [TM]	265 Sharpedo [TM]	118 Shelgon [TM]	115 Shellder [TM]	260 Shellos [TM]	190 Shieldon [TM]
		146 Shiinotic [TM]	204 Silvally [TM]	208 Skarmory [TM]	179 Sliggoo [TM]	038 Slowbro [TM]	039 Slowking [TM]
		037 Slowpoke [TM]	249 Sneasel [TM]	036 Snorlax [TM]	246 Snorunt [TM]	258 Snubbull [TM]	291 Solgaleo [TM]
		073 Spearow [TM]	022 Spinarak [TM]	105 Spinda [TM]	185 Starmie [TM]	184 Staryu [TM]	172 Steenee [TM]
		122 Stoutland [TM]	169 Stufful [TM]	031 Sudowoodo [TM]	139 Surskit [TM]	131 Sylveon [TM]	160 Talonflame [TM]
		287 Tapu Bulu [TM]	288 Tapu Fini [TM]	285 Tapu Koko [TM]	286 Tapu Lele [TM]	137 Tauros [TM]	106 Tentacool [TM]
		107 Tentacruel [TM]	194 Tirtouga [TM]	225 Togedemaru [TM]	223 Torkoal [TM]	005 Torracat [TM]	012 Toucannon [TM]
		114 Toxapex [TM]	235 Trapinch [TM]	197 Trevenant [TM]	206 Trubbish [TM]	011 Trumbeak [TM]	173 Tsareena [TM]
		224 Turtonator [TM]	203 Type: Null [TM]	128 Umbreon [TM]	256 Vanillish [TM]	255 Vanillite [TM]	257 Vanilluxe [TM]
		124 Vaporeon [TM]	236 Vibrava [TM]	029 Vikavolt [TM]	077 Vullaby [TM]	266 Wailmer [TM]	267 Wailord [TM]
		250 Weavile [TM]	088 Whimsicott [TM]	094 Whiscash [TM]	136 Wigglytuff [TM]	182 Wimpod [TM]	040 Wingull [TM]
		110 Wishiwashi [TM]	296 Xurkitree [TM]	013 Yungoos [TM]	068 Zubat [TM]	205 Zygarde [TM]	
Ghost	Confuse Ray	254 Alolan Ninetales [1]	253 Alolan Vulpix [12]	201 Chinchou [17]	112 Corsola [E]	070 Crobat [17]	155 Feebas [E]
		248 Froslass [32]	061 Gastly [19]	063 Gengar [19]	069 Golbat [17]	062 Haunter [19]	202 Lanturn [17]
		268 Lapras [7]	292 Lunala [13]	166 Magby [26]	167 Magmar [26]	168 Magmortar [26]	213 Minior [10]
		066 Misdreavus [14]	145 Morelull [25]	277 Murkrow [E]	196 Phantump [1]	089 Psyduck [E]	001 Rowlet [E]
		102 Sableye [31]	146 Shiinotic [26]	185 Starmie [40]	184 Staryu [40]	106 Tentacool [E]	197 Trevenant [1]
		128 Umbreon [17]	068 Zubat [17]				
Psychic	Confusion	044 Alakazam [1, 16]	270 Alolan Exeggutor [1]	243 Bruxish [9]	019 Butterfree [1, 11]	054 Drowzee [9]	127 Espeon [1, EV]
		269 Exeggcute [27]	090 Golduck [10]	055 Hypno [1, 9]	043 Kadabra [1, 16]	292 Lunala [1]	216 Metagross [1]
		215 Metang [1, EV]	300 Necrozma [1]	176 Oranguru [1]	089 Psyduck [10]	038 Slowbro [14]	039 Slowking [14]
		037 Slowpoke [14]	286 Tapu Lele [1]				
Normal	Constrict	023 Ariados [1]	065 Drifblim [1]	064 Drifloon [1]	293 Nihilego [1]	022 Spinarak [1]	106 Tentacool [7]
		107 Tentacruel [1, 7]					
	Conversion	217 Porygon [1]	218 Porygon2 [1]	219 Porygon-Z [1]			
	Conversion 2	217 Porygon [1]	218 Porygon2 [1]	219 Porygon-Z [1]			
	Copycat	030 Bonsly [1]	210 Cleffa [13]	032 Happiny [5]	134 Igglybuff [11]	242 Mimikyu [1]	279 Riolu [19]
		105 Spinda [5]	031 Sudowoodo [1]				
Dragon	Core Enforcer	205 Zygarde [ZC]					
Psychic	Cosmic Power	181 Castform [E]	211 Clefairy [34]	290 Cosmoem [1, EV]	292 Lunala [1]	213 Minior [36]	291 Solgaleo [1]
		184 Staryu [49]					
Grass	Cotton Guard	087 Cottonee [37]					
	Cotton Spore	087 Cottonee [17]	088 Whimsicott [1]				
Fighting	Counter	229 Alolan Geodude [E]	015 Alolan Rattata [E]	251 Alolan Sandshrew [E]	030 Bonsly [36]	294 Buzzwole [43]	033 Chansey [E]
		178 Goomy [E]	032 Happiny [E]	271 Jangmo-o [E]	165 Kangaskhan [E]	280 Lucario [6]	104 Lycanroc (Midnight Form) [1, EV]
		095 Machop [E]	056 Makuhita [E]	079 Mankey [E]	132 Mudbray [36]	133 Mudsdale [42]	035 Munchlax [E]
		147 Paras [E]	200 Pyukumuku [17]	279 Riolu [6]	232 Sandile [E]	275 Scyther [E]	260 Shellos [E]
		190 Shieldon [E]	249 Sneasel [E]	036 Snorlax [E]	031 Sudowoodo [36]		
Normal	Covet	045 Alolan Meowth [E]	210 Cleffa [E]	123 Eevee [1, E]	274 Emolga [E]	052 Growlithe [E]	134 Igglybuff [E]
		079 Mankey [1]					
Water	Crabhammer	059 Crabrawler [37]					
Fairy	Crafty Shield	241 Klefki [23]	301 Magearna [1]				
Fighting	Cross Chop	226 Elekid [E]	006 Incineroar [66]	097 Machamp [47]	096 Machoke [47]	095 Machop [39]	166 Magby [E]
		056 Makuhita [E]	079 Mankey [22]	080 Primeape [22]	089 Psyduck [E]	279 Riolu [E]	
Poison	Cross Poison	023 Ariados [55]	070 Crobat [1, EV]	147 Paras [E]	148 Parasect [1]	022 Spinarak [47]	

Type	Move Name	Pokémon					
Dark	Crunch	284 Aerodactyl [33]	050 Alolan Grimer [32]	051 Alolan Muk [32]	016 Alolan Raticate [24]	015 Alolan Rattata [22]	142 Araquanid [38]
		192 Archen [35]	193 Archeops [35]	117 Bagon [25]	243 Bruxish [28]	195 Carracosta [21]	264 Carvanha [36]
		028 Charjabug [25]	188 Cranidos [E]	141 Dewpider [32]	240 Garchomp [1, EV]	247 Glalie [41]	259 Granbull [39]
		052 Growlithe [39, E]	027 Grubbin [22]	014 Gumshoos [39]	299 Guzzlord [37]	092 Gyarados [39]	121 Herdier [24]
		165 Kangaskhan [37]	233 Krokorok [28]	234 Krookodile [28]	120 Lillipup [22]	004 Litten [E]	104 Lycanroc (Midday Form) [40]
		104 Lycanroc (Midnight Form) [40]	220 Pancham [39]	221 Pangoro [42]	279 Riolu [E]	103 Rockruff [40]	119 Salamence [25]
		232 Sandile [28]	265 Sharpedo [40]	118 Shelgon [25]	204 Silvally [50]	036 Snorunt [41]	246 Snorunt [41]
		258 Snubbull [49, E]	291 Solgaleo [37]	122 Stoutland [24]	194 Tirtouga [21]	235 Trapinch [22]	013 Yungoos [34]
		205 Zygarde [51]					
Normal	Crush Claw	251 Alolan Sandshrew [E]	076 Braviary [46]	165 Kangaskhan [E]	103 Rockruff [E]	075 Rufflet [46]	204 Silvally [25]
		249 Sneasel [E]	203 Type: Null [25]				
Ghost	Curse	245 Absol [E]	284 Aerodactyl [E]	229 Alolan Geodude [E]	050 Alolan Grimer [E]	251 Alolan Sandshrew [E]	030 Bonsly [E]
		195 Carracosta [35]	112 Corsola [E]	188 Cranidos [E]	123 Eevee [E]	269 Exeggcute [E]	061 Gastly [12]
		063 Gengar [12]	178 Goomy [E]	062 Haunter [12]	268 Lapras [E]	138 Miltank [E]	242 Mimikyu [E]
		066 Misdreavus [E]	035 Munchlax [E]	196 Phantump [28]	200 Pyukumuku [25]	098 Roggenrola [E]	001 Rowlet [E]
		260 Shellos [E]	190 Shieldon [E]	208 Skarmory [E]	038 Slowbro [1]	039 Slowking [1]	037 Slowpoke [1]
		036 Snorlax [E]	031 Sudowoodo [E]	194 Tirtouga [35]	223 Torkoal [22]	197 Trevenant [28]	206 Trubbish [E]
		266 Wailmer [E]	068 Zubat [E]				
Normal	Cut	298 Kartana [1]					
Dark	Dark Pulse (TM97)	245 Absol [TM]	164 Alolan Marowak [TM]	045 Alolan Meowth [55, TM]	051 Alolan Muk [TM]	254 Alolan Ninetales [TM]	016 Alolan Persian [69, TM]
		018 Alolan Raticate [TM]	015 Alolan Rattata [TM]	253 Alolan Vulpix [TM]	264 Carvanha [TM]	070 Crobat [TM]	207 Gartoudor [TM]
		061 Gastly [36, TM]	063 Gengar [44, TM]	247 Glalie [TM]	183 Golisopod [TM]	299 Guzzlord [TM]	092 Gyarados [TM]
		062 Haunter [44, TM]	278 Honchkrow [75, TM]	006 Incineroar [TM]	233 Krokorok [TM]	234 Krookodile [TM]	280 Lucario [TM]
		078 Mandibuzz [46, TM]	242 Mimikyu [TM]	066 Misdreavus [TM]	067 Mismagius [TM]	277 Murkrow [TM]	300 Necrozma [TM]
		220 Pancham [TM]	221 Pangoro [TM]	196 Phantump [TM]	219 Porygon-Z [TM]	102 Sableye [TM]	232 Sandile [TM]
		265 Sharpedo [TM]	208 Skarmory [TM]	249 Sneasel [TM]	197 Trevenant [TM]	206 Trubbish [TM]	128 Umbreon [TM]
		077 Vullaby [46, TM]	250 Weavile [47, TM]				
	Darkest Lariat	006 Incineroar [1, EV]					
Fairy	Dazzling Gleam (TM99)	042 Abra [TM]	044 Alakazam [TM]	254 Alolan Ninetales [1, TM, EV]	034 Blissey [TM]	171 Bounsweet [TM]	101 Carbink [TM]
		033 Chansey [TM]	201 Chinchou [TM]	212 Clefable [TM]	211 Clefairy [TM]	174 Comfey [TM]	087 Cottonee [TM]
		083 Cutiefly [31, TM]	054 Drowzee [TM]	127 Espeon [TM]	061 Gastly [TM]	063 Gengar [TM]	259 Granbull [TM]
		062 Haunter [TM]	055 Hypno [TM]	135 Jigglypuff [TM]	043 Kadabra [TM]	241 Klefki [TM]	202 Lanturn [TM]
		292 Lunala [TM]	301 Magearna [TM]	242 Mimikyu [TM]	213 Minior [TM]	066 Misdreavus [TM]	067 Mismagius [TM]
		145 Morelull [TM]	293 Nihilego [TM]	198 Nosepass [TM]	009 Primarina [TM]	199 Probopass [TM]	084 Ribombee [35, TM]
		102 Sableye [TM]	146 Shiinotic [TM]	258 Snubbull [TM]	185 Starmie [TM]	184 Staryu [TM]	172 Steenee [TM]
		131 Sylveon [TM]	287 Tapu Bulu [TM]	288 Tapu Fini [TM]	285 Tapu Koko [TM]	286 Tapu Lele [TM]	106 Tentacool [TM]
		107 Tentacruel [TM]	173 Tsareena [TM]	088 Whimsicott [TM]	136 Wigglytuff [TM]	296 Xurkitree [TM]	
Normal	Defense Curl	229 Alolan Geodude [1]	231 Alolan Golem [1]	230 Alolan Graveler [1]	251 Alolan Sandshrew [1]	252 Alolan Sandslash [1]	117 Bagon [E]
		034 Blissey [1]	030 Bonsly [E]	033 Chansey [1]	211 Clefairy [13]	134 Igglybuff [3]	135 Jigglypuff [3]
		222 Komala [1]	301 Magearna [1]	138 Miltank [5]	213 Minior [3]	035 Munchlax [4]	218 Porygon2 [1]
		036 Snorlax [4]	031 Sudowoodo [E]	225 Togedemaru [5]	266 Wailmer [E]	136 Wigglytuff [1]	
Flying	Defog	192 Archen [E]	076 Braviary [32]	064 Drifloon [E]	143 Fomantis [E]	298 Kartana [1]	078 Mandibuzz [32]
		001 Rowlet [E]	075 Rufflet [32]	275 Scyther [E]	288 Tapu Fini [38]	077 Vullaby [32]	068 Zubat [E]
Ghost	Destiny Bond	264 Carvanha [E]	081 Delibird [E]	064 Drifloon [E]	248 Froslass [1, 61]	061 Gastly [40]	063 Gengar [50]
		062 Haunter [50]	242 Mimikyu [E]	066 Misdreavus [E]	196 Phantump [39]	186 Sandygast [E]	197 Trevenant [39]
Fighting	Detect	245 Absol [33]	163 Cubone [E]	123 Eevee [E]	298 Kartana [53]	280 Lucario [1]	056 Makuhita [E]
		279 Riolu [E]	102 Sableye [14]				
Ground	Dig	071 Alolan Diglett [31]	072 Alolan Dugtrio [35]	028 Charjabug [37]	239 Gabite [40]	240 Garchomp [40]	238 Gible [31]
		027 Grubbin [28]	233 Krokorok [32]	234 Krookodile [32]	232 Sandile [31]	235 Trapinch [19]	029 Vikavolt [37]
		205 Zygarde [10]					
Normal	Disable	044 Alakazam [18]	050 Alolan Grimer [12]	051 Alolan Muk [12]	253 Alolan Vulpix [E]	243 Bruxish [20]	181 Castform [E]
		064 Drifloon [E]	054 Drowzee [5]	061 Gastly [E]	090 Golduck [19]	055 Hypno [1, 5]	135 Jigglypuff [14]
		043 Kadabra [18]	165 Kangaskhan [E]	089 Psyduck [19]	162 Salazzle [1]	038 Slowbro [19]	039 Slowking [19]
		037 Slowpoke [19]	246 Snorunt [E]	022 Spinarak [E]	105 Spinda [E]	287 Tapu Bulu [1]	136 Wigglytuff [1]
Fairy	Disarming Voice	008 Brionne [1, 8]	212 Clefable [1]	211 Clefairy [1]	135 Jigglypuff [11]	156 Milotic [11]	024 Pichu [E]
		007 Popplio [8]	009 Primarina [1, 9]	131 Sylveon [1]	225 Togedemaru [E]		

Type	Move Name	Pokémon					
Electric	Discharge	229 Alolan Geodude [34]	231 Alolan Golem [40]	230 Alolan Graveler [40]	028 Charjabug [43]	201 Chinchou [34]	227 Electabuzz [36]
		228 Electivire [36]	226 Elekid [33]	274 Emolga [50]	125 Jolteon [37]	202 Lanturn [37]	047 Magnemite [37]
		048 Magneton [43]	049 Magnezone [43]	198 Nosepass [31]	025 Pikachu [34]	217 Porygon [40]	218 Porygon2 [40]
		219 Porygon-Z [40]	199 Probopass [31]	285 Tapu Koko [48]	225 Togedemaru [29]	296 Xurkitree [47]	
Water	Dive	262 Relicanth [26]	266 Wailmer [41]	267 Wailord [44]	110 Wishiwashi [30]		
Normal	Dizzy Punch	060 Crabominable [25]	059 Crabrawler [25]	165 Kangaskhan [34]	020 Ledyba [E]	138 Miltank [E]	105 Spinda [23]
	Double Hit	165 Kangaskhan [19]	175 Pinsir [22]	276 Scizor [49]	275 Scyther [49]	204 Silvally [55]	249 Sneasel [E]
		203 Type: Null [55]					
Fighting	Double Kick	163 Cubone [E]	052 Growlithe [E]	125 Jolteon [17]	132 Mudbray [15]	133 Mudsdale [15]	295 Pheromosa [1]
Normal	Double Slap	157 Alomomola [13]	034 Blissey [12]	008 Brionne [33]	033 Chansey [12]	212 Clefable [1]	211 Clefairy [10]
		207 Garbodor [14]	135 Jigglypuff [17]	082 Oricorio [23]	024 Pichu [E]	152 Politoed [1]	149 Poliwag [15]
		150 Poliwhirl [15]	151 Poliwrath [1]	007 Popplio [29]	009 Primarina [33]	161 Salandit [21]	162 Salazzle [21]
		172 Steenee [1, EV]	206 Trubbish [14]	173 Tsareena [1]	136 Wigglytuff [1]		
Normal	Double Team (TM32)	042 Abra [TM]	245 Absol [19, TM]	284 Aerodactyl [TM]	044 Alakazam [TM]	071 Alolan Diglett [TM]	072 Alolan Dugtrio [TM]
		270 Alolan Exeggutor [TM]	229 Alolan Geodude [TM]	231 Alolan Golem [TM]	230 Alolan Graveler [TM]	050 Alolan Grimer [TM]	164 Alolan Marowak [TM]
		045 Alolan Meowth [TM]	051 Alolan Muk [TM]	254 Alolan Ninetales [TM]	046 Alolan Persian [TM]	026 Alolan Raichu [TM]	016 Alolan Raticate [TM]
		015 Alolan Rattata [TM]	251 Alolan Sandshrew [TM]	252 Alolan Sandslash [TM]	253 Alolan Vulpix [TM]	157 Alomomola [TM]	142 Araquanid [TM]
		053 Arcanine [TM]	192 Archen [8, TM]	193 Archeops [8, TM]	023 Ariados [TM]	117 Bagon [TM]	093 Barboach [TM]
		191 Bastiodon [TM]	170 Bewear [TM]	034 Blissey [TM]	099 Boldore [TM]	030 Bonsly [TM]	171 Bounsweet [TM]
		076 Braviary [TM]	008 Brionne [TM]	243 Bruxish [TM]	019 Butterfree [TM]	294 Buzzwole [TM]	101 Carbink [TM]
		195 Carracosta [TM]	264 Carvanha [TM]	181 Castform [TM]	297 Celesteela [TM]	033 Chansey [TM]	028 Charjabug [TM]
		201 Chinchou [TM]	212 Clefable [TM]	211 Clefairy [TM]	210 Cleffa [TM]	116 Cloyster [TM]	174 Comfey [TM]
		112 Corsola [TM]	087 Cottonee [TM]	060 Crabominable [TM]	059 Crabrawler [TM]	188 Cranidos [TM]	070 Crobat [TM]
		163 Cubone [TM]	083 Cutiefly [TM]	002 Dartrix [TM]	003 Decidueye [TM]	081 Delibird [TM]	141 Dewpider [TM]
		263 Dhelmise [TM]	282 Dragonair [TM]	283 Dragonite [TM]	244 Drampa [TM]	281 Dratini [TM]	065 Drifblim [TM]
		064 Drifloon [TM]	054 Drowzee [TM]	123 Eevee [TM]	227 Electabuzz [TM]	228 Electivire [TM]	226 Elekid [TM]
		274 Emolga [19, TM]	127 Espeon [TM]	269 Exeggcute [TM]	074 Fearow [TM]	155 Feebas [TM]	108 Finneon [TM]
		126 Flareon [TM]	159 Fletchinder [TM]	158 Fletchling [TM]	237 Flygon [TM]	143 Fomantis [TM]	248 Froslass [1, 5, TM]
		239 Gabite [TM]	207 Garbodor [TM]	240 Garchomp [TM]	061 Gastly [TM]	261 Gastrodon [TM]	063 Gengar [TM]
		238 Gible [TM]	100 Gigalith [TM]	130 Glaceon [TM]	247 Glalie [1, 5, TM]	069 Golbat [TM]	153 Goldeen [TM]
		090 Golduck [TM]	183 Golisopod [TM]	180 Goodra [TM]	178 Goomy [TM]	259 Granbull [TM]	052 Growlithe [TM]
		027 Grubbin [TM]	014 Gumshoos [TM]	299 Guzzlord [TM]	092 Gyarados [TM]	272 Hakamo-o [TM]	032 Happiny [TM]
		057 Hariyama [TM]	062 Haunter [TM]	121 Herdier [TM]	278 Honchkrow [TM]	055 Hypno [TM]	134 Igglybuff [TM]
		006 Incineroar [TM]	271 Jangmo-o [TM]	135 Jigglypuff [TM]	125 Jolteon [TM]	043 Kadabra [TM]	165 Kangaskhan [TM]
		298 Kartana [TM]	241 Klefki [TM]	222 Komala [TM]	273 Kommo-o [TM]	233 Krokorok [TM]	234 Krookodile [TM]
		202 Lanturn [TM]	268 Lapras [TM]	129 Leafeon [TM]	021 Ledian [TM]	020 Ledyba [TM]	086 Lilligant [TM]
		120 Lillipup [TM]	004 Litten [TM]	280 Lucario [TM]	109 Lumineon [TM]	292 Lunala [TM]	144 Lurantis [TM]
		111 Luvdisc [TM]	104 Lycanroc (Midday Form) [TM]	104 Lycanroc (Midnight Form) [TM]	097 Machamp [TM]	096 Machoke [TM]	095 Machop [TM]
		166 Magby [TM]	301 Magearna [TM]	167 Magmar [TM]	168 Magmortar [TM]	047 Magnemite [TM]	048 Magneton [TM]
		049 Magnezone [TM]	056 Makuhita [TM]	078 Mandibuzz [TM]	079 Mankey [TM]	113 Mareanie [TM]	140 Masquerain [TM]
		216 Metagross [TM]	215 Metang [TM]	156 Milotic [TM]	138 Miltank [TM]	242 Mimikyu [5, TM]	213 Minior [TM]
		066 Misdreavus [TM]	067 Mismagius [TM]	145 Morelull [TM]	132 Mudbray [TM]	133 Mudsdale [TM]	035 Munchlax [TM]
		277 Murkrow [TM]	300 Necrozma [TM]	293 Nihilego [TM]	198 Nosepass [TM]	176 Oranguru [TM]	082 Oricorio [TM]
		187 Palossand [TM]	220 Pancham [TM]	221 Pangoro [TM]	147 Paras [TM]	148 Parasect [TM]	177 Passimian [TM]
		041 Pelipper [TM]	085 Petilil [TM]	196 Phantump [TM]	295 Pheromosa [TM]	024 Pichu [TM]	025 Pikachu [23, TM]
		010 Pikipek [TM]	175 Pinsir [TM]	152 Politoed [TM]	149 Poliwag [TM]	150 Poliwhirl [TM]	151 Poliwrath [TM]
		007 Popplio [TM]	217 Porygon [TM]	218 Porygon2 [TM]	219 Porygon-Z [TM]	009 Primarina [TM]	080 Primeape [TM]
		199 Probopass [TM]	089 Psyduck [TM]	200 Pyukumuku [TM]	189 Rampardos [TM]	262 Relicanth [TM]	084 Ribombee [TM]
		279 Riolu [TM]	103 Rockruff [TM]	098 Roggenrola [TM]	001 Rowlet [TM]	075 Rufflet [TM]	102 Sableye [TM]
		119 Salamence [TM]	161 Salandit [TM]	162 Salazzle [TM]	232 Sandile [TM]	186 Sandygast [TM]	276 Scizor [TM]
		275 Scyther [37, TM]	154 Seaking [TM]	265 Sharpedo [TM]	118 Shelgon [TM]	115 Shellder [TM]	260 Shellos [TM]
		190 Shieldon [TM]	146 Shiinotic [TM]	204 Silvally [TM]	208 Skarmory [TM]	179 Sliggoo [TM]	038 Slowbro [TM]
		039 Slowking [TM]	037 Slowpoke [TM]	249 Sneasel [TM]	036 Snorlax [TM]	246 Snorunt [5, TM]	258 Snubbull [TM]
		291 Solgaleo [TM]	073 Spearow [TM]	022 Spinarak [TM]	105 Spinda [TM]	185 Starmie [TM]	184 Staryu [TM]
		172 Steenee [TM]	122 Stoutland [TM]	169 Stufful [TM]	031 Sudowoodo [TM]	139 Surskit [TM]	131 Sylveon [TM]
		160 Talonflame [TM]	288 Tapu Fini [TM]	285 Tapu Koko [TM]	286 Tapu Lele [TM]	137 Tauros [TM]	106 Tentacool [TM]
		107 Tentacruel [TM]	194 Tirtouga [TM]	225 Togedemaru [TM]	223 Torkoal [TM]	005 Torracat [TM]	012 Toucannon [TM]
		114 Toxapex [TM]	235 Trapinch [TM]	197 Trevenant [TM]	206 Trubbish [TM]	011 Trumbeak [TM]	173 Tsareena [TM]
		224 Turtonator [TM]	203 Type: Null [TM]	128 Umbreon [TM]	256 Vanillish [43]	255 Vanillite [TM]	257 Vanilluxe [TM]
		124 Vaporeon [TM]	236 Vibrava [TM]	029 Vikavolt [TM]	077 Vullaby [TM]	266 Wailmer [TM]	267 Wailord [TM]

Type	Move Name	Pokémon					
Normal	Double Team (TM32)	250 Weavile [TM]	088 Whimsicott [TM]	094 Whiscash [TM]	136 Wigglytuff [TM]	182 Wimpod [TM]	040 Wingull [TM]
		110 Wishiwashi [TM]	296 Xurkitree [TM]	013 Yungoos [TM]	068 Zubat [TM]	205 Zygarde [TM]	
	Double-Edge	245 Absol [E]	229 Alolan Geodude [40]	231 Alolan Golem [50]	230 Alolan Graveler [50]	016 Alolan Raticate [39]	015 Alolan Rattata [31]
		117 Bagon [49]	170 Bewear [56]	034 Blissey [1, 54]	030 Bonsly [43]	264 Carvanha [E]	297 Celesteela [73]
		033 Chansey [1, 54]	188 Cranidos [E]	163 Cubone [43]	123 Eevee [37]	238 Gible [E]	052 Growlithe [E]
		135 Jigglypuff [45]	165 Kangaskhan [E]	021 Ledian [47]	020 Ledyba [40]	138 Miltank [E]	213 Minior [43]
		132 Mudbray [E]	035 Munchlax [E]	198 Nosepass [E]	177 Passimian [36]	262 Relicanth [50]	119 Salamence [63]
		232 Sandile [E]	118 Shelgon [56]	190 Shieldon [E]	204 Silvally [80]	036 Snorlax [E]	258 Snubbull [E]
		105 Spinda [46]	169 Stufful [46]	031 Sudowoodo [43]	203 Type: Null [80]	266 Wailmer [E]	136 Wigglytuff [1]
		110 Wishiwashi [41]					
Dragon	Draco Meteor	270 Alolan Exeggutor [T]	117 Bagon [T]	282 Dragonair [T]	283 Dragonite [T]	244 Drampa [T]	281 Dratini [T]
		237 Flygon [T]	239 Gabite [T]	240 Garchomp [T]	238 Gible [T]	180 Goodra [T]	178 Goomy [T]
		299 Guzzlord [T]	272 Hakamo-o [T]	271 Jangmo-o [T]	273 Kommo-o [T]	119 Salamence [T]	118 Shelgon [T]
		204 Silvally [T]	179 Sliggoo [T]	224 Turtonator [T]	236 Vibrava [T]	205 Zygarde [T]	
	Dragon Breath	284 Aerodactyl [E]	192 Archen [31]	193 Archeops [31]	117 Bagon [13]	244 Drampa [29]	281 Dratini [E]
		155 Feebas [E]	237 Flygon [1]	238 Gible [E]	180 Goodra [18]	178 Goomy [18]	271 Jangmo-o [E]
		119 Salamence [13]	118 Shelgon [13]	179 Sliggoo [18]	236 Vibrava [1, EV]	205 Zygarde [1]	
	Dragon Claw (TM02)	284 Aerodactyl [TM]	192 Archen [48, TM]	193 Archeops [56, TM]	117 Bagon [29, TM]	170 Bewear [TM]	283 Dragonite [TM]
		244 Drampa [TM]	237 Flygon [1, TM, EV]	239 Gabite [33, TM]	240 Garchomp [33, TM]	238 Gible [27, TM]	299 Guzzlord [TM]
		272 Hakamo-o [43, TM]	271 Jangmo-o [41, TM]	273 Kommo-o [43, TM]	234 Krookodile [TM]	221 Pangoro [TM]	119 Salamence [29, TM]
		161 Salandit [TM]	162 Salazzle [TM]	118 Shelgon [29, TM]	204 Silvally [TM]	224 Turtonator [TM]	203 Type: Null [TM]
	Dragon Dance	117 Bagon [E]	093 Barboach [E]	282 Dragonair [61]	283 Dragonite [61]	281 Dratini [51, E]	237 Flygon [1]
		092 Gyarados [45]	272 Hakamo-o [53]	271 Jangmo-o [49]	273 Kommo-o [59]	268 Lapras [E]	205 Zygarde [EC]
	Dragon Hammer	270 Alolan Exeggutor [1, EV]					
	Dragon Pulse	192 Archen [E]	117 Bagon [E]	244 Drampa [41]	281 Dratini [E]	155 Feebas [E]	180 Goodra [47]
		178 Goomy [42]	268 Lapras [E]	280 Lucario [60]	161 Salandit [48]	162 Salazzle [56]	179 Sliggoo [47]
		224 Turtonator [41]	205 Zygarde [63]				
	Dragon Rage	117 Bagon [E]	282 Dragonair [15]	283 Dragonite [15]	244 Drampa [21]	281 Dratini [15]	239 Gabite [1, 7]
		240 Garchomp [1, 7]	238 Gible [7]	299 Guzzlord [1]	092 Gyarados [36]	161 Salandit [13]	162 Salazzle [13]
	Dragon Rush	117 Bagon [E]	282 Dragonair [47]	283 Dragonite [47]	244 Drampa [E]	281 Dratini [41, E]	237 Flygon [47]
		239 Gabite [49]	240 Garchomp [55]	238 Gible [37]	299 Guzzlord [73]		
	Dragon Tail (TM82)	270 Alolan Exeggutor [TM]	193 Archeops [TM]	282 Dragonair [33, TM]	283 Dragonite [33, TM]	244 Drampa [TM]	281 Dratini [31, TM]
		237 Flygon [29, TM]	240 Garchomp [TM]	180 Goodra [TM]	299 Guzzlord [23, TM]	092 Gyarados [TM]	272 Hakamo-o [17, TM]
		271 Jangmo-o [17, TM]	273 Kommo-o [17, TM]	234 Krookodile [TM]	156 Milotic [24, TM]	189 Rampardos [TM]	119 Salamence [1, TM]
		162 Salazzle [TM]	039 Slowking [TM]	224 Turtonator [TM]	205 Zygarde [TM]		
Fighting	Drain Punch	020 Ledyba [E]					
Fairy	Draining Kiss	174 Comfey [7]	083 Cutiefly [16]	248 Froslass [23]	241 Klefki [18]	111 Luvdisc [9]	084 Ribombee [16]
		131 Sylveon [20]	286 Tapu Lele [1]				
Psychic	Dream Eater (TM85)	042 Abra [TM]	245 Absol [TM]	044 Alakazam [TM]	270 Alolan Exeggutor [TM]	164 Alolan Marowak [TM]	045 Alolan Meowth [TM]
		254 Alolan Ninetales [TM]	046 Alolan Persian [TM]	034 Blissey [TM]	243 Bruxish [TM]	019 Butterfree [TM]	033 Chansey [TM]
		212 Clefable [TM]	211 Clefairy [TM]	210 Cleffa [TM]	087 Cottonee [TM]	083 Cutiefly [TM]	065 Drifblim [TM]
		064 Drifloon [TM]	054 Drowzee [TM]	127 Espeon [TM]	269 Exeggcute [TM]	248 Froslass [TM]	061 Gastly [33, TM]
		063 Gengar [39, TM]	032 Happiny [TM]	062 Haunter [39, TM]	278 Honchkrow [TM]	055 Hypno [TM]	134 Igglybuff [TM]
		135 Jigglypuff [TM]	043 Kadabra [TM]	268 Lapras [TM]	086 Lilligant [TM]	292 Lunala [59, TM]	242 Mimikyu [TM]
		066 Misdreavus [TM]	067 Mismagius [TM]	145 Morelull [43, TM]	277 Murkrow [TM]	176 Oranguru [TM]	085 Petilil [TM]
		196 Phantump [TM]	217 Porygon [TM]	218 Porygon2 [TM]	219 Porygon-Z [TM]	084 Ribombee [TM]	102 Sableye [TM]
		146 Shiinotic [49, TM]	038 Slowbro [TM]	039 Slowking [TM]	037 Slowpoke [TM]	249 Sneasel [TM]	105 Spinda [TM]
		185 Starmie [TM]	197 Trevenant [TM]	128 Umbreon [TM]	250 Weavile [TM]	088 Whimsicott [TM]	136 Wigglytuff [TM]
Flying	Drill Peck	081 Delibird [25]	074 Fearow [41]	277 Murkrow [E]	010 Pikipek [27]	208 Skarmory [E]	073 Spearow [36]
		012 Toucannon [34]	011 Trumbeak [32]				
Ground	Drill Run	074 Fearow [1, 45]					
Dragon	Dual Chop	239 Gabite [1, EV]	240 Garchomp [1]	097 Machamp [33]	096 Machoke [33]	095 Machop [31]	
Fighting	Dynamic Punch	294 Buzzwole [59]	060 Crabominable [45]	059 Crabrawler [45]	226 Elekid [E]	097 Machamp [57]	096 Machoke [57]
		095 Machop [45]	166 Magby [E]	056 Makuhita [E]	151 Poliwrath [32]		
Ground	Earth Power	071 Alolan Diglett [28]	072 Alolan Dugtrio [30]	192 Archen [E]	093 Barboach [E]	112 Corsola [47]	237 Flygon [26]
		198 Nosepass [37]	187 Palossand [47]	199 Probopass [37]	186 Sandygast [45]	235 Trapinch [26, E]	236 Vibrava [26]

Type	Move Name	Pokémon					
Ground	Earthquake (TM26)	284 Aerodactyl [TM]	071 Alolan Diglett [39, TM]	072 Alolan Dugtrio [47, TM]	270 Alolan Exeggutor [TM]	229 Alolan Geodude [TM]	231 Alolan Golem [TM]
		230 Alolan Graveler [TM]	164 Alolan Marowak [TM]	251 Alolan Sandshrew [TM]	252 Alolan Sandslash [TM]	192 Archen [TM]	193 Archeops [TM]
		093 Barboach [32, TM]	191 Bastiodon [TM]	170 Bewear [TM]	034 Blissey [TM]	099 Boldore [TM]	294 Buzzwole [TM]
		195 Carracosta [TM]	297 Celesteela [TM]	033 Chansey [TM]	112 Corsola [TM]	060 Crabominable [TM]	059 Crabrawler [TM]
		188 Cranidos [TM]	163 Cubone [TM]	263 Dhelmise [TM]	283 Dragonite [TM]	244 Drampa [TM]	228 Electivire [TM]
		237 Flygon [33, TM]	239 Gabite [TM]	240 Garchomp [TM]	261 Gastrodon [TM]	238 Gible [TM]	100 Gigalith [TM]
		247 Glalie [TM]	180 Goodra [TM]	259 Granbull [TM]	014 Gumshoos [TM]	299 Guzzlord [TM]	092 Gyarados [TM]
		272 Hakamo-o [TM]	057 Hariyama [TM]	006 Incineroar [TM]	271 Jangmo-o [TM]	165 Kangaskhan [TM]	222 Komala [TM]
		273 Kommo-o [TM]	233 Krokorok [48, TM]	234 Krookodile [54, TM]	280 Lucario [TM]	097 Machamp [TM]	096 Machoke [TM]
		095 Machop [TM]	168 Magmortar [TM]	056 Makuhita [TM]	079 Mankey [TM]	216 Metagross [TM]	215 Metang [TM]
		138 Miltank [TM]	213 Minior [TM]	132 Mudbray [38, TM]	133 Mudsdale [47, TM]	035 Munchlax [TM]	300 Necrozma [TM]
		198 Nosepass [TM]	176 Oranguru [TM]	187 Palossand [TM]	221 Pangoro [TM]	177 Passimian [TM]	175 Pinsir [TM]
		152 Politoed [TM]	150 Poliwhirl [TM]	151 Poliwrath [TM]	080 Primeape [TM]	199 Probopass [TM]	189 Rampardos [TM]
		262 Relicanth [TM]	279 Riolu [TM]	098 Roggenrola [TM]	119 Salamence [TM]	232 Sandile [43, TM]	186 Sandygast [TM]
		265 Sharpedo [TM]	190 Shieldon [TM]	038 Slowbro [TM]	039 Slowking [TM]	037 Slowpoke [TM]	036 Snorlax [TM]
		258 Snubbull [TM]	291 Solgaleo [TM]	169 Stufful [TM]	031 Sudowoodo [TM]	137 Tauros [TM]	194 Tirtouga [TM]
		223 Torkoal [TM]	235 Trapinch [33, TM]	197 Trevenant [TM]	224 Turtonator [TM]	236 Vibrava [33, TM]	266 Wailmer [TM]
		267 Wailord [TM]	094 Whiscash [34, TM]	110 Wishiwashi [TM]	013 Yungoos [TM]	205 Zygarde [55, TM]	
Normal	Echoed Voice (TM49)	245 Absol [TM]	071 Alolan Diglett [TM]	072 Alolan Dugtrio [TM]	231 Alolan Golem [TM]	164 Alolan Marowak [TM]	045 Alolan Meowth [TM]
		046 Alolan Persian [TM]	026 Alolan Raichu [TM]	034 Blissey [TM]	008 Brionne [TM]	033 Chansey [TM]	212 Clefable [TM]
		211 Clefairy [TM]	210 Cleffa [TM]	174 Comfey [TM]	163 Cubone [TM]	002 Dartrix [TM]	003 Decidueye [TM]
		244 Drampa [1, TM]	123 Eevee [TM]	127 Espeon [TM]	074 Fearow [TM]	126 Flareon [TM]	130 Glaceon [TM]
		014 Gumshoos [TM]	272 Hakamo-o [TM]	032 Happiny [TM]	134 Igglybuff [TM]	271 Jangmo-o [TM]	135 Jigglypuff [TM]
		125 Jolteon [TM]	273 Kommo-o [TM]	268 Lapras [TM]	129 Leafeon [TM]	104 Lycanroc (Midday Form) [TM]	104 Lycanroc (Midnight Form) [TM]
		301 Magearna [TM]	138 Miltank [TM]	066 Misdreavus [TM]	067 Mismagius [TM]	293 Nihilego [TM]	220 Pancham [TM]
		221 Pangoro [TM]	041 Pelipper [TM]	295 Pheromosa [TM]	024 Pichu [TM]	025 Pikachu [TM]	010 Pikipek [7, TM]
		152 Politoed [TM]	007 Popplio [TM]	009 Primarina [TM]	103 Rockruff [TM]	001 Rowlet [TM]	038 Slowbro [TM]
		039 Slowking [TM]	037 Slowpoke [TM]	073 Spearow [TM]	131 Sylveon [TM]	287 Tapu Bulu [TM]	288 Tapu Fini [TM]
		285 Tapu Koko [TM]	286 Tapu Lele [TM]	012 Toucannon [1, 7, TM]	011 Trumbeak [1, 7, TM]	128 Umbreon [TM]	124 Vaporeon [TM]
		266 Wailmer [TM]	267 Wailord [TM]	136 Wigglytuff [TM]	040 Wingull [TM]	013 Yungoos [TM]	
Electric	Eerie Impulse	202 Lanturn [1]	296 Xurkitree [29]				
Normal	Egg Bomb	270 Alolan Exeggutor [27]	034 Blissey [42]	033 Chansey [42]			
Electric	Electric Terrain	228 Electivire [1, 65]	048 Magneton [1]	049 Magnezone [1]	024 Pichu [E]	285 Tapu Koko [1]	225 Togedemaru [37]
		296 Xurkitree [53]					
Electric	Electro Ball	201 Chinchou [9]	227 Electabuzz [22]	228 Electivire [22]	226 Elekid [22]	274 Emolga [26]	202 Lanturn [1, 9]
		047 Magnemite [29]	048 Magneton [29]	049 Magnezone [29]	025 Pikachu [13]	285 Tapu Koko [58]	
	Electroweb	027 Grubbin [E]	022 Spinarak [E]				
Dark	Embargo (TM63)	042 Abra [TM]	044 Alakazam [TM]	050 Alolan Grimer [TM]	045 Alolan Meowth [TM]	051 Alolan Muk [TM]	046 Alolan Persian [TM]
		016 Alolan Raticate [TM]	015 Alolan Rattata [TM]	243 Bruxish [TM]	263 Dhelmise [TM]	065 Drifblim [TM]	064 Drifloon [TM]
		248 Froslass [TM]	061 Gastly [TM]	063 Gengar [TM]	062 Haunter [TM]	278 Honchkrow [TM]	006 Incineroar [TM]
		043 Kadabra [TM]	233 Krokorok [22, TM]	234 Krookodile [22, TM]	301 Magearna [TM]	078 Mandibuzz [50, TM]	242 Mimikyu [TM]
		066 Misdreavus [TM]	067 Mismagius [TM]	277 Murkrow [TM]	300 Necrozma [TM]	176 Oranguru [TM]	082 Oricorio [TM]
		187 Palossand [TM]	221 Pangoro [TM]	219 Porygon-Z [34, TM]	102 Sableye [TM]	232 Sandile [22, TM]	249 Sneasel [TM]
		077 Vullaby [50, TM]	250 Weavile [1, TM]				
Fire	Ember	117 Bagon [4]	181 Castform [10]	126 Flareon [1, EV]	159 Fletchinder [1, EV]	052 Growlithe [6]	006 Incineroar [1]
		004 Litten [1]	166 Magby [5]	167 Magmar [1, 5]	168 Magmortar [1, 5]	119 Salamence [1, 4]	161 Salandit [5]
		162 Salazzle [1, 5]	118 Shelgon [1, 4]	160 Talonflame [1]	223 Torkoal [1]	005 Torracat [1]	224 Turtonator [1]
Normal	Encore	042 Abra [E]	253 Alolan Vulpix [E]	008 Brionne [19]	211 Clefairy [1]	210 Cleffa [4]	087 Cottonee [E]
		274 Emolga [38]	020 Ledyba [E]	095 Machop [E]	079 Mankey [E]	024 Pichu [E]	149 Poliwag [E]
		007 Popplio [18]	009 Primarina [19]	089 Psyduck [E]	162 Salazzle [1]	105 Spinda [E]	225 Togedemaru [E]
	Endeavor	164 Alolan Marowak [49]	016 Alolan Raticate [44]	015 Alolan Rattata [34]	192 Archen [38]	193 Archeops [40]	087 Cottonee [44]
		059 Crabrawler [E]	163 Cubone [41]	165 Kangaskhan [E]	149 Poliwag [E]	189 Rampardos [1, EV]	110 Wishiwashi [49]
Normal	Endure	071 Alolan Diglett [E]	229 Alolan Geodude [E]	251 Alolan Sandshrew [E]	157 Alomomola [E]	117 Bagon [E]	191 Bastiodon [36]
		030 Bonsly [E]	294 Buzzwole [23]	033 Chansey [E]	174 Comfey [E]	112 Corsola [35]	163 Cubone [E]
		123 Eevee [E]	178 Goomy [E]	027 Grubbin [E]	032 Happiny [E]	057 Hariyama [42]	165 Kangaskhan [43]
		120 Lillipup [E]	056 Makuhita [37]	138 Miltank [E]	198 Nosepass [E]	147 Paras [E]	085 Petilil [E]
		024 Pichu [E]	149 Poliwag [E]	200 Pyukumuku [E]	279 Riolu [1]	275 Scyther [E]	190 Shieldon [33]
		208 Skarmory [E]	169 Stufful [E]	031 Sudowoodo [E]	139 Surskit [E]	223 Torkoal [E]	235 Trapinch [E]
		224 Turtonator [21]					

Type	Move Name	Pokémon					
Grass	Energy Ball (TM53)	042 Abra [TM]	044 Alakazam [TM]	270 Alolan Exeggutor [TM]	171 Bounsweet [TM]	019 Butterfree [TM]	181 Castform [TM]
		297 Celesteela [TM]	174 Comfey [TM]	087 Cottonee [35, TM]	083 Cutiefly [TM]	002 Dartrix [TM]	003 Decidueye [TM]
		263 Dhelmise [41, TM]	244 Drampa [TM]	269 Exeggcute [TM]	143 Fomantis [TM]	061 Gastly [TM]	063 Gengar [TM]
		062 Haunter [TM]	043 Kadabra [TM]	129 Leafeon [TM]	086 Lilligant [TM]	144 Lurantis [TM]	301 Magearna [TM]
		140 Masquerain [TM]	067 Mismagius [TM]	145 Morelull [TM]	176 Oranguru [TM]	187 Palossand [TM]	147 Paras [TM]
		148 Parasect [TM]	177 Passimian [TM]	085 Petilil [35, TM]	196 Phantump [TM]	009 Primarina [TM]	084 Ribombee [TM]
		001 Rowlet [TM]	186 Sandygast [TM]	146 Shiinotic [TM]	172 Steenee [TM]	287 Tapu Bulu [TM]	286 Tapu Lele [TM]
		197 Trevenant [TM]	173 Tsareena [TM]	029 Vikavolt [TM]	088 Whimsicott [TM]	296 Xurkitree [TM]	
Normal	Entrainment	142 Araquanid [62]	141 Dewpider [48]	111 Luvdisc [E]	220 Pancham [42]	221 Pangoro [1, 45]	085 Petilil [37]
Fire	Eruption	223 Torkoal [E]					
Normal	Explosion (TM64)	270 Alolan Exeggutor [TM]	229 Alolan Geodude [36, TM]	231 Alolan Golem [44, TM]	230 Alolan Graveler [44, TM]	050 Alolan Grimer [TM]	051 Alolan Muk [TM]
		099 Boldore [55, TM]	030 Bonsly [TM]	101 Carbink [TM]	297 Celesteela [TM]	116 Cloyster [TM]	112 Corsola [TM]
		065 Drifblim [60, TM]	064 Drifloon [50, TM]	269 Exeggcute [TM]	207 Garbodor [59, TM]	061 Gastly [TM]	063 Gengar [TM]
		100 Gigalith [55, TM]	247 Glalie [TM]	062 Haunter [TM]	301 Magearna [TM]	047 Magnemite [TM]	048 Magneton [TM]
		049 Magnezone [TM]	216 Metagross [TM]	215 Metang [TM]	213 Minior [50, TM]	190 Nosepass [TM]	199 Probopass [TM]
		098 Roggenrola [40, TM]	115 Shellder [TM]	204 Silvally [TM]	031 Sudowoodo [TM]	223 Torkoal [TM]	206 Trubbish [47, TM]
		224 Turtonator [53, TM]	256 Vanillish [TM]	255 Vanillite [TM]	257 Vanilluxe [TM]		
Psychic	Extrasensory	253 Alolan Vulpix [31, E]	244 Drampa [37]	269 Exeggcute [47]	176 Oranguru [E]	286 Tapu Lele [48]	
	Extreme Speed	053 Arcanine [34]	281 Dratini [E]	280 Lucario [65]	205 Zygarde [ZC]		
Normal	Facade (TM42)	042 Abra [TM]	245 Absol [TM]	284 Aerodactyl [TM]	044 Alakazam [TM]	071 Alolan Diglett [TM]	072 Alolan Dugtrio [TM]
		270 Alolan Exeggutor [TM]	229 Alolan Geodude [TM]	231 Alolan Golem [TM]	230 Alolan Graveler [TM]	050 Alolan Grimer [TM]	164 Alolan Marowak [TM]
		045 Alolan Meowth [TM]	051 Alolan Muk [TM]	254 Alolan Ninetales [TM]	046 Alolan Persian [TM]	026 Alolan Raichu [TM]	016 Alolan Raticate [TM]
		015 Alolan Rattata [TM]	251 Alolan Sandshrew [TM]	252 Alolan Sandslash [TM]	253 Alolan Vulpix [TM]	157 Alomomola [TM]	142 Araquanid [TM]
		053 Arcanine [TM]	192 Archen [TM]	193 Archeops [TM]	023 Ariados [TM]	117 Bagon [TM]	093 Barboach [TM]
		191 Bastiodon [TM]	170 Bewear [TM]	034 Blissey [TM]	099 Boldore [TM]	030 Bonsly [TM]	171 Bounsweet [TM]
		076 Braviary [TM]	008 Brionne [TM]	243 Bruxish [TM]	019 Butterfree [TM]	294 Buzzwole [TM]	101 Carbink [TM]
		195 Carracosta [TM]	264 Carvanha [TM]	181 Castform [TM]	297 Celesteela [TM]	033 Chansey [TM]	028 Charjabug [TM]
		201 Chinchou [TM]	212 Clefable [TM]	211 Clefairy [TM]	210 Cleffa [TM]	116 Cloyster [TM]	174 Comfey [TM]
		112 Corsola [TM]	087 Cottonee [TM]	060 Crabominable [TM]	059 Crabrawler [TM]	188 Cranidos [TM]	070 Crobat [TM]
		163 Cubone [TM]	083 Cutiefly [TM]	002 Dartrix [TM]	003 Decidueye [TM]	081 Delibird [TM]	141 Dewpider [TM]
		263 Dhelmise [TM]	282 Dragonair [TM]	283 Dragonite [TM]	244 Drampa [TM]	281 Dratini [TM]	065 Drifblim [TM]
		064 Drifloon [TM]	054 Drowzee [TM]	123 Eevee [TM]	227 Electabuzz [TM]	228 Electivire [TM]	226 Elekid [TM]
		274 Emolga [TM]	127 Espeon [TM]	269 Exeggcute [TM]	074 Fearow [TM]	155 Feebas [TM]	108 Finneon [TM]
		126 Flareon [TM]	159 Fletchinder [TM]	158 Fletchling [TM]	237 Flygon [TM]	143 Fomantis [TM]	248 Froslass [TM]
		239 Gabite [TM]	207 Garbodor [TM]	240 Garchomp [TM]	061 Gastly [TM]	261 Gastrodon [TM]	063 Gengar [TM]
		238 Gible [TM]	100 Gigalith [TM]	130 Glaceon [TM]	247 Glalie [TM]	069 Golbat [TM]	153 Goldeen [TM]
		090 Golduck [TM]	183 Golisopod [TM]	180 Goodra [TM]	178 Goomy [TM]	259 Granbull [TM]	052 Growlithe [TM]
		027 Grubbin [TM]	014 Gumshoos [TM]	299 Guzzlord [TM]	092 Gyarados [TM]	272 Hakamo-o [TM]	032 Happiny [TM]
		057 Hariyama [TM]	062 Haunter [TM]	121 Herdier [TM]	278 Honchkrow [TM]	055 Hypno [TM]	134 Igglybuff [TM]
		006 Incineroar [TM]	271 Jangmo-o [TM]	135 Jigglypuff [TM]	125 Jolteon [TM]	043 Kadabra [TM]	165 Kangaskhan [TM]
		241 Klefki [TM]	222 Komala [TM]	273 Kommo-o [TM]	233 Krokorok [TM]	234 Krookodile [TM]	202 Lanturn [TM]
		268 Lapras [TM]	129 Leafeon [TM]	021 Ledian [TM]	020 Ledyba [TM]	086 Lilligant [TM]	120 Lillipup [TM]
		004 Litten [TM]	280 Lucario [TM]	109 Lumineon [TM]	292 Lunala [TM]	144 Lurantis [TM]	111 Luvdisc [TM]
		104 Lycanroc (Midday Form) [TM]	104 Lycanroc (Midnight Form) [TM]	097 Machamp [TM]	096 Machoke [TM]	095 Machop [TM]	166 Magby [TM]
		167 Magmar [TM]	168 Magmortar [TM]	047 Magnemite [TM]	048 Magneton [TM]	049 Magnezone [TM]	056 Makuhita [TM]
		078 Mandibuzz [TM]	079 Mankey [TM]	113 Mareanie [TM]	140 Masquerain [TM]	216 Metagross [TM]	215 Metang [TM]
		156 Milotic [TM]	138 Miltank [TM]	242 Mimikyu [TM]	213 Minior [TM]	066 Misdreavus [TM]	067 Mismagius [TM]
		132 Mudbray [TM]	133 Mudsdale [TM]	035 Munchlax [TM]	277 Murkrow [TM]	300 Necrozma [TM]	293 Nihilego [TM]
		198 Nosepass [TM]	176 Oranguru [TM]	082 Oricorio [TM]	187 Palossand [TM]	220 Pancham [TM]	221 Pangoro [TM]
		147 Paras [TM]	148 Parasect [TM]	177 Passimian [TM]	041 Poliooer [TM]	085 Petilil [TM]	196 Phantump [TM]
		295 Pheromosa [TM]	024 Pichu [TM]	025 Pikachu [TM]	175 Pinsir [TM]	152 Politoed [TM]	149 Poliwag [TM]
		150 Poliwhirl [TM]	151 Poliwrath [TM]	007 Popplio [TM]	217 Porygon [TM]	218 Porygon2 [TM]	219 Porygon-Z [TM]
		009 Primarina [TM]	080 Primeape [TM]	199 Probopass [TM]	089 Psyduck [TM]	189 Rampardos [TM]	262 Relicanth [TM]
		084 Ribombee [TM]	279 Riolu [TM]	103 Rockruff [TM]	098 Roggenrola [TM]	001 Rowlet [TM]	075 Rufflet [TM]
		102 Sableye [TM]	119 Salamence [TM]	161 Salandit [TM]	162 Salazzle [TM]	232 Sandile [TM]	186 Sandygast [TM]
		276 Scizor [TM]	275 Scyther [TM]	154 Seaking [TM]	265 Sharpedo [TM]	118 Shelgon [TM]	115 Shellder [TM]
		260 Shellos [TM]	190 Shieldon [TM]	204 Silvally [TM]	208 Skarmory [TM]	179 Sliggoo [TM]	038 Slowbro [TM]
		039 Slowking [TM]	037 Slowpoke [TM]	249 Sneasel [TM]	036 Snorlax [TM]	246 Snorunt [TM]	258 Snubbull [TM]
		291 Solgaleo [TM]	073 Spearow [TM]	022 Spinarak [TM]	105 Spinda [TM]	185 Starmie [TM]	184 Staryu [TM]
		172 Steenee [TM]	122 Stoutland [TM]	169 Stufful [TM]	031 Sudowoodo [TM]	139 Surskit [TM]	131 Sylveon [TM]

Type	Move Name	Pokémon					
Normal	Facade (TM42)	160 Talonflame [TM]	287 Tapu Bulu [TM]	288 Tapu Fini [TM]	285 Tapu Koko [TM]	286 Tapu Lele [TM]	137 Tauros [TM]
		106 Tentacool [TM]	107 Tentacruel [TM]	194 Tirtouga [TM]	225 Togedemaru [TM]	223 Torkoal [TM]	005 Torracat [TM]
		114 Toxapex [TM]	235 Trapinch [TM]	197 Trevenant [TM]	206 Trubbish [TM]	173 Tsareena [TM]	224 Turtonator [TM]
		203 Type: Null [TM]	128 Umbreon [TM]	256 Vanillish [TM]	255 Vanillite [TM]	257 Vanilluxe [TM]	124 Vaporeon [TM]
		236 Vibrava [TM]	029 Vikavolt [TM]	077 Vullaby [TM]	266 Wailmer [TM]	267 Wailord [TM]	250 Weavile [TM]
		088 Whimsicott [TM]	094 Whiscash [TM]	136 Wigglytuff [TM]	182 Wimpod [TM]	040 Wingull [TM]	110 Wishiwashi [TM]
		296 Xurkitree [TM]	013 Yungoos [TM]	068 Zubat [TM]	205 Zygarde [TM]		
Fairy	Fairy Lock	241 Klefki [1]					
	Fairy Wind	087 Cottonee [1]	083 Cutiefly [4]	241 Klefki [5]	084 Ribombee [1, 4]	131 Sylveon [1, EV]	
Normal	Fake Out	045 Alolan Meowth [9]	046 Alolan Persian [1, 9]	081 Delibird [E]	057 Hariyama [10]	165 Kangaskhan [7]	004 Litten [E]
		056 Makuhita [10]	024 Pichu [E]	102 Sableye [21]	161 Salandit [E]	249 Sneasel [E]	105 Spinda [E]
		225 Togedemaru [E]					
Dark	Fake Tears	030 Bonsly [1]	210 Cleffa [E]	087 Cottonee [E]	123 Eevee [E]	134 Igglybuff [E]	246 Snorunt [E]
		258 Snubbull [E]	105 Spinda [E]	077 Vullaby [E]			
Normal	False Swipe (TM54)	245 Absol [TM]	164 Alolan Marowak [TM]	294 Buzzwole [TM]	163 Cubone [27, TM]	002 Dartrix [TM]	003 Decidueye [TM]
		074 Fearow [TM]	143 Fomantis [TM]	240 Garchomp [TM]	183 Golisopod [TM]	272 Hakamo-o [TM]	271 Jangmo-o [TM]
		298 Kartana [7, TM]	273 Kommo-o [TM]	144 Lurantis [TM]	301 Magearna [TM]	220 Pancham [TM]	221 Pangoro [TM]
		147 Paras [TM]	148 Parasect [TM]	295 Pheromosa [TM]	175 Pinsir [TM]	001 Rowlet [TM]	276 Scizor [13, TM]
		275 Scyther [13, TM]	249 Sneasel [TM]	073 Spearow [TM]	287 Tapu Bulu [TM]	285 Tapu Koko [1, TM]	250 Weavile [TM]
Flying	Feather Dance	002 Dartrix [46]	003 Decidueye [49]	277 Murkrow [E]	082 Oricorio [20]	010 Pikipek [33]	001 Rowlet [39]
		073 Spearow [E]	012 Toucannon [44]	011 Trumbeak [40]			
Normal	Feint	245 Absol [1]	045 Alolan Meowth [50]	046 Alolan Persian [65]	171 Bounsweet [E]	226 Elekid [E]	180 Goodra [1]
		280 Lucario [11]	056 Makuhita [E]	177 Passimian [E]	295 Pheromosa [19]	025 Pikachu [21]	175 Pinsir [E]
		279 Riolu [11]	102 Sableye [E]	276 Scizor [1, 61]	275 Scyther [61]	265 Sharpedo [1]	208 Skarmory [20]
		249 Sneasel [E]	235 Trapinch [29]				
Dark	Feint Attack	245 Absol [E]	071 Alolan Diglett [E]	045 Alolan Meowth [22]	046 Alolan Persian [22]	253 Alolan Vulpix [23]	030 Bonsly [19]
		237 Flygon [1]	134 Igglybuff [E]	166 Magby [12]	167 Magmar [12]	168 Magmortar [12]	056 Makuhita [E]
		078 Mandibuzz [23]	242 Mimikyu [23]	277 Murkrow [35, E]	176 Oranguru [22]	196 Phantump [19]	175 Pinsir [E]
		102 Sableye [19]	249 Sneasel [10]	258 Snubbull [E]	073 Spearow [E]	105 Spinda [10]	031 Sudowoodo [19]
		235 Trapinch [1]	197 Trevenant [19]	128 Umbreon [20]	236 Vibrava [1]	077 Vullaby [23]	250 Weavile [10]
		110 Wishiwashi [9]	068 Zubat [E]				
Bug	Fell Stinger	023 Ariados [1]	294 Buzzwole [1]	147 Paras [E]	139 Surskit [E]	225 Togedemaru [53]	
Fighting	Final Gambit	071 Alolan Diglett [E]	015 Alolan Rattata [E]	079 Mankey [50]	080 Primeape [1, 57]	279 Riolu [50]	
Fire	Fire Blast (TM38)	245 Absol [TM]	284 Aerodactyl [TM]	229 Alolan Geodude [TM]	231 Alolan Golem [TM]	230 Alolan Graveler [TM]	050 Alolan Grimer [TM]
		164 Alolan Marowak [TM]	051 Alolan Muk [TM]	053 Arcanine [TM]	117 Bagon [TM]	191 Bastiodon [TM]	034 Blissey [TM]
		181 Castform [35, TM]	297 Celesteela [TM]	033 Chansey [TM]	212 Clefable [TM]	211 Clefairy [TM]	210 Cleffa [TM]
		188 Cranidos [TM]	163 Cubone [TM]	282 Dragonair [TM]	283 Dragonite [TM]	244 Drampa [TM]	281 Dratini [TM]
		126 Flareon [TM]	159 Fletchinder [TM]	237 Flygon [TM]	239 Gabite [TM]	240 Garchomp [TM]	238 Gible [TM]
		180 Goodra [TM]	259 Granbull [TM]	052 Growlithe [TM]	299 Guzzlord [TM]	092 Gyarados [TM]	032 Happiny [TM]
		134 Igglybuff [TM]	006 Incineroar [TM]	135 Jigglypuff [TM]	165 Kangaskhan [TM]	004 Litten [TM]	097 Machamp [TM]
		096 Machoke [TM]	095 Machop [TM]	166 Magby [43, TM]	167 Magmar [55, TM]	168 Magmortar [55, TM]	035 Munchlax [TM]
		189 Rampardos [TM]	119 Salamence [TM]	161 Salandit [TM]	162 Salazzle [TM]	118 Shelgon [TM]	190 Shieldon [TM]
		038 Slowbro [TM]	039 Slowking [TM]	037 Slowpoke [TM]	036 Snorlax [TM]	258 Snubbull [TM]	291 Solgaleo [TM]
		160 Talonflame [TM]	137 Tauros [TM]	223 Torkoal [TM]	005 Torracat [TM]	224 Turtonator [TM]	136 Wigglytuff [TM]
	Fire Fang	284 Aerodactyl [1]	053 Arcanine [1]	117 Bagon [E]	126 Flareon [20]	240 Garchomp [1]	259 Granbull [1]
		052 Growlithe [21]	006 Incineroar [15]	120 Lillipup [E]	004 Litten [15]	103 Rockruff [E]	119 Salamence [1]
		232 Sandile [E]	204 Silvally [1]	258 Snubbull [1, E]	122 Stoutland [1]	005 Torracat [15]	
	Fire Pledge	006 Incineroar [T]	004 Litten [T]	005 Torracat [T]			
	Fire Punch	042 Abra [E]	283 Dragonite [1]	054 Drowzee [E]	228 Electivire [1]	226 Elekid [E]	061 Gastly [E]
		095 Machop [E]	166 Magby [29]	167 Magmar [29]	168 Magmortar [29]		
	Fire Spin	126 Flareon [25]	052 Growlithe [E]	166 Magby [15]	167 Magmar [15]	168 Magmortar [15]	223 Torkoal [13]
		224 Turtonator [E]					
Bug	First Impression	183 Golisopod [1, EV]					
Ground	Fissure	071 Alolan Diglett [43]	072 Alolan Dugtrio [53]	093 Barboach [44]	268 Lapras [E]	260 Shellos [E]	190 Shieldon [E]
		036 Snorlax [E]	223 Torkoal [E]	235 Trapinch [47]	266 Wailmer [E]	094 Whiscash [52]	

Type	Move Name	Pokémon					
Normal	Flail	229 Alolan Geodude [E]	045 Alolan Meowth [E]	251 Alolan Sandshrew [E]	253 Alolan Vulpix [E]	093 Barboach [E]	170 Bewear [19]
		030 Bonsly [5]	171 Bounsweet [29]	101 Carbink [35]	201 Chinchou [31, E]	112 Corsola [50]	123 Eevee [E]
		155 Feebas [50]	108 Finneon [E]	139 Fletchinder [10]	138 Fletchling [10]	153 Goldeen [13]	100 Goodra [20]
		178 Goomy [28]	222 Komala [26]	202 Lanturn [33]	111 Luvdisc [26]	091 Magikarp [30]	147 Paras [E]
		024 Pichu [E]	175 Pinsir [E]	262 Relicanth [1]	154 Seaking [13]	179 Sliggoo [28]	105 Spinda [50]
		169 Stufful [19]	031 Sudowoodo [1, 5]	160 Talonflame [16]	194 Tirtouga [E]	225 Togedemaru [E]	223 Torkoal [42]
		235 Trapinch [E]	224 Turtonator [17]				
Fire	Flame Burst	052 Growlithe [28]	166 Magby [22]	167 Magmar [22]	168 Magmortar [22]	161 Salandit [24]	162 Salazzle [24]
		223 Torkoal [E]					
	Flame Charge (TM43)	164 Alolan Marowak [TM]	053 Arcanine [TM]	297 Celesteela [TM]	126 Flareon [TM]	159 Fletchinder [38, TM]	138 Fletchling [34, TM]
		052 Growlithe [TM]	006 Incineroar [TM]	004 Litten [TM]	166 Magby [TM]	167 Magmar [TM]	168 Magmortar [TM]
		010 Pikipek [TM]	161 Salandit [TM]	162 Salazzle [TM]	204 Silvally [TM]	291 Solgaleo [TM]	160 Talonflame [39, TM]
		223 Torkoal [TM]	005 Torracat [TM]	012 Toucannon [TM]	011 Trumbeak [TM]	224 Turtonator [TM]	203 Type: Null [TM]
	Flame Wheel	164 Alolan Marowak [1, 11]	052 Growlithe [17]	223 Torkoal [18]			
Fire	Flamethrower (TM35)	245 Absol [TM]	284 Aerodactyl [TM]	270 Alolan Exeggutor [TM]	229 Alolan Geodude [TM]	231 Alolan Golem [TM]	230 Alolan Graveler [TM]
		050 Alolan Grimer [TM]	164 Alolan Marowak [TM]	051 Alolan Muk [TM]	053 Arcanine [TM]	117 Bagon [44, TM]	191 Bastiodon [TM]
		034 Blissey [TM]	181 Castform [TM]	297 Celesteela [TM]	033 Chansey [TM]	212 Clefable [TM]	211 Clefairy [TM]
		210 Cleffa [TM]	188 Cranidos [TM]	163 Cubone [TM]	282 Dragonair [TM]	283 Dragonite [TM]	244 Drampa [TM]
		281 Dratini [TM]	228 Electivire [TM]	126 Flareon [TM]	159 Fletchinder [TM]	237 Flygon [TM]	239 Gabite [TM]
		240 Garchomp [TM]	238 Gible [TM]	180 Goodra [TM]	259 Granbull [TM]	052 Growlithe [34, TM]	299 Guzzlord [TM]
		092 Gyarados [TM]	032 Happiny [TM]	134 Igglybuff [TM]	006 Incineroar [44, TM]	135 Jigglypuff [TM]	165 Kangaskhan [TM]
		273 Kommo-o [TM]	004 Litten [46, TM]	097 Machamp [TM]	096 Machoke [TM]	095 Machop [TM]	166 Magby [40, TM]
		167 Magmar [49, TM]	168 Magmortar [49, TM]	035 Munchlax [TM]	189 Rampardos [TM]	119 Salamence [49, TM]	161 Salandit [40, TM]
		162 Salazzle [44, TM]	118 Shelgon [49, TM]	190 Shieldon [TM]	204 Silvally [TM]	038 Slowbro [TM]	039 Slowking [TM]
		037 Slowpoke [TM]	036 Snorlax [TM]	258 Snubbull [TM]	291 Solgaleo [TM]	160 Talonflame [TM]	137 Tauros [TM]
		223 Torkoal [34, TM]	005 Torracat [42, TM]	224 Turtonator [29, TM]	136 Wigglytuff [TM]		
	Flare Blitz	164 Alolan Marowak [53]	126 Flareon [45]	052 Growlithe [45, E]	006 Incineroar [55]	004 Litten [43]	166 Magby [E]
		291 Solgaleo [61]	160 Talonflame [1]	005 Torracat [51]			
Normal	Flash	145 Morelull [8]	146 Shiinotic [1, 8]				
Steel	Flash Cannon (TM91)	071 Alolan Diglett [TM]	072 Alolan Dugtrio [TM]	191 Bastiodon [TM]	099 Boldore [TM]	297 Celesteela [37, TM]	263 Dhelmise [TM]
		100 Gigalith [TM]	241 Klefki [TM]	273 Kommo-o [TM]	280 Lucario [TM]	301 Magearna [41, TM]	047 Magnemite [31, TM]
		048 Magneton [33, TM]	049 Magnezone [33, TM]	216 Metagross [TM]	215 Metang [TM]	300 Necrozma [TM]	199 Probopass [TM]
		098 Roggenrola [TM]	276 Scizor [TM]	190 Shieldon [TM]	204 Silvally [TM]	208 Skarmory [TM]	291 Solgaleo [23, TM]
		185 Starmie [TM]	184 Staryu [TM]	012 Toucannon [TM]	224 Turtonator [TM]	256 Vanillish [TM]	255 Vanillite [TM]
		257 Vanilluxe [TM]	029 Vikavolt [TM]				
Dark	Flatter	045 Alolan Meowth [E]	054 Drowzee [E]	078 Mandibuzz [19]	277 Murkrow [E]	102 Sableye [E]	286 Tapu Lele [53]
		077 Vullaby [19]					
Fairy	Fleur Cannon	301 Magearna [49]					
Dark	Fling (TM56)	042 Abra [TM]	044 Alakazam [TM]	229 Alolan Geodude [TM]	231 Alolan Golem [TM]	230 Alolan Graveler [TM]	050 Alolan Grimer [26, TM]
		164 Alolan Marowak [37, TM]	051 Alolan Muk [26, TM]	026 Alolan Raichu [TM]	251 Alolan Sandshrew [TM]	252 Alolan Sandslash [TM]	170 Bewear [TM]
		034 Blissey [34, TM]	243 Bruxish [TM]	294 Buzzwole [TM]	033 Chansey [34, TM]	212 Clefable [TM]	211 Clefairy [TM]
		210 Cleffa [TM]	174 Comfey [TM]	060 Crabominable [TM]	059 Crabrawler [TM]	188 Cranidos [TM]	163 Cubone [33, TM]
		081 Delibird [TM]	283 Dragonite [TM]	244 Drampa [TM]	054 Drowzee [TM]	227 Electabuzz [TM]	228 Electivire [TM]
		226 Elekid [TM]	274 Emolga [TM]	143 Fomantis [TM]	248 Froslass [TM]	207 Garbodor [TM]	240 Garchomp [TM]
		063 Gengar [TM]	090 Golduck [TM]	183 Golisopod [TM]	259 Granbull [TM]	014 Gumshoos [TM]	299 Guzzlord [TM]
		272 Hakamo-o [TM]	032 Happiny [TM]	057 Hariyama [TM]	062 Haunter [TM]	055 Hypno [TM]	134 Igglybuff [TM]
		006 Incineroar [TM]	135 Jigglypuff [TM]	043 Kadabra [TM]	165 Kangaskhan [TM]	273 Kommo-o [TM]	233 Krokorok [TM]
		234 Krookodile [TM]	021 Ledian [TM]	020 Ledyba [TM]	280 Lucario [TM]	144 Lurantis [TM]	097 Machamp [TM]
		096 Machoke [TM]	095 Machop [TM]	166 Magby [TM]	167 Magmar [TM]	168 Magmortar [TM]	056 Makuhita [TM]
		079 Mankey [TM]	138 Miltank [TM]	242 Mimikyu [TM]	035 Munchlax [41, TM]	300 Necrozma [TM]	176 Oranguru [TM]
		187 Palossand [TM]	220 Pancham [TM]	221 Pangoro [TM]	177 Passimian [39, TM]	041 Pelipper [28, TM]	295 Pheromosa [TM]
		024 Pichu [TM]	025 Pikachu [TM]	175 Pinsir [TM]	152 Politoed [TM]	150 Poliwhirl [TM]	151 Poliwrath [TM]
		080 Primeape [1, TM]	089 Psyduck [TM]	189 Rampardos [TM]	279 Riolu [TM]	102 Sableye [TM]	161 Salandit [TM]
		162 Salazzle [TM]	276 Scizor [TM]	038 Slowbro [TM]	039 Slowking [TM]	249 Sneasel [TM]	036 Snorlax [TM]
		258 Snubbull [TM]	105 Spinda [TM]	172 Steenee [TM]	169 Stufful [TM]	031 Sudowoodo [TM]	287 Tapu Bulu [TM]
		288 Tapu Fini [TM]	286 Tapu Lele [TM]	225 Togedemaru [TM]	173 Tsareena [TM]	224 Turtonator [TM]	250 Weavile [28, TM]
		088 Whimsicott [TM]	136 Wigglytuff [TM]	296 Xurkitree [TM]			
Fairy	Floral Healing	174 Comfey [37]					
	Flower Shield	174 Comfey [1]					

Type	Move Name	Pokémon					
Flying	Fly (TM76)	284 Aerodactyl [TM]	193 Archeops [TM]	076 Braviary [TM]	297 Celesteela [TM]	070 Crobat [TM]	081 Delibird [TM]
		283 Dragonite [TM]	244 Drampa [45, TM]	065 Drifblim [TM]	074 Fearow [TM]	159 Fletchinder [TM]	158 Fletchling [TM]
		237 Flygon [TM]	069 Golbat [TM]	278 Honchkrow [TM]	292 Lunala [TM]	078 Mandibuzz [TM]	277 Murkrow [TM]
		082 Oricorio [TM]	041 Pelipper [TM]	010 Pikipek [TM]	075 Rufflet [TM]	119 Salamence [1, TM, EV]	208 Skarmory [TM]
		073 Spearow [TM]	160 Talonflame [TM]	285 Tapu Koko [TM]	012 Toucannon [TM]	011 Trumbeak [TM]	236 Vibrava [TM]
		077 Vullaby [TM]	040 Wingull [TM]	068 Zubat [TM]			
Fighting	Focus Blast (TM52)	044 Alakazam [TM]	231 Alolan Golem [TM]	164 Alolan Marowak [TM]	051 Alolan Muk [TM]	026 Alolan Raichu [TM]	252 Alolan Sandslash [TM]
		193 Archeops [TM]	170 Bewear [TM]	034 Blissey [TM]	195 Carracosta [TM]	212 Clefable [TM]	060 Crabominable [TM]
		059 Crabrawler [TM]	283 Dragonite [TM]	244 Drampa [TM]	227 Electabuzz [TM]	228 Electivire [TM]	207 Garbodor [TM]
		063 Gengar [TM]	090 Golduck [TM]	183 Golisopod [TM]	180 Goodra [TM]	259 Granbull [TM]	272 Hakamo-o [TM]
		057 Hariyama [TM]	055 Hypno [TM]	006 Incineroar [TM]	271 Jangmo-o [TM]	165 Kangaskhan [TM]	273 Kommo-o [TM]
		234 Krookodile [TM]	021 Ledian [TM]	280 Lucario [TM]	292 Lunala [TM]	097 Machamp [TM]	096 Machoke [TM]
		095 Machop [TM]	301 Magearna [TM]	167 Magmar [TM]	168 Magmortar [TM]	056 Makuhita [TM]	079 Mankey [TM]
		138 Miltank [TM]	133 Mudsdale [TM]	176 Oranguru [TM]	221 Pangoro [TM]	177 Passimian [TM]	295 Pheromosa [TM]
		175 Pinsir [TM]	152 Politoed [TM]	151 Poliwrath [TM]	080 Primeape [TM]	189 Rampardos [TM]	279 Riolu [TM]
		038 Slowbro [TM]	039 Slowking [TM]	036 Snorlax [TM]	291 Solgaleo [TM]	169 Stufful [TM]	287 Tapu Bulu [TM]
		286 Tapu Lele [TM]	197 Trevenant [TM]	224 Turtonator [TM]	250 Weavile [TM]	136 Wigglytuff [TM]	205 Zygarde [TM]
Normal	Focus Energy	016 Alolan Raticate [1, 7]	015 Alolan Rattata [7]	023 Ariados [1]	117 Bagon [21]	294 Buzzwole [1]	264 Carvanha [8]
		188 Cranidos [6]	163 Cubone [17]	065 Drifblim [13]	064 Drifloon [13]	074 Fearow [32]	057 Hariyama [1]
		165 Kangaskhan [E]	097 Machamp [1, 3]	096 Machoke [1, 3]	095 Machop [3]	166 Magby [E]	056 Makuhita [1]
		079 Mankey [1]	177 Passimian [11]	175 Pinsir [1]	080 Primeape [1]	189 Rampardos [1, 6]	119 Salamence [21]
		232 Sandile [E]	276 Scizor [5]	275 Scyther [5]	265 Sharpedo [1, 8]	118 Shelgon [21]	190 Shieldon [E]
		073 Spearow [29]	235 Trapinch [E]				
Fighting	Focus Punch	294 Buzzwole [73]	226 Elekid [E]	165 Kangaskhan [E]	020 Ledyba [E]	056 Makuhita [E]	079 Mankey [E]
		258 Snubbull [E]					
Normal	Follow Me	211 Clefairy [16]	279 Riolu [E]				
Fighting	Force Palm	057 Hariyama [13]	056 Makuhita [13]	279 Riolu [15]	169 Stufful [E]		
Normal	Foresight	284 Aerodactyl [E]	002 Dartrix [19]	003 Decidueye [19]	165 Kangaskhan [E]	268 Lapras [E]	280 Lucario [1]
		097 Machamp [9]	096 Machoke [9]	095 Machop [9]	056 Makuhita [E]	079 Mankey [E]	089 Psyduck [E]
		279 Riolu [1]	001 Rowlet [18]	102 Sableye [4]	249 Sneasel [E]	139 Surskit [E]	
Grass	Forest's Curse	196 Phantump [35]	197 Trevenant [35]				
Dark	Foul Play	045 Alolan Meowth [E]	278 Honchkrow [45]	241 Klefki [27]	233 Krokorok [40]	234 Krookodile [42]	277 Murkrow [45]
		176 Oranguru [36]	220 Pancham [E]	102 Sableye [41]	232 Sandile [37]	077 Vullaby [E]	
Ice	Freeze-Dry	253 Alolan Vulpix [E]	081 Delibird [E]	247 Glalie [1, EV]	268 Lapras [E]	257 Vanilluxe [1]	
Grass	Frenzy Plant	003 Decidueye [T]					
Ice	Frost Breath (TM79)	254 Alolan Ninetales [TM]	251 Alolan Sandshrew [TM]	252 Alolan Sandslash [TM]	253 Alolan Vulpix [TM]	142 Araquanid [TM]	243 Bruxish [TM]
		116 Cloyster [TM]	060 Crabominable [TM]	059 Crabrawler [TM]	081 Delibird [TM]	141 Dewpider [TM]	248 Froslass [TM]
		130 Glaceon [TM]	247 Glalie [37, TM]	183 Golisopod [TM]	268 Lapras [TM]	113 Mareanie [TM]	246 Snorunt [37, TM]
		114 Toxapex [TM]	256 Vanillish [TM]	255 Vanillite [TM]	257 Vanilluxe [TM]		
Normal	Frustration (TM21)	042 Abra [TM]	245 Absol [TM]	284 Aerodactyl [TM]	044 Alakazam [TM]	071 Alolan Diglett [TM]	072 Alolan Dugtrio [TM]
		270 Alolan Exeggutor [TM]	229 Alolan Geodude [TM]	231 Alolan Golem [TM]	230 Alolan Graveler [TM]	050 Alolan Grimer [TM]	164 Alolan Marowak [TM]
		045 Alolan Meowth [TM]	051 Alolan Muk [TM]	254 Alolan Ninetales [TM]	046 Alolan Persian [TM]	026 Alolan Raichu [TM]	016 Alolan Raticate [TM]
		015 Alolan Rattata [TM]	251 Alolan Sandshrew [TM]	252 Alolan Sandslash [TM]	253 Alolan Vulpix [TM]	157 Alomomola [TM]	142 Araquanid [TM]
		053 Arcanine [TM]	192 Archen [TM]	193 Archeops [TM]	023 Ariados [TM]	117 Bagon [TM]	093 Barboach [TM]
		191 Bastiodon [TM]	170 Bewear [TM]	034 Blissey [TM]	099 Boldore [TM]	030 Bonsly [TM]	171 Bounsweet [TM]
		076 Braviary [TM]	008 Brionne [TM]	243 Bruxish [TM]	019 Butterfree [TM]	294 Buzzwole [TM]	101 Carbink [TM]
		195 Carracosta [TM]	264 Carvanha [TM]	181 Castform [TM]	297 Celesteela [TM]	033 Chansey [TM]	028 Charjabug [TM]
		201 Chinchou [TM]	212 Clefable [TM]	211 Clefairy [TM]	210 Cleffa [TM]	116 Cloyster [TM]	174 Comfey [TM]
		112 Corsola [TM]	087 Cottonee [TM]	060 Crabominable [TM]	059 Crabrawler [TM]	188 Cranidos [TM]	070 Crobat [TM]
		163 Cubone [TM]	083 Cutiefly [TM]	002 Dartrix [TM]	003 Decidueye [TM]	081 Delibird [TM]	141 Dewpider [TM]
		263 Dhelmise [TM]	282 Dragonair [TM]	283 Dragonite [TM]	244 Drampa [TM]	281 Dratini [TM]	065 Drifblim [TM]
		064 Drifloon [TM]	054 Drowzee [TM]	123 Eevee [TM]	227 Electabuzz [TM]	228 Electivire [TM]	226 Elekid [TM]
		274 Emolga [TM]	127 Espeon [TM]	269 Exeggcute [TM]	074 Fearow [TM]	155 Feebas [TM]	108 Finneon [TM]
		126 Flareon [TM]	159 Fletchinder [TM]	158 Fletchling [TM]	237 Flygon [TM]	143 Fomantis [TM]	248 Froslass [TM]
		239 Gabite [TM]	207 Garbodor [TM]	240 Garchomp [TM]	061 Gastly [TM]	261 Gastrodon [TM]	063 Gengar [TM]
		238 Gible [TM]	100 Gigalith [TM]	130 Glaceon [TM]	247 Glalie [TM]	069 Golbat [TM]	153 Goldeen [TM]
		090 Golduck [TM]	183 Golisopod [TM]	180 Goodra [TM]	178 Goomy [TM]	259 Granbull [TM]	052 Growlithe [TM]
		027 Grubbin [TM]	014 Gumshoos [TM]	299 Guzzlord [TM]	092 Gyarados [TM]	272 Hakamo-o [TM]	032 Happiny [TM]
		057 Hariyama [TM]	062 Haunter [TM]	121 Herdier [TM]	278 Honchkrow [TM]	055 Hypno [TM]	134 Igglybuff [TM]
		006 Incineroar [TM]	271 Jangmo-o [TM]	135 Jigglypuff [TM]	125 Jolteon [TM]	043 Kadabra [TM]	165 Kangaskhan [TM]
		298 Kartana [TM]	241 Klefki [TM]	222 Komala [TM]	273 Kommo-o [TM]	233 Krokorok [TM]	234 Krookodile [TM]

Type	Move Name	Pokémon					
Normal	**Frustration (TM21)**	202 Lanturn [TM]	268 Lapras [TM]	129 Leafeon [TM]	021 Ledian [TM]	020 Ledyba [TM]	086 Lilligant [TM]
		120 Lillipup [TM]	004 Litten [TM]	280 Lucario [TM]	109 Lumineon [TM]	292 Lunala [TM]	144 Lurantis [TM]
		111 Luvdisc [TM]	104 Lycanroc (Midday Form) [TM]	104 Lycanroc (Midnight Form) [TM]	097 Machamp [TM]	096 Machoke [TM]	095 Machop [TM]
		166 Magby [TM]	301 Magearna [TM]	167 Magmar [TM]	168 Magmortar [TM]	047 Magnemite [TM]	048 Magneton [TM]
		049 Magnezone [TM]	056 Makuhita [TM]	078 Mandibuzz [TM]	079 Mankey [TM]	113 Mareanie [TM]	140 Masquerain [TM]
		216 Metagross [TM]	215 Metang [TM]	156 Milotic [TM]	138 Miltank [TM]	242 Mimikyu [TM]	213 Minior [TM]
		066 Misdreavus [TM]	067 Mismagius [TM]	145 Morelull [TM]	132 Mudbray [TM]	133 Mudsdale [TM]	035 Munchlax [TM]
		277 Murkrow [TM]	300 Necrozma [TM]	293 Nihilego [TM]	198 Nosepass [TM]	176 Oranguru [TM]	082 Oricorio [TM]
		187 Palossand [TM]	220 Pancham [TM]	221 Pangoro [TM]	147 Paras [TM]	148 Parasect [TM]	177 Passimian [TM]
		041 Pelipper [TM]	085 Petilil [TM]	196 Phantump [TM]	295 Pheromosa [TM]	024 Pichu [TM]	025 Pikachu [TM]
		010 Pikipek [TM]	175 Pinsir [TM]	152 Politoed [TM]	149 Poliwag [TM]	150 Poliwhirl [TM]	151 Poliwrath [TM]
		007 Popplio [TM]	217 Porygon [TM]	218 Porygon2 [TM]	219 Porygon-Z [TM]	009 Primarina [TM]	080 Primeape [TM]
		199 Probopass [TM]	089 Psyduck [TM]	189 Rampardos [TM]	262 Relicanth [TM]	084 Ribombee [TM]	279 Riolu [TM]
		103 Rockruff [TM]	098 Roggenrola [TM]	001 Rowlet [TM]	075 Rufflet [TM]	102 Sableye [TM]	119 Salamence [TM]
		161 Salandit [TM]	162 Salazzle [TM]	232 Sandile [TM]	186 Sandygast [TM]	276 Scizor [TM]	275 Scyther [TM]
		154 Seaking [TM]	265 Sharpedo [TM]	118 Shelgon [TM]	115 Shellder [TM]	260 Shellos [TM]	190 Shieldon [TM]
		146 Shiinotic [TM]	204 Silvally [TM]	208 Skarmory [TM]	179 Sliggoo [TM]	038 Slowbro [TM]	039 Slowking [TM]
		037 Slowpoke [TM]	249 Sneasel [TM]	036 Snorlax [TM]	240 Snorunt [TM]	258 Snubbull [TM]	291 Solgaleo [TM]
		073 Spearow [TM]	022 Spinarak [TM]	105 Spinda [TM]	185 Starmie [TM]	184 Staryu [TM]	172 Steenee [TM]
		122 Stoutland [TM]	169 Stufful [TM]	031 Sudowoodo [TM]	139 Surskit [TM]	131 Sylveon [TM]	160 Talonflame [TM]
		287 Tapu Bulu [TM]	288 Tapu Fini [TM]	285 Tapu Koko [TM]	286 Tapu Lele [TM]	137 Tauros [TM]	106 Tentacool [TM]
		107 Tentacruel [TM]	194 Turtonator [TM]	225 Togedemaru [TM]	223 Torkoal [TM]	005 Torracat [TM]	012 Toucannon [TM]
		114 Toxapex [TM]	235 Trapinch [TM]	197 Trevenant [TM]	206 Trubbish [TM]	011 Trumbeak [TM]	173 Tsareena [TM]
		224 Turtonator [TM]	203 Type: Null [TM]	128 Umbreon [TM]	256 Vanillish [TM]	255 Vanillite [TM]	257 Vanilluxe [TM]
		124 Vaporeon [TM]	236 Vibrava [TM]	029 Vikavolt [TM]	077 Vullaby [TM]	266 Wailmer [TM]	267 Wailord [TM]
		250 Weavile [TM]	088 Whimsicott [TM]	094 Whiscash [TM]	136 Wigglytuff [TM]	182 Wimpod [TM]	040 Wingull [TM]
		110 Wishiwashi [TM]	296 Xurkitree [TM]	013 Yungoos [TM]	068 Zubat [TM]	205 Zygarde [TM]	
	Fury Attack	076 Braviary [1, 5]	002 Dartrix [33]	003 Decidueye [33]	074 Fearow [11]	153 Goldeen [24]	078 Mandibuzz [1, 5]
		010 Pikipek [21]	175 Pinsir [E]	001 Rowlet [29]	075 Rufflet [5]	154 Seaking [24]	208 Skarmory [17]
		073 Spearow [11]	012 Toucannon [24]	011 Trumbeak [24]	077 Vullaby [5]		
Bug	**Fury Cutter**	251 Alolan Sandshrew [11]	143 Fomantis [1]	183 Golisopod [1, 4]	298 Kartana [1]	144 Lurantis [1]	147 Paras [17]
		148 Parasect [17]	276 Scizor [25]	275 Scyther [25]	235 Trapinch [E]		
Normal	**Fury Swipes**	045 Alolan Meowth [14]	046 Alolan Persian [14]	015 Alolan Rattata [E]	251 Alolan Sandshrew [20]	023 Ariados [23]	090 Golduck [13]
		006 Incineroar [33]	004 Litten [29]	079 Mankey [5]	080 Primeape [5]	089 Psyduck [13]	102 Sableye [11]
		249 Sneasel [16]	022 Spinarak [22]	005 Torracat [33]	250 Weavile [16]		
Psychic	**Future Sight**	245 Absol [1, 53]	044 Alakazam [43]	093 Darboach [39]	101 Castform [E]	081 Delibird [E]	054 Drowzee [61]
		127 Espeon [25]	055 Hypno [1, 61]	043 Kadabra [43]	268 Lapras [E]	176 Oranguru [46]	089 Psyduck [E]
		037 Slowpoke [E]	094 Whiscash [45]				
Poison	**Gastro Acid**	299 Guzzlord [53]	200 Pyukumuku [29]				
Steel	**Gear Up**	301 Magearna [1]					
Grass	**Giga Drain**	297 Celesteela [31]	087 Cottonee [26]	263 Dhelmise [23]	269 Exeggcute [E]	143 Fomantis [E]	129 Leafeon [25]
		145 Morelull [29]	187 Palossand [36]	147 Paras [38]	148 Parasect [44]	085 Petilil [26]	186 Sandygast [36]
		146 Shiinotic [31]	287 Tapu Bulu [14]	068 Zubat [E]			
Normal	**Giga Impact (TM68)**	245 Absol [TM]	284 Aerodactyl [81, TM]	044 Alakazam [TM]	072 Alolan Dugtrio [TM]	270 Alolan Exeggutor [TM]	231 Alolan Golem [TM]
		164 Alolan Marowak [TM]	051 Alolan Muk [TM]	254 Alolan Ninetales [TM]	046 Alolan Persian [TM]	026 Alolan Raichu [TM]	016 Alolan Raticate [TM]
		252 Alolan Sandslash [TM]	053 Arcanine [TM]	193 Archeops [TM]	023 Ariados [TM]	191 Bastiodon [TM]	170 Bewear [TM]
		034 Blissey [TM]	076 Braviary [TM]	243 Bruxish [TM]	019 Butterfree [TM]	294 Buzzwole [TM]	195 Carracosta [TM]
		297 Celesteela [TM]	033 Chansey [TM]	212 Clefable [TM]	116 Cloyster [TM]	060 Crabominable [TM]	070 Crobat [TM]
		003 Decidueye [TM]	263 Dhelmise [TM]	283 Dragonite [TM]	244 Drampa [TM]	065 Drifblim [TM]	227 Electabuzz [TM]
		228 Electivire [62, TM]	127 Espeon [TM]	074 Fearow [TM]	126 Flareon [TM]	237 Flygon [TM]	248 Froslass [TM]
		207 Garbodor [TM]	240 Garchomp [TM]	261 Gastrodon [TM]	063 Gengar [TM]	100 Gigalith [TM]	130 Glaceon [TM]
		247 Glalie [TM]	069 Golbat [TM]	090 Golduck [TM]	183 Golisopod [TM]	180 Goodra [TM]	259 Granbull [TM]
		299 Guzzlord [TM]	092 Gyarados [TM]	057 Hariyama [TM]	121 Herdier [47, TM]	278 Honchkrow [TM]	055 Hypno [TM]
		006 Incineroar [TM]	125 Jolteon [TM]	165 Kangaskhan [TM]	298 Kartana [TM]	241 Klefki [TM]	273 Kommo-o [TM]
		234 Krookodile [TM]	202 Lanturn [TM]	268 Lapras [TM]	129 Leafeon [TM]	021 Ledian [TM]	086 Lilligant [TM]
		120 Lillipup [40, TM]	280 Lucario [TM]	109 Lumineon [TM]	292 Lunala [TM]	144 Lurantis [TM]	097 Machamp [TM]
		301 Magearna [TM]	167 Magmar [TM]	168 Magmortar [TM]	048 Magneton [TM]	049 Magnezone [TM]	078 Mandibuzz [TM]
		140 Masquerain [TM]	216 Metagross [TM]	156 Milotic [TM]	138 Miltank [TM]	213 Minior [TM]	067 Mismagius [TM]
		133 Mudsdale [TM]	300 Necrozma [TM]	176 Oranguru [TM]	187 Palossand [TM]	221 Pangoro [TM]	148 Parasect [TM]
		177 Passimian [50, TM]	041 Pelipper [TM]	295 Pheromosa [TM]	175 Pinsir [TM]	152 Politoed [TM]	151 Poliwrath [TM]

Type	Move Name	Pokémon					
Normal	Giga Impact (TM68)	217 Porygon [TM]	218 Porygon2 [TM]	219 Porygon-Z [TM]	009 Primarina [TM]	080 Primeape [TM]	199 Probopass [TM]
		189 Rampardos [TM]	262 Relicanth [TM]	119 Salamence [TM]	276 Scizor [TM]	275 Scyther [TM]	154 Seaking [TM]
		265 Sharpedo [TM]	146 Shiinotic [TM]	204 Silvally [TM]	038 Slowbro [TM]	039 Slowking [TM]	036 Snorlax [35, TM]
		291 Solgaleo [73, TM]	185 Starmie [TM]	122 Stoutland [59, TM]	131 Sylveon [TM]	160 Talonflame [TM]	287 Tapu Bulu [TM]
		288 Tapu Fini [TM]	285 Tapu Koko [TM]	286 Tapu Lele [TM]	137 Tauros [63, TM]	107 Tentacruel [TM]	225 Togedemaru [TM]
		223 Torkoal [TM]	197 Trevenant [TM]	173 Tsareena [TM]	224 Turtonator [TM]	203 Type: Null [TM]	128 Umbreon [TM]
		257 Vanilluxe [TM]	124 Vaporeon [TM]	029 Vikavolt [TM]	267 Wailord [TM]	250 Weavile [TM]	088 Whimsicott [TM]
		094 Whiscash [TM]	136 Wigglytuff [TM]	296 Xurkitree [TM]	205 Zygarde [TM]		
	Glare	244 Drampa [13]	205 Zygarde [1]				
Grass	Grass Knot (TM86)	042 Abra [TM]	044 Alakazam [TM]	270 Alolan Exeggutor [TM]	026 Alolan Raichu [TM]	016 Alolan Raticate [TM]	015 Alolan Rattata [TM]
		034 Blissey [TM]	171 Bounsweet [TM]	297 Celesteela [TM]	033 Chansey [TM]	212 Clefable [TM]	211 Clefairy [TM]
		210 Cleffa [TM]	174 Comfey [34, TM]	087 Cottonee [TM]	002 Dartrix [TM]	003 Decidueye [TM]	263 Dhelmise [TM]
		244 Drampa [TM]	054 Drowzee [TM]	127 Espeon [TM]	269 Exeggcute [TM]	143 Fomantis [TM]	032 Happiny [TM]
		055 Hypno [TM]	134 Igglybuff [TM]	135 Jigglypuff [TM]	043 Kadabra [TM]	233 Krokorok [TM]	234 Krookodile [TM]
		129 Leafeon [TM]	086 Lilligant [TM]	144 Lurantis [TM]	301 Magearna [TM]	216 Metagross [TM]	215 Metang [TM]
		145 Morelull [TM]	293 Nihilego [TM]	220 Pancham [TM]	221 Pangoro [TM]	147 Paras [TM]	148 Parasect [TM]
		177 Passimian [TM]	085 Petilil [TM]	196 Phantump [TM]	024 Pichu [TM]	025 Pikachu [TM]	001 Rowlet [TM]
		146 Shiinotic [TM]	038 Slowbro [TM]	039 Slowking [TM]	037 Slowpoke [TM]	185 Starmie [TM]	172 Steenee [TM]
		287 Tapu Bulu [TM]	288 Tapu Fini [TM]	285 Tapu Koko [TM]	286 Tapu Lele [TM]	225 Togedemaru [TM]	197 Trevenant [TM]
		173 Tsareena [TM]	088 Whimsicott [TM]	136 Wigglytuff [TM]	296 Xurkitree [TM]	205 Zygarde [TM]	
	Grass Pledge	002 Dartrix [T]	003 Decidueye [T]	001 Rowlet [T]			
	Grass Whistle	171 Bounsweet [E]	087 Cottonee [E]	129 Leafeon [17]	085 Petilil [E]		
	Grassy Terrain	174 Comfey [46]	269 Exeggcute [E]	287 Tapu Bulu [1]			
Psychic	Gravity	033 Chansey [E]	211 Clefairy [49]	032 Happiny [E]	134 Igglybuff [E]	300 Necrozma [31]	199 Probopass [1]
		098 Roggenrola [E]					
Normal	Growl	071 Alolan Diglett [4]	072 Alolan Dugtrio [1, 4]	164 Alolan Marowak [1]	045 Alolan Meowth [1]	046 Alolan Persian [1]	034 Blissey [1]
		008 Brionne [1, 4]	033 Chansey [1]	211 Clefairy [1]	163 Cubone [1]	002 Dartrix [1, 4]	003 Decidueye [1, 4]
		123 Eevee [1]	074 Fearow [1]	159 Fletchinder [1]	158 Fletchling [1]	006 Incineroar [1, 4]	268 Lapras [1]
		004 Litten [4]	138 Miltank [3]	066 Misdreavus [1]	067 Mismagius [1]	082 Oricorio [4]	041 Pelipper [1]
		025 Pikachu [5]	010 Pikipek [3]	007 Popplio [4]	009 Primarina [1, 4]	001 Rowlet [4]	038 Slowbro [1, 5]
		039 Slowking [5]	037 Slowpoke [5]	073 Spearow [1]	160 Talonflame [1]	005 Torracat [1, 4]	012 Toucannon [1, 3]
		011 Trumbeak [1, 3]	266 Wailmer [4]	267 Wailord [1, 4]	040 Wingull [1]	110 Wishiwashi [1]	
	Growth	174 Comfey [13]	087 Cottonee [4]	263 Dhelmise [1]	143 Fomantis [14]	086 Lilligant [1]	144 Lurantis [1, 14]
		145 Morelull [E]	147 Paras [33]	148 Parasect [37]	085 Petilil [4]	196 Phantump [8]	197 Trevenant [1, 8]
		088 Whimsicott [1]					
Ghost	Grudge	253 Alolan Vulpix [44]	061 Gastly [E]	242 Mimikyu [E]	066 Misdreavus [50]	196 Phantump [E]	
Psychic	Guard Split	042 Abra [E]	101 Carbink [27]	293 Nihilego [1]	190 Shieldon [E]	105 Spinda [E]	
	Guard Swap	042 Abra [E]	181 Castform [E]	054 Drowzee [E]	208 Skarmory [E]	194 Tirtouga [E]	128 Umbreon [45]
Normal	Guillotine	298 Kartana [73]	175 Pinsir [50]	029 Vikavolt [25]			
Poison	Gunk Shot	050 Alolan Grimer [40]	051 Alolan Muk [40]	207 Garbodor [54]	206 Trubbish [45]		
Flying	Gust	019 Butterfree [1, EV]	065 Drifblim [1, 8]	064 Drifloon [8]	108 Finneon [17]	109 Lumineon [1, 17]	078 Mandibuzz [1]
		140 Masquerain [17]	235 Trapinch [E]	077 Vullaby [1]	088 Whimsicott [10]	040 Wingull [E]	068 Zubat [E]
Steel	Gyro Ball (TM74)	229 Alolan Geodude [TM]	231 Alolan Golem [TM]	230 Alolan Graveler [TM]	251 Alolan Sandshrew [34, TM]	252 Alolan Sandslash [TM]	294 Buzzwole [TM]
		101 Carbink [TM]	297 Celesteela [TM]	263 Dhelmise [14, TM]	065 Drifblim [TM]	064 Drifloon [TM]	247 Glalie [TM]
		299 Guzzlord [TM]	135 Jigglypuff [35, TM]	301 Magearna [TM]	047 Magnemite [47, TM]	048 Magneton [59, TM]	049 Magnezone [59, TM]
		216 Metagross [TM]	215 Metang [TM]	138 Miltank [41, TM]	213 Minior [TM]	300 Necrozma [TM]	177 Passimian [TM]
		291 Solgaleo [TM]	185 Starmie [TM]	184 Staryu [24, TM]	225 Togedemaru [TM]	223 Torkoal [TM]	136 Wigglytuff [TM]
Ice	Hail (TM07)	245 Absol [TM]	254 Alolan Ninetales [TM]	251 Alolan Sandshrew [42, TM]	252 Alolan Sandslash [TM]	253 Alolan Vulpix [TM]	157 Alomomola [TM]
		093 Barboach [TM]	034 Blissey [TM]	008 Brionne [TM]	101 Carbink [TM]	264 Carvanha [TM]	181 Castform [20, TM]
		033 Chansey [TM]	201 Chinchou [TM]	116 Cloyster [TM]	112 Corsola [TM]	060 Crabominable [TM]	081 Delibird [TM]
		282 Dragonair [TM]	283 Dragonite [TM]	281 Dratini [TM]	155 Feebas [TM]	108 Finneon [TM]	248 Froslass [54, TM]
		261 Gastrodon [TM]	130 Glaceon [37, TM]	247 Glalie [54, TM]	153 Goldeen [TM]	090 Golduck [TM]	183 Golisopod [TM]
		180 Goodra [TM]	092 Gyarados [TM]	032 Happiny [TM]	165 Kangaskhan [TM]	202 Lanturn [TM]	268 Lapras [TM]
		109 Lumineon [TM]	111 Luvdisc [TM]	113 Mareanie [TM]	156 Milotic [TM]	041 Pelipper [TM]	152 Politoed [TM]
		149 Poliwag [TM]	150 Poliwhirl [TM]	151 Poliwrath [TM]	007 Popplio [TM]	009 Primarina [TM]	089 Psyduck [TM]
		200 Pyukumuku [TM]	262 Relicanth [TM]	154 Seaking [TM]	265 Sharpedo [TM]	115 Shellder [TM]	260 Shellos [TM]
		204 Silvally [TM]	038 Slowbro [TM]	039 Slowking [TM]	037 Slowpoke [TM]	249 Sneasel [TM]	246 Snorunt [50, TM]
		185 Starmie [TM]	184 Staryu [TM]	106 Tentacool [TM]	107 Tentacruel [TM]	114 Toxapex [TM]	203 Type: Null [TM]
		256 Vanillish [42, TM]	255 Vanillite [40, TM]	257 Vanilluxe [42, TM]	124 Vaporeon [TM]	266 Wailmer [TM]	267 Wailord [TM]
		250 Weavile [TM]	094 Whiscash [TM]	182 Wimpod [TM]	040 Wingull [TM]	110 Wishiwashi [TM]	

Type	Move Name	Pokémon					
Fighting	Hammer Arm	170 Bewear [36]	294 Buzzwole [47]	188 Cranidos [E]	226 Elekid [E]	299 Guzzlord [43]	165 Kangaskhan [E]
		216 Metagross [1, EV]	138 Miltank [E]	221 Pangoro [1, 70]	169 Stufful [32]	031 Sudowoodo [50]	
Normal	Harden	030 Alolan Grimer [4]	031 Alolan Muk [1, 4]	099 Boldore [1, 4]	030 Bonsly [E]	294 Buzzwole [1]	101 Carbink [1]
		297 Celesteela [1]	112 Corsola [1]	261 Gastrodon [1, 4]	100 Gigalith [1, 4]	027 Grubbin [E]	018 Metapod [1, EV]
		198 Nosepass [4]	187 Palossand [1]	175 Pinsir [11]	200 Pyukumuku [1]	262 Relicanth [1]	098 Roggenrola [4]
		186 Sandygast [1]	260 Shellos [4]	184 Staryu [1]	031 Sudowoodo [E]	256 Vanillish [1, 4]	255 Vanillite [4]
		257 Vanilluxe [1, 4]	182 Wimpod [E]				
Ice	Haze	070 Crobat [40]	281 Dratini [E]	064 Drifloon [E]	155 Feebas [E]	061 Gastly [E]	069 Golbat [40]
		153 Goldeen [E]	278 Honchkrow [1]	113 Mareanie [E]	277 Murkrow [11]	149 Poliwag [E]	001 Rowlet [E]
		155 Surskit [15]	288 Tapu Fini [1]	106 Tentacool [E]	200 Trubbish [E]	124 Vaporeon [33]	068 Zubat [35]
		205 Zygarde [44]					
Rock	Head Smash	192 Archen [E]	112 Corsola [E]	188 Cranidos [46]	293 Nihilego [73]	189 Rampardos [58]	262 Relicanth [1, 56]
		031 Sudowoodo [54]	224 Turtonator [E]				
Normal	Headbutt	071 Alolan Diglett [E]	117 Bagon [17]	099 Boldore [1, 10]	030 Bonsly [E]	181 Castform [15]	188 Cranidos [1]
		163 Cubone [11]	054 Drowzee [13, 29]	100 Gigalith [1, 10]	247 Glalie [28]	259 Granbull [19]	272 Hakamo-o [25]
		055 Hypno [13, 29]	271 Jangmo-o [25]	273 Kommo-o [25]	293 Nihilego [19]	189 Rampardos [1]	098 Roggenrola [10]
		119 Salamence [17]	118 Shelgon [17]	190 Shieldon [E]	038 Slowbro [23]	039 Slowking [23]	037 Slowpoke [23]
		246 Snorunt [28]	258 Snubbull [19]	031 Sudowoodo [E]			
	Heal Bell	033 Chansey [E]	032 Happiny [E]	138 Miltank [48]	258 Snubbull [E]		
	Heal Block	241 Klefki [50]	204 Silvally [1]	203 Type: Null [85]			
Psychic	Heal Pulse	157 Alomomola [17]	034 Blissey [38]	033 Chansey [38]	210 Cleffa [E]	134 Igglybuff [E]	280 Lucario [51]
		111 Luvdisc [E]	038 Slowbro [1, 68]	039 Slowking [1, 58]	037 Slowpoke [58]	288 Tapu Fini [1]	
	Healing Wish	157 Alomomola [1, 57]	034 Blissey [50]	033 Chansey [50]	211 Clefairy [55]	085 Petilil [E]	
	Heart Stamp	111 Luvdisc [22]	138 Miltank [E]				
	Heart Swap	301 Magearna [89]					
Fire	Heat Wave	052 Growlithe [41, E]	004 Litten [E]	223 Torkoal [45]			
Steel	Heavy Slam	231 Alolan Golem [1, 60]	191 Bastiodon [58]	297 Celesteela [67]	263 Dhelmise [50]	299 Guzzlord [59]	057 Hariyama [54]
		095 Machop [E]	056 Makuhita [46]	132 Mudbray [31]	133 Mudsdale [34]	098 Roggenrola [E]	190 Shieldon [46]
		036 Snorlax [50]	266 Wailmer [53]	267 Wailord [1, 65]			
Normal	Helping Hand	157 Alomomola [1, 53]	033 Chansey [E]	174 Comfey [1]	087 Cottonee [31]	123 Eevee [1]	127 Espeon [1]
		126 Flareon [1]	130 Glaceon [1]	052 Growlithe [12]	032 Happiny [E]	121 Herdier [12]	125 Jolteon [1]
		129 Leafeon [1]	120 Lillipup [12]	301 Magearna [1]	056 Makuhita [E]	138 Miltank [E]	082 Oricorio [10]
		085 Petilil [31]	200 Pyukumuku [5]	122 Stoutland [12]	131 Sylveon [1]	128 Umbreon [1]	124 Vaporeon [1]
		110 Wishiwashi [6]					
Ghost	Hex	245 Absol [E]	164 Alolan Marowak [17]	253 Alolan Vulpix [26]	181 Castform [E]	065 Drifblim [27]	064 Drifloon [27]
		061 Gastly [43]	063 Gengar [55]	062 Haunter [55]	066 Misdreavus [23]	246 Snorunt [E]	106 Tentacool [40]
		107 Tentacruel [44]					
Normal	Hidden Power (TM10)	042 Abra [TM]	245 Absol [TM]	284 Aerodactyl [TM]	044 Alakazam [TM]	071 Alolan Diglett [TM]	072 Alolan Dugtrio [TM]
		270 Alolan Exeggutor [TM]	229 Alolan Geodude [TM]	231 Alolan Golem [TM]	230 Alolan Graveler [TM]	050 Alolan Grimer [TM]	164 Alolan Marowak [TM]
		045 Alolan Meowth [TM]	051 Alolan Muk [TM]	254 Alolan Ninetales [TM]	046 Alolan Persian [TM]	026 Alolan Raichu [TM]	016 Alolan Raticate [TM]
		015 Alolan Rattata [TM]	251 Alolan Sandshrew [TM]	252 Alolan Sandslash [TM]	253 Alolan Vulpix [TM]	157 Alomomola [TM]	142 Araquanid [TM]
		053 Arcanine [TM]	192 Archen [TM]	193 Archeops [TM]	023 Ariados [TM]	117 Bagon [TM]	093 Barboach [TM]
		191 Bastiodon [TM]	170 Bewear [TM]	034 Blissey [TM]	099 Boldore [TM]	030 Bonsly [TM]	171 Bounsweet [TM]
		076 Braviary [TM]	008 Brionne [TM]	243 Bruxish [TM]	019 Butterfree [TM]	294 Buzzwole [TM]	101 Carbink [TM]
		195 Carracosta [TM]	264 Carvanha [TM]	181 Castform [TM]	297 Celesteela [TM]	033 Chansey [TM]	028 Charjabug [TM]
		201 Chinchou [TM]	212 Clefable [TM]	211 Clefairy [TM]	210 Cleffa [TM]	116 Cloyster [TM]	174 Comfey [TM]
		112 Corsola [TM]	087 Cottonee [TM]	060 Crabominable [TM]	059 Crabrawler [TM]	188 Cranidos [TM]	070 Crobat [TM]
		163 Cubone [TM]	083 Cutiefly [TM]	002 Dartrix [TM]	003 Decidueye [TM]	081 Delibird [TM]	141 Dewpider [TM]
		263 Dhelmise [TM]	282 Dragonair [TM]	283 Dragonite [TM]	244 Drampa [TM]	281 Dratini [TM]	065 Drifblim [TM]
		064 Drifloon [TM]	054 Drowzee [TM]	123 Eevee [TM]	227 Electabuzz [TM]	228 Electivire [TM]	226 Elekid [TM]
		274 Emolga [TM]	127 Espeon [TM]	269 Exeggcute [TM]	074 Fearow [TM]	155 Feebas [TM]	108 Finneon [TM]
		126 Flareon [TM]	159 Fletchinder [TM]	158 Fletchling [TM]	237 Flygon [TM]	143 Fomantis [TM]	248 Froslass [TM]
		239 Gabite [TM]	207 Garbodor [TM]	240 Garchomp [TM]	061 Gastly [TM]	261 Gastrodon [16, TM]	063 Gengar [TM]
		238 Gible [TM]	100 Gigalith [TM]	130 Glaceon [TM]	247 Glalie [TM]	069 Golbat [TM]	153 Goldeen [TM]
		090 Golduck [TM]	183 Golisopod [TM]	180 Goodra [TM]	178 Goomy [TM]	259 Granbull [TM]	052 Growlithe [TM]
		027 Grubbin [TM]	014 Gumshoos [TM]	299 Guzzlord [TM]	092 Gyarados [TM]	272 Hakamo-o [TM]	032 Happiny [TM]
		057 Hariyama [TM]	062 Haunter [TM]	121 Herdier [TM]	278 Honchkrow [TM]	055 Hypno [TM]	134 Igglybuff [TM]
		006 Incineroar [TM]	271 Jangmo-o [TM]	135 Jigglypuff [TM]	125 Jolteon [TM]	043 Kadabra [TM]	165 Kangaskhan [TM]
		298 Kartana [TM]	241 Klefki [TM]	222 Komala [TM]	273 Kommo-o [TM]	233 Krokorok [TM]	234 Krookodile [TM]
		202 Lantern [TM]	268 Lapras [TM]	129 Leafeon [TM]	021 Ledian [TM]	020 Ledyba [TM]	086 Lilligant [TM]
		120 Lillipup [TM]	004 Litten [TM]	280 Lucario [TM]	109 Lumineon [TM]	292 Lunala [TM]	144 Lurantis [TM]

Type	Move Name	Pokémon					
Normal	Hidden Power (TM10)	111 Luvdisc [TM]	104 Lycanroc (Midday Form) [TM]	104 Lycanroc (Midnight Form) [TM]	097 Machamp [TM]	096 Machoke [TM]	095 Machop [TM]
		166 Magby [TM]	301 Magearna [TM]	167 Magmar [TM]	168 Magmortar [TM]	047 Magnemite [TM]	048 Magneton [TM]
		049 Magnezone [TM]	056 Makuhita [TM]	078 Mandibuzz [TM]	079 Mankey [TM]	113 Mareanie [TM]	140 Masquerain [TM]
		216 Metagross [TM]	215 Metang [TM]	156 Milotic [TM]	138 Miltank [TM]	242 Mimikyu [TM]	213 Minior [TM]
		066 Misdreavus [TM]	067 Mismagius [TM]	145 Morelull [TM]	132 Mudbray [TM]	133 Mudsdale [TM]	035 Munchlax [TM]
		277 Murkrow [TM]	300 Necrozma [TM]	293 Nihilego [TM]	198 Nosepass [TM]	176 Oranguru [TM]	082 Oricorio [TM]
		187 Palossand [TM]	220 Pancham [TM]	221 Pangoro [TM]	147 Paras [TM]	148 Parasect [TM]	177 Passimian [TM]
		041 Pelipper [TM]	085 Petilil [TM]	196 Phantump [TM]	295 Pheromosa [TM]	024 Pichu [TM]	025 Pikachu [TM]
		010 Pikipek [TM]	175 Pinsir [TM]	152 Politoed [TM]	149 Poliwag [TM]	150 Poliwhirl [TM]	151 Poliwrath [TM]
		007 Popplio [TM]	217 Porygon [TM]	218 Porygon2 [TM]	219 Porygon-Z [TM]	009 Primarina [TM]	080 Primeape [TM]
		199 Probopass [TM]	089 Psyduck [TM]	189 Rampardos [TM]	262 Relicanth [TM]	084 Ribombee [TM]	279 Riolu [TM]
		103 Rockruff [TM]	098 Roggenrola [TM]	001 Rowlet [TM]	075 Rufflet [TM]	102 Sableye [TM]	119 Salamence [TM]
		161 Salandit [TM]	162 Salazzle [TM]	232 Sandile [TM]	186 Sandygast [TM]	276 Scizor [TM]	275 Scyther [TM]
		154 Seaking [TM]	265 Sharpedo [TM]	118 Shelgon [TM]	115 Shellder [TM]	260 Shellos [16, TM]	190 Shieldon [TM]
		146 Shiinotic [TM]	204 Silvally [TM]	208 Skarmory [TM]	179 Sliggoo [TM]	038 Slowbro [TM]	039 Slowking [1, TM]
		037 Slowpoke [TM]	249 Sneasel [TM]	036 Snorlax [TM]	246 Snorunt [TM]	258 Snubbull [TM]	291 Solgaleo [TM]
		073 Spearow [TM]	022 Spinarak [TM]	105 Spinda [TM]	185 Starmie [TM]	184 Staryu [TM]	172 Steenee [TM]
		122 Stoutland [TM]	169 Stufful [TM]	031 Sudowoodo [TM]	139 Surskit [TM]	131 Sylveon [TM]	160 Talonflame [TM]
		287 Tapu Bulu [TM]	288 Tapu Fini [TM]	285 Tapu Koko [TM]	286 Tapu Lele [TM]	137 Tauros [TM]	106 Tentacool [TM]
		107 Tentacruel [TM]	194 Tirtouga [TM]	225 Togedemaru [TM]	223 Torkoal [TM]	005 Torracat [TM]	012 Toucannon [TM]
		114 Toxapex [TM]	235 Trapinch [TM]	197 Trevenant [TM]	206 Trubbish [TM]	011 Trumbeak [TM]	173 Tsareena [TM]
		224 Turtonator [TM]	203 Type: Null [TM]	128 Umbreon [TM]	256 Vanillish [TM]	255 Vanillite [TM]	257 Vanilluxe [TM]
		124 Vaporeon [TM]	236 Vibrava [TM]	029 Vikavolt [TM]	077 Vullaby [TM]	266 Wailmer [TM]	267 Wailord [TM]
		250 Weavile [TM]	088 Whimsicott [TM]	094 Whiscash [TM]	136 Wigglytuff [TM]	182 Wimpod [TM]	040 Wingull [TM]
		110 Wishiwashi [TM]	296 Xurkitree [TM]	013 Yungoos [TM]	068 Zubat [TM]	205 Zygarde [TM]	
Ground	High Horsepower	132 Mudbray [24]	133 Mudsdale [24]	036 Snorlax [57]			
Fighting	High Jump Kick	295 Pheromosa [67]	279 Riolu [E]	173 Tsareena [49]			
Dark	Hone Claws	076 Braviary [14]	242 Mimikyu [41]	075 Rufflet [14]	249 Sneasel [25]	250 Weavile [25]	
Normal	Horn Attack	153 Goldeen [8]	154 Seaking [8]	287 Tapu Bulu [8]	137 Tauros [8]		
	Horn Drill	153 Goldeen [37]	268 Lapras [E]	154 Seaking [40]			
Grass	Horn Leech	196 Phantump [54]	287 Tapu Bulu [32]	197 Trevenant [1, 54]			
Normal	Howl	253 Alolan Vulpix [E]	052 Growlithe [E]	120 Lillipup [E]	104 Lycanroc (Midday Form) [12]	104 Lycanroc (Midnight Form) [12]	103 Rockruff [12]
Flying	Hurricane	181 Castform [45]	283 Dragonite [1, 81]	244 Drampa [E]	092 Gyarados [48]	082 Oricorio [50]	041 Pelipper [1, 55]
		088 Whimsicott [46]	040 Wingull [43]				
Water	Hydro Cannon	009 Primarina [T]					
	Hydro Pump	157 Alomomola [1, 65]	117 Bagon [E]	093 Barboach [E]	008 Brionne [51]	195 Carracosta [61]	264 Carvanha [E]
		181 Castform [35]	201 Chinchou [45]	116 Cloyster [1]	153 Goldeen [E]	090 Golduck [46]	092 Gyarados [42]
		202 Lanturn [51]	268 Lapras [47]	111 Luvdisc [46]	156 Milotic [44]	041 Pelipper [1, 50]	149 Poliwag [38]
		150 Poliwhirl [48]	007 Popplio [43]	009 Primarina [55]	089 Psyduck [40]	262 Relicanth [46]	115 Shellder [61]
		185 Starmie [1]	184 Staryu [53]	139 Surskit [E]	288 Tapu Fini [58]	106 Tentacool [46]	107 Tentacruel [52]
		194 Tirtouga [50]	124 Vaporeon [45]	266 Wailmer [49]	267 Wailord [58]	110 Wishiwashi [54]	
Normal	Hyper Beam (TM15)	245 Absol [TM]	284 Aerodactyl [65, TM]	044 Alakazam [TM]	072 Alolan Dugtrio [TM]	270 Alolan Exeggutor [TM]	231 Alolan Golem [TM]
		164 Alolan Marowak [TM]	051 Alolan Muk [TM]	254 Alolan Ninetales [TM]	046 Alolan Persian [TM]	026 Alolan Raichu [TM]	016 Alolan Raticate [TM]
		252 Alolan Sandslash [TM]	053 Arcanine [TM]	193 Archeops [TM]	023 Ariados [TM]	191 Bastiodon [TM]	170 Bewear [TM]
		034 Blissey [TM]	076 Braviary [TM]	019 Butterfree [TM]	195 Carracosta [TM]	297 Celesteela [TM]	033 Chansey [TM]
		212 Clefable [TM]	116 Cloyster [TM]	174 Comfey [TM]	070 Crobat [TM]	263 Dhelmise [TM]	282 Dragonair [75, TM]
		283 Dragonite [75, TM]	244 Drampa [TM]	281 Dratini [61, TM]	065 Drifblim [TM]	227 Electabuzz [TM]	228 Electivire [TM]
		127 Espeon [TM]	074 Fearow [TM]	126 Flareon [TM]	237 Flygon [43, TM]	248 Froslass [TM]	207 Garbodor [TM]
		240 Garchomp [TM]	261 Gastrodon [TM]	063 Gengar [TM]	100 Gigalith [TM]	130 Glaceon [TM]	247 Glalie [TM]
		069 Golbat [TM]	090 Golduck [TM]	180 Goodra [TM]	259 Granbull [TM]	299 Guzzlord [TM]	092 Gyarados [54, TM]
		057 Hariyama [TM]	278 Honchkrow [TM]	055 Hypno [TM]	006 Incineroar [TM]	125 Jolteon [TM]	165 Kangaskhan [TM]
		241 Kiefki [TM]	273 Kommo-o [TM]	234 Krookodile [TM]	202 Lanturn [TM]	268 Lapras [TM]	129 Leafeon [TM]
		021 Ledian [TM]	086 Lilligant [TM]	280 Lucario [TM]	109 Lumineon [TM]	292 Lunala [73, TM]	144 Lurantis [TM]
		097 Machamp [TM]	301 Magearna [TM]	167 Magmar [TM]	168 Magmortar [62, TM]	048 Magneton [TM]	049 Magnezone [TM]
		078 Mandibuzz [TM]	140 Masquerain [TM]	216 Metagross [60, TM]	215 Metang [50, TM]	156 Milotic [TM]	138 Miltank [TM]
		242 Mimikyu [TM]	213 Minior [TM]	067 Mismagius [TM]	300 Necrozma [TM]	221 Pangoro [TM]	148 Parasect [TM]
		177 Passimian [TM]	041 Pelipper [TM]	295 Pheromosa [TM]	175 Pinsir [TM]	152 Politoed [TM]	151 Poliwrath [TM]

Type	Move Name	Pokémon					
Normal	**Hyper Beam (TM15)**	217 Porygon [TM]	218 Porygon2 [67, TM]	219 Porygon-Z [67, TM]	080 Primeape [TM]	199 Probopass [TM]	189 Rampardos [TM]
		262 Relicanth [TM]	119 Salamence [TM]	276 Scizor [TM]	275 Scyther [TM]	154 Seaking [TM]	265 Sharpedo [TM]
		204 Silvally [TM]	038 Slowbro [TM]	039 Slowking [TM]	036 Snorlax [TM]	291 Solgaleo [TM]	185 Starmie [TM]
		122 Stoutland [TM]	131 Sylveon [TM]	160 Talonflame [TM]	287 Tapu Bulu [TM]	288 Tapu Fini [TM]	285 Tapu Koko [TM]
		286 Tapu Lele [TM]	137 Tauros [TM]	107 Tentacruel [TM]	223 Torkoal [TM]	235 Trapinch [43, TM]	197 Trevenant [TM]
		224 Turtonator [TM]	128 Umbreon [TM]	257 Vanilluxe [TM]	124 Vaporeon [TM]	236 Vibrava [43, TM]	029 Vikavolt [TM]
		267 Wailord [TM]	250 Weavile [TM]	088 Whimsicott [TM]	094 Whiscash [TM]	136 Wigglytuff [TM]	296 Xurkitree [TM]
		205 Zygarde [TM]					
	Hyper Fang	016 Alolan Raticate [16]	015 Alolan Rattata [16]	014 Gumshoos [43]	013 Yungoos [37]		
	Hyper Voice	008 Brionne [37]	244 Drampa [49]	135 Jigglypuff [41]	010 Pikipek [37]	152 Politoed [48]	007 Popplio [32]
		009 Primarina [38]	012 Toucannon [50]	011 Trumbeak [45]			
Psychic	**Hypnosis**	270 Alolan Exeggutor [1]	045 Alolan Meowth [E]	253 Alolan Vulpix [E]	064 Drifloon [E]	054 Drowzee [1]	269 Exeggcute [1]
		155 Feebas [E]	061 Gastly [1]	063 Gengar [1]	062 Haunter [1]	055 Hypno [1]	292 Lunala [1]
		187 Palossand [27]	152 Politoed [1]	149 Poliwag [8]	150 Poliwhirl [1, 8]	151 Poliwrath [1]	089 Psyduck [E]
		186 Sandygast [27]	105 Spinda [19]	296 Xurkitree [43]	068 Zubat [E]		
Ice	**Ice Ball**	251 Alolan Sandshrew [7]	252 Alolan Sandslash [1]	081 Delibird [E]	149 Poliwag [E]		
	Ice Beam (TM13)	245 Absol [TM]	164 Alolan Marowak [TM]	254 Alolan Ninetales [1, TM]	016 Alolan Raticate [TM]	015 Alolan Rattata [TM]	253 Alolan Vulpix [36, TM]
		157 Alomomola [TM]	142 Araquanid [TM]	093 Barboach [TM]	191 Bastiodon [TM]	034 Blissey [TM]	008 Brionne [TM]
		243 Bruxish [TM]	195 Carracosta [TM]	264 Carvanha [TM]	181 Castform [TM]	033 Chansey [TM]	201 Chinchou [TM]
		212 Clefable [TM]	211 Clefairy [TM]	116 Cloyster [TM]	112 Corsola [TM]	060 Crabominable [TM]	188 Cranidos [TM]
		163 Cubone [TM]	081 Delibird [TM]	141 Dewpider [TM]	282 Dragonair [TM]	283 Dragonite [TM]	244 Drampa [TM]
		281 Dratini [TM]	155 Feebas [TM]	108 Finneon [TM]	248 Froslass [TM]	261 Gastrodon [TM]	130 Glaceon [TM]
		247 Glalie [TM]	153 Goldeen [TM]	090 Golduck [TM]	183 Golisopod [TM]	180 Goodra [TM]	092 Gyarados [TM]
		135 Jigglypuff [TM]	165 Kangaskhan [TM]	202 Lanturn [TM]	268 Lapras [32, TM]	109 Lumineon [TM]	292 Lunala [TM]
		111 Luvdisc [TM]	301 Magearna [TM]	113 Mareanie [TM]	140 Masquerain [TM]	156 Milotic [TM]	138 Miltank [TM]
		035 Munchlax [TM]	041 Pelipper [TM]	295 Pheromosa [TM]	152 Politoed [TM]	149 Poliwag [TM]	150 Poliwhirl [TM]
		151 Poliwrath [TM]	007 Popplio [TM]	217 Porygon [TM]	218 Porygon2 [TM]	219 Porygon-Z [TM]	009 Primarina [TM]
		089 Psyduck [TM]	189 Rampardos [TM]	262 Relicanth [TM]	154 Seaking [TM]	265 Sharpedo [TM]	115 Shellder [52, TM]
		260 Shellos [TM]	190 Shieldon [TM]	204 Silvally [TM]	179 Sliggoo [TM]	038 Slowbro [TM]	039 Slowking [TM]
		037 Slowpoke [TM]	249 Sneasel [TM]	036 Snorlax [TM]	246 Snorunt [TM]	185 Starmie [TM]	184 Staryu [TM]
		139 Surskit [TM]	288 Tapu Fini [TM]	137 Tauros [TM]	106 Tentacool [TM]	107 Tentacruel [TM]	194 Tirtouga [TM]
		114 Toxapex [TM]	256 Vanillish [36, TM]	255 Vanillite [35, TM]	257 Vanilluxe [36, TM]	124 Vaporeon [TM]	266 Wailmer [TM]
		267 Wailord [TM]	250 Weavile [TM]	094 Whiscash [TM]	136 Wigglytuff [TM]	040 Wingull [TM]	110 Wishiwashi [TM]
	Ice Fang	284 Aerodactyl [1]	243 Bruxish [E]	264 Carvanha [25]	130 Glaceon [20]	247 Glalie [23]	259 Granbull [1]
		092 Gyarados [27]	120 Lillipup [E]	265 Sharpedo [25]	204 Silvally [1]	246 Snorunt [23]	258 Snubbull [1, E]
		122 Stoutland [1]					
	Ice Hammer	060 Crabominable [37]					
	Ice Punch	042 Abra [E]	294 Buzzwole [1]	060 Crabominable [1, EV]	081 Delibird [E]	054 Drowzee [E]	226 Elekid [E]
		061 Gastly [E]	095 Machop [E]	249 Sneasel [E]	169 Stufful [E]		
	Ice Shard	254 Alolan Ninetales [1]	253 Alolan Vulpix [10]	081 Delibird [E]	248 Froslass [1, 10]	130 Glaceon [25]	247 Glalie [1, 10]
		268 Lapras [10]	115 Shellder [28]	249 Sneasel [47, E]	246 Snorunt [10]	255 Vanillite [E]	
	Icicle Crash	251 Alolan Sandshrew [E]	252 Alolan Sandslash [1]	116 Cloyster [50]	249 Sneasel [E]		
	Icicle Spear	251 Alolan Sandshrew [E]	252 Alolan Sandslash [1, EV]	112 Corsola [E]	115 Shellder [13, E]	256 Vanillish [1]	255 Vanillite [1]
		257 Vanilluxe [1]					
	Icy Wind	253 Alolan Vulpix [15]	081 Delibird [E]	248 Froslass [14]	130 Glaceon [1, EV]	247 Glalie [14]	249 Sneasel [14]
		246 Snorunt [14]	105 Spinda [E]	256 Vanillish [13]	255 Vanillite [13]	257 Vanilluxe [13]	250 Weavile [14]
Psychic	**Imprison**	050 Alolan Grimer [E]	254 Alolan Ninetales [1]	253 Alolan Vulpix [39]	241 Klefki [36]	066 Misdreavus [E]	196 Phantump [E]
		102 Sableye [E]	204 Silvally [1]	203 Type: Null [15]	255 Vanillite [E]		
Fire	**Incinerate**	224 Turtonator [13]					
	Inferno	223 Torkoal [50]					
Bug	**Infestation (TM83)**	270 Alolan Exeggutor [TM]	050 Alolan Grimer [TM]	051 Alolan Muk [TM]	142 Araquanid [1, 5, TM]	023 Ariados [8, TM]	019 Butterfree [TM]
		083 Cutiefly [TM]	141 Dewpider [5, TM]	269 Exeggcute [TM]	207 Garbodor [TM]	061 Gastly [TM]	261 Gastrodon [TM]
		063 Gengar [TM]	180 Goodra [TM]	178 Goomy [TM]	062 Haunter [TM]	021 Ledian [TM]	020 Ledyba [TM]
		113 Mareanie [TM]	140 Masquerain [TM]	242 Mimikyu [TM]	187 Palossand [TM]	221 Pangoro [TM]	084 Ribombee [TM]
		186 Sandygast [TM]	260 Shellos [TM]	179 Sliggoo [TM]	022 Spinarak [8, TM]	139 Surskit [TM]	106 Tentacool [TM]
		107 Tentacruel [TM]	114 Toxapex [TM]	206 Trubbish [TM]			
Grass	**Ingrain**	297 Celesteela [1]	112 Corsola [E]	269 Exeggcute [E]	143 Fomantis [19]	144 Lurantis [19]	145 Morelull [22]
		085 Petilil [E]	196 Phantump [13]	146 Shiinotic [1, 22]	197 Trevenant [13]	296 Xurkitree [19]	
Psychic	**Instruct**	176 Oranguru [32]					
Electric	**Ion Deluge**	201 Chinchou [47]	228 Electivire [1]	274 Emolga [E]	202 Lanturn [54]	296 Xurkitree [67]	

Type	Move Name	Pokémon					
Steel	Iron Defense	251 Alolan Sandshrew [23]	191 Bastiodon [19]	099 Boldore [20]	297 Celesteela [59]	028 Charjabug [49]	112 Corsola [29]
		060 Crabominable [42]	059 Crabrawler [42]	100 Gigalith [20]	183 Golisopod [36]	272 Hakamo-o [38]	271 Jangmo-o [37]
		241 Klefki [E]	273 Kommo-o [38]	301 Magearna [57]	216 Metagross [52]	215 Metang [47]	132 Mudbray [29]
		133 Mudsdale [29]	300 Necrozma [59]	187 Palossand [32]	199 Probopass [1, 4]	279 Riolu [E]	098 Roggenrola [20]
		186 Sandygast [32]	276 Scizor [37]	115 Shellder [49]	190 Shieldon [19]	194 Tirtouga [E]	223 Torkoal [38]
		224 Turtonator [25]	255 Vanillite [E]				
	Iron Head	284 Aerodactyl [1, 57]	071 Alolan Diglett [35]	072 Alolan Dugtrio [41]	251 Alolan Sandshrew [30]	191 Bastiodon [51]	297 Celesteela [29]
		188 Cranidos [E]	163 Cubone [E]	238 Gible [E]	301 Magearna [1]	177 Passimian [E]	276 Scizor [50]
		190 Shieldon [42]	204 Silvally [1]	291 Solgaleo [7]	203 Type: Null [50]		
	Iron Tail	188 Cranidos [E]	281 Dratini [E]	274 Emolga [E]	155 Feebas [E]	238 Gible [E]	178 Goomy [E]
		052 Growlithe [E]	299 Guzzlord [29]	166 Magby [E]			
Fighting	Jump Kick	295 Pheromosa [31]					
	Karate Chop	226 Elekid [E]	097 Machamp [1, 7]	096 Machoke [1, 7]	095 Machop [7]	166 Magby [E]	079 Mankey [8]
		220 Pancham [12]	221 Pangoro [12]	080 Primeape [8]			
Psychic	Kinesis	044 Alakazam [1, EV]	043 Kadabra [1, EV]				
Dark	Knock Off	042 Abra [E]	050 Alolan Grimer [29]	051 Alolan Muk [29]	192 Archen [E]	057 Hariyama [19]	020 Ledyba [E]
		097 Machamp [21]	096 Machoke [21]	095 Machop [21, E]	056 Makuhita [19]	102 Sableye [26]	161 Salandit [E]
		106 Tentacool [E]	194 Tirtouga [E]	077 Vullaby [E]	040 Wingull [E]		
Ground	Land's Wrath	205 Zygarde [26]					
	Laser Focus	298 Kartana [29]	280 Lucario [1]				
Normal	Last Resort	123 Eevee [41]	127 Espeon [41]	126 Flareon [41]	130 Glaceon [41]	032 Happiny [E]	121 Herdier [42]
		134 Igglybuff [E]	125 Jolteon [41]	129 Leafeon [41]	120 Lillipup [36]	035 Munchlax [1, 57]	122 Stoutland [51]
		131 Sylveon [41]	128 Umbreon [41]	124 Vaporeon [41]	013 Yungoos [E]		
Fire	Lava Plume	126 Flareon [37]	166 Magby [33]	167 Magmar [36]	168 Magmortar [36]	223 Torkoal [25]	
Grass	Leaf Blade	002 Dartrix [42]	003 Decidueye [44]	143 Fomantis [23]	298 Kartana [43]	129 Leafeon [45]	144 Lurantis [23]
		001 Rowlet [36]					
	Leaf Storm	270 Alolan Exeggutor [47]	269 Exeggcute [E]	143 Fomantis [E]	085 Petilil [46]	172 Steenee [45]	173 Tsareena [45]
	Leafage	002 Dartrix [1]	003 Decidueye [1]	143 Fomantis [5]	144 Lurantis [1, 5]	001 Rowlet [1]	287 Tapu Bulu [1]
Bug	Leech Life (TM28)	251 Alolan Sandshrew [TM]	252 Alolan Sandslash [TM]	142 Araquanid [33, TM]	023 Ariados [TM]	294 Buzzwole [29, TM]	070 Crobat [35, TM]
		083 Cutiefly [TM]	141 Dewpider [29, TM]	143 Fomantis [TM]	069 Golbat [35, TM]	183 Golisopod [TM]	006 Incineroar [TM]
		004 Litten [TM]	144 Lurantis [TM]	242 Mimikyu [TM]	147 Paras [TM]	148 Parasect [TM]	084 Ribombee [TM]
		161 Salandit [TM]	162 Salazzle [TM]	022 Spinarak [TM]	005 Torracat [TM]	182 Wimpod [TM]	068 Zubat [31, TM]
Grass	Leech Seed	297 Celesteela [19]	174 Comfey [4]	087 Cottonee [8]	269 Exeggcute [11]	086 Lilligant [1]	145 Morelull [E]
		147 Paras [E]	085 Petilil [8]	196 Phantump [23]	287 Tapu Bulu [26]	197 Trevenant [23]	088 Whimsicott [1]
Normal	Leer	245 Absol [1, 4]	164 Alolan Marowak [13]	192 Archen [1]	193 Archeops [1]	117 Bagon [7]	170 Bewear [1]
		076 Braviary [1]	264 Carvanha [1]	060 Crabominable [1, 9]	059 Crabrawler [9]	188 Cranidos [1, E]	163 Cubone [13]
		282 Dragonair [1]	283 Dragonite [1]	281 Dratini [1]	227 Electabuzz [1]	228 Electivire [1]	226 Elekid [1]
		074 Fearow [1, 4]	248 Froslass [1]	247 Glalie [1]	052 Growlithe [8]	014 Gumshoos [1, 3]	092 Gyarados [21]
		272 Hakamo-o [1, 5]	121 Herdier [1]	006 Incineroar [11]	271 Jangmo-o [5]	165 Kangaskhan [1]	273 Kommo-o [1, 5]
		233 Krokorok [1]	234 Krookodile [1]	120 Lillipup [1]	004 Litten [11]	104 Lycanroc (Midday Form) [1]	104 Lycanroc (Midnight Form) [1]
		097 Machamp [1]	096 Machoke [1]	095 Machop [1]	166 Magby [1]	167 Magmar [1]	168 Magmortar [1]
		078 Mandibuzz [1]	079 Mankey [1]	220 Pancham [1]	221 Pangoro [1]	177 Passimian [4]	295 Pheromosa [1]
		080 Primeape [1]	189 Rampardos [1]	103 Rockruff [1]	075 Rufflet [1]	102 Sableye [1]	119 Salamence [1, 7]
		232 Sandile [1]	276 Scizor [1]	275 Scyther [1]	265 Sharpedo [1]	118 Shelgon [1, 7]	115 Shellder [20]
		208 Skarmory [1]	249 Sneasel [1]	246 Snorunt [1]	073 Spearow [4]	122 Stoutland [1]	169 Stufful [1]
		005 Torracat [11]	077 Vullaby [1]	250 Weavile [1]	013 Yungoos [3]		
Ghost	Lick	061 Gastly [1]	063 Gengar [1]	259 Granbull [13]	062 Haunter [1]	006 Incineroar [1, 8]	120 Lillipup [E]
		004 Litten [8]	035 Munchlax [1, 12, E]	036 Snorlax [12, E]	258 Snubbull [13]	005 Torracat [1, 8]	
Psychic	Light Screen (TM16)	042 Abra [TM]	044 Alakazam [TM]	270 Alolan Exeggutor [TM]	026 Alolan Raichu [TM]	157 Alomomola [TM]	034 Blissey [46, TM]
		171 Bounsweet [TM]	243 Bruxish [TM]	101 Carbink [60, TM]	033 Chansey [46, TM]	028 Charjabug [TM]	212 Clefable [TM]
		211 Clefairy [TM]	210 Cleffa [TM]	174 Comfey [TM]	112 Corsola [TM]	083 Cutiefly [TM]	002 Dartrix [TM]
		003 Decidueye [TM]	282 Dragonair [TM]	283 Dragonite [TM]	244 Drampa [17, TM]	281 Dratini [TM]	054 Drowzee [TM]
		227 Electabuzz [26, TM]	228 Electivire [26, TM]	226 Elekid [26, TM]	274 Emolga [34, TM]	127 Espeon [TM]	269 Exeggcute [TM]
		155 Feebas [TM]	248 Froslass [TM]	247 Glalie [TM]	090 Golduck [TM]	027 Grubbin [TM]	032 Happiny [TM]
		055 Hypno [TM]	134 Igglybuff [TM]	135 Jigglypuff [TM]	125 Jolteon [TM]	043 Kadabra [TM]	241 Klefki [TM]
		021 Ledian [12, TM]	020 Ledyba [12, TM]	086 Lilligant [TM]	292 Lunala [TM]	097 Machamp [TM]	096 Machoke [TM]
		095 Machop [TM]	301 Magearna [TM]	047 Magnemite [13, TM]	048 Magneton [13, TM]	049 Magnezone [13, TM]	216 Metagross [TM]
		215 Metang [TM]	156 Milotic [TM]	242 Mimikyu [TM]	213 Minior [TM]	145 Morelull [TM]	300 Necrozma [TM]
		293 Nihilego [TM]	176 Oranguru [TM]	147 Paras [TM]	148 Parasect [TM]	024 Pichu [TM]	025 Pikachu [53, TM]
		009 Primarina [TM]	089 Psyduck [TM]	200 Pyukumuku [TM]	084 Ribombee [TM]	001 Rowlet [TM]	276 Scizor [TM]
		275 Scyther [TM]	146 Shiinotic [TM]	038 Slowbro [TM]	039 Slowking [TM]	037 Slowpoke [TM]	246 Snorunt [TM]

Type	Move Name	Pokémon					
Psychic	Light Screen (TM16)	291 Solgaleo [TM]	185 Starmie [TM]	184 Staryu [46, TM]	172 Steenee [TM]	131 Sylveon [33, TM]	287 Tapu Bulu [TM]
		288 Tapu Fini [TM]	285 Tapu Koko [TM]	286 Tapu Lele [TM]	114 Toxapex [TM]	173 Tsareena [TM]	256 Vanillish [TM]
		255 Vanillite [TM]	257 Vanilluxe [TM]	029 Vikavolt [TM]	088 Whimsicott [TM]	130 Wigglytuff [TM]	258 Xurkitree [TM]
Water	Liquidation	142 Araquanid [57]	112 Corsola [E]	141 Dewpider [45]	183 Golisopod [48]	113 Mareanie [49]	194 Tirtouga [E]
		114 Toxapex [58]					
Normal	Lock-On	241 Klefki [E]	047 Magnemite [41]	048 Magneton [49]	049 Magnezone [49]	198 Nosepass [43]	217 Porygon [45]
		218 Porygon2 [45]	219 Porygon-Z [45]	199 Probopass [43]	098 Roggenrola [E]		
Fighting	Low Kick	030 Bonsly [8]	227 Electabuzz [8]	228 Electivire [1, 8]	226 Elekid [8]	097 Machamp [1]	096 Machoke [1]
		095 Machop [1]	079 Mankey [1]	295 Pheromosa [1]	080 Primeape [1]	279 Riolu [E]	031 Sudowoodo [1, 8]
Fighting	Low Sweep (TM47)	170 Bewear [TM]	294 Buzzwole [TM]	003 Decidueye [TM]	054 Drowzee [TM]	227 Electabuzz [TM]	228 Electivire [TM]
		090 Golduck [TM]	057 Hariyama [TM]	055 Hypno [TM]	006 Incineroar [TM]	222 Komala [TM]	233 Krokorok [TM]
		234 Krookodile [TM]	280 Lucario [TM]	144 Lurantis [TM]	097 Machamp [13, TM]	096 Machoke [13, TM]	095 Machop [13, TM]
		167 Magmar [TM]	168 Magmortar [TM]	056 Makuhita [TM]	079 Mankey [TM]	132 Mudbray [TM]	133 Mudsdale [TM]
		220 Pancham [TM]	221 Pangoro [1, 57, TM]	177 Passimian [TM]	295 Pheromosa [TM]	151 Poliwrath [TM]	080 Primeape [TM]
		279 Riolu [TM]	102 Sableye [TM]	249 Sneasel [TM]	172 Steenee [TM]	169 Stufful [TM]	173 Tsareena [TM]
		250 Weavile [TM]					
Normal	Lucky Chant	181 Castform [E]	211 Clefairy [37]	174 Comfey [E]	112 Corsola [23]	269 Exeggcute [E]	111 Luvdisc [13]
		301 Magearna [9]	067 Mismagius [1]	024 Pichu [E]			
Bug	Lunge	142 Araquanid [45]	294 Buzzwole [53]	141 Dewpider [37]	295 Pheromosa [47]	139 Surskit [E]	
Fighting	Mach Punch	021 Ledian [15]	020 Ledyba [15]	166 Magby [F]			
Psychic	Magic Coat	245 Absol [E]	292 Lunala [43]	217 Porygon [56]	218 Porygon2 [1, 56]	219 Porygon-Z [1, 56]	
	Magic Room	241 Klefki [44]					
Grass	Magical Leaf	171 Bounsweet [21]	210 Cleffa [16]	174 Comfey [10]	129 Leafeon [20]	067 Mismagius [1]	085 Petilil [19]
		172 Steenee [21]	173 Tsareena [21]				
Steel	Magnet Bomb	047 Magnemite [7]	048 Magneton [1, 7]	049 Magnezone [1, 7]	199 Probopass [1, 10]		
Electric	Magnet Rise	229 Alolan Geodude [E]	047 Magnemite [43]	048 Magneton [53]	049 Magnezone [53]	216 Metagross [1]	215 Metang [1]
		217 Porygon [23]	218 Porygon2 [23]	219 Porygon-Z [23]	199 Probopass [1]	225 Togedemaru [25]	255 Vanillite [E]
	Magnetic Flux	049 Magnezone [1]	199 Probopass [1]				
Ground	Magnitude	071 Alolan Diglett [14]	072 Alolan Dugtrio [14]	093 Barboach [20]	132 Mudbray [E]	198 Nosepass [E]	262 Relicanth [E]
		098 Roggenrola [E]	094 Whiscash [20]				
Normal	Me First	245 Absol [41, E]	015 Alolan Rattata [E]	159 Fletchinder [46]	158 Fletchling [41]	090 Golduck [1]	280 Lucario [37]
		066 Misdreavus [E]	220 Pancham [E]	295 Pheromosa [50]	175 Pinsir [E]	232 Sandile [E]	037 Slowpoke [E]
		160 Talonflame [49]					
Normal	Mean Look	245 Absol [E]	050 Alolan Grimer [E]	070 Crobat [32]	061 Gastly [8]	063 Gengar [8]	069 Golbat [32]
		062 Haunter [8]	066 Misdreavus [19]	277 Murkrow [41]	102 Sableye [46, E]	232 Sandile [E]	287 Tapu Bulu [1]
		288 Tapu Fini [1]	285 Tapu Koko [1]	286 Tapu Lele [1]	128 Umbreon [37]	077 Vullaby [E]	068 Zubat [29]
Psychic	Meditate	054 Drowzee [21]	226 Elekid [E]	055 Hypno [21]	095 Machop [E]	079 Mankey [E]	
Grass	Mega Drain	297 Celesteela [13]	087 Cottonee [13]	263 Dhelmise [5]	086 Lilligant [1]	145 Morelull [15]	187 Palossand [18]
		085 Petilil [13]	186 Sandygast [18]	146 Shiinotic [15]	088 Whimsicott [1]		
Normal	Mega Kick	132 Mudbray [43]	133 Mudsdale [55]	169 Stufful [E]			
Normal	Mega Punch	294 Buzzwole [37]	165 Kangaskhan [25]	166 Magby [F]			
Bug	Megahorn	245 Absol [E]	153 Goldeen [45]	154 Seaking [1, 54]	022 Spinarak [E]	287 Tapu Bulu [53]	
Dark	Memento	071 Alolan Diglett [E]	050 Alolan Grimer [48]	051 Alolan Muk [57]	087 Cottonee [E]	064 Drifloon [E]	066 Misdreavus [E]
		200 Pyukumuku [49]	260 Shellos [E]				
Steel	Metal Burst	252 Alolan Sandslash [1]	191 Bastiodon [43]	102 Sableye [E]	190 Shieldon [37]	291 Solgaleo [43]	
	Metal Claw	071 Alolan Diglett [1]	072 Alolan Dugtrio [1]	251 Alolan Sandshrew [14, E]	252 Alolan Sandslash [1]	238 Gible [E]	280 Lucario [1]
		216 Metagross [1]	215 Metang [1, EV]	300 Necrozma [1]	147 Paras [E]	276 Scizor [21]	208 Skarmory [9]
		249 Sneasel [22]	291 Solgaleo [1]	250 Weavile [22]	182 Wimpod [E]		
	Metal Sound	071 Alolan Diglett [E]	191 Bastiodon [1, 10]	297 Celesteela [23]	263 Dhelmise [18]	241 Klefki [12]	280 Lucario [24]
		047 Magnemite [25]	048 Magneton [25]	049 Magnezone [25]	190 Shieldon [10]	204 Silvally [45]	208 Skarmory [42]
		291 Solgaleo [13]	203 Type: Null [45]				
	Meteor Mash	211 Clefairy [50]	216 Metagross [44]	215 Metang [44]			
Normal	Metronome	033 Chansey [E]	212 Clefable [1]	211 Clefairy [31]	210 Cleffa [E]	032 Happiny [E]	035 Munchlax [1]
		258 Snubbull [E]					
	Milk Drink	138 Miltank [11]					
	Mimic	030 Bonsly [15]	210 Cleffa [E]	135 Jigglypuff [38]	242 Mimikyu [19]	258 Snubbull [E]	031 Sudowoodo [15]
	Mind Reader	301 Magearna [33]	149 Poliwag [E]	151 Poliwrath [43]	279 Riolu [E]	139 Surskit [E]	
Normal	Minimize	050 Alolan Grimer [21]	051 Alolan Muk [21]	034 Blissey [23]	033 Chansey [23]	212 Clefable [1]	211 Clefairy [25]
		065 Drifblim [1]	064 Drifloon [1]	184 Staryu [31]			

Type	Move Name	Pokémon					
Psychic	Miracle Eye	044 Alakazam [23]	043 Kadabra [23]	216 Metagross [29]	215 Metang [29]		
	Mirror Coat	157 Alomomola [E]	142 Araquanid [50]	112 Corsola [45]	141 Dewpider [40]	155 Feebas [E]	130 Glaceon [33]
		049 Magnezone [1]	293 Nihilego [43]	260 Shellos [E]	106 Tentacool [E]	256 Vanillish [47]	255 Vanillite [44]
		257 Vanilluxe [50]					
Flying	Mirror Move	074 Fearow [18]	078 Mandibuzz [1, 70]	277 Murkrow [E]	082 Oricorio [43]	010 Pikipek [E]	073 Spearow [18]
		285 Tapu Koko [38]	077 Vullaby [64]				
Steel	Mirror Shot	241 Klefki [34]	301 Magearna [25]	047 Magnemite [23]	048 Magneton [23]	049 Magnezone [23]	300 Necrozma [1]
		256 Vanillish [26]	255 Vanillite [26]	257 Vanilluxe [26]			
Ice	Mist	253 Alolan Vulpix [20]	157 Alomomola [E]	201 Chinchou [E]	112 Corsola [E]	244 Drampa [E]	281 Dratini [E]
		155 Feebas [E]	268 Lapras [4]	041 Pelipper [12]	149 Poliwag [E]	260 Shellos [E]	139 Surskit [25]
		288 Tapu Fini [1]	256 Vanillish [16]	255 Vanillite [16]	257 Vanilluxe [16]	266 Wailmer [22]	267 Wailord [22]
		040 Wingull [12, E]	110 Wishiwashi [E]				
Fairy	Misty Terrain	008 Brionne [55]	210 Cleffa [E]	134 Igglybuff [E]	007 Popplio [46]	009 Primarina [60]	131 Sylveon [29]
		288 Tapu Fini [1]					
	Moonblast	253 Alolan Vulpix [E]	008 Brionne [42]	101 Carbink [50]	211 Clefairy [46]	083 Cutiefly [E]	292 Lunala [47]
		145 Morelull [39]	007 Popplio [36]	009 Primarina [44]	146 Shiinotic [44]	131 Sylveon [37]	288 Tapu Fini [1]
		286 Tapu Lele [58]	088 Whimsicott [50]				
Ghost	Moongeist Beam	292 Lunala [1, EV]					
Fairy	Moonlight	211 Clefairy [43]	269 Exeggcute [E]	292 Lunala [31]	145 Morelull [11]	300 Necrozma [1]	102 Sableye [E]
		146 Shiinotic [11]	128 Umbreon [33]				
Normal	Morning Sun	127 Espeon [33]	052 Growlithe [E]	300 Necrozma [1]	291 Solgaleo [31]		
Ground	Mud Bomb	071 Alolan Diglett [25]	072 Alolan Dugtrio [25]	093 Barboach [13]	033 Chansey [E]	261 Gastrodon [11]	032 Happiny [E]
		132 Mudbray [E]	149 Poliwag [41]	150 Poliwhirl [53]	089 Psyduck [E]	260 Shellos [11]	094 Whiscash [13]
	Mud Shot	093 Barboach [E]	238 Gible [E]	153 Goldeen [E]	027 Grubbin [E]	149 Poliwag [28, E]	150 Poliwhirl [32]
		262 Relicanth [E]	115 Shellder [E]	139 Surskit [E]	235 Trapinch [E]		
	Mud Sport	093 Barboach [6]	155 Feebas [E]	261 Gastrodon [1, 2]	153 Goldeen [E]	111 Luvdisc [E]	132 Mudbray [3]
		133 Mudsdale [1, 3]	200 Pyukumuku [1]	262 Relicanth [1, 6]	260 Shellos [2]	037 Slowpoke [E]	206 Trubbish [E]
		094 Whiscash [1, 6]					
Water	Muddy Water	093 Barboach [35, E]	261 Gastrodon [41]	180 Goodra [38]	178 Goomy [38]	262 Relicanth [E]	260 Shellos [37]
		179 Sliggoo [38]	288 Tapu Fini [48]	106 Tentacool [E]	124 Vaporeon [37]	094 Whiscash [39]	110 Wishiwashi [E]
Ground	Mud-Slap	071 Alolan Diglett [10]	072 Alolan Dugtrio [10]	093 Barboach [1]	099 Boldore [17]	028 Charjabug [1, 7]	237 Flygon [5]
		261 Gastrodon [1]	100 Gigalith [17]	153 Goldeen [E]	027 Grubbin [7]	014 Gumshoos [23]	233 Krokorok [19]
		234 Krookodile [19]	120 Lillipup [E]	132 Mudbray [1]	133 Mudsdale [1]	262 Relicanth [E]	098 Roggenrola [17]
		232 Sandile [19]	260 Shellos [1]	235 Trapinch [5]	236 Vibrava [5]	029 Vikavolt [1, 7]	094 Whiscash [1]
		013 Yungoos [22]					
Normal	Multi-Attack	204 Silvally [1, EV]					
Fire	Mystical Fire	067 Mismagius [1]					
Dark	Nasty Plot	045 Alolan Meowth [38]	254 Alolan Ninetales [1]	046 Alolan Persian [44]	002 Dartrix [55]	003 Decidueye [60]	054 Drowzee [53, E]
		278 Honchkrow [35]	055 Hypno [1, 53]	004 Litten [E]	078 Mandibuzz [14]	066 Misdreavus [E]	176 Oranguru [25]
		024 Pichu [13]	219 Porygon-Z [1]	279 Riolu [47]	001 Rowlet [46]	102 Sableye [E]	161 Salandit [32]
		162 Salazzle [32]	039 Slowking [36]	077 Vullaby [14]	250 Weavile [20]	068 Zubat [E]	
Normal	Natural Gift	033 Chansey [E]	174 Comfey [22]	087 Cottonee [E]	244 Drampa [25]	123 Eevee [E]	269 Exeggcute [37, E]
		159 Fletchinder [31]	158 Fletchling [29]	032 Happiny [E]	138 Miltank [E]	035 Munchlax [49, E]	147 Paras [E]
		085 Petilil [E]	036 Snorlax [E]	160 Talonflame [31]	255 Vanillite [E]		
Normal	Nature Power (TM96)	270 Alolan Exeggutor [TM]	229 Alolan Geodude [TM]	231 Alolan Golem [TM]	230 Alolan Graveler [TM]	099 Boldore [TM]	030 Bonsly [TM]
		171 Bounsweet [TM]	101 Carbink [TM]	174 Comfey [TM]	112 Corsola [TM, E]	087 Cottonee [TM]	002 Dartrix [TM]
		003 Decidueye [TM]	244 Drampa [TM]	269 Exeggcute [TM, E]	108 Finneon [TM]	143 Fomantis [TM]	100 Gigalith [TM]
		129 Leafeon [TM]	086 Lilligant [TM]	144 Lurantis [TM]	145 Morelull [TM]	176 Oranguru [TM]	147 Paras [TM]
		148 Parasect [TM]	085 Petilil [TM]	196 Phantump [TM]	084 Ribombee [TM]	098 Roggenrola [TM]	001 Rowlet [TM]
		146 Shiinotic [TM]	172 Steenee [TM]	031 Sudowoodo [TM]	287 Tapu Bulu [TM]	288 Tapu Fini [TM]	285 Tapu Koko [TM]
		286 Tapu Lele [TM]	223 Torkoal [TM]	197 Trevenant [TM]	173 Tsareena [TM]	088 Whimsicott [TM]	296 Xurkitree [TM]
Fairy	Nature's Madness	287 Tapu Bulu [43]	288 Tapu Fini [43]	285 Tapu Koko [43]	286 Tapu Lele [43]		
Dark	Night Daze	292 Lunala [37]					
Ghost	Night Shade	023 Ariados [15]	061 Gastly [15]	063 Gengar [15]	062 Haunter [15]	292 Lunala [7]	277 Murkrow [21]
		102 Sableye [6]	022 Spinarak [15]				
Dark	Night Slash	245 Absol [29]	072 Alolan Dugtrio [1]	045 Alolan Meowth [49]	046 Alolan Persian [61]	251 Alolan Sandshrew [E]	278 Honchkrow [1, 55]
		298 Kartana [31]	079 Mankey [E]	300 Necrozma [23]	276 Scizor [45]	275 Scyther [45, E]	265 Sharpedo [1, 62]
		208 Skarmory [53]	022 Spinarak [E]	250 Weavile [35]			
Ghost	Nightmare	061 Gastly [47]	063 Gengar [61]	062 Haunter [61]	055 Hypno [1]	242 Mimikyu [E]	
Normal	Noble Roar	272 Hakamo-o [48]	271 Jangmo-o [45]	273 Kommo-o [51]	291 Solgaleo [59]	267 Wailord [1]	

Type	Move Name	Pokémon					
Electric	Nuzzle	274 Emolga [15]	025 Pikachu [29]	225 Togedemaru [21]			
Normal	Odor Sleuth	053 Arcanine [1]	052 Growlithe [10]	014 Gumshoos [13]	121 Herdier [1, 5]	120 Lillipup [5]	104 Lycanroc (Midday Form) [18]
		104 Lycanroc (Midnight Form) [18]	035 Munchlax [1]	103 Rockruff [18]	122 Stoutland [1, 5]	013 Yungoos [13]	
Ghost	Ominous Wind	181 Castform [E]	065 Drifblim [20]	064 Drifloon [20]	248 Froslass [1, EV]	140 Masquerain [1]	066 Misdreavus [E]
		001 Rowlet [E]					
Dragon	Outrage	282 Dragonair [67]	283 Dragonite [67]	244 Drampa [53]	281 Dratini [55]	238 Gible [E]	180 Goodra [1, 55]
		259 Granbull [1, 67]	052 Growlithe [43]	272 Hakamo-o [58]	006 Incineroar [60]	271 Jangmo-o [53]	105 Kangaskhan [46]
		273 Kommo-o [67]	234 Krookodile [60]	004 Litten [46]	079 Mankey [47]	080 Primeape [53]	005 Torracat [55]
		205 Zygarde [80]					
Fire	Overheat (TM50)	053 Arcanine [TM]	126 Flareon [TM]	159 Fletchinder [TM]	158 Fletchling [TM]	259 Granbull [TM]	052 Growlithe [TM]
		006 Incineroar [TM]	004 Litten [TM]	166 Magby [TM]	167 Magmar [TM]	168 Magmortar [TM]	079 Mankey [TM]
		080 Primeape [TM]	161 Salandit [TM]	162 Salazzle [TM]	258 Snubbull [TM]	160 Talonflame [TM]	223 Torkoal [TM]
		005 Torracat [TM]	012 Toucannon [TM]	224 Turtonator [49, TM]			
Normal	Pain Split	157 Alomomola [E]	170 Bewear [49]	301 Magearna [65]	242 Mimikyu [50]	066 Misdreavus [32]	200 Pyukumuku [33]
		169 Stufful [41]					
Dark	Parting Shot	045 Alolan Meowth [E]	220 Pancham [45]	221 Pangoro [48]	204 Silvally [85]		
Normal	Pay Day	045 Alolan Meowth [30]					
Dark	Payback (TM66)	245 Absol [TM]	284 Aerodactyl [TM]	050 Alolan Grimer [TM]	045 Alolan Meowth [TM]	051 Alolan Muk [TM]	254 Alolan Ninetales [TM]
		046 Alolan Persian [TM]	253 Alolan Vulpix [18, TM]	170 Bewear [23, TM]	243 Bruxish [TM]	294 Buzzwole [TM]	264 Carvanha [TM]
		116 Cloyster [TM]	060 Crabominable [TM]	059 Crabrawler [29, TM]	188 Cranidos [TM]	070 Crobat [TM]	263 Dhelmise [TM]
		065 Drifblim [16, TM]	064 Drifloon [16, TM]	108 Finneon [TM]	143 Fomantis [TM]	248 Froslass [TM]	207 Garbodor [TM]
		061 Gastly [26, TM]	063 Gengar [28, TM]	247 Glalie [TM]	069 Golbat [TM]	183 Golisopod [TM]	259 Granbull [51, TM]
		014 Gumshoos [TM]	299 Guzzlord [TM]	092 Gyarados [TM]	272 Hakamo-o [TM]	057 Hariyama [TM]	062 Haunter [28, TM]
		121 Herdier [TM]	278 Honchkrow [TM]	271 Jangmo-o [TM]	222 Komala [TM]	273 Kommo-o [TM]	233 Krokorok [TM]
		234 Krookodile [TM]	280 Lucario [TM]	109 Lumineon [TM]	144 Lurantis [TM]	097 Machamp [TM]	096 Machoke [TM]
		095 Machop [TM]	078 Mandibuzz [TM]	079 Mankey [TM]	113 Mareanie [TM]	242 Mimikyu [TM]	066 Misdreavus [37, TM]
		067 Mismagius [TM]	132 Mudbray [TM]	133 Mudsdale [TM]	277 Murkrow [TM]	176 Oranguru [TM]	220 Pancham [TM]
		221 Pangoro [TM]	177 Passimian [TM]	041 Pelipper [19, TM]	152 Politoed [TM]	151 Poliwrath [TM]	080 Primeape [TM]
		189 Rampardos [TM]	279 Riolu [TM]	102 Sableye [TM]	161 Salandit [TM]	162 Salazzle [TM]	232 Sandile [TM]
		265 Sharpedo [TM]	115 Shellder [TM]	204 Silvally [TM]	208 Skarmory [TM]	249 Sneasel [TM]	258 Snubbull [43, TM]
		172 Steenee [TM]	122 Stoutland [TM]	169 Stufful [23, TM]	287 Tapu Bulu [TM]	137 Tauros [24, TM]	106 Tentacool [TM]
		107 Tentacruel [TM]	225 Togedemaru [TM]	114 Toxapex [TM]	206 Trubbish [TM]	173 Tsareena [TM]	224 Turtonator [TM]
		203 Type: Null [TM]	128 Umbreon [TM]	077 Vullaby [TM]	250 Weavile [TM]	013 Yungoos [TM]	068 Zubat [TM]
Flying	Peck	076 Braviary [1]	002 Dartrix [1, 8]	003 Decidueye [1, 8]	074 Fearow [1]	159 Fletchinder [10]	158 Fletchling [10]
		153 Goldeen [1]	113 Mareanie [5]	277 Murkrow [1]	082 Oricorio [6]	010 Pikipek [1]	001 Rowlet [8]
		075 Rufflet [1]	154 Seaking [1]	208 Skarmory [1]	073 Spearow [1]	160 Talonflame [1, 10]	012 Toucannon [1]
		114 Toxapex [1, 5]	011 Trumbeak [1]				
Normal	Perish Song	245 Absol [1, 57, E]	163 Cubone [E]	061 Gastly [E]	134 Igglybuff [E]	268 Lapras [27]	066 Misdreavus [46]
		277 Murkrow [E]	152 Politoed [1]	007 Popplio [E]			
Grass	Petal Blizzard	174 Comfey [25]	086 Lilligant [50]	144 Lurantis [1, EV]			
Grass	Petal Dance	174 Comfey [40]	086 Lilligant [46]				
Ghost	Phantom Force	263 Dhelmise [54]	065 Drifblim [1, 65]	292 Lunala [61]	067 Mismagius [1]	196 Phantump [45]	197 Trevenant [45]
Bug	Pin Missile	023 Ariados [41]	183 Golisopod [41]	125 Jolteon [25]	113 Mareanie [45]	022 Spinarak [36]	225 Togedemaru [45]
		114 Toxapex [51]					
Normal	Play Nice	157 Alomomola [1]	171 Bounsweet [5]	244 Drampa [1]	135 Jigglypuff [9]	025 Pikachu [7]	172 Steenee [1, 5]
Fairy	Play Rough	245 Absol [E]	046 Alolan Persian [1]	171 Bounsweet [E]	174 Comfey [49]	244 Drampa [E]	259 Granbull [43]
		121 Herdier [52]	241 Klefki [43]	222 Komala [E]	120 Lillipup [45]	242 Mimikyu [46]	258 Snubbull [37]
		122 Stoutland [63]	136 Wigglytuff [1]				
Flying	Pluck	192 Archen [15]	193 Archeops [15]	002 Dartrix [24]	003 Decidueye [24]	074 Fearow [1]	078 Mandibuzz [1, 10]
		082 Oricorio [E]	010 Pikipek [15]	001 Rowlet [22]	012 Toucannon [16]	011 Trumbeak [16]	077 Vullaby [10]
Poison	Poison Fang	050 Alolan Grimer [18]	051 Alolan Muk [18]	243 Bruxish [E]	264 Carvanha [32]	070 Crobat [27]	069 Golbat [27]
		265 Sharpedo [34]	204 Silvally [1]	068 Zubat [25]			
Poison	Poison Gas	050 Alolan Grimer [1]	051 Alolan Muk [1]	054 Drowzee [17]	207 Garbodor [1]	055 Hypno [17]	161 Salandit [1]
		162 Salazzle [1]	206 Trubbish [1]				
Poison	Poison Jab (TM84)	050 Alolan Grimer [TM]	051 Alolan Muk [TM]	251 Alolan Sandshrew [TM]	252 Alolan Sandslash [TM]	142 Araquanid [TM]	023 Ariados [50, TM]
		294 Buzzwole [TM]	028 Charjabug [TM]	116 Cloyster [TM]	141 Dewpider [TM]	143 Fomantis [TM]	240 Garchomp [TM]
		063 Gengar [TM]	153 Goldeen [TM]	183 Golisopod [TM]	027 Grubbin [TM]	299 Guzzlord [TM]	057 Hariyama [TM]
		062 Haunter [TM]	273 Kommo-o [TM]	280 Lucario [TM]	144 Lurantis [TM]	097 Machamp [TM]	096 Machoke [TM]
		095 Machop [TM]	056 Makuhita [TM]	079 Mankey [TM]	113 Mareanie [37, TM]	293 Nihilego [TM]	221 Pangoro [TM]

Type	Move Name	Pokémon					
Poison	**Poison Jab (TM84)**	196 Phantump [TM]	295 Pheromosa [TM]	151 Poliwrath [TM]	080 Primeape [TM]	279 Riolu [TM]	102 Sableye [TM]
		161 Salandit [TM]	162 Salazzle [TM]	154 Seaking [1, TM]	265 Sharpedo [TM]	249 Sneasel [TM]	022 Spinarak [43, TM]
		106 Tentacool [31, TM]	107 Tentacruel [32, TM]	225 Togedemaru [TM]	114 Toxapex [37, TM]	197 Trevenant [TM]	029 Vikavolt [TM]
		250 Weavile [TM]					
	Poison Powder	019 Butterfree [13]	087 Cottonee [22]	269 Exeggcute [21]	145 Morelull [E]	147 Paras [6]	148 Parasect [1, 6]
	Poison Sting	023 Ariados [1]	113 Mareanie [1]	022 Spinarak [1]	106 Tentacool [1]	107 Tentacruel [1]	114 Toxapex [1]
	Poison Tail	178 Goomy [E]					
Bug	**Pollen Puff**	084 Ribombee [1, EV]					
Normal	**Pound**	050 Alolan Grimer [1]	051 Alolan Muk [1]	157 Alomomola [1]	034 Blissey [1]	008 Brionne [1]	033 Chansey [1]
		211 Clefairy [1]	210 Cleffa [1]	054 Drowzee [1]	108 Finneon [1]	207 Garbodor [1]	032 Happiny [1]
		055 Hypno [1]	134 Igglybuff [5]	135 Jigglypuff [5]	109 Lumineon [1]	293 Nihilego [1]	082 Oricorio [1]
		007 Popplio [1]	009 Primarina [1]	162 Salazzle [1]	206 Trubbish [1]		
Ice	**Powder Snow**	251 Alolan Sandshrew [5]	253 Alolan Vulpix [1]	181 Castform [10]	248 Froslass [1]	247 Glalie [1]	246 Snorunt [1]
		255 Vanillite [E]					
Rock	**Power Gem**	046 Alolan Persian [32]	099 Boldore [1, EV]	101 Carbink [46]	112 Corsola [41]	100 Gigalith [1]	213 Minior [38]
		066 Misdreavus [55]	067 Mismagius [1]	300 Necrozma [43]	293 Nihilego [37]	198 Nosepass [25]	199 Probopass [25]
		102 Sableye [36]	039 Slowking [1]	184 Staryu [37]			
Psychic	**Power Split**	141 Dewpider [E]	293 Nihilego [1]	139 Surskit [E]			
	Power Swap	253 Alolan Vulpix [E]	127 Espeon [45]	269 Exeggcute [E]	166 Magby [E]	285 Tapu Koko [1]	
	Power Trick	042 Abra [E]	095 Machop [E]				
Dark	**Power Trip**	234 Krookodile [1]	079 Mankey [E]	220 Pancham [E]	232 Sandile [E]		
Grass	**Power Whip**	263 Dhelmise [59]	180 Goodra [50]	296 Xurkitree [59]			
Fighting	**Power-Up Punch**	294 Buzzwole [1]	060 Crabominable [22]	059 Crabrawler [22]	280 Lucario [15]		
Normal	**Present**	033 Chansey [E]	210 Cleffa [E]	081 Delibird [1]	032 Happiny [E]	134 Igglybuff [E]	138 Miltank [E]
		024 Pichu [E]	258 Snubbull [E]	225 Togedemaru [E]			
Psychic	**Prismatic Laser**	300 Necrozma [73]					
Normal	**Protect (TM17)**	042 Abra [TM]	245 Absol [TM]	284 Aerodactyl [TM]	044 Alakazam [TM]	071 Alolan Diglett [TM]	072 Alolan Dugtrio [TM]
		270 Alolan Exeggutor [TM]	229 Alolan Geodude [TM]	231 Alolan Golem [TM]	230 Alolan Graveler [TM]	050 Alolan Grimer [TM]	164 Alolan Marowak [TM]
		045 Alolan Meowth [TM]	051 Alolan Muk [TM]	254 Alolan Ninetales [TM]	046 Alolan Persian [TM]	026 Alolan Raichu [TM]	016 Alolan Raticate [TM]
		015 Alolan Rattata [TM]	251 Alolan Sandshrew [TM]	252 Alolan Sandslash [TM]	253 Alolan Vulpix [TM]	157 Alomomola [21, TM]	142 Araquanid [TM]
		053 Arcanine [TM]	192 Archen [TM]	193 Archeops [TM]	023 Ariados [TM]	117 Bagon [TM]	093 Barboach [TM]
		191 Bastiodon [1, TM]	170 Bewear [TM]	034 Blissey [TM]	099 Boldore [TM]	030 Bonsly [TM]	171 Bounsweet [TM]
		076 Braviary [TM]	008 Brionne [TM]	243 Bruxish [TM]	019 Butterfree [TM]	294 Buzzwole [TM]	101 Carbink [TM]
		195 Carracosta [11, TM]	264 Carvanha [TM]	181 Castform [TM]	297 Celesteela [TM]	033 Chansey [TM]	028 Charjabug [TM]
		201 Chinchou [TM]	212 Clefable [TM]	211 Clefairy [TM]	210 Cleffa [TM]	116 Cloyster [1, TM]	174 Comfey [TM]
		112 Corsola [TM]	087 Cottonee [TM]	060 Crabominable [TM]	059 Crabrawler [TM]	188 Cranidos [TM]	070 Crobat [TM]
		163 Cubone [TM]	083 Cutiefly [TM]	002 Dartrix [TM]	003 Decidueye [TM]	081 Delibird [TM]	141 Dewpider [TM]
		263 Dhelmise [TM]	282 Dragonair [TM]	283 Dragonite [TM]	244 Drampa [9, TM]	281 Dratini [TM]	065 Drifblim [TM]
		064 Drifloon [TM]	054 Drowzee [TM]	123 Eevee [TM]	227 Electabuzz [TM]	228 Electivire [TM]	226 Elekid [TM]
		274 Emolga [TM]	127 Espeon [TM]	269 Exeggcute [TM]	074 Fearow [TM]	155 Feebas [TM]	108 Finneon [TM]
		126 Flareon [TM]	159 Fletchinder [TM]	158 Fletchling [TM]	237 Flygon [TM]	143 Fomantis [TM]	248 Froslass [TM]
		239 Gabite [TM]	207 Garbodor [TM]	240 Garchomp [TM]	061 Gastly [TM]	261 Gastrodon [TM]	063 Gengar [TM]
		238 Gible [TM]	100 Gigalith [TM]	130 Glaceon [TM]	247 Glalie [32, TM]	069 Golbat [TM]	153 Goldeen [TM]
		090 Golduck [TM]	183 Golisopod [TM]	180 Goodra [1, 9, TM]	178 Goomy [9, TM]	259 Granbull [TM]	052 Growlithe [TM]
		027 Grubbin [TM]	014 Gumshoos [TM]	299 Guzzlord [TM]	092 Gyarados [TM]	272 Hakamo-o [1, 13, TM]	032 Happiny [TM]
		057 Hariyama [TM]	062 Haunter [TM]	121 Herdier [TM]	278 Honchkrow [TM]	055 Hypno [TM]	134 Igglybuff [TM]
		006 Incineroar [TM]	271 Jangmo-o [13, TM]	135 Jigglypuff [TM]	125 Jolteon [TM]	043 Kadabra [TM]	165 Kangaskhan [TM]
		298 Kartana [TM]	241 Klefki [TM]	222 Komala [TM]	273 Kommo-o [1, 13, TM]	233 Krokorok [TM]	234 Krookodile [TM]
		202 Lanturn [TM]	268 Lapras [TM]	129 Leafeon [TM]	021 Ledian [TM]	020 Ledyba [TM]	086 Lilligant [TM]
		120 Lillipup [TM]	004 Litten [TM]	280 Lucario [TM]	109 Lumineon [TM]	292 Lunala [TM]	144 Lurantis [TM]
		111 Luvdisc [TM]	104 Lycanroc (Midday Form) [TM]	104 Lycanroc (Midnight Form) [TM]	097 Machamp [TM]	096 Machoke [TM]	095 Machop [TM]
		166 Magby [TM]	301 Magearna [TM]	167 Magmar [TM]	168 Magmortar [TM]	047 Magnemite [TM]	048 Magneton [TM]
		049 Magnezone [TM]	056 Makuhita [TM]	078 Mandibuzz [TM]	079 Mankey [TM]	113 Mareanie [TM]	140 Masquerain [TM]
		216 Metagross [TM]	215 Metang [TM]	156 Milotic [TM]	138 Miltank [TM]	242 Mimikyu [TM]	213 Minior [TM]
		066 Misdreavus [TM]	067 Mismagius [TM]	145 Morelull [TM]	132 Mudbray [TM]	133 Mudsdale [TM]	035 Munchlax [TM]
		277 Murkrow [TM]	300 Necrozma [TM]	293 Nihilego [TM]	198 Nosepass [TM]	176 Oranguru [TM]	082 Oricorio [TM]
		187 Palossand [TM]	220 Pancham [TM]	221 Pangoro [TM]	147 Paras [TM]	148 Parasect [TM]	177 Passimian [TM]
		041 Pelipper [1, TM, EV]	085 Petilil [TM]	196 Phantump [TM]	295 Pheromosa [TM]	024 Pichu [TM]	025 Pikachu [TM]
		010 Pikipek [TM]	175 Pinsir [TM]	152 Politoed [TM]	149 Poliwag [TM]	150 Poliwhirl [TM]	151 Poliwrath [TM]
		007 Popplio [TM]	217 Porygon [TM]	218 Porygon2 [TM]	219 Porygon-Z [TM]	009 Primarina [TM]	080 Primeape [TM]

ALOLA REGION POKÉDEX · HOW TO COMPLETE THE ALOLA POKÉDEX · CHAMPION'S GUIDE TO ALOLA · ADVENTURE DATA

Type	Move Name	Pokémon					
Normal	Protect (TM17)	199 Probopass [TM]	089 Psyduck [TM]	200 Pyukumuku [TM]	189 Rampardos [TM]	262 Relicanth [TM]	084 Ribombee [TM]
		279 Riolu [TM]	103 Rockruff [TM]	098 Roggenrola [TM]	001 Rowlet [TM]	075 Rufflet [TM]	102 Sableye [TM]
		119 Salamence [1, TM]	161 Salandit [TM]	162 Salazzle [TM]	232 Sandile [TM]	186 Sandygast [TM]	276 Scizor [TM]
		275 Scyther [TM]	154 Seaking [TM]	265 Sharpedo [TM]	118 Shelgon [1, TM, EV]	115 Shellder [16, TM]	260 Shellos [TM]
		190 Shieldon [1, TM]	146 Shiinotic [TM]	204 Silvally [TM]	208 Skarmory [TM]	179 Sliggoo [9, TM]	038 Slowbro [TM]
		039 Slowking [TM]	037 Slowpoke [TM]	249 Sneasel [TM]	036 Snorlax [TM]	246 Snorunt [32, TM]	258 Snubbull [TM]
		291 Solgaleo [TM]	073 Spearow [TM]	022 Spinarak [TM]	105 Spinda [TM]	185 Starmie [TM]	184 Staryu [TM]
		172 Steenee [TM]	122 Stoutland [TM]	169 Stufful [TM]	031 Sudowoodo [TM]	139 Surskit [TM]	131 Sylveon [TM]
		160 Talonflame [TM]	287 Tapu Bulu [TM]	288 Tapu Fini [TM]	285 Tapu Koko [TM]	286 Tapu Lele [TM]	137 Tauros [TM]
		100 Tentacool [TM]	107 Tentacruel [TM]	194 Tirtouga [11, TM]	225 Togedemaru [TM]	223 Torkoal [30, TM]	005 Torracat [TM]
		012 Toucannon [TM]	114 Toxapex [TM]	235 Trapinch [TM]	197 Trevenant [TM]	206 Trubbish [TM]	011 Trumbeak [TM]
		173 Tsareena [TM]	224 Turtonator [9, TM]	203 Type: Null [TM]	128 Umbreon [TM]	256 Vanillish [TM]	255 Vanillite [TM]
		257 Vanilluxe [TM]	124 Vaporeon [TM]	236 Vibrava [TM]	029 Vikavolt [TM]	077 Vullaby [TM]	266 Wailmer [TM]
		267 Wailord [TM]	250 Weavile [TM]	088 Whimsicott [TM]	094 Whiscash [TM]	136 Wigglytuff [TM]	182 Wimpod [TM]
		040 Wingull [TM]	110 Wishiwashi [TM]	298 Xurkitree [TM]	013 Yungoos [TM]	068 Zubat [TM]	205 Zygarde [TM]
Psychic	Psybeam	044 Alakazam [21]	019 Butterfree [17]	201 Chinchou [E]	054 Drowzee [25]	127 Espeon [20]	108 Finneon [E]
		153 Goldeen [E]	055 Hypno [25]	043 Kadabra [21]	020 Ledyba [E]	301 Magearna [1]	066 Misdreavus [28]
		147 Paras [E]	217 Porygon [7]	218 Porygon2 [7]	219 Porygon-Z [7]	089 Psyduck [E]	022 Spinarak [E]
		105 Spinda [14]	139 Surskit [E]	286 Tapu Lele [14]			
Normal	Psych Up (TM77)	042 Abra [TM]	245 Absol [TM]	044 Alakazam [TM]	270 Alolan Exeggutor [TM]	045 Alolan Meowth [TM]	254 Alolan Ninetales [TM]
		046 Alolan Persian [TM]	253 Alolan Vulpix [TM]	157 Alomomola [TM]	034 Blissey [TM]	030 Bonsly [TM]	019 Butterfree [TM]
		101 Carbink [TM]	181 Castform [TM]	033 Chansey [TM]	212 Clefable [TM]	211 Clefairy [TM]	210 Cleffa [TM]
		174 Comfey [TM]	083 Cutiefly [TM]	244 Drampa [TM]	065 Drifblim [TM]	064 Drifloon [TM]	054 Drowzee [33, TM]
		127 Espeon [29, TM]	269 Exeggcute [TM]	108 Finneon [TM]	248 Froslass [TM]	061 Gastly [TM]	063 Gengar [TM]
		090 Golduck [36, TM]	183 Golisopod [TM]	032 Happiny [TM]	062 Haunter [TM]	278 Honchkrow [TM]	055 Hypno [33, TM]
		134 Igglybuff [TM]	135 Jigglypuff [TM]	043 Kadabra [TM]	241 Klefki [TM]	222 Komala [36, TM]	109 Lumineon [TM]
		292 Lunala [TM]	111 Luvdisc [TM]	047 Magnemite [TM]	048 Magneton [TM]	049 Magnezone [TM]	078 Mandibuzz [TM]
		140 Masquerain [TM]	216 Metagross [TM]	215 Metang [TM]	156 Milotic [TM]	138 Miltank [TM]	242 Mimikyu [TM]
		213 Minior [TM]	066 Misdreavus [TM]	067 Mismagius [TM]	277 Murkrow [TM]	176 Oranguru [18, TM]	217 Porygon [TM]
		218 Porygon2 [TM]	219 Porygon-Z [TM]	009 Primarina [TM]	089 Psyduck [34, TM]	200 Pyukumuku [TM]	262 Relicanth [TM]
		084 Ribombee [TM]	102 Sableye [TM]	038 Slowbro [62, TM]	039 Slowking [54, TM]	037 Slowpoke [54, TM]	249 Sneasel [TM]
		291 Solgaleo [TM]	105 Spinda [41, TM]	185 Starmie [TM]	184 Staryu [TM]	031 Sudowoodo [TM]	139 Surskit [TM]
		131 Sylveon [45, TM]	287 Tapu Bulu [TM]	288 Tapu Fini [TM]	285 Tapu Koko [TM]	286 Tapu Lele [TM]	128 Umbreon [TM]
		077 Vullaby [TM]	250 Weavile [TM]	136 Wigglytuff [TM]			
Psychic	Psychic (TM29)	042 Abra [TM]	044 Alakazam [38, TM]	270 Alolan Exeggutor [TM]	026 Alolan Raichu [1, TM, EV]	157 Alomomola [TM]	023 Ariados [46, TM]
		034 Blissey [TM]	243 Bruxish [TM]	019 Butterfree [TM]	101 Carbink [TM]	033 Chansey [TM]	212 Clefable [TM]
		211 Clefairy [TM]	210 Cleffa [TM]	112 Corsola [TM]	083 Cutiefly [TM]	065 Drifblim [TM]	064 Drifloon [TM]
		054 Drowzee [49, TM]	227 Electabuzz [TM]	228 Electivire [TM]	226 Elekid [TM]	127 Espeon [37, TM]	269 Exeggcute [TM]
		248 Froslass [TM]	207 Garbodor [TM]	061 Gastly [TM]	063 Gengar [TM]	090 Golduck [TM]	032 Happiny [TM]
		062 Haunter [TM]	278 Honchkrow [TM]	055 Hypno [49, TM]	134 Igglybuff [TM]	135 Jigglypuff [TM]	043 Kadabra [38, TM]
		241 Klefki [TM]	268 Lapras [TM]	280 Lucario [TM]	292 Lunala [TM]	166 Magby [TM]	167 Magmar [TM]
		168 Magmortar [TM]	216 Metagross [38, TM]	215 Metang [38, TM]	242 Mimikyu [TM]	213 Minior [TM]	066 Misdreavus [TM]
		067 Mismagius [TM]	035 Munchlax [TM]	277 Murkrow [TM]	300 Necrozma [TM]	293 Nihilego [TM]	176 Oranguru [43, TM]
		187 Palossand [TM]	196 Phantump [TM]	152 Politoed [TM]	149 Poliwag [TM]	150 Poliwhirl [TM]	151 Poliwrath [TM]
		217 Porygon [TM]	218 Porygon2 [TM]	219 Porygon-Z [TM]	009 Primarina [TM]	089 Psyduck [TM]	084 Ribombee [TM]
		102 Sableye [TM]	186 Sandygast [TM]	038 Slowbro [49, TM]	039 Slowking [45, TM]	037 Slowpoke [45, TM]	036 Snorlax [TM]
		291 Solgaleo [TM]	022 Spinarak [40, TM]	105 Spinda [TM]	185 Starmie [TM]	184 Staryu [42, TM]	286 Tapu Lele [TM]
		197 Trevenant [TM]	128 Umbreon [TM]	088 Whimsicott [TM]	136 Wigglytuff [TM]		
	Psychic Fangs	243 Bruxish [41]	264 Carvanha [E]	120 Lillipup [E]			
	Psychic Terrain	176 Oranguru [E]	286 Tapu Lele [1]				
	Psycho Cut	245 Absol [37]	044 Alakazam [28]	054 Drowzee [E]	043 Kadabra [28]	298 Kartana [67]	300 Necrozma [37]
		105 Spinda [E]					
	Psycho Shift	042 Abra [E]	277 Murkrow [E]	105 Spinda [E]			
Psychic	Psyshock (TM03)	042 Abra [TM]	044 Alakazam [TM]	270 Alolan Exeggutor [17, TM]	254 Alolan Ninetales [TM]	026 Alolan Raichu [TM]	212 Clefable [TM]
		211 Clefairy [TM]	210 Cleffa [TM]	054 Drowzee [57, TM]	127 Espeon [TM]	090 Golduck [TM]	055 Hypno [57, TM]
		043 Kadabra [TM]	241 Klefki [TM]	292 Lunala [TM]	216 Metagross [TM]	215 Metang [TM]	300 Necrozma [TM]
		293 Nihilego [TM]	176 Oranguru [TM]	217 Porygon [TM]	218 Porygon2 [TM]	219 Porygon-Z [TM]	089 Psyduck [TM]
		038 Slowbro [TM]	039 Slowking [TM]	037 Slowpoke [TM]	291 Solgaleo [TM]	185 Starmie [TM]	131 Sylveon [TM]
		286 Tapu Lele [32, TM]					

Type	Move Name	Pokémon					
Psychic	Psywave	243 Bruxish [25]	061 Gastly [E]	066 Misdreavus [1]	067 Mismagius [1]	293 Nihilego [13]	184 Staryu [13]
		286 Tapu Lele [8]					
Dark	Punishment	245 Absol [E]	045 Alolan Meowth [E]	134 Igglybuff [E]	078 Mandibuzz [28]	079 Mankey [29]	138 Miltank [E]
		080 Primeape [30]	102 Sableye [24]	204 Silvally [65]	249 Sneasel [44, E]	203 Type: Null [65]	077 Vullaby [28]
		250 Weavile [44]					
Poison	Purify	200 Pyukumuku [21]					
Dark	Pursuit	245 Absol [10]	284 Aerodactyl [E]	071 Alolan Diglett [E]	050 Alolan Grimer [E]	016 Alolan Raticate [13]	015 Alolan Rattata [13]
		060 Crabominable [1, 13]	059 Crabrawler [13]	188 Cranidos [10]	274 Emolga [16]	074 Fearow [1, 8]	014 Gumshoos [1, 7]
		278 Honchkrow [1]	120 Lillipup [E]	079 Mankey [12]	216 Metagross [23]	215 Metang [23]	035 Munchlax [E]
		277 Murkrow [5]	147 Paras [E]	080 Primeape [12]	189 Rampardos [1, 10]	232 Sandile [E]	276 Scizor [9]
		275 Scyther [9]	204 Silvally [10]	208 Skarmory [E]	249 Sneasel [E]	036 Snorlax [E]	073 Spearow [8]
		022 Spinarak [E]	137 Tauros [15]	203 Type: Null [10]	128 Umbreon [1, EV]	040 Wingull [26]	013 Yungoos [7]
		068 Zubat [E]					
	Quash (TM60)	050 Alolan Grimer [TM]	045 Alolan Meowth [TM]	051 Alolan Muk [TM]	046 Alolan Persian [1, TM]	016 Alolan Raticate [TM]	015 Alolan Rattata [TM]
		278 Honchkrow [65, TM]	006 Incineroar [TM]	222 Komala [TM]	277 Murkrow [65, TM]	176 Oranguru [11, TM]	082 Oricorio [TM]
		187 Palossand [TM]	220 Pancham [E]	221 Pangoro [TM]	200 Pyukumuku [TM]	102 Sableye [44, TM]	039 Slowking [TM]
Normal	Quick Attack	245 Absol [1, 7]	026 Alolan Raichu [1]	016 Alolan Raticate [1, 4]	015 Alolan Rattata [4]	192 Archen [1]	193 Archeops [1]
		081 Delibird [E]	123 Eevee [13]	227 Electabuzz [1]	228 Electivire [1]	226 Elekid [1]	274 Emolga [4]
		127 Espeon [13]	126 Flareon [13]	159 Fletchinder [1, 6]	158 Fletchling [6]	130 Glaceon [13]	125 Jolteon [13]
		129 Leafeon [13]	280 Lucario [1]	104 Lycanroc (Midday Form) [1]	140 Masquerain [1, 6]	177 Passimian [E]	025 Pikachu [10]
		175 Pinsir [E]	279 Riolu [1]	276 Scizor [1]	275 Scyther [1]	249 Sneasel [8]	073 Spearow [E]
		139 Surskit [6]	131 Sylveon [13]	160 Talonflame [1, 6]	285 Tapu Koko [1]	235 Trapinch [E]	128 Umbreon [13]
		124 Vaporeon [13]	250 Weavile [1, 8]	040 Wingull [19]	068 Zubat [E]		
Fighting	Quick Guard	192 Archen [25]	193 Archeops [25]	070 Crobat [51]	158 Fletchling [E]	069 Golbat [51]	280 Lucario [33]
		104 Lycanroc (Midday Form) [1]	095 Machop [E]	220 Pancham [E]	177 Passimian [E]	295 Pheromosa [1]	275 Scyther [E]
		068 Zubat [43]					
Bug	Quiver Dance	019 Butterfree [47]	083 Cutiefly [41]	086 Lilligant [28]	140 Masquerain [1, 52]	295 Pheromosa [1]	084 Ribombee [49]
Normal	Rage	117 Bagon [1]	243 Bruxish [E]	264 Carvanha [4]	163 Cubone [23]	259 Granbull [35]	165 Kangaskhan [22]
		233 Krokorok [1]	234 Krookodile [1]	080 Primeape [1, EV]	119 Salamence [1]	232 Sandile [1]	265 Sharpedo [1, 4]
		118 Shelgon [1]	204 Silvally [5]	258 Snubbull [31]	137 Tauros [5]	203 Type: Null [5]	
Bug	Rage Powder	019 Butterfree [35]	147 Paras [49]	148 Parasect [59]	022 Spinarak [E]		
Water	Rain Dance (TM18)	042 Abra [TM]	245 Absol [TM]	284 Aerodactyl [TM]	044 Alakazam [TM]	050 Alolan Grimer [TM]	164 Alolan Marowak [TM]
		045 Alolan Meowth [TM]	051 Alolan Muk [TM]	254 Alolan Ninetales [TM]	046 Alolan Persian [TM]	026 Alolan Raichu [TM]	016 Alolan Raticate [TM]
		015 Alolan Rattata [TM]	253 Alolan Vulpix [TM]	157 Alomomola [TM]	142 Araquanid [TM]	117 Bagon [TM]	093 Barboach [TM]
		191 Bastiodon [TM]	034 Blissey [TM]	076 Braviary [TM]	008 Brionne [TM]	243 Bruxish [TM]	019 Butterfree [TM]
		195 Carracosta [56, TM]	264 Carvanha [TM]	181 Castform [20, TM]	033 Chansey [TM]	028 Charjabug [TM]	201 Chinchou [TM]
		212 Clefable [TM]	211 Clefairy [TM]	210 Cleffa [TM]	116 Cloyster [TM]	112 Corsola [TM]	060 Crabominable [TM]
		059 Crabrawler [TM]	188 Cranidos [TM]	070 Crobat [TM]	081 Delibird [TM]	141 Dewpider [TM]	263 Dhelmise [TM]
		282 Dragonair [TM]	283 Dragonite [TM]	244 Drampa [TM]	281 Dratini [TM]	065 Drifblim [TM]	064 Drifloon [TM]
		054 Drowzee [TM]	123 Eevee [TM]	227 Electabuzz [TM]	228 Electivire [TM]	226 Elekid [TM]	274 Emolga [TM]
		127 Espeon [TM]	074 Fearow [TM]	155 Feebas [TM]	108 Finneon [13, TM]	126 Flareon [TM]	248 Froslass [TM]
		239 Gabite [TM]	207 Garbodor [TM]	240 Garchomp [TM]	061 Gastly [TM]	261 Gastrodon [22, TM]	063 Gengar [TM]
		238 Gible [TM]	130 Glaceon [TM]	247 Glalie [TM]	069 Golbat [TM]	153 Goldeen [TM]	090 Golduck [TM]
		183 Golisopod [TM]	180 Goodra [25, TM]	178 Goomy [25, TM]	259 Granbull [TM]	027 Grubbin [TM]	092 Gyarados [51, TM]
		032 Happiny [TM]	057 Hariyama [TM]	062 Haunter [TM]	121 Herdier [TM]	278 Honchkrow [TM]	055 Hypno [TM]
		134 Igglybuff [TM]	135 Jigglypuff [TM]	125 Jolteon [TM]	043 Kadabra [TM]	165 Kangaskhan [TM]	241 Klefki [TM]
		202 Lanturn [TM]	268 Lapras [22, TM]	129 Leafeon [TM]	120 Lillipup [TM]	280 Lucario [TM]	109 Lumineon [13, TM]
		111 Luvdisc [TM]	097 Machamp [TM]	096 Machoke [TM]	095 Machop [TM]	047 Magnemite [TM]	048 Magneton [TM]
		049 Magnezone [TM]	056 Makuhita [TM]	078 Mandibuzz [TM]	079 Mankey [TM]	113 Mareanie [TM]	140 Masquerain [TM]
		216 Metagross [TM]	215 Metang [TM]	156 Milotic [47, TM]	138 Miltank [TM]	066 Misdreavus [TM]	067 Mismagius [TM]
		035 Munchlax [TM]	277 Murkrow [TM]	176 Oranguru [TM]	220 Pancham [TM]	221 Pangoro [TM]	177 Passimian [TM]
		041 Pelipper [TM]	024 Pichu [TM]	025 Pikachu [TM]	175 Pinsir [TM]	152 Politoed [TM]	149 Poliwag [18, TM]
		150 Poliwhirl [18, TM]	151 Poliwrath [TM]	007 Popplio [TM]	217 Porygon [TM]	218 Porygon2 [TM]	219 Porygon-Z [TM]
		009 Primarina [TM]	080 Primeape [TM]	089 Psyduck [TM]	200 Pyukumuku [TM]	189 Rampardos [TM]	262 Relicanth [TM]
		279 Riolu [TM]	075 Rufflet [TM]	102 Sableye [TM]	119 Salamence [TM]	276 Scizor [TM]	275 Scyther [TM]
		154 Seaking [TM]	265 Sharpedo [TM]	118 Shelgon [TM]	115 Shellder [TM]	260 Shellos [22, TM]	190 Shieldon [TM]
		204 Silvally [TM]	179 Sliggoo [25, TM]	038 Slowbro [55, TM]	039 Slowking [TM]	037 Slowpoke [49, TM]	249 Sneasel [TM]
		036 Snorlax [TM]	246 Snorunt [TM]	258 Snubbull [TM]	073 Spearow [TM]	105 Spinda [TM]	185 Starmie [TM]
		184 Staryu [TM]	122 Stoutland [TM]	139 Surskit [TM]	131 Sylveon [TM]	288 Tapu Fini [TM]	285 Tapu Koko [TM]
		137 Tauros [TM]	106 Tentacool [TM]	107 Tentacruel [TM]	194 Tirtouga [48, TM]	114 Toxapex [TM]	206 Trubbish [TM]

Type	Move Name	Pokémon					
Water	Rain Dance (TM18)	203 Type: Null [TM]	128 Umbreon [TM]	256 Vanillish [TM]	255 Vanillite [TM]	257 Vanilluxe [TM]	124 Vaporeon [TM]
		029 Vikavolt [TM]	077 Vullaby [TM]	266 Wailmer [TM]	267 Wailord [TM]	250 Weavile [TM]	094 Whiscash [TM]
		136 Wigglytuff [TM]	182 Wimpod [TM]	040 Wingull [TM]	110 Wishiwashi [TM]	296 Xurkitree [TM]	068 Zubat [TM]
Normal	Rapid Spin	251 Alolan Sandshrew [9]	171 Bounsweet [9]	081 Delibird [E]	263 Dhelmise [1]	222 Komala [11]	295 Pheromosa [1]
		115 Shellder [E]	105 Spinda [E]	185 Starmie [1]	184 Staryu [7]	172 Steenee [1, 9]	106 Tentacool [E]
		223 Torkoal [10]	173 Tsareena [1, 9]				
Grass	Razor Leaf	171 Bounsweet [13]	087 Cottonee [19]	002 Dartrix [15]	003 Decidueye [15]	143 Fomantis [10]	298 Kartana [13]
		129 Leafeon [1, EV]	144 Lurantis [1, 10]	001 Rowlet [15]	172 Steenee [1, 13]	173 Tsareena [1, 13]	
Water	Razor Shell	183 Golisopod [26]	115 Shellder [32]				
	Razor Wind	245 Absol [49]	244 Drampa [E]	159 Fletchinder [27]	158 Fletchling [25]	276 Scizor [33]	275 Scyther [33, E]
		204 Silvally [70]	073 Spearow [F]	160 Talonflame [27]	203 Type: Null [70]		
Normal	Recover	044 Alakazam [31]	112 Corsola [8]	261 Gastrodon [54]	043 Kadabra [31]	113 Mareanie [33]	156 Milotic [27]
		217 Porygon [18]	218 Porygon2 [18]	219 Porygon-Z [18]	200 Pyukumuku [37]	102 Sableye [F]	260 Shellos [46]
		185 Starmie [1]	184 Staryu [10]	114 Toxapex [33]			
	Recycle	207 Garbodor [1, 3]	241 Klefki [40]	035 Munchlax [1]	217 Porygon [34]	218 Porygon2 [34]	206 Trubbish [3]
Psychic	Reflect (TM33)	042 Abra [TM]	044 Alakazam [26, TM]	270 Alolan Exeggutor [TM]	026 Alolan Raichu [TM]	142 Araquanid [TM]	171 Bounsweet [TM]
		243 Bruxish [TM]	101 Carbink [18, TM]	212 Clefable [TM]	211 Clefairy [TM]	210 Cleffa [TM]	112 Corsola [TM]
		083 Cutiefly [TM]	054 Drowzee [TM]	127 Espeon [TM]	269 Exeggcute [7, TM]	259 Granbull [TM]	055 Hypno [TM]
		134 Igglybuff [TM]	135 Jigglypuff [TM]	043 Kadabra [26, TM]	241 Klefki [TM]	021 Ledian [12, TM]	020 Ledyba [12, TM]
		292 Lunala [TM]	301 Magearna [TM]	047 Magnemite [TM]	048 Magneton [TM]	049 Magnezone [TM]	216 Metagross [TM]
		215 Metang [TM]	213 Minior [TM]	300 Necrozma [TM]	293 Nihilego [TM]	176 Oranguru [TM]	196 Phantump [TM]
		009 Primarina [TM]	200 Pyukumuku [TM]	084 Ribombee [TM]	249 Sneasel [TM]	250 Snubbull [TM]	291 Solgaleo [TM]
		185 Starmie [TM]	184 Staryu [TM]	172 Steenee [TM]	131 Sylveon [TM]	287 Tapu Bulu [TM]	288 Tapu Fini [TM]
		285 Tapu Koko [TM]	286 Tapu Lele [TM]	225 Togedemaru [TM]	197 Trevenant [TM]	173 Tsareena [TM]	250 Weavile [TM]
		136 Wigglytuff [TM]	296 Xurkitree [TM]				
	Reflect Type	181 Castform [E]	061 Gastly [E]	184 Staryu [35]	107 Tentacruel [1]		
Normal	Refresh	157 Alomomola [E]	034 Blissey [9]	033 Chansey [9]	112 Corsola [13]	123 Eevee [20]	032 Happiny [9]
		268 Lapras [E]	156 Milotic [1, 7]	149 Poliwag [E]	089 Psyduck [E]	288 Tapu Fini [26]	
Psychic	Rest (TM44)	042 Abra [TM]	245 Absol [TM]	284 Aerodactyl [TM]	044 Alakazam [TM]	071 Alolan Diglett [TM]	072 Alolan Dugtrio [TM]
		270 Alolan Exeggutor [TM]	229 Alolan Geodude [TM]	231 Alolan Golem [TM]	230 Alolan Graveler [TM]	050 Alolan Grimer [TM]	164 Alolan Marowak [TM]
		045 Alolan Meowth [TM]	051 Alolan Muk [TM]	254 Alolan Ninetales [TM]	046 Alolan Persian [TM]	026 Alolan Raichu [TM]	016 Alolan Raticate [TM]
		015 Alolan Rattata [TM]	251 Alolan Sandshrew [TM]	252 Alolan Sandslash [TM]	253 Alolan Vulpix [TM]	157 Alomomola [TM]	142 Araquanid [TM]
		053 Arcanine [TM]	192 Archen [TM]	193 Archeops [TM]	023 Ariados [TM]	117 Bagon [TM]	093 Barboach [25, TM]
		191 Bastiodon [TM]	170 Bewear [TM]	034 Blissey [TM]	099 Boldore [TM]	030 Bonsly [TM]	171 Bounsweet [TM]
		076 Braviary [TM]	008 Brionne [TM]	243 Bruxish [TM]	019 Butterfree [TM]	294 Buzzwole [TM]	101 Carbink [TM]
		195 Carracosta [TM]	264 Carvanha [TM]	181 Castform [TM]	297 Celesteela [TM]	033 Chansey [TM]	028 Charjabug [TM]
		201 Chinchou [TM]	212 Clefable [TM]	211 Clefairy [TM]	210 Cleffa [TM]	116 Cloyster [TM]	174 Comfey [TM]
		112 Corsola [TM]	087 Cottonee [TM]	060 Crabominable [TM]	059 Crabrawler [TM]	188 Cranidos [TM]	070 Crobat [TM]
		163 Cubone [TM]	083 Cutiefly [TM]	002 Dartrix [TM]	003 Decidueye [TM]	081 Delibird [TM]	141 Dewpider [TM]
		263 Dhelmise [TM]	282 Dragonair [TM]	283 Dragonite [TM]	244 Drampa [TM]	281 Dratini [TM]	065 Drifblim [TM]
		064 Drifloon [TM]	054 Drowzee [TM]	123 Eevee [TM]	227 Electabuzz [TM]	228 Electivire [TM]	226 Elekid [TM]
		274 Emolga [TM]	127 Espeon [TM]	269 Exeggcute [TM]	074 Fearow [TM]	155 Feebas [TM]	108 Finneon [TM]
		126 Flareon [TM]	159 Fletchinder [TM]	158 Fletchling [TM]	237 Flygon [TM]	143 Fomantis [TM]	248 Froslass [TM]
		239 Gabite [TM]	207 Garbodor [TM]	240 Garchomp [TM]	061 Gastly [TM]	261 Gastrodon [TM]	063 Gengar [TM]
		238 Gible [TM]	100 Gigalith [TM]	130 Glaceon [TM]	247 Glalie [TM]	069 Golbat [TM]	153 Goldeen [TM]
		090 Golduck [TM]	183 Golisopod [TM]	180 Goodra [TM]	178 Goomy [TM]	259 Granbull [TM]	052 Growlithe [TM]
		027 Grubbin [TM]	014 Gumshoos [55, TM]	299 Guzzlord [TM]	092 Gyarados [TM]	272 Hakamo-o [TM]	032 Happiny [TM]
		057 Hariyama [TM]	062 Haunter [TM]	121 Herdier [TM]	278 Honchkrow [TM]	055 Hypno [TM]	134 Igglybuff [TM]
		006 Incineroar [TM]	271 Jangmo-o [TM]	135 Jigglypuff [30, TM]	125 Jolteon [TM]	043 Kadabra [TM]	165 Kangaskhan [TM]
		298 Kartana [TM]	241 Klefki [TM]	273 Kommo-o [TM]	233 Krokorok [TM]	234 Krookodile [TM]	202 Lanturn [TM]
		268 Lapras [TM]	129 Leafeon [TM]	021 Ledian [TM]	020 Ledyba [TM]	086 Lilligant [TM]	120 Lillipup [TM]
		004 Litten [TM]	280 Lucario [TM]	109 Lumineon [TM]	292 Lunala [TM]	144 Lurantis [TM]	111 Luvdisc [TM]
		104 Lycanroc (Midday Form) [TM]	104 Lycanroc (Midnight Form) [TM]	097 Machamp [TM]	096 Machoke [TM]	095 Machop [TM]	166 Magby [TM]
		167 Magmar [TM]	168 Magmortar [TM]	047 Magnemite [TM]	048 Magneton [TM]	049 Magnezone [TM]	056 Makuhita [TM]
		078 Mandibuzz [TM]	079 Mankey [TM]	113 Mareanie [TM]	140 Masquerain [TM]	216 Metagross [TM]	215 Metang [TM]
		156 Milotic [TM]	138 Miltank [TM]	242 Mimikyu [TM]	213 Minior [TM]	066 Misdreavus [TM]	067 Mismagius [TM]
		145 Morelull [TM]	132 Mudbray [TM]	133 Mudsdale [TM]	035 Munchlax [TM]	277 Murkrow [TM]	300 Necrozma [TM]
		293 Nihilego [TM]	198 Nosepass [16, TM]	176 Oranguru [TM]	082 Oricorio [TM]	187 Palossand [TM]	220 Pancham [TM]
		221 Pangoro [TM]	147 Paras [TM]	148 Parasect [TM]	177 Passimian [TM]	041 Pelipper [TM]	085 Petilil [TM]
		196 Phantump [TM]	295 Pheromosa [TM]	024 Pichu [TM]	025 Pikachu [TM]	010 Pikipek [TM]	175 Pinsir [TM]
		152 Politoed [TM]	149 Poliwag [TM]	150 Poliwhirl [TM]	151 Poliwrath [TM]	007 Popplio [TM]	217 Porygon [TM]

Type	Move Name	Pokémon					
Psychic	Rest (TM44)	218 Porygon2 [TM]	219 Porygon-Z [TM]	009 Primarina [TM]	080 Primeape [TM]	199 Probopass [16, TM]	089 Psyduck [TM]
		200 Pyukumuku [TM]	189 Rampardos [TM]	262 Relicanth [41, TM]	084 Ribombee [TM]	279 Riolu [TM]	103 Rockruff [TM]
		098 Roggenrola [TM]	001 Rowlet [TM]	075 Rufflet [TM]	102 Sableye [TM]	119 Salamence [TM]	161 Salandit [TM]
		162 Salazzle [TM]	232 Sandile [TM]	186 Sandygast [TM]	276 Scizor [TM]	275 Scyther [TM]	154 Seaking [TM]
		265 Sharpedo [TM]	118 Shelgon [TM]	115 Shellder [TM]	260 Shellos [TM]	190 Shieldon [TM]	146 Shiinotic [TM]
		204 Silvally [TM]	208 Skarmory [TM]	179 Sliggoo [TM]	038 Slowbro [TM]	039 Slowking [TM]	037 Slowpoke [TM]
		249 Sneasel [TM]	036 Snorlax [28, TM]	246 Snorunt [TM]	258 Snubbull [TM]	291 Solgaleo [TM]	073 Spearow [TM]
		022 Spinarak [TM]	105 Spinda [TM]	185 Starmie [TM]	184 Staryu [TM]	172 Steenee [TM]	122 Stoutland [TM]
		169 Stufful [TM]	031 Sudowoodo [TM]	139 Surskit [TM]	131 Sylveon [TM]	160 Talonflame [TM]	137 Tauros [19, TM]
		106 Tentacool [TM]	107 Tentacruel [TM]	194 Tirtouga [TM]	225 Togedemaru [TM]	223 Torkoal [TM]	005 Torracat [TM]
		012 Toucannon [TM]	114 Toxapex [TM]	235 Trapinch [TM]	197 Trevenant [TM]	206 Trubbish [TM]	011 Trumbeak [TM]
		173 Tsareena [TM]	224 Turtonator [TM]	203 Type: Null [TM]	128 Umbreon [TM]	256 Vanillish [TM]	255 Vanillite [TM]
		257 Vanilluxe [TM]	124 Vaporeon [TM]	236 Vibrava [TM]	029 Vikavolt [TM]	077 Vullaby [TM]	266 Wailmer [29, TM]
		267 Wailord [29, TM]	250 Weavile [TM]	088 Whimsicott [TM]	094 Whiscash [25, TM]	136 Wigglytuff [TM]	182 Wimpod [TM]
		040 Wingull [TM]	110 Wishiwashi [TM]	296 Xurkitree [TM]	013 Yungoos [46, TM]	068 Zubat [TM]	205 Zygarde [TM]
Normal	Retaliate	164 Alolan Marowak [59]	163 Cubone [47]	052 Growlithe [32]	121 Herdier [33]	120 Lillipup [29]	122 Stoutland [36]
	Return (TM27)	042 Abra [TM]	245 Absol [TM]	284 Aerodactyl [TM]	044 Alakazam [TM]	071 Alolan Diglett [TM]	072 Alolan Dugtrio [TM]
		270 Alolan Exeggutor [TM]	229 Alolan Geodude [TM]	231 Alolan Golem [TM]	230 Alolan Graveler [TM]	050 Alolan Grimer [TM]	164 Alolan Marowak [TM]
		045 Alolan Meowth [TM]	051 Alolan Muk [TM]	254 Alolan Ninetales [TM]	046 Alolan Persian [TM]	026 Alolan Raichu [TM]	016 Alolan Raticate [TM]
		015 Alolan Rattata [TM]	251 Alolan Sandshrew [TM]	252 Alolan Sandslash [TM]	253 Alolan Vulpix [TM]	157 Alomomola [TM]	142 Araquanid [TM]
		053 Arcanine [TM]	192 Archen [TM]	193 Archeops [TM]	023 Ariados [TM]	117 Bagon [TM]	093 Barboach [TM]
		191 Bastiodon [TM]	170 Bewear [TM]	034 Blissey [TM]	099 Boldore [TM]	030 Bonsly [TM]	171 Bounsweet [TM]
		076 Braviary [TM]	008 Brionne [TM]	243 Bruxish [TM]	019 Butterfree [TM]	294 Buzzwole [TM]	101 Carbink [TM]
		195 Carracosta [TM]	264 Carvanha [TM]	181 Castform [TM]	297 Celesteela [TM]	033 Chansey [TM]	028 Charjabug [TM]
		201 Chinchou [TM]	212 Clefable [TM]	211 Clefairy [TM]	210 Cleffa [TM]	116 Cloyster [TM]	174 Comfey [TM]
		112 Corsola [TM]	087 Cottonee [TM]	060 Crabominable [TM]	059 Crabrawler [TM]	188 Cranidos [TM]	070 Crobat [TM]
		163 Cubone [TM]	083 Cutiefly [TM]	002 Dartrix [TM]	003 Decidueye [TM]	081 Delibird [TM]	141 Dewpider [TM]
		263 Dhelmise [TM]	282 Dragonair [TM]	283 Dragonite [TM]	244 Drampa [TM]	281 Dratini [TM]	065 Drifblim [TM]
		064 Drifloon [TM]	054 Drowzee [TM]	123 Eevee [TM]	227 Electabuzz [TM]	228 Electivire [TM]	226 Elekid [TM]
		274 Emolga [TM]	127 Espeon [TM]	269 Exeggcute [TM]	074 Fearow [TM]	155 Feebas [TM]	108 Finneon [TM]
		126 Flareon [TM]	159 Fletchinder [TM]	158 Fletchling [TM]	237 Flygon [TM]	143 Fomantis [TM]	248 Froslass [TM]
		239 Gabite [TM]	207 Garbodor [TM]	240 Garchomp [TM]	061 Gastly [TM]	261 Gastrodon [TM]	063 Gengar [TM]
		238 Gible [TM]	100 Gigalith [TM]	130 Glaceon [TM]	247 Glalie [TM]	069 Golbat [TM]	153 Goldeen [TM]
		090 Golduck [TM]	183 Golisopod [TM]	180 Goodra [TM]	178 Goomy [TM]	259 Granbull [TM]	052 Growlithe [TM]
		027 Grubbin [TM]	014 Gumshoos [TM]	299 Guzzlord [TM]	092 Gyarados [TM]	272 Hakamo-o [TM]	032 Happiny [TM]
		057 Hariyama [TM]	062 Haunter [TM]	121 Herdier [TM]	278 Honchkrow [TM]	055 Hypno [TM]	134 Igglybuff [TM]
		006 Incineroar [TM]	271 Jangmo-o [TM]	135 Jigglypuff [TM]	125 Jolteon [TM]	043 Kadabra [TM]	165 Kangaskhan [TM]
		298 Kartana [TM]	241 Klefki [TM]	222 Komala [TM]	273 Kommo-o [TM]	233 Krokorok [TM]	234 Krookodile [TM]
		202 Lanturn [TM]	268 Lapras [TM]	129 Leafeon [TM]	021 Ledian [TM]	020 Ledyba [TM]	086 Lilligant [TM]
		120 Lillipup [TM]	004 Litten [TM]	280 Lucario [TM]	109 Lumineon [TM]	292 Lunala [TM]	144 Lurantis [TM]
		111 Luvdisc [TM]	104 Lycanroc (Midday Form) [TM]	104 Lycanroc (Midnight Form) [TM]	097 Machamp [TM]	096 Machoke [TM]	095 Machop [TM]
		166 Magby [TM]	301 Magearna [TM]	167 Magmar [TM]	168 Magmortar [TM]	047 Magnemite [TM]	048 Magneton [TM]
		049 Magnezone [TM]	056 Makuhita [TM]	078 Mandibuzz [TM]	079 Mankey [TM]	113 Mareanie [TM]	140 Masquerain [TM]
		216 Metagross [TM]	215 Metang [TM]	156 Milotic [TM]	138 Miltank [TM]	242 Mimikyu [TM]	213 Minior [TM]
		066 Misdreavus [TM]	067 Mismagius [TM]	145 Morelull [TM]	132 Mudbray [TM]	133 Mudsdale [TM]	035 Munchlax [TM]
		277 Murkrow [TM]	300 Necrozma [TM]	293 Nihilego [TM]	198 Nosepass [TM]	176 Oranguru [TM]	082 Oricorio [TM]
		187 Palossand [TM]	220 Pancham [TM]	221 Pangoro [TM]	147 Paras [TM]	148 Parasect [TM]	177 Passimian [TM]
		041 Pelipper [TM]	085 Petilil [TM]	196 Phantump [TM]	295 Pheromosa [TM]	024 Pichu [TM]	025 Pikachu [TM]
		010 Pikipek [TM]	175 Pinsir [TM]	152 Politoed [TM]	149 Poliwag [TM]	150 Poliwhirl [TM]	151 Poliwrath [TM]
		007 Popplio [TM]	217 Porygon [TM]	218 Porygon2 [TM]	219 Porygon-Z [TM]	009 Primarina [TM]	080 Primeape [TM]
		199 Probopass [TM]	089 Psyduck [TM]	189 Rampardos [TM]	262 Relicanth [TM]	084 Ribombee [TM]	279 Riolu [TM]
		103 Rockruff [TM]	098 Roggenrola [TM]	001 Rowlet [TM]	075 Rufflet [TM]	102 Sableye [TM]	119 Salamence [TM]
		161 Salandit [TM]	162 Salazzle [TM]	232 Sandile [TM]	186 Sandygast [TM]	276 Scizor [TM]	275 Scyther [TM]
		154 Seaking [TM]	265 Sharpedo [TM]	118 Shelgon [TM]	115 Shellder [TM]	260 Shellos [TM]	190 Shieldon [TM]
		146 Shiinotic [TM]	204 Silvally [TM]	208 Skarmory [TM]	179 Sliggoo [TM]	038 Slowbro [TM]	039 Slowking [TM]
		037 Slowpoke [TM]	249 Sneasel [TM]	036 Snorlax [TM]	246 Snorunt [TM]	258 Snubbull [TM]	291 Solgaleo [TM]
		073 Spearow [TM]	022 Spinarak [TM]	105 Spinda [TM]	185 Starmie [TM]	184 Staryu [TM]	172 Steenee [TM]
		122 Stoutland [TM]	169 Stufful [TM]	031 Sudowoodo [TM]	139 Surskit [TM]	131 Sylveon [TM]	160 Talonflame [TM]
		287 Tapu Bulu [TM]	288 Tapu Fini [TM]	285 Tapu Koko [TM]	286 Tapu Lele [TM]	137 Tauros [TM]	106 Tentacool [TM]
		107 Tentacruel [TM]	194 Tirtouga [TM]	225 Togedemaru [TM]	223 Torkoal [TM]	005 Torracat [TM]	012 Toucannon [TM]
		114 Toxapex [TM]	235 Trapinch [TM]	197 Trevenant [TM]	206 Trubbish [TM]	011 Trumbeak [TM]	173 Tsareena [TM]

Type	Move Name	Pokémon					
Normal	Return (TM27)	224 Turtonator [TM]	203 Type: Null [TM]	128 Umbreon [TM]	256 Vanillish [TM]	255 Vanillite [TM]	257 Vanilluxe [TM]
		124 Vaporeon [TM]	236 Vibrava [TM]	029 Vikavolt [TM]	077 Vullaby [TM]	266 Wailmer [TM]	267 Wailord [TM]
		250 Weavile [TM]	088 Whimsicott [TM]	094 Whiscash [TM]	136 Wigglytuff [TM]	182 Wimpod [TM]	040 Wingull [TM]
		110 Wishiwashi [TM]	296 Xurkitree [TM]	013 Yungoos [TM]	068 Zubat [TM]	205 Zygarde [TM]	
	Revelation Dance	082 Oricorio [40]					
Fighting	Revenge	015 Alolan Rattata [E]	004 Litten [E]	097 Machamp [19]	096 Machoke [19]	095 Machop [19]	056 Makuhita [E]
		079 Mankey [E]	175 Pinsir [15]	224 Turtonator [E]	250 Weavile [1]	013 Yungoos [E]	
	Reversal	071 Alolan Diglett [E]	015 Alolan Rattata [E]	294 Buzzwole [1]	060 Crabominable [33]	059 Crabrawler [33]	052 Growlithe [19]
		057 Hariyama [50]	121 Herdier [38]	271 Jangmo-o [E]	165 Kangaskhan [50]	120 Lillipup [33]	104 Lycanroc (Midnight Form) [1]
		056 Makuhita [43]	079 Mankey [F]	138 Miltank [E]	177 Passimian [46]	024 Pichu [E]	279 Riolu [29]
		275 Scyther [E]	122 Stoutland [42]	225 Togedemaru [F]			
Normal	Roar (TM05)	284 Aerodactyl [9, TM]	231 Alolan Golem [TM]	254 Alolan Ninetales [TM]	046 Alolan Persian [TM]	016 Alolan Raticate [TM]	253 Alolan Vulpix [7, TM]
		053 Arcanine [1, TM]	192 Archen [TM]	193 Archeops [TM]	117 Bagon [TM]	191 Bastiodon [TM]	170 Bewear [TM]
		188 Cranidos [TM]	283 Dragonite [TM]	244 Drampa [TM]	126 Flareon [TM]	239 Gabite [TM]	240 Garchomp [TM]
		238 Gible [TM]	130 Glaceon [TM]	259 Granbull [27, TM]	052 Growlithe [1, TM]	014 Gumshoos [TM]	092 Gyarados [TM]
		272 Hakamo-o [TM]	121 Herdier [29, TM]	006 Incineroar [19, TM]	271 Jangmo-o [TM]	125 Jolteon [TM]	165 Kangaskhan [TM]
		273 Kommo-o [TM]	233 Krokorok [TM]	234 Krookodile [TM]	268 Lapras [TM]	129 Leafeon [TM]	120 Lillipup [26, TM]
		004 Litten [18, TM]	280 Lucario [TM]	292 Lunala [TM]	104 Lycanroc (Midday Form) [26, TM]	104 Lycanroc (Midnight Form) [26, TM]	132 Mudbray [TM]
		133 Mudsdale [TM]	220 Pancham [TM]	221 Pangoro [TM]	189 Rampardos [TM]	279 Riolu [TM]	103 Rockruff [26, TM]
		119 Salamence [TM]	232 Sandile [TM]	265 Sharpedo [TM]	118 Shelgon [TM]	190 Shieldon [TM]	204 Silvally [TM]
		208 Skarmory [TM]	258 Snubbull [25, TM]	291 Solgaleo [TM]	122 Stoutland [29, TM]	169 Stufful [TM]	287 Tapu Bulu [TM]
		285 Tapu Koko [TM]	005 Torracat [19, TM]	224 Turtonator [TM]	203 Type: Null [TM]	124 Vaporeon [TM]	266 Wailmer [TM]
		267 Wailord [TM]					
Rock	Rock Blast	229 Alolan Geodude [30]	231 Alolan Golem [34]	230 Alolan Graveler [34]	099 Boldore [14]	112 Corsola [31]	100 Gigalith [14]
		300 Necrozma [19]	198 Nosepass [28]	199 Probopass [28]	098 Roggenrola [14]	115 Shellder [E]	190 Shieldon [E]
		012 Toucannon [1]	206 Trubbish [E]	011 Trumbeak [1]			
Normal	Rock Climb	229 Alolan Geodude [E]	238 Gible [E]	104 Lycanroc (Midday Form) [45]	104 Lycanroc (Midnight Form) [45]	103 Rockruff [45]	232 Sandile [E]
Rock	Rock Polish (TM69)	284 Aerodactyl [TM]	229 Alolan Geodude [6, TM]	231 Alolan Golem [1, 6, TM]	230 Alolan Graveler [1, 6, TM]	050 Alolan Grimer [TM]	051 Alolan Muk [TM]
		192 Archen [TM]	193 Archeops [TM]	191 Bastiodon [TM]	099 Boldore [TM]	030 Bonsly [TM]	101 Carbink [TM]
		195 Carracosta [TM]	112 Corsola [TM]	188 Cranidos [TM]	207 Garbodor [TM]	100 Gigalith [TM]	273 Kommo-o [TM]
		104 Lycanroc (Midday Form) [TM]	104 Lycanroc (Midnight Form) [TM]	216 Metagross [TM]	215 Metang [TM]	213 Minior [TM]	300 Necrozma [TM]
		198 Nosepass [TM]	187 Palossand [TM]	199 Probopass [TM]	189 Rampardos [TM]	262 Relicanth [TM]	103 Rockruff [TM]
		098 Roggenrola [TM]	186 Sandygast [TM]	190 Shieldon [TM]	031 Sudowoodo [TM]	194 Tirtouga [TM]	
Rock	Rock Slide (TM80)	245 Absol [TM]	284 Aerodactyl [73, TM]	071 Alolan Diglett [TM]	072 Alolan Dugtrio [TM]	229 Alolan Geodude [TM]	231 Alolan Golem [TM]
		230 Alolan Graveler [TM]	050 Alolan Grimer [TM]	164 Alolan Marowak [TM]	051 Alolan Muk [TM]	251 Alolan Sandshrew [TM]	252 Alolan Sandslash [TM]
		192 Archen [45, TM]	193 Archeops [51, TM]	117 Bagon [TM]	191 Bastiodon [TM]	170 Bewear [TM]	034 Blissey [TM]
		099 Boldore [30, TM]	030 Bonsly [33, TM]	076 Braviary [TM]	294 Buzzwole [TM]	101 Carbink [TM]	195 Carracosta [51, TM]
		297 Celesteela [TM]	033 Chansey [TM]	112 Corsola [TM]	060 Crabominable [TM]	059 Crabrawler [TM]	188 Cranidos [TM]
		163 Cubone [TM]	263 Dhelmise [TM]	283 Dragonite [TM]	244 Drampa [TM]	228 Electivire [TM]	237 Flygon [15, TM]
		239 Gabite [TM]	240 Garchomp [TM]	261 Gastrodon [TM]	238 Gible [TM]	100 Gigalith [30, TM]	183 Golisopod [TM]
		180 Goodra [TM]	178 Goomy [TM]	259 Granbull [TM]	299 Guzzlord [TM]	272 Hakamo-o [TM]	057 Hariyama [TM]
		271 Jangmo-o [TM]	165 Kangaskhan [TM]	222 Komala [TM]	273 Kommo-o [TM]	233 Krokorok [TM]	234 Krookodile [TM]
		280 Lucario [TM]	104 Lycanroc (Midday Form) [34, TM]	104 Lycanroc (Midnight Form) [34, TM]	097 Machamp [TM]	096 Machoke [TM]	095 Machop [TM]
		168 Magmortar [TM]	056 Makuhita [TM]	079 Mankey [TM]	216 Metagross [TM]	215 Metang [TM]	138 Miltank [TM]
		213 Minior [TM]	132 Mudbray [TM]	133 Mudsdale [TM]	035 Munchlax [TM]	300 Necrozma [TM]	198 Nosepass [22, TM]
		176 Oranguru [TM]	187 Palossand [TM]	220 Pancham [TM]	221 Pangoro [TM]	177 Passimian [TM]	196 Phantump [TM]
		175 Pinsir [TM]	151 Poliwrath [TM]	080 Primeape [TM]	199 Probopass [22, TM]	189 Rampardos [TM]	262 Relicanth [TM]
		279 Riolu [TM]	103 Rockruff [34, TM]	098 Roggenrola [27, TM]	075 Rufflet [TM]	119 Salamence [TM]	232 Sandile [TM]
		186 Sandygast [TM]	118 Shelgon [TM]	190 Shieldon [TM]	204 Silvally [TM]	208 Skarmory [TM]	179 Sliggoo [TM]
		036 Snorlax [TM]	291 Solgaleo [TM]	105 Spinda [TM]	169 Stufful [TM]	031 Sudowoodo [33, TM]	287 Tapu Bulu [TM]
		137 Tauros [TM]	194 Tirtouga [45, TM]	223 Torkoal [TM]	235 Trapinch [15, TM]	197 Trevenant [TM]	203 Type: Null [TM]
		236 Vibrava [15, TM]	094 Whiscash [TM]	205 Zygarde [TM]			
Fighting	Rock Smash	060 Crabominable [1, 5]	059 Crabrawler [5]	183 Golisopod [1, 7]	177 Passimian [8]	010 Pikipek [9]	012 Toucannon [1, 9]
		011 Trumbeak [1, 9]					

Type	Move Name	Pokémon					
Rock	Rock Throw	229 Alolan Geodude [16]	231 Alolan Golem [16]	230 Alolan Graveler [16]	192 Archen [5]	193 Archeops [1, 5]	030 Bonsly [12]
		101 Carbink [5]	104 Lycanroc (Midday Form) [15]	104 Lycanroc (Midnight Form) [15]	198 Nosepass [10]	103 Rockruff [15]	031 Sudowoodo [1, 12]
		194 Tirtouga [E]					
Rock	Rock Tomb (TM39)	245 Absol [TM]	284 Aerodactyl [TM]	071 Alolan Diglett [TM]	072 Alolan Dugtrio [TM]	229 Alolan Geodude [TM]	231 Alolan Golem [TM]
		230 Alolan Graveler [TM]	050 Alolan Grimer [TM]	164 Alolan Marowak [TM]	051 Alolan Muk [TM]	192 Archen [TM]	193 Archeops [TM]
		117 Bagon [TM]	093 Barboach [TM]	191 Bastiodon [TM]	170 Bewear [TM]	034 Blissey [TM]	099 Boldore [TM]
		030 Bonsly [26, TM]	076 Braviary [TM]	294 Buzzwole [TM]	101 Carbink [TM]	195 Carracosta [TM]	033 Chansey [TM]
		112 Corsola [TM]	060 Crabominable [TM]	059 Crabrawler [TM]	188 Cranidos [TM]	163 Cubone [TM]	283 Dragonite [TM]
		228 Electivire [TM]	237 Flygon [TM]	239 Gabite [TM]	240 Garchomp [TM]	261 Gastrodon [TM]	238 Gible [TM]
		100 Gigalith [TM]	183 Golisopod [TM]	259 Granbull [TM]	014 Gumshoos [TM]	299 Guzzlord [TM]	272 Hakamo-o [TM]
		057 Hariyama [TM]	121 Herdier [TM]	271 Jangmo-o [TM]	165 Kangaskhan [TM]	273 Kommo-o [TM]	233 Krokorok [TM]
		234 Krookodile [TM]	120 Lillipup [TM]	280 Lucario [TM]	104 Lycanroc (Midday Form) [23, TM]	104 Lycanroc (Midnight Form) [23, TM]	097 Machamp [TM]
		096 Machoke [TM]	095 Machop [TM]	168 Magmortar [TM]	056 Makuhita [TM]	078 Mandibuzz [TM]	079 Mankey [TM]
		216 Metagross [TM]	215 Metang [TM]	138 Miltank [TM]	213 Minior [TM]	132 Mudbray [TM]	133 Mudsdale [TM]
		035 Munchlax [TM]	300 Necrozma [TM]	198 Nosepass [TM]	187 Palossand [TM]	220 Pancham [TM]	221 Pangoro [TM]
		177 Passimian [TM]	175 Pinsir [TM]	151 Poliwrath [TM]	080 Primeape [TM]	199 Probopass [TM]	189 Rampardos [TM]
		262 Relicanth [15, TM]	279 Riolu [TM]	103 Rockruff [23, TM]	098 Roggenrola [TM, E]	075 Rufflet [TM]	102 Sableye [TM]
		119 Salamence [TM]	232 Sandile [TM]	186 Sandygast [TM]	265 Sharpedo [TM]	118 Shelgon [TM]	190 Shieldon [TM]
		208 Skarmory [TM]	036 Snorlax [TM]	291 Solgaleo [TM]	105 Spinda [TM]	122 Stoutland [TM]	169 Stufful [TM]
		031 Sudowoodo [26, TM]	287 Tapu Bulu [TM]	137 Tauros [TM]	194 Tirtouga [TM]	223 Torkoal [TM]	235 Trapinch [TM]
		224 Turtonator [TM]	236 Vibrava [TM]	077 Vullaby [TM]	266 Wailmer [TM]	267 Wailord [TM]	094 Whiscash [TM]
		013 Yungoos [TM]					
Psychic	Role Play	054 Drowzee [E]	043 Kadabra [41]	105 Spinda [E]			
Fighting	Rolling Kick	226 Elekid [E]	095 Machop [E]				
Rock	Rollout	229 Alolan Geodude [10]	230 Alolan Graveler [10]	030 Bonsly [E]	195 Carracosta [1, 5]	135 Jigglypuff [20]	222 Komala [1]
		138 Miltank [19]	213 Minior [8]	035 Munchlax [36]	198 Nosepass [E]	036 Snorlax [36]	246 Snorunt [E]
		031 Sudowoodo [E]	194 Tirtouga [5]	225 Togedemaru [9]	206 Trubbish [E]	266 Wailmer [10]	267 Wailord [1, 10]
Flying	Roost (TM19)	284 Aerodactyl [TM, E]	192 Archen [TM]	193 Archeops [TM]	076 Braviary [TM]	019 Butterfree [TM]	294 Buzzwole [TM]
		070 Crobat [TM]	083 Cutiefly [TM]	002 Dartrix [TM]	003 Decidueye [TM]	283 Dragonite [1, TM]	244 Drampa [TM]
		274 Emolga [TM, E]	074 Fearow [36, TM]	159 Fletchinder [25, TM]	158 Fletchling [21, TM]	237 Flygon [TM]	069 Golbat [TM]
		278 Honchkrow [TM]	021 Ledian [TM]	020 Ledyba [TM]	292 Lunala [TM]	078 Mandibuzz [TM]	140 Masquerain [TM]
		277 Murkrow [TM, E]	082 Oricorio [30, TM]	041 Pelipper [39, TM]	295 Pheromosa [TM]	010 Pikipek [19, TM]	084 Ribombee [TM]
		001 Rowlet [TM]	075 Rufflet [TM]	119 Salamence [TM]	276 Scizor [TM]	275 Scyther [TM]	208 Skarmory [TM]
		073 Spearow [32, TM]	160 Talonflame [25, TM]	285 Tapu Koko [TM]	012 Toucannon [21, TM]	011 Trumbeak [21, TM]	236 Vibrava [TM]
		029 Vikavolt [TM]	077 Vullaby [TM, E]	040 Wingull [33, TM, E]	068 Zubat [TM]		
Ground	Rototiller	072 Alolan Dugtrio [1]	132 Mudbray [8]	133 Mudsdale [1, 8]	147 Paras [E]	287 Tapu Bulu [38]	
Normal	Round (TM48)	042 Abra [TM]	245 Absol [TM]	284 Aerodactyl [TM]	044 Alakazam [TM]	071 Alolan Diglett [TM]	072 Alolan Dugtrio [TM]
		270 Alolan Exeggutor [TM]	229 Alolan Geodude [TM]	231 Alolan Golem [TM]	230 Alolan Graveler [TM]	050 Alolan Grimer [TM]	164 Alolan Marowak [TM]
		045 Alolan Meowth [TM]	051 Alolan Muk [TM]	254 Alolan Ninetales [TM]	046 Alolan Persian [TM]	026 Alolan Raichu [TM]	016 Alolan Raticate [TM]
		015 Alolan Rattata [TM]	251 Alolan Sandshrew [TM]	252 Alolan Sandslash [TM]	253 Alolan Vulpix [TM]	157 Alomomola [TM]	142 Araquanid [TM]
		053 Arcanine [TM]	192 Archen [TM]	193 Archeops [TM]	023 Ariados [TM]	117 Bagon [TM]	093 Barboach [TM]
		191 Bastiodon [TM]	170 Bewear [TM]	034 Blissey [TM]	099 Boldore [TM]	030 Bonsly [TM]	171 Bounsweet [TM]
		076 Braviary [TM]	008 Brionne [TM]	243 Bruxish [TM]	019 Butterfree [TM]	294 Buzzwole [TM]	101 Carbink [TM]
		195 Carracosta [TM]	264 Carvanha [TM]	181 Castform [TM]	297 Celesteela [TM]	033 Chansey [TM]	028 Charjabug [TM]
		201 Chinchou [TM]	212 Clefable [TM]	211 Clefairy [TM]	210 Cleffa [TM]	116 Cloyster [TM]	174 Comfey [TM]
		112 Corsola [TM]	087 Cottonee [TM]	060 Crabominable [TM]	059 Crabrawler [TM]	188 Cranidos [TM]	070 Crobat [TM]
		163 Cubone [TM]	083 Cutiefly [TM]	002 Dartrix [TM]	003 Decidueye [TM]	081 Delibird [TM]	141 Dewpider [TM]
		263 Dhelmise [TM]	282 Dragonair [TM]	283 Dragonite [TM]	244 Drampa [TM]	281 Dratini [TM]	065 Drifblim [TM]
		064 Drifloon [TM]	054 Drowzee [TM]	123 Eevee [TM]	227 Electabuzz [TM]	228 Electivire [TM]	226 Elekid [TM]
		274 Emolga [TM]	127 Espeon [TM]	269 Exeggcute [TM]	074 Fearow [TM]	155 Feebas [TM]	108 Finneon [TM]
		126 Flareon [TM]	159 Fletchinder [TM]	158 Fletchling [TM]	237 Flygon [TM]	143 Fomantis [TM]	248 Froslass [TM]
		239 Gabite [TM]	207 Garbodor [TM]	240 Garchomp [TM]	061 Gastly [TM]	261 Gastrodon [TM]	063 Gengar [TM]
		238 Gible [TM]	100 Gigalith [TM]	130 Glaceon [TM]	247 Glalie [TM]	069 Golbat [TM]	153 Goldeen [TM]
		090 Golduck [TM]	183 Golisopod [TM]	180 Goodra [TM]	178 Goomy [TM]	259 Granbull [TM]	052 Growlithe [TM]
		027 Grubbin [TM]	014 Gumshoos [TM]	299 Guzzlord [TM]	092 Gyarados [TM]	272 Hakamo-o [TM]	032 Happiny [TM]
		057 Hariyama [TM]	062 Haunter [TM]	121 Herdier [TM]	278 Honchkrow [TM]	055 Hypno [TM]	134 Igglybuff [TM]
		006 Incineroar [TM]	271 Jangmo-o [TM]	135 Jigglypuff [22, TM]	125 Jolteon [TM]	043 Kadabra [TM]	165 Kangaskhan [TM]
		298 Kartana [TM]	241 Klefki [TM]	222 Komala [TM]	273 Kommo-o [TM]	233 Krokorok [TM]	234 Krookodile [TM]
		202 Lanturn [TM]	268 Lapras [TM]	129 Leafeon [TM]	021 Ledian [TM]	020 Ledyba [TM]	086 Lilligant [TM]
		120 Lillipup [TM]	004 Litten [TM]	280 Lucario [TM]	109 Lumineon [TM]	292 Lunala [TM]	144 Lurantis [TM]

Type	Move Name	Pokémon					
Normal	Round (TM48)	111 Luvdisc [TM]	104 Lycanroc (Midday Form) [TM]	104 Lycanroc (Midnight Form) [TM]	097 Machamp [TM]	096 Machoke [TM]	095 Machop [TM]
		166 Magby [TM]	301 Magearna [TM]	167 Magmar [TM]	168 Magmortar [TM]	047 Magnemite [TM]	048 Magneton [TM]
		049 Magnezone [TM]	056 Makuhita [TM]	078 Mandibuzz [TM]	079 Mankey [TM]	113 Mareanie [TM]	140 Masquerain [TM]
		216 Metagross [TM]	215 Metang [TM]	156 Milotic [TM]	138 Miltank [TM]	242 Mimikyu [TM]	213 Minior [TM]
		066 Misdreavus [TM]	067 Mismagius [TM]	145 Morelull [TM]	132 Mudbray [TM]	133 Mudsdale [TM]	035 Munchlax [TM]
		277 Murkrow [TM]	300 Necrozma [TM]	293 Nihilego [TM]	198 Nosepass [TM]	176 Oranguru [TM]	082 Oricorio [TM]
		187 Palossand [TM]	220 Pancham [TM]	221 Pangoro [TM]	147 Paras [TM]	148 Parasect [TM]	177 Passimian [TM]
		041 Pelipper [TM]	085 Petilil [TM]	196 Phantump [TM]	295 Pheromosa [TM]	024 Pichu [TM]	025 Pikachu [TM]
		010 Pikipek [TM]	175 Pinsir [TM]	152 Politoed [TM]	149 Poliwag [TM]	150 Poliwhirl [TM]	151 Poliwrath [TM]
		007 Popplio [TM]	217 Porygon [TM]	218 Porygon2 [TM]	219 Porygon Z [TM]	009 Primarina [TM]	080 Primeape [TM]
		199 Probopass [TM]	089 Psyduck [TM]	189 Rampardos [TM]	262 Relicanth [TM]	084 Ribombee [TM]	279 Riolu [TM]
		103 Rockruff [TM]	098 Roggenrola [TM]	001 Rowlet [TM]	075 Rufflet [TM]	102 Sableye [TM]	119 Salamence [TM]
		161 Salandit [TM]	162 Salazzle [TM]	232 Sandile [TM]	186 Sandygast [TM]	276 Scizor [TM]	275 Scyther [TM]
		154 Seaking [TM]	265 Sharpedo [TM]	118 Shelgon [TM]	115 Shellder [TM]	260 Shellos [TM]	190 Shieldon [TM]
		146 Shiinotic [TM]	204 Silvally [TM]	208 Skarmory [TM]	179 Sliggoo [TM]	038 Slowbro [TM]	039 Slowking [TM]
		037 Slowpoke [TM]	249 Sneasel [TM]	036 Snorlax [TM]	246 Snorunt [TM]	258 Snubbull [TM]	291 Solgaleo [TM]
		073 Spearow [TM]	022 Spinarak [TM]	105 Spinda [TM]	185 Starmie [TM]	184 Staryu [TM]	172 Steenee [TM]
		122 Stoutland [TM]	169 Stufful [TM]	031 Sudowoodo [TM]	139 Surskit [TM]	131 Sylveon [TM]	160 Talonflame [TM]
		287 Tapu Bulu [TM]	288 Tapu Fini [TM]	285 Tapu Koko [TM]	286 Tapu Lele [TM]	137 Tauros [TM]	106 Tentacool [TM]
		107 Tentacruel [TM]	194 Tirtouga [TM]	225 Togedemaru [TM]	223 Torkoal [TM]	005 Torracat [TM]	012 Toucannon [TM]
		114 Toxapex [TM]	235 Trapinch [TM]	197 Trevenant [TM]	206 Trubbish [TM]	011 Trumbeak [TM]	173 Tsareena [TM]
		224 Turtonator [TM]	203 Type: Null [TM]	128 Umbreon [TM]	256 Vanillish [TM]	255 Vanillite [TM]	257 Vanilluxe [TM]
		124 Vaporeon [TM]	236 Vibrava [TM]	029 Vikavolt [TM]	077 Vullaby [TM]	266 Wailmer [TM]	267 Wailord [TM]
		250 Weavile [TM]	088 Whimsicott [TM]	094 Whiscash [TM]	136 Wigglytuff [TM]	182 Wimpod [TM]	040 Wingull [TM]
		110 Wishiwashi [TM]	296 Xurkitree [TM]	013 Yungoos [TM]	068 Zubat [TM]	205 Zygarde [TM]	
Fighting	Sacred Sword	298 Kartana [1]					
Normal	Safeguard (TM20)	042 Abra [TM]	044 Alakazam [TM]	254 Alolan Ninetales [1, TM]	026 Alolan Raichu [TM]	251 Alolan Sandshrew [TM]	252 Alolan Sandslash [TM]
		253 Alolan Vulpix [34, TM]	157 Alomomola [45, TM]	142 Araquanid [TM]	053 Arcanine [TM]	034 Blissey [TM]	171 Bounsweet [TM]
		243 Bruxish [TM]	019 Butterfree [25, TM]	101 Carbink [70, TM]	033 Chansey [TM]	212 Clefable [TM]	211 Clefairy [TM]
		210 Cleffa [TM]	174 Comfey [TM]	112 Corsola [TM]	087 Cottonee [TM]	083 Cutiefly [TM]	002 Dartrix [TM]
		003 Decidueye [TM]	282 Dragonair [53, TM]	283 Dragonite [53, TM]	244 Drampa [33, TM]	281 Dratini [45, TM]	054 Drowzee [TM]
		108 Finneon [29, TM]	143 Fomantis [TM]	248 Froslass [TM]	247 Glalie [TM]	052 Growlithe [TM]	272 Hakamo-o [TM]
		032 Happiny [TM]	055 Hypno [TM]	134 Igglybuff [TM]	271 Jangmo-o [TM]	135 Jigglypuff [TM]	043 Kadabra [TM]
		165 Kangaskhan [TM]	241 Klefki [TM]	273 Kommo-o [TM]	268 Lapras [43, TM]	021 Ledian [12, TM]	020 Ledyba [12, TM]
		086 Lilligant [TM]	109 Lumineon [29, TM]	292 Lunala [TM]	144 Lurantis [TM]	111 Luvdisc [49, TM]	113 Mareanie [TM]
		156 Milotic [37, TM]	242 Mimikyu [TM]	213 Minior [TM]	145 Morelull [TM]	293 Nihilego [31, TM]	176 Oranguru [TM]
		082 Oricorio [TM, E]	085 Petilil [TM]	196 Phantump [TM]	200 Pyukumuku [13, TM]	262 Relicanth [TM]	084 Ribombee [TM]
		001 Rowlet [TM]	276 Scizor [TM]	275 Scyther [TM]	146 Shiinotic [TM]	038 Slowbro [TM]	039 Slowking [TM]
		037 Slowpoke [TM]	246 Snorunt [TM]	291 Solgaleo [TM]	105 Spinda [TM]	172 Steenee [TM]	131 Sylveon [TM]
		287 Tapu Bulu [TM]	288 Tapu Fini [TM]	285 Tapu Koko [TM]	286 Tapu Lele [TM]	106 Tentacool [TM]	107 Tentacruel [TM]
		114 Toxapex [TM]	197 Trevenant [TM]	173 Tsareena [TM]	088 Whimsicott [TM]	136 Wigglytuff [TM]	205 Zygarde [5, TM]
Ground	Sand Attack	071 Alolan Diglett [1]	072 Alolan Dugtrio [1]	099 Boldore [1, 7]	123 Eevee [5]	127 Espeon [5]	126 Flareon [5]
		237 Flygon [1]	239 Gabite [1, 3]	240 Garchomp [1, 3]	238 Gible [3]	100 Gigalith [1, 7]	130 Glaceon [5]
		183 Golisopod [1]	014 Gumshoos [1, 10]	057 Hariyama [1, 4]	125 Jolteon [5]	233 Krokorok [1, 7]	234 Krookodile [1, 7]
		129 Leafeon [5]	120 Lillipup [E]	104 Lycanroc (Midday Form) [1, 4]	104 Lycanroc (Midnight Form) [1, 4]	056 Makuhita [4]	187 Palossand [1, 9]
		103 Rockruff [4]	098 Roggenrola [7]	161 Salandit [E]	232 Sandile [7]	186 Sandygast [9]	208 Skarmory [6]
		131 Sylveon [5]	235 Trapinch [1]	206 Trubbish [E]	128 Umbreon [5]	124 Vaporeon [5]	236 Vibrava [1]
		182 Wimpod [1]	013 Yungoos [10]				
	Sand Tomb	072 Alolan Dugtrio [1, EV]	030 Bonsly [E]	237 Flygon [12]	239 Gabite [19]	240 Garchomp [19]	238 Gible [19, E]
		233 Krokorok [13]	234 Krookodile [13]	187 Palossand [14]	232 Sandile [13]	186 Sandygast [14]	031 Sudowoodo [E]
		235 Trapinch [12]	236 Vibrava [12]				
Rock	Sandstorm (TM37)	245 Absol [TM]	284 Aerodactyl [TM]	071 Alolan Diglett [TM]	072 Alolan Dugtrio [TM]	229 Alolan Geodude [TM]	231 Alolan Golem [TM]
		230 Alolan Graveler [TM]	164 Alolan Marowak [TM]	192 Archen [TM]	193 Archeops [TM]	093 Barboach [TM]	191 Bastiodon [TM]
		034 Blissey [TM]	099 Boldore [42, TM]	030 Bonsly [TM]	101 Carbink [TM]	195 Carracosta [TM]	181 Castform [TM]
		033 Chansey [TM]	112 Corsola [TM]	188 Cranidos [TM]	163 Cubone [TM]	283 Dragonite [TM]	237 Flygon [36, TM]
		239 Gabite [13, TM]	240 Garchomp [1, 13, TM]	261 Gastrodon [TM]	238 Gible [13, TM]	100 Gigalith [42, TM]	014 Gumshoos [TM]
		092 Gyarados [TM]	272 Hakamo-o [TM]	271 Jangmo-o [TM]	165 Kangaskhan [TM]	273 Kommo-o [TM]	233 Krokorok [44, TM]
		234 Krookodile [48, TM]	216 Metagross [TM]	215 Metang [TM]	138 Miltank [TM]	213 Minior [TM]	132 Mudbray [TM]
		133 Mudsdale [TM]	035 Munchlax [TM]	293 Nihilego [TM]	198 Nosepass [34, TM]	082 Oricorio [TM]	187 Palossand [60, TM]

Type	Move Name	Pokémon					
Rock	Sandstorm (TM37)	199 Probopass [34, TM]	189 Rampardos [TM]	262 Relicanth [TM]	098 Roggenrola [33, TM]	232 Sandile [40, TM]	186 Sandygast [54, TM]
		276 Scizor [TM]	190 Shieldon [TM]	204 Silvally [TM]	208 Skarmory [TM]	036 Snorlax [TM]	031 Sudowoodo [TM]
		137 Tauros [TM]	194 Tirtouga [TM]	235 Trapinch [36, TM]	203 Type: Null [TM]	236 Vibrava [36, TM]	094 Whiscash [TM]
		013 Yungoos [TM]	205 Zygarde [35, TM]				
Water	Scald (TM55)	157 Alomomola [TM]	142 Araquanid [TM]	093 Barboach [TM]	008 Brionne [TM]	243 Bruxish [TM]	195 Carracosta [TM]
		264 Carvanha [TM]	181 Castform [TM]	201 Chinchou [TM]	112 Corsola [TM]	060 Crabominable [TM]	059 Crabrawler [TM]
		141 Dewpider [TM]	155 Feebas [TM]	108 Finneon [TM]	261 Gastrodon [TM]	153 Goldeen [TM]	090 Golduck [TM]
		183 Golisopod [TM]	092 Gyarados [TM]	202 Lanturn [TM]	109 Lumineon [TM]	111 Luvdisc [TM]	113 Mareanie [TM]
		140 Masquerain [TM]	156 Milotic [TM]	041 Pelipper [TM]	152 Politoed [TM]	149 Poliwag [TM]	150 Poliwhirl [TM]
		151 Poliwrath [TM]	007 Popplio [TM]	009 Primarina [TM]	089 Psyduck [TM]	262 Relicanth [TM]	154 Seaking [TM]
		265 Sharpedo [TM]	260 Shellos [TM]	038 Slowbro [TM]	039 Slowking [TM]	037 Slowpoke [TM]	185 Starmie [TM]
		184 Staryu [TM]	139 Surskit [TM]	288 Tapu Fini [TM]	106 Tentacool [TM]	107 Tentacruel [TM]	194 Tirtouga [TM]
		114 Toxapex [TM]	124 Vaporeon [TM]	266 Wailmer [TM]	267 Wailord [TM]	094 Whiscash [TM]	182 Wimpod [TM]
		040 Wingull [TM]	110 Wishiwashi [TM]				
Normal	Scary Face	284 Aerodactyl [1]	050 Alolan Grimer [E]	016 Alolan Raticate [1, EV]	192 Archen [11]	193 Archeops [11]	023 Ariados [12]
		117 Bagon [39]	076 Braviary [19]	264 Carvanha [29]	188 Cranidos [19]	126 Flareon [29]	061 Gastly [E]
		238 Gible [E]	259 Granbull [1]	014 Gumshoos [35]	092 Gyarados [33]	272 Hakamo-o [21]	006 Incineroar [49]
		271 Jangmo-o [21]	273 Kommo-o [21]	233 Krokorok [36]	234 Krookodile [36]	004 Litten [39]	104 Lycanroc (Midday Form) [37]
		104 Lycanroc (Midnight Form) [37]	097 Machamp [53]	096 Machoke [53]	095 Machop [43]	140 Masquerain [22]	216 Metagross [35]
		215 Metang [35]	177 Passimian [18]	189 Rampardos [19]	103 Rockruff [37]	075 Rufflet [19]	119 Salamence [42]
		232 Sandile [34]	265 Sharpedo [29]	118 Shelgon [42]	190 Shieldon [E]	204 Silvally [30]	258 Snubbull [1]
		073 Spearow [E]	022 Spinarak [12]	287 Tapu Bulu [20]	137 Tauros [11]	005 Torracat [46]	203 Type: Null [30]
		077 Vullaby [E]	013 Yungoos [31]				
	Scratch	245 Absol [1]	045 Alolan Meowth [1]	046 Alolan Persian [1]	251 Alolan Sandshrew [1]	090 Golduck [1]	006 Incineroar [1]
		004 Litten [1]	079 Mankey [1]	242 Mimikyu [1]	147 Paras [1]	148 Parasect [1]	080 Primeape [1]
		089 Psyduck [1]	102 Sableye [1]	161 Salandit [1]	249 Sneasel [1]	005 Torracat [1]	250 Weavile [1]
	Screech	229 Alolan Geodude [E]	050 Alolan Grimer [37]	045 Alolan Meowth [17]	051 Alolan Muk [37]	046 Alolan Persian [17]	243 Bruxish [36]
		264 Carvanha [18]	201 Chinchou [E]	112 Corsola [E]	188 Cranidos [42]	070 Crobat [1]	163 Cubone [E]
		227 Electabuzz [42]	228 Electivire [42]	226 Elekid [36]	237 Flygon [22]	069 Golbat [1]	090 Golduck [22]
		272 Hakamo-o [33]	271 Jangmo-o [33]	273 Kommo-o [33]	020 Ledyba [E]	166 Magby [E]	047 Magnemite [35]
		048 Magneton [39]	049 Magnezone [39]	079 Mankey [40]	066 Misdreavus [E]	035 Munchlax [20]	277 Murkrow [E]
		147 Paras [E]	010 Pikipek [25]	080 Primeape [44]	089 Psyduck [22]	189 Rampardos [51]	279 Riolu [24]
		265 Sharpedo [18]	115 Shellder [E]	190 Shieldon [E]	249 Sneasel [32]	285 Tapu Koko [20]	106 Tentacool [37]
		107 Tentacruel [40]	012 Toucannon [30]	011 Trumbeak [29]	128 Umbreon [29]	236 Vibrava [22]	250 Weavile [32]
	Secret Power	253 Alolan Vulpix [E]	054 Drowzee [E]	089 Psyduck [E]			
Grass	Seed Bomb	270 Alolan Exeggutor [1]	297 Celesteela [47]				
Fighting	Seismic Toss	033 Chansey [E]	057 Hariyama [34]	097 Machamp [15]	096 Machoke [15]	095 Machop [15]	056 Makuhita [31]
		079 Mankey [15]	138 Miltank [E]	177 Passimian [E]	175 Pinsir [8]	080 Primeape [15]	
Normal	Self-Destruct	229 Alolan Geodude [24]	231 Alolan Golem [24]	230 Alolan Graveler [24]	030 Bonsly [E]	213 Minior [22]	035 Munchlax [E]
		031 Sudowoodo [E]	206 Trubbish [E]				
Ghost	Shadow Ball (TM30)	042 Abra [TM]	245 Absol [TM]	044 Alakazam [TM]	050 Alolan Grimer [TM]	164 Alolan Marowak [TM]	045 Alolan Meowth [TM]
		051 Alolan Muk [TM]	046 Alolan Persian [TM]	016 Alolan Raticate [TM]	015 Alolan Rattata [TM]	157 Alomomola [TM]	034 Blissey [TM]
		019 Butterfree [TM]	181 Castform [TM]	033 Chansey [TM]	212 Clefable [TM]	211 Clefairy [TM]	210 Cleffa [TM]
		112 Corsola [TM]	070 Crobat [TM]	003 Decidueye [TM]	263 Dhelmise [36, TM]	244 Drampa [TM]	065 Drifblim [40, TM]
		064 Drifloon [36, TM]	054 Drowzee [TM]	123 Eevee [TM]	127 Espeon [TM]	126 Flareon [TM]	248 Froslass [42, TM]
		061 Gastly [29, TM]	063 Gengar [33, TM]	130 Glaceon [TM]	247 Glalie [TM]	069 Golbat [TM]	259 Granbull [TM]
		032 Happiny [TM]	062 Haunter [33, TM]	121 Herdier [TM]	278 Honchkrow [TM]	055 Hypno [TM]	134 Igglybuff [TM]
		135 Jigglypuff [TM]	125 Jolteon [TM]	043 Kadabra [TM]	165 Kangaskhan [TM]	129 Leafeon [TM]	120 Lillipup [TM]
		280 Lucario [TM]	292 Lunala [23, TM]	301 Magearna [TM]	078 Mandibuzz [TM]	140 Masquerain [TM]	216 Metagross [TM]
		215 Metang [TM]	138 Miltank [TM]	242 Mimikyu [TM]	066 Misdreavus [41, TM]	067 Mismagius [TM]	035 Munchlax [TM]
		277 Murkrow [TM]	176 Oranguru [TM]	187 Palossand [41, TM]	177 Passimian [TM]	196 Phantump [TM]	217 Porygon [TM]
		218 Porygon2 [TM]	219 Porygon-Z [TM]	009 Primarina [TM]	102 Sableye [39, TM]	186 Sandygast [41, TM]	204 Silvally [TM]
		038 Slowbro [TM]	039 Slowking [TM]	037 Slowpoke [TM]	249 Sneasel [TM]	036 Snorlax [TM]	246 Snorunt [TM]
		258 Snubbull [TM]	105 Spinda [TM]	122 Stoutland [TM]	139 Surskit [TM]	131 Sylveon [TM]	288 Tapu Fini [TM]
		286 Tapu Lele [TM]	197 Trevenant [TM]	128 Umbreon [TM]	124 Vaporeon [TM]	077 Vullaby [TM]	250 Weavile [TM]
		088 Whimsicott [TM]	136 Wigglytuff [TM]	068 Zubat [TM]			
	Shadow Bone	164 Alolan Marowak [27]					
	Shadow Claw (TM65)	245 Absol [TM]	071 Alolan Diglett [TM]	072 Alolan Dugtrio [TM]	045 Alolan Meowth [TM]	046 Alolan Persian [TM]	016 Alolan Raticate [TM]
		015 Alolan Rattata [TM]	251 Alolan Sandshrew [TM]	252 Alolan Sandslash [TM]	192 Archen [TM]	193 Archeops [TM]	117 Bagon [TM]

Type	Move Name	Pokémon					
Ghost	Shadow Claw (TM65)	170 Bewear [TM]	076 Braviary [TM]	002 Dartrix [TM]	003 Decidueye [TM]	263 Dhelmise [TM]	244 Drampa [TM]
		239 Gabite [TM]	240 Garchomp [TM]	063 Gengar [TM]	238 Gible [TM]	090 Golduck [TM]	183 Golisopod [TM]
		299 Guzzlord [TM]	272 Hakamo-o [TM]	062 Haunter [TM]	006 Incineroar [TM]	271 Jangmo-o [TM]	165 Kangaskhan [TM]
		222 Komala [TM]	273 Kommo-o [TM]	233 Krokorok [TM]	234 Krookodile [TM]	004 Litten [TM]	280 Lucario [TM]
		292 Lunala [TM]	242 Mimikyu [37, TM]	300 Necrozma [TM]	220 Pancham [TM]	221 Pangoro [TM]	196 Phantump [TM]
		089 Psyduck [TM]	279 Riolu [TM]	001 Rowlet [TM]	075 Rufflet [TM]	102 Sableye [29, TM]	119 Salamence [TM]
		161 Salandit [TM]	162 Salazzle [TM]	118 Shelgon [TM]	204 Silvally [TM]	249 Sneasel [TM]	005 Torracat [TM]
		197 Trevenant [1, TM, EV]	203 Type: Null [TM]	250 Weavile [TM]			
	Shadow Punch	063 Gengar [1, EV]	062 Haunter [1, EV]				
	Shadow Sneak	050 Alolan Grimer [E]	023 Ariados [19]	242 Mimikyu [14]	066 Misdreavus [E]	102 Sableye [10]	022 Spinarak [19]
Normal	Sharpen	101 Carbink [8]	217 Porygon [1]				
Ice	Sheer Cold	253 Alolan Vulpix [50]	247 Glalie [1, 61]	268 Lapras [50]	256 Vanillish [58]	255 Vanillite [53]	257 Vanilluxe [1, 67]
Normal	Shell Smash	195 Carracosta [40]	116 Cloyster [1]	213 Minior [45]	115 Shellder [56]	194 Tirtouga [38]	223 Torkoal [47]
		224 Turtonator [37]					
Fire	Shell Trap	224 Turtonator [45]					
Steel	Shift Gear	301 Magearna [1]					
Electric	Shock Wave	201 Chinchou [E]	227 Electabuzz [15]	228 Electivire [15]	226 Elekid [15]	274 Emolga [22, E]	285 Tapu Koko [14]
		296 Xurkitree [13]					
Ground	Shore Up	187 Palossand [54]	186 Sandygast [50]				
Bug	Signal Beam	201 Chinchou [28]	108 Finneon [E]	153 Goldeen [E]	202 Lanturn [29]	217 Porygon [29]	218 Porygon2 [29]
		219 Porygon-Z [29]	022 Spinarak [E]	139 Surskit [E]	235 Trapinch [E]	296 Xurkitree [31]	
	Silver Wind	019 Butterfree [19]	083 Cutiefly [13]	108 Finneon [49]	021 Ledian [20]	020 Ledyba [19, E]	109 Lumineon [59]
		140 Masquerain [32]	295 Pheromosa [23]	084 Ribombee [13]	275 Scyther [E]		
	Simple Beam	089 Psyduck [E]					
Normal	Sing	034 Blissey [31]	008 Brionne [28]	033 Chansey [31]	212 Clefable [1]	211 Clefairy [7]	210 Cleffa [7]
		134 Igglybuff [1]	135 Jigglypuff [1]	222 Komala [E]	268 Lapras [1]	007 Popplio [25]	009 Primarina [28]
		136 Wigglytuff [1]					
	Sketch	058 Smeargle [1, 11, 21, 31, 41, 51, 61, 71, 81, 91]					
Psychic	Skill Swap	042 Abra [E]	101 Carbink [40]	083 Cutiefly [E]	054 Drowzee [E]	269 Exeggcute [E]	066 Misdreavus [E]
		131 Sylveon [25]	286 Tapu Lele [26]				
Normal	Skull Bash	297 Celesteela [53]	163 Cubone [E]	153 Goldeen [E]	262 Relicanth [E]	265 Sharpedo [51]	287 Tapu Bulu [58]
		223 Torkoal [E]					
Flying	Sky Attack	277 Murkrow [E]	208 Skarmory [E]	073 Spearow [E]			
	Sky Drop (TM58)	284 Aerodactyl [49, TM]	076 Braviary [50, TM]	283 Dragonite [TM]	292 Lunala [TM]	041 Pelipper [TM]	075 Rufflet [50, TM]
		208 Skarmory [TM]	285 Tapu Koko [TM]	029 Vikavolt [TM]			
Fighting	Sky Uppercut	272 Hakamo-o [1, EV]	273 Kommo-o [1]	220 Pancham [48]	221 Pangoro [52]	279 Riolu [E]	
	Slack Off	038 Slowbro [36]	037 Slowpoke [36]				
Normal	Slam	188 Cranidos [E]	263 Dhelmise [45]	282 Dragonair [21]	283 Dragonite [21]	281 Dratini [21]	222 Komala [21]
		025 Pikachu [37]	031 Sudowoodo [1, EV]	194 Tirtouga [E]			
	Slash	245 Absol [22]	045 Alolan Meowth [33]	046 Alolan Persian [37]	251 Alolan Sandshrew [26]	252 Alolan Sandslash [1]	076 Braviary [28]
		143 Fomantis [32]	239 Gabite [28]	240 Garchomp [28]	238 Gible [25]	183 Golisopod [21]	144 Lurantis [32]
		242 Mimikyu [32]	300 Necrozma [7]	220 Pancham [20]	221 Pangoro [20]	147 Paras [27]	148 Parasect [29]
		075 Rufflet [28]	276 Scizor [29]	275 Scyther [29]	265 Sharpedo [1, EV]	208 Skarmory [39]	249 Sneasel [35]
Grass	Sleep Powder	019 Butterfree [13]	269 Exeggcute [23]	145 Morelull [18]	085 Petilil [10]	146 Shiinotic [18]	
Normal	Sleep Talk (TM88)	042 Abra [TM]	245 Absol [TM]	284 Aerodactyl [TM]	044 Alakazam [TM]	071 Alolan Diglett [TM]	072 Alolan Dugtrio [TM]
		270 Alolan Exeggutor [TM]	229 Alolan Geodude [TM]	231 Alolan Golem [TM]	230 Alolan Graveler [TM]	050 Alolan Grimer [TM]	164 Alolan Marowak [TM]
		045 Alolan Meowth [TM]	051 Alolan Muk [TM]	254 Alolan Ninetales [TM]	046 Alolan Persian [TM]	026 Alolan Raichu [TM]	016 Alolan Raticate [TM]
		015 Alolan Rattata [TM]	251 Alolan Sandshrew [TM]	252 Alolan Sandslash [TM]	253 Alolan Vulpix [TM]	157 Alomomola [TM]	142 Araquanid [TM]
		053 Arcanine [TM]	192 Archen [TM]	193 Archeops [TM]	023 Ariados [TM]	117 Bagon [TM]	093 Barboach [TM]
		191 Bastiodon [TM]	170 Bewear [TM]	034 Blissey [TM]	099 Boldore [TM]	030 Bonsly [TM]	171 Bounsweet [TM]
		076 Braviary [TM]	008 Brionne [TM]	243 Bruxish [TM]	019 Butterfree [TM]	294 Buzzwole [TM]	101 Carbink [TM]
		195 Carracosta [TM]	264 Carvanha [TM]	181 Castform [TM]	297 Celesteela [TM]	033 Chansey [TM]	028 Charjabug [TM]
		201 Chinchou [TM]	212 Clefable [TM]	211 Clefairy [TM]	210 Cleffa [TM]	116 Cloyster [TM]	174 Comfey [TM]
		112 Corsola [TM]	087 Cottonee [TM]	060 Crabominable [TM]	059 Crabrawler [TM]	188 Cranidos [TM]	070 Crobat [TM]
		163 Cubone [TM]	083 Cutiefly [TM]	002 Dartrix [TM]	003 Decidueye [TM]	081 Delibird [TM]	141 Dewpider [TM]
		263 Dhelmise [TM]	282 Dragonair [TM]	283 Dragonite [TM]	244 Drampa [TM]	281 Dratini [TM]	065 Drifblim [TM]
		064 Drifloon [TM]	054 Drowzee [TM]	123 Eevee [TM]	227 Electabuzz [TM]	228 Electivire [TM]	226 Elekid [TM]
		274 Emolga [TM]	127 Espeon [TM]	269 Exeggcute [TM]	074 Fearow [TM]	155 Feebas [TM]	108 Finneon [TM]
		126 Flareon [TM]	159 Fletchinder [TM]	158 Fletchling [TM]	237 Flygon [TM]	143 Fomantis [TM]	248 Froslass [TM]
		239 Gabite [TM]	207 Garbodor [TM]	240 Garchomp [TM]	061 Gastly [TM]	261 Gastrodon [TM]	063 Gengar [TM]

Type	Move Name	Pokémon					
Normal	Sleep Talk (TM88)	238 Gible [TM]	100 Gigalith [TM]	130 Glaceon [TM]	247 Glalie [TM]	069 Golbat [TM]	153 Goldeen [TM, E]
		090 Golduck [TM]	183 Golisopod [TM]	180 Goodra [TM]	178 Goomy [TM]	259 Granbull [TM]	052 Growlithe [TM]
		027 Grubbin [TM]	014 Gumshoos [TM]	299 Guzzlord [TM]	092 Gyarados [TM]	272 Hakamo-o [TM]	032 Happiny [TM]
		057 Hariyama [TM]	062 Haunter [TM]	121 Herdier [TM]	278 Honchkrow [TM]	055 Hypno [TM]	134 Igglybuff [TM, E]
		006 Incineroar [TM]	271 Jangmo-o [TM]	135 Jigglypuff [TM]	125 Jolteon [TM]	043 Kadabra [TM]	165 Kangaskhan [TM]
		298 Kartana [TM]	241 Klefki [TM]	222 Komala [TM]	273 Kommo-o [TM]	233 Krokorok [TM]	234 Krookodile [TM]
		202 Lanturn [TM]	268 Lapras [TM, E]	129 Leafeon [TM]	021 Ledian [TM]	020 Ledyba [TM]	086 Lilligant [TM]
		120 Lillipup [TM]	004 Litten [TM]	280 Lucario [TM]	109 Lumineon [TM]	292 Lunala [TM]	144 Lurantis [TM]
		111 Luvdisc [TM]	104 Lycanroc (Midday Form) [TM]	104 Lycanroc (Midnight Form) [TM]	097 Machamp [TM]	096 Machoke [TM]	095 Machop [TM]
		166 Magby [TM]	167 Magmar [TM]	168 Magmortar [TM]	047 Magnemite [TM]	048 Magneton [TM]	049 Magnezone [TM]
		056 Makuhita [TM]	078 Mandibuzz [TM]	079 Mankey [TM, E]	113 Mareanie [TM]	140 Masquerain [TM]	216 Metagross [TM]
		215 Metang [TM]	156 Milotic [TM]	138 Miltank [TM, E]	242 Mimikyu [TM]	213 Minior [TM]	066 Misdreavus [TM]
		067 Mismagius [TM]	145 Morelull [TM]	132 Mudbray [TM]	133 Mudsdale [TM]	035 Munchlax [TM]	277 Murkrow [TM]
		300 Necrozma [TM]	293 Nihilego [TM]	198 Nosepass [TM]	176 Oranguru [TM]	082 Oricorio [TM]	187 Palossand [TM]
		220 Pancham [TM]	221 Pangoro [TM]	147 Paras [TM]	148 Parasect [TM]	177 Passimian [TM]	041 Pelipper [TM]
		085 Petilil [TM]	196 Phantump [TM]	295 Pheromosa [TM]	024 Pichu [TM]	025 Pikachu [TM]	010 Pikipek [TM]
		175 Pinsir [TM]	152 Politoed [TM]	149 Poliwag [TM]	150 Poliwhirl [TM]	151 Poliwrath [TM]	007 Popplio [TM]
		217 Porygon [TM]	218 Porygon2 [TM]	219 Porygon-Z [TM]	009 Primarina [TM]	080 Primeape [TM]	199 Probopass [TM]
		089 Psyduck [TM, E]	200 Pyukumuku [TM]	189 Rampardos [TM]	262 Relicanth [TM, E]	084 Ribombee [TM]	279 Riolu [TM]
		103 Rockruff [TM]	098 Roggenrola [TM]	001 Rowlet [TM]	075 Rufflet [TM]	102 Sableye [TM]	119 Salamence [TM]
		161 Salandit [TM]	162 Salazzle [TM]	232 Sandile [TM]	186 Sandygast [TM]	276 Scizor [TM]	275 Scyther [TM]
		154 Seaking [TM]	265 Sharpedo [TM]	118 Shelgon [TM]	115 Shellder [TM]	260 Shellos [TM]	190 Shieldon [TM]
		146 Shiinotic [TM]	204 Silvally [TM]	208 Skarmory [TM]	179 Sliggoo [TM]	038 Slowbro [TM]	039 Slowking [TM]
		037 Slowpoke [TM, E]	249 Sneasel [TM]	036 Snorlax [33, TM]	246 Snorunt [TM]	258 Snubbull [TM]	291 Solgaleo [TM]
		073 Spearow [TM]	022 Spinarak [TM]	105 Spinda [TM]	185 Starmie [TM]	184 Staryu [TM]	172 Steenee [TM]
		122 Stoutland [TM]	169 Stufful [TM]	031 Sudowoodo [TM]	139 Surskit [TM]	131 Sylveon [TM]	160 Talonflame [TM]
		287 Tapu Bulu [TM]	288 Tapu Fini [TM]	285 Tapu Koko [TM]	286 Tapu Lele [TM]	137 Tauros [TM]	106 Tentacool [TM]
		107 Tentacruel [TM]	194 Tirtouga [TM]	225 Togedemaru [TM]	223 Torkoal [TM, E]	005 Torracat [TM]	012 Toucannon [TM]
		114 Toxapex [TM]	235 Trapinch [TM]	197 Trevenant [TM]	206 Trubbish [TM]	011 Trumbeak [TM]	173 Tsareena [TM]
		224 Turtonator [TM]	203 Type: Null [TM]	128 Umbreon [TM]	256 Vanillish [TM]	255 Vanillite [TM]	257 Vanilluxe [TM]
		124 Vaporeon [TM]	236 Vibrava [TM]	029 Vikavolt [TM]	077 Vullaby [TM]	266 Wailmer [TM, E]	267 Wailord [TM]
		250 Weavile [TM]	088 Whimsicott [TM]	094 Whiscash [TM]	136 Wigglytuff [TM]	182 Wimpod [TM]	040 Wingull [TM]
		110 Wishiwashi [TM]	296 Xurkitree [TM]	013 Yungoos [TM]	068 Zubat [TM]	205 Zygarde [TM]	
Poison	Sludge	207 Garbodor [18]	260 Shellos [E]	206 Trubbish [18]			
	Sludge Bomb (TM36)	071 Alolan Diglett [TM]	072 Alolan Dugtrio [TM]	270 Alolan Exeggutor [TM]	050 Alolan Grimer [TM]	051 Alolan Muk [TM]	016 Alolan Raticate [TM]
		015 Alolan Rattata [TM]	023 Ariados [TM]	070 Crobat [TM]	269 Exeggcute [TM]	207 Garbodor [29, TM]	061 Gastly [TM]
		261 Gastrodon [TM]	063 Gengar [TM]	069 Golbat [TM]	183 Golisopod [TM]	180 Goodra [TM]	178 Goomy [TM]
		259 Granbull [TM]	299 Guzzlord [TM]	062 Haunter [TM]	233 Krokorok [TM]	234 Krookodile [TM]	113 Mareanie [TM]
		216 Metagross [TM]	215 Metang [TM]	145 Morelull [TM]	293 Nihilego [TM]	187 Palossand [TM]	220 Pancham [TM]
		221 Pangoro [TM]	147 Paras [TM]	148 Parasect [TM]	161 Salandit [TM]	162 Salazzle [TM]	232 Sandile [TM]
		146 Shiinotic [TM]	179 Sliggoo [TM]	258 Snubbull [TM]	022 Spinarak [TM]	106 Tentacool [TM]	107 Tentacruel [TM]
		223 Torkoal [TM]	114 Toxapex [TM]	206 Trubbish [29, TM]	068 Zubat [TM]		
	Sludge Wave (TM34)	072 Alolan Dugtrio [TM]	050 Alolan Grimer [TM]	051 Alolan Muk [TM]	016 Alolan Raticate [TM]	263 Dhelmise [TM]	207 Garbodor [TM]
		261 Gastrodon [TM]	183 Golisopod [TM]	180 Goodra [TM]	178 Goomy [TM]	299 Guzzlord [TM]	113 Mareanie [TM]
		293 Nihilego [TM]	161 Salandit [TM]	162 Salazzle [TM]	179 Sliggoo [TM]	106 Tentacool [43, TM]	107 Tentacruel [48, TM]
		114 Toxapex [TM]	206 Trubbish [TM]	205 Zygarde [TM]			
Rock	Smack Down (TM23)	284 Aerodactyl [TM]	229 Alolan Geodude [18, TM]	231 Alolan Golem [18, TM]	230 Alolan Graveler [18, TM]	164 Alolan Marowak [TM]	192 Archen [TM]
		193 Archeops [TM]	191 Bastiodon [TM]	099 Boldore [23, TM]	030 Bonsly [TM]	294 Buzzwole [TM]	101 Carbink [12, TM]
		195 Carracosta [31, TM]	297 Celesteela [7, TM]	188 Cranidos [TM]	163 Cubone [TM]	003 Decidueye [TM]	207 Garbodor [TM]
		100 Gigalith [23, TM]	299 Guzzlord [TM]	057 Hariyama [TM]	234 Krookodile [TM]	097 Machamp [TM]	096 Machoke [TM]
		095 Machop [TM]	056 Makuhita [TM]	079 Mankey [TM]	198 Nosepass [TM]	177 Passimian [TM]	010 Pikipek [TM]
		175 Pinsir [TM]	080 Primeape [TM]	199 Probopass [TM]	189 Rampardos [TM]	262 Relicanth [TM]	098 Roggenrola [23, TM]
		190 Shieldon [TM]	036 Snorlax [TM]	031 Sudowoodo [TM]	194 Tirtouga [31, TM]	012 Toucannon [TM]	114 Toxapex [TM]
		011 Trumbeak [TM]	224 Turtonator [TM]				
Steel	Smart Strike (TM67)	023 Ariados [TM]	297 Celesteela [TM]	116 Cloyster [TM]	153 Goldeen [TM]	298 Kartana [TM]	268 Lapras [TM]
		300 Necrozma [TM]	154 Seaking [TM]	287 Tapu Bulu [TM]	288 Tapu Fini [TM]	137 Tauros [TM]	
Normal	Smelling Salts	057 Hariyama [30]	095 Machop [E]	056 Makuhita [28]	079 Mankey [E]	258 Snubbull [E]	105 Spinda [E]
Poison	Smog	126 Flareon [33]	061 Gastly [E]	166 Magby [1]	167 Magmar [1]	168 Magmortar [1]	161 Salandit [16]
		162 Salazzle [16]	223 Torkoal [4]	224 Turtonator [5]			
Normal	Smokescreen	166 Magby [8]	167 Magmar [8]	168 Magmortar [1, 8]	223 Torkoal [15]		

Type	Move Name	Pokémon					
Dark	Snarl (TM95)	245 Absol [TM]	050 Alolan Grimer [TM]	051 Alolan Muk [TM]	046 Alolan Persian [TM]	016 Alolan Raticate [TM]	015 Alolan Rattata [TM]
		053 Arcanine [TM]	264 Carvanha [TM]	244 Drampa [TM]	183 Golisopod [TM]	259 Granbull [TM]	052 Growlithe [TM]
		299 Guzzlord [TM]	121 Herdier [TM]	270 Honchkrow [TM]	006 Incineroar [TM]	233 Krokorok [TM]	234 Krookodile [TM]
		120 Lillipup [TM]	104 Lycanroc (Midday Form) [TM]	104 Lycanroc (Midnight Form) [TM]	078 Mandibuzz [TM]	277 Murkrow [TM]	221 Pangoro [TM]
		103 Rockruff [TM]	102 Sableye [TM]	232 Sandile [TM]	265 Sharpedo [TM]	204 Silvally [TM]	249 Sneasel [TM]
		258 Snubbull [TM]	291 Solgaleo [TM]	122 Stoutland [TM]	287 Tapu Bulu [TM]	128 Umbreon [TM]	077 Vullaby [TM]
		250 Weavile [TM]					
	Snatch	045 Alolan Meowth [E]	015 Alolan Rattata [E]	158 Fletchling [E]	035 Munchlax [50]	161 Salandit [E]	249 Sneasel [40]
		250 Weavile [40]					
Normal	Snore	093 Barboach [25]	262 Relicanth [E]	037 Slowpoke [E]	036 Snorlax [28]	258 Snubbull [E]	266 Wailmer [E]
		094 Whiscash [25]					
Water	Soak	157 Alomomola [33]	142 Araquanid [1]	201 Chinchou [E]	108 Finneon [54]	153 Goldeen [40]	090 Golduck [31]
		109 Lumineon [1, 66]	111 Luvdisc [42]	041 Pelipper [1]	089 Psyduck [31]	200 Pyukumuku [41]	154 Seaking [46]
		288 Tapu Fini [20]	266 Wailmer [E]	267 Wailord [1]	040 Wingull [E]	110 Wishiwashi [46]	
Normal	Soft-Boiled	034 Blissey [16]	033 Chansey [16]				
Grass	Solar Beam (TM22)	270 Alolan Exeggutor [TM]	053 Arcanine [TM]	023 Ariados [TM]	034 Blissey [TM]	171 Bounsweet [TM]	019 Butterfree [TM]
		181 Castform [TM]	297 Celesteela [TM]	033 Chansey [TM]	212 Clefable [TM]	211 Clefairy [TM]	210 Cleffa [TM]
		174 Comfey [TM]	087 Cottonee [46, TM]	002 Dartrix [TM]	003 Decidueye [TM]	263 Dhelmise [TM]	244 Drampa [TM]
		269 Exeggcute [43, TM]	237 Flygon [TM]	143 Fomantis [41, TM]	207 Garbodor [TM]	100 Gigalith [TM]	259 Granbull [TM]
		032 Happiny [TM]	134 Igglybuff [TM]	135 Jigglypuff [TM]	165 Kangaskhan [TM]	129 Leafeon [TM]	021 Ledian [TM]
		020 Ledyba [TM]	086 Lilligant [TM]	292 Lunala [TM]	144 Lurantis [TM]	301 Magearna [TM]	168 Magmortar [TM]
		110 Macguerain [TM]	138 Miltank [TM]	213 Minior [TM]	145 Morelull [TM]	035 Munchlax [TM]	300 Necrozma [TM]
		147 Paras [TM]	148 Parasect [TM]	085 Petilil [TM]	196 Phantump [TM]	217 Porygon [TM]	218 Porygon2 [TM]
		219 Porygon-Z [TM]	084 Ribombee [TM]	001 Rowlet [TM]	146 Shiinotic [TM]	036 Snorlax [TM]	258 Snubbull [TM]
		291 Solgaleo [47, TM]	022 Spinarak [TM]	172 Steenee [TM]	139 Surskit [TM]	160 Talonflame [TM]	287 Tapu Bulu [TM]
		137 Tauros [TM]	223 Torkoal [TM]	235 Trapinch [TM]	197 Trevenant [TM]	173 Tsareena [TM]	224 Turtonator [TM]
		236 Vibrava [TM]	029 Vikavolt [TM]	088 Whimsicott [TM]	136 Wigglytuff [TM]	296 Xurkitree [TM]	
	Solar Blade	144 Lurantis [47]					
Normal	Sonic Boom	237 Flygon [1]	301 Magearna [1]	047 Magnemite [17]	048 Magneton [17]	049 Magnezone [17]	022 Spinarak [E]
		236 Vibrava [1]					
Electric	Spark	229 Alolan Geodude [12]	231 Alolan Golem [12]	230 Alolan Graveler [12]	093 Barboach [E]	028 Charjabug [16]	201 Chinchou [23]
		274 Emolga [13]	027 Grubbin [16]	202 Lanturn [23]	047 Magnemite [19]	048 Magneton [19]	049 Magnezone [19]
		198 Nosepass [19]	025 Pikachu [26]	199 Probopass [19]	285 Tapu Koko [8]	225 Togedemaru [17]	029 Vikavolt [16]
		296 Xurkitree [1]					
Water	Sparkling Aria	009 Primarina [1, EV]					
Psychic	Speed Swap	026 Alolan Raichu [1]	083 Cutiefly [E]	274 Emolga [E]	295 Pheromosa [73]		
Bug	Spider Web	142 Araquanid [1, 8]	023 Ariados [32]	141 Dewpider [8]	022 Spinarak [29]		
Normal	Spike Cannon	116 Cloyster [13]	112 Corsola [20]	113 Mareanie [29]	114 Toxapex [29]		
Ground	Spikes	116 Cloyster [28]	081 Delibird [E]	241 Klefki [15]	208 Skarmory [28]	246 Snorunt [E]	206 Trubbish [E]
		182 Wimpod [E]					
Grass	Spiky Shield	225 Togedemaru [49]					
Ghost	Spirit Shackle	003 Decidueye [1, EV]					
Normal	Spit Up	050 Alolan Grimer [E]	141 Dewpider [E]	065 Drifblim [34]	064 Drifloon [32]	135 Jigglypuff [25]	222 Komala [6]
		202 Lanturn [1, EV]	113 Mareanie [E]	041 Pelipper [33]	186 Sandygast [E]	260 Shellos [E]	
Ghost	Spite	050 Alolan Grimer [E]	045 Alolan Meowth [E]	253 Alolan Vulpix [E]	061 Gastly [5]	063 Gengar [1, 5]	183 Golisopod [13]
		062 Haunter [1, 5]	066 Misdreavus [5, E]	067 Mismagius [1]	249 Sneasel [E]		
Normal	Splash	171 Bounsweet [1]	210 Cleffa [E]	289 Cosmog [1]	081 Delibird [E]	155 Feebas [1]	108 Finneon [E]
		111 Luvdisc [E]	091 Magikarp [1]	242 Mimikyu [1]	149 Poliwag [E]	172 Steenee [1]	173 Tsareena [1]
		266 Wailmer [1]	267 Wailord [1]				
Grass	Spore	145 Morelull [36]	147 Paras [22]	148 Parasect [22]	146 Shiinotic [40]		
Normal	Spotlight	212 Clefable [1]	211 Clefairy [1]	145 Morelull [46]	146 Shiinotic [53]	105 Spinda [E]	185 Starmie [1]
Rock	Stealth Rock	229 Alolan Geodude [28]	231 Alolan Golem [30]	230 Alolan Graveler [30]	099 Boldore [36]	030 Bonsly [E]	101 Carbink [21]
		100 Gigalith [36]	104 Lycanroc (Midday Form) [29]	104 Lycanroc (Midnight Form) [29]	213 Minior [24]	300 Necrozma [53]	293 Nihilego [59]
		198 Nosepass [E]	103 Rockruff [29]	098 Roggenrola [30]	190 Shieldon [E]	208 Skarmory [E]	031 Sudowoodo [E]
Bug	Steamroller	231 Alolan Golem [10]	299 Guzzlord [19]				

Type	Move Name	Pokémon					
Steel	Steel Wing (TM51)	284 Aerodactyl [TM, E]	192 Archen [TM, E]	193 Archeops [TM]	076 Braviary [TM]	070 Crobat [TM]	002 Dartrix [TM]
		003 Decidueye [TM]	283 Dragonite [TM]	244 Drampa [TM]	074 Fearow [TM]	159 Fletchinder [55, TM]	158 Fletchling [48, TM]
		237 Flygon [TM]	069 Golbat [TM]	278 Honchkrow [TM]	078 Mandibuzz [TM]	277 Murkrow [TM]	082 Oricorio [TM]
		041 Pelipper [TM]	010 Pikipek [TM]	001 Rowlet [TM]	075 Rufflet [TM]	119 Salamence [TM]	276 Scizor [TM]
		275 Scyther [TM, E]	204 Silvally [TM]	208 Skarmory [34, TM]	073 Spearow [TM, E]	160 Talonflame [60, TM]	285 Tapu Koko [TM]
		012 Toucannon [TM]	011 Trumbeak [TM]	236 Vibrava [TM]	077 Vullaby [TM, E]	040 Wingull [TM]	068 Zubat [TM, E]
Bug	Sticky Web	023 Ariados [58]	022 Spinarak [50]	139 Surskit [38]			
Normal	Stockpile	050 Alolan Grimer [E]	015 Alolan Rattata [E]	141 Dewpider [E]	065 Drifblim [25]	064 Drifloon [25]	207 Garbodor [23]
		299 Guzzlord [1]	135 Jigglypuff [25]	222 Komala [6]	202 Lanturn [1, EV]	113 Mareanie [E]	035 Munchlax [28]
		041 Pelipper [33]	186 Sandygast [E]	260 Shellos [E]	206 Trubbish [23]		
	Stomp	188 Cranidos [E]	299 Guzzlord [7]	165 Kangaskhan [E]	138 Miltank [8]	132 Mudbray [17]	133 Mudsdale [17]
		295 Pheromosa [13]	037 Slowpoke [E]	172 Steenee [29]	173 Tsareena [29]		
Ground	Stomping Tantrum	164 Alolan Marowak [43]	163 Cubone [37]	299 Guzzlord [31]	079 Mankey [43]	080 Primeape [48]	169 Stufful [E]
Rock	Stone Edge (TM71)	245 Absol [TM]	284 Aerodactyl [TM]	072 Alolan Dugtrio [TM]	229 Alolan Geodude [42, TM]	231 Alolan Golem [54, TM]	230 Alolan Graveler [54, TM]
		050 Alolan Grimer [TM]	164 Alolan Marowak [TM]	051 Alolan Muk [TM]	192 Archen [TM]	193 Archeops [TM]	191 Bastiodon [TM]
		099 Boldore [48, TM]	294 Buzzwole [TM]	101 Carbink [49, TM]	195 Carracosta [TM]	297 Celesteela [TM]	112 Corsola [TM]
		060 Crabominable [TM]	059 Crabrawler [TM]	188 Cranidos [TM]	283 Dragonite [TM]	237 Flygon [TM]	239 Gabite [TM]
		240 Garchomp [TM]	261 Gastrodon [TM]	238 Gible [TM]	100 Gigalith [48, TM]	259 Granbull [TM]	299 Guzzlord [TM]
		092 Gyarados [TM]	057 Hariyama [TM]	233 Krokorok [TM]	234 Krookodile [TM]	280 Lucario [TM]	104 Lycanroc (Midday Form) [48, TM]
		104 Lycanroc (Midnight Form) [48, TM]	097 Machamp [TM]	213 Minior [TM]	300 Necrozma [TM]	198 Nosepass [40, TM]	187 Palossand [TM]
		220 Pancham [TM]	221 Pangoro [TM]	175 Pinsir [TM]	080 Primeape [TM]	199 Probopass [40, TM]	189 Rampardos [TM]
		262 Relicanth [TM]	103 Rockruff [48, TM]	098 Roggenrola [36, TM]	119 Salamence [TM]	232 Sandile [TM]	186 Sandygast [TM]
		190 Shieldon [TM]	291 Solgaleo [TM]	031 Sudowoodo [47, TM]	287 Tapu Bulu [TM]	137 Tauros [TM]	194 Tirtouga [TM]
		223 Torkoal [TM]	224 Turtonator [TM]	094 Whiscash [TM]	205 Zygarde [TM]		
Psychic	Stored Power	211 Clefairy [28]	210 Cleffa [E]	123 Eevee [E]	300 Necrozma [13]	176 Oranguru [15]	
Fighting	Storm Throw	220 Pancham [E]	175 Pinsir [36]				
Normal	Strength	097 Machamp [1, EV]					
Grass	Strength Sap	145 Morelull [32]	146 Shiinotic [35]				
Bug	String Shot	023 Ariados [1]	017 Caterpie [1]	028 Charjabug [1, 4]	027 Grubbin [4]	022 Spinarak [1]	029 Vikavolt [1, 4]
	Struggle Bug	083 Cutiefly [10]	183 Golisopod [1]	084 Ribombee [1, 10]	182 Wimpod [1]		
Grass	Stun Spore	019 Butterfree [13]	087 Cottonee [10]	083 Cutiefly [7]	269 Exeggcute [19]	140 Masquerain [26]	145 Morelull [E]
		147 Paras [6]	148 Parasect [1, 6]	085 Petilil [22]	084 Ribombee [1, 7]		
Fighting	Submission	097 Machamp [37]	096 Machoke [37]	095 Machop [33]	175 Pinsir [33]	151 Poliwrath [1, EV]	
Normal	Substitute (TM90)	042 Abra [TM]	245 Absol [TM]	284 Aerodactyl [TM]	044 Alakazam [TM]	071 Alolan Diglett [TM]	072 Alolan Dugtrio [TM]
		270 Alolan Exeggutor [TM]	229 Alolan Geodude [TM]	231 Alolan Golem [TM]	230 Alolan Graveler [TM]	050 Alolan Grimer [TM]	164 Alolan Marowak [TM]
		045 Alolan Meowth [TM]	051 Alolan Muk [TM]	254 Alolan Ninetales [TM]	046 Alolan Persian [TM]	026 Alolan Raichu [TM]	016 Alolan Raticate [TM]
		015 Alolan Rattata [TM]	251 Alolan Sandshrew [TM]	252 Alolan Sandslash [TM]	253 Alolan Vulpix [TM]	157 Alomomola [TM]	142 Araquanid [TM]
		053 Arcanine [TM]	192 Archen [TM]	193 Archeops [TM]	023 Ariados [TM]	117 Bagon [TM]	093 Barboach [TM]
		191 Bastiodon [TM]	170 Bewear [TM]	034 Blissey [TM]	099 Boldore [TM]	030 Bonsly [TM]	171 Bounsweet [TM]
		076 Braviary [TM]	008 Brionne [TM]	243 Bruxish [TM]	019 Butterfree [TM]	294 Buzzwole [TM]	101 Carbink [TM]
		195 Carracosta [TM]	264 Carvanha [TM]	181 Castform [TM]	297 Celesteela [TM]	033 Chansey [TM]	028 Charjabug [TM]
		201 Chinchou [TM]	212 Clefable [TM]	211 Clefairy [TM]	210 Cleffa [TM]	116 Cloyster [TM]	174 Comfey [TM]
		112 Corsola [TM]	087 Cottonee [TM]	060 Crabominable [TM]	059 Crabrawler [TM]	188 Cranidos [TM]	070 Crobat [TM]
		163 Cubone [TM]	083 Cutiefly [TM]	002 Dartrix [TM]	003 Decidueye [TM]	081 Delibird [TM]	141 Dewpider [TM]
		263 Dhelmise [TM]	282 Dragonair [TM]	283 Dragonite [TM]	244 Drampa [TM]	281 Dratini [TM]	065 Drifblim [TM]
		064 Drifloon [TM]	054 Drowzee [TM]	123 Eevee [TM]	227 Electabuzz [TM]	228 Electivire [TM]	226 Elekid [TM]
		274 Emolga [TM]	127 Espeon [TM]	269 Exeggcute [TM]	074 Fearow [TM]	155 Feebas [TM]	108 Finneon [TM]
		126 Flareon [TM]	159 Fletchinder [TM]	158 Fletchling [TM]	237 Flygon [TM]	143 Fomantis [TM]	248 Froslass [TM]
		239 Gabite [TM]	207 Garbodor [TM]	240 Garchomp [TM]	061 Gastly [TM]	261 Gastrodon [TM]	063 Gengar [TM]
		238 Gible [TM]	100 Gigalith [TM]	130 Glaceon [TM]	247 Glalie [TM]	069 Golbat [TM]	153 Goldeen [TM]
		090 Golduck [TM]	183 Golisopod [TM]	180 Goodra [TM]	178 Goomy [TM]	259 Granbull [TM]	052 Growlithe [TM]
		027 Grubbin [TM]	014 Gumshoos [TM]	299 Guzzlord [TM]	092 Gyarados [TM]	272 Hakamo-o [TM]	032 Happiny [TM]
		057 Hariyama [TM]	062 Haunter [TM]	121 Herdier [TM]	278 Honchkrow [TM]	055 Hypno [TM]	134 Igglybuff [TM]
		006 Incineroar [TM]	271 Jangmo-o [TM]	135 Jigglypuff [TM]	125 Jolteon [TM]	043 Kadabra [TM]	165 Kangaskhan [TM]
		298 Kartana [TM]	241 Klefki [TM]	222 Komala [TM]	273 Kommo-o [TM]	233 Krokorok [TM]	234 Krookodile [TM]
		202 Lanturn [TM]	268 Lapras [TM]	129 Leafeon [TM]	021 Ledian [TM]	020 Ledyba [TM]	086 Lilligant [TM]
		120 Lillipup [TM]	004 Litten [TM]	280 Lucario [TM]	109 Lumineon [TM]	292 Lunala [TM]	144 Lurantis [TM]
		111 Luvdisc [TM]	104 Lycanroc (Midday Form) [TM]	104 Lycanroc (Midnight Form) [TM]	097 Machamp [TM]	096 Machoke [TM]	095 Machop [TM]

350

Type	Move Name	Pokémon					
Normal	Substitute (TM90)	166 Magby [TM]	301 Magearna [TM]	167 Magmar [TM]	168 Magmortar [TM]	047 Magnemite [TM]	048 Magneton [TM]
		049 Magnezone [TM]	056 Makuhita [TM]	078 Mandibuzz [TM]	079 Mankey [TM]	113 Mareanie [TM]	140 Masquerain [TM]
		216 Metagross [TM]	215 Metang [TM]	156 Milotic [TM]	138 Miltank [TM]	242 Mimikyu [TM]	213 Minior [TM]
		066 Misdreavus [TM]	067 Mismagius [TM]	145 Morelull [TM]	132 Mudbray [TM]	133 Mudsdale [TM]	035 Munchlax [TM]
		277 Murkrow [TM]	300 Necrozma [TM]	293 Nihilego [TM]	198 Nosepass [TM]	176 Oranguru [TM]	082 Oricorio [TM]
		187 Palossand [TM]	220 Pancham [TM]	221 Pangoro [TM]	147 Paras [TM]	148 Parasect [TM]	177 Passimian [TM]
		041 Pelipper [TM]	085 Petilil [TM]	196 Phantump [TM]	295 Pheromosa [TM]	024 Pichu [TM]	025 Pikachu [TM]
		010 Pikipek [TM]	175 Pinsir [TM]	152 Politoed [TM]	149 Poliwag [TM]	150 Poliwhirl [TM]	151 Poliwrath [TM]
		007 Popplio [TM]	217 Porygon [TM]	218 Porygon2 [TM]	219 Porygon-Z [TM]	009 Primarina [TM]	080 Primeape [TM]
		199 Probopass [TM]	089 Psyduck [TM]	200 Pyukumuku [TM]	189 Rampardos [TM]	262 Relicanth [TM]	084 Ribombee [TM]
		279 Riolu [TM]	103 Rockruff [TM]	098 Roggenrola [TM]	001 Rowlet [TM]	075 Rufflet [TM]	102 Sableye [TM]
		119 Salamence [TM]	161 Salandit [TM]	162 Salazzle [TM]	232 Sandile [TM]	186 Sandygast [TM]	276 Scizor [TM]
		275 Scyther [TM]	154 Seaking [TM]	265 Sharpedo [TM]	118 Shelgon [TM]	115 Shellder [TM]	260 Shellos [TM]
		190 Shieldon [TM]	146 Shiinotic [TM]	204 Silvally [TM]	208 Skarmory [TM]	179 Sliggoo [TM]	038 Slowbro [TM]
		039 Slowking [TM]	037 Slowpoke [TM]	249 Sneasel [TM]	036 Snorlax [TM]	246 Snorunt [TM]	258 Snubbull [TM]
		291 Solgaleo [TM]	073 Spearow [TM]	022 Spinarak [TM]	105 Spinda [TM]	185 Starmie [TM]	184 Staryu [TM]
		172 Steenee [TM]	122 Stoutland [TM]	169 Stufful [TM]	031 Sudowoodo [TM]	139 Surskit [TM]	131 Sylveon [TM]
		160 Talonflame [TM]	287 Tapu Bulu [TM]	288 Tapu Fini [TM]	285 Tapu Koko [TM]	286 Tapu Lele [TM]	137 Tauros [TM]
		106 Tentacool [TM]	107 Tentacruel [TM]	194 Tirtouga [TM]	225 Togedemaru [TM]	223 Torkoal [TM]	005 Torracat [TM]
		012 Toucannon [TM]	114 Toxapex [TM]	235 Trapinch [TM]	197 Trevenant [TM]	206 Trubbish [TM]	011 Trumbeak [TM]
		173 Tsareena [TM]	224 Turtonator [TM]	203 Type: Null [TM]	128 Umbreon [TM]	256 Vanillish [TM]	255 Vanillite [TM]
		257 Vanilluxe [TM]	124 Vaporeon [TM]	236 Vibrava [TM]	029 Vikavolt [TM]	077 Vullaby [TM]	266 Wailmer [TM]
		267 Wailord [TM]	250 Weavile [TM]	088 Whimsicott [TM]	054 Whiscash [TM]	136 Wigglytuff [TM]	182 Wimpod [TM]
		040 Wingull [TM]	110 Wishiwashi [TM]	296 Xurkitree [TM]	013 Yungoos [TM]	068 Zubat [TM]	205 Zygarde [TM]
Dark	Sucker Punch	245 Absol [45, E]	071 Alolan Diglett [22]	072 Alolan Dugtrio [22]	016 Alolan Raticate [29]	015 Alolan Rattata [25]	023 Ariados [28]
		030 Bonsly [40]	002 Dartrix [37]	003 Decidueye [38]	061 Gastly [22]	063 Gengar [22]	183 Golisopod [31]
		062 Haunter [22]	278 Honchkrow [1]	165 Kangaskhan [49]	222 Komala [31]	066 Misdreavus [E]	277 Murkrow [55]
		103 Rockruff [E]	001 Rowlet [32]	102 Sableye [E]	022 Spinarak [26]	105 Spinda [28]	031 Sudowoodo [40]
Fire	Sunny Day (TM11)	042 Abra [TM]	245 Absol [TM]	284 Aerodactyl [TM]	044 Alakazam [TM]	071 Alolan Diglett [TM]	072 Alolan Dugtrio [TM]
		270 Alolan Exeggutor [TM]	229 Alolan Geodude [TM]	231 Alolan Golem [TM]	230 Alolan Graveler [TM]	050 Alolan Grimer [TM]	164 Alolan Marowak [TM]
		045 Alolan Meowth [TM]	051 Alolan Muk [TM]	046 Alolan Persian [TM]	016 Alolan Raticate [TM]	015 Alolan Rattata [TM]	251 Alolan Sandshrew [TM]
		252 Alolan Sandslash [TM]	053 Arcanine [TM]	023 Ariados [TM]	117 Bagon [TM]	191 Bastiodon [TM]	034 Blissey [TM]
		030 Bonsly [TM]	171 Bounsweet [TM]	076 Braviary [TM]	019 Butterfree [TM]	101 Carbink [TM]	181 Castform [20, TM]
		033 Chansey [TM]	212 Clefable [TM]	211 Clefairy [TM]	210 Cleffa [TM]	174 Comfey [TM]	112 Corsola [TM]
		087 Cottonee [40, TM]	060 Crabominable [TM]	059 Crabrawler [TM]	188 Cranidos [TM]	070 Crobat [TM]	163 Cubone [TM]
		083 Cutiefly [TM]	002 Dartrix [TM]	003 Decidueye [TM]	263 Dhelmise [TM]	282 Dragonair [TM]	283 Dragonite [TM]
		244 Drampa [TM]	281 Dratini [TM]	065 Drifblim [TM]	064 Drifloon [TM]	054 Drowzee [TM]	123 Eevee [TM]
		127 Espeon [TM]	269 Exeggcute [TM]	074 Fearow [TM]	126 Flareon [TM]	159 Fletchinder [TM]	158 Fletchling [TM]
		237 Flygon [TM]	143 Fomantis [46, TM]	239 Gabite [TM]	207 Garbodor [TM]	240 Garchomp [TM]	061 Gastly [TM]
		063 Gengar [TM]	238 Gible [TM]	130 Glaceon [TM]	069 Golbat [TM]	180 Goodra [TM]	178 Goomy [TM]
		259 Granbull [TM]	052 Growlithe [TM]	032 Happiny [TM]	057 Hariyama [TM]	062 Haunter [TM]	121 Herdier [TM]
		278 Honchkrow [TM]	055 Hypno [TM]	134 Igglybuff [TM]	006 Incineroar [TM]	135 Jigglypuff [TM]	125 Jolteon [TM]
		043 Kadabra [TM]	165 Kangaskhan [TM]	241 Klefki [TM]	222 Komala [TM]	129 Leafeon [37, TM]	021 Ledian [TM]
		020 Ledyba [TM]	086 Lilligant [TM]	120 Lillipup [TM]	004 Litten [TM]	280 Lucario [TM]	292 Lunala [TM]
		144 Lurantis [55, TM]	097 Machamp [TM]	096 Machoke [TM]	095 Machop [TM]	166 Magby [36, TM]	167 Magmar [42, TM]
		168 Magmortar [42, TM]	047 Magnemite [TM]	048 Magneton [TM]	049 Magnezone [TM]	056 Makuhita [TM]	078 Mandibuzz [TM]
		079 Mankey [TM]	140 Masquerain [TM]	216 Metagross [TM]	215 Metang [TM]	138 Miltank [TM]	066 Misdreavus [TM]
		067 Mismagius [TM]	145 Morelull [TM]	035 Munchlax [TM]	277 Murkrow [TM]	198 Nosepass [TM]	176 Oranguru [TM]
		220 Pancham [TM]	221 Pangoro [TM]	147 Paras [TM]	148 Parasect [TM]	177 Passimian [TM]	085 Petilil [40, TM]
		196 Phantump [TM]	010 Pikipek [TM]	175 Pinsir [TM]	217 Porygon [TM]	218 Porygon2 [TM]	219 Porygon-Z [TM]
		080 Primeape [TM]	199 Probopass [TM]	189 Rampardos [TM]	084 Ribombee [TM]	279 Riolu [TM]	001 Rowlet [TM]
		075 Rufflet [TM]	102 Sableye [TM]	119 Salamence [TM]	276 Scizor [TM]	275 Scyther [TM]	118 Shelgon [TM]
		190 Shieldon [TM]	204 Silvally [TM]	208 Skarmory [TM]	179 Sliggoo [TM]	038 Slowbro [TM]	039 Slowking [TM]
		037 Slowpoke [TM]	249 Sneasel [TM]	036 Snorlax [TM]	258 Snubbull [TM]	291 Solgaleo [TM]	073 Spearow [TM]
		022 Spinarak [TM]	105 Spinda [TM]	172 Steenee [TM]	122 Stoutland [TM]	031 Sudowoodo [TM]	139 Surskit [TM]
		131 Sylveon [TM]	160 Talonflame [TM]	287 Tapu Bulu [TM]	286 Tapu Lele [TM]	137 Tauros [TM]	223 Torkoal [TM]
		005 Torracat [TM]	012 Toucannon [TM]	235 Trapinch [TM]	197 Trevenant [TM]	206 Trubbish [TM]	011 Trumbeak [TM]
		173 Tsareena [TM]	224 Turtonator [TM]	203 Type: Null [TM]	128 Umbreon [TM]	124 Vaporeon [TM]	236 Vibrava [TM]
		077 Vullaby [TM]	250 Weavile [TM]	088 Whimsicott [TM]	136 Wigglytuff [TM]	296 Xurkitree [TM]	068 Zubat [TM]
		205 Zygarde [TM]					
Steel	Sunsteel Strike	291 Solgaleo [1, EV]					
Normal	Super Fang	016 Alolan Raticate [34]	015 Alolan Rattata [28]	014 Gumshoos [27]	013 Yungoos [25]		

Type	Move Name	Pokémon					
Fighting	Superpower	170 Bewear [62]	076 Braviary [1, EV]	294 Buzzwole [67]	059 Crabrawler [E]	132 Mudbray [45]	133 Mudsdale [60]
		175 Pinsir [47, E]	169 Stufful [50]	287 Tapu Bulu [1]	223 Torkoal [E]	235 Trapinch [40]	
Normal	Supersonic	284 Aerodactyl [1]	019 Butterfree [23]	201 Chinchou [1]	116 Cloyster [1]	070 Crobat [1, 5]	281 Dratini [E]
		237 Flygon [19]	069 Golbat [1, 5]	153 Goldeen [5]	202 Lanturn [1]	021 Ledian [1, 5]	020 Ledyba [5]
		111 Luvdisc [E]	047 Magnemite [1]	048 Magneton [1]	049 Magnezone [1]	041 Pelipper [5]	010 Pikipek [13]
		154 Seaking [1, 5]	115 Shellder [8]	106 Tentacool [4]	107 Tentacruel [1, 4]	012 Toucannon [13]	011 Trumbeak [13]
		236 Vibrava [19]	040 Wingull [5]	068 Zubat [5]			
Water	Surf (TM94)	157 Alomomola [TM]	142 Araquanid [TM]	093 Barboach [TM]	008 Brionne [TM]	243 Bruxish [TM]	195 Carracosta [TM]
		264 Carvanha [TM]	201 Chinchou [TM]	116 Cloyster [TM]	112 Corsola [TM]	141 Dewpider [TM]	263 Dhelmise [TM]
		282 Dragonair [TM]	283 Dragonite [TM]	244 Drampa [TM]	281 Dratini [TM]	155 Feebas [TM]	108 Finneon [TM]
		240 Garchomp [TM]	261 Gastrodon [TM]	153 Goldeen [TM]	090 Golduck [TM]	183 Golisopod [TM]	092 Gyarados [TM]
		057 Hariyama [TM]	121 Herdier [TM]	165 Kangaskhan [TM]	202 Lanturn [TM]	268 Lapras [TM]	109 Lumineon [TM]
		111 Luvdisc [TM]	056 Makuhita [TM]	113 Mareanie [TM]	156 Milotic [TM]	138 Miltank [TM]	035 Munchlax [TM]
		220 Pancham [TM]	221 Pangoro [TM]	041 Pelipper [TM]	152 Politoed [TM]	149 Poliwag [TM]	150 Poliwhirl [TM]
		151 Poliwrath [TM]	007 Popplio [TM]	009 Primarina [TM]	089 Psyduck [TM]	189 Rampardos [TM]	262 Relicanth [TM]
		154 Seaking [TM]	265 Sharpedo [TM]	115 Shellder [TM]	260 Shellos [TM]	204 Silvally [TM]	038 Slowbro [TM]
		039 Slowking [TM]	037 Slowpoke [TM]	249 Sneasel [TM]	036 Snorlax [TM]	185 Starmie [TM]	184 Staryu [TM]
		122 Stoutland [TM]	288 Tapu Fini [TM]	137 Tauros [TM]	106 Tentacool [TM]	107 Tentacruel [TM]	194 Tirtouga [TM]
		114 Toxapex [TM]	124 Vaporeon [TM]	266 Wailmer [TM]	267 Wailord [TM]	250 Weavile [TM]	094 Whiscash [TM]
		182 Wimpod [TM]	110 Wishiwashi [TM]				
Normal	Swagger (TM87)	042 Abra [TM]	245 Absol [TM]	284 Aerodactyl [TM]	044 Alakazam [TM]	071 Alolan Diglett [TM]	072 Alolan Dugtrio [TM]
		270 Alolan Exeggutor [TM]	229 Alolan Geodude [TM]	231 Alolan Golem [TM]	230 Alolan Graveler [TM]	050 Alolan Grimer [TM]	164 Alolan Marowak [TM]
		045 Alolan Meowth [TM]	051 Alolan Muk [TM]	254 Alolan Ninetales [TM]	046 Alolan Persian [TM]	026 Alolan Raichu [TM]	016 Alolan Raticate [TM]
		015 Alolan Rattata [TM]	251 Alolan Sandshrew [TM]	252 Alolan Sandslash [TM]	253 Alolan Vulpix [TM]	157 Alomomola [TM]	142 Araquanid [TM]
		053 Arcanine [TM]	192 Archen [TM]	193 Archeops [TM]	023 Ariados [TM]	117 Bagon [TM]	093 Barboach [TM]
		191 Bastiodon [24, TM]	170 Bewear [TM]	034 Blissey [TM]	099 Boldore [TM]	030 Bonsly [TM]	171 Bounsweet [TM]
		076 Braviary [TM]	008 Brionne [TM]	243 Bruxish [TM]	019 Butterfree [TM]	294 Buzzwole [TM]	101 Carbink [TM]
		195 Carracosta [TM]	264 Carvanha [22, TM]	181 Castform [TM]	297 Celesteela [TM]	033 Chansey [TM]	028 Charjabug [TM]
		201 Chinchou [TM]	212 Clefable [TM]	211 Clefairy [TM]	210 Cleffa [TM]	116 Cloyster [TM]	174 Comfey [TM]
		112 Corsola [TM]	087 Cottonee [TM]	060 Crabominable [TM]	059 Crabrawler [TM]	188 Cranidos [TM]	070 Crobat [TM]
		163 Cubone [TM]	083 Cutiefly [TM]	002 Dartrix [TM]	003 Decidueye [TM]	081 Delibird [TM]	141 Dewpider [TM]
		263 Dhelmise [TM]	282 Dragonair [TM]	283 Dragonite [TM]	281 Dratini [TM]	065 Drifblim [TM]	064 Drifloon [TM]
		054 Drowzee [45, TM]	123 Eevee [TM]	227 Electabuzz [TM]	228 Electivire [TM]	226 Elekid [TM]	274 Emolga [TM]
		127 Espeon [TM]	269 Exeggcute [TM]	074 Fearow [TM]	155 Feebas [TM]	108 Finneon [TM]	126 Flareon [TM]
		159 Fletchinder [TM]	158 Fletchling [TM]	237 Flygon [TM]	143 Fomantis [TM]	248 Froslass [TM]	239 Gabite [TM]
		207 Garbodor [TM]	240 Garchomp [TM]	061 Gastly [TM]	261 Gastrodon [TM]	063 Gengar [TM]	238 Gible [TM]
		100 Gigalith [TM]	130 Glaceon [EV]	247 Glalie [TM]	069 Golbat [TM]	153 Goldeen [TM]	090 Golduck [TM]
		183 Golisopod [TM]	180 Goodra [EV]	178 Goomy [TM]	259 Granbull [TM]	052 Growlithe [TM]	027 Grubbin [TM]
		014 Gumshoos [TM]	092 Gyarados [TM]	272 Hakamo-o [TM]	032 Happiny [TM]	057 Hariyama [TM]	062 Haunter [TM]
		121 Herdier [TM]	278 Honchkrow [25, TM]	055 Hypno [45, TM]	134 Igglybuff [TM]	006 Incineroar [28, TM]	271 Jangmo-o [TM]
		135 Jigglypuff [TM]	125 Jolteon [TM]	043 Kadabra [TM]	165 Kangaskhan [TM]	298 Kartana [TM]	241 Klefki [TM]
		222 Komala [TM]	273 Kommo-o [TM]	233 Krokorok [25, TM]	234 Krookodile [25, TM]	202 Lanturn [TM]	268 Lapras [TM]
		129 Leafeon [TM]	021 Ledian [TM]	020 Ledyba [TM]	086 Lilligant [TM]	120 Lillipup [TM]	004 Litten [25, TM]
		280 Lucario [TM]	109 Lumineon [TM]	292 Lunala [TM]	144 Lurantis [TM]	111 Luvdisc [TM]	104 Lycanroc (Midday Form) [TM]
		104 Lycanroc (Midnight Form) [TM]	097 Machamp [TM]	096 Machoke [TM]	095 Machop [TM]	166 Magby [TM]	301 Magearna [TM]
		167 Magmar [TM]	168 Magmortar [TM]	047 Magnemite [TM]	048 Magneton [TM]	049 Magnezone [TM]	056 Makuhita [TM]
		078 Mandibuzz [TM]	079 Mankey [19, TM]	113 Mareanie [TM]	140 Masquerain [TM]	216 Metagross [TM]	215 Metang [TM]
		156 Milotic [TM]	138 Miltank [TM]	242 Mimikyu [TM]	213 Minior [TM]	066 Misdreavus [TM]	067 Mismagius [TM]
		145 Morelull [TM]	132 Mudbray [TM]	133 Mudsdale [TM]	035 Munchlax [TM]	277 Murkrow [TM]	300 Necrozma [TM]
		293 Nihilego [TM]	198 Nosepass [TM]	176 Oranguru [TM]	082 Oricorio [TM]	187 Palossand [TM]	220 Pancham [TM]
		221 Pangoro [TM]	147 Paras [TM]	148 Parasect [TM]	177 Passimian [TM]	041 Pelipper [TM]	085 Petilil [TM]
		196 Phantump [TM]	295 Pheromosa [TM]	024 Pichu [TM]	025 Pikachu [TM]	010 Pikipek [TM]	175 Pinsir [TM]
		152 Politoed [27, TM]	149 Poliwag [TM]	150 Poliwhirl [TM]	151 Poliwrath [TM]	007 Popplio [TM]	217 Porygon [TM]
		218 Porygon2 [TM]	219 Porygon-Z [TM]	009 Primarina [TM]	080 Primeape [19, TM]	199 Probopass [TM]	089 Psyduck [TM]
		200 Pyukumuku [TM]	189 Rampardos [TM]	262 Relicanth [TM]	084 Ribombee [TM]	279 Riolu [TM]	103 Rockruff [TM]
		098 Roggenrola [TM]	001 Rowlet [TM]	075 Rufflet [TM]	102 Sableye [TM]	119 Salamence [TM]	161 Salandit [TM]
		162 Salazzle [1, TM]	232 Sandile [25, TM]	186 Sandygast [TM]	276 Scizor [TM]	275 Scyther [TM]	154 Seaking [TM]
		265 Sharpedo [22, TM]	118 Shelgon [TM]	115 Shellder [TM]	260 Shellos [TM]	190 Shieldon [24, TM]	146 Shiinotic [TM]
		204 Silvally [TM]	208 Skarmory [TM]	179 Sliggoo [TM]	038 Slowbro [E]	039 Slowking [41, TM]	037 Slowpoke [TM]
		249 Sneasel [TM]	036 Snorlax [TM]	246 Snorunt [TM]	258 Snubbull [TM]	291 Solgaleo [TM]	073 Spearow [TM]

Type	Move Name	Pokémon					
Normal	Swagger (TM87)	022 Spinarak [TM]	105 Spinda [TM]	185 Starmie [TM]	184 Staryu [TM]	172 Steenee [TM]	122 Stoutland [TM]
		169 Stufful [TM]	031 Sudowoodo [TM]	139 Surskit [TM]	131 Sylveon [TM]	160 Talonflame [TM]	287 Tapu Bulu [TM]
		299 Tapu Fini [TM]	285 Tapu Koko [TM]	286 Tapu Lele [TM]	127 Tauros [48, TM]	106 Tentacool [TM]	107 Tentacruel [TM]
		194 Tirtouga [TM]	225 Togedemaru [TM]	223 Torkoal [TM]	005 Torracat [28, TM]	012 Toucannon [TM]	114 Toxapex [TM]
		235 Trapinch [TM]	197 Trevenant [TM]	206 Trubbish [TM]	011 Trumbeak [TM]	173 Tsareena [1, 5, TM]	224 Turtonator [TM]
		203 Type: Null [TM]	128 Umbreon [TM]	256 Vanillish [TM]	255 Vanillite [TM]	257 Vanilluxe [TM]	124 Vaporeon [TM]
		236 Vibrava [TM]	029 Vikavolt [TM]	077 Vullaby [TM]	266 Wailmer [TM]	267 Wailord [TM]	250 Weavile [TM]
		088 Whimsicott [TM]	094 Whiscash [TM]	136 Wigglytuff [TM]	182 Wimpod [TM]	040 Wingull [TM]	110 Wishiwashi [TM]
		296 Xurkitree [TM]	013 Yungoos [TM]	068 Zubat [TM]	205 Zygarde [TM]		
	Swallow	050 Alolan Grimer [5]	015 Alolan Rattata [5]	065 Drifblim [34]	064 Drifloon [33]	207 Gyrhodor [73]	209 Guzzlord [1]
		135 Jigglypuff [25]	222 Komala [6]	202 Lanturn [1, EV]	113 Mareanie [E]	035 Munchlax [33]	041 Pelipper [33]
		186 Sandygast [E]	260 Shellos [E]	206 Trubbish [23]			
Fairy	Sweet Kiss	210 Cleffa [10]	174 Comfey [19]	108 Finneon [E]	032 Happiny [12]	134 Igglybuff [9]	111 Luvdisc [31]
		024 Pichu [10]					
Normal	Sweet Scent	171 Bounsweet [17]	174 Comfey [31]	083 Cutiefly [21]	143 Fomantis [37]	144 Lurantis [40]	140 Masquerain [1, 9]
		147 Paras [E]	085 Petilil [E]	084 Ribombee [21]	161 Salandit [8]	162 Salazzle [1, 8]	172 Steenee [17]
		139 Surskit [9]	286 Tapu Lele [20]	173 Tsareena [17]			
	Swift	046 Alolan Persian [1, EV]	251 Alolan Sandshrew [17]	264 Carvanha [E]	070 Crobat [24]	123 Eevee [17]	227 Electabuzz [12]
		228 Electivire [12]	226 Elekid [12]	127 Espeon [17]	069 Golbat [24]	021 Ledian [1, 8]	020 Ledyba [8]
		213 Minior [15]	295 Pheromosa [7]	208 Skarmory [23]	185 Starmie [1]	184 Staryu [16]	131 Sylveon [17]
		068 Zubat [23]					
Dark	Switcheroo	046 Alolan Persian [1]	015 Alolan Rattata [E]	192 Archen [E]	087 Cottonee [E]	263 Dhelmise [1]	055 Hypno [1]
		241 Klefki [E]	240 Snorunt [E]				
Normal	Swords Dance (TM75)	245 Absol [25, TM]	270 Alolan Exeggutor [TM]	164 Alolan Marowak [TM]	016 Alolan Raticate [1, TM]	251 Alolan Sandshrew [38, TM]	252 Alolan Sandslash [TM]
		023 Ariados [1, TM, EV]	170 Bewear [TM]	243 Bruxish [TM]	188 Cranidos [TM]	163 Cubone [TM]	002 Dartrix [TM]
		003 Decidueye [TM]	263 Dhelmise [TM]	269 Exeggcute [TM]	159 Fletchinder [TM]	158 Fletchling [TM]	143 Fomantis [TM]
		240 Garchomp [TM]	183 Golisopod [16, TM]	272 Hakamo-o [TM]	006 Incineroar [TM]	271 Jangmo-o [TM]	298 Kartana [37, TM]
		222 Komala [TM]	273 Kommo-o [TM]	129 Leafeon [29, TM]	021 Ledian [TM]	020 Ledyba [TM]	086 Lilligant [TM]
		004 Litten [TM]	280 Lucario [19, TM]	144 Lurantis [TM]	104 Lycanroc (Midday Form) [TM]	104 Lycanroc (Midnight Form) [TM]	242 Mimikyu [TM]
		300 Necrozma [TM]	082 Oricorio [TM]	220 Pancham [TM]	221 Pangoro [TM]	147 Paras [TM]	148 Parasect [TM]
		010 Pikipek [TM]	175 Pinsir [40, TM]	189 Rampardos [TM]	279 Riolu [TM]	001 Rowlet [TM]	276 Scizor [57, TM]
		275 Scyther [57, TM]	204 Silvally [TM]	208 Skarmory [TM]	249 Sneasel [TM]	169 Stufful [TM]	160 Talonflame [TM]
		287 Tapu Bulu [TM]	106 Tentacool [TM]	107 Tentacruel [TM]	005 Torracat [TM]	012 Toucannon [TM]	011 Trumbeak [TM]
		203 Type: Null [TM]	250 Weavile [TM]				
Psychic	Synchronoise	243 Bruxish [44]	054 Drowzee [37]	123 Eevee [E]	055 Hypno [37]	301 Magearna [73]	089 Psyduck [E]
Grass	Synthesis	171 Bounsweet [E]	174 Comfey [28]	002 Dartrix [28]	003 Decidueye [28]	269 Exeggcute [E]	143 Fomantis [28]
		298 Kartana [19]	129 Leafeon [33]	086 Lilligant [1]	144 Lurantis [28]	085 Petilil [17]	001 Rowlet [25]
Normal	Tackle	229 Alolan Geodude [1]	231 Alolan Golem [1]	230 Alolan Graveler [1]	016 Alolan Raticate [1]	015 Alolan Rattata [1]	191 Bastiodon [1]
		170 Bewear [1]	099 Boldore [1]	101 Carbink [1]	181 Castform [1]	017 Caterpie [1]	297 Celesteela [1]
		112 Corsola [1]	002 Dartrix [1]	003 Decidueye [1]	123 Eevee [1]	127 Espeon [1]	155 Feebas [15]
		126 Flareon [1]	159 Fletchinder [1]	158 Fletchling [1]	239 Gabite [1]	240 Garchomp [1]	238 Gible [1]
		100 Gigalith [1]	130 Glaceon [1]	180 Goodra [1]	178 Goomy [1]	259 Granbull [1]	014 Gumshoos [1]
		272 Hakamo-o [1]	057 Hariyama [1]	121 Herdier [1]	271 Jangmo-o [1]	125 Jolteon [1]	241 Klefki [1]
		273 Kommo-o [1]	129 Leafeon [1]	021 Ledian [1]	020 Ledyba [1]	120 Lillipup [1]	111 Luvdisc [1]
		104 Lycanroc (Midday Form) [1]	104 Lycanroc (Midnight Form) [1]	091 Magikarp [15]	047 Magnemite [1]	048 Magneton [1]	049 Magnezone [1]
		056 Makuhita [1]	138 Miltank [1]	213 Minior [1]	035 Munchlax [1]	198 Nosepass [1]	220 Pancham [1]
		221 Pangoro [1]	177 Passimian [1]	196 Phantump [1]	217 Porygon [1]	218 Porygon2 [1]	219 Porygon-Z [1]
		199 Probopass [1]	262 Relicanth [1]	103 Rockruff [1]	098 Roggenrola [1]	001 Rowlet [1]	115 Shellder [1]
		190 Shieldon [1]	204 Silvally [1]	179 Sliggoo [1]	038 Slowbro [1]	039 Slowking [1]	037 Slowpoke [1]
		036 Snorlax [1]	258 Snubbull [1]	105 Spinda [1]	184 Staryu [1]	122 Stoutland [1]	169 Stufful [1]
		131 Sylveon [1]	160 Talonflame [1]	137 Tauros [1]	225 Togedemaru [1]	197 Trevenant [1]	224 Turtonator [1]
		203 Type: Null [1]	128 Umbreon [1]	124 Vaporeon [1]	013 Yungoos [1]		
Bug	Tail Glow	296 Xurkitree [1]					
	Tail Slap	253 Alolan Vulpix [E]					
Normal	Tail Whip	164 Alolan Marowak [1, 3]	026 Alolan Raichu [1]	016 Alolan Raticate [1]	015 Alolan Rattata [1]	253 Alolan Vulpix [4]	034 Blissey [5]
		033 Chansey [5]	163 Cubone [3]	123 Eevee [1]	274 Emolga [7]	127 Espeon [1]	126 Flareon [1]
		130 Glaceon [1]	153 Goldeen [1]	090 Golduck [1, 4]	259 Granbull [1]	125 Jolteon [1]	165 Kangaskhan [10]
		129 Leafeon [1]	024 Pichu [5]	025 Pikachu [1]	089 Psyduck [4]	154 Seaking [1]	258 Snubbull [1]
		131 Sylveon [1]	137 Tauros [3]	128 Umbreon [1]	124 Vaporeon [1]		

Type	Move Name	Pokémon					
Flying	Tailwind	284 Aerodactyl [E]	076 Braviary [37]	019 Butterfree [41]	064 Drifloon [E]	159 Fletchinder [51]	158 Fletchling [45, E]
		020 Ledyba [E]	078 Mandibuzz [37]	277 Murkrow [50]	082 Oricorio [E]	041 Pelipper [1, 44]	010 Pikipek [E]
		075 Rufflet [37]	160 Talonflame [55]	077 Vullaby [37]	088 Whimsicott [28]		
Normal	Take Down	284 Aerodactyl [41]	093 Barboach [E]	191 Bastiodon [15]	214 Beldum [1]	170 Bewear [30]	034 Blissey [27]
		264 Carvanha [43]	033 Chansey [27]	201 Chinchou [39]	188 Cranidos [15]	123 Eevee [25]	239 Gabite [15]
		240 Garchomp [15]	238 Gible [15]	052 Growlithe [23]	014 Gumshoos [31]	121 Herdier [15]	202 Lanturn [43]
		120 Lillipup [15]	111 Luvdisc [34]	216 Metagross [1]	215 Metang [1]	213 Minior [29]	177 Passimian [22]
		189 Rampardos [15]	262 Relicanth [31]	098 Roggenrola [E]	115 Shellder [E]	190 Shieldon [15]	204 Silvally [40]
		122 Stoutland [15]	169 Stufful [28]	137 Tauros [41]	206 Trubbish [25]	203 Type: Null [40]	110 Wishiwashi [25]
		013 Yungoos [28]					
Dark	Taunt (TM12)	042 Abra [TM]	245 Absol [13, TM]	284 Aerodactyl [TM]	044 Alakazam [TM]	050 Alolan Grimer [TM]	045 Alolan Meowth [25, TM]
		051 Alolan Muk [TM]	046 Alolan Persian [25, TM]	016 Alolan Raticate [TM]	015 Alolan Rattata [TM]	192 Archen [TM]	193 Archeops [TM]
		191 Bastiodon [1, 6, TM]	170 Bewear [TM]	243 Bruxish [TM]	294 Buzzwole [31, TM]	264 Carvanha [TM]	174 Comfey [TM]
		087 Cottonee [TM]	070 Crobat [TM]	054 Drowzee [TM]	228 Electivire [TM]	274 Emolga [TM]	159 Fletchinder [TM]
		158 Fletchling [TM]	248 Froslass [TM]	061 Gastly [TM]	063 Gengar [TM]	247 Glalie [TM]	069 Golbat [TM]
		183 Golisopod [TM]	259 Granbull [TM]	014 Gumshoos [TM]	092 Gyarados [TM]	272 Hakamo-o [TM]	062 Haunter [TM]
		278 Honchkrow [TM]	055 Hypno [TM]	006 Incineroar [TM]	271 Jangmo-o [TM]	043 Kadabra [TM]	273 Kommo-o [TM]
		233 Krokorok [TM]	234 Krookodile [TM]	004 Litten [TM]	104 Lycanroc (Midday Form) [TM]	104 Lycanroc (Midnight Form) [1, TM]	168 Magmortar [TM]
		078 Mandibuzz [TM]	079 Mankey [TM]	242 Mimikyu [TM]	066 Misdreavus [TM]	067 Mismagius [TM]	277 Murkrow [31, TM]
		198 Nosepass [TM]	176 Oranguru [8, TM]	082 Oricorio [TM]	221 Pangoro [65, TM]	177 Passimian [TM]	295 Pheromosa [TM]
		080 Primeape [TM]	199 Probopass [TM]	200 Pyukumuku [9, TM]	103 Rockruff [TM]	102 Sableye [TM]	161 Salandit [TM]
		162 Salazzle [TM]	232 Sandile [TM]	265 Sharpedo [56, TM]	190 Shieldon [6, TM]	208 Skarmory [TM]	249 Sneasel [1, TM]
		258 Snubbull [TM]	169 Stufful [TM]	031 Sudowoodo [TM]	160 Talonflame [TM]	287 Tapu Bulu [TM]	288 Tapu Fini [TM]
		285 Tapu Koko [TM]	286 Tapu Lele [TM]	005 Torracat [TM]	224 Turtonator [TM]	128 Umbreon [TM]	256 Vanillish [22, TM]
		255 Vanillite [22, TM]	257 Vanilluxe [22, TM]	077 Vullaby [TM]	250 Weavile [1, TM]	088 Whimsicott [TM]	182 Wimpod [TM]
		013 Yungoos [TM]	068 Zubat [TM]				
Normal	Tearful Look	030 Bonsly [22]	031 Sudowoodo [22]	110 Wishiwashi [22]			
	Teeter Dance	171 Bounsweet [25]	086 Lilligant [10]	082 Oricorio [26]	105 Spinda [32]	172 Steenee [25]	173 Tsareena [25]
	Telekinesis	044 Alakazam [33]	043 Kadabra [33]				
Psychic	Teleport	042 Abra [1]	044 Alakazam [1]	290 Cosmoem [1]	289 Cosmog [23]	043 Kadabra [1]	292 Lunala [1]
		291 Solgaleo [1]					
Dark	Thief (TM46)	042 Abra [TM]	245 Absol [TM]	284 Aerodactyl [TM]	044 Alakazam [TM]	071 Alolan Diglett [TM]	072 Alolan Dugtrio [TM]
		270 Alolan Exeggutor [TM]	050 Alolan Grimer [TM]	164 Alolan Marowak [TM]	045 Alolan Meowth [TM]	051 Alolan Muk [TM]	046 Alolan Persian [TM]
		026 Alolan Raichu [TM]	016 Alolan Raticate [TM]	015 Alolan Rattata [TM]	251 Alolan Sandshrew [TM]	252 Alolan Sandslash [TM]	053 Arcanine [TM]
		023 Ariados [TM]	030 Bonsly [TM]	019 Butterfree [TM]	264 Carvanha [TM]	181 Castform [TM]	174 Comfey [TM]
		060 Crabominable [TM]	059 Crabrawler [TM]	188 Cranidos [TM]	070 Crobat [TM]	163 Cubone [TM]	083 Cutiefly [TM]
		081 Delibird [TM]	263 Dhelmise [TM]	065 Drifblim [TM]	064 Drifloon [TM]	054 Drowzee [TM]	227 Electabuzz [TM]
		228 Electivire [TM]	226 Elekid [TM]	269 Exeggcute [TM]	074 Fearow [TM]	159 Fletchinder [TM]	158 Fletchling [TM]
		207 Garbodor [TM]	061 Gastly [TM]	063 Gengar [TM]	069 Golbat [TM]	259 Granbull [TM]	052 Growlithe [TM]
		014 Gumshoos [TM]	299 Guzzlord [TM]	062 Haunter [TM]	278 Honchkrow [TM]	055 Hypno [TM]	043 Kadabra [TM]
		165 Kangaskhan [TM]	241 Klefki [TM, E]	233 Krokorok [TM]	234 Krookodile [TM]	021 Ledian [TM]	020 Ledyba [TM]
		097 Machamp [TM]	096 Machoke [TM]	095 Machop [TM]	166 Magby [TM]	167 Magmar [TM]	168 Magmortar [TM]
		078 Mandibuzz [TM]	079 Mankey [TM]	140 Masquerain [TM]	242 Mimikyu [TM]	066 Misdreavus [TM]	067 Mismagius [TM]
		277 Murkrow [TM]	300 Necrozma [TM]	221 Pangoro [TM]	147 Paras [TM]	148 Parasect [TM]	177 Passimian [TM]
		041 Pelipper [TM]	196 Phantump [TM]	010 Pikipek [TM]	175 Pinsir [TM]	152 Politoed [TM]	149 Poliwag [TM]
		150 Poliwhirl [TM]	151 Poliwrath [TM]	217 Porygon [TM]	218 Porygon2 [TM]	219 Porygon-Z [TM]	080 Primeape [TM]
		189 Rampardos [TM]	084 Ribombee [TM]	102 Sableye [TM]	161 Salandit [TM]	162 Salazzle [TM]	232 Sandile [TM]
		276 Scizor [TM]	275 Scyther [TM]	265 Sharpedo [TM]	208 Skarmory [TM]	249 Sneasel [TM]	258 Snubbull [TM]
		073 Spearow [TM]	022 Spinarak [TM]	105 Spinda [TM]	031 Sudowoodo [TM]	139 Surskit [TM]	160 Talonflame [TM]
		285 Tapu Koko [TM]	286 Tapu Lele [TM]	106 Tentacool [TM]	107 Tentacruel [TM]	225 Togedemaru [TM]	012 Toucannon [TM]
		197 Trevenant [TM]	206 Trubbish [TM]	011 Trumbeak [TM]	077 Vullaby [TM]	250 Weavile [TM]	088 Whimsicott [TM]
		040 Wingull [TM]	013 Yungoos [TM]	068 Zubat [TM]			
Ground	Thousand Arrows	205 Zygarde [ZC]					
	Thousand Waves	205 Zygarde [ZC]					

Type	Move Name	Pokémon					
Normal	Thrash	071 Alolan Diglett [E]	164 Alolan Marowak [33]	192 Archen [50]	193 Archeops [61]	117 Bagon [E]	093 Barboach [E]
		170 Bewear [43]	076 Braviary [1, 70]	264 Carvanha [E]	188 Cranidos [E]	163 Cubone [31]	238 Gible [E]
		057 Growlithe [6]	014 Gumshoos [51]	289 Guzzlord [47]	092 Gyarados [1]	006 Incineroar [38]	222 Komala [46]
		233 Krokorok [52]	004 Litten [32]	079 Mankey [33]	177 Passimian [29]	175 Pinsir [43]	080 Primeape [35]
		103 Rockruff [E]	075 Rufflet [64]	232 Sandile [46]	105 Spinda [55]	169 Stufful [37]	137 Tauros [50]
		005 Torracat [37]	266 Wailmer [E]	094 Whiscash [1, EV]	013 Yungoos [43]		
Dark	Throat Chop	006 Incineroar [1]	249 Sneasel [E]				
Electric	Thunder (TM25)	245 Absol [TM]	229 Alolan Geodude [TM]	231 Alolan Golem [TM]	230 Alolan Graveler [TM]	164 Alolan Marowak [TM]	045 Alolan Meowth [TM]
		046 Alolan Persian [TM]	026 Alolan Raichu [TM]	191 Bastiodon [TM]	034 Blissey [TM]	181 Castform [TM]	033 Chansey [TM]
		201 Chinchou [TM]	212 Clefable [TM]	211 Clefairy [TM]	188 Cranidos [TM]	282 Dragonair [TM]	283 Dragonite [TM]
		244 Drampa [TM]	281 Dratini [TM]	065 Drifblim [TM]	064 Drifloon [TM]	227 Electabuzz [55, TM]	220 Electivire [55, TM]
		226 Elekid [43, TM]	274 Emolga [TM]	248 Froslass [TM]	063 Gengar [TM]	180 Goodra [TM]	259 Granbull [TM]
		092 Gyarados [TM]	135 Jigglypuff [TM]	125 Jolteon [45, TM]	165 Kangaskhan [TM]	202 Lanturn [TM]	268 Lapras [TM]
		292 Lunala [TM]	047 Magnemite [TM]	048 Magneton [TM]	049 Magnezone [TM]	079 Mankey [TM]	138 Miltank [TM]
		242 Mimikyu [TM]	066 Misdreavus [TM]	067 Mismagius [TM]	035 Munchlax [TM]	293 Nihilego [TM]	198 Nosepass [TM]
		176 Oranguru [TM]	024 Pichu [TM]	025 Pikachu [58, TM]	217 Porygon [TM]	218 Porygon2 [TM]	219 Porygon-Z [TM]
		080 Primeape [TM]	199 Probopass [TM]	189 Rampardos [TM]	190 Shieldon [TM]	036 Snorlax [TM]	258 Snubbull [TM]
		291 Solgaleo [TM]	185 Starmie [TM]	184 Staryu [TM]	122 Stoutland [TM]	285 Tapu Koko [TM]	286 Tapu Lele [TM]
		137 Tauros [TM]	225 Togedemaru [TM]	029 Vikavolt [TM]	136 Wigglytuff [TM]	296 Xurkitree [TM]	
	Thunder Fang	284 Aerodactyl [1]	053 Arcanine [1]	259 Granbull [1]	125 Jolteon [20]	120 Lillipup [E]	103 Rockruff [E]
		119 Salamence [1]	232 Sandile [E]	204 Silvally [1]	258 Snubbull [1, F]	122 Stoutland [1]	
	Thunder Punch	042 Abra [E]	229 Alolan Geodude [22]	231 Alolan Golem [22]	230 Alolan Graveler [22]	294 Buzzwole [1]	283 Dragonite [1]
		054 Drowzee [E]	227 Electabuzz [23]	220 Electivire [25]	226 Elekid [25]	001 Gastly [E]	095 Machop [E]
		166 Magby [E]	168 Magmortar [1]	024 Pichu [E]	169 Stufful [E]	296 Xurkitree [23]	
	Thunder Shock	026 Alolan Raichu [1]	227 Electabuzz [1, 5]	228 Electivire [1, 5]	226 Elekid [5]	274 Emolga [1]	125 Jolteon [1, EV]
		047 Magnemite [5]	048 Magneton [1, 5]	049 Magnezone [1, 5]	024 Pichu [1]	025 Pikachu [1]	285 Tapu Koko [1]
		225 Togedemaru [1]	296 Xurkitree [1]				
	Thunder Wave (TM73)	042 Abra [TM]	245 Absol [TM]	044 Alakazam [TM]	026 Alolan Raichu [TM]	034 Blissey [TM]	181 Castform [TM]
		033 Chansey [TM]	028 Charjabug [TM]	201 Chinchou [6, TM]	212 Clefable [TM]	211 Clefairy [TM]	210 Cleffa [TM]
		282 Dragonair [1, 5, TM]	283 Dragonite [1, 5, TM]	244 Drampa [TM]	281 Dratini [5, TM]	065 Drifblim [TM]	064 Drifloon [TM]
		054 Drowzee [TM]	227 Electabuzz [19, TM]	228 Electivire [19, TM]	226 Elekid [19, TM]	274 Emolga [TM]	248 Froslass [TM]
		259 Granbull [TM]	027 Grubbin [TM]	092 Gyarados [TM]	032 Happiny [TM]	121 Herdier [TM]	278 Honchkrow [TM]
		055 Hypno [TM]	134 Igglybuff [TM]	135 Jigglypuff [TM]	125 Jolteon [33, TM]	043 Kadabra [TM]	241 Klefki [TM]
		202 Lanturn [1, 6, TM]	120 Lillipup [TM]	292 Lunala [TM]	301 Magearna [TM]	047 Magnemite [11, TM]	048 Magneton [11, TM]
		049 Magnezone [11, TM]	138 Miltank [TM]	242 Mimikyu [TM]	066 Misdreavus [TM]	067 Mismagius [TM]	145 Morelull [TM]
		277 Murkrow [TM]	300 Necrozma [TM]	293 Nihilego [TM]	198 Nosepass [13, TM]	024 Pichu [18, TM]	025 Pikachu [18, TM]
		217 Porygon [TM]	218 Porygon2 [TM]	219 Porygon-Z [TM]	199 Probopass [13, TM]	146 Shiinotic [TM]	204 Silvally [TM]
		038 Slowbro [TM]	039 Slowking [TM]	037 Slowpoke [TM]	258 Snubbull [TM]	291 Solgaleo [TM]	185 Starmie [TM]
		184 Staryu [TM]	122 Stoutland [TM]	285 Tapu Koko [TM]	225 Togedemaru [TM]	203 Type: Null [TM]	029 Vikavolt [TM]
		136 Wigglytuff [TM]	296 Xurkitree [7, TM]				
	Thunderbolt (TM24)	245 Absol [TM]	229 Alolan Geodude [TM]	231 Alolan Golem [TM]	230 Alolan Graveler [TM]	164 Alolan Marowak [TM]	045 Alolan Meowth [TM]
		046 Alolan Persian [TM]	026 Alolan Raichu [1, TM]	191 Bastiodon [TM]	034 Blissey [TM]	181 Castform [TM]	033 Chansey [TM]
		028 Charjabug [TM]	201 Chinchou [TM]	212 Clefable [TM]	211 Clefairy [TM]	188 Cranidos [TM]	282 Dragonair [TM]
		283 Dragonite [TM]	244 Drampa [TM]	281 Dratini [TM]	065 Drifblim [TM]	064 Drifloon [TM]	227 Electabuzz [49, TM]
		228 Electivire [49, TM]	226 Elekid [40, TM]	274 Emolga [TM]	248 Froslass [TM]	207 Garbodor [TM]	001 Gastly [TM]
		063 Gengar [TM]	180 Goodra [TM]	178 Goomy [TM]	259 Granbull [TM]	027 Grubbin [TM]	092 Gyarados [TM]
		062 Haunter [TM]	121 Herdier [TM]	135 Jigglypuff [TM]	125 Jolteon [TM]	165 Kangaskhan [TM]	202 Lanturn [TM]
		268 Lapras [TM]	120 Lillipup [TM]	292 Lunala [TM]	301 Magearna [TM]	168 Magmortar [TM]	047 Magnemite [TM]
		048 Magneton [TM]	049 Magnezone [TM]	079 Mankey [TM]	138 Miltank [TM]	242 Mimikyu [TM]	066 Misdreavus [TM]
		067 Mismagius [TM]	035 Munchlax [TM]	293 Nihilego [TM]	198 Nosepass [TM]	176 Oranguru [TM]	024 Pichu [TM]
		025 Pikachu [42, TM]	217 Porygon [TM]	218 Porygon2 [TM]	219 Porygon-Z [TM]	080 Primeape [TM]	199 Probopass [TM]
		189 Rampardos [TM]	190 Shieldon [TM]	204 Silvally [TM]	179 Sliggoo [TM]	036 Snorlax [TM]	258 Snubbull [TM]
		291 Solgaleo [TM]	185 Starmie [TM]	184 Staryu [TM]	122 Stoutland [TM]	285 Tapu Koko [TM]	286 Tapu Lele [TM]
		137 Tauros [TM]	225 Togedemaru [TM]	029 Vikavolt [1, TM, EV]	136 Wigglytuff [TM]	296 Xurkitree [37, TM]	
Normal	Tickle	157 Alomomola [E]	210 Cleffa [E]	087 Cottonee [E]	123 Eevee [E]	274 Emolga [E]	155 Feebas [E]
		108 Finneon [E]	268 Lapras [E]	095 Machop [E]	293 Nihilego [1]	024 Pichu [E]	200 Pyukumuku [E]
		286 Tapu Lele [38]	106 Tentacool [E]	225 Togedemaru [E]	266 Wailmer [E]	094 Whiscash [1]	

Type	Move Name	Pokémon					
Dark	Torment (TM41)	042 Abra [TM]	245 Absol [TM]	284 Aerodactyl [TM]	044 Alakazam [TM]	050 Alolan Grimer [TM]	045 Alolan Meowth [TM]
		051 Alolan Muk [TM]	046 Alolan Persian [TM]	016 Alolan Raticate [TM]	015 Alolan Rattata [TM]	192 Archen [TM]	193 Archeops [TM]
		191 Bastiodon [TM]	243 Bruxish [TM]	264 Carvanha [TM]	116 Cloyster [TM]	070 Crobat [TM]	054 Drowzee [TM]
		228 Electivire [TM]	248 Froslass [TM]	061 Gastly [TM]	063 Gengar [TM]	247 Glalie [TM]	069 Golbat [TM]
		259 Granbull [TM]	014 Gumshoos [TM]	092 Gyarados [TM]	062 Haunter [TM]	278 Honchkrow [TM]	055 Hypno [TM]
		006 Incineroar [TM]	043 Kadabra [TM]	241 Klefki [32, TM]	233 Krokorok [10, TM]	234 Krookodile [10, TM]	004 Litten [TM]
		168 Magmortar [TM]	078 Mandibuzz [TM]	066 Misdreavus [TM]	067 Mismagius [TM]	277 Murkrow [61, TM]	198 Nosepass [TM]
		220 Pancham [TM]	221 Pangoro [TM]	295 Pheromosa [TM]	199 Probopass [TM]	102 Sableye [TM]	161 Salandit [TM]
		162 Salazzle [1, TM]	232 Sandile [10, TM]	265 Sharpedo [TM]	190 Shieldon [TM]	208 Skarmory [TM]	249 Sneasel [TM]
		258 Snubbull [TM]	031 Sudowoodo [TM]	287 Tapu Bulu [TM]	288 Tapu Fini [TM]	285 Tapu Koko [TM]	286 Tapu Lele [TM]
		005 Torracat [TM]	128 Umbreon [TM]	077 Vullaby [TM]	250 Weavile [TM]	013 Yungoos [TM]	068 Zubat [TM]
Poison	Toxic (TM06)	042 Abra [TM]	245 Absol [TM]	284 Aerodactyl [TM]	044 Alakazam [TM]	071 Alolan Diglett [TM]	072 Alolan Dugtrio [TM]
		270 Alolan Exeggutor [TM]	229 Alolan Geodude [TM]	231 Alolan Golem [TM]	230 Alolan Graveler [TM]	050 Alolan Grimer [TM]	164 Alolan Marowak [TM]
		045 Alolan Meowth [TM]	051 Alolan Muk [TM]	254 Alolan Ninetales [TM]	046 Alolan Persian [TM]	026 Alolan Raichu [TM]	016 Alolan Raticate [TM]
		015 Alolan Rattata [TM]	251 Alolan Sandshrew [TM]	252 Alolan Sandslash [TM]	253 Alolan Vulpix [TM]	157 Alomomola [TM]	142 Araquanid [TM]
		053 Arcanine [TM]	192 Archen [TM]	193 Archeops [TM]	023 Ariados [TM]	117 Bagon [TM]	093 Barboach [TM]
		191 Bastiodon [TM]	170 Bewear [TM]	034 Blissey [TM]	099 Boldore [TM]	030 Bonsly [TM]	171 Bounsweet [TM]
		076 Braviary [TM]	008 Brionne [TM]	243 Bruxish [TM]	019 Butterfree [TM]	294 Buzzwole [TM]	101 Carbink [TM]
		195 Carracosta [TM]	264 Carvanha [TM]	181 Castform [TM]	297 Celesteela [TM]	033 Chansey [TM]	028 Charjabug [TM]
		201 Chinchou [TM]	212 Clefable [TM]	211 Clefairy [TM]	210 Cleffa [TM]	116 Cloyster [TM]	174 Comfey [TM]
		112 Corsola [TM]	087 Cottonee [TM]	060 Crabominable [TM]	059 Crabrawler [TM]	188 Cranidos [TM]	070 Crobat [TM]
		163 Cubone [TM]	083 Cutiefly [TM]	002 Dartrix [TM]	003 Decidueye [TM]	081 Delibird [TM]	141 Dewpider [TM]
		263 Dhelmise [TM]	282 Dragonair [TM]	283 Dragonite [TM]	244 Drampa [TM]	281 Dratini [TM]	065 Drifblim [TM]
		064 Drifloon [TM]	054 Drowzee [TM]	123 Eevee [TM]	227 Electabuzz [TM]	228 Electivire [TM]	226 Elekid [TM]
		274 Emolga [TM]	127 Espeon [TM]	269 Exeggcute [TM]	074 Fearow [TM]	155 Feebas [TM]	108 Finneon [TM]
		126 Flareon [TM]	159 Fletchinder [TM]	158 Fletchling [TM]	237 Flygon [TM]	143 Fomantis [TM]	248 Froslass [TM]
		239 Gabite [TM]	207 Garbodor [39, TM]	240 Garchomp [TM]	061 Gastly [TM]	261 Gastrodon [TM]	063 Gengar [TM]
		238 Gible [TM]	100 Gigalith [TM]	130 Glaceon [TM]	247 Glalie [TM]	069 Golbat [TM]	153 Goldeen [TM]
		090 Golduck [TM]	183 Golisopod [TM]	180 Goodra [TM]	178 Goomy [TM]	259 Granbull [TM]	052 Growlithe [TM]
		027 Grubbin [TM]	014 Gumshoos [TM]	299 Guzzlord [TM]	092 Gyarados [TM]	272 Hakamo-o [TM]	032 Happiny [TM]
		057 Hariyama [TM]	062 Haunter [TM]	121 Herdier [TM]	278 Honchkrow [TM]	055 Hypno [TM]	134 Igglybuff [TM]
		006 Incineroar [TM]	271 Jangmo-o [TM]	135 Jigglypuff [TM]	125 Jolteon [TM]	043 Kadabra [TM]	165 Kangaskhan [TM]
		298 Kartana [TM]	241 Klefki [TM]	222 Komala [TM]	273 Kommo-o [TM]	233 Krokorok [TM]	234 Krookodile [TM]
		202 Lanturn [TM]	268 Lapras [TM]	129 Leafeon [TM]	021 Ledian [TM]	020 Ledyba [TM]	086 Lilligant [TM]
		120 Lillipup [TM]	004 Litten [TM]	280 Lucario [TM]	109 Lumineon [TM]	292 Lunala [TM]	144 Lurantis [TM]
		111 Luvdisc [TM]	104 Lycanroc (Midday Form) [TM]	104 Lycanroc (Midnight Form) [TM]	097 Machamp [TM]	096 Machoke [TM]	095 Machop [TM]
		166 Magby [TM]	167 Magmar [TM]	168 Magmortar [TM]	047 Magnemite [TM]	048 Magneton [TM]	049 Magnezone [TM]
		056 Makuhita [TM]	078 Mandibuzz [TM]	079 Mankey [TM]	113 Mareanie [21, TM]	140 Masquerain [TM]	216 Metagross [TM]
		215 Metang [TM]	156 Milotic [TM]	138 Miltank [TM]	242 Mimikyu [TM]	213 Minior [TM]	066 Misdreavus [TM]
		067 Mismagius [TM]	145 Morelull [TM]	132 Mudbray [TM]	133 Mudsdale [TM]	035 Munchlax [TM]	277 Murkrow [TM]
		300 Necrozma [TM]	293 Nihilego [TM]	198 Nosepass [TM]	176 Oranguru [TM]	082 Oricorio [TM]	187 Palossand [TM]
		220 Pancham [TM]	221 Pangoro [TM]	147 Paras [TM]	148 Parasect [TM]	177 Passimian [TM]	041 Pelipper [TM]
		085 Petilil [TM]	196 Phantump [TM]	295 Pheromosa [TM]	024 Pichu [TM]	025 Pikachu [TM]	010 Pikipek [TM]
		175 Pinsir [TM]	152 Politoed [TM]	149 Poliwag [TM]	150 Poliwhirl [TM]	151 Poliwrath [TM]	007 Popplio [TM]
		217 Porygon [TM]	218 Porygon2 [TM]	219 Porygon-Z [TM]	009 Primarina [TM]	080 Primeape [TM]	199 Probopass [TM]
		089 Psyduck [TM]	200 Pyukumuku [45, TM]	189 Rampardos [TM]	262 Relicanth [TM]	084 Ribombee [TM]	279 Riolu [TM]
		103 Rockruff [TM]	098 Roggenrola [TM]	001 Rowlet [TM]	075 Rufflet [TM]	102 Sableye [TM]	119 Salamence [TM]
		161 Salandit [29, TM]	162 Salazzle [29, TM]	232 Sandile [TM]	186 Sandygast [TM]	276 Scizor [TM]	275 Scyther [TM]
		154 Seaking [TM]	265 Sharpedo [TM]	118 Shelgon [TM]	115 Shellder [TM]	260 Shellos [TM]	190 Shieldon [TM]
		146 Shiinotic [TM]	204 Silvally [TM]	208 Skarmory [TM]	179 Sliggoo [TM]	038 Slowbro [TM]	039 Slowking [TM]
		037 Slowpoke [TM]	249 Sneasel [TM]	036 Snorlax [TM]	246 Snorunt [TM]	258 Snubbull [TM]	291 Solgaleo [TM]
		073 Spearow [TM]	022 Spinarak [TM]	105 Spinda [TM]	185 Starmie [TM]	184 Staryu [TM]	172 Steenee [TM]
		122 Stoutland [TM]	169 Stufful [TM]	031 Sudowoodo [TM]	139 Surskit [TM]	131 Sylveon [TM]	160 Talonflame [TM]
		287 Tapu Bulu [TM]	288 Tapu Fini [TM]	285 Tapu Koko [TM]	286 Tapu Lele [TM]	137 Tauros [TM]	106 Tentacool [TM]
		107 Tentacruel [TM]	194 Tirtouga [TM]	225 Togedemaru [TM]	223 Torkoal [TM]	005 Torracat [TM]	012 Toucannon [TM]
		114 Toxapex [21, TM]	235 Trapinch [TM]	197 Trevenant [TM]	206 Trubbish [36, TM]	011 Trumbeak [TM]	173 Tsareena [TM]
		224 Turtonator [TM]	203 Type: Null [TM]	128 Umbreon [TM]	256 Vanillish [TM]	255 Vanillite [TM]	257 Vanilluxe [TM]
		124 Vaporeon [TM]	236 Vibrava [TM]	029 Vikavolt [TM]	077 Vullaby [TM]	266 Wailmer [TM]	267 Wailord [TM]
		250 Weavile [TM]	088 Whimsicott [TM]	094 Whiscash [TM]	136 Wigglytuff [TM]	182 Wimpod [TM]	040 Wingull [TM]
		110 Wishiwashi [TM]	296 Xurkitree [TM]	013 Yungoos [TM]	068 Zubat [TM]	205 Zygarde [TM]	

Type	Move Name	Pokémon					
Poison	**Toxic Spikes**	116 Cloyster [1]	207 Garbodor [1, 7]	113 Mareanie [13]	293 Nihilego [29]	022 Spinarak [E]	106 Tentacool [13]
		107 Tentacruel [13]	114 Toxapex [1, 13]	206 Trubbish [7]			
	Toxic Thread	023 Ariados [63]	022 Spinarak [54]				
Normal	**Transform**	209 Ditto [1]					
	Tri Attack	072 Alolan Dugtrio [1]	048 Magneton [1, EV]	049 Magnezone [1]	217 Porygon [50]	218 Porygon2 [50]	219 Porygon-Z [50]
		199 Probopass [1, EV]	204 Silvally [75]	073 Spearow [E]	203 Type: Null [75]		
	Trick	044 Alakazam [46]	043 Kadabra [46]	102 Sableye [E]	105 Spinda [E]		
Psychic	**Trick Room (TM92)**	042 Abra [TM]	044 Alakazam [TM]	270 Alolan Exeggutor [TM]	243 Bruxish [TM]	101 Carbink [TM]	174 Comfey [TM]
		054 Drowzee [TM]	127 Espeon [TM]	269 Exeggcute [TM]	061 Gastly [TM]	063 Gengar [TM]	062 Haunter [TM]
		055 Hypno [TM]	043 Kadabra [TM]	232 Lunala [TM]	301 Magearna [TM]	242 Mimikyu [TM]	066 Misdreavus [TM]
		067 Mismagius [TM]	300 Necrozma [TM]	293 Nihilego [1M]	176 Oranguru [50, TM]	196 Phantump [TM]	217 Porygon [TM]
		218 Porygon2 [TM]	219 Porygon-Z [1, TM]	038 Slowbro [TM]	039 Slowking [TM]	037 Slowpoke [TM]	291 Solgaleo [TM]
		105 Spinda [TM]	185 Starmie [TM]	197 Trevenant [TM]	088 Whimsicott [TM]		
Fighting	**Triple Kick**	295 Pheromosa [43]					
Grass	**Trop Kick**	173 Tsareena [1, EV]					
Normal	**Trump Card**	123 Eevee [45]	165 Kangaskhan [E]	301 Magearna [97]	260 Shellos [E]	039 Slowking [49]	
Bug	**Twineedle**	115 Shellder [E]	022 Spinarak [E]	225 Togedemaru [E]			
Dragon	**Twister**	117 Bagon [E]	282 Dragonair [1, 11]	283 Dragonite [1, 11]	244 Drampa [5]	281 Dratini [11]	238 Gible [E]
		092 Gyarados [74]	156 Milotic [14]	040 Wingull [E]			
Normal	**Uproar**	015 Alolan Rattata [E]	269 Exeggcute [1]	237 Flygon [40]	165 Kangaskhan [E]	010 Pikipek [E]	232 Sandile [E]
		073 Spearow [E]	105 Spinda [37]	254 Vanillish [1, 10]	255 Vanillite [10]	257 Vanilluxe [1, 10]	236 Vibrava [40]
Bug	**U-turn (TM89)**	045 Alolan Meowth [TM]	046 Alolan Persian [TM]	016 Alolan Raticate [TM]	015 Alolan Rattata [TM]	192 Archen [41, TM]	193 Archeops [45, TM]
		076 Braviary [TM]	019 Butterfree [TM]	174 Comfey [TM]	070 Crobat [TM]	083 Cutiefly [TM]	003 Decidueye [1, TM]
		274 Emolga [TM]	074 Fearow [TM]	108 Finneon [42, TM]	159 Fletchinder [TM]	158 Fletchling [TM]	237 Flygon [TM]
		069 Golbat [TM]	014 Gumshoos [TM]	006 Incineroar [TM]	222 Komala [TM]	021 Ledian [TM]	020 Ledyba [TM]
		004 Litten [TM]	109 Lumineon [48, TM]	078 Mandibuzz [TM]	079 Mankey [TM]	140 Masquerain [TM]	213 Minior [TM]
		082 Oricorio [TM]	177 Passimian [TM]	041 Pelipper [TM]	295 Pheromosa [TM]	010 Pikipek [TM]	080 Primeape [TM]
		084 Ribombee [TM]	075 Rufflet [TM]	276 Scizor [TM]	275 Scyther [TM]	204 Silvally [TM]	073 Spearow [TM]
		160 Talonflame [TM]	285 Tapu Koko [TM]	225 Togedemaru [TM]	005 Torracat [TM]	012 Toucannon [TM]	011 Trumbeak [TM]
		173 Tsareena [TM]	203 Type: Null [TM]	236 Vibrava [TM]	077 Vullaby [TM]	088 Whimsicott [TM]	040 Wingull [TM]
		110 Wishiwashi [TM]	013 Yungoos [TM]	068 Zubat [TM]			
Fighting	**Vacuum Wave**	298 Kartana [1]	279 Riolu [E]	275 Scyther [1]			
	Venom Drench	051 Alolan Muk [1, EV]	023 Ariados [1]	113 Mareanie [41]	293 Nihilego [53]	196 Phantump [E]	200 Pyukumuku [E]
		161 Salandit [45]	162 Salazzle [51]	114 Toxapex [44]	068 Zubat [E]		
Poison	**Venoshock (TM09)**	050 Alolan Grimer [TM]	051 Alolan Muk [TM]	016 Alolan Raticate [TM]	023 Ariados [TM]	243 Bruxish [TM]	019 Butterfree [TM]
		070 Crobat [43, TM]	207 Garbodor [TM]	061 Gastly [TM]	063 Gengar [TM]	069 Golbat [43, TM]	183 Golisopod [TM]
		062 Haunter [TM]	113 Mareanie [25, TM]	293 Nihilego [23, TM]	147 Paras [TM]	148 Parasect [TM]	161 Salandit [37, TM]
		162 Salazzle [39, TM]	276 Scizor [TM]	022 Spinarak [TM]	106 Tentacool [TM]	107 Tentacruel [TM]	114 Toxapex [25, TM]
		206 Trubbish [TM]	224 Turtonator [TM]	068 Zubat [37, TM]			
Normal	**Vice Grip**	028 Charjabug [1]	027 Grubbin [1]	175 Pinsir [1]	029 Vikavolt [1]		
Grass	**Vine Whip**	174 Comfey [1]					
Fighting	**Vital Throw**	294 Buzzwole [19]	057 Hariyama [22]	097 Machamp [25]	096 Machoke [25]	095 Machop [25]	056 Makuhita [22]
		220 Pancham [27]	221 Pangoro [27]	177 Passimian [E]	175 Pinsir [18]		
Electric	**Volt Switch (TM72)**	229 Alolan Geodude [TM]	231 Alolan Golem [TM]	230 Alolan Graveler [TM]	026 Alolan Raichu [TM]	028 Charjabug [TM]	201 Chinchou [TM]
		227 Electabuzz [TM]	228 Electivire [TM]	226 Elekid [TM]	274 Emolga [42, TM]	027 Grubbin [TM]	125 Jolteon [TM]
		202 Lanturn [TM]	301 Magearna [TM]	047 Magnemite [TM]	048 Magneton [TM]	049 Magnezone [TM]	198 Nosepass [TM]
		024 Pichu [TM]	025 Pikachu [TM]	199 Probopass [TM]	285 Tapu Koko [TM]	225 Togedemaru [TM]	029 Vikavolt [TM]
		296 Xurkitree [TM]					
	Volt Tackle	024 Pichu [E] ♦	025 Pikachu [T]				
Fighting	**Wake-Up Slap**	157 Alomomola [29]	211 Clefairy [22]	248 Froslass [37]	057 Hariyama [38]	135 Jigglypuff [27]	097 Machamp [27]
		096 Machoke [27]	095 Machop [27]	056 Makuhita [34, E]	138 Miltank [50]	149 Poliwag [35]	150 Poliwhirl [43]
		291 Solgaleo [1]					
Water	**Water Gun**	093 Barboach [9]	008 Brionne [1]	243 Bruxish [1]	195 Carracosta [1]	181 Castform [10]	201 Chinchou [12]
		108 Finneon [6]	090 Golduck [1, 7]	202 Lanturn [12]	268 Lapras [1]	109 Lumineon [1, 6]	111 Luvdisc [4]
		156 Milotic [1]	041 Pelipper [1]	149 Poliwag [5]	150 Poliwhirl [1, 5]	007 Popplio [1]	009 Primarina [1]
		089 Psyduck [7]	262 Relicanth [1, 10]	115 Shellder [1]	038 Slowbro [9]	039 Slowking [9]	037 Slowpoke [9]
		185 Starmie [1]	184 Staryu [4]	288 Tapu Fini [1]	194 Tirtouga [1]	124 Vaporeon [1, EV]	266 Wailmer [7]
		267 Wailord [1, 7]	094 Whiscash [1, 9]	040 Wingull [1]	110 Wishiwashi [1]		
	Water Pledge	008 Brionne [T]	007 Popplio [T]	009 Primarina [T]			

♦ For Pichu to inherit the Egg Move Volt Tackle, one of the Pokémon you leave at the Pokémon Nursery must be holding a Light Ball. You can find a Light Ball in Resolution Cave's interior, and wild Pikachu are sometimes found holding them.

Type	Move Name	Pokémon					
Water	Water Pulse	157 Alomomola [25]	093 Barboach [17]	243 Bruxish [E]	201 Chinchou [E]	112 Corsola [E]	281 Dratini [E]
		108 Finneon [22]	261 Gastrodon [1, 7]	153 Goldeen [16]	090 Golduck [16]	268 Lapras [14]	109 Lumineon [22]
		111 Luvdisc [17]	156 Milotic [1, EV]	041 Pelipper [15]	149 Poliwag [E]	089 Psyduck [16]	154 Seaking [16]
		115 Shellder [E]	260 Shellos [7]	038 Slowbro [28]	039 Slowking [28]	037 Slowpoke [28]	105 Spinda [E]
		288 Tapu Fini [8]	106 Tentacool [16]	107 Tentacruel [16]	194 Tirtouga [E]	255 Vanillite [E]	124 Vaporeon [17]
		266 Wailmer [19]	267 Wailord [19]	094 Whiscash [17]	040 Wingull [15]	110 Wishiwashi [E]	
	Water Sport	157 Alomomola [1]	093 Barboach [6]	141 Dewpider [1]	153 Goldeen [1]	090 Golduck [1]	111 Luvdisc [E]
		140 Masquerain [1, 14]	156 Milotic [1, 4]	041 Pelipper [1]	149 Poliwag [1, E]	150 Poliwhirl [1]	089 Psyduck [1]
		200 Pyukumuku [1]	262 Relicanth [E]	154 Seaking [1]	139 Surskit [14]	094 Whiscash [1, 6]	040 Wingull [E]
		110 Wishiwashi [E]					
	Water Spout	266 Wailmer [33]	267 Wailord [33]				
	Waterfall (TM98)	157 Alomomola [TM]	142 Araquanid [TM]	093 Barboach [TM]	008 Brionne [TM]	243 Bruxish [TM]	195 Carracosta [TM]
		264 Carvanha [TM]	201 Chinchou [TM]	141 Dewpider [TM]	282 Dragonair [TM]	283 Dragonite [TM]	281 Dratini [TM]
		155 Feebas [TM]	108 Finneon [TM]	261 Gastrodon [TM]	153 Goldeen [32, TM]	090 Golduck [TM]	183 Golisopod [TM]
		092 Gyarados [TM]	202 Lanturn [TM]	268 Lapras [TM]	109 Lumineon [TM]	111 Luvdisc [TM]	156 Milotic [TM]
		152 Politoed [TM]	149 Poliwag [TM]	150 Poliwhirl [TM]	151 Poliwrath [TM]	007 Popplio [TM]	009 Primarina [TM]
		089 Psyduck [TM]	262 Relicanth [TM]	154 Seaking [32, TM]	265 Sharpedo [TM]	185 Starmie [TM]	184 Staryu [TM]
		288 Tapu Fini [TM]	106 Tentacool [TM]	107 Tentacruel [TM]	194 Tirtouga [TM]	124 Vaporeon [TM]	266 Wailmer [TM]
		267 Wailord [TM]	094 Whiscash [TM]	182 Wimpod [TM]	110 Wishiwashi [TM]		
Normal	Weather Ball	181 Castform [25]	064 Drifloon [E]	143 Fomantis [E]	246 Snorunt [E]	257 Vanilluxe [1]	
Water	Whirlpool	157 Alomomola [49]	093 Barboach [E]	201 Chinchou [E]	263 Dhelmise [27]	108 Finneon [38]	268 Lapras [E]
		109 Lumineon [42]	115 Shellder [40]	288 Tapu Fini [14]	194 Tirtouga [E]	266 Wailmer [13]	267 Wailord [13]
Normal	Whirlwind	284 Aerodactyl [E]	076 Braviary [1, 57]	019 Butterfree [29]	188 Cranidos [E]	057 Hariyama [16]	056 Makuhita [16]
		078 Mandibuzz [1, 57]	140 Masquerain [1, 48]	035 Munchlax [E]	277 Murkrow [E]	075 Rufflet [55]	208 Skarmory [E]
		036 Snorlax [E]	073 Spearow [E]	287 Tapu Bulu [1]	077 Vullaby [55]	068 Zubat [E]	
Rock	Wide Guard	284 Aerodactyl [E]	229 Alolan Geodude [E]	157 Alomomola [1, 61]	142 Araquanid [1]	195 Carracosta [25]	297 Celesteela [1]
		059 Crabrawler [E]	299 Guzzlord [1]	292 Lunala [67]	097 Machamp [1]	056 Makuhita [E]	113 Mareanie [17]
		198 Nosepass [E]	147 Paras [E]	199 Probopass [1]	098 Roggenrola [E]	190 Shieldon [E]	291 Solgaleo [67]
		169 Stufful [E]	194 Tirtouga [25]	114 Toxapex [17]	224 Turtonator [E]	182 Wimpod [E]	040 Wingull [E]
Electric	Wild Charge (TM93)	231 Alolan Golem [TM]	026 Alolan Raichu [TM]	053 Arcanine [TM]	034 Blissey [TM]	033 Chansey [TM]	028 Charjabug [TM]
		201 Chinchou [TM]	227 Electabuzz [TM]	228 Electivire [TM]	226 Elekid [TM]	274 Emolga [TM]	259 Granbull [TM]
		052 Growlithe [TM]	027 Grubbin [TM]	121 Herdier [TM]	134 Igglybuff [TM]	135 Jigglypuff [TM]	125 Jolteon [TM]
		202 Lanturn [TM]	120 Lillipup [TM]	047 Magnemite [TM]	048 Magneton [TM]	049 Magnezone [TM]	024 Pichu [TM]
		025 Pikachu [50, TM]	036 Snorlax [TM]	258 Snubbull [TM]	291 Solgaleo [TM]	105 Spinda [TM]	122 Stoutland [TM]
		285 Tapu Koko [32, TM]	137 Tauros [TM]	225 Togedemaru [41, TM]	029 Vikavolt [TM]	136 Wigglytuff [TM]	296 Xurkitree [TM]
Fire	Will-O-Wisp (TM61)	245 Absol [TM]	164 Alolan Marowak [23, TM]	053 Arcanine [TM]	065 Drifblim [TM]	064 Drifloon [TM]	126 Flareon [TM]
		159 Fletchinder [TM]	248 Froslass [28, TM]	061 Gastly [TM]	063 Gengar [TM]	052 Growlithe [TM]	062 Haunter [TM]
		006 Incineroar [TM]	004 Litten [TM]	292 Lunala [TM]	166 Magby [TM]	167 Magmar [TM]	168 Magmortar [TM]
		242 Mimikyu [TM]	066 Misdreavus [TM]	067 Mismagius [TM]	196 Phantump [31, TM]	102 Sableye [TM]	161 Salandit [TM]
		162 Salazzle [TM]	160 Talonflame [TM]	223 Torkoal [TM]	005 Torracat [TM]	197 Trevenant [31, TM]	224 Turtonator [TM]
Flying	Wing Attack	284 Aerodactyl [1]	192 Archen [1]	193 Archeops [1]	076 Braviary [1, 10]	070 Crobat [13]	283 Dragonite [1, EV]
		069 Golbat [13]	278 Honchkrow [1]	277 Murkrow [15, E]	041 Pelipper [1, 8]	075 Rufflet [10]	275 Scyther [21]
		040 Wingull [8]	068 Zubat [13]				
Normal	Wish	157 Alomomola [37]	210 Cleffa [E]	123 Eevee [E]	134 Igglybuff [E]	222 Komala [E]	024 Pichu [E]
		105 Spinda [E]	225 Togedemaru [E]				
Water	Withdraw	195 Carracosta [1]	116 Cloyster [1]	115 Shellder [4]	038 Slowbro [1, EV]	287 Tapu Bulu [1]	288 Tapu Fini [1]
		285 Tapu Koko [1]	286 Tapu Lele [1]	194 Tirtouga [1]	223 Torkoal [7]		
Psychic	Wonder Room	090 Golduck [51]	066 Misdreavus [E]	293 Nihilego [67]	176 Oranguru [E]	007 Popplio [E]	089 Psyduck [43]
		037 Slowpoke [E]					
Grass	Wood Hammer	270 Alolan Exeggutor [37]	222 Komala [41]	242 Mimikyu [1]	196 Phantump [49]	031 Sudowoodo [1]	287 Tapu Bulu [1]
		197 Trevenant [49]					
Normal	Work Up (TM01)	071 Alolan Diglett [TM]	072 Alolan Dugtrio [TM]	045 Alolan Meowth [TM]	046 Alolan Persian [TM]	251 Alolan Sandshrew [TM]	252 Alolan Sandslash [TM]
		170 Bewear [TM]	034 Blissey [TM]	076 Braviary [TM]	008 Brionne [TM]	294 Buzzwole [TM]	181 Castform [TM]
		033 Chansey [TM]	212 Clefable [TM]	211 Clefairy [TM]	210 Cleffa [TM]	060 Crabominable [TM]	059 Crabrawler [TM]
		002 Dartrix [TM]	003 Decidueye [TM]	244 Drampa [TM]	123 Eevee [TM]	127 Espeon [TM]	074 Fearow [TM]
		126 Flareon [TM]	159 Fletchinder [TM]	158 Fletchling [TM]	130 Glaceon [TM]	259 Granbull [TM]	014 Gumshoos [TM]
		272 Hakamo-o [29, TM]	032 Happiny [TM]	057 Hariyama [TM]	121 Herdier [20, TM]	134 Igglybuff [TM]	006 Incineroar [TM]
		271 Jangmo-o [29, TM]	135 Jigglypuff [TM]	125 Jolteon [TM]	165 Kangaskhan [TM]	222 Komala [TM]	273 Kommo-o [29, TM]
		129 Leafeon [TM]	120 Lillipup [19, TM]	004 Litten [E]	280 Lucario [42, TM]	292 Lunala [TM]	097 Machamp [TM]
		096 Machoke [TM]	095 Machop [TM]	056 Makuhita [TM]	079 Mankey [TM]	138 Miltank [TM]	242 Mimikyu [TM]

Type	Move Name	Pokémon					
Normal	Work Up (TM01)	035 Munchlax [TM]	176 Oranguru [TM]	082 Oricorio [TM]	220 Pancham [10, TM]	221 Pangoro [1, 10, TM]	177 Passimian [TM]
		010 Pikipek [TM]	151 Poliwrath [TM]	007 Popplio [TM]	009 Primarina [TM]	080 Primeape [TM]	279 Riolu [TM]
		001 Rowlet [TM]	075 Rufflet [TM]	204 Silvally [TM]	036 Snorlax [TM]	250 Snubbull [TM]	291 Solgaleo [TM]
		073 Spearow [TM]	105 Spinda [TM]	122 Stoutland [20, TM]	169 Stufful [TM]	131 Sylveon [TM]	160 Talonflame [TM]
		287 Tapu Bulu [TM]	285 Tapu Koko [TM]	137 Tauros [29, TM]	225 Togedemaru [TM]	005 Torracat [TM]	012 Toucannon [TM]
		011 Trumbeak [TM]	224 Turtonator [TM]	203 Type: Null [TM]	128 Umbreon [TM]	124 Vaporeon [TM]	136 Wigglytuff [TM]
		013 Yungoos [TM]					
Grass	Worry Seed	087 Cottonee [E]	269 Exeggcute [33]	085 Petilil [E]			
Normal	Wrap	174 Comfey [16]	263 Dhelmise [9]	282 Dragonair [1]	283 Dragonite [1]	281 Dratini [1]	156 Milotic [1]
		106 Tentacool [10]	107 Tentacruel [10]	296 Xurkitree [1]			
	Wring Out	299 Guzzlord [67]	300 Necrozma [67]	106 Tentacool [49]	107 Tentacruel [1, 56]		
Bug	X-Scissor (TM81)	245 Absol [TM]	251 Alolan Sandshrew [TM]	252 Alolan Sandslash [TM]	142 Araquanid [TM]	023 Ariados [TM]	028 Charjabug [31, TM]
		070 Crobat [TM]	141 Dewpider [TM]	143 Fomantis [TM]	183 Golisopod [TM]	027 Grubbin [25, TM]	272 Hakamo-o [TM]
		271 Jangmo-o [TM]	298 Kartana [47, TM]	273 Kommo-o [TM]	129 Leafeon [TM]	144 Lurantis [1, TM]	242 Mimikyu [TM]
		300 Necrozma [TM]	221 Pangoro [TM]	147 Paras [54, TM]	148 Parasect [66, TM]	175 Pinsir [29, TM]	276 Scizor [41, TM]
		275 Scyther [41, TM]	204 Silvally [35, TM]	208 Skarmory [TM]	249 Sneasel [TM]	022 Spinarak [TM]	197 Trevenant [TM]
		203 Type: Null [35, TM]	029 Vikavolt [TM]	250 Weavile [TM]			
Normal	Yawn	123 Eevee [E]	014 Gumshoos [47]	222 Komala [16]	120 Lillipup [E]	089 Psyduck [E]	262 Relicanth [35]
		260 Shellos [E]	038 Slowbro [1]	039 Slowking [1]	037 Slowpoke [1]	036 Snorlax [20]	223 Torkoal [E]
		013 Yungoos [40]					
Electric	Zap Cannon	047 Magnemite [49]	048 Magneton [1, 63]	049 Magnezone [1, 63]	198 Nosepass [43]	217 Porygon [62]	218 Porygon2 [1, 62]
		219 Porygon-Z [1, 62]	199 Probopass [43]	029 Vikavolt [41]	296 Xurkitree [73]		
Psychic	Zen Headbutt	245 Absol [E]	117 Bagon [34]	188 Cranidos [37]	054 Drowzee [41]	090 Golduck [25]	055 Hypno [41]
		216 Metagross [32]	215 Metang [32]	138 Miltank [29]	035 Munchlax [E]	176 Oranguru [29]	089 Psyduck [25]
		189 Rampardos [43]	262 Relicanth [E]	102 Sableye [34]	119 Salamence [35]	118 Shelgon [35]	038 Slowbro [32]
		039 Slowking [32]	037 Slowpoke [32, E]	291 Solgaleo [19]	287 Tapu Bulu [48]	137 Tauros [35]	266 Wailmer [E]
		094 Whiscash [1]	068 Zubat [E]				
Electric	Zing Zap	225 Togedemaru [33]					

Pokémon Abilities Reverse Lookup

If you are looking for a Pokémon with a particular Ability in Alola, you have turned to the right pages! These lists contain all of the Pokémon you must obtain to complete the Alola Pokédex, sorted by Ability. Remember that Pokémon species can have two normal Abilities, as well as a Hidden Ability, so you may see the same Pokémon listed multiple times in these lists.

ALOLA REGION POKÉDEX

HOW TO COMPLETE THE ALOLA POKÉDEX

CHAMPION'S GUIDE TO ALOLA

ADVENTURE DATA

Adaptability
123 Eevee
155 Feebas
014 Gumshoos
280 Mega Lucario
219 Porygon-Z
013 Yungoos

Aerilate
175 Mega Pinsir
119 Mega Salamence

Aftermath
065 Drifblim
064 Drifloon
207 Garbodor
206 Trubbish

Analytic
047 Magnemite
048 Magneton
049 Magnezone
217 Porygon
218 Porygon2
219 Porygon-Z
185 Starmie
184 Staryu

Anger Point
060 Crabominable
059 Crabrawler
233 Krokorok
234 Krookodile
079 Mankey
080 Primeape
232 Sandile
137 Tauros

Anticipation
093 Barboach
123 Eevee
094 Whiscash

Arena Trap
235 Trapinch

Aura Break
205 Zygarde

Battery
028 Charjabug

Battle Armor
163 Cubone
203 Type: Null

Beast Boost
294 Buzzwole
297 Celesteela
299 Guzzlord
298 Kartana
293 Nihilego
295 Pheromosa
296 Xurkitree

Berserk
244 Drampa

Big Pecks
158 Fletchling
078 Mandibuzz
077 Vullaby

Blaze
006 Incineroar
004 Litten
005 Torracat

Bulletproof
272 Hakamo-o
271 Jangmo-o
273 Kommo-o

Chlorophyll
087 Cottonee
269 Exeggcute
129 Leafeon
086 Lilligant
085 Petilil
088 Whimsicott

Clear Body
214 Beldum
101 Carbink
216 Metagross
215 Metang
106 Tentacool
107 Tentacruel

Cloud Nine
244 Drampa
090 Golduck
089 Psyduck

Comatose
222 Komala

Competitive
134 Igglybuff
135 Jigglypuff
156 Milotic
136 Wigglytuff

Compound Eyes
019 Butterfree

Contrary
143 Fomantis
144 Lurantis
105 Spinda

Corrosion
161 Salandit
162 Salazzle

Cursed Body
164 Alolan Marowak
248 Froslass
063 Gengar

Cute Charm
212 Clefable
211 Clefairy
210 Cleffa
134 Igglybuff
135 Jigglypuff
156 Milotic
169 Stufful
131 Sylveon
136 Wigglytuff

Damp
090 Golduck
147 Paras
148 Parasect
152 Politoed
149 Poliwag
150 Poliwhirl
151 Poliwrath
089 Psyduck

Dancer
082 Oricorio

Dazzling
243 Bruxish

Defeatist
192 Archen
193 Archeops

Defiant
076 Braviary
079 Mankey
080 Primeape

Disguise
242 Mimikyu

Download
217 Porygon
218 Porygon2
219 Porygon-Z

Drizzle
041 Pelipper
152 Politoed

Drought
223 Torkoal

Dry Skin
147 Paras
148 Parasect

Early Bird
165 Kangaskhan

Effect Spore
145 Morelull
147 Paras
148 Parasect
146 Shiinotic

Electric Surge
285 Tapu Koko

Emergency Exit
183 Golisopod

Flame Body
159 Fletchinder
166 Magby
167 Magmar
168 Magmortar
160 Talonflame

Flare Boost
065 Drifblim
064 Drifloon

Flash Fire
053 Arcanine
126 Flareon
052 Growlithe

Flower Veil
174 Comfey

Fluffy
170 Bewear
169 Stufful

Forecast
181 Castform

Forewarn
054 Drowzee
055 Hypno

Friend Guard
211 Clefairy
210 Cleffa
032 Happiny
134 Igglybuff
135 Jigglypuff

Frisk
270 Alolan Exeggutor
196 Phantump
197 Trevenant
136 Wigglytuff

Full Metal Body
291 Solgaleo

Fur Coat
046 Alolan Persian

Gale Wings
159 Fletchinder
158 Fletchling
160 Talonflame

Galvanize
229 Alolan Geodude
231 Alolan Golem
230 Alolan Graveler
235 Trapinch

Gluttony
050 Alolan Grimer
051 Alolan Muk
016 Alolan Raticate
015 Alolan Rattata
035 Munchlax
036 Snorlax

Gooey
180 Goodra
178 Goomy
179 Sliggoo

Grassy Surge
287 Tapu Bulu

Guts
126 Flareon
057 Hariyama
097 Machamp
096 Machoke
095 Machop
056 Makuhita

Harvest
270 Alolan Exeggutor
269 Exeggcute
196 Phantump
197 Trevenant

Healer
157 Alomomola
034 Blissey
033 Chansey

Honey Gather
083 Cutiefly
084 Ribombee

Hustle
016 Alolan Raticate
015 Alolan Rattata
112 Corsola
081 Delibird
075 Rufflet

Hydration
157 Alomomola
093 Barboach
180 Goodra
178 Goomy
268 Lapras
111 Luvdisc
179 Sliggoo
124 Vaporeon
094 Whiscash
040 Wingull

Hyper Cutter
060 Crabominable
059 Crabrawler
175 Pinsir
235 Trapinch

Ice Body
130 Glaceon
247 Glalie
246 Snorunt
256 Vanillish
255 Vanillite
257 Vanilluxe

Illuminate
201 Chinchou
202 Lanturn
145 Morelull
146 Shiinotic
185 Starmie
184 Staryu

Immunity
036 Snorlax

Imposter
209 Ditto

Infiltrator
087 Cottonee
070 Crobat
069 Golbat
088 Whimsicott
068 Zubat

Innards Out
200 Pyukumuku

Inner Focus
042 Abra
044 Alakazam
070 Crobat
054 Drowzee
247 Glalie
069 Golbat
055 Hypno
043 Kadabra
165 Kangaskhan
280 Lucario
132 Mudbray
133 Mudsdale
176 Oranguru
279 Riolu
249 Sneasel
246 Snorunt
128 Umbreon
068 Zubat

Insomnia
023 Ariados
081 Delibird
054 Drowzee
278 Honchkrow
055 Hypno
277 Murkrow
022 Spinarak

Intimidate
053 Arcanine
259 Granbull
052 Growlithe
092 Gyarados
121 Herdier
233 Krokorok
234 Krookodile
140 Masquerain
119 Salamence
232 Sandile
258 Snubbull
122 Stoutland
137 Tauros

Iron Barbs
225 Togedemaru

Iron Fist
060 Crabominable
059 Crabrawler
021 Ledian
220 Pancham
221 Pangoro

Justified
245 Absol
053 Arcanine
052 Growlithe
280 Lucario

Keen Eye
076 Braviary
074 Fearow
104 Lycanroc (Midday Form)
104 Lycanroc (Midnight Form)
041 Pelipper
010 Pikipek
103 Rockruff
075 Rufflet
102 Sableye
208 Skarmory
249 Sneasel
073 Spearow
012 Toucannon
011 Trumbeak
040 Wingull

Klutz
170 Bewear
169 Stufful

Leaf Guard
171 Bounsweet
143 Fomantis
129 Leafeon
086 Lilligant
144 Lurantis
085 Petilil
172 Steenee
173 Tsareena

Levitate
237 Flygon
061 Gastly
062 Haunter
066 Misdreavus
067 Mismagius
236 Vibrava
029 Vikavolt

Light Metal
214 Beldum
216 Metagross
215 Metang
276 Scizor

Lightning Rod
164 Alolan Marowak
163 Cubone
153 Goldeen
024 Pichu
025 Pikachu
154 Seaking
225 Togedemaru

Limber
209 Ditto
113 Mareanie
114 Toxapex

Liquid Ooze
106 Tentacool
107 Tentacruel

Magic Bounce
127 Espeon
245 Mega Absol
102 Mega Sableye

Magic Guard
042 Abra
44 Alakazam
212 Clefable
211 Clefairy
210 Cleffa
043 Kadabra

Magician
241 Klefki

Magnet Pull
229 Alolan Geodude
231 Alolan Golem
230 Alolan Graveler
047 Magnemite
048 Magneton
049 Magnezone
198 Nosepass
199 Probopass

Marvel Scale
282 Dragonair
281 Dratini
156 Milotic

Merciless
113 Mareanie
114 Toxapex

Misty Surge
288 Tapu Fini

Mold Breaker
188 Cranidos
092 Mega Gyarados
220 Pancham
221 Pangoro
175 Pinsir
189 Rampardos

Moody
247 Glalie
058 Smeargle
246 Snorunt

Motor Drive
228 Electivire
274 Emolga

Moxie
092 Gyarados
278 Honchkrow
233 Krokorok
234 Krookodile
175 Pinsir
119 Salamence
232 Sandile

Multiscale
283 Dragonite

Natural Cure
034 Blissey
033 Chansey
174 Comfey
112 Corsola
032 Happiny
196 Phantump
185 Starmie
184 Staryu
197 Trevenant

No Guard
104 Lycanroc (Midnight Form)
097 Machamp
096 Machoke
095 Machop

Oblivious
093 Barboach
266 Wailmer
171 Bounsweet
155 Feebas
161 Salandit
162 Salazzle
038 Slowbro
039 Slowking
037 Slowpoke
172 Steenee
266 Wailmer
267 Wailord
094 Whiscash

Overcoat
116 Cloyster
272 Hakamo-o
271 Jangmo-o
273 Kommo-o
078 Mandibuzz
118 Shelgon
115 Shellder
077 Vullaby

Overgrow
002 Dartrix
003 Decidueye
001 Rowlet

Own Tempo
086 Lilligant
132 Mudbray
133 Mudsdale
085 Petilil
038 Slowbro
039 Slowking
037 Slowpoke
058 Smeargle
105 Spinda

Receiver
177 Passimian

Refrigerate
247 Mega Glalie

Parental Bond
165 Mega Kangaskhan

Pickpocket
249 Sneasel
250 Weavile

Pickup
045 Alolan Meowth
120 Lillipup
035 Munchlax
010 Pikipek
011 Trumbeak

Pixilate
131 Sylveon

Poison Touch
050 Alolan Grimer
051 Alolan Muk

Power Construct
205 Zygarde

Power of Alchemy
050 Alolan Grimer
051 Alolan Muk

Prankster
087 Cottonee
241 Klefki
277 Murkrow
279 Riolu
102 Sableye
088 Whimsicott

Pressure
245 Absol
284 Aerodactyl
266 Wailmer
267 Wailord
250 Weavile

Prism Armor
300 Necrozma

Psychic Surge
286 Tapu Lele

Queenly Majesty
173 Tsareena

Quick Feet
259 Granbull
125 Jolteon

Rain Dish
145 Morelull
041 Pelipper
146 Shiinotic
139 Surskit
106 Tentacool
107 Tentacruel
040 Wingull

Rattled
045 Alolan Meowth
046 Alolan Persian
030 Bonsly
259 Granbull
020 Ledyba
091 Magikarp
258 Snubbull
031 Sudowoodo

Receiver
177 Passimian

Regenerator
157 Alomomola
112 Corsola
113 Mareanie
038 Slowbro
039 Slowking
037 Slowpoke
114 Toxapex

RKS System
204 Silvally

Rock Head
284 Aerodactyl
164 Alolan Marowak
117 Bagon
030 Bonsly
163 Cubone
262 Relicanth
118 Shelgon
031 Sudowoodo

Rough Skin
264 Carvanha
239 Gabite
240 Garchomp
238 Gible
265 Sharpedo

Run Away
017 Caterpie
123 Eevee
120 Lillipup
258 Snubbull

Sand Force
071 Alolan Diglett
072 Alolan Dugtrio
099 Boldore
261 Gastrodon
100 Gigalith
240 Mega Garchomp
198 Nosepass
199 Probopass
098 Roggenrola
260 Shellos

Sand Rush
121 Herdier
104 Lycanroc (Midday Form)
115 Shellder
122 Stoutland

Sand Stream
100 Gigalith

Sand Veil
071 Alolan Diglett
072 Alolan Dugtrio
239 Gabite
240 Garchomp
238 Gible
187 Palossand
186 Sandygast

Sap Sipper
244 Drampa
180 Goodra
178 Goomy
138 Miltank
179 Sliggoo

Schooling
110 Wishiwashi

Scrappy
121 Herdier
165 Kangaskhan
138 Miltank
220 Pancham
221 Pangoro
122 Stoutland

Serene Grace
034 Blissey
033 Chansey
032 Happiny
114 Toxapex

Shadow Shield
292 Lunala

Shadow Tag
063 Mega Gengar

Shed Skin
282 Dragonair
281 Dratini
018 Metapod

Sheer Force
117 Bagon
076 Braviary
188 Cranidos
057 Hariyama
056 Makuhita
189 Rampardos
075 Rufflet
137 Tauros
012 Toucannon
235 Trapinch

Shell Armor
116 Cloyster
268 Lapras
120 Lillipup
038 Mega Slowbro
115 Shellder
223 Torkoal
224 Turtonator

Shield Dust
017 Caterpie
083 Cutiefly
084 Ribombee

Shields Down
213 Minior

Skill Link
116 Cloyster
010 Pikipek
115 Shellder
012 Toucannon
011 Trumbeak

Slush Rush
251 Alolan Sandshrew
252 Alolan Sandslash

Sniper
023 Ariados
074 Fearow
073 Spearow
022 Spinarak

Snow Cloak
254 Alolan Ninetales
251 Alolan Sandshrew
252 Alolan Sandslash
253 Alolan Vulpix
248 Froslass
130 Glaceon
256 Vanillish
255 Vanillite

Snow Warning
254 Alolan Ninetales
253 Alolan Vulpix
257 Vanilluxe

Solid Rock
195 Carracosta
194 Tirtouga

Soul-Heart
301 Magearna

Soundproof
191 Bastiodon
272 Hakamo-o
271 Jangmo-o
273 Kommo-o
190 Shieldon

Speed Boost
264 Carvanha
265 Sharpedo

Stakeout
014 Gumshoos
013 Yungoos

Stall
102 Sableye

Stamina
132 Mudbray
133 Mudsdale

Static
227 Electabuzz
226 Elekid
274 Emolga
024 Pichu
025 Pikachu

Steadfast
280 Lucario
104 Lycanroc (Midday Form)
097 Machamp
096 Machoke
095 Machop
279 Riolu
103 Rockruff
275 Scyther

Steelworker
263 Dhelmise

Stench
206 Trubbish
207 Garbodor

Sticky Hold
261 Gastrodon
260 Shellos
206 Trubbish

Storm Drain
108 Finneon
261 Gastrodon
109 Lumineon
260 Shellos

Strong Jaw
243 Bruxish
014 Gumshoos
265 Mega Sharpedo
013 Yungoos

Sturdy
229 Alolan Geodude
231 Alolan Golem
230 Alolan Graveler
191 Bastiodon
099 Boldore
030 Bonsly
101 Carbink
195 Carracosta
290 Cosmoem
100 Gigalith
047 Magnemite
048 Magneton
049 Magnezone
198 Nosepass
199 Probopass
262 Relicanth
008 Roggenrola
190 Shieldon
208 Skarmory
031 Sudowoodo
194 Tirtouga
225 Togedemaru

Super Luck
245 Absol
278 Honchkrow
277 Murkrow

Surge Surfer
026 Alolan Raichu

Swarm
023 Ariados
027 Grubbin
021 Ledian
020 Ledyba
276 Scizor
275 Scyther
022 Spinarak

Sweet Veil
171 Bounsweet
083 Cutiefly
084 Ribombee
172 Steenee
173 Tsareena

Swift Swim
195 Carracosta
155 Feebas
108 Finneon
153 Goldeen
090 Golduck
109 Lumineon
111 Luvdisc
091 Magikarp
149 Poliwag
150 Poliwhirl
151 Poliwrath
089 Psyduck
262 Relicanth
154 Seaking
139 Surskit
194 Tirtouga

Synchronize
042 Abra
044 Alakazam
127 Espeon
043 Kadabra
128 Umbreon

Tangled Feet
105 Spinda

Tangling Hair
071 Alolan Diglett
072 Alolan Dugtrio

Technician
045 Alolan Meowth
046 Alolan Persian
276 Mega Scizor
276 Scizor
275 Scyther
058 Smeargle

Telepathy
176 Oranguru

Thick Fat
016 Alolan Raticate
015 Alolan Rattata
057 Hariyama
056 Makuhita
138 Miltank
035 Munchlax
036 Snorlax

Tinted Lens
019 Butterfree

Torrent
008 Brionne
007 Popplio
009 Primarina

Tough Claws
284 Mega Aerodactyl
216 Mega Metagross

Trace
044 Mega Alakazam
217 Porygon
218 Porygon2

Triage
174 Comfey

Unaware
212 Clefable
289 Cosmog
200 Pyukumuku

Unburden
065 Drifblim
064 Drifloon

Unnerve
284 Aerodactyl
170 Bewear
140 Masquerain

Vital Spirit
081 Delibird
227 Electabuzz
228 Electivire
226 Elekid
120 Lillipup
104 Lycanroc (Midnight Form)
166 Magby
167 Magmar
168 Magmortar
079 Mankey
080 Primeape
103 Rockruff

Volt Absorb
201 Chinchou
125 Jolteon
202 Lanturn

Water Absorb
142 Araquanid
201 Chinchou
141 Dewpider
202 Lanturn
268 Lapras
152 Politoed
149 Poliwag
150 Poliwhirl
151 Poliwrath
124 Vaporeon

Water Bubble
142 Araquanid
141 Dewpider

Water Compaction
187 Palossand
186 Sandygast

Water Veil
108 Finneon
153 Goldeen
109 Lumineon
154 Seaking
266 Wailmer
267 Wailord

Weak Armor
099 Boldore
207 Garbodor
078 Mandibuzz
098 Roggenrola
208 Skarmory
256 Vanillish
255 Vanillite
257 Vanilluxe
077 Vullaby

White Smoke
223 Torkoal

Wimp Out
182 Wimpod

Wonder Skin
243 Bruxish

ALOLA REGION POKé-EX

HOW TO COMPLETE THE ALOLA POKéDEX

CHAMPION'S GUIDE TO ALOLA

ADVENTURE DATA

Pokémon Weakness Chart

These weakness charts provide you with a handy reference to check which move types a particular Pokémon is weak to when you are battling against it. It also tells you which move types the Pokémon may be immune to. Note that a Pokémon's Ability may affect how weak or resistant it is to certain move types. Look out for types highlighted in green or orange—these weaknesses and immunities may change depending on which Ability your opponent has!

Key to Tables

4× Pokémon has 4× weakness to this type. Any other weak types deal 2× damage.

* Ability increases resistance to certain move types, though it does not make the Pokémon entirely immune to them.

Ability grants immunity to a type (also marked in green). Pokémon without that Ability will not share this immunity.

Ability causes a weakness to a type (also marked in orange) that the Pokémon is not otherwise weak to.

Alola Dex No.	Pokémon	Type		Ability		Hidden Ability	Weak to these move types					Immune to these move types
042	Abra	Psychic		Synchronize	Inner Focus	Magic Guard	Bug	Ghost	Dark			
245	Absol	Dark		Pressure	Super Luck	Justified	Fighting	Bug	Fairy			Psychic
245	Absol (Mega Absol)	Dark		Magic Bounce			Fighting	Bug	Fairy			Psychic
284	Aerodactyl	Rock	Flying	Rock Head	Pressure	Unnerve	Water	Electric	Ice	Rock	Steel	Ground
284	Aerodactyl (Mega Aerodactyl)	Rock	Flying	Tough Claws			Water	Electric	Ice	Rock	Steel	Ground
044	Alakazam	Psychic		Synchronize	Inner Focus	Magic Guard	Bug	Ghost	Dark			
044	Alakazam (Mega Alakazam)	Psychic		Trace			Bug	Ghost	Dark			
157	Alomomola	Water		Healer	Hydration	Regenerator	Grass	Electric				
142	Araquanid	Water	Bug	Water Bubble*		Water Absorb	Electric	Flying	Rock			Water
053	Arcanine	Fire		Intimidate	Flash Fire	Justified	Water	Ground	Rock			Fire
192	Archen	Rock	Flying	Defeatist			Water	Electric	Ice	Rock	Steel	Ground
193	Archeops	Rock	Flying	Defeatist			Water	Electric	Ice	Rock	Steel	Ground
023	Ariados	Bug	Poison	Swarm	Insomnia	Sniper	Fire	Flying	Psychic	Rock		
117	Bagon	Dragon		Rock Head		Sheer Force	Ice	Dragon	Fairy			
093	Barboach	Water	Ground	Oblivious	Anticipation	Hydration	4×Grass					Electric
191	Bastiodon	Rock	Steel	Sturdy		Soundproof	4×Fighting	4×Ground	Water			Poison
214	Beldum	Steel	Psychic	Clear Body		Light Metal	Fire	Ground	Ghost	Dark		Poison
170	Bewear	Normal	Fighting	Fluffy	Klutz	Unnerve	Fire	Fighting	Flying	Psychic	Fairy	Ghost
034	Blissey	Normal		Natural Cure	Serene Grace	Healer	Fighting					Ghost
099	Boldore	Rock		Sturdy	Weak Armor	Sand Force	Water	Grass	Fighting	Ground	Steel	
030	Bonsly	Rock		Sturdy	Rock Head	Rattled	Water	Grass	Fighting	Ground	Steel	
171	Bounsweet	Grass		Leaf Guard	Oblivious	Sweet Veil	Fire	Ice	Poison	Flying	Bug	
076	Braviary	Normal	Flying	Keen Eye	Sheer Force	Defiant	Electric	Ice	Rock			Ground Ghost
008	Brionne	Water		Torrent			Grass	Electric				
243	Bruxish	Water	Psychic	Dazzling	Strong Jaw	Wonder Skin	Grass	Electric	Bug	Ghost	Dark	
019	Butterfree	Bug	Flying	Compound Eyes		Tinted Lens	4×Rock	Fire	Electric	Ice	Flying	Ground
294	Buzzwole	Bug	Fighting	Beast Boost			4×Flying	Fire	Psychic	Fairy		
101	Carbink	Rock	Fairy	Clear Body		Sturdy	4×Steel	Water	Grass	Ground		Dragon
195	Carracosta	Water	Rock	Solid Rock*	Sturdy	Swift Swim	4×Grass	Electric	Fighting	Ground		
264	Carvanha	Water	Dark	Rough Skin		Speed Boost	Grass	Electric	Fighting	Bug	Fairy	Psychic
181	Castform	Normal		Forecast			Fighting					Ghost
181	Castform (Rainy Form)	Water		Forecast			Grass	Electric				
181	Castform (Snowy Form)	Ice		Forecast			Fire	Fighting	Rock	Steel		
181	Castform (Sunny Form)	Fire		Forecast			Water	Ground	Rock			
017	Caterpie	Bug		Shield Dust		Run Away	Fire	Flying	Rock			
297	Celesteela	Steel	Flying	Beast Boost			Fire	Electric				Poison Ground
033	Chansey	Normal		Natural Cure	Serene Grace	Healer	Fighting					Ghost
028	Charjabug	Bug	Electric	Battery			Fire	Rock				
201	Chinchou	Water	Electric	Volt Absorb[1]	Illuminate	Water Absorb[2]	Grass	Ground				Water[2] Electric[1]
212	Clefable	Fairy		Cute Charm	Magic Guard	Unaware	Poison	Steel				Dragon
211	Clefairy	Fairy		Cute Charm	Magic Guard	Friend Guard	Poison	Steel				Dragon
210	Cleffa	Fairy		Cute Charm	Magic Guard	Friend Guard	Poison	Steel				Dragon
116	Cloyster	Water	Ice	Shell Armor	Skill Link	Overcoat	Grass	Electric	Fighting	Rock		
174	Comfey	Fairy		Flower Veil	Triage	Natural Cure	Poison	Steel				Dragon
112	Corsola	Water	Rock	Hustle	Natural Cure	Regenerator	4×Grass	Electric	Fighting	Ground		
290	Cosmoem	Psychic		Sturdy			Bug	Ghost	Dark			
289	Cosmog	Psychic		Unaware			Bug	Ghost	Dark			
087	Cottonee	Grass	Fairy	Prankster	Infiltrator	Chlorophyll	4×Poison	Fire	Ice	Flying	Steel	Dragon

Alola Dex No.	Pokémon	Type		Ability	Hidden Ability	Weak to these move types						Immune to these move types		
060	Crabominable	Fighting	Ice	Hyper Cutter	Iron Fist	Anger Point	Fire	Fighting	Flying	Psychic	Steel	Fairy			
059	Crabrawler	Fighting		Hyper Cutter	Iron Fist	Anger Point	Flying	Psychic	Fairy						
188	Cranidos	Rock		Mold Breaker		Sheer Force	Water	Grass	Fighting	Ground	Steel				
070	Crobat	Poison	Flying	Inner Focus		Infiltrator	Electric	Ice	Psychic	Rock			Ground		
163	Cubone	Ground		Rock Head	Lightning Rod	Battle Armor	Water	Grass	Ice				Electric		
83	Cutiefly	Bug	Fairy	Honey Gather	Shield Dust	Sweet Veil	Fire	Poison	Flying	Rock	Steel		Dragon		
002	Dartrix	Grass	Flying	Overgrow			Ice	Fire	Poison	Flying	Rock		Ground		
003	Decidueye	Grass	Ghost	Overgrow			Fire	Ice	Flying	Ghost	Dark		Normal	Fighting	
081	Delibird	Ice	Flying	Vital Spirit	Hustle	Insomnia	Rock	Fire	Electric	Steel			Ground		
141	Dewpider	Water	Bug	Water Bubble*		Water Absorb	Electric	Flying	Rock				Water		
263	Dhelmise	Ghost	Grass	Steelworker			Fire	Ice	Flying	Ghost	Dark		Normal	Fighting	
071	Diglett (Alola Form)	Ground	Steel	Sand Veil	Tangling Hair	Sand Force	Fire	Water	Fighting	Ground			Electric	Poison	
209	Ditto	Normal		Limber		Imposter	Fighting						Ghost		
282	Dragonair	Dragon		Shed Skin		Marvel Scale	Ice	Dragon	Fairy						
283	Dragonite	Dragon	Flying	Inner Focus		Multiscale	Ice	Rock	Dragon	Fairy			Ground		
244	Drampa	Normal	Dragon	Berserk	Sap Sipper	Cloud Nine	Ice	Fighting	Dragon	Fairy			Grass	Ghost	
281	Dratini	Dragon		Shed Skin		Marvel Scale	Ice	Dragon	Fairy						
065	Drifblim	Ghost	Flying	Aftermath	Unburden	Flare Boost	Electric	Ice	Rock	Ghost	Dark		Normal	Fighting	Ground
064	Drifloon	Ghost	Flying	Aftermath	Unburden	Flare Boost	Electric	Ice	Rock	Ghost	Dark		Normal	Fighting	Ground
054	Drowzee	Psychic		Insomnia	Forewarn	Inner Focus	Bug	Ghost	Dark						
072	Dugtrio (Alola Form)	Ground	Steel	Sand Veil	Tangling Hair	Sand Force	Fire	Water	Fighting	Ground			Electric	Poison	
121	Dunsparce	Normal		Run Away	Adaptability	Rattled	Fighting						Ghost		
227	Electabuzz	Electric		Static		Vital Spirit	Ground								
228	Electivire	Electric		Motor Drive		Vital Spirit	Ground						Electric		
226	Elekid	Electric		Static		Vital Spirit	Ground								
274	Emolga	Electric	Flying	Static		Motor Drive	Ice	Rock					Electric	Ground	
127	Espeon	Psychic		Synchronize		Magic Bounce	Bug	Ghost	Dark						
269	Exeggcute	Grass	Psychic	Chlorophyll		Harvest	Bug	Fire	Ice	Poison	Flying	Ghost	Dark		
270	Exeggutor (Alola Form)	Grass	Dragon	Frisk		Harvest	Ice	Poison	Flying	Bug	Dragon	Fairy			
074	Fearow	Normal	Flying	Keen Eye		Sniper	Electric	Ice	Rock				Ground	Ghost	
155	Feebas	Water		Swift Swim	Oblivious	Adaptability	Grass	Electric							
108	Finneon	Water		Swift Swim	Storm Drain	Water Veil	Grass	Electric					Water		
126	Flareon	Fire		Flash Fire		Guts	Water	Ground	Rock				Fire		
159	Fletchinder	Fire	Flying	Flame Body		Gale Wings	Rock	Water	Electric				Ground		
158	Fletchling	Normal	Flying	Big Pecks		Gale Wings	Electric	Ice	Rock				Ground	Ghost	
237	Flygon	Ground	Dragon	Levitate			Ice	Dragon	Fairy				Electric	Ground	
143	Fomantis	Grass		Leaf Guard		Contrary	Fire	Ice	Poison	Flying	Bug				
248	Froslass	Ice	Ghost	Snow Cloak		Cursed Body	Fire	Rock	Ghost	Dark	Steel		Normal	Fighting	
239	Gabite	Dragon	Ground	Sand Veil		Rough Skin	Ice	Dragon	Fairy				Electric		
207	Garbodor	Poison		Stench	Weak Armor	Aftermath	Ground	Psychic							
240	Garchomp	Dragon	Ground	Sand Veil		Rough Skin	Ice	Dragon	Fairy				Electric		
240	Garchomp (Mega Garchomp)	Dragon	Ground	Sand Force			Ice	Dragon	Fairy				Electric		
061	Gastly	Ghost	Poison	Levitate			Psychic	Ghost	Dark				Normal	Fighting	Ground
261	Gastrodon (East Sea)	Water	Ground	Sticky Hold	Storm Drain	Sand Force	Grass						Water	Electric	
063	Gengar	Ghost	Poison	Cursed Body			Ground	Psychic	Ghost	Dark			Normal	Fighting	
063	Gengar (Mega Gengar)	Ghost	Poison	Shadow Tag			Ground	Psychic	Ghost	Dark			Normal	Fighting	
229	Geodude (Alola Form)	Rock	Electric	Magnet Pull	Sturdy	Galvanize	Ground	Water	Grass	Fighting					
238	Gible	Dragon	Ground	Sand Veil		Rough Skin	Ice	Dragon	Fairy				Electric		
100	Gigalith	Rock		Sturdy	Sand Stream	Sand Force	Water	Grass	Fighting	Ground	Steel				
130	Glaceon	Ice		Snow Cloak		Ice Body	Fire	Fighting	Rock	Steel					
247	Glalie	Ice		Inner Focus	Ice Body	Moody	Fire	Fighting	Rock	Steel					
247	Glalie (Mega Glalie)	Ice		Refrigerate			Fire	Fighting	Rock	Steel					
069	Golbat	Poison	Flying	Inner Focus		Infiltrator	Electric	Ice	Psychic	Rock			Ground		
153	Goldeen	Water		Swift Swim	Water Veil	Lightning Rod	Grass	Electric					Electric		
090	Golduck	Water		Damp	Cloud Nine	Swift Swim	Grass	Electric							
231	Golem (Alola Form)	Rock	Electric	Magnet Pull	Sturdy	Galvanize	Ground	Water	Grass	Fighting					
183	Golisopod	Bug	Water	Emergency Exit			Electric	Flying	Rock						
180	Goodra	Dragon		Sap Sipper	Hydration	Gooey	Ice	Dragon	Fairy				Grass		
178	Goomy	Dragon		Sap Sipper	Hydration	Gooey	Ice	Dragon	Fairy				Grass		
259	Granbull	Fairy		Intimidate	Quick Feet	Rattled	Poison	Steel					Dragon		

Alola Dex No.	Pokémon	Type		Ability	Hidden Ability	Weak to these move types						Immune to these move types		
230	Graveler (Alola Form)	Rock	Electric	Magnet Pull	Sturdy	Galvanize	ⓍGround	Water	Grass	Fighting				
050	Grimer (Alola Form)	Poison	Dark	Poison Touch	Gluttony	Power of Alchemy	Ground					Psychic		
052	Growlithe	Fire		Intimidate	Flash Fire	Justified	Water	Ground	Rock			Fire		
027	Grubbin	Bug		Swarm			Fire	Flying	Rock					
014	Gumshoos	Normal		Stakeout	Strong Jaw	Adaptability	Fighting					Ghost		
299	Guzzlord	Dark	Dragon	Beast Boost			ⓍFairy	Ice	Fighting	Bug	Dragon	Psychic		
092	Gyarados	Water	Flying	Intimidate		Moxie	ⓍElectric	Rock				Ground		
092	Gyarados (Mega Gyarados)	Water	Dark	Mold Breaker			Grass	Electric	Fighting	Bug	Fairy	Psychic		
272	Hakamo-o	Dragon	Fighting	Bulletproof	Soundproof	Overcoat	ⓍFairy	Ice	Flying	Psychic	Dragon			
032	Happiny	Normal		Natural Cure	Serene Grace	Friend Guard	Fighting					Ghost		
057	Hariyama	Fighting		Thick Fat*	Guts	Sheer Force	Flying	Psychic	Fairy					
062	Haunter	Ghost	Poison	Levitate			Psychic	Ghost	Dark			Normal	Fighting	Ground
121	Herdier	Normal		Intimidate	Sand Rush	Scrappy	Fighting					Ghost		
278	Honchkrow	Dark	Flying	Insomnia	Super Luck	Moxie	Electric	Ice	Rock	Fairy		Ground	Psychic	
055	Hypno	Psychic		Insomnia	Forewarn	Inner Focus	Bug	Ghost	Dark					
134	Igglybuff	Normal	Fairy	Cute Charm	Competitive	Friend Guard	Poison	Steel				Ghost	Dragon	
006	Incineroar	Fire	Dark	Blaze			Water	Fighting	Ground	Rock		Psychic		
271	Jangmo-o	Dragon		Bulletproof	Soundproof	Overcoat	Ice	Dragon	Fairy					
135	Jigglypuff	Normal	Fairy	Cute Charm	Competitive	Friend Guard	Poison	Steel				Ghost	Dragon	
125	Jolteon	Electric		Volt Absorb		Quick Feet	Ground					Electric		
043	Kadabra	Psychic		Synchronize	Inner Focus	Magic Guard	Bug	Ghost	Dark					
165	Kangaskhan	Normal		Early Bird	Scrappy	Inner Focus	Fighting					Ghost		
165	Kangaskhan (Mega Kangaskhan)	Normal		Parental Bond			Fighting					Ghost		
298	Kartana	Grass	Steel	Beast Boost			ⓍFire	Fighting				Poison		
241	Klefki	Steel	Fairy	Prankster		Magician	Fire	Ground				Poison	Dragon	
222	Komala	Normal		Comatose			Fighting					Ghost		
273	Kommo-o	Dragon	Fighting	Bulletproof	Soundproof	Overcoat	ⓍFairy	Ice	Flying	Psychic	Dragon			
233	Krokorok	Ground	Dark	Intimidate	Moxie	Anger Point	Water	Grass	Ice	Fighting	Bug	Fairy	Electric	Psychic
234	Krookodile	Ground	Dark	Intimidate	Moxie	Anger Point	Water	Grass	Ice	Fighting	Bug	Fairy	Electric	Psychic
202	Lanturn	Water	Electric	Volt Absorb¹	Illuminate	Water Absorb²	Grass	Ground				Water²	Electric¹
268	Lapras	Water	Ice	Water Absorb	Shell Armor	Hydration	Grass	Electric	Fighting	Rock		Water		
129	Leafeon	Grass		Leaf Guard		Chlorophyll	Fire	Ice	Poison	Flying	Bug			
021	Ledian	Bug	Flying	Swarm	Early Bird	Iron Fist	ⓍRock	Fire	Electric	Ice	Flying	Ground		
020	Ledyba	Bug	Flying	Swarm	Early Bird	Rattled	ⓍRock	Fire	Electric	Ice	Flying	Ground		
086	Lilligant	Grass		Chlorophyll	Own Tempo	Leaf Guard	Fire	Ice	Poison	Flying	Bug			
120	Lillipup	Normal		Vital Spirit	Pickup	Run Away	Fighting					Ghost		
004	Litten	Fire		Blaze			Water	Ground	Rock					
280	Lucario	Fighting	Steel	Steadfast	Inner Focus	Justified	Fire	Fighting	Ground			Poison		
280	Lucario (Mega Lucario)	Fighting	Steel	Adaptability			Fire	Fighting	Ground			Poison		
109	Lumineon	Water		Swift Swim	Storm Drain	Water Veil	Grass	Electric				Water		
292	Lunala	Psychic	Ghost	Shadow Shield			ⓍGhost	ⓍDark				Normal	Fighting	
144	Lurantis	Grass		Leaf Guard		Contrary	Fire	Ice	Poison	Flying	Bug			
111	Luvdisc	Water		Swift Swim		Hydration	Grass	Electric						
104	Lycanroc (Midday Form)	Rock		Keen Eye	Sand Rush	Steadfast	Water	Grass	Fighting	Ground	Steel			
104	Lycanroc (Midnight Form)	Rock		Keen Eye	Vital Spirit	No Guard	Water	Grass	Fighting	Ground	Steel			
097	Machamp	Fighting		Guts	No Guard	Steadfast	Flying	Psychic	Fairy					
096	Machoke	Fighting		Guts	No Guard	Steadfast	Flying	Psychic	Fairy					
095	Machop	Fighting		Guts	No Guard	Steadfast	Flying	Psychic	Fairy					
166	Magby	Fire		Flame Body		Vital Spirit	Water	Ground	Rock					
301	Magearna	Steel	Fairy	Soul-Heart			Fire	Ground				Poison	Dragon	
091	Magikarp	Water		Swift Swim		Rattled	Grass	Electric						
167	Magmar	Fire		Flame Body		Vital Spirit	Water	Ground	Rock					
168	Magmortar	Fire		Flame Body		Vital Spirit	Water	Ground	Rock					
047	Magnemite	Electric	Steel	Magnet Pull	Sturdy	Analytic	ⓍGround	Fire	Fighting			Poison		
048	Magneton	Electric	Steel	Magnet Pull	Sturdy	Analytic	ⓍGround	Fire	Fighting			Poison		
049	Magnezone	Electric	Steel	Magnet Pull	Sturdy	Analytic	ⓍGround	Fire	Fighting			Poison		
056	Makuhita	Fighting		Thick Fat*	Guts	Sheer Force	Flying	Psychic	Fairy					
078	Mandibuzz	Dark	Flying	Big Pecks	Overcoat	Weak Armor	Electric	Ice	Rock	Fairy		Ground	Psychic	
079	Mankey	Fighting		Vital Spirit	Anger Point	Defiant	Flying	Psychic	Fairy					
113	Mareanie	Poison	Water	Merciless	Limber	Regenerator	Electric	Ground	Psychic					

Alola Dex No.	Pokémon	Type		Ability	Hidden Ability	Weak to these move types						Immune to these move types		
164	Marowak (Alola Form)	Fire	Ghost	Cursed Body	Lightning Rod	Rock Head	Water	Ground	Rock	Ghost	Dark		Normal	Electric	Fighting
140	Masquerain	Bug	Flying	Intimidate		Unnerve	⓫Rock	Fire	Electric	Ice	Flying		Ground		
045	Meowth (Alola Form)	Dark		Pickup	Technician	Rattled	Fighting	Bug	Fairy				Psychic		
216	Metagross	Steel	Psychic	Clear Body		Light Metal	Fire	Ground	Ghost	Dark			Poison		
216	Metagross (Mega Metagross)	Steel	Psychic	Tough Claws			Fire	Ground	Ghost	Dark			Poison		
215	Metang	Steel	Psychic	Clear Body		Light Metal	Fire	Ground	Ghost	Dark			Poison		
018	Metapod	Bug		Shed Skin			Fire	Flying	Rock						
156	Milotic	Water		Marvel Scale	Competitive	Cute Charm	Grass	Electric							
138	Miltank	Normal		Thick Fat*	Scrappy	Sap Sipper	Fighting						Grass	Ghost	
242	Mimikyu	Ghost	Fairy	Disguise			Ghost	Steel					Normal	Fighting	Dragon
213	Minior (Meteor Form)	Rock	Flying	Shields Down			Water	Electric	Ice	Rock	Steel		Ground		
066	Misdreavus	Ghost		Levitate			Ghost	Dark					Normal	Fighting	Ground
067	Mismagius	Ghost		Levitate			Ghost	Dark					Normal	Fighting	Ground
145	Morelull	Grass	Fairy	Illuminate	Effect Spore	Rain Dish	⓬Poison	Fire	Ice	Flying	Steel		Dragon		
132	Mudbray	Ground		Own Tempo	Stamina	Inner Focus	Water	Grass	Ice				Electric		
133	Mudsdale	Ground		Own Tempo	Stamina	Inner Focus	Water	Grass	Ice				Electric		
051	Muk (Alola Form)	Poison	Dark	Poison Touch	Gluttony	Power of Alchemy	Ground						Psychic		
035	Munchlax	Normal		Pickup	Thick Fat*	Gluttony	Fighting						Ghost		
277	Murkrow	Dark	Flying	Insomnia	Super Luck	Prankster	Electric	Ice	Rock	Fairy			Ground	Psychic	
300	Necrozma	Psychic		Prism Armor*			Bug	Ghost	Dark						
293	Nihilego	Rock	Poison	Beast Boost			⓫Ground	Water	Psychic	Steel					
254	Ninetales (Alola Form)	Ice	Fairy	Snow Cloak		Snow Warning	⓬Steel	Fire	Poison	Rock			Dragon		
108	Nosepass	Rock		Sturdy	Magnet Pull	Sand Force	Water	Grass	Fighting	Ground	Steel				
176	Oranguru	Normal	Psychic	Inner Focus	Telepathy		Bug	Dark					Ghost		
082	Oricorio (Baile Style)	Fire	Flying	Dancer			⓬Rock	Water	Electric				Ground		
082	Oricorio (Pa'u Style)	Psychic	Flying	Dancer			Electric	Ice	Rock	Ghost	Dark		Ground		
082	Oricorio (Pom-Pom Style)	Electric	Flying	Dancer			Ice	Rock					Ground		
082	Oricorio (Sensu Style)	Ghost	Flying	Dancer			Electric	Ice	Rock	Ghost	Dark		Normal	Fighting	Ground
187	Palossand	Ghost	Ground	Water Compaction		Sand Veil	Water	Grass	Ice	Ghost	Dark		Normal	Electric	Fighting
220	Pancham	Fighting		Iron Fist	Mold Breaker	Scrappy	Flying	Psychic	Fairy						
221	Pangoro	Fighting	Dark	Iron Fist	Mold Breaker	Scrappy	⓬Fairy	Fighting	Flying				Psychic		
147	Paras	Bug	Grass	Effect Spore	Dry Skin	Damp	⓬Fire	⓬Flying	Ice	Poison	Bug	Rock	Water		
148	Parasect	Bug	Grass	Effect Spore	Dry Skin	Damp	⓬Fire	⓬Flying	Ice	Poison	Bug	Rock	Water		
177	Passimian	Fighting		Receiver			Flying	Psychic	Fairy						
041	Pelipper	Water	Flying	Keen Eye	Drizzle	Rain Dish	⓬Electric	Rock					Ground		
046	Persian (Alola Form)	Dark		Fur Coat	Technician	Rattled	Fighting	Bug	Fairy				Psychic		
085	Petilil	Grass		Chlorophyll	Own Tempo	Leaf Guard	Fire	Ice	Poison	Flying	Bug				
196	Phantump	Ghost	Grass	Natural Cure	Frisk	Harvest	Fire	Ice	Flying	Ghost	Dark		Normal	Fighting	
295	Pheromosa	Bug	Fighting	Beast Boost			⓬Flying	Fire	Psychic	Fairy					
024	Pichu	Electric		Static		Lightning Rod	Ground						Electric		
025	Pikachu	Electric		Static		Lightning Rod	Ground						Electric		
010	Pikipek	Normal	Flying	Keen Eye	Skill Link	Pickup	Electric	Ice	Rock				Ground	Ghost	
175	Pinsir	Bug		Hyper Cutter	Mold Breaker	Moxie	Fire	Flying	Rock						
175	Pinsir (Mega Pinsir)	Bug	Flying	Aerilate			⓬Rock	Fire	Electric	Ice	Flying		Ground		
152	Politoed	Water		Water Absorb	Damp	Drizzle	Grass	Electric					Water		
149	Poliwag	Water		Water Absorb	Damp	Swift Swim	Grass	Electric					Water		
150	Poliwhirl	Water		Water Absorb	Damp	Swift Swim	Grass	Electric					Water		
151	Poliwrath	Water	Fighting	Water Absorb	Damp	Swift Swim	Grass	Electric	Flying	Psychic	Fairy		Water		
007	Popplio	Water		Torrent			Grass	Electric							
217	Porygon	Normal		Trace	Download	Analytic	Fighting						Ghost		
218	Porygon2	Normal		Trace	Download	Analytic	Fighting						Ghost		
219	Porygon-Z	Normal		Adaptability	Download	Analytic	Fighting						Ghost		
009	Primarina	Water	Fairy	Torrent			Grass	Electric	Poison				Dragon		
080	Primeape	Fighting		Vital Spirit	Anger Point	Defiant	Flying	Psychic	Fairy						
199	Probopass	Rock	Steel	Sturdy	Magnet Pull	Sand Force	⓬Fighting	⓬Ground	Water				Poison		
089	Psyduck	Water		Damp	Cloud Nine	Swift Swim	Grass	Electric							
200	Pyukumuku	Water		Innards Out		Unaware	Grass	Electric							
026	Raichu (Alola Form)	Electric	Psychic	Surge Surfer			Ground	Bug	Ghost	Dark					
189	Rampardos	Rock		Mold Breaker		Sheer Force	Water	Grass	Fighting	Ground	Steel				
016	Raticate (Alola Form)	Dark	Normal	Gluttony	Hustle	Thick Fat*	⓬Fighting	Bug	Fairy				Psychic	Ghost	

Alola Dex No.	Pokémon	Type		Ability		Hidden Ability	Weak to these move types						Immune to these move types		
015	Rattata (Alola Form)	Dark	Normal	Gluttony	Hustle	Thick Fat*	4x Fighting	Bug	Fairy				Psychic	Ghost	
262	Relicanth	Water	Rock	Swift Swim	Rock Head	Sturdy	4x Grass	Electric	Fighting	Ground					
084	Ribombee	Bug	Fairy	Honey Gather	Shield Dust	Sweet Veil	Fire	Poison	Flying	Rock	Steel		Dragon		
279	Riolu	Fighting		Steadfast	Inner Focus	Prankster	Flying	Psychic	Fairy						
103	Rockruff	Rock		Keen Eye	Vital Spirit	Steadfast	Water	Grass	Fighting	Ground	Steel				
098	Roggenrola	Rock		Sturdy	Weak Armor	Sand Force	Water	Grass	Fighting	Ground	Steel				
001	Rowlet	Grass	Flying	Overgrow			4x Ice	Fire	Poison	Flying	Rock		Ground		
075	Rufflet	Normal	Flying	Keen Eye	Sheer Force	Hustle	Electric	Ice	Rock				Ground	Ghost	
102	Sableye	Dark	Ghost	Keen Eye	Stall	Prankster	Fairy						Normal	Fighting	Psychic
102	Sableye (Mega Sableye)	Dark	Ghost	Magic Bounce			Fairy						Normal	Fighting	Psychic
119	Salamence	Dragon	Flying	Intimidate		Moxie	4x Ice	Rock	Dragon	Fairy			Ground		
119	Salamence (Mega Salamence)	Dragon	Flying	Aerilate			4x Ice	Rock	Dragon	Fairy			Ground		
161	Salandit	Poison	Fire	Corrosion		Oblivious	4x Ground	Water	Psychic	Rock					
162	Salazzle	Poison	Fire	Corrosion		Oblivious	4x Ground	Water	Psychic	Rock					
232	Sandile	Ground	Dark	Intimidate	Moxie	Anger Point	Water	Grass	Ice	Fighting	Bug	Fairy	Electric	Psychic	
251	Sandshrew (Alola Form)	Ice	Steel	Snow Cloak		Slush Rush	4x Fire	4x Fighting	Ground				Poison		
252	Sandslash (Alola Form)	Ice	Steel	Snow Cloak		Slush Rush	4x Fire	4x Fighting	Ground				Poison		
186	Sandygast	Ghost	Ground	Water Compaction		Sand Veil	Water	Grass	Ice	Ghost	Dark		Normal	Electric	Fighting
276	Scizor	Bug	Steel	Swarm	Technician	Light Metal	4x Fire						Poison		
276	Scizor (Mega Scizor)	Bug	Steel	Technician			4x Fire						Poison		
275	Scyther	Bug	Flying	Swarm	Technician	Steadfast	4x Rock	Fire	Electric	Ice	Flying		Ground		
154	Seaking	Water		Swift Swim	Water Veil	Lightning Rod	Grass	Electric					Electric		
265	Sharpedo	Water	Dark	Rough Skin		Speed Boost	Grass	Electric	Fighting	Bug	Fairy		Psychic		
265	Sharpedo (Mega Sharpedo)	Water	Dark	Strong Jaw			Grass	Electric	Fighting	Bug	Fairy		Psychic		
118	Shelgon	Dragon		Rock Head		Overcoat	Ice	Dragon	Fairy						
115	Shellder	Water		Shell Armor	Skill Link	Overcoat	Grass	Electric							
260	Shellos (East Sea)	Water		Sticky Hold	Storm Drain	Sand Force	Grass	Electric					Water		
190	Shieldon	Rock	Steel	Sturdy		Soundproof	4x Fighting	4x Ground	Water				Poison		
146	Shiinotic	Grass	Fairy	Illuminate	Effect Spore	Rain Dish	4x Poison	Fire	Ice	Flying	Steel		Dragon		
204	Silvally (Type: Bug)	Bug		RKS System			Fire	Flying	Rock						
204	Silvally (Type: Dark)	Dark		RKS System			Fighting	Bug	Fairy				Psychic		
204	Silvally (Type: Dragon)	Dragon		RKS System			Ice	Dragon	Fairy						
204	Silvally (Type: Electric)	Electric		RKS System			Ground								
204	Silvally (Type: Fairy)	Fairy		RKS System			Poison	Steel					Dragon		
204	Silvally (Type: Fighting)	Fighting		RKS System			Flying	Psychic	Fairy						
204	Silvally (Type: Fire)	Fire		RKS System			Water	Ground	Rock						
204	Silvally (Type: Flying)	Flying		RKS System			Electric	Ice	Rock				Ground		
204	Silvally (Type: Ghost)	Ghost		RKS System			Ghost	Dark					Normal	Fighting	
204	Silvally (Type: Grass)	Grass		RKS System			Fire	Ice	Poison	Flying	Bug				
204	Silvally (Type: Ground)	Ground		RKS System			Water	Grass	Ice				Electric		
204	Silvally (Type: Ice)	Ice		RKS System			Fire	Fighting	Rock	Steel					
204	Silvally (Type: Normal)	Normal		RKS System			Fighting						Ghost		
204	Silvally (Type: Poison)	Poison		RKS System			Ground	Psychic							
204	Silvally (Type: Psychic)	Psychic		RKS System			Bug	Ghost	Dark						
204	Silvally (Type: Rock)	Rock		RKS System			Water	Grass	Fighting	Ground	Steel				
204	Silvally (Type: Steel)	Steel		RKS System			Fire	Fighting	Ground				Poison		
204	Silvally (Type: Water)	Water		RKS System			Grass	Electric							
208	Skarmory	Steel	Flying	Keen Eye	Sturdy	Weak Armor	Fire	Electric					Poison	Ground	
179	Sliggoo	Dragon		Sap Sipper	Hydration	Gooey	Ice	Dragon	Fairy				Grass		
038	Slowbro	Water	Psychic	Oblivious	Own Tempo	Regenerator	Grass	Electric	Bug	Ghost	Dark				
038	Slowbro (Mega Slowbro)	Water	Psychic	Shell Armor			Grass	Electric	Bug	Ghost	Dark				
039	Slowking	Water	Psychic	Oblivious	Own Tempo	Regenerator	Grass	Electric	Bug	Ghost	Dark				
037	Slowpoke	Water	Psychic	Oblivious	Own Tempo	Regenerator	Grass	Electric	Bug	Ghost	Dark				
058	Smeargle	Normal		Own Tempo	Technician	Moody	Fighting						Ghost		
249	Sneasel	Dark	Ice	Inner Focus	Keen Eye	Pickpocket	4x Fighting	Fire	Bug	Rock	Steel	Fairy	Psychic		
036	Snorlax	Normal		Immunity	Thick Fat*	Gluttony	Fighting						Ghost		
246	Snorunt	Ice		Inner Focus	Ice Body	Moody	Fire	Fighting	Rock	Steel					
258	Snubbull	Fairy		Intimidate	Run Away	Rattled	Poison	Steel					Dragon		
291	Solgaleo	Psychic	Steel	Full Metal Body			Fire	Ground	Ghost	Dark			Poison		

Alola Dex No.	Pokémon	Type		Ability	Hidden Ability	Weak to these move types						Immune to these move types	
073	Spearow	Normal	Flying	Keen Eye		Sniper	Electric	Ice	Rock			Ground	Ghost
022	Spinarak	Bug	Poison	Swarm	Insomnia	Sniper	Fire	Flying	Psychic	Rock			
105	Spinda	Normal		Own Tempo	Tangled Feet	Contrary	Fighting					Ghost	
185	Starmie	Water	Psychic	Illuminate	Natural Cure	Analytic	Grass	Electric	Bug	Ghost	Dark		
184	Staryu	Water		Illuminate	Natural Cure	Analytic	Grass	Electric					
172	Steenee	Grass		Leaf Guard	Oblivious	Sweet Veil	Fire	Ice	Poison	Flying	Bug		
122	Stoutland	Normal		Intimidate	Sand Rush	Scrappy	Fighting					Ghost	
169	Stufful	Normal	Fighting	Fluffy	Klutz	Cute Charm	Fire	Fighting	Flying	Psychic	Fairy	Ghost	
031	Sudowoodo	Rock		Sturdy	Rock Head	Rattled	Water	Grass	Fighting	Ground	Steel		
139	Surskit	Bug	Water	Swift Swim		Rain Dish	Electric	Flying	Rock				
131	Sylveon	Fairy		Cute Charm		Pixilate	Poison	Steel				Dragon	
160	Talonflame	Fire	Flying	Flame Body		Gale Wings	4×Rock	Water	Electric			Ground	
287	Tapu Bulu	Grass	Fairy	Grassy Surge			4×Poison	Fire	Ice	Flying	Steel	Dragon	
288	Tapu Fini	Water	Fairy	Misty Surge			Grass	Electric	Poison			Dragon	
285	Tapu Koko	Electric	Fairy	Electric Surge			Poison	Ground				Dragon	
286	Tapu Lele	Psychic	Fairy	Psychic Surge			Poison	Ghost	Steel			Dragon	
137	Tauros	Normal		Intimidate	Anger Point	Sheer Force	Fighting					Ghost	
106	Tentacool	Water	Poison	Clear Body	Liquid Ooze	Rain Dish	Electric	Ground	Psychic				
107	Tentacruel	Water	Poison	Clear Body	Liquid Ooze	Rain Dish	Electric	Ground	Psychic				
194	Tirtouga	Water	Rock	Solid Rock*	Sturdy	Swift Swim	4×Grass	Electric	Fighting	Ground			
225	Togedemaru	Electric	Steel	Iron Barbs	Lightning Rod	Sturdy	4×Ground	Fire	Fighting			Electric	Poison
218	Torkoal	Fire		White Smoke	Drought	Shell Armor	Water	Ground	Rock				
005	Torracat	Fire		Blaze			Water	Ground	Rock				
012	Toucannon	Normal	Flying	Keen Eye	Skill Link	Sheer Force	Electric	Ice	Rock			Ground	Ghost
114	Toxapex	Poison	Water	Merciless	Limber	Regenerator	Electric	Ground	Psychic				
235	Trapinch	Ground		Hyper Cutter	Arena Trap	Sheer Force	Water	Grass	Ice			Electric	
197	Trevenant	Ghost	Grass	Natural Cure	Frisk	Harvest	Fire	Ice	Flying	Ghost	Dark	Normal	Fighting
206	Trubbish	Poison		Stench	Sticky Hold	Aftermath	Ground	Psychic					
011	Trumbeak	Normal	Flying	Keen Eye	Skill Link	Pickup	Electric	Ice	Rock			Ground	Ghost
173	Tsareena	Grass		Leaf Guard	Queenly Majesty	Sweet Veil	Fire	Ice	Poison	Flying	Bug		
224	Turtonator	Fire	Dragon	Shell Armor			Ground	Rock	Dragon				
203	Type: Null	Normal		Battle Armor			Fighting					Ghost	
128	Umbreon	Dark		Synchronize		Inner Focus	Fighting	Bug	Fairy			Psychic	
256	Vanillish	Ice		Ice Body	Snow Cloak	Weak Armor	Fire	Fighting	Rock	Steel			
255	Vanillite	Ice		Ice Body	Snow Cloak	Weak Armor	Fire	Fighting	Rock	Steel			
257	Vanilluxe	Ice		Ice Body	Snow Warning	Weak Armor	Fire	Fighting	Rock	Steel			
124	Vaporeon	Water		Water Absorb		Hydration	Grass	Electric				Water	
236	Vibrava	Ground	Dragon	Levitate			4×Ice	Dragon	Fairy			Electric	Ground
029	Vikavolt	Bug	Electric	Levitate			Fire	Rock				Ground	
077	Vullaby	Dark	Flying	Big Pecks	Overcoat	Weak Armor	Electric	Ice	Rock	Fairy		Ground	Psychic
253	Vulpix (Alola Form)	Ice		Snow Cloak		Snow Warning	Fire	Fighting	Rock	Steel			
266	Wailmer	Water		Water Veil	Oblivious	Pressure	Grass	Electric					
267	Wailord	Water		Water Veil	Oblivious	Pressure	Grass	Electric					
250	Weavile	Dark	Ice	Pressure		Pickpocket	4×Fighting	Fire	Bug	Rock	Steel	Fairy	Psychic
088	Whimsicott	Grass	Fairy	Prankster	Infiltrator	Chlorophyll	4×Poison	Fire	Ice	Flying	Steel	Dragon	
094	Whiscash	Water	Ground	Oblivious	Anticipation	Hydration	4×Grass					Electric	
136	Wigglytuff	Normal	Fairy	Cute Charm	Competitive	Frisk	Poison	Steel				Ghost	Dragon
182	Wimpod	Bug	Water	Wimp Out			Electric	Flying	Rock				
040	Wingull	Water	Flying	Keen Eye	Hydration	Rain Dish	4×Electric	Rock				Ground	
110	Wishiwashi (Solo Form)	Water		Schooling			Grass	Electric					
110	Wishiwashi (School Form)	Water		Schooling			Grass	Electric					
296	Xurkitree	Electric		Beast Boost			Ground						
013	Yungoos	Normal		Stakeout	Strong Jaw	Adaptability	Fighting					Ghost	
068	Zubat	Poison	Flying	Inner Focus		Infiltrator	Electric	Ice	Psychic	Rock		Ground	
205	Zygarde (10% Forme)	Dragon	Ground	Aura Break	Power Construct		4×Ice	Dragon	Fairy			Electric	
205	Zygarde (50% Forme)	Dragon	Ground	Aura Break	Power Construct		4×Ice	Dragon	Fairy			Electric	
205	Zygarde (Complete Forme)	Dragon	Ground	Power Construct			4×Ice	Dragon	Fairy			Electric	

Type Matchup Chart

Types are assigned both to moves and to the Pokémon themselves. These types can greatly affect the amount of damage dealt or received in battle, so if you learn how they line up against one another, you'll give yourself an edge in battle.

If your Pokémon has two types, the strengths and weaknesses of both types will be used to calculate that Pokémon's weaknesses and strengths. If both types share the same weakness, the Pokémon will take four times the damage. (For example, Grass types and Ice types are both weak to Fire, and each will take 2× damage from a Fire-type move. A Grass- and Ice-type Pokémon will be twice as weak, and take 4× the damage from a Fire-type move.) However, two resistances can combine in the same way. (Fire types and Water types are both resistant to Fire-type attacks, taking only 1/2 the usual damage. A Fire- and Water-type Pokémon would be twice as resistant, and only take 1/4 the usual damage from a Fire-type move.) Finally, a strength and weakness will cancel each other out. (Grass types take 2× damage from Fire-type attacks, and Water types take 1/2 damage from Fire-type attacks. A Grass- and Water-type Pokémon will simply take normal damage from a Fire-type attack, not more or less.)

Key

Symbol	Meaning	Multiplier
◉	Very effective "It's super effective!"	× 2
No icon	Normal damage	× 1
▲	Not too effective "It's not very effective…"	× 1/2
×	No effect "It doesn't affect…"	× 0

Type Matchup

Defending Pokémon's Type →, Attacking Pokémon's Move Type ↓

Move \ Def	Normal	Fire	Water	Grass	Electric	Ice	Fighting	Poison	Ground	Flying	Psychic	Bug	Rock	Ghost	Dragon	Dark	Steel	Fairy
Normal													▲	×			▲	
Fire		▲	▲	◉		◉						◉	▲		▲		◉	
Water		◉	▲	▲					◉				◉		▲			
Grass		▲	◉	▲				▲	◉	▲		▲	◉		▲		▲	
Electric			◉	▲	▲				×	◉					▲			
Ice		▲	▲	◉		▲			◉	◉					◉		▲	
Fighting	◉					◉		▲		▲	▲	▲	◉	×		◉	◉	▲
Poison				◉				▲	▲				▲	▲			×	◉
Ground		◉		▲	◉			◉		×		▲	◉				◉	
Flying				◉	▲		◉					◉	▲				▲	
Psychic							◉	◉			▲					×	▲	
Bug		▲		◉			▲	▲		▲	◉			▲		◉	▲	▲
Rock		◉				◉	▲		▲	◉		◉					▲	
Ghost	×										◉			◉		▲		
Dragon															◉		▲	×
Dark							▲				◉			◉		▲		▲
Steel		▲	▲		▲	◉							◉				▲	◉
Fairy		▲					◉	▲							◉	◉	▲	

Ineffective status conditions and moves depending on type

Type	Effect
Fire	• Immune to the Burned condition
Grass	• Immune to Leech Seed • Immune to powder and spore moves
Electric	• Immune to the Paralysis condition
Ice	• Immune to the Frozen condition • Take no damage from hail • Immune to Sheer Cold
Poison	• Immune to the Poisoned and Badly Poisoned conditions, even when switched in with Toxic Spikes in play • Nullify Toxic Spikes so no other Pokémon will be Poisoned when switching in. (Note: if the Poison-type Pokémon is also a Flying type, has the Levitate Ability, or holds an Air Balloon, this nullifying effect will not occur.)
Ground	• Immune to Thunder Wave* • Take no damage from sandstorms
Flying	• Cannot be damaged by Spikes when switching in • Immune to the Poisoned and Badly Poisoned conditions, when switching in with Toxic Spikes in play
Rock	• Take no damage from sandstorms • Sp. Def goes up in a sandstorm
Ghost	• Cannot be affected by moves and Abilities that prevent Pokémon from fleeing from battle
Dark	• Immune to the effect of status moves used by Pokémon with the Prankster Ability
Steel	• Take no damage from sandstorms • Immune to the Poisoned and Badly Poisoned conditions, even when switched in with Toxic Spikes in play

*Types usually don't have effects on status moves, but Thunder Wave won't work against Ground-type Pokémon.